the **BERKELEY** guides

## CRITICAL ACCLAIM FOR THE BERKELEY GUIDES

"Planet-wise instruction for [the] cash conscious . . . for the price, the time of your life."
—*Details*

"[The Berkeley Guides are] brimming with useful information for the low-budget traveler—material delivered in a fresh, funny, and often irreverent way."
—*The Philadelphia Inquirer*

"The [Berkeley Guides] are deservedly popular because of their extensive coverage, entertaining style of writing, and heavy emphasis on budget travel . . . If you are looking for tips on hostels, vegetarian food, and hitchhiking, there are no books finer."
—*San Diego Union-Tribune*

"[The Berkeley Guides] offer straight dirt on everything from hostels to look for and beaches to avoid to museums least likely to attract your parents . . . they're fresher than Harvard's Let's Go series."
—*Seventeen*

"The [Berkeley Guides] give a rare glimpse into the real cultures of Europe, Canada, Mexico, and the United States . . . with in-depth historical backgrounds on each place and a creative, often poetical style of prose."
—*Eugene Weekly*

"The new On the Loose guides are more comprehensive, informative and witty than Let's Go."
—*Glamour*

"The Berkeley Guides have more and better maps, and on average, the nuts and bolts descriptions of such things as hotels and restaurants tend to be more illuminating than the often terse and sometimes vague entries in the 'Let's Go' guides."
— *San José Mercury News*

"The well-organized guides list can't miss sights, offbeat attractions and cheap thrills, such as festivals and walks. And they're fun to read."
— *New York Newsday*

"Reading (these guides) is a lot like listening to a first-hand report from a friend...They're also just plain fun to read."
— *Greensboro News & Record*

"Written for the young and young at heart...you'll find this thick, fact-filled guide makes entertaining reading."
— *St. Louis Dispatch*

"...bright articulate guidebooks. The irreverent yet straightforward prose is easy to read and offers a sense of the adventures awaiting travelers off the beaten path."
— *Portland Oregonian*

THE BERKELEY GUIDES are printed using soy-based ink on 100% recycled paper, including 50% post-consumer fiber and 100% de-inked newspapers, magazines and catalogs. What's the use of traveling if there's nothing left to see?

**THE BERKELEY GUIDES**

California 1996

Central America (2nd Edition)

Eastern Europe (3rd Edition)

Europe 1996

France 1996

Germany & Austria 1996

Great Britain & Ireland 1996

Italy 1996

London 1996

Mexico 1996

Pacific Northwest & Alaska (2nd Edition)

Paris 1996

San Francisco 1996

# the BERKELEY guides

# california '96

On the Loose
On the Cheap
Off the Beaten Path

WRITTEN BY BERKELEY STUDENTS IN COOPERATION WITH THE ASSOCIATED STUDENTS OF THE UNIVERSITY OF CALIFORNIA

ISBN 0-679-02978-8

## THE BERKELEY GUIDE TO CALIFORNIA

**Editor:** Jennifer Wedel
**Managing Editors:** Nicole Harb, Kristina Malsberger, Sharron Wood
**Executive Editor:** Scott McNeely
**Creative Director:** Fabrizio La Rocca
**Cartographer:** David Lindroth, Inc.; Eureka Cartography
**Text Design:** Tigist Getachew
**Cover Design:** Fabrizio La Rocca
**Cover Art:** Poul Lange (3-D art), © Mark S. Wexler (photo in frame), Paul D'Innocenzo (still life)

## SPECIAL SALES

The Berkeley Guides and Fodor's Travel Publications are available at special discounts for bulk purchases for sales promotions or premiums. Special editions, including personalized covers, excerpts of existing guides, and corporate imprints, can be created in large quantities for special needs. For more information, contact your local bookseller or write to Special Markets, Fodor's Travel Publications, 201 E. 50th Street, New York, NY 10022. Inquiries from Canada should be directed to your local Canadian bookseller or sent to Random House of Canada, Ltd., Marketing Dept., 1265 Aerowood Drive, Mississauga, Ontario L4W 1B9. Inquiries from the United Kingdom should be sent to Fodor's Travel Publications, 20 Vauxhall Bridge Road, London SW1V 2SA, England.

MANUFACTURED IN THE UNITED STATES OF AMERICA

10 9 8 7 6 5 4 3 2 1

# Contents

## 4 THE NORTH COAST 113



## 5 THE CASCADES 157



## 6 THE GOLD COUNTRY 193



## 7 THE SIERRA NEVADA AND SAN JOAQUIN VALLEY 225



## 8 THE CENTRAL COAST 267

# What the Berkeley Guides Are All About

**Four years ago, a motley bunch of U.C. Berkeley students launched a new series** of guidebooks—*The Berkeley Guides.* Since then, we've been busy writing and editing 13 books to destinations across the globe, from California, Mexico, and Central America to Europe and Eastern Europe. Along the way our writers have weathered bus plunges, rabies, and guerrilla attacks, landed bush planes above the Arctic Circle, gotten lost in the woods (proverbially and literally), and broken bread with all sorts of peculiar characters—from Mafia dons and Hell's Angel bikers to tofu-eating, tie-dye wearing, Jerry Garcia mourning attorneys. And don't forget about the train station sleep-ins, voodoo bus schedules, and drive-by shootings.

Coordinating the efforts of 65 U.C. Berkeley writers back at the office is an equally daunting task (have you ever tried to track manuscript from Morocco?). But that's the whole point of *The Berkeley Guides*: to bring you the most up-to-date info on prices, the latest budget-travel trends, the newest restaurants and hostels, where to catch your next train—all written and edited by people who know what cheap travel is all about.

You see, it's one of life's weird truisms that the more cheaply you travel, the more you inevitably experience. If you're looking for five-star meals, air-conditioned tour buses, and reviews of the same old tourist traps, you're holding the wrong guidebook. Instead, *The Berkeley Guides* give you an in-depth look at local culture, detailed coverage of small towns and off-beat sights, bars and cafés where tourists rarely tread, plus no-nonsense practical info that deals with the real problems of real people (where to get aspirin at 3 AM, where to launder those dirty socks).

Coming from a community as diverse as Berkeley, we also wanted our guides to be useful to everyone, so we tell you if a place is wheelchair accessible, if it provides resources for gay and lesbian travelers, and if it's safe for women traveling solo. Many of us are Californians, which means most of us like trees and mountain trails. It also means we emphasize the outdoors in every *Berkeley Guide* and include lots of info about hiking and tips on protecting the environment. To minimize our impact on the environment, we print our books on recycled paper using soy-based inks.

Most important, these guides are for travelers who want to see more than just the main sights. We find out what local people do for fun, where they go to eat, drink, or just hang out. Most guidebooks lead you down the tourist trail, ignoring important local issues, events, and culture. In *The Berkeley Guides* we give you the information you need to understand what's going on around you, whether it's the controversy over logging the North Coast or the progress in the rebuilding of South Central.

We've done our best to make sure the information in *The Berkeley Guides* is accurate, but time doesn't stand still: prices change, places go out of business, currencies get devalued. Call ahead when it's really important, and try not to get too stressed out.

# Thanks to You

**Lots of people helped us put together this year's edition of *The Berkeley Guide to* ***California.* Some are listed below, but many others—whom our writers met briefly on buses, in motels, and in hostels—also helped out. We would like you to help us update this book and give us feedback from the road. Drop us a line—a postcard, a scrawled note on some toilet paper, whatever—and we'll be happy to acknowledge your contribution below. Our address is 515 Eshleman Hall, University of California, Berkeley, CA 94720.

Special thanks go to Jim Algeo (Moaning Caverns); Paula Ananda (Healdsburg); Katherine "Petunia" Audley and Eric Gilmore (Mill Valley); Lorena Barros (L.A.); Steph Bornstien (S.F.); Jeff Bratcher (Santa Barbara); Philip and Noah Craft (L.A.); Robert Dickinson (Berkeley); Christi Ehrlich (Oakland); Jessie Figueroa (Sacramento); Matt Fischer (Berkeley); Mitch Ginsburg (Israel); Alexis Goltra (Virginia); Paul Grant (London, England); Oren Harman (Israel); David Henschel (Manhattan Beach); Jeff Irvin (Flagstaff and Page, AZ); John at the Hollywood International Hostel (L.A.); Chris Johnson (Arcata); Mara Katz (S.F.); David Kallinger (Berkeley); Nikki Korfanta (Fresno); Rob Krochmal (L.A.); Ava Montgomery (Orleans); Michael Moore (Tucson, AZ); Chris Murphy (L.A.); John Olmstead (Nevada City); Eric Pankonin (Berkeley); Mary Phulps (Sonoma); Al Porter (Anza-Borrego Desert State Park); Michael Richards; Kathleen Rodriguez and Mellissa Aragon (Honeydew); Matt Rolufs (S.F.); David Rosnow (S.F.); Fred Rozendal (San Rafael); the wonderful Aimy Seabrook (Portland); Patricia Shea (San Rafael); Jane Sperling (S.F.); Meg Stalcup (Oakland); Ann Titus (Death Valley National Park); John Vrilakas (Santa Cruz); Arthur Webster (Joshua Tree National Park); Bill and Kathi Wojtkowski (Monterey); Art Yanez (L.A.); Eugenio Zanett and Tom (L.A.).

# Berkeley Bios

**Behind every restaurant blurb, write-up, lodging review, and introduction in this** book lurks a student writer. You might recognize the type—perpetually short on time, money, and clean underwear. These Berkeley students spent the summer traveling around the state, completely revising and updating *The Berkeley Guide to California.* Every two weeks they sent their manuscript back to an editor in Berkeley, who whipped it into shape faster than you can say "sleep deprivation."

## The Writers

**Laura Burgardt**—proud Oakland native—was skeptical of spending the summer in Southern California. But after personally investigating sleek nightspots and sunsets over the Pacific, she found out San Diego is a pretty cool place to spend some time. Next Laura took off across the desert in a borrowed 4 × 4 (thanks, Mom) to update coverage of the Grand Canyon, where she almost learned-the-hard-way to fill up the gas tank *before* setting off across the Arizona and Utah deserts. Determined to put off joining the "real world" that everyone says is inevitable, Laura will spend the next couple years making plans for grad school and doing what her Latin American Studies degree most qualifies her for: traveling.

Despite the difficulties of getting stuck in an unseasonable May blizzard, **Kelly Green** found both of her brief assignments—to a snowbound Lake Tahoe and a sticky-hot Santa Cruz—to be a welcome change from her regular 9-to-5 job as an editor (just don't tell her boss she's moonlighting). She longs to breathe that sweet, unrecirculated air again someday . . .

**Danna Harman** from Jerusalem, Israel (via lots of other places and en route to graduate school in England for a master's degree in Islamic Studies), failed the written part of California's driving test twice before she was allowed to drive her borrowed car off into the wild blue yonder—or the Central Coast, whichever. She made her way north along Highway 1 in search of the best tacos in Santa Barbara, the funkiest gay club in San Luis Obispo, the *least* interesting cabin in the Gold Country (that would be Mark Twain's), and the most decadent activities in Reno (this she had no trouble with). If anyone should find her worn-out, much-loved Berkeley sweatshirt (possibly on some windswept Central Coast beach), send it this way.

Sporting his tackiest clothes, **Ray Klinke** was dispatched by the *Berkeley Guides* to Las Vegas. Fueled by equal parts fascination and distaste (as well as all-you-can-eat buffets), he combed the casinos in search of hidden bargains, loose slots, and an elusive Elvis impersonator known as Eddie DeWayne. Along the way, he improved his card-counting abilities, learned the "don't piss off the pit boss" lesson, and spent enough time at Circus Circus to acquire a fierce phobia of clowns. Severely discombobulated by the end of his stay, Ray found sanctuary in a secluded café far from the Strip, for which he is eternally grateful, and left Vegas seriously questioning the prospects for survival of a culture that erects shrines to Liberace and reveres the wit of Buddy Hackett.

Ever since her freshman year at Berkeley, **Kristina Malsberger** has been haunted by the words "You're from Napa; you pick out the wine." Needless to say, she jumped at the chance to receive a proper viticultural education while writing up the Wine Country and Santa Rosa. Somewhere between her 53rd and 54th glass, Kristina decided to relocate to the Burgundy countryside, change her name to "Chardonnay," and spend the rest of her natural life becoming rich and mellow with age.



A native of Argentina, **Sonia Perel** had traveled extensively outside the States before her *Berkeley Guides* assignment in Los Angeles; she had not, however, been behind the wheel of a car in years and her knowledge of movie-star trivia had gotten quite hazy. But, each day of her itinerary, years of anti-L.A. brainwashing peeled away as she sped down flat luminescent roads, munched fresh mangoes, and stumbled upon expansive art collections. L.A. was higher in contrasts, lower in gloss, than she had been led to believe. Sonia plans to be gainfully employed someday, but she's not holding her breath.

**Alan Covington Phulps,** a California native, has gone through at least 20 jobs—from dish-washing to bicycle messengering—to afford the luxuries of travel and rock climbing. He spent years traveling through North America and Asia before he realized that there's no place like home when home is California. After accepting his assignment with the *Berkeley Guides*, Alan bought a precarious '72 Volkswagen van and took off into the high country of the Sierra Nevada and Cascades to discover first-hand California's best hiking, rock-climbing, summer skiing, mountain biking, fishing . . . and greasy spoons. It's a dirty job, but somebody had to do it.

Joyfully leaving the dusty words of the English canon behind him, **Michael Rozendal** took to the road looking for inspiration and (elusive) organic markets in the southern deserts and on the northern coasts of California. Along the way, he slept under the stars in Death Valley, got drenched while rafting down the Trinity River at sunset, and spent the 4th of July watching fireworks with a multigenerational clan of hippies. When he wasn't chasing roadrunners in the Mojave, eating snow peas in the Sagely City of 10,000 Buddhas, or soaking in the carbonated waters of Vichy Springs, he was engaging in careful, scientific analysis of the North Coast's microbreweries. On his journeys, Michael realized that he could live life instead of just reading about it, and he's ready to strike out on the road again before returning to the ivory tower.

**Jim Stanley,** a native of Southern California, is trying to forget his experience near L.A. He now lives in San Francisco, anxiously awaiting the next *Star Wars* film.

After writing for the Berkeley Guides three years running while working full-time as a managing editor for the series, an overworked **Sharron Wood** says "No more!". Of course, she doesn't really mean it, especially since this year's assignment gave her the opportunity to explore the North Coast's famed and gorgeous Redwood National and State Parks. She'll be back next year for more.

We'd also like to put in a word for the writers of *The Berkeley Guide to San Francisco 1996,* whose work appears in the San Francisco and Bay Area chapters: **Alice Chang, Kelly Green, Danna Harman, Emily Hastings, Ray Klinke, Baty Landis, Cynthia Leung, David Walter,** and **Sharron Wood.** Thanks also to **Shayna Samuels**, one of the writers of *The Berkeley Guide to Mexico 1996*, for sparing Laura Burgardt a trip to Tijuana.

# The Editor

Just looking at that singular noun, Editor, makes **Jennifer Wedel** (pronounced like ladle or cradle, *not* like needle or beetle or pedal or mettle) shake with both fear and joy. Taking sick pleasure in the fact that she is one of few *non*-native Californians in the office, Jennifer escaped mentally to Lake Josephine, Minnesota, when the task of editing the California book overwhelmed her sometimes-fragile sensibilities. Jennifer would especially like to thank Jen Brewer, her co-editor in spirit and editor of the forthcoming *Berkeley Guide to New York City.* Having survived this baptism by fire, Jennifer will soon endure another, more literal one when she moves to Tucson, AZ, deep in the hellish heart of the Sonoran Desert. "The things you do for love," she has been heard muttering to her computer screen.

In addition, thanks go to the Random House folks who helped us with cartography, page design, and production: Bob Blake, Ellen Browne, Denise DeGennaro, Janet Foley, Tigist Getachew, Tracy Patruno, Fabrizio La Rocca, and Linda Schmidt.

# Northern California

O R E
Six Rivers National Forest
Crescent City
Yreka
Klamath
Redwood National Park
Klamath R.
Mt. Shasta
Klamath National Forest
Arcata
Eureka
Fortuna
Lake Shasta
Redding
Trinity National Forest
Eel R.
Red Bluff
Garberville
Leggett
Mendocino National Forest
Sacramento Valley
Fort Bragg
Mendocino
Ukiah
Clear Lake
Point Arena
PACIFIC OCEAN
Santa Rosa
Napa
Petaluma
Sonoma
Novato
Point Reyes National Seashore
Berkeley
SAN FRANCISCO
Oakland
Fremont
San Mateo
Santa Cruz
199
97
96
3
299
36
44
5
101
1
128
505
116
12
29
680
280
0
50 miles
0
75 km

# Northern California

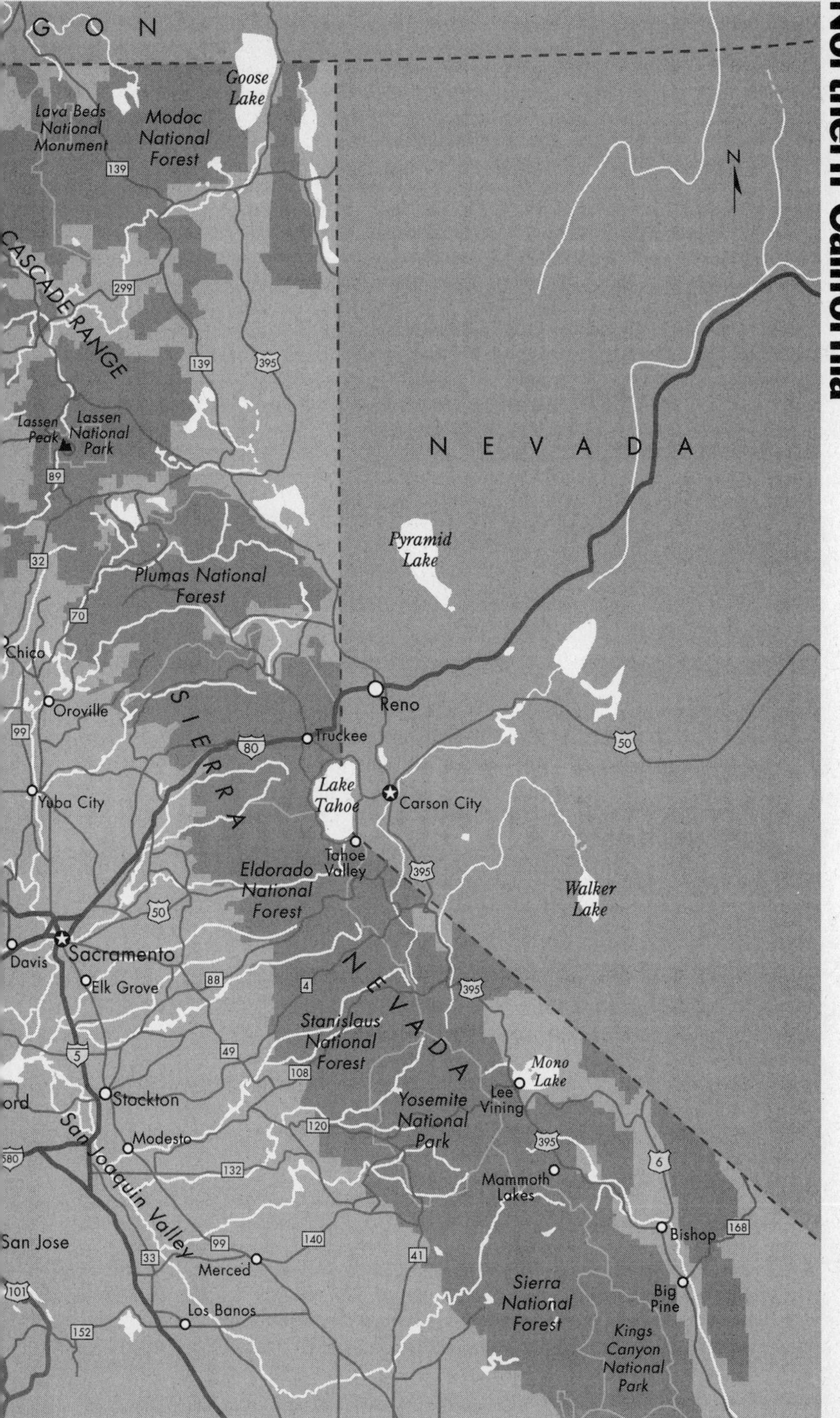

GON
Goose Lake
Lava Beds National Monument
Modoc National Forest
139
CASCADE RANGE
299
139
395
Lassen Peak
Lassen National Park
89
NEVADA
Pyramid Lake
32
Plumas National Forest
70
Chico
Oroville
SIERRA
Reno
99
80
Truckee
50
Lake Tahoe
Carson City
Yuba City
Tahoe Valley
395
Eldorado National Forest
Walker Lake
50
Davis
Sacramento
Elk Grove
88
4
NEVADA
395
Stanislaus National Forest
5
49
108
Mono Lake
Lee Vining
Stockton
Yosemite National Park
ord
San Joaquin Valley
120
Modesto
395
580
132
6
Mammoth Lakes
Bishop
168
San Jose
99
140
33
Merced
41
Big Pine
Sierra National Forest
101
Los Banos
152
Kings Canyon National Park
N

# Southern California

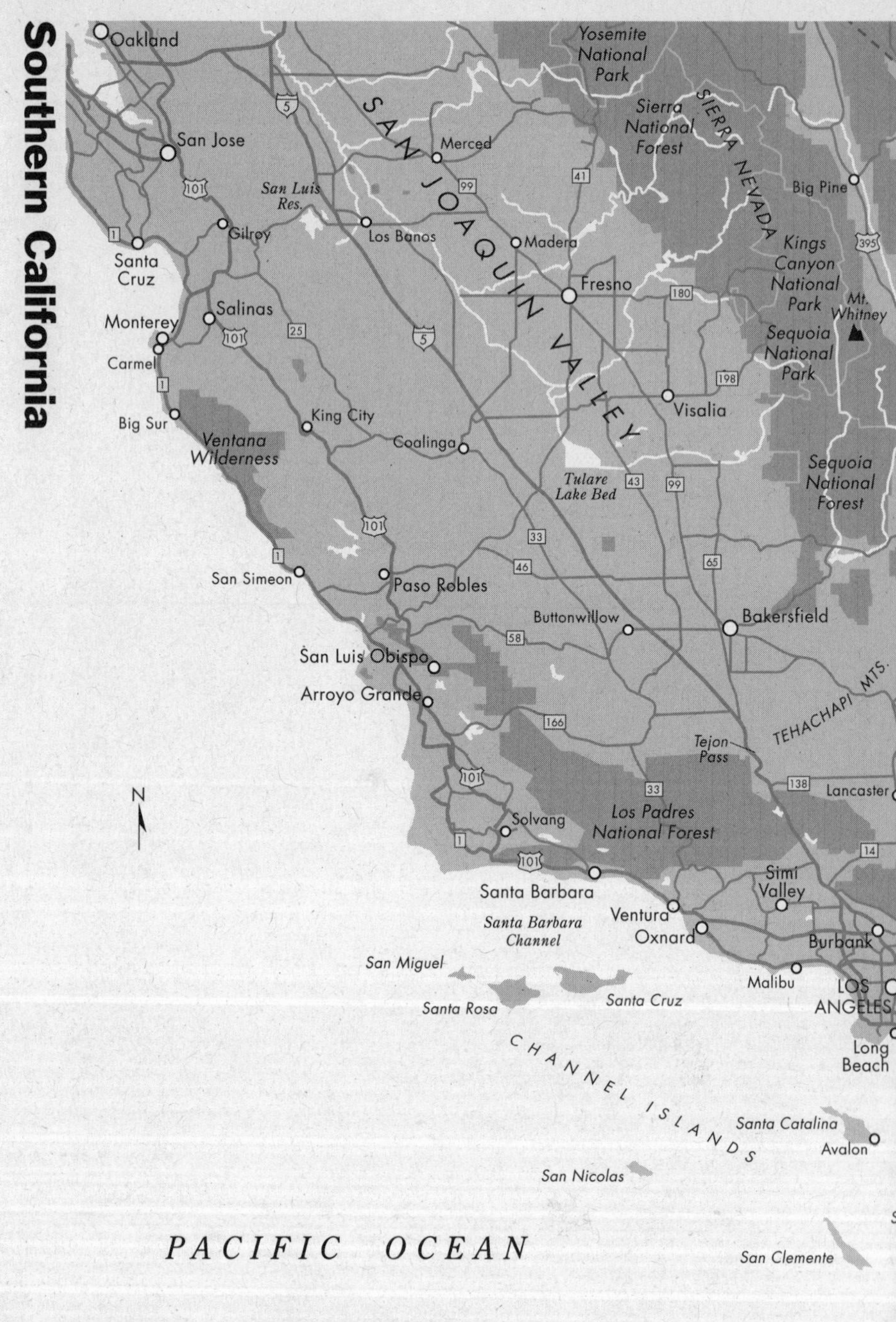

Oakland
San Jose
Santa Cruz
Gilroy
Monterey
Carmel
Salinas
Big Sur
Ventana Wilderness
King City
San Luis Res.
Los Banos
Merced
Madera
Fresno
SAN JOAQUIN VALLEY
Yosemite National Park
Sierra National Forest
SIERRA NEVADA
Big Pine
Kings Canyon National Park
Mt. Whitney
Sequoia National Park
Sequoia National Forest
Visalia
Coalinga
Tulare Lake Bed
San Simeon
Paso Robles
Buttonwillow
Bakersfield
San Luis Obispo
Arroyo Grande
TEHACHAPI MTS.
Tejon Pass
Lancaster
Solvang
Los Padres National Forest
Santa Barbara
Santa Barbara Channel
Ventura
Oxnard
Simi Valley
Burbank
Malibu
LOS ANGELES
Long Beach
San Miguel
Santa Rosa
Santa Cruz
CHANNEL ISLANDS
Santa Catalina
Avalon
San Nicolas
San Clemente
PACIFIC OCEAN
N
0
50 miles
0
75 km

# Southern California

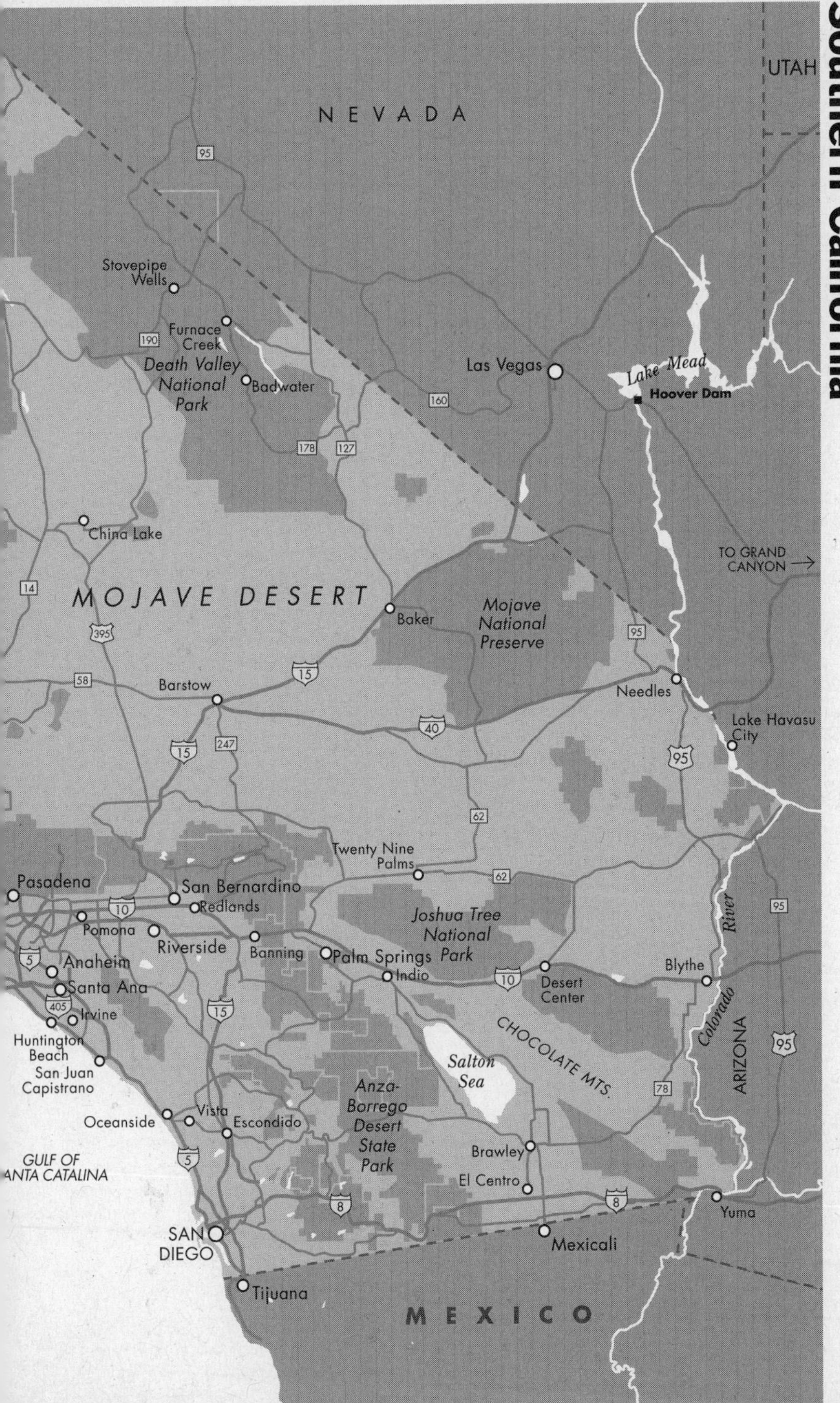

NEVADA
UTAH
95
Stovepipe Wells
Furnace Creek
190
Death Valley National Park
Badwater
Las Vegas
Lake Mead
Hoover Dam
160
178
127
China Lake
14
MOJAVE DESERT
Baker
Mojave National Preserve
TO GRAND CANYON
395
95
58
Barstow
15
Needles
40
Lake Havasu City
15
247
95
62
Twenty Nine Palms
62
Pasadena
San Bernardino
Redlands
10
Pomona
Riverside
Banning
Palm Springs
Joshua Tree National Park
Indio
95
River
5
Anaheim
Santa Ana
405
Irvine
15
10
Desert Center
Blythe
Huntington Beach
San Juan Capistrano
CHOCOLATE MTS.
Salton Sea
Colorado
ARIZONA
95
78
Anza-Borrego Desert State Park
Oceanside
Vista
Escondido
GULF OF
ANTA CATALINA
5
Brawley
El Centro
8
8
Yuma
SAN DIEGO
Mexicali
Tijuana
MEXICO

# Introduction

By Laura Burgardt

**The world sees California through the fun-house lens of Hollywood, and it looks** marvelous. Easy sex, stretch limos bigger than houses, surfers, and new Beatniks with neatly clipped goatees—these images of the state abound in movies and on commercials, TV shows, and music videos. Trends in fashion, sport, and language seem to flow magically out of this state and into the other 49; as a wry Jimmy Carter said in 1977, "Whatever starts in California unfortunately has an inclination to spread.' But like Oz, E.T., and Elvis impersonators, the California of popular conception is based in fantasy rather than fact. Sure, some Californians say "like totally, dude" and resemble a member of the *Melrose Place* cast: Hollywood's clichés have to come from somewhere. But California's population defies stereotypes: This is the most ethnically diverse state in the country, projected soon after the year 2000 to become the first in the nation with a minority of European-Americans.

Arrive in California expecting one giant beach and you'll be shocked. The state's terrain is as varied as its people, from the arid desert of Death Valley, the lowest point in the United States at 282 feet below sea level, to the jagged spine of the Sierra Nevada, with snow-covered peaks reaching higher than 12,000 feet. Almost the entire region north and east of Sacramento, the state capital, is national forest, where towering thousand-year-old redwood trees form cathedral-like glens. Near the Oregon border, Mt. Shasta is either a dormant volcano—one in a Pacific Rim chain that also includes Lava Beds National Monument and Lassen Volcanic National Park—or a mystical world power point, depending on who you ask. The sun-warmed Central Valley has been pressed into service as the nation's breadbasket; mile after mile of farmlands and orchards line the highways running north from Mexico. To the east, the national parks of the Sierra Nevada hold bubbling hot springs, strange rock formations, and fields of golden poppies. There's no way to absorb the whole state in one trip, though you'll probably wish you could. Believe it or not, at some point in your journey you're likely to stumble upon a vista so stunning you won't know whether to shout or cry. It's that beautiful.

The legend of California's beauty traces all the way back to Spanish explorers who named the land after an earthly paradise described in a popular 16th-century novel. Spain didn't settle California until 1769, when Father Junípero Serra built the first of 21 missions extending from San Diego to Sonoma. But the state remained on the fringes of the New Spain and later Mexico; in 1823 the settler population, mostly *rancheros,* numbered only 3,200. A second legend—gold—would usher in the first "boom" period in California history. The United States claimed the territory from Mexico in 1849, just weeks after carpenter James Marshall discovered the precious nuggets in the foothills of the Sierra Nevada. The news spread fast, and more than 100,000 men descended on the state, tossing social conventions right out the window in favor of boozin', whorin', and grubbin' for gold. The extravagant spending of miners who hit pay dirt helped to make cities out of tin-roof settlements like San Francisco, and the completion of the Transcontinental Railroad in 1869 made it easier for the rest of the country to come out and join in the free-for-all.

The development of the southern half of the state was not nearly as sudden as the north's Gold Rush. Using an "if-you-build-it-they-will-come" mentality, a rail line was extended to Los Angeles in 1876. Railroad companies used every available marketing strategy—from pamphlets to free lunches and brass-band concerts—to convince speculators and tourists that the desolate "cow counties" had something to offer. The Rush of the 1880s was on, this time not for metal but for golden sun and citrus. Forty years later, a second southern boom involved a similar concept, but with interstate freeways and a wider range of industrial giants. The advertising campaign—playing up Southern California's Spanish past and using images of an exotic Mediterranean-style paradise—caused outsiders to confuse Southern California with the whole state; even today, the motion picture industry happily promotes the "sunny California" image—and the world has bought it, big time.

In the minds of millions of Americans, California is still the place where you can discard the baggage of the past and go about the earnest business of re-creating yourself. Just because you come from a family of Southern Baptists (or multimillionaires, or circus performers) doesn't mean you can't move three thousand miles away and embrace Sufism or take up method acting. The motion picture industry is an obvious draw, but it's almost matched in income potential by Silicon Valley, an area just south of San Francisco where computer giants IBM and Apple were born. California's promise has lured a cast of thousands, which explains the decades-old joke defining "Old Settlers" as anyone's who's been in the state for more than two years.

The cult of the individual has reached its apogee in California, and the body is its temple. Nowhere else do people devote so much energy to maintaining their physical and emotional selves, whether they're running up and down mountains or ingesting awful-tasting things that are supposed to make them smarter, fitter, or more in tune with their inner child. If these measures fail to add the desired muscle tone or take off the unwanted pounds, there's always a trip to the plastic surgeon.

But California is not a seamlessly perfect state, physically or otherwise. The state has been battered by drought, fires, floods, earthquakes, and even flies, which have caused over $10 million in crop damage annually in the Central Valley since 1993. These disasters come as California crawls out of a recession, aggravated by defense-industry downsizing that is expected to continue for the next few years at the rate of 30,000 jobs annually. Economists are forecasting renewed growth, but no one's taking any chances: For the first time, Americans leaving the state outnumber those coming in. However, immigrants streaming across the southern border, and from every other imaginable country, more than make up the difference. Many residents, fighting to keep their piece of a shrinking pie, are looking to anti-immigrant laws to "Save Our State" despite xenophobic intonations.

Californians aren't just blaming the immigrants: There seems to be enough blame to go around for everyone. Last year Pete Wilson, governor and presidential hopeful, convinced the University of California to scrap its 30-year-old affirmative action program, and an initiative on the 1996 ballot proposes to ban racial preferences in all public institutions. The state already spends more on prisons than on higher education, and despite only a minor increase in the crime rate, a "get-tough-on-crime" attitude has seized California. The 1994 "three-strikes-and-you're-out" law, which gives mandatory life sentences to third-time felons, will add more than 200,000 inmates in the next 10 years to what is already the world's third-largest prison system (China's is first, the United States' second).

As if the border gates and prison walls weren't enough, many Californians would probably fence off their whole city, or more: The rivalry between Northern and Southern California has gone so far as an initiative (in 1992) to split the state in half. Though the measure was largely symbolic, the sparring continues. Nowhere is the split between north and south more pronounced than in politics. The south is one of the most conservative regions in the nation, the rock on which Reagan and Nixon built their presidencies. The north, on the other hand, has a long history of radicalism, from hippies and student protesters and Black Panthers to the election of the country's first openly gay city official in San Francisco.

Despite a growing sense of pessimism, Californians stay and tourists come to this state precisely because it offers everything imaginable—and then some. This is where both humanity and nature show off all their possibilities, whether dreadful or breathtakingly beautiful. So if you can afford it, rent a car, rip off the roof, pop in some tunes, and hit the road. Soon you'll find yourself with the same rapturous look you see on the faces of many long-term residents. It's a look that comes from the realization that amid all this beauty little really matters, that it's okay to freak out and lose your shit, and that, yes, you might even discover yourself here.

# BASICS 1

By Laura Burgardt, Danna Harman, Sonia Perel, Alan Covington Phulps, and Michael Rozendal

**If you've ever traveled with anyone before, you know the two types of people in the** world: the planners and the nonplanners. You also know that travel brings out the very worst in both groups: Left to their own devices, the planners will have you goose-stepping from attraction to attraction on a cultural blitzkrieg, while the nonplanners will invariably miss the flight, the bus, and the point. This Basics chapter offers you a middle ground, providing enough information to help plan your trip without saddling you with an itinerary or invasion plan. Keep in mind that companies go out of business, prices inevitably go up, and sooner or later you're going to miss a train connection. If it's predictability you want, stay home.

## Planning Your Trip

### WHEN TO GO

If *Baywatch* taught you everything you know about California's climate, you're probably going to be disappointed. Summer temperatures in Southern California do hover pleasantly in the 80s, and the inland areas do see their share of 100° days; but the northern coasts only rarely see temperatures higher than 70°, and winter temperatures all over the state can dip below 50°. The litmus test to determine seasons: If it's raining, it must be winter. Summers are very dry and hot in many parts of the state, but the scenic coastal towns are often shrouded with fog in these months. Mid- to late spring and early to mid-fall—when fog gives way to sun, tourist hordes abate, and prices plummet—are the optimum times to travel along the coast.

**FESTIVALS** Californians will celebrate anything, anytime, anyplace, so don't be surprised by ridiculous festivals like the North Coast's **World Championship Crab Race** (Crescent City, tel. 707/464–3174). Ethnicity, culture, and diversity are among the more celebrated things in these parts. Only the major events are highlighted below; look in individual chapters for smaller festivals. Call the California Division of Tourism (tel. 800/862–2543) for a free copy of the Events Calendar, and check out *The Festival Hopper's Guide to California and Nevada* (Creative Chaos, $13), by Darrin and Julie Craig, which lists more than 450 affairs.

JANUARY 1: The **Tournament of Roses Parade** attracts thousands; people sleep overnight on the streets of Pasadena (near Los Angeles) in order to claim a prime slab of concrete. Their efforts hardly seem heroic compared to those of the glue-gun wielders who affix more than 25 million flowers to the mammoth floats. For more information, contact Pasadena's Tournament of Roses Headquarters (391 S. Orange Grove Blvd., Pasadena 91184, tel. 818/449–4100).

JANUARY–APRIL: January marks the start of the **whale-watching** season, which takes place all along the coast, as gray whales migrate from Arctic feeding grounds in order to mate and calve off the coast of Baja California. The best spot to watch from land is the Point Reyes National Seashore (tel. 415/663–1200) north of San Francisco, but the view from a boat is even better. The California Division of Tourism (*see below*) offers a list of tour operators from Fort Bragg to San Diego.

FEBRUARY: **Chinese New Year** celebrations in San Francisco's Chinatown begin in mid-February and culminate with the big parade on March 2. For info, contact the Chinese Chamber of Commerce (730 Sacramento St., San Francisco 94108, tel. 415/982–3000). Los Angeles also sees the new year kick-off with a parade; contact L.A.'s Chinese Chamber of Commerce (977E N. Broadway, Los Angeles 90012, tel. 213/617–0396) for more info.

MARCH: Don't forget Hollywood's prom night, the **Academy Awards** ceremony, held in downtown Los Angeles (usually the last week of March). You can't get in without an invitation, but you can freely gawk at the movie stars from bleachers set up outside. Contact the Academy (tel. 310/247–3000).

MARCH–JULY: Catch the **Grunion Run** if you're in Southern California. The nighttime fish-breeding orgy allows voyeurs to observe wiggling, ecstatic grunions, the only fish species that comes ashore to mate. Not all Southern California beaches turn on the grunions, so check with state beaches or the Cabrillo Marine Museum (tel. 310/548–7563) in San Pedro, which sponsors grunion-peeping programs.

APRIL–JUNE: The **Renaissance Pleasure Faire** (tel. 800/52–FAIRE) is a gathering of fun-loving Elizabethans (suspiciously similar in appearance to modern day Deadheads), who re-create Shakespearean England in San Bernardino. For Northern California dates—usually later in the year—contact the main office (tel. 909/880–6211).

MAY: California's huge Latino and Chicano communities celebrate **Cinco de Mayo,** which commemorates Mexico's victory over the French at Puebla in 1862. Festivities pop up statewide on the weekends surrounding May 5; the most impressive celebrations take place in San Francisco, Los Angeles, and San Diego.

Toward the end of the month, San Francisco's **Bay to Breakers** features thousands of athletes and comedians who show up in running shorts, G-strings, or wacky costumes to run from, you guessed it, the bay side of the city to the ocean (about 7½ mi). You can get information from the San Francisco Examiner Promotion Department (Box 429200, San Francisco 94142, tel. 415/777–7771).

JUNE: Santa Barbara's **Summer Solstice Celebration** (tel. 805/965–3396) gives new meaning to the word *counterculture*. The festivities, held each year on the Saturday closest to June 21, feature a parade with no motorized vehicles whatsoever. Members of the human train dress every which way (including loose) and act truly strange.

The **San Francisco Lesbian, Gay, Bisexual, Transgender Pride Celebration** (San Francisco Pride for short) in San Francisco and the **Los Angeles Gay and Lesbian Pride Parade** in West Hollywood kick off what has been officially allocated Gay Pride month. Both are rollicking bashes with costumes and floats. Contact Gay Freedom Day Parade (Box 513, San Francisco 94114, tel. 415/864–3733) or Los Angeles Gay and Lesbian Pride Parade (7925 Santa Monica Blvd., West Hollywood 90046, tel. 213/656–6553).

JULY: The **Gilroy Garlic Festival** (Box 2311, Gilroy 95021, tel. 408/842–1625), near the end of the month, is a huge, aromatic celebration and mass gorging on one of the tastiest plants around.

JULY–AUGUST: During the **International Surf Festival,** amateurs shred on raspy waves along Los Angeles's South Bay beaches. Contact the L.A. County Department of Harbors and Beaches (tel. 310/305–9546) for information.

SEPTEMBER: Held at the end of the month, the **Valley of the Moon Vintage Festival** is the state's oldest celebration of wine-making. Drink, stomp grapes, and be merry. Contact the Vintage Festival Association (Box 652, Sonoma 95476, tel. 707/996–2109).

OCTOBER: To prepare for Halloween, Half Moon Bay sponsors the **Art and Pumpkin Festival** (tel. 415/726–9652) the third weekend of October, with crafts and the Great Pumpkin Parade. Linus never misses it.

OCTOBER 31: Traditionally, this huge, raucous, queers-only **Halloween** party has taken place on the closed-off streets of San Francisco's Castro district, but at press time, a change of venue was being considered due to overcrowding and excessive gawking. Check local papers or ask around as the holiday approaches, and prepare to dress to the nines.

NOVEMBER: The creator of Pasadena's **Doo Dah Parade** (Box 2392, Pasadena 91102, tel. 818/449–3689) freely admits that this Rose Parade spoof was conceived over a few beers with crestfallen friends who weren't allowed to participate in the respected flower fest. Today the Doo Dah has grown to alarmingly oddball proportions.

DECEMBER: Many coastal cities have **Christmas Boat Parades,** with tugboats, yachts, and military ships festively lit to usher in the holiday. Newport Beach's scenic nautical parade runs for six nights before Christmas in the harbor. Contact the Newport Chamber of Commerce (1470 Jamboree Rd., Newport Beach 92660, tel. 714/644–8211).

## TOURIST OFFICES

Aside from offering the usual glossy tourist brochures, state and local tourist offices can answer general questions about travel in their areas or refer you to other organizations. If you write for information, you may want to request brochures on specialized interests, such as boating, horseback riding, or biking, which may not be included in a generic information package. The **California Division of Tourism** mails out a tourist package that includes general information on various sights and activities throughout the state. *801 K St., Suite 1600, Sacramento 95814, tel. 916/322–2881 or 800/862–2543 to order package.*

**OFFICES ABROAD** Foreign visitors who want some "official" tourist information about the United States can check with the **U.S. Travel and Tourism Administration (USTTA)** (Dept. of Commerce, 14th and Constitution Aves. NW, Washington, DC 20230, tel. 202/482–3811). The USTTA has offices in Canada (Suite 602, 480 University Ave., Toronto, Ont. M5G 1V2, tel. 416/595–5082; 1095 W. Pender St., 20th floor, Vancouver, BC postal code V6E 2M6, tel. 604/685–1930), the United Kingdom (Box 170, Ashford, Kent TN24 0ZX, tel. 0171/495–4466), and Australia (APO GPO Box 478, Sydney 2001, tel. 02/233–4055).

## BUDGET TRAVEL ORGANIZATIONS

**Council on International Educational Exchange (Council)** is a private, nonprofit organization that administers work, volunteer, academic, and professional programs worldwide. Its travel division, **Council Travel,** is a full-service travel agency specializing in student, youth, and budget travel. They offer discounted airfares, rail passes, accommodations, guidebooks, budget tours, and travel gear. They also issue the ISIC, GO25, and ITIC identity cards (*see* Student ID Cards, *below*), as well as Hostelling International cards. Forty-one Council Travel offices serve the budget traveler in the United States, and there are about a dozen overseas. Council also puts out a variety of publications, including the free *Student Travels* magazine, a gold mine of travel tips (including information on work- and study-abroad opportunities). *205 E. 42nd St., New York, NY 10017, tel. 212/661–1414.*

**Educational Travel Center (ETC)** books low-cost flights to destinations within the continental United States and around the world. Their best deals are on flights leaving the Midwest, especially Chicago. ETC also issues Hostelling International cards. For details request their free brochure, *Taking Off. 438 N. Frances St., Madison, WI 53703, tel. 608/256–5551.*

**STA Travel,** the world's largest travel organization catering to students and young people, has over 100 offices worldwide and offers low-price airfares to destinations around the globe, as well as rail passes, car rentals, tours, you name it. STA issues the ISIC and the GO25 youth cards (*see* Student ID Cards, *below*), both of which prove eligibility for student airfares and other travel discounts. Call 800/777–0122 or the nearest STA office for more information.

**Student Flights, Inc.** sells rail passes, travel guide books, and ISE cards (*see* Student ID Cards, *below*); they specialize in student and faculty airfares. *5010 E. Shea Blvd., Scottsdale, AZ 85254, tel. 602/951–1177 or 800/255–8000.*

**Y's Way International.** This network of YMCA overnight centers offers low-cost accommodations (average overnight rate of $26) in the United States to travelers of all ages. Their booklet, "The Y's Way," details locations, reservation policies, and package tours. *224 E. 47th St., New York, NY 10017, tel. 212/308–2899.*

**Hostelling International (HI),** formerly the IYHF, is the umbrella group for a number of national youth hostel associations. HI offers single-sex dorm-style beds ("couples" rooms and family accommodations are available at certain hostels) and self-service kitchen facilities at nearly 5,000 locations in more than 70 countries around the world. Membership in any HI national hostel association (*see below*), open to travelers of all ages, allows you to stay in HI-affiliated hostels at member rates (about $10–$25 a night). Members also have priority if the hostel is full and are eligible for discounts on rail and bus travel around the world.

A one-year membership runs about $25 for adults (renewal $20) and $10 for those under 18. A one-night guest membership is about $3. Family memberships are available for $35, and a lifetime membership will set you back $250. Handbooks listing current hostels and discounts are available from some national associations; one covers Europe and the Mediterranean, while another covers Africa, the Americas, Asia, and Australasia ($13.95 each). *733 15th St. NW, Suite 840, Washington, DC 20005, tel. 202/783–6161 or 800/444–6111.*

National branches of Hostelling International include **Hostelling International–American Youth Hostels (HI–AYH)** (733 15th St., Suite 840, Washington, DC 20005, tel. 202/783–6161 or

## Council Travel Offices in the United States

***ARIZONA:** Tempe (tel. 602/966–3544). **CALIFORNIA:** Berkeley (tel. 510/848–8604), Davis (tel. 916/752–2285), La Jolla (tel. 619/452–0630), Long Beach (tel. 310/598–3338), Los Angeles (tel. 310/208–3551), Palo Alto (tel. 415/325–3888), San Diego (tel. 619/270–6401), San Francisco (tel. 415/421–3473 or 415/566–6222), Santa Barbara (tel. 805/562–8080). **COLORADO:** Boulder (tel. 303/447–8101), Denver (tel. 303/571–0630). **CONNECTICUT:** New Haven (tel. 203/562–5335). **FLORIDA:** Miami (tel. 305/670–9261). **GEORGIA:** Atlanta (tel. 404/377–9997). **ILLINOIS:** Chicago (tel. 312/951–0585), Evanston (tel. 708/475–5070). **INDIANA:** Bloomington (tel. 812/330–1600). **LOUISIANA:** New Orleans (tel. 504/866–1767). **MASSACHUSETTS:** Amherst (tel. 413/256–1261), Boston (tel. 617/266–1926), Cambridge (tel. 617/497–1497 or 617/225–2555). **MICHIGAN:** Ann Arbor (tel. 313/998–0200). **MINNESOTA:** Minneapolis (tel. 612/379–2323). **NEW YORK:** New York (tel. 212/661–1450, 212/666–4177, or 212/254–2525). **NORTH CAROLINA:** Chapel Hill (tel. 919/942–2334). **OHIO:** Columbus (tel. 614/294–8696). **OREGON:** Portland (tel. 503/228–1900). **PENNSYLVANIA:** Philadelphia (tel. 215/382–0343), Pittsburgh (tel. 412/683–1881). **RHODE ISLAND:** Providence (tel. 401/331–5810). **TEXAS:** Austin (tel. 512/472–4931), Dallas (tel. 214/363–9941). **UTAH:** Salt Lake City (tel. 801/582–5840). **WASHINGTON:** Seattle (tel. 206/632–2448 or 206/329–4567). **WASHINGTON, DC** (tel. 202/337–6464). For U.S. cities not listed, call tel. 800/2–COUNCIL.*

800/444–6111); **Hostelling International–Canada (HI–C)** (400-205 Catherine St., Ottawa, Ont. K2P 1C3, tel. 613/237–7884 or 800/663-5777); **Youth Hostel Association of England and Wales (YHA)** (Trevelyan House, 8 St. Stephen's Hill, St. Albans, Herts. AL1 2DY, England, tel. 01727/855–215); **Australian Youth Hostels Association (YHA)** (Level 3, 10 Mallett St., Camperdown, New South Wales 2050, tel. 02/565–1699); and **Youth Hostels Association of New Zealand (YHA)** (Box 436, Christchurch 1, tel. 03/379–9970).



## STUDENT ID CARDS

Students traveling in California should not expect big discounts from student ID cards—except possibly on air travel. Still, it's a good thing to have along for those occasional discounts on admission prices, bus travel, and club cover charges.

The **International Student Identity Card (ISIC)** entitles students to special fares on local transportation and discounts at museums, theaters, sports events, and other attractions. Buy the card in the U.S. (for a mere $18) and you'll receive $3,000 in emergency medical coverage at no extra charge! But wait—there's more: Limited hospital coverage is also included in the one-low-price. Buy now and receive, as a bonus, access to a 24-hour international, toll-free hotline for assistance in medical, legal, and financial emergencies. Too good to be true, you say? If

### *STA Offices*

***UNITED STATES • CALIFORNIA:** Berkeley (tel. 510/642–3000), Los Angeles (tel. 213/934–8722), San Francisco (tel. 415/391–8407), Santa Monica (tel. 310/394–5126), Westwood (tel. 310/824–1574). **MASSACHUSETTS:** Boston (tel. 617/266–6014), Cambridge (tel. 617/576–4623). **NEW YORK:** Columbia University (tel. 212/854–2224), West Village (tel. 212/627–3111). **PENNSYLVANIA:** Philadelphia (tel. 215/382–2928). **WASHINGTON:** Seattle (tel. 206/633–5000). **WASHINGTON, DC** (tel. 202/887–0912).*

***INTERNATIONAL • AUSTRALIA:** Adelaide (tel. 08/223–2426); Brisbane (tel. 07/221–9388), Cairns (tel. 070/314199), Darwin (tel. 089/412955), Melbourne (tel. 03/349–2411), Perth (tel. 09/227–7569), Sydney (tel. 02/212–1255). **AUSTRIA:** Graz (tel. 0316/32482), Innsbruck (tel. 0512/588997), Linz (tel. 0732/775893), Salzburg (tel. 0662/883252), Vienna (tel. 0222/401480 or 0222/5050–1280). **DENMARK:** Copenhagen (tel. 031/35–88–44). **FRANCE:** Paris (tel. 01/43–25–00–76). **GERMANY:** Berlin (tel. 030/281–6741), Frankfurt (tel. 069/430191 or 069/703035), Hamburg (tel. 040/442363). **GREECE:** Athens (tel. 01/32–21–267). **ITALY:** Bologna (tel. 051/261802), Florence (tel. 055/289721), Genoa (tel. 010/564366), Milan (tel. 02/5830–4121), Naples (tel. 081/552–7960), Rome (tel. 06/467–9291), Venice (tel. 041/520–5660). **NETHERLANDS:** Amsterdam (tel. 020/626–2557). **NEW ZEALAND:** Auckland (tel. 09/309–9995), Christchurch (tel. 03/379–9098), Wellington (tel. 04/385–0561). **SPAIN:** Barcelona (tel. 03/487–9546), Madrid (tel. 01/541–7372). **SWEDEN:** Göteborg (tel. 031/774–0025). **SWITZERLAND:** Lausanne (tel. 0121/617–58–11), Zurich (tel. 01/297–11–11). **TURKEY:** Istanbul (tel. 01/252–59–21). **UNITED KINGDOM:** London (tel. 0171/937–9962).*

you've bought this book, it probably is: Medical coverage doesn't apply within the U.S. (*see* fine print). On the bright side, even domestic travelers still get access to the 24-hour hotline. Cards are available through Council Travel or STA in the United States; in Canada, **Travel CUTS** (187 College St., Toronto, Ont. M5T 1P7, tel. 416/979–2406) issues cards for C$15. In the United Kingdom, students with valid university IDs can purchase the ISIC at any student union or student-travel company.

**Go 25,** issued to travelers ages 12 to 25, provides services and benefits similar to those of the ISIC. The $10 card is available from those same organizations that sell its aforementioned student-only counterpart. When applying, bring a passport-size photo and your passport as proof of your age. The **International Student Exchange Card (ISE),** available to students and faculty members for $18, offers comparable benefits. They also give you a $10 discount on flights within the U.S. and a $50 discount on many international flights. *5010 E. Shea Blvd., Suite A104, Scottsdale, AZ 85254, tel. 602/951–1177 or 800/255–8000, fax 602/951–1216.*

## MONEY

**HOW MUCH IT WILL COST** California is one of the country's most desirable places to live. Unfortunately this means that the state has one of the highest costs of living in the nation. After transportation (car rental, while convenient, is not cheap; long-distance bus travel, while less expensive, is neither cheap nor convenient), food and lodging will probably be the biggest expenses. If you buy food in markets and camp or stay in hostels, expect to spend $20–$30 per person daily; staying in hotels and eating in restaurants is difficult to swing in California without dropping upwards of $45 each day. Luckily, cheap nighttime entertainment is easy to come by. Many of the more low-key bars have DJ dancing or even live music with no cover, or will maybe ask for $2 or $3 at the door.

**TRAVELER'S CHECKS** They look like play money, have the purchasing power of real money, and—best of all—can be replaced if lost or stolen. To be reimbursed, you *must* produce the purchase agreement and a record of the checks' serial numbers, so it's a good idea to keep those documents separate from your checks.

**American Express** card members can purchase traveler's checks through many banks (1% commission) or order them by phone (free for gold-card holders, 1% commission for green-card holders). AmEx also issues **Traveler's Cheques for Two,** which can be signed and used by either you or your companion. Lost or stolen checks are often refunded in as little as 24 hours. At their Travel Services offices (about 1,500 around the world) you can buy and cash traveler's checks, write a personal check in exchange for traveler's checks, report lost or stolen checks, exchange foreign currency, and pick up mail. *Tel. 800/221–7282 in the U.S. and Canada.*

*If you don't have an AmEx gold card, you can still get American Express Traveler's Checks free with an AAA membership. Talk to the cashier at your local AAA office (*see box *A Driver's Dream,* below*).*

The following brands (and occasional others) can be exchanged for cash at banks, select hotels, tourist offices, American Express offices, or currency-exchange offices, usually for a 1%–2% commission. **Citicorp** (tel. 800/645–6556 in the U.S. or 813/623–1709 collect outside the U.S.) traveler's checks are available from Citibank and other banks worldwide. For 45 days from date of check purchase, purchasers have access to the 24-hour International S.O.S. Assistance Hotline and an emergency message center. **MasterCard International** (tel. 800/223–7373 in the U.S. or 609/987–7300 collect from outside the U.S.) traveler's checks are offered through banks, credit unions, and foreign-exchange booths. **Visa** (tel. 800/227–6811 in the U.S. and Canada or 813/623–1709 collect from outside the U.S.) traveler's checks are available in U.S. dollars, British pounds, and various other currencies.

**GETTING MONEY ON THE ROAD** Virtually all U.S. banks belong to a network of **ATMs** (automated teller machines), which gobble up bank cards and spit out cash 24 hours a day. ATMs can increasingly be found in convenience stores and supermarkets, where you can pay for the purchase with the card and get cash back. A **Visa** or **MasterCard** can also be used to access cash through certain ATMs (provided you have a PIN for the card), but fees for this service are usually higher than bank-card fees. If an ATM machine is not available, cash advances from Visa and MasterCard can still be had—you just have to actually go *in* the bank. Commission for this handy-dandy service varies from about 3% to almost 10%.

**American Express** cardholders can cash personal checks up to $1,000 at American Express offices. **Express Cash** allows AmEx cardholders to withdraw up to $1,000 in a seven-day period (21 days outside the U.S.) from their personal checking accounts (gold cardholders can receive up to $2,500). Each transaction carries a 2% fee, with a minimum charge of $2 and a maximum of $6. Apply for a PIN and link your accounts at least two to three weeks before departure. Call 800/528–4800 for an application.

**GETTING MONEY FROM HOME** Provided there is money at home to be had, there are at least three ways to get it. (1) Have it sent through a large **commercial bank** that has a branch in the town where you're staying. Unless you have an account with that bank, though, you'll have to initiate the transfer at your own bank, and the process will be even slower and more expensive than usual. (2) An **American Express *MoneyGram*℠** (tel. 800/926–9400 or 303/980–3340 collect from overseas) can be a dream come true if you can convince someone back home to go to an American Express MoneyGram agent and fill out the necessary forms. You don't have to be an AmEx cardholder to use this service: Simply hand over your credit card (for transfers under $1,000) or lay down cash and, as quick as 10 minutes later, it's ready to be picked up. Fees vary according to the amount of money sent but average 3%–10%. You have to show ID when picking up the money. (3) Have funds sent through **Western Union** (tel. 800/325–6000). MasterCard and Visa holders can have money sent up to the card's credit limit. If not, have someone take cash, a certified cashier's check, or a healthy MasterCard or Visa to a Western Union office. The money will reach its destination in minutes but may not be available for several more hours or days, depending on the whim of local authorities.

## WHAT TO PACK

As little as possible. Besides the usual suspects—clothes, toiletries, camera, a Walkman, and a good book—bring along a day pack or some type of smaller receptacle for stuff; it'll come in handy not only for day excursions but also for those places where you plan to stay for only one or two days. You can check heavy, cumbersome bags at the train or bus station (or leave it at your motel or hostel) and just carry the essentials while you are out and about.

**CLOTHING** Smart—and not terribly fashion-conscious—travelers will bring two outfits and learn to wash clothes by hand regularly. At the very least, bring comfortable, easy-to-clean clothes. Californians are, by and large, casual dressers. If you're traveling in summer, pack one pair of pants and a heavy sweatshirt for colder nights (especially in the mountains and along the coast). Pack a raincoat and/or umbrella for the inevitable. If you plan to spend most of your

### *Making the Most of Your Parents' Credit Card*

***Even if you have no job, no credit, no cards, and no respect, you can still tap into services offered by the Visa Assistance Center if one of your parents has a Visa Gold or Business card and you are a dependent of 22 years or less and at least 100 miles from home. Write down the card number in a safe, memorable place and call the center for emergency cash service, emergency ticket replacement and lost-luggage assistance, medical and legal assistance, and an emergency message service. Helpful, multilingual personnel await your call 24 hours a day, seven days a week. In the U.S. call 800/847–2911; from overseas call 410/581—9994 collect.***

time outdoors, a fleece jacket and a nylon shell to keep out the wind are indispensable. Shoes can be your biggest friend or your worst foe: A sturdy pair of walking shoes or hiking boots plus another, spare pair of shoes will allow you to switch off and give your barkin' dogs a rest. Consider taking a pair of heavy-duty sport sandals like Tevas—you can bike, hike, or walk in water in them, and they'll protect your feet on communal shower floors.

## WOMEN TRAVELERS

Unfortunately, not everyone is as open-minded about independent women as they should be—solo women travelers often have to put on a tough, surly exterior to avoid unwelcome advances. Hitchhiking alone is a bad idea, and women who stop to pick up roadside hitchers should also exercise caution. Though large cities like San Francisco and Los Angeles are full of women's organizations and resource networks, keep in mind that the liberal bent of the state's urban centers goes only so far. Physical and verbal harassment definitely occur here, particularly if you stand out.

**PUBLICATIONS** For a complete listing of women's periodicals, presses, and cafés, try the ***Directory of Women's Media*** ($30), published by the National Council for Research on Women (530 Broadway, 10th floor, New York, NY 10012, tel. 212/274–0730). Major travel publications for women include ***Women Travel: Adventures, Advice, and Experience*** ($12.95), published by Prentice Hall and available at bookstores. Over 70 countries receive some sort of coverage in the form of journal entries and short articles. As far as practical travel information goes, it offers few details on prices, phone numbers, and addresses. Thalia Zepatos's ***A Journey of One's Own*** ($13), available at most bookstores, is fun to read but has little information on specific countries or regions. Still, it's a good resource for general travel information.

**ORGANIZATIONS** **Women Welcome Women (WWW)** is a nonprofit organization aimed at bringing together women of all nationalities. WWW can get you in touch with women around the globe who are interested in every variety of women's issues. *Contact F. Alexander, 8/A Chestnut Ave., High Wycombe, Buckinghamshire HP11 1DJ, England, tel. 01494/439–481.*

In Los Angeles, the **Commission on Assaults Against Women** (6043 Hollywood Blvd., tel. 213/462–1281) provides a 24-hour rape-and-battery hotline (tel. 310/392–8381). Call **S.F. Women Against Rape** (tel. 415/861–2024 or 415/647–7273 for 24-hour hotline) if you're in San Francisco and need help. The **Women's Needs Center** (1825 Haight St., San Francisco 94117, tel. 415/487–5607) and the **West Side Women's Health Center** (1705 Ocean Park Blvd., Santa Monica 90405, tel. 310/450–2191) are medical clinics for women. The **Young Women's Christian Association (YWCA)** (620 Sutter St., San Francisco, tel. 415/775–6502; 3345 Wilshire Blvd., Suite 300, Los Angeles, tel. 213/365–2991) offers social-service programs and accommodation referrals for women.

## TRAVELERS OF COLOR

California has a rich mix of ethnicities, but everyone in this so-called melting pot does not always live in harmony—as attested by the 1992 riots in Los Angeles. Cities tend to be divided into ethnic sections where all are not always welcome. Check the white pages of the phone book for organizations that cater to the needs of a specific ethnic group, or check with local universities for relevant student organizations.

The **National Association for the Advancement of Colored People (NAACP)** has its western regional office in Los Angeles (4929 Wilshire Blvd., Suite 360, 90010, tel. 213/931–6331). The **Black Women's Resource Center** (518 17th St., Suite 202, Oakland 94612, tel. 510/763–9501) offers information and referrals and publishes a newsletter on issues of interest to African-American women. The **United States African-American Chamber of Commerce** (117 Broadway, Suite 119, Oakland, tel. 510/444–5741) and the **Los Angeles Black Chamber of Commerce** (3860H Amberly Dr., Inglewood, tel. 310/412–1991) provide lists of businesses operated by African Americans. **La Raza Information Referral Center** (474 Valencia St., Suite 100, San Francisco, tel. 415/863–0764) provides all types of referrals and other service information for Latinos. Similar information in Los Angeles is provided by the **Chicano Resource**

**Center** (4801 E. 3rd St., East L.A. Library, tel. 213/223–2475). Japanese travelers may want to contact the **Japanese Community Culture Center of Northern California** (1840 Sutter St., San Francisco, tel. 415/567–5505). In the San Francisco Bay Area, you'll find the **Oakland Chinese Community Council** (168 11th St., tel. 510/839–2022), which tracks local public affairs. In L.A., the **Los Angeles Chinese Chamber of Commerce** (977 N. Broadway, Suite E, tel. 213/617–0396) provides information on Chinese cultural events and can refer callers to other service organizations.



## GAY AND LESBIAN TRAVELERS

Though gay bashing definitely occurs even on the streets of San Francisco, gay men and women enjoy a certain amount of freedom in California. San Francisco and Los Angeles have large gay communities served by many organizations, bookstores, cafés, and the like. Publications on gay issues and organizations include the *Sentinel,* a statewide weekly with a political focus; and the *Advocate,* a well-known national bimonthly gay magazine. Many cities have community centers that serve as meeting places; check phone books and individual chapters in this book. Palm Springs and Guerneville, in particular, are popular destinations for gay visitors. The **Gay Switchboard** (tel. 510/841–6224) is a referral service in the San Francisco Bay Area that provides crisis support and information on social events and emergency housing.

The **International Gay Travel Association (IGTA)** (Box 4974, Key West, FL 33041, tel. 800/448–8550) is a nonprofit organization with worldwide listings of travel agencies, gay-friendly hotels, gay bars, and travel services aimed at gay travelers. One of the best gay and lesbian travel newsletters is ***Out and About*** (tel. 800/929–2268), with listings of gay-friendly hotels and travel agencies plus health cautions for travelers with HIV. Guidebooks that cover all of North America include the ***Damron Address Book*** ($14), which focuses on gay male travel and lists services and entertainment options; and ***The Women's Traveller*** ($11), which lists resources for lesbians. For either publication, write to Box 422458, San Francisco 94142, or call 415/255–0404.

## TRAVELERS WITH DISABILITIES

Accessibility may soon have an international symbol if an initiative begun by the Society for the Advancement of Travel for the Handicapped (SATH) catches on. A bold, underlined, capital **H** is the symbol that SATH is publicizing for hotels, restaurants, and tourist attractions to indicate that the property has some accessible facilities. While awareness of the needs of travelers with disabilities increases every year in the United States, budget opportunities are harder to find. Always ask if discounts are available, either for you or for a companion. In addition, plan your trip and make reservations far in advance, since companies that provide services for people with disabilities go in and out of business regularly.

**Twin Peaks Press** (Box 129, Vancouver, WA 98666, tel. 360/694–2462 or 800/637–2256 for orders only) specializes in books for the disabled, such as *Travel for the Disabled,* which offers helpful hints as well as a comprehensive list of guidebooks and facilities geared to the disabled. Their *Directory of Travel Agencies for the Disabled* lists more than 350 agencies throughout the world. Each is $19.95 plus $3 ($4.50 for both) shipping and handling. Whenever possible, reviews in this book will indicate if rooms are wheelchair-accessible. Most large hotel chains, such as **Embassy Suites, Radisson,** and the cheaper **Motel 6** can accommodate wheelchair users but rarely offer discounts. **Best Western** sometimes discounts rooms for the disabled, but the offers vary from hotel to hotel. **Red Roof Inns** (tel. 800/843–7663 in U.S. and Canada) have wheelchair-accessible rooms and special alarm systems for deaf and blind guests.

**GETTING AROUND** The **American Public Transit Association** (tel. 202/898–4000) in Washington, DC, has information on transportation options in all U.S. cities for travelers with disabilities. Most major airlines are happy to help travelers with disabilities make flight arrangements, provided they receive notification 48 hours in advance. **Amtrak** (tel. 800/872–7245 or 800/523–6590 TYY) offers a 25% discount on one-way coach fares for travelers with disabilities who show written proof of disability. If notified when reservations are made, Amtrak will provide assistance for travelers at stations. **Greyhound-Trailways** (tel. 800/752–4841 or

800/345–3109 TDD) allows a disabled traveler and a companion to ride for the price of a single fare. No advance notice is required, although you will need to show proof of disability (such as a doctor's letter) to receive the special fare.

Some major car-rental companies are able to supply hand-controlled vehicles with a minimum of 24 hours' advance notice. Given a day's notice, **Avis** (tel. 800/331–1212) will install hand-controlled mechanisms at no extra charge. **Hertz** (tel. 800/654–3131 or 800/654–2280 TDD) asks for 48 hours' advance notice and a $25 cash or credit-card deposit to do the same. **National** (tel. 800/328–4567 or 800/328–6323 TDD) and **Thrifty** (tel. 800/367–2277) have hand-controlled cars at certain locations and ask for at least two days' notice to serve mobility-impaired renters.

**ORGANIZATIONS** **Outdoors Forever** (Box 4832, East Lansing, MI 48823, tel. 517/337–0018) is a nonprofit organization that works to make the outdoors more accessible to people with physical limitations. Call or write for more information about their magazine, *Outdoors Forever,* or their publications on equipment, techniques, and organizations that plan outings. **Mobility International USA (MIUSA)** (Box 10767, Eugene, OR 97440, tel. and TDD 503/343–1284) is a nonprofit organization that coordinates exchange programs for disabled people around the world. MIUSA also offers information on accommodations and organized study programs for members ($20 annually).

The national park system offers the **Golden Access Passport,** a free, lifetime entry pass that exempts travelers with disabilities and their families or friends from all entry fees and 50% of use fees for camping and parking in federal parks and wildlife refuges. You aren't allowed to register by mail or phone, but you can apply in person with medical proof of disability at all National Park Service and Forest Service offices, Forest Service ranger station offices, national parks that charge fees, Bureau of Land Management Offices, and Fish and Wildlife Service offices. For info, contact the **Outdoor Recreation Information Center** (915 2nd Ave., Suite 442, Seattle, WA 98174, tel. 206/220–7450).

# Info for Foreign Visitors

## PASSPORTS AND VISAS

**CANADA** Canadian citizens must show proof of citizenship and identity to enter the United States (a passport, birth certificate with raised seal, or voter registration card is preferred). Passport applications, available at any post office or passport office, cost C$35 and take one to two weeks to process. For additional information while in the United States, contact the **Canadian Embassy** (501 Pennsylvania Ave. NW, Washington, DC 20001, tel. 202/682–1740).

**UNITED KINGDOM** You need a valid 10-year, £15 passport to enter the United States. Application forms, which take about four weeks to process, are available from the **Passport Office** (Clive House, 70 Petty France, London SW1H 9HB, tel. 0171/279–4000 or 0171/279–3434 for recorded info), or from most travel agents, main post offices, and regional passport offices. A British Visitor Passport is not acceptable.

Visas are required for visits of more than 90 days. Apply four weeks in advance to a travel agent or the **U.S. Embassy Visa and Immigration Department** (5 Upper Grosvenor St., London W1A 2JB, tel. 0171/499–9000 for general info, 0171/499–7010 for visa info) or, for residents of Northern Ireland, to the **U.S. Consulate General** (Queen's House, Queen St., Belfast BT1 6E0, tel. 1232/328–239). Visas can be given only to holders of 10-year passports—although visas in expired passports remain valid. Submit a completed Nonimmigrant Visa Application (Form 156), a copy of your passport, a photograph, and evidence of your intended departure from the United States after a temporary visit.

**AUSTRALIA** Australian citizens need a valid passport and visa to enter the United States. Passports cost AUS$77 for adults. People younger than 18 may purchase a five-year passport for AUS$38. Applications are available at any post office or passport office, or call toll-free in Australia 008/02–60–22 weekdays for additional information. While in the United States,

Australians may obtain additional information from the **Embassy of Australia** (1601 Massachusetts Ave. NW, Washington, DC 20036, tel. 202/797–3000).

**NEW ZEALAND** New Zealand citizens need a valid passport to enter the United States. Ten-year passports, which cost NZ$55 and take about three weeks to process, are available from the **New Zealand Passport Office** (Documents of National Identity Division, Department of Internal Affairs, Box 10526, Wellington, tel. 04/474–8100), as well as regional passport offices and post offices. To stay more than 90 days, you'll also need a visa; contact the American embassy or consulate nearest you. In the United States, you can get more information from the **New Zealand Embassy** (37 Observatory Circle NW, Washington, DC 20008, tel. 202/328–4800).

## INTERNATIONAL FLIGHTS

**FROM CANADA** **Air Canada** (tel. 800/776–3000) has nonstop flights from Calgary, Toronto, and Montreal to Los Angeles's airport (LAX) and San Francisco's (SFO). **United** (tel. 800/538–2929) schedules flights from Vancouver, Calgary, and Toronto to LAX and SFO. **Canadian Airlines International** (tel. 800/426–7000) serves LAX and SFO from Vancouver. **Delta** (tel. 800/241–4141) flies nonstop from Calgary, Vancouver, and Edmonton to LAX and SFO.

**FROM THE U.K.** **British Airways** (tel. 800/247–9297), which offers youth fares, sometimes has special fares on its nonstop flights from Heathrow to L.A. and San Francisco. **United** (tel. 800/538–2929) also flies nonstop from Heathrow to L.A. and San Francisco. **American** (tel. 800/433–7300) flies nonstop from Heathrow to L.A., and to San Francisco with a stop in Chicago. **Delta** (tel. 800/241–4141) flies nonstop from Heathrow to LAX and SFO, and from Gatwick and Manchester to L.A., San Francisco, and San Diego—via Atlanta, Georgia, or Cincinnati, Ohio.

**FROM AUSTRALIA AND NEW ZEALAND** **Qantas** (tel. 800/227–4500) and **Air New Zealand** (tel. 800/262–1234) fly from Sydney and Auckland to L.A., while **United** (tel. 800/241–6522) flies nonstop to SFO and LAX from Auckland and Sydney, and from Melbourne (via Auckland) to SFO and LAX. **Japan Airlines** (tel. 800/525–3663) flies from Australia and New Zealand to LAX and SFO with a stopover in Tokyo.

## CUSTOMS AND DUTIES

Visitors 21 and older can bring into the United States: (1) 200 cigarettes or 100 non-Cuban cigars or 2 kilograms of smoking tobacco; (2) one U.S. liter of alcohol; (3) duty-free gifts to a value of $400 (including the value of any tobacco, cigars, or alcohol). Also, you may ship gifts valued up to $100 duty-free. Forbidden are meat and meat products, seeds, plants, and fruits. Avoid illegal drugs like the plague.

**CANADIAN CUSTOMS** Exemptions for returning Canadians range from $20 to $500, depending on how long you've been out of the country. Above these limits, you'll be taxed about 15%. Duty-free limits are: up to 50 cigars, 200 cigarettes, 400 grams of tobacco, and 1.14 liters of liquor—all must be declared in writing upon arrival at customs and must be with you or in your checked baggage. To mail back gifts, label the package "Unsolicited Gift–Value under C$60." For more scintillating details, call the automated information line of the **Revenue Canada Customs, Excise and Taxation Department** (2265 St. Laurent Blvd. S, Ottawa, Ont., K1G 4K3, tel. 613/993–0534 or 613/991–3881) and request a copy of the Canadian Customs brochure "I Declare/Je Déclare."

**U.K. CUSTOMS** Travelers age 17 or over who return to the United Kingdom may bring back the following duty-free goods: 200 cigarettes or 100 cigarillos or 50 cigars or 250 grams of tobacco; one liter of alcohol over 22% volume or two liters of alcohol under 22% volume, plus two liters of still table wine; 60 ml of perfume and 250 ml of toilet water; and other goods worth up to £136. For further information or a copy of "A Guide for Travellers," which details standard customs procedures and allotments, contact **HM Customs and Excise** (Dorset House, Stamford St., London SE1 9PY, tel. 0171/928–3344).

**AUSTRALIAN CUSTOMS** Australian travelers 18 and over may bring back, duty free: one liter of alcohol; 250 grams of tobacco products (equivalent to 250 cigarettes or cigars); and other articles worth up to $AUS400. If you're under 18, your duty-free allowance is $AUS200. To avoid paying duty on goods you mail back to Australia, mark the package: "Australian goods returned."

**NEW ZEALAND CUSTOMS** Travelers over age 17 are allowed, duty-free: 200 cigarettes or 250 grams of tobacco or 50 cigars or a combo of all three up to 250 grams; 4.5 liters of wine or beer and one 1,125-ml. bottle of spirits; and goods with a combined value up to NZ$700. If you want more details, ask for the pamphlet "Customs Guide for Travellers" from a New Zealand consulate (*see below*).

## CONSULATES

This information is for Californian locations of consulates only. For other locations, look in the Business section of the White Pages for the city you are in, or call information for that city.

**Canada.** *In Los Angeles: 300 S. Grand Ave., Suite 1000, 90071, tel. 213/346–2701. Open weekdays 8:30–12:30 and 1:30–4:30.*

**United Kingdom.** *In Los Angeles: 11766 Wilshire Blvd., Suite 850, 90025, tel. 310/477–3322. In San Francisco: 1 Sansome St., Suite 850, 94104, tel. 415/981–3030. Both open weekdays 8:30–5.*

**Australia.** *In Los Angeles: 611 N. Larchmont Blvd., 90004, tel. 213/469–4300. In San Francisco: 1 Bush St., Suite 700, 94104, tel. 415/362–6160. Both open weekdays 8:45–5.*

**New Zealand.** *In Los Angeles: 12400 Wilshire Blvd., Suite 1150, 90025, tel. 310/207–1605. In San Francisco: 1 Maritime Plaza, Suite 700, 94111, tel. 415/399–1455. Both open weekdays 9–5.*

## WORKING IN THE UNITED STATES

In order to work legally in the United States, you must have a social-security number, which is the birthright of U.S. citizens. Obtaining a green card, which entitles foreigners to work and reside in the United States, is a long shot for most visitors. If you're caught working illegally you will be deported and perhaps permanently denied entrance into the United States. Another option is to participate in an **Exchange Visitor Program (EVP)** (*see* Work Programs, *below*).

*The "Au-Pair in America" program is offered by the American Institute for Foreign Study (102 Greenwich Ave., Greenwich, CT 06830, tel. 203/869–9090 or 800/727–2437, ext. 6127).*

**WORK PROGRAMS** Exchange-visitor programs are authorized by the U.S. government to provide foreign students with legal jobs. Most jobs are big on restrictions and short on money. An excellent resource is Council's ***Work, Study, Travel Abroad: The Whole World Handbook*** ($13.95), which gives the lowdown on scholarships, grants, fellowships, study abroad programs, and work exchanges. The U.K.-based Vacation Work Press (9 Park East End, Oxford OX1 1HJ, England, tel. 01865/241–978) publishes two other first-rate guides: ***Directory of Overseas Summer Jobs*** (£9) and Susan Griffith's ***Work Your Way Around the World*** (£12). The first lists over 45,000 jobs worldwide; the latter has fewer listings but makes a more interesting read.

Canadians should contact **Travel CUTS** (*see* Budget Travel Organizations, *above*), which offers a version of the CIEE program to Canadian students who want to work abroad for up to six months. For British travelers, **British Universities North America Club (BUNAC)** (16 Bowling Green Lane, London EC1R OBD, tel. 0171/251–3472) operates in conjunction with Council (*see* Student ID Cards, *above*) to provide temporary work permits. The **Camp America** program run by the American Institute for Foreign Studies (Dept. WW 37A, Queens Gate, London SW7 5HR, England, tel. 0171/581–7373) places visitors in camps throughout the United States, including some in California.

**VOLUNTEER WORK** If you can afford to work for nothing, more power to you. And the first call you should make is to the **CIEE Voluntary Service Department,** which can get you a job in the United States as a teacher, house builder, archaeological dig helper, whatever. An excellent resource is Council's ***Volunteer!*** ($12.95 plus $1.50 postage), a guide to opportunities worldwide. *205 E. 42nd St., New York, NY 10017, tel. 212/661–1414, ext. 1139.*

**Service Civil International (SCI)** and **International Voluntary Service (IVS)** work for peace and international understanding through two- to three-week work camps in the United States ($50) and Europe ($100–$150). Applicants must be 16 or older. Send for a free brochure. *5474 Walnut Level Rd., Crozet, VA 22932, tel. 804/823–1826.*

Long- and short-term jobs in the great outdoors as a host or interpretive guide in one of California's many state parks attract thousands of people each year. Contact the **California Department of Parks and Recreation** (Box 942896, Sacramento, CA 94296–0001, tel. 916/653–6995) or call **Sierra Club Service Trips** (tel. 415/923–5222) for information.

### PHONES AND MAIL

**INTERNATIONAL CALLS** Calls between the United States and Canada are not considered international calls and can be dialed as regular long-distance numbers. To call any other country, dial 011, the country code, the city code (dropping the initial zero if there is one), then the telephone number. If you get stuck and want help, dial 00 for a long-distance operator. The country code for the United Kingdom is 44, for Ireland 353, for Australia 61, and for New Zealand 64. When calling, remember to account for time differences from Pacific Standard Time (PST): the United Kingdom and Ireland are eight hours ahead; New Zealand is 19 hours ahead; and Australia, with three time zones, is 16–18 hours ahead. The cheapest times (PST) to call England are 6 PM–7 AM; for New Zealand it's 11 PM–10 AM, and for Australia 3 AM–2 PM. A three-minute call from anywhere in the United States during the evening will cost about $2.33 (England), $3.37 (New Zealand), or $3.08 (Australia). For the exact rate, call the **AT&T** long-distance operator (tel. 00), **U.S. Sprint** (tel. 800/877–4646), or **MCI** (tel. 800/444–3333).

**SENDING MAIL HOME** International rates for sending letters to destinations beyond the North American continent begin at 60¢ for the first half ounce and $1 for the first full ounce. Add 40¢ per half ounce for letters heavier than 1 ounce. Rates are slightly cheaper for mail to Canada (52¢ for the first ounce). You can also stop by any post office and buy ready-to-mail aerograms. For 50¢ you get paper, envelope, and postage all in one. Post cards cost 35–50¢. Allow one to two weeks' delivery time for international mail.

## Coming and Going

When your travel plans are still in the fantasy stage, start studying the travel sections of major Sunday newspapers: Courier companies, charter flights, and fare brokers often list incredibly cheap flights. (For info on travel into California via bus or train, *see* Getting Around, *below*). Travel agents are another obvious resource, as they have access to computer networks that show the lowest fares before they're even advertised. However, budget travelers are the bane of travel agents, whose commission is based on the ticket prices. That said, agencies on or near college campuses—try STA or Council Travel (*see* Budget Travel Organizations, *above*)—actu-

### *Mail on the Road*

***You can receive mail (including packages) from your squeeze back home in care of General Delivery at any post office. Have the sender indicate the city and zip code of a specific post office in a specific city. Most post offices are open weekdays 9–5 and Saturday morning and will hold mail for up to 30 days before returning it to the sender.***

ally cater to this pariah class and can help you find cheap deals. **APEX** (advance purchase excursion) tickets bought directly from the airline or from a travel agent are the simplest way to go if you know exactly when you want to leave and it's not tomorrow (or the next day). Simply ask for the APEX fare when making a reservation: Regular APEX fares normally apply to tickets bought at least 21 days in advance; you can get Super-APEX fares if you know your travel plans at least one month in advance. Here's the catch: If you cancel or change your plans, you'll pay a penalty, anywhere from $50 to $100.

Some tips on airline reservations: If the reservation clerk tells you the least expensive seats are no longer available on a flight, ask to be put on a waiting list. If the airline doesn't keep waiting lists for the lowest fares, call on subsequent mornings and ask about cancellations and last-minute openings—airlines sometimes add additional cut-rate tickets at the last moment to fill seats. When setting travel dates, remember that off-season fares can be as much as 50% lower, and fares vary even among days of the week. If you paid more than you'd like for a ticket, scan the ads in newspaper travel sections for last-minute deals and lower fares; airlines claiming the "lowest fares" will sometimes refund the difference in ticket price.

*Flexibility is the key to getting a serious bargain on airfare. If you can play around with your departure date, destination, amount of luggage, and return date, you can save some cash.*

A useful resource is Michael McColl's ***The Worldwide Guide to Cheap Airfares,*** an in-depth account of how to find cheap tickets and generally beat the system. If you don't find it at your local bookstore, you can mail a check for $14.95 plus $2.50 for shipping and handling to Insider Publications (2124 Kittredge St., 3rd Floor, Berkeley, CA 94704), or call 800/782–6657 and order with a credit card.

## CONSOLIDATORS AND BUCKET SHOPS

Consolidator companies, also known as bucket shops, buy blocks of tickets at wholesale prices from airlines trying to fill flights. Check out any consolidator's reputation with the Better Business Bureau before starting; most are perfectly reliable, but better safe than sorry. If everything works as planned, you'll save 10%–40% on the published APEX fare.

There are several drawbacks, however: Consolidator tickets are often not refundable, and the flights to choose from often feature indirect routes, long layovers in connecting cities, and undesirable seating assignments. If your flight is delayed or canceled, you'll also have a tough time switching airlines. As with charter flights, you risk taking a huge loss if you change your travel plans. If possible, pay with a credit card, so that if your ticket never arrives you don't have to pay. Bucket shops generally advertise in newspapers—be sure to check restrictions, refund possibilities, and payment conditions. One last suggestion: Confirm your reservation with the airline both before and after you buy a consolidated ticket. This not only decreases the chance of fraud, but also ensures that you won't be the first to get bumped if the airline overbooks. For more details, contact one of the following consolidators.

**Discount Travel International** (169 W. 81st St., New York, NY 10024, tel. 212/362–3636) books courier and charter flights, and has reduced-fare tickets. **Globe Travel** (507 5th Ave.,

### *Bikes in Flight*

***California is a great place to hit the road on two wheels, and most airlines will accommodate by shipping bikes as luggage, provided they are dismantled and put into a box. Call to see if your airline sells bike boxes (about $5; bike bags are at least $100), although you can often pick them up free at bike shops. International travelers can substitute a bike for a piece of checked luggage for free; otherwise, it will cost about $100. Domestic and Canadian airlines charge a $25–$50 fee.***

Suite 604, New York, NY 10017, tel. 800/969–4562) has consolidated tickets to "any place you want." **UniTravel** (1177 N. Warson, St. Louis, MO 63132, tel. 800/325–2222) offers good deals to Europe and a handful of destinations within the United States.

### STANDBY AND THREE-DAY-ADVANCE-PURCHASE

Flying standby is almost a thing of the past. The idea is to purchase an open ticket and wait for the next available seat on the next available flight to your chosen destination. Yet most airlines have dumped standby policies in favor of three-day-advance-purchase youth fares, which are open only to people under 25 and (as the name states) can only be purchased within three days of departure. Return flights must also be booked no more than three days prior to departure. If you meet the above criteria, expect 10%–50% savings on published APEX fares.

There are also a number of brokers that specialize in discount and last-minute sales, offering savings on unsold seats on commercial carriers and charter flights, as well as tour packages. If you're desperate to get to California by Wednesday, try **Last Minute Travel Club** (tel. 617/267–9800).

### CHARTER FLIGHTS

Generally speaking, a charter company either buys a block of tickets on a regularly scheduled commercial flight and sells them at a discount (the prevalent form in the United States) or leases the whole plane and then offers relatively cheap fares to the public (most common in the United Kingdom). Despite a few potential drawbacks—including infrequent flights, restrictive return-date requirements, lickety-split payment demands, frequent bankruptcies—charter companies often offer the cheapest tickets around, especially during high season when APEX fares are most expensive. Make sure you find out a company's policy on refunds should a flight be canceled by either yourself or the airline. Summer charter flights fill up fast and should be booked a couple months in advance. You can minimize risks by checking the company's reputation with the Better Business Bureau and taking out enough trip-cancellation insurance to cover the operator's potential failure.

Charter companies to try include **DER Tours** (Box 1606, Des Plains, IL 60017, tel. 800/782–2424), **MartinAir** (tel. 800/627–8462), **Tower Air** (tel. 800/34–TOWER), and **Travel CUTS** (*see* Budget Travel Organizations, *above*). The previous list of charter companies is by no means exhaustive; check newspaper travel sections for more extensive listings. Council Travel and STA (*see* Budget Travel Organizations, *above*) also offer exclusively negotiated discount airfares on scheduled airlines.

## Staying in California

### GETTING AROUND

If you've glanced at a map, you already know that California is large. The easiest way to see as much of the state as possible is by car; a car will also help you stray from the well-traveled tourist track. However, buses can get you between major and medium-sized cities, and Amtrak trains will take you up the coast and inland—although air travel is sometimes cheaper than the train.

**BY CAR** Besides being the most efficient way to navigate this monster state, a car allows you to explore the back roads where mass transportation fears to tread. Renting a car can be economical, but take your own car if you plan to drive for more than a week or two. **I–5** is the fastest route for traveling north–south through the state, but the scenery is flat and uneventful, save for the occasional cow. **Highway 1** is a beautiful but slow drive that hugs the coast north of Santa Barbara all the way up into Oregon. **U.S. 101,** which lies between the two, and ends in Leggett when it meets Highway 1, is a compromise in scenery and time. The rolling hills are sometimes pretty, but less spectacular than those you'll see on Highway 1; and it takes about eight hours to travel between Los Angeles and San Francisco, compared to six hours on I–5. The north–south route for people who don't like other people is **U.S. 395,** which starts near San Bernardino and climbs north along the eastern slope of the Sierra Nevada, cuts into Nevada and back into northeast California on its way to southeast Oregon. East–west interstate freeways include **I–80** in the north, a fast freeway that can see a lot of messy commute traffic; it heads east from San Francisco through Sacramento and Lake Tahoe on its way across the entire country. In the south, there is I–15, which starts in Los Angeles and travels east through Barstow and the Mojave Desert to Las Vegas; **I–10** shoots east out of Los Angeles into southern Arizona and the great beyond.

➢ **DRIVE-AWAY SERVICES** • This can be one of the cheapest ways to get around the United States. If you have a current driver's license, are older than 21, and have about $200 for a deposit, you get the keys to a car that someone needs delivered to a specific Point B from a specific Point A. You just worry about gas money and keeping the car clean. Drive-away services usually have time, routing, and mileage limits—these are sometimes very strict. There are services and agents in most major cities; look under "Automobile and Truck Transporting" and "Drive-Away Services" in the Yellow Pages and shop around.

➢ **CAR RENTALS** • National car-rental agencies include **Alamo** (tel. 800/327–9633), **Budget** (tel. 800/527–0700), **Dollar** (tel. 800/800–4000), and **Thrifty** (tel. 800/367–2277). Most charge about $25–$45 a day (often with unlimited mileage) to renters over 25 with a major credit card. In the off-season, a week's rental with unlimited mileage can be as low as $120. Expect to pay more ($10–$20 a day) for the privilege of being under 25 years old; no company rents to anyone under 21. The 21-to-24 set does best at **Enterprise** (tel. 800/325–8007), which charges only $8 extra a day. Reserving a car a few days in advance and renting it for a week or more may get you a better guaranteed rate. Some companies charge nothing to return the car to another location, others charge $100–$150 extra. Optional insurance ($9–$12 a day) is a good idea, but check with your credit-card company first to see if you're already covered. American Express provides automatic car-insurance coverage if you charge your rental, but be sure to read the small print. Companies like **Rent-a-Wreck** (tel. 800/535–1391), which specializes in cheaper, older, and uglier cars, sometimes undercut the national companies on rates—but make sure the lower rental cost is not eclipsed by added mileage charges or limits, and make doubly sure that the company will provide you with a replacement in case the car breaks down.

**BY BUS** **Greyhound** (tel. 800/231– 2222) offers bus service along U.S. I–5, U.S. 101, and I–80, as well as to a few offshoot towns. The cheapest fares are during low season (Jan.–June and Sept.–Nov.). Their **Ameripass,** valid on all U.S. routes, can be purchased in advance in cities throughout the U.S.; spontaneous types can also buy it up to 45 minutes before the bus leaves from the terminal. The pass allows unlimited travel within a limited time period: seven days ($179), 15 days ($289), or 30 days ($399). Foreign visitors can get slightly lower rates. **Green Tortoise** (*see* Funky Deals *box, below*) is usually a better option than Greyhound.

## *A Driver's Dream*

***If you're going to be traveling in California by car, becoming a member of the Automobile Association of America (AAA) or one of its affiliates is the best investment you can make. Membership generally costs $58 for the first year and $41 annually thereafter, though rates vary from state to state. Members receive free maps and tour books, personalized itinerary plans, free emergency road service, and discounts at hotels, motels, and some restaurants. If you belong to any type of auto club abroad, AAA may honor your membership; otherwise consider joining while you're here. 1000 AAA Dr., Heathrow, FL 32746, tel. 800/222–4357.***

**BY TRAIN** **Amtrak** (tel. 800/USA–RAIL) has two main routes in the state. The *Coast Starlight* runs north–south from Los Angeles to Seattle, stopping at cities in between and offering bus connections to outlying towns. Although the name implies that tracks skim the coastline, the *Starlight* does so only south of San Luis Obispo and skips the spectacular scenery of Big Sur. The other route is the *San Joaquin* line, a bus-train combination running north–south between Bakersfield and Emeryville, with stops at cities in the San Joaquin Valley. Round-trip fare on the *San Joaquin* is $69; the trip takes around six hours from end to end. Fare on the *Starlight* from S.F. to L.A. runs $72–$142 round-trip, depending upon availability, and takes about 12 hours each way. Because of the huge distances involved, train travel in the United States is not as speedy, popular, or economical as in Europe. Reservations are not required, but the *Coast Starlight* tends to fill up, so book ahead. Trains have dining cars on board, but it's cheaper to bring your own food.

The **All-Aboard Pass** is good for people who plan their itinerary in advance. The pass, which is actually a booklet of tickets, allows Amtrak riders special fares for three stops made in 45 days of travel within a region. For travel in or through California, request the All-Aboard Pass for the western United States (about $199, $179 off-season), and choose your own route. Ticket agents need to know your dates of travel and intended destinations for ticketing, so call in advance. Amtrak also provides free but limited shuttle services for pass-holders whose routes don't connect. **USARailPass** works to the advantage of the foreign budget traveler (it's not available to U.S. or Canadian citizens) because it requires no formal itinerary, works on any of Amtrak's U.S. routes, and allows for spontaneous planning (within a specified time period). Fifteen-day passes start at $200, $340 peak-season; 30-day passes $225, $425 peak-season. Buy them at an international travel agency before entering the United States. In the United States, purchase the pass at any Amtrak station (international passport required for purchase).

**BY PLANE** If you're short on time and long on desire to see California's major cities, air travel is the quickest and cheapest option. Round-trip tickets between Los Angeles and the Bay Area can cost as little as $70, provided you fulfill certain requirements such as giving two weeks' advance notice. **Southwest Airlines** (tel. 800/I–FLY–SWA) usually has the lowest fares.

**Council Travel** (*see* Budget Travel Organizations, *above*) offers the USAir Pass to students only, and allows you to fly between three U.S. cities for $385. The Visit America pass is available to foreign visitors only; it entitles the holder to one-direction travel with three stops in a 60-day period for $200–$300. However, you must purchase it *before* arriving in the U.S. Talk to a budget travel agency in your home country. **Delta** (tel. 800/221–1212) offers the Discover America Pass to foreign visitors. The pass consists of a coupon book (three coupons at $439,

## *Funky Deals on Wheels*

***Green Tortoise is among the least rapid, most memorable ways to traverse California. From Venice Beach to Yreka (and a lot of destinations outside the state), the Tortoise's camper coaches wend their way along a dot-to-dot map of natural (and unnatural) attractions—including Santa Barbara, Berkeley, Yosemite, and Mt. Shasta. Often compared to youth hostels on wheels, the buses feature foam mattresses for sleeping, and communally cooked vegetarian food is included in the price of the trip. Green Tortoise also makes longer treks (e.g., to Mexico, Baja California, Central America, Alaska, the Grand Canyon, and the east coast). Selected fares: San Francisco–L.A., $30; San Francisco–Santa Cruz, $10; Seattle, Washington–L.A., $69, $79 in peak-season. For a free pamphlet, write or call Green Tortoise Adventure Travel, 494 Broadway, San Francisco, tel. 415/821–0803 or 800/867–8647 outside the 415 and 510 area codes. Reservations are recommended for most journeys.***

four at $549, five at $659 and six at $769); a coupon is required for each flight taken including any connecting flights. Booklets are good for flights in a 60-day period to U.S. cities served by Delta. These passes must be purchased before you arrive in the States.

**BY BIKE** Bicycling through California is perhaps the cheapest, most environmentally sound, and—depending on your physical shape—most enjoyable way to see the state. Campgrounds cost less for cyclers, and hostels sometimes make room for you even if they're full. Some highways, including stretches of U.S. 101 and Highway 1, accommodate bicyclists, but the best routes are the less crowded roads that parallel or branch off the highways. **Backroads Bicycling Touring** (1516 5th St., Berkeley 94710, tel. 510/527–1888) offers trips around California, Baja, and the Grand Canyon starting at $189 and up. If you go on your own and plan to bike only part of the way, **Amtrak** will transport you and your bike ($5 handling fee) on the *Coast Starlight* route. They provide the bike box but require you to disassemble the bike. ***Bicycling the Pacific Coast*** (The Mountaineers; $15), by Tom Kirkendall and Vicky Spring, explores the coastal route from Canada to Mexico.

**HITCHING** There is no California law against hitchhiking, but neither is there a specific penal code stating that it is legal. Simply put, do not hitchhike where you see signs that the activity is illegal (in major cities, on freeway on- or off-ramps, along any roadway with more than one lane in each direction); exercise caution in other areas. Different police officers in the same area sometimes have a different understanding of the legality involved, so don't hesitate to challenge a citation—politely, of course. Hitching is easiest in rural communities, especially in Northern California and in national and state parks. It is safer to travel with a friend—especially if you're female—but you'll get a ride faster if you're alone. Women should avoid getting into a van or into any vehicle with more than one man inside. Be discriminating and trust your instincts. For a safer alternative, check ride boards at youth hostels or universities. With either option, be prepared to contribute towards gas costs.

*Watch out for the devilish three-leaf stems of poison oak indigenous to California (their red leaves are a dead giveaway in fall). You can buy preventative lotions at most sporting goods stores; otherwise, wash your skin with soap and cold water if you touch the stuff, and don't scratch.*

**HIKING** With its scenic landscapes, diverse terrain, and gentle climate, California is a hiker's haven. The Pacific Crest Trail runs from Mexico to Canada through the Sierra Nevada mountain range, and countless other trails traverse the state. **Wilderness Press** (2440 Bancroft Way, Berkeley 94704, tel. 510/843–8080) publishes excellent guides on hiking in California, including the ***High Sierra Hiking Guide,*** complete with topographical maps, for about $12. **Sierra Club** headquarters (730 Polk St., San Francisco 94109, tel. 415/923–5660) has info about hiking trips and operates a bookstore with an extensive selection of guides.

## FOOD

As befits a place of such ethnic and cultural diversity, California can offer an amazing variety of cuisine within a few city blocks (especially in L.A. and San Francisco). Mexican restaurants are a safe bet for cheap, fresh, high-quality food throughout the state—in fact, this could easily be considered California's specialty. Be wary, however, of Asian restaurants in small towns; their quality varies widely. Vegetarians will have little trouble finding meatless meals in most areas. For the cheapest food, try supermarkets, which charge no sales tax (restaurants do). The budget-minded should also take advantage of lunch specials and early-evening "happy hours." On the pricier side, "California cuisine" is known for its artful presentation, fresh ingredients, and minimalistic portions. Assume that restaurants reviewed in this guide accept credit cards, unless otherwise noted.

## WHERE TO SLEEP

Budget lodging may be ubiquitous or nonexistent, depending on where you are in California. Apart from a quiet beach or the back seat of your Plymouth, the cheapest options are youth hostels, which charge $10–$15 per person, and campgrounds (sometimes free in national forests, or $4–$20 per site). Hotels and motels usually start at $30 for a double. Bed-and-breakfasts are not the money savers they are in Europe, and in fact usually cost more than nice motels.

*Throughout the book, the lodging price categories refer to the cost of a double room excluding tax. Likewise, in the Food sections, the price categories refer to the cost of a main course with a non-alcoholic drink. If you're a soda addict or insist on a king-size bed, all bets are off.*

**HOTELS AND MOTELS** About $30–$50 will get you a double room with a private bath in an average hotel. Single travelers often have to pay the double rate. Budget chains—including Motel 6 and E-Z 8—permeate the state and can be a reliable and relatively cheap option ($20 and up for a double), although they're usually bland. Hotels and motels are cheapest in the off-season and sometimes offer package deals. With the **Entertainment Card,** a promotion run through many credit-card companies, you can get a 50% discount on many moderate to expensive hotels across the country, including about 300 in California. The card costs $49 per year; call 800/548–1116 to enroll. Also look for AAA discounts (*see box* A Driver's Dream, *above*). Assume that hotels reviewed in the book take credit cards unless otherwise noted.

**BED-AND-BREAKFASTS** Bed-and-breakfasts are usually out of the budget range, but if you want to splurge for a homey and more personal touch, spend your money here rather than at a large, swanky hotel. B&Bs start as low as $55 in some areas but usually average $80 and up for a double, with occasional discounts on longer stays. The room price includes breakfast, which can range from a Danish and coffee to a five-course feast. Rooms are often without telephones and televisions and sometimes have a shared bath. **Bed and Breakfast International** (Box 282910, San Francisco 94128, tel. 415/696–1690) is a reservation service for more than 500 B&Bs in California and Nevada.

**HOSTELS** Hostels affiliated with **American Youth Hostels (AYH),** the American branch of **Hostelling International (HI)** (733 15th St. NW, Suite 840, Washington, DC 20005, tel. 202/783–6161 or 800/444–6111), offer a certain welcome predictability, but private hostels are often cheaper and filled with a more eclectic crowd. HI is the granddaddy of hostel associations, offering single-sex dorm-style beds ("couples" rooms and family accommodations are sometimes available) and kitchen facilities at nearly 5,000 locations in 70 countries around the world. Membership in AYH allows you to stay in any HI hostel at member rates (about $10–$15 per night). Non-U.S. citizens who are members of their own national hostel associations receive membership privileges at AYH hostels as well. Those with no affiliation are almost always allowed to stay at HI hostels, but they pay a higher rate (usually about $3–$5 more), and members have priority if a hostel is full. A one-year membership is available to travelers of all ages and runs about $25 for adults (renewal $20) and $10 for those under 18. Family memberships are available for $35, and a lifetime membership will set you back $250.

AYH's facilities vary widely, from lighthouse cabins to small three- or four-bed in-home operations. There are strict rules: Alcohol, drugs, and smoking are forbidden, curfews are enforced, and each visitor is responsible for a simple chore. The maximum stay is three days unless an extension is granted. In high season it's a good idea to book ahead. Some hostels allow you to use your sleeping bag, although officially they require a sleep sack that can be rented for about $1 a night. All hostels have a kitchen, common room, and often useful listings of cheap things to do in the area. A real pain in the butt is the lockout that most hostels institute from 9 AM to 5 PM, during which all guests must leave the premises. AYH publishes a U.S. handbook (free, $3 if you order by mail) that details the location and amenities of each hostel. For more info, contact one of the following:

**AYH-California.** *308 Mason St., San Francisco 94102, tel. 415/788–2525; Los Angeles Council, 1434 2nd St., Santa Monica 90401, tel. 310/393–6263.*

**Hostelling International–Canada (HI–C).** *400-205 Catherine St., Ottawa, Ont. K2P 1C3, tel. 613/237–7884 or 800/663-5777.*

**Youth Hostel Association of England and Wales (YHA).** *Trevelyan House, 8 St. Stephen's Hill, St. Albans, Herts. AL1 2DY, England, tel. 01727/855–215.*

**Australian Youth Hostels Association (YHA).** *Level 3, 10 Mallett St., Camperdown, New South Wales 2050, tel. 02/565–1699.*

**Youth Hostels Association of New Zealand (YHA).** *Box 436, Christchurch 1, tel. 3/379–9970.*

**Y's Way International** (224 E. 47th St., New York, NY 10017, tel. 212/308–2899) is a network of YMCA and YWCA overnight centers offering low-cost accommodations—anything from dorms to makeshift high-school gymnasiums—at an average overnight rate of $26. Age limits and prices vary, so contact the YMCA in the area you'll be visiting. Some offer special rates for lengthy stays. Ys in California include Berkeley/Albany YMCA (2001 Allston Way, Berkeley 94704, tel. 510/848–6800), the Glendale YMCA near L.A.—for men only—(140 N. Louise St., Glendale 91206, tel. 818/240–4130), San Diego ASY (500 W. Broadway, San Diego 92101, tel. 619/232–1133), and San Francisco Central YMCA (220 Golden Gate Ave., San Francisco 94102, tel. 415/885–0460).

**UNIVERSITY/STUDENT HOUSING** During summer, universities often rent out dorm rooms by the night or the week; however, it's usually under the pretense that you're there on some sort of school-related business. A good line in such a circumstance is to say you're thinking of attending school there. Generally, universities are not a real bargain. Dorms are dreary and costs are high: $30–$40 for a single or double. This book lists, in individual chapters, some universities that offer housing. If you're interested in one not listed, contact the university's housing office.

**LODGING ALTERNATIVES** Formed in the aftermath of World War II, **Servas** (11 John St., New York, NY 10038, tel. 212/267–0252) is a membership organization that enables you to stay with host families around the globe. California listings are plentiful, but Servas is *not* for tourists or weekend travelers. Peace-minded individuals who want more than a free bed can write or call for an application and an interview. Membership is $55 per year, and a one-time deposit of $25 is required.

## CAMPING

California was made for camping. Most of the state's forests, mountains, deserts, and coastal areas have designated public and private campgrounds whose sites range from primitive (meaning no running water and pit toilets) to annoyingly developed (overrun by RVs and arcades). Prices vary accordingly—anywhere from free (for some walk-in campgrounds) to $18 for a public site, more for a private site. For general info about camping, the **Sierra Club** (*see* Hiking, in Getting Around, *above*) has a good selection of guidebooks and group tours. For a guide to more than 15,000 campgrounds, splurge on a copy of ***California Camping*** (Foghorn Press, $18), by Tom Stienstra.

### Vacations with a Vengeance

***Eco-travel is on the rise; organizations that combine tourism with ecological or political awareness are popping up all over California. Coastwalk (1389 Cooper Rd., Sebastopol 95472, tel. 707/829–6689) takes groups on four- to six-day hiking and camping trips along the California Coastal Trail while promoting environmental awareness. The Student Conservation Association (Box 550, Charlestown, NH 03603, tel. 603/543–1700) offers 12-week internships where you can lead hikes for the park service or work with wildlife researchers. It's free, and SCA provides lodging, transportation, and a stipend. Earthwatch (Box 403BC, Watertown, MA 02272, tel. 800/776–0188) offers two-week expeditions that let you explore national parks ($90 a day), study dolphins in Monterey ($100 a day), and more. Fees cover your living expenses, and both projects offer academic credit.***

**CAMPING GEAR** Before packing loads of camping gear, seriously weigh how much camping you will actually do versus the hassle of hauling around a tent, sleeping bag, stove, and accoutrements. Also consider climate in choosing what to bring. A great place to get equipment, outdoor publications, and useful free pamphlets is **Recreational Equipment, Inc. (REI)** (1700 45th St. E, Sumner, WA 98352, tel. 800/426–4840), with locations up and down the West Coast. Request a free catalog by calling the toll-free number. **The North Face** (tel. 206/622–4111 or 800/362–4963) has factory outlets in large cities, where supplies and gear are much cheaper than at their regular stores. Call for outlet locations.

Essential camping supplies include a good sleeping bag (preferably stuffed with Qualofil, which provides warmth when sopping wet); a quality backpack (external-frame packs are better suited to rough terrain, but are more awkward and less flexible than internal frames); and lightweight, waterproof clothes (layered synthetics are most effective). Tents, which can be expensive, are desirable but not obligatory; a bivouac "bivvy" bag (a water-repellent shell that fits over a sleeping bag) can do the trick, or you can find semi-sheltered areas and risk the rain. Other odds and ends you probably want to have are matches in a waterproof container, a rain poncho, a multiblade knife, something for banging in tent pegs (your shoe will work if it's sturdy enough), a mess kit, water bottle, a water filter or purifying pills, a can/bottle opener, a small cookstove, extra rope, a flashlight or candle lantern, toilet paper, and extra batteries. Always carry a first-aid kit with lots of adhesive bandages, gauze, aspirin, antibacterial ointment (Neosporin is a good brand), and an emergency procedures guide. Optionals include an elastic bandage, hydrogen peroxide, tweezers, sunscreen, moleskin with tape for blisters, and a sewing kit.

*Any water that comes from lakes or streams should be purified if you plan on drinking or cooking with it. Purification pills and filters are available at most sporting goods stores, but boiling is the safest and cheapest method.*

**OFF-ROAD CAMPING** On state park lands, camping is legal only at designated campgrounds, though the *Official Guide to State Parks*, available from the California State Park System (*see below*), lists certain "on-route" spots where you can pull your vehicle off to the side of the road and sleep inside. But there are almost 20 million national forest acres and more than 17 million Bureau of Land Management acres in California—that's two-fifths of the state—that allow free, dispersed camping. With the exception of some national forest campgrounds and towns, these lands are backcountry—no piped-in water, no picnic tables, few paved or maintained roads, maybe an occasional outhouse. Some BLM areas may be the local hot-spot for off-road vehicles, but for the most part, national forest and BLM lands are pristine and peaceful. Please be careful to keep it that way. Permits are required for open fires and most camping in wilderness areas (*see below*). For info on BLM lands, write or call the Bureau of Land Management, 2800 Cottage Way, Sacramento 95825, tel. 916/979–2800 (for contact information for national and state parks and national forests, *see below*).

**PROTECTING THE ENVIRONMENT** Wilderness permits, which outline backpacking rules and help limit the number of people on a trail, are usually required if you plan on any backcountry exploration. They're free and obtainable by mail or at the point of entry to your park (usually no more than a day before you plan to hike). Consult each park individually for their regulations on trail quotas and mail-in permits. Even if you don't get one, keep in mind some general rules: Always travel on trails and, if possible, camp at previously used sites to avoid trampling vegetation and causing soil erosion. Also, don't camp closer than 100 feet to any road, trail, or water source. Hang your food and other smelly items slightly away from camp to deter bears, and always pack out your garbage; bury human waste 8 inches deep, at least 200 feet from water, your camp, and trails. To wash anything, use only biodegradable soap, and never wash directly in a stream or lake—do it at least 100 feet from the water's edge. Very few parks allow you to build fires in the wilderness; if you must, get a free fire permit at the nearest ranger station (these are required for any kind of open flame, including cookstoves), and make sure to put the fire out completely.

## NATIONAL AND STATE PARKS

National-park campgrounds are well kept but often crowded. National forests, which are "multiple-use land" areas, have less spectacular but also comparatively uncrowded campgrounds. State parks (usually historically or geologically significant and smaller than national parks) lie somewhere in between in terms of quality of the scenery and campground maintenance. Many campgrounds do not accept reservations, but those in popular spots will take bookings eight weeks in advance. Call MISTIX (tel. 800/365–2267 for national parks, or 800/444–7275 for state parks or national forests) for reservations. Avoid camping or reserve way ahead on Labor Day, Memorial Day, July 4, and any other three-day weekend.

For information on California's eight national parks (Lassen Volcanic, Redwood, Sequoia, Kings Canyon, Yosemite, Death Valley, Joshua Tree, and the Channel Islands) and various national monuments, call the **National Park Service** (Western Region Information Office, Fort Mason, Bldg. 201, San Francisco 94123, tel. 415/556–0560). To find out about national forests, contact the **U.S. Forest Service** (Pacific Southwest Region, 630 Sansome St., San Francisco 94111, tel. 415/705–2874). For information on state parks, such as Big Basin Redwoods near Santa Cruz or Anza Borrego Desert near San Diego, call the **California State Park System** (tel. 916/653–6995). These offices are open 9:30–4:30, although you'll probably get a recording during off-hours with some useful information.

National and state parks charge a $4–$6 entrance fee per car, even if you don't plan on camping. This gives you entry to the parks for seven days, and you can come or go as you please. If you're walking or biking in, the fee will be about $2–$3. If you plan on visiting many parks, consider a **Golden Eagle Pass** ($25), available through the mail from the National Park Service or at the entrance to each national park. These are valid for one year from the date of purchase.

## OUTDOOR ACTIVITIES

**HIKING** California's beautiful scenery and temperate climate make for some of the nation's best hiking. The Sierras, the Cascades, Big Sur, the southern deserts, and the North Coast offer options (the most notable being the Pacific Crest Trail, which zigzags from Mexico to Canada along the length of California) for days or months of hiking. Pick up **California Hiking** (Foghorn Press, $19) for the low-down on trails. For more information, *see* Getting Around, *above.*

*If you plan on rubbing shoulders with Mother Nature, Avon "Skin So Soft" moisturizer is the best mosquito repellent in the world. Check the phone book under "Avon."*

**BIKING** Road bikers have long pinpointed Highway 1, the coastal road running from Canada to Mexico along the Pacific, as one of America's great rides. But throughout the state, the stunning scenery makes for wonderful biking. Large cities, resort towns, and national parks rent bikes for about $25 a day, and have set aside special routes or trails. While road biking is popular all over the state, mountain bikers should particularly consider trips to the Eastern Sierra, the Angeles and Plumas national forests, the Cascades, Santa Cruz, Big Sur, and Marin County. For more information, *see* Getting Around by Bike, *above.*

**ROCK CLIMBING** In the past few years more and more Californians have been trying to learn this difficult and somewhat scary sport. Favorite spots include Yosemite National Park in the Sierra Nevada, Joshua Tree National Park, Stoney Point in Los Angeles's San Fernando Valley, and Pinnacles National Monument in the Salinas Valley, although climbs of all levels can be found throughout the state. For equipment, advice, and names of climbing schools contact **REI** (*see* Camping, *above*).

**WHITE-WATER RAFTING AND KAYAKING** Rafting and kayaking have become popular and exciting activities in the spring and summer on the Tuolumne River in Yosemite and on the American River north of Sacramento. Outfitters have also sprung up around the Klamath, Trinity, and Eel rivers, offering half-day to multi-day trips on Class II–Class IV rapids. Check individual chapters for companies and prices, but expect to pay about $40 per half day and $90 for a full-day excursion. The price usually includes lunch and transportation.

**SURFING AND WINDSURFING** One of California's biggest con jobs has been the image of blonde babes and dudes surfing and swimming in warm Pacific waters. The truth is that the water around some of California's most popular surfing towns (Santa Cruz, for example) is cold enough to freeze the balls off a brass monkey. Most surfing is restricted to the Bay Area, Santa Cruz, and, of course, infamous Southern California (from Santa Barbara into Baja California). For tips on starting, try Doug Werner's ***Surfer's Start-Up*** (Pathfinder Publishing; $10). Serious windsurfers will want to make a pilgrimage to the Bay Area, which has some of the finest conditions (and competitions) in the country.

**SKIING AND SNOWBOARDING** California offers some of the finest nordic and alpine skiing in the country. Head to Lake Tahoe (*see* Chapter 6), Mammoth Lakes (*see* Chapter 7), Mt. Shasta (*see* Chapter 5), or Big Bear Lake (*see* Chapter 10) for the best trails. Downhill skiing, however, is a rich person's sport: Lift tickets cost around $30–$40, and equipment rental is about $20–$25. Try going midweek, when resorts and lodges offer lower prices and special deals. If surfing-cum-skateboarding on snow is your thing, try the popular sport of snowboarding. Most resorts in California now allow boards, and you can rent the boots and gear for about the same price as skiing equipment. For details check the ***Skier's Guide to California*** (Gulf Publishing Co.; $16), by Nadine Nardi Davidson.

## BEACHES

Those who expect California to have the palm-dotted, serene waters of the tropics will be startled to find beaches with a harsh, violent beauty instead. The coast south of Santa Barbara more or less upholds the *Baywatch* image (prominent lifeguard stands and loads of Beautiful People in skimpy beachwear), but even here the water is rarely warm (about 65°). Farther north, only the foolish and the bold swim in the ocean; doing so means contending with chilly water, deadly undercurrents, and the occasional shark. There are a few safe havens, such as Santa Cruz. Along the Central Coast, beaches give way to the majestic cliffs of Big Sur. Summertime is when most people hit the sand, but don't expect to catch rays on the Central Coast, which is at its foggiest and dampest then. For a really thorough tan, check out Dave Patrick's ***California's Nude Beaches*** (Bold Type, Inc.; $16).

## CRIME AND PUNISHMENT

California's legal drinking age is 21, and it's strictly enforced in cities and college towns. It's essential to carry picture identification such as a passport or driver's license, or you may not be allowed into places that serve alcohol. Drinking and driving is a big no-no. In addition to putting yourself and others in danger, you may get pulled over by the police. If the alcohol content in your blood exceeds the legal .08% limit, you'll be arrested, your license will be suspended, and you'll face fines starting at about $400. Attitudes toward drugs largely depend on the company you keep. One thing is certain: California courts do not have a positive outlook on the subject. Carrying 1 ounce of marijuana is a misdemeanor punishable by up to one year in jail. Possession or sale of hash, cocaine, heroin, or more than an ounce of marijuana is a felony and punishable by more than a year in jail, although first-time offenders are often placed in drug-treatment programs in lieu of prison. How strictly the laws are enforced depends largely on the county in which you're arrested.

## FURTHER READING

A little research before or during your trip can help you make sense or nonsense out of California. Reference works, often pitched to specific kinds of travelers, are legion. Outdoor adventurers should check out the *California Coastal Access Guide* (University of California Press), which provides maps and information about the wildlife along the coast, or *The Pacific Crest Trail* (Wilderness Press), a guide to the southern section of the trail (*see* Hiking, in Getting Around, *above*). Indoor types might prefer Jack Erickson's *Brewery Adventures in the Wild West* (Red Brick Press).

Besides travel guides, there are countless books on California's culture and politics. Marc Reiser's *Cadillac Desert* explores the significance of water to the history of the state, Mike

Davis's excellent *City of Quartz* treats L.A.'s status as a symbol of cultural possibility and political oppression. *The Mayor of Castro Street,* Randy Shilts's biography of late San Francisco Supervisor Harvey Milk (killed together with Mayor George Moscone in 1978), provides insight into the development and politicization of S.F.'s gay community. An even better sense of California emerges from the pages of Joan Didion's essays (try *The White Album* or *Slouching Toward Bethlehem),* Tom Wolfe's *The Electric Kool-Aid Acid Test,* and *West of the West: Imagining California,* an excellent collection of fiction and nonfiction.

*Americans and the California Dream* by Kevin Starr and *California: An Interpretive History* by Walton Bean are good general California history books, the former concentrating on social and cultural aspects, the latter on politics. In addition, many 20th-century American classics are set in California: John Steinbeck's *Grapes of Wrath* and *Cannery Row* (Monterey), Raymond Chandler's *The Big Sleep* (L.A.), Nathaniel West's *Day of the Locust* (L.A.), and Jack Kerouac's *The Subterraneans* (S.F.) are just a few. More recent titles, like Armistead Maupin's *Tales of the City* series (S.F.) and the surrealistic *Vineland* by Thomas Pynchon (North Coast) make good reading on a long Amtrak ride.

As for film, great images of different parts of the state, from *Play It Again Sam's* San Francisco to *Bagdad Café*'s Mojave Desert, can be found at revival houses throughout the country. Leaving aside the more obvious ones (*L.A. Story, The Player, Boyz N the Hood*), a few are essential background: Laslo Benedek's *The Wild One,* starring Marlon Brando as an early Hell's Angel; *American Graffiti,* a vision of youth culture straight out of George Lucas's native Modesto; Billy Wilder's *Sunset Boulevard,* the classic film noir portrayal of the darker side of 1940's Hollywood; Roman Polanski's *Chinatown*; and two films by Amy Heckerling that say a mouthful about Southern California, *Fast Times at Ridgemont High* (1982) and *Clueless* (1995).

# SAN FRANCISCO 2

**San Francisco, love child of the West, remains a proud oasis for people and events** divergent from the norm. On the tiny tip of a peninsula that separates the Pacific Ocean from San Francisco Bay, this hilly, eminently explorable city continues to go about its business with dignity and aplomb, through ubiquitous fog, ever-impending earthquakes, Be-Ins, Love-Ins, and one of the world's most severe AIDS epidemics. Whatever's hit the streets, from the drinking and whoring of the gold prospectors to the living and loving of the country's largest lesbian and gay population, has left reminders of its presence in nooks and crannies all over the city. You've just got to find them: a task that will be a joy, especially if the weather holds.

*Sure, San Francisco is in California, but you're going to freeze your buns off in summer unless you bring some warm clothes.*

Without a doubt, San Francisco is one of the world's most beautiful cities, and upon arrival almost every traveler already knows what he or she wants to see—the Golden Gate Bridge, Alcatraz, cable cars, twisty Lombard Street, and the impossibly steep hills. But don't settle for coffee-table San Francisco: The city has a whole lot more to offer. San Francisco's compactness and density beg you to explore on foot, so take advantage—just wear sturdy shoes and prepare for lots of climbing. Everywhere you go, you'll find something unexpected—a view continuously changing amid tricks of fog and sunlight; a friendly exchange between an aging hippie and a leather-clad skinhead; a Victorian home smack in the midst of a warehouse district. And it all happens so quickly—one minute you're marveling at the frenetic pace of Financial District workers, and the next you're strolling through Chinese herb shops and produce markets. Ten minutes after downing a cappuccino and biscotti in a noisy North Beach café, you're gazing at the Golden Gate Bridge from the water's edge.

Indeed, the city's greatest strength is its astonishing diversity. When you get on a bus and hear snatches of Mandarin, Thai, Spanish, Vietnamese, and Arabic; when city officials ride in the Gay Freedom Day parade not as a token gesture but because they're gay; when in certain neighborhoods you draw dirty looks because you're wearing a suit and tie—you know you're not in Kansas anymore.

San Francisco

Golden Gate Bridge
Fort Point National Historic Site
101
Golden Gate National Recreation Area
PACIFIC OCEAN
The Presidio
1
Baker Beach
Phelan Beach
Lands End
Lincoln Park
Palace of the Legion of Honor
SEACLIFF
W. Pacific Ave.
Lake St.
Clement St.
Point Lobos
Cliff House
Geary Blvd.
43rd Ave.
34th Ave.
25th Ave.
19th Ave.
Park Presidio Blvd.
8th Ave.
Arguello Blvd.
Balboa St.
Turk
RICHMOND
Fulton St.
Golden Gate Park
Kennedy Dr.
Middle Dr.
Martin Luther King Jr. Dr.
Slanyan St.
COLE VALLEY
Lincoln Way
Judah St.
28th Ave.
Lawton St.
Funston Ave.
7th Ave.
Ocean Beach
Great Highway
SUNSET
Noriega St.
Ortega St.
19th Ave.
Clarendon Ave.
Quintara St.
41st Ave.
Sunset Blvd.
PARKSIDE
McCoppin Square
Taraval St.
14th Ave.
Dewey Blvd.
Larsen Park
Vicente St.
Mt. Davidson
Stern Grove
Portola Dr.
Yerba Buena Ave.
San Francisco Zoo
Sloat Blvd
Monterey Blvd.
Ocean Ave.
Miramar Ave.
Harding Park
Lake Merced
Skyline Blvd.
Lake Merced Blvd.
San Francisco State Univ.
Font Blvd.
Junipero Serra Blvd.
Holloway Ave.
Garfield St.
INGLESIDE
Plymouth Ave.
280
Fort Funston
35
Brotherhood Way
N
0
1 mile
0
1 km

San Francisco
San Francisco Bay
Pier 39
TO ALCATRAZ ISLAND
Marina Green
Fort Mason
Fisherman's Wharf
Aquatic Park
MARINA
Bay St.
NORTH BEACH
Coit Tower
Columbus
TELEGRAPH HILL
RUSSIAN HILL
Hyde St.
Lombard St.
101
Ave.
(tunnel)
Ferry Building
San Francisco-Oakland Bay Bridge
CHINATOWN
Grant Ave.
Powell St.
FINANCIAL DISTRICT
PACIFIC HEIGHTS
Broadway
Washington St.
Sacramento St.
California St.
NOB HILL
Gough St.
Van Ness Ave.
UNION SQUARE
80
1st St.
2nd St.
Pine St.
Bush St.
Post St.
Geary St.
JAPAN TOWN
Laguna St.
Divisadero St.
Mission St.
3rd St.
Franklin St.
Turk St.
4th St.
5th St.
SOUTH BEACH
Steiner St.
6th St.
St.
China Basin
Golden Gate Ave.
WESTERN ADDITION
Market St.
SOMA
Fulton St.
Alamo Square
Fell St.
Oak St.
Folsom
Harrison
Bryant
Townsend St.
10th St.
9th St.
Brannan St.
7th St.
Haight St.
Central Skyway
Buena Vista Park
Duboce Ave.
280
Castro St.
Potrero Ave.
Central Basin
17th St.
Harrison St.
Mariposa St.
Market St.
CASTRO
Mission Dolores Park
MISSION
20th St.
South Van Ness Ave.
POTRERO
Pennsylvania Ave.
Indiana St.
3rd St.
Dolores St.
Guerrero St.
Valencia St.
Mission St.
San Francisco General Hospital
25th St.
NOE VALLEY
César Chavez (Army) St.
Islais Cr. Channel
Diamond St.
BERNAL HEIGHTS
India Basin
Oakdale Ave.
GLEN PARK
Bosworth St.
Fwy.
Silver Ave.
Quesada Ave.
Felton Ave.
Hunters Point
Alemany Blvd.
Excelsior Ave.
Mission St.
Persia Ave.
Moscow St.
John McLaren Park
Mansell St.
Gilman Ave.
Jamestown Ave.
France Ave.
Geneva Ave.
South Basin
Candlestick Park
TO COW PALACE
TO SAN FRANCISCO INTERNATIONAL AIRPORT

# Basics

**A good all-purpose source of info is the front-matter of** the San Francisco Yellow Pages, called the **Access Pages,** which lists community organizations, public-transit information, maps, descriptions of famous attractions, and a calendar of events. The best city map—available at most bookstores, convenience stores, liquor stores, and MUNI stations for $2—is the **MUNI Street and Transit Map,** which shows all transit lines and labels all the neighborhoods in the city.

**AMERICAN EXPRESS** AmEx has four offices in San Francisco that offer travel services and cash personal checks for cardholders. For lost or stolen traveler's checks, call 800/221–7282. *Main Office: 237 Post St., btw Grant Ave. and Stockton St., tel. 415/981–5533. Open weekdays 9–5, Sat. 9–2.*

**MEDICAL AID** The **Haight-Ashbury Free Medical Clinic** (558 Clayton St., at Haight St., tel. 415/487–5632) offers free medical service by appointment only (call or come in), but donations are appreciated. It's open Monday–Thursday 1–9, Friday 1–5. To get prescriptions filled after hours, head for one of the chain drugstores. **Walgreen's** offers 24-hour prescription service at two San Francisco locations (498 Castro St., tel. 415/861–3136; 3201 Divisadero St., tel. 415/931–6417).

**PUBLICATIONS** San Francisco's daily morning newspaper is the ***Chronicle***; its afternoon "competition" is the ***Examiner.*** The two merge in a single Sunday edition, which you might want to purchase for its "Datebook" section—commonly called the "Pink Section"— listing cultural and entertainment events for the coming week. Alternative (and far superior) free papers include the weekly ***Bay Guardian,*** a useful and popular compendium of cultural listings, general-interest features, local political commentary, and personal ads.

*If you're tuning in to San Francisco radio, check out Berkeley's KALX (90.7 FM), an alternative college station run by an all-volunteer staff. The University of San Francisco's KUSF (90.3 FM) plays new and ethnic music. Try listener-sponsored KPFA (94.1 FM) for national news, classical music, world music, reggae, rap, and blues.*

**RESOURCES FOR GAYS AND LESBIANS** The **Lavender Youth Recreation and Information Center** (127 Collingwood St., at 18th St., tel. 415/703–6150, hotline 415/863–3636 or 800/246–7743) is a social and support organization for lesbians, gays, and transgenders aged 23 and younger. **Communities United Against Violence** (973 Market St., Suite 500, tel. 415/777–5500, 24-hr emergency hotline 415/333–HELP) provides crisis counseling and referrals for victims of antigay violence. The free weekly newspaper the ***Bay Times*** comes out every two weeks and has a left-of-center orientation. It serves as an information network for the gay, lesbian, and bisexual communities, listing clubs, 12-step meetings, political organizations, and gay business classifieds.

**VISITOR INFORMATION** For pretrip planning, write to the **San Francisco Convention and Visitors Bureau** to receive free information about hotels, restaurants, and shopping. *201 3rd St., Suite 900, 94103, tel. 415/974–6900. 3 blocks from Montgomery St. BART/MUNI. Open weekdays 8:30–5.*

## Get the Spins

***You might have to lug' your laundry a ways to reach the Brainwash Laundromat (7722 Folsom St., btw 7th and 8th Sts., tel. 415/861–FOOD), but once the clothes are in the machine you can drink a beer or a glass of wine, relax over a pizza or sandwich, and listen to live music four nights a week. It's a fine place to exchange your deepest thoughts about powder vs. liquid.***

Once you're in San Francisco, stop in for maps and brochures at the **Visitor Information Center** in the lower level of Hallidie Plaza, next to the Powell Street BART station at Powell and Market streets. *Tel. 415/391-2000. Open weekdays 9-5:30, Sat. 9-3, Sun. 10-2.*

## COMING AND GOING

**BY PLANE** **San Francisco International Airport** (tel. 415/876-7809), the big cheese of Northern California airports, lies about 10 miles south of the city on U.S. 101. All the major domestic airlines and many international ones fly to SFO, as it's called, including United, Delta, USAir, and Continental. The airport has two **currency exchange** offices, both located in the international terminal. Here you'll also find **baggage storage** (near the Air France ticket desk, tel. 415/877-0422), open 7 AM-11 PM. Charges are based on the size of the luggage; an average bag runs $3.50 per day. Lockers (15 by 24 inches, 31 inches deep) cost $1 in quarters per 24 hours. Look for **Travelers Aid Visitor Information** booths in the domestic and international terminals, with information on transportation and lodging, and other special services for the traveler.

➢ **AIRPORT TRANSIT** • The best public transit to and from SFO is **SamTrans Bus 7B** or **7F.** Both lines travel between the airport and San Francisco's Transbay Terminal (board in front of the terminal at Mission and Fremont Sts.). They run every half-hour from about 5:45 AM to 1:15 AM. Express Bus 7F costs $2 and takes 35 minutes; you're restricted to one small carry-on bag. Bus 7B costs $1, takes 55 minutes, and has no luggage restrictions. For more info, call 800/660-4BUS.

Most people, though, feel it's well worth 10 bucks in order to be picked up at their doorstep by a private shuttle. Vans will whisk you to the airport anytime, day or night. Fare from San Francisco to SFO usually runs a mere $10-$11; from other Bay Area cities to SFO or Oakland Airport, you'll pay $10-$25. There's often a reduced rate for two or more people. If you board the shuttle at a major hotel, you could save up to $10. The **Super Shuttle** chain (tel. 415/558-8500) serves SFO from San Francisco and the Peninsula, as does the reliable **Quake City** (tel. 415/255-4899), an employee-owned business with friendly drivers. **BayPorter Express** (tel. 415/467-1800) runs from the East and South bays to SFO, Oakland, and San Jose, and from San Francisco to Oakland.

**BY CAR** From the north, you can reach San Francisco via U.S. 101, which merges with Highway 1 (Pacific Coast Highway) and shoots right over the Golden Gate Bridge ($3) and into the city. From the south, you can either head north on I-5 to I-580 west, north on U.S. 101, or north on Highway 1. From the east, you'll take either I-580 or I-80 west, over the Bay Bridge ($1). For car rental information, *see* Getting Around by Car, *below.*

**BY BUS** **Green Tortoise Adventure Travel** (494 Broadway, San Francisco 94133, tel. 415/285-2441) is *the* cheap, fun alternative to humdrum bus travel. Only on Green Tortoise does your journey from Seattle (24 hrs, $49 one-way) feature a cookout ($3) and skinny-dipping. Buses come equipped with sleeping pads, kitchens, and stereos. You can catch almost all of Green Tortoise's routes from here: Regularly scheduled runs (*also see box* Funky Deals on Wheels, in Chapter 1) go to the Bay Area from L.A. (12 hrs, $30), Eugene (17 hrs, $39), and Portland (20 hrs, $39). All fares are for one-way travel and must be paid in cash, with traveler's checks, or with a money order. Reservations are advised.

**Greyhound** (tel. 800/231-2222) travels to and from San Francisco all day; major destinations include Seattle (20-26 hrs, $62 one-way), Los Angeles (11-12 hrs, $35 one-way), and Santa Cruz (2-4 hrs, $14 one-way). In San Francisco, Greyhound operates out of the **Transbay Terminal** (1st and Mission Sts., tel. 415/495-1569), where many MUNI lines (*see* Getting Around by Bus, *below*) begin. The terminal is prone to gunfire, so it's not a bad idea to plan your arrival for daytime. You'll find Greyhound on the third floor. **Luggage storage** is available for $1.50 per day on the third floor; you pay for one day up front and for the rest when you pick up your bags.

➢ **REGIONAL BUS LINES** • **AC Transit** (tel. 510/839-2882) buses travel between San Francisco and the East Bay 24 hours a day, while **SamTrans** (tel. 800/660-4BUS) services downtown San Francisco from San Mateo County, south of the city. **Golden Gate Transit** (tel. 415/923–2000) runs north from the city to Marin, Napa, and Sonoma counties. Fares and schedules vary. For more information, *see* Chapters 3 and 4.

**BY TRAIN** Several **Amtrak** (tel. 800/USA–RAIL) lines, including the *Zephyr* from Chicago via Denver, the *Coast Starlight* from San Diego and Seattle, and the *Capitol* from Sacramento and the San Joaquin Valley, stop at four East Bay stations: in Richmond (16th St. and MacDonald Ave., adjoining Richmond BART), Berkeley (foot of 3rd St. and University Ave.—you can board, but you can't buy tickets here), Emeryville (5885 Landregan St.), and Oakland (245 2nd St., at Jack London Square). From the Emeryville station, a connecting Amtrak bus runs to San Francisco's Ferry Building (31 Embarcadero, at the foot of Market St.). Fares vary according to the time of year and other factors; round trip to Seattle (24 hrs one-way) runs $88–$176, to Los Angeles (12 hrs one-way) $78–$146.

➢ **REGIONAL TRAIN LINES** • **CalTrain** (tel. 800/660–4BUS) offers regular service from San Francisco (4th and Townsend Sts.) to downtown San Jose (65 Cahill St.) on double-decker trains. One-way fare is $4.50 and the trip takes 1½ hours; trains leave hourly between 5 AM and 10 PM. Along the way, the trains stop at a number of Peninsula cities (including Palo Alto) and Santa Clara. Bikes are allowed on the trains.

## GETTING AROUND

**BY CAR** No, it's not L.A., but no one's going to mistake San Francisco driving for a relaxing spin down a country back road. Common frustrations include high Golden Gate Bridge tolls, traffic jams at any time of day or night, and a notable lack of places to leave the damn car once you've arrived at your destination.

➢ **RENTAL CARS** • The city's relatively small size, combined with a comprehensive public transit system, might persuade you to skip cars altogether. But if you do opt for your own wheels, your best bet is always to rent at one of the airports; Oakland Airport in particular has good deals. If you can't make it to an airport, almost all the rental car agencies have offices in downtown San Francisco, within 5 or 6 blocks of Union Square; look in the Yellow Pages for listings (*also see* Getting Around, in Chapter 1). Unfortunately, all Bay Area companies require a credit card for deposit purposes.

*Welcome to San Francisco—hope you left your car behind. If you ever find a parking space, it might be on the side of a sheer precipice. Remember to curb your wheels, set the emergency brake, and, if you're in a stick-shift, leave the car in gear.*

➢ **PARKING** • Plenty of lots and garages offer parking by the hour or by the day. Pay close attention to rates, as they can get quite steep, especially around prime tourist country like Fisherman's Wharf. In the Union Square area, you can expect to find a parking place at the large **Sutter-Stockton Garage** (444 Stockton St., tel. 415/982–7275). They charge a graduated rate—$3 for three hours, $8 for five hours, and $18 for 24 hours. The cheapest lot near Fisherman's Wharf ($2 an hour) is the **Wharf Garage** (350 Beach St., btw Taylor and Mason Sts.). Near North Beach and Chinatown, try the lot at the **corner of Sansome and Pacific**; on weekends they have a flat $4 fee, which you pay on the honor system.

**BY BUS** **MUNI** (tel. 415/673–MUNI), San Francisco's bus and streetcar service, runs buses as often as every five minutes in certain well-traveled parts of town. Between 1 AM and 5 AM, only nine lines run every 30 minutes. Adult fare is $1 and includes a one-hour transfer; youth, senior, and disabled fare is 35¢. Short-term **Passport** passes allow unlimited access to MUNI (including cable cars) for one day ($6), three days ($10), or one week ($15). Get a one-day pass on board; others can be bought at the Powell and Market cable-car turnaround.

*For great views, take the California Street cable car or the Hyde and Powell line. On the latter, you get a gander at Alcatraz and pass right by Lombard Street, the crookedest street in the world.*

➢ **CABLE CARS** • San Francisco's cable cars were the world's first large-scale mechanized street transportation. If you can handle throngs of tourists, the cable cars are actually pretty groovy. They run at a pace straight out of the early

1900s (the cables that propel the cars move at 9½ mph), so if you're Type A, take the bus. Fare is $2, though a MUNI Passport (*see above*) allows you to ride for free. All three lines run from around 6 AM to a little before 1 AM.

**BY BART** Relatively clean and quiet, **Bay Area Rapid Transit (BART)** (tel. 415/992–2278 or 510/465–BART) is a smooth subway system somewhat reminiscent of Disneyland's Monorail. Unlike many subways, its primary purpose is not to get you around within the city but to move you from city to city. Its four lines reach 34 stations, serving San Francisco, Daly City to the south, and the East Bay. BART trains head out on their last run of the day around midnight; you may be able to catch trains at some stations as late as 1:30 AM, but don't bank on it or you may be left stranded. Service starts up again at 4 AM weekdays, 6 AM Saturdays, and 8 AM Sundays. Expect trains every 15–20 minutes; schedules are available at the stations. The cost of a ticket ranges from 90¢ to $3.45, depending on the length of the journey; for example, the 25-minute trip from downtown San Francisco to Berkeley costs $2.10. The disabled get a good discount deal: a $16 ticket for $4. Bearers of BART bicycle permits ($3 for three years) can bring their bikes onto most trains. Call for more info.

**BY TAXI** You can hail a cab in San Francisco, but you may end up standing in the street for hours. Most residents phone. All taxis are metered, but you might be able to negotiate a flat rate to the airport at the driver's discretion. **Veteran's Cab** (tel. 415/552–1300) in San Francisco charges a base fee of $1.70, 30¢ every one-sixth of a mile, and 30¢ per minute of waiting time or traffic delay. Don't forget to tip the driver; 15% is typical.

**BY FERRY** In terms of speed, ferries are comparable to other forms of transport, and they afford lovely views, too. **Golden Gate Ferry** (tel. 415/332–6600) crosses the bay between Marin County (Larkspur Landing, Tiburon, or Sausalito) and the San Francisco Ferry Building (31 Embarcadero, foot of Market St.). Ferries run from about 7 AM to 8 PM; one-way fare, which includes free transfers to Golden Gate Transit buses, is $2.50–$4.25 depending on your destination.

The **Oakland/Alameda Ferry** (tel. 510/522–3300), also known as the **Blue and Gold Fleet,** leaves from Jack London Square in Oakland, or from the Alameda Ferry Dock, and arrives at the San Francisco Ferry Building 30 minutes later. The boat then continues to Pier 39 at Fisherman's Wharf. Ferries begin running from the East Bay at 6 AM on weekdays, 10 AM on weekends and holidays, and leave on their last run at 7:55 PM. From Memorial Day to Labor Day, weekend runs are expanded. One-way adult fare is $3.75, disabled fare $2.50. Ferry stubs serve as transfers to MUNI and AC Transit.

# Where to Sleep

**For an expensive city, San Francisco has a sur**prisingly large assortment of reasonably priced and centrally located accommodations. For a great no-frills deal, stay in one of nine hostels or one of the residential hotels that can be found downtown, in the South of Market (SoMa) area, and North Beach. For a bit more ($30–$50 a night), many small downtown hotels offer charming "European-style" rooms (i.e., the toilet's down the hall). Then there's the specialty hotel, which may cause you to shake your head and sigh, "Only in San Francisco." Where else would you find the leather-and-Levi's gay B&B, or the inn whose nightly accommodations include the "Summer of Love Room" and the "Japanese Tea Garden Room"?

If you don't reserve one to two weeks in advance in summer, you may be exiled to the strip of motels along **Lombard Street** in the Marina district, about a 20-minute bus ride from downtown (on Bus 76) but quite close to Fisherman's Wharf. On Lombard, you'll pay an annoying $50–$70 for a double. Sixth Street in SoMa has its share of "last resort" places, but the neighborhood can be unsafe; if you do want to stay in SoMa—near the Museum of Modern Art and much of the city's more hard-core nightlife—try one of the hostels.

## HOTELS AND MOTELS

**DOWNTOWN** Stay downtown if you want to be surrounded by tall buildings, old architecture (at least, old by California standards), fog, and tourists. Most of the small European-style hotels are here, affirming an ambience that'll make you sure you've time-warped into the '40s. Staying downtown offers the added advantage of easy proximity to North Beach, Fisherman's Wharf, Chinatown, and Union Square. The neighborhood is deserted at night and not particularly safe; keep your wits about you. For a map of Downtown lodging, *see* Exploring, *below*.

➢ **UNDER $40** • **Alexander Inn.** An upscale version of a European-style hotel, the Alexander—2 blocks west of Union Square—has deferential employees, sunny rooms with color TVs and coffeemakers, real wood furniture, and an international clientele. If you're willing to share a bath, you pay a super-low $35 per night (singles and doubles with private bath cost $72). *415 O'Farrell St., at Taylor St., tel. 415/928–6800 or 800/843–8709. From Powell St. BART/MUNI, walk 2 blocks west on Eddy St., 2 blocks north on Taylor St. 76 rooms, most with bath. Reserve 1 week in advance.*

**Hyde Plaza Hotel.** This well-kept, European-style hotel, in limbo between Van Ness Avenue, the Tenderloin, and Nob Hill, offers a good deal: Nightly rates run anywhere from $30 per double to $45 for a room sleeping four, with a weekly rate for a double of about $150. The beautiful old building features an adjoining restaurant. *835 Hyde St., near Sutter St., tel. 415/885–2987. From Montgomery St. BART/MUNI, Bus 2, 3, or 4 west on Sutter St. to Hyde St. 50 rooms, most with shared bath. Laundry, luggage storage.*

**Olympic Hotel.** The Olympic is centrally located near Union Square. The clean, small rooms are basic and functional and the lobby is almost charming (though the building itself is slightly rundown). The hotel seems to appeal to backpackers, both American and from abroad. A single or double with shared bath is $30; rooms with private bath are $45. *140 Mason St., at Ellis St., tel. 415/982–5010. From Powell St. BART/MUNI, walk 1 block west on Eddy St. and ½ block north on Mason St. 120 rooms, half with bath. Laundry. Reserve 1 week in advance in summer.*

**Herbert Hotel.** The proprietor of this residential hotel, a block from Union Square, rents out only a few rooms by the night ($40 for a double with private bath), but you can't beat the weekly rates: $150 for a clean, midsized double with private bath. The hotel doesn't usually take reservations, but if you call ahead and explain your plans, the manager might hold a room for you. *161 Powell St., btw Ellis and O'Farrell Sts., tel. 415/362–1600. From Powell St. BART/MUNI, walk 1½ blocks north on Powell St. 100 rooms, half with bath.*

➢ **UNDER $50** • **Adelaide Inn.** This place is comfortable in a kitschy, Swiss way (you'd expect a cuckoo clock on the mantelpiece, if there was a mantelpiece). Very popular with Europeans, it's minutes from Union Square. Singles run $32–$38, doubles $42–$48, depending on room size and availability. Rates include a continental breakfast. *5 Isadora Duncan Ln., near Taylor St., tel. 415/441–2261. From Montgomery St. BART/MUNI, Bus 38 NW to Geary and Taylor Sts., walk ¾ block north on Taylor St., and turn left. 18 rooms, none with private bath. Kitchen. Reserve in summer.*

**Grant Hotel.** The gaudy red decor won't appear in *Interior Design Monthly* anytime soon, but this hotel's location on Nob Hill, 2 blocks from Union Square and Chinatown, is unbeatable. The rooms have furniture that looks like it came from Grandma's basement, clean bedding, TVs, phones, and private baths—not bad for $49 per double. Try to reserve about a week in advance in summer, or show up in the morning on the day you arrive, when there may be cancellations. *753 Bush St., btw Powell and Mason Sts., tel. 415/421–7540 or 800/522–0979. From Powell St. BART/MUNI, walk 5½ blocks north on Powell St. and turn left. 76 rooms.*

➢ **UNDER $70** • **Brady Acres.** Come to this small, comfortable hotel near the Theater District when you long for the comforts of home. Each room includes a fully equipped kitchenette with microwave, toaster, coffeemaker, and minifridge filled with chocolates and jam; the bathrooms have not only cozy towels but also a variety of shampoos and soaps. Your phone comes with an answering machine and each room has a TV and a radio with cassette player. Singles are $50–$60, doubles $60–$75; ask about weekly specials. *649 Jones St., btw Post and Geary Sts., tel. 415/929–8033 or 800/627–2396. From Montgomery St. BART/MUNI, Bus 38 west to Geary and Jones Sts. 25 rooms. Laundry. Reservations advised in summer.*

**Golden Gate Hotel.** At this small hotel atop Nob Hill, spotless rooms are decorated with wicker, antiques, floral wallpaper, and fresh flowers. Rooms with shared bath ($59 per double) are a better bargain than the slightly larger rooms with private bath ($89 per double). The hotel offers a continental breakfast in the morning and afternoon tea in the front sitting room, where you'll meet a pretty diverse bunch of globetrotters. *775 Bush St., btw Powell and Mason Sts., tel. 415/392–3702. Follow directions to Grant Hotel (see above). 23 rooms, half with bath. Reserve 2–3 weeks in advance in summer.*

➢ **UNDER $85 • Amsterdam.** For a Victorian bed-and-breakfast two blocks from Nob Hill, this is a sweet deal: $69 for two people (rates are lower off-season). The recently renovated rooms have cable TV and most have private bath; you'll pay $50 if you're willing to share a bath. When the temperature drops to a windy 50° on an August night, you'll be stoked on the cozy reading room. And when the sun shines, your complimentary breakfast is served on the patio. *749 Taylor St., btw Sutter and Bush Sts., tel. 415/673–3277 or 800/637–3444. From Montgomery St. BART/MUNI, Bus 2, 3, or 4 west on Sutter St. 34 rooms.*

**CIVIC CENTER** The area around the Civic Center should be a great place to stay: Davies Symphony Hall, the Opera House, and a host of theaters are all within easy walking distance, and many of the city's public transport lines converge here. Sadly, the Civic Center is also incredibly sleazy, especially at night, due to an active drug scene. Solo travelers, especially women, should avoid the triangle formed by Market, Larkin, and Geary streets. For a map of Civic Center lodging, *see* Exploring, *below.*

➢ **UNDER $45 • Aida Hotel.** Tourists from all over the world crash at this centrally located hotel a block from Civic Center BART. For $37 a night you get a clean double with TV and phone (bath down the hall); for $8 more your room will have a private bath. Since there are 174 rooms, you can probably get something at the last minute even during high season. *1087 Market St., at 7th St., tel. 415/863–4141. From Civic Center BART/MUNI, walk 1 block NE on Market St. Free breakfast, luggage storage.*

➢ **UNDER $55 • Albergo Verona.** In a neighborhood that's central but dicey, this beautifully renovated turn-of-the-century hotel is a safe haven that attracts all sorts of international travelers. Rooms, some with private bath, are a good deal at $40–$50 per double. Also here are 14 dorm spaces in two-, four-, and six-person rooms, which rent for $17 per person; all rates include morning coffee and doughnuts. *317 Leavenworth St., at Eddy St., tel. 415/771–4242 or 800/422–3646. From Powell St. BART/MUNI, walk 4 blocks west on Eddy St. 67 rooms.*

➢ **UNDER $100 • Phoenix Hotel.** In the nether regions of the Tenderloin, the Phoenix has built a reputation among young hipsters. Bands like the Red Hot Chili Peppers, NRBQ, Simple Minds, and Living Colour have stayed here; and original work by Bay Area artists spices up the alternately tropical and Southwestern design scheme. The hotel is joined at the hip, as it were, to Miss Pearl's Jam House (*see* Food, *below*). In high season, you'll pay $89 for a single or double, but rates go down as much as $20 in winter, depending on demand. If you seek a quiet night, ask at the front desk for earplugs (where you'll also find complimentary condoms and dental floss). *601 Larkin St., at Eddy St., tel. 415/776–1380. From Powell St. BART/MUNI, Bus 31 west on Eddy St. 44 rooms. Wheelchair access.*

**NORTH BEACH** North Beach is a great place to stay: It's near downtown, Chinatown, and Fisherman's Wharf; and no part of the city feels more classically San Franciscan. Many of the city's best restaurants and cafés are here, too. Unfortunately, you'll have to search hard for something affordable. For a map of North Beach lodging, *see* Exploring, *below.*

➢ **UNDER $40 • Europa Hotel.** Sandwiched between two establishments boasting of "totally, completely, entirely nude girls," this place tries hard to be a bastion of morality. The security entrance (guests are buzzed in) and lengthy list of rules make it fairly safe, though it looks divey—and some strange characters were spied wandering the incense-scented halls. If you don't mind street noise, ask for a room with a view of Broadway and Columbus. Doubles go for $30. *310 Columbus Ave., at Broadway, tel. 415/391–5779. From Montgomery St. BART/MUNI, Bus 15 north to Columbus Ave. and Broadway. 76 rooms, none with bath.*

➢ **UNDER $65 • San Remo Hotel.** A short walk from both Fisherman's Wharf and North Beach, the lovely San Remo is an incredible bargain in a pricey area: $55–$65 for a double with shared bath. The hotel boasts helpful management, beautiful redwood furnishings, stained-glass windows, and quiet, spotless rooms. *2237 Mason St., btw Francisco and Chestnut Sts., tel. 415/776–8688. From Montgomery St. BART/MUNI, Bus 15 north to Chestnut St., walk 1 block west.*

**THE MARINA** The Marina is a quiet, safe residential neighborhood popular with young folks busy climbing the corporate ladder. It's a long walk from North Beach, Chinatown, and downtown, but the views of the bay and the Golden Gate Bridge from the nearby waterfront are tremendous. Unfortunately, most of the lodging in this area lies along busy Lombard Street, lined with run-down motels, gas stations, and cheap restaurants. For a map of Marina hotels, *see* Exploring, *below.*

➢ **UNDER $85** • **Marina Motel.** If you decide to stay in the Marina, head straight for the Spanish-style stucco facade of the Marina Motel, where doubles ($70) are slightly cheaper than at other motels nearby; prices rise during peak season. About half the rooms have kitchens. *2576 Lombard St., btw Broderick and Divisadero Sts., tel. 415/921–9406. From Montgomery St. BART/MUNI, Bus 30 north to Broderick and Chestnut Sts., walk 1 block south, and turn left. 45 rooms.*

**HAIGHT AND WESTERN ADDITION** Rock bands (the Dead, Janis Joplin), poets (Allen Ginsberg), psycho cult families (the Mansons), and runaway flower children have all settled in the Haight at one time or another, and it remains a fun, eclectic neighborhood. Staying here offers great insights on how the postcollege set lives in San Francisco, and it's close to other fine districts like the Castro and the Mission. Caution is advised around lower Haight Street at night. For a map of Haight and Western Addition lodging, *see* Exploring, *below.*

➢ **UNDER $20** • **Sappho's.** Just arrived in town and need a safe, affordable room in a single-sex environment? Then head immediately to Sappho's. This women's residence, a seven-bedroom Victorian house on the edge of the Western Addition, is a secure, welcoming space for single women who need a temporary home for the night or the week or the month (monthly rates in effect Oct.–Apr.). Not only does a bed in a two- or three-person room cost but $20 a night, the management also provides resources to help you find work and permanent housing. Certain rules apply—no men upstairs, limited smoking areas, clean up after yourself—but they're all meant to enhance the feeling of comfort and cooperation, as is the meditation garden outside. *859 Fulton St., near Fillmore St., tel. 415/775–3243. From Civic Center BART/MUNI, Bus 5 west on McAllister St. to Fillmore St.*

*If you get lucky you might share quarters at Sappho's with an all-girl punk band or lesbian movie directors in town for the film festival.*

➢ **UNDER $50** • **Metro Hotel.** This hotel, whose neon sign lights up a major Western Addition through street, is a good mid-range lodging option. The whole place was recently redone and its 23 rooms are large and comfortable. Try to get a room in back, away from street noise. Singles and doubles cost $45; add $10 for a third person. *319 Divisadero St., btw Oak*

## *Zen and the Art of Sleeping*

***If you have an honest interest in enlightenment and you're not just looking for a cheap place to crash, the San Francisco Zen Center, between the Civic Center and the lower Haight, has a few rooms for visitors. You get a spotless, nicely furnished room overlooking a courtyard ($30–$40 for a single, $40–$50 for a double with shared bath), plus a hearty breakfast. This working temple also offers a guest-student program ($10 a night) in which you adhere to the center's meditation, work, and meal schedules for one to six weeks. You should reserve in advance, especially during summer. 300 Page St., at Laguna St., tel. 415/863–3136. From Market St. downtown, Bus 7 or 71 west to Page and Laguna Sts.***

*and Page Sts., tel. 415/861–5364. From Market St. downtown, Bus 7 or 71 west to Divisadero and Haight Sts.; walk north 1½ blocks. Reservations advised in summer.*

➢ **UNDER $100 • The Red Victorian.** At this immensely popular Haight Street relic, each room is decorated according to a particular theme. You can crash in the Japanese Tea Garden Room ($96), the Summer of Love Room, or the Skylight Room (painted in deep jewel tones, with a skylight in the ceiling; $86). Some rooms are more gimmicky than others, but it's clear from the moment you walk in that the proprietors take great care with every aspect of this place. *1665 Haight St., btw Belvedere and Cole Sts., tel. 415/864–1978. From Market St. downtown, Bus 7 or 71 west to Haight and Cole Sts. 18 rooms, most with shared bath. Reservations advised in summer.*

**CASTRO DISTRICT** As the United States' most prominent gay neighborhood, the Castro naturally offers a wide variety of gay-and lesbian-friendly accommodations. Reserve way, way, way in advance for the Gay and Lesbian Freedom Day Parade weekend (end of June). For a map of Castro lodging, *see* Exploring, *below*.

➢ **UNDER $50 • Twin Peaks.** Firm beds and clean bathrooms compensate for the generic motel decor. Doubles are $38 ($45 with private bath); weekly rates are $135–$170, depending on room size. *2160 Market St., btw Church and Sanchez Sts., tel. 415/621–9467. MUNI K, L, or M Streetcar to Church St., walk 1 block SW on Market St. 60 rooms.*

➢ **UNDER $85 • 24 Henry.** This charming B&B caters to a mostly gay and lesbian clientele. The management is friendly, the rooms are colorful and cozy, the showers are big enough for two, and a complimentary breakfast is served in the Victorian-style parlor. Doubles are $75–$95 per night. *24 Henry St., btw 14th and 15th Sts., tel. 415/864–5686 or 800/900–5686. MUNI J Streetcar to 16th and Church Sts., walk 3 blocks west to Noe St., 3 blocks north to Henry St. Reservations advised.*

➢ **UNDER $100 • The Black Stallion.** The city's only leather-and-Levi's B&B provides an immaculate, comfortable home base from which to explore the Castro. The hotel has nine rooms ($85–$110), all with shared bath, featuring gorgeous woodwork and one working fireplace. *635 Castro St., at 19th St., tel. 415/863–0131. Kitchen, sundeck. Reservations a must in summer.*

**MISSION DISTRICT** This lively neighborhood is home not only to the city's Latino communities, but also to a sizable multi-ethnic population of young, politically radical types. It's not the safest part of San Francisco, but intellectually it's an exciting place to be. For a map of Mission district hotels, *see* Exploring, *below*.

➢ **UNDER $20 • Curtis Hotel.** The Mission has its share of shady characters, but this hotel works hard to keep the riffraff out. They also offer a sweet deal: A clean single with shared bath is just $85 a week (no doubles); talk to the owner about shorter stays. If you get too wild, the owner will throw you back out on the street. Yikes. *559 Valencia St., near 16th St., tel. 415/621–9337. From 16th St./Mission BART, walk 1 block west on 16th St., left on Valencia. 60 rooms, none with bath. Key deposit ($2).*

## HOSTELS

Perhaps due to the dearth of other budget accommodations, San Francisco's hostels are extremely popular; you should make reservations before you arrive in the city. In a pinch, you could also try Albergo Verona (*see* Civic Center, *above*), which charges $17 for one of 14 dorm spaces. Unless otherwise noted, all the hostels listed below have 24-hour receptions, and do not have curfews or lockouts.

**AYH Hostel at Union Square.** A block from Union Square, this huge hostel sleeps more than 220 people in rooms with one to four beds ($14, $17 for nonmembers). The interior is bright and pleasant, and the hostel includes such amenities as a TV room, a kitchen (with microwaves, toasters, and refrigerators), a smoking room, and other common spaces. Bulletin boards offer info on nightlife and San Francisco attractions. About 40% of the rooms are set aside for reservations, which must be made at least 48 hours in advance ($14 deposit). You can stay a maximum of six days in high season, 14 days otherwise. *312 Mason St., btw O'Farrell and Geary Sts., tel. 415/788–5604. From Powell St. BART/MUNI, walk 1½ blocks north on Powell St., 1 block west on O'Farrell St., turn right. Wheelchair access.*

**European Guest House.** A good choice for those wanting to take advantage of SoMa nightlife, this midsize hostel offers decent, if unspectacular, lodging in one 15-bed room ($10 per person), four-person dorms ($12 per person), or rooms sleeping two ($14 per person). It's got a rooftop sundeck, a common room, and a kitchen. *761 Minna St., tel. 415/861–6634. Near Mission St., btw 8th and 9th Sts. From Civic Center BART/MUNI, walk 2 blocks south on 8th St., turn right onto Minna. Deposit ($5), laundry.*

**Fort Mason International Hostel.** This AYH hostel, perched above the waterfront, will dazzle you with its views of the bay and the Golden Gate Bridge. The rules and regulations are tedious and complex, however, so pay close attention: It's almost impossible to stay here unless you reserve ahead. Reservations (by phone or in person) must be made at least 24 hours ahead with a credit card, or by sending the cost of your first night's stay at least two weeks prior to your arrival with the names and genders of those in your party, as well as the dates you intend to stay. Get here *early* if you don't have a reservation. Beds are $13–$14 a night for both members and nonmembers. During summer you can stay a maximum of 14 nights. You've got to perform a chore each day, and smoking is not allowed. Whew. *Bldg. 240, Box A, San Francisco 94123, tel. 415/771–7277. From Transbay Terminal, MUNI Bus 42 to Van Ness Ave. and Bay St.; turn right on Bay St. and follow signs. 150 beds. Lockout 11–3. Reception open daily 7–2 and 3–midnight. Bike and luggage storage, common room, free linen, kitchen, laundry.*

**Globetrotter's Inn.** Its lack of restrictions (curfew, chores, etc.) and its small size—it sleeps only 39—are among the strengths of this independent hostel on the edge of the down-and-out Tenderloin. It's not as new or sunny as some of the others, but the staff has done its best, putting artwork on the walls and creating a comfortable common space with a TV, plants, and a 24-hour kitchen. A space in a double or in a four- or six-person dorm goes for $12; single rooms are $24. *225 Ellis St., btw Mason and Taylor Sts., tel. 415/346–5786. From Powell St. BART/MUNI, walk ½ block north on Powell St., 1½ blocks west on Ellis St. Reception open 8–1 and 5–9. Key deposit ($5), laundry.*

**Grand Central Hostel.** The transformation of a centrally but seedily located flophouse into this hostel has been snazzily accomplished. The 122 rooms (dorms $12 a night, $75 a week; singles $20 a night; doubles $30 a night) come with an exercise room, TV rooms, unlimited free coffee, all kinds of social events, free linen, a pool table, a jukebox, and table tennis. All guests must have passports and travel documents to stay here. *1412 Market St., at 10th St., tel. 415/703–9988. From Van Ness MUNI, walk 1 block NE on Market St. 21-day maximum stay.*

**Green Tortoise Guest House.** Green Tortoise is smack-dab in the middle of hip North Beach, just blocks from the Financial District and Chinatown. Cool Eurobackpackers inhabit most of the rooms, which are clean, spacious, and rarely vacant—call ahead. A single bunk is only $12, a private double $35. *494 Broadway, btw Montgomery and Kearny Sts., tel. 415/834–9060. 5 blocks north of TransAmerica Pyramid. From Montgomery St. BART/MUNI, Bus 15 or 9X north. 40 rooms. Complimentary breakfast, common rooms, kitchen, laundry, sauna.*

**Interclub Globe Hostel.** Intended for international travelers (though passport-carrying Americans are not turned away), this SoMa hostel has few rules and a warm, relaxed atmosphere—not to mention a pool table and a sundeck with a great view of the city. Guests sleep four to a room, and each room has a bathroom; two floors are reserved for nonsmokers. A bed is $15 in summer, $12 other times. At the adjoining canteen you can get dinner for under $5. *10 Hallam Pl., near Folsom St. btw 7th and 8th Sts., tel. 415/431–0540. From Civic Center BART/MUNI, walk 3 blocks south on 8th St., left on Folsom St. 100 beds. Laundry.*

**Pacific Tradewinds.** The antithesis of an institutional hostel, this homey place in Chinatown has only four rooms (28 beds total), plus a friendly common space and a kitchen. There's no official lockout (although they like people to be gone during the afternoon), and if you want to come in after midnight, the proprietors will lend you a key ($10 deposit). Ask them about cheap restaurants and other attractions in the area. Beds are usually $14 a night, but this fluctuates. If you stay seven nights, you only pay for six; in summer, they ask that you pay the week in advance. *680 Sacramento St., near Kearny St., tel. 415/433–7970. From Montgomery St. BART/MUNI, Bus 15 north on Kearny St. Reception open 8 AM–midnight.*

**San Francisco International Student Center.** Small, homey, and right in the middle of the hip SoMa area, the center has 16 rooms with three to five beds ($13 a night, $84 a week) in each, a small kitchen, a sunny rooftop, and a common room. The center rents rooms to students only; Americans must present passports and travel documents. *1188 Folsom St., near 8th St., tel. 415/255–8800. From Civic Center BART/MUNI, walk 3 blocks south on 8th St. to Folsom. Reception open 9 AM–11 PM.*

# Food

**San Francisco has more than 4,000 restaurants to satisfy** everyone from lobster lovers to tofu fanatics. Waves of Asian and Latino immigrants have brought the city a tasty cavalcade of good-deal taquerías, Chinese restaurants, gracious Thai and Vietnamese establishments, reasonably priced sushi houses, and Korean and Mongolian barbecue joints. These places come equipped with a seemingly endless selection of restaurant reviews, dutifully pasted up in almost every window. Don't assume this little strip of paper means the place is any good, however. Always check the date of the review, since writers frequently update their impressions and restaurants regularly change owners and chefs. One of the more reliable reviewers is Jim Wood, who writes for the *Examiner.*

## DOWNTOWN

Downtown abounds with old, classic restaurants that evoke San Francisco's golden years, and lunch counters that still feature blue-plate specials and chocolate malteds. Some newer haunts cater to a high-rolling Financial District clientele, and the occasional health-food joint attempts to keep all those executives from succumbing to heart disease at a young age. The **International Food Fair** (24 Ellis St., at Market St.) probably contains the highest concentration of cheap eats in all of downtown: Persian, Greek, Burmese, Korean, Mexican, Japanese, Chinese, and American fast-food concessions rub shoulders, offering $3–$5 lunch specials.

*One way to keep dining costs low is to make lunch your biggest meal, and thus take advantage of the cheap lunch specials available all over town.*

➢ **UNDER $5 • Specialty's.** This quartet of tiny takeout stands bakes 14 kinds of bread, including potato-cheese, herb, nine-grain, and carrot-curry, on which they will make any of 40—count 'em, 40—fresh sandwiches ($3–$7). If you don't feel like eating on the sidewalk, head over to the rooftop garden at Crocker Galleria (cnr Kearny and Post Sts.) and relax. *312 Kearny St., btw Bush and Pine Sts.; 22 Battery St., at Market St.; 150 Spear St., btw Mission and Howard Sts.; 1 Post St., at Market St. Tel. 415/896–BAKE for daily specials, 415/512–9550 for phone orders. Open weekdays 6–6. No credit cards.*

➢ **UNDER $10 • 101 Restaurant.** This highly respected Vietnamese restaurant in the downtrodden Tenderloin serves up a tasty *chao tom* (shrimp and sugarcane; $8) or *ga xao lang* (coconut chicken and lemongrass curry; $5.25). At lunch they have a $4.75 special with soup, an imperial roll, and your choice of barbecued beef, chicken, or pork. *101 Eddy St., at Mason St., tel. 415/928–4490. Open Mon.–Sat. 11–9.*

**Café Bastille.** Come here for neat little French appetizers like onion soup, pâté, or baked goat cheese on eggplant ($3–$5) in a happening Gallic atmosphere. For a more substantial meal, they've got sandwiches ($5–$7) and crêpe dinners ($6.50). The café gets fun and friendly, especially when the live jazz is going Wednesday–Saturday. *22 Belden Pl., btw Pine and Bush Sts. and Kearny and Montgomery Sts., tel. 415/986–5673. Open Mon.–Thurs. 11–10, Fri. 11–11, Sat. 11 AM–2 AM.*

➢ **UNDER $15 • Yank Sing.** The tasteful, modern setting makes this a great place to feast on *dim sum* (small dumplings that you choose from passing carts and pay for by the plate). A meal should cost $10–$15 per person, but watch out: Let your appetite run away with you and next thing you know your pants are unbuttoned, your head is nodding, stacks of plates are sliding off the table, and the waiter's handing you a bill the size of Beijing. *427 Battery St., at Clay St., tel. 415/362–1640. Open weekdays 11–3, weekends 10–4.*

## CIVIC CENTER

Along with museums and theaters, this area also offers a number of restaurants for every price range. To grab a bite on your way to—or a cuppa joe after—the opera, walk along **Hayes** and **Grove streets** between Franklin and Laguna—the area is a prime example of gentrification in progress, with cafés and restaurants sprouting up all over the place. Stay alert around here at night.

➢ **UNDER $5** • **Main Squeeze.** This space-age juice bar on Polk Street, innovatively designed with industrial materials molded into postmodern pieces of fruit, specializes in juices ($2.75–$3.75), but also has a decent breakfast and lunch menu that's 100% vegetarian, partially vegan, and includes focaccia sandwiches ($4–$5) and healthy soups ($2.50). *1515 Polk St., at California St., tel. 415/567–1515. Open Mon.–Sat. 8–6, Sun. 9–7.*

➢ **UNDER $10** • **Ananda Fuara.** Escape from grimy Market Street to this vegetarian restaurant and its soothing sky-blue walls. Servers in flowing saris sway past the tables, bearing entrées like curry with rice and chutney ($7) or various sandwiches ($5). The massive Brahma burrito ($5) will keep you full all day. *1298 Market St., at 9th St., tel. 415/621–1994. Open Mon.–Sat. 8–8 (Wed. only until 3 PM). Wheelchair access. No credit cards.*

**Moishe's Pippic.** This Chicago-style Jewish deli will satisfy the corned-beef pangs of relocated, alienated East Coasters. They've got it all: kosher salami, hot dogs, corned beef, chopped liver, pastrami, tongue, bagels and lox, matzo ball soup, Polish sausage, knishes . . . It'll almost make living in California bearable. Hot dogs start at $2.50, sandwiches at $5. *425A Hayes St., at Gough St., tel. 415/431–2440. Open weekdays 8–4, Sat. 9:30–4. No credit cards.*

**Racha Café.** In a city brimming with Thai restaurants, this is an exceptional choice for both the food and the service. Try the spicy mint chicken (around $6) or the tasty vegetables with peanut sauce ($5.50). *771 Ellis St., at Polk St., tel. 415/885–0725. Open daily 11–9:30. Wheelchair access.*

*A little sister to Stars, one of the city's most highly touted (and priciest) restaurants, is Stars Café (500 Van Ness Ave., tel. 415/861–4344), where you get similarly inventive California cuisine for about half what it costs at the main restaurant next door.*

➢ **UNDER $15** • **Golden Turtle.** Here you can consume some of San Francisco's best Vietnamese food in high style, among carved-wood pieces that look like they belong in an Asian art collection. The barbecued quail is excellent ($5), and a number of vegetarian dishes, such as spicy lemongrass vegetable curry ($9), round out the menu. *2211 Van Ness Ave., btw Broadway and Vallejo St., tel. 415/441–4419. Open Tues.–Sun. 11–3 and 5–11.*

➢ **UNDER $20** • **Miss Pearl's Jam House.** Miss Pearl's live reggae and calypso music (Thursday–Saturday nights) and Soul-Food Sunday gospel performances attract a young, lively crowd. You'll have to traipse through a scuzzy neighborhood to get here, but once you arrive you can eat poolside (weekends only; the pool belongs to the attached Phoenix Hotel) or in the Jamaican-style dining room. In addition to a selection of Caribbean entrées ($12–$18), the restaurant serves inventive appetizers like corn and machego cheese *arepas* (fritters) with smoked tomato salad ($5). *601 Eddy St., at Larkin St., tel. 415/775–5267. Open Wed.–Thurs. 6 PM–10 PM, Fri.–Sat. 6 PM–11 PM, Sun. 11–2:30 and 5:30–10.*

## CHINATOWN

Finding something to eat in Chinatown will probably be one of your easiest and most pleasurable projects. Steer clear of the glaringly tourist-oriented restaurants (where you have to ask for chopsticks). For extra adventure, go to a place with no English on the menu, close your eyes, and point to something.

➢ **UNDER $5** • **Lucky Creation.** This small restaurant in the heart of Chinatown serves fantastic meatless fare. From its green sign to its green tabletops and green menus, Lucky Creation is loud and clear about aiming to please the vegetarian palate. And it's cheap. Mixed vegetables over rice go for $3.75, and braised eggplant in a clay pot will run you just $4. *854 Washington St., near Stockton St., tel. 415/989–0818. Open Thurs.–Tues. 11–9:30. No credit cards.*

➢ **UNDER $10** • **Chef Jia's.** Next door to the ever-popular House of Nanking (*see below*), Chef Jia's manages to survive, indeed thrive, because of its top-notch Hunan and Mandarin cuisine. The onion cakes ($1.50) and the spicy yams in garlic sauce ($4) are both awe-inspiring. It's noisy and crowded, and the decor leaves a bit to be desired, but the food will make you forget about all that. *925 Kearny St., btw Jackson and Columbus Sts., tel. 415/398–1626. Open daily 11–10. No credit cards.*

**House of Nanking.** This Chinatown standby offers excellent Shanghai-style home cooking at relatively low prices. The space is tiny and constantly packed with locals and tourists alike, the decor is nonexistent, and the waiters keep you on your toes. Ask for the delicious shrimp cakes in peanut sauce ($4.50)—they're not on the menu—or try the chicken Nanking ($5), a version of General Tsuo's piquant chicken. *919 Kearny St., btw Jackson and Columbus Sts., tel. 415/421–1429. Open weekdays 11–10, Sat. noon–10, Sun. 4–10. No credit cards.*

## NORTH BEACH

This Italian neighborhood wows the hungry visitor with strong coffee, fresh pasta, spicy sausages, and the highest concentration of restaurants in the city. Both Columbus Avenue and Grant Avenue—north of Columbus—are lined with reliable, reasonably priced Italian eateries. At **Molinari Delicatessen** (373 Columbus Ave., at Vallejo St., tel. 415/421–2337) you can get reasonably priced homemade pastas, cheeses, wine, bread, and anything else decadent and Italian you can think of—perfect for a picnic in Washington Square Park. If you overindulge, go to the nearby Church of Saints Peter and Paul to atone for your gastronomic sins.

➢ **UNDER $5** • **San Francisco Art Institute Café.** Usually the only way you can eat with a view like this is by dressing up, subjecting yourself to a snotty waitstaff, and dishing out large amounts of cash: Here's the exception. A couple of steep blocks up Russian Hill from North Beach, this café offers a superlative garden burger, regular burgers, and sandwiches for only $4. *800 Chestnut St., 1½ blocks uphill (west) from Columbus Ave., tel. 415/749–4567. Open weekdays 9–9, Sat. 9–4 in winter; Mon.–Sat. 9–2 in summer. No credit cards.*

### This Pearl Is No Ugly Duckling

***Politicians can open their mouths wider than tiny Swan Oyster Depot (1517 Polk St., btw California and Sacramento Sts., tel. 415/673–1101), which consists of nothing more than a lunch counter, a few stools, and the best damn seafood in town. Swan Oyster Depot is run by a genial bunch of beefy guys who seem to like nothing better than providing you with a bowl of New England clam chowder, an Anchor Steam beer, and a plate of sourdough bread. That'll cost about $5, but don't be surprised if you find yourself ordering a half-dozen oysters from Point Reyes and cracked Dungeness crab. Such gluttony will set you back $20, but you just won't care. The Depot is open until 5:30 Monday–Saturday, closed all day Sunday.***

➢ **UNDER $10** • **Bocce Café.** For about $6–$8 at this high-ceilinged restaurant, hidden away from the craziness of North Beach, you'll get a large, fresh Caesar or chicken salad, or a large individual pizza, or a choice of five types of pasta topped with a choice of about 15 sauces (including mussels, feta, olive, and tomato), or risotto with wild mushrooms, or an oven dish like lasagna. In warm weather, you can eat in the garden to the sounds of live jazz. *478 Green St., at Grant Ave., tel. 415/981–2044. Open daily 11:30–11 (Fri.–Sat. until 11:30).*

**Mario's Bohemian Cigar Store and Café.** With about 10 tables and a big wooden bar, this old-time Italian establishment has been packing 'em in and feeding 'em cups of strong, syrupy espresso, glasses of Chianti, and beers for the last 50 years. You can also get a fine sandwich (meatball, roasted eggplant, Italian sausage, chicken, etc.) on homemade focaccia for $5–$6. The windows face onto Washington Square Park and the Church of Saints Peter and Paul, in case you didn't already feel like you were in Italy. *566 Columbus Ave., at Union St., tel. 415/ 362–0536. Open Mon.–Sat. 10 AM–midnight, Sun. 10 AM–11 PM. No credit cards.*

*For cheap and unusual picnic food, head to San Francisco's colorful neighborhood markets: You'll find great produce in the Mission, Asian specialties on Clement Street in the Richmond district, and Italian delicatessens in North Beach.*

➢ **UNDER $15** • **The Gold Spike.** It opened as a candy store in 1927—conveniently manufacturing bathtub gin on the side. These days, this quirkily decorated, utterly unpretentious restaurant serves up delicious entrées like eggplant and chicken parmigiano and sautéed calamari ($7–$10). *527 Columbus Ave., btw Union and Green Sts., tel. 415/986–9747. Open Mon.–Tues. and Thurs.–Fri. 5–10, weekends 5–10:30.*

## FISHERMAN'S WHARF AND THE MARINA

Steer clear of the mediocre, high-priced seafood restaurants that compete for tourist bucks all along the wharf. The best dining experience you could have here would involve a loaf of sourdough, some cooked shrimp, a bottle of wine, and a perch on the pier. South of the wharf, lots of upscale restaurants, from grills to sushi spots to California-cuisine eateries, line **Chestnut** and **Union streets.**

➢ **UNDER $10** • **Angkor Palace.** Excellent Cambodian food—a must if you like fish—is served in a fantasy-blue dining room by waiters in traditional Cambodian clothing. The stir-fried mushrooms and steamed baby eggplant (both $5) are especially tasty. The nonadventurous can request chairs, but you should really take off your shoes and sit on the floor. *1769 Lombard St., at Octavia St., tel. 415/931–2830. Open daily 5–10:30. Wheelchair access.*

**Buena Vista Café.** This brass-and-wood bar just down the road from Fisherman's Wharf at the Hyde Street cable-car turnaround serves burgers and sandwiches ($4–$7.50), as well as Irish coffee, which the establishment claims to have introduced to America. While the tourists are sometimes packed in elbow to elbow, dignity manages to endure. *2765 Hyde St., tel. 415/ 474–5044. Open weekdays 9 AM–2 AM, weekends 8 AM–2 AM. No credit cards.*

**Eagle Café.** Lifted whole from its former location 2 blocks away and dropped onto Pier 39's upper story, this bar/restaurant is authentically rustic, unlike the rest of this area. Windows and patio tables offer a view of the waterfront, Fisherman's Wharf, and Alcatraz. It's a good place to eat a bowl of clam chowder ($4) or a burger ($5) and plan your escape from Fisherman's Wharf. After lunch, the Eagle becomes a bar only. *Upper level, Pier 39, tel. 415/433–3689. Kitchen open Mon.–Sat. 7:30–2:30, Sun. 7:30–3. Wheelchair access. No credit cards.*

➢ **UNDER $25** • **Greens.** Tucked away in Fort Mason, this place will make cynics re-evaluate their idea of vegetarian dining. No macaroni and cheese or carrot sticks here—Greens serves state-of-the-art vegetarian food in a beautifully spacious, gallery-like setting with a romantic bay view. Soups, salads, and breads are all highly recommended, but be prepared for small portions and haughty waiters. Sunday brunch is probably the best deal here; full dinners cost around $20. *Fort Mason, Bldg. A, tel. 415/771–6222. Open Tues.–Fri. 11:30–1:45 and 5:30–9:30, weekends 11:30–2:15 and 6–9:15.*

## JAPANTOWN

In the **Japan Center** (1737 Post St., btw Geary and Fillmore Sts.), Japantown's heart, a bunch of decent restaurants spanning a wide range of price categories display their fare via shiny photos or shellacked plastic replicas. If nothing there piques your interest, explore the surrounding streets for older, perhaps shabbier places that might turn out to be gems. The cheapest option of all is to visit the Japanese market **Maruwa** (open Mon.–Sat. 10–7, Sun. 10–6) on the corner of Post and Webster streets. Along with fruits and vegetables and all manner of Japanese products, the delicatessen offers sushi, rice and noodle dishes, and individual cuts of meat.

➢ **UNDER $10** • **Isobune.** At this touristy but fun sushi restaurant you can pack in around a large table and pluck your sushi off little boats that bob in the water before you. Kimono-clad chefs deftly mold the sushi and replenish the boats' cargo as swiftly as it disappears. Prices range from $1.20 for two pieces of octopus or fried tofu sushi to $2.50 for two pieces of salmon roe or red clam. It may not be the best sushi you'll ever eat, but it's good at the price. *Japan Center, 1737 Post St., near Geary Blvd., tel. 415/563–1030. Open daily 11:30–10. Wheelchair access.*

**Mifune.** A steady stream of Asian, American, and Asian-American patrons slurp cheap, tasty udon and soba noodles and *donburi* (one-bowl meals atop rice) in the simple dining room. The noodles come with various soups, meats, and vegetables and cost anywhere from $3.50 in plain broth to $8.50 with jumbo shrimp. *Japan Center, 1737 Post St., tel. 415/922–0337. Open daily 11–9:30. Wheelchair access.*

## UPPER AND LOWER HAIGHT

The Haight abounds with good breakfast places, full to the brim with the youth of today—in case you can't tell, they're the ones wearing black and sunglasses, smoking, looking like hell, and sucking on coffee like it's the primal life force. For dinner the Haight offers a few trendy hot spots and a preponderance of pizza joints, which provide the necessary carbohydrates to propel you to the next bar.

➢ **UNDER $10** • **Crescent City Café.** Every so often, we at the *Berkeley Guides* find a restaurant we like so much that we don't want to review it. The situation is especially grave in the case of this New Orleans–style café, which has just six small tables and maybe a dozen counter seats. Whatever you do, please do not come for brunch on weekends for Andouille hash ($5.75) and hefty plates of pork chops and eggs ($6). Another bad deal is the Thursday-night barbecued-rib special ($8). Do us a favor and order your po-boy catfish sandwich ($6) to go. *1418 Haight St., at Masonic St., tel. 415/863–1374. Open daily 8–4 and 5–10.*

**Kan Zaman.** This trendy Mediterranean restaurant attracts a crowd every night. Patrons sit on big floor pillows in a dimly lit room, listening to hypnotic Middle Eastern music, and indulge in hummus ($2.75), baba ghanoush ($2.75), and spinach pies ($3). If you need that final push to reach a dreamlike state, fork over $7 for a huge hookah (a traditional water pipe), which is brought to your table with your choice of tobacco (try the apple). On Friday and Saturday nights the Fat Chance Belly Dance troupe does its seductive thing. *1793 Haight St., at Shrader St., tel. 415/751–9656. Open Mon. 5 PM–midnight, Tues.–Fri. noon–midnight, weekends noon–2 AM. No credit cards.*

**Kate's Kitchen.** Kate's is the biggest thing to hit Haight Street since LSD. The crowd here might be grungy, but the food is positively wholesome, and the decor evokes some cheery breakfast nook. A chummy staff brings you specials like a big plate of lemon/cornmeal pancakes with fresh fruit and syrup ($5–$7) or an omelet with cilantro pesto, tomatoes, feta, and roasted chilies ($7). They serve big sandwiches and creative lunches, too. Expect lines on weekends. *471 Haight St., btw Fillmore and Webster Sts., tel. 415/626–3984. Open Tues.–Fri. 8 AM–2:45 PM, weekends 9–3:45.*

**Ya, Halla!** This new Middle Eastern restaurant hasn't yet attracted attention, possibly because it's on a particularly grimy stretch of lower Haight Street. Beat the crowds while you can for some of the freshest, most delicious falafel and hearty main dishes ($4–$8) around. *494 Haight St., at Fillmore St., tel. 415/522–1509. Open daily 11–11. Wheelchair access.*

➢ **UNDER $15** • **Cha Cha Cha.** You'll enjoy the skillfully prepared *tapas* (appetizers) and the wild pseudo-Catholic icons on the walls—but you'll wait all night for a table at this Caribbean joint. Entrées range from $10 to $15, but it's de rigueur to stick to a variety of tapas, like fried plantains with black beans and sour cream ($5.25) or shrimp sautéed in Cajun spices ($6.75). To wash it all down you'll want plenty of sangria (which can also help your potential two-hour wait for a table fly by in a veritable blur). *1801 Haight St., at Shrader St., tel. 415/386–7670. Open weekdays 11:30–3 and 5–11 (Fri. until 11:30), weekends 10–4 and 5–11. No credit cards.*

**Ganges.** Those who think vegetarian meals are dull or tasteless should come to this small Indian restaurant whose delicious, extra-spicy Surti cuisine contains no meat, no fish, and only homemade cheeses. If you order the "number one" package (raita, papadum, chapati, chutneys, appetizer, rice, vegetable, curry, and dessert), you can have a feast for less than $15. À la carte curry dishes like *chana masala* (a garbanzo-bean delicacy) and stuffed zucchini cost $5.50. Friday and Saturday nights musicians play sitar and tabla. *775 Frederick St., btw Stanyan and Arguello Sts., tel. 415/661–7290. Open Tues.–Sat. 5–10.*

## CASTRO DISTRICT

The Castro teems with cute, slightly pricey restaurants, many with outdoor patios for optimum people-watching. Brunch seems to be the Castro's favorite meal, followed closely by after-hours dining: You won't have to travel far for a mimosa or a late-night diner.

➢ **UNDER $5** • **Amazing Grace.** This cafeteria-style, no-nonsense vegetarian restaurant offers an inventive and tasty array of dishes that changes daily. An order of Moroccan vegetables with couscous or a tofu loaf with cashew and mushroom sauce will run you $4.25. *216 Church St., at Market St., tel. 415/626–6411. Open Mon.–Sat. 11–10. Wheelchair access. No credit cards.*

**Hot 'n' Hunky.** This pink, perky little place with a preponderance of Marilyn Monroe posters on the wall is a Castro institution for thick, juicy burgers, served until midnight on weekdays, 1 AM on weekends. Ordering burgers with names like The Macho Man (three patties; $4.25), I Wanna Hold Your Ham (with ham and Swiss; $4), and Ms. Piggy (with cheddar and bacon; $4) is half the fun. *4039 18th St., near Castro St., tel. 415/621–6365. No credit cards.*

➢ **UNDER $10** • **La Méditerranée.** This small, personable restaurant on the edge of the Castro serves great Middle Eastern and Greek food, including dolmas, salads, hummus, baba ghanoush, and Levant sandwiches (appetizers $4–$5; entrées $6–$10). If you can't decide, get the combination plate—two meaty phyllo pastries, a Levant sandwich, luleh kabob, and salad ($7). For dessert, try the decadent *datil* ($3.50), a dense roll made of dates, phyllo dough, nuts, and cream. *288 Noe St., at Market St., tel. 415/431–7210. Open Sun. and Tues.–Thurs. 11–10, Fri.–Sat. 11–11.*

**No-Name (Nippon) Sushi.** Everybody calls this small wood-paneled restaurant No-Name Sushi, even though the proprietors did eventually put up a tiny cardboard sign in the window officially dubbing it "Nippon." There's almost always a line out the door for the huge sushi combos at deliciously low prices—try $6–$10 on for size. No alcohol is served. *314 Church St., at 15th St., no phone. Open Mon.–Sat. noon–10. No credit cards.*

## MISSION DISTRICT

In the Mission you can wander from taquería to café to bookstore to taquería again in a salsa-induced state of bliss. Mexican and Central American spots crowd the neighborhood. All of the following restaurants, including the taquerías listed in the box, are accessible from either the 16th Street/Mission BART station or the 24th Street/Mission BART station. Be careful walking around here at night. For a daytime picnic, head to cooperatively owned and run **Rainbow Grocery** (1899 Mission St., tel. 415/863–0620) for organic produce and snacks.

➢ **UNDER $10** • **Esperpento.** Tapas and sangria have lately become very popular as a reasonably priced and festive dinner. When this tapas joint opened in the Mission in 1992, it skyrocketed to instant popularity, as lines out the door on weekends will attest. Brightly lit and decorated with all sorts of surreal, Daliesque touches, it serves delicacies like garlic shrimp ($6.50), red pepper salad ($4), and *tortilla de patatas* (potato and onion pancake; $4.75), as well as huge *paella* (saffron rice) dinners ($26 for two). *3295 22nd St., btw Valencia and Mission Sts., tel. 415/282–8867. Open daily 11 AM–3 PM and Mon.–Sat. 5 PM–10 PM. No credit cards.*

**Ti Couz.** A youngish crowd lines up outside the door, waiting for a taste of the succulent, piping-hot crêpes whipped up at this joint, styled after Breton crêperies in northwest France. A main course, with savory fillings like spinach, mushrooms, and ricotta, will run you $3–$5, while a sweet crêpe will set you back $2–$5. Warm and friendly, Ti Couz is perfect for dinner on a long summer evening or lunch on a rainy afternoon. *3108 16th St., at Valencia St., tel. 415/252–7373. Open weekdays 11–11, Sat. 10 AM–11 PM, Sun. 10–10.*

## SOUTH OF MARKET

If you eat in SoMa, you'll see harried Financial District workers trying to unwind and youthful clubbers fueling up for an evening out on the town. Wander along Folsom Street between 7th and 11th streets, or along 11th and 9th streets between Howard and Harrison streets, and you'll have the SoMa eating scene in the palm of your hand.

### A Cheap Trip South of the Border

*San Francisco and the burrito have a serious love affair going on. For years, storefront taquerías in the Mission district have distributed the steaming tortillas filled with meat, beans, rice, salsa, sour cream, cheese, and/or guacamole, to millions of hungry residents and travelers. For people who lack kitchens and/or money, the hefty concoctions can be a major nutritional staple, capable of sating you completely for around $4. Below are some of the best places to get your burrito fix—or your enchilada, taco, flauta, quesadilla, or tamale fix, for that matter.*

*Casa Sanchez. Renowned all over the Mission for its homemade tortillas, chips, and salsa, Casa Sanchez also has a colorful outdoor patio and filling combo platters for $4–$5. 2778 24th St., tel. 415/282–2400.*

*El Farolito. Stagger in for a burrito ($2.50–$3.50) as late as 3 AM (4 AM Sat.). 2777 Mission St., tel. 415/826–4870.*

*La Cumbre. The carne asada (beef) burritos are so good they can call a vegetarian back to the herd. 515 Valencia St., tel. 415/863–8205.*

*Cancún Taquería. In the middle of the Mission's mayhem, Cancún serves one of the best vegetarian burritos around, chock-full of beans, rice, and thick avocado slices ($3). 2288 Mission St., tel. 415/252–9560.*

*Panchita's. If you happen to have an army to feed, stock up on king-size super burritos ($4) at this Salvadoran hole-in-the-wall with mariachi on the jukebox. 3091 16th St., tel. 415/431–4232.*

➢ **UNDER $10** • **Hamburger Mary's.** The messy burgers ($5–$8) and the cluttered decor go together wonderfully. Come by at 1 in the morning to hang out with clubbers in various states of drunkenness and undress. Veggie options available. *1582 Folsom St., at 12th St., tel. 415/626–5767. Open Tues.–Thurs. 11:30 AM–1 AM, Fri.–Sat. 10 AM– 2 AM, Sun. 10 AM–1 AM. Wheelchair access.*

**Manora's Thai Cuisine.** The branch on Folsom is trendier than most Thai restaurants in the city, and big crowds wait at the bar before being seated. The Mission location is smaller and less crowded. At either branch, the fresh, attractive dishes (garlic quail, $7.50; spicy Japanese eggplant with prawns, $7) are worth a wait. *1600 Folsom St., at 12th St., tel. 415/861–6224. Other location: 3226 Mission St., at 29th St., tel. 415/550–0856. Both open weekdays 11:30–2:30 and 5:30–10:30, Sat. 5:30–10:30, Sun. 5–10. Both have wheelchair access.*

➢ **UNDER $15** • **South Park Café.** Only minutes away from seedy streets and empty warehouses lies South Park, which could easily double as a refined European town square. You can gnaw on *boudin noir* (blood sausage; $10) and *frites* ($1.75) at the South Park Café and pretend you're in Paris. This French-style bistro opens at 8 AM for fresh croissants and coffee, and stays open for country-cooked lunches ($5–$10) and dinners ($6–$15). *108 South Park Ave., btw 2nd and 3rd and Bryant and Brannan Sts., tel. 415/495–7275. Open for coffee weekdays 8 AM–10 PM, for meals weekdays 11:30–2:30 and 6–10, Sat. 6–10.*

# Cafés

San Franciscans strongly believe in the connection between coffee and the arts. Early converts to the café-as-muse philosophy include renegades Jack Kerouac and Allen Ginsberg, who held all manner of performances at the still-pumping Caffè Trieste in North Beach. With its European-style park and tiny streets, North Beach is still a popular place to grab a demitasse on a rainy day, especially if you have someone to hold hands with under the table. Post-modern hipsters, however, may be more comfortable in the Haight or in the Mission.

**Café Flore.** The Castro's premier gay hangout, Flore is a hotbed of activity day and night, drawing pseudoartists, political activists, and trendy boys from all over. If you can't find a place at one of the outside tables, strike an attractive pose and loiter until someone makes room for you—sharing tables is de rigueur. Expect noise and commotion and, in the middle of it all, an incredibly attractive someone sipping a chamomile tea and looking furtively your way. *2298*

## Late-Night Bites

***So many occasions call for a big meal at 3 AM . . .***

***Clown Alley. Burgers, fries, and shakes in North Beach. Open until 3 Friday and Saturday. 42 Columbus Ave., at Jackson St., tel. 415/421–2540.***

***Grubstake. Decent breakfasts and thick, messy burgers in the Civic Center. Open until 4. 1525 Pine St., tel. 415/673–8268.***

***Lori's Diner. Earnestly nostalgic '50s diner-type food downtown. Open 24 hours. 336 Mason St., tel. 415/392–8646***

***Orphan Andy's. Cute all-night diner in the Castro. 3991 17th St., tel. 415/864–9795.***

***Sparky's. The menu has shades of Denny's, but the atmosphere is strictly Doc Martens. In the Castro District. Open 24 hours. 242 Church St., tel. 415/626–8666.***

*Market St., at Noe St., tel. 415/621–8579. Open Sun.–Thurs. 7:30 AM–11:30 PM, Fri.–Sat. 7:30 AM–midnight.*

**Caffè Trieste.** This is the legendary North Beach home of the Beat generation; it was here that Kerouac and the gang oozed cool from every pore. The café doesn't seem to have changed a bit. It's smoky as ever, with decor straight out of the '50s and an opera-spouting jukebox. The delicious coffee drinks are $3.50, though the pastry selection is poor. Saturday afternoons at 1:30 PM, the owner's family serenades guests with anything from old Italian tunes to opera. *601 Vallejo St., at Grant Ave., tel. 415/392–6739. Open daily 6:30 AM–11:30 PM (Fri.–Sat. until midnight).*

**Gathering Caffè.** The small marble tables and black-and-white checkered floor evoke a tiny Florentine jazz bar, not a San Francisco café, only 3 blocks from the "Girls! Girls! Girls!" of Broadway. *1326 Grant Ave., at Green St., tel. 415/433–4247. Open daily 11 AM–11:30 PM (Fri.–Sat. until midnight).*

*Jazz afficionados take note: The Gathering charges no cover for its nightly live music—you'll just pay an extra 50¢ for your coffee drink.*

**The Horse Shoe.** Here you'll find more disaffected youths with tattoos, piercings, and time on their hands than perhaps anywhere else in the city. Come for a strong cuppa joe and enjoy a shouted conversation over the blasting music, peruse the millions of flyers on the walls seeking band members or advertising artistic events, or toy with the idea of just a small tattoo. *566 Haight St., near Steiner St., tel. 415/626–8852. Open daily 7:30 AM–1 AM.*

**La Bohème.** Across the street from BART, this Mission district institution has supplied locals with hearty breakfasts (fruit and granola, poached eggs, bagels) for years. Day and night, a steady stream of jazz or Stevie Wonder flows from the stereo while a multiracial, all-ages clientele gathers around large, antique-looking tables. *3318 24th St., at Mission St., tel. 415/285–4122. Open weekdays 5 AM–11 PM, weekends 7 AM–11 PM.*

**Red Dora's Bearded Lady.** A self-proclaimed "dyke café (everybody welcome)," this small coffeehouse in the Mission is a visible expression of San Francisco's energetic queer culture. It's decorated with votive candles and mismatched furniture; a variety of contemporary music blasts inside, but you can always escape to the lovely garden in back. Spoken-word and musical performances often take place Fridays and Saturdays at 8 PM after the café closes, but call ahead to confirm. *485 14th St., at Guerrero St., tel. 415/626–2805. Open weekdays 7–7, weekends 9–7.*

# Exploring San Francisco

**Though the hills make walking** tough, you can only really become acquainted with San Francisco on foot. You haven't experienced the city until you've climbed through other people's backyards on hidden stairway streets and gotten lost for a day or two in Golden Gate Park. When your dogs get tired, as they inevitably will on the dizzying hills, hop a bus for a higher-speed version of the San Francisco scene. You can get a MUNI transportation map at most liquor and grocery stores for $2; carry it with you and when you're all worn out you should be able to find a line to take you someplace interesting. The 30 Stockton bus transports you through the thick of downtown and through North Beach, skirts the Victorian homes on Russian Hill, and continues on to the Palace of Fine Arts, the Exploratorium, and the Presidio; the route then plows through the heart of Chinatown on its way back to Market Street. For a taste of the Bay Area's more natural offerings, head out of town to Marin County or the San Mateo County Coast (*see* Chapter 2).

## MAJOR SIGHTS

With the exception of Fisherman's Wharf, which bludgeons visitors with its banality, San Francisco's major sights are major for a reason. Even the most jaded travelers can't help but sigh

# Downtown San Francisco

**Sights ●**

Ansel Adams Center, **47**

Cable Car Museum, **12**

Cartoon Art Museum, **46**

Chinatown Gate, **28**

Chinese Telephone Exchange, **16**

Circle Gallery, **44**

City Hall, **57**

City Lights Bookstore, **9**

Coit Tower, **7**

Embarcadero Center, **20**

Ferry Building, **22**

Glide Memorial Methodist Church, **38**

Golden Gate Fortune Cookie Factory, **18**

Grace Cathedral, **23**

Haas-Lilienthal House, **11**

Jackson Square, **14**

Japan Center, **32**

Justin Herman Plaza, **21**

Kabuki 8 Theatres, **29**

Kabuki Hot Springs, **30**

Lombard Street, **4**

Louise M. Davies Symphony Hall, **56**

Painted Ladies, **51**

Palace of Fine Arts, **1**

Peace Plaza, **31**

Portsmouth Square, **17**

San Francisco Museum of Modern Art, **49**

South Park, **50**

Tin Hou Temple, **15**

Transamerica Pyramid, **19**

Transbay Terminal, **45**

Union Square, **43**

United Nations Plaza, **62**

# Downtown San Francisco

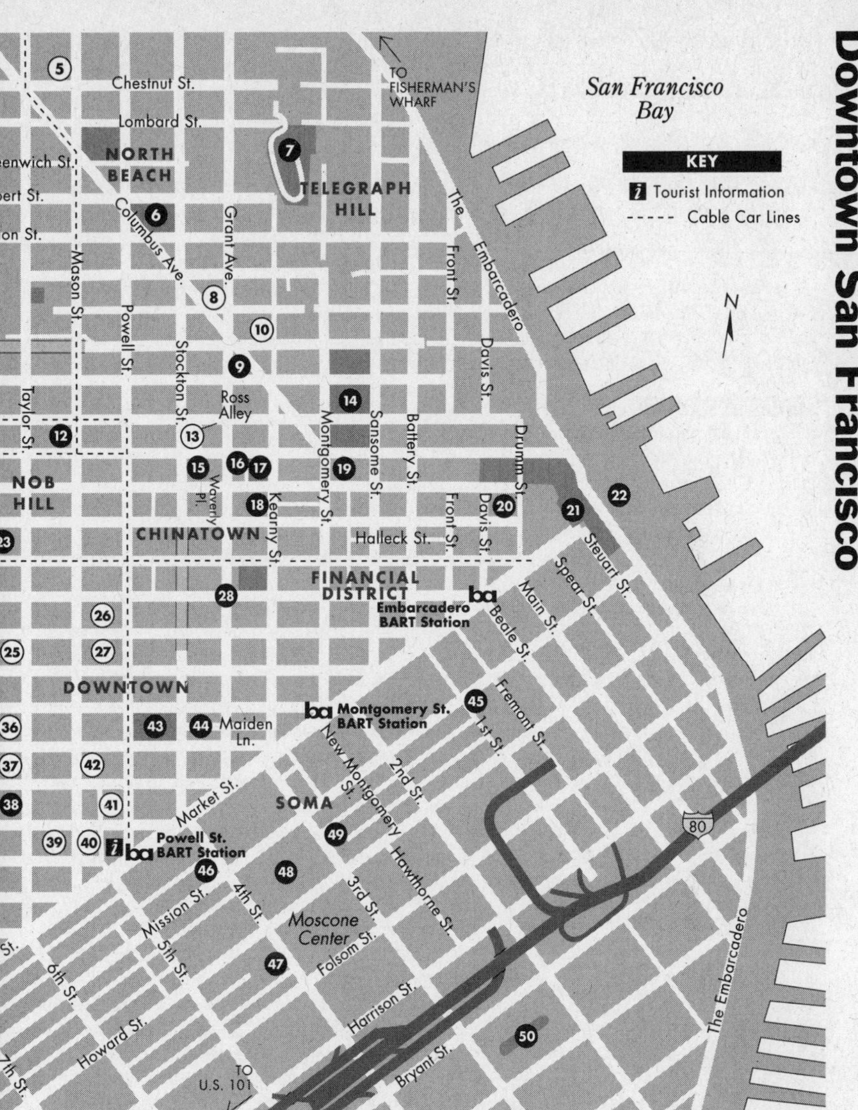


Veteran's Building, **54**

War Memorial Opera House, **55**

Washington Square, **6**

Yerba Buena Gardens, **48**

**Lodging** ○

Adelaide Inn, **36**

Aida Hotel, **63**

Albergo Verona, **34**

Alexander Inn, **37**

Amsterdam, **25**

AYH Hostel at Union Square, **42**

Brady Acres, **35**

Europa Hotel, **8**

European Guest House, **59**

Ft. Mason International Hostel, **3**

Globetrotter's Inn, **39**

Golden Gate Hotel, **27**

Grand Central Hostel, **58**

Grant Hotel, **26**

Green Tortoise Guest House, **10**

Herbert Hotel, **41**

Hyde Plaza Hotel, **24**

Interclub Globe Hostel, **60**

Marina Motel, **2**

Olympic Hotel, **40**

Pacific Tradewinds, **13**

Phoenix Hotel, **33**

San Francisco International Student Center, **61**

San Francisco Zen Center, **53**

San Remo Hotel, **5**

Sappho's, **52**

reverently at the sight of the Golden Gate Bridge looming overhead. The Alcatraz tour, for all its hype, explores such a truly fascinating place—on such a genuinely stark, scary island—that it doesn't come off as idiotic. This is the city's true appeal: Despite myriad merchants' best efforts to flog tourist schlock, the spirit of San Francisco refuses to yield, and the real city pulses through the neon surface.

**GOLDEN GATE BRIDGE** More than a mile long, the bridge to end all bridges has come to symbolize San Francisco more than any other monument. This masterpiece of design and engineering, which links San Francisco to its wealthy neighbor, Marin County, has withstood wind, fog, and the combined weight of more than 200,000 people who showed up all at once to celebrate the the suspension bridge's 50th birthday back in 1987. The "Golden" Gate is painted International Orange for visibility in fog—so the seagulls don't crash into it. Of course, you'll want to cross over. Bus 28 will drop you at the toll plaza, from which point you can hoof it or hitch. The walk across and back takes about an hour and the wind can be freezing.

**ALCATRAZ ISLAND** Known as "the Rock," Alcatraz Island served for 60 years as the nation's most notorious federal penitentiary, holding high-risk prisoners—including Al Capone, Robert "The Birdman" Stroud, and Machine Gun Kelly—in its isolated maw. The prison closed in 1963; six years later, a group of Native Americans occupied the island in an attempt to reclaim it, declaring that a 1868 federal treaty allows Native Americans to use all federal territory not actively being used by the government. After almost two years, the U.S. government forced them off, none too gently. Today the island is part of the national park system, and tourists visit its grounds in hordes.

The Red and White Fleet (tel. 415/546–2896 for info or 415/546–2700 for tickets) ferries you to the island; the $9 pricetag includes the round-trip ferry ride, an interpretive talk by a park ranger, and an audiocassette tour of the prison itself (tapes are available in several languages, and the average tour takes about 2½ hrs). You can skip the cassette tour and pay only $5.75, but the tape, which features former inmates and guards talking about their experiences on Alcatraz, is one of the best parts of the experience. Ferries leave 9:30 AM–2:15 PM (until 4:15 June–August); you'll need Visa, MasterCard, or American Express to reserve tickets by phone, and you'll pay a $2 service fee. If you're buying tickets in person, especially during summer, go to the ferry ticket office (open 8:30–5) at Pier 41. You should reserve or buy tickets *several* days in advance, especially in summer. To reach Pier 41, take Bus 32 from the Ferry Building downtown. All tours are wheelchair accessible.

**FISHERMAN'S WHARF** Once the domain of Italian fishermen, the wharf is now San Francisco's prize tourist trap, whose sole purpose is to make you spend money. You'll only see fishermen here if you arrive in the misty early-morning hours (around 5 AM) to watch the boats unload. Otherwise, it's schlock city. Jefferson Street, the wharf's main drag, is now packed with expensive seafood restaurants, tacky souvenir shops, and ripoff "museums" like the **Wax Museum, Ripley's Believe It or Not!,** the **Guinness Museum of World Records, The Haunted Gold Mine,** and the **Medieval Dungeon.** Each can be yours for the low admission price of $6–$9. The only thing that remains fairly authentic here is the array of seafood stands along Jefferson Street. Buy clam chowder ($3–$4) or a half-pound of shrimp ($6) from one of the sidewalk vendors and a loaf of sourdough bread ($2.50–$3) from **Boudin Bakery** (156 Jefferson St., tel. 415/928–1849) and eat on one of the piers, watching cruise ships and fishing boats glide in and out of the harbor. Then hightail it out of there to catch a ferry to Alcatraz (*see above*) or Angel Island (*see* Marin County, in Chapter 3), or walk over to Fort Mason (*see* The Marina, *below*) to check out its museums.

*You'll get a great view of the Golden Gate Bridge from the Maritime Museum. Walk all the way out on the museum's pier and you'll see the bridge, picture perfect, in one direction and the city looking like a toy in the other.*

If you must stick around the wharf, check out the **Maritime Museum** (Beach St., at foot of Polk St., tel. 415/929–0202), housed in an art-deco building and displaying all sorts of artifacts from San Francisco's maritime history. The museum is free, but if you have $2 to spare you might have more fun exploring one of the old ships at Hyde Street Pier, between the Cannery and Ghirardelli Square. Among the vessels docked there are the ***Balclutha,*** a 100-year-old square-rigger, and the ***Eureka,*** an old ferry that now holds a classic car collection.

Three shopping complexes girdle the wharf: **Pier 39,** the **Cannery,** and **Ghirardelli Square.** Owned by Texas's billionaire Bass brothers, Pier 39 is a bland imitation of a fin-de-siècle New England seaport village—the shopping mall of your worst nightmares. Pier 39's one redeeming quality is the confab of sea lions that took over several of the marina docks next to the development a few years ago and have refused to leave. The owners wanted them removed—killed, if necessary—until they realized the barking sea mammals were attracting more tourists. To shake the "I'm-being-ripped-off" feeling that accompanies any visit to Pier 39, eat at the **Eagle Café** (*see* Food, *above*).

A former Del Monte peach-canning factory, the **Cannery** (Jefferson, Leavenworth, Beach, and Hyde Sts., tel. 415/771–3112) is now a gallery of chic boutiques. Chocolate is no longer made on-site at **Ghirardelli Square** (900 North Point St., tel. 415/775–5500), but you can buy it here in bars or, semiliquefied, atop a huge, tasty ice cream sundae ($5.50). To reach Fisherman's Wharf, take Bus 32 from the Ferry Building downtown. Or fulfill your other tourist obligation by taking a cable car from Powell Street (*see* Getting Around, *above*) to the end of the line (a nice metaphor for Fisherman's Wharf).

**COIT TOWER** The 210-foot concrete observation tower on Telegraph Hill offers one of the best bay views in the city. Heiress Lillie Hitchcock Coit (1843–1929) left the funds to build the tower, which memorializes San Francisco's volunteer firefighters. An eccentric San Francisco legend, Coit was a cross-dresser—in men's clothes she could gain access to the city's most interesting realms—who literally chased fire engines around town.

*Tumbling down the east side of the hill from Coit Tower, Greenwich and Filbert streets turn into wood and brick public steps that go through lush private gardens. Walk down the Filbert steps to Napier Lane, a tiny wooden path surrounded by riots of flowers.*

The walls inside the tower lobby are covered with Depression-era murals in the style of Diego Rivera, painted by local artists on the government dole. Free descriptive tours of the murals are given every Saturday at 11 AM; call 415/557–4266 for more information. The elevator inside the tower will take you to the top ($3) for a 360° view of the bay. Come at sunset if it's one of San Francisco's rare sunny days; the crowd is thinner then and the view is spectacular. *Tel. 415/362–0808. From Market and 3rd Sts. downtown, Bus 30 or 45 to Washington Square; walk 2 blocks east on Union St., left on Kearny St. Or Bus 39 from Fisherman's Wharf. Tower open daily 10–6:30.*

**GOLDEN GATE PARK** The western keyhole to San Francisco is Golden Gate Park—1,000 acres of plant life, museums, Dutch windmills, sporting events, open-air performances, and even a herd of bison. Much larger and more beautiful than New York's Central Park, Golden Gate Park has the added bonus of blustery Ocean Beach and the Pacific Ocean at its far western end. Bordered on the east by Haight Street, the park has always been a natural hangout for that neighborhood's countercultural denizens: Hippie historians should note that Ken Kesey and friends celebrated the first **Human Be-In** here on January 14, 1966. The park has also hosted the Grateful Dead, Jefferson Airplane, Peter Gabriel's WOMAD (World of Music and Dance), and Pearl Jam, to name only a few.

*On Sundays, John F. Kennedy Drive, the main thoroughfare, is closed to car traffic; flocks of bikers, in-line skaters, and skateboarders take over the park. Hang out by the Conservatory and watch some expert bladers do their thing.*

Once a stretch of sand dunes, Golden Gate Park today is home to blue gum eucalyptus, Monterey pine, and Monterey cypress trees, not to mention one of the world's foremost horticultural displays. The **Strybing Arboretum and Botanical Gardens** (off Martin Luther King, Jr. Dr., near the museum complex, tel. 415/ 661–1316) has 70 dazzling acres of plants, featuring some 5,000 specimens arranged by country of origin, genus, and fragrance. Admission is free. The nearby **Japanese Tea Garden** (tel. 415/752–4227), with its koi ponds and 18th-century Buddha, is the United States' oldest; the garden is open daily 9–6:30 and you must pay $2 to enter (though it's free before 9:30 AM). The park's first building was the delicate Victorian **Conservatory** (off Kennedy Dr., near east entrance, tel. 415/752–8080); a knockoff of London's Kew Gardens, it features a tropical garden and exotic orchids.

Golden Gate Park is bordered by Stanyan Street, the Great Highway, Lincoln Way, and Fulton Street. Several places near the park rent bikes and Rollerblades. **Park Cyclery** (1749 Waller St., at Stanyan St., tel. 415/752–8383) has mountain bikes for $5 an hour or $30 a day. **Skate Pro Sports** (27th Ave., at Irving St., tel. 415/752–8776), near a less-traveled part of the park, offers a good deal on blades: $20 a day, including pads and a helmet. To get to the park from downtown or the Civic Center, take Bus 5, 71, or 73.

**THE PRESIDIO** A huge chunk of prime waterfront land stretching from the western end of the Marina district all the way to Golden Gate Bridge, the Presidio was one of the country's oldest military installations. The land was turned over to the National Park Service in 1994, though it remains to be seen how much will be developed and how much will remain open space: Enjoy the 1,500 acres of rolling hills, forests, and attractive old military buildings while you can. The **Officers' Club** in the main post area contains one adobe wall reputed to date from 1776, the year the base was founded. The best way to get acquainted with the Presidio is to take a ranger-led walk; they usually happen on the weekends. To speak to a ranger in the **visitor center,** call 415/556–0865 between 10 AM and 3 PM.

The views from the Presidio out over the bay are terrific. The easiest way to get here is to drive north toward the bay on Van Ness, turn left on Lombard, and then follow signs. Otherwise, take Bus 38 from Montgomery Street BART/MUNI to Geary Boulevard and Presidio Avenue, then switch to Bus 43, which travels into the Presidio.

## NEIGHBORHOODS

The best way to experience San Francisco's neighborhoods is to plunk yourself down in one and walk till you drop, preferably into a chair on a café patio. You can look at a map and plan your walks, or skip the map, start off in an interesting spot, and just go for what looks good. Certain parts of the city lend themselves especially well to the latter mode of exploration, in which you surrender to the whims of the streets: You won't need to look for special places because they'll emerge spontaneously in the course of your wanderings. One such area is the **Mission–Noe Valley–Castro.** Get off BART at 16th and Mission streets, and head west on 16th or south on Mission or Valencia. Either direction will guarantee that you'll see scenes of neighborhood life, funky shops, and enough cafés and restaurants to keep you fueled up. If you're near the waterfront, try the same method in **North Beach** and **Chinatown.**

**DOWNTOWN** For better or worse, Downtown is the grand old San Francisco of tea dances, cocktail hours, fedoras, and big winter overcoats. All you have to do is look up at the old architectural details and you could forget what decade it is. The modern face of downtown is still big, though perhaps not so grand—big consumerism, big banking, big poverty, big cafeterias, and waitresses with big hair. It's typical cosmopolitan walking territory, with all the fascinating and horrifying elements of urban American life.

➢ **UNION SQUARE** • Union Square is the physical heart—though not the soul—of the city, especially for tourists who come to shop, browse the galleries, attend the theater, then sleep in one of the posh hotels. The square, bordered by Powell, Post, Stockton, and Geary streets, was named in honor of Union-boosting rallies held prior to the Civil War. But some San Franciscans would rather attribute the square's name to huge labor-organization demonstrations held here in the 1930s; these at one point effectively shut down the city for a week. Today, Union Square consists of a park encircled by the city's most elegant stores and boutiques, including Neiman-Marcus, Saks, Chanel, Tiffany, Cartier, Hermès, and Gump's. The park can be a relaxing place to rest after a hard day's window-shopping, if you don't mind pigeons and homeless folks as your companions. By nightfall it gets a little seedy, and it might be time to hop a MUNI bus out of here.

**Maiden Lane,** a short alley off the east side of Union Square, was once the lair of the "cribs" or brothels that formed the center of a notorious and violent red-light district. Now it's a shopping arcade for the thick-walleted and the site of San Francisco's only Frank Lloyd Wright building, the **Circle Gallery** (140 Maiden Ln., tel. 415/989–2100), which served as the prototype for the Guggenheim Museum in New York.

Heading south on Powell Street from Union Square, you'll come to the intersection of Market and Powell streets. Here lie the cable-car turnaround, the Powell Street BART station, and the **San Francisco Visitor Information Center** (*see* Basics, *above*), tucked below the street in the submerged Hallidie Plaza. Market Street is also home to a string of cheap fast-food joints.

*Everyone passes by the corner of Market and Powell: proselytizers, street musicians, artists, punks, young professionals, flower vendors, protesters, and tourists in matching jogging suits.*

➢ **TRANSAMERICA PYRAMID** • Located in San Francisco's Financial District, where the towers of wealth block all sun at street level, the pyramid (600 Montgomery St., btw Clay and Washington Sts.) is *the* distinguishing pointy feature of the San Francisco skyline. You can ride the elevator to the 27th-floor observation deck for free, for a bird's-eye view down Columbus Avenue and of Coit Tower.

Nearby **Jackson Square** (Jackson St., btw Montgomery and Sansome Sts.), lined with expensive antique shops and upholstery stores, has some of the only buildings surviving from the days when this area was overrun with brothels and saloons. The old-time atmosphere of gentility and calm (see what happens when you renovate?) contrasts markedly with the greed-and-skyscrapers feel of the rest of the Financial District.

➢ **THE EMBARCADERO** • The Embarcadero, Spanish for "wharf," looks more like a string of office buildings than anything vaguely maritime. One exception is the **Ferry Building** at the end of Market Street, with its 230-foot clock tower; an excellent landmark, this is also the place to catch the ferry for Sausalito (*see* Getting Around, *above*). Dominating the Embarcadero is the **Embarcadero Center,** a conglomeration of four nearly identical towers chockablock with shops, restaurants, and a movie theater. Between the center and the Ferry Building stretches **Justin Herman Plaza,** a favorite haunt of the white-collar bag-lunch crowd and young skateboarders who favor long expanses of brick and concrete. Here, Jean Dubuffet's mammoth stainless-steel sculpture *La Chiffonière* poses like a Napoleonic Pillsbury doughboy. Armand Vallaincourt's huge building-block fountain looks a little too much like prehistoric plumbing, but you can play in it even when the water is streaming through.

**CIVIC CENTER** The Civic Center is the locus of city government and home to many cultural events including dance, opera, and theater. It's also where a good percentage of San Francisco's homeless have camped out since the 1940s. **City Hall,** built in classic beaux arts stYie, dominates the scene with its bronze rotunda. Joe DiMaggio and Marilyn Monroe got married here on January 15, 1954. In 1960, protesters were washed down the central stairway with giant firehoses while hearings of the House Un-American Activities Committee went on inside. And it was here in 1978 that conservative former city supervisor Dan White shot and killed Mayor George Moscone and Supervisor Harvey Milk, who was the first openly gay elected official in the United States. Has this building seen some crazy times or what?

Surrounding City Hall are many of the city's cultural mainstays. On Van Ness Avenue, the **Louise M. Davies Symphony Hall** and the **War Memorial Opera House** offer San Franciscans their fill of high culture. The **Veterans Building,** at McAllister and Van Ness, houses the Herbst Theatre, where you can catch concerts, readings, and lectures (*also see* After Dark, *below*). In 1996, the Opera House will close for renovations, but volunteers conduct 75-minute tours of the other two buildings every Monday on the hour and half-hour from 10 to 2, leaving from Davies Symphony Hall's Grove Street entrance. If you're exploring on foot, head to **Hayes Street** between Franklin and Webster streets, where you'll find several blocks lined with specialty shops, art galleries, cafés, and restaurants.

Across from City Hall on the south side is the large plaza where protest marches usually culminate in rallies (including a few 200,000-people-plus ones during the Persian Gulf War) and an occasional riot. Leading away from City Hall toward Market Street is the **United Nations Plaza,** commemorating the U.N.'s founding in San Francisco in 1945. A dramatic statue of South American hero Simón Bolivar presides over the plaza.

➢ **POLK GULCH** • Once the gay heart of San Francisco, Polk Gulch now ranks second to that most prominent gay neighborhood, the Castro. The gulch is part yuppie hangout, part urban blight. It's a good place to buy roasted coffee for yourself and Spandex undies for cousin Bob back east. Two of Polk Street's big industries—drug sales and prostitution—don't exactly make it a prowling-ground for tour buses. Rumor has it that the call boys get more expensive by the block—the most expensive is the stretch from Bush to Pine streets; the bargain basement is around Geary Street. Bus 19 from Civic Center BART/MUNI runs up Polk Street on its way to Ghirardelli Square at Fisherman's Wharf.

**CHINATOWN** The real appeal of San Francisco's Chinatown—possibly the most famous immigrant community in the world—is its street life; so go in hungry and energetic, with open eyes and ears. Despite all the tourists, Chinatown steadfastly remains a residential area, where the largest Chinese community outside Asia has made its home for 140 years. The original immigrants were refugees from the Opium Wars who came to San Francisco seeking their fortune during the Gold Rush.

*Don't miss the huge annual Chinese New Year festival, held over a couple of weeks coinciding with the lunar new year—usually in early February. Come early to get a spot for the final parade—a riotous celebration of Asian culture, featuring floats, firecrackers, and lion dancers.*

To reach Chinatown, take Bus 45 from Market and Third streets downtown. You'll know you're in the 16-block neighborhood when the street signs are in Chinese. The best way to enter is through the dragon-crowned **Chinatown Gate** on Grant Avenue at Bush Street, when the sense of being in a different world is suddenly palpable. Or enter through **Portsmouth Square** on Washington Street at Kearny Street, where dozens of old Chinese men gather in groups, gambling or shooting the breeze.

**Grant Avenue,** the main tourist thoroughfare, is crowded with souvenir shops, restaurants, and intricate red, green, and gold lampposts. The old **Chinese Telephone Exchange** building, now the Bank of Canton, stands at 743 Washington Street, at Grant Avenue. Operators here had to memorize all their customers' names and speak English as well as five Chinese dialects. Many Chinatown diehards eschew Grant and stay on **Stockton Street,** packed with grocery stores, bakeries, and trade and service shops. In between these two main drags lie several narrow alleys worth exploring.

*Park yourself in a café and watch the twentysomething crowd try to capture the spirit of their famous Beat predecessors, whom James Baldwin called "uptight, middle-class white people, imitating poverty, trying to get down, to get with it . . . doing their despairing best to be funky."*

One of the most interesting streets is **Waverly Place,** off Sacramento and Washington streets between Grant and Stockton. You might recognize the name as that of a character in Amy Tan's *The Joy Luck Club*; it's also known as the "street of painted balconies." Chinese temples line Waverly Place, including the **Tin Hou Temple** (125 Waverly Pl., top floor), purportedly the city's oldest. Don't miss nearby **Ross Alley,** between Grant and Stockton and Jackson and Washington streets, home of the **Golden Gate Fortune Cookie Factory** (56 Ross Alley), where you can get cookies with risqué fortunes: Slip them to whomever you'd like to see blush.

**NORTH BEACH** Walk north on Columbus Avenue from the Columbus and Broadway intersection (one of San Francisco's best-known red-light districts) and you'll find yourself in the heart of the legendary Italian neighborhood where the Beat movement was born. Nowadays North Beach offers an incredible selection of restaurants, delis, and cafés, not to mention a lingering aura of the alternative culture that thrived here during the 1950s. Poets and writers like Jack Kerouac, Lawrence Ferlinghetti, and Allen Ginsberg came to North Beach around 1953 to write, play music, and generally promote a lifestyle that emphasized Eastern religion, free love, drugs, and crazy new means of artistic expression. Ferlinghetti's **City Lights Bookstore** (261 Columbus Ave.) continues to publish and sell alternative, little-known literature, as well as stuff by the Beats, who hardly qualify as alternative anymore, having since been anthologized to high heaven.

Those looking to immerse themselves in Beat history can poke around **Vesuvio** (255 Columbus Ave., tel. 415/362–3370), a bar just across the alley from City Lights, where the boys undoubtedly consumed more than one glass of red. Also visit **Caffè Trieste** (*see* Cafés, *above*), which fueled the Beats with their favorite legal amphetamine, a strong shot of espresso; the clientele, some 35 years later, still looks pretty beat. Continue the pilgrimage with a hefty walk over to Russian Hill, where you can lay a poem or a lit stick of incense in front of **29 Russell Street** (btw Larkin and Hyde Sts. and Union and Green Sts.), where Kerouac crashed with Neal and Carolyn Cassady for a time in the early '50s. (His relationship with Neal is immortalized in his popular tome *On the Road,* but *The Subterraneans* better evokes Kerouac's North Beach days.)

**Washington Square,** off Columbus between Filbert and Union streets, is the heart of North Beach. Bordered by bakeries and coffee shops, the square attracts an eclectic crowd of old-time Italian residents, noisome bums, and tourists. Come here early in the morning to see dozens of old Chinese women practicing tai chi in the fog. To reach the square, take Bus 30 or 45 from Market and 3rd streets downtown.

**NOB HILL AND RUSSIAN HILL** The most classically elitist of San Francisco's elite districts is Nob Hill, the city's high-society hub for more than a century. The hill has great views that even the downtrodden will enjoy, assuming they can drag their sorry selves up here. North of Nob Hill lies **Russian Hill,** originally a burial ground for Russian seal hunters and traders, which today features a combination of old Victorian homes and new highrises, and even more of San Francisco's upper crust.

A steep walk (or an expensive cable-car ride) north from Union Square, Nob Hill was once home to the city's biggest entrepreneurs; now the city's poshest hotels are located here. Ignore the doormen's suspicious looks as you nose around the lobbies of the **Fairmont Hotel,** at California and Mason streets; the **Mark Hopkins,** across California Street from the Fairmont; and the **Stanford Court Hotel,** at California and Powell streets. See how many times you can ride up and down the Fairmont's glass elevator before the management ever-so-politely suggests that you scram.

➢ **CABLE CAR MUSEUM** • On your way from Nob Hill to Russian Hill, check out this small museum, stocked with photographs, scale models, vintage cars, and other memorabilia from the cable car's 121-year history. From an adjacent overlook you can gawk at the brawny cables that haul the cars up- and downhill, or watch the cables turn from an underground viewing room. *1201 Mason St., at Washington St., tel. 415/474–1887. Admission free. Open daily 10–5.*

➢ **GRACE CATHEDRAL** • A nouveau Gothic structure that took 53 years to build, the cathedral is essentially a poured-concrete replica of an old European-style cathedral. The gilded bronze doors at the east entrance were made from casts of Ghiberti's *Gates of Paradise* on the Baptistry in Florence. For a truly sublime experience, come for the singing of **vespers** every Thursday at 5:15 PM; an all-male choir will lift you out of the muck of your petty little world and leave you feeling almost sanctified. *1051 Taylor St., at California St., tel. 415/776–6611. From Embarcadero BART/MUNI, Bus 1 to Sacramento and Jones streets. Admission and guided tours free; donations accepted.*

➢ **LOMBARD STREET** • Since you've made it all the way up Russian Hill, don't miss the chance to do some strenuous walking around the well-maintained streets of San Francisco's wealthy. The most famous is undoubtedly **Lombard Street** between Hyde and Leavenworth, the block-long "crookedest street in America" and the recent site of the hipster house on MTV's *Real World.* If you're a lowly pedestrian, be careful negotiating this heavily trafficked route.

**THE MARINA** Stretching over a gorgeous strip of waterfront between **Fort Mason** and the **Presidio** (*see* Major Sights, *above*) and bordered to the south by **Union Street,** the Marina provides a home for San Francisco's yuppies. Even if it's not your scene, you'll possibly find yourself wandering **Chestnut Street** at some point, perhaps for a meal after visiting Fort Mason or upon escaping Fisherman's Wharf.

➢ **FORT MASON** • A series of warehouses built on piers on the Marina's eastern border, Fort Mason was once an army command post; now it's a nexus of artistic, cultural, and environmental organizations as well as small specialty museums. The **African American Historical and Cultural Society** and the **Mexican Museum** (*see* Museums, *below*), among others, are here. Although it's fairly quiet most days, Fort Mason is well worth a trip. Read through the newsletter that details what's going on this month; you can pick up a copy at one of the museums.

The renowned (and expensive) vegetarian restaurant **Greens** (*see* Food, *above*) is tucked into one of the warehouses. If you're too immobilized after eating to even think about a museum tour, relax at the **Book Bay Bookstore** (Fort Mason, Bldg. C, tel. 415/771–1076), where you can still get a book for a quarter. From Fisherman's Wharf, Fort Mason is about a 10-minute walk west: go down Beach Street past the Municipal Pier, climb the forested hill past the hostel, and as you descend on the other side you'll see Fort Mason spread out on the waterfront. *General information: tel. 415/979–3010. Buses 22, 28, 30, 42, 47, and 49.*

**PACIFIC HEIGHTS** The defining characteristics of Pacific Heights—the posh, high-altitude neighborhood stretching up from Van Ness and west to the Presidio—are its Victorian mansions, spared in the 1906 postquake fire that ravaged the rest of the city east of Van Ness. A good place to start your tour of Victorian Pacific Heights is at the **Haas-Lilienthal House,** the only one open to the public. Modest compared to the mansions that once stood along Van Ness, the 1886 Queen Anne-style house is now the property of **The Foundation for San Francisco's Architectural Heritage** (2007 Franklin St., near Washington St., tel. 415/441–3000), headquartered here. The trick is, in order to step inside and see the original furnishings, you must spend $5 to join an hour-long, docent-led tour. These leave Wednesdays noon–3:15 and Sundays 11–4, whenever a small group is gathered. Meet here at 12:30 PM on Sundays for a $5 walking tour covering the surrounding blocks of Victorians and Edwardians.

**JAPANTOWN** Modern Japantown spans the area north of Geary Street between Fillmore and Laguna streets. It's dominated by a massive and somewhat depressing shopping complex called **Japan Center.** The community was much larger before it dispersed during World War II, at which time the U.S. government began "relocating" Japanese Americans to remote internment camps.

Japan Center's **Peace Plaza** and five-story **Pagoda** were designed by architect Yoshiro Taniguchi in a gesture of goodwill from the people of Japan. The plaza is landscaped with traditional Japanese-style gardens and reflecting pools, and is the site of many traditional festivals throughout the year (*see* Festivals, *below*). Several shops in the area sell Japanese wares, and you'll find a number of good restaurants (*see* Food, *above*).

To relax after a day of sightseeing, try a Japanese steam bath at the **Kabuki Hot Springs** (1750 Geary Blvd., tel. 415/922–6000 for appointments), where you can use the steam room, sauna, and hot and cold baths (all sex-segregated) for $10, or get a 25-minute shiatsu massage and unlimited bath use for $35. The bath is reserved for women on Sunday, Wednesday, and Friday; men have access the rest of the week. Also in Japan Center, the **Kabuki 8 Theaters** (1881 Post St., tel. 415/931–9800) show first-run films in a high-tech complex. From the Montgomery Street BART/MUNI Station, Bus 2, 3, 4, or 38 will deposit you in Japantown.

**THE HAIGHT** East of Golden Gate Park sits the Haight-Ashbury district, the name of which still strikes fear in the hearts of suburban parents everywhere. The Haight began its career as a center for the counterculture in the late 1950s and early 1960s, when some Beat writers, several more or less illustrious fathers of the drug culture, and bands like the Grateful Dead and Jefferson Airplane moved in. There went the neighborhood. Attracted by the experimental, liberal atmosphere, several hundred thousand blissed-out teenagers soon converged on the Haight to drop their body weight in acid, play music, sing renditions of "Uncle John's Band" for days at a time, and generally do things for which they would feel incredibly silly 20 years later. But like the '60s themselves, the Haight's atmosphere of excitement and idealism was pretty much washed up by 1970 or so. Nowadays, the Haight is a semipunk hangout where '90s young people do things that frighten their formerly hippie parents.

**HOME SWEET HOME FOR THE PARAGONS OF COUNTERCULTURE:**

- *Janis Joplin: 112 Lyon St., btw Page and Oak Sts.*
- *The Grateful Dead: 710 Ashbury St., at Waller St.*
- *The Manson family: 636 Cole St., at Haight St.*
- *Jefferson Airplane: 2400 Fulton St., at Willard St.*

Since 1970, the stretch of Haight Street between Divisadero and Stanyan streets—often called "upper" Haight to distinguish it from the neighborhood at the foot of the hill (*see below*)—has gone through various stages of seediness and gentrification. With no little irony, its countercultural spirit survives largely in terms of the goods you can buy—like bongs, leather harnesses, and rave wear. The youthful slackers who live here still try to maintain an aura of rebelliousness, and neohippies still strum guitars on street corners—but the revolution is nowhere in sight. You can still buy drugs at the intersection of Haight Street and Golden Gate Park; in fact, it's pretty rare to walk through the Haight *without* being offered 'shrooms, green kind buds, or doses.

**LOWER HAIGHT AND WESTERN ADDITION** The hip, alternative Haight of the '60s isn't dead, it's just relocated. Full of disaffected youths and bedraggled Victorian houses, the lower Haight—between Fillmore and Steiner streets—is a new breeding ground for a community of angry youth, eccentrics of all ages, mental cases, and—perhaps an amalgam of all three—aspiring artists and writers. At night, the street is loud with the din of '70s funk or '90s hiphop blaring from the doorway of **Nickie's BBQ** (460 Haight St., tel. 415/621–6508), which overflows with sweaty, dancing youth of all races. If you're looking for a more laid-back scene, skirt the ornery drunks and drug dealers and head for **Toronado** (*see* Bars, *below*). During daylight, the **Horse Shoe Coffee House** (*see* Cafés, *above*) is a meeting place for neopsychedelic artists and trust-fund poets.

This colorful haven of new subcultures is itself subverted, however, by the very real poverty of its neighboring district to the north, the Western Addition. Though best explored during daylight hours, the Western Addition is worth checking out as a real-life community struggling with a legacy of poverty and discrimination. The main commercial drag is **Fillmore Street** between

## *Chilling by the Ocean*

***Step off the bus at Ocean Beach in your bikini, all sunscreened and ready to catch some rays, and you might be in for a big shock. No matter how hot the weather—San Francisco does see a few 95° days every year—the water will quickly cool you off to an icy shade of blue. Residents learn to use the beach for things other than swimming—like meditating, kite-flying, running, and exercising dogs. Luckily, Ocean Beach is more than just sand and water. Its attractions include Cliff House, a restaurant and historic San Francisco landmark perched on the cliffs, and the National Park Service office, where you can pick up information on the Golden Gate National Recreation Area. Across the plaza from the park office is the Musée Mécanique, a quirky museum stuffed with antique mechanical carnival attractions (player pianos, marionette shows, fortune tellers, etc.). Bring a pocketful of quarters to play with all the gadgets. North of Cliff House lie the ruins of the Sutro Baths. This huge complex of fresh- and saltwater pools, modeled after ancient Roman baths, torn down in 1966. People still climb around on the baths' foundations, trying to get a look at sea lions. To reach Ocean Beach take the N Judah Streetcar from any downtown underground MUNI station.***

***Baker Beach, below the Presidio, is quieter. It offers beautiful views of the Marin Headlands, the Golden Gate Bridge, and the bay. One end sees families, tourists, fishermen, and wealthy homeowners taking their dogs for a walk; the end nearest the bridge is a nude beach. Take Bus 1 from Clay and Drumm streets near the Embarcadero, and transfer to Bus 29 heading into the Presidio.***

# The Haight, Castro, and Mission Districts

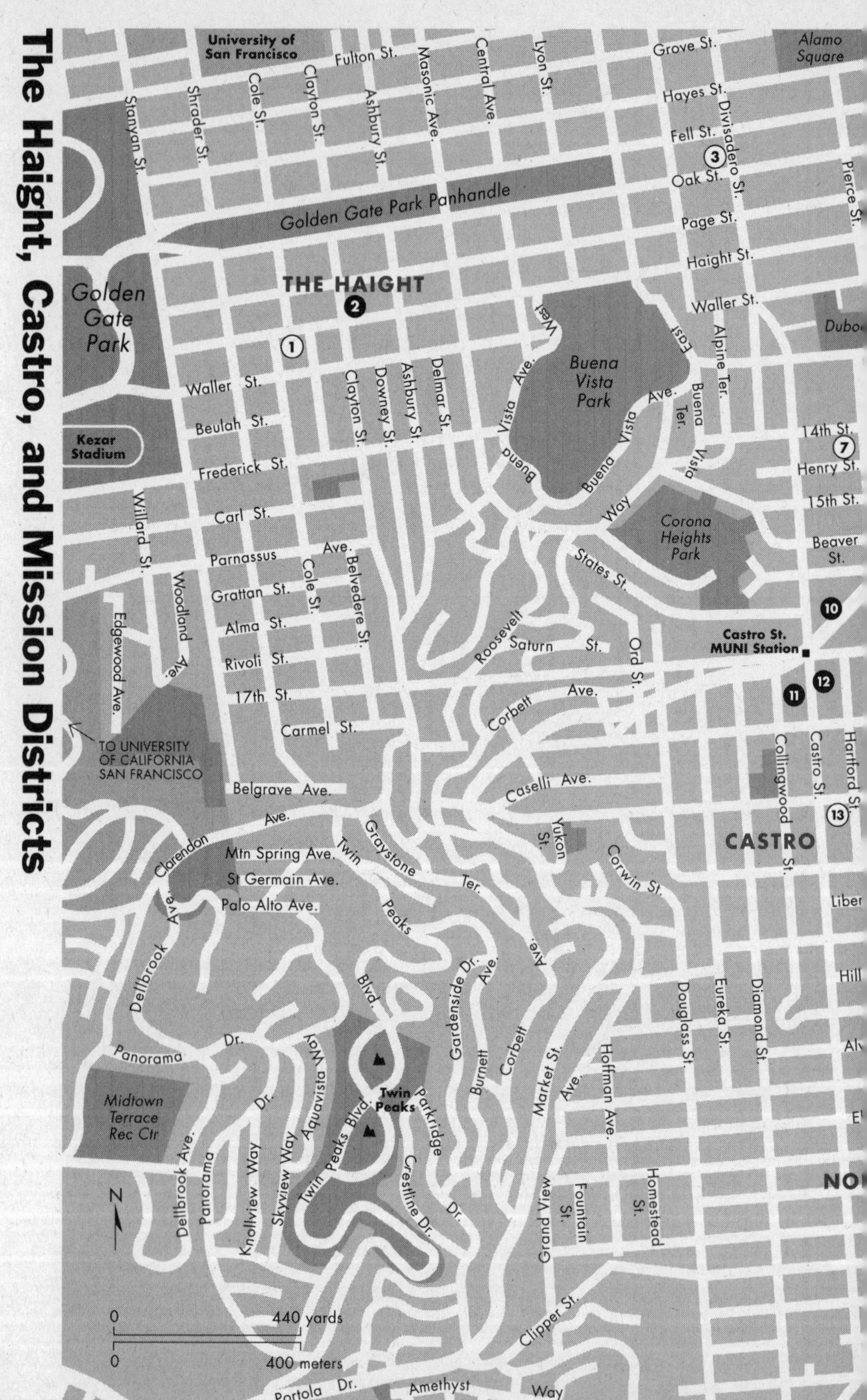

# The Haight, Castro, and Mission Districts

**Sights** ●

Café Flore, **9**
Castro Theatre, **12**
Haight-Ashbury Free Medical Clinic, **2**
Harvey Milk Plaza, **11**
Mission Dolores, **14**
The NAMES Project, **10**
Painted Ladies, **4**
Women's Building, **16**

**Lodging** ○

24 Henry, **7**
Black Stallion, **13**
Curtis Hotel, **15**
Metro Hotel, **3**
Red Victorian, **1**
San Francisco Zen Center, **6**
Sappho's, **5**
Twin Peaks, **8**

Oak Street and Geary Boulevard. If you're interested in African-American literature or history, make a beeline for the outstandingly comprehensive **Marcus Books** (1712 Fillmore St., btw Post and Sutter Sts., tel. 415/346–4222). Nearby, at the corner of Octavia and Bush streets, a half-dozen eucalyptus trees and a memorial plaque mark the former residence of Mary Ellen Pleasant (1816–1904), the hero of the Western Addition. Rumored to be a madam, a murderer, a witch, or some combination thereof, Pleasant was most renowned for her business savvy, profits from which financed the western leg of the Underground Railroad.

➢ **PAINTED LADIES** • The most famous row of houses in San Francisco is situated across from Alamo Square, a block west of Fillmore Street. The six beautifully restored, brightly painted Victorians sit side by side on a steep street with the downtown skyline looming majestically beyond. To snap the obligatory picture, take MUNI Bus 6, 7, 66, or 71 from downtown to Haight and Steiner streets, and walk north on Steiner to Hayes Street.

**CASTRO DISTRICT** To get to the Castro, simply follow the trail of rainbow flags and pink triangle bumper stickers. Since the early 1970s, the area around Castro Street has been attracting gay men and women from around the world. Before the AIDS epidemic, it was known as a spot for open revelry, with disco music pumping 24 hours a day. Today, the community is less carefree than since the first days of open gay pride, but, especially on weekends, it still bustles with people on the streets, in the bars, and at the gyms, socializing and checking one another out.

*On November 27, 1978, Milk and then-Mayor George Moscone were assassinated by Dan White, a disgruntled former supervisor. That night, 40,000 San Franciscans gathered at the plaza and proceeded to City Hall, where the murder took place, in a candlelight march. The procession is repeated every year on the anniversary of the event.*

The heart of the district is **Castro Street,** between Market and 19th streets. At the southwest corner of Market and Castro, where the K, L, and M MUNI streetcar lines stop, is **Harvey Milk Plaza,** named in honor of California's first openly gay elected official. All the shops, bars, and cafés in the neighborhood cater to the gay community. Travel agencies bill themselves as gay and lesbian vacation experts and card shops have names such as **Does Your Mother Know . . .** (4079 18th St., tel. 415/864–3160). The **Castro Theater** (*see* After Dark, *below*) is an impressive, art deco repertory house that hosts the much-loved International Lesbian and Gay Film Festival each summer. The Castro is also a good area to pick up information on gay and, to a lesser extent, lesbian resources—try **A Different Light Bookstore** (489 Castro St., near 18th St.,

## *Gay and Lesbian San Francisco*

***San Francisco promotes the fact that it is a gay city, the gayest in the world, even. Some neighborhood populations are as much as 95% gay, and it is feasible here for lesbian women and gay men to go about their lives dealing almost exclusively with other gays and lesbians, both in business and in pleasure. Gays and lesbians are the city's most prominent special-interest group and many hold public office, ranging from the Board of Supervisors to the Police Commission to the Municipal Court.***

***San Francisco's most concentrated gay neighborhood is the Castro district, followed closely by Polk Gulch. Although there isn't a lesbian neighborhood per se, many young lesbians gravitate to the Mission. Bernal Heights seems to attract slightly older women-loving women, while the more upwardly mobile lesbian set heads to Noe Valley. Valencia Street in the Mission is home to the greatest concentration of women-oriented shops, though it is not nearly the "dyke enclave" it was in the 1980s.***

tel. 415/431–0891), with its extensive collection of lesbian and gay literature. Look for special interest listings, abundant free publications, and advertisements for clubs or events in neighborhood shop windows.

The Castro is filled with unique gift shops and boutiques, especially those selling men's clothing. At **Man Line** (516 Castro St., tel. 415/863–7811), you can buy Keith Haring earrings and a rainbow-striped robe for yourself, and a decorative wine bottle holder and an American flag in a red, white, and Roy G. Biv rainbow motif for your home. Don't step into **Jaguar** (4057 18th St., tel. 415/863–4777) until you're prepared to be confronted with a foot-long silicon fist and other "objects of art" and books on how to use them. Not for the faint of heart.

The social hub of the neighborhood is east of Harvey Milk Plaza at **Café Flore** (*see* Cafés, *above*), where the eyes turn and the gossip mills churn. Closer to Castro Street, **The Café** (*see* Bars, *below*), is the only bar in the area where women represent a majority of the clientele. At the intersection of Castro and Market streets, **Twin Peaks** (401 Castro St., tel. 415/864–9470) has the distinction of being the first gay bar in the city with clear glass windows, a celebration of the fact that gay bars no longer feared arbitrary and frequent police raids. Note that Castro area bars get going in the afternoon. Why waste any time?

If you're in the city around the end of June, come to the Castro to witness one of San Francisco's craziest parties—the **San Francisco Lesbian, Gay, Bisexual, Transgender Pride Celebration** (tel. 415/864–3733), which attracts tens of thousands of participants. The Castro is also the traditional home of the city's other big bash—Halloween. At press time, however, a change of venue was being considered due to overcrowding and the recent influx of gawking "breeders" (*also see* Festivals, *below*).

➢ **NAMES PROJECT FOUNDATION** • For a sobering reminder of the continuing crisis facing the gay community, drop by the NAMES Project Foundation's **Visitor Center and Panel-making Workshop,** where panels from the now famous NAMES Quilt—a tribute to those who have died of AIDS—are displayed. The full quilt contains more than 30,000 panels. For those who are interested in creating a panel, the foundation provides sewing machines, fabric, company, and support, as well as a weekly "quilting bee" (Wednesdays 7–10 PM), if you need to brush up on your sewing skills. *2362A Market St., tel. 415/863–1966. Visitor center open daily 12–5.*

➢ **TWIN PEAKS** • Looming high above the Castro, Twin Peaks is one of the few places in the city where you can see both the bay and the ocean, and everything in between. Naturally, it's one of the prime make-out spots in San Francisco. If you surface long enough to look at the view, you'll have to admit it's truly spectacular—definitely worth the hassle of getting here on public transportation. When the Spanish came to this area in the 18th century, they named the peaks *Los Pechos de la Choca* (the Breasts of the Indian Maiden). Just another example of missionaries hard at work converting the heathens. To reach Twin Peaks, take MUNI Bus 37 west from Castro and Market streets.

**MISSION DISTRICT** Unplagued by fog, the sunny Mission district—named after Mission Dolores (*see below*)—was once San Francisco's prime real estate, first for the native Ohlone people and then for Spanish missionaries. Over the years in this district Scandinavian, German, Irish, and Italian populations have given way to immigrants from Mexico and Central America, and the community today is low-income and primarily Latino, though it also includes a significant contingent of bohemians, artists, and radicals of all ethnicities. The neighborhood is a colorful and usually friendly place to hang out, but it can also be dangerous. Women won't feel comfortable walking alone here at night, and while you can actually find a parking space, you might think twice about leaving your car.

The neighborhood provides a bounty of cheap food, in the form of huge burritos and succulent tacos made up fresh in

*You'll see murals all over the Mission, many done in the tradition of Mexican painters like Diego Rivera. Look for the one near the 24th Street/ Mission BART station that seems to depict BART being built on the backs of the people. Another spectacular mural covers the Women's Building (18th St., btw Valencia and Guerrero Sts.), honoring women throughout time and from every culture.*

numerous storefront taquerías (*see box* A Cheap Trip South of the Border, in Food, *above*). You'll quickly learn the distinction between genuine Mexican fast food and Taco Bell, if you don't know it already. The area also abounds with specialty bookstores, alternative theater companies, and an increasing variety of bars, some of which offer live music, poetry readings, and dance spaces. Two BART stations (one at Mission and 16th Street and the other at Mission and 24th) put you right in the heart of all the activity.

A good place to discover the Mission district's offbeat side is Valencia Street (a block west of Mission Street), lined with cafés, secondhand furniture and clothing stores, galleries, and bookstores. Check out **Epicenter** (475 Valencia St., tel. 415/431–2725), an anarchist-oriented community center with a huge selection of new and used punk albums. Nearby is the **Women's Building** (3543 18th St., tel. 415/431–1180), a meeting place for progressive and radical political groups. Valencia Street is also the site of several good new and used bookstores, including the feminist **Old Wives' Tales** (1009 Valencia St., tel. 415/821–4675). Also check out **Good Vibrations** (1210 Valencia St., tel. 415/974–8980), a collectively owned, user-friendly vibrator and sex-toy store; and **Botanica Yoruba** (998 Valencia St., at 21st St., tel. 415/826–4967), where you can pick up incense, herbs, and spiritual advice.

➢ **MISSION DOLORES** • Though it's made of humble adobe, the oldest building in San Francisco has survived some powerful earthquakes and fires. Commissioned by Junípero Serra to honor San Francisco de Asis (St. Francis of Assisi), it was nicknamed Dolores by the Spanish after a nearby stream, *Arroyo de Nuestra Señora de los Dolores* (Stream of Our Lady of the Sorrows). Mission Dolores is both the simplest architecturally and the least restored of all the California missions, with a bright ceiling painted in a traditional Native American design by local Costanoans. The mission bells still ring on holy days, and the cemetery next door is the permanent home of a few California celebrities, including San Francisco's first mayor, Don Francisco de Haro. For the $1 admission fee you get an informative pamphlet on the history of the mission, access to a small museum with old artifacts, and as much time as you like in the mission and the fascinating old cemetery. *16th and Dolores Sts., tel. 415/621–8203. Admission: $1. Open daily 9–4.*

**SOUTH OF MARKET** Until recently, SoMa—the area bordered by Mission Street, Townsend Street, the Embarcadero, and 12th Street—was merely a nondescript stretch of abandoned factories. Now, thanks to a resurgent art and theater scene and a happening nightlife, the region is coming alive. The South of Market nightlife scene centers around **Folsom Street,** where the city's predilection for loud music combines nicely with cheap warehouse space and a lack of neighbors to disturb, creating a heathen's haven of dance clubs (*see* Clubs, *below*).

The brand-new Yerba Buena Gardens and the San Francisco Museum of Modern Art (*see below*) are the stars of the SoMa arts scene, both figuratively and literally. Smaller, hipper galleries are relocating to the neighborhood as fast as they can, borrowing light from the big names to draw attention to themselves. To test this theory, wander *behind* the SFMOMA and try to count the warehouse-cum-gallery spaces within a 3-block radius. Progress continues apace: 1995 saw the **California Historical Society**'s relocation to 678 Mission Street, at 3rd Street (tel. 415/567–1848); a Children's Center should open in 1996, and the Mexican Museum, now in cramped Fort Mason quarters, will make its new home here around 1998.

*Old-fashioned, sunny, and smack in the middle of warehouse-riddled SoMa, South Park (off 2nd and 3rd Sts., btw Bryant and Brannan Sts.) is perfect for those postmodern moments when you feel like you've spent the whole day on the set of the movie "Mad Max."*

South of Market also attracts bargain hunters with its outlet stores and warehouses; by day, shoppers are out in force hunting leather fashions, beauty products, work clothes, office supplies, and anything else you can think of. At **660 Center** (660 3rd St., btw Brannan and Townsend Sts., tel. 415/227–0464), you'll find the ultimate bargain basement—22 outlet stores under one roof.

➢ **YERBA BUENA GARDENS** • On the east side of this 8.3-acre arts space and garden complex, the **Center for the Arts** (tel. 415/978–2787) houses galleries and a high-tech multimedia theater, both meant to celebrate the Bay Area's multicultural nature. Admission to the galleries is $4, $2 students. Critics suggest the multicultural emphasis might be to the exclusion of mainstream arts. Others smirk at the money spent building the center: a whopping $41 million. *701 Mission St., tel. 415/978–2787.*

Aside from the performing and visual arts, Yerba Buena Gardens offers a welcome respite from the frenzy of downtown—yet it's just a couple blocks southeast of the Montgomery Street BART station. Take a walk along the paths of the grassy, spacious esplanade to the Martin Luther King, Jr. Memorial: 12 glass panels, all behind a shimmering waterfall, engraved with quotes from Dr. King in English and in the languages of San Francisco's various sister cities.



## MUSEUMS

Although San Francisco has been trying to build a name for itself as a city graced with big, impressive institutions of art—note the newly relocated Museum of Modern Art and the renovated California Palace of the Legion of Honor—the increasing attention to the arts in general is a boon to the smaller, funky spaces that fit more naturally into the city's eclectic cultural landscape. The city's fine arts collection is divided between the M.H. de Young Museum and the California Palace of the Legion of Honor.

*A number of the city's hoity-toitiest museums and galleries are a part of the SoMa landscape. And then there's the Cartoon Art Museum (814 Mission St., at 4th St., tel. 415/546–3922), which will teach you all you ever wanted to know about the history of cartoons, comics, and underground comix for an admission price of $3.50 ($2.50 students).*

**African American Museum.** Aimed at disseminating African-American culture, this place offers a contemporary art gallery with works by African and African-American artists; an intriguing gift shop selling jewelry and crafts; and a historical archive and research library. In addition, the museum has performing-arts classes and lecture series. *Fort Mason Center, Bldg. C, tel. 415/441–0640. Donation requested. Open Wed.–Sun. noon–5.*

**Ansel Adams Center.** If you're even remotely interested in serious photography, come here. The West Coast's largest repository of art photography, the Ansel Adams Center has five rotating exhibits, one of which is devoted to Adams's work. Adams himself founded the Friends of Photography, a national group that created the center, which now serves photographers with publications, awards, an incredible bookstore, and an educational series taught by famous shutterbugs. Its 1993 Annie Leibovitz retrospective put it on the pop-culture map. *250 4th St., btw Howard and Folsom Sts., tel. 415/495–7000. Admission: $4, $3 students. Open Tues.–Sun. 11–5 (until 8 first Thurs. of month).*

**Asian Art Museum.** Housed in the same building as the M.H. de Young (*see below*), this is the West Coast's largest Asian museum, with more than 12,000 pieces representing every major period of Asian art—from nearly every region of Asia. Highlights include the oldest known dated Buddha image (AD 338) and superb collections of jade and ancient Chinese ceramics. *John F. Kennedy and Tea Garden Drs., Golden Gate Park, tel. 415/668–8921. Admission: $5, $3 students; free first Wed. of month, first Sat. of month until noon. Open Wed.–Sun. 10–5 (until 8:45 first Wed. of month).*

**California Academy of Sciences.** This huge natural-history complex houses one of the country's best natural history museums, subdivided into blockbuster sights including the **Steinhart Aquarium** and **Morrison Planetarium.** One big draw is the aquarium's **Fish Roundabout,** which places you in an underwater world of 14,500 different creatures. The living coral reef, with fish, giant clams, tropical sharks, and a rainbow of hard and soft corals, is super-cool. Go mid-morning so you can watch the penguins and dolphins at feeding time. If your imagination inextricably links San Francisco with temblors, try the shuddery earthquake floor in the **Space and Earth Hall.** *Btw John F. Kennedy and Martin Luther King, Jr. Drs., Golden Gate Park, tel. 415/750–7000; laser shows at planetarium, tel. 415/750–7138. Admission: $7 to museum and aquarium, $4 students (free first Wed. of month); $2.50 to planetarium; $7 to laser shows. Open daily 10–5.*

**Exploratorium.** Come here for the ultimate fourth-grade field trip you never took—it's a great place to learn about science and technology in a big, drafty warehouse. The 650-plus exhibits, many of them computer-assisted, strongly emphasize sensual interaction, making this place especially popular with people on hallucinogenic drugs. Advance reservations are required for the excellent crawl-through **Tactile Dome.** *3601 Lyon St., btw Marina Blvd. and Lombard St., tel. 415/561–0360. Admission: $8.50, $6.50 students, $4.50 disabled; free first Wed. of month. Open Tues.–Sun. 10–5 (Wed. until 9:30); Memorial Day and Labor Day 10–5.*

**Legion of Honor.** San Francisco's European fine arts are on display, once again, in the newly reopened California Palace of the Legion of Honor, overlooking the Pacific Ocean. The collection, while not exactly stunning, does include some fine late-19th-century pieces, including one of Monet's *Water Lilies* and several Rodin sculptures, including a cast of *The Thinker. In Lincoln Park, enter at 34th Ave. and Clement St., tel. 415/750–3600. Admission: $6. Open Tues.–Sun. 10–5 (until 8:45 first Sat. of month).*

**M. H. de Young Memorial Museum.** San Francisco's big, mainstream museum is best known for its substantial, 20-plus-gallery survey collection of American art, from paintings and sculpture to decorative arts, textiles, and furniture. Some pieces date as far back as 1670, and the artists represented include Sargent, Whistler, Church, and Wood. Classical and tribal arts are also on display. Docent-led tours depart on the hour. *Btw John F. Kennedy Dr. and 8th Ave., Golden Gate Park, tel. 415/750–3600 or 415/863–3330 for recorded info. Admission: $5, free first Wed. of month. Open Wed.–Sun. 10–4:45 (Wed. until 8:45), additional open hrs during special exhibitions.*

**Mexican Museum.** A unique center exploring Mexican and Chicano culture in the United States, this museum—boasting a 9,000-item permanent collection—has had to make do with a relatively small space. Yet it has scored the likes of Diego Rivera and Frida Kahlo exhibits, as well as less mainstream shows with themes like Chicano graffiti art. *Fort Mason Center, Bldg. D, tel. 415/441–0404. Admission: $3, $2 students; free first Wed. of month. Open Wed.–Sun. noon–5 (until 8 first Wed. of month).*

**San Francisco Museum of Modern Art.** SFMOMA's new brick-and-stone home is dominated by a huge, cylindrical skylight trimmed in black and white stone. The space is twice that of the museum's prior home at the War Memorial Veterans Building, where it opened in 1935 as the West Coast's first museum devoted to 20th-century art. The excellent permanent collection includes works by Jackson Pollock, Jasper Johns, Frida Kahlo, Henri Matisse, and Frank Stella, as well as a healthy representation of contemporary photography. *151 3rd St., tel. 415/357–4000. Admission: $7, $3.50 students; free first Tues. of month, half-price Thurs. 6–9. Open Tues.–Sun. 11–6 (Thurs. until 9). Closed major holidays.*

## CHEAP THRILLS

The **Midsummer Music Festival** at Stern Grove offers 10 Sunday afternoons of free symphony, opera, jazz, dance, and pop to an appreciative crowd of picnickers. In order to get the most out of the concerts, be sure to bring a blanket, food, drinks, and your friends. The amphitheater is in a beautiful eucalyptus grove; concerts start at 2 PM, but you'll want to show up around noon. *Sloat Blvd., at 19th Ave., tel. 415/252–6252. MUNI 23, 28, K, or M.*

The **Anchor Brewing Company** (1705 Mariposa St., tel. 415/863–8350) offers free brewery tours, including a history of the brewery, a step-by-step explanation of the brewing process, and, yep, free samples at the end. Tours run twice a day June–August, and once a day the rest of the year. You *must* make reservations three to four weeks in advance.

All the world's a stage, and the **San Francisco Shakespeare Festival** (tel. 415/666–2221) brings a free play to Liberty Tree Meadow (west of the Conservatory) in Golden Gate Park every Saturday and Sunday at 1:30 from Labor Day through the first weekend in October. Call for details.

**San Francisco Mime Troupe.** This agitprop ensemble stages scathing political comedies and musicals—free! They appear in Golden Gate Park and other Bay Area parks between July 4 and Labor Day. Bring a picnic and spend a terrifically entertaining sunny afternoon. *Tel. 415/285–1717.*

Ever been to church and come away humming, tapping your toes, and with the phone number of the stranger you sat next to? You may not see a single religious icon at the Sunday morning "celebration" at **Glide Memorial United Methodist Church,** presided over by a beaming Reverend Cecil Williams in his colorful robe. Instead of organ music, a funky band and choir give parishioners reason to stand up and groove when the spirit moves them. Celebrations at Glide attract all ethnicities, classes, and sexual orientations. Bobby McFerrin often comes to Glide; Bill Clinton and Maya Angelou stopped in when they were in town. The Rev. Williams is also a famous community activist in San Francisco. Celebrations occur every Sunday morning at 9 and 11. Try to arrive a few minutes early. *330 Ellis St., at Taylor St., tel. 415/ 771–6300. Near Powell St. BART/MUNI.*



## FESTIVALS

➢ **JANUARY** • During the one-day **Tet Festival** in late January, the streets around Civic Center come alive with performances by Vietnamese, Cambodian, and Laotian singers and dancers, and numerous booths sell Southeast Asian delicacies. Call 415/885–2743 for more information.

➢ **FEBRUARY** • **Chinese New Year and Golden Dragon Parade.** Celebrate the dawn of the Year of the Rat with North America's largest Chinese community. The Chinatown Chamber of Commerce (730 Sacramento St., San Francisco, tel. 415/982–3000) has the lowdown on cultural events, which take place during the last two weeks of February. The justly famous Golden Dragon Parade—1996's is March 2 at 6 PM—sparkles with firecrackers and a riot of colorful costumes.

➢ **APRIL** • **Cherry Blossom Festival.** Japantown hosts this cultural festival, which extends over two weekends and incorporates such Japanese traditions as the tea ceremony, taiko drum performances, and martial arts and cooking demonstrations. The festivities conclude with a 2½-hour parade. *Tel. 415/563–2313.*

**San Francisco International Film Festival.** The oldest film festival in the United States features 14 straight days of films and seminars and many opportunities to mingle with the creative minds behind them. Screenings take place at the Kabuki 8 and the Castro Theatre in San Francisco, the Pacific Film Archive in Berkeley, and at theaters in the South Bay and Marin County. *Tel. 415/929–5000. Admission: $7.50 per program, $5.50 students, seniors, and disabled.*

➢ **MAY** • San Francisco's Mission district explodes with *felicidad* on the weekend nearest May 5, during the two-day **Cinco de Mayo** fiesta (tel. 415/647–8622) extolling Mexico's independence from France. Later in the month, on Memorial Day Weekend, the Mission celebrates **Carnaval** (tel. 415/826–1401) with dance, music, arts and crafts, and a parade.

**Bay to Breakers.** Listed in the *Guinness Book of Records* as the world's largest foot race, this zany 7½-mile race pits world-class runners against costumed human centipedes and huge safe-sex condom caravans. The half-comical, half-serious event takes place the third Sunday in May and attracts more than 100,000 people. *Tel. 415/777–7770.*

➢ **JUNE** • Summer brings out all the neighborhood celebrations, including the **Haight Street Fair** (tel. 415/661–8025), the **Polk Street Fair** (tel. 415/346–4561), the **North Beach Festival** (tel. 415/403–0666), and the **Union Street Spring Festival** (tel. 415/346–4561), all of which feature craft booths, music, and food.

**San Francisco Lesbian, Gay, Bisexual, Transgender Pride Celebration.** Known as San Francisco Pride for short (tel. 415/864–3733), this is San Francisco at its fabulous queer best. June also brings the much-loved and internationally famous **Lesbian and Gay Film Festival** (tel. 415/ 703–8650).

➢ **JULY** • **Fourth of July Waterfront Festival.** San Francisco Bay is illuminated every 4th with fireworks along the waterfront between Aquatic Park and Pier 39. Festivities start in the afternoon with musical performances by Bay Area musicians. *Tel. 415/777–8498.*

➢ **SEPTEMBER** • **San Francisco Blues Festival.** This two-day event draws some mighty big names—for mighty big bucks—and is a must for blues enthusiasts. Past performers have included John Mayall and the Robert Cray Band. The 1996 festival takes place September 22–23; one-day tickets are $16.50 in advance, $20 at the door; two-day tickets are $28, advance purchase only. A free kickoff concert happens at Justin Herman Plaza September 21. *Great Meadow, Fort Mason, tel. 415/826–6837 or 415/979–5588 for recorded info.*

➢ **OCTOBER • Halloween.** Traditionally, this huge, raucous, queers-only party has taken place on the Castro's closed-off streets, but at press time, a change of venue was being considered due to overcrowding and the recent influx of gawking "breeders." Check local papers or ask around as the holiday approaches. And if you aren't dressed to the nines, don't even bother.

# After Dark

**San Francisco nightlife leans toward the** casual, though you can wear incredibly expensive clothes and sneer at your fellow patrons over $10 martinis if you really want to. Look in the *S.F. Weekly* or the *Bay Guardian* for possibilities; you'll find about a hundred different choices, costing from next to nothing to a whole lot of money. The *Bay Times* is the best source for gay- and lesbian-oriented entertainment listings. Bars and clubs (and liquor stores) are all supposed to close by 2 AM, but several clubs stay open until the wee hours for those who just can't stop dancing.

**BARS** **Elbo Room.** This stylish Mission watering hole becomes unmanageably popular as the night progresses. Upstairs, live jazz and hip-hop acts, as well as occasional DJs, attract the crowds. Plus, the drinks are cheap enough ($2–$3) to keep you around until closing. *647 Valencia St., near 17th St., tel. 415/552–7788.*

**Mad Dog in the Fog.** This British-style pub in the heart of lower Haight is frequented by people who don't mind communicating in screams over loud grunge music and cold, frothy beer. You can also play darts here, and during the day you might get lucky and enjoy a moment of peace on the back patio. *530 Haight St., btw Fillmore and Steiner Sts., tel. 415/626–7279.*

**The Noc Noc.** This lower-Haight bar features an interior that looks like a postmodern cave—complete with chunky Flintstones-style furniture—not to mention a healthy variety of beers, a couple kinds of wine and sake, and all manner of tunes passing through the speakers. It's a favorite of visiting Europeans. *557 Haight St., btw Fillmore and Steiner Sts., tel. 415/861–5811.*

**Place Pigalle.** The vibes are hip and European at this sleek, low-key, French-owned wine bar and gallery space in the Western Addition. Stop in for a glass of wine or stay for the evening; there's live jazz Thursday through Saturday nights, and occasional spoken-word performances during the week. *520 Hayes St., btw Octavia and Laguna Sts., tel. 415/552–2671. Cover: up to $3. Wheelchair access.*

**Specs'.** One of the classic North Beach hangouts for the perennially half-sloshed, this is a jovial, divey, no-attitude sort of place where, if the conversation sucks, you can gaze all night at the quirky memorabilia on the walls. *12 Saroyan Pl., tel. 415/421–4112. In the alley across Columbus Ave. from City Lights Books.*

**The Toronado.** A narrow, dark dive in the Haight with lots of folks in leather, the Toronado features one of the city's widest selections of microbrewed beer, and the jukebox plays a refreshing mix of kitschy country-and-western and grunge. *547 Haight St., btw Fillmore and Steiner Sts., tel. 415/863–2276.*

**Tosca.** This lovely, cavernous establishment in North Beach is renowned for its liqueur-laced coffee drinks, its beautiful old espresso machine, its opera-only jukebox, and its celebrity patrons (including Francis Ford Coppola and Mikhail Baryshnikov). *242 Columbus Ave., at Broadway, tel. 415/391–1244. Wheelchair access.*

**Zeitgeist.** This is the original no-frills biker bar, for every kind of biker. In the afternoons, it fills with bike messengers relating the day's near encounters with the Big Grille in the Sky; by night the BMW motorcycle crowd clogs the outdoor deck. The 'Geist is trendier and younger than your average Hell's Angels hangout. *199 Valencia St., at Duboce Ave., tel. 415/255–7505.*

➢ **GAY AND LESBIAN** • **The Café.** This large, lively bar with mirrored walls and neon lights caters mainly to lesbians, although gay men also frequent the place. If there's no room on the dance floor, you can hang out on the balcony and watch the Castro strut by. *2367 Market St., near Castro St., tel. 415/861–3846.*

**The Detour.** Minimally decorated with a chain-link fence and pool table, this bar caters to a youngish leather-queen wanna-be crowd sporting goatees. The urgent techno-house music causes the sexual frustration level in the room to skyrocket. If you forget the address, listen for the music, since the black-on-black sign is impossible to see at night. *2348 Market St., btw Castro and Noe Sts., tel. 415/861–6053.*

**QT.** At the "Quick Trick" you can cozy up to hustlers and drag queens in an unassuming atmosphere. There's live music Friday and Saturday nights, and free male strip shows, both professional and amateur, on Sundays and Tuesdays. Legend has it that the owner gave Anita Baker her start. *1312 Polk St., btw Bush and Pine Sts., tel. 415/885–1114.*

**CLUBS** Dance clubs range from the cheap, local, and casual to the expensive, pretentious, and trendy. On the low end, some local bars will just stick a DJ in a corner and clear the tables away—instant disco. For the most eclectic and underground clubs, look in smaller retail and record shops for flyers advertising one-night extravaganzas that take place in changing locations. The *S.F. Weekly, the Bay Guardian,* and *Klub* magazine are also good resources. Always call ahead; clubs can change as quickly as fashion fades.

➢ **STRAIGHT** • **Bahia Cabana.** A multigenerational, international crowd gets its samba fix at this colorful downtown supper club with mural-covered walls. Wednesdays it's reggae; other nights feature Afro-Brazilian music and shows by local dance troupes. *1600 Market St., at Franklin St., tel. 415/282–4020 or 415/861–4202. Cover: $5–$10.*

**DNA Lounge.** A dependable choice for late-night dancing (until 4 AM nightly) and eclectic acts that range from bands to tattoo/piercing shows. You can hear a diverse range of live sounds (from accordion to industrial) early in the evening, but it's the leather-jacket SoMa crowd that dances until the wee hours of the morning. *375 11th St., at Harrison St., tel. 415/626–1409. Cover: $5.*

*Don't get bowling-ball wax on your leather jacket at the Park Bowl (1855 Haight St., tel. 415/752–2366) on Rock 'n Bowl nights, which feature that quintessentially American pastime accompanied by that quintessentially American music, all in one alley.*

**Nickie's BBQ.** Red vinyl booths and Christmas lights decorate this racially mixed, unpretentious lower-Haight hole-in-the-wall. Everything from funk and Latin to hip-hop and reggae booms through the speakers every night except Monday. *460 Haight St., btw Webster and Fillmore Sts., tel. 415/621–0249. Cover: $3–$5.*

➢ **MIXED** • **1015 Club.** This SoMa spot hosts various clubs on a nightly basis. Fridays, "Dakota" (tel. 415/431–1200) captures the history of disco in three rooms: deep funk and tribal beats in the basement, '70s disco in the Gold Room, and high house in the main dance pit. Dress up for this one. Saturdays, "Release" (415/337–7457) keeps you going with '70s funk and disco, high house, and acid jazz. Call for a complete listing of club nights. *1015 Folsom St., btw 6th and 7th Sts., tel. 415/431–0700. Cover: about $10.*

**The Box.** This Thursdays-only SoMa club plays hard-core hip-hop, funk, and house, and you'll find minimal attitude here because everybody's sweating on the dance floor. Go-go boxes mounted on the wall showcase dancers with breathtaking bodies at full throttle. This is technically a gay club, run by lesbians, but the multicultural crowd includes straights too. Simply put, it's a very popular club and everybody wants to go. The city's most accomplished DJs and club dance troupes appear here. *715 Harrison St., btw 3rd and 4th Sts. Cover: $6. Wheelchair access.*

**DV8.** This is the hippest of the hip: From private parties to roaming dance clubs, you can almost never go wrong at this SoMa warehouse. Come on Saturdays for "Star 69," a new, primarily gay dance party, and move it all night to deep house tunes. *540 Harrison St., near 1st St., tel. 415/957–1730.*

**The EndUp.** Venues change as fickle hipsters try to keep up with trends, but The EndUp always has a sweaty crowd gettin' down. Come at 6 AM Sunday for the Tea Dance: $3 for all the dancing you can handle until 2 AM Monday morning. Call the info line for details. *401 6th St., at Harrison St., tel. 415/487–6277. Cover: $7–$10.*

➢ **GAY AND LESBIAN • Club Townsend.** This dance mecca hosts "Pleasuredome," San Francisco's most popular gay and lesbian club, on Sunday nights. The crowd is mostly male, but "Club Universe" on Saturdays and "Club King" on Wednesdays are less gender-specific. All three are flashy and groovy; don't bother showing up if you can't take the loud, deep sounds of house music. *177 Townsend St., btw 2nd and 3rd Sts., tel. 415/974–6020. Cover: $7–$10.*

**The Stud.** It's a San Francisco legend and a good watering hole—dress up or come as you are—any night of the week. Thursdays, the Stud hosts "Junk," a thrash-dance club for lesbians; Wednesdays it's "oldies" and a beer bust; and Sundays it's "80something," a new-wave dance party. *399 Harrison St., at 9th St., tel. 415/863–6623. Cover: up to $6.*

**LIVE MUSIC** San Francisco has an eclectic and extensive music scene. Sometimes you'll catch hugely talented bands for free in parks, bars, cafés, and the occasional alley. On the other hand, you could pay $15–$20 to see bands on the verge of MTV stardom play at the **Warfield** (982 Market St., btw 5th and 6th Sts., tel. 415/775–7722) or the historic, recently reopened **Fillmore** (1805 Geary St., at Fillmore St., tel. 415/346–6000).

*Bottom of the Hill's Sunday all-you-can-eat barbecues ($3) draw mammoth crowds.*

➢ **ROCK • Bottom of the Hill.** This neighborhood space at the bottom of Potrero Hill showcases up-and-coming local bands. Hang out here a few nights in a row and you'll get a comprehensive sense of the local music scene. *1233 17th St., at Texas St., tel. 415/626–4455. Cover: $3–$6.*

**Paradise Lounge.** The quality of music varies widely (to put it kindly) at this hip SoMa cocktail lounge, but with three stages to choose from and a constant flow of people, it's a reliable weekend destination. Upstairs you can play a game of pool, listen to low-key music, or participate in a poetry reading. *1501 Folsom St., at 11th St., tel. 415/861–6906. Cover: $3–$5.*

➢ **JAZZ • Café du Nord.** The specialty at this club, which can get horribly overcrowded, is jazz you can afford. You'll see good local bands, play pool, and stare at young San Franciscans in their finest duds, nodding their heads and snapping their fingers. *2170 Market St., btw Church and Sanchez Sts., tel. 415/861–5016. Cover: $3–$5.*

**Club 181.** A gorgeous old jazz club that was closed in the '80s, the 181 recently reopened its doors to a whole new crowd. With a sizable clientele of jet-setting Euro-types and rich kids, this has become the chic place for twentysomethings to see, be seen, and eat dinner. Dress up for a great jazz or hip-hop show. *181 Eddy St., near Taylor St., tel. 415/673–8181. Cover: $5–$10.*

**Noe Valley Ministry.** An adventurous booking policy embracing experimental jazz, blues, and world music draws serious talent into this no-smoke/occasional-drink church that moonlights as a theater. *1021 Sanchez St., btw 23rd St. and Elizabeth St., tel. 415/282–2317. Cover: $8–$15.*

## Free Verse

***The spoken-word scene, with its historic Beat connection, is enjoying a renaissance in cafés and bars throughout the Bay Area. In case you didn't know, the genre encompasses poetry, antipoetry, monologues, howls, grunts, screams, and even readings of cereal boxes. The Blue Monkey (1777 Steiner St., btw Sutter and Post Sts., tel. 415/929–7117) has mostly poetry, with some music and storytelling, at 7:30 PM on Tuesdays; Café International (508 Haight St., at Fillmore St., tel. 415/552–7390) offers readings—often with an ethnic bent—at 9 PM on Fridays.***

**Up and Down Club.** Sleek deco digs and live jazz make this SoMa spot the lounge of choice for those who like to pretend San Francisco is New York City. Upstairs you'll find a DJ laying down tracks, but little room to dance. *1151 Folsom St., btw 7th and 8th Sts., tel. 415/626–2388. Closed Tuesdays. Cover: $5; free Wed.*

➢ **BLUES** • **Grant and Green Blues Club.** This dark, smoky bar hosts some raucous blues shows—a welcome change in North Beach, where too many folks sit stiffly in coffeehouses discussing obscure lit-crits over bottles of wine. *1731 Grant Ave., at Green St., tel. 415/693–9565. Cover: $2–$5.*

**Slim's.** This club, owned by Boz Skaggs, features all types of American roots music. Blues and jazz prevail, but on the right night you might catch funk, gospel, reggae, or rock. *333 11th St., btw Folsom and Harrison Sts., tel. 415/621–3330. Cover: $7–$12.*

➢ **CLASSICAL** • The **San Francisco Symphony** plays from September to May. The 1996 season includes Milhaud's *La Création du Monde,* Berlioz's *Symphonie Fantastique,* and Stravinsky's *Canticum Sacrum* and *Symphony of Psalms.* Tickets cost $9 (for a rear view) and up; seats in the second-tier balcony are $22. *Davies Symphony Hall, Van Ness Ave. at Grove St., tel. 415/864–6000.*

The **San Francisco Opera** puts on quality performances during its regular season (early September to mid-December) and a short summer season, often hurling scads of money into one truly knockout performance each year (usually Wagner). Ticket prices range from $20 to about half your weekly paycheck; the cheapest seats will sell out first, so plan in advance. Student rush tickets ($20) go on sale two hours before the show. The War Memorial Opera House (301 Van Ness Ave.) is closed until 1997; until then, performances will be staged at Bill Graham Memorial Civic Auditorium (cnr Grove and Polk Sts.) and the Orpheum Theater (1192 Market St., near 8th St.). *Box office: 199 Grove St., at Van Ness Ave., tel. 415/864–3330.*

**MOVIE HOUSES** **Castro Theatre.** The most beautiful place to see a film in San Francisco, the Castro shows a wide selection of rare, foreign, and offbeat movies. It specializes in Audrey Hepburn and Bette Davis flicks and other camp classics of gay culture, as well as new releases of interest to lesbian and gay viewers. The kitschy man who comes up out of the floor playing the Würlitzer organ is guaranteed to make you giggle. *429 Castro St., btw Market and 18th Sts., tel. 415/621–6120.*

**The Red Vic.** It's the only theater in town with couches. How cool. Films range from the artsy to the cultish to the rare, and you can order herbal tea or coffee to accompany your yeasted popcorn. *1727 Haight St., btw Cole and Shrader Sts., tel. 415/668–3994.*

**THEATER** While it doesn't carry the national reputation of New York, Los Angeles, or Chicago, San Francisco has a diverse and affordable theater scene. **ACT** (345 Mason St., tel. 415/749–2228) is the city's premier local repertory company, but what San Francisco does best—as usual—is experimental theater, with an emphasis on multimedia visual arts and solo performers. Look through the *S.F. Weekly,* the *Bay Guardian,* or the Sunday *Chronicle-Examiner's* "Pink Section" for special events.

**Magic Theater** (Fort Mason Center, Bldg. D, tel. 415/441–8822) is the city's standby for the mildly experimental, showcasing innovative, modern American works. **Theater Artaud** (450 Florida St., at 17th St., tel. 415/621–7797) regularly programs avant-garde dance, drama, and multimedia work in a cavernous warehouse space. **Theater Rhinoceros** (2926 16th St., near Mission St., tel. 415/861–5079) is dedicated to all kinds of gay theater.

**Beach Blanket Babylon** is the longest-lived musical revue in history. It features high production values, impeccable timing, well-practiced musicians, polished performers, extra-large headgear, and a zesty, zany script that changes often to incorporate topical references and characters. Twenty-plus bucks is a high price to pay, but BBB is notable for spending a significant portion of its profits on local charities. If you're under 21 you can only attend Sunday matinees. Make reservations well in advance. *Fugazi Hall, 678 Green St., tel. 415/421–4222. Shows Wed.–Sun.*

# SAN FRANCISCO BAY AREA 3

Y

**You're standing on Telegraph Hill, maybe even perched on the phallic tip of Coit** Tower. It's a sunny day, there's a light wind off the bay, and San Francisco looks like the center of the world. "Ah," you say to yourself, like so many before you, "beautiful San Francisco. There's no other." Yet something is amiss. You've been to Fisherman's Wharf and Alcatraz. You've cruised North Beach and made your pilgrimage to City Lights. You've driven down Lombard Street, had a burrito in the Mission, and snapped a photo of the Haight-Ashbury street sign. You've got some great stories to tell future grandkids, but at the moment you're asking yourself anxiously: What next?

Luckily, a host of adventures awaits you in the San Francisco Bay Area—encompassing Marin, Sonoma, and Napa counties to the north; Berkeley and Oakland to the east; and Palo Alto, San Jose, and the San Mateo County Coast to the south. There's no doubt San Francisco is beautiful, but there are a few things the city just doesn't have—from the hip-hop Oaktown beat and the hippie parade in Berkeley to the rugged beauty of Marin and the sleepy seaside charm of Half Moon Bay on the south coast. And whether you're looking for a day on the beach or a weekend in the Wine Country, a New Age healing session or a grungy blues band, odds are good that you'll find it somewhere in the surrounding Bay Area. Most of the places covered here are within easy reach of San Francisco—by car or on public transportation—and can be covered in day trips or short overnight forays.

## Berkeley

**Berkeley and the University of California may** not be synonymous, but they're so interdependent that it's difficult to tell where one stops and the other begins. You won't find many knapsack-toting students in the upscale neighborhoods that buffer the north and east sides of campus, but for the most part Berkeley is a student town, dominated by the massive U.C. campus and its 30,000 enrollees. Because of its offbeat, countercultural reputation, the university attracts every sort of person imaginable—from artists, anarchists, and hypergenius intellectuals to superjocks, sorority girls, and fashion slaves, not to mention the stubbornly apathetic and the piously ideological. But anyone who has watched the documentary *Berkeley in the Sixties* might be surprised to find out that the city ain't what it used to be. Sure, Berkeley is still a breeding ground for alternative social trends, and political

*Most recently, Berkeley attracted national publicity due to the presence of the Naked Guy, a Cal student who was expelled for attending class in the nude—hey, at least he attended class.*

# The San Francisco Bay Area

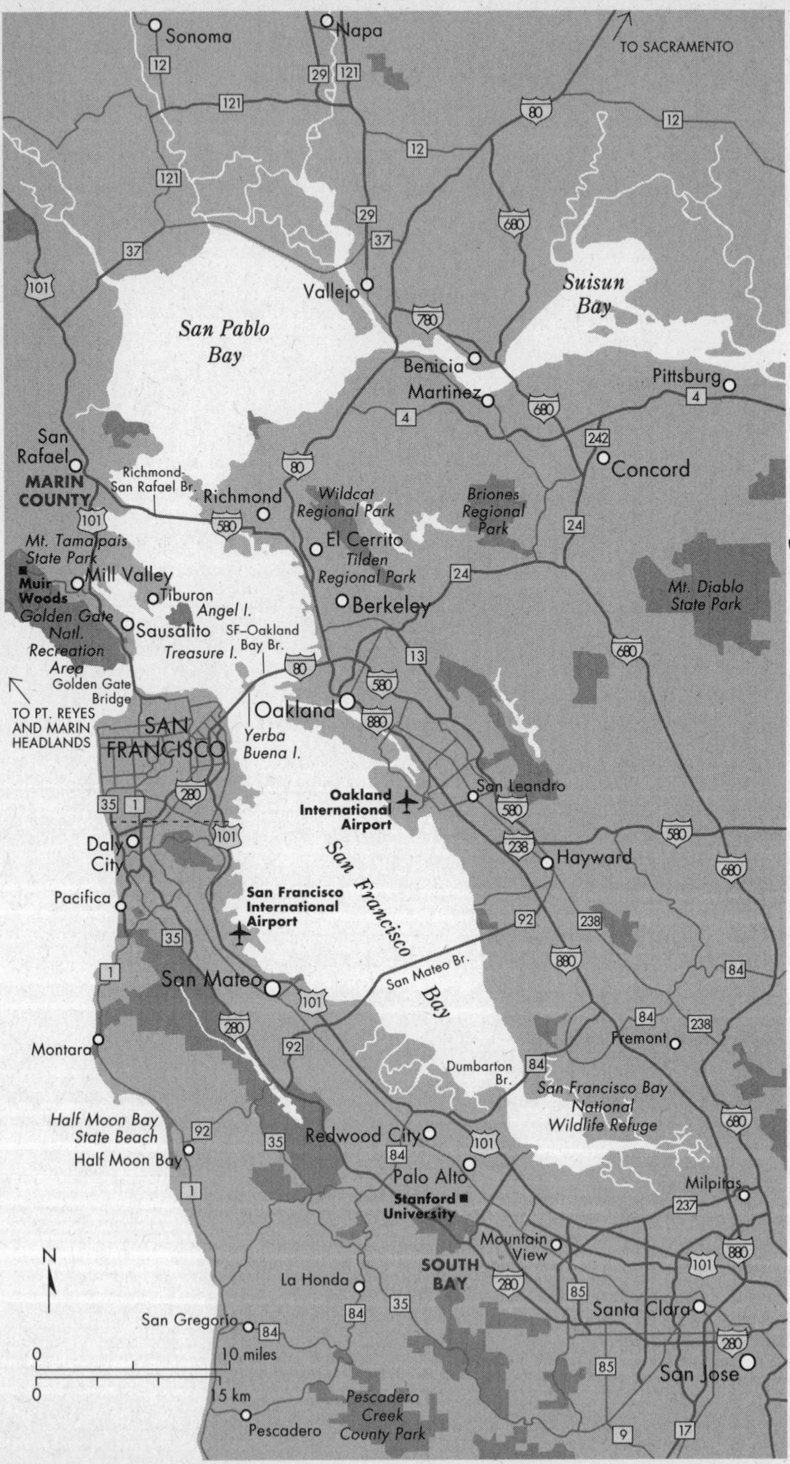

Sonoma
Napa
TO SACRAMENTO
Vallejo
Suisun Bay
San Pablo Bay
Benicia
Martinez
Pittsburg
Concord
San Rafael
MARIN COUNTY
Richmond-San Rafael Br.
Richmond
Wildcat Regional Park
Briones Regional Park
El Cerrito
Tilden Regional Park
Mt. Tamalpais State Park
Muir Woods
Mill Valley
Tiburon
Angel I.
Berkeley
Mt. Diablo State Park
Golden Gate Natl. Recreation Area
Sausalito
SF–Oakland Bay Br.
Treasure I.
Golden Gate Bridge
TO PT. REYES AND MARIN HEADLANDS
SAN FRANCISCO
Oakland
Yerba Buena I.
Oakland International Airport
San Leandro
Daly City
Hayward
Pacifica
San Francisco International Airport
San Francisco Bay
San Mateo
San Mateo Br.
Montara
Dumbarton Br.
Fremont
San Francisco Bay National Wildlife Refuge
Half Moon Bay State Beach
Half Moon Bay
Redwood City
Palo Alto
Stanford University
Milpitas
Mountain View
SOUTH BAY
La Honda
Santa Clara
San Gregorio
San Jose
0 10 miles
0 15 km
Pescadero Creek County Park
Pescadero
N

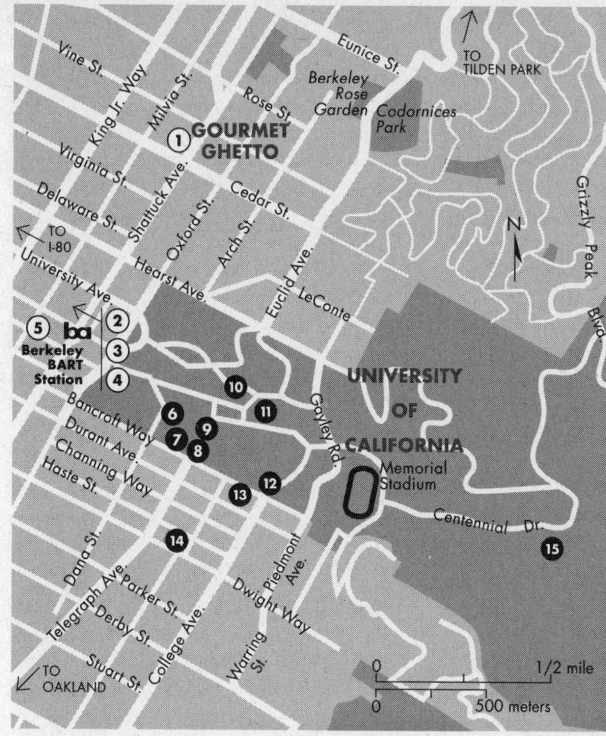


**Sights ●**
Campanile, **11**
Main (Doe) Library, **10**
People's Park, **14**
Phoebe Hearst Museum of Anthropology, **12**
Sather Gate, **9**
Sproul Plaza, **8**
Student Union Building, **7**
U.C. Botanical Gardens, **15**
University Art Museum, **13**
Zellerbach Hall, **6**

**Lodging ○**
Campus Motel, **2**
Capri Motel, **3**
French Hotel, **1**
Travel Inn, **4**
YMCA, **5**

posters and protesters are still a common feature of the landscape. But with the 1994 election of a conservative mayor, Shirley Dean, there's been a "cool it" reaction against the city's free-for-all reputation.

Southside, the area south of campus, is dominated by chaotic **Telegraph Avenue,** while Northside, the area (surprise) north of campus, is more refined, consisting of peaceful residential areas and Berkeley's **Gourmet Ghetto,** home of the famed Chez Panisse and other pricey restaurants. The Berkeley Hills, rising north and east of campus, offer the huge **Tilden Regional Park** and several impressive smaller gardens.

## COMING AND GOING

**BY CAR** From San Francisco, cross the Bay Bridge (no toll this direction) and take **I–80** east. Exit east at University Avenue, which eventually dead-ends at the west side of campus near Shattuck Avenue and downtown. For Telegraph Avenue and the traditional campus entrance, from University Avenue turn right on Shattuck Avenue and left on Durant Avenue, and then look for parking; Telegraph Avenue is a quarter-mile ahead. Unless there's heavy traffic, the trip takes 30–40 minutes. Parking is a serious problem, but there's a **parking garage** on Durant just west of Telegraph; look for it on the right side of the street.

**BY BUS** It's easier to reach Berkeley on BART, but if crossing under the bay gives you the creeps, **AC Transit** (tel. 800/559–INFO) offers daily service from both Oakland and San Francisco. The F and T buses run from San Francisco's Transbay Terminal (1st and Mission Sts.) to Berkeley ($2.20) until 2 AM, and Bus N travels 24 hours. Within Berkeley, Bus 51 travels from the Marina (*see* Cheap Thrills, *below*) east on University Avenue past the Berkeley BART station, past campus, and south on College Avenue into Oakland.

**BY TRAIN** **Amtrak** stops both in Berkeley (3rd St. and University Ave.)—you can board, but you can't buy tickets—and in nearby Emeryville (5885 Landegran St.), where connecting buses travel into San Francisco.

**BY BART** Take **Bay Area Rapid Transit (BART)** (tel. 510/465–BART) from San Francisco or Oakland to the downtown Berkeley station on Shattuck Avenue. One-way fare from San Francisco is $2.10, and the trip takes about 25 minutes. From the station, you can make the 10-minute walk to Telegraph up Bancroft Way (to the south), or the five-minute walk to the campus's west entrance on Center Street.

## WHERE TO SLEEP

Lodging in Berkeley is either shabby or downright expensive—sometimes both. Most budget motels are on **University Avenue,** west of campus. Your life isn't necessarily in danger here, but expect a general air of seediness (i.e., red velvet curtains, the reek of cheap perfume). It's best to stick to the campus end of University; the farther west you go on the avenue, the shoddier the surroundings become. In a pinch, the **Capri Motel** (1512 University Ave., at Sacramento St., tel. 510/845–7090) has drab but neat singles ($40) and doubles ($50).

In mid-May, when thousands of graduating Berkeley students don their caps and gowns, reservations for motels and hotels become *absolutely* essential. Most of the nicer places sell out four to five months in advance. Reservations are also a good idea in late August, when incoming freshmen and their hovering parents invade town. Add 12% tax to the prices listed below.

There are no youth hostels in Berkeley, but the **YMCA** (2001 Allston Way, tel. 510/848–6800)—open to both men and women—is cheap and within easy reach of Berkeley's sights. Its 80 dorm-style rooms, with shared bath, go for $25 a night ($27 if you stay only one night) and are available on a first-come, first-served basis. After 14 days, you're eligible to stay on at around $100 a week.

➢ **UNDER $60** • **Campus Motel.** This place is located right on noisy University Avenue, but it *is* close to campus (6 blocks west) and the rooms are neat and clean. All rooms have cable TV and coffee makers. Singles are $45, doubles $50. *1619 University Ave., btw McGee Ave. and California St., tel. 510/841–3844. 23 rooms.*

**Travel Inn.** This pink motel is cheap (singles $40, doubles $47), clean, and far enough from the street to escape traffic noise. The rooms are spacious and the management is friendly. *1461 University Ave., btw Sacramento and Acton Sts., tel. 510/848–3840. 3 blocks south of North Berkeley BART. 42 rooms.*

➢ **UNDER $100** • **French Hotel.** Doubles at this little Euro inn in North Berkeley go for $85 (they have one room for $68), but the location is prime. All rooms have a small, sunny patio, and most come with a complimentary breakfast. The surrounding neighborhood, nicknamed the "Gourmet Ghetto," overflows with bookstores and great restaurants. *1538 Shattuck Ave., btw Cedar and Vine Sts., tel. 510/548–9930.*

**UNIVERSITY HOUSING** **University Summer Visitor Housing** (tel. 510/642–4444) offers dorm accommodations on the Berkeley campus for $38–$48 per night. Rooms are nothing to write home about (bed, desk, chair, phone), but you get access to a comfy lounge with piano, and a downstairs rec room with pool table, ping pong, and a vending machine. Reservations are required. If you call early enough (a month before you arrive), you can probably live in the dorms all summer (June–Aug. 9), if you want to pay that much.

The student-owned and -operated coops are also open during summer to students from any college; inquire and make reservations at the **University Students' Cooperative Association** (2424 Ridge Rd., tel. 510/848–1936). Finally, if cleanliness is not a top priority, most of U.C. Berkeley's **fraternities** rent rooms in the summer, usually for around $500 for the whole summer. Scout the neighborhood on foot (Piedmont Avenue, between Bancroft and Dwight ways, is considered "Fraternity Row"), and knock on any door with a FOR RENT sign; ask to look around (one look at the kitchen and bathrooms should tell you whether the place is livable).

## FOOD



Berkeleyans take their food very seriously. California cuisine, designer fuel for the yuppie generation, got its start here. It's based on the idea that fresh, home-cultivated ingredients (no matter how costly) are vital to the success of a dish, and that portions are to be savored, not shoveled in. This concept has reached its apex at the world-famous restaurant **Chez Panisse** (1517 Shattuck Ave., tel. 510/548–5525), which serves stunning five- to six-course meals for upwards of $65 per person. The area surrounding Chez Panisse, on Shattuck Avenue near Cedar and Vine, has become known as the **Gourmet Ghetto,** because it contains a number of high-quality restaurants, cafés, and specialty shops. A better bet for budget travelers is **Telegraph Avenue** between Dwight Way and the U.C. campus. Here you'll find a high concentration of super-cheap restaurants serving fast food with a Berkeley twist (heaping green salads and gourmet sandwiches are far more common than burgers). West of campus, along **University Avenue,** there's a string of small restaurants, mostly Asian and Indian.

➢ **UNDER $5** • Several food carts park along Bancroft Avenue where Telegraph ends, selling everything from bagels and smoothies to Japanese food, burritos, and stuffed potatoes. For the cheapest Chinese food in Berkeley, head to **Chinese Express** (2488 Channing Way, at Telegraph Ave., tel. 510/845–3766), where each entrée from the 20-dish buffet goes for $1. For pizza with an "eat it or screw you" attitude, stop by **Blondie's** (2340 Telegraph Ave., tel. 510/548–1129), a popular place with street freaks and bleary-eyed students in need of a $2 pepperoni fix at 1 AM (until 2 AM Friday and Saturday). On Durant Avenue just east of Telegraph, in the **Durant Food Court,** 10 small places, including American, Chinese, Japanese, and Mexican, vie to serve you a big meal for about $3.50.

**Café Intermezzo.** This Berkeley institution indisputably serves the biggest and best salads around. Order one salad ($4–$5) and share with a friend. It comes with homemade dressing and includes a bookend-sized slab of fresh honey-wheat bread. Or try one of the mammoth sandwiches on inch-thick slices of the same bread ($4.50). *2442 Telegraph Ave., at Haste St., tel. 510/849–4592. Open daily 8:30 AM–10 PM. Wheelchair access.*

**Juice Bar Collective.** Smack in the middle of the Gourmet Ghetto, the Juice Bar offers fresh and organic sandwiches as well as hot dishes like spinach lasagna ($3–$4). But their focus, as the name suggests, is conjuring up fruit smoothies like the Sunset ($3.25), made with bananas, orange juice, and yogurt. *2114 Vine St., tel. 510/548–8473. Open Mon.–Sat. 10–4:30. Wheelchair access.*

➢ **UNDER $10** • **Blue Nile.** This Ethiopian eatery serves everything from thick split-pea stew and pepper-cooked beef to *tej* (honey wine) and freshly blended fruit shakes. The space is small and intimate, decorated with wicker furniture and Ethiopian knickknacks. Silverware is available, but you're encouraged to eat with your fingers, using *injera* (unleavened bread) to scoop up the food. Plates are about $6–$8 for dinner, $5 for lunch. *2525 Telegraph Ave., btw Dwight Way and Parker St., tel. 510/540–6777. Open Mon.–Sat. 11–10. Wheelchair access.*

**Cha Am.** This airy restaurant—one of Berkeley's best Thai spots—feels removed from Shattuck Avenue, though its window seats overlook the street. Try the *dom-ka gai* (chicken and coconut soup; $6) or the mixed seafood plate with chili, garlic, and vegetables ($8.75). *1543 Shattuck Ave., at Cedar St., tel. 510/848–9664. 7 blocks north of Berkeley BART. Open weekdays 11:30–4 and 5–9:30 (Fri. until 10), Sat. noon–4 and 5–10, Sun. 5–9:30.*

**Chester's Café.** Looking out over the bay from Chester's sunny deck is one of the best ways to start a lazy weekend morning. Weekend specials include eggs Juneau (poached eggs and smoked salmon on an English muffin topped with Hollandaise sauce; $7.50). If you wake up on the lunch side of brunch, console yourself with warm chicken salad with sautéed red, yellow, and green bell peppers ($7). *1508B Walnut Ave., at Vine St., tel. 510/849–9995. Open Mon.–Sat. 8 AM–9 PM, Sun. 8–5.*

**Kabana.** This Pakistani restaurant has wonderful spicy food. Vegetarians should try the *tinda* (herbed and spiced summer squash, with rice or spicy flat bread; $5.50). The tropical wall mural and friendly waitstaff brighten the sparse atmosphere. *1106 University Ave., at San Pablo Ave., tel. 510/845–3355. Open Tues.–Sun. 11–9:30. Wheelchair access. No credit cards.*

**Saul's.** In the midst of the Gourmet Ghetto, this is the closest thing to a New York deli in the East Bay. Shelves of Manischewitz products line the entryway, and a glass deli counter displays bowls of chopped liver, sauerkraut, and whole smoked fish. Sandwiches ($5–$8) are stuffed with pastrami, corned beef, brisket, or tongue. Jewish specialties include knishes ($3), potato latkes with sour cream and applesauce ($6 for three), and matzo-ball soup ($3.50). Saul's gets noisy and crowded during peak hours; avoid the lunch-hour wait by getting your food to go. *1475 Shattuck Ave., at Vine St., tel. 510/848–3354. 8 blocks north of Berkeley BART. Open daily 8–9:30.*

**Zachary's Chicago Pizza Inc.** People rave about the spinach and mushroom special (medium, $16.50), but whatever the topping, your stuffed pizza pie will come with a wall of bready crust and a layer of stewed tomatoes. The place is always packed, and they don't take reservations, but you can place your order so the pizza will be ready when your table is. Both locations are near bookstores and boutiques, so you can browse while you wait. At lunch time, grab a thin slice for $1.75–$2. *1853 Solano Ave., btw Colusa and Fresno Aves., tel. 510/525–5950. Other location: 5801 College Ave., near Rockridge BART in Oakland, tel. 510/655–6385. Both open Sun.–Thurs. 11–10, Fri. and Sat. 11–10:30. Both have wheelchair access.*

➢ **UNDER $20 • Chez Panisse Café.** The café upstairs from the world-famous Chez Panisse restaurant serves many of the same dishes for half the price. You can make same-day lunch reservations, but for dinner just go early and expect to wait an hour or more for a table. Try Heidi's garden salad with goat cheese ($6) or the delicious prosciutto, garlic, and goat cheese calzone ($14.50). The café feels like a wealthy professor's living room, and patrons sport everything from jeans to suits and evening wear. *1517 Shattuck Ave., at Cedar St., tel. 510/548–5049. 7 blocks north of Berkeley BART. Open Mon.–Thurs. 11:30–3 and 5–10:30, Fri. and Sat. 11:30–4 and 5–11:30.*

**CAFES** Without its cafés, the People's Republic of Berkeley would collapse. Students would have nowhere to see and be seen while "studying," skate punks would have nowhere to hang out while cutting class, and artists and poets would have no place to share their angst. Luckily, within a square mile of the U.C. campus, no fewer than 50 cafés peacefully co-exist. Smokers should take note: In 1994, Berkeley banned smoking in all indoor *and* outdoor cafés.

*The Red Café (1941A University Ave., at Grant St., tel. 510/843–8607), one of a few as yet undiscovered by students, has a welcoming atmosphere, a full kitchen serving mostly vegetarian fare ($3–$6), smooth coffee, and occasional live jazz on weekends.*

**Caffè Mediterraneum.** Featured in the film *The Graduate,* the Med has nurtured countless bursts of inspiration and the occasional failed revolution. Frequented by lifelong Berkeleyans rather than students, the Med serves espresso drinks and desserts; a small kitchen (open daily 7–3) serves omelets, sandwiches, and pasta at reasonable prices. The café—but not the second-floor bathroom—is wheelchair accessible. *2475 Telegraph Ave., btw Haste St. and Dwight Way, tel. 510/549–1128. Open daily 7 AM–11 PM.*

**Caffè Strada.** There's very little indoor seating, but the sprawling outdoor patio attracts a good mix of architecture students, frat and sorority types, and visiting foreigners. It's a social spot, so don't expect to get much work done. Instead, bring a newspaper, relax in the sun, and eavesdrop while you sip your latte ($1.50) and munch on your pastry ($1–$2). *2300 College Ave., at Bancroft Way, tel. 510/843–5282. Open daily 7 AM–11:30 PM.*

**The Musical Offering.** With its airy interior and constant stream of classical music, this café caters to a tweedy and mature crowd. Coffees, sandwiches, vegetarian fare, and soups are sold in front, classical CDs and cassettes in back. The smoked trout salad will set you back $6; a latte is $1.50. Shopper's hint: Buy a CD or tape on the composer's birthday and receive a 20% discount. *2430 Bancroft Way, near Telegraph Ave., tel. 510/849–0211. Café open daily 8–8, music store open daily 10–9.*

## WORTH SEEING



**TELEGRAPH AVENUE** When most people think of Berkeley, they think of Telegraph, which begins at the campus and runs south into Oakland. The first 5 blocks of this colorful and congested avenue are full of cafés, bookstores, art shops, harried students, long-haired hippies, homeless buskers, lunatics, metaphysical warriors, and wide-eyed tourists. Every day—rain or shine—troops of street vendors line the street, selling everything from handmade jewelry and imported crafts to crystals, incense, and tie-dyed T-shirts. New Age prophets offer tarot and numerology readings to passersby while baggy-jeaned hip-hop fans skateboard down the sidewalks. Telegraph today is a unique blend of '60s and '90s counterculture, and the two elements blend nicely.

*If you're lucky you may cross paths with the Bubble Lady (poet and bubble-maker Julia Vinograd), Rare (lunatic and sports-trivia fiend), the Hate Man (high heels, lipstick, and a professed hatred of everyone and everything), and any of the other wacked-out denizens who give Berkeley its odd appeal.*

Shops along Telegraph come and go, but neighborhood landmarks include **Rasputin's Records** (2350 Telegraph Ave., at Durant Ave., tel. 510/848–9005) and well-stocked **Amoeba** (2455 Telegraph Ave., at Haste St., tel. 510/549–1125), both of which feature that rare medium: vinyl. Book lovers should check out **Cody's Books** (2454 Telegraph Ave., at Haste St., tel. 510/845–7852) and **Moe's** (2476 Telegraph Ave., btw Haste St. and Dwight Way, tel. 510/849–2087). Cody's hosts regular readings and has probably the largest selection of new books in the area, while Moe's has four stories of used and rare books. For candles, incense, black-light posters and, other, er, recreational needs, stop by local head shop **Annapurna** (2416 Telegraph Ave., at Channing Way, tel. 510/841–6187).

**U.C. BERKELEY** Established in 1868 as the first branch of the statewide University of California system, the "Cal" campus retains some of the beauty and gentility of its early years (especially in the old brick and stone buildings scattered around campus), some of the fire of the revolutionary '60s (check out Sproul Plaza at noon), and some of the apathy of the 1980s (also visible on Sproul at noon). For a map, stop by the **Student Union Building** on the west side of Sproul Plaza (*see below*). In the lobby there's a small visitor center (tel. 510/642–3361) staffed by students. Free student-led tours of campus, held on Monday, Wednesday, and Friday at 10 AM and 1 PM, start from a second visitor center (101 University Hall, tel. 510/642–5215), at the corner of University Avenue and Oxford Street on the west side of campus.

**Sproul Plaza,** just north of the Telegraph and Bancroft intersection, is where the Free Speech Movement began in 1964. Look inside **Sproul Hall** (the imposing administration building overlooking the plaza) for a display of photographs from this first demonstration, in which 3,000 students surrounded a police car that was holding a man arrested for distributing political flyers. Today, Sproul Plaza is a source of endless entertainment for locals and tourists alike, where some of Berkeley's most famous loonies get a chance to match wits. Here's your chance to debate foreign policy or the existence of God with street philosophers of all stripes. **Lower Sproul Plaza,** just west of Sproul Plaza, is the site of sporadic free noon concerts as well as weekend jam sessions by a ragtag group of bongo drummers. Bring your own pot and kettle and join in, or just hang and listen. **Zellerbach Hall,** on Lower Sproul, brings more professional productions to campus; check the box office for upcoming events.

*On Sproul Plaza, watch The Hate Man, in bra and high heels, heckling an evangelist who's preaching damnation and hellfire to fornicators and sodomites.*

North of Sproul Plaza, pass over Strawberry Creek and through **Sather Gate,** the main entrance to campus until expansion in the 1960s. Head uphill (to the right) to find Sather Tower, more commonly known as the **Campanile,** a 307-foot clock tower modeled after the one in Venice's Piazza San Marco. The carillon is played weekdays at 7:50 AM, noon, and 6 PM, Saturdays at noon and 6, and on Sundays at 2 for an extended 45 minutes (concerts are suspended during final exam periods). You can watch the noon performances from the observation deck (open Mon.–Sat. 10–3:30, Sun. 10–1:45), which is reached via a brief elevator ride (50¢). Even if you miss the show, the Bay Area views from here are stunning.

Kroeber Hall houses the **Phoebe Hearst Museum of Anthropology,** with rotating exhibits that cover everything from ancient America to Neolithic China. Also on display are artifacts used by Ishi, the lone survivor of California's Yahi tribe, who was brought to live at the U.C. campus in 1911, after gold miners slaughtered the rest of his tribe. *Tel. 510/642–3681. Admission: $2. Open Wed.–Sun. 10–4:30 (Thurs. until 9).*

**UNIVERSITY ART MUSEUM** This low-key cement building with balcony galleries houses the largest university-owned collection in the country, mostly contemporary European and American works. The works displayed are confoundingly diverse and may include anything from a 16th-century altar panel to a passel of sugar candy pastel Bibles made by a Berkeley MFA candidate. One of the museum's most impressive collections is a room full of violently colorful paintings by the abstract expressionist Hans Hoffman. You can wander through the peaceful outdoor sculpture garden for free, and there's a café with pricey but good food. The attached **Pacific Film Archive** (2621 Durant Ave., near College Ave., tel. 510/642–1124) caters to hard-core film enthusiasts with an impressive collection of rare titles. *2626 Bancroft Way, tel. 510/642–0808. Admission: $6, $4 students and seniors, free Thurs. 11–noon and 5–9. Open Wed.–Sun. 11–5 (Thurs. until 9).*

**U.C. BOTANICAL GARDEN** Notable for the diversity of its collection, the garden contains more than 10,000 species of plants from habitats around the world, from South African deserts to Himalayan forests. If you make it to the top, you'll be rewarded with a view of the San Francisco Bay, framed in green. Located in Strawberry Canyon, the garden is especially colorful in spring, when the extensive rhododendron collection is in full bloom. *Centennial Dr., tel. 510/642–3343. From Berkeley BART, Bus 65; or Hill Service Shuttle (50¢) from Hearst Mining Circle on campus; or walk 15 min uphill from Memorial Stadium. Admission free. Open daily 9–4:45. Tours weekends at 1:30.*

## CHEAP THRILLS

Telegraph Avenue is a haven for street musicians. In particular, look for **Spirit of '29,** a local Dixieland blues and jazz ensemble distinguished by what so many other street players lack—harmony. They're not very punctual, but about once a week they set up on the corner of Telegraph and Bancroft and let loose; try calling 510/883–0650 for more info on where to find them. As always, a small donation is encouraged.

### People's Park

***Just east of Telegraph, between Haste Street and Dwight Way, People's Park was originally created by students in 1969 from a fenced-off and abandoned asphalt lot. When the university tried to replace the park with a dormitory, thousands of students and locals converged here and refused to leave. The university reacted by erecting a chain-link fence around the park; ensuing protests ended in the death of one man, the use of tear gas on Sproul Plaza, and the 17-day occupation of Berkeley by the National Guard. Over the years, the park decayed while activists and university and city officials argued. There isn't that much to do here; you can play basketball or volleyball on the new, much-disputed courts. The homeless and activists are still here; check out the elaborately graffitied bathrooms covered with murals, poetry, anti-government statements, and witty slogans like "Kill the Narks in People's Park."***

Warm, windy days were meant to be spent at the **Berkeley Marina,** on the water a half-mile west of I–80. Take in the sweeping views of San Francisco, Alcatraz Island, and the Golden Gate Bridge from the marina's pier and from adjacent **César E. Chavez Park,** then flop down on the grass and watch local kids flying their dragon kites. On the first full weekend of every month, you can catch a free spin around the bay with the **Cal Sailing Club** (tel. 510/287–5905); wear warm, waterproof clothing, and prepare to get wet. To reach the marina from Berkeley BART, take Bus 51 west.

North of the Berkeley campus on Euclid Street, between Bayview Place and Eunice Street, you'll find the multilevel **Berkeley Rose Garden,** an amphitheater with roses, benches aplenty, more roses, and a panoramic bay view. It's an attractive spot for a picnic or a moment of solitude. To get there from campus, walk north on Euclid Street for 15 minutes; from Berkeley BART, take Bus 65 north.

## AFTER DARK

Like everything else in Berkeley, nightlife is eclectic and casual. Needless to say, you'll mingle with plenty of college students just about everywhere you go. The campus paper, the *Daily Californian,* regularly lists all student-oriented events, most of which are free or dirt cheap. The free weekly *East Bay Express* contains a complete events calendar for the East Bay, including films, lectures, readings, and musical events. For dancing, head across the Bay Bridge to San Francisco; Berkeley's dance club scene is so low-key as to be almost nonexistent—try Larry Blake's (*see below*) in a pinch.

**BARS** **The Albatross.** This no-nonsense, no-attitude pub attracts both students and working folk. The cheap beer ($1.25) tastes even better with the free popcorn, and there's a cozy fireplace and a whole row of dart boards. *1822 San Pablo Ave., btw Hearst Ave. and Delaware St., tel. 510/849–4714.*

**Bison Brewing Company.** Five blocks south of the U.C. Berkeley campus, Bison is the local watering hole for Berkeley's pierced and tattooed set. The homemade stout, ale, and cider will thrill the beer enthusiast, and there's live music Thursday through Saturday ($1–$2 cover), ranging from blues to Irish folk. Happy hour (weekdays 4–6) features $1.75 pints and attracts huge crowds. *2598 Telegraph Ave., at Parker St., tel. 510/841–7734. Wheelchair access.*

**Jupiter.** This spacious, down-to-earth wine-and-beer bar across from Berkeley BART has 20 microbrews on tap, a terraced patio, and live music Thursday–Saturday (no cover). Get a beer at the bar and try to make a game out of finding an empty table. *2181 Shattuck Ave., near Center St., tel. 510/843–8277.*

**Triple Rock Brewery.** At this popular microbrewery, 3 blocks north of Berkeley BART, '50s-era posters and knickknacks line the walls. Look for grad students talking shop, frat and sorority types pounding homemade ale (in light, red, or dark), and office workers unwinding from a stressful day. *1920 Shattuck Ave., at Hearst Ave., tel. 510/843–2739. Wheelchair access.*

**LIVE MUSIC** **924 Gilman Street.** This all-ages, alcohol-free cooperative features hard-core local garage bands and occasional big-name acts. The music is loud and aggressive, the crowd young, sweaty, tattooed, and not afraid to throw themselves around. Most shows cost $5, and you have to buy a $2 membership (valid for a year) to get in the first time. *924 Gilman St., at 8th St., tel. 510/525–9926.*

**Ashkenaz.** There's a different live beat here every night, from African and Cajun to Bulgarian folk. You can take dance lessons first, or just come and wing it. You won't find any brain-dead ravers here, only a devoted group of older locals and students out to broaden their cultural horizons. *1317 San Pablo Ave., tel. 510/525–5054. Cover: $5–$8. Wheelchair access.*

**Larry Blake's.** This restaurant and blues joint opened in the late 1940s, and since then it's become a Berkeley institution. The upstairs dining room serves decent food to a yuppie crowd, and the cramped basement downstairs—a no-frills bar with sawdust on the floor—hosts some of the best blues acts in the area, plus the occasional alternative rock band. *2367 Telegraph Ave., at Durant Ave., tel. 510/848–0886. Cover: $5 and up.*

**The Starry Plough.** This popular Irish pub near the Berkeley–Oakland border offers an eclectic mix of folk music and not-too-extreme rock bands, usually for about $5. Join the older, politically left crowd for a pint or two of Guinness, Bass, or Anchor Steam and a game of darts. *3101 Shattuck Ave., at Prince St., Berkeley, tel. 510/841–2082. From Ashby BART, walk 1 block east on Prince St. Cover: up to $6. Wheelchair access.*

*Join both the pros and the amateurs at the Starry Plough on Monday nights at 7 PM for free Irish dance lessons.*

## OUTDOOR ACTIVITIES

Berkeley's **Tilden Regional Park** boasts two of the highest points in the East Bay hills—Volmer Peak (1,913 ft) at the southern end and Wildcat Peak (1,250 ft) to the north. The hike to Wildcat Peak from Inspiration Point (a vista point/parking lot; follow signs from within the park) is just a moderate sweat-breaker. In fact, the trail, called **Nimitz Way,** is 4½ miles of wheelchair-accessible road. The hike should take a good two hours, during which you'll have plenty of time to absorb the view of the bay and the San Pablo and Briones reservoirs. For more hiking info, contact the **Environmental Education Center** (north end of park, tel. 510/525–2233), open Tuesday–Sunday 10–5. Nimitz Way is also popular with mountain bikers. If you want to tackle it on two wheels, the friendly, intelligent folks at **Missing Link Bicycle Co-op** (1988 Shattuck Ave., at University Ave., tel. 510/843–7471) will rent you a mountain bike for $20 a day.

*Rumor has it that Lake Anza is a popular spot for skinny-dipping under a full moon.*

If you don't mind sharing a small lakeside beach with a bunch of toddlers in Mickey Mouse swimsuits, Tilden's **Lake Anza** (tel. 510/848–3028), with clean water and sandy beaches, makes a good swimming hole. A changing facility is open when the lifeguards are on duty (mid-May–mid-Oct., daily 11–6). While the lifeguards are around, adults pay $2; at all other times you swim for free and at your own risk.

To reach the park on weekends, take Bus 67 from Berkeley BART to the end of the line; on weekdays, Bus 65 takes you from BART to the edge of the park. Bikes are allowed on both of these buses, summer only. If you're driving, take University Avenue east from I–80, go left on Oxford Street, right on Rose, and left on Spruce to the top of the hill. Cross Grizzly Peak Boulevard, make an immediate left on Canon Drive, and follow signs. The park is open 5 AM–10 PM.

# Oakland

**If you expect Oakland to dazzle you like San Francisco,** save the $2 BART fare for a cup of coffee. Oakland isn't glitzy or chic; it's a predominantly working-class community where people go about their business and have a hell of a good time on Saturday night. It's the home of the West Coast Blues and, more recently, the Oaktown school of rap and funk, whose practitioners include local artists MC Hammer, Digital Underground, Too Short, Tony! Toni! Tone!, Oaktown 3-5-7, and Tupac Shakur. Okay, so it's a bit dirty and slummy, but in an odd way, that's the root of Oakland's appeal.

*If you think Oakland's African American hip-hop and rap club scene is a new phenomenon, think again. In the 1940s, West 7th Street was home to some of the most famous nightclubs on the West Coast, where Earl "Fatha" Hines and Dinah Washington played to packed crowds.*

Oakland is a primary U.S. shipping port and a major West Coast rail terminus. On the downside, the city has had economic hardships, and for years has been notorious for its high crime rate. Though the downtown area has seen a slew of urban renewal projects, the empty storefronts and failed developments remain, and the streets can be very dangerous at night.

But there's a lot to discover here, most within easy reach of a BART station or AC Transit bus. Wander through the untouristy **Chinatown** (downtown between 7th, 10th, Broadway, and Alice streets), and afterwards grab a coffee in the trendier areas around Grand or Piedmont Avenue. If the city is fraying your nerves, head for the hills to the east, and get an idea of what the topography was like when the Ohlone Native Americans first lived here 2,000 years ago.

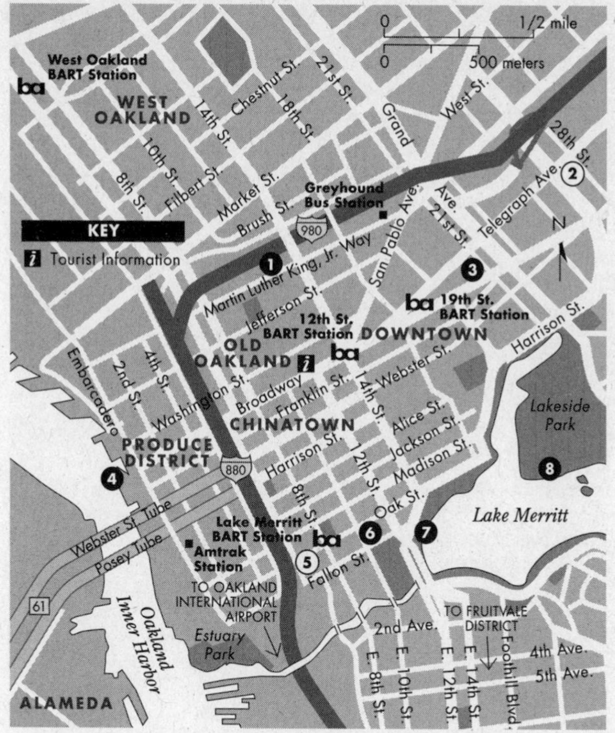


**Sights ●**

Camron-Stanford House, **7**

Jack London Square, **4**

Oakland Museum, **6**

Paramount Theatre, **3**

Preservation Park, **1**

Sailboat House, **8**

**Lodging ○**

Avondale Residence Hotel, **2**

Civic Center Lodge, **5**

## BASICS

The **Oakland Convention and Visitors' Bureau** (1000 Broadway, Suite 200, tel. 510/ 839–9000), open weekdays 8:30–5, is geared toward convention-goers, but the staff is happy to answer all inquiries. Pick up a copy of their small pamphlet, "The Official Visitors Guide," which lists dozens of museums, historical attractions, and community events. To reach the bureau, take BART to 12th Street Station, and walk south on Broadway to 11th Street. For recorded info on the arts, theater, sports, and other entertainment, call 510/835–2787.

Free walking tours are available early May through October from the **City of Oakland Walking Tours** (tel. 510/238–3234) promptly at 10 AM; call for current itineraries. The **Port of Oakland** (tel. 510/272–1200) runs free, 90-minute boat tours of Oakland Harbor every month; call ahead for reservations.

## COMING AND GOING

If you're coming by car from San Francisco, take **I–580** to **I–880** south to the Grand Avenue exit for Lake Merritt, or to the Waterfront and Downtown exits for Jack London Square and downtown, respectively. Depending on traffic, the trip takes 30–45 minutes. Once you get to town, Oakland's individual neighborhoods are best explored on foot, even though the city covers a huge geographical area.

**BY PLANE** **Oakland International Airport** (1 Airport Dr., off Hegenberger Rd., tel. 510/ 577–4000) is a small airport, easily accessed on public transportation from points throughout the Bay Area, and less hectic and crowded than San Francisco International. It's often much cheaper to fly into, particularly on **Southwest** (tel. 800/I–FLY–SWA), which has more than 80 flights in and out, many of which go to Los Angeles.

➢ **AIRPORT TRANSIT** • For $2 in exact change, the **Air-BART Shuttle** (tel. 510/562–7700) runs every 15 minutes (Mon.–Sat. 6 AM–midnight, Sun. 8:30–midnight) between the airport and the Coliseum BART station, where you can catch a BART train to Berkeley, San Francisco, or Oakland proper. Otherwise, AC Transit Bus 58 travels between the airport and Jack London Square, stopping at Lake Merritt and near the Coliseum BART station on the way. A taxi to downtown Berkeley should cost about $30–$35.

**BY BUS** **AC Transit** (tel. 800/559–INFO) runs from Oakland to points throughout the Bay Area (several lines run 24 hours). The fare is $1.25, and 60¢ for seniors and the disabled. Transfers (25¢) are good for 90 minutes. Lines designated by letters, instead of numbers, go over the Bay Bridge to San Francisco's **Transbay Terminal** (1st and Mission Sts.); the F and T run until 2 AM and the N runs all night. Fare to San Francisco is $2.20, $1.10 for the disabled. Within Oakland, Bus 40 travels from near Jack London Square north on Broadway into Berkeley, then past the U.C. campus to Berkeley BART. Bus 12 travels from 12th Street BART past Lakeside Park, around Lake Merritt, and east on Grand Avenue.

**Greyhound** (2103 San Pablo Ave., at 20th St., tel. 800/231–2222) travels to and from Oakland. Fare to San Francisco is $3 one-way; buses leave once an hour from around 2:15 AM to 11:25 PM. One-way fare to Los Angeles is $29.

**BY TRAIN** Oakland's brand-new **Amtrak** station (245 2nd St., tel. 510/238–4320 or 800/USA–RAIL for reservations) is centrally located near downtown at Jack London Square, less than a mile from 12th Street/Civic Center BART. Both the *Capitol* from Sacramento and the long-distance *Coast Starlight* pass through the station.

**BY BART** Oakland has eight **BART** stations, but the only ones near downtown are 12th Street, 19th Street, and Lake Merritt. BART runs daily until 1:30 AM (though stations close as soon as the last train goes through, which may be as early as midnight). Expect trains every 15–20 minutes. The 15-minute ride from San Francisco's Embarcadero Station to Oakland's MacArthur Station costs $1.85. For more info, call 510/465–BART.

**BY FERRY** The **Oakland/Alameda Ferry** (tel. 510/522–3300), also known as the **Blue and Gold Fleet,** runs between Oakland's Jack London Square and San Francisco's Pier 39 or the Ferry Building 4–5 times daily for about $4 one-way.

## WHERE TO SLEEP

Oakland's budget lodging scene isn't a pretty sight, price-wise or safety-wise. Hotels are either geared toward businesspeople on expense accounts, or they're in grimy, scary neighborhoods. If you're sniffing around for a budget bed, you should probably go back to Berkeley. Of course, if you're desperate, there are hundreds of faceless chain motels with rooms ($50–$75) in downtown Oakland (near Lake Merritt) and around the airport.

**Avondale Residence Hotel.** On a residential street, not far from downtown Oakland, the Avondale offers singles only at an unbeatable price: $20–$30 for a room with private bath. The manager is extremely gracious, but the neighborhood can get a bit noisy at night. You should also be careful here, even though the neighborhood is safer than some other parts of Oakland. *540 28th St., tel. 510/832–9769. From MacArthur BART, Bus 40 or walk 7 blocks south on Telegraph Ave., then turn right.*

**Civic Center Lodge.** The lodge is within easy reach of the waterfront, Lake Merritt, and the downtown bars and restaurants. It offers basic, no-frills doubles for $48; singles are $38. *50 6th St., tel. 510/444–4139. From Lake Merritt BART, walk 3 blocks down Oak St. to 6th St., turn left. 32 rooms.*

**CAMPING** You can camp at one of the 75 sites at **Anthony Chabot Regional Park,** east of downtown in the Oakland Hills. Tent sites are $13 a night, hookups $18; you have to fork over a $5 reservation charge for either. The campground has showers and is about a mile from Lake Chabot; a 9-mile trail meanders around the lake. You need your own wheels to get here. *Tel. 510/562–CAMP. From I–80, I–580 east to Redwood Road exit, turn left, follow Redwood Road 4½ mi to park gate (it's another 2½ mi to campground).*

## FOOD

From Southern-style shacks to El Salvadoran holes-in-the-wall, Oakland is loaded with cheap and colorful eateries. Because the city's population is so diverse, you can find just about every type of cuisine imaginable. The center for Asian food is **Chinatown,** downtown between 7th, 10th, Broadway, and Alice streets. The **Fruitvale** district, accessed by the Fruitvale BART station, has dozens of cheap Mexican and Central American restaurants. It's safest to restrict your visits here to the daylight hours. If you don't feel like having an adventure along with your meal, two long avenues in Oakland offer a wide selection of familiar delis, burger joints, and gringo burrito shops. From downtown Oakland, Bus 59 or 59A will take you north on Broadway to **Piedmont Avenue**; for **College Avenue,** take BART to Rockridge.

➢ **UNDER $5** • **Taqueria Morelia.** Come here for one of the area's best quesadillas ($1.50–$2), a fried tortilla oozing cheese, chopped tomatoes, and cilantro. Locals of all ages flow between the restaurant and adjacent dive bar, Talk of the Town, carrying plastic baskets of tacos and burritos ($2.50–$4 each) and cheap beer. *4481 E. 14th St., near High St., tel. 510/535–6030. About 7 blocks SE of Fruitvale BART. Open Mon.–Wed. 10–10, Thurs. and Sun. 10 AM–11 PM, Fri. and Sat. 10 AM–midnight.*

➢ **UNDER $10** • **Asmara Restaurant.** Colorful baskets and rugs suspended from the ceiling cheer up this East African restaurant in North Oakland. Sample three excellent entrées in the combination platter, either meat ($5.50 lunch, $8 dinner) or vegetarian ($5.50 lunch, $7.50 dinner). The red lentil is the most flavorful of the vegetarian dishes. Food is served family-style with injera bread and a notable lack of utensils—use your fingers. *5020 Telegraph Ave., near 51st St., tel. 510/547–5100. Open Mon., Wed.–Fri. 11–11, weekends noon–11. Wheelchair access.*

**Barney's Gourmet Hamburger.** This Rockridge joint specializes in gourmet burgers, like the Parisian, served on a baguette with bleu cheese ($5). The prices are reasonable and the portions enormous. They even cater to those trying to avoid red meat—you can order your burger with grilled chicken instead. Round off your meal with an order of fries and a chocolate malt. *5819 College Ave., near Chabot Ave., tel. 510/601–0444. Open Mon.–Thurs. 11–9:30, Fri.–Sat. 11–10, Sun. 11–9:30. Other locations: 4162 Piedmont Ave., Oakland, tel. 510/655–7180; 1591 Solano Ave., Albany, tel. 510/526–8185; 4138 24th St., at Castro St., San Francisco, tel. 415/282–7770.*

**Lucy's Creole Kitchen.** At this sunny, friendly diner, you'll find some of the best southern seafood west of the Mississippi River Delta. Daily lunch specials like jambalaya ($6) or smothered short ribs ($7.50) attract crowds from the neighborhood. And let's not forget the spicy crab burger ($4.50) and catfish with fries, coleslaw, or potato salad ($6.25). *1601 San Pablo Ave., at 16th St., tel. 510/763–6706. 7 blocks SW of 19th St. BART. Open Mon.–Thurs. 7:30–5. Wheelchair access. No credit cards.*

**Nan Yang.** Although it's in Oakland's Chinatown, Nan Yang serves authentic Burmese cuisine. The atmosphere is less than intimate, but the service is fast and cordial. Stick with Burmese specialties rather than the supplementary Chinese dishes. Especially tasty are the curry chicken noodle soup ($5.50), the ginger salad ($4.75), and the curry shrimp ($6.50). *301 8th St., at Harrison St., tel. 510/465–6924. Open Tues.–Thurs. 11–9, Fri.–Sat. 11–9:30, Sun. noon–9. Wheelchair access. Other location: 6408 College Ave., at Claremont Ave., tel. 510/655–3298.*

**Tin's Teahouse.** On the edge of Oakland's Chinatown, Tin's serves great dim sum for about $5 per person. Feast on shark's fin dumplings, chicken buns, stuffed bell peppers, taro triangles or steamed rice-noodle crêpes. *701 Webster St., at 7th St., tel. 510/832–7661. Open Mon., Wed.–Fri. 9–3, weekends 8:30–8:30.*

## WORTH SEEING

**JACK LONDON SQUARE** Although born in San Francisco, Jack London spent his early years in Oakland before shipping out on the adventures that inspired *The Call of the Wild, The*

*Locals get a kick out of wandering around at 3 AM in the Produce District (one block east of Jack London Square) to watch the vendors setting up shop. After you've taken in the scene, walk down to the 24-hour, but otherwise undistinguishable, Jack London Inn Coffeeshop (on Embarcadero and Broadway) for some pancakes.*

*Sea Wolf,* and *The Cruise of the Snark.* In an effort to cash in on this legacy, Oakland created this collection of waterfront boutiques and restaurants on the Oakland Embarcadero, best avoided unless you have an unusual obsession with Jack London. If you're really interested in Jack the writer, you'll better enjoy the collection of his letters, manuscripts, and photographs in the public library's **Oakland History Room** (125 14th St., tel. 510/238–3222).

**LAKE MERRITT** A 155-acre oasis in the middle of urban Oakland, the synthetic lake is surrounded by a park filled with shady trees, meandering paths, and old men feeding the ducks. **Lakeside Park** (tel. 510/238–3091), on the north shore, has picnic facilities, Japanese and herb gardens, frequent music events, the oldest bird sanctuary in the United States, and boat rentals at the **Sailboat House** (tel. 510/444–3807). For $6–$8 an hour (plus a $10 deposit) you can paddle or canoe on the lake; sailboats are $6–$12 an hour ($20 deposit). Otherwise, take a tour of the lake aboard the *Merritt Queen,* a replica of a Mississippi River steamboat ($1). If you prefer to remain on shore, a 3½-mile paved walking path circles the lake. **Grand Avenue,** which shoots off from the northern tip of the lake past the art-deco Grand Lake Theater, is also a good place for a stroll, with a number of reasonably good ethnic restaurants and cafés.

Each June, Lake Merritt is the site of Oakland's **Festival at the Lake** (tel. 510/286–1061), the East Bay's largest urban fair, and the **Juneteenth Festival** (tel. 510/238–3866). Year-round, it's a nice place for an afternoon nap or stroll and easily reached from downtown. Walk a quarter-mile southeast from the 12th Street or 19th Street BART station downtown, or go directly to the Lake Merritt BART station. Nearby, you can tour the **Camron-Stanford House** (1418 Lakeside Dr., near 14th St., tel. 510/836–1976), the only remaining Victorian building in this formerly bourgeois neighborhood. Tours ($2; free first Sunday of month) are offered Wednesday 11–4 and Sunday 1–5.

**MORMON TEMPLE** It's hard to tell whether this is a place of worship or a forgotten Disneyland attraction. The Mormons have received a lot of flak for believing the Garden of Eden may be in Mississippi, for building their temples near major freeways to attract distraught souls, for barring women from many church services, and for spending millions of dollars on elaborate, marble-covered temples. Come see for yourself. Free tours of the outside only are given daily 9–9. Pick up a souvenir in the visitor center, or watch the 15-minute video about Joseph Smith and the gang. *4766 Lincoln Ave., tel. 510/531–1475. From Hwy. 13 (Warren Fwy.), exit Lincoln Ave., or Bus 46 from Oakland Coliseum BART.*

**OAKLAND MUSEUM** The three permanent collection halls at the Oakland Museum are devoted to the art, history, and ecology of the Golden State. Extensive mixed-media exhibits

## A Different Beat

***Like San Francisco and Berkeley, Oakland has a reputation for being a center of alternative culture and revolutionary politics. The militant and still widely debated Black Panther Party began here. In the 1970s, the city was headquarters for the Symbionese Liberation Army, who kidnapped Patty Hearst and demanded as part of her ransom that food be distributed to Oakland's poor. Even the city's most famous literary figure, Jack London, was steeped in controversy—an ardent socialist and debauched trouble maker, he wanted California to secede from the U.S. (although that's hard to detect in those two novels about dogs).***

document the rise and fall of the Ohlone people (the region's first inhabitants), and tackle the issues of urban violence and Oakland's subsequent deterioration. The changing shows in the art hall feature work by California artists. Be sure to visit the museum's terraced gardens and the nearby Estuary Park, a 22-acre sculpture garden. *1000 Oak St., tel. 510/238–3401. 1 block east of Lake Merritt BART. Admission free. Open Wed.–Sat. 10–5, Sun. noon–7.*



**PARAMOUNT THEATRE** First-time visitors to Oakland are generally surprised by the art-deco architecture around the 19th Street BART station. Some buildings have fallen into disrepair, but the Paramount Theatre still hosts dance, music, and film, and is an architectural masterpiece. If you can't attend a show, you'll still be able to afford the tour ($1), offered the first and third Saturday of each month at 10 AM. For concert information, thumb through the free weekly *East Bay Express* or call the box office. *2025 Broadway, tel. 510/465–6400. 1½ blocks north of 19th St. BART.*

**PRESERVATION PARK** As a busy transportation hub and the last stop for the Transcontinental Railway, Old Oakland boomed in the late 1800s. Those years saw the construction of some of the finest Victorian homes in the West, 14 of which have been restored at Preservation Park (cnr Martin Luther King Dr. and 13th St.), an idyllic cul-de-sac lined with Queen Anne cottages and colonial revival homes. Sitting near the fountain, you could almost believe that it truly is the turn of the century—except for I–980 traffic noise from just over the hedges. Most of the buildings are private office spaces and are off-limits to the public (unless, oops, you accidentally went into the wrong one).

## AFTER DARK

Music, especially blues and jazz, is an integral part of the Oakland scene. For this reason, you may want to venture into that seedy bar or unassuming nightclub down the street—you know, the kind of places Mom warned you about. There's no telling what kind of magic may be going on inside. For a complete listing of cultural events, thumb through the *East Bay Express* calendar section, a free weekly available at most newsstands and cafés. The **White Horse Inn** (6551 Telegraph Ave., at 66th St., tel. 510/652–3820) has DJ dancing Thursday–Saturday under a gleaming disco ball. The scene is low-key, friendly, and primarily gay and lesbian, though other orientations are welcome so long as they behave themselves.

**BARS** **The Alley.** Where else can you can sit at a piano and sing along with your drunken compadres? The Alley has been in business since the late 1940s and has the clientele to prove it. Dark, musty, and unassuming, it's a great place to hang out with low-key locals. Nightly piano music begins at 9; drinks are $3–$5. *3325 Grand Ave., 3 blocks east of Lake Merritt, tel. 510/444–8505.*

**George and Walt's.** A stylish, somewhat sterile place, G&W is filled with smoke, pool tables, sports-laden conversation, and comfortable booths. On weekends you should probably steer clear unless you don't mind crowds of U.C. Berkeley students. *5445 College Ave., 3 blocks south of Rockridge BART, tel. 510/653–7441.*

**Pacific Coast Brewing Company.** In Old Oakland, this brew pub serves four homebrews and 16 other beers on tap. It's popular with the thirtysomething crowd and a bit yuppie, but the beers are top rate. Lunch is served daily 11:30–3 and dinner Tuesday–Saturday until 9; the burgers, grilled specialties, and salads range from $3 to $10. Drinks are around $3. *906 Washington St., near 10th St., tel. 510/836–2739.*

**LIVE MUSIC** In the years following World War II, Oakland gave birth to the gritty, hurts-so-bad-I'm-gonna-die music known as the West Coast blues. Even after 50 years, it still flourishes in clubs and bars all over Oakland. Dedicated to the preservation of blues, jazz, and gospel, the **Bay Area Blues Society** (tel. 510/836–2227) sponsors shows and festivals year-round and is a wellspring of information about West Coast blues.

➢ **BLUES** • **Eli's Mile High Club.** The reputed birthplace of West Coast blues remains a consistently good bet, highlighting promising local acts as well as more renowned performers. It's a small, basic club with a pool table, soul food, and live music Thursday–Sunday. The kitchen opens around 6:30 and music starts by 9. *3629 Martin Luther King Jr. Way, tel. 510/655–6661. Cover: $3–$8.*

**The Fifth Amendment.** High-quality blues and jazz acts play to a largely African-American crowd of professionals, students, and neighborhood old-timers. Dress up a bit for some absolutely searing music. *3255 Lakeshore Ave., at Lake Park Way, tel. 510/832–3242. Cover: $5–$10.*

➢ **JAZZ • Kimball's East.** In Emeryville, a small community tucked in between Berkeley and Oakland, this excellent jazz and supper club books big-name jazz musicians Wednesday through Sunday. Downstairs, Kimball's Carnival draws big names in Latin jazz and Caribbean music, with an audience of mostly older professional types. *5800 Shellmound St., near I–80, tel. 510/658–2555. Cover: $10–$25.*

**Yoshi's.** Yoshi's is an historic Bay Area joint that serves up sushi and jazz with sophisticated style. The clientele knows its music—past acts have included Cecil Taylor, Anthony Braxton, and Ornette Coleman. Visit while you can—Yoshi's is considering closing its doors, and may or may not relocate to Jack London Square. *6030 Claremont Ave., 3 blocks north of Rockridge BART, tel. 510/652–9200. Cover: $5–$30.*

## OUTDOOR ACTIVITIES

While the tourist hordes head to Muir Woods to see California redwoods, you can slip away to **Redwood Regional Park** in the Oakland Hills. The park's original trees were mowed down at the start of the California gold rush, so the trees you'll see are youngsters—not even 100 years old. But unlike Muir Woods, where the trails sport guard rails and a few too many tourists, Redwood offers an environment rough enough to let you know you're not at the mall. From the Skyline Gate entrance, take the 3-mile (one-way) **Stream Trail,** which, after a steep (and often hot and dry) descent to the valley floor, meanders through the redwoods. To return to the Skyline Gate entrance from the valley floor, simply pick any trail heading up and to the right; you'll soon connect with the West Ridge Trail, which will lead you back to the park entrance. For mountain-bikers, the park offers a moderately difficult, 9-mile bike loop on **East and West Ridge** trails, accessible from the Redwood Gate. Here and at the Skyline Gate entrances, you'll find free trail maps. *Tel. 510/ 635–0135, ext. 2578. From I–580, Hwy. 24 east to Hwy. 13 south. Exit north on Joaquin Miller Rd., turn left on Skyline Blvd.; Skyline Gate entrance is about 4 mi further on the right. For Redwood Gate, I–580 east, exit at 35th Ave./MacArthur Blvd. east; park entrance is 2 mi past Skyline Boulevard. Parking: $3 weekends, roadside parking free.*

# South Bay

**A wannabe philosopher once said that mid**dle America begins but a few miles away from San Francisco. Indeed, just south of the San Francisco International Airport, you'll notice a rapid proliferation of shopping malls, industrial parks, tract homes, and brightly lit clusters of fast-food restaurants. Before you know it, the winding streets and frenetic energy of San Francisco seem miles away. But life does not end in suburbia—the region has quite a few interesting, amusing, or just plain weird attractions that San Francisco snobs thoroughly underrate (or don't know about). The cities that stretch south from San Francisco—on the finger of land wedged between the San Francisco Bay and the Pacific—include Palo Alto, home to Stanford University, and San Jose, the most populous city in northern California.

The South Bay's best-kept secret, however, is the secluded San Mateo County Coast—more than 75 miles of curvy coastline and gently undulating hills stretching south from Pacifica, just south of San Francisco, to Año Nuevo State Park, about 30 miles north of Santa Cruz. Along the way are long, empty beaches; small towns just beginning to awaken to their potential as tourist destinations; and redwood groves filled with great hiking trails. The only bummer here is the weather: While the inland areas like La Honda and Pescadero are always pleasantly warm, the beaches more often than not are windswept and chilly—better for a brisk walk than sunbathing. If you want to make your stay here last a while, consider the coast's two gorgeous hostels, Point Montara Lighthouse HI-Hostel in Montara and, farther south, Pigeon Point Lighthouse Youth Hostel near Pescadero. Either one could easily make a claim to be the best lodging deal in the Bay Area.

**BASICS** The **Palo Alto Chamber of Commerce** (325 Forest Ave., tel. 415/324–3121) has maps of the city, as well as limited information on sights, restaurants, and lodging. The **San Jose Convention and Visitors Bureau** (150 W. San Carlos St., tel. 408/283–8833) is open weekdays 8–5:30, weekends 11–5. Call the **San Jose Events Hotline** (tel. 408/295–2265) anytime for listings of community events and after-dark diversions.

The friendly staff at the **Half Moon Bay Chamber of Commerce** (520 Kelly Ave., Half Moon Bay, tel. 415/726–8380), open weekdays 10–4, will give you more info than you ever wanted on Half Moon Bay, as well as a smattering of maps and brochures for the entire coast. The **State Parks District Office** (95 Kelly Ave., Half Moon Bay, tel. 415/726–8800), open weekdays 8–5, is your best source for short descriptions of the coastal parks from Montara to Año Nuevo.

**COMING AND GOING**

➢ **BY CAR** • **I–280** (a.k.a. the Junipero Serra Freeway) is more scenic than the industry-laden **U.S. 101,** though both connect San Francisco with Palo Alto, Santa Clara, and San Jose. Avoid rush hours, when traffic is bumper to bumper, especially on U.S. 101. From Oakland or Berkeley, take I–880 south for San Jose, or I–880 south to Highway 84 and the Dumbarton Bridge for Palo Alto. I–280 also provides access to the San Mateo County Coast via the east–west **Highway 92** (a.k.a. Half Moon Bay Road), which runs from the interstate to Half Moon Bay and **Coastal Highway 1,** the region's only north–south thoroughfare. The only other major road on the San Mateo County Coast is the east–west **Highway 84** (a.k.a. La Honda Road), which connects San Gregorio with La Honda before meeting up with I–280.

➢ **BY BUS** • San Francisco's BART trains don't travel beyond Daly City, but **SamTrans** (tel. 800/660–4BUS) runs buses regularly throughout San Mateo County. They leave from the Daly City BART station, downtown San Francisco, and San Francisco International Airport, and go to Palo Alto and as far south as Año Nuevo. While most run weekdays only, some heavily trafficked routes run every day; call SamTrans and they'll plot your journey for you. Fares are $1–$2 (35¢–$2 for the disabled). No transfers are issued, and bikes are only allowed on SamTrans buses at the discretion of the driver. From Daly City BART, south of San Francisco, Bus 1L ($1) takes off for Half Moon Bay about five times daily on weekends. From Half Moon Bay, Bus 96C ($1) makes two trips a day south to Waddel Creek, just past Año Nuevo State Reserve.

➢ **BY TRAIN** • **CalTrain** (tel. 800/660–4BUS) offers regular service from San Francisco (4th and Townsend Sts.) to downtown San Jose (65 Cahill St.), with stops in Palo Alto and Santa Clara. The one-way trip from S.F. to San Jose is $4.50 and takes 1½ hours; trains leave hourly between 5 AM and 10 PM, more frequently during commute hours. Bikes are allowed on CalTrain.

# Palo Alto

Palo Alto (about 30 miles south of San Francisco) is mostly known as the home of Stanford University, and it's certainly worth the drive just to check out the beautiful 8,200-acre campus. Off U.S. 101, **University Avenue** is Palo Alto's main drag; west of El Camino Real it'll metamorphose into **Palm Drive,** Stanford's entrance and main thoroughfare. University Avenue and its side streets are loaded with restaurants, music shops, galleries, boutiques, and bookstores. All are disappointingly upscale for a student shopping district, but at least the streets are punctuated by pleasant little plazas with benches and plants.

*The Barbie Hall of Fame (433 Waverly St., at University Ave., tel. 415/326–5841) houses 16,000 of the plastic bombshells. Just about every fashion and lifestyle trend of the past few decades can be seen in these halls for a $4 admission fee.*

If you're curious about what a $20,000-a-year education would look like, swing through the Stanford University campus and check out the sights. Nicknamed "The Farm" because the land was once a stud farm, Stanford consists of look-alike mustard-colored buildings that combine Romanesque squatness with the ranchy feel of a Spanish mission, giving the campus an austere and refined flavor; the more disenchanted of its enrollees, however, refer to it as an oversized Taco Bell.

Palm Drive will take you to the **Quad,** the heart of campus and a popular student hangout. You can pick up free maps or take a guided walking tour from the information office (tel. 415/723–2560) here. The plaza is dominated by the Romanesque **Memorial Church,** best known for its Venetian mosaics. At the entrance to the quad, the grassy **Memorial Court** has a couple of Auguste Rodin statues—dedicated to Stanford men who died for their country—that depict 14th-century English martyrs "at the moment of painful departure from their families and other citizens." Just to the south of the quad, the 280-foot **Hoover Tower,** home of the ultra-conservative Hoover Institution for the Study of War, Revolution, and Peace, thrusts mightily into the sky. For a 360° view of campus and parts of Palo Alto, pay $2 to climb to the tower's observation deck.

The **Rodin Sculpture Garden** is as near as you can get to Stanford's Museum of Art, seriously damaged in the 1989 earthquake and closed at least until June 1997. The 20 or so works by French sculptor Auguste Rodin (1840–1917) are clustered in a small area to the left of the museum. Check out the particularly intense *Gates of Hell*; the giant iron doors are the scene of lots of wild action. Descriptive tours are given at 2 PM Wednesday and on weekends; call for details. *Museum Way and Lomita Dr., tel. 415/723–3469. From Palm Dr., turn right on Museum Way, 1 block past Campus Dr.*

*Palo Alto's requisite dive bar is Antonio's Nut House (321 California Ave., at Birch St., tel. 415/321–2550), where you can get Guinness on tap ($3), peanuts from the gorilla cage, and drinks until 2 AM—a rarity around Stanford.*

Even if you're only vaguely interested in science, make the trek up Sand Hill Road (west from campus toward I–280) to the **Stanford Linear Accelerator.** The 2-mile-long atom smasher is amazing—thousands of house-size machines, dials, diodes, and mussy scientists who get excited when you mention n-orbits and electrons. Reserve space in advance for the twice weekly, free two-hour tour, which includes a slide show and lecture (days and times vary); it's geared toward lay people and is extremely interesting. *2575 Sand Hill Rd., east of I–280 in Menlo Park, tel. 415/926–2204.*

The sprawling campus is best explored by bike, and the biking is even better in the foothills west of the university. For rentals, try **Campus Bike Shop,** which can get you rolling on a mountain bike for $20 or a three-speed for $10 a day. You must leave a deposit equal to the cost of the bike. *551 Salvatierra St., on campus, tel. 415/325–2945.*

**WHERE TO SLEEP** **Coronet Motel.** Traffic on El Camino Real makes it noisy, but the Coronet wins points for location and value. It's only a few blocks from the university, and Stanford

## Dying to Get to Colma

***If you're driving to the South Bay on I–280, be sure to stop in the small city of Colma, a modern-day necropolis filled with cemeteries and macabre graveyard art. In 1914, San Francisco's mayor ordered most city cemeteries to relocate their occupants to Colma, since the city needed the land for its more active (and tax-paying?) residents. Since then, no new cemeteries have been created within San Francisco's city limits. The Colma Town Hall (1198 El Camino Real, at Serramonte Blvd., tel. 415/997–8300) offers a self-guided tour of the city's cemeteries ($2.50), from the prestigious Cypress Lawn to the eerie Pet's Rest, littered with flea collars and dog toys. Look for the graves of Dodge City's Wyatt Earp and former Yankee pitcher Lefty O'Doul.***

Shopping Center is a short drive away. Doubles go for $40 and the rooms—some with kitchenette—are comfortable, if not exactly modern. *2455 El Camino Real, btw California Ave. and Page Mill Rd., tel. 415/326–1081. From U.S. 101, west on Embarcadero Rd., turn left on El Camino Real. 21 rooms.*

**Stanford Arms Motel.** This blue-and-white, rustic-looking motel is less generic than most others in its price range, and it's conveniently located near the Stanford campus. The rooms are clean, if tired-looking; singles cost $42 and doubles are about $44 ($10 extra for rooms with kitchenette). *115 El Camino Real, at Harvard St. in Menlo Park, tel. 415/325–1428. From U.S. 101, Embarcadero Rd. west to El Camino Real, turn left. 14 rooms.*

➢ **HOSTELS** • **Hidden Villa Hostel.** In the Los Altos Hills between Palo Alto and San Jose, this is an actual working farm—complete with animals and an organic garden. Set in a 1,500-acre canyon, the hostel offers easy access to hiking trails and peaceful dirt roads. Large rustic dorm-style cabins dot the canyon, each with communal bathroom facilities. HI members pay $10 a night, nonmembers $13. Unfortunately, public transportation doesn't come anywhere near here, and you need to bring your own food. *26870 Moody Rd., Los Altos, tel. 415/949–8648. From San Francisco, take I–280 south past Palo Alto to the El Monte/Moody Rd. exit, turn right (SW) on El Monte Ave., left on Moody Rd. at stop sign, and go 1.7 mi. Reception open 7:30 AM–9:30 AM and 4:30 PM–9:30 PM. Closed June–Aug.*

**FOOD** **University Avenue** is one long food court, with cutesy, yuppified restaurants everywhere you look. You'll pay just enough more than usual for your burrito, your burger, or your beer to make it annoying. For excellent sushi at a decent price, try **Sushi Ya** (380 University Ave., btw Waverly and Bryant Sts., tel. 415/322–0330). **Jing Jing** (443 Emerson St., off University Ave., tel. 415/328–6885) is a Chinese restaurant popular in these parts for its spicy dishes (most under $10). **Oasis Beer Garden** (241 El Camino Real, Menlo Park, tel. 415/326–8896), a grubby but immensely popular hangout, serves tasty burgers and sandwiches ($4–$7).

# San Jose

People are too hard on San Jose. True, Northern California's largest city is marked by the mini-mall sprawl you'll find all over middle-class America. Despite this, though, San Jose has an oddly comfortable and cosmopolitan feel to it. Encircled by mountain ranges, buffered by city parks and gardens, San Jose is home to museums, symphonies, and wineries as well as industrial parks, computer companies, and corporate headquarters.

The new billion-dollar **downtown** is a good place to start exploring. Hop on the **Light Rail** (tel. 408/321–2300) that connects San Jose State University on one end with the Center for Performing Arts on the other (fare is $1.10). Its numerous stops should give you a good overview of the city center, which is architecturally interesting in its—generally successful—attempt to meld existing Old West themes with modern styles and materials (note the traditional small-town clock tower built from marble and stainless steel). Cruising the heart of downtown, around the intersection of Market and San Carlos streets, you'll see a number of pedestrian plazas and a host of museums, including **The Tech** (145 W. San Carlos St., across from Convention Center, tel. 408/279–7150), a hands-on technology museum that definitely inspires appreciation for the wizardry of the computer age. **Plaza Park** (S. Market St., in front of Fairmont Hotel) is a pleasant grassy strip that runs for 2 blocks, complete with benches and a fountain you can play in, where water shoots up out of grates in the ground.

The **Winchester Mystery House** is a 160-room Victorian mansion built by rifle heiress Sarah Winchester, after a fortune teller told her that as long as she continued to build her house, she wouldn't die. Admission is a steep $12.50, but the house is genuinely cool. *525 S. Winchester Blvd., btw Stevens Creek Blvd. and I–280, tel. 408/247–2001.*

The **Rosicrucian Egyptian Museum and Planetarium** houses one of the most impressive collections of Egyptian, Assyrian, and Babylonian artifacts west of the Nile. Truly fascinating are the animal and human mummies, the underground tomb, and the decorative wall reliefs. The planetarium shows here also hold their own; call 408/947–3634 for show times and ticket prices. *1342 Naglee Ave., at Park Ave., tel. 408/947–3636. Exit I–880 at Alameda East, turn right on Naglee Ave. Admission: $6, $4 under 18. Open daily 9–5, last entry 4:35.*

If you want to be where most of San Jose is during summer, though, head straight for Santa Clara's **Great America** amusement park. It now specializes in movie-theme attractions like the new Top Gun Jet Coaster and the Days of Thunder racing simulator, and sports a handful of water rides, as well as the stand-up Vortex coaster, built a few years ago for a whopping $5 million. To shave a few bucks of the admission price, call and ask about any current discount schemes (usually involving a Coke can or a token from some fast-food restaurant). *Great America Pkwy., Santa Clara, tel. 408/998–1800. Take Great America Pkwy. exit off U.S 101, about 10 mi north of San Jose. Admission: $26. Open spring and fall weekends; summer, daily 10–9 (Sat. until 11).*

**WHERE TO SLEEP** The **Sanborn Park Hostel,** west of San Jose, is one of the most beautiful in California, perfectly situated for hikers and easily reached by public transportation. The main cottage, a wooden cabin that dates from 1908, is surrounded by a dense redwood forest. Hostelers stay in a large rec hall and have access to a volleyball court, grill, laundry facilities, and the standard HI kitchen with pots and pans, all for $7.50 per night for members or $9.50 for nonmembers. It's a busy place, but they try to find room for anyone who shows up. You need to bring your own food, though, as the only restaurants and grocery stores are in downtown Saratoga, 4 miles away. *15808 Sanborn Rd., Saratoga, tel. 408/741–0166. I–280 south to Saratoga/Sunnyvale exit, turn right, go 5½ mi to Hwy. 9. Turn right (toward Big Basin), go 2½ mi, turn left at SANBORN SKYLINE COUNTY PARK sign, go 1 mi, and turn right. Or, Santa Clara County Transit Bus 54 from Sunnyvale CalTrain station, get off at Saratoga post office, and call hostel for a ride. Curfew 11 PM, lockout 9–5. Reception open 5 PM–11 PM. Linen rental (50¢). Wheelchair access.*

**FOOD** Make a beeline for the incredible Cambodian cuisine at **Chez Sovan** (923 Oakland Rd., 1 block north of Hedding and 13th Sts., tel. 408/287–7619), open weekdays 11–3. The lunch-only menu includes a selection of ginger-cooked meats and vegetables, coconut and leek soups, and other traditional Cambodian specials. Most dishes start at around $5. **Taco Al Pastor** (400 Bascom Ave., at San Carlos St., tel. 408/275–1619) has been serving good, cheap Mexican food for more than 15 years. You can fill up on the excellent homemade burritos and tacos for under $5.

# The San Mateo County Coast

## PACIFICA AND MONTARA

Two particularly sleepy seaside towns on a coastline known for its lack of energy, Pacifica and Montara—about 15 and 20 minutes south of San Francisco, respectively—are great places for a quick escape from urban chaos. The "historic" section of Pacifica, located on the northernmost outpost of town, is full of bungalow-style homes that once served as weekend retreats for

### *The Wall of Garbage*

***Californians generate more garbage per capita than any other group of people in the world, and this museum gives you some dramatic ways to feel guilty about it. The massive 100-foot "Wall of Garbage" exhibit represents merely one second's worth of what the country is continually throwing out. At least there's the Recycling Hall, where a huge magnet separates steel and iron from a mountain of tin cans. 1601 Dixon Landing Rd., Milpitas, tel. 408/432–1234. Take Dixon Landing exit off I–880, 5 mi north of San Jose; the recyclery is visible from the freeway. Admission free. Open weekdays 7:30–5.***

wealthy San Franciscans. Pacifica's small commercial district, to the south, is an eclectic combination of old mom-and-pop shops and upscale specialty stores, the latter suggesting that the town is growing a little weary of its backwater authenticity and wants to start attracting some of San Francisco's yuppie business. Bridging past and present are the old paved boardwalk and fishing pier, which serve the same purpose today that they have all along. Come here to smell the salt water, feed the pigeons, and watch the local fishermen ply their trade; the pier also affords brilliant views of San Francisco and Marin County.

*Pacifica has the feel of a town in transition, striving to become the Sausalito of the future. It's the sort of place where you'll find a deteriorating garage next to a brand-spanking-new ristorante Italiano.*

Pacifica's beaches lie south of town, and they're the attractions that lure most San Franciscans down this way. About two miles south of old Pacifica is **Rockaway Beach.** Two large dollops of sand on either end of this gorgeous cove are just large enough for half a dozen sunbathers, and your only other company will be a handful of surfers and fishermen. Immediately south of Rockaway you'll come to the more popular **Pacifica State Beach,** a long, sandy beach favored by surfers and sun worshipers.

Just a few miles farther removed from the city, Montara is pretty much all beach—its commercial district nearly nonexistent. **Gray Whale Cove State Beach** (tel. 415/728–5336), a half-mile north of town, is an American anomaly: a government-supported clothing-optional beach. Entrance to the spectacular, secluded cove is $5. Immediately south of the Montara city limits in Moss Beach, the rich tide pools of the **James V. Fitzgerald Marine Reserve** stretch along the coast for 4 miles. Go at low tide to check out abalone, barnacles, and maybe an octopus or two; but remember, this is a reserve, so look, but don't touch.

**WHERE TO SLEEP** **Marine View Motel.** With roomy doubles ($42) that boast enough carpeted floor space for at least six, this motel is run-down but acceptably clean. It's an easy walk to old town and the beach, but the noise from Highway 1 is slightly annoying. *2040 Francisco Blvd., tel. 415/355–9042. 14 rooms. Wheelchair access.*

➢ **HOSTEL** • **Point Montara Lighthouse HI-Hostel.** This functioning lighthouse and its adjoining hostel are perched on a cliff half a mile south of Montara State Beach just off Highway 1. The attraction of Point Montara Lighthouse reaches well beyond the usual audience for hostels: Expect anyone from San Franciscans on a weekend break to German travelers on a cross-country trek, and look for a few 40- and 50-year-olds scattered among the twentysomethings. The comfortable living room has a fireplace; and there's a communal kitchen, a dining area, and even an outdoor redwood hot tub ($5 per person for a half hour, two-person minimum). Beds go for $11 to members, $14 for nonmembers; and everyone must do a small chore. Reservations can be made anywhere from three days to six months in advance and are advised for summer weekends. *Hwy. 1 and 16th St., tel. 415/728–7177. From Daly City BART, SamTrans Bus 1L or 1C southbound; ask to be let off at 14th St. 45 beds. Curfew 11 PM. lockout 9:30–4:30. Reception open 7:30–9:30 and 4:30–9:30. Laundry. Deposit of first-night fee required for reservations.*

**FOOD** Pacifica's and Montara's budget eating scene consists almost exclusively of low-end ethnic restaurants. In Pacifica's old town, head straight to Francisco Boulevard, just west of Highway 1, where you'll find **Pacifica Thai Cuisine** (1966 Francisco Blvd., tel. 415/355–1678), featuring traditional specialties like chicken curry in coconut milk ($5.50). In Montara, **A Coastal Affair** (Hwy. 1, at 8th St., tel. 415/728–5229), ⅓-mile north of the Point Montara Lighthouse Hostel, is a combination craft gallery and café with excellent espresso drinks ($1.75–$2.75) and freshly made sandwiches (about $4).

**OUTDOOR ACTIVITIES** If you're looking for something a bit more challenging than lying on the beach, **San Pedro Valley County Park** has a number of mellow hiking trails through rolling green hills. In winter and spring, try the **Brooks Falls Overlook Trail,** a half-mile path with views of a three-tiered, 275-foot waterfall. To reach the park from Highway 1 in Pacifica, turn east on Linda Mar Boulevard; when it dead-ends, turn right onto Oddstad Boulevard; the park entrance and visitor center (tel. 415/355–8289) are 50 yards up on the right.

## HALF MOON BAY

Famous for growing Halloween pumpkins and Christmas trees, Half Moon Bay is an easygoing seaside town 28 miles south of San Francisco on Highway 1 (known here as the Cabrillo Highway). With its small-town rural feel, natural beauty, and wealth of activities (well, compared to the other dinky villages around here), it's the most inviting of the coastal communities. The small downtown area centers around **Main Street,** parallel to Highway 1, and is cluttered with crafts stores, produce markets, flower gardens, cafés, and straightforward burger joints.

If lolling on the beach is more your speed, head to the popular **Half Moon Bay State Beach,** actually a series of beaches covering more than 2 miles. To avoid the $5 parking fee, make the ⅓-mile walk from downtown. It will probably get unpleasantly cold near the water before too long, a perfect excuse to trek 2 miles inland along Highway 92 and sample—free of charge—the local wines at **Obester Winery** (tel. 415/726–9463), open daily 10–5.

Half Moon Bay hosts dozens of annual festivals, any one of which you could plan a visit around. The largest and most popular one is the annual **Art and Pumpkin Festival,** held the weekend after Columbus Day. The high-spirited festival includes live music, local foods, crafts, vendors, a children's parade, and pie-eating and pumpkin-carving contests. Other yearly events include the riotous **Human Race** every May, in which entrants use every wacky scheme they can devise to carry other contestants along the course. For more information, contact the Half Moon Bay Chamber of Commerce.

**WHERE TO SLEEP** A visit to the Half Moon Bay area can be relatively cheap if you camp or stay in either of the beautiful nearby youth hostels, Point Montara Lighthouse HI-Hostel (*see* Pacifica and Montara, *above*), 4 miles north, or Pigeon Point Lighthouse Youth Hostel (*see* Pescadero, *below*), 30 miles south. Otherwise, the options for affordable lodging in the area are almost nonexistent. **Cameron's Inn** (1410 S. Cabrillo Hwy. (Hwy. 1), tel. 415/726–5705) has three clean, simple doubles with a distinctly European feel. Big beds and fine art prints lend some style to the rooms, all of which share a common bath. You'll drift off to the sound of big-rigs downshifting on the highway, but at $50 on weekdays and $60 on weekends, it's about as cheap as you'll find in the area. If all else fails, the 20-room **Ramada Inn** (3020 Hwy. 1, tel. 415/726–9700 or 800/2–RAMADA) on the north end of town has doubles starting at $72 weekdays, $98 weekends, including breakfast.

➢ **CAMPING** • **Half Moon Bay State Beach.** Close to downtown, these 55 characterless, first-come first-served sites ($14) attract teenage partyers and weekend-warrior types, especially during summer. Though you'll fall asleep to the sound of waves and arise to the smell of sea salt, it's hardly the great outdoors. *95 Kelly Ave., west of Hwy. 1, tel. 415/726–8820. Cold showers, fire pits, flush toilets, food lockers, picnic tables.*

**FOOD** Half Moon Bay has everything from reasonably priced health-food counters to way-outta-range seafood restaurants. The best of the former is the **Healing Moon Natural Foods Market** (523 Main St., tel. 415/726–7881); if you're not looking for groceries, serve yourself a cup of soup and eat it on the peaceful patio. Despite its chain-restaurant exterior, **3 Amigos** (200 N. Cabrillo Hwy., on Hwy. 1 at Kelly Ave., tel. 415/726–6080) offers tasty, cheap Mexican food (veggie burritos $3) daily until midnight. At the **Flying Fish Grill** (99 San Mateo Rd., cnr Hwy. 92 and Main St., tel. 415/712–1125), you'll find reasonably priced seafood (a rarity around here) in a casual environment. Chow down on clam chowder ($3) and a variety of deep-fried and grilled fresh fish ($7–$10).

**OUTDOOR ACTIVITIES** Since it occupies a prime spot between the ocean and the hills, Half Moon Bay is a great place to pursue both land and water sports. You'll also find plenty to do at Pacifica and Montara to the north and Año Nuevo State Reserve to the south, all within an hour's drive.

If you want to spend an hour or so racing a steed along the beach, contact **Sea Horse Ranch** or **Friendly Acres Ranch** (tel. 415/726–2362). A 1½-hour ride on the beach will run you $30; a one-hour trail ride goes for $22. The two ranches—owned by the same people—are just north of Half Moon Bay on Highway 1, about 500 yards from each other. Call ahead and ask where you can pick up $5 discount coupons (usually available at supermarkets or Travelodge).

If you have a yen to sail out of Pillar Point Harbor in search of rock cod or salmon, **Huck Finn Sportfishing** (tel. 415/726–7133 or 800/572–2934 outside of northern California) on the harbor offers full-day expeditions starting at $40 (tackle and license about $5 extra). Huck Finn will also take you out on whale-watching trips ($20) in season; January through March is the prime time to catch sight of the California gray whale migration.

## SAN GREGORIO TO AÑO NUEVO STATE RESERVE

The desolate stretch of coastline between Half Moon Bay and Santa Cruz is nearly deserted year-round, and for good reason. The beaches here are colder, more windblown, and less spectacular than their counterparts to the north and south; the opportunities for outdoor exploration on foot or bike are scarcer than in places like Big Basin Redwoods State Park; the choice of affordable food and lodging is limited; and the number of worthwhile "sights," depending on your criteria, can be almost negligible. But the very fact that the area is so empty makes up for all this. With the exception of Año Nuevo State Reserve during elephant-seal mating season, there's almost nothing you can do here that will require advance planning. The rich tide pools at Pescadero State Beach, the cliff-hugging Pigeon Point Lighthouse Hostel, and the sky-high trees lining Highway 84 through La Honda all make this chunk of coast extremely worthwhile for people taking the slow road up or down the California shore.

**SAN GREGORIO** Although not much of a destination in itself, San Gregorio is a worthwhile stop if you're traveling the coast between Santa Cruz and Half Moon Bay. The drive to this hitching post of a town, at the junction of Highways 1 and 84, is half the fun, even if you don't come via the coast road. Highway 84 (also known as La Honda Road) heads west from I–280 and is for the strong of stomach only; a roller-coaster ride on a highway so thick with redwoods it barely sees the light of day. The road spits you out at the isolated **San Gregorio State Beach,** where you can lie back and soak up some rays, or, more likely, throw on a sweater and battle the wind as you watch the fog roll in. Stock up on supplies at the eclectic **San Gregorio General Store** (tel. 415/726–0565; open daily 9–7), 1 mile east of Highway 1 on Highway 84. It doubles as the town saloon and community center, and you might even catch some Bulgarian bluegrass or Irish R&B if you show up on the right weekend night.

**LA HONDA** If you're getting tired of relentlessly magnificent coastal scenery, the densely forested, mountainous community of La Honda (on Hwy. 84, 11 mi east of Hwy. 1) is the perfect antidote. About the size of a postage stamp, La Honda seems almost lost in the shadow of countless giant sequoias and redwoods. The town consists of **Pioneer Market** (tel. 415/747–9982), where you can stock up on camping supplies and sandwiches ($3.50); the **Clear Water Café** (tel. 415/742–9600), open daily until 8, offering barbecued chicken sandwiches ($4.50) and espresso drinks (about $2); a post office; and **Apple Jack's Tavern** (La Honda Rd., tel. 415/747–0331), a scruffy bar you shouldn't miss, no matter what time of day you're pass-

### *The Merry Pranksters*

***In the early 1960s La Honda was home to one of the hippie era's most renowned groups of psychedelic crazies, the Merry Pranksters. Led by the multi-talented bohemian Ken Kesey, author of such acclaimed novels as One Flew Over the Cuckoo's Nest, the Merry Pranksters spent several years on a La Honda farm exploring "states of non-ordinary reality" (i.e., dropping acid, eating mushrooms, and smoking dope). When La Honda became too limiting, they outfitted an old school bus with Day-Glo paint and filming equipment, and set off to travel across the country, a journey made famous by Tom Wolfe in his novel The Electric Kool-Aid Acid Test.***

ing through town. Open weekdays noon–2 AM and weekends 10 AM–2 AM, Apple Jack's is today's version of an Old West saloon: The men drink their whiskey straight up, the women are loud and boisterous, and a brawl seems ready to erupt at any minute. You'll feel equally comfortable pulling up on a Harley Davidson or on a horse.

➢ **WHERE TO SLEEP** • If you want to pitch a tent, the most developed sites are in **Portola State Park** (just south of Pescadero Creek County Park; *see below*) and **Memorial County Park** (Pescadero Rd., west of La Honda), while **Pescadero Creek County Park** (take Hwy. 84 west from La Honda, turn left on Alpine Rd.) has more primitive, secluded hike-in campgrounds. Memorial is a thick old-growth forest that offers 135 quiet sites ($12), all with picnic tables, fire pits, and hot showers. Although popular with car campers on summer weekends, the first-come, first-served campground is sparsely visited at other times. The 53 campsites ($14) at Portola State Park have running water, showers, fire pits, and picnic tables. Reserve through MISTIX (tel. 800/444–PARK). For a spot at one of Pescadero Creek's 15 hike-in sites ($7), located in dense second-growth forest along the river, contact the rangers at Portola State Park (tel. 415/948–9098).

**PESCADERO** More than 100 years ago, all the wooden buildings in the small fishing village of Pescadero were painted white with paint that washed up on shore when the clipper ship *Carrier Pigeon* crashed into the rocks off Pigeon Point, a few miles south of town. Today, the bank, bakery, general store, and other shops that populate Pescadero retain their whitewashed uniformity, giving this town, in the flatlands a mile inland from the coast on Pescadero Road, a calming, subdued ambience.

After you've rambled around the 3 blocks that make up Pescadero's commercial district, head straight to **Duarte's Tavern** (202 Stage Rd., at Pescadero Rd., tel. 415/879–0464; open daily 7 AM–9 PM), a combination bar and restaurant that's been run by four generations of Duartes since 1894. The homey restaurant serves everything from peanut butter and jelly sandwiches ($3) to lamb chops ($14), but it's most famous for its cream of artichoke soup ($4), fresh seafood plates ($6–$20), and homemade pies ($3).

On the coast just west of town, you'll find **Pescadero State Beach,** a long, sandy expanse with some vibrant tide pools, perfect for checking out the Pacific's aquatic community. Immediately north of the beach is the **Pescadero Marsh Reserve** (tel. 415/879–2170), a protected area favored by ornithologists. Free guided walks leave from the parking lot Saturdays at 10:30 AM and Sundays at 1 PM year-round.

Charming **Butano State Park** (tel. 415/879–0173), 5 miles south of Pescadero on Cloverdale Road, has 20 miles of trails on 2,700 acres. You can reach the park from Highway 1 south of Pescadero State Beach; there's a $5 parking fee. The beautiful **Little Butano Creek Trail,** about a half mile from the entrance, takes you 3 miles along a creek and past old-growth redwoods. Mountain bikes are forbidden on the park's trails, but you can ride on any of the fire roads. Your best bet is to park at the entrance gate near the corner of Cloverdale and Canyon roads, about a mile north of the main park entrance, and ride the Butano Fire Road. If you're in pretty good shape you can take it all the way to the Olmo Fire Road, which leads back to the park's main road, and pedal back to your car.

➢ **WHERE TO SLEEP** • If you want a bed, a shower, the beach, or all three, the **Pigeon Point Lighthouse Youth Hostel,** perched on a small bluff 5 miles south of Pescadero State Beach, is definitely *the* place to go. With four bungalow-style dorms overlooking miles of unblemished coast, and an outdoor hot tub ($3 per person per half-hour), the Pigeon Point Hostel tends to enchant its guests and destroy their will to leave—perhaps accounting for the three-night maximum stay. A night in any of the 54 comfortable beds costs $10 ($13 for nonmembers); and all the guests must do a chore during their stay. *Pigeon Point Rd. and Hwy. 1, tel. 415/879–0633. From Daly City BART, SamTrans Bus 96C. Curfew 11 PM, lockout 9:30–4:30. Reception open 7:30–9:30 and 4:30–9:30 PM. Free lighthouse tours. Reservations advised. Wheelchair access.*

In **Butano State Park** (*see above*), 27 drive-in campsites ($14) and 18 hike-in sites ($7) lie peacefully among the redwoods waiting patiently for the few visitors who venture this way. The drive-in sites have fire rings, picnic tables, and food lockers; none of the sites has showers. Reservations can be made through MISTIX (tel. 800/444–PARK) up to eight weeks in advance, but are usually unnecessary.



**ANO NUEVO STATE RESERVE** Named by explorer Sebastian Viscaino on New Year's Day 1603, the Punta del Año Nuevo is one of the few places in the world where you can safely view live elephant seals close up. Not only that, if you're here between December and March, you get to see them do the wild thing. During mating season, you'll need to make reservations up to eight weeks in advance through MISTIX (tel. 800/444–PARK), and you can only visit the reserve on one of their 2½-hour guided walks ($4, plus $4 parking fee). If you're lucky, you may also catch sight of migrating gray whales during the mating season.

*Since drag queen Divine kicked the bucket some years ago, this may be your only chance to watch overfed, under-exercised, 200-pound-plus honking balls of blubber perform their mating rituals. Don't miss it.*

At other times of the year, you can check out the elephant seals resting on the rocks by obtaining a free visitor's permit when you show up (parking is still $4). The path to the beach from the parking lot is 1½ miles long; and if you come in spring, you'll be treated to the sight of thousands of colorful wildflowers. The reserve, 22 miles north of Santa Cruz, is on Highway 1 and can be reached on SamTrans Bus 96C (*see* Coming and Going in the South Bay, *above*).

# Marin County

**Just across the Golden Gate** Bridge, Marin is the state's richest county, an upscale playground for children old enough to remember Woodstock. Everywhere you turn, you'll see an odd combination of hippie ideals and yuppie wealth: expensive estates buffered by ragged log cabins, Porsches and BMWs parked next to aging Volvo station wagons and VW vans.

The reason so many '60s-refugees-turned-'80s-success-stories want to live here—and the reason you'll want to visit despite the price tag—is Marin's incredible natural beauty. The county encompasses stunning ocean views, thick redwood forests, and rural back roads tempered by sheep ranches and country farms. You could spend a lifetime hiking in Muir Woods and the Point Reyes National Seashore, and it's hard to act blasé about the view from **Coastal Highway 1,** no matter how many times you've driven the road.

*Filmmaker George Lucas and out-there musician Todd Rundgren are a couple of the cultural heroes who live in Marin County.*

Marin's upscale, touristed bayside towns, like Tiburon and Sausalito, are tougher for the budget traveler to love. You'll have to pick your way through an ostentatious show of wealth to find a cheap organic grocery store where you can stock up on supplies for your hike; a sunny field hospitable to hackysack players; or an unpretentious restaurant that serves reasonably priced seafood. But these things do exist—and once you find them, you'll consider never leaving.

**BASICS** The **Marin County Convention and Visitors Bureau** distributes the free *Weekender Magazine,* which lists cultural events in the area. *Marin Center, on Ave. of the Flags in San Rafael, tel. 415/472–7470. Open weekdays 8:30–5.*

The **West Marin Chamber of Commerce** has a free newsletter, "The Coastal Traveler," with great info on out-of-the-way beaches, bike rides, and backpacking trips. *Mailing Address: Box 1045, Point Reyes Station 94956. Street Address: 70 2nd St., Point Reyes Station, tel. 415/663–9232. 2 mi north of Olema on Hwy. 1. Open Mon.–Sat. 9–5.*

**COMING AND GOING** Even the most bucolic corners of Marin are little more than two hours from San Francisco. However, once you're there, getting around Marin on public transportation can be a big drag. Luckily, locals know this, and hitchhiking is a semi-accepted mode of transit. As always, exercise caution and use your street sense. Traffic is a problem year-round, especially on summer weekends and holidays. The Golden Gate Bridge turns into a gigantic parking lot every rush hour, and the Sunday traffic on Highway 1 will remind you of what "painfully slow" and "brain-numbing headache" really mean.

From San Francisco, head north on **U.S. 101** and cross the **Golden Gate Bridge** (no toll this direction). For Sausalito, take the Sausalito exit and go south on Bridgeway to the municipal parking lot near the center of town. Farther north on U.S. 101, you'll see exits for Tiburon (take Tiburon Blvd.) and San Rafael. For Mill Valley, **Highway 1,** and West Marin, follow U.S. 101 north to the Stinson Beach/Highway 1 exit. For Mill Valley, turn right on Miller Avenue at the stop light. Or take Highway 1 north, and as it winds uphill you'll pass turnoffs for Muir Woods and Mt. Tamalpais. Keep going to get to Stinson Beach (1 hr) and Point Reyes (1½ hrs).

➢ **BY BUS** • **Golden Gate Transit** (tel. 415/455–2000 from Marin, 415/923–2000 from San Francisco, or 707/541–2000 from Sonoma County) provides service to Marin County. Buses connect San Francisco with the inland cities of Sausalito, Mill Valley, Tiburon, and San Rafael every half-hour during the week. Many buses run weekdays only, dawn to dusk, but some routes (including the 20 and 50) run on weekends and as late as 4 AM. There is no direct service from San Francisco to coastal Highway 1; on weekends, you can take Bus 80 (which is the most direct) or Bus 50 from San Francisco to San Rafael, then transfer to Bus 65, which stops in Inverness, Point Reyes, Olema, and Stinson Beach. Bus 20 will take you to Marin City where you can catch Bus 63 directly to Stinson Beach. Within San Francisco, buses leave from the Transbay Terminal; fares range from $2 to $4.50. During non-commute hours, bikes are allowed on Bus 40 (El Cerrito del Norte BART–San Rafael) and Bus 80 to Stinson Beach.

➢ **BY FERRY** • If you're sick of Bay Area traffic, or just in the mood for a change of pace, pack a thermos of coffee and a warm jacket, and hop on one of the commuter ferries from San Francisco to Marin County. **Golden Gate Ferry** (tel. 415/332–6600) crosses the bay between Marin County and the San Francisco Ferry Building (on the Embarcadero, at the bottom of Market St.) from 7 AM to 8 PM. It's $4.25 to the **Sausalito Ferry Dock** (south end of Bridgeway); the trip takes 30 minutes. The 50-minute journey to the **Larkspur Ferry Terminal** (101 E. Sir Francis Drake Blvd.) costs $2.50, $4.25 weekends and holidays. Tickets include free transfers for Golden Gate Transit buses (*see above*). The **Red and White Fleet** (tel. 415/546–BOAT or 800/229–2784) leaves from Pier 43½ at Fisherman's Wharf for the Sausalito Ferry Dock ($5.50, 20–30 min). The fleet also runs commuter services to Tiburon ($5.50) and excursion trips to Angel Island ($9) and Alcatraz ($5.75). A number of these ferries leave from Pier 41; call for details.

# Marin Headlands

For a quick taste of what Marin County has to offer nature freaks, cross the Golden Gate Bridge, exit at Alexander Avenue, and drive up Conzelman Road to the Marin Headlands. Consisting of several small but steep bluffs overlooking the San Francisco Bay and the Pacific Ocean, the undeveloped, 1,000-acre headlands are a great place to while away the afternoon. Snap a few photos (though the fog often obscures the view), or just clamber over the decaying WWII-era gun emplacements. Hundreds of hiking and biking trails meander along the wind-beaten hills and cliffs. Rangers sometimes lead mountain-biking tours; call or stop by the **visitor center** (Field and Bunker Rds., follow signs from Conzelman Rd., tel. 415/331–1540) for details on this and other activities in the headlands.

Most weekends—especially in summer—the area crawls with locals, but the farther north you hike, the fewer people you'll encounter. From the visitor center parking lot, head up the closed-off road (*not* the left stairway) on the **Coastal Trail.** After about 2 miles, turn right onto the **Wolf Ridge Trail,** and head up the grassy hill (alias Wolf Ridge) for 1.6 miles to the top. When you're ready to stop gazing at the Tennessee Valley, continue for .7 miles down the verdant leeward side of the hill until it hooks up with the **Miwok Trail,** which you follow south, back to the visitor center.

**WHERE TO SLEEP** **Golden Gate AYH-Hostel.** Set amid the beaches and forest of the headlands in historic Fort Barry, the hostel, built in 1907, has a common room with fireplace, a communal kitchen, laundry room, and tennis court. Beds cost $10 a night and are often available at the last minute, but call at least a week in advance if you have your heart set on staying. Recently opened "family rooms" sleep up to four people, so couples may get their own room on slow nights. Membership is not required. If you're coming from San Francisco, catch Golden Gate Transit Bus 10 or 50 from the Transbay Terminal and ask to be let off at the bottom of the Alexander Avenue off-ramp; from there it's still a hefty 4-mile hike to the headlands. Sundays only, MUNI Bus 43 goes from the Transbay Terminal all the way up to the Marin Headlands Visitor Center, a block from the hostel. *Ft. Barry, Bldg. 941, tel. 415/331-2777. From U.S. 101, Alexander Ave. exit, cross under freeway, and make first right after* MARIN HEADLANDS *sign. 1 mi farther, turn right on McCullough Rd., left on Bunker Rd., and follow sign to visitor center (hostel is just uphill). 101 beds. No curfew, lockout 9:30–3:30. Reception open 7:30* AM*–9:30* PM*. Key deposit ($10).*



# Sausalito

Only a few miles north of San Francisco, Sausalito flourished during the 1880s and 1890s as a small whaling town, infamous for its saloons, gambling dens, and bordellos. Even after it was suburbanized in the 1940s, the town continued to attract an offbeat and raffish element as an artists' colony and seaside playground. Over the years, however, Sausalito's wharf rats have been replaced with another type of rat—lawyers and investment bankers—and this is now a bland, wealthy resort town, popular with yachters and San Francisco's upwardly mobile crowd. If you have unlimited time to explore the Bay Area, Sausalito is worth a gander, but don't go out of your way. Parking is next to impossible, the shops and restaurants are shockingly expensive, and you'll have to dodge camera-toting tourists who fill the sidewalks and streets.

*After dark, a rowdy over-thirty crowd congregates at Sausalito's No Name Bar (757 Bridgeway, tel. 415/332-1392) to enjoy free live jazz, blues, or Dixieland music Wednesday–Sunday.*

At the south end of Bridgeway, Sausalito's main thoroughfare, is the **Sausalito Ferry Terminal,** where the commuter boat from San Francisco docks. Perhaps the most interesting thing to do in Sausalito is to wander among the unusual houseboats docked in the marinas. Some look like little more than barges, others so houselike it's hard to believe they float.

**WHERE TO SLEEP** Don't even bother. Unless you have $80–$100 to blow on a room, Sausalito is a traveler's nightmare. The only reasonable alternative is the **Golden Gate AYH-Hostel** (*see* Marin Headlands, *above*), 15 minutes away in the Marin Headlands.

**FOOD** Restaurants and cafés line Bridgeway, but they're generally overpriced and touristy. Expect to pay at least $15–$20 for seafood and waterfront vistas. Save your cash and visit **Hamburgers** (737 Bridgeway, tel. 415/332-9471), a lunch-only hole-in-the-wall doing a few variations on the hamburger ($4–$5) and fries ($1.50) theme. For a meal with a view, head to the top floor of **Village Fair** (777 Bridgeway) and **Café Sausalito** (tel. 415/332-6579), where you'll find affordable fare and phenomenal views of San Francisco and Angel Island. If you head one block inland to **Caledonia Street,** you'll find better bargains without the tourist brouhaha. **Stuffed Croissant** (43 Caledonia St., tel. 415/332-7103) is *the* stop for picnic-packers attempting to avoid Sausalito's overpriced restaurants. The tiny mom-and-pop deli offers sandwiches ($4–$5.50), soups, and decadent desserts. Still, your best bet is to pack a lunch and picnic in the grassy area between Bridgeway and the bay.

# Tiburon and Angel Island

Little Tiburon, a peninsula jutting into the bay just north of Sausalito, has a relaxed atmosphere and great views of Angel Island and San Francisco, but the small cluster of gift shops and pricey boutiques along the waterfront will seem cutesy and cloying before long. To rise above the tourist schlock on Main Street (both literally and figuratively), head up the hill to **Old St. Hilary's Historic Preserve,** which stands in a field of wildflowers on a lonely perch above town.

The white, wooden Victorian church is run by the Landmarks Society as a historical and botanical museum. *Esperanza and Alemany Sts., tel. 415/435–1853. Admission free. Open April–Oct., Wed. and Sun. 1–4.*

The main reason to come to Tiburon, though, is to catch a 15-minute ferry ride to **Angel Island,** where you can explore sandy beaches, eucalyptus groves, and old military installations, all crammed into a 750-acre state park within spitting distance of the Golden Gate Bridge. **Ayala Cove,** the area around the ferry landing, is congested with picnickers taking advantage of tables and barbecue grills. The 5-mile perimeter road that rings the island, offering access to plenty of scenic and historic sites, is also heavily traveled. But it's easy to escape the crowds. Try the **Sunset Trail,** immediately southeast of the park headquarters at Ayala Cove. Two miles of ascending switchbacks afford stunning views of San Francisco to the west as you circle the 781-foot summit of Mt. Caroline Livermore. A **visitor center** at Ayala Cove (tel. 415/ 435–5390) distributes leaflets about the island for a quarter.

For the ultimate isolated picnic, schlepp your stuff about a mile from Ayala Cove to **Camp Reynolds,** which functioned as an army camp from the Civil War to World War II. Plenty of people linger at the Commanding Officer's House along the road, but about a quarter-mile past the old army barracks, at the water's edge, you'll find empty picnic tables and an outstanding close-up view of the Golden Gate Bridge. On the other side of the island is the **Immigration Station,** where immigrants (mostly Asian) were detained when trying to enter the United States between 1910 and 1940. A few poems written by despairing immigrants are etched into the walls.

Ferries (tel. 415/435–2131) leave for Angel Island from Tiburon's Main Street pier at 10, 11, 1, and 3 on summer weekdays, and every hour from 10 to 5 on spring and summer weekends. Boats depart from Angel Island 20 minutes after they dock. Round-trip fares are $5, plus $1 for bicyles, no cars allowed. Ferries also leave from Fisherman's Wharf in the summer.

**WHERE TO SLEEP** Other than camping on Angel Island, an attractive option, Tiburon is a tired budget traveler's nightmare. Nine showerless, hike-in environmental campsites ($9) are scattered around Angel Island—sites 3 and 4, with views of the Golden Gate Bridge, are the most popular; Sites 1 and 2, surrounded by pine trees and with a view of the East Bay, offer more privacy and shelter from the wind. Reserve a few weeks ahead for a weekend stay; on weekdays, you can almost always get a site on the same day. *Tel. 415/435–1915 for info or 800/444–PARK for reservations. Barbecue grills, drinking water, pit toilets.*

**FOOD** One of the least expensive waterfront restaurants is **Sam's Anchor Café** (27 Main St., tel. 415/435–4527), where hearty breakfast dishes are $7–$9; try the Hangtown Fry omelet ($7.50) with oysters, bacon, scallions, and cheese if you're feeling adventurous. Fresh seafood dishes are $8–$16, burgers run $7–$9, sandwiches $5.50 and up. Sam's is also the center of Tiburon's nightlife.

# Mill Valley

Off U.S. 101 at the Stinson Beach/Highway 1 exit, Mill Valley is a community of millionaires and mountain-bikers set amid the California redwoods on the eastern slope of Mt. Tamalpais—a laid-back, sleepy town where people have paid dearly for their solitude and want to keep it that way. There aren't any official tourist sights, but a drive through the hills and forested canyons will explain why this is some of the Bay Area's most coveted real estate. If you want a break from driving, turn off on **Tennessee Valley Road** and follow it to its end. From there you can hike or bike the dirt path that gently descends to the beach where, in 1853, the steamship *Tennessee* wrecked in dangerous surf, giving the valley its name.

After you return to Mill Valley along Miller Avenue (the freeway exit road), stop by the **Depot Bookstore and Café** (87 Throckmorton Ave., at Miller St., tel. 415/383–2665), which faces the small central plaza. You can enjoy an espresso drink, a salad, or a pita sandwich ($4–$6) and browse through the adjoining bookstore. After sunset, locals mosey over to the **Sweetwater** (153 Throckmorton Ave., at Miller Ave., tel. 415/388–2820), where on any given night bluesman Roy Rogers or Huey Lewis might show up to jam. This tiny club is a Bay Area institution, attracting some of the finest blues and R&B talents in the country.

**FOOD** Head to **Stefano's Pizza** (8 E. Blithedale Ave., at Throckmorton Ave., tel. 415/ 383–9666) for a large, super-tasty slice of thin pizza ($2–$3) served by a guy who actually speaks Italian. If you're anxious to get an early start on the day, funky **Mama's Royal Café** (393 Miller Ave., tel. 415/388–3261) serves an unbeatable breakfast. Specialties include *huevos rancheros* ($6) and *huevos con nopales* (eggs with cactus; $6). The café, full of thrift-store artifacts and psychedelic murals, has promised to reinstate live music in the evenings now that Mill Valley has relaxed its law against same—call for details.



# San Rafael

Unassuming San Rafael, between the foot of Mt. Tamalpais and San Rafael Hill, would perhaps attract more day-trippers from foggy San Francisco if people realized it's almost always several degrees warmer here than elsewhere in the Bay Area. In fact, that's exactly why the town was founded in the first place. In 1817, when Native Americans at San Francisco's Mission Dolores started dying at an alarming rate, missionaries built a hospital here so they could receive care in a more hospitable climate. The original buildings of the **Mission San Rafael Arcangel** were torn down in the 1870s, but a replica of the chapel (5th and A Sts.), built of stuccoed concrete instead of the original adobe, now sits next to a gift shop selling Catholic kitsch. A block away from the chapel, **4th Street** is the town's main drag, lined with used bookstores, a large contingent of department stores, and cafés. The best of the last is **Jazzed** (816 4th St., at Lincoln Ave., tel. 415/455-8077). At this smoke- and alcohol-free club, closed Monday, enjoy a light meal ($5–$7) or creative coffee concoction (about $2) while listening to the free live jazz performances.

If you're tired of suburbia, drive 4 miles east on San Pedro Road to **China Camp State Park,** a beautiful 1,600-acre wilderness area that has remained undeveloped and unpublicized. Remnants of an old Chinese fishing village are still visible, and the oak knolls and saltwater marshes are great for hiking and camping (*see* Where to Sleep, *below*). You pay $3 in day-use fees to park your car. From the parking lot at China Camp Point, you can hike 5 miles along the well-marked **Shoreline Trail.** The **Bay View Trail,** a steeper schlepp but wonderfully uncrowded, is a favorite of rangers. Pick up a trail map from the ranger station about a mile from the park entrance on North San Pedro Road.

**WHERE TO SLEEP** San Rafael has one of the few hotels in Marin County that you might actually be able to afford. The **Panama Hotel** (4 Bayview St., tel. 415/457–3993) offers individually decorated rooms (all with TV), a restaurant whose menu will make your mouth water, and a beautiful outdoor area draped with wisteria. Most amazing, the prices are reasonable (at least for this area): Rooms without bath start at $45 (with bath $70 and up). If you can't get a room in the Panama, the **San Rafael Inn** (865 E. Francisco Blvd., tel. 415/454–9470), with 32 wheelchair-accessible rooms, isn't a bad back-up; the rooms are clean, and a pool and Jacuzzi are available. Singles and doubles (all with TV) are $48–$54; tack on about $5 on weekends and holidays.

➢ **CAMPING** • **China Camp State Park.** At this 1,600-acre park 4 miles northeast of San Rafael you can pitch your tent at one of 30 walk-in campsites near San Pablo Bay. The sites ($14 a night, $12 off-season) aren't far from the parking lot, or from each other, but they're well sheltered by oak trees. And you get hot water to boot. Call MISTIX (tel. 800/444–PARK) to reserve. *Tel. 415/456–0766. Take N. San Pedro Rd. exit east from U.S. 101 in San Rafael, and follow signs. Fire pits, flush toilets, showers. Parking: $3.*

**FOOD** Compared to most of Marin County, San Rafael has a down-to-earth restaurant scene, with lots of cafés, Mexican joints, and other ethnic eateries lining 4th Street downtown. At the **San Rafael Station Café** (1013 B St., tel. 415/456–0191), locals hang out on weekends reading the paper and ingesting phenomenal amounts of cholesterol. Omelets of every persuasion run $5–$8, and sandwiches are $3.50–$7.50. People all over the Bay Area also rave over

**Royal Thai** (610 3rd St., tel. 415/485–1074), which serves up no-frills seafood and curry dishes (under $10) in a restored Victorian house.

# Muir Woods and Mt. Tamalpais

**MUIR WOODS NATIONAL MONUMENT** Judging from the crowded parking lot and tacky gift shop, the Muir Woods National Monument looks like just another overtouristed attraction to be avoided. This 550-acre park, however, contains one of the most majestic groves of redwoods in the world, some more than 250 feet tall and 800 years old. Muir Woods has been preserved by the federal government since 1908, as a result of John Muir's (1838–1914) campaign to save old-growth forests from destruction. It's crowded and a favorite destination of the older set, so try to visit on a weekday morning, or even a rainy day. Neither picnicking nor camping is allowed in the park, but snacks are available at the gift shop, along with every type of redwood souvenir imaginable. The **visitor center** (tel. 415/388–2595) organizes free nature walks through the woods; call for current schedules. The weather here is usually cool and often damp, so dress warmly. The woods lie off U.S. 101, 17 miles northwest of San Francisco. Take the Stinson Beach/Highway 1 exit and follow signs. The monument is open daily 8 AM–sunset, and parking is free.

To rid yourself of the crowds, escape to the rugged, unpopulated trails that meander along cool, fern-filled ridges high above the canyon. The **Ocean View Trail** ascends for 1.3 miles before connecting with the **Lost Trail,** which hooks up with **Fern Creek Trail,** taking you back to the parking lot. The moderate hike is 3 miles round-trip and passes some of the park's most impressive stands of redwoods. For a more spectacular view and workout, head up the **Ben Johnson Trail** from the same spot. You'll climb up through the forest for 2 miles (the last half-mile is quite steep) until you reach the top of a hill with a wonderful view of several canyons and the Pacific.

**MUIR BEACH** If you stick to Highway 1 instead of following the turnoff to Muir Woods, you come to Muir Beach, a quiet strip of sand cluttered with odd-shaped pieces of driftwood and hundreds of tidal pools. It's strikingly scenic and attracts folks looking to get away and relax—not the Budweiser and volleyball crowd you'll find at Stinson, 6 miles farther on.

If you really want to get a feel for Marin's landscape, park your car at Muir Beach and hike the difficult **Coastal Trail,** which leads up a steep hill overlooking the ocean and crawls around a series of deserted coves and valleys for 4 miles. Return the same way and reward yourself with a pint of Guinness and ploughman's lunch in front of the fire at the **Pelican Inn** (Hwy. 1 at Muir Beach, tel. 415/383–6000 or 415/383–6005). The restaurant serves everything from fish-and-chips ($8) to prime rib ($17) and Yorkshire pudding ($2), along with a healthy sampling of British ales and bitters; the kitchen closes between 3 and 6 in the afternoon.

**MT. TAMALPAIS STATE PARK** Not to belittle the beauty of Muir Woods, but it's a place you could take your grandma (and many people do). To see Marin at its most powerful, go to the source—Mt. Tamalpais. The Coastal Miwok Native Americans revered Mt. Tam as a spiritual center, and you'll be hard-pressed not to feel it yourself as you wander the forested slopes. With more than 50 miles of trails, Mt. Tam is now home to explorers of a different sort, hiking and biking around the forested canyons and up to the 2,571-ft. summit. The **summit** can be reached by car (look for the turnoff opposite Pantoll station); the gates are open dawn–dusk, and the view of the ocean and Marin's golden hillsides and lakes should not be missed.

A good starting point for your exploration is **Pantoll Ranger Station** (tel. 415/388–2070), where you can buy a $1 topographic trail map. Mountain-biking is big here, and the map distinguishes the fire trails (where biking is allowed) from the walking trails (where biking nets you a fat $100-plus fine). One beautiful and strenuous hike, the 2-mile **Steep Ravine Trail,** takes you down a series of ladders from Pantoll to the Steep Ravine cabins (*see below*). Parking is $5 in the Pantoll parking lot, but you can park for free anywhere along the road—just make sure you are completely outside the white sideline. The place is packed on weekends, so you'll have trouble parking if you're not there before noon.

➢ **WHERE TO SLEEP** • You can camp at one of Pantoll's 15 walk-in sites ($14) or at its hike-and-bike site ($3 per person), or arrange for a site at the more primitive **Steep Ravine** campground and cabins off the coast highway. Steep Ravine's six walk-in campsites go for $9 per night, and the cabins (for up to five people), with indoor wood stove and outdoor barbecue, go for $30 per night. If you can deal with a pit toilet, this place is absolutely unbeatable—just you and a few other guests sharing almost the entire dramatic coast as far as the eye can see. Unfortunately, Steep Ravine is not an unknown gem, and the cabins book up well in advance. Reservations for Pantoll and Steep Ravine can be made through MISTIX (tel. 800/444–PARK).

# Stinson Beach

Six treacherous miles north of Muir Beach on Highway 1 lies Stinson Beach, one of northern California's most popular coastal towns. It's loaded with rickety wooden houses and friendly general stores, and its 3-mile-long beach has a beach-bum and barbecue appeal that's hard to find north of Santa Cruz. Despite Stinson's isolated location, chilly waters, and the threat of sharks, hordes of surfers and sun worshipers descend upon this town of 1,200. Even if you're not planning to surf or swim, the 20-minute (10-mile) drive from Muir Woods to Stinson, past towering cliffs and jagged granite peaks, is incredible. Traffic can be a problem on summer weekends, but there are plenty of scenic overlooks along the way to cushion the blow of bumper-to-bumper traffic.

The **Livewater Surfshop** (3450 Hwy. 1, tel. 415/868–0333) rents body boards ($8 a day), wet suits ($10 a day), and surfboards ($25 a day) year-round. If you're hungry, stop off at the **Parkside Café** (43 Arenal St., tel. 415/868–1272), with good burgers at the cheapest prices in town ($5–$6). Turn west at the stop sign on Highway 1 and you'll run right into it.

For a different slice of nature, walk down to **Red Rocks Beach,** where extremely low tides reveal caves containing natural hot springs. Be prepared—the locals are likely to be protective of their turf and entirely naked. Even when the caves are concealed by water, the beach is peopled by nudists. Leave your inhibitions in the car and bring some strong sunscreen. To get here, drive ¾ mile south of Stinson Beach and park in the big gravel lot you'll see on the right (it's often full on sunny weekends), then look for the path leading down to the beach.

**WHERE TO SLEEP** Stinson Beach is full of nauseatingly quaint bed-and-breakfasts that cost upwards of $90 a night. Instead, head to the **Stinson Beach Motel** (3416 Hwy. 1, tel. 415/868–1712), which has inviting doubles with private bath starting at $50. The nearest camping is at Steep Ravine or at Pantoll on Mt. Tamalpais (*see above*).

# Bolinas

Bolinas works hard to avoid notice. The town lies at the end of an unmarked road running west from Highway 1 (the first left you can make after circling the estuary). Every time the state tries to post street signs and mileage markers, the raffish residents tear them down. If you breeze into town to wander Main Street and do some shopping, you'll feel barely tolerated by the locals who loathe the idea of tacky, Sausalito-style development. You might brave the cold stares to witness the town's **Fourth of July** festivities, which have included outrageous parades and a tug-of-war with Stinson Beach (the loser ends up in the muddy mouth of the estuary between the two towns).

*One local described Bolinas as the "zen-purity, earth-magnet, long-hair, free-to-do-what-you-want place to be, man," but a walk past the town's million-dollar homes makes you wonder how much residents really champion the ideals of the '60s.*

Despite the elitism, you'll still find a few VW buses and bearded hippies strumming their guitars on street corners. The **Bolinas People's Store** (14 Wharf Rd., tel. 415/868–1433) is famous for its fresh, high-quality local produce, grown by the same sweaty hippies who once gave the town so much of its character. The only nightlife in town is **Smiley's Schooner Saloon** (41 Wharf Rd., tel. 415/868–1311), ostensibly the oldest continually operated saloon in California. Huddled around its pool table and jukebox are an odd combination of suit-and-tie professional and tie-dyed alternative fringe. For a bite to eat, go next door to the **Bolinas Bay Bakery and Café** (20 Wharf Rd., tel. 415/868–0211), which offers fresh baked goods, pasta salads, and pizza. Many items feature locally grown organic ingredients.

# Point Reyes National Seashore

With its lush grazing land and rambling farms, Point Reyes could easily pass for the Scottish Highlands or western Ireland—minus the pubs. And exploring the Point Reyes National Seashore—a 66,500-acre mosaic of marshes, ferocious cliffs, and undisturbed beaches—you'll feel a lot farther than 30 miles away from San Francisco. Even though it's isolated, Point Reyes, a hammerhead-shaped peninsula jutting out 10 miles into the ocean, is a manageable day trip from San Francisco, about 1½ hours each way. There are hundreds of hiking trails on the peninsula and, if you want to spend the night, four backpackers' campgrounds and an excellent hostel. Crowds are a problem on summer weekends, but otherwise it's generally deserted—an ideal escape for nature lovers and misanthropes alike. The peninsula erupts with wildflowers from mid-February through July; and though winter sees a lot of rain, that's when the rivers and ponds teem with life and the gray whales migrate south.

Twelve miles north of Bolinas on Highway 1, past the block-long town of Olema, look for a sign marking the turnoff for Point Reyes at the end of the block of stores, and head for the **Bear Valley Visitor Center** (tel. 415/663–1092). This is the best place to begin your exploration; you can sign up for ranger-led interpretive hikes or get trail maps and camping permits. A short walk away, look for the replica of a typical Coastal Miwok village, built on the ruins of a 400-year-old Miwok farming settlement. Also nearby is the **Bear Valley Trail,** a lightly traveled, 4-mile hike through the woods and down to a secluded beach. If you can't make it out to Point Reyes Lighthouse, the trail offers a good overview of the peninsula.

Two miles farther, Bear Valley Road (which turns into Sir Francis Drake Boulevard) passes through the quiet town of **Inverness.** Coming across this town's Czech restaurants and architecture, with its oddly colored, intricately carved wooden houses, can be disorienting after miles of uncluttered coast, but the town's Eastern European flavor is definitely real. In 1935, after a freighter ran aground in San Francisco Bay, a number of its Czech deckhands jumped ship and ended up here. Ever since, dozens of Czech families have settled in Inverness, bringing their culture and their cuisine.

A quarter-mile north of windswept **Drake's Beach,** west of Inverness at the end of Sir Francis Drake Boulevard, a sign directs you to the **Point Reyes Lighthouse** (tel. 415/669–1534), 6 miles to the west. It's open Thursday–Monday 10–4:30, though closed during particularly windy weather, and admission is free. From the small parking lot, a steep trail leads down to the lighthouse, and a dozen or so trails traverse the surrounding cliffs. The hike to **Chimney Rock,** ¾ mile away, is one of the most scenic; look for the trailhead in the parking lot.

**COMING AND GOING** From San Francisco, take U.S. 101 north and cross the Golden Gate Bridge. If speed is more important than scenery, exit at Sir Francis Drake Boulevard and follow it 21 miles to the coast. Eventually, you'll end up 2 miles north of Olema on Highway 1. Otherwise, take the Stinson Beach/Highway 1 exit and enjoy the curvy, 30-mile scenic drive along the coast. For bus information, *see* Coming and Going, in Marin County, *above.*

**WHERE TO SLEEP** Dozens of B&Bs line Highway 1 near Point Reyes, but you'll pay anywhere from $85 to $120 for a night in one of these excessively charming cottages. There are a few hotels in the area, but they, too, charge over $70 a night.

A much better option is the **Point Reyes AYH-Hostel,** 8 miles west of the Bear Valley Visitor Center, popular with foreign travelers and locals alike. The two common rooms have wood-burning stoves and loads of reading material. Dorm beds cost $10 per night ($12 for nonmembers). Reservations are advised; if you want them to hold a bed, either call and use a Visa or MasterCard, or mail a check. Golden Gate Transit (*see* Coming and Going, in Marin County, *above*) stops at the visitor center, but you'll have to hitch or walk the remaining 8 miles to the hostel. *Box 247, Point Reyes Station 94956, tel. 415/663–8811. From Hwy. 1, left (west) in Olema on Bear Valley Rd. 1 block beyond stop sign; 1½ mi farther, left at LIGHTHOUSE/BEACHES/HOSTEL sign, left after 6 mi on Crossroads Rd. 44 beds. Curfew 10 PM, lockout 9:30–4:30. Reception open 7:30–9:30 and 4:30–9:30. Kitchen, linen rental.*

➢ **CAMPING** • To reserve one of Point Reyes' backpackers-only campsites up to a month in advance in Point Reyes, call the visitor information center (tel. 415/663–1092); trails lead from here to the campgrounds. Located in isolated wilderness areas, all sites have picnic tables and pit toilets, but none has running water or allows fires, so bring plenty of supplies, a camp stove, and warm clothing.

**Coast Camp** is a 3-mile hike from the youth hostel parking lot (*see above*) or a 9-mile trek from the visitor center, but you'll sleep within a stone's throw of the ocean at any of the 15 sites. People tend to avoid **Glenn Camp** because it's 5 miles from the nearest road. Surrounded by trees in a quiet valley, its 12 sites feel thoroughly apart from the reek of civilization. The 16 sites at **Sky Camp** are the most popular. You'd have to hike a steep 2½ miles from the visitor center, but the ranger can direct you to a pullout up the road that's a gentler 1-mile hike. The campground is perched on a small mountain ridge with outstanding views of the peninsula and seashore. **Wildcat Camp,** a 6½-mile hike from the nearest road, is accessible only to the rugged, and its 12 sites are scattered in a dense thicket, so privacy is never a problem.

Six miles east of Point Reyes on Sir Francis Drake Boulevard, **Samuel P. Taylor State Park** (tel. 415/488–9897) has 60 sites that go for $14 per night (hike/bike $3 per person, day use $5). They feature—blessing of all blessings—hot showers (50¢ for 5 minutes). Reservations can be made through MISTIX (tel. 800/444–PARK); during summer, even weekdays get booked up. If you do get in, you're in for a treat of the redwood variety. Think about taking the hike up to Barnaby Peak (4–5 hrs round-trip). Golden Gate Transit Bus 65 stops at the park on weekends and holidays.

**FOOD** There aren't too many places to eat inside the Point Reyes National Seashore, so stock up in San Francisco or at the **Bovine Bakery** (Hwy. 1, 2 mi north of Olema, tel. 415/663–9420). They have excellent, reasonably priced sandwiches, pastries, and breads—the perfect makings for a picnic. The most popular picnic stop, however, is Inverness's **Perry's Delicatessen** (12301 Sir Francis Drake Blvd., near Vallejo Ave., tel. 415/663–1491). For less than $6 you can brown-bag one of their shrimp sandwiches or take some pasta salad to go.

# The Wine Country

**The Wine Country is only 50 miles northeast** of San Francisco, an easy and highly recommended day trip if you have a car. You don't have to be a wine connoisseur to enjoy a visit to this region—even philistines appreciate the rustic beauty of the area and the opportunity to get a free buzz. Many of the wineries will pour you glass after glass of free samples. Choose carefully, though: A number of Napa Valley wineries charge a $2 or $3 tasting fee, which can add up if you're making the rounds. In some places, you may have to take a tour or watch a film before you can get to the tasting; but luckily, the tours are usually interesting (especially in the smaller wineries).

*Remember that it doesn't always work to just drop in at a winery, especially if you want to take a tour. At some of the smaller places, you may need an appointment.*

Most vineyards are concentrated in the Napa and Sonoma valleys, but the Wine Country actually stretches north through Santa Rosa into Lake and Mendocino counties. Vintners have been making wine here for well over 100 years, but it was only in 1976, when a cabernet sauvignon from Stag's Leap won a blind taste test in Paris, that Californians began boasting and people all over the world began buying. Since then, production has skyrocketed: 25 years ago there were only about 25 wineries; now there are more than 200.

Napa Valley has the greatest number, but its wineries are also the most expensive and pretentious. Once upon a time, visitors were greeted with open arms—and flowing bottles—by jolly

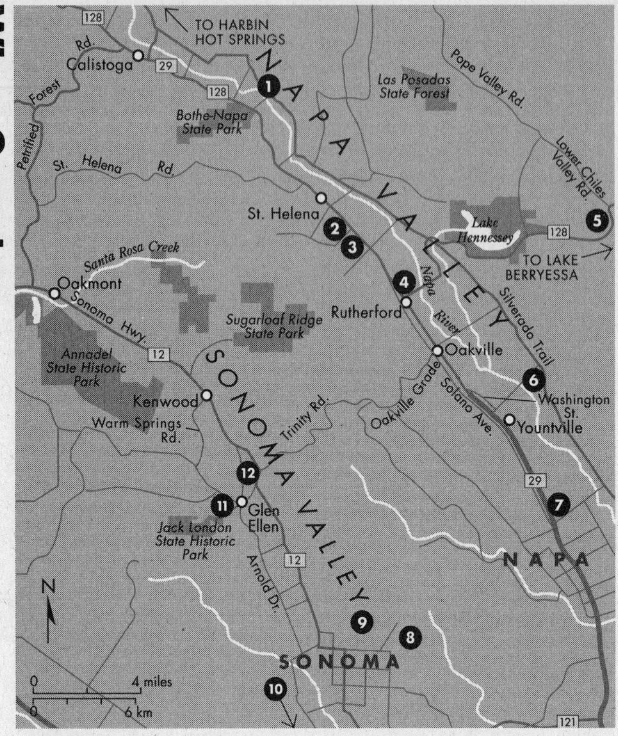


**Wineries ●**
Beaulieu Vineyards, **4**
Benzinger, **11**
Buena Vista, **8**
Cline Cellars, **10**
Nichelini, **5**
Prager Port Works, **2**
Ravenswood, **9**
S. Anderson, **6**
Sutter Home Winery, **3**
Trefethen Vineyards, **7**
Wellington, **12**
Wermuth, **1**

vintners thankful for even a trickle of business. These days, you'll have to search out Napa's tiniest wineries to get this kind of reception. A better option for budget travelers is to make a beeline for Sonoma Valley, which draws fewer tourists and is home to a greater share of rustic, family-owned and -operated vineyards. In both valleys, the farther you stray from the main drag, the better off you'll be.

If you need a break from the wineries, you can luxuriate in the hot springs, mud baths, and mineral baths of Calistoga, loiter in the lovely Spanish mission and old adobes of Sonoma, or browse through the small museums devoted to former residents Jack London and Robert Louis Stevenson, both of whom wrote about the area. Be forewarned, though: An overnight stay can take a monster-size bite out of your budget. Lodging tends to be more expensive than in San Francisco, and food is pricey as well. You can survive cheaply by eating at roadside produce stands, drinking free wine, and sleeping in a state park. Otherwise, expect to pay through the nose.

## BASICS

**VISITOR INFORMATION** Before you go (or once you arrive), you may want to call the **Napa Chamber of Commerce** (1556 1st St., tel. 707/226–7455), open weekdays 9–5, which can help you organize your trip and provide you with more maps than you'll ever need. The **Sonoma Valley Visitors' Bureau** (453 1st St. E, Sonoma, tel. 707/996–1090), open weekdays 9–7 and weekends until 6, offers friendly advice on what to see and do in the "other" valley. Additionally, most wineries carry the *California Visitor's Review,* a free weekly that has maps and winery information.

**WHEN TO GO** During the autumn harvest season you'll see some real action in the wine cellars. In both spring and fall, wildflowers bloom amid the endless rows of manicured vines. Try to avoid the Wine Country in summer, when the dry, dusty region becomes even drier and dustier, and the crowds can be suffocating.

**COMING AND GOING** If you do go to the Wine Country in summer, stay off gridlocked Highway 29 as much as possible and explore the less crowded and more scenic **Silverado Trail,** which runs parallel to Highway 29 a mile to the east.

➢ **BY CAR** • Though traffic is heavy, the best way to reach the Wine Country is by car. From San Francisco, take **U.S. 101** north over the Golden Gate Bridge and connect with **Highway 37** east near Ignacio. From here take **Highway 121** north to **Highway 12** north for Sonoma, or follow Highway 121 as it curves east toward **Highway 29** for Napa. If you're only visiting Napa or are coming from the East Bay, it's quicker to take **I–80** north and exit to Highway 37 west in Vallejo, which joins up with Highway 29 north to Napa. Traffic is heaviest on weekends and during commute hours, but even at the worst times it shouldn't take more than two hours.

➢ **BY BUS** • **Golden Gate Transit** (tel. 415/923–2000 or 707/541–2000) provides bus service from San Francisco and Marin County to towns throughout Sonoma County. Bus 90 goes from San Francisco to Sonoma (1½ hrs, $4.50) two or three times a day. **Greyhound** has service from San Francisco's Transbay Terminal once daily to Napa (2½ hrs, $15 one-way) and Middletown (4¼ hrs, $17 one-way), twice daily to Sonoma (3–4 hrs, change in Vallejo, $15 one-way). Tickets are usually cheaper if you buy seven days in advance.

**GETTING AROUND** Quaint and tempting as the **Napa Valley Wine Train** (1275 McKinstry St., Napa, tel. 707/253–2111) may sound, it's more of a restaurant than a means of transportation—no stopping for a taste of the grape. If you're still interested, $24 buys you a joyride to St. Helena and back. Some people tour the Napa Valley by balloon, but this extravagance costs upwards of $150 per person.

➢ **BY CAR** • For the 26-mile grand tour through the Wine Country's major towns and vineyards, take **Highway 29** north from Napa to Calistoga, head west for 12 miles toward Fulton and U.S. 101 on the **Petrified Forest Trail,** drive 4 miles south on **U.S. 101** to Santa Rosa, and then take **Highway 12** south to Sonoma.

➢ **BY BUS** • **Sonoma County Transit** (tel. 707/576–7433) connects all cities in Sonoma County. Buses run daily (some until 10 PM). Fares are less than $2 to most places (ask for student and disabled discounts); buses can get you within walking distance of a few wineries. **Napa Valley Transit** (tel. 707/255–7631) travels between Napa and Yountville ($1).

➢ **BY BIKE** • Biking is perhaps the best way to see the Wine Country. Within each region, the wineries tend to be grouped close together, making them easy to see on two wheels. Bicyclists should stick to the Silverado Trail. Riding on Highway 29 means a greater risk of being run over by tipsy drivers, especially on summer weekends. **Napa Valley Cyclery** (4080 Byway E, at Salvador Ave., tel. 707/255–3380 or 800/707–BIKE), at the northern end of town, rents bikes for $6 an hour or $20 a day. They offer biking maps and tour suggestions, so squeeze as much information from them as possible before heading out.

# Sonoma Valley

The town of **Sonoma** may have recently grown into an upscale bedroom community for San Francisco commuters, but behind the trendy restaurants and chic clothing boutiques lies a rich history. It was here that Father Junipero Serra built the last and northernmost of the California missions, **Mission San Francisco Solano** (1st and Spain Sts., tel. 707/938–1519), now a museum housing a collection of 19th-century watercolors by Chris Jorgenson; the $2 admission fee is also good at Lachryma Montis and the army barracks. Just east of the mission lies grassy **Sonoma Plaza,** the epicenter of Sonoma life. Around the plaza, many adobe buildings remain from the days of Spanish and Mexican rule, including old army barracks and the restored **Toscana Hotel** (20 E. Spain St., tel. 707/938–5889). Three blocks west of the plaza lie **Sonoma State Historical Park** and **Lachryma Montis** (3rd St. W, off W. Spain St., tel. 707/938–1519), the ornate home of the last Mexican governor, General Vallejo. Admission to the grounds (open daily 10–5) is $2.

Nearby in **Glen Ellen,** north of Sonoma off Highway 12, look for the **Jack London State Historic Park.** Tired of drinking and brawling on the Oakland waterfront, London (1876–1916) came here to build his dream home, Wolf House. The house was torched by an arsonist before it was finished, but the impressive stone foundations remain, along with the architects' drawings of what the house would have looked like. A shady half-mile walk through the oak trees takes you from the Jack London Museum to his grave and the ruins of his home. *Tel. 707/ 938–5216. From Hwy. 12, take Glen Ellen turnoff and follow signs. Parking: $5. Museum open daily 10–5. Park open daily 9:30–7.*

**WHERE TO SLEEP** Beds don't come cheap in the Sonoma Valley. Your best bet is camping—otherwise, you'll probably want to make the half-hour drive to Santa Rosa for an affordable room. Even at Sonoma's least expensive motel, the **El Pueblo Motel** (896 W. Napa St., on Hwy. 12, tel. 707/996–3651 or 800/900–8844), a clean, generic double will run you a whopping $70 weekdays, $80 weekends ($58 daily in winter). They do have a great swimming pool, and the motel is close to the central square and several wineries.

Since prices are comparable, consider staying at one of Sonoma's B&Bs. **Hollyhock House** (1541 Denmark St., off 8th St. E, tel. 707/938–1809) is an old, two-story farmhouse on a quiet country road, with roosters, geese, and a flower garden worthy of Monet. The three doubles cost $80–$90 on summer weekends ($55 in winter), but you can lower the price by staying more than one weekend night or coming on a weekday. In Glen Ellen, **Jack London Lodge** (13740 Arnold Dr., at London Ranch Rd., tel. 707/938–8510) offers comfortable doubles with antique decor for $75; $55–$60 off-season. The lodge has a pool, saloon, and a decent restaurant. A small continental breakfast is included on weekends and in summer. Reservations are strongly advised, especially in summer.

➢ **CAMPING** • **Sugarloaf State Park.** Only 8 miles north of Sonoma on Highway 12, Sugarloaf has 50 campsites scattered around a large meadow (dry and uninviting in summer). There are 25 miles of trails for hiking, biking, and horseback riding. If you hike up the trail to your left as you enter the park, you're likely to see deer, especially around sunset when they come out for early evening grazing. Campsites cost $14 ($12 in winter). In summer and on weekends it's a good idea to reserve through MISTIX (tel. 800/444–PARK). *Tel. 707/833–5712. From Sonoma, Hwy. 12 north to Adobe Canyon Rd., which ends at the park. Day use fee ($5), drinking water, flush toilets.*

**FOOD** Sonoma is *the* place to get your fill of gourmet-pesto-this and roasted-goat-that. Fortunately, there are some options for those unable to lay out huge sums of cash: Put together a picnic at the **Sonoma Farmer's Market** Friday 9–noon in Depot Park. An additional market is held in the plaza Tuesday evenings from 4:30 until dusk. For the best breakfast deal in town, go to the **Feed Store Café and Bakery** (529 1st St. W. off central plaza, tel. 707/938–2122): from 7 to 11:30 AM you can get a two-egg breakfast, fruity granola, oat bran pancakes, or orange-brandy French toast for less than $5.

Head down the alley east of the plaza to lively **Murphy's Irish Pub** (464 1st St. E, tel. 707/935–0660) for homemade lamb stew served with mushy peas ($5.50) and a pint of stout ($3). For a Mexican fix, the roadside **Cocina Cha Cha Cha** (897 W. Napa St., tel. 707/996–1735) is open daily until 9 PM and serves crisp tacos with ground beef for only 99¢. Two people can easily split the enormous burrito grande, filled with the works and topped with a homemade spicy sauce ($6.75).

## The Bear Flag Republic

***For a short period in 1846, Sonoma belonged not to Mexico, Spain, or the United States, but to the lesser-known Bear Flag Republic. The Republic was the brainchild of Captain John C. Frémont and a ragtag group of Yankee trappers, who decided to resolve tensions between the Mexican government and non-Mexican immigrants by throwing the Mexican commander in prison and creating their own country. The republic evaporated a few months later when the U.S. Navy arrived, but the bear remains on the California state flag.***

For an excellent sit-down meal, trek out to the one-street town of Glen Ellen, where you'll find the **Sonoma Mountain Grill** (13690 Arnold Dr., tel. 707/938–2370), open Monday and Wednesday–Friday 11–9, weekends 9–9. The fresh fish special, with a heaping salad, vegetables, and rice, is the most expensive thing on the menu ($12–$14), but it's well worth it; with an appetizer, it could feed two.

**WINERIES** Sonoma Valley is home to some 30 wineries and 6,000 acres of vineyards. It was here that California began its upstart drive to compete with old-world wineries, when Count Agoston Haraszthy planted the first European vines in 1857. You can easily spend a leisurely day driving up Highway 12 through the 17-mile-long valley, stopping to sip a little wine, learn a little history, have a picnic, and laze around in the sun.

**Benziger.** You're encouraged to roam the beautiful grounds, enjoy the fragrant rose gardens, picnic in any spot you choose, and indulge in many a free taster. Guided tram tours are available, though not required for tasting. Hooray. *1883 London Ranch Rd., Glen Ellen, tel. 707/935–3000. From Hwy. 12, take Glen Ellen (Arnold Dr.) turnoff and follow signs for Jack London State Park. Open daily 10–5. Wheelchair access.*

**Buena Vista.** Count Agoston Haraszthy, the "father of California wine," brought thousands of European grapevine cuttings to the United States in the mid-1800s to start this winery. The guided tour (2 PM) covers his colorful life as well as the history of the vineyard. Free tastings happen in the impressive, ivy-covered main building—definitely try the pinot noir and the Carneros Estate chardonnay. *18000 Old Winery Rd., Sonoma, tel. 800/926–1266. From plaza, E. Napa St. east, turn left on Old Winery Rd. Open July–Sept., daily 10:30–5; Oct.–June, daily 10:30–4:30.*

**Cline Cellars.** You drive through grapevines and roses on the way to the tasting room, in an old farmhouse dating from the mid-1800s. At the tasting bar, you can try four of the six wines, as well as homemade mustards, for free. You can picnic on the porch beside one of six ponds fed by neighboring hot springs. *24737 Arnold Dr. (Hwy. 121), Sonoma, tel. 707/935–4310. Btw Hwys. 12 and 37. Open daily 10–6. Wheelchair access.*

**Ravenswood.** This small stone winery in the Sonoma hills has a relaxed, intimate feel. Better yet, the jovial staff does not seem to care how many wines you taste. Their motto is *Nulla Vinum Flaccidum* (No Wimpy Wines) and their merlots and zinfandels are definitely worth writing home about. Bring a picnic to savor on the terrace, or try their barbecued chicken or ribs with bread, coleslaw, and potato salad ($6–$7.25), available on summer weekends only. *18701 Gehricke Rd., Sonoma, tel. 707/938–1960. From plaza, take Spain St. east, left on 4th St. E, right onto Lovall Valley Rd., left on Gehricke Rd. Open daily 10–4:30. Wheelchair access.*

**Wellington.** Run by a father-son team, this new and tiny winery is still obscure enough to escape the tourist hordes. The down-to-earth tasting room has a small terrace and a view of the Sonoma Mountains. Tastings of their delicious wines are unlimited—be sure to try the Estate Chardonnay, a combination of fruit and clove flavors that tastes like liquid Christmas. *11600 Dunbar Rd., Glen Ellen, tel. 707/939–0708. From Sonoma, Hwy. 12 north 7 mi, exit left at Dunbar Rd. Open Thurs.–Mon. noon–5. Wheelchair access.*

# Napa Valley

While Sonoma is cheaper and more welcoming, it's Napa Valley, about a 20-minute drive east of Sonoma on Highway 121, that lures most visitors to the Wine Country. When the traffic backs up for miles on Highway 29, it's clear that Napa Valley has become one of the Bay Area's biggest tourist attractions north of Fisherman's Wharf. The scenery is still beautiful and the wine (in some cases) still free, but the Napa Valley is losing some of its old-time charm with each trampling tourist.

The quiet town of **St. Helena,** 16 miles north of Napa on Highway 29, may be fraught with tourists, but the grocery stores and pharmacies (and a no-frills rural appeal) make this a good rest stop on your way up the valley. St. Helena is also home to the **Silverado Museum** (1490 Library Ln., off Adams St., tel. 707/963–3002), which houses a collection of photographs, letters, and manuscripts of former Napa Valley resident Robert Louis Stevenson. The museum is open Tuesday–Sunday noon–4 PM.

Wine may take center stage in the Napa Valley, but a fair share of hedonists come here solely for a peaceful soak in the valley's hot springs and mud baths, most located in or near **Calistoga.** Though you'd perhaps hesitate to throw yourself in a roadside ditch and roll around in the muck, folks in the Wine Country believe that mud baths and sulfur springs heal all manner of ills. Poverty is not one of them: You'll pay a pretty penny for a day of pampering. On the bright side, you can spend the night at any of several resorts for a decent price, and get free access to mineral pools and Jacuzzis.

**WHERE TO SLEEP** Although some of the most expensive lodging in the Wine Country is here in the posh Napa Valley, budget travelers can survive by camping or checking into one of Napa's lower-end motels. Always call at least three weeks in advance in summer.

➢ **NAPA** • The **Silverado Motel** (500 Silverado Trail, tel. 707/253–0892) offers tacky but cleanish rooms for $38 weekdays, $55 weekends ($38 daily in winter). The **Napa Valley Budget Inn** (3380 Solano Ave., off Hwy. 29, tel. 707/257–6111) has bland but clean doubles starting at $52 ($76 on Friday or Saturday). The swimming pool is perfect after a long day at the wineries, many of which are within biking distance. At the **Wine Valley Lodge** (200 S. Coombs St., Napa, tel. 707/224–7911), comfy doubles cost $50 on weekdays, $75 on weekends, and one room is wheelchair accessible. Amenities include a pool and a barbecue.

➢ **CALISTOGA** • Pleasure-seekers planning to hit both the wineries and the hot springs should consider staying in Calistoga. If you want to stay on the main drag, the **Calistoga Inn** (1250 Lincoln Ave., tel. 707/942–4101) has clean, simple bed-and-breakfast rooms with shared baths and full-size beds for $49 ($60 Fri.–Sat.). If you can't spend the night without a color TV, try the **Holiday House** (3514 Hwy. 128, tel. 707/942–6174), 3 miles north of Calistoga; watch for the white picket fence. From the outside it looks like you're pulling into a friend's house; the three rooms ($50), though, are strictly Motel 6.

➢ **CAMPING** • Camping is the only budget option in Napa. Unfortunately, there isn't any public transportation to the campgrounds; unless you have a car, you'll have to hitchhike, walk, or bike back to civilization. If you're getting desperate and don't mind driving, head 20 miles east from Rutherford on Highway 128 to Lake Berryessa. The lake is divided into seven campgrounds, including **Pleasure Cove** (tel. 707/966–2172) and **Spanish Flat** (tel. 707/966–7700). Altogether you'll find 225 tent sites near the water for around $16 a night. Crowds aren't usually a problem, but the area around the lake is barren, dusty, and very hot during the summer—a place to crash cheaply for a night, not to discover nature. Reservations are advised for summer weekends.

**Bothe-Napa State Park.** This is the Wine Country's most attractive campground, situated in the Napa foothills amid redwoods, madrone, and tan oaks only 5 miles north of St. Helena and its wineries. The sites are reasonably private, and the park is one of the few with a swimming pool ($3 separate fee), much used on hot summer days. The fee is $14 (half-price disabled camping pass available through MISTIX) and reservations are suggested in summer, especially on weekends. For reservations call MISTIX (tel. 800/444–PARK). *Tel. 707/942– 4575. From St. Helena, north on Hwy. 29. 48 sites. No cooking facilities, day use fee ($5), flush toilets, hot showers. Wheelchair access.*

**FOOD** The best way to eat well in gourmet-friendly Napa without losing your shirt is to stock up at one of the area's makeshift farmers' markets (*see below*), where you'll find a bevy of fresh produce at reasonable prices. If you're spending the day in Calistoga, cruise down to **Calistoga Drive-In Taquería** (1207 Foothill Blvd., tel. 707/942–0543), at the west end of Lincoln Avenue. A veggie burrito here runs $3.50, and the tortillas and chips are great. The restaurant is wheelchair accessible.

Fine California cuisine—with fair portions for the price—can be had at the **Calistoga Inn** (1250 Lincoln Ave., tel. 707/942–4101). Try the grilled lemon-chicken sausage with sauerkraut, roasted potatoes, and coleslaw ($7.25), or the award-winning ales and lagers—only $2 during happy hour (weekdays 4–5:30). **The Diner** (6476 Washington St., Yountville, tel. 707/944–2626) serves huge plates of American or Mexican food for lunch and dinner, or specialty eggs and pancakes for breakfast. Most meals are in the $7–$10 range, but portions are generous (couples should consider splitting an appetizer and a main course). **Green Valley Café and Trattoria** (1310 Main St., St. Helena, tel. 707/963–7088) ain't cheap, but it is remarkably unpretentious, offering tasty pasta entrées like pesto pasta with green beans and potatoes ($9.25) or smoked salmon tortellini ($10.75). Locals come for the $5 sandwiches (lunch only), served in a casual, diner-like atmosphere.

➢ **MARKETS AND DELICATESSENS** • **Napa Valley Farmers' Market.** This market is held on Tuesdays in Napa and Fridays in St. Helena, with fruits and veggies, cheese, eggs, honey, dressings, cut flowers, baked goods, and countless other edibles. *Napa: West St., btw 1st and Pearl Sts., tel. 707/963–7343. Just west of Cinedome Theatre, which has free parking. Open May–Oct., Tues. 7:30–noon. St. Helena: Old Railroad Depot, tel. 707/963–7343. East on Adams St. off Hwy. 29, left at stop sign, and 1 block up on right. Open May–Oct., Fri. 7:30–11:30 AM.*

**Pometta's Deli.** This place is famous for its barbecued chicken platters ($7), but you can also get box lunches to go ($9.50–$12.50). Especially good is the vegetarian sandwich (about $4), stuffed with avocado, provolone, zucchini, and jalapeños. The restaurant has indoor and outdoor seating and—wonder of wonders—tournament horseshoe pits (free). *Hwy. 29, at Oakville Grade in Oakville, tel. 707/944–2365. Open daily 9–5.*

**WINERIES** With literally hundreds of wineries crammed into the 35-mile-long Napa Valley, it's difficult to decide which ones to visit. Some, like **Sutter Home Winery** (277 Hwy. 29, St. Helena, tel. 707/963–3104), right on the main drag, are packed with drunken revelers, while others, like **Trefethen Vineyards** (1160 Oak Knoll Ave., Napa, tel. 707/255–7700), draw a sedate crowd able to hold forth about a wine's bouquet and tannins. If you're irked by the idea of paying a $3 tasting fee, you'll have to choose carefully.

**Beaulieu Vineyards.** Affectionately known as "BV," Beaulieu has supplied wine to President Eisenhower and Queen Elizabeth, among others. Yet this large winery is far from snooty. The staff greets you with a glass of wine at the door of the tasting room and encourages you to indulge in free samples. If you like dessert wine, be sure to taste the lovely muscat. Free half-

## How to Taste like a Master

***If you want to pass yourself off as a wine aficionado (as opposed to a freeloading swiller), you'll need to know some rules of tasting. First of all, move from light wines to dark, so as not to "clutter your palate." Begin by vigorously swirling an ounce of wine in your glass—put your hand over the glass to hold in the aromas (as well as the wine, if you're new to the swirling business). Raise the glass to your nose and inhale deeply. In young wines, you smell only the grapes (for example, the smell of the pinot noir grape might remind you of black cherries); with aging, the wine becomes more complex, emitting a whole "bouquet" of aromas (in pinot, that can include violets, vanilla, a spicy pepper, or even leather). Next, take a sip—you're encouraged to slurp, because air helps you taste the wine. Swish the wine around in your mouth to pick up the more subtle flavors. Before downing the rest of your glass, notice the aftertaste (or "finish"), and then decide what you think. ("It's a cheeky little wine, reminiscent of running naked through verdant pastures.")***

*In the 1920s, European countries signed a treaty agreeing that only the French could use the name champagne. Those were Prohibition days in the United States, and since we were convinced we'd never again produce alcohol, we never signed the treaty. Thus, Americans can still legally make champagne, but many vintners play it safe and call their products "sparkling wines."*

hour tours cover the winemaking process and BV's 100-year history. *1960 Hwy. 29, Rutherford, tel. 707/963–2411. Open daily 10–5. Wheelchair access.*

**Nichelini.** Napa's oldest family-owned winery (since 1890) lies 11 miles east of Rutherford and is worth every minute of the beautiful drive. Outside, under the shade of walnut trees and next to an old Roman grape press (which looks like a giant garlic press), you can sample several wines for free. Picnic to the strains of traditional Italian music on a hill overlooking the countryside. *Hwy. 128, St. Helena, tel. 707/963–0717 or 800/WE-TASTE. Open May–Oct., weekends 10–6; Nov.–Apr., weekends 10–5.*

**Prager Port Works.** Owner Jim Prager and the family dog Eno (short for "Enology") know the meaning of hospitality. This rustic winery doesn't even produce enough cases a year to be classified as "small." ("That makes us 'tiny,'" quips Jim.) Tastings run $3, but the fee can be applied toward a bottle of Prager's special port ($35), available only at the winery. The homey garden provides a quiet break from the Highway 29 crowds. *1281 Lewelling Ln., St. Helena, tel. 707/963–PORT or 800/969–PORT. On Hwy. 29, next to Sutter Home. Open daily 10:30–4:30, or whenever the last person leaves. Wheelchair access.*

**S. Anderson.** Tours are given twice daily, frequently by John Anderson, son of the late Stan (as in "S.") Anderson. He does a wonderful job guiding you through his vineyards and candlelit stone wine caves, modeled after those in the Champagne region of France. The caves hold over 400,000 bottles of sparkling wine, awaiting their "turn" (champagne bottles are turned by hand in a labor-intensive process that removes the yeast). The tour, with tasting, costs $3, but it's more than worth it. Plan for over an hour—John doesn't need much prompting to extend the visit. *1473 Yountville Crossroad, Yountville, tel. 707/944–8642 or 800/4–BUBBLY. From Hwy. 29 in Yountville, take Madison exit and follow signs for Yountville Crossroad. Open daily 10–5; tours at 10:30 and 2:30.*

**Wermuth.** Vintner Ralph Wermuth—philosopher, mad scientist, stand-up comedian—presides over the tiny tasting room and is more entertaining than a barrel of monkeys. Free tastings of Gamay are accompanied by chocolate chips to "bring out the flavor," while the dry colombard is paired with that gourmet standby, Cheez-Its. *3942 Silverado Trail, Calistoga, tel. 707/942–5924. From Hwy. 29 north, Hwy. 128 east to Silverado Trail; continue north past Bale Ln. and look for sign on right. Open Tues.–Sun. 11–5.*

**HOT SPRINGS** The majority of the Napa Valley's mud and mineral baths are located in the offbeat town of Calistoga, at the northern end of the valley. The town's bubbling mineral spring became a spa in 1859, when entrepreneur Sam Brannan slurred together the word California with the name of New York's Saratoga Springs resort; Calistoga has been attracting health seekers ever since. Unfortunately, most visitors are loaded and willing to pay up the wazoo to get their wazoo steam-wrapped. Prices at the Calistoga spas are uniformly steep, varying by only a couple of dollars. Be sure to pick up 10%-off coupons at the **Calistoga Chamber of Commerce** (1458 Lincoln Ave., tel. 707/942–6333), open Monday–Saturday 10–5, Sunday 10–4.

A cheaper option is open-air bathing at rustic retreats like Harbin Hot Springs or White Sulphur Springs. You won't get to play human mud pie at the outdoor spas, but you can bathe in natural springs and hike through rolling grounds far from the buzz of urbanity. These resorts offer many of the same amenities as the Calistoga spas, and you can get an affordable room for the night to boot. If you opt for one of the indoor spas, call ahead for a reservation. Most accept walk-ins, but nothing is more stressful than being turned away from the massage you've been aching for.

**Golden Haven Hot Springs.** A favorite with hetero couples, Golden Haven is the only Calistoga spa to offer private co-ed mud baths (sorry lovebirds, there's still an attendant). The full treatment (mud bath, mineral Jacuzzi, blanket wrap, and 30-minute massage) will run you $64 per person. If you're too relaxed to make it past the front door, you can crash in one of their rooms for $59 ($49 Sept.–June), which includes use of the swimming pool and hot mineral pool. *1713 Lake St., Calistoga, tel. 707/942–6793. From Lincoln Ave. east, left on Stevenson St., right on Lake St. Open daily 9–9.*

*They say "clothing optional," but you're going to feel pretty out of place if you wear anything but a smile into the pools at Harbin Hot Springs. If you have the cash and the curiosity, get "watsu-ed"—an underwater shiatsu massage that's a house specialty.*

**Harbin Hot Springs.** Forty minutes north of Calistoga, this 1,200-acre community is run by the Heart Consciousness Church, a group that advocates holistic health and spiritual renewal. The retreat, popular with gay men, has three natural mineral pools, varying in temperature from tepid to *very* hot, and a cold, spring-fed "plunge" pool, all open 24 hours. There's also an acclaimed massage school, whose graduates would be happy to show you their stuff ($46 per hour, $60 for 90 minutes). If you bring your own food, you're welcome to use the communal, vegetarian kitchen. Otherwise, a vegetarian restaurant serves breakfast (under $8) and dinner ($8–$12). Beds in the ramshackle dorm rooms start at $23 ($35 on weekends), and you have to provide your own sheets or sleeping bag. Private rooms with shared bath are $60 ($90 on weekends). There are somewhat shabby campsites along the creek and in nearby meadows ($14 per person, $23 Fri.–Sat., $17 Sun.). To use the pools, you must pay $5 for a one-month membership, plus an additional day-use fee ($12 Mon.–Thurs., $17 Fri.–Sun.). *Tel. 707/987–2477 or 800/622–2477 (Northern California only). Hwy. 29 north to Middletown, turn left at junction for Hwy. 175, right on Barnes St.; go 1½ mi to Harbin Springs Rd. and turn left. Rides can be arranged for those taking Greyhound.*

**Lincoln Avenue Spa.** Their Body Mud Treatment ($38) is the ideal alternative for those squeamish about wallowing in mud someone else has already wallowed in: You get your choice of mud (herbal, sea, or mint) slathered over your body, a relaxing nap on the steam table, and a soothing facial mask. *1339 Lincoln Ave., Calistoga, tel. 707/942–5296. Open daily 9–9.*

**White Sulphur Springs.** If you're planning to stay the night in Napa Valley, this St. Helena resort is a bargain. For $65 you get access to 300 acres of land, plenty of hiking and biking trails, a Jacuzzi, a natural mineral bath; *and* you get a decent room for the night, either in the rustic, dormitory-style carriage house or in the inn, where each room has a half-bath. It's a day and night of decadence for the price of an hour or two at some of Calistoga's spas. An even cheaper option is to stop by during the day 9 AM–6 PM and use the facilities for $15. If you only want to be there for an hour or two, the management will usually knock down the price—just ask. *3100 White Sulphur Springs Rd., St. Helena, tel. 707/963–8588. From Hwy. 29 north, turn left on Spring St. in St. Helena and go 2.8 mi. Note: Do NOT take Sulphur Springs Rd. from Hwy. 29.*

**OUTDOOR ACTIVITIES** If you're spending the day in Calistoga, pay a visit to **Robert Louis Stevenson State Park** off Highway 29, 9 miles northeast of Calistoga. Here you can hike to the bunkhouse of the Silverado Mine, where the impoverished author honeymooned with his wife, Fanny Osbourne, in the summer of 1880. The stay inspired Stevenson's *The Silverado Squatters.* The park's 3,000 acres on top of Mt. St. Helena are largely undeveloped; picnicking is permitted but overnight camping is not.

**Skyline Wilderness Park.** Perhaps the best way to experience the beauty of the Napa Valley is to get out and hike, preferably on Skyline's 2½-mile Lake Marie Trail, which runs along a shady creek and past overgrown orchards and ruined stone dairies. Swimming in Lake Marie isn't allowed, but you can try your luck fishing for bluegill and bass. *2201 Imola Ave, tel. 707/252–0481. Open Mon.–Thurs. 9–8, Fri.–Sun. 8–8; shorter hrs in winter.*

# THE NORTH COAST 4

By Michael Rozendal, with Sharron Wood

**Between San Francisco and the Oregon border lie some 400 miles of rugged** coastline, presided over by legions of enormous, mystical trees. The inhabitants of small towns dotting the coast are divided between those who live for the trees, and those who live by cutting them down. In either case, the North Coast is defined by the giant redwoods, and the trip through Northern California is well worth it if only to pass some time among these ancient beings—which often measure 60 feet around the base and rise to a height of several hundred feet. There's a magical quality to the light in a redwood forest. John Steinbeck described it well when he said that a day in the shadow of the towering redwoods consists of a prolonged dawn followed by a prolonged dusk, with little straight daylight in between.

*Some of these trees are older than Christianity, and you'll find more than a few locals who'd look to the trees for spirituality before they'd ever look to a Bible.*

The camping in this part of the state is excellent, especially around Patrick's Point near **Arcata,** in the **Jedediah Smith Redwoods,** north of **Crescent City,** and in the isolated Northern Coast Ranges. But it's also worth hanging around the towns, getting to know the people and lifestyles up here. There's something about the lack of high-rise buildings and the proximity of uncharted wilderness that brings out the friendly side in most folks. You can explore the coast on either Highway 1 or U.S. 101, which separate north of San Francisco to become the two main roads through the region. **Highway 1** winds right along the jagged coastline and is one of the most dramatic drives in the United States. North of Westport, Highway 1 leaves the Pacific and heads east to join U.S. 101. The land for the next 73 miles is so rugged that the state has never extended the highway along the coast. This isolated region, known as the **Lost Coast,** is accessible only by a series of winding, treacherous roads that meander through virgin (never logged) redwood forests and open grazing lands overlooking black-sand beaches.

**U.S. 101,** which parallels Highway 1 before joining it at Leggett, is a faster route that takes you through turn-of-the-century farming towns, vineyards, and the impressive **Avenue of the Giants** near Garberville. Here you can touch the Dyerville Giant, the fourth-largest redwood in the world, which stretches across the fern-filled forest floor (it fell in 1990). Farther north on U.S. 101, Arcata is home to Humboldt State University. It's like a mini-Berkeley, with tofu burritos, repertory film houses, and plenty of live music. This is a great launching point for adventures north into the stunning **Redwood National Forest** or east into the thickly forested wilderness and numerous pristine river valleys of the Northern Coast Ranges.

The **Redwood Empire Association** (785 Market St., 15th Floor, San Francisco 94103, tel. 415/543–8334), open weekdays 9–5, has a wealth of info on attractions, activities, and

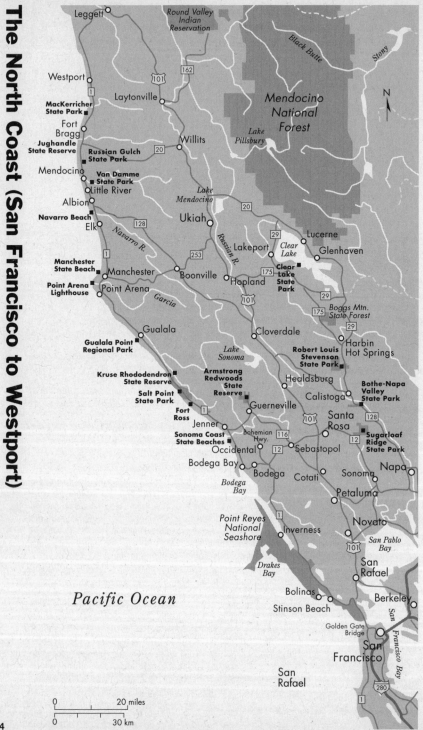


Leggett
Round Valley Indian Reservation
Black Butte
Stony
162
101
Westport
1
Laytonville
Mendocino National Forest
N
MacKerricher State Park
Fort Bragg
Lake Pillsbury
Jughandle State Reserve
Russian Gulch State Park
20
Willits
Mendocino
Van Damme State Park
Little River
Lake Mendocino
Albion
20
Navarro Beach
Ukiah
Elk
128
Navarro R.
Russian R.
29
Lucerne
Lakeport
Clear Lake
Glenhaven
1
253
Manchester State Beach
Manchester
Boonville
Hopland
175
Clear Lake State Park
Point Arena Lighthouse
Point Arena
Garcia
101
29
175
Boggs Mtn. State Forest
29
Gualala
Cloverdale
Gualala Point Regional Park
Harbin Hot Springs
Lake Sonoma
Robert Louis Stevenson State Park
Kruse Rhododendron State Reserve
Armstrong Redwoods State Reserve
Healdsburg
Salt Point State Park
Bothe-Napa Valley State Park
Calistoga
Fort Ross
1
Guerneville
101
Santa Rosa
128
Jenner
Sonoma Coast State Beaches
Bohemian Hwy.
116
Sugarloaf Ridge State Park
12
Occidental
12
Sebastopol
Bodega Bay
Bodega
Cotati
Sonoma
Napa
Bodega Bay
Petaluma
1
Point Reyes National Seashore
Inverness
Novato
San Pablo Bay
101
Drakes Bay
San Rafael
Pacific Ocean
Bolinas
Stinson Beach
Berkeley
San Francisco Bay
Golden Gate Bridge
San Francisco
San Rafael
280
1
0
20 miles
0
30 km

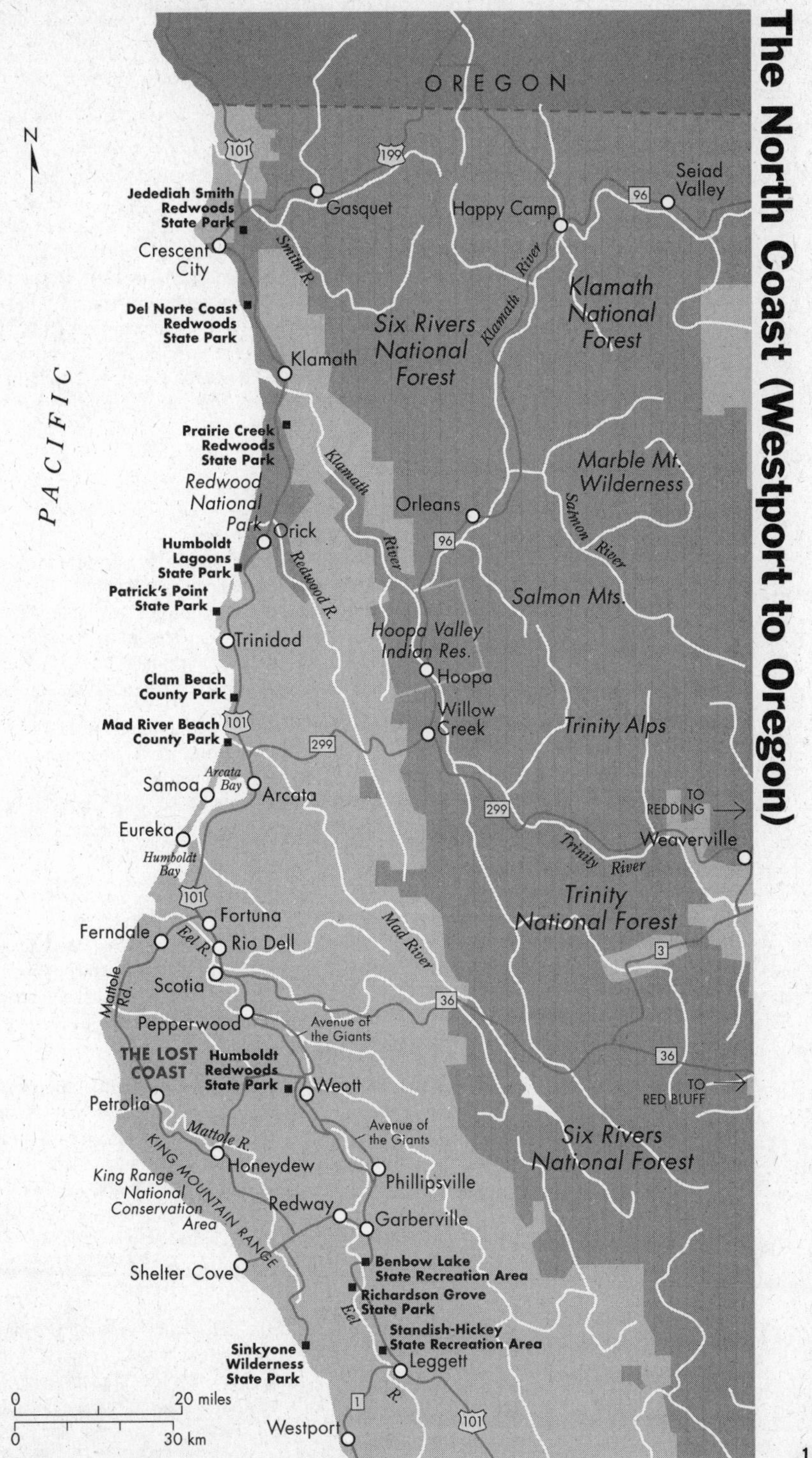

The North Coast (Westport to Oregon)
OREGON
PACIFIC
N
101
199
96
Seiad Valley
Gasquet
Happy Camp
Jedediah Smith Redwoods State Park
Crescent City
Smith R.
Klamath River
Klamath National Forest
Del Norte Coast Redwoods State Park
Six Rivers National Forest
Klamath
Prairie Creek Redwoods State Park
Klamath River
Marble Mt. Wilderness
Salmon River
Redwood National Park
Orleans
Orick
Humboldt Lagoons State Park
Redwood R.
Patrick's Point State Park
Salmon Mts.
Hoopa Valley Indian Res.
Trinidad
Hoopa
Clam Beach County Park
Willow Creek
Mad River Beach County Park
299
Trinity Alps
Arcata Bay
Samoa
Arcata
TO REDDING
Eureka
Weaverville
Trinity River
Humboldt Bay
Trinity National Forest
Fortuna
Ferndale
Eel R.
Rio Dell
Mad River
3
Scotia
Mattole Rd.
36
Pepperwood
Avenue of the Giants
THE LOST COAST
Humboldt Redwoods State Park
Weott
TO RED BLUFF
Petrolia
Avenue of the Giants
Mattole R.
Six Rivers National Forest
Honeydew
KING MOUNTAIN RANGE
King Range National Conservation Area
Phillipsville
Redway
Garberville
Shelter Cove
Benbow Lake State Recreation Area
Richardson Grove State Park
Eel R.
Standish-Hickey State Recreation Area
Sinkyone Wilderness State Park
Leggett
0
20 miles
1
0
30 km
Westport

regional history. Their 48-page booklet is $3 if you send away for it, but free if you stop by the office, located near the Powell Street BART station in San Francisco.

## WHEN TO GO

Along the North Coast, you should abandon your preconceptions about traditional seasons. While the words winter, spring, summer, and fall have some value dividing the year into 3-month periods, there are only two true seasons here—rainy and dry. Showers are usually concentrated December–February, though you should come prepared for rain November–April. If you're willing to brave the chance of rain to see the annual whale migrations, January–March can be a prime time to travel. The coast's proximity to the Pacific Ocean keeps temperatures in the cool to comfortable range year-round. This can be exhilarating on clear days in spring and fall—or deeply depressing in summer, when you may wish you'd brought ear muffs to the fog-enshrouded beach instead of a swim suit. One of the best times to see the coast is late spring, when the rolling hills are still a lush green dotted with colorful wildflowers and the summer waves of fog and tourists have yet to begin. If you're heading inland, keep in mind that temperature variations are usually more extreme: summers are seasonally hot and winter lows sometimes fall below freezing.

## COMING AND GOING

**BY CAR** The best way to explore the North Coast is by car, particularly if you want to stray from Highway 1 and U.S. 101. Much of the region is mountainous and remote, and the distances you'll cover are tremendous. Make sure you have decent tires, and be prepared for rock slides, hairpin turns, road work, and intimidating logging trucks. On summer weekends, the tourists are out in force along Highway 1—you can spend up to 90 minutes traveling 20 miles on the narrow, difficult roads. On U.S. 101, traffic is usually not too bad north of Santa Rosa.

**BY BUS** Amtrak sticks to inland I–5, so your only choice for public transit is the bus. **Greyhound** (tel. 800/231–2222) runs along U.S. 101 from San Francisco all the way to Seattle. The trip from San Francisco to Eureka, the North Coast's most important transport hub, costs $41 (about 8 hrs one-way). Buses arrive at the **Eureka depot** (1603 4th St., at Q St., tel. 707/442–0370), open weekdays 8:30–1:30 and 2:30–5:30, Saturday 9–noon. From here, buses depart for Crescent City (2 hrs one-way, $16). The driver will stop at towns along the way if you specify your destination when buying the ticket.

A livelier option is **Green Tortoise** (tel. 415/956–7500 or 800/867–8647; *see box* Funky Deals on Wheels, in Chapter 1), which offers a six-day Northern California Parks Loop for $199, plus $51 for food. The loop departs from San Francisco three times each summer, and covers Lassen Volcanic National Park and Mt. Shasta (*see* Chapter 5), Crater Lake in southern Oregon, and Redwood National and State Parks (*see below*). Itineraries are flexible, so you may get them to swing by other parks and forests along the way.

**BY BIKE** Nearly all of U.S. 101 from Ukiah to the Oregon border is bikeable, though you'll have to share the road with RVs, passenger cars, and logging trucks. During summer, a tailwind makes it easy to pedal south through Humboldt County on U.S. 101, and you'll find a parade of other riders in Day-Glo colors out to enjoy the amazing scenery. The rainy season here can last up to 8 months, so plan a summer trip unless you don't mind getting very, very wet. Don't even think of riding on the cliff-hugging Highway 1 unless you have lots of experience. The best source of info for biking the North Coast is the free "District 1 Bicycle Touring Guide," available from **CalTrans** (Box 3700, 1656 Union St., Eureka 95502, tel. 707/445–6600). The pamphlet contains info on routes, campgrounds, bike shops, and attractions.

**HITCHING** Hitching is always risky business in California, but along the North Coast you'll still find some of the "Hail fellow, well met" spirit that made hitchhiking the hippies' favorite form of transportation. You might have a hard time getting a ride out of San Francisco or Santa Rosa, but it gets easier once you leave the urban areas behind. Have fun, but don't be lulled into a situation you'll regret by friendly overtures or good sinsimilla. The best places to get picked up are small towns near the entrances to Highway 1 or U.S. 101. You can also check the ride boards at Sonoma State University in Santa Rosa or Humboldt State University and the Arcata co-op in Arcata.



# Coastal Highway 1

**After it crosses the Golden Gate Bridge, Highway 1** follows the rugged Northern California coast for close to 200 miles before turning inland and joining U.S. 101 in **Leggett.** The dramatic shoreline here has nothing to do with popular conceptions of sunny California beaches. Instead you'll find natural beauty of the stark and chilling variety—the kind that Alfred Hitchcock captured in *The Birds,* filmed in **Bodega Bay.** The twisting highway and foggy weather, especially in July and August, can make your drive positively eerie. (Early spring and late fall are the best times to catch a clear day.) Some of the most beautiful spits of sand lie at the base of jagged cliffs nearly impossible to descend, and the forest extends right to the shore in many places.

*Locals use inland temperatures as an inverted sign of the weather on the coast—if it's really hot in Willits or Ukiah, odds are it'll be foggy at the beach.*

The road passes through a number of carefully maintained, photogenic towns before reaching **Fort Bragg,** pretty much the only place on the coast that doesn't look like storybook-land. A feasible, if long, day trip is to set out from San Francisco in the early morning, drive up the coast for a late lunch in upscale **Mendocino,** and return to the Bay Area in the evening on U.S. 101. The drive on Highway 1 from San Francisco all the way to Leggett takes a minimum of 7 hours (longer in foggy weather). Take your time, though. The forested hillsides and rough cliffs along the road make for great hiking, and a night spent camping in any of the coastal state parks could be the most memorable of your trip.

Of course, you can't exactly hide this kind of beauty from the more than three million people living in the San Francisco Bay Area. The slow-moving traffic over windswept switchbacks on summer weekends testifies to the area's popularity with everyone from vacationing yuppies to RV trekkers. Nearly all the coastal campgrounds are booked up in advance in summer, and the fragile natural surroundings are endangered by overuse—that's why beach access is often restricted to certain hours. Even greater changes have been wrought by wealthy urbanites from the Bay Area, who have developed some of the best-situated property. Highway 1 has been tamed by city dollars, or so it seems in comparison to the pristine Lost Coast farther north. Still, if you're in a position to splurge on a night in a rustic inn or bed-and-breakfast (some charge upwards of $90 per night), this is one of the best places in California to do it; and it's likely that the desk clerk will know about karma and bodywork, too.

Driving is by far the easiest way to see Highway 1. On the other hand, the **Mendocino Transit Authority** (tel. 707/884–3723 or 800/696–4MTA) provides daily bus service from Point Arena to Santa Rosa (3½ hrs one-way, $6.25); weekday routes service Gualala–Ukiah, Gualala–Fort Bragg, and Mendocino–Santa Rosa. Call ahead for schedule info; they only run one bus a day in each direction. The **Fort Bragg and Mendocino Coast Chamber of Commerce** (332 N. Main St., Fort Bragg, tel. 707/961–6300 or 800/726–2780), open Monday–Saturday 9–5, has maps, brochures, and lodging referrals for the Mendocino County coast from Gualala to Sinkyone Wilderness State Park.

## Bodega Bay

With its rusty schooners, crooked streets, and aging wooden houses, Bodega Bay at first sight looks like a crusty old harbor town, the kind of place that should be full of the smells and sights of the sea. So it is, to a certain extent, but instead of wizened fishermen and old saloons, you're more likely to find real estate agents, overpriced seafood, and developers doing their best to transform this natural harbor into a high-class resort. Luckily, developers can't take credit for the abundant natural beauty. A walk out on the headland leads through tall grasses—and wildflowers in spring and summer—to rocky cliffs; from the top, you can sometimes see migrating whales in the spring and fall. Sturdy shoes will enable you to climb down the rocks along the ocean trail to check out the tide pools. If you're in town at the end of April, try to catch the **Bodega Bay Fisherman's Festival** (tel. 707/875–3422), where clergymen stand starboard blessing the fishing fleet, and a crafts fair and boat parade take place on the harbor.

Sportfishing is popular in Bodega Bay, and plenty of charter services vie to take you out on the water. Several also offer whale-watching trips from January to April. For a friendly charter try the **Boat House** (1445 Hwy. 1, tel. 707/875–3495), which runs daily outings for salmon ($45) and rock cod ($40), plus whale-watching trips ($25) on weekends from late December to mid-April. If surfing's more your thing, talk to Bob Miller at **North Coast Surf Plus** (913 Hwy. 1, tel. 707/875–3944; open daily 10–6). He can report on current wave conditions, set you up with a wet suit and surfboard or body board ($13 each per day), or a sailboard ($25 per day). He also offers three-hour lessons, with all-day board and wet suit included ($75 for one person, $120 for two). For those who just want to hang out by the ocean, **South Salmon Creek State Beach** is 5 miles north of town on Highway 1 (turn left on Bean St. just south of Salmon Creek Bridge). Like many area beaches, this one forbids swimming. For more info on the area and a small local map, stop by the **Bodega Bay Visitor Information Center** (850 Hwy. 1, tel. 707/875–3422), open Sunday–Thursday 10–4, Friday–Saturday 10–5.

*Longing to howl at the moon? Gather with the locals for a drum party (bring your own drum) under every full moon at South Salmon Creek State Beach.*

**WHERE TO SLEEP** The cheapest room in town is at the **Bodega Harbor Inn** (1345 Bodega Ave., east of Hwy. 1 at Boat House, tel. 707/875–3594), which overlooks the harbor. Prices start at $48 ($43 in winter) for a simple cabaña-style room trimmed in blue and white. As with everywhere on the coast, book at least a week ahead in summer, or pray for a cancellation. One room is wheelchair accessible.

➢ **CAMPING** • Cold winds whip the coast at night, even in summer, so bring extra blankets and use the driftwood on the beach to build a fire—where it's legal. For more info on campgrounds and day-use beaches in Sonoma County, visit the kiosk at the entrance to Bodega Dunes Campground. If the campgrounds below are full, look for spaces at **Willow Creek** and **Pomo Canyon campgrounds** (*see* Sonoma Coast State Beaches, in Near Bodega Bay, *below*).

**Bodega Dunes Campground.** Part of the Sonoma Coast State Beaches (*see* Near Bodega Bay, *below*), Bodega Dunes has 98 sites ($14 summer, $12 winter) in open stretches of sand and grass. You have to look around to find a secluded spot behind the dunes or in patches of trees, but the beach is nearby. Reserve through MISTIX (tel. 800/444–PARK). *Hwy. 1, 1½ mi north of Bodega Bay, tel. 707/875–3483. Day use $5. Flush toilets, running water, showers.*

**Doran Park.** This county park on a narrow spit of sand at the southern end of Bodega Bay offers sites ($14) on barren beaches with little privacy. For tent camping, try to get the sites lettered A–J, right on the beach. If these are full, try **Shell Campground,** with sites in the dunes and scrub brush. You can fish from the jetty at the end of the park. *Off Hwy. 1 just south of Bodega Bay Lodge, tel. 707/875–3540. 138 sites. Day use $3. Running water, showers, toilets. No reservations.*

**FOOD** If you want good value for your money, skip Lucas Wharf and the Tides, the most touristy spots in town. Locals prefer the restaurants in nearby Occidental (*see* Near Guerneville, in U.S. 101 to Leggett, *below*). Otherwise, a good bet is the **Lucas Wharf Deli** (595 Hwy. 1, tel. 707/875–3562; open daily 10–7), a cheaper arm of the popular restaurant. Highlights here are the crab cioppino (a tomato-based stew), which goes for $5 a pint during crab season (Nov.–June), and the tasty sandwich made with seasonal smoked salmon ($6). The **Sandpiper** (1410 Bay Flat Rd., tel. 707/875–2278) has a bowl of clam chowder that's pricey at $4.50, but if a Bodega Bay fisherman is willing to shell out for it you can trust it's good. Splurge for the Bodega Bay Melt ($10), an open-face crab and shrimp sandwich with melted cheese. It's open daily 7 AM–8 PM (Fri.–Sat. until 8:30 PM).

## NEAR BODEGA BAY

**SONOMA COAST STATE BEACHES** On the drive along Highway 1 to Jenner (*see below*), windswept cliffs lead down to some of California's finest beaches, collectively administered by the California Department of Parks and Recreation (tel. 707/865–2391). Although some rules here may seem rigid (no dogs, gates closed at sunset, et cetera), they're needed to keep the popular beaches in a more or less natural state. You can camp at **Wright's Beach** (6 mi north of Bodega Dunes, tel. 707/875–3483), which has 30 sites ($19) near the ocean, but it's usually overrun by trailers and families. Sites 0–9, which face the sea, fill up fast, so reserve early through MISTIX (tel. 800/444–PARK). On those rare days when the fog lifts, you'll see great sunsets from camp. If you stop at only one beach, make it beautiful, empty **Goat Rock State Beach,** at the northern end of the recreation area. Entrance is free, dogs are allowed, and toilets are provided—what more could you want?

About 5 miles north of Goat Rock Beach are two prime environmental (i.e., walk-in with no water) campsites along the mouth of the Russian River ($9 a night for either). **Willow Creek** has 11 sites set in meadows against a backdrop of alder and willow thickets. **Pomo Canyon** has 22 incredibly green, secluded sites among thickets of berry bushes and stands of redwoods. Both campgrounds are first come, first served and relatively unknown so they may have spots available even on crowded weekends; bring your own wood and don't expect a shower. To reach the campgrounds from Highway 1, turn left onto Willow Creek Road just south of the Russian River bridge; after 1 mile, go left at the small tent sign. Pomo Canyon lies 2 miles further down Willow Creek Road and has two wheelchair-accessible sites.

**JENNER** In the tiny town of Jenner, 10 miles north of Bodega Bay, the Russian River empties into the Pacific, often under the close observation of a colony of seals. Jenner is the start of one of the most dramatic stretches of Highway 1, a series of dizzying switchbacks that takes you up and down coastal mountains and to the brink of some awe-inspiring cliffs. On foggy days, petrified passengers stare steadily ahead, hoping they can somehow help the driver keep the car between the lines. If you need a place to crash, try the **Lazy River Motel** (10624 Hwy. 1, tel. 707/865–1948), where rooms start at $40; you might be able to cut a deal if you're really scraping bottom (though it was in the process of changing hands at press time). For food, the nearby **Sizzling Tandoor** (9960 Hwy. 1, at Willow Creek Rd., tel. 707/865–0625) on the river has wonderful Indian food. Vegetarian entrées are particularly good: Try the saag paneer dinner ($9), a delicate spinach curry over cubes of homemade cheese, served with nan bread and basmati rice. It's open daily 11:30–3 and 5–9:30.

### Friend or Anemone?

***If you've never gone tide pooling before, there are a few things you should know. Tide pools are located in the "intertidal zone," the area that's exposed at low tide; you may want to check a local newspaper or pick up a tide table at a Chamber of Commerce to find the best time of day to go. The rocks around the pools are usually jagged and slippery, so wear tennis shoes, hiking boots, or dive booties. Go ahead and touch most of what you see, but don't detach any creatures from the rocks and keep an eye out for incoming waves. Look for the tiny sea palms—a delicate form of kelp—that inhabit the pools along with starfish and crabs. Don't stick your hands in dark crevices; you might get pinched by a crab or stabbed by a sea urchin quill. If you're into slimy things, anemones are the most fun to touch. Underwater they resemble translucent rubber flowers; out of the water, they close up and are easily squashed—watch your step. MacKerricher State Park (see Near Fort Bragg, below) is a great spot for tide pooling, though almost any ranger can direct you to choice pools all along the coast.***

**SALT POINT STATE PARK** The 6,000-acre Salt Point State Park (tel. 707/847–3221) lies 6½ miles north of **Ft. Ross,** a historical park with a sizable, reconstructed Russian fort as its centerpiece. Salt Point itself is an ocean lover's delight, full of white-sand coves, tidal pools, sandstone cliffs, and headlands. A good place to camp is **Woodside,** 8 miles north of Ft. Ross on the east side of Highway 1, with secluded sites scattered around a dense forest. If you can carry your stuff ¼ mile, the solitude of the 20 walk-in sites ($12) is worth the extra effort. The 70 drive-in sites go for $14 and the 19 hike/bike sites are $3 per person.

Across the highway from Woodside lies **Gerstle Cove,** the start of the **Salt Point Trail,** which meanders for 3 miles north along the coast to **Stump Beach.** Here intrepid swimmers (that is, people as cold-blooded as dinosaurs) enjoy the clear blue waters. The beach is also accessible by car from Highway 1. A good place to explore tide pools is **Fisk Mill Cove,** 2 miles north of Stump Beach on Highway 1, where you'll also find wonderful picnic spots—and toilets. An easy hike leads down the cliffs to the beach from the north parking area. If you park on the highway you can avoid the $3 day-use fee. However, when you pay a day-use fee at any state park, the pass is good for all state park fee areas; Ft. Ross can be a bargain if you stop at Fisk Mill Cove first.

**KRUSE RHODODENDRON STATE RESERVE** Just north of Fisk Mill Cove, on the inland side of Highway 1, you'll see the small entrance sign for Kruse Rhododendron State Reserve. You can wander on the 5-mile **Phillips Gulch Trail**—which winds through second-growth redwood, fir, and oak—or save yourself the effort and take the pleasant 10-minute stroll along the **Rhododendron Loop Trail** instead. Both trails start from the unpaved parking lot near the entrance to the reserve. From May through early June, the 14-foot-tall rhododendron plants are in lavish pink bloom. They're not quite as impressive as their height would suggest, but the bright pink flowers make your hike more colorful. The lazy can drive the almost 2-mile length of the unpaved, one-lane entrance road, which runs through the reserve.

# Gualala, Point Arena, and Elk

At the southern border of Mendocino County, winding Highway 1 calms down in time to enter the 1-block town of Gualala (pronounced wah-LA-la), overlooking the ocean. Gualala is much frequented by coastal residents for its two well-stocked supermarkets (both on Highway 1) and several restaurants. At **Gualala Point** (*see* Camping, *below*), you'll find an isolated beach ($2 day-use fee) at the end of an easy walk through the scrub.

Sixteen miles north of Gualala is the tiny fishing village of Point Arena, a good place for a break from driving. If you're in town between 11 and 3:30 (2:30 in winter), take a $2.50 tour of the 115-foot **Point Arena Lighthouse** (tel. 707/882–2777), the second lighthouse to stand at this location. (The first, built in 1870, did its job efficiently until it was knocked down by the 1906 earthquake.) The tour requires you to climb the equivalent of a six-story building, but on a sunny day you'll be rewarded by an excellent view of the ocean and the point.

Fourteen miles north of Point Arena, you'll pass through the blink-and-miss-it town of Elk, with its old grocery store and cute, modern pub **Bridget Dolan's** (5910 Hwy. 1, tel. 707/877–1820; open daily 5–10), which has local microbrews and Guinness on tap. Here Highway 1 begins a series of hair-raising ascents and descents. Just before you reach the Navarro River Bridge near Albion, 26 miles north of Gualala, you'll find the turnoff for **Navarro Beach** (*see* Camping, *below*) at the end of Navarro Bluff Road. The **Navarro River,** south of Albion, is good for relaxed, do-it-yourself kayaking and canoeing. Access to the mouth of the river is easy and free, but you have to bring your own equipment.

**WHERE TO SLEEP** If you can't camp, try one of the 18 rooms at the inviting **Gualala Hotel** (39301 Hwy. 1, tel. 707/884–3441), where doubles go for $44, ($55 with private bath). With its wood-burning heater, old books and puzzles scattered around the parlor, and first-floor saloon, it's a good place to pretend you just stepped off the stagecoach. For the traditional motel atmosphere and a few more amenities (cable TV, in-room telephone, private bath), your best bet is the **Sea Shell Inn** (135 Main St., Point Arena, tel. 707/882–2000 or 800/982–

4298). Prices for the 32 comfortable rooms start at $40; make reservations if you plan to travel during the busy summer weekends.

➢ **CAMPING** • **Gualala Point Regional Park** (just south of Gualala, tel. 707/785–2377), the northernmost extension of the Sonoma County Regional Parks, has 18 drive-in and 6 walk-in sites ($14, $3 hike/bike) set in a beautiful redwood forest along the peaceful Gualala River. Running water, flush toilets, and full showers crown this prime, rarely full campground. At **Manchester State Beach** (Hwy. 1, 5 mi north of Point Arena at KOA turnoff, tel. 707/882–2463), you can camp in a grassy park studded with sand dunes and wind-twisted Monterey cypress trees. The huge driftwood logs along the beach help make up for the primitive facilities—the 42 drive-in and 9 hike-in sites (both $9) have running water and pit toilets, but no showers. **Navarro Beach** (no phone) used to be free but now charges $5 to camp on the ocean in one of 10 windy, exposed, and extremely small sites. You can legally burn driftwood here to keep warm, and there are pit toilets, but no running water. To reach Navarro from Highway 1, turn west on Navarro Bluff Road, just south of Navarro River Bridge. None of these campgrounds takes reservations.

**FOOD** **Bookends.** A café, bookstore, and gathering spot for residents, this Point Arena culinary haven has great breakfast burritos with eggs or tofu ($3 and up) and homemade muffins and scones ($1). For lunch, pick up a sandwich with all your favorite fixings or a burrito ($4 and up). *215 Main St., Point Arena, tel. 707/882–2287. Open daily 7 AM–9 PM (Fri.–Sat. until 11 PM). Wheelchair access.*

**Gualala Hotel.** From the steamed vegetable plate ($8.50) to the veal scaloppini ($15), all entrées come with salad, soup, and ice cream for dessert. For breakfast, try the hearty homemade corned beef hash, served with two eggs and potatoes ($6). *39301 Hwy. 1, Gualala, tel. 707/884–3441. Open daily 7–2 and 5–9.*

# Mendocino

Perched on a bluff above the ocean an hour north of Gualala, Mendocino looks like the perfect American seaside town, picturesque enough to be the backdrop for *Murder, She Wrote* (it is). Unfortunately, it's also prime territory for hordes of tourists eager to poke around weathered wooden houses, small art galleries, and well-packed general stores. If you want a slice of real Mendocino life, visit in winter, fall, or spring, when the tourists aren't around and the town feels like it must have 30 years ago.

Mendocino has been a popular artists' retreat since the 1950s and '60s, though today the galleries and crafts shops import many of their wares from outside the area. An exception is the **Artists Co-Op** (45270 Main St., upstairs in Sussex Building, tel. 707/937–2217), a laid-back gallery that exclusively features Mendocino artists. It's open daily 10–5, and artists are often on hand to chat.

Most of the action centers around **Main Street,** which runs along the edge of town toward the ocean. At the far end of the street, stop by **Mendocino Jams and Preserves** (440 Main St., tel. 707/937–1037) for free samples of their excellent jams, chutneys, and mustards, all made in small batches at the store. The **Mendocino Ice Cream Company** (45090 Main St., tel. 707/937–5884) sells quarter-pound scoops in waffle cones ($2.50).

*Mendocino is the only town on the North Coast where you'll have trouble parking or have to wait in line for a table at a restaurant.*

If Main Street's too crowded, wander off into **Mendocino Headlands State Park,** the grassy expanse that lies between town and the ocean. December–April, California gray whales pass the coast on their annual migration from the Arctic Ocean and Bering Sea to Baja California. Not only can you spot some of the whales as they pass, but you can learn about them at free nature talks led by park rangers; times for the talks are posted at the **visitor center** (Ford House Museum, btw Kasten and Lansing Sts., tel. 707/937–5397), open daily 11–4. You can hear more about our large mammalian friends at MacKerricher State Park (*see* Near Fort Bragg, *below*) on weekends at 10 AM in season, or any day during the Mendocino/Fort Bragg **Whale Celebration Weeks** in March. For more info, contact the Department of Parks and Recreation, Mendocino District Headquarters (tel. 707/937–5804), 11 miles north of Mendocino.

**WHERE TO SLEEP** Mendocino is filled with cute, pricey bed-and-breakfasts; camping is the only real budget option. If you're determined to stay in town, try to get the one $40 room with a toilet and sink but no shower ($65 with full bath) at the **Sea Gull Inn** (44594 Albion St., tel. 707/937–5204). If you don't mind being 2 miles south of town, the **Fools Rush Inn** (7533 Hwy. 1, tel. 707/937–5339) offers great deals ($49–$59 for two midweek in fall or spring) on their nine well-stocked cabins with kitchen, fireplace, and cable TV. Rates rise in the summer and peak weekends.

➢ **CAMPING** • The 30 sites ($14) at secluded **Russian Gulch State Park** (2 mi north of Mendocino on Hwy. 1, tel. 707/937–5804, 800/444–PARK for reservations) offer tree-lined privacy and coin-operated hot showers (one site is wheelchair-accessible). From the campground you can take the 6-mile Falls Loop Trail past the 36-foot Russian Gulch Falls and around back to camp. The park is closed mid-October–early April. **Van Damme State Park** (*see* Near Mendocino, *below*) is another convenient option for camping close to Mendocino.

**FOOD** Gourmet delis abound in Mendocino, though it is possible to put together a meal for under $5. At the **Mendocino Bakery and Café** (10485 Lansing St., tel. 707/937–0836), try the turkey pot pie ($5) or the spinach lasagna ($4.25); it's open daily 8–8 in summer, until 6 PM in winter. **Mendo Burgers** (tel. 707/937–1111), on the bakery's back patio, has beef, turkey, or veggie burgers ($4) 11–7 daily. **Lu's Kitchen** (45013 Ukiah St., 707/937–4939; open daily 11:30–5) will satisfy your organic vegetarian cravings handsomely with tasty burritos ($4.25) or the hybrid Mediterranean quesadilla ($6). If you want to buy your own supplies, stop downtown at **Corners of the Mouth Natural Foods** (45015 Ukiah St., tel. 707/937–5345), with a good selection of organic produce, juices, prepared foods, and baked goods.

**Mendocino Café.** If you can afford it, splurge on a meal here. The hands-down favorite is the giant Thai burrito, filled with house-smoked meats or tofu, stir-fried veggies, brown rice, and peanut sauce ($7.50). The burrito costs more at dinner, so come early. If you crave seafood, try the innovative fresh fish specials, served with brown rice and vegetables ($15). *10451 Lansing St., tel. 707/937–2422. Open weekdays 11–4 and 5–9, weekends 10–4 and 5–9.*

**OUTDOOR ACTIVITIES** The Mendocino area is great for biking, while **Big River,** bordering Mendocino to the south, provides 8 miles of first-rate canoeing. To get outfitted for either sport, stop in at **Catch a Canoe and Bicycles, Too!** (44850 Comptche-Ukiah Rd., tel. 707/937–0273 or 800/439–5245; open daily 9:30–5); to get here go left on South Big River Road, park where the road ends, and look for it behind Stanford Inn by the Sea. They rent mountain bikes, kayaks (both $10 per hour, $30 per day), and canoes (starting at $12 per hour, $35 per day). All paddle-craft rentals include life jackets and lessons on basic technique. One option for biking is to start in Mendocino and bike 2 miles south on Highway 1 to Van Damme State Park (*see below*) and pedal around the lower portion of the park's **Fern Canyon Trail** (where bikes are allowed). The 10-mile round-trip trek takes about 2 hours.

## NEAR MENDOCINO

**VAN DAMME STATE PARK** Van Damme State Park (tel. 707/937–5804), 2 miles south of Mendocino, has 74 drive-in campsites ($14) and 10 walk-in sites ($9), which often fill up during abalone season (Apr.–June and Aug.–Nov.) and on summer weekends. This is one of the coast's best spots for abalone diving; for info on equipment rental, *see* Outdoor Activities, in Fort Bragg, *below.* Even if you're not here to dive, you'll love the privacy of the sites in the dewy coastal forest, and you'll appreciate the coin-operated hot showers. Reserve sites through MISTIX (tel. 800/444–PARK).

The park's **visitor center** (tel. 707/937–4016) has interesting displays on ocean life and Native American history. The nearby **Pygmy Forest** comprises mile after freaky mile of wizened trees, some more than a century old, that stand only 3 or 4 feet tall. Highly acidic soil and poor drainage work to stunt the trees' growth. This is a good place for Godzilla-like special effects—

bring your camera. To reach the forest by car, turn left on Little River Airport Road ½ mile south of Van Damme State Park and continue 3½ miles to the clearly marked parking area.

# Fort Bragg

If you're almost to the point of overdosing on quaintness, Fort Bragg is a welcome change. This is just about the only "real" town on this make-believe coast. It's not romantic (the ocean is eclipsed by a steam-belching lumber mill), but people here have jobs and spend their locally earned money in working-class bars and restaurants. Appreciate it while you can—the cutesy style (and tourist traffic) of Mendocino, only 10 miles south, has recently begun to creep into Fort Bragg, resulting in a small surge of upscale eateries and a restored historic downtown.

*Fort Bragg is one of the cheapest places in California to indulge in a massage or seek holistic healing. Michelle Peters-Loville (tel. 707/964–0300) only charges $35 for a 30-minute acupressure treatment. She'll work with you on the price if you're short on cash.*

Fort Bragg is the place to stop for camping and outdoor supplies. Try **Payless** (490 S. Main St., tel. 707/964–1214) if you're shopping on the cheap, or the **Outdoor Store** (143 E. Laurel St., tel. 707/964–1407) if you want quality equipment. You'll also find reasonable motels, good and inexpensive food, and entertainment in the area bordered by Main, Oak, Franklin, and Pine streets. In tiny **Noyo Harbor,** just south of downtown Fort Bragg, you can sit on the docks and watch the fishing boats come in, unloading big plastic crates full of the day's catch. For nightlife, everyone travels 3 miles south to the tiny town of Caspar, where the **Caspar Inn** (cnr Caspar Rd. and Caspar St., west of Hwy. 1, tel. 707/964–5565) has been booking great jazz, blues, and rock bands for years. The cover charge is generally $3–$7, except on Sunday (open-mike night) when you get some serious acoustic jam sessions by local talents—for free.

For hiking, follow the signs to **Jughandle State Reserve,** about 3 miles south of Fort Bragg. The highlight here is the Ecological Staircase, a series of five wave-cut terraces created by successive ice ages and seismic activity, each 100 feet higher and 100,000 years older than the one before it.

**WHERE TO SLEEP** The cheapest motel in town is the **E. Colombi Motel** (647 Oak St., tel. 707/964–5773), 5 blocks east of Highway 1. It's a bit out of the way, but the price ($35 for two off-season, $45 on summer weekends) and large rooms make up for the location. For a more luxurious (and wheelchair-accessible) version of Motel Generic, try the **Coast Motel** (18661 Hwy. 1, ¼ mi south of Hwy. 20, tel. 707/964–2852), where rooms start at $36 ($42 in summer). You get a heated pool, cable TV, and—just in case you needed one—a fish-cleaning facility.

**Jughandle Beach Country Bed-and-Breakfast Inn.** It's a bit more money, but a much better choice only 3 miles south of Fort Bragg, next to Jughandle State Reserve. For $75 a night, you get a full gourmet breakfast, a tastefully decorated room with private bath, and owner Sue's expert advice on what to do in the area. She's willing to deal on prices midweek and in the off-season. *32980 Gibney Ln., at Hwy. 1, tel. 707/964–1415.*

**Jughandle Farm.** An even better bargain is this beautiful Victorian farmhouse (look for the small white sign) with a huge, spotless kitchen and shared bathrooms. Sleep on a foam mat or a bed for $18 ($12 students) April–September or for $15 ($10 students) October–March. You have the choice of doing a one-hour chore or paying an extra $5. There are also two cabins ($20–$22 per person, plus chore) that usually rent as doubles. *East side of Hwy. 1, south of Jughandle Beach, tel. 707/964–4630.*

**FOOD** At **Egghead's Restaurant** (326 N. Main St., tel. 707/964–5005), open daily 7 AM–2 PM, the yellow brick road leads to the "Emerald City" bathroom, and Oz memorabilia covers the walls. Try the omelets ($5–$11) or the "Wicked Witch" ($6.25), a ½-lb. spicy turkey burger with a side salad. Expect a wait on weekend mornings. For a huge basket of the best fish 'n' chips in town ($7), join the fishermen and families at **Cap'n Flints** (32250 N. Harbor Dr., in Noyo Fishing Village, tel. 707/964–9447), open daily 11–9 (Fri. and Sat. until 9:30). A great place to kick back with a steaming mocha while contemplating the cosmic implications of Highway 1 is the **Headlands Coffee House** (120 E. Laurel St., tel. 707/964–1987). This cultural center and local gathering place features live music most nights and is one of the few places in town open late (every night except Tues.). If you want to put together your own organic vittles, **Down Home Foods** (115 S. Franklin St., tel. 707/964–4661) offers a full line of supplies, fresh organic carrot juice ($2), and espressos weekdays 10–5:30, weekends 10–5.

**North Coast Brewing Company.** To accompany their regionally celebrated beer, the brewery cooks up burgers ($7–$8), sandwiches ($8), and Texas chili ($6.50), a better bet than the pricey dinner menu in the restaurant next door. During happy hour (Tues.–Fri. 4–6), a pint of beer costs only $1.75 ($2.50 otherwise). Try the medal-winning Scrimshaw Pilsner, or better yet, ask the staff to recommend a brew to match the spices in your dinner order—they are as meticulous about this issue as the finest French sommelier. Free tours of the brewing area are given Tuesday–Friday at 3:30, Saturday at 1:30 and 3:30, though beer tasting is *not* included. Live jazz happens Saturday nights. *444 N. Main St., at Pine St., tel. 707/964–BREW. Open Tues.–Fri. 4 PM–11 PM, Sat. 2 PM–11 PM.*

**Viraporn's Thai Café.** When you're itching for a break from the typical North Coast burgers-and-sandwiches diet, come to this sunny green hut, where excellent vegetarian, vegan, and meat curries go for under $6. The atmosphere is homey ("like sitting in Viraporn's living room") and the food authentic. *Cnr Chestnut and Main Sts., across from Payless Drugs, tel. 707/964–7931. Generally open daily 11:30–2:30 and 5–9:30; call ahead.*

**OUTDOOR ACTIVITIES** Surf fishing is popular at beaches up and down the coast: Marty at the **North Coast Angler** (1260 N. Main St., tel. 707/964–8931) is more than willing to give advice and rent you a rod ($5 a day). For deep-sea fishing, the **Noyo Fishing Center** (32450 N. Harbor Dr., tel. 707/964–7609; open daily 6–noon), in Noyo Harbor, provides the instruction and equipment to help you reel 'em in. The center can get you in touch with skippers who run 5-hour trips for $45.

Abalone diving is great along the coast, but you have to be around between April and November (the season is temporarily suspended in July), and only snorkeling gear (no scuba) is

## Grass Roots Brewing

***Maybe you didn't come to the North Coast for its rolling, golden hills, towering ancient redwoods, or wave-swept beaches. Maybe you came for the microbrewed beer at one of a half-dozen coastal microbreweries. Why are the region's brews so good? Well, big beer companies substitute cheaper corn and rice for malted barley, use chemical stabilizers, and heat-pasteurize their beers to prolong shelf life. Microbreweries offer fresh, unpasteurized brews straight from the source.***

***Working your way up the coast, the first stop north of the Bay Area is the Hopland Brewery (see Near Ukiah, below), where you can take your choice of four quality beers on tap. Continue on to Fort Bragg's excellent North Coast Brewing Company. Finally, skip up U.S. 101 to the Lost Coast Brewing Company (see Food, in Eureka, below) before savoring the Red Nectar Ale produced in Humboldt County (see Arcata, below). Though you can get the inside scoop on each ale from bartenders along the way, pick up a copy of "Celebrator Beer News" ($2) at one of these brew pubs for up-to-date info on microbrew trends throughout the West.***

allowed. **Russian Gulch** (*see* Mendocino, *above*) and Van Damme State Park (*see* Near Mendocino, *above*) are two of the best spots to slip into the ocean in search of abalone. **Sub-Surface Progression** (18600 Hwy. 1, 1 mi south of Fort Bragg, tel. 707/964–3793) rents complete equipment for $25 a day, as well as boogie boards and surfboards ($7.50 a day) if you'd rather catch some waves in Caspar Cove (*see* Fort Bragg intro, *above*).



## NEAR FORT BRAGG

**MACKERRICHER STATE PARK** MacKerricher lies 3½ miles north of Fort Bragg on Highway 1. The blacktop promenade fronting the beach here is good for mountain biking, though it gets rough in places. You'll find tide pools near the boardwalk, and January–April you can walk to the end of Laguna Point and watch the whales go by. The easily hiked **Coast Trail** runs parallel to the promenade along the headlands, with plenty of beach access and 9 miles of spectacular ocean views. At **Lake Cleone,** the park's freshwater lake, you can fish for trout or watch flocks of ducks and geese, who migrate in from Mono Lake each summer. Day use of the park is free; get a map showing all the attractions from the **ranger station** (tel. 707/964–9112) at the entrance, open daily 7 AM–10 PM in summer, erratically in winter.

The campground here has 141 drive-in sites ($14)—most packed close together among the coastal pines—with running water and coin-operated hot showers. The best camping, though, is at the 10 walk-in sites ($14), 50 yards from the parking lot but still fairly secluded. Reserve in summer for the drive-in campsites; the walk-ins are first-come, first-served. There's also a hike/bike site ($3) with room for about 10 people.

# U.S. 101 to Leggett

**While Highway 1 meanders along the coast** north of San Francisco, U.S. 101 takes the inland route, passing through some 100 miles of gentle, oak-covered hills and dilapidated barns before rejoining Highway 1 at Leggett. Once you're north of the Wine Country (*see* Chapter 3), California seems to unfold at a more natural pace. You leave the crowds behind, the land starts to open up—in short, you're in the country now, and lifestyles reflect that fact. This is where you start to see at least as many hunting and taxidermy shops as vegetarian menus and New Age bookstores.

The towns along U.S. 101—Santa Rosa, Cloverdale, Hopland, Willits, Leggett, Garberville—were stagecoach stops a hundred or more years ago, and they're still destinations for migrating urbanites. People with strong ties to the left and the environmental movement have been relocating here since the '60s. Their presence is widely felt, a funky, unpredictable counterpart to the traditional rural sensibility that dominates the region. To further complicate the mix, a new contingent of yuppies is entering the picture (much to the chagrin of locals).

On the way to Leggett, U.S. 101 follows the path of the Russian River, which rolls toward the sea from Lake Mendocino. The four-lane highway is a much faster option than Highway 1 for those in a hurry to get to Oregon, but drivers who stick to the main road entirely miss the most interesting spots, which usually require a short detour. A drive west on Highway 116, for example, will lead you to Guerneville, a popular gay vacation spot and a great base for mellow water sports on the lazy Russian River. To the east, via Highway 175 or 20, is the resort town of Clear Lake, an ideal spot to languish by the water and check out water skiers.

**GETTING AROUND** As with the rest of California, a car is your best bet for touring. Traffic thins out on U.S. 101 north of Santa Rosa, and gas is reasonably inexpensive. On public transportation, it can be a hassle to travel between transit districts. **Sonoma County Transit** (tel. 800/345–7433) runs buses between Sebastopol, Santa Rosa, and Guerneville. Most fares are $1–$2. To the north, the **Mendocino Transit Authority** (tel. 707/462–1422 or 800/696–4682) connects Ukiah with Willits (1 hr, $1.95) six times a day on weekdays, and once a day weekends. For more info on travel through the region, *see* Coming and Going, at beginning of chapter.

# Santa Rosa

When residents of Sonoma County (*see* the Wine Country, in Chapter 3) refer to "the city," they no longer mean San Francisco. Once a small farming community, Santa Rosa—an hour's drive north of San Francisco—has become one of California's fastest-growing suburban areas, with shopping malls, mini-marts, and housing tracts sprouting at an alarming rate. Most of old Santa Rosa was destroyed in the 1906 earthquake, but a section called **Railroad Square** (btw 3rd, 6th, Wilson, and Davis Sts.) has been preserved. Today the square is the most happening part of town, home to a battalion of cafés, restaurants, and bookstores, as well as **Railroad Park**—a pleasant spot during the day, but a potentially dangerous place after dark. Pick up a map at the **Chamber of Commerce** (637 1st St., at Santa Rosa Ave., tel. 707/545–1414), open weekdays 8:30–5, weekends 10–2.

Daytime Santa Rosa is pretty slow, peopled almost exclusively by older folks, but the pace picks up with nightfall. Check out **A'Roma Roasters and Coffee House** (95 5th St., at Wilson St., tel. 707/576–7765) for café cuisine and live jazz, folk, and classical music Wednesday–Saturday. The doors open at 7 AM (8 AM weekends) and things don't quiet down until 11 or midnight. Night owls can head to nearby Railroad Square and **Café This** (122 4th St., tel. 707/576–8126), where the decor is 100% *Clockwork Orange* meets *Pee-Wee's Big Adventure.* The cafe is open nightly 6 PM–3 AM.

**COMING AND GOING** **Greyhound** has service to Santa Rosa from San Francisco's Transbay Terminal (1½ hrs, $11 one-way). You can also get here on **Golden Gate Transit** (tel. 415/923–2000 or 707/541–2000) Bus 80, which runs hourly from San Francisco to Santa Rosa (2 hrs, $4.50) until 11 PM daily. Once you're in town, **Santa Rosa City Bus** (tel. 707/524–5306) can get you around locally for just 85¢.

**WHERE TO SLEEP** Santa Rosa can be a convenient base for day trips east to the Wine Country. **Motel 6** (3145 Cleveland Ave., tel. 707/525–9010) might be just right, with simple doubles ($38) and a pool. Those looking for something a little more stylish should head to **Hotel La Rose** (308 Wilson St., tel. 707/579–3200) on Railroad Square. Beautifully decorated rooms with antiques and a complimentary continental buffet run $65 weekdays, $75–$110 on weekends. If business is slow, you may be able to get a $10 discount.

➢ **CAMPING** • **Spring Lake Regional Park.** Though it's only a few miles from downtown Santa Rosa, the park is secluded and woodsy, with 31 campsites ($14) on a bluff overlooking Spring Lake (Site 14 has the best view). You can swim in the lagoon, row, or fish year-round. *Tel. 707/539–8092. From downtown Santa Rosa, U.S. 101 south to Hwy. 12 east, cross Summerfield Rd., go over hill, and turn left on Newanga Rd. Hot showers. Campground closed Mon.–Thurs. Labor Day–Memorial Day. Reservations advised.*

**FOOD** Santa Rosa has plenty of restaurants that offer good food at affordable prices. On 4th Street, east of the freeway, something is bound to fit your fancy. For a splurge, **Mixx** (135 4th St., at Davis St., tel. 707/573–1344) serves such delicacies as grilled Cajun prawns ($9) and crème brûlée ($5). **Omelette Express** (112 4th St., tel. 707/525–1690) keeps locals coming back with its 40 varieties of omelets, plus burgers and sandwiches ($5–$7). Split the fabulous chicken emerald curry ($10) with your honey at **California Thai** (522 7th St., at B St., tel. 707/573–1441), and you'll forget about the bland suburban-mall atmosphere.

## NEAR SANTA ROSA

**COTATI** This funky, progressive farming community 8 miles south of Santa Rosa is a popular hangout with students from nearby Sonoma State University. Come in mid-June for the **Cotati Jazz Festival** (tel. 707/523–8378; tickets $12 a day) or in August for the **Cotati Accordion Festival** (tel. 707/664–0444). For great down-home pancakes, homemade biscuits, and other breakfast and lunch staples ($3–$7), try **Mom's Boarding House** (8099 La Plaza St., at Old Redwood Hwy., tel. 707/795–3381), open daily until 2 PM. The veggie omelet ($6) is big enough for two. Enormous portions can also be had at **Rafa's** (8230 Old Redwood Hwy., tel. 707/795–7068), a low-key Mexican joint that's packed with locals. Roll up your sleeves, take a deep breath, and order the Rafa's burrito ($13.50), a four-pound monster that's not for the faint of heart.

*Cotati's Inn of the Beginning specializes in trades—used books for lattes.*

**The Inn of the Beginning,** billed as a café/pub-cum-bookstore, not only offers acoustic folk and blues music and poetry readings, but also has darts, a pool table, and a ton of history. Neil Young, Bo Diddley, and Jerry Garcia all played here between 1969 and 1982. Kick back with a pint of "Death and Taxes," a popular dark beer ($2.75), or sample the vegetarian chili ($3). Call for a schedule of events. *8201 Old Redwood Hwy., tel. 707/794–9453. Open daily 9 AM–midnight (Fri.-Sat. until 2 AM). Wheelchair access.*

**SEBASTOPOL** Long famous for its Gravenstein apples, Sebastopol still has the look of a slow-moving agricultural town, despite its suburbanization in the last 10 years. Most folks zoom through en route from Santa Rosa (only 7 miles west on Hwy. 12) to Bodega Bay (*see* Coastal Highway 1, *above*), but those who stop to taste the apples will find a few cafés, bookstores with a liberal attitude, and hometown festivals that bring out Sebastapol's small-town spirit. Everyone from grammar-school kids to the mayor turns out for the **Apple Blossom Parade,** held the last weekend in April. The fruit itself gets its turn in the spotlight during the mid-August **Gravenstein Apple Fair** (tel. 707/829–GRAV), an apple-centric food fest held in **Ragle Park** (Ragle Rd., off Bodega Ave). You can enjoy Sebastapol's harvest year-round by paying a visit to the numerous local farms. The **Chamber of Commerce** (265 S. Main St., tel. 707/823–3032), open weekdays 9–5, stocks the free Farm Trails brouchure, which lists commercial farms selling everything from walnuts to persimmons to bonzai trees.

*For summer fruit and berries, be on the lookout for come-and-go roadside stands, or stop by Sebastopol's farmers' market (tel. 707/522–9305), held Sundays June–October from 10 AM to 1 PM in the Downtown Plaza on McKinley Street, east of Main Street.*

If you're looking to eat something other than apples, try the trendy and tasty fare at **East-West Café** (128 N. Main St., tel. 707/829–2822), open weekdays 7 AM–9 PM, Saturday 8 AM–9 PM, and Sunday until 8 PM. The menu offers adventures in tofu and egg for breakfast, and international organic lunch and dinner fare for $4.50–$8. **Copperfield's Café** (138 N. Main St., tel. 707/829–1286)—open weekdays 8–6, Saturday 9–6, and Sunday 9–5—sells tempting sandwiches ($3–$5) named after writers like Jack Kerouac, Alice Walker, and Dr. Seuss.

# Guerneville and the Russian River

Highway 116 passes through the easygoing resort town of Guerneville on its way from U.S. 101 in Santa Rosa to Jenner on the coast. Even when the coast is wrapped in fog (as it is nearly year-round), it'll probably be sunny in Guerneville, and weekend trekkers from San Francisco and points north will be swimming in the Russian River's warm waters. The river is especially popular with gays and lesbians: Several of the best-known resorts, notably the **Willows** (*see* Where to Sleep, *below*) and the **Russian River Resort** (cnr 4th and Mill Sts., tel. 707/869–0691), are owned and operated by gays and lesbians.

*Twice a year, an influx of estrogen pours into Guerneville—an event known informally as Women's Weekend (tel. 707/869–4522). The festival takes place on the last weekends of April and September, featuring live music, crafts, and lots of bonding for lesbians and straights alike.*

In 1995, the normally benign waters of the Russian River turned into roiling cesspools when heavy rains caused the Russian River to flood twice and submerge Guerneville. The flooding caused millions of dollars of damage, drew national attention, and brought in the National Guard. Luckily, Guerneville—with friendly local cafés and a nearby redwoods reserve—has bounced back and remains a great place to hang out. Though **Johnson's Beach** downtown is packed on summer weekends, if you get here early you can park for free, rent canoes or pedal boats ($5 an hour, $12 a day), and paddle lazily up and down the river. For the true slacker, they also rent inner tubes ($3 a day) that carry you down the river with no effort on your part.

For an only slightly more high-tech float, take a trip ($30, including free shuttle back) with **Burke's Canoe Trips** (tel. 707/887–1222). Though the 10-mile float (reservations advised) only takes about three hours if you paddle straight through, there's no reason not to bring a swimsuit and lunch, and loll away some time at a remote beach along the way. After you've had your fill of water activities, drive 3½ miles east of Guerneville on River Road to **Korbel** (13250 River Rd., tel. 707/887–2294; open daily 9–5) to tour their champagne vineyards and sample a little bubbly at no charge.

Despite Guerneville's small size, it sees quite a number of cultural events. One of the biggest is the two-day **Russian River Jazz Festival**—held every year in September at Johnson's Beach—which features some of the world's finest jazz musicians (tickets are about $30 a day). Seemingly sleepy Guerneville is also home to **Jungle** (16135 Main St., next to Chevron station, tel. 707/869–1400), a full-blown, multilevel dance club that might make you think you're in New York; it's open Thursday–Sunday and the cover is $2–$7.

**BASICS** Pick up a free copy of the monthly paper *We the People* at **Music Corner** (14045 Armstrong Woods Rd., at River Rd., tel. 707/869–0571) for the scoop on local gay and lesbian issues and events. For more info and a crude map of town, visit the **Russian River Chamber of Commerce** (16200 1st St., tel. 707/869–9000), open weekdays 9–5, weekends noon–3.

**WHERE TO SLEEP** In Guerneville, it's almost impossible to find a room during summer without reservations. If you're out of luck, try the first-come, first-served Armstrong Redwoods State Reserve (*see* Camping, *below*), spend a night in nearby Occidental (*see* Near Guerneville, *below*), or drive to one of the campgrounds along the coast (*see* Near Bodega Bay, in Coastal Highway 1, *above*).

**Johnson's Beach Resort.** Right in town, Johnson's has 20 rundown cabins (with kitchen, bath, and TV) crammed haphazardly near the river for $30–$35 a night ($150–$175 a week). If you yearn for that shantytown feel, stay at their crowded campground on the grassy shore ($8 plus $2 per person). *16421 1st St., off Hwy. 116 just west of Guerneville Bridge, tel. 707/869–2022. Closed Oct.–May.*

**Riverlane Resort.** It's right next door to Johnson's and far better-maintained. The 12 cabins (with kitchens and access to a pool, hot tub, and the Russian River) are $45 on weekdays, $55 on weekends and holidays. *1st St., at Church St., tel. 707/869–2323.*

**The Willows.** The best, most pleasant bargain in town, with antique furniture and quiet gardens to lounge in. Doubles with shared bath are $49, including morning pastries, fresh fruit, and coffee. You can camp next to the river here for $18 and still get the free breakfast. The kitchen, showers, hot tub, sauna, pedal boats, and canoes are available at no charge to all guests, and the uninhibited can sunbathe nude on the private beach. *15905 River Rd., ½ mi east of town, tel. 707/869–2824 or 800/953–2828.*

➢ **CAMPING** • **Armstrong Redwoods State Reserve.** Just 2½ miles north of Guerneville, you can camp in the reserve's first-come, first-served Bullfrog Pond Campground (no showers), with 24 drive-in sites ($10) and four hike-in sites ($7) set among the oaks, madrones, and firs. To guarantee yourself a place, check in early in the morning at the ranger's kiosk. You won't be camping in the redwoods, but you can hike down into the much-visited reserve from camp, or explore the backcountry along the moderate 5-mile loop from East Austin Creek Trail to Gilliam Creek Trail and back up East Ridge Trail to Bullfrog Pond. Register with the rangers before entering the backcountry. *Armstrong Woods Rd., 2½ mi from downtown Guerneville, tel. 707/869–2015 or 707/865–2391. Drive-in day use $5, walk-in day use free.*

**FOOD** It's easy to eat well on the cheap in Guerneville, but stopping at that would miss the point—restaurants here are great places to kill time, listen to music, and talk to strangers. There is a Mexican restaurant in town, but those in the know go for the cheaper Mexican fare at the food truck that stops in front of **Safeway** (16405 Main St.) every afternoon and evening; tamales here cost $1.50, extra-large meat burritos $4.50. **Brew Moon** (16248 Main St., tel. 707/869-0201) serves hot java and the best desserts in town. On Friday and Saturday nights, it stays open as long as the place is hopping; on Thursday nights, you can catch open-mike poetry readings.

**Breeze Inn Bar-B-Q.** It does offer a few vegetarian options (fettuccine, corn bread, greens), but the Breeze Inn is famous for its ribs—"slow cooked in our brick oven." A full order (six ribs and two sides) runs $10; a whole slab (12 ribs and four sides) feeds three to four people and costs $19. For orders over $10 they'll deliver free to any local resort or campsite. *15640 River Rd., tel. 707/869-9208 or 707/869-9209. ½ mi east of town on River Rd. Open Wed.-Mon. noon-9. Wheelchair access. No credit cards.*

**Coffee Bazaar.** Put together a customized meal from their selection of coffees, bagel sandwiches ($1.25 and up), and ice cream. Locals lounge here for hours reading the papers. *14045 Armstrong Woods Rd., tel. 707/869-9706. 1 block north of River Rd. Open weekdays 6:45 AM-8 PM, Sat. 8 AM-9 PM, Sun. 8-8. Wheelchair access. No credit cards.*

## NEAR GUERNEVILLE

**OCCIDENTAL** Just 10 miles south of Guerneville on the Bohemian Highway lies the quiet town of Occidental, a popular stop for bicyclists touring the valley and travelers looking to escape Guerneville's bustle. A great bike tour from here is the 25-mile loop on Coleman Valley Road west to Highway 1, south to Bodega Highway, and north up the Bohemian Highway back to Occidental. The strenuous tour climbs several hills on backcountry road before falling to the ocean and following the coast along more-traveled roads.

➢ **WHERE TO SLEEP AND EAT** • Bed down at **Negri's Occidental Lodge** (3610 Bohemian Hwy., tel. 707/874-3623), which has big, airy rooms with comfortable beds, cushy carpeting, and TV ($42, $54 weekends and holidays). If you're on a tight budget, the **Occidental Motel** (cnr Main and Occidental Sts., tel. 707/874-3635) charges $30 for doubles ($43 on weekend and holidays). Both motels have pools. **Juice, Java, and Joy** (14775 3rd St., tel. 707/874-9928; open Tues.-Sun. 9-5) serves gourmet salads and vegetarian sandwiches for under $4, as well as fresh juices and excellent coffee. The **Bohemian Café** (3688 Bohemian Hwy., tel. 707/874-3931) has tasty Belgian waffles and orange French toast ($4.25) for early risers, but the real treats come later in the day: Their California-style pizzas with funky toppings like apples, walnuts, and Brie ($10.50) are big enough to split. Look for live jazz on Friday and Saturday nights. They're open weekdays 8-2 and 5-9, weekends 8 AM-9 PM.

# Healdsburg

At Healdsburg, 14 miles north of Santa Rosa, the southward-moving Russian River crosses U.S. 101 for the last time before heading to the ocean. In hot summer weather, this is a good place to stop for a dip. Get off U.S. 101 at the Healdsburg Avenue exit, cross the bridge, park on the street to avoid parking fees, and walk back across the bridge to the beach. You can rent a canoe ($6 an hour, $20 a day) or inner tube ($1.50 an hour, $4 a day) from **Trowbridge Canoe Trips** (20 Healdsburg Ave., tel. 707/433-7247), open daily 8-6 in summer.

Healdsburg has produced wine since the early 1900s, but only recently has it become a stop on tours of the Wine Country (*see* Chapter 3). Wineries are more spread out here and tourists almost nonexistent compared to nearby Napa. Among the established wineries are **Simi** (16275 Healdsburg Ave., 1 mi north of Dry Creek Rd., tel. 707/433-6981), **Clos du Bois** (19410 Geyserville Ave., east on Independence Ln. from U.S. 101 and left on Geyserville Ave., tel. 707/857-1651), and **Hop Kiln** (6050 Westside Rd., about 6 miles west of U.S. 101, tel. 707/433-6491), known for its stone hop-drying house and excellent zinfandel. All have free tastings, and Simi offers three tours daily. For a smaller, personal tour through the vineyards (two a day), call the **Michel-Schlumberger Winery** (4155 Wine Creek Rd., tel. 707/433-7427) to make an appointment. For more info about local wineries, stop at the **Healdsburg Area Chamber of Commerce** (217 Healdsburg Ave., tel. 800/648-9922), open weekdays 9:30-5 and weekends 10-2.

**FOOD** The **Salami Tree Deli** (304 Center St., on central plaza, tel. 707/433–7224) stocks a good selection of meats, cheeses, beers, and wines, many of which are produced locally; it's open daily 8–6 (Fri. and Sat. until 7). From a stovetop crammed with pots, **El Farolito** (128 Plaza St., ½ block east of central plaza, tel. 707/433–2807) serves up Mexican food so authentic you might have trouble ordering in English. A vegetarian burrito is $3.50, a combination plate (any two items plus rice, beans, and salad) $7.

# Ukiah

The sensible town of Ukiah, 44 miles north of Healdsburg, started life as a rough and rugged lumber village. Its logging roots remain strong, but in recent years it's become an agricultural center specializing in prunes, apples, and grapes. Ukiah is one of the southernmost outposts of Northern California's "green belt," a band of forest that stretches to Oregon and is home to both loggers and environmentalists. The two groups may be in a long-standing feud over land use and lifestyle, but it's not uncommon to see them drinking next to each other at bars.

Though it's no traveler's paradise, Ukiah is a good place to buy supplies or spend a last night in a soft bed before striking out west to the rugged Mendocino coast or east to Clear Lake and Mendocino National Forest. Without straying too far, you can take advantage of nearby **Lake Mendocino** (*see* Near Ukiah, *below*), which offers camping, hiking, boating, and fishing within 20 minutes' drive of downtown. Appealing nightlife is sparse here. The best bet on a Friday or Saturday night is the live acoustic music at **Coffee Critic** (476 N. State St., tel. 707/462–6333), which usually draws a thick crowd of locals.

**WHERE TO SLEEP** If you're not up to camping at Lake Mendocino, Ukiah has a few budget motels along State Street, which runs parallel to U.S. 101 about half a mile to the west and can be accessed from any of the Ukiah exits. The best deal in town is the **Garden Court Motor Inn** (1175 S. State St., tel. 707/462–5646), whose friendly managers offer remarkably clean and comfortable doubles overlooking a quiet garden for $37 ($34 in winter). Also easy on the wallet is the **Lantern Inn** (650 S. State St., tel. 707/462–6601), with doubles for $38 ($33 in winter). Rates climb $5 on holiday weekends.

## *Eco-Wars on the North Coast*

***It may be hard to distinguish a flannel-clad logger from a blue-jeaned activist when you see them in Northern California's small towns, but their superficial similarities belie deep differences. The loggers often come from families that have worked in the timber industry for generations. For them, it's a way of life. The activists, meanwhile, are passionate about conserving trees; many have migrated from urban areas to spend their lives among forests that are disappearing. The conflict centers on the timber industry's practice of clear-cutting (chopping down all the trees in a given area to obtain lumber) and disregard for shrinking supplies of old-growth forests.***

***Though the spotted owl, which lives in old-growth forests, is still in danger, recent debate has focused on the marbled murrelet and the Pacific salmon. These species near the top of the food chain serve as indicators for the overall health of forests, and the diagnosis does not look promising. After the recent flurry of public attention, the Clinton administration attempted to ease tensions with a long-term-use plan for all forests in the Pacific Northwest, but its effects have yet to be felt—no thanks to a Republican-dominated Congress intent on rewriting many long-standing environmental regulations.***

**FOOD** Don't bother with the fast-food chains near U.S. 101; if you head 6 blocks west on Perkins Street to the downtown area, you'll find reasonably priced restaurants with menus that weren't planned by a corporation. **Ellie's Mutt Hut and Vegetarian Café** (732 S. State St., near Gobbi St., tel. 707/468–5376) may sound like a strange combination, but who can resist a restaurant that has both chili dogs ($3) and vegetarian black-bean chili sandwiches ($5) on the menu? To reach the Hut, open weekdays 6 AM–8 PM, exit U.S. 101 at Talmage Road west and go ½ mile north on State Street.

**Super-Taco** (506 E. Perkins St., tel. 707/462–5979), open daily 10–9, has super-size tacos ($1.50) and burritos ($3.75), as well as dinners like *camarones à la diabla* (large, spicy shrimp with rice, beans, and tortillas; $7). To get here, take the Perkins Street exit west off U.S. 101 to the Pear Tree shopping center; it's next to the K-mart. On the south end of town, **Moores' Flour Mill** (1550 S. State St., tel. 707/462–6550; open weekdays 8–6, Sat. 9–6) sells sandwiches priced by weight ($3–$3.75) on fresh-baked bread. You can chow down on the patio next to a giant waterwheel that actually grinds the flour they use in their bread. Moores' also carries vitamins, herbs, homeopathics, a limited supply of organic groceries, and bulk bags of grains, flour, and beans. The friendly, well-stocked **Ukiah Co-Op** (308-B E. Perkins St., tel. 707/462–4778) can amply satisfy your needs for organic and bulk supplies.

**WORTH SEEING** The **Grace Hudson Museum** and adjacent **Sun House** are especially interesting in light of Ukiah's lack of other diversions. The museum features baskets, photographs, and paintings of the indigenous Pomo, as well as rotating exhibitions of Americana. Sun House was home to Grace Hudson and her husband (a doctor who gave up his practice to become a collector-scholar of Native American basketry). Grace painted the scenes of Pomo life that adorn the museum's walls. Half-hour tours of Sun House are given four times daily Wednesday–Sunday. *431 S. Main St., btw Gobbi and Clay Sts., tel. 707/462–3370. 1 block east of State St. Suggested donation: $2. Open Wed.–Sat. 10–4:30, Sun. noon–4:30.*

If you're searching for a more profound peace of mind, visit the **Sagely City of 10,000 Buddhas,** a Buddhist community of over 100 people that, surprisingly, resembles a small suburb. (And yes, the temple walls really are lined with 10,000 tiny Buddha statues.) They stress that only visitors interested in praying or learning more about Buddhism should come: This is not a tourist site, but a place of work, study, and worship. The excellent vegetarian restaurant, open Wednesday–Monday 11–6, charges $3.50–$15 for meals—but again, don't come if you're not serious about the Buddha thing. Be sure to wear "proper attire" (no shorts), and keep in mind that the sexes live separately here—couples should limit public displays of affection. *2001 Talmage Rd., tel. 707/462–0939. From U.S. 101, take Talmage exit east.*

➢ **HOT SPRINGS • Vichy Springs.** For a relaxing splurge make the short trek out to Vichy, purportedly Jack London's favorite retreat. Room start at $130, but for $25 a day ($15 for 2 hrs), you get a mineral hot tub; warm, naturally carbonated mineral baths (about 90°); and 700 acres of hiking and mountain-biking trails. Bathing suits are required. *2605 Vichy Springs Rd., tel. 707/462–9515. From U.S. 101, take Vichy Springs Road exit east for 3 mi.*

**Orr Hot Springs.** Thirty minutes west of Ukiah, Orr has rustic rooms that start at $76 ($92 on weekends) and a community room where you can "camp" for $25 ($30 on weekends). The $15 day-use fee ($9 Mon., when cold pool closes) buys access to a sauna, a cold pool partially built into the hillside, and a hot pool inside a stained-glass gazebo. Clothing is required only in the main building, which has a fully equipped kitchen, wood-paneled dining room, and library. Bring your own food. *13201 Orr Springs Rd., tel. 707/462–6277. From U.S. 101, take North State St. exit, turn north, go ¼ mi to Orr Springs Rd., turn left, and continue 13½ mi.*

## NEAR UKIAH

**LAKE MENDOCINO** The most accessible camping in the Ukiah area is 20 minutes from town at Lake Mendocino (1160 Lake Mendocino Dr., tel. 707/462–7581), popular with families, jet skiers, and anglers. If you want to spend time on the lake, try the **Lake Mendocino Marina** (north end of lake, tel. 707/485–8644), where you can rent jet skis ($55 per hr) or canoes ($15 per hr). The marina is open 8–8 daily in summer; winter hours vary.

**Bu-shay Campground** (164 sites) and **Ky-en Campground** (103 sites), at the lake's north end, are fully developed and have showers. The campgrounds line the golden hills around the lake under a light cover of oaks and madrones, but you won't get much protection from families and their dogs. Of the two, Bu-shay is less crowded. At both you'll pay $12 in summer ($14 for a spot next to the lake) and $8 October–mid-April, when only Ky-en is open. **Che-ka-ka** is a cheaper option in the summer with its 23 sites ($8) among scrub trees on a bluff overlooking the southern end of the lake—but you'll have to rough it without flush toilets or showers. To reach the larger campgrounds and the marina from U.S. 101, take Highway 20 east for 3 miles. Ky-en is south of Highway 20 off the Lake Mendocino Marina exit; Bu-shay is a mile north of Highway 20 off the same exit. For Che-ka-ka, take the Lake Mendocino exit and follow Lake Mendocino Drive east to the lake.

**HOPLAND BREWERY** It's in the middle of nowhere (13 miles south of Ukiah in the town of Hopland, to be precise), but the Hopland Brewery is one of the best-known brew pubs in California. On summer weekends, the beer garden is crowded with bicyclists down from Oregon, motorcyclists out for a ride in the country, and day-tripping Deadheads from the Bay Area. Four types of beer are brewed on the premises: Peregrine Pale Ale, Blue Heron Pale Ale, Red Tail Ale, and Black Hawk Stout. Try the 4-ounce samplers (50¢ each) for a good overview. There's a good selection of meat and veggie sandwiches (around $6), as well as snacks like potato skins ($4). Blues bands play on Saturday nights ($6–$10 cover), giving the maudlin an excuse to cry into their beer and everyone else an excuse to raise hell. Also look for a slew of annual parties, including Oktoberfest (first Sat. of Oct.), Fourth of July, and the Mendocino Brewing Company's anniversary (the weekend nearest Aug. 12). *13351 U.S. 101, tel. 707/744–1361. Open daily 11 AM–midnight (Sat. until 2 AM); shorter hrs in winter.*

*Boontling, a language native to Boonville, is said to have begun as a children's trick on their parents in the 1880s. It later blossomed into a completely usable language that locals used to confuse outsiders. These days, only a few remnants exist: If you need to make a local call, deposit 20¢ into the nearest "Buckey Walters."*

**BOONVILLE** Boonville is a one-street town halfway between Ukiah and the Pacific Ocean in the center of Anderson Valley (Hwy. 253). The first clue that yuppies have arrived is the overpriced golf shirts for sale at the local pub, the **Buckhorn Saloon** (14081 Hwy. 128, tel. 707/895–2337). The eight microbrewed ales here are truly excellent, but the loggers and lefties now look out of place in the sparkling-clean surroundings. The town remains true to its underground politics, though—if you doubt it, pick up a copy of the *Anderson Valley Advertiser*, a local independent newspaper that takes on issues ranging from pot raids to international politics.

**WILLITS** North of Ukiah, U.S. 101 moves into increasingly rugged land. The logging town of Willits, 33 miles north, is fairly unexceptional. It does give the world at least one extraordinary product, though: the Proto Pipe, a solid brass smoking implement with cleverly interlocking pieces that's selling 1,200 units per week—making it a multimillion-dollar industry. While advertisements claim the pipe is for "contemporary tobacco consumption," any Willits police officer can tell you that pipe owners are making their own decisions about what to put in their pipes. At the **Proto Pipe Factory** (275 Franklin St., tel. 707/459–5512), open weekdays 8–5, you can buy a pipe at the low wholesale price of $25 (some stores sell them for twice as much). The factory is located around the side of an unassuming brown warehouse near the end of Franklin Street.

➢ **WHERE TO SLEEP** • The **Skunk Train Motel** (500 S. Main St., tel. 707/459–2302) has 17 clean rooms with TVs, and an unheated pool. Their two budget rooms (no phone) run $25 in winter, $30 in summer; call ahead to check prices (the new managers may up the rates).

➢ **FOOD** • The best reason to stop in Willits is **Tsunami,** with fresh seafood, chicken, and tofu, prepared in French, Japanese, and Cajun styles ($7–$12). They also have wonderful soups (try the zucchini-nutmeg; $3) and monstrous salads ($6–$8). *50 S. Main St., tel. 707/459–4750. Open Mon.–Sat. 9:30–9, Sun. 5 PM–9 PM. No credit cards.*

# Clear Lake

Once you turn east off U.S. 101 toward Lake County you begin to breathe the cleanest air in California. It's also part of the state that most resembles middle America. As you head toward Clear Lake, California's largest natural lake, you'll see recent retirees shooting the breeze on warm summer evenings, and you can't help thinking that Garrison Keillor would feel right at home, for better or for worse. **Lakeport,** the town with the best services and most reasonable prices, feels especially Midwestern.

Coming from points north of Ukiah, turn east off U.S. 101 on Highway 20; coming from Hopland, take Highway 175 east. Along the way you'll probably see trailers loaded with water-ski boats, jet skis, and fishing boats (anglers catch crappie, catfish, and largemouth bass year-round). The 580-acre Clear Lake State Park (*see* Camping, *below*) has plenty of quiet inlets that are wonderful for watching grebes, egrets, cormorants, and other water birds. The nearby Mendocino National Forest (*see* Near Clear Lake, *below*) offers over a million acres for hiking. The truly sedentary can sit and admire the view of **Mt. Konocti,** a volcano rising 4,200 feet above the southern part of the lake. If you'd rather hike, the moderately difficult **Dorn Nature Trail** (3 mi), beginning at the Swim Beach parking lot, has sweeping lake views.

You can rent all the equipment you'd ever need at the dozens of competitively priced shops in Lakeport and around the lake. **On the Waterfront** (60 3rd St., Lakeport, tel. 707/263–6789) rents fishing boats ($40 for 2 hrs) and offers parasailing ($35–$45). If you rent jet skis ($35–$60 an hr) on weekdays, you'll get an extra half hour free for every hour you pay. Pete of **Pete's Sporting Goods** (690 S. Main St., Lakeport, tel. 707/263–4413) is a bit crusty, but if you're extra nice he might advise you on the lake's best fishing spots.

Clear Lake is also prime biking territory. Drop by the **Lake County Visitor Information Center** (875 Lakeport Blvd., Lakeport, tel. 800/525–3743), weekdays 8:30–5:30 or Saturday 10–6, for maps of 11 different regional biking trails. A good one is the 30-mile **Kelseyville Loop,** which begins at Library Park (cnr 3rd and Park Sts. in downtown Lakeport). A moderately easy trail with great views, it takes you through orchards and vineyards to the town of Kelseyville and into Clear Lake State Park. Rent a mountain bike ($25 a day) at **The Bicycle Rack** (350 N. Main St., Lakeport, tel. 707/263–1200).

**WHERE TO SLEEP** Don't even bother with motels. The abundant natural beauty and mild year-round temperatures of Lake County should be appreciated with a tent and a sleeping bag. If you're absolutely determined to sleep indoors, you could do worse than the **Rainbow Lodge Motel** (2569 Lakeshore Blvd., Lakeport, tel. 707/263–4309), where small rooms with a double bed run only $34 even in the heat of summer. The hotel is about 1½ miles north of downtown; follow Main Street until it becomes Lakeshore Boulevard.

➢ **CAMPING** • **Clear Lake State Park.** The 147 sites on the western edge of the lake are close together, but you won't feel like you're sleeping in your neighbor's tent. The campground is full almost every summer weekend, so arrive early to choose between sites in a meadow, near the water, or on a bluff overlooking Soda Bay (where hot springs surface on an island accessible only by boat). Sites 110–112 have the best views. Rates are $14–$19 ($12–$17 off-season); bike sites are $3. *5300 Soda Bay Rd., tel. 707/279–4293 or 800/444–PARK for reservations. From Hwy. 29, take Kelseyville exit and follow signs. Day use: $5.*

**FOOD** In good weather, pull up a chair on the outside deck of one of Lakeport's several waterfront hangouts, or—if you're watching the bucks—buy deli sandwiches ($2–$3) from the well-stocked **Bruno's Foods** (cnr Lakeport and Main Sts., tel. 707/263–7337). Eat on the shore at sunny Library Park (cnr 3rd and Park Sts. in downtown Lakeport), watching people cast their lines from fishing docks. The best fruits and veggies in town are at **Epidendio Produce** (390 S. Main St., tel. 707/263–6321), which is little more than a fruit stand in a semi-permanent building.

**Cottage Coffee Shop.** This indoor-outdoor café serves home cooking of the bland, greasy-spoon variety, but the friendly waitresses treat everyone like regular customers. With a little Tabasco sauce, the Spanish omelet ($5) hits the spot for breakfast; the $3.50 chicken salad sandwich will keep you going until dinner. *1090 N. Main St., Lakeport, tel. 707/263–5071. From Hwy. 29, take 11th St. exit east. Open daily 6 AM–8 PM.*

**Nature's Bounty Herbs and Vegetarian Deli.** The deli offers a variety of pita sandwiches with potato salad, chick peas, or falafel ($2), as well as large green salads ($3.25) and all-you-can-eat soup ($4). Children's drawings adorn the walls, cheerfully advising customers to eat healthfully. *301 N. Main St., tel. 707/263–4575. Open weekdays 11:30–4:30.*

**Park Place.** Perhaps the lake's most popular restaurant, Park Place serves Italian food in a "California cuisine" format. The pasta ($5–$6 lunch, $8–$14 dinner) is made fresh daily. There are plenty of meatless dishes, a great Mediterranean pasta salad ($7), and local beer and wine. Best of all is the lakeside location; sunset is gorgeous on the upstairs open-air deck. *50 3rd St., tel. 707/263–0444. Next to Library Park in downtown Lakeport. Open daily 11–9 (Fri. and Sat. until 10). Wheelchair access.*

## NEAR CLEAR LAKE

**MENDOCINO NATIONAL FOREST** East of U.S. 101 and directly north of Clear Lake on Highway 20 lies the southern edge of huge Mendocino National Forest, where the mountains soar to almost 7,000 feet and the lakes, rivers, and unspoiled wilderness are ideal for a quiet retreat. Here you can fish and hike under pines, fir, and scrub oaks that remain green even in the heat of summer. Campgrounds are never more than $10 a night, and you don't have to worry about crowds, reservations, or noise from RVs, as rough roads prevent all but the most determined Winnebago warriors.

On Road 18N16, which branches off Road 240 a mile south of Sunset Campground (*see* Where to Sleep, *below*), lies the trailhead for the challenging 8-mile **Lakeshore Loop Trail.** This hike takes you up to a ridgetop and down again to the lake. The ranger station up here is only staffed on holiday weekends; otherwise get maps ($3) and info at the **Upper Lake Ranger District** (10025 Elk Mountain Rd., Upper Lake, tel. 707/275–2361), open weekdays 8–4:30, and the **Mendocino National Forest Headquarters** (420 E. Laurel St., Willows 95988, tel. 916/934–3316), open weekdays 8–4:30.

➢ **WHERE TO SLEEP** • As in all national forests, you're allowed to pull to the side of any road and camp for free, though you will need a campfire permit—available gratis from all ranger stations—for any open flame. The narrow, rough road leading to the lake keep most RVs away. If you are up to navigating the gravel-strewn, 11-mile dirt road (unmaintained during winter) that leads to Lake Pillsbury, you'll find marshy inlets great for trout fishing and bird-watching, and plenty of free camping: **Oak Flat Campground** has free sites in a meadow with a good view of the lake. The more developed **Sunset Campground** has shady lakeside spots for $6. *From Hwy. 29 north of Lakeport, take Hwy. 20 west 15 mi, go right on Potter Valley Rd. for 6½ mi, right on Eel River Rd. for 5 mi, and right on Mendocino County Rd. 240 for 11 mi. No reservations.*

If you don't want to brave all 11 miles to Lake Pillsbury, pull into small, shady **Trout Creek Campground** (open in summer only) after just 2 miles of dirt on Road 240, and lie back and listen to the Eel River for the rest of the evening. The 15 thickly wooded sites are distributed on a first-come, first-served basis for $10. There are no showers, but the campground has running water, pit toilets, and a pay phone.

# Leggett

Approximately 50 miles north of Willits, U.S. 101 joins Highway 1 at Leggett. The town consists of little more than a quarter-mile row of buildings along **Drive-Through Tree Road** (parallel to and just west of U.S. 101), but this is where redwood country begins. From here all the way to Crescent City, you'll be faced with the choice of *which* stupendously beautiful grove of ancient or second-growth trees you want to visit.

First in line is the **Standish-Hickey State Recreation Area.** It's not the most densely packed redwood grove, but you'll find an excellent (though much-used) swimming hole a quarter mile west of the picnic area; the $5 day-use fee is good for access to any state park for the day. Several hiking trails traverse the park, including the 2.1-mile **Big Tree Loop Trail,** which starts at the parking lot next to Site 108 and takes you to the biggest tree in the area, the Miles Standish Tree (named for a descendent of the captain of the Mayflower, even though the tree is about 900 years older). The 1.7-mile **Grove Trail Loop** begins on the east side of U.S. 101 north of the gas station and takes you through virgin forest. Campers have a choice of 162 sites ($14 a night) in three campgrounds or eight hike/bike sites ($3 a person), many with huge stone fire-pits and all with tables, food cupboards, and coin-operated hot showers. *69350 U.S. 101, 2 mi north of Leggett, tel. 707/925–6482 or 800/444–PARK for reservations.*

One weekend a year in June, thousands of Harley-Davidson owners converge in the town of Piercy, 11 miles north of Leggett, for the **Redwood Run,** which is sponsored by the Kiwanis Club. The biker reunion features motorcycle shows, relay games, tattoo and leather accessory booths, steak barbecues, and two nights of live rhythm and blues. The $45 ticket includes two nights of camping. For details, call 800/4–FUNRUN.

**WHERE TO SLEEP** The **Eel River Redwoods Hostel** is on a sun-warmed stretch of the Eel River in Mendocino National Forest. Beds are $12 for members of any hosteling association, $14 for others. Little wooden cabins and separate dorm rooms for "guys" and "girls" make you feel like you're in summer camp. Call ahead to reserve private rooms that sleep two, or dorm rooms that sleep seven. Hostelers (and those who pay a $5 day-use fee) have access to Gene's extensively researched day trips in the area, a hammock, inner tubes, a 9-hole Frisbee-golf course, a well-equipped kitchen, and a sauna and Jacuzzi (open 24 hrs). Most nights you can get a meal at the hostel's pub for $5–$8. Free supplies for pancakes are available every morning. Make reservations about a week ahead in summer. *70400 U.S. 101, 2 mi north of Leggett, tel. 707/925–6425. Follow signs for Bell Glen Resort. 43 beds. Reception open 24 hrs. Sheet rental ($1).*

**FOOD** Leggett's **Ne-Bobs Café** (Drive-Through Tree Rd., tel. 707/925–6323) has spunky service and "the best burgers in town" ($3). Count on getting filling, traditional versions of breakfast, lunch, and dinner ($6–$9); open 8–8 daily. If you desperately need supplies before exploring the redwoods, **Garske's Leggett Market** (Drive-Through Tree Rd., tel. 707/925–6779) will cover the necessities, though you'll probably do better in Willits or Garberville.

# U.S. 101 at the Top of the State

**After joining Highway 1 at Leggett, U.S. 101** winds through stunning redwood forests, where you can camp among some of the oldest living things on earth. Starting just south of **Garberville,** the highway follows the course of the Eel River, great for fishing. To the west is the stunning, isolated **Lost Coast.** The 80-mile stretch of road between **Arcata** and **Crescent City** winds past windswept shoreline, lovely deserted beaches, rugged forests, and several of the state's finest parks.

The region is not without its touristy side. In corny, over-hyped sites like the Trees of Mystery in Klamath and Confusion Hill near Richardson Grove State Park (*see* Near Garberville, *below*), you'll see the give-'em-what-they-want brand of American tourism at its worst. But you can easily avoid all that and have a hell of a time. The massive and spectacular Redwood state and national parks alone make the drive worthwhile. Here you'll find the world's tallest trees (the highest redwood

*Maybe it's the old trees, the mountains, the ocean. Maybe it's all the marijuana. Whatever the reason, residents here get into alternative healing practices, spiritual energies, and inner voyages. Learn more about holistic healing in the free publications "Access" and "The Well-Being Directory," available in any Humboldt County town.*

in Tall Tree Grove was last measured at 367 ft), as well as rare Roosevelt elk and thousands of other plants and animals seldom seen elsewhere. It's a great swath of wilderness, and one of the few such places in the state that haven't been overrun by crowds.

With the proximity to this awe-inspiring amount of nature, it's no surprise that almost everybody in the region is either vocally involved in protecting the environment or turning it to profit. Logging, tourism, and agriculture (both legal and otherwise) are some of the major industries in the area; all three work to maintain a small-town atmosphere which can be instantly welcoming or chillingly exclusive, though you'll rarely encounter the latter in your travels along this part of the coast. For transportation info, *see* Coming and Going, at the beginning of the chapter, and Eureka and Arcata, *below.*

# Garberville

Two hundred miles north of San Francisco and 65 miles south of Eureka lies Garberville, the first of a stretch of North Coast towns in which the longhair-to-redneck balance tips slightly in favor of the former. At first glance, Garberville and Redway, 2 miles north on Redwood Drive, don't look like much more than the usual string of motels, supermarkets, and diners designed to serve the river of tourists passing through on their way to more redwoods. But these towns serve as metropolitan centers for the back-to-the-landers who inhabit the Lost Coast to the west, and for residents of Trinity County (*see* Chapter 5) to the east. To get a taste of local life, try a 1½-hour yoga class ($5 minimum donation) at **Standing Wave Yoga Dharma Center** (434 Maple Ln., 1 block east of Redwood Dr., tel. 707/946–2028); class times vary, so call ahead or check the schedule on the door. Instructor Hal welcomes any and all comers (no experience necessary)—just wear loose clothing, come with an empty stomach, and bring a blanket.

*In addition to left-wing news reporting, Garberville's KMUD radio (91.1 FM) plays a wide mix of alternative music—a rarity in these parts.*

The first weekend in August, thousands flock to the Eel River just south of town for **Reggae on the River,** maybe the best reggae festival in the world aside from the Reggae Sunsplash in Jamaica. The 8,000 tickets always go fast, so call by late April or early May to be safe. In 1995, 2-day tickets were $80 (no single-day tickets available). Call the Mateel Community Center (tel. 707/923–3368) in Redway for ticket outlet locations. The **Redwood Transit System** (133 V St., Eureka, tel. 707/443–0826) runs buses twice a day from Garberville to Scotia (80 min, $1.60). From Scotia, buses travel as far north as Trinidad (165 min, $1.60 extra).

**WHERE TO SLEEP** You'd do best to stay at the Eel River Redwoods Youth Hostel (*see* Leggett, *above*), since it's only 24 miles south. On the motel circuit, your cheapest option is 2 miles north of town at the **Budgetwest Redway Inn** (3223 Redwood Dr., tel. 707/923–2660) where comfortable, slightly outdated rooms with air conditioning, phones, and TV with HBO run $34–$40 in winter, $40–$50 in summer. In town, a decent bet is the **Humboldt Redwoods Inn** (987 Redwood Dr., tel. 707/923–2451), where redwood-paneled doubles go for $46 in the winter, $4 more in the summer—but you might negotiate a good deal on a quiet weeknight. You get a comfy bed, TV with HBO, a phone, and access to a swimming pool.

**FOOD** It's no surprise that half the restaurants here cater to ethereal health-food enthusiasts and the other half to loggers looking for meat and potatoes. Almost all the food in town can be found on a short stretch of Redwood Drive near the intersection with Sprowel Creek Road. If you think the loggers have the right idea, try **Café Garberville** (770 Redwood Dr., tel. 707/923–3551; open weekdays 8–8), a "family-oriented" restaurant, where a plate of pork chops and apple sauce with soup, potatoes, and garlic bread costs around $8. Stop off at **Chautauqua Natural Foods** (436 Church St., tel. 707/923–2452; open Mon.–Sat. 10–7, Sun. noon–4), 1 block east of Redwood Drive, for organic produce, vegetarian deli items, herbs, vitamins, and body-care products.

**Mateel Café.** This gourmet restaurant and coffeehouse in Redway, 2½ miles north of Garberville on Redwood Drive, draws locals and travelers from miles around with its elaborate salads ($6.50), stone-baked pizzas (about $11), fresh fish specials ($12–$14), sandwiches ($5–

$7), and vegetarian lasagna ($8.50). You can hang out on the redwood patio sipping a cappuccino ($2) and nibble on one of the chef's special desserts. Check local papers or the Garberville Chamber of Commerce (773 Redwood Dr., tel. 707/923–2613) for discount coupons. *3344 Redwood Dr., next to Redway Liquors, tel. 707/923–2030. Open Mon.–Sat. 11:30–9. Wheelchair access. No credit cards.*

**Woodrose Café.** It's across the street from Café Garberville but on a different culinary planet. Come for huge omelets ($5–$6), bowls of oatmeal with raisins and banana ($3), sandwiches ($3.50 and up), and a new dinner menu every week (entrées $9–$14). You'll find several vegetarian options, some organic ingredients, and *no* beef. *911 Redwood Dr., tel. 707/923–3191. Breakfast served weekdays 8–noon, weekends 8–1; lunch weekdays noon–2:30; dinner Thurs.–Sun. 5:30–9.*

### NEAR GARBERVILLE

**RICHARDSON GROVE** Seven miles south of Garberville on U.S. 101, **Richardson Grove State Park** (tel. 707/247–3318) is an easily accessible redwood stop. Unfortunately, this means the place is usually pretty congested. Four loop trails and a self-guided nature trail wind around the park. The **Woodland Trail** is a gentle 1½-mile hike through redwoods and tan oaks. The **Toumey Trail** (accessible only in summer) takes you 2 miles through redwoods and up to a panorama point. Drive-in campers have a choice between 95 oak-forested or 75 redwood-packed sites ($14), all of which have fire rings, picnic tables, and food lockers, with coin-operated hot showers and toilets nearby. Weekend partyers often fill the campground to capacity, so call MISTIX (tel. 800/444–PARK) for reservations. The day-use fee for hiking is $5.

**BENBOW LAKE** Five miles north of Richardson Grove on U.S. 101, **Benbow Lake State Recreation Area** (tel. 707/923–3238) has 75 campsites with coin-operated hot showers in meadows exposed to the sun. The sites ($14) are secluded and fill less quickly than Richardson Grove; reservations through MISTIX are rarely necessary. If you just want to stop for a swim at the seasonal lake (they take the dam out during the winter), the day-use fee is $5. The day-use area west of U.S. 101 rents canoes ($18 for 3 hrs, $43 a day) and inner tubes ($2 per hr). A popular spring activity is to enjoy a 5-mile float on the Eel River from Richardson Grove north to Benbow.

## The Lost Coast

Because of the rugged terrain, the state of California abandoned hope of extending Highway 1 along the Pacific between Rockport and Eureka, and now this whole region goes by the name Lost Coast. It's true that, in California terms, lack of proximity to a major highway is ample reason for a place to be considered "lost." But this strange, isolated region earns its name in other ways. While California's other coastal areas have been the site of major building and development, the Lost Coast remains in a virtually pristine state. It's comparable in beauty to Big Sur but not nearly as explored, since most tourists head to places that better accommodate their automobiles. Wherever you go on the Lost Coast, you get a sense that you've entered another era—redwood trees perch on cliffs 200 feet above rocky shores and black-sand beaches, with nary a condo unit to spoil the view.

Only about 2,000 people live in the whole region, and many of them moved here as part of the late '60s hippie migration to Northern California. Hang out at the Hideaway (*see* Food, *below*) in Petrolia on a weekend afternoon to get a feel for the quality of life in these parts. The locals aren't too interested in hordes of people invading their home turf, and don't ask people what they do for a living: The question can be a risky one here, in one of the world's most celebrated pot-growing regions. During the '80s, huge pot farms sprang up all over the Lost Coast; the economic boom was big enough to replace the prosperous timber industry that died out (thanks to clear cutting). But since the feds started weeding out pot crops all over California—with a major emphasis on Humboldt County—local pot farmers have become a tad suspicious of outsiders (*also see box* Humboldt Home-Grown, *below*).

**WHERE TO SLEEP** For every cheap motel farther north in Eureka, there's a pricey bed-and-breakfast in Ferndale. If you're on a tight budget, think "camping."

➢ **HONEYDEW** • **Mattole River Resort.** It's fairly luxurious but still reasonably priced, with six 1920s redwood cabins that rent by the night or week. The cabins ($45–$100) have equipped kitchens and hot showers, and you're across the street from the river—good for swimming in summer and fishing (mainly steelhead) in winter. The shady grounds have a few plum and apple trees, as well as grapevines and blackberry bushes, all free for the picking. For $8 a night you can camp in one of six sites, eat the fruit, and take hot showers. They've also got coin-operated washers and dryers. *42354 Mattole Rd., 26 mi west of U.S. 101 and 2¼ mi west of Honeydew, tel. 707/629–3445 or 800/845–4607. Reservations advised.*

➢ **FERNDALE** • **Ferndale Laundromat and Motel.** They're not joking about the "laundromat" part, though noise is luckily not a problem. The two clean rooms (with kitchenettes and TVs) are big enough to sleep five and cost $45 (a few dollars less in winter). Beyond two people, it's an extra $5 per person. Register at the laundromat. *632 Main St., tel. 707/786–9471.*

**Shaw House.** With its extremely ornate architecture and immaculate grounds, the Shaw House is the best place to indulge your Lost Coast B&B fantasies. Robes, slippers, nightshirts, bubble bath, full breakfast, a balcony, and a beautiful room filled with antiques are all only $75 year-round. Norma can deliver excellent advice about exploring Ferndale, and bikes are available for guests. *703 Main St., tel. 707/786–9958.*

➢ **CAMPING** • The best primitive camping is in the **Sinkyone Wilderness State Park,** where all campgrounds lie within walking distance of deserted beaches. Stop at the **Needle Rock Visitor Center** (tel. 707/986–7711)—staffed sporadically during daylight hours—to check in and figure out the best camping area. In foul weather, you can rent one of two unfurnished rooms here that sleep up to four for $14 ($12 in winter). To reach Sinkyone from Garberville (1½ hrs), take Redwood Drive to Redway, then the Briceland Thorne Road west for 25 twisty miles to Four Corners, where you head west on a rough unpaved road for 2½ miles to the visitor center (look for signs). All campgrounds in Sinkyone cost $9 ($7 in winter); require short walks in; and are first-come, first-served (but you should have no problem finding space).

Of Sinkyone's three campgrounds, **Jones Beach** and **Barn Camp,** near the visitor center, are best for beach combing. The three sites at **Bear Harbor,** about 3 miles beyond the visitor center, are popular stops on the Lost Coast Trail (*see* Outdoor Activities, *below*). Either way, the settings are truly stupendous—Roosevelt elk cruise the meadows, streams gurgle down canyons, and cool winds sweep across empty beaches. Not many people get out here (you'll see why as you drive the rutted dirt road), but it's well worth the beating to your car.

Another option is **Usal Beach,** 6 miles north of Westport and 15 miles south of Leggett off Highway 1—watch for the hidden driveway at County Road 431 on the west side of Highway 1. The beach is also accessible from Garberville via Four Corners. Usal's 15 campsites are strung out on the coast road, some among trees, some in an open field, and some next to the beach. There are also 10 campsites ($3 per person) along the **Lost Coast Trail** (*see* Outdoor Activities, *below*) between Bear Harbor and Usal Beach. Pay in advance at the visitor center or Usal Beach.

**FOOD** The Lost Coast escapes most tourist itineraries, so it's not surprising that there's almost nothing to speak of in the way of restaurants. Bring your own supplies or plan on eating many meals at the Hideaway.

➢ **PETROLIA** • The **Petrolia General Store** (40 Sherman St., tel. 707/629–3455) has a range of supplies to help you through the Lost Coast: food, sliced deli meat, beer, wine, candy, and ice cream. It's open Monday–Saturday 9–6, Sunday 11–5:30.

**Hideaway.** You can't help but admire this restaurant/bar on the north side of Petrolia's Mattole Bridge. It features the home cooking of Ed, the owner, who's got an enormous barbecue out back that cooks hindquarters, sides of beef, sometimes even whole hogs. Five bucks gets you a half-foot-long sandwich of Polish kielbasa on sourdough. On weekends there's sometimes an all-you-can-eat barbecue ($7) with meat, potato salad, macaroni, and coleslaw. You can also buy deli meats and cheeses to take with you. On weekends, the Hideaway is quite the local hangout. *Cnr Mattole and Conklin Creek Rds., tel. 707/629–3533. Open daily 10 AM–2 AM (food served until 9 PM).*

*One local disciple of the Hideaway's barbecue dinners claims, "Ed's goal is to make everyone as big as he is"—a prodigious task given Ed's girth.*

➢ **FERNDALE** • Ferndale has several restaurants that cater to wealthy tourists, but you can get a $3 sandwich that won't leave you hungry at the **Ferndale Meat Company** (376 Main St., tel. 707/786–4501; open Mon.–Sat. 8–5). More upscale but still reasonably priced is **Curley's Grill** (460 Main St., tel. 707/786–9696; open daily 11:30–9), with tasty grilled sandwiches ($5–$7) for lunch and dinner. The bright, airy dining room features work of local artists.

**EXPLORING THE LOST COAST** The only ways to enter the Lost Coast are from Highway 1 in the south on the barely maintained, dirt County Road 431; from U.S. 101 at Garberville on the Briceland Thorne Road; from Humboldt Redwoods State Park on the Mattole Road, 3 miles north of Weott; or from Ferndale in the north on the Mattole Road. Once you get into the Lost Coast, almost all roads are marked for the next hamlet along the way; you won't find elaborate sign posts on most intersections. Though you won't need a four-wheel drive to navigate the area, you should come prepared to drive on stretches of unpaved road no matter which route you take.

➢ **HONEYDEW** • The most accessible of the four routes is the beautiful paved road from Humboldt Redwoods, which heads west toward Honeydew, basically a post office and general store. You'll loop around a stunning and desolate stretch of coastline—"Malibu without the people," one local termed it—before passing east through Ferndale and returning to U.S. 101 just south of Eureka. Budget three hours for the 75-mile drive—and bring an extra-heavy sweater, even in summer, if you want to hang out and enjoy the rugged landscape.

➢ **FERNDALE** • On the north end of the Lost Coast, you may recognize the fairy-tale town of **Ferndale** as the backdrop for the 1995 virus-thriller movie *Outbreak.* Painted pink, blue, and yellow (Ferndale is a state historic landmark because of its Victorian homes and storefronts), the architecture seems incongruous in this otherwise undeveloped area. Instead of the grain stores, open markets, and saloons of yesteryear, the town is now full of antique shops, touristy boutiques, and candy stores.

For a look at Ferndale's history—which began in 1852 when the first farmers arrived to use the lush pastures for dairy cattle—stop by the **Ferndale Museum,** definitely worth the $1 admission. *Cnr Shaw and 3rd Sts., tel. 707/786–4466. Open Wed.–Sat. 11–4, Sun. 1–4; also June–Sept., Tues. 11–4. Closed Jan.*

## *Humboldt Home-Grown*

***So you've been wondering where that marvelous eighth of sinsimilla (seedless) marijuana came from? Backwoods botanists in the Lost Coast first produced the world-famous variety in the 1970s and soon succeeded in turning a form of personal recreation into the basis of the local economy. As the price of a pound of quality pot rose in the '70s and '80s (currently it hovers around $5,000), locals remember that Humboldt County was so flooded with $100 bills that the stores ran out of small change. That prosperous era began its decline in 1984 with the arrival of CAMP (Campaign Against Marijuana Planting) and Operation Greensweep—the federal government's domestic Grenada invasion. Growers have adjusted to the permanent CAMP presence by taking their business literally underground, using grow lights in specially designed caves or planting crops on mobile platforms. It's been unofficially estimated that CAMP only gets about 30 percent of the yearly output, making pot a still-lucrative, though illegal, cash crop.***

Ferndale's **Kinetic Sculpture Museum** displays vehicles from past Kinetic Sculpture Races, a Memorial Day weekend event requiring participants to travel in human-powered vehicles over a 38-mile course that traverses roads, dunes, bays, and rivers. Elaborate, ingenious, and comical only begin to describe what you'll see in this museum. *Cnr Main and Shaw Sts., no phone. Open daily 10–5.*

**OUTDOOR ACTIVITIES** The **Lost Coast Trail** winds past 52 miles of untouched coastline in the King Range and Sinkyone Wilderness. From the northern trailhead at Mattole Campground—at the end of Lighthouse Road just south of Petrolia—it takes 3 days to a week to hike the 24 miles to **Shelter Cove** in the south. After a few miles on paved roads, the trail begins again in earnest at **Hidden Valley** and stretches south to Usal Beach. Cooksie Creek, Spanish Flat, and Shipman Creek are good stopping points. The unkempt trail, best hiked in spring or fall when the days are warm and the evenings cool, alternates between ridges with ocean views and dark, fern-filled canyons. You can camp anywhere along the trail, but you'll need a free campfire permit, even if you only plan to use a gas stove. (Though you can probably find propane bottles at most Lost Coast general stores, camping supplies are sparse and you should stock up before leaving the freeways.) Water appears periodically along the way; don't forget to bring a filter or purification tablets. Check in with the **Bureau of Land Management** in Arcata (1695 Heindon Rd., tel. 707/825–2300) or Ukiah (2550 N. State St., tel. 707/468–4000) weekdays 7:45–4:30 to get permits and up-to-date trail info (also check tide tables, as a few points may be impassable during high tides).

# Avenue of the Giants

This 31-mile drive winds through some of the world's largest coastal redwoods—and yes, they are giants. The road runs roughly parallel to U.S. 101 between **Phillipsville,** a few miles north of Garberville, and **Pepperwood,** a few miles south of Scotia. Many of the redwood groves are up to 1,500 years old and are named after individuals and organizations who donated money to protect them. With luck, the trees will still be standing long after their names are forgotten.

Most of the Avenue of the Giants is contained within **Humboldt Redwoods State Park,** a truly amazing place to camp and hike. There's a $5 per vehicle day-use fee for some picnic areas and a couple campsites, but there's no reason to waste the money; almost the whole park is free. The **visitor center** (2 mi south of Weott on Avenue of the Giants, tel. 707/946–2263) has a staff of friendly volunteers and all the redwood-related items you could want, from books to postcards to ready-to-plant seedlings. It's open daily 9–5 March–October (Thurs.–Sun. 10–4 the rest of the year). Brochures for a self-guided auto tour of the park are available here and at both ends of the avenue (donation requested). For a dollar you can also get a map showing hiking and biking trails, campgrounds, and topo lines—well worth it if you plan to do some exploring, especially since the alternative free map is somewhat inaccurate.

Almost all the tourist traffic keeps to the Avenue of the Giants, but if you head west off the avenue onto Mattole Road (5 mi north of visitor center), you'll pass through equally beautiful old-growth stands where no Winnebagos block your view. In fact, you could easily keep yourself occupied for weeks without ever visiting such predictable tourist traps as the nearby **Confusion Hill**—where water appears to flow uphill—and the schlocky shops that sell redwood carvings and slabs of burl. Take a half-mile, self-guided loop trail through the wheelchair-accessible **Founders Grove,** 4 miles north of the visitor center on Avenue of the Giants, and visit the **Dyerville Giant,** which fell in March 1991. At 362 feet, it was the fourth-tallest tree in the world when it was last measured in 1972, and some believe it surpassed the 367-foot record before it toppled. The fact that it's now lying down makes its immensity all the more appreciable.

The **Drury-Chaney Loop** takes you on an easy 1- to 1½-hour round-trip (almost 3 mi) through redwood groves where 6-feet-tall lady ferns cover the forest floor. You'll find the trailhead 17 miles north of the visitor center on Avenue of the Giants, just south of Pepperwood at stop 9 on the auto tour. For a longer hike (9 mi round-trip) that's fairly flat the whole way, try the **Big Tree–Bull Creek Flats Loop,** which runs along both banks of Bull Creek through the **Rockefeller**

**Forest,** the largest tract of uncut old-growth redwoods. Start at either Big Tree or Bull Creek Flats parking area (both on Mattole Rd.), choose your bank, and go. Bridges connect the trails on either side of the creek at both parking areas, though the Bull Creek Flats Bridge is only installed in summer.

**CAMPING** If you want to camp on the Avenue of the Giants, skip the overcrowded Burlington Campground (next to visitor center), and head 5 miles south to **Hidden Springs Campground** (tel. 707/943–3177). The 154 private sites set on a hillside shaded by mixed forest rarely fill up, so you shouldn't need reservations. Better still, stay in one of the 39 sites at **Albee Creek Campground** (tel. 707/946–2472), 4 miles west of Avenue of the Giants on Mattole Road. You can sleep under the redwoods or out in the open, and solar-powered showers let you wash off the grime accumulated since your last ablution. The camp is conveniently located next to some of the best old-growth forest in the park. All developed sites are $14 in summer, $12 in winter. Reservations for all sites in the park can be made through MISTIX (tel. 800/444–PARK).

For those trekking through the area under their own power, the **Marin Hike and Bike Campground**—2 miles north of the visitor center on the Avenue of the Giants—is an ideal spot. For $3 a person you can sleep under the redwoods near the sparkling Eel River; the grounds have picnic tables, flush toilets, and treated water. If you have a small group and don't mind an environmental campsite, see if you can reserve one of the two walk-in sites ($9 each, $7 off-season) at **Baxter Campground.** The secluded sites have fire rings, tables, food-storage boxes, untreated water, and pit toilets. You'll sleep among beautiful redwoods growing alongside a gurgling stream. The campground is 6 miles west of U.S. 101 on Mattole Road. For all trail and environmental camps, you must register at Burlington Campground next to the visitor center.

# Scotia

A few miles north of the Avenue of the Giants is Scotia, a town that looks like it belongs on a movie set. Since its founding in 1869, Scotia has been owned by the Pacific Lumber Company, which runs the churches, the school, and the medical clinic, and provides housing for over 270 families. The largest redwood sawmill in the United States sprawls across town, blowing its whistles throughout the day. The effect is eerie, but the town's close-knit residents don't seem to mind.

*All along the Pacific Lumber tour are cards with pro-logging info, designed to convince visitors that the timber industry is a redwood's best friend. Directions for the tour are printed on an actual souvenir hunk of redwood—by loggers' reckoning a perfectly renewable resource.*

The mill offers a free self-guided tour that's worthwhile for even the staunchest opponent of the timber industry. You see the logs unloaded from trucks, moved through the log pond, stripped of bark with hydro-jets, and whittled into usable lumber—in short, the whole process. The way those huge chunks of old-growth redwood are tossed around like toys may bring a tear to your eye, but you have to be awed by the sheer magnitude of the operation. Pick up passes for the hour-long tour—offered weekdays 8–10:30 and 11:30–2—at the **Scotia Museum** (Main St., ½ mi south of Scotia exit, tel. 707/764–2222, ext. 247). Arrive at the museum by 1:30 since part of the mill shuts down at 2:30, and get earplugs from the gate house at the mill entrance—you'll be sorry if you don't.

**WHERE TO SLEEP** A few blocks north of Scotia in Rio Dell, the **Rio Dell Motel** (53 W. Center St., tel. 707/764–5165) has clean, slightly rickety doubles ($30, sometimes more in summer) with TVs but no phones. In Fortuna, 10 miles north of Scotia on U.S. 101, crash in a pleasant double ($38) with cable TV and a phone at the salmon-pink **Six Rivers Motel** (531 Fortuna Blvd., btw 1st and 2nd Sts., tel. 707/725–1181). For more choices, Eureka and Arcata (*see below*) are only 20–30 minutes north.

**FOOD** Diversity is not Scotia's strong suit, and its food is no exception. If you just want supplies before camping along the Avenue of Giants, Scotia's **Hoby's Market and Deli** (111 Main St., tel. 707/764-5331) is open 5 AM–9 PM daily. If you can't push on 10 miles north to Fortuna for a sit-down meal, try the **Hamburger and Sausage Company** (509 Wildwood Ave., Rio Dell, tel. 707/764–3319), where locals prefer the Big Boy ($4.50), a burger topped with cheese, a hot dog, bacon, and the works; with buffalo meat it's $6.25. Vegetarians are confined to fries or grilled-cheese sandwiches ($1.75).

Fortuna's **Hot Brew** is the best café, gallery, and bistro for miles. Try the huge veggie sandwich ($4 lunch, $7 dinner) filled with hummus, cream cheese, avocado, slivered almonds, lettuce, tomato, and sprouts. The adventurous will get a kick out of the Brew's shots of herbal extract ($1) that run the gamut from "mellow out" to "male vitality." There are live jam sessions by local bands on some Fridays and Saturdays at 9:30 PM. *2020 S. Main St., near Fortuna Blvd., tel. 707/725–2361. Open Mon.–Wed. 6–6, Thurs. 6–9, Fri. 6–11, Sat. 9–11.*

# Eureka

Twenty-five miles north of Scotia, U.S. 101 returns to the shoreline and arrives at Eureka, the most populous city on the North Coast. In 1807, when whaler James T. Ryan shouted "Eureka!" (Greek for "I've found it!") upon making his way through the narrow entrance to Humboldt Bay, he succeeded in giving the future state of California its motto. In 1849, miners traveled here to search the Trinity River for gold, but Eureka's distinction came as a whaling and logging town, and as a Native American lookout post where soldiers were known to go crazy with boredom.

*You'll know you're getting close to Eureka by the stench of its paper-mills. Apparently, locals build up some kind of immunity, but short-term visitors may find themselves wincing and dreaming of nicer-smelling areas.*

With the exception of **Old Town** (btw 1st, 2nd, C, and M Sts.), a neighborhood of restored Victorians worth a quick exploration by car, today's Eureka is a depressing slough of motels, fast-food joints, gas stations, and city-style dreariness. Though you probably won't want to stay long unless you enjoy the peculiar stench that wafts off the paper mill at almost all times, Eureka can be a great place to stock up on supplies and recuperate from the road. If you've been dying for luxury accommodations, it's well worth the money for a night at one of the area's reasonable bed-and-breakfast inns (*see box, below*). If you're simply looking for a place to stop on your drive up U.S. 101, you might do better to push 10 minutes north to Arcata (*see below*), where the scene is more appealing. Otherwise, pick up a free map at the **Eureka Chamber of Commerce** (2112 Broadway, tel. 707/442–3738), open weekdays 9–7, weekends 10–4 (in winter, weekdays 9–5 only).

**GETTING AROUND** **Humboldt Transit System** (133 V St., tel. 707/443–0826) runs buses in Eureka for 75¢. For 60¢ more, the bus will take you as far north as Trinidad (75 min) or as far south as Scotia (90 min). Buses allow bikes, but you'll need to make an appointment at the office to get the $5 lifetime permit.

**WHERE TO SLEEP** Motels are concentrated on Broadway and 4th streets, both of which serve U.S. 101. Most are noisy, grungy places to crash, but for the money they can't be beat. On the south entrance to Eureka along Broadway, try the **Broadway Motel** (1921 Broadway, btw Hawthorne St. and Wasash Ave., tel. 707/443–3156), where you can get an older-looking but reasonably clean room for two with TV, telephone, and tub for $26.50 ($2 more in summer). Within walking distance of Old Town, the **Budget Motel** (11400 4th St., at M St., tel. 707/443–7321) offers fairly clean doubles for $36, with queen beds, cable TV, and phones.

**FOOD** A **farmers' market** convenes 10 AM–1 PM summer Tuesdays in Old Town, and summer Thursdays (same times) at the Eureka Mall (btw Harris and Henderson Sts. east of U.S. 101). More than 60 small farms in Humboldt County participate—this is the place to stock up on fresh fruits and veggies, as well as herbs and honey. If you miss the market but still want some bulk foods, stop by **Eureka Natural Foods** (1626 Broadway, tel. 707/442–6325), open weekdays 9–7, Saturday 9–6, Sunday 10–6. The **Humboldt Bay Coffee Company** (211 F St., tel. 707/444–3961) has the finest mocha ($2.15) in town, made from beans roasted right on the premises. It's open daily 7–7, with extended hours in summer.

**Eureka Seafood Grotto.** It may attract an older crowd, but at least the food's cheap: fish and fries for $5.25 (lunch) or $6.75 (dinner) and oyster stew for $6.25. You can also get clam chowder to go ($3 a pint, $4.50 a quart). *605 Broadway, at 6th St., tel. 707/443–2075. Open Mon.–Sat. 11–10, Sun. noon–9.*

**Lost Coast Brewery and Café.** They brew their own beer and serve great food, attracting crowds of locals and tourists. The batter on the fish 'n' chips ($6.25) is made with the brewery's own ale, and their hearty sandwiches ($5–$8) come with garlic parmesan fries or coleslaw. You can't tour the brewery, but you can sample the beers (at least five are always on tap) for 50¢–75¢ per 2-ounce glass. *617 4th St., btw H and G Sts., tel. 707/445–4480. Open daily 11 AM–1 AM (food served until midnight).*

**Luna's.** The influence of the nearby Pacific is apparent in Luna's surprisingly authentic Mexican food—try the crab tostada ($6.25). Meat eaters should consider the bean platter (refried beans with steak and cheese; $6), served with fresh tortillas. *1134 5th St., btw L and M Sts., tel. 707/445–9162. Open Mon.–Sat. 11–9.*

**Samoa Cookhouse.** Hearty meals here are dished up lumber-camp style on oil-cloth-covered long tables. It's all-you-can-eat for breakfast ($6), lunch ($6.25), and dinner ($11); everyone gets the same meal, so you might want to call ahead to check the daily menu. *45 W. Washington St., tel. 707/442–1602. From U.S. 101, take Hwy. 255 west and follow signs.*

**WORTH SEEING** For an interesting glimpse of historical Eureka, head to the free, wheelchair-accessible **Clarke Memorial Museum** (240 E St., at 3rd St., tel. 707/443–1947), housed in a marble and granite edifice that used to be the Bank of Eureka. It has one of the best Native American displays in California; in addition to the usual arrows and baskets, there's an authentic Yurok dugout boat in the annex. The museum is open Tuesday–Saturday noon–4. For history buffs, the **Blue Ox Millworks** (north end of X St., tel. 707/444–3437 or 800/248–4259) offers a self-guided tour ($5) of a working Victorian sawmill and an entirely animal-powered farm. It's open Monday–Saturday 9–5 and summer Sundays 11–4.

For an history lesson with style, head to the pier at the foot of C Street in Old Town and board the *Madaket* for the **Humboldt Bay Harbor Cruise** (tel. 707/445–1910). For $9.50 March–October, skipper Leroy Zerlang—a Eureka native and tour guide for 20 years—gives you a look at the history of Humboldt Bay, complete with amusing anecdotes. From the ship's decks, you can see harbor seals, Canada geese, cormorants, lumber mills, and shipwrecks.

**OUTDOOR ACTIVITIES** Eureka isn't the most exciting place to enjoy Mother Nature, but you can take a refreshing walk in **Sequoia Park** (W St., take Harris St. east off U.S. 101), a small but dense forest featuring the big trees advertised in its name. **Humboldt Bay** is good for sea kayaking (there are several boat ramps along Waterfront Dr.), and you're not far from beautiful rivers and mountains. The Trinity River, also great for kayaking, is an hour's drive. The 3-mile run from Hayden Flat to Cedar Flat has a Class II–III difficulty. Need outdoor supplies? **Northern Mountain Supply** (125 W. 5th St., Eureka, tel. 707/445–1711) rents sleeping bags ($9–$10 a day), two-person tents ($10–$12 a day), canoes ($30 a day), kayaks ($20–$30 a day), and snowshoes ($10 a day), with significant discounts for multiple-day use. Stop by Mon-

## *B&Bs That Charge Only an Arm*

***The Eureka area is littered with posh bed-and-breakfasts charging upwards of $125 a night, but you won't have to sell your firstborn if you choose a B&B carefully. The Shannon House (2154 Spring St., 4 blocks south of Wabash Ave., tel. 707/443–8130) has three cluttered, kitschy rooms for $65–$75. Dorothy and Bob of the nearby Weaver's Inn (1440 B St., at 14th St., tel. 707/443–8119) are incredibly friendly, and their four rooms are straight out of a storybook, starting at $65 for a small single with shared bath.***

day–Saturday 9:30–7, Sunday 10–5. That said, check prices against Humboldt State University's Center Activities (*see* Arcata, *below*) before you rent or buy.

# Arcata

This beautiful, woodsy town 8 miles north of Eureka makes you feel instantly at home. Most shops, restaurants, and services are within easy walking distance of the town's grassy central plaza (btw G, H, 8th, and 9th Sts.), where you can listen to some pretty good buskers. Across U.S. 101, **Humboldt State University (HSU)** (Plaza Ave., off L. K. Wood Blvd. east of U.S. 101, tel. 707/826–4402) deserves its reputation as a hotbed of environmentalism and has attracted lots of students interested in earning non-traditional degrees.

*One local describes Arcata as the place "where the '60s meet the sea." Smiles and hellos are exchanged routinely on the streets and seem quite sincere, if occasionally pot-induced.*

Seventy-five percent of California's oysters are harvested from Arcata Bay, a fact celebrated in mid-June's **Oyster Festival.** Locals line up to consume the tasty bivalves ($1 each, six for $5) while listening to live folk music. The highlight is the oyster-calling contest (words can't do it justice). Call 707/826–9043 for more info.

**BASICS** The **Arcata Chamber of Commerce** has a small, free map of town and copious quantities of regional info. Pick up the free monthly *North Coast Journal,* which highlights local news and happenings. *1062 G St., at 11th St., tel. 707/822–3619. Open weekdays 10–4, Sat. 9–3.*

**COMING AND GOING** Arcata is the gateway to Redwood National Forest to the north and the mountainous national parks to the east on Highway 299 (*see* The Northern Coast Ranges, *below*). If you're carless and coming from Eureka (20 min, $1.35), take a ride on the **Humboldt Transit System** (133 V St., Eureka, tel. 707/443–0826). The **Arcata and Mad River Transit System** (tel. 707/822–3775) has routes around the city and to the suburbs in the north for a whopping 80¢.

**WHERE TO SLEEP** Besides the hostel, the only affordable option is the **Fairwinds Motel** (1674 G St., at 17th St., tel. 707/822–4824), 6 blocks north of the plaza. Generic doubles cost $42–$55 ($8 less in winter); at least the 27 rooms all face away from the freeway. Also consider camping farther up U.S. 101 (*see* Near Arcata, *below*) or crashing in a cheap motel in Eureka (*see above*).

➢ **HOSTELS** • **Arcata Youth Hostel.** It's an old wooden Victorian with a TV, microwave, barbecue, and five refrigerators. The hostel is only open June 25–August 25, as it's used for student housing the rest of the year. The 18 beds rent for $10 a night (including tax), regardless of whether you're an HI member. If you call ahead or get lucky, there are usually one or two private rooms available ($10 per person). *1390 I St., at 14th St., tel. 707/822–9995. Lockout 9 AM–5 PM. Reception open daily 5 PM–11 PM. Sheet rental ($1). Reservations recommended.*

**FOOD** Arcata has a wide range of inexpensive restaurants that cater to the student community. Most are near the plaza or in the area bordered by 16th, 18th, G, and H streets. A breakfast landmark is **TJ's Classic Café** (1057 H St., near 10th St., tel. 707/822–4650), where the weekday-morning special gives you a choice of eggs and potatoes, pancakes, or French toast for $2.50. The **Wildflower Café and Bakery** (1604 G St., at 16th St., tel. 707/822–0360) has good tempeh and nature burgers ($5) as well as organic specials and a tempting array of desserts. The **Arcata Co-Op** (cnr 8th and I Sts., tel. 707/822–5947) has a great bakery and an excellent selection of produce, cheeses, bulk and prepared foods, and locally produced tofu. They're open Monday–Saturday 9–9, Sunday until 8. A **farmers' market** convenes on Arcata's central plaza Saturday mornings 9 AM–1 PM from May to November.

**¡Hey Juan!** Ignore the name and focus instead on the massive, filling burritos ($4.75) lathered with one of four salsas (be warned that the "death paste" is only for the masochistic). Saturday 10:30–6, all veggie burritos are an unbeatable two-for-one. *1642½ G St., near 16th St., tel. 707/822–8433. Open daily 10:30–11 (Fri. and Sat. until 11:30).*

**Los Bagels.** It's something of a town institution, with outdoor tables, reggae music on the stereo, and a basketball court in back. Expect to see lots of students enjoying the killer bagels (45¢–55¢ each) piled high with toppings (50¢–$2). *1061 I St., near 11th St., tel. 707/822–3150. Open Mon. and Wed.–Fri. 7–6, Sat. 7–5, Sun. 8–3.*

**WORTH SEEING** The **Arcata Community Forest** offers nearly 10 miles of trails (most mountain-bike accessible) through second-growth redwoods. To get here, take 14th Street east over U.S. 101 until it dead-ends in a parking lot within forest boundaries. The Chamber of Commerce (*see* Basics, *above*) has free trail maps, as well as info on the **Arcata Marsh and Wildlife Sanctuary,** a water-treatment experiment headed by HSU professors. The marsh project lets the natural purifying processes of the marshlands erase contaminants from waste-water, allowing the water to be released into the adjoining Humboldt Bay. Foot trails pass throughout the 154-acre facility, allowing prime viewing of the many birds and ducks who call the marsh home. The Audubon Society offers free guided tours of the marsh Saturday morning at 8:30. To reach the marsh, take I Street south to the end.

At the **Finnish Country Sauna and Tubs,** $6.25 gets you a half hour in a private sauna or outdoor hot tub looking out on a relaxing garden and fish pond. At the sauna's Café Mokka Coffeehouse, enjoy the cheapest coffee in town (85¢ for a large), drink hot or cold juice from the juice bar, or browse through stacks of national and international newspapers and magazines. Live acoustic folk music happens here Friday and Saturday nights. *Cnr 5th and J Sts., tel. 707/822–2228. Tubs and coffeehouse open daily noon–11 (Fri. and Sat. until 1 AM).*

The local semi-pro baseball team, the **Humboldt Crabs,** enjoys much community support. If you're around in mid-summer, there are worse ways to spend a few dollars than buying a seat at a Crabs game. Check their schedule at stores, bulletin boards, and restaurants around town.

**AFTER DARK** Arcata is a college town, and its bars and theaters cater to the student population. **The Humboldt Brewing Company** (856 10th St., at I St., tel. 707/826–2739) is a laid-back pub that draws a local crowd for their award-winning microbrewed ales ($2.50 a pint) and a delicious selection of sandwiches ($6.25), burgers ($6), and salads ($4–$8). Live bands often play on Friday and Saturday nights (about $3 cover). **Brewin' Beats** (773 8th St., on the plaza, tel. 707/822–5053) is a truly happening place for eclectic live music Tuesday–Sunday. Cover is generally $3–$5, though on Wednesday and Sundays you can hear acoustic, bluegrass, or jazz for free. **Jambalaya** (915 H St., just off the plaza, tel. 707/822–4766) also has live entertainment almost every night. Weekly open-mike poetry readings and jazz music appeal to an older, artsy crowd, but on weekends the place books more hard-core bands (about $3 cover).

**OUTDOOR ACTIVITIES** Your adventures should begin at Humboldt State's **Center Activities** (2nd floor of University Center, under bookstore, tel. 707/826–3357), open weekdays 10–4 in summer, weekdays 9–6 during the school year. They rent everything from Windsurfers ($18–$28 a day) to canoes and kayaks ($20 a day) to sailboats ($35 a day) to camping, fishing, and snow gear. They've even got soccer balls and basketballs ($1 a day). For weekend rentals (Fri.–Mon.), you'll get great discounts. Humboldt Lagoons State Park (*see below*) is a great place for sailing and windsurfing, and the knowledgeable staff at the center has up-to-date info on area river conditions.

## NEAR ARCATA

**MAD RIVER BEACH** U.S. 101 hugs the coast north of Arcata, passing by a number of wide, windswept beaches, most of which are great for camping. You can't camp at the first one, Mad River Beach County Park (tel. 707/445–7652), but it's close enough to Arcata that you can come here for a brisk morning walk or an afternoon picnic. In mid to late summer, you'll get to tromp through thickets of wildflowers in the dunes, where the Mad River meets the Pacific. Bathrooms are in the boat ramp parking lot. Bring your sweatshirt, as winds range from mild to staggeringly gusty. To get here, take U.S. 101 just north of Arcata to the Guintoli Lane exit, and go west on Janes Road to Upper Bay Road, following the COASTAL ACCESS signs to the end of the narrow country road.

**CLAM BEACH** North of Mad River, Clam Beach County Park (tel. 707/445–7652) is—surprise!—a good place for clamming during low tides. As the water recedes, look for bubbles coming out of the sand, and then dig like hell (with shovel, pitchfork, or hands). David at **Time Flies** (815 J St., at 8th St., tel. 707/822–8331) can give you the scoop on the critters, including the mandatory license ($9 a day, $15 a year) and tips on how to steam your catch. No clamming is allowed May–October because the shellfish can become potentially fatal. Camping costs $8 per vehicle; arrive on foot and avoid the fee. Pit toilets are provided, and the campground's 16 sites are right next to U.S. 101, but at least the beach itself is wide enough that you'll feel like you're away from the highway on a shoreline walk. Sites closest to the parking lot have easy access to cement picnic tables and barbecue pits, but you'll find more privacy if you park along Clam Beach Drive between the two lots and hike through the waist-high scrub to a secluded patch of sand. To get here take Clam Beach exit off U.S. 101.

**PATRICK'S POINT STATE PARK** The campgrounds at Patrick's Point State Park, 20 miles north of Arcata, will make you happy you chose to travel in California. Even on summer weekends, when the three campgrounds (124 sites in all) fill to capacity, your site among the trees feels secluded, though you might have to wait for the coin-operated hot showers. Sites run $14, $12 in winter. There are plenty of hike/bike sites ($3), and 6 miles of trails traverse the grounds. An especially nice walk from the Agate Beach parking lot follows the **Rim Trail** for 2 miles along ocean bluffs. Periodic offshoots take you out to rocky points ideal for whale and sea-lion watching. You can also check out the yearly rituals still performed at the park's reconstructed Yurok village. *4150 Patrick's Point Dr., tel. 707/677–3570. Follow signs from U.S. 101. Day use: $5. Make camping reservations through MISTIX (tel. 800/444–PARK).*

**TRINIDAD** If your tent pole breaks or you get rained out, take refuge in tiny Trinidad at the **Lighthouse Motel** (3360 Patrick's Point Dr., 1½ mi south of U.S. 101, tel. 707/677–3121). Small but clean rooms go for $42—a bargain in this bed-and-breakfast enclave. The backyard boasts a cliff's-edge view of the ocean and a beautifully maintained garden. Owners Bill and Lorie have been known to barbecue with the guests. No credit cards are accepted and there's no smoking in the rooms. In case you forgot to stock up in Arcata, you can grab a tasty lunch for less than $5 at the campy **El-di-vi Caboose** (702 Patrick's Point Dr., 4 mi south of U.S. 101, tel. 707/677–3389), open Monday–Saturday 11–5.

**BIG LAGOON AND HUMBOLDT LAGOONS** A few miles north of Patrick's Point lies **Big Lagoon County Park** (tel. 707/445–7652). The 26 drive-in campsites are set among the trees, but they're not as private as the ones at Patrick's Point. There are no showers, though you will find flush toilets. Do some bird-watching at the lagoon or just take a peaceful walk at the water's edge. Sites cost $10 per night, and day use is $2. About 8 miles further north, U.S. 101 runs through **Humboldt Lagoons State Park** (tel. 707/488–2014). The beautiful beaches and lagoons in the park are free for day use, but you should keep on driving if you're looking for camping—the sole campground in the area ($7) is only accessible by boat.

# Redwood National and State Parks

The mammoth trees that populate the northern coast used to cover almost two million acres of California and Oregon, but as of 1993 only 87,000 acres of old growth remained in California—a sad tribute to the fact that a large tree can be worth as much as $50,000–$60,000 when sold for lumber. Thankfully, 80,000 of the remaining acres of old-growth are within protected parks, most here in Redwood National and State Parks, about an hour north of Eureka on U.S. 101. This is one of the few places on earth where you can enjoy the coastal redwoods, some of which are over 350 feet tall, 20 feet in diameter, and more than 2,000 years old.

Redwood National and State Parks, occupying a narrow strip that runs all the way from Orick to Crescent City, encompass much more than redwoods. So even if you don't know the difference between a redwood and a madrone (and don't care), you can still enjoy the park's wildlife. You're unlikely to have run in with one of the park's mountain lions or black bears, but it's easy to get a look at the abundant Roosevelt elk. More patient types can watch for whales December–March. The best spots for viewing are the Redwood Information Center (*see below*), where a spotting scope helps you get a closer look, and Klamath Overlook and Gold Bluffs Beach. You have a chance of seeing seals or sea lions almost anywhere along the coast—the park rangers can tell you which areas have seen the most activity of late. And, if you know what a pileated woodpecker or a marbled murrelet is, you'll be glad to know that the park is on one of North America's four major bird-migration routes. Dozens of books and pamphlets sold at the two main ranger stations (*see below*) will help you identity the things flapping above your head.

The park is confusingly divided between state and federal jurisdiction, and within the boundaries of Redwood National Park are the following state parks: **Prairie Creek** (tel. 707/488–2171), **Del Norte Coast** (tel. 707/464–9533), and **Jedediah Smith** (tel. 707/458–3310). The easiest way to approach the parks, though, is as one long continuum—just make forays from the highway wherever desire strikes. But, whatever you do, don't stick only to U.S. 101—the largest trees, best wildlife-viewing opportunities, and most secluded inlets lie a few miles off the highway.

**BASICS** Pick up maps, get pointers on trails and campgrounds, and get info on ranger-led programs at one of the two main ranger stations: The **Redwood Information Center** (off U.S. 101, 1 mi south of Orick, tel. 707/488–3461), near the southern park entrance and open daily 8–6 (daily 9–5 off-season); and Crescent City's **Redwood National Park Headquarters** (1111 2nd St., tel. 707/464–6101), open daily 8–5 year-round. The somewhat smaller **Hiouchi Information Center** (off Rte. 199, 10 mi NE of Crescent City, no phone) is only open May–October.

**FEES** Admission to Redwood National Park is free, but you pay $6 per carload in day-use fees for state park facilities, such as picnic grounds or beaches.

**WHEN TO GO** July and August bring flocks of hikers and RV commandos to the park. Temperatures rarely climb above the '60s in this foggy region, though it becomes dramatically warmer as you travel away from the coast. Winter means damp, chilly weather, but it's rarely bitterly cold. Expect temperatures between 30° and 50°, and expect to get wet.

**WHERE TO SLEEP** You didn't come to this neck of the woods to stay in a hotel—you're in the middle of the redwoods after all. Besides, the few roadside motels in Orick and Klamath are downright depressing. The best of the lot is the **Palm Café and Motel** (121130 U.S. 101, tel. 707/488–3381) in Orick. The Astroturf-like carpeting outside won't win any awards, but the rooms are perfectly clean—and not as tacky as you might have expected from the exterior, which sports a palm tree inexplicably growing out of the roof. Doubles are $45 in summer, $35 off-season. Otherwise, continue up the road a few miles to Crescent City (*see below*), where dozens of mostly generic hotels line U.S. 101.

➢ **HOSTELS** • **Redwood Youth Hostel (HI).** Perched above the ocean in Redwood National Park, this turn-of-the-century logger's mansion is a great base from which to explore the nearby beaches and mountains. (Several good trails begin just steps from the front door, and the staff leads nature walks that introduce you to the park's flora, fauna, and Native American history.) The hostel is clean and non-smoking, and has new furniture, a well-equipped kitchen (with separate stoves for vegetarian and meat cooking), and three showers. Some of the six rooms are coed. This is a strictly by-the-book hostel, so expect to do a chore. The atmosphere is friendly; in the evenings, guests gather on the redwood deck or around the wood-burning stove in the living room. Reservations (by check or credit card) are suggested in summer. Beds cost $10 a night. If you're not staying the night, a shower is $3. *14480 U.S. 101, Klamath, tel. 707/482–8265. 30 beds. Curfew 11 PM, strict lockout 9:30–4:30. Reception open daily 4:30 PM–9:30 PM. Sheet rental ($1).*

➢ **CAMPING** • The cheapest option is to take one of the national park's free campsites (tel. 707/464–6101), distributed on a first-come, first-served basis, but they all require up to a half-mile walk in. **Flint Ridge** is off the Coastal Drive near Klamath, and the walk there takes you through coastal growth into a quiet redwood forest. The 10 free sites have picnic tables, fire rings, and water nearby. The five free sites at **Nickel Creek** offer tide-pooling opportunities and ocean views. From Crescent City, drive a few miles south on U.S. 101, turn right on Endert's Beach Road, continue to the end, and follow the signs as you hike in a half mile. Bring your own water and keep your valuables out of sight, as there have been some thefts here. The

10 sites at **DeMartin** are on a grassy prairie a few minutes' walk from the ocean, and have potable water. From U.S. 101, look for signs just north of the Redwood Youth Hostel.

If you want a few more amenities—such as that gift from heaven, hot showers—try the state parks ($14 a night). Reservations are mandatory in summer, so call MISTIX (tel. 800/444–PARK) before setting out. The 25 shoreline sites at **Gold Bluffs Beach Campground** in Prairie Creek Redwoods State Park are exposed, but wind breaks have been put up. There are also three walk-in environmental sites and a hike/bike site here ($3). The huge sandy beach makes this campground particularly nice, as long as you don't mind the cold. Traveling north on U.S. 101, turn left on Davison Road a few miles past Orick; the 8-mile drive down the gravel access road discourages trailers and motor homes. The sites at **Elk Prairie Campground** (near Newton B. Drury Pkwy., off U.S. 101) are close together and attract noisy weekenders, but at least you're among old-growth redwoods. There's also good elk viewing here (hence the name). **Jedediah Smith Redwoods Campground** has 106 beautiful sites along the Smith River. Its accessibility (right off Hwy. 199, which branches off U.S. 101 just north of Crescent City) makes it popular with RVers, though. For info on many more camping options in and around the park, corner any park ranger at the park information offices (*see above*).

**FOOD** Within the park, your food options are severely limited. Smart travelers will stock up on groceries on the north edge of the park in Crescent City or 80 miles south of the park in Eureka. Otherwise, make do at one of the three or so markets off U.S. 101 in Orick, at the southern edge of the park. Perhaps the best stocked is the **Orick Market** (tel. 707/488–3225) on U.S. 101—if you're heading north, it's on your right just past the post office.

*If you've never tried salmon jerky before, get a free sample at Klamath Trading Company, which is connected to Kirstens Klam House in Klamath. At $30–$39 per pound it's pricey stuff, but it makes great trail food.*

About the only restaurants you'll find in the park are a few greasy spoons and hamburger joints in Orick and Klamath. The best of this grim lot is Orick's **Palm Café** (121130 U.S. 101, tel. 707/488–3381), where local loggers eat meat loaf ($4) and mashed potatoes ($1.50). Vegetarians will be hard pressed to find much here. A better but more expensive option is **Rolf's Park Café** (U.S. 101, at Davison Rd., 2 mi north of Orick, tel. 707/488–3841). The European chef cooks up meaty sandwiches ($6–$8.50) for lunch, hearty German entrées ($10–$16) for dinner, and game dishes—their specialty—morning, noon, and night. Breakfast ($6) here is massive: a German farmer's omelet served family style, with ham, bacon, sausage, mushrooms, cheese, potatoes, and pasta. In Klamath, stop off at **Kirstens Klam House Restaurant** (17505 U.S. 101, south of Requa, tel. 707/482–7325 or 707/482–5385), usually open daily 8–8, but sometimes closed in the off-season. Here you'll get big portions of deep-fried or sautéed salmon and chips (around $7). A veggie burger is about $4.25.

**EXPLORING THE REDWOOD PARKS** About 200 miles of trails wind through the park, from old-growth redwood groves that block out almost all light on the forest floor to driftwood-strewn beaches and estuaries. Pick up a hiking map from one of the ranger offices (*see above*) before you set out—many trails are poorly signposted. The Redwood Natural History Association's *Redwood National Park Trail Map* ($1.50) is best.

One of the best hikes in the park is the easy ¾-mile jaunt across shallow creeks to **Fern Canyon** in Prairie Creek Redwoods State Park. You have to drive 8 miles on a dirt road to reach the canyon (take the Davison Road turnoff west from U.S. 101), but it's worth it. The 40-foot high canyon walls are covered with five-finger ferns, which, as their name implies, look like green hands projecting from the canyon's sides—get a breeze going, and you'll think a million green Martians are waving at you.

If you came to Redwood National Parks strictly to see redwoods, you'll want to take the **Stout Grove Trail,** where you'll find some of the oldest and largest trees in the park—some 22 feet in diameter. To get here, drive south on U.S. 101 from Crescent City, turn left on Elk Valley Road, and right on Howland Hill Road to the Stout Grove parking area. More ambitious hikers may want to head to the **Redwood Creek Trailhead** (look for signs pointing south after you turn onto Bald Hills Rd. from U.S. 101). From the parking area you can hike about 8 miles (each way) on a mellow trail that's not too steep. If you get a free permit from the Redwood Information Center (*see above*), you can camp anywhere along the trail.

If you're short on time or energy, a wheelchair-accessible trail leads from Bald Hills Road to the **Lady Bird Johnson Grove.** It's a comfortable 1-mile loop through a beautiful stand of redwoods, perfect for those on a whirlwind tour of the area. Look for the trailhead 2 miles east of U.S. 101 on Bald Hills Road.

*If your tour of the redwood parks is truly of the whirlwind, no-getting-out-of-the-car variety, check out the 45-mile scenic loop that follows U.S. 199 from Crescent City to Howland Hill Road, which will return you to the coast.*

The best place in the park to hang out and watch the wild Roosevelt elk is at Rolf's Park Café. Unfortunately, Rolf's other specialty is elk steak with wild mushroom sauce and cranberries. Even if you won't be here long enough to take a kayak trip, you should make a brief stop to see the park's Roosevelt elk. The field behind Rolf's Park Café (*see* Food, *above*) is so popular with the elk that the park sends rangers out here to explain the habits of the big critters. You're also likely to see the elk along Newton B. Drury Scenic Parkway, accessible from U.S. 101 at the southern end of the park about 6 miles north of Orick, or from U.S. 101 further north, about 4 miles south of Klamath. The rare marbled murrelet, a small seabird that's the latest endangered species to become a pawn in the war to save the old-growth forests, is a more elusive creature. It's more frequently spotted at Lost Man Creek in summer.

**PARK ACTIVITIES** Mountain bikers are prohibited from using most of the trails in the park, but one exception is the moderately difficult 11½-mile **Holter Ridge Bike Trail.** This old logging road, accessible from the end of Bald Hills Road (which leads east from U.S. 101 a few miles north of Orick), passes both old-growth and second-growth redwood trees.

If you forgot your bicycle and your hiking boots, all is not lost. The rangers lead two different **kayaking** trips. The tour of the Klamath River estuary takes place twice a day Friday–Tuesday from mid-July through August. You must register no more than two days in advance at the Redwood Information Center (*see above*), and the trip is free. If you're up for a few small rapids, try the kayak tour of the Smith River, at the north edge of the park. Again, register no more than two days in advance, this time at the Hiouchi Information Center (*see above*). The Smith River trip costs $6 and runs June–July. Both book up fast, and budget cutbacks means the trips might be curtailed—call the ranger stations for the most recent information. If you miss the kayak trips, the **Hiouchi Hamlet** (2100 Rte. 199) in Hiouchi will sell you an inner tube for $12 and buy it back (if it still holds air) for $7, so you can enjoy the Smith River by tube.

# Crescent City

Sixteen miles north of Klamath and 20 miles south of the Oregon border lies Crescent City, the last bastion of fast food and 24-hour supermarkets on the Northern California coast. This is little more than a convenient urban base for trips into Redwood National Park to the south (*see above*) or the Smith River National Recreation Area to the east (*see* the Northern Coast Ranges, *below*).

If you decide to stick around town, there are ways to occupy your time at minimal cost. Head over to **Popeye's Landing** (bottom of B St.) to try your hand at crabbing, a popular sport here thanks to a prolific Dungeness crab population. You can rent a crab pot (a net strung on a set of flexible rings) and bait at the landing ($5 for 3 hrs weekdays, $8 weekends), or a chair ($2 for 3 hrs) in case you get tired of standing. Basically, you just sit on the pier, throw the baited ring into the ocean, and wait for a crab to crawl inside (pull the ring up once in a while to check it). You might find someone at the landing who will cook up your catch for a few bucks and bag it to go (the catch limit is 10 crabs per person). If you'd rather fish for perch, pole rental is $5 for three hours; no fishing license is required.

At low tide April–September, you can walk from the pier across the ocean floor to the **Battery Point Lighthouse** (tel. 707/464–3089) and take a $2 tour Wednesday–Sunday 10–4. A map of the city and copious advice on scenic drives are available at the **Crescent City Chamber of**

**Commerce** (1001 Front St., tel. 707/464–3174 or 800/343–8300), open daily Memorial Day to Labor Day (otherwise weekdays) 9–5.

**WHERE TO SLEEP** The dozens of hotels lining U.S. 101 near Crescent City charge remarkably similar rates: $35–$45 per double in winter, $45–$60 in summer. Possibly the best option in town, especially when winter rates are in effect, is **Curly Redwood Lodge** (701 U.S. 101, on south edge of Crescent City, tel. 707/464-2137). The decor in the huge rooms is so '70s it could be used in a *Brady Bunch* episode. Doubles start at $37 in winter, $59 in summer. The cheaper **Reef Motel** (665 L St., at 7th St., tel. 707/464–3142), smack in the center of town, has tacky brown-and-orange bedspreads and rickety furniture that are somewhat compensated for by friendly owners who do their best to keep this 1952 building from totally disintegrating. Doubles start at $33 in winter, $38.50 in summer. You'll find the shiny, antiseptic **Bayview Inn** (310 U.S. 101, tel. 707/465–2050) just south of Crescent City. Finally, a hotel that *doesn't* charge extra for rooms with a view; doubles start at $45 in winter, $55 in summer.

**FOOD** Crescent City's tiny earthy community eats at **Alias Jones** (983 3rd St., tel. 707/465–6987), open weekdays 7 AM–5:30 PM and Saturday until 3 PM. Try the pesto omelet or the hot zucchini, mushroom, cheese and tomato sandwich (both $6). They also have great salads, burgers, baked goods, and coffee drinks. At the **Good Harvest Café** (700 Northcrest Dr., at U.S. 101, tel. 707/465–6028), locals rave about breakfast (a large order of French toast is $5), but the lunches are just as good (sandwiches are $4.50–$5.75). Vegetarians will have a field day here. It's open Monday–Saturday 7–3, Sunday 8–1. While you're in town, restock your backpack at the small health-food market **Harvest Natural Foods** (265 L St., tel. 707/464–1926), open Monday–Saturday 10–6.

Crescent City is also home to the **Tired Chicken** (1299 9th St., tel. 707/464–4057), probably the only restaurant on earth where you can order a strawberry omelet with cream cheese and Cool Whip, or a hot-dog crêpe with sauerkraut and Velveeta cheese sauce. Despite serving these culinary perversions, this little shack is generally full of off-duty cops and other locals eating less creative omelets and crêpes.

# The Northern Coast Ranges

**The Northern Coast Ranges are** "Bigfoot Country," where the legendary man-ape is sometimes sighted. More frequently sighted are Bigfoot tourist traps, with everything from T-shirts to chain saw–carved sculptures touting the mythical beast. **Bigfoot Days,** the climax of which is the crowning of a Bigfoot king and queen, is the best time to satiate cravings for both Bigfoot hype and small-town culture; the festivities take place in Happy Camp on Labor Day weekend.

The mountainous regions of the **Six Rivers** and **Klamath** national forests are well worth a visit—this is some of the state's most spectacular and unpopulated wilderness, with glacial lakes, salmon-filled rivers, and 8,000-foot mountain peaks where the snow doesn't melt until July. The forest's character ranges from the redwood-dominated coastal communities to the inland forests of fir, pine, madrone, and oak—all of which are supported by water from the six major rivers that flow through the region's deep valleys. You'll find lots of opportunities for fishing, rafting, kayaking, and mountain biking, but best of all is the chance for solitary hiking in wilderness areas untouched by logging. Within Six Rivers National Forest, near the coast, is the **Smith River National Recreation Area,** 315 miles of wild and scenic river. While the beauty of the river and its valley can be awe-inspiring, the chances of your bliss being ruined by crowds are much higher.

Towns are few and far between, and they're small at that. In the northern part of Klamath National Forest, **Happy Camp** makes a convenient launching pad into the Siskiyou or Marble Mountain Wilderness. Still an active gold-mining town, Happy Camp feels a bit like the old California frontier. A helpful ranger station and modern conveniences get you set for the woods. In the south, **Willow Creek** has gas, markets, a few unexceptional eateries, and many rafting companies. The Trinity River flows right through town on its way north through a beautiful valley, and offers opportunities for mellow floats or real action on high-intensity white water. For info on adjacent areas, including Weaverville, Lewiston Lake, Trinity National Forest, and the Yolla Bolly–Middle Eel Wilderness, *see* Chapter 5.



## BASICS

**VISITOR INFORMATION** You can send away for trail maps ($3) and make camping reservations in advance through all the branches of the national forest office headquarters. Each office has general info about the area it covers, but you'll rarely get rangers with good field experience. For that you should go to a national forest substation in the area you wish to explore. As for weather considerations, plan ahead if you're the type, but don't count on the weather to comply (*see* When to Go, *below*).

*Tune in to 91.3 (KIDE)—Hoopa's local station—for a wide range of music that reflects local tastes. Country and western gets major play, but you might also find classical, rock and roll, and talk radio.*

The **Klamath National Forest Headquarters** (1312 Fairlane Rd., Yreka 96097, tel. 916/842–6131), open weekdays 8–5, is just east of I–5 at the south end of Yreka (*see* Chapter 5). There are substations in Etna (tel. 916/467–5757), Fort Jones (tel. 916/468–5351), Happy Camp (tel. 916/493–2243), Klamath River (tel. 916/465–2241), MacDoel (tel. 916/398–4391), and Orleans (tel. 916/627–3291).

**Six Rivers National Forest Headquarters** (1330 Bayshore Way, Eureka 95501, tel. 707/442–1721) has maps ($3), books, and staff on hand weekdays 8–4:30. Six Rivers substations are in Gasquet (tel. 707/457–3131), Mad River (tel. 707/574–6233), Orleans (tel. 916/627–3291), and Willow Creek (916/629–2118). Headquarters for the **Smith River National Recreation Area** are in Gasquet (tel. 707/457–3131).

**WHEN TO GO** Prepare for an almost biblical onslaught of strange weather. Rain (50–70 inches per year), sleet, and hail soak the unprepared, even in summer, and wildfires periodically serve up wilderness barbecue-style. Fall and spring bring more rain, mud slides, the occasional flood, and sometimes even snow. A few areas remain accessible in winter, but the weather is *really* nasty then. While summer temperatures in the valleys average in the 90s, cooler temperatures at higher elevations make long backpacking trips bearable. Snow blocks some high-country trails through July, so be sure to check on trail conditions with the local ranger substations, and carry warm clothing to protect against hypothermia. Late spring, summer, and early fall (through early September) are the best times to visit.

**WHAT TO PACK** Aside from the usual camping gear, bring the means to secure your supplies from hungry bears (*see* Camping, in Chapter 1). Make sure you have a good tarp to lay under your tent in case of rain, and spikes to hold your tent down in heavy wind. Wood abounds, but bring charcoal or fire-starter sticks to get things going in case the wood is wet. Tire chains are a must December–March to get through the mountain passes.

### *Hoopla in Hoopa*

***Twelve miles north of Willow Creek is the Hoopa Valley Indian Reservation, the first land granted to Native Americans in California after the Gold Rush in 1864. The 89,000-acre reservation is shared by both Hoopa and Yurok tribes. Visitors are welcome to view Hoopa dances, but no cameras or video and tape recorders are allowed. For $10, you can tour the restored village and talk to tribe members. Contact the Hoopa Tribal Museum (Hoopa Valley Shopping Center, tel. 916/625–4110).***

## COMING AND GOING

The Northern Coast Ranges are bordered by two major north–south highways: **U.S. 101** on the west and **I–5** on the east. The major east–west thoroughfare is **Highway 299,** which you can reach by turning east from U.S. 101 north of Arcata or west from I–5 at Redding. From Highway 299, you can tour both forests, with the option of detouring into the backcountry, by turning north onto Highway 3 at Weaverville and looping back south on Highway 96, which rejoins Highway 299 at Willow Creek. The trip will take at least 7½ hours of straight driving, so you'll probably want to take advantage of the excellent camping along the way. Don't leave the major roads without good tires and a spare—many forest-service roads are gravel-covered and unmaintained. **Green Belt Stages** (tel. 800/861–6122) runs buses once a day on Highway 299 between Eureka and Redding (4 hrs, $30 round-trip); you can arrange to have the bus let you out at a town along Highway 299 for slightly less.

## WHERE TO SLEEP

**MOTELS** The clean rooms at the **Willow Creek Motel** (Hwy. 96, ¼ mi north of Hwy. 299 in Willow Creek, tel. 916/629–2922 or 916/629–2115) are so quaint they have duck decals on the toilet seats. Air-conditioned doubles with cable TV start at $35. The motel fills up in summer with tourists, and in fall with fishermen, so try to reserve at least 3 days in advance. In Happy Camp, where Indian Creek meets the Klamath River, the **Klamath Inn Motel and RV Park** (110 Nugget Rd., off Hwy. 96, tel. 916/493–2860) has eight doubles with shared bath starting at $33 ($3 more for private bath). In Hoopa, 12 miles north of Willow Creek, the **Best Western Tsewenaldin Inn** (Hwy. 96, at Hoopa Valley Shopping Center, tel. 916/625–4294 or 800/528–1234) has a pool and Jacuzzi, but the rates ($65 for two) should make you think twice.

**CAMPING** Hundreds of developed and backcountry campsites are scattered throughout the national forests, and you almost never have to worry about crowds hampering your appreciation of nature. Free camping is available throughout the national forests: Simply throw down a tent or sleeping bag at least a quarter mile away from any developed campground, after picking up the required (free) campfire permit from any ranger station. If you want to camp in the Smith River National Recreation Area, check out **Grassy Flat** (on Hwy. 199, 4 mi east of Gasquet), situated near the Middle Fork of the Smith River. The 19 ($8) sites are spread through a hardwood forest, and come with fire grills, vault toilets, and drinking water; reservations can be made by calling 800/280–CAMP.

➢ **NEAR WILLOW CREEK** • A convenient and popular campground is **Tish Tang**—8 miles north of Willow Creek (3 mi south of Hoopa) on Highway 96—with 40 river-accessible and first-come, first-served sites ($6) in a dense forest of young firs, maples, and madrones. Though it's open year-round, running water is only available late May–October. The noise from Highway 96 filters down the canyon, but you're fairly secluded. Keep an eye on your stuff; occasional thefts have been reported here. In the oak, madrone, and fir forest of **Grays Falls** (12 mi east of Willow Creek on Hwy. 299), the 33 sites ($6), open mid-May to early September, are equipped with running water and flush toilets, and the area is so lightly used you'll probably feel like you own the place. Site 13 is wheelchair accessible.

➢ **NEAR HAPPY CAMP** • Though the 21 well-shaded sites ($6, $2 day use) set in a stand of fir at **Dillon Creek Campground** (about 25 mi south of Happy Camp, on Hwy. 96) are not the most private spots you could find, easy access and an idyllic, sandy-bottomed swimming hole make the camp well worth a stop during the sweltering summer months. Dillon Creek, with drinking water and toilets, is open May–August. The 18 free sites at **O'Neil Creek** (on Hwy. 96, halfway btw Happy Camp and I–5) are set under towering firs; some of the sites overlook the Klamath River. Open June–mid-November, the campground has vault toilets and only stream water, so remember to filter or boil before drinking.

One of the better campgrounds around, **Sulphur Springs** offers six secluded walk-in sites along Elk Creek in a mixed forest marked by huge, old-growth firs. Moss-covered rocks crowd the edge of the creek, and campers have easy access to a nearby natural hot spring (about 75°). Sulphur Springs has only vault toilets and no drinking water, and is located 15 miles south of

Happy Camp on Elk Creek Road. One mile up the road, **Norcross** has six free sites situated in meadows and second-growth forest with vault toilets and no drinking water. Both Norcross and Sulphur Springs serve as trailheads into the Marble Mountain Wilderness, though you'll have to ford Elk Creek if you start from Norcross. Look for the burned-out chimney between the two campgrounds: It marks a popular swimming hole on Elk Creek.

## FOOD

You'll get a good meal if you're willing to travel to Yreka, Etna, or Weaverville (*see* Chapter 5), but short of that you're looking at mediocrity. In Happy Camp, the **Indian Creek Café** (106 Indian Creek Rd., tel. 916/493–5180), open daily 7 AM–9 PM in summer and until 7 PM in winter, has a 25-page menu that "reads like *Gone With the Wind*"—but while quantity is high, quality suffers, and the cafeteria-style furnishings aren't much to look at. You get fewer options but a friendlier atmosphere at the **Frontier Café** (64118 2nd Ave., Happy Camp, tel. 916/493–2242), open weekdays 5 AM–8 PM and Saturday 7 AM–8 PM. Sample the vegetarian lasagna ($5.50) or taco salad ($5). The best source for supplies is **Larry's Market** (144 Davis Rd., tel. 916/493–2621).

If you're in Willow Creek, stop in for decent, if generic, diner fare at the wheelchair-accessible **Flame Restaurant** (Hwy. 299, just west of Hwy. 96, tel. 916/629–2609), open daily 6 AM–9 PM. Lalo's potatoes (hash browns with sautéed bell pepper, onion, sour cream, cheese, and salsa; $3.50) will sit perfectly with that jug of Gallo burgundy you guzzled around the campfire last night. You'll pay a bit more for the Old West atmosphere at **Cinnabar Sam's** (19 Willow Way, off Hwy. 299, tel. 916/629–3437), where pelts, saws, antlers, and stuffed birds cover the walls. Sandwiches run $4–$10; on Fridays and Saturdays the pub stays open until 10. The bright-green-trimmed **Bob's Shopping Center** (Hwy. 299, west of Hwy. 96, tel. 916/629–2457) is the place to stop if you're gathering groceries before hitting the trail.

## EXPLORING THE NORTHERN COAST RANGES

The "greenbelt" that extends from the Oregon border all the way down to Clear Lake comprises several mountain ranges, national forests, and wilderness areas. Six Rivers National Forest—and the Siskiyou Wilderness—lies to the northwest, Klamath National Forest to the northeast. To the south is Mendocino National Forest (*see* Near Clear Lake, in U.S. 101 to Leggett, *above*), and to the east are Shasta-Trinity National Forest, the Trinity Alps Wilderness, and the Yolla Bolly–Middle Eel Wilderness (*see* Chapter 5). This is all confusing, even on the map, but don't be discouraged.

**KLAMATH NATIONAL FOREST** The 250,000-acre **Marble Mountain Wilderness** in Klamath National Forest is one of the most pristine areas in California, and you don't need a wilderness permit to explore it—though you will need a free campfire permit for any open flame (including camp stoves). This is where the wild things are: bears, mountain lions, quail, foxes, deer, elk, red-tail hawks, bald eagles, and Black Marble Mountain itself, its marble-and-limestone peak rising 7,442 feet out of the snow. The rugged ridges of the wilderness tower over narrow, winding river valleys and isolated highlands filled with meadows and lakes and an extremely diverse population of trees that includes mixed fir, oak, madrone, pine, and mountain hemlock.

➢ **SHORT HIKES** • A short and easily accessible day hike is the **Dillon Creek Trail,** which follows the picturesque and inviting Dillon Creek for a little more than a mile as it flows through a forested valley toward the Klamath River. The sharp-eyed may catch sight of deer, elk, osprey, fox, or even a bear. To reach the trail from the Dillon Creek Campground (*see* Camping, *above*), cross the bridge to the north, walk underneath the bridge, then follow the trail.

For a short, scenic hike through some of the forest's most impressive—and most secluded—stands of ancient Douglas fir, spend some time along Groves Prairie Creek on the mile-long **Groves Prairie Trail.** The flat terrain makes for easy hiking, and the 4,200-foot elevation means that temperatures stay pleasantly cool in summer. To reach the trailhead, head east on Hwy.

299 for 11 miles, turn left on Denny Road (Trinity County Road 402), and after 2 miles turn left onto Forest Service Road 4. After 6.8 miles turn right onto Road 7N04, and after crossing over Groves Prairie Creek (7 miles), turn right onto Road 7N04P, which leads to the picnic area and trailhead.

➢ **LONGER HIKES** • To access the Marble Mountain Wilderness, try the eight free campsites at **Lovers' Camp.** From Highway 3 in Fort Jones, take Scott River Road west for 12 miles, turn south toward Indian Scotty Campground, cross the river, and follow signs to Lovers' Camp. From here, the 5-mile **Canyon Creek Trail** leads west into the Marble Valley, a popular backcountry camping spot. One mile into the Canyon Creek Trail, near the Sky High Lakes, the **Red Rock Trail** forks to the south and continues into high mountain meadows, eventually meeting the Pacific Crest Trail after 6½ miles. In hunting season (fall and winter), avoid Lovers' Camp and its trails, as the area is popular with drunken marksmen.

**SIX RIVERS NATIONAL FOREST** The Six Rivers National Forest stretches like a long finger south from Oregon to the Trinity County line. The forest contains (part of) the 135,000-acre **Siskiyou Wilderness** (the wilderness spills over into Klamath and Siskiyou national forests). Though you won't find the same concentration of lakes and alpine meadows here as in Klamath National Forest's more popular Marble Mountain Wilderness (*see above*), you will almost always be rewarded for your backcountry efforts with some truly superlative views and solitude among the forests and mountains.

In the very northwest corner of the forest, east of Gasquet on Highway 199, the mountains, streams, and canyons of the **Smith River National Recreation Area** surround the green Smith River, one of the last undammed rivers in California. In summer you can arrange to kayak the scenic Smith for just $6 (*see* Park Activities, in Redwood National and State Parks, *above*). The river valleys are truly spectacular, though the area's proximity to the coast and its warm summer weather sometimes mean overcrowding.

➢ **SHORT HIKES** • For an accelerated introduction to the coastal and inland botany of the Smith River National Recreation Area, try the 1-mile round-trip **Myrtle Creek Trail.** This self-guided interpretive trail runs along an old mining ditch near a gurgling stream, passing from a thick redwood forest into a more open pine forest. The trailhead is just off Highway 199 7 miles west from Gasquet; park on the left-hand side just past the South Fork Bridge, cross 199 on foot and walk west 20 yards.

If your interests in the Six Rivers forest lie farther inland, the **Grays Falls Nature Trail** is a perfect self-guided, hands-on introduction to the flora of the Trinity River valley. The trail starts at Grays Falls Campground (*see* Camping, *above*) and runs though oak, fir, madrone, and pine for a little more than a mile before winding down to Grays Falls and a sunny riverside beach.

For a low-intensity hike with big rewards, you can't beat the trek to **Mill Creek Lake.** From Highway 96 about a mile north of Hoopa, take Big Hill Road east 12 miles and follow signs to Mill Creek. It's only about a half-hour hike from the trailhead to the beautiful lake (stocked annually—bring your fishing pole). You need a wilderness permit for this one, so stop in before you go at the Lower Trinity Ranger District (Hwy. 96, ½ mi north of Willow Creek, tel. 916/629–2118), open daily 8–4:30 but closed winter weekends.

➢ **LONGER HIKES** • The **South Kelsey Trail** was created in 1851 as an army supply artery from Crescent City to Fort Jones, 200 miles east. Today, it provides over 16 miles of challenging hiking through the Siskiyou Wilderness. After following the south fork of the Smith River, you reach the 5,775-foot Baldy Peak, from which you can view the Pacific Ocean, the rugged Siskiyou Backbone, the Marble Mountains, and Mount Shasta to the east on a clear day. There's plenty of water along the way, but giardia has been found, so boil or filter it before drinking. You can cover the whole trail to Harrington Lake in a great 3- to 4-day hike. To reach the trailhead from Crescent City, take Highway 199 east 7 miles to South Fork Road (County Rd. 427), turn right, and go 14 miles to Forest Service Road 15 (there's no sign, so watch your mileage). Turn right, go 3 miles, turn left onto Forest Service Road 15N39, and follow signs.

If you want to get a taste of the Siskiyou Wilderness without trekking through the backcountry for days, the **Buck Lake Trail** will take you by towering old-growth firs on the way to a mountain lake where you can enjoy excellent fishing in almost total solitude. From Gasquet, travel 8 miles north on Highway 199, turn right onto Forest Service Road 17N05 for 8½ miles, then left on Road 6N02 for 3½ miles to the Doe Flat Trailhead. Park and take the Doe Flat Trail for a mile to the Buck Lake Trail.

## FOREST ACTIVITIES

**BIKING** Bicycles are not allowed on trails in the wilderness areas, but most backcountry trails in the three forests are great for mountain biking. In summer, use Highway 3 and Highway 96 as takeoff points for bike trips. The roads are not crowded, and cycling through picturesque mining towns like Callahan, Etna, Seiad Valley, and Somes Bar is a great way to travel. The fat biking packet available at the Klamath National Forest ranger station (*see* Visitor Information, *above*) is an excellent resource listing 17 rides. A moderate, scenic 13-mile ride starts at the far end of Elk Creek Bridge in Happy Camp. You follow asphalt and dirt roads to Sulphur Springs Campground (*see* Camping, *above*), where you can go for a swim. If you have mechanical problems, **Shasta Valley Bikes** (215 W. Miner St., Yreka, tel. 916/842–7701), 70 miles east of Happy Camp, charges $25 for a 2-hour tune-up.

**RAFTING** Most people don't want to make the long trek north to the Klamath River in Happy Camp, but if you do you'll be rewarded by 30 miles of rafting over Class II and III rapids. Local guide **Bryan Joosten** (Box 319, Happy Camp 96039, tel. 916/493–2207) takes private parties on two- to three-day trips for $65 a person per day—he'll negotiate day-trips for groups smaller than four if he's not busy. If you want to cut the cost, you can bring your own meals, but his are worth the price. *See* Redwood National and State Parks, *above,* for the lowdown on free ranger-led rafting on the Klamath.

For a guided white-water adventure on the Trinity River, try the **Bigfoot Outdoor Company** (Hwy. 299, behind Cinnabar Sam's in Willow Creek, tel. 916/629–2263 or 800/722–2223). It offers full-day trips for $70 (including lunch) and half-day trips for $39. You can also rent rafts for self-guided Class I and II tours (starting at $36 per day); the staff will recommend good spots. **Tish Tang Gorge** is a 3½-hour Class II run beginning at Big Rock outside of Willow Creek, and ending at the Tish Tang Campground (*see* Camping, *above*). Bigfoot also rents inflatable kayaks ($25 per person) and other river gear, and you can arrange for shuttle service to a put-in point (so you can end up at your car) for $6–$15.

# THE CASCADES 5

By Alan Covington Phulps

**Overlooked by everyone from international tourists to longtime California residents,** the north inland expanse of pine forests, alpine mountains, and dormant volcanoes is perhaps the best place in the state to get away from the crowds and into the great outdoors. To the east the Sierra Nevadas gradually melt into the Cascade range, to the west the forests and mountain lakes of the coast ranges play host to Bigfoot, and looming over it all is the mystical Mt. Shasta, whose shadow stretches across the Sacramento Valley. There's never a dull vista—except when you're traveling up I–5, the major highway that runs north–south through the region.

While the oppressively hot mining and shipping towns along I–5, including Red Bluff, Redding, and Yreka, make convenient bases, you'll want to leave the Sacramento Valley as soon as possible and head into the mountains. East of Red Bluff, you can imbibe microbrewed beer with Cal State students in Chico, or opt for solitary hiking or biking in the gentle mountains of the Plumas National Forest. West of Red Bluff lies backpacker's paradise: The Yolla Bolly–Middle Eel Wilderness beckons with absolute seclusion and pristine mountain streams.

*The sheer variety of people and backgrounds makes you wonder how north staters live together peacefully. You'll rub shoulders with loggers, New Agers, farmers, neo-hippies, mountain folk, hyper-educated "flatlanders" (city dwellers who move to the mountains), miners, and more.*

The Cascade Range, formed by volcanic eruptions, begins in Northern California and climbs through Oregon and onward into Washington. It is part of the "Ring of Fire," a virtually contiguous chain of andesitic volcanoes that circle the Pacific Ocean from South America, on through to Alaska, Japan, the Philippines, and New Zealand. Almost as an apology for Redding's dreariness, the area east of it—including Lassen Volcanic National Park and Lava Beds National Monument—offers an unforgettable taste of the desolate but subtly beautiful volcanic landscape that marks northeastern California. Lava Beds gives you the chance to be a kid again—you can explore miles of deserted caves on your own with just a flashlight in hand. To the west lies the dramatic Trinity Alps Wilderness; and in the north, Mount Shasta City is home to New Agers eager to explore the mountain's mysterious powers.

The weather in this region is as diverse as the landscape. Moving from west to east it becomes dryer and dryer. The Trinity Alps' coastal proximity keeps them wet and their elevation keeps them snow-capped year round. The Sacramento Valley is dryer and in the summer temperatures often soar over 100°. The western Cascades are dryer than the Trinities, but also stay snow-capped year round. East of the Cascades lies the high desert of Nevada.

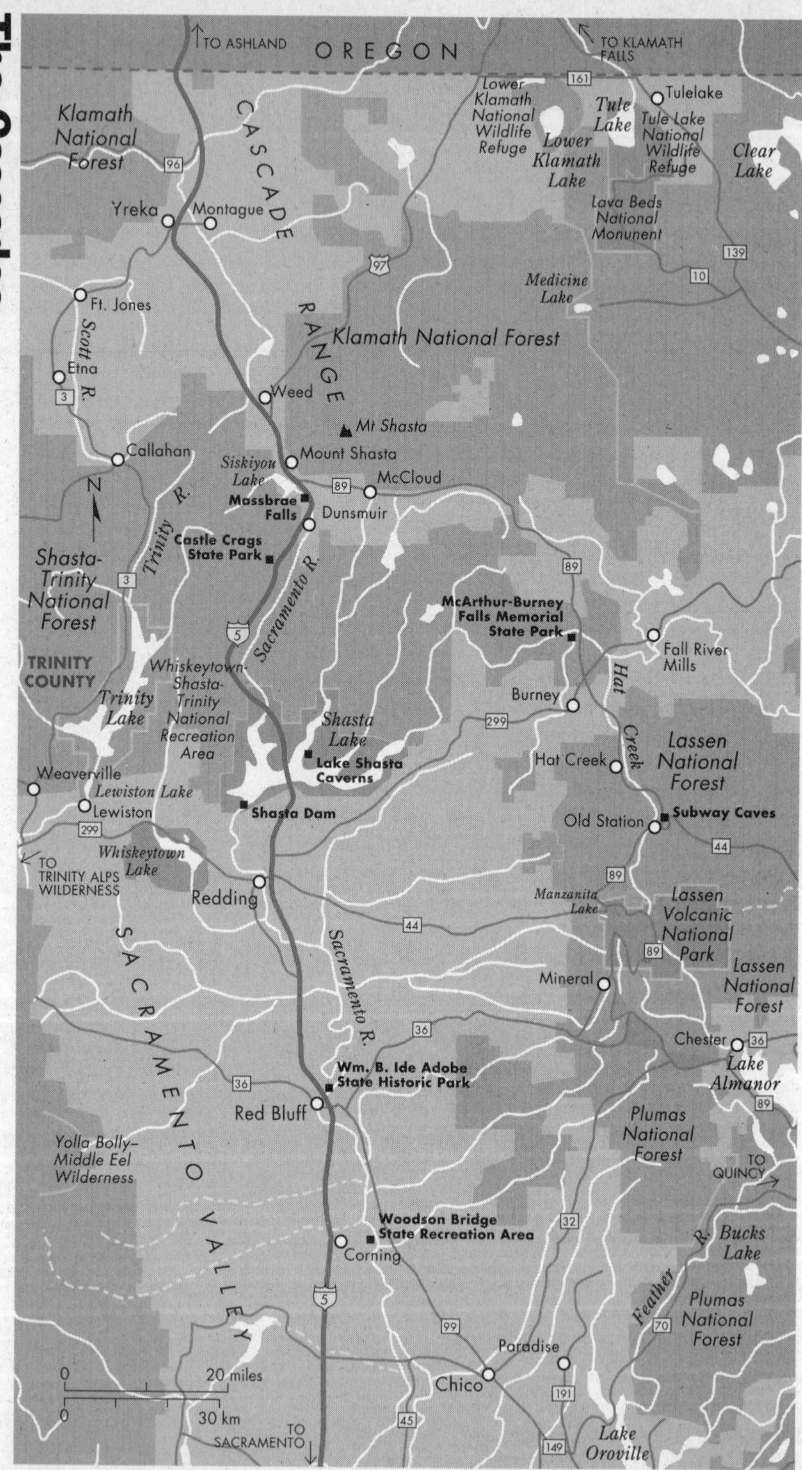
TO ASHLAND
OREGON
TO KLAMATH FALLS
161
Lower Klamath National Wildlife Refuge
Tule Lake
Tulelake
Tule Lake National Wildlife Refuge
Lower Klamath Lake
Clear Lake
Klamath National Forest
96
CASCADE RANGE
Yreka
Montague
Lava Beds National Monument
97
139
10
Medicine Lake
Ft. Jones
Scott R.
Klamath National Forest
Etna
3
Weed
Mt Shasta
Callahan
Siskiyou Lake
Mount Shasta
89
McCloud
N
Mossbrae Falls
Dunsmuir
Trinity R.
Castle Crags State Park
Shasta-Trinity National Forest
Sacramento R.
89
3
McArthur-Burney Falls Memorial State Park
5
Fall River Mills
TRINITY COUNTY
Whiskeytown-Shasta-Trinity National Recreation Area
Hat Creek
Trinity Lake
Shasta Lake
Burney
299
Lassen National Forest
Hat Creek
Lake Shasta Caverns
Weaverville
Lewiston Lake
Lewiston
Shasta Dam
Old Station
Subway Caves
299
44
Whiskeytown Lake
TO TRINITY ALPS WILDERNESS
89
Redding
Manzanita Lake
Lassen Volcanic National Park
44
Sacramento R.
SACRAMENTO VALLEY
89
Lassen National Forest
Mineral
36
Chester
36
Lake Almanor
Wm. B. Ide Adobe State Historic Park
36
89
Red Bluff
Plumas National Forest
Yolla Bolly–Middle Eel Wilderness
TO QUINCY
Woodson Bridge State Recreation Area
32
Feather R.
Bucks Lake
Corning
5
Plumas National Forest
70
99
Paradise
0
20 miles
Chico
191
0
30 km
45
TO SACRAMENTO
149
Lake Oroville

## COMING AND GOING

**BY CAR** From the southland or the Bay Area, bomb straight up that monotonous, god-awful concrete icon to rapid transit, **I–5,** which runs the length of the state. You may not see any noteworthy scenery along the way, but at least you'll get to the mountains quickly. It should take about 3 hours to reach Chico from San Francisco, 3½ hours to reach Redding, and 4½ hours to arrive at Mount Shasta. The Oregon border is less than an hour north of Shasta. If you're driving, getting around the north state is relatively hassle-free. With the exception of the occasional trundling logging truck, traffic is rare, and except for Highway 89 in Lassen Volcanic National Park—which is often shut down November–June—road closures are rare.

➢ **CAR RENTALS** • Redding offers the biggest selection of rental agencies, including **Avis** (tel. 916/221–2855 or 800/331–1212) and **Hertz** (tel. 916/221–4620 or 800/654–3131). The agencies are concentrated at the Redding Municipal Airport and near the corner of Cypress and Hilltop avenues. **California Compacts Rent-a-Car** has outlets in Mount Shasta (tel. 916/926–2519) and at a car wash in Yreka (tel. 916/842–7379).

**BY BUS** **Greyhound** (tel. 916/241–2070 or 800/231–2222) serves Marysville, Chico, Red Bluff, Redding, Weed, and Yreka along I–5, en route from San Francisco to Seattle and points beyond. From San Francisco, expect to cough up $34 one-way to Redding or $28 one-way to Chico. You'll pay $31 one-way to Red Bluff; and from here Mt. Lassen Motor Transit (*see* Coming and Going, in Red Bluff, *below*) can get you near Lassen Volcanic National Park. **Green Tortoise** (*see box* Funky Deals on Wheels, in Chapter 1) makes a stop in Redding, an access point for Lassen Volcanic National Park, Lake Shasta, and Shasta National Forest.

**BY TRAIN** **Amtrak** (tel. 800/USA–RAIL) travels between San Francisco and Seattle, stopping in Chico, Redding, Dunsmuir, and Klamath Falls. The best option for those traveling round-trip is to ride the train to Sacramento and then take the Amtrak bus to Chico ($37 for the entire round-trip) or Redding ($47 round-trip). If you leave the Bay Area in the morning, you'll be in Redding by afternoon. On the other hand, the six-hour train trip straight to Redding will cost $70–$92 round-trip. On top of that, the train leaves after sundown and you arrive in Redding in the middle of the night—desirable only if you find dark, empty train stations in the middle of nowhere exciting. Verify departure times and prices before you go.

# Chico

**A simple trip on Highway 99 north from Sacramento or** south from Red Bluff allows you to dodge the monotony of I–5. Better yet, it delivers you to the friendly town of Chico (also accessible from Highway 32 east off I–5), home of one of the liveliest branches of the California State University system and gateway to the Plumas National Forest. During the school year, activity in agricultural Chico revolves around the Cal State campus, north of downtown. The town is slow and sleepy in the hot summers, although more students each year are staying behind to liven things up. *Playboy* once rated Chico the top party school in the nation, largely because of **Pioneer Days,** an annual fest of tremendous proportions. But after riots and violence in the late '80s, Pioneer Days had the life squeezed out of it. Still, a quick tour of the downtown bar scene will reassure you that the collegiate taste for beer and parties hasn't dried up.

The **Chico Chamber of Commerce** (500 Main St., at 5th St., tel. 916/891–5556 or 800/852–8570), open weekdays 9–5:30 and May–September on Saturdays 10–3, stocks the "Visitor Guide," a seasonal listing with maps, hot spots, sights, and strolls. Be sure to ask for the free tourist map of Chico. The *Chico News and Review,* free every Thursday and available all over town (gas stations, grocery stores, et cetera), has a great weekly calendar.

## COMING AND GOING

Both **Greyhound** (717 Wall St., 1 block east of Main St. btw 7th and 8th Sts., tel. 916/343–8266 or 800/231–2222) and **Amtrak** (W. 5th and Orange Sts., tel. 800/USA–RAIL) have makeshift stations in Chico, unstaffed except when buses or trains arrive and depart. If you want to travel around the area, though, you're better off in a car. Your chances of catching a

*The sign at the Underground (325 Main St., btw 4th and 5th Sts., tel. 916/342–3500), Chico's "rock and roll department store," asks SHOWER? WHY BOTHER? Their olfactious alternative: aroma enhancer oil for $2 a bottle.*

ride out of Chico are pretty good when the university is in session (end of Aug. to mid-May). Check the ride board on campus.

A map of Chico's skewed and often one-way streets is essential to avoid frustration on your visit. Pick one up at the Chamber of Commerce (*see above*). You can get by in the downtown and university areas on foot, though the heat of a summer day might have you looking for an oasis. Chico is generally safe, but walking alone at night around campus, Bidwell Park, and the downtown bars is not advisable.

Chico is also a great town for bicycling: It's mostly flat, and bike lanes give you plenty of room on city streets. Just carry lots of water in summer, and walk your bike on campus or the police get ornery (a ticket is guaranteed). You can rent bikes at **Campus Bicycles** (*see* Outdoor Activities, *below*) and the city buses, run by the **Chico Area Transit System** (tel. 916/893–5252), have bike racks on the back. Buses can take you away from downtown to the outer reaches of Bidwell Park, as well as to some neighboring towns. The fare is 60¢ within the city.

## WHERE TO SLEEP

The best of the average motel scene includes $35 rooms at **Motel 6** (665 Manzanita Ct., off Cohasset St. at Hwy. 99 behind Holiday Inn, tel. 916/345–5500); and $36 rooms at **Motel Orleans** next door (655 Manzanita Ct., tel. 916/345–2533). In general, downtown is the best place to look for budget lodging; try the clean, well-maintained **Thunderbird Lodge** (715 Main St., btw 7th and 8th Sts., tel. 916/343–7911), which gives you a wheelchair-accessible $35 room near most of what Chico has to offer. There are several cheaper motels nearby, but the sacrifice in quality may not be worth the five bucks you'll save. Prices go up $10 for graduation weekend in May. Remember to add 10% tax to the room price.

**CAMPING** **Woodson Bridge State Recreation Area.** About a half-hour drive from town, this private campground is as close to Chico as any you'll find. Its 100 or so enormous sites ($15–$17), among the oaks along the Sacramento River, put plenty of space between you and other campers. Unfortunately, the sites have full hookups, which means summer weekends and holidays are noisy. The bathrooms can be nasty (crawling with earwigs); opt for one of the two showers. *Tel. 916/839–2151. Take Hwy. 99 north about 20 mi and turn left at CORNING/5 FREEWAY sign; go 3 mi and turn right.*

## FOOD

Most of the worthwhile restaurants in town are conveniently in the downtown area. **Big Al's Drive-In** (1844 Esplanade, btw Main St. and Broadway, tel. 916/342–2722), open daily 10–10:30, serves burgers and a delight known as a "triple-thick" milkshake ($1.25–$2.25)—try fresh banana and peanut-butter chocolate chip. For late-night fare (until midnight Mon.–Wed. and until 3 AM Thurs.–Sat.), head to the new **Pizza Face** (128 W. 2nd St., tel. 916/345–FACE), a restaurant with a conscience: part of your $2 for a slice goes to support charities. Breakfast downtown is a very Chico thing to do. Two popular and affordable spots are **Cory's** (230 W. 3rd St., tel. 916/345–2955), with homemade cinnamon bread, wonderful omelets, and strong coffee; and **Oy Vey Café** (146 W. 2nd St., tel. 916/891–6710), which serves bagels with veggie cream cheese ($1.75) and the "Jewish Nightmare" omelet ($5), filled with ham or sausage and cheese. Cory's is closed on Mondays and summer Sundays. There are plenty of major grocery stores around town, but for organic and bulk foods, stop by **Chico Natural Foods** (818 Main St., at 8th St., tel. 916/891–1713), open 8–9 Monday–Saturday, Sunday 10–6. Better yet, if you're in town on Wednesday (7 AM–1 PM) or Saturday (5–8 PM), shop at the **Farmer's Market** (2nd St., at Wall St., tel. 916/893–FARM).

**Cafe Sandino.** Organic ingredients make this yuppie vegetarian (mostly vegan) restaurant a valued oasis in the vast beef-eating desert of Northern California. The spicy tofu tamale ($7), the Del Sol tamale (with artichoke hearts, olives, and sun-dried tomatoes; $7.50), and the tofu and veggie burgers ($7–$8) should satisfy even the carnivores in your group. *817 Main St., btw W. 8th and 9th Sts., tel. 916/894–6515. 3 blocks from central plaza. Open Mon.–Sat. 11:30–3 and 5:30–9 (Fri. and Sat. until 9:30). Wheelchair access.*

**CAFES** For a more bohemian scene, try two excellent coffeehouses: the upbeat **Mana Java** (138 Broadway, btw 1st and 2nd Sts., tel. 916/343–1844) and the stylish **Café Sienna** (128 Broadway, btw 1st and 2nd Sts., tel. 916/345–7745). Both serve killer house coffee ($1), while Sienna features live bands Thursday–Saturday at 8 PM and Sundays at 11 AM. Mana Java is open until 9 PM weekdays, 11 on Friday, and 8 on weekends. Sienna keeps later hours: until 11 PM in summer, until midnight during the school year.

## WORTH SEEING

Chico's "parents," General John and Annie Bidwell, were pioneers known for their hospitality and generosity. Their legacy is all around—from the land the university occupies to the innumerable trees that shade the town on hot days. If you are dying to get out of the sun, tour the **Bidwell Mansion,** their Italian villa–style home. The mansion has hosted such historical figures as General Sherman (who was known to complain about the lack of alcohol in the mansion) and John Muir. Tours are $2 and last 45 minutes. *525 Esplanade, at 1st Ave., tel. 916/895–6144. Open weekdays 10–5. Tours on the hour 10–4.*

The best way to enjoy Chico, though, is to head straight for **Bidwell Park** (take 1st St. exit off Hwy. 99 south, go 1 mi to Esplanade and turn left), with plenty of urban swimming, biking, and Rollerblading. It's deluged by families on summer weekends. **One Mile** and **Five Mile** are swimming beaches along Big Chico Creek, located (not surprisingly) 1 and 5 miles from downtown. For a real Chico experience, head to **Upper Park** beyond Five Mile, where bathers and tanners go au naturel. The farther you get from Chico, the less prevalent clothing becomes (Bear Hole, Salmon Hole, and Brown Hole, in ascending order of nakedness). Otherwise, grab your mountain bike (and required helmet) and head onto the dirt logging roads in Upper Park or the nearby **Skyway,** which leads east from Chico.

One of Chico's biggest claims to fame is its renowned **Sierra Nevada Brewing Company.** Free tours walk you through the mishmashing, boiling, fermenting, and bottling routine—complimentary samples of their award-winning brews are highly recommended but not mandatory. Tours start Tuesday–Friday at 2:30 PM and Saturdays every half hour noon–3 PM. *1075 E. 20th St., tel. 916/345–2739.*

## AFTER DARK

During summer and fall, the popular Friday night **Concerts in the Downtown City Plaza** feature excellent jazz, rock, bluegrass, and classical musicians. On Tuesday nights, the plaza features local alternative bands—ranging from the noisy garage stuff to the up-and-coming local pride: The Mother Hips. For Saturday listings call 916/345–6500; for Tuesday shows ring 916/899–0491.

**Tower Books** (211 Main St., tel. 916/893–2665), open daily 9 AM–midnight, is where everyone shoots the breeze after hours, thumbing through magazines, checking out new releases, and running into old friends. The **Pageant Theater** (351 E. 6th St., 2 blocks from central plaza, tel. 916/343–0663) shows foreign and domestic films at out-of-this-world prices: tickets are $4 ($2.50 on Monday).

**BARS** The city of Chico recently put a cap on bars in the downtown area—not for lack of popularity, but because the main strip is already one huge bar. The scene seems divided by factions—fraternities and hippies—but with this many bars, at least there's no lack of choice. Loyalties shift rapidly, but some of the most popular watering holes are funky **Juanita's** (126 W. 2nd St., tel. 916/893–4125), which showcases local bands on weekends, and trendy **Lasalle's** (229 Broadway, tel. 916/891–4444), popular with students looking for live reggae. The **Sierra Nevada Brewing Company** (*see* Worth Seeing, *above*) doubles as a bar and live music venue. Call to see what bands they've got booked; covers run $5–$10.

**Madison Bear.** This Chico icon is worth a quick peek: Every square inch of wall and ceiling is plastered with some sort of bric-a-brac and by day it resembles an indoor amusement park (teens rule the video games and pool tables). By 8 PM the Bear manages to screen out everyone not over 21 (and in a local fraternity). The window of opportunity here is weekdays during happy hour (3–8 PM), when crowds are small, and micro-brewed pints are $1.50, domestic pitchers $2.99. *316 W. 2nd St., tel. 916/891–1639.*

**Rascals.** Chico's only gay and lesbian bar has a friendly crowd that comes to dance to a live DJ Friday–Sunday 6 PM–2 AM. It gets extra friendly on Sunday 7–10 PM during the "beer bust," when for $5 you can guzzle to your heart's content (or your liver's discontent). *900 Jerry St., at 9th St., tel. 916/893–0900.*

## OUTDOOR ACTIVITIES

**Bidwell Park** (*see* Worth Seeing, *above*) is the center of your outdoor world, with 15 miles of paved biking, jogging, and in-line skating trails. You can rent a bike for $20 a day ($10 for ½ day on weekdays) at **Campus Bicycles** (cnr Main and 5th Sts., on central plaza, tel. 916/345–2081). Pick up their free bike-trail map and check out the **Upper Park** and **North Rim trails,** which give you a good few hours' workout in the dry foothills. After your ride, you can swim in Big Chico Creek (*see* Worth Seeing, *above*). Inner tubing down the river is a major Chico activity. Kegs were recently banned, but many have discovered that coolers fit into inner tubes quite nicely. You can rent the rubbers at **Scotty's Boat Landing** (12609 River Rd., tel. 916/893–2020) for only $2 a day (some assembly required).

Lassen Volcanic National Park (*see below*) is less than two hours away, as are the Plumas National Forest (*see* Near Chico, *below*) and Lake Oroville. **Chico State's Adventure Outings** (tel. 916/898–4011), open Wednesday–Friday in summer, plans day-long and overnight hiking, skiing, and rafting trips. Chico State students get a great bargain, and nonstudents can sign up if space is available. In winter, fine cross-country skiing is just a short drive away near the small towns of Paradise and Inskip.

## NEAR CHICO

**QUINCY** Sixteen miles south of Chico, Highway 70 veers northeast, passes Lake Oroville, and climbs through the striking Feather River canyon, eventually reaching the town of Quincy (a two-hour drive). If you're lucky enough to pass this way in fall, the trees in the canyon put on the West Coast's closest approximation of the East's "changing of the colors." The canyon drive follows the clear, tumbling course of the Feather River, and any pullout provides a great picnic spot. The snowmelt-fed river can be a tad chilly for swimming, but if you're feeling bold . . .

*If you stay at the Feather Bed in Quincy, you may share a room with friendly poltergeists. At this B&B, stories abound about bricks moving out of fireplaces, and sounds of snoring in unoccupied parlors. Many like to believe that the original owners never completely moved out—or on.*

Quincy (elevation 3,500 ft) is an excellent stop for a meal, a night's sleep, or provisioning before you head out to Plumas National Forest or Mt. Lassen to the north. If you have time, check out the **Plumas County Museum** (500 Jackson St., behind courthouse, tel. 916/283–6320), with a display of Maidu basketry and quilts. The free museum is open weekdays 8–5 and, in summer, weekends 10–4.

➢ **WHERE TO SLEEP** • If you've been holding out for a splurge in a Victorian B&B, spend a night at Quincy's **Feather Bed** (542 Jackson St., behind Plumas County Museum, tel. 916/283–0102). This soft and quiet place features claw-foot tubs and big porches where you can while away evenings with iced tea and homemade cookies. Rooms with private baths start at $70. For something cheaper, the modest and homey cabins of the **Pine Hill Motel** (Hwy. 70, just north of downtown, tel. 916/283–1670) are your best bet. All rooms ($37–$47) have private baths and phones, and some have kitchenettes. Ask the friendly owners about what to do in the area. For camping or roughing it, *see* Plumas National Forest, *below.*

➢ **FOOD** • Buy groceries at **Safeway** (20 E. Main St., tel. 916/283–1404) or the **Quincy Natural Foods** co-op (30 Harbison St., tel. 916/283–3528), great for organic and bulk staples. The co-op is open weekdays 10–6:30, Saturday 11–5, Sunday 11–4. Otherwise, the **Morning Thunder Café** (557 Lawrence St., tel. 916/283–1310) serves serious breakfasts daily 7–2. A single, Frisbee-size blueberry pancake ($2.25) might do it for you; if not, consider a three-egg omelet ($5–$6). For dinner, locals are wild about **Moon's** (497 Lawrence St., tel. 916/283–0765), an Italian restaurant with a verdant outdoor patio. House specials include chicken cacciatore ($10) and fresh steamed veggies with brown rice and melted cheese ($8.50). The best lunch choice is **The Loft** (384 W. Main St., tel. 916/283–0126; closed Sun.). Try the huge, juicy burgers with home fries ($4–$6).

**PLUMAS NATIONAL FOREST** In the huge Plumas National Forest, which surrounds Quincy on all sides, the Sierra Nevada range to the south merges with the Cascade range to the north. Though Plumas isn't as uniformly spectacular as national forests in the Sierras, you're bound to get your beauty fix from the massive granite corridors in the Feather River canyon and from a number of dramatic waterfalls—the tallest of which is Feather Falls, at 640 feet. The falls are most impressive during spring; take lots of water and mosquito repellent if you plan to hike the **Feather Falls Trail,** a hilly, 7-mile round-trip hike to the falls (3–4 hrs total); it begins on Trailhead Road, off Lumpkin Road 1 mile west of the town of Feather Falls. Confused? Lost? Get a free map from the **Lake Oroville Visitor Center** (917 Kelly Ridge Rd., tel. 916/538–2219), open daily 9–4:30. To reach the visitor center, follow Highway 162 east from Highway 70 and turn left on Kelly Ridge Road.

Another option is to head west from Quincy on Bucks Lake Road to the **Bucks Lake Recreation Area** (elevation 5,155 ft), a popular boating and fishing spot. Rent a fishing boat from the **Bucks Lake Marina** (tel. 916/283–4243) for $49 a day. You'll need a fishing permit ($8.95), available at the marina's small general store.

If you're looking for a hike, the **Mills Creek Trail** starts about half a mile from the Whitehorse Campground (*see below*) on Bucks Lake Road and follows a relatively flat route for 5½ miles, crossing several streams. As the trail continues through the Bucks Lake Wilderness, the vegetation varies from mixed conifer forest to oaks and red fir, as the landscape changes from mountain meadow to sheer cliff. At the top of the escarpment, the elevation reveals a brilliant view of the forest, and on a clear day, Mt. Lassen is visible. Here the trail intersects with the **Pacific Crest Trail,** which leads onward to either Mexico or Canada.

Mountain-bike routes literally cover Plumas National Forest. One easy trail is the **Summit–Bucks Creek Loop,** which starts at Bucks Creek Road, about 12 miles west of Quincy, just past the Bucks Summit OHV staging area. The 3.8-mile ride gives you great views of the Bucks Lake Wilderness. For more biking, ask for route maps (free) at a ranger station. But bring your bike—you can't rent in or around Plumas. In winter, the gentle hills and meadows here are perfect for cross-country skiing. Rent skis ($10 a day) or snowshoes ($15 a day) from Quincy's **Sierra Mountain Sports** (501 W. Main St., tel. 916/283–2323).

➢ **CAMPING** • As with all national forests, camping is free anywhere within Plumas's boundaries. You'll need a free campfire permit, however, which is good throughout the summer. Pick it up at the **Quincy Ranger District** (39696 Hwy. 70, 4 mi north of Quincy, tel. 916/283–0555), open weekdays 8–4:30, or the **Plumas National Forest Supervisor's Office** (159 Lawrence St., Quincy, tel. 916/283–2050), open weekdays 8–5. Both offices have info on the forest and its dozens of campgrounds, as well as a $3 map marking roads, trails, campsites, and other points of interest.

Two miles north of Belden on Highway 70, about 25 miles west of Quincy, you'll find three campgrounds along **Caribou Road** (look for the Caribou Café and General Store). Sites at all three go for $11 a night and are first-come, first-served. There are several turn-outs by the river between these campgrounds in which many people camp for free. The secluded, tree-lined campgrounds, open April–October, have access to a trout-fishing creek. Scrub off your grime for $2 in the hot showers at the Caribou Café.

About 10 miles farther east on Highway 70 you'll see signs for **Hallstead Campground** on your right. Here, 20 summer-only wooded sites with flush toilets go for $9 a night. A quarter mile east from the campground is the **Twain General Store** (Twain Store Rd., off Hwy. 70, tel. 916/283–2130), where you can take a hot shower for $2.

The **Whitehorse Campground,** 15 miles west of Quincy on Bucks Lake Road, has 20 huge sites ($11) in a beautiful cedar grove, with pit toilets, fire pits, tables, and running water. Several smaller nearby lakes, such as **Snake Lake,** also have campgrounds (no drinking water)—ask at the Quincy ranger station about availability.

# Red Bluff

**Of all the towns in the Sacramento Valley,** this probably isn't the one you want to spend much time in. And it might seem like most locals in Red Neck—sorry, we mean Red Bluff—would prefer that you didn't. For this very reason, Red Bluff makes an interesting stop anyway. This is also the best place to shop for essentials before heading eastward off the beaten path.

Like many Northern California towns built on ranching, mining, or logging, Red Bluff retains a mix of Victorian gentility and Old West roughness, with some modern suburban mediocrity thrown in for good measure. Unlike some of the towns around it, Red Bluff got its start in 1850 as a shipping center, with steamer service on the Sacramento River to San Francisco. Inquire at the Chamber of Commerce about the tour of historical homes—it's a relaxing way to fritter away a summer evening and recover from daytime temperatures that often exceed 100°.

For a real taste of local culture, check out April's **Red Bluff Round-Up** (tel. 916/527–8700), the world's largest two-day rodeo. There's also a four-day bull and gelding sale in January, when you'll be hard-pressed to find a vacant room. The **Red Bluff–Tehama County Chamber of Commerce** (100 Main St., tel. 916/527–6220), open weekdays 8:30–5 (Fri. until 4:30), has info on the whole area. If you're heading west off I–5 toward Weaverville, north toward Mt. Shasta, or east to Mt. Lassen, stop here for brochures and maps.

## COMING AND GOING

**Mt. Lassen Motor Transit** (22503 Sunbright Ave., 3½ mi south of Antelope Blvd., tel. 916/529–2722) offers sporadic trips from Red Bluff to Reno (4 hrs, $23 one-way). They'll also take you to Mineral, near the entrance to Lassen Volcanic National Park (2 hrs, $6.50 one-way), though from there you're on your own as far as getting around the park. They pick up at the **Greyhound** station (Montgomery Rd., tel. 916/527–0434 or 800/231–2222) at 8 AM sharp Monday–Saturday. For info on Greyhound buses, *see* Coming and Going, at the beginning of the chapter. When all is said and done, it's easier to reach Lassen in a rental car. **Enterprise Rent-a-Car** (570 Antelope Blvd., at Chester St., tel. 916/529–0177) offers a weekend special (Fri.–Mon.), including 450 free miles, starting at $15 a day.

Red Bluff lies mainly to the west of I–5. The town centers around the intersection of **Main Street,** which runs north–south (paralleling I–5), and **Antelope Boulevard,** which runs east–west. Antelope Boulevard heads east toward Highway 36, the main road to Mt. Lassen. The town's famed Victorian neighborhoods are to the west of Main Street, within walking distance of the business district.

## WHERE TO SLEEP

There's a cluster of nondescript budget motels (all with pools) off Main Street and Antelope Boulevard on either side of I–5. The quiet **Lamplighter Lodge** (210 S. Main St., near Chamber of Commerce, tel. 916/527–1150) has huge, tasteful rooms with queen-size beds, free breakfast, HBO for $35. **King's Lodge** (38 Antelope Blvd., tel. 916/527–6020 or 800/426–5655) has doubles that overlook the Sacramento River for $37. Though it sits on the highway, **Motel Orleans** (5 John Sutter Sq., off S. Main St., tel. 916/527–6130 or 800/626–1900) has spacious rooms facing away from the road. A double costs $35; for $39 you get a queen bed and—luxury of luxuries—a bathtub. The **Sky Terrace Motel** (99 Main St., south of Willow St., tel. 916/527–8700) wins the prize for the cheapest rooms—and the rudest management—with clean and spacious singles at $25, including free cable. Add 10% city tax to all prices.

**CAMPING** Unless you want to stay at Chico's Woodson Bridge State Recreation Area, head for Red Bluff's **Lake Red Bluff Campground,** next to the Tehama-Colusa Fish Facility (*see* Worth Seeing, *below*). The 30 large sites ($10) have access to the Sacramento River and great fishing. The site has flush toilets, towels, fire rings, and drinking water, but be prepared for dusty and exposed sites in the hot summer months. Also come armed with mosquito repellent. *South end of Sole Rd., off Antelope Blvd., tel. 916/824–5169. Closed Dec.–Mar.*

## FOOD

As one Red Bluff resident put it, "they kill you with food" at **The Feedbag** (200 S. Main St., tel. 916/527–3777), open Monday–Saturday 6:30 AM–8 PM and Sunday 7:30–3. The thing here is breakfast, and be sure to ask for apricot or boysenberry syrup with your huge flapjack pancake ($1.25). Szechuan and Mandarin lunch specials at the **Great Wok Restaurant** (490 Antelope Blvd., tel. 916/529–5558) run $3.50–$4, and they've got vegetarian selections—a comparative rarity here in beef country. For a drive-thru Chinese meal, head to **Egg Roll King** (55 Antelope Blvd., tel. 916/529–2888), open daily 11–9:30. They never use MSG, and you can't beat the hot garlic shrimp special ($3.75), served with fried rice and an egg roll.

**Francisco's** (480 Antelope Blvd., tel. 916/527–5311) is a good bet for Mexican food. Try the Memo Special ($5.50), a quesadilla with lettuce and chili; or the Cuco Special ($6), a tostada with spiced meat, shrimp, or vegetarian chili. The **Snack Box** (257 Main St., tel. 916/529–0227), open daily 7–2, tries a little too hard for the "quaint" look, but it serves one of the best breakfasts around. Omelets are $5–$6, and a stack of buttermilk pancakes that hangs over the plate is $3.25. Expect a wait on weekends, especially after church lets out. You can buy fresh produce at the **farmer's market** (Red Bluff Shopping Center, Main St., at Luther Rd.), held June–October every Saturday and Wednesday 8–noon.

## WORTH SEEING

Red Bluff likes to think of itself as a "traditional" town. Sometimes, that just means that everyone gets married at 18 and the confederate flag still flies high. For a more romantic image of the city's traditionalism, take a stroll down its few streets and drop by **Moore's Blacksmith Shop** (742 Oak Rd., at Jackson St., tel. 916/527–4501) to watch horses being shod, or do a little antique hunting on Main Street between Antelope and Walnut streets. **Eli's Bargain Center** (418 Walnut St., tel. 916/527–1395) will astound you with its vast collection of contemporary Americana, from roller skates ($12) to leather attachés ($75). At the **Kelly-Griggs House Museum** (311 Washington St., tel. 916/527–1129), open Thursday–Sunday 2–4, informative docents lead you on a tour (donation requested) through renovated rooms with antique furnishings and Victorian-garbed mannequins. The Ishi Room contains artifacts relating to Ishi, the last of the Yahi Native Americans of eastern Tehama County.

*Stroll by the Carousel Corner (342 Ash St.) and chat with Bob Grootveld, who carves carousel horses. He has an "electric camel" in his workshop that was a precursor to the exercise bike and was actually in the exercise room on the Titanic.*

Take a dip in the Sacramento River at **William B. Ide Adobe State Historic Park.** Ide led a group of settlers in 1846 against the Mexican government and for a few weeks was president of the Bear Flag Republic. The U.S. government and its troops soon put an end to that, and he settled on this bend in the Sacramento River. The shade from the huge oaks is welcome, and the colors at dusk will make you appreciate Mr. Ide's choice of a homestead. *3040 Adobe Rd., tel. 916/529–8599. From I-5 north of Red Bluff, take Wilcox Golf Rd. exit and follow signs. Admission free. Open daily 8–5.*

Watch salmon and steelhead swim upstream on their spawning runs at the **Tehama-Colusa Fish Facility.** Over 34,000 salmon pass through the facility yearly, though the best viewing time is September–December, during the fall and winter runs, when you'll see more of the determined suckers than you ever thought possible. In the off-season, though, it's a bit like waiting for Godot. The official fish-count phone line (tel. 916/527–1408) gives daily and year-to-date statistics. *Sale Ln., south off Antelope Blvd., east side of I–5, tel. 916/527–3043.*

## AFTER DARK

Don't get your hopes up for a wild night life; bars are few and far between, and they're all either a little bit honkey-tonk or a little bit rock and roll. If you have your heart set on a night out, try the **Palomino Room** (723 Main St., tel. 916/527–5470), where the locals are likely to stop talking, turn their heads, and shamelessly stare a minute when a tourist struts in. They offer free live entertainment (country and western) most nights and showcase local comedians on Thursdays ($5 cover). The **Brunswick** (343 Walnut St., tel. 916/527–1992), built in 1886, is the place to shoot pool, reacquaint yourself with classic rock, and rub shoulders with locals. On summer Mondays at 8 PM, catch an old-fashioned band concert at the **Red Bluff City Park,** near the Chamber of Commerce.

## OUTDOOR ACTIVITIES

If you want to get out onto the Sacramento River, trout, steelhead, salmon, catfish, and bass are here for the casting. Get your permit ($8.95 a day), tackle, and gear at **Sports Wild** (333 Walnut St., tel. 916/527–3225), where rods start at $20. If you'd rather float through an afternoon, **Jellys Ferry Raft Rentals** (21785 Bend Ferry Rd., off Jellys Ferry Rd., tel. 916/527–3016) rents rafts from $20 a day. You can drift quietly for several miles and then be picked up at a pull-out station for free.

## NEAR RED BLUFF

**YOLLA BOLLY–MIDDLE EEL WILDERNESS** Blessed with the most provocative name around, the 147,070-acre Yolla Bolly–Middle Eel Wilderness is perfect for an escape from civilization. About 70 miles from Red Bluff and 230 miles from San Francisco, the wilderness spans the northern sector of Mendocino National Forest, the southern portion of Shasta-Trinity National Forest, and the southeastern part of Six Rivers National Forest. Yolla Bolly means "snow-covered" and Bolly "high peak" in the Wintu Indian language, apt names when you look up and notice snow-capped **Mount Linn** (elevation 8,092 ft) and its smaller neighbors, **Harvey Peak** (7,361 ft) and **Solomon Peak** (7,581 ft). The wilderness, lush with pine, offers a welcome change from overdeveloped campgrounds, crowded trails, and the din of motorized vehicles. If you're willing to rough it (even good drinking water is scarce in summer), the wilderness will overwhelm you with its stunning mountain peaks, streams, high-altitude lakes, fir and pine trees, and incredible wildflowers (at their height in July).

To access the northwest region of the wilderness, use the **Ides Cove Trailhead,** 56 miles from Corning; for the southeast region, use the **Green Springs Trailhead,** 65 miles away. For Ides Cove, take Corning/Paskenta Road (County Rd. A9) west to Paskenta, make a right at the fork on Road M2 to Cold Springs Station, and take another right at the fork on Road M22. For Green Springs, follow the directions above, but take a left at the Cold Springs fork on M2 and follow it to the trailhead. The trip involves lots of narrow dirt roads and intimidating logging trucks.

The Ides Cove Trailhead offers access to the **Ides Cove Loop National Recreation Trail.** Day hikers should try the moderate 5- to 6-mile loop that passes by **Square Lake,** a popular fishing hole, and then heads north to Burnt Camp and east back to the trailhead, where you can camp for free. More serious hikers will want to do the full loop, which continues past Square Lake to **Long Lake** (with dispersed camping) and meets the **Thomes Trail.** The loop then moves north and east, passing Burnt Camp before heading back. The moderately strenuous trip (about 12–14 mi) is a great all-day or overnight hike, but bring plenty of water.

➢ **BASICS** • Get weather and hiking info, a free campfire permit, and a topo map of the area ($3) at the **Corning Ranger District,** in the small town of Corning, about 20 miles south of Red Bluff on I-5. Maps are also available by mail (Box 1019, Corning 96021). Be sure to sign in at trailhead registries or at the ranger station, leaving a record of when you enter the wilderness and when you plan to leave it. *Corning Rd., ½ mi west of I-5, tel. 916/824–5196. Open weekdays 8–4:30.*

➢ **WHEN TO GO** • The lower altitudes of the wilderness are accessible year-round, but everything above 6,000 feet is snowed in October–June. Still, June and July are the best months to go: Streams and lakes are at their highest levels, wildflowers are in bloom, and the weather is most consistently cooperative then. You can usually visit May–October, but water becomes scarce in fall. At all times, you'll need to bring a water-purifying system, and pack in (and out) everything else you need. The rough logging roads that traverse the wilderness are almost never plowed in winter, so you'll probably be out of luck then.

➢ **CAMPING** • If you want to camp near the wilderness, drive to **Kingsley Glade Campground** (open June–Oct.), off Road M2 about 5 miles south of Cold Springs on Road 24NO1. It's free, and you'll find tables, fire rings, pit toilets, and piped water. A moderate 5-mile hike leads from the adjacent trailhead to **Thomes Creek,** one of the best spots in the area for trout fishing and swimming. The **Ides Cove Campground,** also blessed with rings, pit toilets, and piped water, is the most accessible free campground, less than a mile west of Cold Springs, off Road M2 (take Road M22 for 7 miles). The road is unpaved but well-maintained and suitable for most vehicles.

# Lassen Volcanic National Park

**A link in a volcanic mountain** chain that includes Lava Beds National Monument and Oregon's Crater Lake to the north, Lassen Volcanic National Park is one of the finest and most accessible places to explore the glories of mud pots, plug domes, sulfur springs, calderas, and lava pinnacles. For some reason, Lassen has escaped wide renown, despite its fascinating terrain and crystalline alpine lakes. Overshadowed by its big-name neighbors Yosemite and Yellowstone, Lassen happily remains one of the least crowded national parks. Its empty landscape (shaped by a now-dormant volcano) may make you think you've landed on another planet, but you'll wonder why you never made the trip earlier.

*With its sweet piney air, anywhere around the 10,457-foot Mt. Lassen volcano is a great place to take a deep breath—except around the malodorous geothermal sulfur works.*

Only one 32-mile road (Hwy. 89) runs through Lassen. This leaves most of the park for hiking, the primary activity here. Snow sometimes blocks the road all the way through June, but when the conditions are right, you'll find spectacular hiking, camping, cross-country skiing, and car touring. And whether your pleasure is fishing in Manzanita Lake or Hat Creek, snow tubing in Mineral, cross-country skiing on the Emigrant Trial, walking through subway-size subterranean lava tubes, exploring the rotten-egg reek of sulfur geysers at Bumpass Hell, or heading off in the backcountry to Cinder Cove and Butte Lake, you'll do it all in wonderful solitude.

## BASICS

**VISITOR INFORMATION** All visitors receive the *Lassen Park Guide,* which includes detailed info on camping, fishing, hiking, backpacking, naturalist programs, and wheelchair access. The guide describes each of the 67 points of interest along Highway 89 as it goes through the center of the park. **Lassen Park Headquarters** (38050 Hwy. 36 East, tel. 916/595–4444), just west of the town of Mineral on Highway 36 near the park's main entrance, is open weekdays 8–4:30 year-round and weekends in summer; hours can fluctuate, though, so call ahead. Come here to get reports on campground availability and hiking conditions. The park entrance fee, good for seven days, is $5 per vehicle, $3 if you bike in.

Near the north entrance to the park, the **Loomis Museum and Seismograph Station** (tel. 916/595–4444), open daily 9–5 July–September, also offers visitor info. The nearby **Manzanita Lake Ranger Station** (tel. 916/335–7373) is not open to the public, but you should call here or Lassen Park Headquarters (*see above*) to report an emergency. For road conditions, call 916/225–3028.

**WHEN TO GO** Lassen is open year-round, though Highway 89, the only road through the park, usually closes from mid-October until Memorial Day due to snow pack. On the plus side, just outside the park, winter sees great snow tubing, sledding, snowshoeing, and cross-country skiing. In summer, hiking, camping, and water recreation predominate. Spring wildflowers and autumn leaves round out the seasons. Even when it's boiling outside, you'll want a jacket if you climb to the top of the peak.

**GENERAL STORES** Provisions near the park are slim. The best bet is the **Mineral Lodge County Store** (Hwy. 36, tel. 916/595–4422), open daily 8 AM–9 PM. It stocks only basic groceries and a few camping supplies at high prices. The **Manzanita Lake Camper Store** (tel. 916/335–7557), at the north end of the park, stocks groceries, camping supplies, gasoline, propane, soup, and sandwiches. Again, expect to pay a bit more than you're used to for the convenience. You can also shower (50¢ for 4 min) and wash and dry your clothes ($2 per load) here, as well as rent bikes ($11 per day). If you're coming from the valley, Red Bluff (*see above*) is the best place to stock up.

## COMING AND GOING

**Mt. Lassen Motor Transit** (*see* Coming and Going, in Red Bluff, *above*) is your only hope for public transport to the park, and even that only gets you to Mineral, near the southern entrance on Highway 36, 1 mile west of Highway 89. The cost is $6.50 each way; the bus leaves Red Bluff Monday–Saturday mornings at 8 AM, arriving in Mineral in the late morning. Unfortu-

### *Mt. Lassen Blows Its Top*

***On Memorial Day 1914, Mt. Lassen issued the first in a string of eruptions that would continue almost seven years. The early rumblings were small affairs; 150 had been counted by March 1915, but no lava had been emitted. Then, on May 19, 1915, lava began welling up within the crater. Three days later, the volcano erupted in its largest explosion in recorded history, sending debris 30,000 feet into the air and a 1,000-foot-wide river of lava (still visible from Manzanita Lake) down the east and west sides of the mountain. Northeast of the peak, a section of trees 1 mile wide and 3 miles long was blown completely flat by the explosion. (Called the "Devastated Area," the patch has since been reforested, though the name remains.) The crater rumbled on and off until early 1921.***

***When the eruptions stopped, the lava on top cooled quickly, in essence plugging up the volcano (hence its classification as a "plug-dome volcano"). Lassen is by no means extinct, though—by some assessments it's still the most likely volcano in the country to erupt. Most days, if you hike up to the peak and down into the crater, you can see steam rising out of vents in the floor.***

nately, you won't find any transportation within the park, except your car, bike, or feet; and the Motor Transit does not allow bikes on board. If you're driving from Red Bluff, follow Highway 36 east for 48 miles to the park's southern entrance just beyond Mineral. From Redding, follow Highway 44 east for 49 miles to the park's northern entrance at Manzanita Lake.



## WHERE TO SLEEP

Most visitors who don't camp stay just outside the park, or in nearby towns like Red Bluff or Redding off I–5, Burney on Highway 299, and Chester on Highway 36.

**Hat Creek Resort.** This well-known fishing resort has been around for decades. In winter there's cross-country skiing across the road, and in summer Hat Creek bubbles through. You can stay in the seven-room motel ($45) or, in summer, rent a cabin sleeping two ($50) that will remind you of places you've seen in antique black-and-white photos. The cabins have kitchens. Many of the resort's loyalists reserve a year ahead, but you may get lucky by just showing up. *Hwy. 89, 11 mi NE of park's north entrance, tel. 916/335–7121.*

**Lassen Mineral Lodge.** This 20-room motel has a swimming pool, tennis courts, a restaurant, a bar, a general store, and a ski shop that's open 8–5 when there's snow (cross-country skis rent for $14 a day, $11 for motel guests). According to the owner, most guests are European, and they reserve way in advance: In summer and on winter holidays, you should secure a place a month or two ahead. Singles start at $40, doubles at $45. *Hwy. 36, in Mineral, 9 mi from park's south entrance, tel. 916/595–4422. Wheelchair access.*

**Rim Rock Ranch.** The Padillas, who own and run the Rim Rock Ranch and General Store, are sweet enough to restore your faith in humanity, and their lodge is in a peaceful meadow with mountains nearby. A room for two runs as little as $30 a night, and a cabin with kitchen, bath, and linens (no maid service) costs $36 a night for one to two people, $48 for three to four. Mr. Padilla can give you inside tips on good fishing spots. Happily, reservations are rarely needed. *13275 Hwy. 89, Old Station, tel. 916/335–7114. 14 mi NE of park's northern entrance.*

**CAMPING** Backcountry camping is free with a wilderness permit, available at park headquarters, the Manzanita Lake Ranger Station, or the Loomis Museum (*see* Visitor Information, *above*). You can also apply for a permit by mail (Box 100, Mineral, CA 96063–0100). Applications are granted immediately in person, but for reservations, call park headquarters (tel. 916/595–4444) and allow two weeks for processing. There are also seven developed campgrounds in Lassen, all of which are distributed on a first-come, first-served basis.

➢ **INSIDE THE PARK** • **Manzanita Lake Campground** ($10), just inside the park's northern entrance, is the largest and most accessible of Lassen's developed campgrounds. It's set in a grove adjacent to Manzanita Lake. You can hike from the nearby trailhead to Chaos Crags Lake (*see* Hiking, *below*) and when you return get a hot shower at the Manzanita Lake Camper Store (*see* General Stores, *above*). When the park gets snowed in, Manzanita Lake is the first campground to get dug out.

Near the southern entrance, **Southwest Walk-In** ($8) is for tents only. Most sites are on a wooded ridge with great views east to Mt. Canard. Across the road from the Lassen Summer Chalet (*see* Food, *below*), Southwest offers flush toilets, piped water, tables, and firepits. If it's open, though, a better choice is **Summit Lake** ($10 at Northern campground; $8 at Southern), 12 miles from Manzanita in the heart of the park. Not as many people come here, even though the tree-lined sites are quite large and secluded. Plus, you're near Summit Lake and the trails into the park's less populated eastern sector (*see* Hiking, *below*).

➢ **NEAR THE PARK** • There are over 40 official campsites in **Lassen National Forest** (which surrounds the park), and all but the group campgrounds cost $10 or less per night. In the northern area of the forest, near McArthur-Burney Falls, the 46 sites at **Cave Campground** ($9 a night; open year-round) sit just across the road from the Subway Caves and lava tubes (*see* Hat Creek and Burney Falls, in Near Lassen, *below*), 15 miles from the park's northern entrance. The tree-lined campground isn't super-private, but the light, large sites are more attractive than those at **Hat Creek Campground,** a few miles south on Highway 89. You shouldn't have trouble finding a spot at Hat Creek's 73 sites ($9). Naturally, the creek and its great fishing are not far off.

If you want to stay on the park's southern side, check out the 32 sites ($9) at **Gurnsey Creek Campground,** off Highway 89, 14 miles west of Chester. Rarely crowded and usually quiet, well-shaded Gurnsey Creek remains cool even in summer. In addition to the official forest campgrounds, you're free to pull off on any road and set up camp (14 days is the maximum stay in one spot). Backcountry exploration is allowed with wilderness permits, but campers should keep an eye on the unpredictable winter weather and heed avalanche warnings.

## FOOD

**INSIDE THE PARK** Picnicking is your best bet, so stock up in a nearby town before you enter the park. Otherwise, the **Lassen Summer Chalet Café** (tel. 916/595–3376), at the park's southern entrance, offers burgers, sandwiches, and breakfasts for less than $5 and an outdoor patio with views of Brokeoff Mountain and Diamond Peak. It's open May–October, daily 8–6 (Fri. and Sat. until 8). Unfortunately, you won't find a grocery store here. The Manzanita Lake Camper Store (*see* General Stores, *above*) has a self-service food area in the best mini-mart tradition, at high mini-mart prices.

**NEAR THE PARK** Besides the restaurants in distant Red Bluff and Redding, there are a few places to eat closer to the park. The **Mineral Lodge Restaurant and Bar** (tel. 916/595–4422), on Highway 36, 9 miles west of the southern park entrance, serves up basic American fare. It's nothing special, but the owner says European visitors can't get enough of the country-fried steak, fried chicken, and vegetarian lasagna ($9–$13), all served with soup or salad. The restaurant is open daily 8–10 for breakfast and 5–10 for dinner.

About 25 miles east of the park on Highway 36 (10 mi west of Chester) is the **Black Forest Lodge Restaurant** (on Hwy. 36, in Mill Creek, tel. 916/258–2941), open Tuesday–Sunday 8 AM–9 PM. Large portions and German specialties like sauerbraten ($14) and wiener schnitzel ($13.25) are the draw here. With owners named Otto and Hildegard Schleicher, the food's got to be authentic. A stone's throw farther east on Highway 36 is the **St. Bernard Lodge** (tel. 916/258–3382), with homemade bread, chili ($5), soup ($3), a full bar, and large portions. For what the owner swears is a low-calorie burger alternative, you can try the half-pound buffalo burger ($6.50). The lodge is open Thursday–Monday 8 AM–9 PM.

## EXPLORING MT. LASSEN

**NATURALIST PROGRAMS** The park offers free naturalist programs on the stars, volcanic activity, Native American ways, and flora and fauna. The guided tours, hikes, and nature walks really do contribute a lot to your understanding of the park. This isn't school; the naturalists do their best to make the programs relevant and fun. One of the programs, "Ooze and Ahs," has you baring your feet and squishing through soft mud near a mountain lake. Programs are usually held late June–late August (January–April for snowshoe programs). Check at park headquarters or one of the ranger stations for current listings (*see* Basics, *above*).

*At the Sulfur Works, in the park's southern sector, extreme heat from subterranean molten lava has dried out the earth. Hot water and acid on the volcanic rock turn the ground brilliant yellows, oranges, purples, and reds. Across the way, mud pots and steam vents are volatile enough to make you wonder if some god is displeased with us.*

**HIKING** A number of popular trails take you past striking volcanic phenomena. The most spectacular is the **Lassen Peak Hike,** a 5-mile round-trip (4 hrs) beginning at 2,000 feet and climbing a strenuous 8,450 feet to the top of the 10,457-foot peak and back. The trail, crowded only by Lassen standards, is totally exposed, so you have to bring sunscreen, a jacket, and plenty of water. Near the top the trail can be snowy, even in July.

A less famous hike beginning near the park's southern entrance, at Road Marker 2, heads up **Brokeoff Mountain.** Brokeoff is 1,200 feet shorter than Lassen, and the path to its peak isn't nearly as traveled. What's more, the trail (7 mi round-trip, 4½ hrs) is tree-shaded until the very top, so you get virtually the same amazing view without the extremes of wind and sun along the way. The hike to **Chaos Crags Lake** (2–3 hrs round-trip) starts near the Manzanita Lake Campground, and meanders through mixed conifer to the edge of the sub-alpine zone at the southwest flank of the 300-year-old remains of a chaotic rock fall. It's uphill going, but a chorus of shy frogs greets you at the lake.

Also worthwhile is the 3-mile **Bumpass Hell Trail** (2–3 hrs round-trip), which features the park's largest thermal areas, hot springs, steam vents, and boiling mud pots. One of the easiest trails is the scenic **Manzanita Lake Hike.** Figure a half-hour to an hour for the 1-mile walk around the lake. The park also has the wheelchair-accessible, self-guided, ½-mile **Devastation Trail,** beginning just south of Emigrant Pass, with sweeping views of the dramatic terrain.

Those wanting extended backcountry hikes to Butte Lake, Snag Lake, Horseshoe Lake, or Juniper Lake in the park's eastern sector should head to the **Summit Lake Trailhead** near the Summit Lake Campground (*see above*). The moderately strenuous 8-mile (each way) trail east to Horseshoe Lake gives you access to the **Pacific Crest Trail,** which runs north–south through the park and to the **Caribou Wilderness** at the park's eastern edge. Remember to get your free wilderness permit from the ranger station before heading out.

**SCENIC DRIVES** Driving through the park on Highway 89 is strictly a summer activity, as snow closes the north–south road in winter. If anyone tells you it's just a bunch of scenery, drive through anyway; it is, but what scenery. The list of road markers in the *Lassen Park Guide* (*see* Basics, *above*) details the peaks, lakes, and volcanic topography. The 30-plus-mile drive will take you a couple of hours thanks to winding, hilly roads. If you're driving I–5 and you want a lazy scenic route through the region, take Highway 36 out of Red Bluff or Highway 44 out of Redding to meet Highway 89, which meanders slowly through the park. The detour will take you an extra three hours or so.

## PARK ACTIVITIES

In addition to biking the 30-mile stretch of Highway 89 that runs through the park, you can try bird-watching, swimming in Manzanita Lake, or fishing (license required). The best fishing opportunity is outside the park in Hat Creek, which gets stocked regularly. See Mr. Padilla at the Rim Rock Ranch (*see* Where to Sleep, *above*) for tackle and tips. Unfortunately, there are no rental facilities for boats or anything else (except cross-country ski equipment), so make do with what you've got.

**SKIING** The winter *Lassen Park Guide* lists touring routes for Nordic skiers and snowshoers. Especially popular are the **Manzanita Lake** area, off Highway 44 at the north end of the park, and the **Lassen Winter Sports Area** (west of the Southwest Information Center). The moderate 10-mile **Manzanita Creek Trail,** which climbs to the base of Crescent Cliffs, and the easier 6-mile **Emigrant Trail,** which ascends a portion of Table Mountain, are two well-marked treks that depart from Manzanita Lake. Remember that winter weather can be extreme—there's always the danger of avalanche. Snow campers should check in with a ranger to be sure they have the necessary equipment, including extra food in case of an emergency. The Lassen Mineral Lodge (*see* Where to Sleep, *above*) will rent you a complete cross-country get-up (skis, boots, and poles) for $15 a day. And they can point you to trails (all free) suited to your ability level.

**SNOWSHOEING** Naturalist-led snowshoe walks, which emphasize the park's winter ecology and geologic history, are held at 1:30 in the afternoon Saturday and Sunday throughout winter, and daily during holiday periods. Snowshoes are provided free of charge, although a donation is requested for their upkeep.

**SNOW TUBING AND SLEDDING** Next to the Lassen Mineral Lodge in Mineral (*see* Where to Sleep, *above*) is a beautiful slope popular with sledders and snow tubers. The process for using it is a little screwy: Since no one can afford to assume responsibility for the land (the liability risk is too great), people have to buy (instead of rent) sleds and inner tubes and then sell them back at the end of the day. The Lassen Mineral Lodge sells sledding disks for $15 (buyback is $10); and the Chevron across the street sells inner tubes for $10 and buys them back (if they still hold air) for $5.

## NEAR LASSEN

**LASSEN NATIONAL FOREST** The 1.2-million-acre Lassen National Forest, which surrounds the park, supports three significant wilderness areas: **Caribou Wilderness** to the east, **Ishi Wilderness** to the south, and **Thousand Lakes Wilderness** to the north. These California Wilderness areas are so little trampled that wilderness permits are not yet required. The Thousand Lakes Wilderness (only a wee bit of an exaggeration) is the most accessible of the three; and you don't need a backcountry permit to camp here or to use the 22 miles of maintained trails, which wind through volcanic formations, stands of pine and fir, and, of course, plenty of lakes.

Two trailheads mark the main roads through the Thousand Lakes Wilderness. Whichever one you take, stop in first at a ranger station to pick up a trail map. Turning west off Highway 89 at the Ashpan Snowmobile Park (a few miles south of Old Station), you can follow Forest Service Road 16 for 11 miles to the turnoff for Magee Trailhead (Road 32N48 north). From here, the **Magee Peak Trail** runs for 3.7 difficult miles over Magee Peak (8,550 ft) to Magee Lake. At the peak, you'll see the Sacramento Valley to the south and the Northern Coast Ranges to the west. After only about 5 miles on Forest Service Road 16 from Highway 89, Road 32N45 leads north to the **Bunchgrass Trailhead.** From here you can take an easier hike (3½ mi) to Durbin Lake, passing recent lava flows (about 500 years old) on the way. For maps, trail descriptions, and other details contact the **Hat Creek Ranger District Office** (Fall River Mills, off Hwy. 299 15 mi NE of Burney, tel. 916/336–5521), open weekdays 8–4:30.

**HAT CREEK AND BURNEY FALLS** North of the park on Highway 89, you'll find world-class stream fishing along Hat Creek. Pick up fishing permits and equipment in nearby Burney if you don't have them already. You can bring a flashlight and explore the long, subway-size corridors at **Subway Caves** (near junction of Hwys. 44 and 89, north of Old Station). These were once rivers of molten lava. When the surface cooled and hardened, the lava underneath continued to flow and then finally drained, leaving caves in its wake. Even on baking summer days, the lava tubes feel like a refrigerator, so bring a jacket.

**McArthur–Burney Falls Memorial State Park** (Hwy. 89, 6 mi north of Hwy. 299 junction, tel. 916/335–2777) features one attraction (the 129-foot falls) and about a thousand kitschy items commemorating it. The falls are quite spectacular (and refreshing on a hot day), but crowds make this a less-than-relaxing picnic spot. It's $5 to drive your car in, but if you park outside you can walk in for free, take the 1-mile loop trail to check out the falls, and leave without feeling suckered. If some strange urge possesses you to camp at the **McArthur–Burney Falls Campground,** the 112 sites are $14 May–September, $12 otherwise. They're full all summer, so you have to reserve through MISTIX (tel. 800/444–PARK) and pay their $7 "convenience charge," thus completing the process of being bent over the barrel.

# Redding

**After the straight-as-an-arrow monotony of I–5,** many travelers are seduced by the fast-food joints, gas stations, and motels that beckon from the Hilltop Drive/Cypress Avenue exit. Then Redding is seared into their memory by the heat, which shoots past 100° nearly all summer long. Redding is much more than that exhaust-clogged intersection. In fact, after minuscule towns like Williams, Willows, Corning, and Cottonwood, the sprawling city of about 60,000 starts to look like Los Angeles. After all, this is the transport hub of Northern California.

Despite Redding's size and low prices, there's not a hell of a lot to keep you around for any length of time. The city is most useful as a base for trips out into the surrounding wilderness; you can rent bikes, boats, fishing gear, rafts, and just about anything else here. The **Redding Convention and Visitors Bureau** (777 Auditorium Dr., west of I–5 on Hwy. 299, tel. 916/225–

4100 or 800/874–7562) has info on Redding but little on the surrounding area. It's open weekdays 8–5 and weekends 9–5 (closed Sun. Oct.–Mar.). You can pick up a $1 map to help you navigate the confusing city streets.

*Ask native Californians about Redding and they'll probably say, "Redding. Yeah. I got a taco/went to the bathroom/got gas there once—it was hot."*



## COMING AND GOING

Redding is about three hours north of Sacramento on I–5, four hours north of San Francisco (I–80 east to I–505 north to I–5), and 2½ hours south of the Oregon border. For bus and train travel, *see* Coming and Going, at the beginning of the chapter. The **Greyhound** station (1315 Butte St., at Pine St. next to downtown mall, tel. 916/241–2531 or 800/231–2222) offers small 25¢ lockers. The **Amtrak** station (west of downtown mall on SW cnr of California and Yuba Sts., tel. 800/USA–RAIL) is unstaffed.

Within the city, I–5 is your best compass, pointing north toward Mt. Shasta. The Sacramento River winds through the center of town, heading roughly northwest–southeast. Cypress Avenue to the south and Highway 299 to the north are the main east–west drags. The municipal bus service, **The Ride,** is run by the Redding Area Bus Authority (tel. 916/241–2877). Fare is 60¢ for anywhere within Redding. Buses run weekdays 6:30–6:30, Saturday 9:30–6:30.

## WHERE TO SLEEP

Don't expect anything in the way of character. The good news is that you can get a clean double room for under $30 (not including the 10% room tax). On Hilltop Drive, which runs parallel to I–5 just to the east, there's a good selection of national chains. The motels on Market and Pine streets, off Highway 299 west of I–5, vary greatly in quality and price. Try the friendly **Shasta Lodge** (1245 Pine St., tel. 916/243–6133) for tidy doubles at $32. Across the street, the **Stardust Inn** (1200 Pine St., tel. 916/241–6121) has pretty much the same rooms for $27.50. If you can get a hold of a free *California Traveler Discount Guide* (available at chambers of commerce and visitor centers) bring it to the **Colony Inn** (2731 Bechelli Ln., off I–5 at Cypress exit, tel. 916/223–1935 or 800/354–5222). With a coupon, you'll get a room with queen-size bed, bathtub, and free Showtime for $29 ($35–$40 otherwise). If you can go without a telephone and pool, save a few dollars at **Roberts Motel** (2171 Market St., tel. 916/243–0256), where small but clean singles start at $22. There's camping 15 minutes west of town at Whiskeytown Lake and 20 minutes north at Shasta Lake (*see* Near Redding, *below*).

## FOOD

There are as many major grocery stores as there are car dealerships in Redding. For organic and bulk food, shop at **Orchard Nutrition** (221 Locus St., tel. 916/244–9141). If you're in town on Tuesday or Saturday 7–noon, visit the fine **Farmers Market** (take Hilltop Dr. exit of I–5 to Shasta Mall parking lot). Redding's size brings with it a decent array of budget dining options. **The Silver Saddle** (401 E. Cypress, tel. 916/223–6588) is a good place for that cheap, home-style power breakfast ($5) with a pancake, egg twins, triplet sausage links, hashbrowns, and toast. **C. R. Gibbs' Alehouse** (2300 Hilltop Dr., at Cypress Ave., tel. 916/221–2335) has 99¢ appetizers (quesadillas, spicy french fries, shrimp or oyster shooters) and $2 margaritas during happy hour (daily 4:30–7). For coffee (try the $2.50 raspberry mocha), make a beeline for the café **Serendipity** (236 Hartnell Ave., at Cypress Ave., tel. 916/223–4497), open weekdays 7 AM–7 PM, Saturday 8–4, Sunday 9–3.

**Buzz's Crab Stand.** It may not sound like much—and, well, don't expect it to look like much—but man does this place dish out the fish and chips, be it red snapper ($2.99), calamari ($5.95), or salmon ($6.95). *2159 East St., at Cypress Ave., tel. 916/243–2120. Open daily 11–9. Wheelchair access.*

**El Papagayo.** Like many Mexican restaurants in these parts, El Papagayo lacks that staffed-by-Mexicans authenticity, but it's the local choice for quality burritos and enchiladas. The burrito supreme ($7) is a two-meat monster. Vegetarians can feel good about the beans, prepared with canola oil. *460 N. Market St., north of river, tel. 916/243–2493. Open daily 11–10 (until 9 in winter). Wheelchair access.*

**Kona's Polynesian Sizzlin' Grill and Grog.** The dinner menu has three choices: all-you-can-eat salad bar ($5), all-you-can-eat stir-fry ($7.50), or all-you-can-eat stir-fry and salad bar ($9). For stir-fry, you fill your bowl with raw meats or veggies, and it's cooked before your eyes. During lunch, you only get one trip to the grill ($5.50, $7.50 with salad). Sake and plum wine ($2) will lubricate your imagination. *1844 Park Marina Dr., across from visitor center, tel. 916/243–1996. Open daily 11–10. Wheelchair access.*

## WORTH SEEING

Although there's certainly a lot worth seeing *around* Redding, even locals admit that nothing is actually *in* Redding. If you find yourself with an afternoon to kill, visit the museums in **Caldwell Park,** along the Sacramento River Trail (*see* Outdoor Activities, *below*). The curators of the **Redding Museum of Art and History** (56 Quartz Hill Rd., Caldwell Park, tel. 916/243–8801) consistently snag high-quality shows, featuring the stories of California's Wintu and Pit River tribes, as well as the area's pioneers. The museum is open Tuesday–Sunday 10–5; admission is $1. A short walk away, fun and excitement await at the **Carter House Natural Science Museum** (48 Quartz Hill Rd., tel. 916/243–5457), open Tuesday–Sunday 10–5. The energetic volunteer staff oversees almost 40 species of live animals, natural-history exhibits, and interactive displays. Admission is $1.

One of the few local outposts of culture is the **Redding Book Store** (1712 California St., at Placer St., tel. 916/246–2171). Just when you thought you'd have to break down and buy the *National Enquirer,* this place saves the day with a huge selection of books and over a thousand magazines (everything from *High Times* to *The Village Voice*). To get here, take Highway 299 west from I–5 and head south on Market Street.

## AFTER DARK

For a listing of movies, theater, special events, and what little nightlife there is in Redding, read the "Spectrum," which the city's newspaper, *The Record Searchlight,* publishes every Thursday. Your best bet is to catch up on those movies you meant to see last year at the **UA Cascade Theater** (1731 Market St., south of Hwy. 299, tel. 916/365–4591). Tickets are $1.50 Monday–Thursday and $2 Friday–Sunday. Locals pack the **British Pub** (2600 Churn Creek Rd., tel. 916/222–1638) every Thursday for live blues, pool and darts, and a great beer list. On weekends the British Pub joins the Modern Rock revolution with alternative and hip-hop DJs. The **Post Office Saloon** (1636 Market St., Downtown Redding Mall, tel. 916/246–2190) draws a regular crowd with live blues and rock bands and cheap domestic beer.

## OUTDOOR ACTIVITIES

Rafting or canoeing on the **Sacramento River** is inviting on a hot summer's day, and in winter snow is only an hour's drive away in Lassen Volcanic National Park (Hwy. 44 takes you to the Manzanita Lake entrance). **Park Marina Raft Rentals** (2515 Park Marina Dr., tel. 916/246–8388) will set you up with a two-person raft ($29) for a lazy 12-mile, four-hour float downriver. They even provide shuttle service back to the parking area. No boats are rented after 1:30 PM. **Alpine Outfitters** (950 Hilltop Dr., tel. 916/221–7333) has skis ($20 a day), Rollerblades ($12 a day), bikes ($15–$20 a day), and assorted camping equipment. They'll give you plenty of info on hiking and rafting in the area.

**HIKING AND BIKING** Put on your walking shoes or rent a bike and hit the flat, 6-mile **Sacramento River Trail,** which runs from the west end of Lake Redding Drive to the south end of Diestelhorst Bridge. Caldwell Park and its museums (*see* Worth Seeing, *above*) lie along the trail. You walk on either side of the river, and cross between the two on a curious footbridge. In summer, the tree-lined path is mercifully cooler than the rest of town. Women tend to hike in pairs for safety.

**SWIMMING** You can swim in the Sacramento River, but the water comes from the bottom of the 602-foot Shasta Dam and is damn cold, so you might want to head to Whiskeytown (*see below*) or consider some less natural options. For a standard approach to water, head for the **Redding Plunge** (Caldwell Park, tel. 916/225–4095), a municipal pool open weekdays 1–4:30 and weekends noon–5. But if slithering down a water slide seems like the best way to combat the valley heat, try **Waterworks Park** (151 N. Boulder Dr., tel. 916/246–9550). From I-5, go west about 2 miles on Highway 299. Entrance is $12.50 per day, $10.50 with a coupon from the *Golden California* visitor's guide. The park is open daily 10–8 from Memorial Day to Labor Day.

## NEAR REDDING

**WHISKEYTOWN LAKE** Eight miles west of Redding on Highway 299 is Whiskeytown Lake, created by the diversion of water from the Trinity River to California's Central Valley. John F. Kennedy dedicated Whiskeytown Dam just a few months before his assassination in 1963. Find your own place to plunge into the lake, or drive to the swimming areas at **Brandy Creek** (J.F.K. Memorial Dr., on south shore) or **Oak Bottom** (Hwy. 299, 2.6 mi west of visitor center). You can get fishing permits ($8.95) and rent canoes ($8 for 4 hrs) or pedal boats ($6 for 4 hrs) at the **Oak Bottom Marina** (tel. 916/359–2269).

Avoid the crowded and dreary campground at Oak Bottom; instead go for one of the free primitive sites back in the hills, all accessible by car. Check in at the **Whiskeytown Visitor Information Center** (Hwy. 299 at Brandy Creek turnoff, tel. 916/246–1225), open daily 9–6, for a free map of the lake and a schedule of ranger-guided activities. Get your free backcountry camping permit a little farther toward Brandy Creek at the **park headquarters** (tel. 916/241–6584, ext. 221)—if you show up after hours, ring the intercom buzzer. The best backcountry option is the camp at **Crystal Creek** at the far eastern edge of the park. It has a pit toilet, and crowds are never a problem. Get a hot shower back at the Oak Bottom Campground (75¢ for 5 min), or deal with the free cold outdoor showers at Brandy Creek.

For an easy and scenic hike following the lakeshore, take the **Davis Gulch Trail** (1½–2 hrs round-trip). You'll find the well marked trailhead on the road to Brandy Creek, less than a mile south of the Whiskeytown Dam. There's also great mountain biking here. Pick up a free copy of "Mountain Bike Riding at Whiskeytown" at the visitor center. The steep and narrow **Boulder Creek Loop** (8.5 mi, 1–2 hrs) climbs 1,100 feet for great views. Begin at the Carr Powerhouse, off Highway 299 at the northwest end of the lake.

**SHASTA LAKE** The sprawling Shasta Lake, 10 miles north of Redding on I-5, is billed as a "full service" lake (i.e., lots of annoying jet skis, motorboats, and all-terrain vehicles). It also offers great fishing for rainbow trout, brown trout, and salmon, and supports 12 pairs of resident bald eagles, the largest nesting population in California. You can rent patio boats, fishing boats, and jet skis at the 11 marinas and resorts around the lake, but expect to pay an arm and a leg. It might be worth it, though, just to catch a glimpse of Merle Haggard's houseboat.

The drive to the monstrous **Shasta Dam** at the southern end of the lake (take Central Valley/Shasta Dam exit west from I-5 and go 6 mi) affords great views of the second-largest dam in the country (602 ft by 3,460 ft), exceeded only by the Grand Coulee Dam in Washington. The **visitor center** (tel. 916/275–4463), open daily 8:30–5, has an exhibit showing what it took to build the dam. Take the informative and fascinating free tour, offered hourly 9–4; you ride in an elevator from the top of the dam all the way to the bottom.

If you don't mind an old-fashioned tourist trap, try the two-hour **Lake Shasta Caverns** tour (tel. 916/238–2341). It starts at a store filled with gaudy souvenirs, continues by boat across the lake and by bus up a genuinely thrilling narrow road, and includes a walk through some fascinating limestone and marble caverns. The tour is marred only by inane commentary; Mother Nature's work seems eloquent enough. Take the O'Brien exit from I-5 and follow the signs;

*Unless you're going into Samwel Cave with rappelling equipment, find out from the ranger where the 75-foot pit is and stay clear (one skeleton has already been found at the bottom by anthropologists).*

tours run daily and cost $12, $10 with a coupon in *Recreation '95* (available at the Shasta Lake info center).

Follow Gilman Road southeast 2 miles from McCloud Bridge Campground (*see* Camping, *below*) and you'll reach the unmarked trail to **Samwel Cave** (the road turns sharply to the left and the narrow path leads down and away to the right). It's a half-mile to the cave mouth, where you can gambol for free around a large room (bring a flashlight). If you have the foresight to ask at the info center and pay a $10 deposit, you can get a key that lets you into deeper chambers and recesses, but it involves quite a bit of crawling on your belly, and you *must* have a headlamp or at least a flashlight (bring two just in case). The rock formations in the cave aren't as spectacular as those in Lake Shasta Caverns (*see above*), but here your visit doesn't cost anything. Pick up a free copy of "A Spelunker's Guide to Samwel Cave" at the info center.

➢ **BASICS** • You'll find many maps at the well-heeled **Shasta Lake Information Center,** as well as pamphlets on local sights. If you're headed to Samwel Cave (*see above*), don't forget to ask for the key. *From I–5, take Mountain Gate/Wonderland exit east, tel. 916/275–1589. Open daily 8:30–4.*

➢ **CAMPING** • If you feel like roughing it, any of the 370 miles of shoreline offer free camping, though you'll need a campfire permit May–October. **Gregory Beach** and **Beehive** are two good spots at the north end of the lake. There's also developed camping, though RVs and boaters flock to these sites. Try the **McCloud Bridge Campground** (Gilman Rd., 17 mi east off I–5), with 20 sites ($9) and flush toilets along a narrow finger on the northeast shore of the lake.

# Trinity County

**Trinity County's entire population**—less than 15,000—is smaller than that of many universities. But instead of occupying cramped and crowded city blocks, the county is spread out over 3,222 forested, lake-dotted, snow-peaked square miles. Locals, living mostly along Highway 299, run the gamut from artists who find the locale inspirational to loggers, miners, and retirees. You won't find a stoplight or parking meter anywhere.

*Don't leave the Trinity Alps without taking a trip downriver, either by raft or by inner tube. Along with the requisite cooler, bring along something to pan for gold with: The shores of the Trinity literally glimmer with flakes of the coveted metal.*

Two scenic roads run through the area. The **Trinity Heritage Scenic Byway** begins in Weaverville and heads 111 miles northeast on Highway 3—past Lewiston, Trinity Lake, Coffee Creek, and other mining towns. Look for mountains scarred by gold-rush hydraulic mining (hillsides were literally washed away by huge water hoses in order to efficiently locate the gold). You can pick up a self-guided auto tour map with 20 designated stops at the Weaverville ranger office (*see below*). The newer **Trinity Scenic Byway** follows Highway 299 through Whiskeytown, Weaverville, and the Old La Grange Mining Area toward Arcata (*see* Chapter 4). Pick up free maps at any visitor center along Highway 299.

The county seat, Weaverville, is a gold-rush town with a brick- and wood-fronted Main Street. Here you can procure ingredients for a macrobiotic diet and meet friendly folks willing to talk about their good fortune to be living in such a pristine, comfortable place. Of course, you'll also meet the contingent of laid-off loggers prominent in so many of these towns. Don't let the depressed economy scare you away from the spectacular land hereabouts. At least in Weaverville, for every disgruntled logger, you also meet someone creative, well-read, and eager to regale you with local stories.

About 15 miles from Weaverville, the blink-and-miss-it town of Lewiston still looks much as it did during the gold rush—most of the district is included in the National Registry of Historic

Landmarks. The Trinity River (warm, gentle, and shallow here) runs through town, making Lewiston a perfect spot to pull out your rod and begin your quest for king salmon.

In fact, if hiking, camping, rafting, fishing, or mountain biking is your thing, you've come to the right place. The half-million-acre **Trinity Alps Wilderness** does not permit mountain bikes or other mechanized vehicles, but for this reason the wilderness plays host to some of the finest backpacking in the state. The **Trinity River,** which flows along Highway 299 west from Weaverville, is a designated Wild Scenic River and offers prime territory for rafting and kayaking, but you might find its secluded, sandy beaches and warm waters more conducive to lazing around and skinny dipping than wave running. This is also one of the best places in the continental United States for fly-fishing—not to mention gold dredging, if you're feeling lucky.

**BASICS** The **Trinity County Chamber of Commerce** is a great source of information for the whole area. If possible, talk to Dale Lackey, an expert angler who writes books on the outdoors and knows all about fishing, hiking, and rafting in the Trinity Alps. And you won't find a more enthusiastic talker than Kathy (if she's there). She can give you a walking-tour brochure directing you to Weaverville's 116 points of historic interest or pamphlets for car touring in the surrounding area. *317 Main St., Weaverville, tel. 916/623–6101 or 800/421–7259. Open summer, daily 9–5; off-season, weekdays 9–5.*

**COMING AND GOING** The only north–south thoroughfare in Trinity County is Highway 3, once the California–Oregon wagon trail for early pioneers. From the north, Highway 3 can be accessed off I–5 from Yreka. To the south, Highway 3 meets Highway 36 just south of Hayfork in the lower county. Highway 36 traverses the county and can be picked up out of Red Bluff from I–5 in the east or just south of Fortuna from Highway 101 in the west. A better and more scenic east-west route is Highway 299, accessed from Redding in the east or Arcata in the west. Greyhound and Amtrak both serve Yreka, Redding, Red Bluff, and Arcata, but do not travel through the county. If you're footloose and fancy-free you might consider hitchhiking, which is easy and common in these parts. Many portions of the road have little or no shoulder, so be sure to find a commodious spot where your ride will be able to pull over safely.

# Weaverville

If you've just passed through a few of this region's depressed logging towns, Weaverville, 45 miles west of Redding on Highway 299, will come as a breath of fresh air. It's been hit as hard as any place by the reduction in logging, but tourist dollars are helping the community stay on its feet. Stores like **Badger Paw Indiancrafts** (Court and Center Sts., north off Hwy. 299, tel. 916/623–6336), which offers exquisite art created by locals, cater to the wealthy traveler. Most objects are probably well beyond your means, but you can find a few nice gifts for under $20. You'll see plenty of small galleries, jewelry stores, and artists' studios if you walk around the downtown area.

## *A Temple Amongst the Forest Beneath the Clouds*

***Weaverville boasts California's oldest active Taoist temple. In the 19th century the Joss House (Oregon and Main Sts., tel. 916/623–5284), also known as the Temple Amongst the Forest Beneath the Clouds, served the indentured Chinese mining population, who burned offerings at the altar to increase their luck. The tour ($2) leaves much to be desired, but the temple, open Wednesday–Sunday, is in great condition—most of the gold, silk, and brightly painted wood objects look as brilliant as they did when they were shipped from China a century ago.***

*Bar-room brawls around closing time (2 AM) must be frightfully common at the Diggins Saloon on Main Street—you'll get warned about them more than once in this otherwise sleepy gold-rush town.*

Though it's a tiny town, Weaverville's location at the junction of Highways 3 and 299 makes it a hub for travel through the Northern Coast Ranges (*see* Chapter 4), especially the spectacular Trinity Alps (*see below*). The **Hays Book Store** (106 Main St., tel. 916/623–2516) has topo maps, hiking guides, and postcards, and **Brady's Sport Shop** (203 S. Main St., at Court Ham St., tel. 916/623–3121) carries basic camping and fishing gear. Also check out the **Bookseller** (220 Main St., tel. 916/623–2232), with a wonderfully eclectic collection. If you happen to be passing through at the beginning of July, Weaverville has a huge **Fourth of July** celebration, starting July 1 and lasting for four event-packed days. The street dances, fireworks, demolition derby, and rodeo draw hundreds of people from miles around.

**WHERE TO SLEEP** For a campground near Weaverville, follow Highway 3 north out of town, go left on East Weaver Creek Road just past the little airport, and continue for 2 miles. You'll see the **East Weaver Creek Campground** on your left, with 10 sites ($5) and pit toilets in a pine forest next to the creek. It's beautiful and noticeably cooler than downtown. Your best bet for access to the Trinity Alps Wilderness is **Pigeon Point Campground,** set on the Trinity River off Highway 299 about 10 miles west of town. The 10 sites ($2) have tables and firepits, but there's no potable water or showers. Arrive early to get one of the beautiful riverside spots.

**49er Motel.** A model gold mine and miner stand in front of this place, making it more distinctive than the run-of-the-mill motels around here. Inside, though, the rooms are pretty much the same as everywhere else—dull and boxy but clean. Doubles are $36 in summer, $34 in winter, including use of the pool and free continental breakfast. *718 Main St., east of downtown, tel. 916/623–4937. 13 rooms.*

**Weaverville Hotel.** This 19th-century hotel has managed to retain its warm, old-time feeling—some of the eight rooms even have claw-foot tubs and views of the old Weaverville bandstand. Doubles start at $32. Get the friendly proprietor, Emilie Brady, talking about what to do in Weaverville; she'll charm the socks off you. *203 Main St., downtown, tel. 916/623–3121. Check in at Brady's Sport Shop downstairs.*

**FOOD** Unlike many small towns in Northern California, Weaverville can actually satisfy your appetite without knocking you out with bacon grease. The **Mountain Market Place** (222 Main St., tel. 916/623–2656) is a vegetarian (largely vegan) grocery and deli open weekdays 9–6 and Saturday 10–5. Get a tasty vegetarian burrito ($3) and a large fruit smoothie ($3) and enjoy them on the small back porch. A great place to go for a burger ($4–$5) and brew ($2–$3 a pint) is the **Brewery Restaurant and Bar** (401 S. Main St., tel. 916/623–3000), open daily 6 AM–9 PM.

**La Grange Café.** You'll get a sizable, tasty dinner at this relaxed Weaverville establishment. Residents love Duane's chicken (sautéed chicken breast with mushroom and wine sauce over California wheat berries; $9). Dinners ($7–$13) come with fresh sautéed vegetables, bread, and soup or salad. If gazpacho is the soup du jour, order it. *315 N. Main St., tel. 916/623–5325. Open Mon.–Thurs. 11–9, Fri. and Sat. 11–10. Wheelchair access.*

**Mustard Seed Café.** Come to this small yellow house for the best, healthiest breakfast in town. The bright, homey café offers wonderful homemade granola served with fresh blueberries and bananas ($4.50) and a fresh-fruit plate with yogurt and cinnamon-date bread ($5.50), as well as omelets and other eggy dishes ($4–$6). Lunch salads and sandwiches go for $5–$7. *Main St., next to Joss House, tel. 916/623–2922. Open Mon.–Sat. 7 AM–3 PM, Sun. 8–3.*

# Lewiston

As dinky, historic California towns go, down-to-earth Lewiston, off Highway 299 between Redding and Weaverville, is a pretty inviting one. You can picnic along the Trinity River, poke around the antiques in the **Country Peddler** (Turnpike and Deadwood Rds., tel. 916/778–3325 or

916/778–3876), check out the work of local artisans at **Jeannie's Corner** (Turnpike and Deadwood Rds., tel. 916/778–3296), or take a walking tour along historic **Deadwood Road,** which boasts a whopping 20 structures listed in the National Register of Historic Places. In mid- to late May, 200 vendors set up along Deadwood Road for Lewiston's **Peddler's Faire** (tel. 916/778–0506).

At **Lewiston Lake,** just south of Trinity Lake (follow Trinity Dam Blvd. to the end and turn right), you can hike, bike, camp, fish, and bird-watch. The 6-mile lakeside trail from Mary Smith Campground (*see* Where to Sleep, *below*) to Ackerman Campground on the northwest shore is perfect for hikers and bikers who want to get a quick lay of the land. It's even wheelchair accessible. Bald eagles and osprey nest in the area, and if you bring a good pair of binoculars, you may see them fighting over a trout or two. You can rent patio boats ($15 per hr, 4 hr minimum) and fishing boats ($7 per hr, 4 hr minimum) at the **Pine Cove Marina** (255 Star Hwy., tel. 916/778–3770). Pick up fishing licenses, rods, and tackle at the **Trinity Fly Shop** (Old Lewiston Rd., tel. 916/623–6757), a mile from Highway 299 in Lewiston (first Lewiston exit coming east from Weaverville, second heading west from Redding).

*If you've ever wanted a free, private winery tour, this is your chance. Alpen Cellars, Trinity County's only vineyard, is a small family venture specializing in white Riesling, gewürztraminer, chardonnay, and pinot noir. Winemaker Keith Groves loves to show visitors around and will give you a taste or two of his vintages. Call 916/266–3363 for an appointment.*



**WHERE TO SLEEP** The sites at the four Forest Service campgrounds along the western shore of Lewiston Lake all go for less than $10. Close to downtown Lewiston, **Mary Smith Campground,** open May–October, has 18 sites ($7) on the lake's forested, hilly southern banks. You'll find vault toilets, but there's no potable water. Besides camping, the only cheap option is the **Lewiston Valley Motel** (Trinity Dam Blvd., tel. 916/778–3942), a sort of Motel 6 in a log cabin, where doubles go for $39 in summer, $35 in winter.

**FOOD** **Lewiston Hotel.** It doesn't put up travelers, but it's still the town's centerpiece, thanks to its restaurant and bar. The walls and ceilings are covered with knickknacks accumulated over the last 120 years, the bar specializes in microbrews ($1.75–$2.50 a bottle), and the humorous menu features several versions of embellished Lewiston history. Dishes like Recently Deceased Fish and Vegetarian à la Birkenstock ($7–$16) come with soup, salad, and homemade bread. *Deadwood Rd., tel. 916/778–3823. Restaurant open Wed.–Sun. 6 PM–10 PM, bar open 3 PM–1 AM.*

**Serendipity.** It's cheaper than the Lewiston Hotel, and a bit healthier. The menu features creative sandwiches and pastas ($3–$5) and the best darn lemonade this side of the Mississippi ($1.25). Check out the adjacent used-paperback bookstore; it's one of the best in the area. *Deadwood and Turnpike Rds., tel. 916/ 778–3856.*

# The Trinity Alps Wilderness

Relative to the Sierra Nevada and the neighboring Cascade ranges, the Trinity Alps don't stand as large. But other Californian ranges have nothing on the Trinities: The area is replete with glaciers, rushing rivers, boisterous waterfalls, granite peaks, alpine lakes, and, in spring, fields of glorious wildflowers. All of this is encompassed by lush fir and ponderosa pine forest. The only thing the area seems to be lacking is mobs of tourists. Only 45 miles west of Redding, just north of Highway 299, the Trinity Alps Wilderness has been discovered by surprisingly few. Days of brilliant solitude are waiting to be found on its backcountry trails and along its warm Trinity and Salmon Rivers—not to say you won't encounter other warm-blooded company. The Trinity Alps Wilderness hosts the highest concentration of black bears in California—one per square mile. But, think of it this way: If you don't have a predator, you're not in wilderness. Also look out for wolverines, mountain lions, and, oh yes, Big Foot.

**BASICS** Snowpack reaches 10–20 feet in winter and keeps trails closed through late June. In summer, temperatures climb above 90° in higher elevations and up to 110° in lower elevations. Even in the heat of summer, thunderstorms break out and cool things down; bring rain gear. At night, temperatures can dip into the low 40s, even in August.

Visitors in the east should contact the **Weaverville Ranger District** office on Highway 299 for necessary wilderness permits, current trail and weather conditions, trail maps, and other literature. *Main St., just north of downtown, tel. 916/623–2121. Open summer, Mon.–Sat. 8–4:30; off-season, weekdays 8–4:30.*

The **Big Bar Ranger District,** on Highway 299 at the southern edge of the Trinity Alps, is your best bet for weather and trail reports, as well as free self-serve backcountry permits after hours. You can also ask for rafting, trail, fishing, and biking suggestions here. *Hwy. 299, at Big Bar, 20 mi west of Weaverville, tel. 916/623–6106. Open weekdays 8–4:30.*

**WHERE TO SLEEP** The only indoors lodging worth mentioning is in Redding, Weaverville, and Lewiston (*see above*). But once in the vicinity of the alps, you'll want to sleep outside anyway. There are no established campgrounds within the Trinity Alps Wilderness, though with wilderness and fire permits in hand, the entire area becomes a bedroom. There are plenty of streams, creeks, and river from which to obtain water. For developed campgrounds, *see* Weaverville and Lewiston, *above.*

**FOOD** If you forgot to stock your food in Redding, Arcata or Weaverville, you should turn around. In Trinity Center it will cost you over $5 for a gloomy burger and $8–$10 for the chicken or steak at the **Sasquach** (Mary Ave. and Airport Rd., tel. 916/266–3250), open daily 5–10 PM. In Coffee Creek, 8 miles north, **The Country Store** (Derrick Flat Loop Rd., tel. 916/266–3233) has a decent selection of food but prices are high. In Big Bar, at the **Outpost Coffee Shop** (off Hwy. 299, tel. 916/623–5434), the menu is only as inspiring as its name, except for the whopping stack of pancakes ($4). Stop by daily 8–3.

## *Grin and Bear It*

***Whether it causes you excitement or fear, the fact of the matter is that black bears roam the mountains and forests of Northern California. And even if you like the idea of seeing one, you should take certain precautions. First and foremost, always put your food and all "odorous" items (like toothpaste or suntan lotion) in sealed plastic bags. Store the bags in a secure place (food lockers, bear-proof containers, your trunk), or hang them from a thin branch at least 10 feet off the ground and well away from the tree trunk and your tent. The latest ranger-approved method is a counterweight system, where you balance the loot with a rock. Ranger stations have detailed illustrations.***

***The surest way not to run into a bear while hiking is to make plenty of noise as you go. Any ursine beings will, in all likelihood, make themselves scarce when they hear your approach. If you do encounter a bear, keep a safe distance, avoid sudden movements, do not tease or play with it, and never get between a mother and her cubs. Make a slow detour, keeping upwind so the bear will smell you and (hopefully) avoid you. Experts disagree on how to respond if a bear starts to chase you; the U.S. Forest Service recommends climbing a tree, making lots of noise and throwing objects to scare the bear away, or, as a last resort, "playing opossum." Finally, respect bears' intelligence; despite Yogi's self-aggrandizement, the average bear is actually pretty damn smart, and can discern your whereabouts and the location of your food without too much trouble.***

**EXPLORING THE TRINITY ALPS** For serious outdoor adventures, the Trinity Alps Wilderness beckons irresistibly, with over 60 alpine lakes and soaring cliffs, many visible from miles around. After you check in at the Weaverville Ranger District (*see* Basics, *above*) for up-to-date info, a $3 topo map, and free backcountry and fire permits, you're good to go.

➢ **HIKING** • To truly explore the Trinity Alps, hikers should budget at least one week in the backcountry. For day- and weekend-trippers there are many options to choose from. A wonderful all-day hike past alpine streams, falls, and meadows leads to **Canyon Creek Lakes.** From Weaverville, take Highway 299 west 7 miles to Canyon Creek Road north (at Junction City), and follow the creek about 15 miles to the trailhead. From there it's a moderate 7-mile hike (3–4 hrs) to the lakes, with a 2,500-foot gain in altitude. If it's too late in the day to start, or you just want to camp somewhere secluded, **Ripstein Campground** is high on a ridge above Canyon Creek, a quarter-mile back toward Junction City. There's no water, but sites are free and there are pit toilets. Bears are a real presence here, so hang your food when you camp and don't leave yummy-smelling things in your car or tent (*see box* Grin and Bear It, *above*).

For a less adventurous hike—an easy day trip if you don't want to camp—take Highway 3 about 40 miles north of Weaverville to the Eagle Creek Loop, 6 miles north of Coffee Creek, and follow signs to the **Stoddard Lake Trailhead,** 6 miles away. From here it's a moderate 3½-mile hike to Stoddard Lake. Another popular hike begins 30 miles north of Weaverville near Trinity Center and goes 2 miles to **Big Boulder Lake,** and then another mile to **Little Boulder Lake.** The lakes are surrounded by virgin forests and granite cliffs, and there are plenty of quiet places to pitch a tent.

For a more strenuous day or overnight trip (10 mi and a 2,500 ft ascent), take the **Bear Creek Loop Trail** off of Bear Creek Loop Road, 15 miles north of Trinity Center. If you have five to seven days to spare, try the 30-mile **Caribou Lake Trail,** which leads 4,000 feet up through the heart of the alps, carpeted with Douglas fir, ponderosa pine, manzanita, and huckleberry oak. About 8 miles north of Trinity Center on Highway 3, look for Coffee Creek Road and proceed west 19 miles to the trailhead at Big Flat Campground.

➢ **RAFTING** • One of the best ways to see this pristine area is by taking a float down the Trinity River. **Trinity River Rafting** (Trinity River Inn, Hwy. 299, Big Flat, tel. 916/623–3033 or 800/307–4837) offers guided trips (half day $39, full day $59) on Class II and III rapids from Pigeon Point, about 10 miles west of Weaverville. The same trips are available by kayak for $5 extra. You can also take self-guided trips on Class I and II rapids for $19 per person, including boat, paddles, life jacket and shuttle service. A cheaper option is to ask around for inner tubes; a good put-in spot is Junction City or Helena. Don't go farther west than Pigeon Point, though; the water gets too rough.

# Mt. Shasta and the Upper State

**"Lonely as God and white** as a winter moon, Mt. Shasta starts up sudden and solitary from the heart of the great black forests of Northern California." The beleaguered forests may not be as pristine now as they were when author Joaquin Miller wrote those words in 1873, but the last hundred or so years haven't really made a dent in the mystic mountain. On a clear day, you can see the 14,162-foot dormant volcano from a hundred miles south. Native Americans valued Mt. Shasta as the home of the Great Spirit, and many people—particularly those who don't think Waterford when you say crystal—remain convinced of its spiritual powers (*see box* The New Age of Mt. Shasta, *below*).

*The local Indians believed that Shasta was a tepee of the Great Spirit. Out of respect, they religiously avoided stepping above the timber line.*

Mt. Shasta dominates the top of California, a region that seems to be more familiar to Oregonians and Washingtonians than to folks from the Golden State. But the tropical Mossbrae Falls in Dunsmuir and the sprawling Scott Valley—not to mention its excellent Etna Brewery—merit a visit. The Oregon Shakespearean Festival is over the border and through the mountain pass in Ashland. If you really want to launch yourself into the unknown, head east on Highways 89 and 161 to Tulelake and the Lava Beds National Monument; the spare but richly detailed high-desert landscape may thrill you more than the state's more famous attractions.

Most travelers will want to head to the north state from late spring to early fall, when the snow has largely melted, the roads are clear, the wildflowers are in bloom, and the trout are jumping. The far north is also wonderful in winter, though: Rip up some turf on your cross-country skis, go bird-watching at Klamath Basin, or do some cold-weather spelunking at Lava Beds.

**COMING AND GOING** Many of the towns mentioned below (including Dunsmuir, Mount Shasta, Yreka, and Ashland) lie along I–5. If you're not driving, **Amtrak** (tel. 800/USA–RAIL) has a station 10 minutes south of Mount Shasta in Dunsmuir (5750 Sacramento Ave., at Pine St.); one-way fare from San Francisco (8 hrs) is $61. **Greyhound** (tel. 800/231–2222) will make a freeway stop at Mount Shasta but won't take you into town. One-way fare from San Francisco is $42.

A car or bicycle is imperative if you want to venture very far east or west of I–5. The drive from Mount Shasta to Tulelake takes less than two hours. From I–5 at Weed, take Highway 97 northeast to Highway 161 east, at the Oregon border. After about 15 minutes, you'll hit Highway 139, on which you can head south 4 miles to Tulelake and another couple miles to the turnoff for Lava Beds National Monument. Of course, it could take considerably longer than two hours, depending on how often you stop to watch the great blue herons, western grebes, pelicans, cormorants, and (during January and February) hundreds of bald eagles in the Klamath Basin National Wildlife Refuge.

# Mount Shasta

At the foot of the venerable mountain, the city of Mount Shasta embraces both the good old boys and the funky New Agers. In fact, unlike most of the Cascades region, Mount Shasta is more crystals and channeling than rifles and power saws. One tourist brochure lists "metaphysical points of interest," including the Buddhist monastery, Shasta Abbey, Panther Meadows, and "other locations you are led to" on the mountain.

*The volcano is only dormant, meaning it will eventually erupt; but as one tourist brochure soothingly explains, "There has never been an unexpected eruption at an instrumented (i.e., monitored) volcano, and there should be ample time to capture the family cat and get Granny into the car."*

You'll get a great view of Mt. Shasta from **Black Butte,** which sits next to the volcano like some smaller, darker alter ego. John Muir once called the 6,325-foot dome Muir's Peak. It takes about three hours to hike the trail to the top; bring warm clothes if you want to hang out there. To get to the butte, you can take Lake Street, which will turn into Everitt Memorial Highway north of town, and do your Zen best to find the trailhead from the confusing signs; but a surer bet is to buy the $3 topo map from the Fifth Season (*see* Outdoor Activities, *below*), which shows all the logging roads leading to the trailhead.

The free **Sisson Museum** (1 N. Old Stage Rd., take Hatchery Rd. west across I–5, tel. 916/926–5508), open daily 10–5 in summer and weekdays 1–4 in winter, features changing exhibits about old-time school days, geology, weather, and Native Americans (though they focus disproportionately on the history of the region since white settlement). You can observe the latest tremors on a seismograph and play a piano once owned by pioneer Elda McCloud. Next door at the **Mount Shasta Fish Hatchery** (tel. 916/926–2215), open daily 8–4, walk among the hatching and rearing ponds out back to see (and smell) trout in all stages of development. Admission is free, though you may end up buying some fish food.

Mount Shasta's **Fourth of July** celebration draws thousands of people from miles around, with a parade, a run, and fireworks that radiate out across Lake Siskiyou. To reach town from I–5, take the central Mount Shasta exit east toward the mountain. This is Lake Street, which crosses Mount Shasta Boulevard; the two roads form the main axes of the town.

**BASICS** The helpful staff at the **Mount Shasta Convention and Visitor Bureau** (300 Pine St., at Lake St., tel. 800/926–4865), open Monday–Saturday 9–5 and Sunday 10–2, can give you info as well as a copy of *Siskiyou County Living* and *After Five,* free entertainment monthlies that cover the whole northern part of the state. The **Mt. Shasta Ranger District** (204 Alma St., off N. Mount Shasta Blvd., tel. 916/926–4511) is open daily 8–4:30 in summer, weekdays 8–4:30 in winter. The nearby **McCloud Ranger District** (Hwy. 89, tel. 916/964–2184) is open weekdays 8–4:30 and Saturdays 9–3.

**WHERE TO SLEEP** The **Evergreen Lodge** (1312 S. Mt. Shasta Blvd., tel. 916/926–2143) has 20 drab rooms, a pool, and a hot tub. Doubles are $34, and for $42 you get a fully equipped kitchenette. Another decent option is the **Shasta Lodge Motel** (724 N. Mt. Shasta Blvd., north of Lake St., tel. 916/926–2815), where your queen bed and bathtub cost $36.

➢ **HOSTELS** • **Alpenrose Cottage Hostel.** This is easily the best lodging choice in town. Betty Brown operates an independent hostel in her beautiful house at the foot of Mt. Shasta. For $13 a night, you get a large deck facing the mountain, a shared kitchen with a microwave, and a common room with TV. Couples can reserve a private room with a queen bed for $23. Read Betty's funny signs all around the house, exchange a book in the small collection, or do some work to cover the cost of your bed if you can't afford it. *204 E. Hinckley St., tel. 916/926–6724. From downtown, walk north 20 min on N. Mount Shasta Blvd., go right at KOA sign on E. Hinckley St. 14 beds. Curfew 11 PM. Reception open daily 8–noon and 5–11. Laundry, linen rental ($1), showers ($2).*

➢ **CAMPING** • Camping costs from nothing to about $8 at the 13 recreation sites in the McCloud and Mt. Shasta ranger districts. Your best bet lies straight up Everitt Memorial Highway: **Panther Meadows,** a free, wooded walk-in campground with vault toilets and picnic tables, offers 10 tents-only sites. At 7,400 feet, Panther Meadows is an important meeting ground for all sorts of New Agers. Bring plenty of drinking water; there's none here. If you can't get into Panther Meadows, drive back down to **McBride Springs,** 4½ miles northeast of down-

## The New Age of Mt. Shasta

***Angel connections, crystal magnetics, ascensions, chadra clearings, aura charging—it's all happening here, folks. Why Mt. Shasta? In a nutshell, many are convinced that the mountain is the center of a powerful energy vortex. Native American legend pays tribute to Shasta's potency; and some say the mountain's bowels support lost civilizations, like the Lemurians, hidden descendants of a 400,000-year-old race from the continent of Mu, which is thought to have sunk into the Pacific Ocean. Through yoga, massage, meditation, and retreats, New Agers hope to tap into Shasta's powers, or at least connect with their own inner selves.***

***Shasta has played host to its share of mystical events. The well-known St. Germain Foundation contends that in 1930, founder Guy W. Ballard met the "ascended master" on the mountain and was taken back in time to be taught archetypal truths. In 1987 the Harmonic Convergence, a celebration of planetary union and a new phase of universal harmony, was held here. If a visit to the mountain also does something mysterious to you, perhaps you should seek enlightenment with Shasta's New Agers. Pick up a free copy of the monthly "Heart Dance, Bringing Us Together," available all around town.***

town on Everitt Memorial Highway. The nine sites ($6), set in a sparse forest, have vault toilets, tables, and drinking water. No reservations are necessary for either campground. Another option is to head to **Lake Siskiyou** (*see* Outdoor Activities, *below*), or check the camping options at **Castle Crags State Park** (*see below*) or at the McCloud Ranger District, about 12 miles east of Mount Shasta (*see* Basics, *above*).

**FOOD** If you're passing through on your way up the mountain, down the river, or into the forest, set aside time to grub in Mount Shasta. The **Bagel Café and Natural Bakery** (105 E. Alma St., just east of N. Mount Shasta Blvd., tel. 916/926–1414), open daily 6:30 AM–9 PM, does all its own baking and has a fresh juice bar. Try the whole-wheat vegetarian pizza ($2.50) or the veggie super burrito ($5.50). The bulletin board is a good source of flyers and posters about all things New Age. **Coffee & Confusion** (408 N. Mount Shasta Blvd., tel. 916/926–3977), open daily 7 AM–10 PM, has $3 breakfast specials, $4 lunch specials, and a fancy selection of caffeinated brews (85¢–$2.25). The only confusion at this high-ceilinged café is the name: Coffee & Confusion is also called Pat's Café.

**The Pasta Shop** (418 N. Mount Shasta Blvd., tel. 916/926–4118), open Monday–Saturday 9–6, makes its own pasta fresh daily (without eggs) and serves generous portions with marinara sauce ($4.75), sundried tomato and basil sauce ($5.25), or plain to go ($2.75 per lb). **The Avalon Square Cafe** (401 N. Mount Shasta Blvd., tel. 916/926–4998), open weekdays 8–5, weekends 8–2, bakes great cinnamon rolls ($1.25), whips up beautiful smoothies ($2.25), and fashions amazing smoked salmon with pesto sandwiches ($5.25). While health-conscious is the watchword in Mount Shasta, you can find things like red meat if you look hard. If you're carbo-loading to attack the mountain, **Mike and Tony's** (501 S. Mount Shasta Blvd., tel. 916/926–4792) will fuel you up with ravioli, spaghetti, and steaks ($6–$18). The restaurant is open Monday, Tuesday, and Thursday 4–9, Friday–Saturday 4–10, and Sunday 1–9. If you're just looking to stock up on supplies, the **Mountain Song Natural Food Market** (134 Morgan Way, next to Thrifty's, tel. 916/926–3391) has organic produce and other healthy items. For a hefty sandwich on the way to a hike or a picnic, **Cervelli's Market** (625 S. Mount Shasta Blvd., tel. 916/926–4110), open daily 8–8, does you right. The Blade Special (roast beef and jack cheese on a sourdough roll with all the trimmings) is $3.

**OUTDOOR ACTIVITIES** With hiking, biking, mountaineering, skiing, swimming, and kayaking, Shasta is prime for all those commune-with-nature urges. For every kind of equipment, try the **Fifth Season** (300 N. Mount Shasta Blvd., at Lake St., tel. 916/926–3606). Crampons and ice axes rent for $12 a day, snowshoes for $9 a day, mountain bikes for $24 a day, cross-country ski packages for $9 a day, and downhill getups for $12 a day. The store also rents sleeping bags ($15 for 2–3 days) and tents ($28 for 2–3 days). Call 916/926–5555 for their daily report on mountain conditions.

➢ **HIKING** • There's hiking galore around Shasta, but the big daddy is the 14,000-foot-plus behemoth itself. While there is no real trail to Shasta's summit, from June to September you can follow the path blazed by climbers on the mountain's south face: the **Avalanche Gulch** route from Bunny Flat (7,000 ft). It's possible to do the 12-mile round-trip from Bunny Flat to the summit and back in a day (8–12 hrs), but the elevation gain is over 7,000 feet (very strenuous), and you'll need crampons and ice axes most of the year. Those who wish to camp can do so at Horse Camp, where drinking water and toilets are available, or Helen Lake, which is usually dry or snowed over. You can get the required hiking and camping permits May 15–October 15 from the Mt. Shasta and McCloud ranger stations (*see* Basics, *above*). Day-use permits may be self-issued at both locations, and in the off-season, all permits can be self-issued from the Mt. Shasta office. Be sure to bring extra clothes and food; Mt. Shasta's unpredictable weather can leave you stranded on the mountain. Check the ranger station or the Fifth Season (*see above*) for conditions before you go.

➢ **BIKING** • You'll find miles of great mountain biking in the Shasta area, much of it on old logging roads. An indispensable resource is the $3.50 Mount Shasta Area Mountain Biker Map, a topographical map developed by a local rider and sold at the visitor center (*see above*). Or just head up 1 mile toward the mountain on Everitt Memorial Highway, turn left on the dirt road past the high school, follow signs to McBride Springs, and go off on the labyrinthine logging roads, which are great for moderate rides. Stop by Fifth Season (*see above*) for rentals, more maps, and local riding wisdom. **Mt. Shasta Ski Park** (*see below*) lets you chairlift to the top in summer ($7) daily 10–4. You can rent bikes here and zoom down the ski runs once up top.

➢ **ROCK CLIMBING** • For backpackers, climbers, and mountaineers, **Shasta Mountain Guides** (1938 Hill Rd., tel. 916/926–3117) runs a $65 one-day crash course to familiarize you with ice axe, crampon, and belay climbing. They also offer guided expeditions to the summit, which take two to 2½ days and cost $225–$285. They'll can customize programs for people with special needs. For the beginner, Mt. Shasta Ski Park (*see below*) has a 24-foot artificial climbing tower with shoes, harness, and assistance for $8 an hour.

➢ **RAFTING** • White-water enthusiasts should contact **Turtle River Rafting Company** (tel. 916/926–3223), which offers everything from relaxing one-day float trips on Class II-plus rivers ($76–$86) to tough one- to three-day trips on Class V waters ($196–$336). **Living Water Recreation** (tel. 916/926–5446) runs cheaper all-day excursions on the easy Class I–II section of the Klamath River ($60 per day) or the moderate Class II–III runs of the Upper Sacramento River ($70 per person).

➢ **WATER SPORTS** • **Lake Siskiyou** is a good choice for camping and water activities. For $1 per person per day, you can lounge on the lake's shore or take a dip; pedal boats and canoes rent for $5 an hour and toy kayaks are $3 an hour. More than 300 sites ($13) are amply spaced among the pines, and hot showers are at your disposal. For reservations and details, contact **Lake Siskiyou Camp-Resort** (tel. 916/926–2618). To get here from I–5, take the central Mount Shasta exit, go west on Hatchery Lane, turn left at the stop sign, bear right onto W. A. Barr Road, and go 3½ miles.

For a lesser-known, uncrowded spot, turn south toward **Castle Lake** just before you reach the Lake Siskiyou Camp-Resort entrance (look for the sign on W. A. Barr Road). About 7 miles into the mountains you'll reach a great spot for an alpine picnic or free lakeside camping (more than 200 feet from the water's edge). A dozen free sites lie to your left just before you reach the lake.

➢ **SKIING** • Cross-country skiing is very popular near Lake Siskiyou and on Mt. Shasta. The Fifth Season (*see above*) rents equipment ($9 a day). Although skiing at **Mt. Shasta Ski Park** (104 Siskiyou Ave., tel. 916/926–8610) is very popular and an integral part of the local economy in the winter, relative to Tahoe or Bend in Oregon, it isn't that great—two short lifts, high intermediate at best. All-day lift tickets are $26, ski rentals are $17, and snowboard rentals are $16–$22. Call 916/926–8686 for snow conditions. To get here, head 10 miles east from town on Highway 89 and follow the signs. The park is open daily 9–4 and Wednesday–Sunday 4–10 for night skiing. The season lasts November–April during a typical year.

## NEAR MOUNT SHASTA

**MCCLOUD** This small town east of Mount Shasta on Highway 89 is known for hosting popular square-dance events. You can check the schedule at **McCloud Dance Country** (Main and Colombero Sts., tel. 916/964–2252), a turn-of-the-century dance hall and school, but don't expect anyone to explain the cryptic notes ("Arizona, A-2, DBD, intro C-1 workshops" is one night's line-up). It's free to watch, but a little do-si-do will run you $10. **McCloud Falls** makes a good swimming hole, and the $8-a-night, 37-site campground is well forested, though crowded in summer. To get there, follow Highway 89 east for 6 miles and turn right at the RIVER ACCESS, FOWLERS CAMPGROUND sign.

*McCloud used to be owned entirely by McCloud River Lumber Company. If they didn't like you, they'd take up your section of wooden sidewalk until you behaved (so says a longtime north-state resident).*

➢ **WHERE TO SLEEP AND EAT** • **Stoney Brook Inn Bed-and-Breakfast** (309 W. Colombero St., NE off Hwy. 89, tel. 916/964–2300 or 800/369–6118) is one of the few B&Bs in California that qualify as "budget." Two people can get a private room with shared bath for only $36, and the price includes unlimited use of the outdoor spa and Finnish sauna, as well as a veggie breakfast. The adjacent restaurant, **Simply Vegetarian,** has an organic salad bar ($5.50) and healthy vegan entrées like pasta primavera and baked polenta ($8). It's open for dinner Wednesday–Sunday in summer. Groups can rent dorm beds for $14 a night—the price includes access to the spa and breakfast. Room 10 has wheelchair access.

**DUNSMUIR** Its tourist brochures are geared to retirees, and a quick trip through the tidy streets attests to the slow-and-steady pace of life in Dunsmuir, south of Mount Shasta on I–5. The town originally flourished with the coming of the railroad, and its life seemed charmed until the summer of 1991, when a train car carrying chemicals used in making pesticides jumped the tracks and landed in the Sacramento River. The extensive pollution killed many fish in the river, and halted all recreational fishing in the Sacramento near Dunsmuir for years. Dunsmuir residents and the Department of Fish and Game happily advertise that the river is now back to health and open for business again. Call the **Chamber of Commerce** (4841 Dunsmuir Rd., tel. 916/235–2177), open weekdays 9–5 in summer, until 2 in winter, for more info. They can customize your drive, hike, or fishing trip.

The water certainly looks pristine enough, especially around **Mossbrae Falls.** You won't believe it until you go there yourself, but these are the most impressive falls this side of Kauai. Getting there is a little complicated but definitely worth the trouble: Follow Dunsmuir Avenue north out of downtown and make a left on Scarlett Road (under the archway to Shasta Retreat). Park at the railroad tracks and walk north along the tracks about a mile; trains do run here so watch out. When you see a bridge up ahead, look for paths leading down the hill to your right (about 150 feet shy of the bridge). Standing on the river's edge you'll be facing the falls.

➢ **WHERE TO SLEEP AND EAT** • The **Oak Tree Inn** (6604 Dunsmuir Ave., south end of town, tel. 916/235–2884) has a roadside flower garden that stops passing cars. Clean motel rooms run $42 for a king-size bed. **Shelby's** (5843 Dunsmuir Ave., tel. 916/235–0654) offers a welcome I–5 dining treat: fresh, non-greasy food. Soup and salad is $3.50, and an avocado melt goes for $5. Breakfast and lunch are served daily, dinner Wednesday–Sunday only.

**CASTLE CRAGS STATE PARK** Castle Crags State Park (Box 80, Castella 96017, tel. 916/235–2684) is home to magnificent, soaring granite crags that actually startle you as you drive north on I–5 (the park lies right off the interstate, south of Dunsmuir). Hiking on the crags is popular with north staters. "You can spend a lifetime up there," one regular said. If you only have a day, don't miss **Summit Dome Trail,** beginning at the Vista Point parking lot, a moderately strenuous 3½-mile hike that takes you virtually to the top of the crags. Experienced climbers have been known to scamper the last unmarked ¼ mile up the granite dome. Either way, you'll get awesome views of Mt. Shasta and the upper Sacramento River valley. Summit Dome is also an access point for the **Pacific Crest Trail.** Day use of the park is $5 (free on bike or foot).

The campground ($14 a night) has 64 spacious, forested sites with hot showers. The only detracting feature is the drone of I–5, but don't blame the park—it was here first. Sites 45–58 are farthest from the freeway. There are also six environmental (walk-in) sites with pit toilets and no running water ($7 a night), with parking close by. Call MISTIX (tel. 800/444–PARK) for reservations. For even cheaper and more secluded camping, follow the park road a few miles past the main campground entrance until you enter the national forest. Then just take one of the small logging roads and camp for free anywhere. If you decide to strike out on your own, though, you'll need a permit.

*At Stewart Mineral Springs, the water is said to be so powerful at pulling toxins from your body that if you rub your skin while bathing, you may break out in a rash, or worse.*

**STEWART MINERAL SPRINGS** With all of Mt. Shasta's volcanic potency, you'd think there'd be more hot springs and what-all around here. In fact, the area has only one developed mineral springs, but fortunately, it's set up nicely for the budget traveler, in a stunningly tranquil, remote location. You can camp on a wooded hillside for $10, rent an authentic tepee (sleeping five) for only $15 a night, or sleep in a real room for two ($35), or in a cabin ($45). There are no picnic tables or fire rings, but there's plenty of space and you won't be turned away. You'll have access to a sauna, shower, sundeck, and cold creek pool (a $5 day-use fee gets you the same amenities). You pay separately to use the mineral baths themselves ($12 a day if you're staying the night, $15 otherwise). A Karuk medicine man occasionally offers purification sweats; call for dates. *4617 Stewart Springs Rd., tel. 800/322–9223. Take I–5 10 mi north from Mount Shasta through Weed. Exit on Edgewood: follow signs to Stewart Springs Rd., and go 4 mi.*

# Yreka

By the time you get to Yreka (pronounced Why-REEK-a), about 40 miles north of Mount Shasta on I–5, you'll probably be tired of seeing yet another sign welcoming you to yet another "historic town" begot during the gold rush. But Yreka is a good place to stop for a good, cheap meal and gas if you're on your way north to Oregon, or headed south for the Scott Valley or Mt. Shasta. It's also worth a second look for the interesting **Siskiyou County Museum,** which has well-presented exhibits on pioneer history, gold mining, and fur trapping. An outdoor wing, which closes at 4:30, offers more tangible historical relics—transplanted original structures from around the county, including a mid-1800s homesteader house, a steam locomotive, a frontier church, and a general store (still using the old cash register to ring up your jawbreakers). *910 S. Main St., tel. 916/842–3836. Take central Yreka exit to Main St. and turn left. Admission: $1. Open Tues.–Sat. 9–5.*

*Like palindromes? The Yreka Bakery has been tripping out locals for years.*

If you're curious about old steam engines and have an itch for a slow-moving, 3½-hour round-trip journey with some great views of Mt. Shasta, take a ride on the **Blue Goose Excursion Train.** The train chugs through the hinterlands of Shasta Valley to the little town of Montague, which has stayed small and sleepy despite the hundreds of tourists who disembark there several days a week during summer. You'll have an hour's stopover for lunch and browsing. The train conductors and even the loudspeaker commentary manage to avoid being overly annoying. *300 E. Miner St., tel. 916/842–4146. From I–5, east at central Yreka exit. Fare: $9. Runs mid-June–early Sept. Departs 10 AM. Reserve in advance.*

**WHERE TO SLEEP** You should be able to find a generic motel for about $30–$35 along Main Street, which runs parallel to I–5. Yreka's motels are all clean and comfortable, with zilcho personality. Add 8% tax. The **Ben Ber Motel** (1210 S. Main St., tel. 916/842–2791 or 800/767–4147) has 36 rooms surrounding its pool. For only $33 in summer ($30–$32 in winter), two people can share a king-size bed. **Motel 6** (1785 S. Main St., tel. 916/842–4111) offers a pool and 102 rooms that all look like other boxy, shag carpeted, ill-decorated abodes. Singles are $31, doubles $37.

**FOOD** Many I–5 travelers (including the California Highway Patrol) frequent **Grandma's House** (123 E. Center St., at I–5, tel. 916/842–5300), open daily 6 AM–10 PM. You can eat your traditional bacon-and-eggs breakfast ($5) or broiled chicken sandwich ($6) surrounded by astonishing, campy decor. A better choice is **Nature's Kitchen** (412 S. Main St., tel. 916/842–1136), open Monday–Saturday for breakfast and lunch, Thursday–Saturday for dinner. Much of the menu at this simple, healthy place is vegetarian. Try the tuna-salad sandwich (certified dolphin-safe) for $4, or the chili veggie burger for $5.50.

## NEAR YREKA

**SCOTT VALLEY** Driving through the 28 miles of beautiful farmland that make up Scott Valley (take Hwy. 3 southwest from Yreka), you'll see one knockout landscape after another. **Fort Jones** was originally an outpost for white settlers who feared the Rogue Indians. In 1852, a fort was established in the town of Etna (originally named Rough and Ready) to protect the area from the Rogue River Indians. The Indians gave such a fight that Ulysses S. Grant was declared AWOL after failing to take command (he returned later with a good excuse). Check out the **Etna Brewing Company, Inc.** (131 Callahan St., off Main St., tel. 916/467–5277), which offers free tours and tasting Saturday 1–5. It's pretty much a two-person operation (in the same building that housed a pre-Prohibition brewery)—casual enough that they'll probably give you a quick tour and samples on a weekday, especially if you call ahead to warn them you're coming.

➢ **WHERE TO SLEEP AND EAT** • A couple blocks west along Main Street you'll find **Sengthong's** (434 Main St., tel. 916/467–5668), a highly regarded Thai-Vietnamese restaurant. The dishes are pricey—hot spiced prawns go for $14, spring rolls for $11—but well worth it if your taste buds have had just about enough diner food. The restaurant is open for dinner Wednesday–Sunday. To stay the night, try the **Marble View Motel** (12425 Main St., Fort Jones, tel. 916/468–2394), just north of Fort Jones on Highway 3, where six tidy, spacious rooms for two go for $32 each (no tax) and there's plenty of scenery to fill your window. Marble View does not accept credit cards.

**ASHLAND** The **Oregon Shakespeare Festival,** held from mid-February through October, has turned Ashland (40 mi North of Yreka) into a staging area for theater of all kinds, from experimental to traditional, though you'll still see a healthy share of the outdoor Elizabethan productions that spawned the festival more than a half-century ago. The flat, pale-green hills make a pretty backdrop for the theatrical whirl. And while you'll find Puck's Donuts, the Romeo Inn, and other allusions to the Bard here, Oregonian sensibilities have prevented Ashland's "Disneyfication." On the whole, it has the feel of a college town—with cafés, bookstores, and a thriving student life (Southern Oregon State College is here).

In addition to the festival, there are several other ways to entertain yourself in Ashland, many free and radiating from the theater district. **Lithia Park** is a shady spot for picnicking or strolling. Look for a slew of events here under the umbrella term **Festival Noons.** These include lectures by actors, directors, and scholars, music by past and contemporary composers, and dance performances. Tickets for Festival Noons are $4 and must be purchased at the Festival Box Office (*see box, below*). Performances begin (surprise) at noon. For free, you can attend the **Talks in the Park,** each an informal hour of questions and answers with directors, costume designers, stage managers, actors, composers, and other theater folk. Talks begin at noon Tuesday–Sunday in Bankside Park, just outside Gate 1 of the Elizabethan Theater. Backstage tours of the theater ($8) can be arranged at the Festival Box Office. The **Ashland Chamber of Commerce** (110 E. Main St., at Pioneer St., tel. 503/482–3486), open weekdays 9–5, can give you more festival info, as well as supplying a free town map and calendar of events.

➢ **WHERE TO SLEEP** • Hotel rates can climb $10–$20 during summer and holidays. Try the lovely old **Columbia Hotel** (262½ E. Main St., tel. 503/482–3726) downtown if you

## *All the World's a Stage*

***The oldest such event in America, Ashland's Oregon Shakespeare Festival has grown to include eleven repertory plays each year (four by Shakespeare), which are performed in three separate theaters, all located in the same courtyard: the beautiful, outdoor Elizabethan Theatre (which has surprisingly good acoustics), the indoor Angus Bowmer Theatre, and the smaller Black Swan stage. Two plays go on daily at 2 PM, and two more at 8:30 PM. Call or stop by the box office for a free schedule. Productions ($13–$29) sell out quickly, but there are always people standing near the Festival Box Office (15 S. Pioneer St., 1 block south of Main St., tel. 503/482–4331; closed Mon.) trying to sell tickets. Standing-room tickets ($9) for the play of the night at the Elizabethan Theatre are a good bet if you're blowing through town and need a Shakespeare fix. Only 20 standing-room tickets are available for each sold-out performance. Get to the box office early (9 AM) to score one. If you aren't able to get a ticket, come around 7 PM to the box office area: actors perform free Elizabethan mini-dramas and musical sets outside before the 8:30 show.***

want something with character. Two people can stay in a simple room with a country-floral motif for $39–$46. Rooms with private bath run $54–$74. The 24 rooms can book up two to three months ahead for summer weekends, so try to call ahead. Besides the hostel, the only other way to spend a cheap night here is to camp. **Jackson Hot Springs Resort** (2253 Hwy. 99, 2 mi north of Ashland, tel. 503/482–3776) allows camping ($13 a tent) on a kept lawn, offering little privacy from other campers and the nearby highway. But you also get a shower, laundry facilities, mineral pool, and mineral hot tubs ($6 an hour for one person; $9 a hour for two). Another option is **Emigrant Lake County Park** (tel. 503/482–5935), about 5 miles east of Ashland on Highway 66. The 42 first-come, first-served sites are $12 a night. You get hot showers, though most spaces lack privacy. Set on an exposed hillside overlooking the lake, the sites can get hot and dusty in summer, but are green in spring and fall.

**Ashland Hostel.** Yreka's nicest budget lodgings are in a big old house with a well-kept garden and reasonably priced dorm beds ($13, $11 for HI members). There are 39 beds, but they do fill up, so send a check to reserve a space (it should arrive 7 days ahead of your stay). There's Foosball (25¢), a piano, and a washer ($1) and dryer (75¢). You can get a shower for $2 if you're just passing through. *150 N. Main St., Ashland 97520, 2 blocks west of the plaza, tel. 503/482–9217. Reception open 8–10 and 5–midnight, check-in by 11 PM.*

➢ **FOOD** • For a great selection of organic, bulk, and nutritional foods, shop at the **Ashland Community Food Store Co-Op** (37 3rd St., off E Main St., tel. 503/482–2237), open Monday–Saturday 8 AM–9 PM, Sunday 9 AM–9 PM. The **Ashland Bakery-Café** (38 E. Main St., tel. 503/482–2117), open Tuesday–Sunday 7 AM–8:30 PM and Monday 7–4, makes a $7 chicken sandwich with ortega chilis on sourdough. **The Beanery** (1602 Ashland St., at Walker St., tel. 503/488–0700), a hip café, makes tasty cheese ravioli ($3.50). On Thursday–Saturday nights you'll get a bit of free live music—anything from folk to rock to '30s tunes. **Geppetto's** (345 E. Main St., tel. 503/482–1138), open daily 8 AM–9 PM, serves a savory marinated herb, vegetable, and cheddar omelet ($6.25), and has a fine dinner menu as well.

# Tulelake

Tulelake resembles a small ghost town, but it's just about the only significant outpost of civilization in the northeast corner of California. (By the way, a tule, pronounced "toolie," is a type of bulrush found in marshes.) The town has a curious mixture of ingredients: more millionaires per capita (according to one resident) than you would think possible, their fortunes built on horseradish and potatoes; one flashing red traffic light; and a large core of well-educated locals (the University of California does genetic crop experiments up here, sometimes amid controversy . . . coincidence or conspiracy?). Once you leave I-5 (take Hwy. 97 northeast to Hwy. 161 east to Hwy. 139 south), the sense of the place will hit you: Tulelake sits in the middle of land that is at once desolate and magnificent, with wide-open gray-blue skies.

The town's proximity to Lava Beds National Monument, Klamath Basin National Wildlife Refuge, and Medicine Lake (*see* Near Lava Beds, *below*) makes it the best (and last) place to stock up on groceries and fill your tank. It's also a fine place to take in a local festival: The **Tulelake Horseradish and Sportsmen's Festival** is held each June, the **Waterfowl Festival** happens in October, and the **Tulelake Butte Valley Fair,** attracting big names from the country-and-western music scene and tens of thousands of visitors, is held the first and second weeks in September. For more info, call the **Tulelake Visitor Center** (Main St., in library, tel. 916/667–2291) Monday–Thursday 10–5.

**WHERE TO SLEEP AND EAT** Before leaving town, don't forget to stock up on horseradish products at the tiny but potent **Mezzetta's Tulelake Horseradish Co.** (619 Main St., tel. 916/667–5319; closed Sun.), by the town's lonely flashing red light. **Mike and Wanda's** (429 Modoc Ave., tel. 916/667–3226) has sandwiches and burgers ($5) and fresh-baked pizza ($7–$13) made with quality (though a bit bland) ingredients; they're open Monday–Saturday 6 AM–10 PM and Sunday until 1 PM. The **Ellis Motel** (tel. 916/667–5242), 1 mile north of town on Highway 139 and situated in lovely farmland, charges $35–$40 for standard rooms; they fill up fast during duck season (mid-Oct.–mid-Jan.), so reserve ahead.

# Klamath Basin

The **Klamath Basin National Wildlife Refuges,** a complex of six waterfront refuges, is partly contained in Northern California but extends well into southern Oregon. Klamath Basin is on the Pacific Flyway, the main north–south migration highway for myriad waterfowl; the birds draw naturalists, bird-watchers, and photographers, as well as hunters. At times during the fall migration (late Aug.–early Nov.) more than a million birds land at Klamath Refuge. The most accessible sections for California travelers are the **Lower Klamath** and **Tule Lake National Wildlife refuges.** Both are easily reached—you skirt the Lower Klamath Refuge driving east on Highway 161, and the Tule Lake Refuge is just southwest of the town of Tulelake—and both have auto-tour routes. Park alongside the road and pull out your binoculars, along with the free checklist of birds you get at the visitor center (*see below*).

*The bald eagle has staged an incredible comeback thanks to the Endangered Species Act of 1973, which banned DDT and encouraged recovery programs like the one at Klamath Basin. The bird was taken off the endangered species list in summer 1994.*

In winter (Nov.–late Mar.) the area is home to 500–1,000 bald eagles. Especially in January and February, you're pretty much guaranteed to see them, even if you're not searching. The **Visitor Center and Refuge Headquarters** (tel. 916/667–2231) can give you up-to-date info on the birds' whereabouts. It's open weekdays 8–4:30, weekends and holidays 8–4. To get here, take East-West Road 5 miles west out of Tulelake, turn left on Hill Road (at the T-junction), and look for the building on your right.

While serious hikers will have to drive 9 miles south to Lava Beds National Monument (*see below*), those who want a bird's-eye view of the marshes should head up the **Sheepy Ridge Wildlife Trail** (behind the visitor center), which runs a steep ¼ mile up a volcanic ridge to a cliff face. You'll see raptors, a yellow-bellied marmot or two, and maybe even a rattlesnake—stay cool, don't panic, and move slowly away. If you happen to have a canoe strapped to the car, the Tule Lake Refuge offers a 2-mile marked canoe trail amid a tule marsh. There's no place to rent a boat in the area, so if you have your heart set on canoeing, drive north on Highway 97 about 15 miles to the **Upper Klamath Refuge,** off Highway 140; you can rent a canoe ($20 half-day; $30 all day) at the Rocky Point Resort (28121 Rocky Point Rd., South Shore of Upper Klamath Lake, tel. 503/356–2287). For more info, call the **Klamath Ranger District** (1936 California Ave., Klamath Falls, OR, tel. 503/883–6717).

# Lava Beds National Monument

*Eight miles south of Tulelake on Highway 139, keep your eyes open for a monument at the site of a Japanese-American internment camp. During World War II, it was the home of 18,789 refugees, forcibly detained here by the U.S. government in an outstanding show of paranoia after the bombing of Pearl Harbor.*

Tucked way up in the northeast corner of the state—west of Highway 139 and south of Tulelake—and consequently not on many tourists' itineraries, Lava Beds' spectacular terrain is *ripe* for exploration. The land is harsh, scarred repeatedly by volcanic activity, but it's what's under the ground that should draw you to this subtly beautiful and often desolate place. The Lava Beds offer dozens of caves to wander through (and 250 more that are rarely explored). You can explore many caves by yourself—borrow lights for free at the visitor center (*see below*), wear hard-soled boots, and buy the useful but silly-looking "bump hats" ($3.25) to protect your head.

This land was the site of the Modoc Indian War: For five months in 1873 Modoc leader Captain Jack used the rough terrain and maze-like lava trails, known as the Stronghold, to fend off a well-fortified U.S. Army. On **Captain Jack's Stronghold Historic Trail** at the north end of the park, you can learn about the Modocs' impressive resistance, and see how the terrain provided perfect natural fortifications for a Modoc force of fewer than 60 to hold off a U.S. Army 20 times its size. Get the excellent interpretive booklet (25¢, available at the trailhead) and take the short half-mile walk or a longer 1½-mile trail through the stronghold.

**BASICS** The park entry fee is $4 per vehicle, valid for seven days of use. The **visitor center,** at the park's south end on Forest Service Road 10, has maps and plenty of info on which caves are okay to explore on your own. Between June and September, the center organizes daily (except Sunday)—and free—two-hour guided walks and a 1- to 1½-hour guided cave tour. *Box 867, Tulelake 96134, tel. 916/667–2282. Open daily 8–6 (until 5 in winter).*

**WHERE TO SLEEP** The **Lava Beds National Monument Campground,** across from the visitor center at the south end of the park, has 40 sites suitable for tents or trailers. For $10 a night, the rangers promise: "No showers, hookups, dump stations, stores, gas, fast food, or pop machines! Plenty of clean air, crystal-clear cold drinking water, and beautiful open space." The campground is free in winter, but all water is turned off.

If the Lava Beds sites are full (this rarely happens), you can camp in the unspoiled backcountry at Lava Beds year-round and for free. Of course, keep in mind the hardships of the terrain and the unpredictability of the weather. Register first at the visitor center, and bring your own water. Rattlesnakes are common. Otherwise, drive 24 miles to Medicine Lake (*see below*) and pitch a tent there. For a shower ($2), make the trek to Tulelake (*see above*) and its **Shady Lanes Trailer Park and Laundromat** (795 Modoc Ave., tel. 916/667–2617).

**EXPLORING THE PARK** The majority of caves open to the public are near the visitor center along **Cave Loop Drive.** Each takes ½–1½ hours to explore—except for **Mushpot Cave,** just outside the visitor center's door; it's a well-lighted place (literally) to get acquainted with basic lava-tube formations. Other cool caverns include **Sentinel Cave,** one of the longest of the lot, with two entrances about a quarter mile apart. **Catacombs** is the most technically challenging—you'll run into a host of small crawl spaces and claustrophobic niches. For a warm-up, try **Golden Dome** or **Hercules Leg.** Two other must-sees in the park are **Fern Cave,** a Modoc spiritual site with pictographs on the wall and a stunning floor of ferns, and **Crystal Cave** (open Dec.–Mar.), full of ice crystals, frozen waterfalls, and the like. Both caves can be seen on arranged tours only. They're free, but tours fill up fast, so call the visitor center well ahead of your trip. If you can do the planning, it's definitely worth it.

Otherwise, there's hiking in the lava wonderland outside. Climb **Schonchin Butte,** a ¾-mile path up a volcanic cinder cone with fantastic wildflowers in late spring. At the top you get to tour the functioning fire lookout and take in an outstanding view (on a clear day you can see mountains in Oregon, 130 miles away). You'll find the ½-mile dirt road to the trailhead off the park's main road, about 5 miles north of the visitor center (follow signs). Another great hike (1⅓ mi), departing from the main road in the park's southern sector, takes you down into **Skull Cave,** the largest in diameter in the park—the ceiling reaches 80 feet in places. You descend to a floor of ice and it's pretty trippy. Most of the caves average a constant 56°, winter or summer, but Skull and Merrill Caves are just below freezing, so dress warmly.

Just northeast of the park proper is **Petroglyph Point,** a prominent butte that used to be an island in a dried-up part of Tule Lake. The original carvings—mostly geometric forms, with the occasional fertility figure or two if you look closely—are estimated to be 2,500–4,500 years old. Unfortunately, vandals have added to the ancient work in recent years, though it's not too difficult to pick out the "real" carvings.

## NEAR LAVA BEDS

**MEDICINE LAKE HIGHLANDS** Fourteen miles south of the Lava Beds visitor center, at the Highway 97 T-junction, follow signs 24 miles west to Medicine Lake, a tree-rimmed mountain lake so beautiful you'll find it hard to believe it's this near the desolate Lava Beds. Four campgrounds surround the lake, with 74 sites total ($7 a night). There's potable water and pit toilets but no showers. The third one down the road, **Medicine Campground,** is the nicest, and has easy access to the lake (not to mention its own small beach). The ranger's trailer is a mile west down the gravel road past the campgrounds. There's no guaranteeing the ranger will be in, but that's where to go with any questions. In a real pinch (or for info prior to coming), contact the **Double Head Ranger District** (Hwy. 139, in Tulelake, tel. 916/667–2246).

Medicine Lake makes a great fishing and swimming hole. Bring all necessary equipment; you can't rent anything here. The **Medicine Lake Day Use Picnic Area** has a swimming area cordoned off from boats; to get here, follow the myriad signs. Hikers will want to head to nearby **Glass Mountain,** where a marked ½-mile trail takes you to an immense obsidian flow covering the mountain's peak. If you have all day, make your way up over the obsidian portion of Glass Mountain; it doesn't get more wild or secluded than this. The way isn't steep, but there isn't a trail and the volcanic glass can be difficult to negotiate at times—wear good boots and register with a ranger if you plan to do serious trekking.

# THE GOLD COUNTRY 6

By Danna Harman

B

**Before high-tech firms, agribusiness, and Hollywood, what made California the** Golden State was, of course, the precious metal itself. James Marshall's discovery of gold in Coloma in 1848 brought a tidal wave of migrants to California and ushered the territory into the Union. Nearby Sacramento soon became the state capital and today remains a place where old California competes with the state's new definition of self. The original boom has long since subsided (though even today, you'll still find a few hopefuls out panning), and the state's population centers have shifted elsewhere. Bustling 19th-century metropolises like Columbia and Nevada City have been reduced to sleepy hamlets proffering a few antiques shops, or "Wild West" museum pieces that feel like a chunk out of Disneyland. If you're interested in what passes for ancient history in California, the towns on Highway 49—in particular, **Auburn, Nevada City,** and **Columbia**—have preserved it laboriously.

Most Californians, though, simply pass through Gold Country en route to a night of modern-day mining: gambling under the bright lights of **Reno**'s casinos. But a wealth of treasures await the intrepid Gold Country explorer: Besides being a cradle of California history, this region is a haven for those seeking a taste of the great outdoors. Claustrophobes from coastal cities find room to breathe while rafting on the Yuba, American, and Stanislaus rivers (easily accessible from towns like Coloma and Columbia); hiking and biking in the foothills; or skiing in the world-class resorts farther east in **Lake Tahoe.** The Tahoe and Eldorado national forests cover much of the region, encompassing 19th-century immigration routes and historic gold mines.

## Sacramento

**Like most state capitals, Sacramento** gets little respect. It's been the seat of California's government since 1854, and it's long been the center of the state's major industry, agriculture. Sacramento has a strong sense of its past, but unlike some of the state's quainter centers of historical self-consciousness, this is a modern city—with ethnic diversity, crime, poverty, an active arts scene, a vocal gay and lesbian community, and a basketball franchise (the Sacramento Kings) that's still a few lottery picks away from respectability. Even so, most Californians persist in thinking of Sacramento as a sleepy backwater town. And as you pass through on your way from the Bay Area to Reno, Tahoe, or the Sierra Nevada, you, too, will have the opportunity to ignore America's 41st-largest city. But Sacramento is a friendly, tree-lined town, where the bars open at 6 AM, the motels and restaurants won't destroy your budget, and the coffeehouses are full all day.

# Sacramento

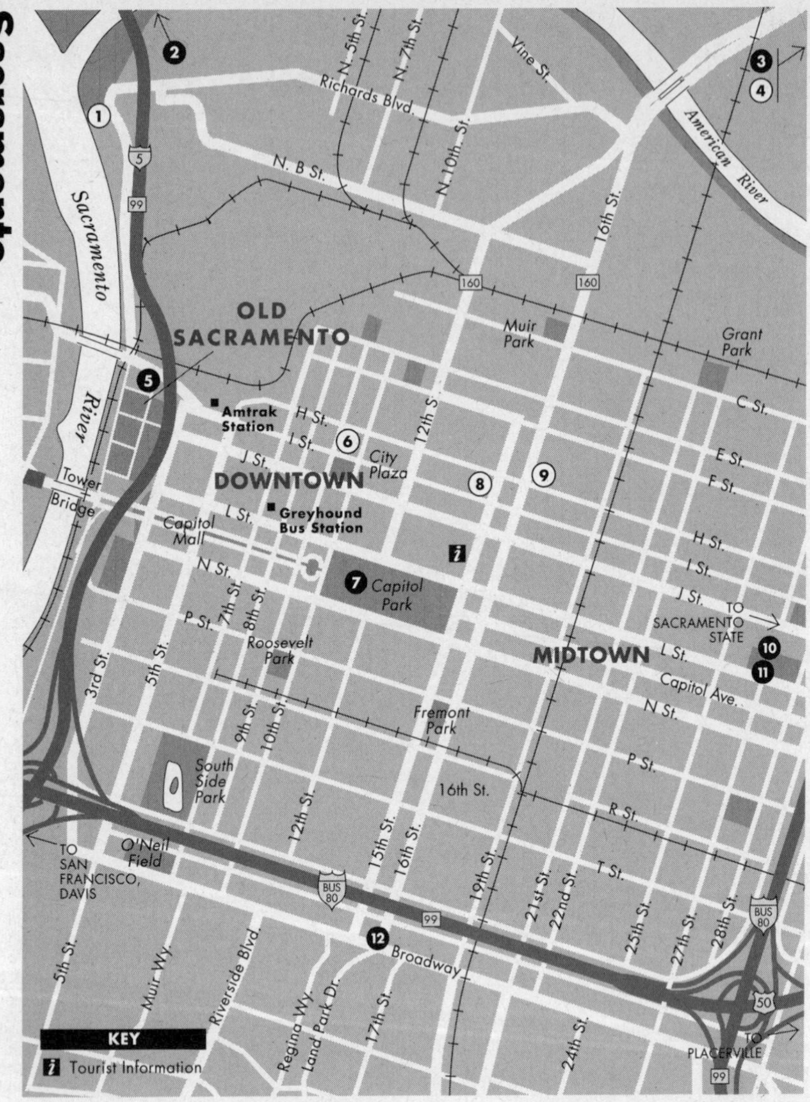


**Sights ●**
Cal Expo, **3**
California State Capitol, **7**
California State Indian Museum, **10**
California State Railroad Museum, **5**
Discovery Park (American River Bike Trail), **2**
Sutter's Fort, **11**
Tower Theater, **12**

**Lodging ○**
Americana Lodge, **8**
Executive Inn, **4**
Mansion View Lodge, **9**
Motel Orleans, **1**
Sacramento Home Hostel, **6**

## BASICS

Pick up info and brochures at the **Sacramento Convention and Visitors Bureau** (1421 K St., at 15th St., tel. 916/264–7777), open weekdays 8–5. If you're down by the river, the **Old Sacramento Visitor Center** (1104 Front St., at K St., tel. 916/442–7644) has lots of the same and is open daily 9–5. For current happenings, check the comprehensive listings in the *Sacramento News & Review,* free at newsstands, and in the *Sacramento Bee*'s "Ticket" section, a weekend entertainment guide published every Friday.

Sacramento's gay and lesbian community is served by *Mom . . . Guess What?,* available at all Tower Books locations (1600 Broadway is the central one), around Sacramento State University (6000 J St.), and at the **Lambda Community Center** (1931 L St., at 20th St., tel. 916/442–0185).

## COMING AND GOING

**BY CAR** **I–80** will take you from San Francisco to Sacramento (1½–2 hrs), but it bypasses the city center to the north, so take the **I–80 Business Loop** to get downtown. Merging with the business loop as it cuts east–west through town, **U.S. 50** heads east toward Placerville and Tahoe. For Reno (about 2 hrs), stay on I–80. If you're traveling north to south, **I–5** and **Highway 99** merge as they pass through the city. Outside town, I–5 is a faster thoroughfare (and the direct route to places like L.A., Portland, Seattle, et cetera), but Highway 99 serves more Central Valley cities. Try to avoid the freeways during commute hours (6–9 AM and 4–7 PM).

**BY BUS** Sacramento is a hub for **Greyhound** buses traveling throughout the state. Round-trip fare to San Francisco is $17, and it takes about 2½ hours each way. The station (715 L St., at 7th St., tel. 800/231–2222) is open 24 hours, and lockers are available. **Yolo Bus Commuter Lines** (10th and N Sts., tel. 916/371–2877) serves Davis (daily) and Woodland (Mon.–Sat.) for $1. Express buses cost $1.50. Buses start running around 6:30 AM and stop around 7:30 PM.

**BY TRAIN** Sacramento's **Amtrak** station is served by many different lines, so call for fares and departure times. Round-trip to San Francisco (2½ hrs each way) costs $17; round-trip fares to Los Angeles (15 hrs one-way) or Seattle (21 hrs one-way) are $68 and $88, respectively. Reservations are required and lockers are available. *401 I St. (enter at 5th and I Sts.), tel. 800/USA–RAIL. Open daily 5 AM–11:30 PM.*

## GETTING AROUND

Sacramento orients itself around its major highways (*see* Coming and Going by Car, *above*), which collectively form a large "H." Most of what you'll want to do in town falls in the top half of the "H" (the part shown on our map), an area arranged in a grid of numbered and lettered streets. **Old Sacramento,** home to most of the museums and tourist traps, is at the west end of this area, near I–5 and the Sacramento River. **Downtown** and the capitol are just east of Old Sac (within walking distance), and **Midtown** is still farther east. North of H Street, some parts of Midtown are a bit iffy; be alert at night. Bus lines crisscross the city, and a light rail connects downtown with the suburban area east of the city.

**BY CAR** Downtown and Old Sac form an annoying maze of one-way streets, and parking can be hard to find. Consider parking in one of the large garages connected to the shopping mall on L Street between 5th and 4th streets (about 50¢ an hour). For rentals, try **Enterprise Rent-a-Car** in Midtown (1401 16th St., tel. 916/444–7600). Their rates are pretty good, they rent to the 21-to-25 age group for an extra $7 a day, and they have $15-a-day weekend specials (including 450 free miles, plus free delivery and pick-up).

**BY BUS** **Regional Transit** covers the whole city and its environs, but service is substantially curtailed late at night and on weekends. Buses and light-rail vehicles start rolling at 6 AM daily; some routes run until about 11 PM, but others stop as early as 6 PM. Call 916/321–BUSS for detailed info, or pick up a $1 map at the **Regional Transit Office** (1013 K St., at Crest Theater ticket booth). Basic one-way tickets are $1.25, but rides are only 25¢ in the Central Business

District 9 AM–3:30 PM, after 6 PM, and all day weekends and holidays. Exact change is required. A $3 daily pass, good for unlimited rides, is available from bus drivers. The main downtown light-rail station is at 7th and K streets. You can take your bike on the bus or light rail with a $5 permit (get it at 1400 29th St. or 1013 K St.) at all times except during peak hours (weekdays 6–9 AM and 3:30–6 PM).

## WHERE TO SLEEP

The sheer number of affordable places makes it easy to find a bed, but keep in mind that room tax is 11% throughout Sacramento County. One hidden bargain is the extremely comfortable, if business-oriented, **Executive Inn,** out by the Cal Expo. At least while they're remodeling, single or double rooms start at $40, and if you have an Entertainment Card (*see* Where to Sleep, in Chapter 1) they'll let you have one for just $33. The inn offers a pool, hot tub, and laundry area, and your room comes with HBO, kitchenette, and free breakfast (if you wake up in time). *2030 Arden Way, tel. 916/929–5600. Take Arden Way exit off Hwy. 160 or off I–80 Business Loop, and head east to Hurley Ave.; it's behind Century Theater. Wheelchair access.*

**DOWNTOWN** Staying near the capitol gives you easy access to Sacramento's main attractions. A stone's throw from the old Governor's Mansion, the **Americana Lodge** (818 15th St., at I St., tel. 916/444–3980) has rooms in pretty good shape, some with king beds. Best of all, there's a small pool. Singles are $37, doubles $42. Two blocks away, the **Mansion View Lodge** (711 16th St., at H St., tel. 916/443–6631) has clean rooms for about the same price; singles $36, doubles $42.

**RICHARDS BOULEVARD** Though it's less convenient to Sacramento's main sights, this area is quieter and safer than downtown, and the motels tend to have cleaner rooms, better paint jobs, and more up-to-date "decor." The best deal is probably at the **Motel Orleans** (228 Jibboom St., west of I–5 at Richards Blvd. exit, tel. 916/443–4811), where singles are $40 and doubles start at $50, with a $5 discount for AAA members. The wheelchair-accessible rooms have quilted bedspreads and plush furniture; plus, there's a pool and laundry room. Discovery Park and the head of the American River Bike Trail (*see* Outdoor Activities, *below*) are nearby.

**HOSTEL** The brand-new **Sacramento Hostel,** in the heart of downtown, charges $15 ($12 with HI card) for a comfy bed in this renovated Victorian mansion. Keep in mind it's a nonsmoking hostel. *900 H St., at 9th St., tel. 916/443–1691. 68 beds, 1 "VIP" room with bath ($8.50 extra). Curfew 11 PM (some exceptions), lockout 9:30 AM–5 PM. Reception open 7:30–9:30 and 5–10. Laundry, linen ($1), luggage storage. Wheelchair access.*

## FOOD

Sacramento is a great place for cheap food. Check the *Sacramento Bee* "Ticket" (every Friday) for listings and ratings of dozens of local restaurants. If the weather's nice, pick up lunch at the **Sacramento Natural Foods Co-op** (1900 Alhambra Blvd., at S St., tel. 916/455–2667) and treat yourself to a picnic in Capitol Park (btw 10th, 15th, L, and N Sts.). The co-op is also a good place to stock up for camping trips.

**DOWNTOWN** If you wander around the capitol (try J St. between 9th and 13th Sts.), you should have no trouble finding something affordable with either outdoor seating or air-conditioning. Old Sacramento, the tourist center to the west, tends to be pricier and tackier.

**Espresso Metro.** The fresh soups and salads ($2.50) and the sandwiches (around $4) at this bustling downtown café draw big lunchtime crowds. Beer and wine are served, and on occasional Thursday nights there's live music (from jazz to Brazilian). *1030 K St., at 11th St., tel. 916/444–8129. Open daily 7 AM–6 PM (Thurs.–Sat. until 10 PM).*

**J's Café.** This narrow diner serves food that could make you forget you're in California (well, the word "avocado" does appear on the menu *once*). It gets crowded at lunch time, so try to wait until off-hours to chow down on the excellent burgers and omelets (both about $4–$5). *1004 J St., at 10th St., tel. 916/446–7456. Open weekdays 6:30 AM–9 PM.*

**The Torpedo Place.** This tiny, slightly out of the way Mexican-food stand serves some of the best burritos in town (about $3–$4), most involving some pig product. There's seating at the counter and at a few outdoor tables. *300 12th St., tel. 916/443–7118. Off Hwy. 160 south as you enter downtown. Open Mon.–Sat. 6 AM–2 PM.*



**MIDTOWN** Some of the grooviest eateries are scattered around Midtown, especially on 18th and 19th Streets between Capitol and I Streets. **Beatniks Acoustic Café** (1216 20th St., at L St., tel. 916/443–9520) has vegan fare (curry over rice; $3) *and* ham sandwiches ($3.50), plus live acoustic music and occasional poetry readings. Beatniks is open daily 11–11 (Fri. and Sat. until 2 AM).

**Greta's Café.** This busy deli and bakery is a local institution, with a progressive clientele, mouthwatering desserts, and delicious soups, salads, and sandwiches ($5 or less). Try the buttermilk pancakes ($2.50) for breakfast, then move on to the black-bean chili ($4.50) or the focaccia sandwiches ($2.50) later in the day. *1831 Capitol Ave., at 19th St., tel. 916/442–7382. Open weekdays 6:30 AM–4 PM, weekends 7:30 AM–4 PM.*

**CAFES** At any time of the day or evening, you can find Sacramentans slacking off in one of several popular coffee spots. The original **Java City** (1800 Capitol Ave., at 18th St., tel. 916/444–5282) is open until 11 on weekdays and midnight on weekends, and is always packed. **New Helvetia** (1215 19th St., at L St., tel. 916/441–1106) is an old fire station that's metamorphosed into a meeting place for the young, hip, and eccentric. The bustling **Tower Café** (1518 Broadway, at 16th St., tel. 916/441–0222) offers the usual fare, and is a prime spot for people watching.

## WORTH SEEING

If today Sacramento is known as a rather pedestrian political center, in days of old it was famed as a bustling railroad hub. Of course, prior to any of this, diverse Native American tribes inhabited the Central Valley—until pioneer families staked their claim, forcing Indian resettlement. Sacramento's museums, easily visited in an afternoon, nicely highlight its patchwork history.

**CALIFORNIA STATE CAPITOL BUILDING** There's always something impressive about capitols. This 1869 structure was extensively restored in the early 1980s with a lavish 120-foot-high interior rotunda. Free tours are given hourly 9–4 on weekdays. Sit in the gallery and watch the Assembly flail at the budget, or visit the annex's Committee Room 4203, where Black Pan-

### All You Can Eat

***It's the sweetest phrase a budget traveler will ever read: all-you-can-eat buffet. Your mind races with thoughts of never having to eat again, of patrons cheering you on from the next table, of the management filing for Chapter 11. Even if you're not Homer Simpson, an all-you-can-eat special gives your travel diet a refreshing elasticity.***

***Marline's Vegetable Patch (1119 8th St., btw K and L Sts., tel. 916/448–3327), a spacious downtown lunch spot, gives vegetarians their fill of highly imaginative fare for $6.50. In Old Sacramento, Annabelle's (200 J St., at 2nd St., tel. 916/448–6239) offers an Italian buffet for $4. For Chinese all-you-can-chow, try New Lu-Shan (403 J St., at 4th St., tel. 916/444–2543), which charges $4.75 for lunch, $5.95 for dinner. Barbecue lovers should stop by the Union Restaurant (117 J St., near 2nd St., tel. 916/448–6467), where $13 gets you salad, veggies, and french fries plus all the beef ribs your stomach can hold.***

ther leaders asserted their right to bear arms. Pick up a map and info in the basement (Room B-27). *10th St. and Capitol Mall, near L St., tel. 916/324–0333. Open daily 9–5.*

**CALIFORNIA STATE RAILROAD MUSEUM** This immensely popular museum successfully conveys the awesome amount of work that went into building the first transcontinental railway, completed in 1869 near Ogden, Utah. The museum pays too much attention to the four financiers who controlled the project, but the exhibits don't entirely gloss over the physical toil and loss of life, suffered mainly by Chinese laborers. The best displays, though, have to do with the railroad culture that emerged in the second half of the last century. Check out the well-restored train cars, several of which you can board. Though it's expensive, this is probably the most worthwhile stop in Old Sacramento. *111 I St., at 2nd St., tel. 916/323–9280. Admission: $5. Open daily 10–5, last entry at 4:30.*

**CALIFORNIA STATE INDIAN MUSEUM** This small, slightly out-of-the-way museum next to Sutter's Fort is worth the hour or so it will take to absorb its dense and memorable exhibits. The museum does a good job of conveying what life in the region was like before the white invasion, while still portraying Native American communities as alive and thriving in present-day California. Call ahead for tours led by Native American volunteers, and for info on special activities, among them Honored Elders Day (in May) and the Native American Film Festival (in November). *2618 K St., btw 26th and 27th Sts., tel. 916/324–0971. Admission: $2. Open daily 10–5.*

**SUTTER'S FORT** Founded in 1839, Sacramento's original settlement retains something of its bold military character—though it's difficult to imagine these white adobe structures as distant outposts for adventurous white folks when the site now stands in the middle of a populous, multicultural city. You will either be annoyed or delighted by the living-history characters roaming around in summer. *27th and L Sts., tel. 916/445–4422. Admission: $2 ($5 in summer). Open daily 10–5, last tour at 4:30.*

## CHEAP THRILLS

The landmark **Tower Theater** (16th St. and Broadway, tel. 916/443–1982) shows art films as well as mainstream releases. Across the street, students, punks, activists, musicians, and old-car freaks fill the aisles at **Tower Books** (tel. 916/444–6688) until midnight daily. During summer months, you can catch free outdoor showings of old movies for free on Thursday nights at the **49 Scene** park in Old Sacramento (Front and I Sts.). Call 916/558–3912 for show times and further info.

*On K Street between the convention center and the mall, the K Street Fair takes place every Thursday evening May–October. Merchants tote their wares outside, and live bands play.*

**FESTIVALS** After a glitzy spell, the **California State Fair** (tel. 916/263–3000), which runs from mid-August through early September, has thankfully returned to its agricultural roots. The weather is always oppressively hot, but it's worth it for the opportunity to fondle the animals, who show up to vie for such titles as Supreme Dairy Goat Total Performer. Take I–80 Business Loop to the Cal Expo.

The **Sacramento Jazz Jubilee,** a 21-year-old international festival featuring blues, zydeco, and country-infused R&B, happens every Memorial Day weekend. Concerts are held in Old Sac, at the Cal Expo, and at the Radisson Hotel. Tickets come in the form of badges ($10–$75) that admit you to a certain number of events; it's best to order them in advance. Room rates go up during the jubilee. Call 916/372–5277 for info.

## AFTER DARK

**BARS** For a straight beer joint, try the **Rubicon Brewing Company** (2004 Capitol Ave., at 20th St., tel. 916/448–7032), a favored hangout for jocks, ski bums, students, and office types looking to kick back. A pint of their India Pale Ale costs $2.50. On the downside, they close at midnight on weekends and even earlier during the week. The **Press Club** (2030 P St., at 21st St., tel. 916/444–7914) hosts good blues music with little or no cover and is packed most nights of the week; it also has a happy hour from 6 to 10 *in the morning,* great for those nights when you don't make it home. A collegiate crowd frequents the **Pine Cove** (502 29th St., at E St., tel. 916/446–3624), which has been around since 1953. Their prices reflect it, with 75¢ beers and $4 pitchers.



**CLUBS** Both the free *Magpie Weekly* (look for it at cafés and newsstands) and the *Sacramento Bee* "Ticket" list dance clubs in the area, though some of their descriptions are too brief to be helpful. The best venue for alternative music is the **Cattle Club** (7042 Folsom Blvd., at 65th St., tel. 916/386–0390), a small all-ages dance club out by Sacramento State. The club publishes a great newsletter, *Alive and Kicking,* that lists upcoming shows; pick one up at Tower Records (cnr 16th St. and Broadway, tel. 916/444–3000). The dance floor at **Faces** (2000 K St., at 20th St., tel. 916/448–7798), Sacramento's largest gay club, attracts a mixed, very trendy crowd. Lesbians hang at the **Buffalo Club** (1831 S St., at 19th St., tel. 916/442–1087), a small, refreshingly low-key spot with pool tables and DJ-dancing on weekends.

### OUTDOOR ACTIVITIES

**BIKING** The **American River Bike Trail,** with several truly pretty stretches, starts near Discovery Park and runs along the river some 30 miles to Folsom. The trail is one of the city's most popular attractions; if you avoid nighttime riding and join the trail around Sac State, you'll avoid some questionable areas and enjoy a green and scenic ride. Solar phones are located along the trail. You can rent bikes for $15 a day at **City Bicycle Works** (2419 K St., at 25th St., tel. 916/447–2453).

**RAFTING** Rafting on the American River during the long, hot summer is a Sacramento tradition. Unless you're a seasoned veteran or are with an experienced guide, stick to the south fork. You can rent equipment from **American River Raft Rentals** (11257 S. Bridge St., Rancho Cordova, tel. 916/635–6400), where four-person rafts go for $30, including life vests and paddles. For another $2.50, you can get a bus ride back when you're done. Dozens of rental outfits will take you on a guided full-day trip for about $75 during the week, $100 on weekends. Check the Yellow Pages under "River Trips."

## Near Sacramento

### DAVIS

You've been cruising I–80 and have soured on Denny's and Target malls. Exit at the neat and trim college town of Davis, set among acres of flat farmland just 12 miles southwest of Sacramento—it may be just what you need. The University of California at Davis is the state's top school for agricultural studies and, as college towns go, it's got more Birkenstocks and bike helmets than Doc Martens and skateboards. The student crowd hangs at the cafés and bookstores in the central business district just east of campus—between B and G streets, bordered by 1st and 5th streets. Have coffee at grad-student hangout **Delta of Venus** (122 B St., at 2nd St., tel. 916/753–8639), or **Coffee and Classics** (132 E St., at 2nd St., tel. 916/758–7358), a used bookstore and coffeehouse in the Mansion Square complex. **Newsbeat** (231 E St., near 3rd St., tel. 916/756–6247) offers an excellent selection of magazines and newspapers from around the world. **Recycle Records** (205 F St., at 2nd St., tel. 916/756–4943) has used records and is a good place to find out about musical happenings.

The big event in Davis is **Picnic in the Park,** which takes place—rain or shine—every Wednesday (May–Oct. 4:30–8:30 PM, Nov.–Apr. 2–6 PM) in **Central Park** (around B and 3rd Sts.). Local merchants hawk ethnic foods, and everyone else chills out listening to live music. Even larger and more impressive, though, is the Saturday morning **farmers' market,** also in Central Park, where vendors from all over the area converge to sell everything from strawberries to live quail. For quieter distractions, head to the southern edge of campus to Davis's impressive

**arboretum** and picnic or nap near the artificially controlled still-water stream. To reach the arboretum from I–80, take the U.C. Davis exit and follow signs from campus.

**WHERE TO SLEEP** While lodging is cheaper in Sacramento, Davis has a couple of attractive options. Right off the I–80 Davis exit, the **Davis Inn** (1111 Richards Blvd., tel. 916/756–0910) has sparkling, well-appointed rooms, a movie channel, and a pool. A double with one bed is $40, with two beds $48. Nearer to campus, Pat Loomis's **Davis B&B Inn** (422 A St., at Russell St., tel. 916/753–9611) is a homey bed-and-breakfast staffed by U.C. students. The 18 wheelchair-accessible rooms, most with TVs and wood floors, run $52–$62, depending on the number of people and beds.

**FOOD** In addition to the cafés listed above, Davis has several good restaurants. Try the **Crêpe Bistro** (234 E St., at 3rd St., tel. 916/753–2575), which specializes in crêpes stuffed with fillings like spinach, chicken, and white wine ($4–$6), or the highly recommended ratatouille ($6). The outside tables, with umbrellas and candles, are great on warm summer nights. For Mexican food, head out to **Dos Coyotes** (1411 W. Covell Blvd., at Sycamore Ln., tel. 916/753–0922), in the northwest section of town, where a mahimahi burrito with chips and salsa goes for less than $6. Located just off the interstate, **Murder Burger** (978 Olive Dr., tel. 916/756–2142; closed Wed.) serves up a mean patty for $5.

**AFTER DARK** While Davis is not much of a drinking mecca (especially for a college town), there are a few decent bars. The best of the bunch is **Sudwerk** (2001 2nd St., at Pole Line Rd., tel. 916/758–8700), a microbrewery with four year-round and two seasonal brews on tap, and local rock and jazz bands Thursday–Saturday nights. There's a $1 cover on Thursdays only—but the beer prices go down at the same time.

## SACRAMENTO RIVER DELTA

The delta is a lazy labyrinth of a thousand or so miles of rivers, streams, and canals connecting Stockton (*see* The San Joaquin Valley, in Chapter 7) and Sacramento with the San Francisco Bay. The delta's waterways are popular with people from nearby cities and suburbs in search of a little fishing, swimming, or boating. Yet the year-round population here is eerily sparse, the culture provincial, the landscape pretty dull, and the summer weather painfully hot. The delta does make a much more scenic drive than I–80, and as you make the 30- to 40-mile trek on Highway 160 between Sacramento and San Francisco you'll be surprised at how quickly you find yourself in a place that feels several time zones and decades away.

*The delta's towns are quiet and underinhabited in a way that might make you feel as though you've taken a wrong turn.*

The biggest town in the area is **Rio Vista,** where you'll find visitor info at the Chamber of Commerce (185 Main St., tel. 707/374–2700), shops, banks, and even a supermarket. This is the place to be if you're without a tent come nightfall. The tinier towns of **Locke, Walnut Grove,** and **Isleton** are more historically interesting: All three once hosted thriving Chinese communities that left a curious legacy of Old West and Far East. There's not much left of Walnut Grove (though amateur archaeologists and historians may want to take a wander); a 1915 fire forced the community to relocate. Isleton is fairly quiet, though it plays host to a popular crawdad festival in June (*see* Food, *below*).

Locke—which emerged as a major Chinese community in the early part of this century—is probably the delta's main tourist attraction. What's left of the town is a block-long area on Main Street that includes **Joe Shoong's Chinese School,** where local kids still study Chinese after school; **Al the Wop's** restaurant and bar (tel. 916/776–1800), which has been operating since 1915 and comes complete with dollar bills on the ceiling, steak dinners on the menu, and country music on the jukebox; and the **Dai Loy Museum** (tel. 916/776–1684), an old gambling house that serves as a historical guide to the delta; it's open afternoons Wednesday–Sunday. At **Yuen Chong Market,** pick up a great map ($2.70) listing all the marinas, harbors, campgrounds, and recreational areas.

**GETTING AROUND** The best ways to tour the delta are by car or boat, though biking is an option if you can stand the heat. It's easy to travel the short distances from town to town, marina to marina, and to most of the 70 islands that make up the region. From the Bay Area, take I–80 east to the Highway 4 turnoff near Hercules, and go east to Highway 160, which follows the Sacramento River through the delta. Heading northeast on Highway 160, you'll soon run into Isleton, Walnut Grove, and Locke. From Sacramento, take I–5 south to the turnoff for Highway 160. From Stockton, Highways 4 and 12 lead west into the delta; Highway 12 goes right through Rio Vista, situated about 6 miles northwest of Isleton.



**WHERE TO SLEEP** The most exciting place to sleep in the delta is on a rented houseboat—a sort of floating RV that cruises up and down the waterways. Prices are steep, but with a large group you may be able to afford a week's rental. At **Herman and Helen's Marina** in Stockton (get off I–5 at 8-Mile Rd. and go west to end, tel. 209/951–4634), weekly rates run from $500 to $3,200, depending on the season and size of the vessel. A cheaper option is to camp near the water at **Brannan Island State Park** (tel. 916/777–6671), 3 miles south of Rio Vista on Highway 160. The 102 sites (some with wheelchair access) go for $14 per vehicle, $12 from September to mid-May. In summer, reserve through MISTIX (tel. 800/444–PARK). There are eight tent sites ($15) at **Vieira's Resort** (15476 Hwy. 160, tel. 916/777–6661), a little over a mile west of Isleton on Highway 160. Vieira's also rents six cabins with kitchens ($40 in winter, $45 in summer), and there's a private beach with a boat ramp and dock.

**FOOD** During the annual **Crawdad Festival**—held on Father's Day weekend in June—Isleton rises from the dead. Sample a heaping portion fresh from the river at **Ernie's Restaurant and Saloon** (212 2nd St., tel. 916/777–6510), at $6 for an appetizer or $10 for a full plate (enough for two). Also in Isleton, **Rogelio's** (34 Main St., tel. 916/777–5878) specializes in Mexican, Italian, and Chinese food. Some lunch entrées, including the chicken tostadas, go for less than $4. In the adjoining bar, you can score free hors d'oeuvres (and cheap drinks) weekdays 2–7 PM.

In Rio Vista, **Foster's Bighorn** (143 Main St., tel. 707/374–2511) gives you a hearty meat-and-potatoes dinner for $10–$15 (lunch sandwiches go for $5–$8). For a $2 short stack of pancakes, try the **Striper** (210 Main St., tel. 707/374–5513) just down the street. The cheapest meals can be had at **Granny's** (310 Hwy. 12, tel. 707/374–2019), a drive-up stand in Rio Vista that'll sell you a 40¢ cup of coffee and a wide selection of burgers ($1.75–$3). If you have cooking equipment, load up at nearby **Lira's Supermarket** (609 Hwy. 12, tel. 707/374–5399).

**OUTDOOR ACTIVITIES** Because temperatures hover in the high 90s most of the summer, a dip in the icy-cold river is the first outdoor option you'll want to consider. It's legal, and free, to swim in the delta as long as you're within 200 feet of shore. If you're looking for a nice beach and large picnic area, take 2nd Street south out of Rio Vista toward **Sandy Beach County Park** (tel. 707/374–2097), which charges $3 per vehicle for day use, $5–$10 for camping. The delta's waterways are also popular with anglers; for advice and the required licenses, try **The Trap** (660 Hwy. 12, tel. 707/374–5554) in Rio Vista. Down the road, **Haps Bay** (84 Main St., tel. 707/374–2372) rents all sorts of fishing gear.

# The Gold Country

**Cutting a 350-mile swath down Highway 49,** from Sierra City in the north to Yosemite in the south, the Gold Country encompasses wineries, caverns, rushing rivers, and the remnants of old frontier towns. The region's Native Americans—who were some of the last holdouts to white encroachment in the West—lived here for at least 2,000 years before James Marshall picked up a shiny rock from under John Sutter's sawmill. "Boys," he said to the millworkers in his thick New Jersey accent, "I believe I have found a gold mine." So began the mass migration of 49ers to the foothills of the Sierra Nevada. Cornish, Peruvian and Chinese hopefuls joined up with Missourians and Bostonians arriving by covered wagon, all hoping to make their fortune. Even at the height of the rush, though, few actually struck it rich. And by the end of the century, increasingly inaccessible deposits and rising production costs—coupled with environmental opposition and sinking gold value—closed most of the mines. The boomtowns busted, and the Wild West faded into nostalgia.

*As miners rushed to the gold, gamblers, saloonkeepers, barbers, and prostitutes followed close behind—creating boomtowns out of formerly sleepy hamlets that lay along rail lines and rivers. When the boom "busted" and folks hightailed it to the coast, only ghost towns were left in their wake.*

The historical ambiance that pervades Gold Country is embodied on the main streets of the towns along Highway 49, filled with commemorative plaques, plank sidewalks, and carriage-ride tours. But the actual drive along Highway 49 is almost more spectacular than most of the stops, particularly during early spring, when the flowers are in bloom. Because they sit on major east–west thoroughfares, **Auburn** and **Placerville** are easy access points for quick forays into the region, heavy on motels, fast food, and other conveniences. The tiny towns of **Volcano** and **Columbia** are far better preserved, but a little harder to reach and dull at night. Towns like **Nevada City** (to the north) and **Sonora** (to the south) strike a balance, feeling different enough from home, but giving you some options for eating, sleeping, and hanging out.

If you couldn't care less where Mark Twain lived or how a mine shaft works, head for the great outdoors, where your fun won't be spoiled by docents or chambers of commerce. Rollins and Scotts Flat reservoirs, both near Grass Valley, offer excellent boating and fishing. Farther south, **Auburn State Recreation Area** boasts some of the best mountain-biking trails in the region, and the American River is rife with rafting and river sports. For more rugged hiking, camping, fishing, and biking, check out the Tahoe and Eldorado national forests.

## BASICS

**VISITOR INFORMATION** Tourist offices include the **Amador County Chamber of Commerce** (125 Peak St., Jackson, tel. 209/223–0350); the **Calaveras Lodging and Visitors Association** (1211 S. Main St., Angels Camp, tel. 800/225–3764); the **El Dorado County Chamber of Commerce** (542 Main St., Placerville, tel. 916/621–5885); the **Nevada City Chamber of Commerce** (132 Main St., tel. 916/265–2692); the **Grass Valley Chamber of Commerce** (248 Mill St., tel. 916/273–4667); the **Placer County Visitor Information Center** (13460 Lincoln Way, Suite A, Auburn, tel. 916/887–2111); and the **Tuolumne County Visitors' Bureau** (55 W. Stockton Rd., Sonora, tel. 209/533–4420 or 800/446–1333).

For maps and hiking info, as well as backcountry and fire permits, head to the **Tahoe National Forest Headquarters,** right outside Nevada City (631 Coyote St., at Hwy. 49, tel. 916/265–4531). Farther south, the **Eldorado National Forest Headquarters** (3070 Camino Heights Dr., tel. 916/644–6048) is 5 miles east of Placerville on Highway 50.

**WHEN TO GO** Consider planning your trip around one of the many Gold Country music festivals, including the **Annual Father's Day Weekend Bluegrass Festival,** held on the third weekend of June in Grass Valley/Nevada City. For info on these and other festivals, contact **Foggy Mountain Music** (tel. 916/273–6676) in Grass Valley or the **Nevada County Arts Council** (tel. 916/274–7867). To see the pioneers' mode of transport in action, come to Placerville in mid-June for the **Wagon Train Parade** down Main Street; call 916/621–5885 for more info.

**COMING AND GOING** **Highway 49** is the north–south backbone of the region, with Placerville (east of Sacramento on **U.S. 50**) roughly in the middle. The route is divided into northern Gold Country (Placerville and north) and southern Gold Country (points south of Placerville). Most of the larger towns on Highway 49 are also served by east–west roads that lead back to the coast and out into the Sierra Nevada. **I–80** meets Highway 49 at Auburn, and continues east to Reno. **Highway 20** goes through Grass Valley and Nevada City, **Highway 4** through Angels Camp and Murphys, **Highway 88** through Jackson, and **Highway 108** through Sonora and Jamestown. Highway 49 can be slow going due to tight curves and periodic 35-mph speed limits.

Though it's difficult, touring Gold Country without a car is not out of the question. **Amtrak** (tel. 800/USA–RAIL) runs once a day to Sonora, with a bus change in Riverbank, from San Francisco (4½ hrs one-way, $41 round-trip) and Los Angeles (12 hrs one-way, $73 round-trip).

# The Gold Country

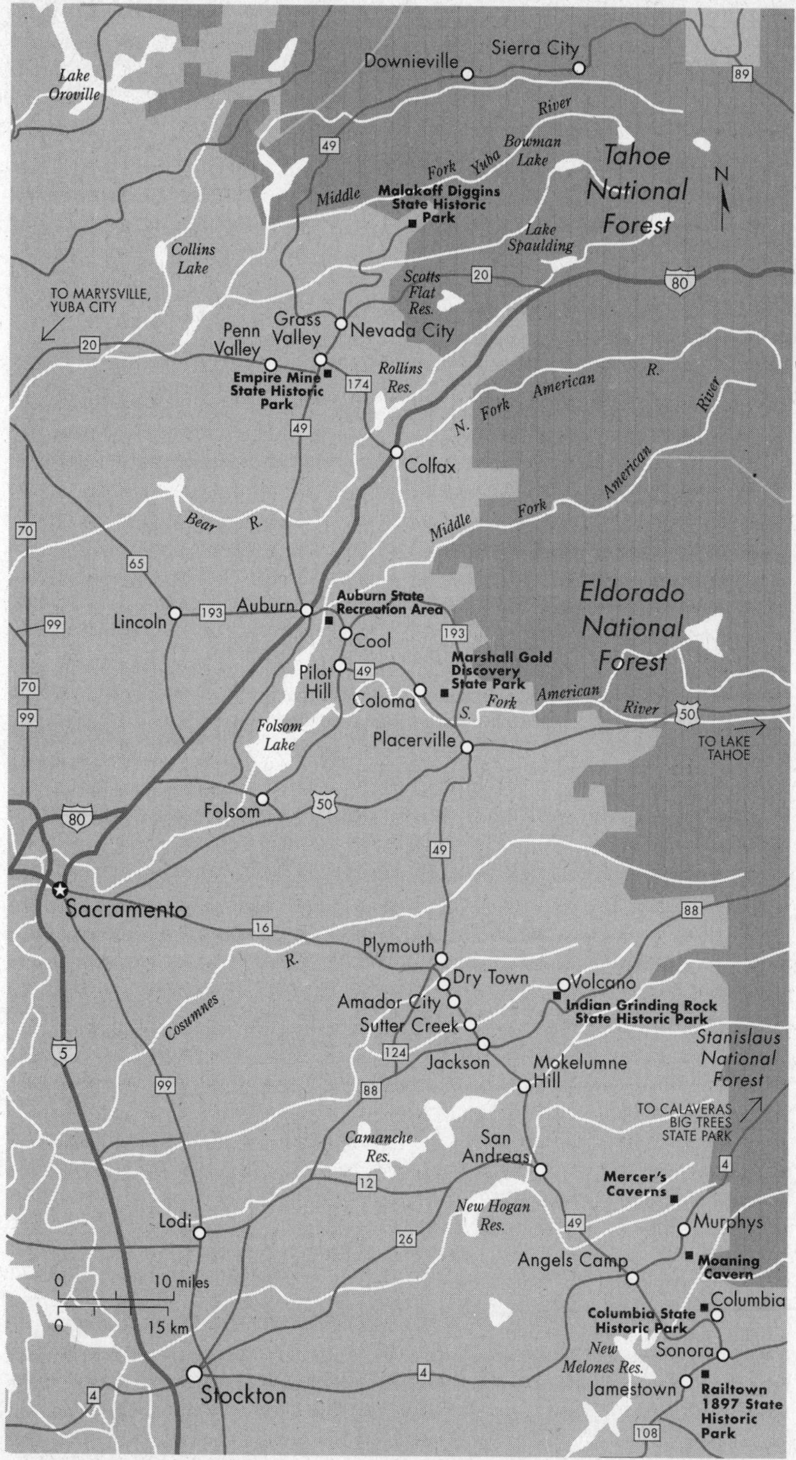

Lake Oroville
Downieville
Sierra City
89
River
49
Bowman Lake
Tahoe National Forest
Middle Fork Yuba
Malakoff Diggins State Historic Park
N
Collins Lake
Lake Spaulding
Scotts Flat Res.
20
80
TO MARYSVILLE, YUBA CITY
Grass Valley
Nevada City
Penn Valley
20
Empire Mine State Historic Park
174
Rollins Res.
N. Fork American R.
River
49
Colfax
Middle Fork American
Bear R.
70
65
Eldorado National Forest
Auburn State Recreation Area
Lincoln
193
Auburn
99
Cool
193
Marshall Gold Discovery State Park
Pilot Hill
49
Coloma
S. Fork American River
70
99
Folsom Lake
Placerville
50
TO LAKE TAHOE
Folsom
50
80
49
Sacramento
16
88
Plymouth
R.
Dry Town
Volcano
Amador City
Indian Grinding Rock State Historic Park
Cosumnes
Sutter Creek
Stanislaus National Forest
124
Jackson
Mokelumne Hill
5
99
88
TO CALAVERAS BIG TREES STATE PARK
Camanche Res.
San Andreas
4
12
Mercer's Caverns
New Hogan Res.
Lodi
49
Murphys
26
Angels Camp
Moaning Cavern
0 10 miles
0 15 km
Columbia
Columbia State Historic Park
New Melones Res.
Sonora
4
Jamestown
Railtown 1897 State Historic Park
Stockton
4
108

From Sonora, **Tuolumne County Transit** will get you to Columbia and Jamestown ($1.50 one-way). For the northern Gold Country, Amtrak runs a bus from San Francisco to Grass Valley three times a day (4½ hrs, $33 round-trip) and a train-bus combination to Placerville three times daily ($24 round-trip). **Greyhound** (tel. 800/231–2222) also runs frequent buses from San Francisco to Placerville (4 hrs, $48 round-trip with 14-day advance purchase).

# Northern Gold Country

**PLACERVILLE** Back in the bad old days, Placerville was known as Hangtown in honor of the notorious brand of frontier justice practiced here. Today, it's mostly known as the last major town on U.S. 50 heading east toward Tahoe. If you decide to make this your principle Gold Country stop, you'll likely be disappointed. Main Street boasts only an old bell tower, a few bookstores, and an effigy of a desperado above the **Hangman's Tree** bar. But this may be your only chance to sample the town's legendary oyster omelet, the Hangtown Fry—try the **Bell Tower Café** (423 Main St., tel. 916/626–3483). If you're not into spending $6.50 for this odd, and possibly stomach-turning, concoction that's been trying to win status as the state meal for years, try **The Apple Cellar** (325 Main St., tel. 916/642–1700) or **Sweetie Pies** (577 Main St., tel. 916/642–0128), cuter-than-thou establishments that serve light lunches (under $10) and heaping portions of fresh baked pies ($2–$3).

Placerville makes a good base for both river sports on the American River and for visiting nearby historic Coloma (8 mi north). Placerville is also the ideal place to pick up some home-grown fruit. **Graham's Shed** (1095 Cold Springs Rd., tel. 916/622–2612) grows and sells some of the best fruit in the county (cherries, apples, oranges, peaches, and walnuts). At **Apple Hill Orchards,** northeast of town (exit U.S. 50 at Carson, Camino, or Cedar Grove), family farms open their gates during apple season (Sept.–Dec.).

➢ **WHERE TO SLEEP** • A half-mile stretch of Broadway offers several places to stay in the $35–$45 range; the cheapest is the **Gold Trail Motor Lodge** (1970 Broadway, tel. 916/622–2906) with doubles for $34 ($38 weekends), minus a few bucks if you have an AAA card. In old town, try **Milton's Cary House** (300 Main St., tel. 916/622–4271), where doubles start at $45. Camping in nearby Eldorado National Forest is a good option; check at the ranger station (*see* Visitor Information, in Basics, *above*) for details. At **Sly Park** recreation area (tel. 916/644–2545), 12 miles east of Placerville (from Hwy. 50, exit Sly Park Rd.; follow signs for 5 mi), you can hike or bike around **Jenkinson Lake** ($5 day-use fee) and camp for $13 a night.

**COLOMA** Just north of Placerville on Highway 49, Coloma offers access to the south fork of the American River, which is filled all summer long with rafts, kayaks, and inner tubes. The site of James Marshall's fateful and fortuitous gold find, Coloma is mostly contained within **Marshall Gold Discovery State Historic Park,** which is home to a museum (tel. 916/622–1116) and several gold-related exhibits along the river. Here you can picnic, cavort in the water, or take a moderately strenuous 1.5-mile hike past historic structures along **Monument Loop.** The park has recently added a 3-mile scenic trail along Monroe Ridge, which provides close-up shots of colorful wildflowers and panoramas of the river and Lotus Valley. **Gold Hill,** the site of a tea and silk colony believed to be the first Japanese settlement in North America, is also here. The best swimming is at North Beach. If you've worked up an appetite with all that hiking, you can get fresh pie ($1.85) and root beer ($1) at the park's **Schulze House.** *Discovery Park: Hwy. 49, tel. 916/622–3470. Day use: $5 per car (main museum and all exhibits included). Park open daily 8–sunset; museum open daily 10–5 (reduced hrs in winter).*

History gives way to water at the **American River Resort** (6019 New River Rd., tel. 916/622–6700). The riverside campgrounds are expensive at $24 for a two-person site ($28 for sites right on the river), but they're near the best swimming and fishing around. **Mother Lode River Trips** (1680 Hwy. 49, 5 mi north of Coloma, tel. 916/626–4187 or 800/427–2387) runs 4½-hour rafting excursions on the south fork for $65 per person during the week, $79 on weekends, plus $10 extra for lunch.

➢ **CAMPING** • In addition to the American River Resort (*see above*), **Camp Lotus** (Bassi Rd., exit Hwy. 49 at Lotus Rd., tel. 916/622–8672), open March–October, offers secluded camping and modern facilities for $7 per person, with a $21 minimum per site (slightly lower weekdays). **Gold Rush Ranch** (5383 Hwy. 49, 5 mi north of Coloma, tel. 916/885–9001) is a larger, more elaborate affair, with a lake, 50 miles of hiking and mountain-biking trails, a general store, a full bar and restaurant, and live music under the stars every summer weekend. Sites ($15–$20) are interspersed among the trees, and bathrooms are modern. Day use is $5.



**AUBURN** Auburn, at the junction of Highway 49 and I-80, is somewhat suburbanized. But, being the largest and oldest Gold Country town, it also has a fairly well-preserved spirit-of-'49 flavor. Check out the **Placer County Courthouse and Museum** (101 Maple St., tel. 916/889–6500), an impressive Greco-Roman structure with a new museum depicting century-old life in Placer County. The **Bernhard Museum Complex** (291 Auburn-Folsom Rd., near High St., tel. 916/889–4156), a 19th-century Victorian house, re-creates the era's domestic realm. Both museums charge $1 admission and are closed Mondays and holidays.

*Early settlers of the Gold Country abandoned their identities as they headed out west. A traditional song from the era asked: "What was your name in the States? Was it Murphy, or Allen, or Bates? Did you have trouble or strife? Did you murder your wife? What was your name in the States?"*

➢ **WHERE TO SLEEP AND EAT** • The nondescript **Foothills Motel** (13431 Bowman Rd., tel. 916/885–8444) charges $42–$48 for a double room. A whole slew of motels, off I-80 at the Foresthill exit, offer more of the same should the Foothills be booked. Camp for $9 in the Auburn State Recreation Area at **Lake Clementine,** about 2 miles from Auburn off the Auburn-Foresthill Road; reserve through MISTIX (tel. 800/444–PARK).

When you get hungry, grab some *machaca con huevos* (shredded beef with scrambled eggs on a tortilla; $6.50) at **Café Delicias** (1591 Lincoln Way, tel. 916/885–2050). For all-you-can-eat Mongolian barbecue, head over to **Sum's** (958 Lincoln Way, tel. 916/889–8948).

➢ **OUTDOOR ACTIVITIES** • The massive **Auburn State Recreation Area** (tel. 916/885–4527 or 916/988–0205) has camping ($7–$19 per site), hiking, swimming, boating, rafting, fishing, and some of the best mountain-biking trails in Northern California. The 10-mile **Omstead Loop** trail, starting behind the fire station in **Cool** on Highway 49, is one of the most beautiful and popular trails. Another good trail for both hiking and biking is the **Stagecoach Trail,** which runs from Russel Road in Auburn to the old Foresthill bridge on the north fork of the American River. Unfortunately, the nearest place to rent a bike is **Cycletime** (4255 Rocklin Rd., tel. 916/624–2453), about 10 miles west in Rocklin; rates are $25 a day.

The recreation area's prime location between the north and middle forks of the **American River** makes it ideal for rafting and water sports, but the rough waters call for experienced navigators. If you're a beginner, it's best to stick to the south fork of the river, near Coloma (*see above*). As you explore the recreation area, be careful not to trespass on the gold claims some folks have staked out here; invade their space, and they'll treat you like they did claim-jumpers in 1849. For info and maps, stop in at the **Department of Parks and Recreation Headquarters,** 2 miles out of Auburn en route to Cool on Highway 49.

**GRASS VALLEY** On the 23-mile drive from Auburn to Grass Valley along Highway 49, you'll shake the familiar vista of fast-food franchises and shopping centers and begin to see the rolling hills that characterize the heart of northern Gold Country. Formerly the center of the so-called second gold rush in 1850, Grass Valley today is a well-groomed little town featuring saloons, antiques stores, and restaurants—all proudly proclaiming to have been in continuous operation since the 1850s. The **North Star Mining Museum** (tel. 916/273–4255), at the south end of Mill Street, houses a large display of mining equipment and artifacts. The museum is closed during the winter; in summer, there's no admission fee but donations are accepted.

Just outside town on East Empire Street is **Empire Mine State Historic Park.** The biggest and richest mine in the area, the Empire remained open until the 1950s. These days, $2 buys you entrance to the museum and grounds; tours of the mine and the **Bourn Mansion** (open hours vary for both); and same-day admittance to **Malakoff Diggins State Historic Park** (*see* Nevada

City, *below*), which otherwise costs $5. Tours give you a good sense of the often wretched existence led by the miners and, conversely, the relatively luxurious life led by the mine owners. If you're not that interested in mining, you can picnic on the grounds for free.

➢ **WHERE TO SLEEP** • Grass Valley may be your best bet in the region for an affordable night's sleep. Try the motels on South Auburn Street, including the **Coach 'n' Four** (628 S. Auburn St., tel. 916/273–8009), where doubles go for $46 during the week and $60 on weekends. If you're on a looser budget, the comfortable **Holiday Lodge** (1221 E. Main St., tel. 916/273–4406) has doubles starting at $60. You may also want to try camping at Rollins Lake Resort (*see* Outdoor Activities, *below*) or **Greenhorn Park** (tel. 916/272–6100). The latter is heavy on the amenities, and convenient if you're coming from Grass Valley (take a left off Hwy. 174 on Greenhorn Access Rd.). Sites are $16 ($19 on the lakefront).

➢ **FOOD** • Grass Valley's specialty is pasties, Cornish baked delicacies that can be found at places like **Marshall's Pasties** (203 Mill St., tel. 916/272–2844), where you can sample ones filled with apples, ham and cheese, or sausage for less than $3. For something more elaborate, check out the popular **Tofanelli's** (302 W. Main St., tel. 916/272–1468), where lunch runs around $7, dinner around $10. For breakfast, savor the breakfast burrito ($5.25) out on Tofanelli's large, new patio. The popular **Main Street Café and Bar** (213 W. Main St., tel. 916/477–6000) is the place for a pint ($3) and live blues and rock Wednesday–Saturday.

➢ **OUTDOOR ACTIVITIES** • A favorite springtime wildflower hike is the **Bridgeport Buttermilk Bend Trail** by the Bridgeport covered bridge, 11 miles out of Grass Valley (west on Hwy. 20 to Penn Valley, then north on Pleasant Valley Rd.). Call the ranger station (tel. 916/432–2546) for more on the latest trail conditions. Halfway between Grass Valley and Colfax on Highway 174, **Rollins Lake Resort,** on Rollins Reservoir, offers a host of camping, swimming, fishing, and waterskiing options. Four separately operated campgrounds and recreation areas are located on different parts of the shoreline, but they all charge $5 for day use, $10 for boat launch ($3 and $5, respectively, after 5 PM), and $16 for tent camping (some river sites $19).

**NEVADA CITY** During its Gold Rush heyday, Nevada City boasted a population virtually equal to that of San Francisco—over a century later, it's even smaller (and better preserved) than its southern neighbor Grass Valley. Nonetheless, there's more to do here than in Grass Valley, just 4 miles away on Highway 49. Refugees from California's coastal cities have given Nevada City a livelier ambiance than most nearby towns, and you're likely to find a poetry reading, a jazz concert, or a theater production going on as you pass through. Many events take place in the **Miner's Foundry** (325 Spring St., tel. 916/265–5040); pick up a schedule of festivals and performances at the Chamber of Commerce (*see* Visitor Information, in Basics, *above*).

If you want to soak up Gold Country history, just walk up and down Broad Street. Stick your head into the old **Nevada Theatre** (401 Broad St.) and the **National Hotel** (211 Broad St.), the oldest continuously operating hotel in California. For a complete list of entertainment and activities, check out a weekly local rag called "The Prospector"; it's inserted in Thursday's edition of *The Union,* or you can find it in the lobbies of most hotels.

After you've worn out Broad Street, drive 11 miles north of Nevada City to the **North Columbia Schoolhouse Cultural Center** (17894 Tyler Foote Rd., tel. 916/265–2826), the hub of activity for a flourishing artists' community that began in the '70s with the likes of Gary Snyder and Allen Ginsberg. These free souls bought up cheap property and started their own mini back-to-the-land movement, building their own homes and organizing craft shows. Most weekends bring live music, art exhibits, and theater presentations to the town's outdoor amphitheater and the cultural center, which also hosts a renowned **Storytelling Festival** the third week in July.

➢ **WHERE TO SLEEP** • Cheap lodging is hard to come by here. Doubles at the comfortable **Northern Queen Inn** (400 Railroad Ave., tel. 916/265–5824) start at $55 and they fill up quickly. The charming old **National Hotel** (*see above,* tel. 916/265–4551) has a few basic rooms for $42 (no TVs, and bathrooms are down the hall), but they, too, fill quickly. Your best bet is to take advantage of the nearby campgrounds (*see* Outdoor Activities, *below*).

➢ **FOOD** • **Cowboy Pizza** (315 Spring St., tel. 916/265–2334), a popular local haunt, is open Wednesday–Sunday 4–9; reservations are a good idea. Specialties like the Greek veggie pizza ($16), made with fresh French-bread crust, will more than satisfy two people. South of the town center (take Pine St. to Zion St., then go west 4 blocks), **Earth Song Café** (135 Argall Way, tel. 916/265–8025 or 916/265–9392) serves scrumptious, strictly vegetarian fare weekdays 11–8:30, weekends 11–9. You'll be surprised at how well a carrot milkshake ($3) goes with grilled tofu over cornbread ($6). The attached market is open daily 8 AM–9 PM and is the place to go for organic produce, fresh bread, and granola. For homemade ice cream, head out to **Nevada City Specialties** (308½ Broad St., tel. 916/265–3723); it's closed Tuesdays. For a "damn fine cup of coffee, conversation, and culture (of questionable value)," try hip **Mekka** (237 Commercial St., tel. 916/478–1517), where the local long-hairs hang out.



➢ **AFTER DARK** • **Chief Crazy Horse Inn** (230 Commercial St., tel. 916/265–9933) has a pool table and offers blues and rock Wednesday–Saturday. Young people hang out at the **Mad Dogs and Englishmen Pub** (211 S. Spring St., tel. 916/265–8173), a darts-and-pints bar with live music and dancing on weekends. The **Nevada City Brewing Company** (75 Bost Ave., tel. 916/265–2446), which gives tours Friday 3–5 and summer Saturdays 1–5, has some of the best microbrewed beer in the Gold Country. At the **Nevada City Winery** (321 Spring St., tel. 916/265–9463), open daily noon–5, you can sample wine for free while you look out over the production area.

➢ **OUTDOOR ACTIVITIES** • Biking and hiking are big here, particularly on the dirt roads around town. The **Banner Mountain Trail** is a 10-mile, 800-foot climb starting at the cross of Sacramento Street and the freeway; ride past the Northern Queen Inn to Gracie Road, then follow signs. The **Augustine Agony** trail, an 1,800-foot climb, is for advanced bikers; ride up Cement Hill Road, turn right at Augustine Road, then keep left all the way down to the South Yuba River. For some light and scenic exercise, drive 7 miles north on Highway 49 to the **South Yuba Independence Trail.** After about a 10-minute hike on this relaxing, wheelchair-accessible trail, you'll get a good view of the Yuba River—but the big payoff comes about half a mile later when you get to the falls. Follow the wooden ramps down to the bottom, picnic on the rocks, and take a dip if you can stand the cold water.

Just northeast of Nevada City lies **Malakoff Diggins State Historic Park.** This 600-foot-deep canyon is a monument to the technological achievement and ecological devastation of hydraulic mining. Before outraged Sacramento Valley farmers managed to get a judgment against the mining company in 1884, $3 million in gold was produced here. The park's **museum** is open daily 10–5, weekends only during winter. You can wander along several trails or take a tour—included in the $5 day-use fee—daily during summer (weekends only in winter). The main attraction here, though, is good camping ($10 per car; reserve through MISTIX, tel. 800/444–PARK). From Nevada City, go north 11 miles on Highway 49 to Tyler Foote Road and follow the signs about 15 miles to the park entrance. Slightly closer to Nevada City and ideal for fishing and hiking is **Scotts Flat Reservoir** (5 mi east of Nevada City on Hwy. 20, tel. 916/265–5302). You can rent boats here ($28 for 4 hrs). Campsites with all the amenities go for $16 (4-person maximum), $19 if you want to be next to the lake.

# Southern Gold Country

**JACKSON** Though it's not as well preserved as some of the smaller Gold Country towns, Jackson makes a good base for quick day trips to smaller towns, such as spruced-up **Sutter Creek** (4 mi north on Hwy. 49); sleepy, unpretentious **Mokelumne Hill** (8 mi south on Hwy. 49); or tiny, engaging **Volcano** (13 mi east of Jackson on Hwy. 88). Nine miles out of Jackson (toward Volcano on Hwy. 88) is the popular **Chaw'se Indian Grinding Rock State Historic Park** (tel. 209/296–7488), a 135-acre park featuring a reconstructed Miwok village and the Chaw'se Regional Indian Museum. The park has 23 campsites, complete with brand-new, wheelchair-accessible bathrooms and showers, at $14 a night ($12 in the winter). If you're not camping, you can still hike around the park and visit the **museum** (open weekdays 11–3, weekends 10–4) for $5. Evening ranger programs are free; ask at the museum for more info. In Jackson itself, check out **St. Sava Serbian Orthodox Church** (724 N. Main St.), in the middle of a dramatic, terraced cemetery. It's the mother church of Serbian orthodoxy in the United States.

➢ **WHERE TO SLEEP** • You can get an inexpensive room at the 130-year-old **National Hotel** (2 Water St., tel. 209/223–0500) any night except Saturday. Rooms with shared bath go for $25 (private bath, $45). For $125, you can stay in the Bordello Room, complete with mirrored canopy bed and a claw-foot tub (but no paid companions). If you prefer ESPN and swimming pools to the hotel that once hosted Will Rogers and Herbert Hoover, head north on Highway 49 to the **Jackson Holiday Lodge** (850 Hwy. 49, tel. 209/223–0486), where rooms start at $46 and include free continental breakfast.

➢ **FOOD** • Locals flock to **Mel and Faye's Drive-In** (tel. 209/223–0853), on the southbound side of Highway 49 near the center of town. Here you can get a heaping plate of corn beef hash and eggs ($5) as early at 4:45 AM; later in the day, try the highly touted New York steak dinner ($9), served until 10 PM. Two miles up Highway 49 in Martell is **Antonio's** (12496 Depot Rd., tel. 209/223–4664), packed Tuesday–Saturday with folks sucking down the finest margaritas for miles around. Try the enchilada dinner, with rice, beans, and salad for $9.

**ANGELS CAMP** Mark Twain set his popular short story "The Celebrated Jumping Frog of Calaveras County" in Angels Camp, where Highway 49 joins the east–west Highway 4. Homage is paid to the Missouri-born satirist in the form of the annual **Calaveras County Fair and International Jumping Frog Jubilee.** Held the third weekend in May at the fairgrounds (2 mi south of town on Hwy. 49), the festival includes carnival rides, a rodeo, and music to put you in the mood for the big frog contest. Admission is $7–$9 a day. The **Sierra Skies Festival,** held in early June on the same grounds, is a two-day mountaintop party featuring country, rock, and blues bands. Tickets are $19–$22 a day. You can pick up brochures and info at the Calaveras Lodging and Visitors Association (*see* Visitor Information, in Basics, *above*).

➢ **WHERE TO SLEEP AND EAT** • The **Gold Country Inn Motel** (720 S. Main St., tel. 209/736–4611) has standard, clean doubles for $51, including one with wheelchair access. **Tuttletown Recreation Area** (tel. 209/536–9094), 1 mile south of New Melones Reservoir (*see* Outdoor Activities, *below*), has 250 sites not far from the water for $10.

Angels Camp has few restaurants, and even fewer of them stay open for dinner. Luckily there's a 24-hour **Golden West Restaurant** (730 S. Main St., tel. 209/736–0170) that serves a reliable chicken-fried steak dinner ($6). A few blocks north, **Mike's Pizza** (294 Main St., tel. 209/736–9246) will deliver free to your motel and has burgers and sandwiches (most under $5) in addition to pizza.

➢ **OUTDOOR ACTIVITIES** • For boating, fishing, waterskiing, and swimming, go south a couple miles on Highway 49 to the Beacon station and follow signs for **New Melones Reservoir,** a large artificial lake created by the damming of the Stanislaus River. Bass, crappie, catfish, and trout can be pulled from the reservoir; if you don't have the required license, you can pick one up for $25 (good for one year) at **Vern's Liquors and Sporting Goods** (324 S. Main St., tel. 209/736–2205), whose shelves look like a confiscated-property room at the Bureau of Alcohol, Tobacco, and Firearms. There's nowhere close by to rent fishing equipment, but Vern'll sell you some. **O.A.R.S.** (tel. 209/736–4677) runs rafting trips on the Stanislaus River that leave from the reservoir turnoff on Highway 49. Full-day trips (including transportation back to Angels Camp) cost $79 on weekdays, $89 on weekends.

**MURPHYS** A short drive east of Angels Camp on Highway 4 is the meticulously restored town of Murphys, a little upscale for lodging and other practicalities but a nice place to spend a day. If the summer heat is beating down on you, take a dip in **Murphys Creek,** a block from tree-lined Main Street. Otherwise, stop by the **Aeolian Harp** (147 Main St., tel. 209/728–2852), an offbeat music store stocked with unusual instruments and all kinds of info about local music events. Across the way at the **Nugget Restaurant** (75 Big Trees Rd., tel. 209/728–2608), you can grab a cheeseburger ($5) and wash it down at the adjacent bar.

The **Old Timers Museum** (470 Main St., tel. 209/728–1160) is a unique conglomeration of curios and photos periodically donated by the town's residents—thus creating an ongoing autobiography of Murphys. The museum is open weekends 11–4, and donations are requested. One of Murphys's biggest attractions is **Mercer's Caverns** (tel. 209/728–2101), about a mile north of Main Street on the old Sheep Ranch Road. Discovered in 1885 by a gold prospector, the caverns contain some awesome crystalline stalactites and stalagmites. They're open daily 9–5 from Memorial Day through September, weekends and holidays 11–4 during the off-season. Admission is $5, including a 45-minute tour.

Fifteen miles out of Murphys (head east on Hwy. 4) is **Calaveras Big Trees State Park.** The Miwok and Washo Indians had been living around these giant sequoia groves for years before an enterprising promoter—feeling the pinch of waning mining fortunes in Murphys—began touring the country with a 116-foot strip of bark from one of the trees: A tourist attraction was born. The North Grove offers easy (wheelchair-accessible) hikes, while the South Grove is the place to go if you want a feel for the wilderness. Guides for the park's trails, which crisscross 6,000 acres of land, are available at the visitor center; day use is $5. Camping is available in the north grove and at Squaw Hollow ($14)—reserve through MISTIX (tel. 800/444–PARK). Both campsites and trails are liable to be closed from late November until late April due to snow. Call the park (209/795–2334) for updates.

**COLUMBIA** In 1854, the raucous mining town of Columbia came within 2 votes of beating out Sacramento for state capital. Twenty years and $87 million worth of gold later, Columbia's population had nearly vanished, leaving the town (2 mi north of Sonora on Parrotts Ferry Road) to suffer the humiliation of being turned into a state historic park. One of the best preserved of the Gold Rush towns, this could well be *the* place to visit or to avoid, depending on your attitude toward Gold Country nostalgia. In addition to stagecoach rides and elegant hotels, Columbia offers a restored schoolhouse that's worth a quick visit. At the end of Main Street (horse-drawn vehicles only), you can drink cheap beer in the old **St. Charles Saloon** (tel. 209/533–4656) next to a lot of heavily tattooed locals and a few German tourists.

For one of the most beautiful drives in the area, take **Parrotts Ferry Road** (County Rd. E18) north toward Highway 4. As you wind through the hills, you'll catch a great view of the Stanislaus River and New Melones Reservoir. About 2 miles north of town, a turnoff leads down to a spot where you can take a warm-water dip (look for the DAY USE ONLY sign). Another 1½ miles north, the no-longer-so-secret watering hole can be found at the end of the **Natural Bridges Trail.** Look for the sign for the trail, park your car, hike down a quarter-mile, and swim under the amazing caverns. Locals are less than thrilled to have their hangout written up in guidebooks, so be cool and don't leave any trash behind. **Zephyr Whitewater Expeditions** (tel. 209/532–6249 or 800/431–3636) leads rafting trips down nearby rivers; one-day trips start at $95. Camping around here is expensive: **Marble Quarry RV Park** (11551 Yankee Hill Rd., tel. 209/532–9539) has sites—complete with TV hookups—for $22–$25.

A mile or so north of the Natural Bridges Trail is the famous **Moaning Cavern,** whose opening is large enough to store the Statue of Liberty. For $45, you get a guided three-hour spelunking tour of the prehistoric cave, including the popular rappel, in which you descend 180 feet by rope (reservations required). For $27, you can just rappel—a lot of money for a few minutes, but the rush might just be worth it (you must be older than 12). For $6.25 take the traditional, no-thrills, 45-minute tour of the main chamber, going down into the cave by spiral staircase. Wear closed shoes. *Parrotts Ferry Rd., tel. 209/736–2708. Open summer, weekdays 9–6, weekends and holidays 10–5; winter, daily 10–5.*

**SONORA AND JAMESTOWN** At the junction of Highways 49 and 108, Sonora is larger and more crowded than most towns in the region. As you walk down Washington Street, the main drag, you'll recognize the trademark elements—Western-style storefronts, second-story porches, and old hotels—that have made this a popular movie location. It's also a pleasant stopover en route to Stanislaus National Forest or Yosemite (*see* Chapter 7). Pick up a map at the Tuolumne County Visitors' Bureau (*see* Visitor Information, in Basics, *above*) and wander around.

A couple miles southwest on Highway 49, small Jamestown (or Jimtown, as it's sometimes called) is named after a certain Colonel George F. James, who used to make a habit of passing out free champagne. This is also Hollywood's favorite "Wild West" movie set. **Railtown 1897 State Historic Park** (end of 5th Ave., tel. 209/984–3953) preserves the remnants of the region's glorious rail culture. The other tourist attraction in Jamestown is the prospecting tour; recent rains have replenished the streams, so you may strike it even richer. **Gold Prospecting Expeditions** (18170 Main St., tel. 209/984–4653) guarantees that anyone who goes on a trip of at least 2 hours ($30 for one person, $60 for families of up to five) and follows their instructions will find some gold.

➢ **WHERE TO SLEEP** • A bunch of motels lie on Highway 108 between Jamestown and Sonora, but your best lodging bets are in Sonora itself. The **Gunn House** (286 S. Washington St., tel. 209/532–3421), the first two-story structure built in town, retains a certain antique charm despite the televisions in its 20 rooms. Small doubles start at $45, with continental breakfast and use of the pool. Otherwise, camp at **Moccasin Point** (tel. 209/852–2396) on Don Pedro Lake for $13, or at **Pine Mountain Lake** (tel. 209/962–8625) for $12. Both are east of Chinese Camp off Highway 120.

➢ **FOOD** • In Sonora, **Alfredo's** (123 S. Washington St., tel. 209/532–8332) has the best Mexican food in the county; most dishes (except for seafood) are in the $7–$10 range. The nearby **Bagel Bin** (83 N. Washington St., tel. 209/533–1904) has fresh, doughy bagels for 60¢. If you're in a meat-and-potatoes mood, come to **Wilma's Café** (275 S. Washington St., tel. 209/532–9957). A half-order of hearty barbecued spare ribs is $7.50; top 'em off with homemade peach pie ($3). In Jamestown, the hot spot for breakfast and lunch is the **Country Kitchen** (18231 Main St., tel. 209/984–3326), located in an old wood building in the center of town. It's open daily 5 AM–5 PM.

➢ **AFTER DARK** • There are several bars on a 2-block stretch of South Washington Street in Sonora, including the **Brass Rail** (131 S. Washington St., tel. 209/533–1700), where you can hear live blues and ol' time rock on the weekends, and sing karaoke during the week. For a more raucous scene, or a game of pool, try **Bill's Sports Bar** (31 S. Washington St., tel. 209/533–1063). In nearby Jamestown, **Lulu's Saloon** (18201 Main St., tel. 209/984–3678) will impress you with its huge collection of lamps. Folks from all over the county come to hear the live blues and country music on Saturday nights.

# Lake Tahoe

**Straddling the border of California and** Nevada on the northern flank of the Sierra Nevada range, Lake Tahoe is one of the West Coast's most popular outdoor playgrounds. During spring and summer, when temperatures hover in the 70s, the lake (about a 3½-hour drive east of San Francisco on I–80) offers boating, fishing, waterskiing, and jet skiing; and the mountains surrounding Tahoe Basin satiate the desires of even the most demanding hikers, bikers, equestrians, and anglers. During the winter season (usually December–April, sometimes extending into May), attention shifts to downhill and cross-country skiing and snowboarding. The West Coast's number-one ski area, Tahoe has earned a worldwide reputation for its "extreme" conditions, provided by the sheer cliffs and steep faces of the Sierra Nevada.

Given the array of pleasures, it's no wonder Lake Tahoe draws up to 100,000 tourists at peak periods. On weekends, the traffic on I–80 between the Bay Area and Lake Tahoe has to be seen to be believed. A common way to explore the lake is to drive around its 72-mile perimeter. On an average day the trip takes about three hours, but plan on traffic slowing you down on summer weekends and holidays, and in winter when there's snow on the roads. If the slow driving starts to annoy you, stop at a few scenic lookouts (especially Emerald Bay on the west shore) and disappear down a hiking path or two.

*Besides being deep and blue, Lake Tahoe is also damn cold. You can swim in it, but most visitors just dip their feet in and scamper back to shore. On the other hand, a quick dip is said by locals to be the best way to cure a hangover.*

At regular intervals around the lake is a series of small towns—some charming, some tacky, all dependent on the tourist industry for their survival. Although it's a somewhat subjective division, the lake's locales are usually designated as belonging to either the north shore or the south shore. Thanks largely to the popularity of the ski resort at Squaw Valley, the north shore—including **Truckee** along I–80 and **Tahoe City** at the northwest corner of the lake—is the domain of Tahoe's young, energetic set, dedicated to spending as much time as possible exploring the

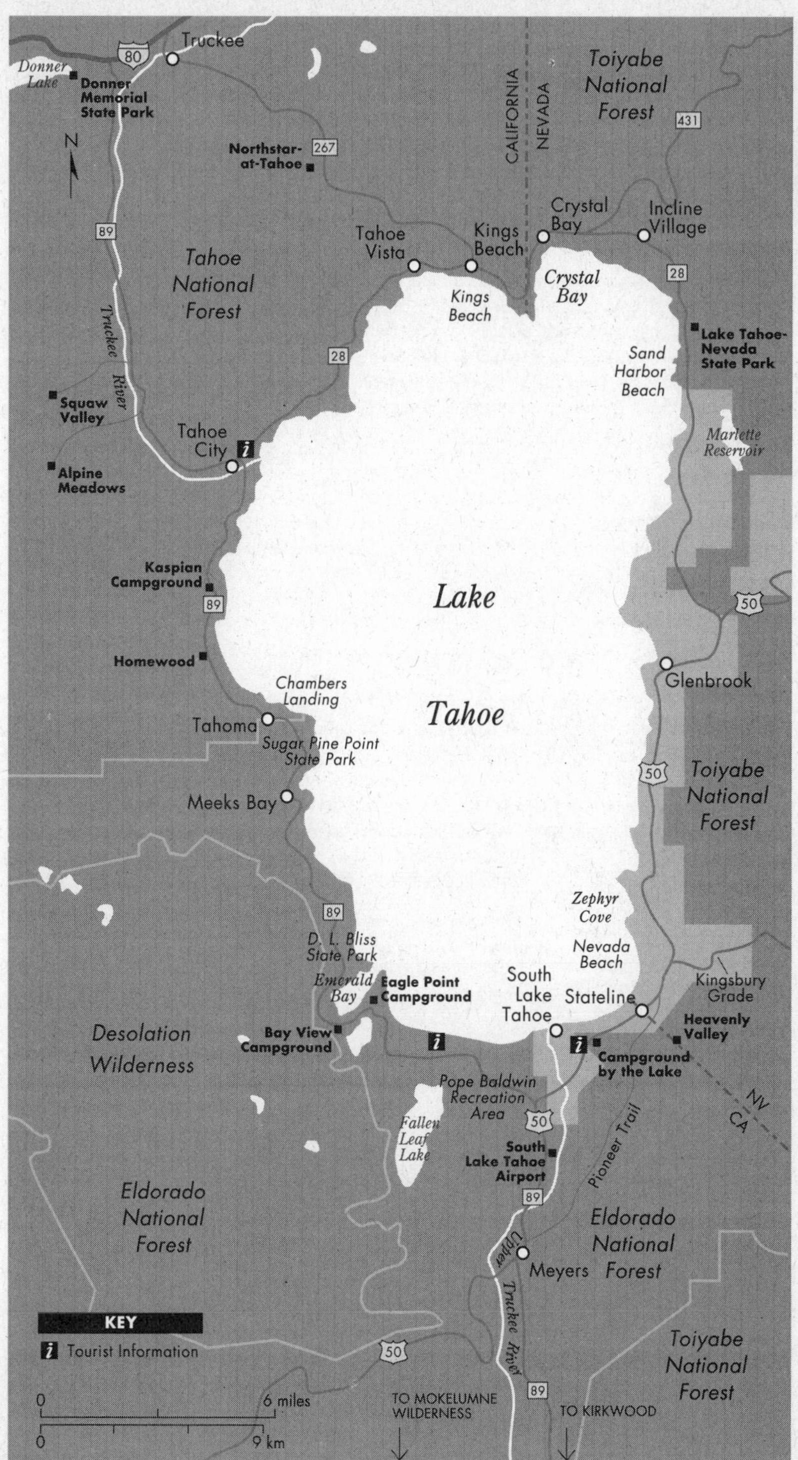

Truckee
80
Donner Lake
Donner Memorial State Park
Toiyabe National Forest
431
CALIFORNIA
NEVADA
N
Northstar-at-Tahoe
267
89
Tahoe National Forest
Tahoe Vista
Kings Beach
Crystal Bay
Incline Village
28
Kings Beach
Crystal Bay
Truckee River
28
Lake Tahoe-Nevada State Park
Sand Harbor Beach
Squaw Valley
Tahoe City
Marlette Reservoir
Alpine Meadows
Kaspian Campground
89
Lake Tahoe
50
Homewood
Glenbrook
Chambers Landing
Tahoma
Sugar Pine Point State Park
50
Toiyabe National Forest
Meeks Bay
89
Zephyr Cove
D. L. Bliss State Park
Nevada Beach
Emerald Bay
Eagle Point Campground
South Lake Tahoe
Stateline
Kingsbury Grade
Heavenly Valley
Desolation Wilderness
Bay View Campground
Campground by the Lake
NV
CA
Pope Baldwin Recreation Area
50
Fallen Leaf Lake
South Lake Tahoe Airport
Pioneer Trail
89
Eldorado National Forest
Eldorado National Forest
Meyers
Upper Truckee River
KEY
Tourist Information
50
Toiyabe National Forest
89
0
6 miles
0
9 km
TO MOKELUMNE WILDERNESS
TO KIRKWOOD

great outdoors and as little time as possible in the restaurants, hotels, and upscale resorts where most of them find employment. The south shore, on the other hand, caters primarily to families. The city of **South Lake Tahoe** is packed to the gills with restaurants, motels, and rental shops. The pace never flags in summer, and in winter popular ski areas like Heavenly keep the town jumping. Butting up against the east side of South Lake Tahoe is the imaginatively named town of **Stateline,** Nevada, a jumble of brightly lit casinos and tacky gift shops.

## BASICS

For the lowdown on equipment rental and what to pack for a day on the ski slopes, *see* Skiing, *below.* If you're just looking to load up on tourist brochures, the **North Lake Tahoe Chamber of Commerce** (245 Hwy. 89, Tahoe City, tel. 916/581–6900) lies between the Lucky supermarket and the Bank of America across from the Tahoe City "Y" (a Y-shaped intersection that's impossible to miss). You can also contact the **South Lake Tahoe Chamber of Commerce** (3066 U.S. 50, tel. 916/541–5255) or **Truckee-Donner Visitor Information** (Donner Pass Rd., Truckee, tel. 916/587–2757), at the Truckee Transit Depot in Old Town.

**Lake Tahoe Forest Service Visitor Center.** In addition to the usual tourist info, the center offers a great location, with beach access and self-guided nature trails. The staff will tell you all you want to know about the lake's natural and human history. This is also the place to pick up campfire and wilderness permits for the Desolation and Mokelumne wilderness areas. Permits are free, but only a limited number are available. Depending on funding, the visitor center may be closed on certain days of the week—call ahead. *Hwy. 89, btw Emerald Bay and South Lake Tahoe, tel. 916/573–2674. Open summer, daily 8–5:30; closed winter.*

## COMING AND GOING

**BY CAR** Both routes to Lake Tahoe take 3–3½ hours from the Bay Area when road and traffic conditions are at their best. To reach the north shore, follow I–80 east all the way to Truckee. For the south shore, take U.S. 50 east from Sacramento, which leads directly to South Lake Tahoe. You won't be allowed into the mountains without chains if it snows; bring your own or you'll have to pay inflated prices for a set near the CalTrans checkpoint. Even if you brought your own, consider paying the small fee (about $10) to let someone else put them on for you. You will see swarms of jumpsuit-clad people with numbers on their backs at every checkpoint waiting to perform this service.

*For recorded info on road conditions, call CalTrans at 800/427–ROAD.*

If snow doesn't slow you down, traffic might, especially on Friday and Sunday afternoons, and especially during summer and on holiday weekends. If you must drive to Tahoe on Friday, wait until 7 or 8 PM. Traffic is usually worst on I–80, so consider taking U.S. 50, even if you're headed for the north shore.

**BY BUS** **Greyhound** (tel. 800/231–2222) runs four buses a day between San Francisco and Truckee (5–6 hrs, $32) and the same number between Truckee and Reno (1 hr, $8). If you're headed to the south shore, Greyhound makes the trip between San Francisco and South Lake Tahoe (5½ hrs, $29) three times a day. Both Amtrak and Greyhound use the **Transit Depot** (Donner Pass Rd., in Old Town Truckee, tel. 916/587–3822), a safe place to wait for connections or pick up info at the tourist office. There are a few coin-operated lockers here. In South Lake Tahoe, the Greyhound station (tel. 702/588–4645) is in back of **Harrah's Hotel and Casino,** on U.S. 50 1½ miles south of the South Lake Tahoe "Y."

*Although the journey over the mountains can be painfully slow at times, the train ride between the Bay Area and Tahoe, especially the final climb up steep mountain passes, has spectacular scenery.*

**BY TRAIN** **Amtrak** (tel. 800/USA–RAIL) runs two train/bus routes a day between Emeryville and Truckee (transfer in Sacramento, 6 hrs, $49). If you're coming from San Francisco, take the free bus from the CalTrain Station at 4th and Townsend streets to the Emeryville Amtrak Station (5885 Landregan St., at Powell St.). Amtrak also has four trains a week traveling the hour-long route between Truckee and Reno ($12 one-way). All trains arrive at the Truckee Transit Depot (*see* Coming and Going by Bus, *above*). Another train/bus combination serves South Lake Tahoe (transfer in Sacramento, 6 hrs, $33).

**BY PLANE** You can reach the tiny **South Lake Tahoe Airport** (off Hwy. 89, about 15 min south of South Lake Tahoe, tel. 916/541–4080) by air from San Francisco. **TWA** (tel. 800/221–2000) makes the trip for about $180 round-trip. Also check potentially cheaper flights into **Reno Cannon International Airport** (*see below*).

## GETTING AROUND

Three intersecting highways form a loop around the lake: **Highway 89** (a.k.a. Emerald Bay Road) skirts the western shore of the lake between Tahoe City and South Lake Tahoe; **U.S. 50** (a.k.a. Lake Tahoe Boulevard) intersects Highway 89 in South Lake Tahoe and follows the lake's eastern shore; and **Highway 28** (a.k.a. North Lake Boulevard or Lake Shore Boulevard) runs along the north part of the shore back into Tahoe City. The intersections of Highways 28 and 89 in Tahoe City and Highway 89 and U.S. 50 in South Lake Tahoe are commonly referred to as the **Tahoe City "Y"** and the **South Lake Tahoe "Y,"** respectively.

**Tahoe Area Regional Transit (TART)** (tel. 916/581–6365 or 800/736–6365 outside California) has buses, most equipped with ski and bike racks, that serve the north and west shores of Lake Tahoe, including Squaw Valley. The fare is $1. The **South Tahoe Area Ground Express (STAGE)** (tel. 916/573–2080) runs 24 hours within South Lake Tahoe; the fare is $1.25.

## WHERE TO SLEEP

You face a mind-boggling number of options in choosing a place to stay in the Tahoe area. Hostels, motels, condos, cabins, and campgrounds abound everywhere you look. If you're just passing through for a night or two in summer, a motel or campground is the cheapest and most convenient alternative. But if you're coming for a week in winter to ski with a group of friends, consider a condo or cabin: Contact the **Lake Tahoe Visitors' Authority** (1156 Ski Run Blvd., South Lake Tahoe, tel. 916/544–5050 or 800/AT–TAHOE) or the **Tahoe North Visitors' and Convention Bureau** (tel. 916/583–3494 or 800/TAHOE–4U) to find out about weekend or weekly rentals. You should be able to find a basic two- to four-person condo for about $75 a night or $425 a week in the off-season, with prices rising roughly 10% in summer. No matter where you stay, reserve as far ahead as possible. On holidays and summer weekends everything is completely packed, despite the fact that most places raise their prices indiscriminately at these times.

In general, prices at all but the finest hotels are flexible, and prices on weekends and holidays rise substantially. The quickest way to find a cheap place to crash is to head to U.S. 50 between South Lake Tahoe and Stateline—cruise the strip and keep your eyes open for the neon. As a last resort, look for cheap deals at the casinos on the Nevada side of both the south and north shores.

**SOUTH SHORE** **El Nido Motel.** If you're seeking comfort at a reasonable price, the El Nido should end your search. Its excellent amenities include a hot tub and small, modern rooms with TV, VCR, and telephone. Flawlessly clean doubles start at $40 on weekdays, $50 on summer weekends; in winter prices are about $10 lower. Call for details on winter ski packages. *2215 Lake Tahoe Blvd. (U.S. 50), tel. 916/541–2711. About 3½ mi west of California–Nevada border. 21 rooms.*

**Emerald Motel.** The rooms are ordinary, but the motel is far enough away from the crowded downtown area to provide a modicum of peace and quiet. Clean doubles with color TV, microwave, and small refrigerator start at $35 on weekdays and $45 on weekends; some rooms also have small kitchenettes, and for about $10 more you can reserve the room with a fireplace. Ask for special rates (negotiable) for stays of four nights or more. *515 Emerald Bay Rd. (Hwy. 89), tel. 916/544–5515. 1 mi north of South Lake Tahoe "Y." 9 rooms.*

**NORTH SHORE** **Northwood Pines Motel.** Yes, it's shabby and generic. But it's also priced right and centrally located (about 8 miles northeast of Tahoe City), especially if you're in Tahoe to explore the north shore's ski areas. Aging doubles cost $40 on weekdays and $55 on weekends; weekly rates start at $160. *8489 Trout St., tel. 916/546–9829. Take North Lake Blvd. (Hwy. 28) northeast, turn left on Bear St., right on Trout St. 9 rooms.*

**Tamarack Lodge Motel.** The Tamarack, about a mile north of the lake in Tahoe City, sits in a clearing surrounded by pines and is within walking distance of the beach. Escape the crowds in a clean and comfortable wood-paneled double, starting at $45 weekdays and $50 weekends; another $5 gets a room with a kitchenette. *2311 North Lake Blvd. (Hwy. 28), tel. 916/583–3350. 21 rooms.*

**HOSTELS** **Doug's Mellow Mountain Retreat.** Billed as "The Perfect Place to Chill Out," this laid-back private hostel resembles a frat house, with team flags on the wall, beds in every square inch of available bedroom space, and drab brown furniture. But Doug's a friendly guy, and he'll let you sit in front of the fireplace and watch movies, use his kitchen, and have barbecues on the deck. He'll even pick you up from the Greyhound station at Harrah's if you call ahead. Doug's house, in a quiet residential neighborhood, is centrally located (about a mile from Heavenly and from the casinos). Beds are $13 and the rooms are co-ed. *3787 Forest St., just west of CA–NV border, tel. 916/544–8065. From South Lake Tahoe, U.S. 50 east, right on Wildwood Rd., left on Forest St. 15 beds in 3 rooms. No curfew, no lockout. Reception hours flexible.*

**Squaw Valley Hostel.** This privately run hostel, within walking distance of the Squaw Valley ski area, opens only during winter, usually from November 15 to April 15. During the week a dorm bed runs $20; on weekends rates go up to $25, and it's next to impossible to get a room unless you call ahead and are blessed with luck. *1900 Squaw Valley Rd., tel. 916/583–7771. From Truckee, Hwy. 89 south, right on Squaw Valley Rd. 100 beds in 9 rooms.*

**CAMPING** For obvious reasons, all campgrounds close in winter. Free camping in the Tahoe area is restricted, but still available at some lesser-known primitive spots around the lake. Ask the Forest Service (*see* Basics, *above*) for directions, maps, and tips on other free spots. If Bay View (*see below*) on the south shore doesn't appeal, check out the north shore's **Blackwood Canyon.** From Highway 89 south of Tahoe City, look for a sign to BLACKWOOD CANYON on the right. After 2½ miles, veer to the right on an unmarked dirt road, and camp anywhere you please.

➢ **SOUTH SHORE** • The most conveniently located, though certainly not the most picturesque, spot on the south shore is the **Campground by the Lake** (Rufus Allen Blvd., at U.S. 50, tel. 916/542–6096), a spacious campground with 170 sites shaded by young pines. Sites go for $17 and are surprisingly isolated, considering how close you are to downtown South Lake Tahoe (the campground lies between Stateline and the South Lake Tahoe "Y," where U.S. 50 meets the lake). Reservations are necessary only on holiday weekends.

Two inviting campgrounds are just south of Emerald Bay on Highway 89. **Bay View,** on the inland side of Highway 89, has 12 primitive sites amid the pines, with picnic tables and fire pits but no drinking water. A stopping-off point for journeys into Desolation Wilderness, it imposes a two-night limit on stays; but for those two nights you'll sleep for free. If all the sites in Bay View are full, head just up the road to beautiful **Eagle Point** (Hwy. 89, 1 mi south of Emerald Bay, tel. 916/541–3030 or 800/444–PARK for reservations). Here you'll find 100 well-spaced sites ($14)—all with fire pits, barbecues, drinking water, picnic tables, food lockers, and access to bathrooms and showers—on a hillside covered with brush and pines. Some sites offer incredible views of Emerald Bay.

➢ **NORTH SHORE** • **William Kent Campground** (off Hwy. 89, tel. 916/573–2600 or 800/444–PARK for reservations) is a 95-site National Forest campground set well off the highway, 2 miles south of Tahoe City. William Kent lies in a moderately dense pine forest, and is within walking distance of the lake. Just down the road to the south, the **Kaspian Campground** (tel. 916/544–5994) is specially equipped for wheelchair travelers. For a complete listing of campgrounds, contact the Lake Tahoe Forest Service Visitor Center (*see* Basics, *above*).

## FOOD

Though the south shore is more noticeably jam-packed than the north, you'll find hundreds of restaurants all around the lake, serving everything from fast food to lobster dinners. On the south shore, eateries are concentrated along U.S. 50 between South Lake Tahoe and Stateline, Nevada. In Stateline itself, you can get cheap (if generic) food at all-you-can-eat casino buffets. On the north shore, there's a heap of restaurants in downtown Truckee (especially on Donner Pass Road) and on Highway 28 in Tahoe City. For fresh organic produce and bulk foods, head to **Grass Roots** (2040 Dunlap Dr., at South Lake Tahoe "Y," tel. 916/541–7788) on the south shore. **The Mustard Seed** (7411 North Lake Blvd., Tahoe Vista, tel. 916/546-3525), a small health food shop on the north shore, is another good bet.

*If you're looking to splurge on local seafood, try Fresh Ketch Lakeside Restaurant (2433 Venice Dr. E, in Tahoe Keys Marina in South Lake Tahoe, tel. 916/541–5683), or Jake's on the Lake (Boatworks Marina, near Tahoe City "Y," tel. 916/583–0188). A meal at either will run you around $20.*

**SOUTH SHORE** **Ernie's Coffee Shop.** An unpretentious greasy spoon serving breakfast and lunch only, Ernie's serves better than average coffee-shop brew, and it's bottomless, to boot. Meals range from the standard two-egg-and-toast breakfast ($4) to more adventurous creations like the tostada omelet ($6.50). *1146 Emerald Bay Rd. (Hwy. 89), South Lake Tahoe, tel. 916/541–2161. ¼ mi south of South Lake Tahoe "Y." Open daily 6 AM–2 PM.*

**Los Tres Hombres Cantina.** This typical Californianized Mexican restaurant has good, if not highly creative, food. Standard burritos ($7) and fajitas ($11) are accompanied by a couple of specialties, including fish tacos ($8). *765 Emerald Bay Rd. (Hwy. 89), tel. 916/544–1233. ½ mi NW of South Lake Tahoe "Y." Open daily 11:30–10:30.*

*Weekdays from 4 to 6 PM is "Fiesta Hour" at Los Tres Hombres, with $1.75 pints of beer, $3 double well drinks, and free chips and salsa.*

**Sprouts.** At South Lake Tahoe's vegetarian paradise, you can feast on great veggie sandwiches ($4–$6), rice and vegetable plates ($4.25–$4.75), tempeh burgers ($4.50), and incredible fruit smoothies ($2.50–$3). They also have a wide selection of microbrewed beers ($2.25–$3.75). The restaurant itself is small and cheery, with a few wooden tables and a small outdoor patio. *3123 Harrison Ave. (U.S. 50), South Lake Tahoe, tel. 916/541–6969. Btw Stateline and South Lake Tahoe "Y," just west of where U.S. 50 meets the lake. Open Mon.–Sat. 8 AM–9 PM, Sun. 8–7. Wheelchair access.*

**NORTH SHORE** **Bridgetender Tavern and Grill.** Housed in an old wooden cabin with high-beam ceilings and trees growing through the roof, the Bridgetender is the north shore's best burgers-and-beer joint. Huge beef patties ($4) and tasty veggie burgers ($6) are both served with hefty french fries. During the day you can sit on a patio overlooking the Truckee River; at night patrons come inside to sip beer and shoot pool. *30 Emerald Bay Rd. (Hwy. 89), Tahoe City, tel. 916/583–3342. Next to bridge at Tahoe City "Y." Open daily 11–11.*

**Coyote's Mexican Grill.** Whether you sit on the sun-drenched patio or in the tranquil south-western dining room, you're bound to like the tasty grub at this woman-owned and -operated, self-service Mexican eatery. Aside from the regular old burritos, tacos, and quesadillas—all under $6—Coyote's also features specialties like tequila-and-lime fajitas ($7.25) and mesquite chicken ($6). Afterward, head to the adjoining Café Luna for a cappuccino and a slice of carrot cake. *521 N. Lake Blvd. (Hwy. 28), Tahoe City, tel. 916/583–6653. ½ mi east of Tahoe City "Y." Open daily 10–10; café open daily 7:30 AM–9 PM.*

## AFTER DARK

Events on the south shore are covered in *Lake Tahoe Action and Adventures,* a free weekly entertainment magazine put out by the *Tahoe Daily Tribune,* available at most motels. Check the free *North Tahoe/Truckee Week* for nightlife on the north shore.

**SOUTH SHORE** Considering the number of people on the streets by day, the south shore is surprisingly quiet by night. What limited action there is takes place on the Nevada side of the border in Stateline, where you'll find a number of casinos and the usual array of shows and "revues." Back in California, about 3 miles west of the Nevada border, **Hoss Hogs** (2543 U.S. 50, tel. 916/541–8328) has an unbelievable collection of beer paraphernalia—labels, posters, hats, mirrors, etc.—and live blues and rock on a tiny stage almost every night of the week. On summer nights you can sit out on the patio and listen to live music and play volleyball. **The Brewery at Lake Tahoe** (3542 U.S. 50, tel. 916/544–BREW), 1½ miles west of the California–Nevada border, is one of several microbreweries that have cropped up around the lake in the last few years. Its proximity to Heavenly ski resort makes it a popular place to relax and have a beer after a hard day on the slopes.

*In summer the Brewery has live music on the patio. Rumor has it that a flaming-stick juggler even makes an appearance on occasion.*

**NORTH SHORE** Tahoe City is without a doubt the center of the lake's nightlife, whether you're looking for a rowdy bar or a mellow patio to kick back on. Loud, crowded, and filled with hard-drinking youth scoping one another out, **Humpty's** (877 North Lake Blvd., 1 mi NE of Tahoe City "Y," tel. 916/583–4867) features the best live music in the area most nights (cover $2–$7); Humpty's closes on Tuesdays. At the **Blue Water Brewery** (850 North Lake Blvd., behind Safeway in Tahoe City, tel. 916/581–2583) you can suck down microbrews, munch on some beer chili ($6) or fish-and-chips in beer batter ($7.50), and shoot a game of pool; live bands play Wednesday–Saturday nights.

## SKIING

Whether you prefer downhill or cross-country, you've come to the right place. Unbelievably sheer faces, narrow chutes, and huge cliffs have attracted a new breed of downhill skier bent on pushing the sport to extremes. But novices shouldn't be intimidated: With more than 24 ski resorts, Lake Tahoe offers ample opportunity for beginners and experts alike on downhill and cross-country slopes. Tahoe, like most ski resorts these days, is also a super-popular venue for snowboarding.

**WHAT TO PACK** The type of gear you'll need depends in large part on the weather: Tahoe's temperatures can dictate several layers of sweaters or shorts and a T-shirt. Don't underestimate the danger of sunburn, since even on a cold day the sun is dangerous when it reflects off snow. Required clothing usually includes thermal underwear, thin wool socks, gloves or mittens, a wool hat, sunglasses, goggles, a turtleneck, a cotton or wool sweater, "powder" or "stretch" pants, and either a vinyl shell or a down jacket. Depending on conditions you might also want to pack sun block, a ski mask, waterproof boots, and a visor or baseball cap.

**EQUIPMENT RENTAL** You'll save money by renting from any of the hundreds of rental stores crowding the lake's major roads, but if you choose to rent from the higher-priced shops run by the ski resorts, it'll be easier to get an adjustment, repair, or replacement midday. If you choose the former option, the best deal anywhere is the south shore's **Don Cheepo's** (3349 U.S. 50, about ¾ mi west of Heavenly, tel. 916/544–0356), which offers full downhill and cross-country rental packages (skis, boots, and poles) for $10, or the unbelievably low price of $7.60 if you produce a coupon (scattered around local motels and tourist info centers). Snowboards rent for $25, including boots—a very competitive price.

Of north-shore rental outfits, **Porter's** has the lowest rates (full ski packages $10–$14, snowboards $15–$22) and three locations, including one in Tahoe City (501 North Lake Blvd., just east of Tahoe City "Y," tel. 916/583–2314) and one in Truckee (in Crossroads Center on Hwy. 89, south of I–80, tel. 916/587–1500).

**DOWNHILL** The "Big Five" ski resorts—**Squaw Valley** (on Hwy. 89, 8 mi south of Truckee, tel. 916/583–6955 for snow report), **Alpine Meadows** (Off Hwy. 89, 2 mi south of Squaw Valley, tel. 916/581–8374 for snow report), **Northstar-at-Tahoe** (Hwy. 267, 7 mi south of Truckee, tel. 916/562–1330 for snow report), **Heavenly Valley** (West entrance off Lake Tahoe Boulevard, in South Lake Tahoe, tel. 916/541–7544 for snow report), and **Kirkwood** (Hwy. 88 east, off Hwy. 89 south from South Lake Tahoe, tel. 209/258–3000 for snow report)—all charge in the neighborhood of $40 a day, but if you're careful you can avoid ever paying these prices. Buying multiple-day tickets will save you $3–$7 per day; also scour local papers, motels, gas stations, and supermarkets for discounts and deals.

Beginners and intermediate skiers can save money and still get their money's worth at one of the smaller, less expensive resorts, some of which even offer midweek discounts. With outstanding views of the lake and a wide variety of terrain, **Homewood** (Hwy. 89, btw Tahoe City and South Lake Tahoe, tel. 916/525–2900 for snow report) has lift tickets for $25 weekdays and $29 on weekends and holidays; on Wednesdays two people can ski for $12.50 each. The cheapest Tahoe skiing, however, can be had at **Donner Ranch** (Soda Springs/Norden exit off I–80, tel. 916/426–3635 for snow report), with lift tickets starting at $10 on weekdays and $20 on weekends. If you're skiing here, rent your equipment elsewhere: ski packages start at $22, some of the highest prices around.

**CROSS-COUNTRY SKIING** You'll have no problem finding a trail to suit your abilities at Tahoe's 13 cross-country ski areas, the most famous of which is the north shore's **Royal Gorge** (Soda Springs/Norden exit south from I–80, tel. 916/426–3871), the largest cross-country ski resort in the United States. You can choose from 200 miles of trails running along a ridge above the north fork of the American River; fees are $16.50. The award for best cross-country deal on the south shore goes to **Hope Valley** (Hwy. 88 east, off Hwy. 89, tel. 916/694–2266), located in a beautiful valley of the Toiyabe National Forest on the grounds of Sorenson's Resort. It offers 60 miles of trails for all levels—FREE.

## SUMMER ACTIVITIES

Lake Tahoe offers opportunities for just about every fair-weather sport imaginable. An abbreviated list would include hiking, biking, fishing, sailing, waterskiing, jet skiing, rock climbing, hot-air ballooning, parasailing, horseback riding, and river rafting. Of course many of the more exotic adventures are pricey, but Tahoe is a great place to splurge. Check tourist offices (*see* Basics, *above*) for more detailed information about all these sports. If you're looking to rent equipment for just about any sport, **Don Cheepo's** (*see* Equipment Rental, in Skiing, *above*) carries everything from water skis to backpacks and other camping supplies.

### *The Big Five*

***All of Tahoe's "Big Five" resorts have different pluses and minuses. If you're in a group with divided loyalties, Northstar-at-Tahoe, Squaw, and Kirkwood offer both downhill and cross-country skiing. Squaw Valley is the unofficial home of "extreme" skiing, but 70% of the mountain is suited to beginning and novice skiers, including much of the high-elevation terrain, where views of the lake are best. With its high elevation, nearby Alpine Meadows gets locals' votes for the best spring skiing. Northstar-at-Tahoe has the best views of any north-shore ski area, great tree skiing, and two wind-protected bowls that get excellent powder after a snowstorm.***

***On the south shore, Heavenly is officially the largest ski area in the United States: The good news is you get 4,300 acres of skiable terrain, a 3,500-foot vertical drop, and 25 lifts scattered over nine peaks; the bad news is lift lines approach those at Disneyland. A tip: lines are usually shorter at Heavenly's Nevada base, 3 miles up Kingsbury Grade from Lake Tahoe Boulevard. Heavenly has a righteous beginner's package ($40 for 4 hrs of instruction, a novice's lift ticket, and skis). With the highest base elevation (7,800 ft) in the Lake Tahoe Basin, laid-back Kirkwood boasts the driest snow, which experienced skiers know means the best powder.***

**HIKING** Almost every acre in the Lake Tahoe Basin is protected by some national, state, or local agency. **Tahoe National Forest** lies to the northwest, **Eldorado National Forest** to the southwest, and **Toiyabe National Forest** to the east. What this means for visitors is a whole lot of hiking trails, from easy scenic walks to strenuous climbs over mountain passes. The Lake Tahoe Forest Service Visitor Center (*see* Basics, *above*) has a complete list of day hikes.

For a woodsy, uncrowded day hike, try the **Mt. Tallac Trail,** ½ mile north of the Lake Tahoe Forest Service Visitor Center (follow the marked asphalt road opposite Baldwin Beach to the trailhead parking lot). A moderate hike takes you 2 miles through a beautiful pine forest to Cathedral Lake. For a serious day-long trek (with no potable water along the way), continue on the trail another 3 miles as it climbs past a series of boulder fields to the peak of Mt. Tallac, the highest point in the basin at 9,735 feet. At the top you'll find excellent views of the lake and Desolation Wilderness. The trip up and back should take seven to eight hours.

*If you suffer from hay fever, come to Tahoe prepared for battle. In the height of summer, pollen falls through the air like so many snowflakes.*

If you're looking to do extensive backcountry camping, you're going to have a hard time choosing where to go. Off the southwest corner of the lake, the 63,473-acre **Desolation Wilderness,** filled with granite peaks, glacial valleys, subalpine forests, and more than 80 lakes, is the most beautiful and popular backcountry destination in the area. South of the lake, **Mokelumne Wilderness,** straddling the border of Eldorado and Stanislaus national forests, has terrain similar to Desolation without the crowds. Before you enter any wilderness area, either for a day or for an extended visit, it's crucial to pick up a wilderness permit from the Lake Tahoe Forest Service Visitor Center (*see* Basics, *above*)—if you don't you may actually be kicked off the trails.

**BIKING** Lake Tahoe has everything from mellow lakeshore trails to steep fire roads and tricky single-track trails. Several paved, gently sloped paths skirt the lakeshore: Try the 3.4-mile **Pope Baldwin Bike Path** in South Lake Tahoe, at the Pope Baldwin Recreational Center; the **West Shore Bike Path,** which extends about 10 miles south from Tahoe City to Sugar Pine Point State Park near the town of Tahoma; or the bike path along the **Truckee River** between Alpine Meadows and Tahoe City on the north shore. For experienced riders only, the famous **Flume Trail** traverses a 24-mile trail past several lakes and along a ridge with sweeping views of Lake Tahoe. The trail begins at the parking lot of Lake Tahoe–Nevada State Park, just north of Spooner Junction on the lake's eastern shore (take Highway 28 east from Tahoe City).

If you like the idea of riding downhill all day, **Northstar-at-Tahoe** (*see* Skiing, *above*) opens a number of its ski runs for mountain biking June–September. An all-day ticket goes for $15 (bike rental $30, including helmet). **Squaw Valley** (*see* Skiing, *above*) allows mountain bikers to ride its tram up 2,000 feet, but limits the number of ski runs you can come down on. A single tram ride costs $17, unlimited rides $25; bikes rent for $17 per half day, $24 per full day (including helmet).

➢ **BIKE RENTALS** • Dozens of shops around Tahoe rent mountain bikes, generally for $4–$6 an hour or $15–$22 a day. On the south shore there's **Anderson's Bicycle Rental** (Hwy. 89, at 13th St., tel. 916/541–0500), conveniently located a half mile from the U.S. Forest Service Bike Trail. Slightly cheaper is **Don Cheepo's** (*see* Equipment Rental, in Skiing, *above*), near the east end of the Pope Baldwin Bike Path. On the north shore try **Porter's** (501 North Lake Blvd., tel. 916/583–2314), on Highway 28 just east of the Tahoe City "Y."

**BEACHES** Dozens of beaches are scattered around the lake's shore, most charging $2–$5 for parking. Two of the best include **Chamber's Landing** near Tahoe City, a favorite of young north shore locals; and **Baldwin Beach,** a gorgeous and usually uncrowded sand beach between South Lake Tahoe and Emerald Bay. **Nevada Beach,** a more populated spot just across the Nevada border in Stateline, has great mountain views. **Sand Harbor,** a crescent-shaped beach off Highway 28 on the northeastern shore, is ideal for sunsets.

**WATER SPORTS** Despite Lake Tahoe's often frigid waters, there's no lack of rental outfits specializing in sailing, waterskiing, jet skiing, boating, windsurfing, kayaking, canoeing, sport fishing, and parasailing. Prices fluctuate a bit but in general, sailboats go for $30–$35 an hour, $85–$95 a day; Jet Skis run $35–$70 an hour; Windsurfers rent for $10–$15 an hour, $30–$40 a half day; and canoes go for $10–$15 an hour, $30–$40 a half day. Parasailing rides, which usually last about 15 minutes, range from $35 to $50.

Shop around before you plunk down a sizable chunk of change. On the south shore, **South Shore Parasailing and Paradise Watercraft Rentals** (tel. 916/541–6166), with motorboats, canoes, kayaks, and other toys, is one of several shops operating out of **Ski Run Marina,** off U.S. 50 about a half mile west of the California–Nevada border. On the north shore, you'll find rental outfits in the **Sunnyside Marina,** about 2 miles south of Tahoe City on Highway 89.

**FISHING** Like nearly everything in Tahoe, fishing options are abundant. Obviously, the most convenient spot is (can you guess?) **Lake Tahoe,** stocked occasionally with rainbow trout by the folks at the Fish and Wildlife Service (to find the section of the lake most recently stocked, call 916/355–7040 or 916/351–0832). Also popular is the stretch of the **Truckee River** between Truckee and Tahoe City—just pick a spot and cast your line. Wherever you fish, licenses ($9 a day, $24 a year) are required by law and available from most sporting-goods shops. For sport fishing on the lake, contact **Tahoe Sportfishing** (tel. 916/541–5448) in the Ski Run Marina or **Let's Go Fishing** (tel. 916/541–5566) in South Lake Tahoe. Half-day trips generally start at $50–$55, full-day trips at $70–$75.

## NEAR LAKE TAHOE

**DONNER MEMORIAL STATE PARK** To learn about the ill-fated Donner party, some of whom were forced to eat their traveling companions during the journey over the Sierra Nevada in the winter of 1847, head for **Donner Memorial State Park** (follow signs off I–80 a few miles west of Truckee, tel. 916/582–7892). The 25-minute slide show at the park's **Emigrant Trail Museum** tells the party's story from a human-interest perspective, but conspicuously lacks the gory details you might hunger for. A snowball's throw away, the **Donner Monument** stands atop a 22-foot-high base, marking the depth of the snow that fateful winter. The park's secluded campsites, spread out along the east shore of Donner Lake, are popular with local anglers. The 100-plus sites ($14), with full facilities, can accommodate up to eight people each.

# Reno

**As you cross the state border and approach Nevada's second-**largest city, the billboards and neon lights leave little doubt in your mind as to the town's main attraction. Though more than half of Reno's workforce draws a paycheck from some source other than the gambling industry, most tourists don't come here to check out the planetarium. The city's history as a center of legalized vice is longer than that of Las Vegas. Well before Bugsy Siegel built his Flamingo, Pappy Smith and Bill Harrah had opened major casinos in Reno, where gambling had flourished—though not always legally—since the days of railroad construction. Now eclipsed in many respects by Las Vegas, Reno continues to have a distinctive character. While Vegas offers a Disneyland for the internationally rich and infamous, Reno preaches the gospel of unearned wealth to the middle class.

People like to portray Reno as a kinder, gentler version of Vegas, congenial to small bankrolls and shy neophytes. But dirt-cheap hotels and low table minimums are, if anything, a bit scarcer here, particularly on the weekends. The reason to choose Reno is not for friendlier baccarat dealers but for its location. Set just over the Sierra, near Lake Tahoe, Donner Lake, and Pyramid Lake, Reno has much cooler weather than Las Vegas; and if you do manage to catch some sleep here, you'll wake up to a gorgeous view of snowcapped mountains outside your hotel window. At the end of your stay, there's always the possibility of marriage. If you have 10 or fewer guests (not including the bride and groom), the **Park Wedding Chapel** (136 S. Virginia St., tel. 702/323–1770) will take care of the whole event for $60.

The **Reno Visitor Center** (300 N. Center St., tel. 800/FOR–RENO), in the lobby of the National Bowling Center, offers hotel information and makes reservations for sightseeing tours and casino shows. It's open daily 8–5. You can also get information at the **Tourist Center** (354 N. Virginia St., tel. 702/333–6739); besides gaming coupons, they will also give you free dice

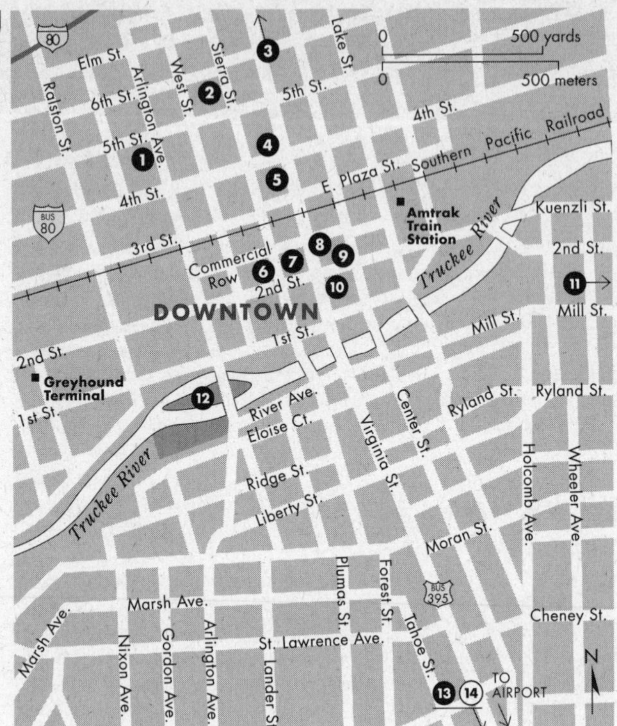


**Sights ●**
Fleischmann Planetarium, **3**
Wingfield Park, **12**

**Lodging ○**
Romance Inn, **14**

**Hotel-Casinos ●**
Circus Circus, **2**
Eldorado, **5**
Flamingo Hilton, **6**
Harrah's, **9**
Nevada Club, **8**
Nugget, **7**
Peppermill, **13**
Reno Hilton, **11**
Silver Legacy, **4**
Sundowner, **1**
Virginian, **10**

(for good luck) and then try and rope you into watching a video on land in southern Nevada. Even if you're not interested in buying real estate, go for the video—you get various gifts (like show tickets) just for sitting through it. Finally, you can also get most info you may need at the registration desks of the big hotel-casinos.

## COMING AND GOING

**BY CAR** Reno lies on **I–80,** two hours and change from Sacramento and just under 4 hours from the Bay Area. You can't possibly miss the city, whose sudden appearance in the distance a few miles after you cross the Nevada border can be quite spectacular, particularly at sunrise. Most of the major casinos are easily spotted from a few miles away. For downtown, take the Virginia Street exit, which is also the business loop of **U.S. 395,** the road serving Reno from points north and south. Be sure to carry chains during winter, as the highway can be treacherous in the higher altitudes between Auburn and Truckee. If you have car trouble, **Grand Auto Supply** (801 W. 5th St., tel. 702/329–5353 or 1501 S. Virginia St., tel. 702/786–7219) is open when you need them: Monday–Saturday 8–8, Sunday 9–6.

**BY BUS** At the 24-hour **Greyhound Terminal** (155 Stevenson St., tel. 702/322–2970 or 800/231–2222 for reservations), buses arrive regularly from San Francisco ($26 round-trip for 5-night maximum stay) and Sacramento ($21 round-trip for 3-night maximum stay). Smaller companies also run gambling tour buses, maybe the least expensive way to get to Reno from the Bay Area: Companies like **Lucky Tours** (1111 Mission St., San Francisco, tel. 415/864–1133) offer regular round-trips for about $30, most of which is returned to you in the form of gambling chips. If Lucky Tours is busy, try **Mike Lee Tours** (tel. 415/421–0900), which leaves from S.F.'s Transbay Terminal (*see* Coming and Going, in Chapter 2) and drops you at John Ascuaga's Nugget or Harrah's ($30 round-trip). Check ads in the Sunday "Datebook" section of the *San Francisco Chronicle* or in other Sunday papers.

**BY TRAIN** **Amtrak** (135 E. Commercial Row, at Lake St. downtown, tel. 800/872–7245) runs from San Francisco all the way across the country along I–80, passing through Reno. Westbound trains leave Reno every morning and eastbound trains pull into town around five in the evening. The trains are comfortable and not too expensive if you purchase tickets in advance: Round-trip tickets from S.F. start at $60 (you take a bus from the Transbay Terminal to the Emeryville station); you'll pay the same from Sacramento. However, the trip is slow (in the neighborhood of 7 hours from S.F.), the schedule is limited to once a day, and the fares are always changing. Reserve as early as possible as there are a limited number of lower fares; once they're filled you might be stuck paying close to double. Amtrak passengers can store luggage for free in the station daily 8 AM–4:30 PM (the desk is closed for lunch 11:30 AM–1 PM).

**BY PLANE** Upstart carrier **Reno Air** (tel. 800/736–6747) offers affordable round-trips to the **Reno Cannon International Airport** (2001 E. Plumb Ln., tel. 702/328–6499). With a 21-day advance purchase, a one-way ticket from L.A. costs $48. Their Quick Escapes program offers package deals that include cheap hotel stays, car rentals, and gambling chips. **Southwest** (tel. 800/435–9792) has good deals from the Bay Area; you'll pay $60 round-trip from Oakland or San Jose if you reserve 21 days in advance. The Reno airport is southeast of town on U.S. 395.

## GETTING AROUND

Once you're in its confines, the self-designated "biggest little city in the world" is quite easily navigated on foot, and there's not much reason to touch your car once it's in a validated parking lot at one of the bigger casinos. Most of the action is concentrated downtown between the Truckee River and the interstate, though a few large casinos (the Peppermill, John Ascuaga's Nugget, and the Reno Hilton, formerly Bally's) lie a couple of miles away. The University of Nevada is south on Virginia Street. **RTC/Citifare** (tel. 702/348–7433), the city's attempt at public transit, offers limited bus service (fare is $1). Bus 1, which runs north–south on Virginia Street, operates 24 hours.

Because the main streets are always lit, you might be lulled into feeling safe. However, gangs, drug dealers, and prostitution rings abound. Areas to avoid walking alone in are around 4th and Lake Streets, and 9th and Sutro Streets.

## WHERE TO SLEEP

Reno is packed with hotels and motels in every nook and cranny, but many of the best deals are in the most obvious and imposing places—the downtown hotel-casinos. Even if you're just passing through Reno for the night, you should try to get a room at a place like the **Sundowner** (450 N. Arlington St., tel. 800/648–5490)—which is often the least expensive bet with off-season rooms for $23, and summer rates starting at $33. **Circus Circus** (*see below*) has comparable prices and is a real kick, and the **Virginian** (140 N. Virginia St., tel. 800/874–5558) is also worth checking out. You won't save more than a couple of bucks (if that) by staying in some fleabag in a marginal neighborhood.

The price of lodging (even outside the casinos) also varies considerably from weekday to weekend and from season to season (summer being highest). Reservations are definitely recommended, and remember to figure in the 9% room tax. You can also call the visitor center (*see above*) for room referrals.

*Reno's Romance Inn will rent their ceiling-mirrored waterbed rooms to any two people, or to threesomes at the discretion of the night manager. No pets, please.*

If you shoot your point enough times at the craps table, consider an evening at the ritzy, well-located **Eldorado** (345 N. Virginia St., tel. 800/648–5966). Some of its 800-plus rooms can run as low as $50 for a double during the week; for a few extra bucks you'll get a room in the Skyline Tower, complete with a sitting area and view. Honeymooners and romantic types should check out the various adult hotels, such as the **Romance Inn** (2905 S. Virginia St., tel. 702/826–1515 or 800/662–8812), where rooms are $70–$140 on summer weekdays, depending on how elaborate the room theme is. You'll find a Jacuzzi and a complimentary bottle of wine (tell them you're on your honeymoon and they'll send champagne) in all the rooms.

**Circus Circus.** One of the city's largest and least expensive hotel-casinos, Circus Circus so thoroughly epitomizes the Reno experience that it behooves every traveler to spend the night here at least once. The pace is frenetic at this enormous place—hugely popular among families with kids because of its Midway circus and carnival, which takes up an entire floor. Rooms start as low as $22 for a double at certain times of year; during summer, rates are $42 Sunday–Thursday, $55 on weekends. All 1,600 rooms are spacious and comfortable, but they sell out early and often. *500 N. Sierra St., btw 5th and 6th Sts., tel. 800/648–5010. Luggage storage. Wheelchair access.*

## FOOD

Obscene quantity is the name of the game when it comes to downtown dining. Pound steaks, ham-and-egg specials, and the much-heralded all-you-can-eat buffets are as central to the ambiance of Reno as the slot machines. At the buffets, you can be completely sated for as little as $2–$3. If you find a feeding frenzy unappetizing, Reno has plenty of normal, civilized restaurants, both inside and outside the casinos.

*While you're at the tables, cocktail waitresses will come by to take your liquor orders. Drinks are free, though it's appropriate to tip.*

**CASINO BUFFETS** One caveat is in order: These buffets are designed to lure you into the casinos. After you've dropped 30 bucks at the craps table while waiting for a table, your meal may seem like less of a bargain. This said, the cheapest buffet is at **Circus Circus** (*see* Where to Sleep, *above*)—where the top-priced meal is $4—but you may want to pay two or three dollars extra at a place like the **Eldorado** (345 N. Virginia St., tel. 702/786–5700) for better quality control. The best spread in town is out at the **Peppermill** (2707 S. Virginia St., tel. 800/648–6992), where locals say lunch ($6) is the best deal.

**RESTAURANTS** **Blue Heron.** An island of vegetarianism in a sea of beef buffets, this busy restaurant has sandwiches ($5.50) and an assortment of Mexican and health-food entrées ($6–$7). They use organic products when possible (90% of the time). The portions are substantial, and you'll fill up before you can spend $10. *1091 S. Virginia St., at Vassar St., tel. 702/786–4110. Open Mon.–Thurs. 11–9, Fri. and Sat. 11–10, Sun. 4–8; shorter hrs in winter.*

**Nugget Diner.** Hidden in back of the Nugget, one of the smaller casinos on Virginia Street, this tiny 24-hour diner is a favorite among local carnivores. For $3.50 you get the Awful-Awful, as juicy a half-pound burger as you'll find, served with enough fries to fill the back seat of a Buick. Also check out the 99¢ breakfast special (two pancakes and an egg), served all day, of course. *233 N. Virginia St., btw 2nd and 3rd Sts., tel. 702/323–0716.*

**DESSERT AND COFFEEHOUSES** **Java Jungle** (246 W. 1st St., tel. 702/324–5282) is a trendy, smokeless hangout—popular among college students and business types—that serves a superior cup of coffee to anything you'll get at the tables. The café is open daily until 6 PM. A couple blocks south and east of Java Jungle, the newer **Café Royale** (236 California Ave., at Hill St., tel. 702/322–3939) has outdoor seating, serves sandwiches ($5), and pours some of the strongest coffee around. It's open daily 7 AM–9 PM (Fri. and Sat. until 1 AM).

## WORTH SEEING

No matter what your prejudices, a visit to the casinos is obligatory once you decide to stop in town. Which one you should choose depends on your budget, your tastes, and whether you're here to play or to gawk. Reno's newest addition is the **Silver Legacy** (407 N. Virginia St., tel. 800/MUST-SEE), which features 1,720 rooms, five theme restaurants, the world's largest domed roof, 2,300 slot machines, and a shopping mall. Among the other downtown options, **Harrah's** (219 N. Center St., tel. 800/HARRAHS) is probably the fanciest, and has an amazing sports-book area. If you're willing to drive a couple of miles south on Virginia Street, the **Pep-**

**permill** (*see* Food, *above*) has a certain Las Vegas–style tits-'n'-glitz appeal. To really make your gambling dollar last, try the small **Nevada Club** (224 N. Virginia St., tel. 702/329–1721), where the bet minimums are extremely low (including 25¢ roulette). For that reason, it's a good place to learn the ropes of an unfamiliar game. **Circus Circus** (*see* Where to Sleep, *above*) also has low table minimums, but it's a real madhouse, with very crowded tables.

In many respects, the nicest place to gamble is the **Flamingo Hilton** (255 N. Sierra St., tel. 702/322–1111), where you might find yourself next to a Roy Orbison impersonator (*see* After Dark, *below*) at the roulette wheel. But the most compelling reason to play here is the superior blackjack rules. Because you're allowed to double down on any two cards (*see box* Blackjack Tips, in Chapter 13), and because you're allowed to double after a split, your odds are better here than in other Reno casinos and the game becomes more fun.

While you may experience Reno as a carnivalesque parody of capitalist values, it doesn't take more than a brief conversation with a humorless pit boss to remind you that this is serious big business. For an education in the workings of Nevada's mega-industry, you can take the **"Behind the Scenes" Gaming Tour,** run by the Reno-Tahoe Gaming Academy (300 E. 1st St., Suite 103, tel. 702/329–5665) Monday–Thursday at 12:30 PM. For $5, you get lessons in seven casino games, as well as a chance to observe the pan-optical surveillance system at the Cal Neva Club. Don't take the tour just to learn the games, though, as several hotels offer free lessons. The **Eldorado** (*see* Where to Sleep, *above*) gives lessons on a number of games weekdays 10–7; ask at the promotion booth for details. Head for the marked tables on the floor of the **Flamingo Hilton** (*see above*) weekdays at 11 AM for the lowdown on craps and blackjack.

**CHEAP THRILLS** When you and your wallet have had enough of the casinos, you might want to check out the **Fleischmann Planetarium** (1650 N. Virginia St., tel. 702/784–4812), on the University of Nevada campus. The planetarium, open daily 8 AM–9 PM (9 AM–5 PM in winter), runs shows on the stars ($5, $3 youth) and has an education center where you can measure your weight on Venus. Telescope viewing times are Wednesday, Friday, and Saturday 9:30–10:30 PM, on clear nights only.

Just a few blocks west of Virginia Street along the Truckee River, you'll run into **Wingfield Park,** a nice spot for a picnic and the site of free summer concerts. Even better, take the Pyramid exit off I–80 up to **Pyramid Lake** and put your gambling losses in some perspective. The drive only takes about 35 minutes, but when you see the desolate desert hills that surround the lake, you may think you've traveled to the moon. For $5 you can camp anywhere you like around the lake. The marina next to the ranger station (tel. 702/476–1156) rents Jet Skis and boats.

**FESTIVALS** Reno's annual **Hot August Nights** (tel. 702/829–1955) is a major nostalgia festival, celebrating classic cars and popular symbols of 1950s culture. Visitors drive their pre-1970 cars in a 2,500-vehicle parade, participate in a huge automobile auction, and crowd into the 24-hour Hamburger Haven soda fountain. The town gets decked out in poodle skirts, greased hair, and rolled-up T-shirts, and there's even a prom. Hotel rates go through the roof and rooms become seriously scarce during this early-August celebration.

## AFTER DARK

Top-name entertainers make well-advertised and expensive appearances in the Reno showrooms, particularly on weekends. The big spots are **Harrah's** downtown (*see* Worth Seeing, *above*) and the **Reno Hilton** (2500 E. 2nd St., tel. 800/648–3568). If you're looking for some real casino kitsch, check out the celebrity impersonators at the **Flamingo Hilton** (tel. 702/785–7080 for show reservations); "American Superstars" ($15 cover) features reasonable imitations of Madonna, Sammy Davis Jr., the Temptations, and others.

Beyond the glitz of the casinos, find out who's playing at the **Hacienda del Sol** (2935 S. Virginia St., tel. 702/825–7144), a Mexican cantina out by the Peppermill. The music ranges from blues to Top 40, and admission is free. If you're only going to hit one bar in town, make it **Bad Dolly's** (535 E. 4th St., at Valley Rd., tel. 702/348–1983), a predominantly lesbian bar that's generally hospitable to other orientations. This country-western spot features two-step and line dancing (lessons available on Thursday evenings). Reno has a thriving gay culture and several gay bars, including the **1099 Club** (1099 S. Virginia St., tel. 702/329–1099), where you can catch a drag show most weekend nights as you sip a martini, play pool, and chat with the friendly bartenders. The 1099 Club is open Monday–Wednesday 10 AM–2 AM, Thursday–Saturday 24 hours. Every June, people come from miles around for the annual coronation of a drag emperor and empress at the convention center. Ask at the bars for details.

# THE SIERRA NEVADA AND SAN JOAQUIN VALLEY 7

By Alan Covington Phulps

**To one of the first explorers it was "a specimen of chaos, which has defied the fin-**ishing hand of time." To naturalist John Muir it was "the Range of Light, the most divinely beautiful of all the mountain chains." And for millions of visitors today, the Sierra Nevada—the largest continuous mountain range in the United States—is one of the most spectacular natural settings in the world. Trade in the strip malls of the lowlands for mile-high panoramas and lush alpine scenery; motel swimming pools for crystal-clear mountain lakes; parking lots for windswept meadows; and faceless high-rises for towering peaks and granite cliffs. Only 4 hours east of San Francisco and 3 to 8 hours north of Los Angeles lie **Yosemite National Park, Inyo National Forest, Sequoia** and **Kings Canyon National Parks,** and **Sierra National Forest**—an unparalleled collection of natural wonders 400 miles long and 80 miles wide.

Roughly translated from the Spanish, Sierra Nevada means "snowy mountain range." And indeed, the Sierra's tallest peaks—many topping 14,000 feet—are capped by snow year-round. The weather is subject to drastic fluctuations: Even in summer, clear blue skies can suddenly give way to awesome thunderstorms or hazardous blizzards. In higher altitudes, temperatures can drop below freezing year-round or climb to 90° in summer; in lower altitudes, summer temperatures are likely to soar as high as 110°. The sudden changes in terrain and climate wreaked havoc on early settlers attempting to cross the mighty mountains in their quest for rich farmland or gold, but the same factors provide an exciting, intense environment for well-prepared hikers, campers, and backpackers.

On the whole, the Eastern Sierra is far less crowded than the western slope, except at Mammoth Lakes during ski season and on the Whitney Portal Trail in summer. Those who want solitude should visit the Sierra Nevada in spring or fall, when tourists don't create the hassles they do in summer. If you seek well-developed facilities, the national parks are for you. But if you want to bring your dog on a hike or ride your mountain bike up a peak, head to the national forests or wilderness areas, which have far fewer facilities and regulations. If you don't have a car, you'll have to do some creative travel planning—but no one said traveling on a shoestring would be easy.

Droves of vacationers escape to the Sierra Nevada, but most Californians would agree that the San Joaquin Valley, directly to the west, is a place to escape *from.* Unfortunately, if you plan on getting from one end of the state to the other, chances are good you'll find yourself in Stockton, Merced, Fresno, or another of the valley's sprawling cities. As long as you can stand oppressive heat and omnipresent country music, your stopover doesn't have to be a miserable one; most towns have a rowdy nightlife and some even boast a few cafés. But there's not enough here to keep a visitor interested for long, and the best part of your visit may be that you get to move on to the great Sierra Nevada.

# The Sierra Nevada and San Joaquin Valley

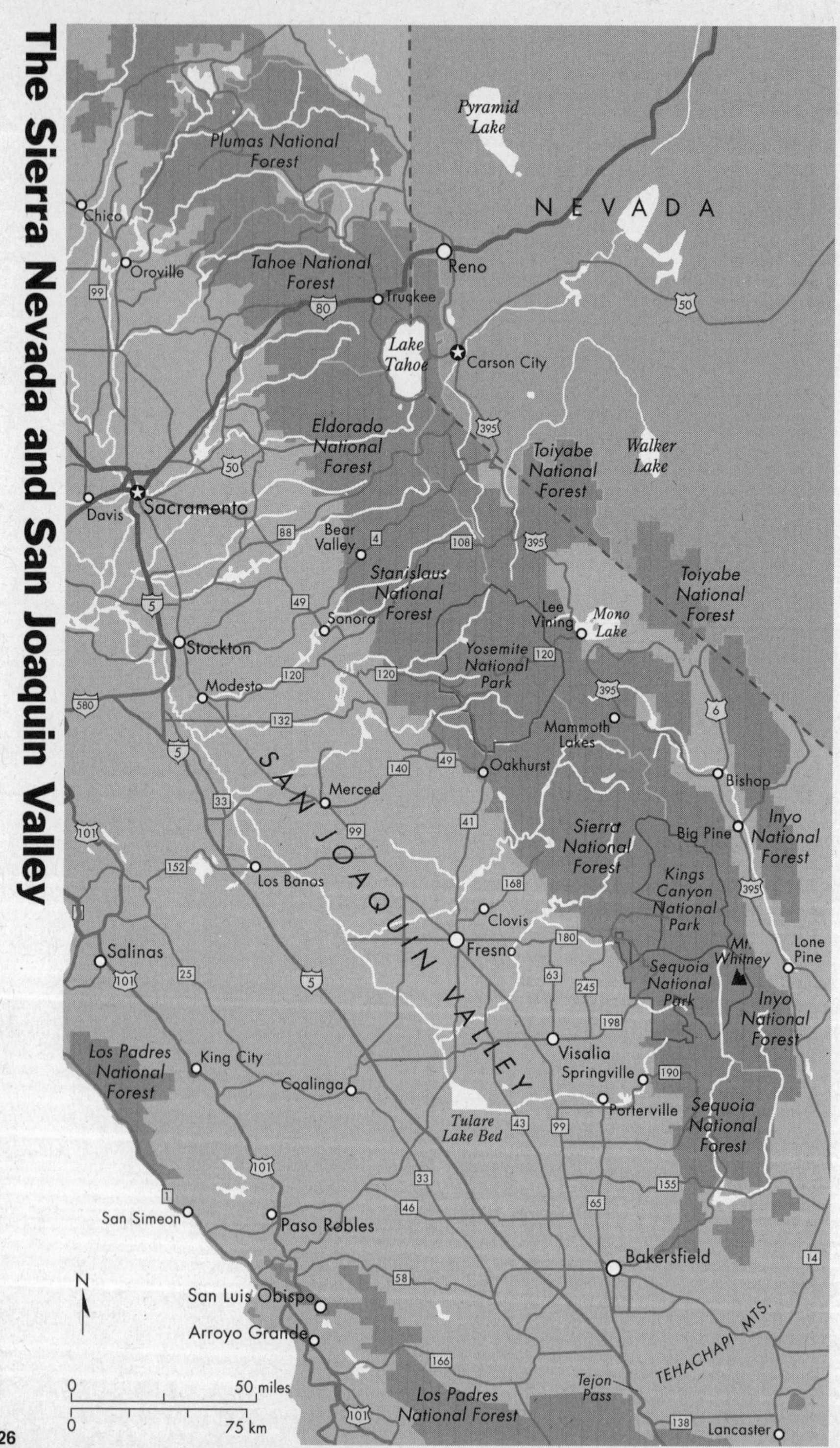

Pyramid Lake
Plumas National Forest
NEVADA
Chico
Oroville
Tahoe National Forest
Reno
Truckee
Lake Tahoe
Carson City
Eldorado National Forest
Toiyabe National Forest
Walker Lake
Davis
Sacramento
Bear Valley
Stanislaus National Forest
Toiyabe National Forest
Lee Vining
Mono Lake
Sonora
Stockton
Yosemite National Park
Modesto
Mammoth Lakes
SAN JOAQUIN VALLEY
Oakhurst
Bishop
Merced
Sierra National Forest
Big Pine
Inyo National Forest
Kings Canyon National Park
Los Banos
Clovis
Fresno
Salinas
Mt. Whitney
Lone Pine
Sequoia National Park
Inyo National Forest
Visalia
Springville
Los Padres National Forest
King City
Coalinga
Porterville
Sequoia National Forest
Tulare Lake Bed
San Simeon
Paso Robles
Bakersfield
San Luis Obispo
Arroyo Grande
TEHACHAPI MTS.
Tejon Pass
Los Padres National Forest
Lancaster
N
0
50 miles
0
75 km

# Yosemite National Park

**For the most part, Yosemite is overdeveloped,** crowded, and expensive—but there is no other place in the world quite like it. Glacial sculpturing and prehistoric activity at the earth's mantle have formed a land so stunning that even the jaded contend it's not to be missed. Slightly smaller than the state of Rhode Island, Yosemite is packed with waterfalls, sheer granite cliffs, lush forests, and generous expanses of alpine meadows. **Yosemite Valley,** the central and most accessible portion of the park, stretches more than 20 miles from the Wawona Tunnel in the west to Curry Village in the east. The valley's major sites are **Half Dome** and **El Capitan**—two breathtaking but treacherous granite formations—as well as the **Yosemite, Nevada,** and **Vernal falls.**

Because the valley is crowded with so much hype, it can be hard to step back and let the beauty soak in. Most people never leave its congested confines—complete with tacky lodges and unsightly gift shops—to explore the rest of the park. That's a big mistake. While it's almost impossible to avoid the valley, consider it a departure point for hikes rather than a destination in itself. The other side of Yosemite—the undisturbed, forested backcountry with its massive granite formations and plunging waterfalls—is where you'll find the real soul of the park. Among the more spectacular nonvalley sights are **Tuolumne Meadows** (pronounced TWA-lo-mee), along Highway 120; the giant sequoias of **Mariposa Grove,** off Highway 41 in the southwest corner of the park; **Glacier Point,** near Badger Pass; and the **Hetch Hetchy Reservoir** (north of Big Oak Flat). These areas are most accessible to backpackers and horseback riders, though numerous turnouts and day-hike areas make them fairly easy to reach from the highway.

If possible, visit during spring or early fall, when crowds are less of a nuisance. Spring (late April–late May) is especially spectacular—the wildflowers are in bloom and the waterfalls are at their peak of sound and fury as snowpack melts in the high country. Of the nearly 4 million people who visit each year, 70% arrive during summer (June–Aug.), when temperatures reach a high of 85° and a low of 40°. During winter (Nov.–Mar.), temperatures drop to a chilly 45° by day and a downright frigid 15° by night. You won't be able to explore the park in winter as easily as you can during summer (Tioga Pass and Glacier Point Road usually close by November due to inclement weather), but when dusted with a blanket of snow, Yosemite will definitely sneak its way into your heart.

*To the Ahwahneechee people, Yosemite was the sacred belly of the world—the divine womb from which nature's wonders were spewed forth in infinite perfection.*

For centuries Yosemite was inhabited by the Ahwahneechee people who lived in settlements in the surrounding mountains. Unfortunately, the Mariposa Battalion, the first group of whites to enter the area (in 1851), saw Yosemite as a prime hunting and fur-trapping ground. By the late 19th century whites had settled (i.e., conquered) the Ahwahneechee and established a lucrative lumber business and trading outpost. We have shepherd and naturalist John Muir to thank that Yosemite Valley is today more than a timber company parking lot: Even in the late-1800s the park was showing signs of wear and tear. By securing the support of some of the nation's most powerful people, Muir played a vital role in having Yosemite declared a national park in 1890.

## BASICS

**VISITOR INFORMATION** Yosemite has two visitor centers; both stock maps and brochures and distribute free wilderness permits (required for overnight camping in the backcountry; *see* Longer Hikes, *below*). For current events in Yosemite, check the *Yosemite Guide,* available at all entrance stations. The **Yosemite Valley Visitor Center** (Shuttle Stops 6 and 9, tel. 209/372–0299) is 6 miles east of the Highway 140 entrance and open daily 8–5 (until 6 in summer). The **Tuolumne Meadows Visitor Center** (tel. 209/372–0263), open daily 9–5 in summer only, is toward the east end of the park, 1 mile east of Tuolumne Meadows on Tioga Pass Road.

It doesn't have much of a tourist desk, but the **Wawona Ranger Station** (south end of Yosemite, on Hwy. 41, tel. 209/372–0563) provides wilderness permits weekdays 8–5. The **Big Oak**

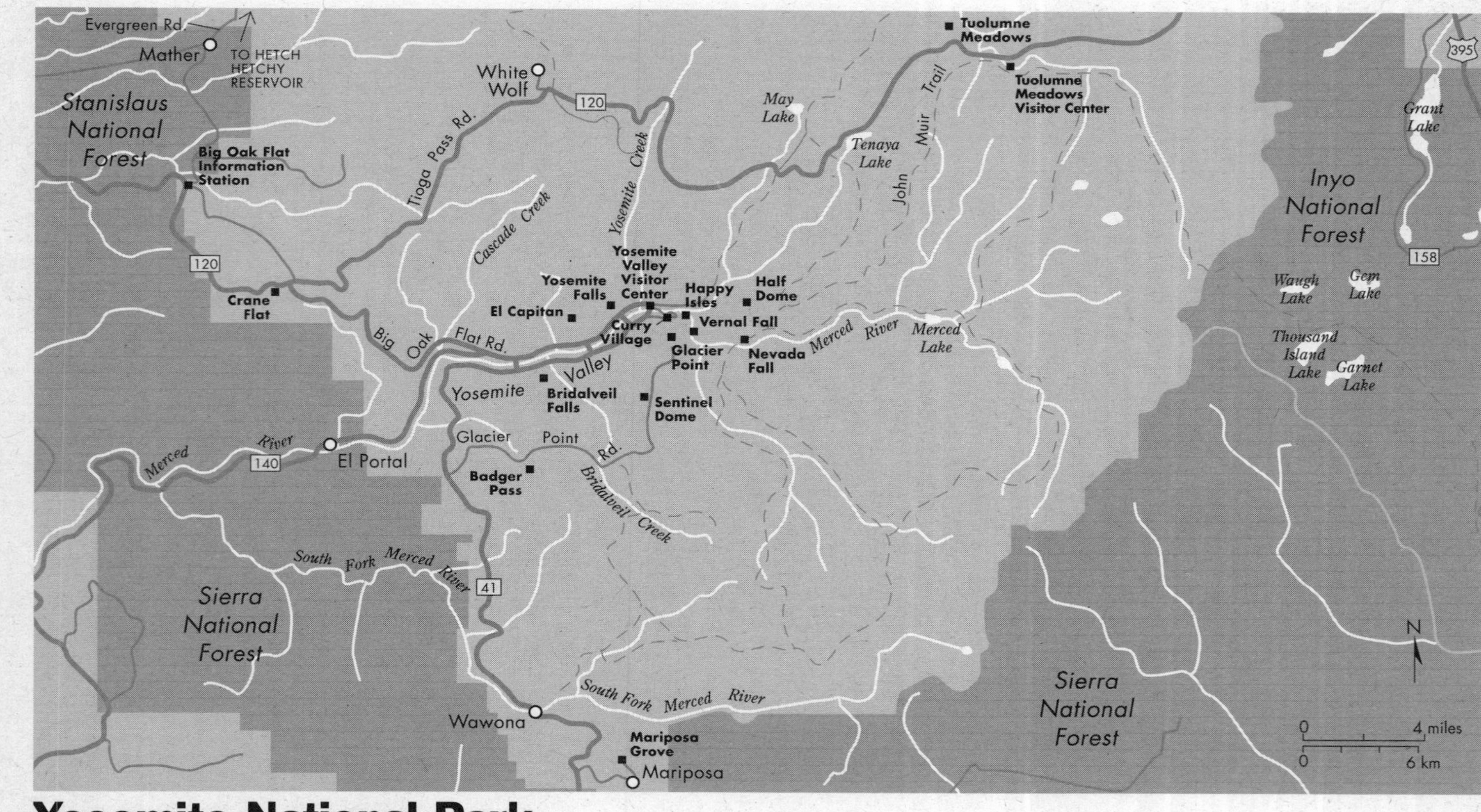


# Yosemite National Park

**Flat Information Station** (tel. 209/372–0615), at the Highway 120 west entrance, is open daily 9–5 in summer and Friday–Sunday the rest of the year. If you're not actually in the park, the **Public Information Service** (Box 577, Yosemite National Park 95389, tel. 209/372–0264) is the place to begin your search for info on Yosemite, though getting through on the phone can be a task. Send an SASE for free brochures and maps, or call weekdays 9–5.

**FEES** The park fee for one week is $5 per car or $3 per hiker, bicyclist, or bus passenger. You can purchase annual passes for $15 that give you unlimited access to the park.

**WHAT TO PACK** Rain gear is important year-round. You may never have to battle one of Yosemite's sudden summertime tempests, but unless you want to be stuck sipping hot chocolate while trying to dry out in a dreary coffee shop, it pays to be prepared. Water-repellent "shell" pants and a warm jacket with polar-fleece lining are a smart idea, and don't forget wool or wick-dry socks—they'll keep you warm even when it's wet. If you plan to camp in winter—you crazy thing, you—you'll need warm clothing, a subzero sleeping bag, and a waterproof (or at least water-resistant) four-season tent. Broken-in hiking boots are a must for exploring the backcountry, and yes, snowshoes or crampons would be a good idea if you want to blaze your own trail. You'll be subject to awful frostbite in the winter without your polar-fleece (or wool) hat and gloves.

**GENERAL STORES** It's best to stop in Oakdale (Hwy. 120), Sonora (Hwy. 108), or Lee Vining (U.S. 395 at Tioga Pass Rd.), before entering the park. Otherwise you're stuck with the grocery and camping stores in pricey Yosemite Village, 5 miles east of Highway 41 in the middle of the park (at Shuttle Stops 3, 5, and 10): The **Village Sport Shop** (tel. 209/372–1286), open from spring to fall, has fishing and camping gear; the **Village Store** (tel. 209/372–1253), open daily 8 AM–10 PM, stocks groceries and basic camping supplies. Just outside the park, the **Wawona Grocery** (Hwy. 41, near south end of park, tel. 209/375–6574), open daily 9–8, also stocks groceries and basic camp gear.

**Badger Pass Sport Shop** (tel. 209/372–8430), open from December to April, has ski clothing and equipment, as well as lotions, waxes, and picnic supplies. It's near Wawona and the Badger Pass ski slopes, off Highway 41 on the south side of the park. In Curry Village, at the far eastern end of Yosemite Valley (Shuttle Stop 14), you'll find a host of stores, including the **Curry Village Mountain Shop** (tel. 209/372–8396), where you can purchase overpriced rock-climbing gear and topographic maps.

**MEDICAL AID** The **Yosemite Medical Clinic** in Yosemite Village offers full medical service and 24-hour emergency care. *Btw visitor center and Ahwahnee Hotel, tel. 209/372–4637. Open weekdays 8–5, weekends 9–noon.*

## COMING AND GOING

**BY CAR** You can reach Yosemite via three routes: **Highway 41** from the south, **Highway 140** from Merced in the west, and **Highway 120** from San Francisco. From San Francisco (4 hrs), take I–580 east to I–205 and connect to Highway 120. From Los Angeles (8 hrs), take I–5 north to Highway 99, then pick up Highway 41 north of Fresno. Highways 41 and 140 terminate in Yosemite Valley, and Highway 120 becomes Tioga Pass Road inside the park. In winter, take Highway 140 from the west, since Highway 120 is usually closed. In spring, the eastern portion of Highway 120 (from the valley past Tuolumne Meadows into Inyo National Forest and Lee Vining) is closed.

From late fall to early spring you should carry snow chains. The highways can get treacherous, and the California Highway Patrol often closes the roads to all traffic without snow gear. If you get stuck, you'll have to buy an expensive set of chains ($60) from a gas station (and boy, do they love it when that happens). For current road and weather conditions, call 209/372–0200 or 800/427–ROAD.

**BY BUS AND TRAIN** There is no direct bus service to Yosemite from San Francisco; all lines stop in either Fresno or Merced, where you have to change coaches. From Merced, a cheap option is **Via Adventures** (tel. 209/384–1315), which runs three buses a day (2½ hrs,

$17 one-way) from Merced's Greyhound station at 16th and N streets. **Amtrak** (tel. 800/USA–RAIL) offers a thruway service that takes you from San Francisco to the park and back for $53. The train stops in Emeryville and in Merced, where you board the bus to Yosemite. From L.A., Amtrak buses run to Merced (through Bakersfield), where you transfer to another bus to reach the park. The round-trip package deal from L.A. is $67. All buses stop at Yosemite Lodge in the valley. **Green Tortoise** (tel. 415/956–7500 or 800/867–8647) runs a 3-day Yosemite Redwoods Tour out of San Francisco that goes through much of the park and surrounding forest. The tour costs $99, plus $21 for food (for more info on Green Tortoise travel, *see box* Funky Deals on Wheels, in Chapter 1).

## GETTING AROUND

Curvy **Tioga Pass Road** (aka **Highway 120**) runs the entire 60-mile east–west length of the park, climbing 8,000 feet in its course. If you're on a bicycle (*see* Biking, *below*), you may want to limit yourself to the valley, since both Highway 41 and Tioga Pass Road are often narrow and steep.

**BY PARK SHUTTLE** Free shuttle buses operate throughout the year, though service hours vary according to season. The **East Valley Loop** travels every 20 minutes, year-round, between Curry Village, Yosemite Village, and the Yosemite Lodge (*see* Where to Sleep, *below*). Starting in mid-April, the shuttle operates 7 AM–10 PM; in winter, hours are reduced to 9 AM–10 PM, and some stops receive no service at all. During ski season a free shuttle leaves Yosemite Lodge for the **Badger Pass** ski area in the morning and returns in the afternoon. Another shuttle ($17.75 round-trip) runs three times daily from mid-May to early October (weather permitting) between Yosemite Lodge and **Glacier Point** (*see* Scenic Drives and Views, *below*). Stops are well marked; just look for the SHUTTLE BUS signs along the main roads. From July until fall, an early-morning backpackers' shuttle ($3.75) runs once daily between Yosemite Lodge and **Crane Flat.** Call a visitor center for schedules.

## WHERE TO SLEEP

Camping is the way to go: Not only are the hotels completely characterless and packed with tourists, they also charge handsomely for the privilege of four thin walls and a sagging bed. Whatever you decide, reservations are highly—repeat: very, very, very highly—recommended; beds and campsites go like hotcakes, especially in summer and fall.

**HOTELS AND CABINS** Hotel reservations can be made up to 366 days in advance and, believe it or not, most places actually fill up that far ahead. Hotel, lodge, and cabin reservations are all handled through **Yosemite Concessions** (5410 E. Home Ave., Fresno 93727, tel. 209/252–4848). Because Yosemite is so mobbed, you probably won't have a choice when it comes to your hotel accommodations. If you can find a single vacancy, consider yourself lucky.

That said, most people prefer the **Yosemite Lodge** (in Yosemite Valley, 5 mi east of Hwy. 140 entrance, tel. 209/372–1274), which has pleasant cabins with shared bath starting at $53 year-round. Each additional person costs an extra $6. Accommodations in **Curry Village** (east end of Yosemite Valley, tel. 209/372–1233) include canvas tent cabins (starting at $33 in winter, $37 in summer) and simple wood cabins ($53 year-round, $72 with private bath). The fee for each extra person in the tent cabins is $5, in the wood cabins $6. Otherwise, look for the shantytown called **Housekeeping Camp** (east end of valley, tel. 209/252–4848) in the valley; here 282 identical cement-and-canvas "tent" units huddle close together, separated only by paper-thin walls. They're not particularly comfortable, but each bare-bones structure houses up to four people for only $39 per night (extra cots are $4 more). The camp is open from mid-March to late October. A grocery store, laundry, bathroom, and showers are nearby.

**CAMPING** Yosemite's developed campgrounds share a number of characteristics: They're all large, flat, near a major road, and shaded by pine trees. Most have picnic tables, fire pits, flush toilets, piped water, and food-storage lockers, but none have direct access to showers (for that, you'll have to head to Housekeeping Camp or Curry Village). All but Tanerac, Yosemite Creek, and Porcupine have wheelchair access. Unfortunately, they're all extremely crowded, especially the ones in the valley. You may get lucky and find an open site during the off-season, but otherwise reservations are a must unless you want to try your luck at one of the first-come, first-served sites. Campground reservations are available up to 8 weeks in advance; contact **MISTIX** (tel. 800/365–CAMP) to secure a place. If you're stuck, show up at one of the reservation kiosks (in Curry Village, Big Oak Flat, Tuolumne Meadows, or Yosemite Village) between 8 and 10 AM, and put your name on the waiting list in case there's a cancellation.

*"During summer months," claims a guidebook to Yosemite, "population density in the campgrounds is higher than in Calcutta's most crowded neighborhoods." The only difference, it seems, is that here you have to make a reservation at least eight weeks in advance.*

In Yosemite Valley, **Upper Pines** is the biggest campground, with 238 tent and RV sites ($14) available March–November. It's conveniently located at Shuttle Stop 15, near trailheads to Mirror Lake and Vernal Fall. Misanthropes be warned: This place gets extremely crowded and the RVs pack together like sardines. Across the street at Shuttle Stop 19, **Lower Pines** is open year-round, with 172 tent and RV sites ($14) sandwiched between the Merced River and Storeman Meadow. Expect the same pack of RVs and families you see at Upper Pines. **Upper River Campground,** between Curry Village and Yosemite Valley at Shuttle Stop 2, is the sole valley campground reserved for tents only. Open April–October, it's notably quieter than its counterparts. Some of the 124 sites ($14) lie near the Merced River. The nicest views (particularly of the Merced River and Yosemite Falls) can be found across the way at **Lower River Campground,** with 126 sites ($14)—but the views may not make up for the hordes of screaming brats who overrun the beach.

Outside the valley, look for **Tuolumne Meadows,** an enormous creekside campground perfect for exploring the eastern side of the park. Its 314 sites ($12) lie along Tioga Pass Road (Hwy. 120) and are usually open July–October. This campground, in some of the park's most beautiful country, attracts its share of day hikers, but it's still one of the last to fill up. **Hodgdon Meadow**—just past the Highway 120 entrance on the west side of the park—allows you to escape the chaos of the valley and still remain within striking distance (30–40 min). It draws nature-loving car campers year-round, except when snow closes the road (sometimes until late spring).

If you can't get a reservation at any of the major campgrounds, there are a few first-come, first-served sites you can try. In particular, check out the valley's only walk-in campground, **Sunnyside,** located about 1 mile west of Yosemite Village on Highway 140. In the '70s, Sunnyside was known to host a certain Bay Area crowd in between Dead shows. Today, it's the favorite of a new kind of subculture: the world's most hardcore rock climbers. Sunnyside has 35 sites ($3 per person) with running water and toilets. For walk-ins outside the valley, try **Tuolumne Meadows** (*see above*), where 25 sites are reserved for backpackers and visitors without vehicles. Tuolumne also reserves half its sites for same-day reservations; check the visitor center (either in the valley or in Tuolumne) for availability. Other walk-ins include **Wawona** (Hwy. 41, south end of park), with 100 sites ($10); **White Wolf** (Tioga Pass Rd., about 10 mi east of Crane Flat), with 87 sites ($10); **Porcupine Flat,** with 52 sites ($6); and **Yosemite Creek,** with 75 sites ($6). The last two are both off Tioga Pass Road east of White Wolf. Keep in mind that all the Tioga Pass Road campgrounds close in winter, usually mid-September or early October to early June. For info on backcountry camping, *see* Longer Hikes, *below.*

## FOOD

If you plan on camping, bring as much food as possible. Prices in Yosemite's stores (*see* Basics, *above*) are considerably higher than in the towns outside the park. A dull variety of American eateries—from fast-food cafeterias to expensive sit-down restaurants—is the only other choice.

The **Yosemite Village** complex, 7 miles east of the Highway 140 entrance, has the largest selection of food in the park. The **Pasta Place** (Shuttle Stop 5, tel. 209/372–8381), open daily 11:30 AM–9 PM, is a cafeteria-style restaurant with basic pasta-with-sauce plates (from $4.60) to choose from. If you have the cash, you might want to stuff yourself with the dinner special

($9–$10): a full pasta plate, Caesar salad, bread, and a large drink. Also in Yosemite Village is **Degnana's Deli** (tel. 209/372–8454), open daily 7 AM–9 PM; they have sandwiches ($4–$5), salads ($2–$4), and picnic supplies. Next door, **Degnana's Pizza and Ice Cream Parlor** (tel. 209/372–8437), open daily 9–9 in summer and daily 10–7 in winter, is the place to grab a slice of cheese pizza ($1.25).

In **Curry Village** (tel. 209/372–8333), on the west side of the valley near Happy Isles, there's a cafeteria, a small pizzeria, and a burger stand. None is particularly appetizing, but the cafeteria does have cheap burgers, sandwiches, and breakfasts (under $5). It's open 7–10 for breakfast, 11:45–1:30 for lunch, and 5:30–8 for dinner between April and October. Don't go out of your way for the pizzeria's merely tolerable slices ($2).

## EXPLORING YOSEMITE

It can take anywhere from one day to the rest of your life to familiarize yourself with Yosemite. Realistically, you'll need at least a few days to venture beyond the crowds. To get a good overview, drive along **Tioga Pass Road** (Hwy. 120), stopping to take a walk or a hike wherever you're inclined: Scores of trails—from relaxing strolls to highly demanding backcountry excursions—meander through the park. Many trailheads are easily reached by shuttle bus (*see* Getting Around, *above*).

**ORIENTATION AND TOURS** The **Yosemite Valley Visitor Center** (*see* Basics, *above*) offers a worthwhile slide program on the park's geography and history. The free 20-minute show runs on the hour 10–3:30 Monday–Saturday and noon–3:30 Sunday. Also look for the center's documentaries on John Muir and Ansel Adams, shown in the late afternoon and evenings (call for schedules). Ranger programs such as nature walks and storytelling last anywhere from 1 to 3 hours and are great ways to learn more about the park.

All kinds of guided bus tours originate in the valley, from 2-hour excursions ($14) along the valley floor (every ½ hr daily 9–4) to a day-long grand tour ($40) of Mariposa Grove and Glacier Point (late spring to early fall). For reservations, contact the **Yosemite Lodge Tour Desk** (tel. 209/372–1274) or go to one of the tour booths at Curry Village, the Ahwahnee Hotel, or the Village Store in Yosemite Village.

**SHORT HIKES** **Yosemite Falls,** also known simply as "The Fall," is the highest waterfall in North America and the fifth-highest in the world. It's divided into the upper falls (1,430 ft), the middle cascades (675 ft), and the lower falls (320 ft). From the parking lot, a ⅕-mile, wheelchair-accessible trail leads to the base, and a second 2-mile trail leads to the lower falls. To reach the top, head to Sunnyside Campground and take the strenuous 3½-mile (one-way) **Yosemite Falls Trail,** which rises over 2,700 feet. The views from the top are breathtaking. If you're not up to the full trek (2–4 hrs round-trip), stop at **Columbia Rock** 1½ miles along the trail. You'll still get a good workout, with dizzying vistas of Half Dome and the valley. Get off at Shuttle Stop 7 and follow signs to the trailhead.

*Don't miss Soda Springs—a potable, naturally carbonated spring on an easy half-mile trail in idyllic Tuolumne Meadows. In 1863, William Brewer of the California Geologic Survey called its water "pungent and delightful," though a more recent visitor said, "It tastes like flat seltzer."*

The easy and popular 3-mile trail around **Mirror Lake** (Shuttle Stop 17), at the east end of the valley, offers some of the best photo opportunities in Yosemite. Beware of camera-toting tourists here: The trail is the gentlest in the park, so nearly everyone takes it. From the Happy Isles Trailhead (Shuttle Stop 16), the difficult 6-mile trail to **Vernal Fall** (317 ft) and **Nevada Fall** (594 ft) takes 2 to 3 hours, but the view from the top is phenomenal. The first half of the trail (aptly named **Mist Trail**) is a great place to soak yourself on a hot day—bring a bathing suit or rain gear, and kiss your hairdo goodbye. A fantastic overnight hike continues past Nevada Fall to Half Dome (*see* Longer Hikes, *below*). If you arrive in Yosemite along Highway 41, your first view of the valley will be at **Bridalveil Falls,** a ragged 620-foot cascade that's often blown by the wind as far as 20 feet from side to side. The Ahwahneechee called it *Pohono* (Puffing Wind). An easy ⅕-mile trail leading to its base starts from the overlook parking lot.

Numerous, relatively uncrowded day hikes begin at **Tuolumne Meadows** (*see* Where to Sleep, *above*), including an easy half-mile trail through the meadow to **Soda Springs,** and a lovely but arduous (3 hrs, 5 mi round-trip) hike that weaves through mountain hemlock and lodgepole pine to emerald **Elizabeth Lake.** If you want to camp, you'll need a permit (*see box, below*).

**LONGER HIKES** There are hundreds of day hikes in Yosemite, but to beat the crowds you'll need to do some serious backpacking in the wilderness, miles away from the stench of civilization. All trails are limited to a certain number of backpackers to prevent overuse, and free wilderness permits are required for overnight stays (*see box, below*). With a permit, you can take any of 70 trails (5–20 miles long) crisscrossing Yosemite's outback. These often involve strenuous climbs along jagged paths no more than a foot wide, and some trails take upward of a week to complete. Fire rings are interspersed along the way, but you'll need to bring your own tent and provisions, including a water filter or iodine tablets to treat stream water. You can rent special 3-pound bear-proof food canisters ($3) from any ranger station. Order maps and a pamphlet of hiking suggestions from the **Yosemite Association Bookstore** (Box 230, Yosemite 95389, tel. 209/379–2648), and pick up topographical maps at the Wilderness Center in Yosemite Village.

If you're in top physical condition, take the hike out of Yosemite Valley to **Half Dome.** Follow the trail to Nevada Fall (*see* Short Hikes, *above*), and continue past Little Yosemite Campground to the Half Dome turnoff; then climb and climb and climb until you've risen nearly 5,000 feet. This trip (10–12 hrs, 17 mi round-trip) is not for those with vertigo or weak wills. You can make it an overnighter by camping at **Little Yosemite Campground,** but you'll need a wilderness permit (*see box, below*). You might leave your pack at the campground and climb the last 8½ miles without extra weight. Truly intrepid hikers have the option of hanging a right, past the Half Dome turnoff, onto the **John Muir Trail** and schlepping 222 miles south to Mt. Whitney.

**Hetch Hetchy,** one of California's largest reservoirs, has irked conservationists since it was built early in the century. Environmentalists like John Muir fought actively against the damming of the Tuolumne River, which, he argued, would irreparably harm the region's wildlife. But politicians in San Francisco wanted mountain-fresh drinking water. Can you guess who won? Today, despite the massive Hetch Hetchy dam, the area retains much of its beauty, and it contains the

## *Bucking the System in Yosemite's Backcountry*

***In the 19th century, visitors used to pay for the privilege of hiking the Yosemite Falls Trail, but the days are long gone when only the wealthy could trek through the park. Now, hordes of wilderness enthusiasts crowd the backcountry every year—so many that in 1972 the park had to institute a permit system to limit the number of backpackers on the trails each day. For the uninitiated, here's how the system works:***

***Half the permits are distributed on a first-come, first-served basis a day in advance at any of the park's six ranger stations. These permits—particularly for popular areas such as the valley and Tuolumne Meadows—go quickly (some in just 5 minutes), so arrive early the day before your hike with a detailed itinerary, including trails and estimated overnight stopping points. Permits are free, but if you're looking to make reservations—available by mail March 1–May 31—you'll need to pay a reservation fee of $3 and send your dates of arrival and departure. You must also include specific trailheads for entry and exit, your main destination in the park, the number in your party, and alternative dates if your first choices aren't available. Write to the Wilderness Office (Box 577, Yosemite 95389, tel. 209/372–0310).***

wonderfully isolated, moderately difficult **Rancheria Falls Trail** (13 mi round-trip), which leads to the eponymous lonely falls. You can do this trail in a day. If you have more time (5 days) and excellent backpacking skills, go for the 52-mile **Rancheria Mountain and Bear Valley Loop,** a strenuous hike that offers a terrific view of the Grand Canyon of the Tuolumne River, as well as plenty of secluded camping around Bear Valley Lake. To reach the Rancheria Falls Trailhead, exit the west side of the park on Tioga Pass Road (Hwy. 120), turn right on Evergreen Road after 1 mile, and continue for 8 miles (you'll see signs).

The area north of the Tuolumne River is wild and pristine—a good place to get away from it all. The numerous trailheads near Tuolumne Meadows are great for backpackers who want to spend at least a few days in the wilderness. Serious hikers should consider the **Tuolumne Grand Canyon Trail** (accessed from either Tuolumne Meadows or Lake Tanaya), a harrowing switchback leading 2 miles down into the canyon, 8 miles across, and 2 miles up the far side. This strenuous hike requires at least 2 full days. Another popular trip out of Tuolumne Meadows from the John Muir Trailhead is an excellent 2- to 3-day hike (about 30 mi round-trip) that leads up to **Vogelsang Lake.** Hike up Lyell Fork on the John Muir Trail to the **Rafferty Creek Trail,** which becomes steep and difficult. This is a popular trip, so get your permits early (*see box, above*).

*On the way to Tuolumne (traveling east on Tioga Pass Road), check out the overlook at Olmstead Point—you get a full view of Cloud's Rest (elev. 9,926) and the eastern side of Half Dome.*

**SCENIC DRIVES AND VIEWS** During summer you can drive up to **Glacier Point** for a spectacular view of the valley and surrounding mountains. The 16-mile road starts at Chinquapin campground (take Hwy. 41 from the south or Hwy. 120 from the west). Better yet, take a shuttle (*see* Getting Around, *above*) to the top and hike **4 Mile Trail** back down into the valley (3 hrs). **Tuolumne Meadows,** the largest subalpine meadow in the High Sierra and the site of several backcountry trailheads, is on Tioga Pass Road, 25 miles west of Lee Vining and U.S. 395. This is a gorgeous part of Yosemite, with delicate meadows surrounded by huge granite formations, and it's normally much less crowded than the valley. Tioga Pass Road is closed during winter, and usually opens by late May or early June.

## PARK ACTIVITIES

For those who want to take it easy, the National Park Service rents binoculars ($3 a day) for **bird-watching.** Free 1½-hour **photography walks,** which lead you to prime spots for shooting Yosemite, leave daily around 8:30 AM from the Yosemite Lodge or the Ahwahnee Hotel. In winter, rangers lead free **snowshoe tours**; you can rent snowshoes ($7 a day) from most lodges. **Horseback rides** originate at the stables near Mirror Lake; a 4-hour trip to Vernal Fall is $44. In summer, you can take a leisurely 3-mile float (they call it "rafting") down the Merced for $12.50. Sign up at the **rafting** area in Curry Village, open daily 10–4. For more info on all these activities, consult the *Yosemite Guide* or check with the visitor center (tel. 209/372–0299).

**BIKING** Bikes are not permitted on any hiking trails, but Yosemite Valley has 8 miles of paved bike paths. Try the spectacular trail to Happy Isles and Mirror Lake, off the road to Curry Village; the easy 3-mile loop takes well under an hour unless you stop for the half-mile walk to Mirror Lake. Rent bikes ($5 an hour, $16 a day) from **Curry Village** (tel. 209/372–8333) or **Yosemite Lodge** (tel. 209/372–1274). Serious bikers should consider the 15-mile round-trip from Tuolumne Meadows to Olmstead Point along Tioga Pass Road. The grades are difficult and the roads narrow, but the views are spine-chilling.

**ROCK CLIMBING** Look around for 2 seconds and you'll understand why Yosemite is a mecca for world-class rock climbers. Basic and intermediate lessons ($120 for one, $85 each for two, $60 each for three to five people) are offered year-round by the **Yosemite Mountaineering School and Guide Service** (tel. 209/372–8344). In summer only, they organize trips from Tuolumne Meadows. Unfortunately, you can't rent equipment in the park without enrolling in a class.

**SKIING** Yosemite's ski season usually lasts from late November or early December to March. Call 209/372–4605 for weather conditions.

➢ **DOWNHILL** • Yosemite has a small ski area, **Badger Pass** (tel. 209/372–8430), that won't pose much of a challenge to accomplished skiers. It's a good place to learn, however, and there are enough relatively uncrowded trails to keep intermediate skiers entertained (three advanced lifts and six intermediate). It's open daily 9–4:30 in winter. Lift tickets cost $25–$30, ski rentals are $18 a day, snowboards $30 a day. Look for Badger Pass 6 miles east of Highway 41 on Glacier Point Road. For 24-hour snow conditions, call 209/372–1000.

➢ **CROSS-COUNTRY** • Yosemite has 90 miles of cross-country trails through the Badger Pass ski area to Glacier Point. A free skiers' shuttle from the valley runs to Badger Pass, departing in the morning and returning in the afternoon. **Glacier Point Road** is a good place to start: Beginners will enjoy the groomed track and advanced skiers will get a workout if they make the whole 21-mile round-trip. The **Cross-Country Ski School** (tel. 209/327-8444) offers 2-hour lessons ($18) and 4-hour lessons ($40, including rentals). A guided overnight trip—with meals and lodging—is $110. Badger Pass (*see above*) has rentals ($9 half day, $13 full day). The **Tuolumne Grove of Giant Sequoias Trail** (3 mi round-trip), which starts at Crane Flat a few miles east of the Big Oak Flat entrance station, has a steep drop, but you get to ski among the largest living things on earth.

# Near Yosemite

## STANISLAUS NATIONAL FOREST

Encompassing a sizable chunk of the Sierra Nevada—more than a million acres in all—just northwest of Yosemite, Stanislaus National Forest offers steep peaks, deep valleys, tranquil meadows, scores of mountain streams and lakes, and free camping (with a fire permit) anywhere within forest boundaries. The backcountry, particularly the **Emigrant** and **Carson-Iceberg wildernesses,** has hiking trails that are significantly less crowded than Yosemite's, and the required permits can be obtained on the day of the hike. Stanislaus is also an excellent choice for mountain biking and fishing (*see* Forest Activities, *below*), besting Yosemite in both number and quality of sites. But although there are plenty of places in Stanislaus to commune with Mother Nature tête-à-tête, those looking to do so should avoid the resort communities of **Pinecrest** and **Lake Alpine** between June and September.

During winter, Stanislaus has cross-country and downhill skiing and snowmobiling, but you'll have to stay in a hotel or by the side of the road; developed campgrounds are open only between May and October. Before you venture into the park, pick up a copy of the free *Summit Passage,* available at the Summit Ranger Station in Pinecrest (*see below*), for detailed descriptions of activities and programs in Stanislaus.

**VISITOR INFORMATION** All ranger stations offer camping and lodging suggestions, hiking and road maps ($3), and free wilderness and campfire permits. The **central station** is in Sonora (19777 Greenley Rd., tel. 209/532–3671). Otherwise, contact **Summit Ranger Station** (Hwy. 108, in Pinecrest, tel. 209/965–3434); **Calaveras Ranger Station** (Hwy. 4, in Hathaway Pines, tel. 209/795–1381); **Groveland Ranger Station** (Hwy. 120, in Groveland, tel. 209/962–7825); or **Mi-Wuk Ranger Station** (Hwy. 108, in Mi-Wuk Village, tel. 209/586–3234). All are open at least 8 AM–4 PM Monday–Saturday (Groveland and Calaveras closed winter Saturdays). On Sundays and holidays, try the Summit and Mi-Wuk stations.

**GENERAL STORES** In the forest, the **Pinecrest Market** (401 Pinecrest Lake Rd., in Pinecrest, tel. 209/965–3661) is well-stocked and has lower prices than others in the area. The market is open summer, daily 7 AM–11 PM; winter, daily 9–6. Beyond this, though, it's best to stock up on the way in. Sonora (*see* Chapter 6), about 10 miles west of Stanislaus on Highway 108, has a few stores that sell camping gear; **Sonora Mountaineering** (173 S. Washington St., tel. 209/532–5621), open Monday–Saturday 9:30–6 and Sunday noon–5, is heads above the rest. For general supplies, head south on Washington Street, Sonora's main thoroughfare, and turn left on Mono Way, where you'll find two shopping centers, a 24-hour **Safeway** and a **Payless** drugstore.

**COMING AND GOING** Three highways traverse Stanislaus in a roughly east–west direction: **Highway 4** to the north, **Highway 108** in the middle, and **Highway 120,** which connects Stanislaus with San Francisco and Yosemite (to the south). Before heading to the high country, check road conditions at the ranger station in Sonora or Calaveras, or call 800/427–ROAD for recorded information—the mountain passes are sometimes closed until late June because of ice and snow. Driving time from San Francisco to Stanislaus (via Hwy. 120) is 3½ hours; from both Stockton (via Hwy. 4) and Modesto (via Hwy. 108) it's 2 hours. **Tuolumne County Transit** (tel. 209/532–0404) runs buses ($1.25) weekdays only from Sonora into Stanislaus National Forest, passing through the towns of Mi-Wuk, Sierra Village, and Twain Harte.

**WHERE TO SLEEP** If none of the following options strike your fancy, the town of Sonora (*see* Chapter 6) has more choices. Within the forest, a number of "resorts" with cabins or cottages allow you to get that rustic feeling without actually camping. One of the cheaper resorts, **Kennedy Meadows** (Hwy. 108, near Sonora, tel. 209/965–3900 or 209/532–9096 in winter) has 18 comfortable cabins for $45–$105. From December to February, **Pinecrest Lake Resort** (Hwy. 108, tel. 209/965–3400) offers a ski package that includes dinner, a lift ticket, and lodging for $50.

Hidden in 20 acres of majestic pines just beyond the forest's western border, the **Mi-Wuk Motor Lodge** (Hwy. 108, Mi-Wuk Village, tel. 209/586–3031 or 800/341–8000) offers doubles with TV, brass beds, and pine furniture for $40–$85 (pricier rooms have Jacuzzis and fireplaces). A new spa, a heated pool, and barbecue equipment are on the premises.

➢ **CAMPING** • To temporarily free yourself from the bonds of civilization, simply find an appealing spot at least 100 feet off any paved road and pitch your tent. If you plan to have a fire of any kind—including a camp stove—you'll need to pick up a fire permit from one of the ranger stations first (*see* Visitor Information, *above*). If this sounds like too much trouble, Stanislaus also has dozens of developed campgrounds, ranging in cost from free to $15.

All developed sites except those at popular **Pinecrest** (near Summit Ranger Station on Hwy. 108) are first come, first served. Should you want to contend for one of Pinecrest's 199 sites ($12.50), open May–October, call the **U.S. Forest Service Reservation Center** (tel. 800/280–CAMP) up to 120 days in advance. But you'd do better—in terms of your pocketbook and your search for quiet beauty—to go elsewhere. For ideas, ask at a ranger station for the free brochure "Camping in Stanislaus Forest."

In a secluded, pine-studded meadow 14 miles east of Pinecrest lies small **Mill Creek Campground** (Hwy. 108, tel. 209/965–3434). Sites are only $4, and it's next to a creek, as promised in the name. Also on Highway 108, **Fraser Flat Campground** (4 mi west of Pinecrest on Hwy. 108, tel. 209/586–3234) is terrific for fishing or just hanging out near the south fork of the Stanislaus River. Sites, including two with wheelchair access, go for $8.

**Carlon Campground.** This quiet, free campground 1 mile west of Yosemite off Highway 120 is a great place to escape the famous park's pricey camps, though during summer it fills quickly with Yosemite overflow. If you cross the bridge just past the entrance and follow the trail along the stream for 30–45 minutes, you'll find a small waterfall and a series of natural pools. *Evergreen Rd., east of Hwy. 120, tel. 209/962–7825. Barbecue pits, chemical toilets, drinking water, picnic tables.*

**FOOD** Expect to encounter standard burger and steak joints in the forest's small smattering of restaurants. The **Mutt House Café** (24262 Hwy. 108, Sugar Pine, tel. 209/586–4067) is one of these, but at least it's cheap. Try the $3 special: a quarter-pound hamburger with all the fixings, surprisingly good french fries, and a drink. Farther up the road, past Mi-Wuk Village, the **Pie in the Sky Pizzeria** (Hwy. 108, Sierra Village, tel. 209/586–4251) caters to truckers in summer and downhill skiers in winter. Pizza and a beer will run you just under $10. Along Highway 4, look for the **Bear Valley Deli** (tel. 209/753–2301), open only from Thanksgiving to Easter; homemade soups cost $5 and sandwiches go for $3–$5. One of the only exceptions to the greasy-spoon norm is **The Strawberry Inn** (31888 Hwy. 108, Strawberry, tel. 209/965–3662). Try a California-style omelet (artichoke hearts, mushrooms, mozzarella, $5.95) for breakfast, but skip dinner, when the food doesn't quite merit the prices.

**EXPLORING STANISLAUS** To get a sense of Stanislaus's often dramatic terrain, take a drive on Highway 4 or Highway 108, both of which traverse the 77-mile-wide forest west to east. Along the way you'll find dozens of turnouts with excellent views and trailheads for day hikes. On Highway 4, stop at **Calaveras Big Trees State Park,** 10 miles into the forest, which has some 150 giant sequoias. You can enjoy them in relative solitude on the 5-mile, 3-hour **South Grove Loop**; the hordes take the easier and shorter **North Grove Loop.** For stellar views of the area, follow Highway 120 to Sonora Pass and hike in either direction up the steep **Pacific Crest Trail.** On clear days, you'll see Mt. Diablo (about 40 mi northeast of San Francisco) to the west and Utah's Salt Lake Desert to the east.

*Be prepared for the humbling effect these tall trees will have on you. As one resident put it, "When you feel too big for your britches, come out here. The redwoods will bring you back down to size."*



If you have a few days for exploring, try one of Stanislaus's three well-preserved wilderness areas. Before setting out, plan a specific route and obtain a wilderness permit and topo maps ($3) from any ranger station. On the eastern fringes of Stanislaus, the 113,000-acre **Emigrant Wilderness** is the most popular, though solitude can still be found among its lakes, rushing streams, granite-walled domes and canyons, and old-growth pine and cedar forests. The **Gianelli Cabin Trail** is a steep half-mile ascent to **Burst Rock,** which offers spectacular views. For some serious backpacking, continue along **Burst Rock Trail** about 7 miles to **Crabtree Trail** and into the great beyond.

The **Mokelumne Wilderness** straddles the border between the Stanislaus and Eldorado national forests; its relatively level landscape generously accommodates easy-to-moderate hikes on trails originating along Highway 4 at **Lake Alpine, Woodchuck Basin,** and **Sandy Meadow.** In contrast, the 160,000-acre **Carson-Iceberg Wilderness,** with its steep ridges, narrow valleys, and lava-formed mountain peaks is less accessible and therefore less popular. Nonetheless, committed hikers enjoy the 8-mile (one-way) **Clark Fork Meadow Trail,** beginning at St. Mary's trailhead on Highway 108 at the eastern edge of the forest, and ending at Clark Fork Road. The truly hard-core hiker can attempt the arduous, all-day climb to **Mt. Disaster Peak** (elev. 10,046). Maps, information, and the required wilderness permits for this hike are available at the Summit Ranger Station (*see* Visitor Information, *above*).

**FOREST ACTIVITIES** Any of Stanislaus's dirt roads are fair game for mountain bikers, but most people stick to the Calaveras Ranger District, off Highway 4. The folks at **Bear Valley Mountain Bikes** (Hwy. 4, Bear Valley, tel. 209/753–2834) rent bikes ($17 half day, $27 full day); you can also purchase a bike trail guide ($3.25) here. A good introduction to the area's bike trails is the 3-mile **Lake Alpine Loop,** which circles Duck Lake. The loop is accessible from Silver Valley campground next to Lake Alpine off Highway 4.

Stanislaus is also one of the Sierra's most popular fishing destinations, with hundreds of streams and lakes stocked with trout. Pick up a list of 20 or so current favorites at the ranger stations. Among the mainstays are the South Fork of the **Stanislaus River** and **Pinecrest Lake,** both on Highway 108; and **Mosquito Lake** and the **Mokelumne River,** both off Highway 4. Bring your own gear, as rental equipment is nonexistent. In winter, **Dodge Ridge Ski Resort** (Hwy. 108, near Pinecrest, tel. 209/965–3474) attracts intermediate skiers to its seven lifts and 29 runs. Lift tickets are $30 and rentals $18. Snowboarders are permitted, but rent equipment elsewhere—Dodge Ridge charges a whopping $40.

## SIERRA NATIONAL FOREST

The proximity of Sierra National Forest to the city of Fresno seems a miracle of sorts. After an hour's drive, the landscape transforms from a vast expanse of car dealerships and tract houses into lakes and coniferous forests, a blessing to valley residents and visitors alike. Unfortunately, this stroke of geological good fortune has resulted in heavy use and extensive development around the bigger lakes and reservoirs, specifically **Bass, Shaver,** and **Huntington lakes.** Still, Sierra National Forest, which lies between Yosemite and Sequoia/Kings Canyon National Parks, is great for a day trip or weekend getaway. Even backpackers craving isolation can find a niche here. In contrast to the extensive development in the western part of the forest, almost the entire eastern half is protected wilderness: the **Ansel Adams Wilderness,** the **Dinkey Lakes Wilderness,** the **John Muir Wilderness,** and the **Kaiser Wilderness.**

The western areas, including **Pine Flat Reservoir** and **Kerckhoff** and **Redinger lakes,** lie at lower elevations and have camping and hiking opportunities year-round. Temperatures climb into the 90s during summer, so try to hit the forest in spring or fall, when both crowds and the blistering sun are less of a problem. The higher elevations (above 5,000 ft) are generally closed November–March due to snow, but by mid-May the camping season is usually in full swing, and lower temperatures make it worth the extra climb. The best time to visit the high country is July–early September, when the snow has melted and the wildflowers are in bloom.

**VISITOR INFORMATION** For info on camping, hiking, and other activities, as well as back-country fire and wilderness permits, stop by one of the ranger stations in the park's western corridor: **Oakhurst/Mariposa Ranger Station** (43060 Hwy. 41, at Batterson Workstation in Oakhurst, tel. 209/683–4665); **Minarets Ranger Station** (in North Fork, tel. 209/877–2218); **Pineridge Ranger District Office** (29688 Aubery Rd., in Prather, tel. 209/855–5360); and **Trimmer/Kings River Ranger Station** (34849 Maxon Rd., near Pine Flat Reservoir, tel. 209/855–8321). All are open weekdays 8–4:30; on weekends, try Minaret or Pineridge. You'll also find a number of smaller ranger stations near major trailheads. If you're coming to Sierra from the west, stop for info at the **Sierra National Forest Supervisor's Office** (1600 Tollhouse Rd./Hwy. 168 in Clovis, tel. 209/297–0706), 15 minutes east of Fresno; it's also open weekdays 8–4:30. For regional road and weather information, call 209/683–4665.

**GENERAL STORES** Shaver Lake and Bass Lake, two overdeveloped resort areas, have sporting-goods shops and grocery stores, as well as restaurants, gas stations, and lodging. In Shaver Lake, locals recommend the **Red Barn** (42300 Tollhouse Rd., tel. 209/841–3341), a glorified hardware/sporting-goods store. Next door you'll find **Monika's Second Time Around** (tel. 209/841–2514), a thrift store chock-full of treasures to barter for. You'll save money, though, by shopping in Fresno or smaller valley towns like Clovis before coming to the mountains. In Clovis, check out the competitive prices at **Peacock Market** (Tollhouse Rd. at Sunnyside Ave., tel. 209/299–6627).

**COMING AND GOING** There's no public transportation into the forest, so forget about it if you don't have a car. Also, Sierra National Forest is accessible only from the west; there are no through roads from U.S. 395 in the east. **Highway 168** (commonly referred to here as Tollhouse Rd.), the primary route from Fresno and nearby Clovis, runs northeast–southwest to Shaver Lake, Dinkey Creek, and Huntington Lake. South of Highway 168, east–west **Highway 180** links Fresno with Pine Flat Lake via Trimmer Springs Road, then continues into Kings Canyon National Park. **Highway 41** runs north from Fresno into the northern end of the forest; Oakhurst, the last major town, is less than 10 miles west of Bass Lake.

**WHERE TO SLEEP** If you lack camping equipment or if weather forces a retreat, **Camp Fresno** (53849 Dinkey Creek Rd., tel. 209/298–5632), 13 miles east of Shaver Lake in Dinkey Creek, rents rustic cabins with electricity and running water at an amazingly reasonable price: In summer, one-bedroom cabins that sleep up to six go for $22 a night, $110 a week; two-bedroom cabins that sleep up to eight fetch $36 a night, $205 a week. They're not particularly clean or comfortable, but at these prices no one seems to mind. Reservations must be made at least a week in advance, and non-Fresno residents can reserve a space only after May 1. The **Mono Hot Springs Resort** (Kaiser Pass Rd., near Mono Hot Springs, tel. 209/449–9054) offers similar accommodations, with the added bonus of a soak in their (human-made, unfortunately) hot springs. Two-person cabins at Mono start at $24.

➢ **CAMPING** • Sierra National Forest offers a variety of camping choices, from dispersed wilderness camping to crowded and loud developed campgrounds. The most popular (and annoying) areas for the latter are the banks of **Shaver, Huntington,** and **Bass lakes,** all of which generally require advance reservations year-round. Call the **U.S. Forest Service Reservation Center** (tel. 800/280–CAMP) for reservations. If you have no specific reason to be near the water, head for one of the smaller, less crowded high-country campgrounds. It's well worth the extra 15-minute drive to escape the din of RV generators and speedboats.

The **Mariposa Ranger District** is ideal as a base for excursions—by foot or car—into Yosemite. Dispersed camping (*also see* Camping, in Chapter 1) is allowed everywhere except around Bass Lake, making Mariposa a good backup in case Yosemite is booked solid. Call the ranger station (*see* Visitor Information, *above*) for info and fire permits. A series of primitive campgrounds (no running water) lines Sky Ranch Road, which extends east from Highway 41 about 5 miles north of Oakhurst. All of these secluded, shady spots provide tables, pit toilets, and barbecue pits. Even better, they're all free and no reservations are needed. The nicest of the seven campgrounds are **Nelder Grove, Big Sandy,** and **Little Sandy.**

In the **Minarets Ranger District** (*see* Visitor Information, *above*), head straight for **Clover Meadow** (Minaret Rd., at Beashore Rd.) and nearby **Granite Creek** (above Clover Meadow, north of Minaret Rd.)—two wonderfully secluded campgrounds on the edge of the Ansel Adams Wilderness. Clover Meadow has seven tent sites ($3) with drinking water, fire pits, tables, and toilets. Granite Creek has 20 free sites with the same amenities but no potable water, and it offers swimming. Plan to stay a few days; the drive is long. To get here from the town of North Fork (7 mi south of Bass Lake), follow the Sierra Vista Scenic Byway north on Minaret Road for about 1½ hours. Both first-come, first-served campgrounds are open June–October.

Secluded campgrounds and dispersed camping opportunities abound in the **High Sierra Ranger District** (tel. 209/877–3138). For true seclusion, try the 44 lovely sites ($12) at **Jackass Meadow Campground** on Florence Lake, off Kaiser Pass Road. Tables, stoves, toilets, and piped drinking water are at your disposal. **Vermilion Campground,** on Edison Lake off Kaiser Pass Road, has 31 sites ($12) with drinking water and nearby swimming. Call ahead (tel. 800/280–CAMP) to reserve at either site, especially on weekends in July and August when these campgrounds crawl with urban assault vehicles.

In the southernmost part of the forest (Pine Flat Reservoir and east along the Kings River), the **Kings River Ranger District** (tel. 209/855–8321) gets frightfully hot in the summer; dispersed camping here would be best in the spring or fall. If you follow Trimmer Springs Road along the Kings River to its end, you'll come across small **Kirch Flat** and **Garnet Dike campgrounds.** These free, no-frills sites lack facilities, but they're terrific escapes from the reservoir crowds; just be sure to pack in plenty of water. Northeast of Pine Flat Reservoir, temperatures drop as you make your way toward the Dinkey Lakes Wilderness off Highway 168. Camping, dispersed or developed, is especially good near the two high-country reservoirs, **Wishon** and **Courtright.**

**FOOD** Your best bet is to stock up on picnic supplies (*see* General Stores, *above*); otherwise you'll find only the occasional greasy spoon with slight variations on the burgers, fries, and black coffee theme. One exception is Shaver Lake's **Sierra House Restaurant** (Hwy. 168, tel. 209/841–3576), open weekdays 11–9 and weekends 11–10; they serve excellent pastas ($9) and monster-size burgers ($6).

**EXPLORING SIERRA NATIONAL FOREST** For weekend boaters, waterskiers, and anglers from the Central Valley, the forest's main attractions are its lakes (*see* Forest Activities, *below*). If water sports don't interest you, there are plenty of other ways to spend your days in the forest.

➢ **MARIPOSA RANGER DISTRICT** • The high-altitude Mariposa Ranger District, which borders Yosemite, contains **Nelder Grove,** home to over 100 giant sequoias. Here you'll find several short hiking trails, including the 1-mile **Shadow of the Giants Trail,** a self-guided hike with signs describing the ecology of giant sequoia trees. To reach Nelder Grove, take Highway 41 north from Oakhurst for 5 miles, turn east on Sky Ranch Road, and follow signs.

➢ **MINARETS RANGER DISTRICT** • In the northeast, the Minarets Ranger District contains a popular 100-mile drive known as the **Sierra Vista Scenic Byway.** From the town of North Fork, the byway makes an inspiring loop up Minaret Road, eventually taking you to Cold Springs Summit at 7,308 feet. The road is only open from June or July to September, and just 75% of it is paved, so make sure your car can take 25 miles of rough driving. You can make the drive in 5 hours, but there are plenty of places to camp and hike along the way. Halfway into the drive, the **Fernandez Trailhead** leads to a series of lakes, including the highly recommended **Madera Lakes,** 4 miles away. To reach the trailhead, take the byway to Clover Meadow Campground and follow signs.

*About a third of the way into the Sierra Vista Scenic Byway, stop at the Mile High Overlook—the views of the Ansel Adams, John Muir, and Kaiser wilderness areas will knock your socks off.*

Back in North Fork, you can learn about Mono Indian culture at the **Mono Indian Museum** (Hwy. 41, North Fork, tel. 209/877–2115), stocked with artifacts and cultural displays. Admission is $2 and the museum is open weekdays 9–4. The short **Mono Wind Nature Trail** (Rd. 209, 2 mi east of North Fork, tel. 209/877–2710) combines plants and flower gardens with exhibits on the culture, history, and gruesome extermination of the Mono. The staff asks that you call before coming, if possible.

➢ **PINERIDGE RANGER DISTRICT** • The Pineridge Ranger District cuts a wide swath through the middle of the forest, extending from Shaver Lake and Redinger Lake in the west to the John Muir and Dinkey Lake wilderness areas in the east. After a slow 45-minute drive from Huntington Lake on Kaiser Pass Road, you'll come to **Mono Hot Springs,** where short trails lead relaxation-seeking backpackers and friendly locals to the hot mineral baths. The **Mono Hot Springs Resort** (*see* Where to Sleep, *above*) offers a synthetic version of the springs, but the natural version is much more satisfying. On the way to Mono, ask at the High Sierra Ranger Station (near Edison Lake, off Hwy. 168, tel. 209/877–3138) about smaller springs, like **Little Eden** (1 mi past ranger station on left side of road just before small bridge). The folks here also issue wilderness permits and offer hiking suggestions for the many trails into the **John Muir Wilderness** from Edison and Florence lakes, a few miles east of Mono Hot Springs. With daunting granite formations, windswept pastures, small lakes, and incredible views, you can't go wrong on any trail, but a good day hike is the 4-mile trek from the Florence Lake Trailhead, on the north end of the lake, to **Crater Lake.**

➢ **KINGS RIVER RANGER DISTRICT** • Encompassing the southern portion of the forest from Shaver Lake in the west to the Dinkey Lakes Wilderness in the east, the terrain here varies widely: Chaparral and woodland vegetation surround **Pine Flat Reservoir** and **Kings River,** two popular water recreation spots; farther north, the elevation increases and the vegetation changes to ponderosa, black oak, and sugar pine, making for shadier and cooler summer camping. **Courtright** and **Wishon reservoirs** lie in the eastern portion of the district; many trails that head east into the high alpine terrain of the John Muir and Dinkey Lakes wildernesses begin here. The **Dinkey Lakes Trailhead,** off Dinkey Lakes Road from Shaver Lake, offers hikers a choice of scenic trails. One popular route is the 7-mile loop through alpine forests and past four lakes: first Dinkey, then Swede, Rainbow, and Mystery.

**FOREST ACTIVITIES** Mountain bikes are allowed on dirt roads but prohibited on hiking trails. You'll find some good, uncluttered roads off the **Sierra Vista Scenic Byway** (*see* Exploring, *above*). In Shaver Lake, **Four-Season** (41781 Tollhouse Rd., tel. 209/841–2224) rents bicycles for $5 an hour or $20 a day. **D&F Pack Station** (on Hwy. 168, ½ mi east of Kinnikinick Campground, tel. 209/893–3220) offers guided horseback rides June–October from Huntington Lake: Two-hour rides ($30) lead to nearby meadows; half-day rides ($50) go to Potter Pass and mountain lakes; and day-long trips ($75) follow the Kaiser Loop Trail (20 mi).

➢ **WATER SPORTS** • From kayaking to jet skiing, water sports are popular all around Sierra National Forest, especially at Bass, Shaver, and Huntington lakes. At Bass Lake, the **Pines Marina** (tel. 209/642–3565) rents Jet Skis ($50 an hour) and pedal boats ($15 an hour). The **Sierra Marina** (tel. 209/841–3324) at Shaver Lake rents fishing boats ($45 a day) and pontoons ($90 a day) April–September. **Rancheria Marina** (tel. 209/893–3234) at Huntington Lake rents fishing boats and pedal boats at comparable rates, as well as kayaks and canoes ($20 for two hours). At Huntington and Shaver lakes, **High Sierra Sailboards** (tel. 209/855–2534) rents Windsurfers ($20 an hour) and offers lessons ($45) for beginners. To run the Class III and IV rapids of Kings River, take a guided tour with **Kings River Expeditions** (tel. 209/233–4881) or **Zephyr River Expeditions** (tel. 209/532–6249), both based at Kirch Flat (*see* Camping, *above*).

➢ **SKIING** • **Sierra Summit** (tel. 209/233–2500), near Huntington Lake, is a downhill ski resort with five lifts. Advanced skiers may find the slopes disappointing, but beginners and intermediates should thoroughly enjoy themselves. Lift tickets are $30 on weekends, $22–$25 during the week. At the bottom of the mountain, the **Sierra Summit Inn** (tel. 209/233–1200) offers basic accommodations from $45 per night. **Goat Meadow,** near the town of Fish Camp, has cross-country trails into the southernmost part of Yosemite National Park. Get detailed maps and trail suggestions at the **Oakhurst Ranger Station** (*see* Visitor Information, *above*). **Tamarack Meadow,** on Highway 168 between Huntington and Shaver lakes, offers miles of marked trails and a plowed parking area. It's managed by the **Pineridge Ranger Station** (tel. 209/855–5360), which sells detailed maps ($3) of the area.

# The Eastern Sierra and Inyo National Forest

**Whether you approach from Yosemite** or Los Angeles, you're bound to be startled by the dramatic and austere beauty of the eastern slope of the Sierra Nevada. Inyo National Forest, which extends from Mono Lake in the north to Bakersfield in the south, is one of California's most diverse and unique national forests—the striking terrain ranges from piñon trees and sage in the lower elevations through mixed coniferous forests at mid-mountain to the lakes and meadows that abound above the timberline. The Eastern Sierra is also pitted with volcanic craters and explorable caves, especially around **Mono Lake,** one of the strangest-looking bodies of water in the world.

*Evidently not everyone feels at home in the wild volcanic landscape of the Eastern Sierra. Witness this entry in the Lee Vining visitor register: "Toto, we're not in Florida anymore. . . And we don't even have any ruby slippers."*

Most visitors are drawn by the resort town of **Mammoth Lakes.** In summer, crowds flock here for biking, backpacking, and fishing; in winter skiers congregate at Mammoth Mountain. The resort is usually overrun from December to April, though in recent years late snows and earthquakes have kept many visitors away. May is a great time to visit, as the town is just about empty. South of Mammoth on U.S. 395, the unavoidable town of **Bishop** provides a jumping-off point for exploring the stark White Mountains or rock climbing in the Owens River Gorge. The only other towns of note are **Lee Vining,** a 3-block-long metropolis with a few shoddy motels and greasy diners (worth mentioning only because it's near Mono Lake and Highway 120), and **Lone Pine,** 61 miles south of Bishop, which offers little more than a great 24-hour coffee shop and a base for folks heading out to nearby **Mt. Whitney**—the highest peak in the lower 48 states.

The hiking and camping season usually begins around May 15, when Highway 120 opens (weather permitting). Day hikers may find that the warm weather and volcanic terrain make for less attractive hiking than on the western side of the Sierra. But the relative absence of crowds here, even in summer, as well as the presence of some of the country's finest hot springs, more than makes up for the dust. Once snow starts falling, the roads become treacherous and the price of accommodations rises. If you can withstand these conditions, however, you'll be treated to some excellent skiing, though it can't compare to Tahoe.

## BASICS

**COMING AND GOING** **U.S. 395** cuts north–south through the Eastern Sierra and Inyo National Forest, connecting the region's major towns: Lee Vining, Mammoth Lakes, Bishop, Big Pine, and Lone Pine.

➢ **BY CAR** • To reach U.S. 395 from L.A., take **Highway 14** north to Mojave, where you pick up U.S. 395 north. From San Francisco, the trip is a bit more difficult. In summer (June/July–Sept./Oct.), it's easiest to access U.S. 395 at Lee Vining via **Highway 120** (Tioga Pass Rd.) through Yosemite. When snow closes Highway 120, the only choice is to take **I–80** east to Sacramento, then **U.S. 50** east to Lake Tahoe, where it meets U.S. 395. Before heading to the Eastern Sierra, check with **CalTrans** (tel. 800/427–ROAD) for road conditions.

Rental cars—including 4-wheel-drive jeeps—are available at **Yosemite Rent-a-Car** (Mammoth and Bishop airports, tel. 619/935–4471 or 800/510–2020), where economy cars rent for about $35 a day, 4-wheel-drives for $60 a day; and **U-Save Auto Rental** (550 Old Mammoth Rd., Mammoth Lakes, tel. 619/934–4168 or 800/272–U–SAV), with economy cars for $36 a day, 4-wheel-drives for $50 a day.

*This is bear territory, and unless your campground has bear-proof containers, you'll need to hang food, deodorant, and toothpaste at least 10 feet out from tree trunks and 12 feet off the ground. Pick up illustrated instructions on the counter-balance method (two sacks roped together and slung over a branch) at any ranger station.*

➢ **BY BUS** • **Greyhound** (tel. 800/231–2222) buses run once a day between Los Angeles and Reno, stopping in Lone Pine, Bishop, Mammoth, and Lee Vining along the way. The L.A.–Bishop leg (8 hrs each way) costs $62 round-trip, the Bishop–Reno leg (5 hrs each way) $66 round-trip. You'll want to spend as little time at the Bishop station as possible; unfriendly sorts hang about.

**CAMPING** In the vast Inyo National Forest, camping outside developed campgrounds, 100 feet from the nearest road or trail (*also see* Camping, in Chapter 1), is permitted above the 1941 watermark in the Mono Lake area and east and west of U.S. 395. Dispersed camping is not allowed in many areas; ask rangers for specifics, but a general rule of thumb is that where there is developed camping, dispersed camping is forbidden. Inquire about the "no fire" areas in Inyo; in any case, you'll need a fire permit, available at any ranger station (*see below*), if you plan to use a stove or build a campfire.

# Mono Lake

At the end of the thrilling 2,700-foot drop from Tioga Pass, where Highway 120 and U.S. 395 intersect, sits one of the eeriest bodies of water in the state. Even if you're short on time, spend a couple hours at Mono Lake. Start at **South Tufa Grove,** 5 miles south of Lee Vining off Highway 120, and follow the short self-guided nature trail. You wander among the spiny, fantastically colored tufa columns, formed when calcium in Mono's freshwater springs encounters carbonates in its salty and alkaline lake water. Normally the columns would remain underwater and out of sight but, since 1940, the level of Mono Lake has dropped 40 feet due to the L.A. water district's siphoning of four of the five streams that once fed the lake. The resulting damage to the lake's ecosystem has made it a favorite cause of California environmentalists—note the SAVE MONO LAKE bumper stickers on old Volvos and Volkswagens around the area. Much effort, and some progress, has been made to replenish the dying lake, which is three times saltier than the ocean, but so far it's been too little too late. Those in the know claim it will be several decades before Mono can once again sustain a hearty animal population. In the meantime, the **Mono Lake Committee** (tel. 619/647–6595) offers hour-long guided canoe trips ($15 per person) on the south shore, weekends mid-June–mid-September. Tours begin at 8, 9:30, and 11 AM; they fill up quickly, so reserve ahead.

Also check out **Navy Beach,** half a mile south of South Tufa Grove, for the most buoyant swimming this side of the Dead Sea. The saline-heavy lake can get crowded on weekends and holidays, but in the summer heat you may not care who's floating next to you. To explore **Panum Crater,** the area's most accessible volcano, take Highway 120 east from U.S. 395 toward Navy Beach for about 4 miles, then go left (north) at the nearly invisible PANUM CRATER sign. Take either the **Plug Trail** or the **Rim Trail,** both short and non-strenuous, and give yourself at least an hour to take in great views of the lake and the volcanic cones south of Mono. Ask at the Mono Basin Visitor Center (*see below*) for a current list of ranger-guided activities, including free sunset tours of creek restoration projects, as well as a 1½-hour discussion of the area's geology, plant life, and history. In winter, when Highway 120 closes, South Tufa Grove, Navy Beach, and Panum Crater are accessible only on cross-country skis.

**VISITOR INFORMATION** The friendly folk at the **Mono Basin Visitor Center and Ranger Station** (U.S. 395, ¼ mi north of Lee Vining, tel. 619/647–3044), open daily 9–5 in summer and 8–4:30 in winter, are helpful with information on Mono Lake happenings. The **Lee Vining Ranger Station** (Hwy. 120, 1 mi west of Lee Vining, tel. 619/647–6525), open weekdays 8–4:30, will help with maps, books, and tips on activities for the region in general.

**WHERE TO SLEEP AND EAT** In Lee Vining, the choices are slim but reasonable. The **Blue Skies Motel** (U.S. 395, at 2nd St., tel. 619/647–6440) is backpacker-friendly and offers standard rooms ($32 in winter, $55 in summer) as well as bare-bones cabins from $25. If you're looking for groceries, you might want to head to Mammoth Lakes (*see below*). For a hot meal, head to **Kellogg's** (U.S. 395, at Main St., tel. 619/647–6470), open 7:30 AM–9 PM, where a huge burger with fries and a salad costs only $6.

➢ **CAMPING** • In warm spring months, you're better off camping. **Lundy Lake Campground** (tel. 619/647–6525), open May–October, is a good spot to fish, hike, or begin a backpacking trip. Trailers are permitted, though, and most folks staying at Lundy have them. The 52 primitive (pit toilets) sites scattered among the trees near Lundy Lake go for $8 a night. Bring water; there's only stream water here. To get here from Lee Vining, take U.S. 395 north to the LUNDY CANYON sign and go west 3 miles. Another camping option is secluded **Sawmill Walk-In** (Hwy. 120, about 10 mi west of Lee Vining), just east of Tuolumne Meadows. It has 12 free walk-in sites, and is set in a meadow surrounded by rocky peaks. Just make sure to bring warm clothing: It gets pretty darn cold at 9,800 feet, even in summer. Sites include tables and vault toilets, but there's no drinking water (just a stream).

**OUTDOOR ACTIVITIES** North of Mono Lake on U.S. 395, **Lundy Canyon** has spectacular hiking trails that wind along alpine lakes, canyons, and jagged mountain ridges. If you follow the mile-long dirt road at the end of Lundy Canyon Road past Lundy Lake, you can pick up the **Lundy Canyon Trail** into the **Hoover Wilderness.** After 5 miles, you'll pass a pair of waterfalls and a number of beaver ponds, and farther on you'll cross Lundy Pass and reach Saddlebag Lake. The trip is 8–10 strenuous miles (4–6 hrs) one-way. For an overnight trip, you can camp at Saddlebag Lake. Otherwise, call **Dial-a-Ride** (tel. 619/872–1901 or 800/922–1930) to pick you up at Saddlebag and take you back to Lundy.

## NEAR MONO LAKE

**BODIE** Desolate and unforgiving ghost-town country lies off U.S. 395 about an hour north of Mono Lake. As you round the first switchback of Bodie Pass (where U.S. 395 makes a 180° turn), look to the right for a small dirt road. Follow it for a half mile, park your car, and walk to deserted **Rattlesnake Gulch,** a mining town that went bust in the 1890s. This is do-it-yourself exploration: No brochures, no tours—just a chunk of history, some startling rock formations and decrepit buildings, and a great view of Mono Lake. A few miles farther north on U.S. 395, you'll meet Highway 270 (sometimes closed in winter). Follow it east for 13 miles (3 of them on difficult dirt roads) to reach **Bodie Ghost Town and State Park** (tel. 619/647–6445), open year-round. It costs $5 to enter, but this is one of the best-preserved ghost towns in the state, complete with a small Chinatown and an abandoned mine shaft. An excellent, free history museum is open daily 9–6 from May to September. Park hours are 8 AM–7 PM in summer, 8–6 in fall and spring, and 9–4 in winter.

*Evidence of Bodie's wild past survives at the museum, where you can see the red light of town harlot Rosa May, which hung in her one-room "crib." She and her colleagues lived and worked on streets ironically nicknamed Maiden Lane and Virgin Alley.*

# Mammoth Lakes

The Mammoth Lakes Basin is a series of glacial lakes, with fishing, boating, and trail access to the John Muir Wilderness. The basin is the Disneyland of the outdoor world, with decent skiing, extraordinary mountain biking, rock climbing, canoeing and kayaking, plus horseback or llama tours, dogsled tours, and even bobsledding. For a literal overview of the area and a gorgeous day hike, try the moderately difficult 4½-mile (one-way) **Duck Pass Trail,** accessible from Coldwater Campground (*see* Where to Sleep, *below*). You have to negotiate a steep pass to reach Duck Lake, but the splendid views along the way should make the burning in your leg muscles subside.

*If you're driving or biking around Mammoth, be sure to check out the extraordinary 17-mile June Lake Loop, off U.S. 395 about 10 miles north of Mammoth. You'll pass a number of high-altitude lakes, including June Lake, in some of the Sierra's most spectacular mountain scenery.*

West of the town of Mammoth Lakes, at the end of Minaret Road (an extension of Hwy. 203), is **Devils Postpile National Monument,** a unique set of uniform rock columns formed by cooling lava less than 100,000 years ago—the blink of an eye in geologic time. From the parking lot, the monument is an easy half mile; after another 2 miles you'll come to the 101-foot **Rainbow Falls.** Nearby **Red's Meadow** affords access to the protected Ansel Adams Wilderness, a long stretch of mountainous terrain running along the western border of Inyo National Forest from Mono Lake to Mammoth. Check with ranger stations for wilderness permits and recommendations for extended backcountry treks.

You'll get an incredible silhouette of the sawtooth **Minarets** at **Minaret Vista,** on Minaret Road past the Mammoth Scenic Loop. The vista is an easy, wheelchair-accessible trek from the parking lot. Bring along your mountain bike or a picnic; there are trails and tables at the vista trailhead.

**VISITOR INFORMATION** The **Mammoth Ranger Station** (Hwy. 203, Main St., 2 mi west of U.S. 395, tel. 619/924–5500), open daily 8–5, offers great guidance for outdoor activities. **Mammoth Lakes Visitors Bureau** (Hwy. 203, Main St., 3 mi west of U.S. 395, tel. 619/934–8006 or 800/367–6572), open daily 8–6 and until 8 on Friday, has maps and suggestions for activities and lodging in town.

*During the annual Jazz Jubilee (tel. 619/934–2478) in July, Mammoth is graced by some of the biggest names in jazz, ragtime, blues, and Dixieland. Tickets cost $25 a day, or $50 for three days. Those with more "classical" interests should check out the Sierra Summer Festival Concert Series (tel. 619/934–2409) in late July/early August. Some concerts are free, and student tickets ($6) are available for others.*

**GETTING AROUND** Mammoth Lakes has a **shuttle bus** (tel. 619/934–2505) between the Mammoth ski area and Devils Postpile ($7 round-trip) that stops at all campgrounds and trailheads along the way. It runs daily June 15–September 15, every 15 minutes 7:30–5:30. During shuttle hours Minaret Road from the Devils Postpile entrance is closed to auto traffic, so the shuttle is the only way to travel between these points, other than walking or biking. Look for the SHUTTLE BUS signs in the Mammoth Mountain parking lot or along the highway. **Dial-a-Ride** (tel. 619/872–1901 or 800/922–1930) lets hikers reserve a one-way shuttle from the end of any trail back to the beginning—ideal if you don't want to trek round-trip.

During winter, the free **Mammoth Area Shuttle** (tel. 619/934–0687) runs every 15 minutes 7–5:30 between Mammoth Village and the mountain. The Red Line stops at the main lodge at Mammoth Mountain and at the visitor center on Main Street (*see above*), where you can get a free shuttle map.

**WHERE TO SLEEP** In Mammoth Lakes, the **ULLR Lodge** (5920 Minaret Rd., tel. 619/934–2454) rents three-person rooms with private baths ($41–$53) and two dorm rooms with shared bath ($12–$16); rates are highest during ski season (Nov.–Apr.). It has a communal kitchen, a common area with a fireplace, and a sauna popular with skiers. This place is packed with young budget travelers—don't expect much privacy. Those looking for quieter accommodations in downtown Mammoth, near skiing and mountain-bike trails, should go to **Zwart House** (76 Lupin Rd., south of Main St., tel. 619/934–2217), which has reasonable rooms (doubles $40 in summer, $50 in winter). Reservations and a deposit are required; the units, which come with a kitchen, private bath, and cable TV, sleep two to eight people (more if someone sleeps on the floor).

Near Mammoth in stunningly beautiful June Lake, the **Fern Creek Lodge** (Hwy. 3, 6 mi west of southern June Lake Loop exit off U.S. 395, tel. 619/648–7722) offers quaint wood cabins starting at $45. Each unit has a kitchen, bath, and TV, and there's a general store at the lodge to boot.

➢ **CAMPING** • **Coldwater Campground.** This popular campground is strewn with boulders, shaded by pine, and close to several chilly lakes and streams favored by anglers. The 77 sites ($11) offer access to several excellent trails, including Duck Pass (*see above*). *Tel. 619/924–5500. From U.S. 395, 8 mi west on Hwy. 203 to Lake Mary Rd. Barbecue pits, drinking water, pit toilets. Open June 12–Sept. 25.*

**Sherwin Creek.** The most secluded campground in the Mammoth Village area offers 87 rustic sites ($10) shaded by pine trees and an occasional aspen grove. The best are the 15 walk-in, tents-only creekside spots; they're usually empty, except on weekends and holidays. The walk-in sites are first come, first served, but other sites can be reserved by calling 800/238–CAMP. *Tel. 619/924–5500. From U.S. 395 3 mi south of Mammoth, take Sherwin Creek Rd. east 3½ mi. Drinking water, fire pits, picnic tables, vault toilets. Open May 13–Sept. 18.*

**FOOD** **The Good Life Café** (126 Old Mammoth Rd., at Tavern Rd., tel. 619/934–1734), open daily 8–3, serves filling breakfasts (full stack of whole-wheat pancakes with fruit, $5). The *chorizo con huevos* (Mexican sausage and eggs, $7) at **Roberto's Café** (271 Old Mammoth Rd., tel. 619/934–3667) is another excellent breakfast option; or stop by later in the day for burritos ($4–$7) or enchiladas ($2.25–$3). Roberto's is open daily 11–8. At **Matsu To Go** (Main Frontage Rd., at Joaquin St., tel. 619/934–8277), open weekdays 11:30–9 and weekends 4:30–9:30, a take-out pint of shrimp fried rice is only $2.50, and chicken teriyaki runs $3.50.

If you're looking for that hearty home-cooking you've come to expect in these parts, **Angels** (Main St., at Sierra Blvd., tel. 619/934–RIBS) does it the right way. Open 11–10 in summer, 5–10 in winter, Angels will barbecue just about anything—but the beer-batter Icelandic cod fish 'n' chips plate ($6.95) might be enough, at least to start. They also have the best beer list for miles. Down the street, the new **Looney Bean Coffee Roasting Company** (Main St., near Napa Auto Parts, tel. 619/934–1345), open daily 6 AM–9 PM (Fri.–Sat. until 11 PM), has the best coffee on U.S. 395, plays upbeat tunes, and is full of conversation you'd actually want to overhear.

**OUTDOOR ACTIVITIES** For equipment rentals and tips on mountain biking, skiing, snowboarding, fishing, or rock climbing, head to **Kittredge Sports** (Main St., at Forest Trail, tel. 619/934–7566).

➢ **MOUNTAIN BIKING** • During summer (late June–Sept.), the **Mammoth Ski Area** (tel. 619/934–0606) converts its peak into the outrageously fun **Mammoth Mountain Bike Park,** open daily 9–6. For $18 a day, you can take the gondola up and zoom down 52 miles of trails—90% of them single-track. Rentals go for $35 a day, but you can save a few bucks by renting in town at Kittredge Sports (*see above*), where bikes rent for $7 an hour or $25 a day. At Mammoth's ranger station (*see* Visitor Information, *above*), grab a free copy of "Mammoth Lakes Bike Trails" for more good trail tips. **Knoll's Trail,** a moderate to strenuous 10-mile loop through pine forests with excellent views, comes highly recommended. The trailhead lies a quarter mile past Shady Rest Campground, just west of the ranger station.

➢ **FISHING** • The Eastern Sierra is the destination of thousands of fishing enthusiasts each year. Their quest: the almighty trout that inhabit the region's countless lakes, rivers, and streams. Though favorite spots differ, mainstays include **Mammoth Lakes,** off Highway 203; **June Lakes,** off Highway 158 between Mono Lake and Mammoth; and the streams of **Rock Creek Canyon,** off Rock Creek Canyon Road between Mammoth and Bishop. Most sporting-goods stores in the area have the required permits ($9 a day), and Kittredge Sports (*see above*) rents equipment.

➢ **SKIING** • **Mammoth Mountain** (tel. 619/934–2571) and **June Mountain** (tel. 619/648–7733) are two of the most popular and crowded ski resorts in California, particularly if there's a good snow pack. Mammoth has far and away the best skiing south of Tahoe. Unfortunately, the resorts aren't cheap. Plan to spend $40 for a lift ticket and at least that much on lodging. Both Mammoth and the more low-key June Mountain allow snowboarders. At **Wave Rave** (3203 Main St., Mammoth Lakes, tel. 619/934–2471), a snowboard and boots rent for $23 a day. Cross-country skiers should contact Mammoth's ranger station (*see* Visitor Information, *above*) for maps of popular routes.

# Bishop

It's hard to miss the looming, barren **White Mountains,** south of Mammoth Lakes on the east side of U.S. 395. Even harder to miss—and, indeed, many have tried—is the town of **Bishop.** Sandwiched between the Eastern Sierra and the White Mountains in the Owens Valley, this boondocks cowtown is straight out of a Merle Haggard song. It's also the commercial hub of the Eastern Sierra, and since passing through is inevitable, take advantage of its facilities and, hell, have a good ol' time. The **White Mountain Ranger Station** (Hwy. 203, 2 mi west of U.S. 395, tel. 619/924–5500), open weekdays 9–4, has maps and other info on the White Mountains and the John Muir Wilderness (*see* Sierra National Forest, *above*).

*On Memorial Day weekend in Bishop, look for the Mule Days celebration, a three-day extravaganza featuring mule rodeos and a parade. One visitor observed, "The town smells like shit for an entire weekend!" As if that's not enough, Bishop hosts the Wild West Weekend on Labor Day, with rodeos, a chili cook-off, and cowboy poetry readings. Yee-haw!*

**WHERE TO SLEEP** The **El Rancho Motel** (274 Lagoon St., tel. 619/872–9251), 1 block from the makeshift Greyhound station, has spacious rooms starting at $30 in winter, $40 in summer; add $8 for a kitchen and refrigerator. The management is friendly and knowledgeable about the area—a real bonus in a town where striking up a conversation with a local can be like pulling teeth. In Bishop Creek Canyon—a stone's throw from Lake Sabrina and trailheads for the John Muir Wilderness—sits **Sabrina Campground** (Hwy. 168, 17 mi south of Bishop, tel. 619/873–2500), one of Inyo National Forest's most unblemished camping spots. The 18 spacious sites ($11) are shaded by aspens and lie on the banks of a tranquil stream; all have tables, fire pits, vault toilets, and drinking water. The campground is open May 15–Sept. 7.

**FOOD** Pricey **Holmes Health Haven** (192 W. Line St., 1 block west of Main St., tel. 619/872–5571) is the only place south of Mammoth that sells organic produce and dried food in bulk. Otherwise, the cheapest options for groceries are one of the two 24-hour **Vons** stores (U.S. 395 on north side of town and U.S. 395 at Eastline St.).

For a hot meal, head to the **Bishop Grill** (281 N. Main St., tel. 619/873–3911), open daily 6 AM–7:30 PM, a meat-and-potatoes diner where the waitress calls you "hon" while refilling your coffee for the 10th time. A burger and fries or a turkey sandwich goes for $3; biscuits and gravy or tasty homemade pie is only $1.50. Next door, **Amigos** (tel. 619/872–2189), open daily 11–9, serves excellent Mexican food. Dinner combos run close to $10, but a filling plate of beans and rice with homemade chips and salsa goes for only $1.50. For coffee and espresso drinks, stop by the huge **Schat's Bakery** (736 N. Main St., tel. 919/873–7156); they also serve homemade shepherd's bread ($2–$5), sandwiches ($4.50–$6), and California's best caramel-filled Dutch waffles ($2.50).

**OUTDOOR ACTIVITIES** If it doesn't have much else, Bishop does have one of the best outdoors stores in the Eastern Sierra. While their specialty is mountaineering supplies, the friendly folk at **Wilson's Eastside Sports** (206 N. Main St., tel. 619/873–7520) also rent mountain bikes ($25 a day) and have loads of tips on other outdoor activities in the area.

*On the Schulman Grove Trail, you can try to guess which tree is the 4,800-year-old "Methuselah," the oldest living tree on the planet—in an effort to protect the old-timer, forest officials keep its identity secret.*

➢ **HIKING •** The desolate White Mountains don't retain much water, so be sure to bring your own if you're thinking of hiking here. One area that explodes with life is the **Ancient Bristlecone Pine Forest,** a thick forest of gnarled, twisted bristlecone pines, among the oldest living things in the world. To reach the easy (4 mi round-trip) **Schulman Grove Trail** through the pine forest, take Highway 168 east from Big Pine (15 mi south of Bishop on U.S. 395) and follow signs for 22 miles north on White Mountain Road to the White Mountain Research Station. Several miles past the grove (on White Mountain Rd.), look for signs to the strenuous, 7½-mile trail leading to the summit of **White Mountain,** the highest peak in the range at 14,246 feet.

Ten miles west of Big Pine is **Big Pine Canyon** and the **Palisade Glacier,** the largest in the Sierra. To get a good view, follow **Big Pine Canyon Trail** 6 miles from the Big Pine Trailhead to **Third Lake,** whose waters appear turquoise because of mineral-rich glacial runoff. You'll have to climb another 2,000 feet (a moderately strenuous 3 miles) to reach the glacier itself. Though you can complete the hike in a day, consider camping at the lake if you have time. The glacial terrain gets dicey; inexperienced hikers should not attempt the last mile and experts should bring crampons and icepicks.

*Located about 50 miles east of Big Pine Canyon and U.S. 395, the Eureka sand dunes are the tallest in California—some reach heights of nearly 700 feet. Fifty plant species thrive here, including three that grow nowhere else in the world. For more information, including directions, see Near Death Valley, in Chapter 12.*

**Rock Creek Canyon,** about 15 miles northwest of U.S. 395 on Rock Creek Canyon Road, provides access to a series of remarkable glacial lakes, canyons, and granite formations. For a good day hike, try the trails from Mosquito Flat to either **Morgan Pass** or the more difficult **Mono Pass,** both about 4 miles each way (6–8 hrs round-trip). For extended trips, the ranger station (*see above*) can give advice and permits.

➢ **ROCK CLIMBING** • The Owens River Gorge is among the best places in the Eastern Sierra for rock climbing, with generous holds and fantastic scenery at 5,000 feet. The time to climb is spring or fall. For the indispensable guide *Owens River Gorge Climbs* ($10), stop by the **Booky Joint** (Minaret Village Shopping Center, Mammoth Lakes, tel. 619/934–3240). To get to the gorge, take the Gorge Road exit east off U.S. 395, 14 miles north of Bishop.

## *Have Some Bubbly on Ma Nature*

***What do you get when you cross volcanic magma with water? Hot springs! You'll find dozens along U.S. 395, many kept secret by locals. One well-known spring is the free Hot Creek Geologic Site. Take the Owens River Road exit from U.S. 395 to the Hot Creek Fish Hatchery, go south on the road behind the airport, then turn left on the dirt road and drive a few miles to the parking area. Find a place on the creek's edge specially dug out for "tubbing it," or swim in the warm waters (avoid restricted areas, though). A more secluded spring is Wild Willy's, 3 miles south of Mammoth on U.S. 395 (left on Benton Crossing Road and right at third cattle crossing; spring is down the slope to your left after 1.2 miles).***

***The Shepherd's Tub used to entertain herders while their flocks were grazing; now two people can soak to their heart's content here in the middle of absolute nowhere. There's a free campsite next door with a fire ring, but you need a fire permit. Take U.S. 395 south from Mammoth past the airport to the road at the little green church (on your left). Drive a mile past Whitmore Pool, and take the gravel road on your left a mile to the bumpy road just before the lone tree (on your right). Follow that for a mile, staying on the main road when it forks. At the second fork, you'll see the tub at the bottom of a dirt road to the left. It's not as hard to find as it sounds on paper, honest. For a complete list of lesser-known sites, check out George Williams's "Hot Springs of the Eastern Sierra" ($10), available at most ranger stations and sporting-goods stores in the region.***

# Mt. Whitney

The biggest attraction in Inyo is Mt. Whitney—the highest peak in the contiguous United States at 14,496 feet. Every year hundreds of hikers make the strenuous 11-mile trek to the summit from the **Whitney Portal Trailhead** (13 mi west of Lone Pine on Whitney Portal Rd.). Reservations and wilderness permits are required May 22–October 15; rangers recommend 3 days for the trip. Send written applications with your name, the size of your group, and your departure date to the **Mt. Whitney Ranger Station** (Box 8, Lone Pine 93545, tel. 619/876–6200). Applications ($3 per person) must be postmarked between March 1 and May 31. If you can't plan that far ahead, show up at the ranger station the morning you want to start the trek and hope for a cancellation (there are at least a few most days). Or approach the mountain from trails originating in Sequoia National Park or Sequoia National Forest, both of which have quotas for accessing the Whitney trails but rarely fill them. These hikes will take a good 7–10 days. If you don't want to climb all the way to the top, you can follow the **Whitney Portal National Recreation Trail** (4 mi) from the lower trailhead at Lone Pine Campground. You'll get a moderate workout and spectacular views of Mt. Whitney, the Alabama Hills, and the Owens Valley. The ranger station (798 N. Main St., Lone Pine), open daily 7–4:30 in the summer and 8–4:30 in the winter, will help with maps and suggestions for surrounding areas.

The one-stoplight tourist town of **Lone Pine** sits in the mountain's shadow, providing little more than food and lodging for the intrepid mountaineers who mob the area. Mt. Whitney is invisible from town, eclipsed by nearer peaks like 12,994-foot **Lone Pine** and **Mt. Williamson,** a mere 120 feet shorter than Whitney.

**WHERE TO SLEEP** Lone Pine's cheapest lodging is at the **Dow Hotel** (310 S. Main St., tel. 619/876–5521), where a room with shared bath is $23 ($35 with private bath). It's a bit shabby, but you get cable TV, Jacuzzi, and a pool.

➢ **CAMPING** • In warmer months, serenity can be yours at one of the 44 sites ($10) of **Whitney Portal Campground** (elev. 8,000 ft)—12 miles north of Lone Pine on Whitney Portal Road—with the desolate Alabama Hills to the north and snow-capped Mount Whitney towering above to the west. On colder nights, try the lower elevation of **Lone Pine Campground,** a few miles east of Whitney Portal, with 43 sites ($7). Both Whitney Portal and Lone Pine have potable water, fire rings, and toilets. For free camping, head for **Tuttle Creek Campground,** which has drinking water but no toilets. To reach the campground, follow directions to Horseshoe Meadow Trailhead (*see* Outdoor Activities, *below*).

**FOOD** If it's after hours, swing by **PJ's Bake 'n' Broil** (446 S. Main St., Lone Pine, tel. 619/876–5796), the quintessential 24-hour coffee shop—no frills and filled with regulars. Go for the homemade soups ($2), the biscuits and gravy ($3), the Alabama Hills Salad with turkey, ham, cheese, and green pepper (half order, $4)—and, of course, the bottomless cup of coffee ($1). The air-conditioning is a definite plus on 100° summer days. Otherwise, try the **Sierra Cantina** (123 N. Main St., Lone Pine, tel. 619/876–5740), open daily 11:30–8 but closed in November. Aside from the usual tacos and tamales ($6), you'll find a burrito enchilada ($6). Better still, go for the all-you-can-eat buffet ($7 lunch, $10 dinner), featuring a build-your-own-taco stand.

**OUTDOOR ACTIVITIES** If hiking steep Mt. Whitney sounds like a nightmare, check out **Taboose Creek,** a popular day-hiking area 10 miles north of Independence off U.S. 395. Better yet, locals highly recommend the trails from **Horseshoe Meadows** (at the end of Horseshoe Meadows Rd.) through the mixed conifer forests of the Golden Trout Wilderness. A popular trip from the Horseshoe Meadows Trailhead follows the **Cottonwood Pass Trail** to Cottonwood Pass (2 mi), Big Whitney Meadow (another 4–5 mi), and finally Rocky Basin Lakes (a strenuous 5 mi more), a spectacular backcountry locale for camping and fishing. To reach the main trailhead, take Whitney Portal Road from Lone Pine to Horseshoe Meadows Road and drive south 20 miles.

Mountain bikers will get a good workout on a scenic 17½-mile loop that affords terrific views of Mt. Whitney. The scenery may look familiar—it's served as backdrop for a multitude of Wild West–type flicks, including 1994's *Maverick.* From Lone Pine, take Whitney Portal Road 2.7

miles west to unpaved **Movie Road,** which will meet **Hogback Road,** also unpaved, and take you back to Whitney Portal.

# Sequoia and Kings Canyon National Parks

**After entering Sequoia and Kings** Canyon National Parks, expect to find yourself looking constantly upward. Not only will the grandiose beauty inspire you to search for a Higher Being, but you'll also be craning your neck to get a view of the giant sequoias for which the southern park is named. You'll have to look up, too, to spot Mt. Whitney, the highest peak in the lower 48 (to climb it, head east to Inyo National Forest; *see above*). Superlatives abound here: Kings Canyon, which separates the two parks, is the deepest in the continental United States. And the parks are almost completely covered with virgin forest, making them exquisite for either day hikes or serious wilderness camping. Best of all, Sequoia and Kings Canyon retain a rustic feeling even in their most developed areas, a pleasant contrast to their congested neighbor Yosemite. You'll find it easy to visit both parks in one trip, as they share the same highways and administrative facilities.

## BASICS

**VISITOR INFORMATION** Upon entrance, all visitors are given a free copy of the *Sequoia Bark,* which contains a detailed map and a list of activities for both parks. The **Cedar Grove Ranger Station** (end of Hwy. 180 in Kings Canyon, tel. 209/565–3793) is open daily 8–5 in summer. The **Foothills Visitor Center** (Hwy. 198 in Sequoia, 1 mi from southern entrance, tel. 209/565–3134) is open daily 8–5 in summer and daily 8–4:30 in winter. The **Grant Grove Visitor Center and Ranger Station** (Hwy. 180, in Kings Canyon, tel. 209/335–2856) is open daily 8–5. The **Lodgepole Visitor Center and Ranger Station** (Generals Hwy., in Sequoia, tel. 209/565–3782) is open daily 9–5 in winter and 8–6 in the summer. If you have trouble getting through to the ranger stations, call general dispatch (tel. 209/565–3341) and they'll transfer you to the right office. For road and weather conditions, call 800/427–ROAD or 209/565–3351. Visitors with disabilities can call 209/565–3134 for info on park facilities and programs.

**FEES AND PERMITS** The entrance fee is $5 per car, or $3 per person if you enter by bus, motorcycle, bicycle, or on foot. This entitles you to a week in both parks.

Visitor centers and ranger stations (*see above*) distribute free **wilderness permits,** required for overnight camping in the backcountry. Permits are issued only for the trails within a particular center's district. After March 1, you can reserve permits at least 2 weeks in advance; after October 1, they're available only on the spot. For an application, write to Wilderness Permit Reservations, Sequoia and Kings Canyon National Parks, Three Rivers 93271. Don't despair if you haven't reserved—even in summer a number of permits are handed out on a first-come, first-served basis. Simply appear in person at the visitor center and sign up. A lot of people try this strategy, so arrive early (7–10 AM). The good news is that Sequoia and Kings Canyon fill their quotas much less frequently than Yosemite, where getting a permit in summer can be as painful as a root canal. Call **Backcountry Information** (tel. 209/565–3708) for weather and trail conditions and permit availability.

**GENERAL STORES** Fresno is the best place to stock up on supplies, but if you miss your chance, **Dixon's Village Market** (40869 Sierra Dr., Hwy. 198, tel. 209/561–4441) in the small town of Three Rivers has the essentials at big-store prices Monday–Saturday 8–7 and Sunday 9–5. Inside the park, your best bets are the **Lodgepole Market** (Generals Hwy., across from visitor center, tel. 209/565–3301) and the **Giant Forest Market** (Generals Hwy., in Giant Forest Village, tel. 209/565–3381, ext. 260), both open daily 8 AM–9 PM. Prices are high—though lower than other in-park stores—but in a jam you can buy what you need.

# Sequoia and Kings Canyon National Parks

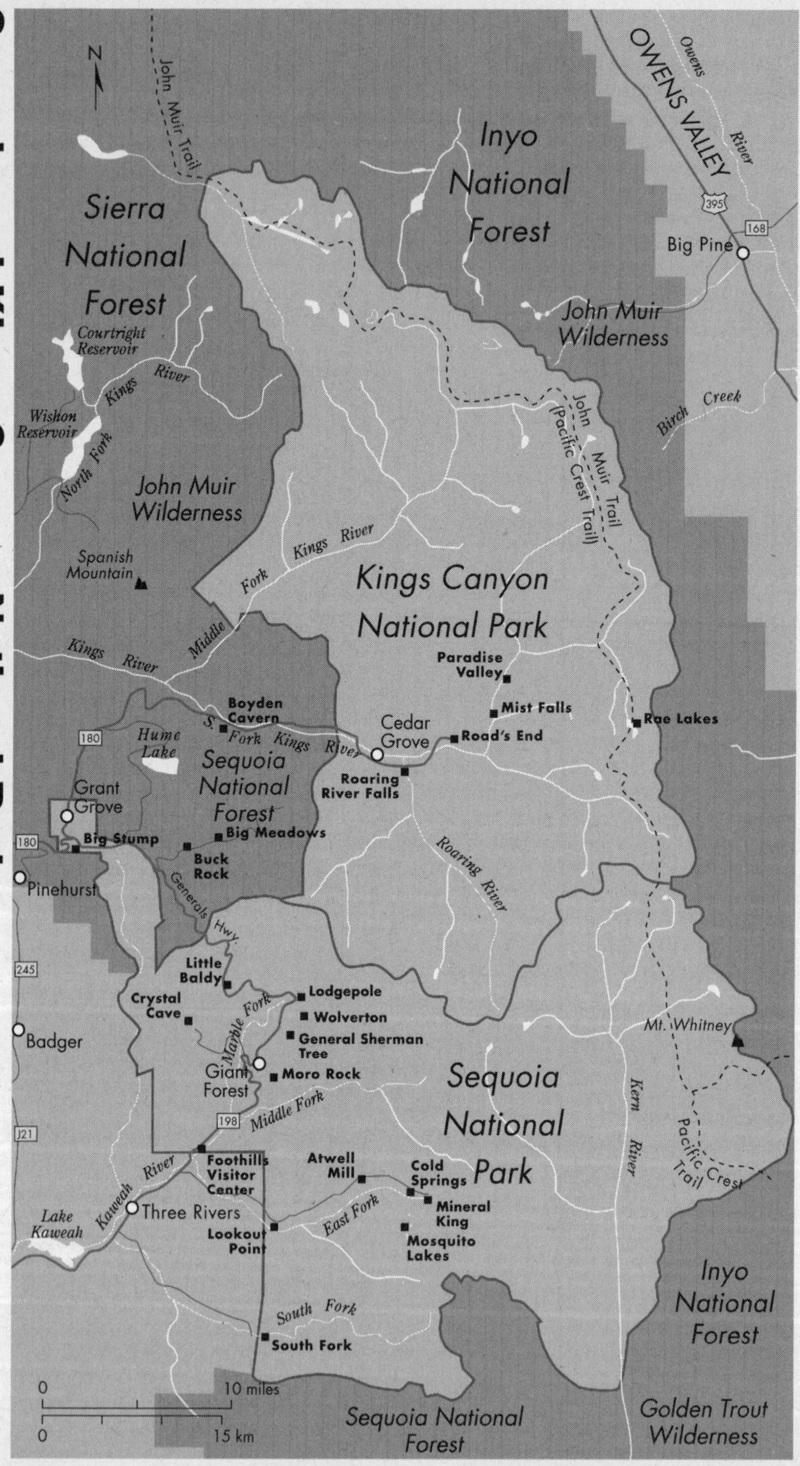
N
John Muir Trail
Inyo National Forest
OWENS VALLEY
Owens River
395
168
Big Pine
Sierra National Forest
Courtright Reservoir
Kings River
Wishon Reservoir
North Fork
John Muir Wilderness
John Muir Wilderness
Birch Creek
John Muir Trail (Pacific Crest Trail)
Spanish Mountain
Middle Fork Kings River
Kings Canyon National Park
Kings River
Paradise Valley
Mist Falls
Rae Lakes
Boyden Cavern
S. Fork Kings River
Cedar Grove
Road's End
180
Hume Lake
Sequoia National Forest
Roaring River Falls
Grant Grove
Big Stump
Big Meadows
Buck Rock
180
Pinehurst
Generals Hwy.
Roaring River
245
Little Baldy
Lodgepole
Crystal Cave
Marble Fork
Wolverton
General Sherman Tree
Badger
Giant Forest
Moro Rock
Mt. Whitney
Sequoia National Park
Middle Fork
198
Kern River
Pacific Crest Trail
J21
Foothills Visitor Center
Atwell Mill
Cold Springs
Mineral King
Kaweah River
Three Rivers
East Fork
Lake Kaweah
Lookout Point
Mosquito Lakes
Inyo National Forest
South Fork
South Fork
0
10 miles
0
15 km
Sequoia National Forest
Golden Trout Wilderness

**WHEN TO GO** Summer in the high country (above 9,000 ft) means mild days, occasional afternoon thundershowers, and nights that can dip below freezing. In the foothills (1,500–3,000 ft), summers are hot and dry. Crowds are a problem during high season, especially in late August when Central Valley residents swarm here to escape 100° temperatures at home. Fall is the best time to visit: The weather is still warm, yet crisp, and there are fewer visitors. During winter, most of the park is blanketed with snow, and while the roads to Cedar Grove (Hwy. 180) and Mineral King (east of Hwy. 198) close, much of the park remains open: Be prepared for freezing temperatures and snowbound campsites, though, and don't forget your snow chains.

## COMING AND GOING

**BY CAR** Both parks are only 1 to 2 hours by car from Fresno and Visalia. **Highway 198** runs roughly east–west between Visalia and Sequoia National Park, entering at the park headquarters at Ash Mountain. The road continues north through Giant Forest to meet **Highway 180** at Lodgepole after about an hour; the switchback-filled stretch where the two roads merge is known as **Generals Highway.** Highway 180 enters Sequoia at the northern Big Stump entrance and provides easy access to Kings Canyon National Park via Grant Grove. It runs primarily east–west from Fresno. In the Central Valley, both roads meet the north–south **Highway 99.** The trip from San Francisco or Los Angeles takes 5–6 hours.

From the Eastern Sierra, no pass leads directly to Kings Canyon or Sequoia. You'll have to come via Yosemite's **Tioga Pass** (Hwy. 120) or skirt the south end of the range below Sequoia National Forest at Bakersfield. If you opt for the northern route, take **Highway 120** west at Lee Vining, then **Highway 41** south from Yosemite Valley to Highway 180 east at Fresno. If you *must* take the hot, godforsaken southern route, pick up **U.S. 395** south to **Highway 14** south to Mojave, where you'll pick up **Highway 58** north to Bakersfield. Highway 99 will then take you north to Fresno, where you connect to Highway 180 east.

## GETTING AROUND

During summer, daytime **shuttles** ($1) run every hour between Lodgepole and Giant Forest Village. Check with the Lodgepole or Grant Grove visitor center for the current schedule—it seemingly changes with the wind. If you've had it with hiking and want a guided motor tour, the best deal is the all-day **Kings Canyon Tour** ($14 per person). Buy tickets and catch the tour bus at the Giant Forest lodge's registration desk.

## WHERE TO SLEEP

Hotels and cabins in both parks are managed by **Sequoia Guest Services** (Box 789, Three Rivers 93271, tel. 209/561–3314), open daily 7–5:30. To reserve a room, call that number directly; during summer most hotels and cabins book 6–10 weeks in advance. Giant Forest, Stony Creek (on Generals Hwy.), and Cedar Grove have the most motels, but they're way overpriced at $60–$90 a night. The cheapest accommodations are **The Rustics**—cabins with no decor to speak of, pit toilets, and kerosene lamps instead of electricity. They do have roofs, wood-burning stoves, and real beds, and they're reasonably priced ($32–$39; $6–$7 for each additional person up to seven). Look for them in Giant Forest (Apr. 29–Oct. 9) and Grant Grove (year-round). Higher-end cabins with real toilets and electricity are available in Grant Grove and Giant Forest for $70–$115 in summer and $58 in winter. They're packed together like a shantytown, but this is certainly more comfortable than sleeping on the rocky ground.

If you want much nicer accommodations for a similar price just outside the park, the **Sierra Lodge** (43175 Sierra Dr., Hwy. 198 in Three Rivers, tel. 209/561–3681), 6 miles west of Foothills park entrance, won't disappoint. Huge, tasteful rooms with private bath, most with a patio or fireplace, go for $42–$70 in winter, $58–$75 in summer (extra person $3). You can swim in the pool, which has terrific views of the foothills. If you're nostalgic for the TV show *Twin Peaks,* try the rarely full **Snowline Lodge** (44138 E. Kings Canyon Rd., Hwy. 180 in Dunlap, tel. 209/336–2300), 8 miles from Big Stump entrance, with small but clean rooms for

$50 and a cabin or large family room that accommodates 4–6 people for $56 ($10 extra for each extra person over two). In the lodge bar, you'll find lots of dark wood, animal heads, and interesting characters.

**CAMPING** From mid-May to Labor Day, the large, crowded **Lodgepole** campground in Sequoia accepts reservations through MISTIX (tel. 800/365–CAMP) up to 8 weeks in advance. The 260 sites ($12), a mixture of tents and small RVs, flank the Kaweah River and provide easy access to the Tokopah Falls Trail (*see* Exploring, *below*). You'll find a few too many noisy families, but for short stays it's not a bad spot. All other campgrounds in Sequoia and Kings Canyon are available on a first-come, first-served basis. Lodgepole, Grant Grove, and Cedar Grove have pay showers.

**South Fork Campground,** in the southwest corner of Sequoia National Park, is the smallest in the area (13 sites, $5) and definitely one of the nicest. RVs and trailers are not permitted, so you won't be bothered by generator-powered televisions. The sites lie in a grove of pine trees, and all have tables and fire pits. There's no potable water, so bring a good supply. Arrive early at this first-come, first-served campground on summer weekends and holidays. *South Fork Dr., 13 mi from Hwy. 198. Open year-round.*

Head north on Highway 198 and east on Mineral King Road in Sequoia and you'll come across two campgrounds pleasantly shaded by pines: **Atwell Mill** (20 mi east of Hwy. 198) and **Cold Springs** (25 mi east of Hwy. 198), both usually open April–November. The curvy road discourages RVs and trailers, making this area quieter than the central campgrounds. The sites, with pit toilets, tables, barbecue pits, and water (after late May only), go for $5 a night.

In Cedar Grove, along Highway 180 deep in the heart of Kings Canyon, **Sentinel Campground** and **Sheep Creek Campground** (both open May–Oct.) offer a total of nearly 200 spacious, well-shaded sites ($10). Neither takes reservations, but if you arrive early you may be able to snag one of the prime spots along Kings River. This is terrific hiking territory: Road's End (where Hwy. 180 dead-ends 5 mi east of the campgrounds) is the starting point for hikes to Mist Falls, Paradise Valley, and the Pacific Crest and John Muir trails (*see* Exploring, *below*). Both campgrounds feature potable water, flush toilets, fire pits, picnic tables, and food-storage lockers—and despite all the people, they still feel isolated. Sentinel is wheelchair accessible.

Just outside park boundaries, there are two excellent free campgrounds in the Sequoia National Forest's Hume Ranger District. Take the road marked BIG MEADOWS off Generals Highway east of Grant Grove. After 4 miles, you'll come to **Buck Rock Campground,** which has five sites with tables, fire pits, and toilets. Two miles farther lies **Big Meadows Campground,** with 25 sites, tables, stoves, and vault toilets. Pack plenty of water; there's none at the sites. Crowds stay away (probably because visitor centers don't steer them here), and the area has fantastic hiking to Mitchell Peak, as well as the best cross-country skiing in the region.

## FOOD

Prices at the markets in Giant Forest, Lodgepole, and Cedar Grove are steep, so stock up before entering (*see* Basics, *above*). Prepared food ranges from greasy and cheap to greasy and expensive. Most resorts have both a cafeteria and a dining room, the former with food under $5 and the latter with food under $15. If you must eat at a resort, try the **Giant Forest Cafeteria** (Hwy. 198, in Giant Forest Village, tel. 209/565–3381, ext. 256), open April–mid-September 6:30 AM–9 PM. A full breakfast is $4–$5; lunch and dinner run $5–$7.

*"Grim" best describes the food situation in Sequoia and Kings Canyon—the only ones who eat well here are campers who bring in their food and the bears who steal it.*

If you're desperate, a few restaurants and sandwich counters cluster in Cedar Grove, Lodgepole, and Grant Grove. Once again, you'll pay too much for a mediocre meal. At the **Cedar Grove Snack Bar** (Hwy. 180, in Cedar Grove Village, tel. 209/565–3617), open daily 7 AM–9 PM May–October, a three-egg omelet with toast and hash browns fetches $5 and a bowl of chili is $3. On Highway 180 in Grant Grove, the **Grant Grove Coffee Shop** serves basic American fare 7 AM–9 PM daily, from burgers and fries ($5) to eggs and hash browns ($4). Box lunches with a sandwich, fruit, and dessert are $7—good for a picnic if you're not up to making your own. Give them at least 8 hours notice for the former.

**Lodgepole Deli.** The best find in the park serves good food at decent prices. Hearty egg-and-sausage breakfasts go for $5, hot and cold sandwiches are $4.50–$5.50, and pizza is $8. Even better, it's next to the **Lodgepole Ice Cream Shop.** *Generals Hwy., Lodgepole, tel. 209/565–3301. Open mid-May–mid-Sept., daily 7 AM–8 PM (ice cream shop open daily noon–8).*

## EXPLORING SEQUOIA AND KINGS CANYON

Altitude in the two parks ranges from less than 1,200 feet to more than 14,000 feet, combining low-elevation chaparral and semi-desert environments with cool, forested high country. Much of the territory here isn't accessible by road, so your best bet is to get out of the car and hike through the backcountry. Even if you're short on time, there are hundreds of easy 1- to 3-hour treks in the area, especially around Mineral King, Giant Forest, Grant Grove, and Cedar Grove. Otherwise, explore Highway 180 and Highway 198, both incredibly scenic though sometimes difficult to navigate (*see* Scenic Drives and Views, *below*).

**ORIENTATION AND TOURS** Foothills, Lodgepole, and Mineral King in Sequoia National Park, and Cedar Grove and Grant Grove in Kings Canyon offer free daily activities in summer that focus on ecology, wildlife, and geology. A complete list, with times, appears in the *Sequoia Bark*; alternately, ask at the visitor centers. In winter, evening programs are offered on Friday and Saturday at Grant Grove and Lodgepole; if conditions permit, rangers also lead snowshoe walks ($1) on weekends and holidays. Reservations are recommended; call the Grant Grove or Lodgepole visitor centers (*see* Visitor Information, *above*).

If you approach Sequoia from the Foothills entrance (Hwy. 198), don't miss **Hospital Rock,** 5 miles north of the visitor center. It has an outdoor display devoted to the Native American population of the Sierra Nevada and a series of pictographs painted by the Monache people, who lived here until 1870. Before tackling the rest of the park, you may also want to take the easy, self-guided .6-mile **Trail for All People,** also called Round Meadow (¼ mi north of Giant Forest on Hwy. 198), which circles a peaceful meadow and features special written exhibits about the ecology of the sequoia groves. The paved trail is gentle enough for wheelchairs to navigate.

**SHORT HIKES** The two parks are oriented around a number of "communities"—developed areas that usually contain a ranger station, grocery store, campground, cafeteria, and trailheads for hikes that range from a quarter mile to 8 miles or more: **Grant Grove** is on the west side of Kings Canyon, where Highway 180 meets the Generals Highway; farther east on Highway 180 is **Cedar Grove.** On the west side of Sequoia, on the Generals Highway, is **Giant Forest,** which also contains **Lodgepole**; **Mineral King** is in the southern part of Sequoia.

➢ **CEDAR GROVE** • Cedar Grove, the other major destination in Kings Canyon, is about an hour's drive (32 mi) east of the popular Grant Grove on Highway 180. On this road, built by convict labor in the 1930s, you can see how stunning the canyon is, particularly the glacier-carved valley. On your way into the area, you'll pass by **Boyden Cavern** (tel. 209/736–2708), a large cave filled with stalagmites and stalactites. To see it, you have to take a sometimes crowded 45-minute tour (on the hour, $5.50)—tours are given June–September, daily 10–5; May and October, daily 11–4.

About 10 miles farther east on Highway 180, just past Cedar Grove Village, a quarter-mile path leads to thunderous **Roaring River Falls,** the canyon's largest waterfall. From here you can stroll along the flat 1½-mile trail (or drive on a paved road) to idyllic **Zumwalt Meadow,** which locals claim is the most beautiful in the Sierra; explore the meadow on an easy 2-mile loop trail. At the end of Highway 180, near the aptly named Road's End, you'll find **Muir Rock,** a popular Kings River swimming hole safe only in late summer. From the Road's End parking lot, you can walk along the south fork of the Kings River for an easy 4½-mile round-trip to refreshing **Mist Falls,** or continue 3 miles farther to **Paradise Valley,** a quiet section of river just begging for a picnic. The moderately strenuous round-trip takes 3 to 5 hours. Beware: Mosquitoes reign here.

➢ **GRANT GROVE** • Grant Grove lies at the western boundary of the parks; you'll pass through it if you come east on Highway 180 from Fresno. This is one of the most developed sections of Kings Canyon, but the short trail around the grove will give you an idea of what it feels like to stand among the monumental giant sequoias, which grow to the size of a city skyscraper (up to 310 ft), weigh up to 2.7 million pounds, and sometimes live as long as 3,200 years. A gentle half-mile trail passes the **General Grant Tree**—the third-largest sequoia in the world and the nation's official Christmas Tree—and the 19th-century **Gamlin Cabin,** once inhabited by a pair of shakers (shingle makers). Also in Grant Grove is the easy mile-long **Big Stump Trail** loop, where you can see firsthand the devastation caused by clear-cutting in the late 19th century. To escape the crowds, check out the **North Grove Trail,** a 3-mile loop (1½ hrs) that starts from the parking lot of the General Grant Tree Trail. About 15 minutes northeast of Grant Grove, off Highway 180 in Sequoia National Forest, **Hume Lake** has a huge Christian camp at its north end, but it's still a nice place to go for a picnic or a swim.

➢ **LODGEPOLE** • Behind the visitor center at Lodgepole, a short nature trail leads down to **Marble Fork** on the Kaweah River, where you'll find a pebbly makeshift beach. The river is normally ice-cold, but you're free—though not encouraged—to swim. A quarter mile north of Lodgepole campground, the 2-mile **Tokopah Falls Trail** (2 hrs) leads up through the hills to the 2,000-foot cascade.

Two miles south of Lodgepole, just off Generals Highway, is the **General Sherman Tree,** the second-largest living thing in the world (a mushroom in Michigan is first—it covers 30 acres). It's 275 feet tall and 102 feet around at the base, and the first branch is nearly 130 feet up. The easy, paved **Congress Trail** (2 mi, 1–2 hrs round-trip) leads from here past some of the park's other well-known giants. Two miles south of the tree lies **Giant Forest,** an overdeveloped resort full of hotels, cafeterias, and convenience stores. The only reason to bother with this place is to access its trailheads. For giant sequoias and a panorama of the Great Western Divide—a dramatic, subsidiary range of the Sierra—head from the Giant Forest Village Trailhead to **Moro Rock** via the **Soldiers Trail Loop** (4.6 mi), a moderate hike of 3 to 4 hours. Eleven miles north of Giant Forest Village on Highway 198, you'll come across Little Baldy Saddle. From here, the **Baldy Trail** climbs 700 feet in 1.7 miles and ends with a stunning view of the surrounding countryside.

Nine miles southwest of Giant Forest, **Crystal Cave** is plagued by crowds during summer, but the 45-minute tour ($4) will appeal to cave buffs and amateur spelunkers. It's only 50° inside, so bring a jacket. The cave lies at the end of a rough 6-mile spur road off Generals Highway; follow signs from Giant Forest. *Tel. 209/565–3134. Open June–Labor Day, daily 10–3; May and Sept., Fri.–Mon. 10–3. 2-hr advance ticket purchase (at Foothills or Lodgepole visitor center) required; no tickets sold at cave).*

*Mineral King is such an idyllic alpine retreat that Disney Studios wanted to convert it into an amusement park in the late 1960s. Conservationists were not enchanted and lobbied against the plan. In 1978, Washington made the area part of Sequoia National Park, thwarting this Hollywood fantasy for good.*

➢ **MINERAL KING** • The southernmost attraction in Sequoia is Mineral King, a secluded, relatively uncongested valley accessible only in summer. Numerous trails lead from here to peaks, meadows, and high lakes, as well as to campgrounds and a ranger station. In particular, the 3.6-mile (one-way) **Mosquito Lakes Trail** winds its way up a series of switchbacks to granite-bound Mosquito Lakes, a secluded area surrounded by a forest of red firs. The **Eagle Lake Trail** (7 mi round-trip), with breathtaking vistas of the southern Sierra, makes a terrific day hike or overnighter. With a permit, you can camp at Eagle Lake (10,000 ft). Both hikes start at the Eagle-Mosquito parking lot; head west to Mosquito Lakes when the trail forks or continue straight for Eagle Lake. To reach Mineral King, take the windy 25-mile Mineral King Road from Highway 198 just north of Three Rivers.

**BACKCOUNTRY TRIPS** Both parks make excellent bases from which to explore the wondrous Sierra Nevada backcountry; for permit information, *see* Basics, *above.* In Kings Canyon, most backpackers depart from Road's End, where you can do the 44½-mile **Rae Lakes Loop,** a strenuous 5- to 7-day trip past alpine lakes that eventually hooks up with the **John Muir** and **Pacific Crest trails.** In Sequoia, you can leave from Lodgepole, the Giant Forest, Buckeye Flat, or trailheads at Mineral King, including Atwell Mill to the west, Franklin Pass to the south, and Sawtooth to the east. Before you choose a path, check in with a visitor center or ranger station (*see* Basics, *above*) for maps, trail suggestions, and wilderness permits, and pick up a copy of the newsletter *Backcountry Basics.*

**SCENIC DRIVES AND VIEWS** From the northern entrance, the winding **Highway 180** descends into Kings Canyon toward Cedar Grove, providing close-up views of daunting cliffs as well as vistas of the entire canyon. Kings Canyon also offers the **Cedar Grove Motor Trail,** a 2.5-mile drive down an old dirt road once used to move livestock into the valley. A booklet (50¢) available at Cedar Grove Visitor Center highlights observation points along the trail.

Between Foothills and Giant Forest, **Generals Highway** (Hwy. 198 outside the park) climbs more than 5,000 feet with 23 switchbacks, giving you a firsthand look at the stunning differences between the dry, chaparral-covered foothills and the high sequoia groves. On a clear day, you get excellent views of the valley, hills, and surrounding peaks.

## PARK ACTIVITIES

**BIKING** Biking on unpaved trails in national parks is illegal, but in Sequoia National Forest between Grant Grove and Cedar Grove, you'll find a moderate—and legal—16½-mile round-trip trail that travels through sequoia groves and provides great views of the **Monarch Divide.** To get to the trailhead from Highway 180 going east, turn right on Hume Lake Road, just past Princess Campground; follow signs to Hume Lake Christian Camp, turn off on the side road leading to public beaches, park on Forest Service Road 13505.

**HORSEBACK RIDING** Guided rides are available in Sequoia at the **Wolverton Pack Station** (btw Lodgepole and Giant Forest, tel. 209/565–3445) or the **Mineral King Pack Station** (on Mineral King Rd., tel. 209/565–3404), and in Kings Canyon at the **Cedar Grove Pack Station** or the **Grant Grove Stables** (tel. 209/565–3464 for both). Most stables open in mid-May and close at the end of September, except for the Cedar Grove Station, which opens in April and runs until late October or early November. Expect to pay around $15–$20 an hour, $60 a day, and $150–$175 (including food) for overnighters.

**FISHING** Still going for that elusive trout? You can cast off along several forks of the **Kaweah** and **Kings Rivers.** Day licenses ($9) and tackle are available at the Lodgepole and Cedar Grove markets (*see* Basics, *above*). You can angle for certain fish year-round, but trout season runs from April through November 15. After your fifth catch (ha!), you have to throw them back.

**CROSS-COUNTRY SKIING** The **Sequoia Ski Touring Center** (Wolverton, tel. 209/565–3435 or 209/565–3381) offers rentals and tours of the limitless backcountry. Similar services are provided by the **Grant Grove Ski Touring Center** (Grant Grove Village, tel. 209/335–2314). The facilities are usually open November–April, but be sure to call for conditions. There's no winter lodging near the Sequoia Ski Touring Center, but temporary facilities—food and ski booths—are set up at Lodgepole Village. Off the Generals Highway, **Big Meadows Nordic Ski Trail** offers 1-mile beginner loops as well as more adventurous treks into Big Meadows. **Grant Grove** and **Giant Forest** also have miles of marked, sometimes groomed routes.

You'll find 52 miles of cross-country trails at **Montecito-Sequoia** (off Hwy. 198, 8 mi south of Hwy. 180, tel. 800/227–9900). It costs $10 a day to use the trails, and ski rentals are $16 a day. The **Montecito-Sequoia Lodge and Resort** (tel. 209/565–3388 or 800/843–8677) offers a midweek winter package: For $59 per person per night, with a 2-night minimum, you get a comfortable, rustic cabin, a delicious breakfast and dinner buffet, access to a spa, ice-skating on the lake, free ski lessons, and a trail pass.

# Near Sequoia and Kings Canyon

## SEQUOIA NATIONAL FOREST

Though Sequoia National Park usually takes credit for the grandeur of *sequoia giganteum,* it is actually the neighboring national forest that holds most of these giants within its boundaries.

Sequoia National Forest is stunning, replete with coniferous trees, massive granite formations, alpine lakes, and trout-filled streams. Beyond this, its main advantage lies in its proximity to the San Joaquin Valley. If you're on a tight schedule, you'll appreciate the fact that the forest is linked by major highways to Bakersfield, Visalia, and beyond—ideal if you're coming from Los Angeles, the Bay Area, or even Yosemite. Of course, Sequoia's proximity to the valley also means crowds are a serious problem between May and September, but most of the RV and ATV enthusiasts seem to cluster around Lake Isabella and the Kern River (*see* Near Bakersfield, *below*). As long as you avoid these areas, the weekenders shouldn't get in your way.

Most of the action takes place in the forest's western and southern portions; backcountry hiking, though, is best in the eastern sector. The **Tule River Ranger District,** in the northwest, extends south to Dome Rock and east to the Kern River. The southern **Greenhorn Ranger District** (which contains Lake Isabella) and the **Hot Springs Ranger District** (which comprises the western forest) are accessible by paved roads and are quite popular in summer. For greater solitude, head east to the **Cannell Meadow Ranger District.** From here you can access the **South Sierra** and **Golden Trout wilderness areas,** as well as scenic **Sherman Pass Road,** the southernmost pass across the towering Sierra Nevada.

**VISITOR INFORMATION** Wilderness permits, maps, hiking suggestions, and a list of park activities are available from all ranger stations. All stations are open weekdays and Saturdays 8–4:30, but hours sometimes change; call for specifics. Stations include the **Cannell Meadow Ranger District Headquarters** (near junction of Hwys. 190 and 155, 10 mi north of Lake Isabella, tel. 619/376–3781); the **Greenhorn Ranger District** (Hwy. 58, tel. 805/871–2223); the **Hot Springs Ranger Station** (Hwy. J22, aka Hot Springs Dr., tel. 805/548–6503); the **Hume Lake Ranger District** (36273 Hwy. 180, 30 mi east of Fresno in Dunlap, tel. 209/338–2251); and the **Tule River Ranger District** (32588 Hwy. 190, Springville, tel. 209/539–2607).

**GENERAL STORES** Before heading into the backcountry, stock up on supplies in Porterville (18 mi west of Springville on Hwy. 190), Fresno, Bakersfield, or Dunlap. A great place to stop is the cheap **Save-Mart Supermarket** (900 W. Henderson Ave., Porterville, tel. 209/781–1447), open 7 AM–midnight; they also have a pharmacy (tel. 209/781–1590). Within the forest, **Ponderosa, Pine Flat,** and **Kennedy Meadows** have small, pricey stores. Don't expect to find your favorite brands: Count your blessings if you can find a six-pack of generic beer and a loaf of stale bread.

**COMING AND GOING** Unless you have a reliable car, save yourself the trouble and turn the page; public transportation into the forest does not exist. If you have wheels, reach Sequoia from Porterville (less than 20 mi west) and other points west (including Hwy. 99) via **Highway 190,** known as the **Western Divide Highway** within Sequoia's boundaries. For the southern Cannell Meadow area, take **Sierra Way** north from Kernville (stop at the ranger station in Kernville before leaving town) to **Sherman Pass Road,** where many wilderness trailheads originate. The Hot Springs area is accessible from the San Joaquin Valley by **Highway J22** (aka **Hot Springs Drive** or **Mountain Road 56**) and from the south and east via Kernville and Sierra Way. Whichever way you go, fill the tank outside the forest; inside, gas prices are criminally high.

**WHERE TO SLEEP** Looking for a hotel? If so, make a beeline for Fresno, Bakersfield, or Visalia. It's hard to believe, but hotels and motels are on Sequoia's endangered species list. In nearby Porterville, try one of the budget chains off Highway 65 or head to the **Sundance Inn** (676 N. Main St., tel. 209/784–7920), which has nicely remodeled doubles ($27) and a pool.

➢ **CAMPING** • Dispersed camping (*also see* Camping, in Chapter 1) is allowed throughout the forest with a fire permit (obtainable at a ranger station), and is especially popular in the secluded **Sherman Pass** area of the Cannell Meadow Ranger District. You can phone the **U.S. Forest Service Reservation Center** (tel. 800/280–CAMP) for reservations at developed campgrounds, but you're unlikely to need them except on holidays and during July and August weekends. Besides, the reservation fee is an astronomical $7.50 per campsite.

If you're coming from Porterville, along Highway 190, the Tule River Ranger District offers six quiet campgrounds. One of the nicest is **Quaking Aspen,** less than a half mile past the end of Highway 190 in a forested area with tall, lichen-covered (you guessed it) aspen trees. The 32 sites ($10), with fire pits, toilets, tables, and drinking water, are usually open May 15–November 15. The campground makes a great base for exploring the Golden Trout Wilderness, and its high altitude (7,200 ft) means cool weather year-round. At **Coy Flat Campground,** 20 miles east of Springville on Highway 190, the 19 sites ($10) give you access to Slate Mountain Peak Trail, 6 steep and strenuous miles to deep snow at the summit. Coy Flat has toilets and potable water.

In the Hot Springs Ranger District, the most convenient campground is **Leavis Flat** ($10), on Hot Spring Road (Hwy. J22) across from California Hot Springs Resort (*see* Exploring, *below*). The low elevation and proximity to the road make this a popular place, so solitude-seekers should head instead to **Redwood Meadow,** on the Western Divide Highway a few miles north of its junction with Sherman Pass Road. Just across the street from the Trail of 100 Giants (*see* Exploring, *below*), this small campground offers the opportunity to sleep under giant sequoias. The 15 sites ($12) have tables, fire pits, and drinking water. **Lower Peppermint,** 10 miles north of Johnsondale on Lloyd Meadow Road, lies near some of the best views of Dome Rock. Despite its popularity, you'll feel isolated here because only tent campers are allowed. The 17 first-come, first-served sites ($10) have tables, fire pits, pit toilets, and piped water. These campgrounds are only open May–October.

**EXPLORING SEQUOIA NATIONAL FOREST** The **Tule River Ranger District** offers superb day hiking and popular access points to the Golden Trout Wilderness, including Lewis Camp, Jerkey, and Summit trailheads. If you can't make the all-day journey to Slate Mountain Peak (*see* Camping, *above*) but still want to study the lay of the land, drive to **Dome Rock** (take marked dirt road 2 mi south of Ponderosa Lodge on Hwy. 190). The ⅛-mile, wheelchair-accessible trail to the top (7,221 ft) is a breeze—and you'll be treated to spectacular views of Slate Mountain to the west, Needles Rock to the northeast, and the Kern Basin to the south. If you're up for a bit more exercise, take the moderate 2½-mile (one-way) trail to **Needles Rock.** Give yourself a good 4 hours for the whole trek—you'll want to explore the fire lookout tower as well as check out views of Mt. Whitney and Kern Basin. Bring plenty of water; it's dry as a bone at the top. To reach the trailhead, take Needles Road (½ mi south of Quaking Aspen Campground) east 3 miles.

*Climbers, get out your gear. The towering granite spires of Needles Rock (8,245 ft) make for exhilarating, world-class high-country climbs. This is where the locals go—which means something in a region where rock faces are in no short supply.*

For more hikes, check out *Upper Tule Hiking Trails* ($2.50), available at the Tule River Ranger Station. Author's choice is the **Coy Flat–Bear Ridge Trail,** a moderate 7-mile, 5-hour hike to an exquisite sequoia grove. The trailhead, accessible from mid-April through October, is near Bear Creek where it meets Coy Flat Campground (*see* Camping, *above*). For some of the best high-altitude hiking in the area, follow signs from Highway 190 to the **Lewis Camp Trailhead:** From here you'll get spectacular views of glacier-carved valleys and you can hike into the pristine Golden Trout Wilderness. A good day trip is the 7-mile loop (4–5 hrs) through Grey Meadow and over the bridge to the other side of Bear Creek on the **Jordan Trail.**

The **Hot Springs Ranger District** features two groups of giant sequoias: the wheelchair-accessible **Trail of 100 Giants** on Western Divide Highway (Hwy. 190) just north of Sherman Pass Road; and the **Deer Creek Grove,** 3 miles south of the ranger station (follow signs). Both have short trails you can easily walk in an hour, even if you're on the verge of cardiac arrest. Despite the name, the ranger district contains only one public hot springs: **California Hot Springs Resort** (42177 Hot Springs Dr., tel. 805/548–6582), just north of the small town of California Hot Springs, lets you soak in hot mineral tubs for only $7 a day. Bring a bathing suit; clothing is not optional here.

The **Cannell Meadow Ranger District** provides trail access to the Dome Land, South Sierra, and Golden Trout wildernesses. The rugged **Dome Land Wilderness,** the southernmost in the Sierra, is covered by piñon and Jeffrey pines. Trailheads are at Big Meadow (Cherry Hill Rd., off Sherman Pass Rd. from Kernville) and Taylor Meadow (southeast of Big Meadow). The **South Sierra Wilderness,** north of Dome Land, is notable for its meadows, granite formations, and diverse topography, ranging from gentle hills to steep peaks. To access its trailheads, take Sherman Pass Road to the Jackass Road turnoff past Black Rock Station and follow signs. The **Golden Trout Wilderness** lies just south of Sequoia National Park. Its pine forests, streams, and meadows are accessible from the trailhead at the Black Rock Station on Sherman Pass Road.

The **Hume Lake Ranger District** in the north (also *see* Sequoia and Kings Canyon National Parks, *above*) offers easy access to the **Jennie Lakes Wilderness,** one of the most pristine retreats south of Yosemite. Trails begin on Big Meadows Road, off Generals Highway. From Big Meadows Station, you can hike 5 moderate-to-strenuous miles (an all-day outing) to **Jennie Lake,** passing the ominous **Bop Out Pass** along the way. To see the Jennie Lakes Wilderness by car, drive along Highway 180 east into Kings River Canyon.

**FOREST ACTIVITIES** Besides enjoying the rigors of high-country hiking, those itching for action can undertake mountain biking or rafting expeditions; the more sedentary can lazily pursue a day of fishing, swimming, or easy biking.

➢ **BIKING** • Bicycles are allowed on almost all forest roads, including fire trails and unimproved dirt roads. The heaviest concentration of trails is in the Hot Springs Ranger District. For an easy pedal, check out **Horse Meadows Road** between Redwood and Holey Meadows campgrounds, off the south end of the Western Divide Highway (Hwy. 190). Serious cyclists can tackle the 6½-mile climb to **Mule Peak,** which offers stunning views. From Horse Meadows, the dirt path follows Horse Meadows Creek north, and the high altitude will make the 1,400-foot ascent feel like 3,000 unless you're already acclimated. For bike rentals ($15 half day, $28 full day), head to Kernville's **Mountain and River Adventures** (11113 Kernville Rd., tel. 619/376–6553).

➢ **FISHING** • Fishing—particularly for trout—is popular along the Tule River, in the high lakes and streams of the Golden Trout and Jennie Lakes wildernesses, and at Hume Lake. You can fish from the last Saturday in April through November 15 near **Coffee Camp** on the Tule River. Pick up a license ($8.75 a day) at any sporting-goods store. Springville (Hwy. 190), the self-proclaimed "Gateway to the Golden Trout Wilderness," is good for supplies; try **Gifford's Market** (35637 Hwy. 190, tel. 209/539–2637).

➢ **RAFTING** • Several companies run raft trips along the Kern River, which boasts Class III and IV rapids. Trips range from 1½-hour outings ($15–$18) to multiple-day adventures ($120–$135). Contact **Chuck Richard's Whitewater** (11200 Kernville Rd., tel. 619/379–4444), which seems to beat the competition by a couple dollars across the board.

➢ **SWIMMING** • Most streams are too shallow or too cold for swimming, but **Coffee Camp,** along Highway 190 just inside forest boundaries, is a blessed exception, offering pools carved into huge granite formations. You pay $5 per vehicle. Huge **Lake Isabella** (*see* Near Bakersfield, *below*) is another option, but you're likely to be sideswiped by a motorboat if you're not paying attention.

# The San Joaquin Valley

**In a state whose image is symbolized by beaches** and movie stars, California's San Joaquin Valley is something of a forgotten land. To many outsiders, the hot, flat, 225-mile stretch of tract homes and mini-malls separating San Francisco and Los Angeles from the Sierra Nevada is a bad dream that reappears periodically in the news as the site of a grisly mass murder or the home of an infectious airborne fungus. The fact remains, though, that this is one of the fastest-growing regions in the state, and no area is so central to the economic health of California. The valley has long supplied agricultural products to the rest of the country, thanks to the labor of migrant workers from the Dust Bowl and Mexico. And its cities have grown spectacularly in recent years, becoming bedroom communities for L.A. and San Francisco commuters. Of course, if neither megasuburbs nor large-scale farming gets you excited, there's not much here to detain you. Most travelers treat the San Joaquin Valley as a vast, unsightly pit stop, stocked with enough cheap fuel and food to get them to their real destinations.

Odds are good that you won't fall in love with this area; but with a healthy sense of the absurd you'll enjoy the time you spend zipping along **I-5** and **Highway 99,** the region's principal thoroughfares. Don't despair if you find yourself in Stockton, Merced, Fresno, or Bakersfield. Head out to the minor-league baseball park, hit a country-western bar, find a comfy room in a chain motel with king beds and a pool, and have an all-American adventure. With the right attitude, you'll be surprised at how much fun it can be.



# Stockton

On the face of it, there's not much reason to visit a place that combines the unmercifully hot weather of Redding with the unmercifully conservative politics of Anaheim. But if you're passing through this inland port—which brought you Maxine Hong Kingston, Chris Isaak, and Pavement (the reigning kings of indie rock)—you'll have no trouble finding a budget motel with a pool or a cheap, authentic Mexican meal. Wandering around the seedy downtown area, where Market and Main streets meet Wilson Way, you'll get a feel for the town as it was before the shopping centers and Bay Area commuters invaded.

*Both redneck capital and bedroom community, Stockton is really two towns in one: the town of gun shows and El Caminos, and the town of malls and 80-mile commutes. It's a little bit country and a little bit Muzak.*

While some people use Stockton as a base for exploring the waterways of the Sacramento River Delta (*see* Chapter 6), you don't have to be a water-sports enthusiast to find something to do here. Head to **Louis Park** and spend a surreal afternoon at the kitschy wonderland of Pixie Woods (*see* Cheap Thrills, *below*). At **Victory Park** you'll find the free **Haggin Museum** (1201 N. Pershing Ave., tel. 209/462–4116), open Tuesday–Sunday 1:30–5, featuring an unusual juxtaposition of antique farm equipment and 19th-century French paintings. If you're in town at the end of April, check out the big **Asparagus Festival** (tel. 209/943–1987), a week-long event that features music, car shows, and enough of the celebrated vegetable to stink up every restroom in town.

**VISITOR INFORMATION** The **Stockton/San Joaquin Convention and Visitors Bureau** has information on the entire region, including a great street map ($1.50) and loads of brochures on lodging, dining, and recreation. *46 W. Fremont St., at Center St., tel. 209/943–1987 or 800/350–1987. Open weekdays 8–5.*

**COMING AND GOING** **I-5** runs north–south through the center of Stockton. **Highway 99** runs north–south along the eastern edge of the city and leads south to Modesto, Merced, Fresno, and Bakersfield. **Highways 4, 26,** and **88** all run east toward the Gold Country (*see* Chapter 6).

## *The Grapes of Wrath*

***California's Central Valley is one of the most productive agricultural regions in the world, but those who work in the fields pay a price for its success. According to the United Farm Workers of America (UFW), 300 million pounds of pesticides are used each year in California, resulting in the poisoning of nearly 300,000 farm workers yearly. The Food and Drug Administration is supposed to regulate hazardous products, yet a third of the pesticides used on grapes are known to cause cancer. In one farm community, the cancer rates were 1,200% higher than the national average. In 1962, César Chavez founded the UFW in hopes the union could address problems like this. His efforts resulted in a grape boycott, which began in 1965 and continues today. Conscientious consumers can ask at stands off the highway for union-friendly fruit or check for the union label at markets.***

**Amtrak** (735 S. San Joaquin St., tel. 209/946–0517) offers trains from Stockton to the Bay Area (2½ hrs each way, $16 round-trip) and down to Bakersfield, with bus service to Los Angeles (7 hrs each way, $66 round-trip). The depot is open daily 8 AM–10:30 PM, but you should spend as little time here as possible: The threat of someone making off with your purse or wallet is all too real. **Greyhound** buses to the Bay Area ($21 round-trip) take as long as trains and are less comfortable. Lockers at the downtown station (121 S. Center St., tel. 209/466–3568 or 800/231–2222), open daily 5:30 AM–10:30 PM, are available for $1 per 24 hours.

**GETTING AROUND** If you don't have a car, a mediocre bus system ($1, transfers free) covers most of the city from 6 AM to 7:30 PM. Bus 6 travels from downtown to University of the Pacific (UOP); Bus 10 will get you from UOP or downtown to the Amtrak Depot. Pick up maps and schedules at the visitor center (*see above*). Most buses are wheelchair accessible. For more info, call the **San Joaquin Regional Transit District** (tel. 209/943–1111).

**WHERE TO SLEEP** One cheap option that requires advance planning is renting a room at **University of the Pacific** (2nd floor, Bannister Hall, UOP, tel. 209/946–2331)—singles are only $20, doubles $25, and all have private showers. Otherwise, budget motels abound near I-5 and Highway 99. The Waterloo Road exit off Highway 99 has some excellent options, including **Motel Orleans** (3951 Budweiser Ct., behind Motel 6, tel. 209/931–9341), with doubles for $40 and a $7 discount for AAA members. It has a pool and wheelchair-accessible rooms. Places off the Waterloo Road exit are more modern than the dives on Wilson Way off Highway 99, but if you're looking for a blast from the past, try the run-down **Crest Motel** (639 N. Wilson Way, tel. 209/466–2431); at $27 for a double, its age can be overlooked. If you're coming in on Greyhound or want to stay downtown, the **Days Inn** (33 N. Center St., tel. 209/948–6151) has comfortable rooms (some with wheelchair access) at $42 for a queen (10% less with AAA card).

**FOOD** Large Asian and Mexican American populations have helped Stockton spice up its standard selection of fast-food chains with cheap, hearty eateries. Still, sometimes it seems like the prime local cuisine is donuts. One donut emporium to try is **MaMa Donuts** (4133 N. El Dorado St., at Willow St., tel. 209/946–4452), where they custom-fill 'em. The health-conscious can load up on fresh produce at Stockton's large **farmers' market,** held 7 AM–11 AM every Saturday beneath the crosstown freeway that connects I-5 and Highway 99. For a quick, tasty meal of sandwiches or burgers (about $3), go to **Manny's California Fresh** (1612 Pacific Ave., at Harding St., tel. 209/463–6415). Near the Greyhound station downtown, popular **Arroyo's Café** (324 S. Center St., at Lafayette St., tel. 209/462–1661) serves great burritos and soft tacos for under $3. On weekend nights you can listen to live Latin music here, but bring a friend: The neighborhood can be questionable after dark.

➢ **UNDER $10** • **Cancun.** Besides being known by locals as a fine Mexican restaurant, Cancun is beautifully decorated with murals of pre-Columbian scenes. The combo plate (rice, beans, and two additional items) runs about $5. *248 N. El Dorado St., at Miner St., tel. 209/465–6810. Open Sun.–Thurs. 11–10:30, Fri.–Sat. 11–3. Wheelchair access.*

**Le Kim's.** This tiny Vietnamese restaurant packs in the crowds during lunch and dinner. Patrons clamor for dishes like the sautéed bean cakes with veggies ($5.25). *631 N. Center St., tel. 209/943–0308. 6 blocks north of Greyhound station. Open Mon.–Sat. 9 AM–10 PM.*

**On Lock Sam.** When you see the ornate bar, you won't believe you're in downtown Stockton. And when you've realized you are indeed in Stockton, you won't believe a meal could be this good. Try the eight-piece foil-wrapped chicken ($7.25) or the mu-shu pork ($6.75). *333 S. Sutter St., btw Sonora and Lafayette Sts., tel. 209/466–4561. Open Mon.–Thurs. 11–9:30, Fri. 11–10:30, Sat. 11:30–10:30, Sun. 11:30–9:30.*

**CHEAP THRILLS** **Pixie Woods.** As you wander around this unusual park, dotted with cement replicas of your favorite fairy-tale characters, you may experience déjà vu: Pixie Woods was the location of one of Spinal Tap's last concerts (*sans* Nigel Tufnel). Set in Louis Park near the San Joaquin River, this is the perfect excursion for the young and twisted at heart. *Tel. 209/937–8206. Pershing exit off I-5, left on Monte Diablo Ave. Admission: $1.50. Open summer, Wed.–Fri. 11–5, weekends 11–6; spring and fall, weekends noon–5; closed late Oct.–Feb.*

**Stockton Ports.** A perennial powerhouse of minor-league baseball, the Ports trace their lineage back to a Stockton team called the Mudville Nine, believed to have been the inspiration for Ernest L. Thayer's poem "Casey at the Bat." Stockton's pride plays at the Billy Hebert Field in Oak Park from early April to August. *Alpine Ave., near California St., tel. 209/944–5943. Admission: $5 (reserved seats, $6).*

**AFTER DARK** Though Stockton's nightlife caters to a conservative sports-bar crowd, other options do exist. If anything exciting is happening in town, you'll probably find out about it at the **Blackwater Café** (912 N. Yosemite St., at Acacia St., tel. 209/943–6938), a casual coffee spot where the young and hip pass evenings sipping stimulants (and depressants). If you're downtown, toss back a few with the loud, colorful crowd at the **Shamrock Bar** (602 E. Market St., btw Main and American Sts., tel. 209/462–2120), which features Irish coffee, two pool tables, and a killer jukebox. Stockton's only full-time gay bar, the **Paradise Club** (10100 Lower Sacramento Rd., tel. 209/477–4724), is somewhat far north and so boring it's barely worth the drive. New to the scene is the **El Dorado Brewing Company** (157 Adams St., off Pacific Ave., tel. 209/948–2537), the city's first microbrewery. For a taste of more typical Stockton culture, try the **El Dorado Bowl** (725 N. El Dorado St., at Flora St., tel. 209/466–9665), where bowlers and pool players have congregated since 1946.

## NEAR STOCKTON

**MODESTO** Less than an hour south of Stockton on Highway 99, Modesto lies deep in the heart of fruit and fertilizer country. Travelers use the town as a gateway to Yosemite and the Sierra Nevada (via Hwy. 132) and usually escape without confronting much of the sizable city. In previous years, the main lure for visitors was **Graffiti Night** (the second or third Saturday in June), a massive celebration of 1950s car culture in the town that inspired native son George Lucas's movie *American Graffiti.* Recent outbursts of gang violence, however, led the city to outlaw the big McHenry Avenue Cruise in 1993, stripping the festival of some of its appeal. As an alternative, catch the minor-league **Modesto A's** (general admission $3) at John Thurman Field (Tuolumne exit from Hwy. 99, left on Neece Dr., tel. 209/529–7368). If you're even the slightest bit hungry, get off the highway to eat at **Portofino Caffè** (521 McHenry Ave., tel. 209/549–7761), which offers delicious six-cheese lasagna ($8 with soup or salad) and amazing desserts ($3.50). For a surprisingly good time and a look at Modesto's definition of hip,

### Buy Me Some Peanuts and Cracker Jacks

***With major-league baseball teams still fighting major-league fall-out from the 1994 baseball strike, minor-league ball teams are enjoying a major surge in popularity. Fans fill bleachers coast to coast looking for a good—and honest—game where the grass is real, the seats are cheap, and most foul balls leave the stadium. Californians have the luxury of a league composed entirely of teams from their state. Though it's only Class A (the highest being AAA), the century-old California League features high-quality baseball played by future stars. (About 25% of major leaguers have done time in "the Cali.") The 10 teams are concentrated in sweltering towns along Highway 99 and I–10, including Stockton (Ports), Modesto (A's), Visalia (Oaks), and Bakersfield (Blaze). Though families, local teenagers, and players' girlfriends (the last two groups sometimes overlap) make up the bulk of the crowd, Cali games are ideal for budget travelers. You get nine innings of baseball for about $4, a glimpse of local culture, and a chance to see some future Hall-of-Famers up close and personal—and, if you're holding the scorecard with the lucky number, you could win a free Jiffy Lube.***

drop by the **J Street Café** (1030 J St., at 11th St., tel. 209/577–8007) for espresso, tasty cake and ice cream ($1–$3), and live music on the weekends.

# Fresno

Forget all the jokes about Fresno being the gateway to Bakersfield: This is the best place to visit in the San Joaquin Valley. Smack in the middle of the Central Valley between Stockton in the north and Bakersfield in the south, Fresno boasts a happening nightlife (by regional standards) and a hip, alternative neighborhood. If you have any time at all, check out the **Tower District** (E. Olive Ave., west of Van Ness Ave.), playground of the city's bohemian, gay, punk, and hippie populations, whose slim numbers force them into an unusually friendly coexistence. The architectural center of the district is the **Tower Theater** (815 E. Olive Ave., tel. 209/485–9050), which books comedy and musical acts; but a better place to enter the scene is down the block at **Java Café** (*see* Food, *below*), where you can pick up copies of the *Fresno Free Press,* the weekly *Metronews,* or *? & Answers,* the local gay and lesbian paper. Other Tower hot spots include **Ragin' Records** (729 E. Olive Ave., tel. 209/485–9926) and **Valentino's Alternative Apparel** (814 E. Olive Ave., tel. 209/233–6900), with the best of L.A.'s Melrose or S.F.'s Haight at half the price. To get to the Tower, take Olive Avenue east from Highway 99, or take McKinley Avenue west from Highway 41, then go left on N. Wishon Avenue.

*Just north of the artsy Tower District, Fat Jerry's Spears of Shiva (1479 N. Maroa Ave., tel. 209/497–5811) specializes in body piercing, scarification, custom-made bondage gear, and other artifacts of the expanding subculture of pain.*

Downtown, the demography and architecture give the area a Mexican feel, while the construction of large office buildings around M and Fresno streets would seem to portend some redevelopment that hasn't yet taken hold. There's not much foot traffic here; most commercial action takes place along **North Blackstone Avenue,** which runs parallel to Highway 41. Shopping centers and multiplex theaters dominate this strip, but you'll also find used-record stores, thrift shops, and a café or two. East of Blackstone on **Shaw Avenue,** a conventional college social scene is sustained by **Cal State Fresno.**

During summer, temperatures hover in the FM-radio range, but if you can stand the outdoors, consider a visit to **Roeding Park** (btw Olive and Belmont Aves., near Olive Ave. exit off Hwy. 99, tel. 209/498–1551), open daily 9 AM–10 PM. While the park can be dangerous at night, the **Chaffee Zoological Gardens** (tel. 209/498–4692), open daily 9–5, gets good reviews from locals. Park entrance is free for pedestrians, $1 for cars; zoo admission is another $4.50.

**VISITOR INFORMATION** The **Fresno Convention and Visitors Bureau** distributes a useful free booklet that includes important phone numbers, public transportation routes, and cheap dining and lodging options. *808 M St., btw Kern and Inyo Sts., tel. 209/233–0836 or 800/788–0836. Open weekdays 8–5.*

**COMING AND GOING** **Highway 99,** the valley's lifeline, runs along Fresno's western edge. **Highway 41,** which extends 90 miles northeast to Yosemite National Park, provides a quick way to get around the sprawling city. If you're coming from L.A., pick up 41 from Highway 99 just south of the city. **Highway 180** runs east to Kings Canyon and Sequoia National Parks, while **Highway 168** goes east to the Shaver Lake area of the Sierra National Forest.

**Greyhound** (1033 Broadway Blvd., tel. 209/268–1829) offers six buses daily to San Francisco (5 hrs, $21 one-way) and 20 daily to L.A. (5½ hrs, $19 one-way). The station, open 5 AM–1 AM, is in an unsafe part of town, but it offers 24-hour lockers for $1. Trains run from Fresno's **Amtrak** station (2650 Tulare St., behind Santa Fe depot, tel. 209/486–7651) to San Francisco (4½ hrs, $39 one-way) and to Bakersfield, with bus connections to Los Angeles (4½ hrs, $38 one-way). The rather unsafe station is open 6 AM–9:20 PM (closed 7–8 PM), but only sells tickets until 9 PM. Passengers can stow luggage behind the ticket counter ($1.50 per piece per day). Another cheap and fast connection to Southern California is **Transportes Inter California** (1333 Broadway Blvd., behind Greyhound station, tel. 209/233–7488), which has three buses daily to L.A. (4 hrs, $21 one-way). Call for information on other Southland destinations (Spanish helpful but not necessary).

**GETTING AROUND** Major north–south routes through town include Blackstone Avenue and Highway 41. Downtown is the only area accessible by foot from the train and bus stations, so if you're car-less, you may want to familiarize yourself with **Fresno Area Express** (tel. 209/498–1122), whose buses run all over town for 75¢ (with one free transfer). Most lines run every 30 minutes (hourly on Sundays); service stops around 7 PM. Important routes include Bus 30 (downtown to N. Blackstone Ave.), Bus 28 (downtown to the Tower District), and Bus 33 (crosstown on Olive Ave. from the Tower to cheap motels on Hwy. 99).

**WHERE TO SLEEP** Your best bet is the Olive Avenue exit off Highway 99, so long as you don't mind sleeping to the clang of the Southern Pacific. Right next to Roeding Park and a little more than a mile down Olive Avenue from the Tower District, a decent **Motel 6** (1240 N. Crystal Ave., tel. 209/237–0855) with HBO and a pool has doubles for $31. The **Golden Penny Inn** (777 N. Parkway Dr., tel. 209/237–2175) lacks a pool, but doubles start at $34. Both motels are wheelchair accessible. There's also a Motel Drive exit off Highway 99, with cheap lodgings right along the tracks, but these motels are dingier than the ones at Olive Avenue. Offerings are sparse downtown, but if you've reached the sleep-or-die state after 22 hours on an excessively intimate bus, try **Motel 7** (888 Broadway Blvd., near Inyo St., tel. 209/485–7550), a block from the station. One bed runs $30, two beds $36.

**FOOD** Thanks to its Mexican American, Southeast Asian, and Armenian communities, Fresno offers some ethnic restaurants worth sticking around for. **Belmont Avenue,** east of Broadway, has popular Thai and Cambodian places, while **West Bullard Avenue** boasts top-rate Armenian spots. **Armenian Cuisine** (742 W. Bullard Ave., at Palm Ave., tel. 209/435–4892) offers hearty meat-and-pilaf dinners ($9–$12) and sandwiches (about $6). Though it sounds like a produce fair, the **Farmers' Market** (Blackstone Ave., at Shaw Ave.), open Wednesday and Saturday mornings, is actually a collection of reasonably priced (around $5) ethnic eateries. In the Tower District, **Piemonte's** (616 Olive Ave., tel. 209/237–2038), open Tuesday–Saturday 9–5:45, is great for take-out sandwiches ($2.50–$4.50).

➢ **UNDER $5** • **Bangkok Restaurant.** Tucked away in a nondescript shopping center, this restaurant offers cheap and tasty Thai food. The basil chicken ($4.50) is the most popular dish, but there are less expensive options, like the broccoli/bean sprout combo ($3.50). *1627 E. Ashlan St., at N. Blackstone Ave., tel. 209/227–9776. Open weekdays 11:30–2:30 and 5–9.*

**Rafael's Sabroso Foods.** Part Mexican deli, part restaurant, and part tortilla factory, Rafael's serves some of the best and cheapest eats in all of Fresno. Enchiladas with rice and beans are $5, and for $4.25 you get the Sabroso burrito with shredded beef or chicken. *94 E. Belmont Ave., near Palm Ave., tel. 209/264–1684. Open Mon.–Sat. 7:30 AM–8 PM, Sun. 7:30–3.*

➢ **UNDER $10** • **Apex.** This new Mediterranean and Caribbean restaurant in the Tower already attracts regular customers who come for the hot seafood salad or the shrimp enchiladas (both $7). *936 E. Olive Ave., tel. 209/266–2739. Open Tues.–Thurs. 11–2 and 5–9, Fri. 11–2 and 5–10, Sat. 5–10, Sun. 9–2.*

**Grandmarie's Chicken Pies.** It's always refreshing to see ol'-timer cowboys and young gay men eating delectable chicken pies together in peace. Chicken pies with gravy, mashed potatoes, and salad are $6; vegetarian chili with cornbread and salad is only $5. It may be worth the price just to see this unofficial museum of America's diner heritage. *861 E. Olive Lane, in the Tower, tel. 209/237–5042. Open weekdays 6 AM–8 PM, Sat. 6–3.*

➢ **CAFES** • In the heart of the Tower District, **Java Café** (805 E. Olive Ave., tel. 209/237–5282) is the city's hippest hangout, but there's less attitude than you might expect. You can sip your espresso ($3) or munch on a sandwich (about $5) on the outdoor patio until 10 on weeknights and midnight on weekends. **City Café** (5048 N. Blackstone Ave., near Shaw Ave., tel. 209/224–4399) is a power-breakfast joint by day and an unlikely hangout for Fresno's young and bored by night (until midnight). Look for photos of former Fresnans like Cher and Tom Seaver on the walls. The newest hot spot in the Tower, **Café Intermezzo** (747 E. Olive Ave., tel. 209/497–1456), has a ceiling painted like the sky and theater and movie posters on the wall. Ingest amazing desserts ($3–$4), fine pizzas ($6–$9), and something from the generous wine and beer lists until 11 PM during the week and midnight on weekends.

**CHEAP THRILLS** On summer Tuesday evenings at 6, head to the Tower District's **street fair.** Or on any evening June–August, head over to the west-facing wall of the **Tower Theater** at sundown (bring a chair) for free movies. You can catch free bluegrass, jazz, or big band concerts Monday evenings in the summer at **Woodward Park,** north of town (cnr Audubon and Friant Rds., Friant exit off Hwy. 41). Ask about the concert schedule at the visitor center.

**Table Mountain Rancheria Casino and Bingo.** For a real taste of local culture, check out the largest gaming facility in the San Joaquin Valley. Thanks to the fact that federal anti-gaming laws do not apply on Indian reservations, you can join the hundreds (often thousands) of Fresnans—not all of them septuagenarians—who flock to this oversized bingo parlor Wednesday–Sunday nights. Spend a few bucks on a couple of games, or buy bingo packs ($5–$10) with potential $500–$1,000 payoffs. There are also blackjack tables and video poker machines at the 24-hour casino if you've got cash to spare. *Tel. 800/541–3637. Friant Rd. exit off Hwy. 41.*

**AFTER DARK** Don't laugh—Fresno has loads of nightlife options. Cheap drinks, dancing, and even live music are easy to find in the Tower District and downtown, though you won't get a bus ride home until morning. Listen to 105.9 FM for info on special events and attractions. Be careful: Not all of Fresno is safe at night, and you may want to avoid walking around downtown or on lower Blackstone Avenue. A good pub is **Butterfield Brewing Company** (777 E. Olive Ave., tel. 209/264–5521) in the Tower, which serves five of their own microbrews for $2.75 a pint (the Bridalveil Ale is a good starter) and hosts jazz and blues on weekends. Fresno's premier gay bar, the **Express** (708 N. Blackstone Ave., at E. Olive Ave., tel. 209/233–1791), offers free barbecue or spaghetti on Sundays and is packed with dancers throughout the week. Try to park your car in the lot, as the bar is in a rough part of town. Expect a $1–$3 cover on Friday and Saturday. Fresno has only one lesbian bar: the **Palace Saloon,** on the far east side of town (4030 E. Belmont Ave., at Cedar Ave, tel. 209/264–8283), with a DJ on Fridays and Saturdays.

Pick up a free mag at **Java Café** (*see* Food, *above*) to find out what's happening at the clubs. For blues, try **Zapp's Park** (1105 N. Blackstone Ave., near Webster St., tel. 209/266–0334), a crowded little bar with live music every night and a $2–$4 cover Friday–Sunday. Pay a $3–$4 cover and join the young and the pierced at **Club Fred** (1426 N. Van Ness Ave, in the Tower, tel. 209/233–3733), a good place to scope out the local alternative music scene.

## NEAR FRESNO

**MERCED** About 70 miles south of Stockton and 55 miles north of Fresno on Highway 99, Merced is the valley's preferred gateway to Yosemite, so thousands of unsuspecting travelers wind up here every year. Most pick up Highway 140 and book right out of town, but Merced has plenty of cheap motels, and it's not the end of the world if you have to spend the night. Motels cluster along Highway 99; the Motel Drive off-ramp is your best bet for good rates, quality, and safety. Try the air-conditioned **Sierra Lodge** (951 Motel Dr., tel. 209/722–3926), with singles for $30, doubles for $38, and a free continental breakfast. The small **Yosemite Gateway Home Hostel** (tel. 209/725–0407), not far from town, has only four beds for $13 each ($10 with AYH card), so reservations are essential. They'll give you directions when you call. One of the most interesting sights in the area (and free to boot) is the **Merced County Courthouse Museum** (21st and N Sts., tel. 209/723–2401), open Wednesday–Sunday 1–4 PM, with everything from old gas pumps to an exotic Taoist shrine (a vestige of the Chinese community that built the Southern Pacific Railroad). If it's not too crowded—it tends not to be—a docent will take you on a free tour.

**VISALIA** A few miles east of Highway 99 on Highway 198 (43 mi south of Fresno), Visalia makes a good pit stop on the way to Sequoia National Park, 55 miles east on Highway 198. You can stock up on groceries on West Mineral King Avenue at the west end of town or on Noble Avenue at the east end. The **Marco Polo Hotel and Restaurant** (4545 W. Mineral King Ave., on Hwy. 198 at Linwood Ave., tel. 209/732–4591) offers small, newly carpeted rooms starting at $30, with balconies, HBO, and a pool. The Indian restaurant on the premises features all-you-can-eat lunch buffets for $5.

Though you can no longer order from your car, the 53-year-old **Mearle's Drive-In** (604 S. Mooney Blvd., tel. 209/734–4447) still serves up sandwiches ($3–$4), diner food ($6 and under), and plenty of ice cream. For an authentic Mexican meal, head to **Colima** (111 E. Main St., tel. 209/733–7078), where great combo plates are less than $7. You wouldn't expect to find a place like **Java Jungle** (208 W. Main St., tel. 209/732–5282) in a town with more cows than people; but even in Visalia would-be urban hipsters have carved a niche. On Saturday nights you can bowl until 2 AM at spacious **Visalia Lanes** (1740 W. Caldwell Ave., tel. 209/625–2100). To make your all-American visit complete, watch the local minor-league team, the Visalia Oaks, play at **Recreation Park** (440 N. Giddings Ave., near downtown north of Hwy. 198, tel. 209/625–0480). Tickets go for $3 ($2 students aged 20 or under).



# Bakersfield

"How many of you who sit and judge me," country singer Dwight Yoakam crooned, "have walked the streets of Bakersfield?" In the past, travelers headed to the Sierra Nevada from Southern California rarely stepped out of their cars as they passed through this maligned city—but more people each year are achieving the moral authority to judge Mr. Yoakam. Despite the heat and the uninspiring oil derricks and shopping centers, Bakersfield's population continues to swell with white folks happy to drive two hours to L.A. every workday in return for mortgage payments that more nearly resemble car insurance premiums in West Hollywood. This conservative town offers little alternative culture, but there are plenty of cheap motels and truck-stop diners, as well as a couple of excellent Basque restaurants. If country music, drive-ins, and girlie bars leave you cold, you can always use Bakersfield as a base for day trips to nearby **Lake Isabella,** the largest freshwater lake in Southern California.

**VISITOR INFORMATION** The helpful staff at the **Kern County Board of Trade** offers guides for food, lodging, and regional transit. *2101 Oak St., at 21st St., tel. 800/500–KERN. Open weekdays 8–5.*

**COMING AND GOING** **Highway 99** runs north–south through town, connecting Bakersfield to L.A. (112 miles south) and Fresno (107 miles north). If you're coming from San Francisco, pick up **Highway 58** off I–5 at Buttonwillow, and follow it 23 miles east into town. East of the city, Highway 58 runs over the Tehachapi Pass into Barstow (136 miles), where you can pick up I–15 and I–40. **Highway 178** goes northeast up the Kern River Canyon toward Lake Isabella and Sequoia National Forest.

**Greyhound** runs 11 buses daily to San Francisco (8–9 hrs each way, $60 round-trip) and 16 buses daily to L.A. (2½–4 hrs each way, $25 round-trip). The station (1820 18th St., at F St. downtown, tel. 805/327–5617 or 800/231–2222) is open daily 7:30 AM–1 AM and has 24-hour lockers for $1. The **Hacienda Café** next door is open 24 hours. **Amtrak** has trains to the San Francisco Bay Area (6½ hrs each way, $66 round-trip). There's no rail service to Los Angeles; Amtrak runs frequent buses (2½–5 hrs each way, $30 round-trip), but you're better off with Greyhound if you're coming from the south. The train station downtown (15th and F Sts., tel. 805/395–3175 or 800/872–7245) is open daily 4:30 AM–8 PM and 9 PM–midnight. Store luggage for free in the baggage room.

**GETTING AROUND** Downtown, roughly the area between F Street and M Street and 15th Street and 24th Street, encompasses the train station, the bus station, and any remnants of character the town might once have possessed. The **Golden Empire Transit District** (cnr 21st St. and Chester Ave., tel. 805/327–7686) hands out transit maps and schedules for city GET buses (75¢, transfers free), which run Monday–Saturday 6:30 AM–7:15 PM.

**WHERE TO SLEEP** Budget accommodations are Bakersfield's main attraction. The Olive Drive exit off Highway 99 (just north of town), and Union and South Union avenues on the east side, are good bets, but the prime location is the intersection of Highway 58 (Rosedale Hwy.) and Highway 99. Here your options include the affordable **E-Z 8 Motel** (2604 Pierce Rd., Pierce Rd. exit off Hwy. 99, tel. 805/322–1901), with comfortable rooms (doubles $29) and a pool where you can splash around with the truckers. Within walking distance of the bus and train stations, the **Downtowner Inn** (1301 Chester Ave., at 13th St., tel. 805/327–7122) is your best bet. Doubles go for $38 and up, and you get free breakfast, HBO, and pool.

**FOOD** Bakersfield specializes in greasy truck-stop food and—believe it or not—Basque food. Several Basque restaurants serve up lavish multi-course meals that feature good, homemade bread, beans, and spicy meats from a broad range of animal organs. If you're partial to the first style of eats, try **Zingo's** (3201 Pierce Rd., tel. 805/321–0627), open 5 AM–10 PM daily, which has pancakes and eggs ($4) for breakfast and a tasty roast beef dinner ($6). **Dewar's** (1120 Eye St., near 12th St., tel. 805/322–0933), an old-fashioned soda fountain and candy shop, has been a town institution since 1909.

➢ **UNDER $10** • **The Garden Spot.** This place offers an all-you-can-eat salad bar ($5.50, $6.50 with soup) that puts Sizzler to shame. The veggies are fresh and the homemade soups good and filling. *3320 Truxtun Ave., at Oak St., tel. 805/323–3236. Open Mon.–Sat. 11–8.*

➢ **UNDER $15** • **Maitia's.** Work up a serious appetite before embarking on the adventure disguised as dinner at this Basque restaurant. You get soup, beans, salad, pickled tongue, spaghetti, *and* a main course (frequent customers swear by the veal and the lamb loin chops). Full dinners run $9–$16. There's also lunch, but it's far less impressive and nearly as pricey ($6–$11). *3535 Union Ave., tel. 805/324–4711. Open weekdays 11–2 and 5:30–10, Sat. 5:30–10, Sun. 4–9.*

**AFTER DARK** A monument to a more glamorous time, the **Hotel Padre** (1813 H St., tel. 805/322–1419) towers above downtown like a lighthouse, with a number of its neon lights burnt out (you may recognize it as Hot Padre or even Hot Pad). It has a popular piano bar, drawing young folks and barflies for serious drinking and Sinatra sing-alongs. A block away, down the alley between 18th and 19th streets, **Guthrie's Alley Cat** (1525 Wall St., tel. 805/324–6328) is probably the hippest bar in town. You'll pay $1.50 for a mug of beer and $2 for well drinks. **Suds Tavern** (1514 Wall St., tel. 805/322–2265) is a 21-and-over rock and blues club with a $3 weekend cover. The Chicano/Latino gay scene centers around **The Cellar** (1927 K St., tel. 805/322–1229), which has a DJ every night, no cover, and cheap beer ($1.50).

## NEAR BAKERSFIELD

**LAKE ISABELLA** Popular with weekend adventurers from the Southland, Lake Isabella—an hour's drive east of Bakersfield on Highway 178—has year-round swimming, fishing, and boating. Marinas and campgrounds line the 38-mile shore, both on Highway 178 past the town of Lake Isabella and on Highway 155 north toward Kernville. The **Lake Isabella Visitor Center** (4875 Ponderosa Dr., off Hwy. 155, tel. 619/379–5646) is open daily 8–5 in summer and weekdays 8–4:30 in winter. **French Gulch Marina** (tel. 619/379–8774), on Highway 155 a couple miles past the junction with Highway 178, rents boats (ski boats $40 per hour) and fishing equipment ($5 a day). You can swim anywhere within 200 feet of the shore, but if you find a cove you'll be protected from the jet skiers who dominate the lake on weekends.

There are several campgrounds on the lake ($14); call 800/280–CAMP for reservations. On the lake side of Highway 178, **Paradise Cove Campground** has some sites for $6 if you're willing to set up your tent next to the parking area. Two nicer campgrounds, off Highway 155 past the visitor center, are quiet, hilly **Hungry Gulch** and **Pioneer Point,** close to the lake but a bit rowdy. For less primitive but no more aesthetically pleasing accommodations, get a room at the **Paradise Cove Lodge** (10700 Hwy. 178, tel. 619/379–2719), past the town of Lake Isabella and right across from the water. Small doubles go for $35 a night; rooms for four are $40.

# THE CENTRAL COAST 8

By Danna Harman

**Whatever you visualize when you think of California, you're likely to find it on the** 360-mile stretch of coastline that runs between San Francisco and Los Angeles. While it does sometimes rain in Pismo Beach, and homeless people do live on the streets of Santa Barbara, you will be struck mostly by the sun-drenched beaches peopled with statuesque blondes and carefree surfers, the treacherous blufftop roads winding their way between gently rolling farmland and the tempestuous Pacific, and the groves of immense redwoods amid which to contemplate nature's wonders. The towns here range from the affluent community of **Santa Barbara** to the south—dominated by conservative retirees and stylish yuppies—to **Santa Cruz** in the north, an ultraliberal refuge for the long of hair and short of respect for traditional social mores. In between the two cities are a handful of small hamlets: student-filled **San Luis Obispo, Monterey** and its world-class aquarium, the old-time beach town of **Avila,** and tiny **San Simeon,** otherwise known as **Hearst Castle.**

*The Central Coast is a land of contrasts, with little to unite its various occupants besides love for its lush, rough-cut shoreline and raging sea.*

Before the Spanish, and later the pioneers, arrived on the rocky shores, the Central Coast was home to a number of Indian tribes who thrived on its rich fauna and diverse sea life. One branch of the Chumash tribe left its mark on caves near Santa Barbara, while another dwelt just off the coast on the ruggedly beautiful Channel Islands. The Esselen Indians were the first to stumble on **Big Sur**'s natural hot springs and later centered their settlements around them (who wouldn't?). The 21 missions dotting the Central Coast were creations of 17th- and 18th-century Portugese and Spanish missionaries, who "borrowed" the Indians' labor to build the missions in an unsuccessful attempt to dominate them through religion. Today, the region retains its stunning natural beauty and continues to enchant folks from all walks of life—from hippies and Hearsts to farmers and the fabulously rich.

The best way to explore the coast is to get yourself a car, some camping equipment, a sturdy pair of shoes, and a map and head straight for **Highway 1.** One of the most scenic stretches of roadway in the country, Highway 1 follows the coast from L.A. to San Francisco. This stretch of highway does have its drawbacks, though, including a limited number of affordable hotels and a dearth of public transportation. The Central Coast is also one of the few parts of California not known for their culinary delights, so you'll do your palate and your wallet a favor by stocking up on picnic supplies. Surprisingly, the best time to explore the coast is not during summer, when the seaboard is frequently blanketed with fog, but in spring or fall, when the mist gives way to clear skies, and temperatures linger in the 70s. If you're just looking to make good time between San Francisco and L.A., you can scurry down the Salinas Valley on **U.S.**

**101** in seven hours, or take the even quicker **I–5** through the San Joaquin Valley for a quick (6 hrs) but tedious trip—but you'll be missing one of the most spectacular chunks of California.

# Santa Cruz

**Originally founded in the late 1800s as a** mission town, Santa Cruz has several identities. Old-time residents, many of Italian descent, still look askance at the liberal students and hippies who have been migrating to the town ever since the University of California opened its "alternative, no-stress" branch here in the 1960s. Although the students, hippies, and New Agers might not dominate this spectacular coastal community numerically, the lifestyles of these three overlapping groups have certainly defined Santa Cruz's cultural landscape. From Volkswagen buses to vegan (no meat, no dairy) restaurants, homeopathic healers to drum circles, Grateful Dead T-shirts to long-hairs smoking dope on the streets, you'll see signs of Santa Cruz's liberal attitude wherever you turn.

*Most of downtown has been rebuilt since the 7.1-magnitude Loma Prieta earthquake of 1989, and many say the squeaky-clean new buildings symbolize a sea change toward conservativism.*

Though subject to the conflicts of any sizable California community, Santa Cruz lives up to its reputation as a happy-dappy beach town better than many. The carnival-like **boardwalk** is Santa Cruz at its flashiest, drawing legions of hormone-crazed teenagers from Salinas and San Jose every weekend. The boardwalk's most popular attraction is the **Giant Dipper,** one of the oldest wooden roller coasters in the world. The harrowing ride affords you a brief panorama of Monterey Bay before it plunges you down toward the beach. If your stomach's not up to such antics, head to Santa Cruz's stunning coast. The rocks off the craggy shore are favored perches for seals, the beaches are thronged by surfers and their retinue, and the hills surrounding the town fade into redwood forests ideal for hiking on or musing over.

## BASICS

**LAUNDRY** **Ultramat,** the hippest laundromat around, eases the pain of doing laundry with the comfort of coffee and assorted noshes. Each load in the washer costs $1.25, and dryers are 25¢ for 10 minutes. You can also take the easy way out and let the folks at Ultramat do all the work for 90¢ a pound (10-pound minimum). *501 Laurel St., at Washington St., tel. 408/426–9274. Open daily 7:30 AM–midnight; last wash at 10:30.*

**LUGGAGE STORAGE** Lockers are available at the **Greyhound** station for $1 a day ($3 for each additional day). *425 Front St., tel. 408/423–1800. Next to Metro Center. Open weekdays 7 AM–11 AM and 2 PM–8 PM, weekends 7–11, 3–4, and 6–7:45.*

**MEDICAL AID** **Westside Community Health Center** (1119 Pacific Ave., Suite 200, at Cathgart St., tel. 408/425–5028) offers general medical care at low cost, based on ability to pay. Appointments are required; Westside is open Monday, Wednesday, and Friday 9–2, and Tuesday 3:30–7:30.

**VISITOR INFORMATION** A friendly staff has tons of free pamphlets, including the mediocre *California Coast* tourist magazine. They can't help with room reservations, however. Maps will set you back $1.50 each. *701 Front St., tel. 408/425–1234. 2 blocks north of Metro Center. Open Mon.–Sat. 9–5, Sun. 10–4.*

## COMING AND GOING

**BY CAR** The most scenic route from either San Francisco, 1½ hours north, or Monterey, an hour south, is along **Highway 1.** San Jose is about 45 minutes away on curvy **Highway 17,** which meets up with I–280, I–880, and U.S. 101, and is the faster drive to San Francisco and the East Bay. Avoid Highway 17 on weekend mornings, though, when the entire Silicon Valley seems to head for the beaches, and at night, when the sharp curves of the road are difficult to navigate.

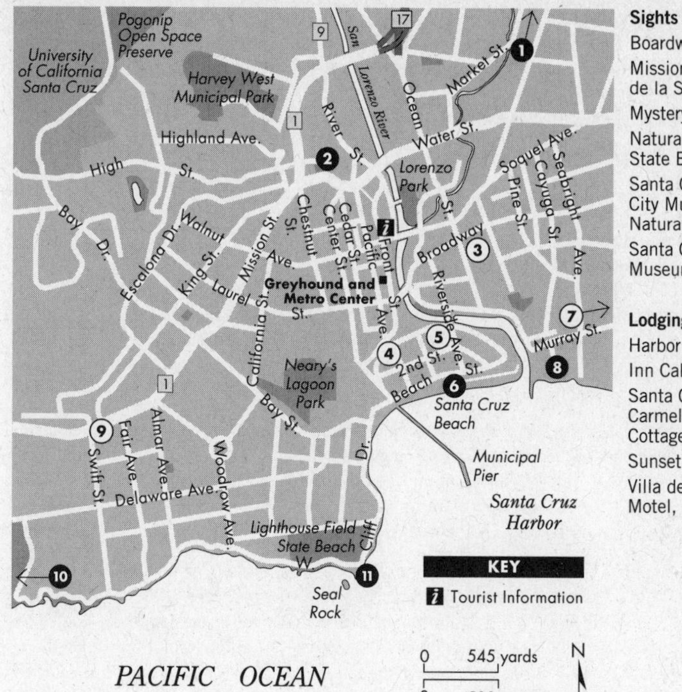


**Sights** ●

Boardwalk, **6**

Mission Exaltación de la Santa Cruz, **2**

Mystery Spot, **1**

Natural Bridges State Beach, **10**

Santa Cruz City Museum of Natural History, **8**

Santa Cruz Surfing Museum, **11**

**Lodging** ○

Harbor Inn, **7**

Inn Cal, **3**

Santa Cruz Carmelita Cottages (HI), **4**

Sunset Inn, **9**

Villa del Mar Motel, **5**

**BY BUS** **Green Tortoise** (tel. 415/956–7500 in California or 800/867–8647)—whose touring buses are known for their casual atmosphere, bunk beds, and "soft areas" made of foam pads and cotton pillows—travels from San Francisco to Los Angeles, stopping in Santa Cruz, once a week. From L.A., buses arrive in the Santa Cruz Safeway parking lot (2018 Mission St.) Monday mornings (13 hrs, $30); buses from San Francisco (3 hrs, $10) arrive in Santa Cruz Fridays at 11 PM. Reserve at least three days in advance, one week ahead in the summer (*also see box* Funky Deals on Wheels, in Chapter 1).

**Greyhound** (425 Front St., at Laurel St., tel. 408/423–1800) has direct service between Santa Cruz and San Francisco six times daily (2 hrs, $14 one-way), and five times daily from Los Angeles (10 hrs, $50 one-way). **Highway 17 Express Bus** (tel. 408/425–8600) has hourly service (every 15 min during commute hours) and is the cheapest way to travel between San Jose and Santa Cruz ($2.25) during the week. Buses stop in Santa Cruz at the junction of Soquel Drive and Highway 1, and in San Jose at the CalTrain station and at the corner of 3rd Street and San Fernando Avenue, one block from San Jose State University.

**BY TRAIN** While you can't get to Santa Cruz directly by train, **CalTrain** (tel. 800/660–4287) does offer daily train service between San Francisco and San Jose (1½ hrs, $4.50). Trains run at least once an hour between 8 AM and 3 PM, more frequently during commute hours. From the San Jose CalTrain station (Cahill and W. San Fernando Sts.), take the **Santa Cruz CalTrain Connector** (tel. 408/425–8600) to the Metro Center (*see* Getting Around by Bus, *below*) in Santa Cruz. The bus leaves every 2 hours on weekdays, less often on weekends; it takes an hour and costs $5.

**HITCHING** Depending on whom you talk to, Santa Cruz is either one of the mellowest or one of the most dangerous places to hitchhike in North America. If you want to give it a go, a good spot to catch a ride north out of town is at the corner of Swift Street and Highway 1 (aka Mission St.) by the LITTER REMOVAL sign (no kidding). Hitching northeast along Highway 17 toward San Jose or south along Highway 1 is more difficult. Try the Ocean Street on-ramp to Highway 17. A less risky idea is the **UCSC rideboard** at Bay Tree Books (the college bookstore, located in the center of campus). The availability of rides varies with the time of year, and some money to cover gas is appreciated, if not expected.

## GETTING AROUND

Santa Cruz lies on the edge of Monterey Bay and is bisected by the San Lorenzo River. The town is full of crooked and confusing streets, so keep a sharp eye on a map. Highway 1 becomes **Mission Street** when it enters Santa Cruz, and resumes its old identity on the way out of town. **Bay Street** and **High Street** both funnel into UCSC, which is located on a hill 2 miles northeast of downtown, while the boardwalk is on **Beach Street** just west of the river. The boardwalk and downtown (which centers around **Pacific Avenue** and **Front Street**) are within comfortable walking distance of each other.

**BY CAR** Except on summer weekends, driving and parking are not difficult here, even downtown. Free 2-hour parking is available along Front and Cedar streets, and on weekends some parking lots are free all day. Possible parking spots include the **Santa Cruz County Building** (701 Ocean St.) and the **River Street Parking Garage** (River St.), which runs shuttles to the beach on weekends (when parking by the boardwalk gets difficult).

**BY BUS** Bus service is efficient and fairly easy to use. The Santa Cruz Metropolitan District Transit (SCMDT), also known as Metro, operates from the **Metro Center** (920 Pacific Ave., at Laurel St.) adjoining the Greyhound Station. Any bus in town will eventually take you to the Metro Center, where you can pick up a copy of "Headways," a free pamphlet that lists all bus routes. The fare is $1, but you can purchase a special all-day pass for $3 on any bus or at the Metro Center. Exact change, in coins or one-dollar bills, is required; change machines are available at the Metro Center. A free shuttle runs between the Metro Center and the boardwalk in summer. *920 Pacific Ave., tel. 408/425–8600 or 408/688–8600. Open daily 7 AM–9 PM. Info booth in lobby open weekdays 8–5.*

**BY BIKE** Biking is the best way to get around Santa Cruz. Many streets have wide bike lanes, and the weather is quite moderate, especially in spring and summer. Bring wheels from home if you can, since renting can be expensive. The imaginatively named **Bicycle Rental Center** (415 Pacific Ave., at Front St., tel. 408/426–8687), 3 blocks north of the boardwalk, has competitive rates of $25 a day.

## WHERE TO SLEEP

The price categories below refer to weekday rates, which often multiply as much as three times on weekends. Winter rates are about $10–$30 lower than in summer. The local youth hostel is definitely the best deal around if you can get a room. Camping in the area is great, as evidenced by the fact that campgrounds fill quickly in summer. If all the campgrounds listed below are full, Big Basin Redwoods State Park (*see* Near Santa Cruz, *below*) is 30–45 minutes away. The dorms at **U.C. Santa Cruz** (tel. 408/459–2611) accept guests from the end of June to the beginning of September, but rooms are plain, far from town and the water, and expensive. A single runs $50, $65 with full board; a double is $40 per person, $55 with full board. The dorms are limited to those on "official" business, so you may want to say you're considering enrolling and sign up for a campus tour.

**HOTELS AND MOTELS** Behind the boardwalk on 2nd Street, 3rd Street, and Riverside Avenue are some fleabag motels that rarely fill up, but you'll find comparably priced places clustered on Mission and Ocean streets that are much more comfortable, and equally convenient if you have a car. In particular, try the **Sunset Inn** (2424 Mission St., tel. 408/423–3471) for clean rooms in a pinch. Weekday rates range from $40 for a double to $85 for a suite that sleeps six.

➢ **UNDER $60** • **Harbor Inn.** In a residential neighborhood 10 minutes southeast of town (though not close to the water), this inviting inn has large cathedral ceilings and doubles (starting at $45 in summer, $35 off-season) with a hodgepodge of old furniture and wooden beds. The antidote to characterless chain motels, the Harbor often fills in summer, so call ahead for reservations. Most rooms have kitchenettes, and larger groups can get a suite ($65–$85, depending on the season). *645 7th Ave., tel. 408/479–9731. From downtown, cross river on Laurel St., right on San Lorenzo Blvd., left on Murray St., left on 7th Ave. Or Bus 65 or 66 to 7th Ave. 19 rooms. Wheelchair access.*

**Inn Cal.** The clean rooms are decorated à la chain motel, but the inn is only 4 blocks from the beach. A double goes for $45 during the week in summer, $55 on weekends; prices drop $10 during winter. *370 Ocean St., at Broadway, tel. 408/458–9220. From Metro Center, Bus 68 or 69 to cnr Ocean St. and Soquel Ave. Reservations advised. Wheelchair access.*

**Villa del Mar Motel.** Its location 1 block away from the boardwalk and beach makes the floral decor forgivable. Singles start as low as $38 and doubles at $42, jumping to $60 and $64, respectively, on summer weekends. *321 Riverside Ave., tel. 408/423–9449. From Metro Center, Bus 7 to cnr Beach and Cliff Sts. 23 rooms. Wheelchair access.*

**HOSTELS** **Santa Cruz Carmelita Cottages (HI).** The cottages are actually a cluster of houses made hosteler-friendly. Located 2 blocks from the boardwalk on Beach Hill, these new accommodations cost $12 for members and $15 for nonmembers. Private doubles are $30, and "family" rooms (three to five people) cost at least $30–$40, depending on the number of beds. Write (Box 1241, Santa Cruz 95061) or call ahead for reservations. *315 Main St., tel. 408/423–8304. From Metro Center, Bus 7 to Main St. 25 beds. Curfew 11 PM, lockout 9–5. Reception open daily 7–9 AM and 5–10 PM. Lockers, sheet rental ($1). Wheelchair access.*

**CAMPING** **Henry Cowell Redwoods State Park.** Fifteen miles north of Santa Cruz, this 111-site campground is buffered by a redwood forest and a stunning series of cliff faces. Things get a little out of hand during summer, when RVs and screaming teens overrun the place, but otherwise this is a camper's paradise. Reserve through MISTIX (tel. 800/444–PARK). Both tent and RV sites are $16 a night. *101 N. Big Trees Park Rd., Felton, tel. 408/335–4598 or 408/438–2396. From Hwy. 1, Hwy. 9 north; from Metro Center, Bus 30. Flush toilets, showers. Closed Dec.–Feb.*

**New Brighton State Beach.** High above the ocean on a large cliff, this popular campground in Capitola, 5 miles southeast of Santa Cruz, offers an incredible view of the coast from some sites. A steep path leads downhill to the soft beach below. Neither the tent nor RV spaces have much privacy, however. Reservations—available through MISTIX (tel. 800/444–PARK)—are a must between May and September, when the place is filled almost every day. Sites go for $16 in summer, $14 in winter. Follow signs from Highway 1. Otherwise, Bus 71 will take you to the corner of Soquel Ave. and Park Ave., but leaves you with a long walk. *1500 Park Ave., tel. 408/475–4850.*

**Sunset State Beach** and **Manresa State Beach.** If New Brighton is booked, try these two scruffy beaches, both about 25 minutes south of Santa Cruz. Sunset has 90 campsites, all with fire rings, picnic tables, and hot showers. Spaces, reserved through MISTIX (tel. 800/444–PARK), are $16 in summer, $14 at other times—and they go quickly on weekends. On the way to Sunset, you'll pass Manresa, which has 60 walk-in sites with the same facilities, prices, and reservation system as Sunset. Sites are on a hill above the beach or set back in a sparse sprinkling of trees with little privacy. *San Andreas Rd. Sunset: tel. 408/724–1266. Manresa: tel. 408/761–1795. Take Hwy. 1 south to San Andreas Rd. exit, right at bottom of ramp, right onto San Andreas Rd.*

**ROUGHING IT** Santa Cruz has a reputation as an easygoing town, but the police nevertheless frown on (and issue citations to) people sleeping in public places. If you're willing to take the risk, try one of the small beaches south of town, along Highway 1. As long as you don't light a campfire or make a lot of noise, you may be left alone.

## FOOD

To say that Santa Cruzians are health conscious is a ferocious understatement. Downtown, reams of cafés, delis, and small restaurants offer health-oriented menus. For fresh produce, much of it organically grown, head to the **farmers' market,** held every Wednesday 2–6 on the corner of Pacific Avenue and Cathcart Street; then trot over to Lorenzo Park (River St., btw Water St. and Soquel Ave.) for a picnic. Also look for the markets and fast-food chains along Mission Street.

➢ **UNDER $5** • For a tasty slice of late-night pizza, there's always **Uppercrust Pizza** (2415 Mission St., tel. 408/423–9010), on the west side of town near the Highway 1 turnoff for Natural Bridges State Beach; it's open until 11 PM Sunday–Thursday, 1 AM on Friday, and midnight on Saturday. For Mexican food in bulk quantities, **Taquería Vallarta** (608 Soquel Ave., 1 block east of Ocean St., tel. 408/457–8226) is the place to go. Enormous burritos ($3 vegetarian, $3.50 carnivore) are served up weekdays 10 AM–midnight and weekends 9 AM–midnight.

**The Bagelry.** This deli warehouse specializes in wacky bagel spreads like the homemade Pink Flamingo (cream cheese with lox and dill, $2.50) and the Luna spread (pesto, ricotta, and almonds, $2). If you're short on cash, try the "three-seed slug"—a flat, wide bagel without the hole (55¢). *320A Cedar St., at Laurel St., tel. 408/429–8049. Other location: 4363 Soquel Dr., tel. 408/462–9888. Both open weekdays 6:30–5:30, Sat. 7:30–5:30, Sun. 7:30–4.*

**Zachary's.** The basic breakfast—two eggs, potatoes, and your choice of homemade breads—sells for a reasonable $3.50 here. If you want something a little more elaborate, the huge stack of pancakes ($3.50) and the family-size omelets ($4 and up) are definitely worth the price. The eating area is usually crowded, but Zachary's outstanding food is worth the wait (except maybe on weekends, when it can take up to an hour to get a table). *819 Pacific Ave., btw Laurel and Maple Sts., tel. 408/427–0646. Open Tues.–Sun. 7–2:30. Wheelchair access.*

➢ **UNDER $10** • **Dolphin Restaurant.** Work your way to the end of Santa Cruz's pier and grab an order of fresh-caught fish and chips ($5) from the outside window of the Dolphin. If you'd rather sit, head to the adjoining restaurant, where, in addition to fried fish, there are burgers ($5.50), hearty clam chowder ($4.25 a bowl), and pasta dishes. *End of pier, tel. 408/426–5830. Open summer, daily 8 AM–11 PM (Fri. and Sat. until midnight; winter hrs vary, so call ahead.*

**King Chwan.** King Chwan has an amazing lunch deal—soup, salad, Chinese entrée, tea, and fortune cookie for $4. A slightly more elaborate combination dinner goes for $6.50. The lighting is bright and the building looks like a large tract house, but for the money you can't complain. *415 Ocean St., across bridge from Front St., tel. 408/429–5898. Open daily 11:30–10. Wheelchair access.*

**Saturn Café.** This is a great place to eat, read, and watch the spaced-out locals. If it's warmth you need, try the lentil chili ($3.50). For greens connoisseurs, the Titan salad ($6.25) is big and satisfying—enough for two to share. Better yet, indulge in the locally famous Chocolate Madness ($4.25), a huge conglomeration of chocolate cookies, chocolate ice cream, chocolate mousse, hot fudge, chocolate chips, and whipped cream. You can sip coffee here while your wash tumbles at the laundromat behind the café. *1230 Mission St., near Laurel St., tel. 408/429–8505. Open weekdays 11:30 AM–midnight, weekends noon–midnight. Wheelchair access. No credit cards.*

**CAFES** In a town with more than 15,000 college students, the absence of nighttime diversions for the under-21 set has fueled a serious café scene. And in addition to being a popular hangout spot for college students, cafés are also frequented by locals looking for a lively debate or a place to read a good book.

**Caffè Pergolesi.** In a big, rambling house downtown graced with a large outside deck, the Perg has all the trappings of a good café—potent house coffee ($1), double-potent espresso drinks ($1–$3), and a large selection of herbal teas (95¢). Try *chai*, a milky Indian spice tea ($2). The small food menu includes veggie lasagna ($5), quiche ($4.50), and sandwiches ($3), as well as the usual bagels ($2) and pastries ($1.50–$2). The crowd is somewhat eclectic, ranging from UCSC students to nouveau-hippies. This is definitely *the* place to play chess. *418A Cedar St., at Elm St., tel. 408/426–1775. Open daily 8 AM–midnight.*

**Herland Book-Café.** Although men are allowed, this bookstore/café was conceived as a safe haven for women. The books, grouped in categories like "Women of the Wild West" or "Women Respond to the Men's Movement," are all female-authored. The café serves coffee (75¢), tea (85¢), espresso drinks ($1.25–$2), and snacks ($1–$3). *902 Center St., at Union St., tel. 408/42–WOMEN. Open Tues.–Sat. 8 AM–10 PM, Sun.–Mon. 10–6.*

**Jahva House.** Located in a large warehouse, the Jahva House is open, airy, and comfortable. Big oriental rugs are strewn on the floors, and ficus trees stand among the outside tables. The incredibly long coffee bar furnishes zillions of different coffees and teas, including organically grown varieties of both. For something extra special, try a Mexican mocha ($2.50), a delicious mix of Mexican hot chocolate, espresso, and steamed milk. Excellent banana bread and slices of pie cost about $3. *120 Union St., near Cedar St., tel. 408/459–9876. Open Mon.–Sat. 6 AM–midnight, Sun. 8–8.*

## WORTH SEEING

Most of Santa Cruz's sights are downtown, within a walkable area. To explore the jagged coast, though, you'll definitely need a car or one heck of a mountain bike. Downtown, the **Pacific Garden Mall** is the center of the action, strewn with specialty stores, antique shops, restaurants, and cafés, and is an easy destination for an afternoon of window-shopping. Two worthwhile bookstores are **Bookshop Santa Cruz** (1520 Pacific Ave., at Locust St., tel. 408/423–0900), a bookstore and café with a humongous selection of books, magazines, and international newspapers; and **Logos** (1117 Pacific Ave., near Lincoln St., tel. 408/427–5100), Santa Cruz's premier used-book and music store.

If you're in the mood for a leisurely afternoon walk, the **Mission de Exaltación de la Santa Cruz** (126 High St.), built between 1857 and 1931, has grounds overrun with colorful gardens and fountains. On the beach near downtown lies the **Santa Cruz Beach Boardwalk,** a little Coney Island by the Pacific, with amusement-park rides, carnival games, kitschy shops, arcades, cotton candy, and plenty of teenage angst. Admission to the boardwalk is free, but the rides cost $2 or $3 a shot. If you do nothing else, ride the Giant Dipper ($3), a fabulous wooden roller coaster with a spectacular view.

**U.C. SANTA CRUZ** Take a quick tour of UCSC, in the thickly forested hills just north of downtown. The **info center** (tel. 408/459–0111) at the campus entrance is open weekdays 8–5 and has maps and tour schedules. Investigate the **limestone quarry** near the campus bookstore—it's a nice spot for a picnic—and take a self-guided tour of the organic growing system at the **Farm and Garden Project** (tel. 408/459–4140). If you park along Meder Avenue at the far west end of campus and catch the free shuttle at Bay and High streets, you can avoid the on-campus parking fee. Otherwise take Bus 41 from the Metro Center to the west entrance of campus.

### State of Kiva

***If you're feeling battered by your journeys around California, Santa Cruz offers the perfect way to enter a state of total relaxation in the form of Kiva, a co-ed, clothing-optional spa favored by locals. For $10 you can spend as many hours as you like drifting into dreamy tranquility in hot tubs, saunas, and cold dips. The spa is open Sunday–Thursday noon–11 PM, Fridays and Saturdays until midnight; the management reserves Sundays 9–noon for women only and gives women a two-for-one discount Monday through Wednesday. 702 Water St., 1 block east of Market St., tel. 408/429–1142.***

**SANTA CRUZ CITY MUSEUM OF NATURAL HISTORY** You'll recognize this place by the huge stone statue of a whale out front. The museum is small, but full of info about the Ohlone Indians—who originally populated the area—and the seals and sea lions that still do. If you're into honeybees, watch thousands encased under glass doing interesting apiarian things. The museum is on the east side of town, near Pleasure Point—a great place to watch local surfers. *1305 E. Cliff Dr., tel. 408/429–3773. From downtown, walk or drive east on Laurel St., cross river, turn right on San Lorenzo St. (which becomes E. Cliff Dr.). Or take Bus 67 from Metro Center. Admission: $2 donation requested. Open Tues.–Fri. 10–5, weekends 1–5.*

**SANTA CRUZ SURFING MUSEUM** At Lighthouse Point on West Cliff Drive, there's a tiny exhibit on surfing—from its Hawaiian origins to the present. The museum is dedicated to the memory of an 18-year-old surfer who drowned in 1965. Also on display is a board bitten by a great white shark in 1987, testimony to the real danger posed by sharks along the coast from Santa Cruz to Pigeon Point. Plop down right outside the lighthouse and watch the surfers on Steamer's Lane, one of the best surf spots in California. Look a little farther out and you'll see Seal Rock, the summertime home of thousands of barking, shiny seals. *Mark Abbott Memorial Lighthouse, W. Cliff Dr., tel. 408/429–3429. Bus 3A or 3B. Admission free. Open Mon., Wed.–Fri. noon–4, weekends noon–5.*

*The path running parallel to West Cliff Drive from the boardwalk to Natural Bridges State Beach is a great place for a walk, jog, or bike ride. The 2-mile jaunt passes innumerable rocky coves and surfing points, and at least one nude beach.*

**NATURAL BRIDGES STATE BEACH** Two miles west of town, the secluded and spectacular Natural Bridges State Beach is the perfect place to escape the overwhelming sensory stimulation of Santa Cruz. As its name implies, the beach features a series of bridge-like rock formations, as well as excellent tidal pools, picnic tables, barbecue pits, and plenty of soft, warm sand to stretch out on. Also on the grounds of the park is a **monarch butterfly colony,** one of only a few places in the world where you can witness the amazing sight of thousands of brightly colored butterflies mating. The mating season usually lasts from mid-October to February, but call ahead for the latest (and to make a reservation for guided walks). Park on Delaware Avenue just east of the park entrance to avoid the parking fee. *W. Cliff Dr., tel. 408/423–4609. From boardwalk, follow W. Cliff Dr. until you see signs. Or Bus 3B from Metro Center. Parking $6. Open daily 8 AM–sunset.*

**MYSTERY SPOT** If you abhor tourist attractions but feel a strange compulsion to "do" at least one, let this be it. This quirky little place lies in the redwoods 3 miles north of Santa Cruz and, in the minds of true believers, is at the center of a mysterious force that makes people taller and compels balls to roll uphill. It's a tacky tourist trap, to be sure, but its gift shop is filled with one-of-a-kind souvenirs and kitschy knickknacks. Your $3 admission also buys you a Mystery Spot bumper sticker. *1953 Branciforte Dr., tel. 408/423–8897. From downtown, go east on Water St., left on Market St., go 2½ mi, then follow signs. Open daily 9:30–4:30.*

## CHEAP THRILLS

For a groovy Santa Cruz experience, go at sunset to **It's Beach,** immediately west of the lighthouse. Almost every day of the year, locals gather here to drum and dance as night falls. Also check out the numerous street performers who line **Pacific Avenue** and the area surrounding the boardwalk during daylight hours.

## FESTIVALS

The **Cabrillo Music Festival,** usually held during the first week of August, has food, symphonic music, and other live entertainment. Call the Santa Cruz Civic Auditorium Box Office (tel. 408/429–3444) for more info. Tickets cost $6–$25 depending on the performance and seating.

**Shakespeare Santa Cruz** (tel. 408/459–2121) is served up against a backdrop of beautiful redwoods during a 6-week UCSC production of the Bard's works mid-July–August on campus. Tickets start at $15 and peak at $21.

Can you think of 1,001 things to do with fungus? If you can't, the people at the **Fungus Fair** will be more than happy to assist you. The fair is held every January at the Santa Cruz City Museum of Natural History (*see* Worth Seeing, *above*). Entrance is $4. Call the museum for more info.

## AFTER DARK

Much of Santa Cruz's nocturnal activity takes place in the cafés and ends early. Nightlife in the traditional sense is decidedly lacking, and those establishments that do cater to the over-21 crowd check ID stringently. The journal *Good Times* (free at cafés and bookstores) comes out every Thursday with a listing of upcoming events. Look for happy hours and reduced cover charges, usually on Wednesday or Thursday nights.

**The Blue Lagoon.** This is Santa Cruz's premier gay and bisexual nighttime hangout. There's a $2 cover on weekends, but it's worth it for some of the best DJ dance music in town. *923 Pacific Ave., across from Metro Center, tel. 408/423–7117.*

**The Catalyst.** It's disparaged by some for its virtual monopoly of the Santa Cruz music scene. Still, the Catalyst attracts a college crowd with local bands nightly and big names on occasion. Covers range from $1 on Thursday nights to $15 for major shows. *1011 Pacific Ave., tel. 408/423–1336.*

**Poet and the Patriot Irish Pub.** This is paradise for UCSC students and Santa Cruz's "artsy" crowd, despite the pricey drinks. The pub has lots of smoke in the air (well, lots by Santa Cruz standards), dart boards on the wall, and Irish beer on tap. In the same building is the Kuumbwa Jazz Center (tel. 408/427–2227), which hosts jazz and blues shows throughout the year. Call for tickets ($2–$14) and schedules. *320 Cedar St., at Laurel St., tel. 408/426–8620.*

**The Red Room.** A true UCSC institution, this run-down dive is darkly lit and usually jammed with students. Don't look for a sign out front; there isn't one. At night the adjacent restaurant becomes a venue for local grunge and punk bands. Some nights you pay a minimal cover. *1003 Cedar St., at Locust St., tel. 408/426–2994.*

## OUTDOOR ACTIVITIES

**HIKING AND MOUNTAIN BIKING** The redwood-filled hills surrounding Santa Cruz provide some of Northern California's best hiking and mountain-biking opportunities. Though it's a bit out of town, real enthusiasts should head directly to **Big Basin Redwoods State Park** (*see* Near Santa Cruz, *below*). Closer to town, **Henry Cowell Redwoods State Park** (*see* Camping, *above*) has hundreds of miles of trails, many of which meander through virgin redwood forests. Bikes are allowed on designated fire and service roads, but not on hiking trails. For a beautiful, albeit sometimes crowded, stroll among some of the park's tallest trees, take the Redwood Grove trail; you'll find the trailhead off Highway 9. For more of a workout, head 4 miles uphill to the observation deck for a beautiful view of the valley (walk up Pipeline Road from the nature center and turn left on Ridge Fire Road). To reach the park from downtown, follow Highway 9 toward Felton.

At the **Forest of Nisene Marks State Park** (Aptos Creek Rd. exit off Hwy. 1, southwest of Santa Cruz, tel. 408/761–3487), you can view the ruins of a Chinese labor camp and hike (2 mi one-way) to the epicenter of the 1989 Loma Prieta earthquake; the trailhead is clearly marked from the main parking lot. Nisene Marks is also a favored locale of mountain bikers; the friendly folks at park headquarters will point you toward trails where bikes are allowed. Bike rentals are available back in town (*see* Getting Around, *above*).

**SURFING** Even though Southern California is reputed to be the state's surfing capital, many locals argue that Santa Cruz has the state's hottest surf spots, the most famous being **Steamer's Lane,** between the boardwalk and the lighthouse. However, beginners would do well to avoid the big breaks, which can be dangerous. For an easier ride head to **Cowell's Beach,** between the boardwalk and Steamer's Lane. If you left your board at home, the **Beach 'n' Bikini**

**Surf Shop** (cnr Beach and Front Sts., near boardwalk, tel. 408/427–2355) rents surfboards ($15), body boards ($10), and wet suits ($10) by the day.

## NEAR SANTA CRUZ

**BIG BASIN REDWOODS STATE PARK** One of the flagships of the California State Park system, Big Basin—23 miles northeast of Santa Cruz off Highway 9—overwhelms you with thousands of acres of gigantic old-growth redwoods, lofty Douglas firs, rushing streams, and flowing waterfalls. All sorts of wildlife call Big Basin home, including black-tailed deer and an occasional fox, bobcat, coyote, or mountain lion. It's quite worthy of at least a day's visit ($5 per car), and more if you groove on the outdoors. So lace up your hiking boots, and go commune with some trees who've been here about 1,500 years longer than you have.

Just past the main entrance you'll come to the **park headquarters** (tel. 408/338–6132), where helpful rangers can give you advice on which trails will best suit your desires and energy level, or simply sell you a map (75¢) and let you go to town. For a relatively easy hike through redwoods, firs, and tan oaks, and past Sempervirens Falls, pick up the **Sequoia Trail** from the south end of the parking lot and follow it to the Skyline-to-Sea Trail, which will take you back to the park headquarters. The 4½-mile walk takes two to three hours.

If you've got a bit more ambition, take the Skyline-to-Sea Trail from the parking lot west to **Berry Creek Falls Trail,** and work your way back to the visitor's center on the **Sunset Trail.** The 10½-mile loop, which affords views of the incredible 75-foot Berry Creek Falls and the Pacific Ocean, takes five to six hours. About a half-mile up the trail, you'll find **Silver Falls** and **Golden Falls,** better for private waterfall play than popular Berry Creek Falls. Here you can wade in the pools, run through the falls themselves, or skip across the creek on the redwood logs.

The truly fit can tackle the 12½-mile **Skyline-to-Sea Trail**—arguably the most scenic hike in the park—which travels over hill and dale all the way to the coast. This is the park's most popular trek, and those who've done it rave about how satisfying it is to reach the water after gazing at it from such a distance earlier in the trail. Leave a second car at the trail's endpoint at Waddell Beach, and either pay scrupulous attention to a map or accept the possibility of getting semi-lost, since several trailheads converge a few miles into the hike. Mountain biking is only allowed on fire roads in the park and unfortunately there aren't any good loops: Your best bet is to follow North Escape Road a short distance from park headquarters to **Gazos Creek Road,** a 14-mile fire trail that stretches to the coast.

➢ **COMING AND GOING** • To reach Big Basin from Santa Cruz, follow Highway 9 north for 25 miles, then follow the signs for another 9 miles from Boulder Creek. If you're coming from the north on I–280, take Highway 85 south from Cupertino to Highway 9 south, then pick up Highway 236 into the park.

➢ **WHERE TO SLEEP** • All Big Basin's 144 drive-in camping sites have picnic tables, fire pits, food lockers, and access to toilets and showers. Most are spread out under the redwoods with lots of room to breathe, and many are situated on the banks of gentle streams. The sites, which fetch $14 in summer, go quickly on weekends; make reservations through MISTIX (tel. 800/444–PARK) up to eight weeks in advance.

Even more lovely are the primitive sites ($7) at Big Basin's trail camps. Though fires in the trail camps are strictly forbidden due to high fire danger, you'll be compensated by the seclusion and privacy of these sites, most less than 2 miles from a trailhead. Call the park headquarters to reserve a few weeks ahead of time, since these sites are also popular. If you can't tear yourself away from the beauty of the park but didn't bring a tent, rent a tent cabin—essentially a shack with a canvas cover and two cots and a wood stove inside—for about $38 for up to eight people. Call 408/338–4745 for more info.

# The Central Coast Drive

**Simone de Beauvoir, Robinson Jeffers,** Jack Kerouac, Henry Miller, Robert Louis Stevenson, John Steinbeck, and Sinclair Lewis number among those who've been inspired by the 131-mile stretch of California coastline between Monterey and San Luis Obispo. Once you get past Monterey, you'll see why people trek down this lovely coast. Since the days when the Esselen people relaxed in Big Sur's hot springs, this has been a place for retreat and self-exploration: William Randolph Hearst built his castle near San Simeon so his son could "get away from it all," and San Francisco's bohemians retreated to tiny Carmel after the 1906 earthquake. Today, New Agers, Buddhists, lovers, scout troops, and reflective souls all converge on Highway 1—carved into the mountains by convict labor in 1937—which twists its way along jagged cliffs, past relentlessly pounding surf, and through ponderous redwood forests.

Outdoor types could easily spend a week on the coast without getting bored, but the lack of budget motels and the dearth of public transportation for travelers *sans* automobile can be a real hardship. If you just want to enjoy some scenery and snap a few photos, you can easily do it in a long day trip from either Los Angeles or San Francisco, though two are preferable. If you decide to go for the gusto and traverse the whole strip, start in Monterey, a heavily touristed and expensive coastal town 48 miles south of Santa Cruz. Heading south, you'll pass through the gorgeous, but very upscale, environs of Carmel before entering the rugged heart of Big Sur. After an intoxicating three or four hours you'll hit San Simeon—home of the ornate Hearst Castle—and, finally, San Luis Obispo, a surprisingly lively college town. Outside San Luis Obispo, Highway 1 meets U.S. 101, continuing south to Santa Barbara and Los Angeles. If you can, make the trip during the week or in late fall or early spring, when hotels and motels chop $5–$10 off their prices.

## COMING AND GOING

**BY CAR** The best way to experience the 131-mile stretch of coastline is to drive it. It's nearly impossible to get lost—the only road is Highway 1. To reach it from the north, take I-280 (from San Francisco) or U.S. 101 to Highway 68 (from San Jose or the Peninsula). If you're coming from Southern California, U.S. 101 meets the highway in San Luis Obispo. In low season, the coastal drive takes less than 6 hours, but summer traffic on Highway 1 can be a mess and will add a good two hours to your driving time.

If you don't have a car, think seriously about renting one. Many agencies will let you pick up a car in Monterey and drop it off in San Luis Obispo, or vice versa, for a "small" fee. In Pacific Grove, near Monterey, try **Rent-a-Wreck** (95 Central Ave., Pacific Grove, tel. 800/548–7888 or 408/373–3356); cars go for about $150 a week with 1,000 free miles; drivers age 21–25 pay $10 extra per week, and the car must be returned to the Pacific Grove location. At last look, **Hertz** (Monterey Peninsula Airport, tel. 800/654–3131), which rents only to those 25 and older, had a round-trip weekly rate of $205 for a compact with unlimited mileage; a one-way rental will run you another $130. One-way from San Francisco to Los Angeles is slightly cheaper, at $285.

**BY BUS** Traveling up and down the entire Central Coast on public transportation is impossible, but with some ingenuity and a lot of patience you can travel between a few towns. In the north, **Monterey-Salinas Transit** (tel. 408/899–2555) runs buses into the heart of Big Sur (*see* Coming and Going, Monterey, *below*); in the south, **Central Coast Area Transit** (tel. 805/541–2228) runs along the coast between San Simeon and San Luis Obispo ($2), but you'll have to transfer. Unfortunately, the San Simeon stop is 4 miles from Hearst Castle.

**BY TRAIN** **Amtrak** (tel. 800/USA–RAIL) runs the *Coast Starlight* line between the San Francisco Bay Area and San Luis Obispo (7 hrs, $58 one-way, $68–$116 round-trip), stopping along the way in San Jose and Salinas. If you like rail travel, it's a cool thing to try; but though parts of the ride give a feel for the Central Coast's beauty, you'll be missing a whole lot of scenic turnoffs.

# The Central Coast

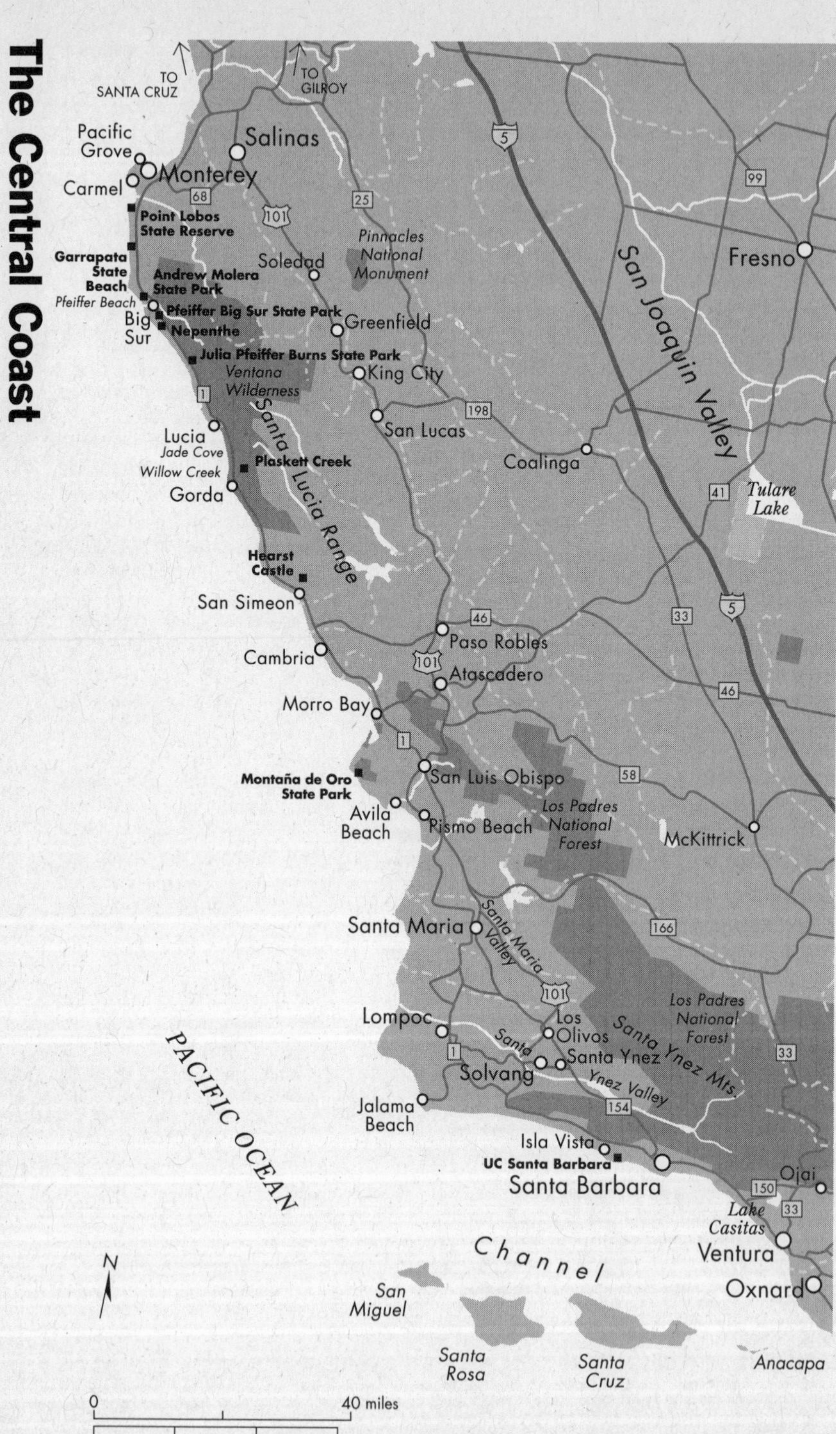

TO SANTA CRUZ
TO GILROY
Pacific Grove
Monterey
Salinas
Carmel
68
101
25
5
99
Point Lobos State Reserve
Garrapata State Beach
Andrew Molera State Park
Soledad
Pinnacles National Monument
Fresno
Pfeiffer Beach
Big Sur
Pfeiffer Big Sur State Park
Nepenthe
Greenfield
Julia Pfeiffer Burns State Park
Ventana Wilderness
King City
San Joaquin Valley
1
Santa Lucia Range
198
San Lucas
Lucia
Jade Cove
Willow Creek
Plaskett Creek
Coalinga
Gorda
41
Tulare Lake
Hearst Castle
San Simeon
46
33
Paso Robles
Cambria
Atascadero
Morro Bay
Montaña de Oro State Park
San Luis Obispo
58
Avila Beach
Pismo Beach
Los Padres National Forest
McKittrick
Santa Maria
Santa Maria Valley
166
Lompoc
Los Olivos
Los Padres National Forest
Santa Ynez Mts.
Santa Ynez
Solvang
Santa Ynez Valley
154
PACIFIC OCEAN
Jalama Beach
Isla Vista
UC Santa Barbara
Santa Barbara
150
Ojai
Lake Casitas
Ventura
Channel
Oxnard
N
San Miguel
Santa Rosa
Santa Cruz
Anacapa
0
40 miles
0
60 km

# Monterey

Monterey is one of California's tackiest and most unabashedly commercial seaside resorts. John Steinbeck (1906–1968) immortalized the busy fishing port in *Cannery Row* and *Sweet Thursday,* describing it as "a poem, a stink, a grating noise, a quality of light, a tone, a habit, a nostalgia, a dream." By the 1950s, however, the sardines were gone, along with much that was poetic. Visitors will still find the fascinating Monterey Bay Aquarium a worthwhile stop; unfortunately, much of the rest of the town has a Disneyland-by-the-sea feel—pricey gift shops sell plastic sardines and lackluster restaurants feature "Steinbeck Specials."

*Jimi Hendrix made rock-and-roll history at the Monterey Fairgrounds in 1969 when he burned his guitar in front of tens of thousands of awestruck fans.*

During summer, the town plays host to the **Monterey Bay Theatrefest** (tel. 408/622–0700), with free outdoor performances on weekend afternoons in the Custom House Plaza. Call for schedules. The world-famous **Monterey Jazz Festival** (tel. 408/373–3366) takes place on the third weekend of September at the Monterey Fairgrounds. Tickets for the 3-day festival start at around $115 and usually sell out a month in advance. During the last week of June, look for big-name artists at the 2-day **Monterey Bay Blues Festival** (tel. 408/394–2652); day tickets cost $15. The **Monterey Peninsula Chamber of Commerce** (380 Alvarado St., tel. 408/649–1770) has information on these events, as well as a free map of the city.

**COMING AND GOING** Greyhound buses have regular service to Monterey from San Francisco (4 hrs, $19 one-way) and Los Angeles (12 hrs, $47 one-way) via Salinas. The Monterey **Greyhound station** (42 Del Monte Ave., tel. 408/373–4735), in a gas station on the eastern end of town, is open daily 7:45 AM–9:50 PM.

**Monterey-Salinas Transit** (tel. 408/899–2555) has regular connections to Carmel, Big Sur, and Salinas from Monterey ($1–$3). All buses depart from the downtown **Monterey Transit Plaza** (cnr Tyler and Pearl Sts.). For Big Sur, take Bus 22; it will get you as far as the Nepenthe restaurant on Highway 1.

**GETTING AROUND** Getting around Monterey is not difficult. From Highway 1, the Pacific Grove/Del Monte Avenue exit will take you straight into downtown. The main drag is north–south **Alvarado Street,** with Fisherman's Wharf at the north end and Cannery Row (and the aquarium) 1½ miles further northwest. Once in town, your best bet for getting around is via **Wave** ($1, transfers free), a shuttle bus with frequent service and stops throughout the downtown/Cannery Row area. There is also a bike/pedestrian path that parallels the shore from the historic downtown area to Fisherman's Wharf and Cannery Row. Because of summer tourism, both parking and crowds are a serious problem for drivers. The most reasonable parking garage downtown (btw Alvarado, Franklin, Washington, and Del Monte Sts.) charges $1 an hour; the meters near Cannery Row charge 25¢ per 30 minutes.

**WHERE TO SLEEP** Monterey is almost devoid of cheap lodging—and unfortunately the lone hostel closed in 1995—but if you're persistent (or if you have a tent) you may be able to scare up something reasonable. A slew of motels along North Fremont Street are close to downtown and accessible via Buses 9 and 10. Across from Del Monte Beach and one block east of the Greyhound station, **Del Monte Beach Inn** (1110 Del Monte Ave., tel. 408/649–4410) is a small bed-and-breakfast offering rooms ($50–$75) tastefully decorated in the English countryside vein.

**Lone Oak Motel.** At this refreshingly tasteful, flawlessly clean motel, the price of a double—$48 weekdays, $80 (ouch!) weekends—includes unlimited access to a new Jacuzzi and sauna room, a great way to unwind after a hard day's traveling. Call ahead, as prices fluctuate. *2221 Fremont St., tel. 408/372–4924. 46 rooms. Wheelchair access.*

**Paramount Motel.** Eight miles north of Monterey in the town of Marina, the Paramount does not accept reservations for its clean, comfortable doubles ($33), so arrive early. *3298 Del Monte Blvd., tel. 408/384–8674. Hwy. 1 north to Del Monte Ave. and drive 5 min; or Bus 12 to Beach Ave. and walk up Del Monte Ave. 6 rooms.*

➢ **CAMPING** • **Laguna Seca.** Most of the 185 campsites here have RV hookups, but a few undeveloped spaces are reserved for tent campers. Considering its location on the grounds of an auto-racing track—the site of various concerts and festivals in summer—the campground is surprisingly scenic. Unfortunately, the sites themselves are pretty ugly and cost $15. Reservations, which must be made at least 5 days in advance, are advised during summer. *Hwy. 68, tel. 408/755–4899 or 408/422–6138. 9 mi east of Monterey off Hwy. 68 (follow signs).*

**Veteran's Memorial Park Campground.** Just 5 minutes from downtown, this first-come, first-served campground lies on a grassy knoll in a quiet valley—pleasant enough if not quite the great outdoors. Forty primitive sites ($15), some shadier and more secluded than others, are packed tightly together. Showers are available, but bring your own food. *Via del Rey, tel. 408/646–3865. Take Hwy. 68 west to Skyline Forest Dr., turn left at stop sign, and drive to bottom of hill; or Bus 3 from Transit Plaza.*

**FOOD** On Tuesdays afternoons, Alvarado Street downtown is closed off for a **farmers' market**; at all other times you can find a plethora of seafood and health-food restaurants here, but unfortunately they're almost all overpriced. The **Bagel Bakery** (201 Lighthouse Blvd., at Reeside Ave., tel. 408/649–1714), open daily 6:30–6, has the best deal in town for breakfast or lunch: Tasty bagels are 40¢–50¢, and you can add whatever toppings suit your fancy, including cream cheese (60¢), Jack or Swiss cheese (35¢), avocado (70¢), and sandwich meat ($1.50). **Rappa's** (end of Fisherman's Pier, tel. 408/372–7562) has a pleasant patio and a $7 lunch menu starring fish and chips. For picnic supplies, head to **Joseph's Patisserie** (435 Alvarado St., at Bonifacio Pl, tel. 408/373–1108); sandwiches run $3–$5.

**Fishwife.** One of the best pasta and seafood restaurants on the peninsula, this casual place is a favorite with locals and travelers in the know. Fish dishes start at $9 and pastas are all less than $9. *1996½ Sunset Dr., Pacific Grove, tel. 408/375–7107. Near Asilomar State Beach. Open Mon., Wed.–Sat. 11–10, Sun. 10–10.*

**Papá Chano's.** This taquería offers tasty, large portions of Mexican basics. Tacos run $2–$3, and for a little more money a burrito ($3.50–$4.50) is a meal in itself. *462 Alvarado St., at Franklin St., tel. 408/646–9587. Open daily 10 AM–11:30 PM.*

**Toastie's Café.** When you walk in you may feel like you're trapped in a pink-lace dollhouse, but the fluffy yogurt-and-buckwheat pancakes ($4) and waffles smothered in blueberries ($4) should win you over. *702 Lighthouse Ave., Pacific Grove, tel. 408/373–7543. West of downtown Monterey. Open Mon.–Sat. 6 AM–3 PM and 5 PM–9 PM, Sun. 7 AM–2 PM.*

**WORTH SEEING** Monterey's main attraction is the justifiably world-famous **Monterey Bay Aquarium** (886 Cannery Row, tel. 408/648–4800), open daily 9:30–6 (10–6 in winter), where you'll find sharks and sea otters in convincingly natural habitats and a 28-foot kelp-forest aquarium. Admission is $11.75. From Highway 1 south, follow signs from the Pacific Grove/Del Monte Avenue exit.

**Cannery Row** lies along the waterfront south of the aquarium, ending at **Fisherman's Wharf.** Both places have seen better days. The Laida Café—an "institution of commercialized love" in Steinbeck's time—is now a bright-yellow ice cream parlor called **Kalisa's** (851 Cannery Row, tel. 408/372–3621); and the lab of Doc Ricketts, a Steinbeck character, is now a nightclub (800 Cannery Row). To drown your sorrows over days gone by, head to **Bargetto Winery** (700 Cannery Row, tel. 408/373–4053), open daily 10:30–6, where you can sip chardonnay and merlot for free. Upstairs, **A Taste of Monterey** (700 Cannery Row, tel. 408/646–5446), also open daily 10:30–6, charges $2 for tasting—but think of it as a fee for the superlative bay views. History buffs can pick up "The Path of History Walking Tour" brochure from the Chamber of Commerce (*see above*) or spend $2 on a guided tour organized by **Monterey State Historic Park** (20 Custom House Plaza, tel. 408/649–7118).

When you've had it with quill pens and adobe walls, head for the water. Beach bums shouldn't waste time at **Monterey State Beach,** where the wind will make you wish you'd worn a sweater. It's nothing compared to fabulous **Asilomar State Beach** (tel. 408/372–4076), which features tide pools and enormous waves crashing on the rocky shore; look for it 2 miles west of Monterey in the quiet town of **Pacific Grove.** Here, between October and March, glimpse thousands of monarch butterflies who make their winter homes in **Washington Park** (cnr Pine Ave. and Alder St.). Pacific Grove is also home to the **Point Pinos Light Station** (Ocean View Blvd., at Point Pinos, tel. 408/ 648–3116), the oldest continuously operating lighthouse on the West Coast. It's open weekends 1–4.

**AFTER DARK** Though Monterey's nightlife could hardly be called raging, there's no need to sit in your tent or motel room and clip your toenails. You'll find a load of gimmicky bars and clubs in the Cannery Row area, but if you prefer to mix with the locals, check out the turquoise cave known as **Viva Monterey Cabaret Café** (414 Alvarado St., tel. 408/646–1415), where the hip set goes to toss down a few, watch local bands, or play pool. With a more laid-back atmosphere, the **Monterey Coffeehouse Bookshop** (472 Alvarado St., tel. 408/647–1822) is a great place to relax after a day at the beach. Browse through the latest literary offerings or foreign language section. The bookshop often has live music or poetry readings—pick up a copy of their "Book Page" newsletter for schedules.

## OUTDOOR ACTIVITIES

➢ **BIKING AND MOPEDS** • **Monterey Moped Adventures** (1250 Del Monte Ave., at Sloat St., tel. 408/ 373–2696) rents beach cruisers ($15 a day) and mopeds ($20 for the first hour, then $10 an hour; $50 a day). A driver's license and deposit are required. For $20 a day you can rent a mountain bike from **Bay Sports** (640 Wave St., 1 block inland from Cannery Row, tel. 408/646–9090) and make tracks for the paved path that stretches from Asilomar State Beach past Lover's Point, Cannery Row, and the wharf. Another great idea is to pedal down 17-Mile Drive (*see box, below*) for free, and on into Carmel or back to Monterey.

➢ **FISHING AND WHALE WATCHING** • For salmon- and tuna-related fun, contact **Chris's Fishing Trips** (tel. 408/375–5951) on Fisherman's Wharf for half-day sportfishing trips ($25–$40); you'll also pay a small fee for equipment. Chris's also offers whale-watching trips ($12–$15) between December and March, when Monterey Bay is filled with the spectacular sight of migrating whales.

### *The Poor Man's 17-Mile Drive*

***Probably the most famous road on the Central Coast, 17-Mile Drive takes you through Pebble Beach, with its immaculate golf courses, multimillion-dollar mansions, and incredibly scenic stretches of coast. You have to pay an immensely annoying $6.50 fee to drive the road in a car, but bicyclists can enter for free through the Pacific Grove gate (take Hwy. 68 or Lighthouse Ave. west to Sunset Dr. and follow signs). Bay Sports (see Outdoor Activities, above) has rentals for $20 a day; you can return the bike to their Carmel location (near south end of drive) for an extra $2.50. If you do decide to use your car, take advantage and explore the roads leading off the 17-Mile Drive. You might receive some less-than-friendly looks, but it's perfectly legal and you'll be treated to up-close views of some high-class homes.***

***If the fee turns you off entirely, there is another option. "The Poor Man's 17-Mile Drive," as locals like to call it, is really only 6 miles long, but it's nearly as dramatic as the real thing (and free). From Monterey, head west on Ocean View Drive (just west of Cannery Row) and follow the road as it bends southward past spectacular Asilomar State Beach. Watch the sun set over wild sand dunes and the untamed Pacific; and look for Lover's Point, a grassy patch overlooking the ocean that's a popular daytime picnic area and nighttime make-out spot.***

➢ **KAYAKING** • The folks at **Monterey Bay Kayaks** (693 Del Monte Ave., 2 blocks north of Fisherman's Wharf, tel. 408/373–KELP) know everything there is to know about the sport and can recommend great takeoff points for exploring Monterey Bay. Day-long rentals ($25) include kayak, oars, wet suit, and on-land instruction.

➢ **SNORKELING AND SCUBA DIVING** • Monterey Bay attracts divers from around the world with its vast kelp beds and magnificent underwater terrain. The bluffs and underwater caves off Ocean View Drive (between the aquarium and Asilomar Beach) are the best scuba and snorkeling spots in the area. **Aquarius Dive Shop** (2040 Del Monte Ave., or 32 Cannery Row, tel. for both 408/375–1933) offers moderately priced equipment rentals for certified divers (about $70 the first day, $35 each additional day). A more feasible option for most people is snorkeling. Aquarius has gear for less than $30—not a high price, considering you'll need a wet suit, boots, gloves, and a hood to brave Monterey Bay's freezing waters. Snorkeling lessons and a tour will set you back $50 more.

# Carmel

Perched on a rocky bluff 8 miles south of Monterey, this quiet, affluent beachfront town doubles as an artists' colony. But don't let the gorgeous coast and shady beaches fool you: Carmel is a strange place—an aloof bastion of conservatism known for its provincial attitudes and some of the most restrictive laws in the nation. Residents make every effort to preserve Carmel's small-town flavor. Downtown establishments do not have street addresses; and when the sun goes down, don't expect to find after-hours food or midnight revelry. No live entertainment is allowed in local drinking holes or restaurants. Instead, Carmel hosts its live shows and movies at the bring-your-own-blanket **Outdoor Forest Theater** (cnr Mountain View Ave. and Santa Rita St., tel. 408/626–1681), located between Highway 1 and downtown.

*There are no sidewalks, no street lighting, and no mail delivery in residential Carmel-by-the-Sea. Locals enjoy this village setting and have chosen to pick up their mail at the post office, where they hang out and exchange gossip, just like in the old days.*

Carmel fancies itself a small and private community, yet it's mercilessly invaded each day by tourists hopping from gift shop to art gallery to "quaint" café. Even more bizarre is the fact that Carmel elected Clint "Go ahead, make my day" Eastwood as its mayor. Above Clint's Hog's Breath Inn restaurant lies the **visitor center** (San Carlos St., btw 5th and 6th Sts., tel. 408/624–2522), open weekdays 9–5, Saturday 10–5, and Sunday noon–4.

**WHERE TO SLEEP** Carmel is *not* cut out for those on a budget. Even the beat-up motels price their rooms as if they were lush suites in an upscale B&B. Your best bet is to camp—either in Carmel itself, north in Monterey, or south along the Big Sur coast. Otherwise, Monterey has a few reasonably priced motels.

**The Homestead.** Right in town, this place fits into the overdone country-inn category—a hotel that goes too far out of its way to be quaint and cozy. However, if you can afford to spend the money, the Homestead is awfully comfortable, and the well-kept garden is an awfully nice place for a stroll. Doubles start at $55 in winter, $65 in summer; four-person cottages are $95. *Lincoln St. and 8th Ave., tel. 408/624–4119. Exit Hwy. 1 at Ocean Ave., then left on Lincoln St. 8 rooms, 4 cottages, some with kitchen. Reservations advised.*

➢ **CAMPING** • **Saddle Mountain.** This well-groomed private campground is the only one within easy reach of Carmel. Fifty developed sites ($20 per night) lie on a terraced hillside. If you don't have camping gear, you can rent a cabin or nifty teepee for $32. The grounds are peaceful and the pool refreshing. *Schulte Rd., tel. 408/624–1617. Take Carmel Valley Rd. off Hwy. 1, turn right at Schulte Rd. Showers available. Reservations advised.*

**FOOD** Unique and expensive are the norms here: Taverns, tearooms, al frescos, and broilers abound—everything except a McDonald's. If you'd rather picnic, head to the **Mediterranean Market** (Ocean Ave. and Mission St., tel. 408/624–2022), where you can create your own sandwich ($5), snack on tasty salads, or buy meats and imported cheeses by the pound. Head to the little park across the street to chow. Two doors down, **Wishart's Bakery** (tel. 408/624–0932) has bagels (60¢) to go with your bowl of homemade soup ($2.75).

**Friar Tuck's.** This friendly, pseudo-English place is down to earth compared to the rest of Carmel. Burgers, salads, and sandwiches run $4–$6. For breakfast, try one of the outstanding omelets ($6.75). *5th Ave. and Dolores St., tel. 408/624–4274. Open daily 6:30 AM–2 PM.*

**WORTH SEEING** Your first stop in Carmel will be the downtown area, easily accessed from Highway 1 via Ocean Avenue. Here you'll find a parade of pricey and often snobby gift shops, boutiques, restaurants, and art galleries (mostly filled with yawn-inducing watercolors). You can pick up a map at the **Carmel Art Association** (Dolores St., btw 5th and 6th Aves., tel. 408/624–6176) that locates over 35 local galleries, many clustered on Dolores Street.

Carmel's **public beach,** at the end of Ocean Avenue, is the place to pick up a game of volleyball or nap in the sand, protected from the blistering sun and howling winds by cypress trees. For a more spectacular and less populated beach, head about a mile south along Scenic Road (off Ocean Ave. just above public beach) until you come around the hairpin curve to **Carmel River State Beach,** known to locals as Oliver's Cove. When you see the view from here, you'll realize how poet Robinson Jeffers remained inspired for so many years—his home, known as the **Tor House** (26304 Oceanview Ave., 2 blocks from Scenic Rd., tel. 408/624–1813), is a stone's throw away. Jeffers, one of Carmel's most famous personalities, built Tor House and the adjacent Hawk Tower from rocks he carried up from the beach himself, creating one of California's most unique "natural" dwellings. Guided tours ($5 and worth it) are available by appointment Fridays and Saturdays 10–3. Otherwise, you get an excellent view of the house from Scenic Road.

The **Carmel Mission** (Rio Rd. and Lasuen Dr., tel. 408/624–3600), founded in 1770 by the busy Padre Serra (who is buried here), includes a stone church, museum, and gardens. Winter hours are Monday–Saturday 9:30–4:30 and Sunday 10:30–4:30; in summer, it's open daily until 7:30 ($1 donations appreciated). To get to the mission take Junipero Avenue south to Rio Road.

**OUTDOOR ACTIVITIES** Hikers should consider the dozens of rambling trails at **Garland Ranch Regional Park** (Carmel Valley Rd., tel. 408/659–4488), 8½ miles east of Highway 1 on Carmel Valley Road. If you've got strong legs and a few hours to spare, take the 5-mile **Lupine Loop** through the meadow and up, up, up on La Mesa and Sky Trail to Snively's Ridge. Besides a watchtower, you'll find one of the best 360° views on the Central Coast.

The main attraction in Carmel for bicyclists is 17-Mile Drive (*see box, above*), or you can pedal south on flat coastal roads for a few miles to Point Lobos. **Bay Sports** (Lincoln St., btw 5th and 6th Aves., tel. 408/625–BIKE) rents hybrid bikes for $20 a day. If you're in good shape, you can ride all the way to Monterey and drop off the bike at their other location for $2.50 (*see* Outdoor Activities, in Monterey, *above*). If you'd rather do your biking in the dirt, there are a few trails at Point Lobos State Reserve (*see* Near Carmel, *below*); ask rangers for details.

## NEAR CARMEL

**POINT LOBOS STATE RESERVE** Point Lobos State Reserve (Hwy. 1, 4 mi south of Carmel, tel. 408/624–4909) is a day-use park where sea lions, harbor seals, and otters frolic; it's also a good spot to watch whales pass by on their southward migration from December to May. It's a great place to stretch your legs: The **Cypress Grove Trail** loops past a rare species of cypress; the **Sea Lion Point Trail** leads to a magnificent series of sea coves; and the **South Shore Trail** takes you to Weston Beach, site of the reserve's best tidal pools. You can park for free across the street from the main entrance on Highway 1; otherwise you pay $6 per vehicle. The park is open daily 9–4:30 in winter and until 6:30 in summer.

The reserve allows up to 15 teams on any given day to dive in **Whaler's Cove** among the otters, seals, and sea lions. Snorkelers and divers must pay a $6 fee; reserve for either activity through MISTIX (tel. 800/444–PARK). Proof of diver certification is required. To rent equipment, contact the Aquarius Dive Shop in Monterey (*see* Outdoor Activities, Monterey, *above*).

**GARRAPATA STATE BEACH** Four and a half miles south of Point Lobos, Garrapata offers a series of loop trails perfect for those who don't like to sweat. **Soberanes Point,** a great place to watch otters playing on offshore rock formations, lies at the end of a short walk. A 1½-mile hike along a redwood-lined creek leads to **Soberanes Canyon.** A bit more rigorous, **Rocky Ridge** slopes steeply on the 3-mile trek up but affords excellent coastal views. You can park along the road near the Soberanes Barn. The trailhead for the point is across the street from the beach; the ones for the canyon and ridge are behind the barn.

# Big Sur

Starting about 8 miles south of Point Lobos, Big Sur is often described as more of a philosophy than a specific acreage. Spanish settlers in the 1770s called this forbidding wilderness *el pais grande del sur* (the big country to the south), which got shortened to Big Sur in the early 1900s. Everyone defines Big Sur differently, but all agree that the region's precipitous cliffs, rocky beaches, and redwood forests make it one of the most dramatic stretches of coastline in the world. The harsh geography, helped along by a core of adamantly protective locals, has precluded development; as a result the area is sparsely populated. The closest thing to a town is the group of stores surrounding the **River Inn** (*see* Where to Sleep, *below*), 22 miles south of Carmel. Locals head over to the inn on Saturday nights to hear live jazz or drum music, and next door, the **Big Sur Pub** (tel. 408/667–2355), open daily until 10 PM, sometimes hosts mariachi bands or guitarists.

Much of Big Sur lies within the 167,000-acre **Ventana Wilderness,** in Los Padres National Forest. Ventana's deep, wide valleys, waterfalls, hot springs, natural pools, perennial streams, and undisturbed wildlife (heaps of deer and more than a few bears) are enough to keep wilderness junkies on a perpetual high. **Big Sur Station** (Hwy. 1, just south of Pfeiffer Big Sur State Park, tel. 408/667–2315), open daily 8–6, is loaded with information on camping and exploring the surrounding wilderness.

**WHERE TO SLEEP** With more than 1,000 campsites up and down the coast, Big Sur is an ideal place to pitch a tent. You can camp for free in **Los Padres National Forest** as long as you hike 100 feet from a paved road and don't light a fire (*also see* Camping, in Chapter 1). Good access roads can be found all along Highway 1: Try Willow Creek Road just north of Gorda or Nacimiento Road about 4 miles south of Lucia. The forest service also runs 11 designated campgrounds ($5) in the area, with fire pits and drinking water. For maps, fire permits, and info contact Big Sur Station (*see above*) or the **U.S. Forest Service District Headquarters** (406 S. Mildred Street, King City 93930).

If you want to sleep indoors, be prepared to pay handsomely for the privilege. If you don't have camping gear, your best option is to rent one of the tent cabins available at private campgrounds for $30–$40. One of the nicest is **Big Sur Campground and Cabins** (tel. 408/667–2322), 3 miles south of Andrew Molera State Park (*see below*), where cabins sleeping two start at $40.

**Deetjen's Big Sur Inn.** This place, consisting of an inn and cabins secluded behind redwoods off Highway 1, is rustic to the core—which means no phones, no TVs, thin walls, old bathrooms, and electricity that could blow out at any moment. Each room has its own name and is uniquely decorated with homey, personal stuff and a down comforter (you'll need it). The atmosphere and the people who run the place are both top-notch, and pleasant hiking trails lie behind the inn. Doubles start at $70, and all proceeds go to the non-profit Preservation Foundation, which runs the place. The on-site restaurant is outta this world. *Hwy. 1, tel. 408/667–2377. 3 mi south of Big Sur Station, 1 mi south of Nepenthe. 20 rooms, some with shared bath. Reservations a must.*

**River Inn.** The first place you hit coming south (22 mi south of Carmel), the inn is comfortable and conveniently located near shops, an overpriced restaurant, and a gas station. The recently renovated rooms are clean, stylish, and typically expensive. Doubles start at $77 in the off-season and $88 in summer. *Hwy. 1, tel. 408/667–2700 or 800/548–3610. 19 rooms. Reservations advised.*

➢ **CAMPING** • **Andrew Molera State Park.** Andrew Molera has more than 4,000 largely undeveloped acres with beach access and camping. Campers pay $3 per person and $1 per dog. Don't try to get by without putting your money in the self-payment box—a ranger *will* come around at 8 AM to collect the cash and hand out tickets to the weasels. The campsites are set against trees in a flat 10-acre meadow, half a mile from the parking area. Beware of staying here on summer weekends, when troops of Cub Scouts and pubescent preteens can make life hell. The tents-only sites are first-come, first-served, but they never turn anyone away. Call Big Sur Station (*see above*) for more info. *West of Hwy. 1, 10 mi south of Palo Colorado Rd.*

**Bottcher's Gap.** If you want to soak up a view of a tremendous valley among the majestic madrones and oaks of the Ventana Wilderness, trek to the 11 free, first-come, first-served campsites in the gorge at Bottcher's Gap. There's no phone, no showers, and (at press time) no running water; but if you come on a weeknight, you'll have all the peace and solitude you could ever want. For the best info on the trails and the campground, call Ranger Larry Born (tel. 408/625–5833). *5 mi south of Garrapata State Beach, go east 8 mi on Palo Colorado Rd.*

**Pfeiffer Big Sur State Park.** Although there are more than 300 RV and tent sites ($16) here, the redwood groves and gurgling stream still make this sprawling campground one of the best places to sleep in Big Sur. For your convenience, there's a general store, a laundromat, and hot showers. It's crowded in summer, and sites should be reserved by calling MISTIX (tel. 800/444–PARK). If you're in the mood to ramble, head south along the river that meanders through the park; a semi-treacherous quarter mile past the last campsite, you'll reach an unspeakably beautiful mountain pool surrounded by 200-foot cliff faces and rocky buttes. *Hwy. 1, tel. 408/667–2315. Fire pits, picnic tables.*

**Julia Pfeiffer Burns State Park.** During summer, weekend warriors deluge the huge redwoods and shady oak trees of this popular park. The jewel here for hikers, bikers, and tent campers is the chance of getting a space at one of two secluded environmental sites ($16), located in a cypress forest on bluffs overlooking the ocean. Even without potable water or flush toilets, these spots book early. Reservations through MISTIX (tel. 800/444–PARK) are advised. For info on both environmental and developed camping, call or stop by Big Sur Station (*see above*). *Hwy. 1, 38 mi south of Carmel.*

**Plaskett Creek.** In a grassy field on the east side of Highway 1, Plaskett Creek offers 43 sites for $15. It's often empty during winter, but reservations through MISTIX (tel. 800/444–PARK) are advised in summer and on holiday weekends. *Hwy. 1, 9½ mi south of Lucia. Drinking water, no showers.*

➢ **ROUGHING IT** • It's illegal to park along Highway 1 and sleep in your car or van, but many people do it anyway because the area is rarely patrolled. People often sleep on the smaller beaches as well. Recently, especially near the southern edge of Big Sur closer to San Simeon, some robberies and beatings have occurred—be careful.

**FOOD** There aren't many restaurants along the Big Sur coast, but you'll come across one or two good finds. The **Center Deli** (Hwy. 1, next to Big Sur post office, tel. 408/667–2225) has groceries, a host of salads, and the cheapest sandwiches around ($3–$5), as well as fruit smoothies ($3) in summer. There's no seating, but you can grab a picnic lunch and eat at a nearby scenic overlook. The **Coast Gallery Café** (above Coast Art Gallery, Hwy. 1, 33 mi south of Carmel, tel. 408/667–2301) is a casual deli with hot sandwiches ($6–$8) and a great view of the coast. The **Big Sur Pub** (next to River Inn; *see above*) has a filling veggie burrito ($5.25) and sandwiches for less than $5.

**Café Kevah.** Part of the Nepenthe restaurant complex, this café has daily brunch and lunch menus with interesting dishes like apple-bread pudding ($6.75) and spicy chicken brochettes ($6.75), as well as the most expensive espresso drinks this side of Paris ($3.50 and up) and a selection of scrumptious pastries ($2.50). The food is overpriced, but what you're really paying for is the fantastic view from the deck. If you want to splurge, head upstairs to the **Nepenthe** dining room, where steaks and seafood start at $12. *Hwy. 1, tel. 408/667–2344. 29 mi south of Carmel. Open weekdays 9–4, weekends 10–5.*

**EXPLORING BIG SUR** Five miles south of Garrapata State Beach, Palo Colorado Road winds its way east from Highway 1 through the Ventana Wilderness for 8 serpentine miles until it ends at **Bottcher's Gap.** From the parking lot, **Skinner's Ridge Trail** climbs 4 miles (roughly 3 hrs) to Devil's Peak, which affords incredible views of Ventana's dramatic wooded peaks and valleys. South off Skinner's Ridge Trail, the 8-hour round-trip hike to **Pico Blanco**—a rugged mountain peak that the Esselen Indians thought of as the top of the world and the site of human creation—offers stunning views but winds through private property. The hike's not legal, but people do it anyway, trekking along the Boy Scout Service Road past the Boy Scout Camp and all the way up **Little Sur Trail.**

Back on Highway 1, south of Palo Colorado Road, look for the **Bixby Creek Bridge,** a 550-foot concrete span built in 1932. Just before the bridge, the circular **Old Coast Road** curves inland for 10 miles and meets back up with Highway 1 opposite the entrance to Andrew Molera State Park. This is California at its rugged best—craggy cliffs, majestic redwoods, and views of the Little Sur River running its way toward the ocean. If you're the four-wheeling type, you'll like the road's gravel- and mud-plagued inclines; a regular old car should be fine if the weather's been dry.

Double back 1½ miles north from Andrew Molera to check out the **Point Sur Light Station** (tel. 408/625–4419), built in 1889 on a strange rock outcropping to prevent shipwrecks along this foggy and rocky stretch of coast. Tours of the lighthouse are available on weekends for $5. Once the site of a Monterey Jack cheese factory and a dairy farm, **Andrew Molera State Park** offers more than 10 miles of hiking and mountain-biking trails. The strenuous hike on the **Ridge Trail** takes you through 4 miles of stunning coastal scenery to the top of a ridge. Take a deep breath and savor the spectacular view of the Pacific before you head down the **Panorama Trail** to the **Bluffs Trail,** which is especially striking in spring when the wildflowers bloom.

About 5 miles south of Andrew Molera State Park, **Pfeiffer Big Sur State Park** (east side of Hwy. 1, tel. 408/667–2315) is one of the most popular camping and hiking spots on the coast, especially during summer. Trails from the parking lot lead to the 60-foot **Pfeiffer Falls,** at the end of a 20-minute hike through groves of huge redwoods. Just south of Pfeiffer on the same side of the highway, Big Sur Station (*see above*) is the starting point for the **Pine Ridge Trail,** a local favorite that leads into the Ventana Wilderness and **Sykes Hot Springs** (*see box, below*).

Sycamore Canyon Road, a mile south of Big Sur Station, is unmarked save for a stop sign. If you can find it, brave the road for 2 miles and you'll land at **Pfeiffer Beach,** a violently turbulent, windswept cove with huge rock formations and an angry ocean that's definitely not suited for swimming. About 2½ miles farther south lies **Nepenthe** (tel. 408/667–2345; *also see* Food, *above*), an expensive restaurant with an extraordinary view (also the last stop of Bus 22 from Monterey).

Head south from Nepenthe to the **Henry Miller Library** (Hwy. 1, ¼ mile south of Nepenthe, tel. 408/667–2574). The library displays the bohemian author's artifacts and has rotating exhibits

## *Sykes Hot Springs*

***If you have 2 or 3 days and backpacking gear on your hands, think seriously about making the 10-mile hike to Sykes Hot Springs, one of the Central Coast's most enticing natural wonders. After a 6- to 7-hour trek up steep ridges and along a river valley crowded with redwoods, you can soak your bones in the thermal spring and sleep under the stars before heading back the next day or continuing on into the depths of the Ventana Wilderness. The trail begins at the Big Sur Station parking lot; register and get a fire permit from the rangers here before heading out.***

on artists and writers associated with Miller or Big Sur. The library is open daily 11–5 in summer, weekends only in winter.

Although not quite as spectacular as Pfeiffer Big Sur State Park, **Julia Pfeiffer Burns State Park** (12 mi south of Big Sur Station, tel. 408/667–2315) has excellent and often less crowded hiking trails. But most people pay the $6 entrance fee to see what was once the most spectacular sight in all of Big Sur, before parking lots, postcards, and crowds demystified some of its natural wonder: **McWay Falls,** which pours 70 feet down into the ocean. From the parking lot, a short half-mile walk leads to a bluff with an incredible view of the creek at the head of the falls.

Three miles south of Julia Pfeiffer, a sign on the right side of the road reads: ESALEN INSTITUTE–RESERVATIONS ONLY. At the end of the road you'll find the world-famous **Esalen Institute** (tel. 408/667–3000), a one-time wacked-out hippie colony that specializes in the "exploration of human value and potentials." Locals tend to scoff, but the institute was one of the first places to introduce Gestalt therapy in the late '60s. Today, Esalen still attracts people from around the world to its skillfully run workshops and self-help sessions, although its gorgeous gardens, pool, and natural hot springs are now closed to the public during the day. To attend one of the outrageously expensive workshops, call the institute. Esalen occasionally rents out extra rooms for $65–$125; the price includes meals and access to the grounds.

*Between 1 AM and 3:30 AM, you can relax naked in Esalen's natural hot springs, perched on a cliff overlooking the Pacific, for just $10—a pleasure that could run you 10 times that much during the day. Call the institute to make reservations.*

The southern stretch of Big Sur—between the tiny towns of Lucia and San Simeon—is both less populated and has a gentler geography than the sometimes violently beautiful north. There's not much to see besides the continually unfolding coastline, but you will come across some choice beaches every now and then. Half a mile south of Plaskett Creek (*see* Where to Sleep, *above*), **Jade Cove** is a secluded, rocky beach with sweeping views both up and down the coast. Just north of Gorda, quiet **Willow Creek** is gorgeous, rocky, and a local favorite.

**OUTDOOR ACTIVITIES** The main activity in Big Sur is hiking (*see* Exploring Big Sur, *above*), but to the dismay of many drivers, lots of people also bicycle along Highway 1. Cyclists should be experienced and familiar with the narrowness of the highway and the lack of road shoulder. One benefit of pedaling the coast is that most of the state parks offer cheap campsites (usually $3) to those on two rather than four wheels.

**Andrew Molera State Park** is the only Big Sur park with single-track trails for mountain biking. Mountain bikers in tip-top shape can take on the steep, strenuous **Ridge Trail,** which is more than 2 miles long and has elevation gains of 1,200 feet. For a more relaxing ride, try the **River** and **Cottonwood trails** (2 mi), both of which wind through the park's meadows. Most trails start at the parking area or a half-mile away at the beach. Elsewhere in Big Sur, you'll have to stick to the fire and service roads, or risk a fine. One possibility is to head up **Nacimiento–Ferguson Road,** 4 miles south of Lucia off Highway 1. Bikes are not allowed to the left into the Ventana Wilderness, but off the right side of the road you'll see a few trails, most of which are quite steep in sections.

# Hearst Castle

Forty-four miles south of Lucia look for **San Simeon,** a small oceanfront town that's famous for one thing and one thing only: Hearst Castle, designed by Julia Morgan and bankrolled by publishing magnate William Randolph Hearst—the model for Orson Welles's *Citizen Kane.* You can sort of see the massive complex from the highway, but for a closer inspection of the eclectic (Greco–Roman/Gothic/Spanish) and fantastically opulent "Enchanted Hill," take one of four guided tours ($14, $25 spring and fall evenings) that leave from the visitor center (*see below*) off Highway 1.

The tours last 1¾ hours, including bus transportation up the private 5-mile road that leads to the site (sit on the right-hand side of the bus for the best views). Although it's pricey, the tour of the ornately decorated rooms, gold-plated indoor pool, flower beds, and sculpture-lined gardens is well worth the money. Most visitors opt for Tour 1, which offers a general overview of the gardens and the main house. All tours cover the ornate interior, lush gardens, and much-photographed indoor and outdoor pools. Reservations are advised, as tickets (tel. 800/444–4445 or 805/927–2005) sell out quickly. Travelers with wheelchairs must make reservations at least 10 days in advance by calling 805/927–2020.

*Throwing a little shindig? You can rent Hearst Castle and the grounds to the tune of $3,000 an hour.*

If you want a sneak preview of your tour or cannot afford the castle's steep admission, check out the free exhibit at the huge **visitor center** (tel. 805/927–2020), off Highway 1 at the bottom of the hill. It documents the history of the Hearst family and the building of the castle, which was begun in 1919 and continued for 28 years. The center is generally open daily 8–5:30, but hours may vary, so call ahead.

**WHERE TO SLEEP** Loads of motels are clustered about 2 miles south of Hearst Castle in a strip known as San Simeon Acres, but they're all overpriced. For a better deal, head 6 miles down Highway 1 into tiny Cambria, where you'll find the **Cambria Palms Motel** (2662 Main St., tel. 805/927–4485) at the south end of the main drag. It's got simple rooms (no phones) with thick walls and cozy beds; the friendly Brits who run the place charge $50 for doubles in summer, $30 off-season. To camp near the beach, head to the unspectacular **San Simeon State Beach Campgrounds** (Hwy. 1, tel. 805/927–2035), which include San Simeon Creek Campground, with 134 modern sites (i.e., with showers) for $16, and Washburn Campground, with 70 primitive sites for $9. San Simeon Creek has some shady trees, while Washburn is on a flat hilltop with no shade and lots of scrub brush. It's wise to reserve through MISTIX (tel. 800/444–PARK), especially on summer weekends.

**FOOD** There's not much to choose from in Cambria and San Simeon. If you see a place that looks good, stop—if you don't, it may be miles before you pass another. **Creekside Gardens Café** (2114 Main St., Cambria, tel. 805/927–8646), open Monday–Saturday 7–2 and Sunday 7–1, is a great place for breakfast, with omelets ($5) and applesauce pancakes ($3.50). At **Robin's** (4095 Burton Dr., off Main St. in Cambria, tel. 805/927–5007), open Monday–Saturday 11–9 and Sunday 5 PM–9 PM, you get home cooking with an ethnic edge. Try the hot-and-spicy tempeh or the fresh pasta Greco with vegetables; both are less than $9.

# San Luis Obispo

Probably the least known of the major Central Coast towns, the inland burg of San Luis Obispo sits 34 miles south of San Simeon and 110 miles north of Santa Barbara, surrounded by rocky hills and volcanic peaks. Half the town is made up of students who attend California Polytechnic State University and nearby Cuesta College, so the population drops dramatically in summer. There's not all that much to do here—Californians sometimes refer to it by its acronym: "SLO." But if you need a place to stop for the night on the drive from San Francisco to L.A., San Luis Obispo is a convenient halfway point, and you can find enough diversions to keep you happily occupied for an evening. Stop in at the **Chamber of Commerce** (1039 Chorro St., at Monterey St., tel. 805/543–1323) for a free map and information on goings-on.

*Not to be missed at the Madonna Inn is the urinal in the men's room—a large waterfall that's activated by lasers (women should knock and look in).*

For starters, check out the tacky pink-and-white **Madonna Inn** (100 Madonna Rd., tel. 805/543–3000), southwest of downtown and visible from U.S. 101. At this popular hotel, no two of the flamboyant rooms are alike. The management won't let you visit the Cave Room (complete with waterfall) or the Old Mill (featuring a working water wheel) unless you have a reservation, but postcards in the lobby detail each of the $77–$210 rooms. When you've had your fill of kitsch, head into San Luis Obispo's long and narrow downtown area, packed with record stores, student-oriented restaurants, cafés, and movie theaters. The main drag, **Higuera Street,** runs roughly east–west, with Palm Street and Marsh Street paralleling it. Intersecting these long commercial avenues, Broad Street to the west and Toro Street to the east form a rectangle within which lie all the downtown sights.

*The gum wall, on Higuera Street between Garden and Broad streets (next to Edgeware Gifts), is the unofficial repository of thousands of people's used gum. You, too, can write your name in Wrigley's or Bubblicious.*

The main attraction is the **Mission San Luis Obispo** (Chorro and Monterey Sts., tel. 805/543—6850), the fifth-oldest of California's 21 historic missions, built in 1772 overlooking San Luis Obispo Creek. Also interesting is the **Ah Louis Store** (800 Palm St., at Chorro St., tel. 805/543–4332), built by its namesake in 1884 to serve the needs of the Chinese laborers who helped build California's railroads. The store still sells a mishmash of things from Asia. On Thursday evenings 6–9 year-round, an excellent **farmers' market** on Higuera Street features fresh produce, hot food, and live music.

**COMING AND GOING** San Luis Obispo lies at the junction of Highway 1 and U.S. 101, both of which run north–south. If you're making the trip from San Francisco to Los Angeles, or vice versa, San Luis Obispo is the perfect halfway point; it's roughly four hours from each city on U.S. 101. If you're looking to find a cheap ride out of town, or somebody to share gas costs with, check the ride board downstairs at the **Cal Poly University Student Union** (Grand Ave. and Perimeter Sts., tel. 805/756–1154).

➢ **BY BUS** • From the San Luis Obispo **Greyhound station** (150 South St., at Parker St., tel. 805/543–2121 or 800/231–2222), buses run north along U.S. 101 to San Francisco (6 hrs, $37 one-way) five times a day, and south to Los Angeles (5½ hrs, $31 one-way) six times a day. The station, where you'll find luggage storage ($1.50 for 24 hrs), is open daily 7:15 AM–9 PM; an overnight locker costs $1. **Green Tortoise** (tel. 800/867–8647) stops in San Luis Obispo at the Denny's restaurant on Los Osos Valley Road; buses to San Francisco ($15) pass through San Luis Obispo early Monday morning, and buses to Los Angeles ($15) pass through early Saturday morning. Call a week ahead to make reservations.

**SLO Transit** (tel. 805/541–BUSS) runs bus service within the city limits (50¢), though service after dark is nearly nonexistent. Bus 3 connects the Greyhound station to downtown, though you can easily walk the quarter-mile.

➢ **BY TRAIN** • **Amtrak's** *Coast Starlight* trains stop at the **San Luis Obispo Depot** (1011 Railroad Ave., at Santa Rosa St., tel. 805/541–0505 or 800/USA-RAIL) once a day in each direction. Going south, you can reach Santa Barbara (2½ hrs, $23 one-way) or Los Angeles (6 hrs, $31 one-way); northbound trains go to Emeryville, where you board a bus to San Francisco (6–6½ hrs, $59 for train and bus). The train is slower and more expensive than the bus, and only travels along the coast between San Luis Obispo and Santa Barbara, yet seats fill up quickly—reserve well in advance. The station's open daily 8:30–5:30. SLO Transit Bus 5 (*see above*) connects the station to downtown.

**WHERE TO SLEEP** If you're in town during graduation week (mid-June) or Mardi Gras (mid-February) you'll be hard pressed to find a double for less than $80. At all other times of the year rooms are plentiful and affordable. Motels are sprinkled around the city, with many concentrated on **Monterey Street** east of Santa Rosa Street. No buses go far enough down Monterey to reach the motels, but you can easily walk from Mission Plaza, a half-mile away. If you can't get into the places listed below, the **Budget Motel** (345 Marsh St., at Archer St., tel. 805/543–6443), a spotless, no-frills place within walking distance of the Greyhound station, has singles for $34, doubles for $45, and $78 suites for those traveling in a convoy.

**Adobe Inn.** Rooms have names instead of numbers (e.g., the Prickly Pear Room) and are decorated in Southwestern style. Spend a night in a comfortable double for $45 in the off-season ($65 on summer weekends) and enjoy a complimentary homemade breakfast the next morning. *1473 Monterey St., tel. 805/549–0321. From Hwy. 1, exit at Grand Ave., right on Monterey St. Reservations advised.*

**Palms Motel.** This collection of bright yellow cottages, in what looks like the proprietors' backyard, is simple, friendly, and low-key—like San Luis Obispo itself. Doubles go for $40 ($25 off-season). *1628 Monterey St., tel. 805/544–8129. ½ mi east of downtown, 2 blocks past Adobe Inn (see above). 3 cottages. Reservations advised.*

➢ **HOSTEL • San Luis Obispo Coast Hostel (HI).** At this recently opened hostel in the foothills near the Cal Poly campus, you'll share the yard with friendly chickens. Sturdy souls who hike or bike in get a $1 discount off the price ($13 HI members; nonmembers pay $3 extra for the first night). Proprietor Elaine Simor organizes free hikes with the Sierra Club on weekends, will rent you a bike for $5 a day, provides tennis rackets for the nearby courts, and will cook you a homemade meal (price varies). *1292 Foothill Blvd., tel. 805/544–4678. From U.S. 101, exit right at California Blvd., right on Foothill Blvd. after ½ mi. 10 beds. Curfew 11 PM (flexible), lockout 9:30–5. Reception open daily 5 PM–10 PM. Laundry, lockers.*

➢ **CAMPING** • There are a number of campgrounds in the semi-arid hills around San Luis Obispo. If you prefer to camp on the beach, head 25 minutes west to Montaña de Oro State Park (*see* Near San Luis Obispo, *below*), or 15 minutes south to Pismo Beach. **Cerro Alto Campground** (tel. 805/466–2636) is run by the Forest Service; to get here from town, take Highway 1 to Morro Bay, then Highway 41 toward Atascadero (watch for signs). The 21 primitive sites ($10) lie in a wooded valley bisected by a narrow stream and are a great base for exploring the nearby mountains. There are pit toilets and all sites are first-come, first-served. The 75 first-come sites ($12) at **El Chorro Regional Park** (tel. 805/781–5219) are in a dry, hot valley with little shade, but they're close to civilization. The park lies 5 miles north of San Luis Obispo off Highway 1, across from the entrance to Cuesta College, and has coin-operated showers, which you won't find at Cerro Alto.

**FOOD** San Luis Obispo is filled with delis and restaurants catering to a student's allowance. **David Muzzio's Market** (870 Monterey St., btw Chorro and Morro Sts., tel. 805/543–0800), open Monday–Saturday 8 AM–6 PM, has groceries and a deli counter with sandwiches ($3) that you can take to Mission Plaza and eat on a bench by San Luis Obispo Creek. If you're looking for tacos ($2) or veggie burritos ($3), head to **Tio Alberto's** (1131 Broad St., tel. 805/546–9646; or 295 Santa Rosa St., tel. 805/542–9321), the best Mexican food stand in town. **Pasta Pronto** (289 Santa Rosa St., tel. 805/541-5110) offers a choice of six pastas and seven sauces ($2.50–$6.50).

**Del Monte Café.** Near the Amtrak depot, this old grocery store has been transformed into an inexpensive, '50s-style diner serving the requisite burgers and fries. The outdoor patio is popular with Cal Poly students on weekends. One of the best dishes is huevos rancheros (eggs, cheese, and beans on a tortilla, $6.50), available weekends only. *1901 Santa Barbara St., tel. 805/541–1901. Open weekdays 6:30 AM–3 PM, Sat. 7:30–3, Sun. 8–1.*

**Hudson's Grill and Bar.** This high-ceilinged eatery has wooden booths and lots of windows. Both the veggie ($5) and the carnivore ($4.50) burgers are good, and you can top off your meal with the brownie sundae ($3) as you watch the game on TV. *1005 Monterey St., downtown, tel. 805/541–5999. Open daily 7 AM–midnight.*

**Woodstock's.** Families and students gather at this local institution to chow down on the best pizza in town; the thick white or wheat crusts (famous for the tomato sauce rolled into the dough) are top-rate. You'll pay around $11 for a large cheese pizza. *1000 Higuera St., at Osos St., tel. 805/541–4420. Open summer, daily 11 AM–midnight (Fri.–Sat. until 1 AM); open 1 hr later in winter.*

**AFTER DARK** San Luis Obispo hops when school's in session (Sept.–May). Pick up a copy of the free weekly *New Times* to check what's on. The action is centered in the commercial district downtown, where many restaurants double as student pubs. **Spike's** (570 Higuera St., tel. 805/544–7157), a burger joint with 48 beers from around the world, is popular with older students. Another favorite, the **S.L.O. Brewing Company** (1119 Garden St., upstairs, tel. 805/543–1843), is a large, airy brick-and-wood microbrewery with live music most Thursday–Saturday nights (cover $2–$4). **Mother's Tavern** (725 Higuera St., tel. 805/541–8733) has live blues and jazz Thursday–Saturday ($3 cover) and swing and big band sounds on other nights (cover varies). **Breezes** (11560 Los Osos Valley Rd., near Madonna Rd., tel. 805/544–8010), located in the Laguna Village Shopping Center, is a raucous gay bar and dance club. The $2–$4 cover also buys your first drink.

For something mellower, check out the popular **Coffee Merchant** (1009 Monterey St., at Osos Rd., tel. 805/543–6701), a small café with wrought-iron chairs and sporadic acoustic music and poetry readings. House coffee is $1 a cup; espresso drinks start at $1. You can have your cuppa in the great outdoors at **Linnaea's Café** (1110 Garden St., tel. 805/541–5888), which has a large patio in the back. On Sundays and some other days the café hosts poetry readings or live music.



## NEAR SAN LUIS OBISPO

**MONTANA DE ORO STATE PARK** This is one of the most beautiful parks on the coast, 12 miles northwest of San Luis Obispo at the end of Los Osos Valley Road. Its 8,000 acres of mostly undeveloped land turn golden (*montaña de oro* means "mountain of gold") every spring when the flowers bloom. You can get a free map at **park headquarters** (tel. 805/528–0513), open daily noon–4 during summer and weekends only in winter; follow signs to the Old Spooner Ranch House from the entrance gate. Troop down to **Spooner's Cove,** once popular with Prohibition-era bootleggers, for a gorgeous vista of crashing waves and a whiff of sea spray. For a more distant view of spume and foam, the **Ocean Bluff Trail,** accessible to bikers and hikers, runs along a bluff overlooking the ocean for a little over 2 miles. The trailhead is down the road from park headquarters.

Montaña de Oro has 50 primitive sites (no showers, chemical toilets) for $9 a night, and four secluded, walk-in environmental sites; bring your own water and prepare for ocean views and total solitude. Reservations are taken for the environmental sites year-round, and from Memorial Day to Labor Day for the other sites; reserve either through MISTIX (tel. 800/444–7275).

# Avila Beach and Pismo Beach

If you follow U.S. 101 for 12 miles south from San Luis Obispo (turn off at San Luis Bay Dr. and follow it to Avila Beach Rd.), you'll hit **Avila Beach.** Just before you cross into town, look for the **Diablo Nuclear Power Plant** exhibit at the **PG&E Community Center** (6588 Ontario Rd., tel. 805/546–5280), which details the history of the power plant, located on the outskirts of town. Diablo is one of the country's most controversial nuclear plants, owing to safety questions raised by its location on top of a major fault line. Drop by and listen to what a siren will sound like in the event of a meltdown. A 3-hour tour of the plant takes you through a simulated control room and the power plant's marine biology lab. Tours are free, but you must call ahead to reserve a space.

Avila Beach has a wonderfully rickety wooden pier and harbor boardwalk. But if the public beach there is too crowded, head up Cave Landing Road (off Avila Beach Rd. on the way back to U.S. 101) to **Pirate's Cove** (officially known as Mallagh Landing), one of the few nude beaches in the area. Both the gay north and the straight southern areas boast warm waters with towering cliffs as backdrop. Nudists claim the cove is one of the most idyllic settings on the California coast, while locals often raise their eyebrows and tell you it's sketchy when asked for directions. Farther down Avila Beach Road, you'll pass **Avila Hot Springs** (250 Avila Beach Rd., tel. 805/595–2359), a developed resort that charges $9 an hour for the use of its hot mineral baths and $7.50 a day to use the regular and hot pools.

**Pismo Beach,** a few miles south of Avila off U.S. 101, is the ultimate "has-been" town. In the 1930s it was one of *the* beachside getaways for Hollywood's elite, including part-time residents Clark Gable and Spencer Tracy. Today, the stars and starlets are gone and the town's once-impressive clam population has been nearly obliterated by overfishing and pollution. But visitors can still enjoy the wide beaches and undulating sand dunes. In fact, Pismo has become one of the least visited and cheapest seaside towns in central California.

Pismo's north end, which lies between wide, sandy Pismo State Beach and an old wooden fishing pier near Price Street, serves as a downtown area. The southern end of town is dominated by the sand dunes, some of which have been designated a state vehicular recreation area, meaning you can drive a car or other motorized vehicle on the beach. If you've got a four-wheel drive, empty your truck, deflate your tires, and go nuts. If you don't have one and you're seriously addicted to adrenaline, you can rent an ATV (starting at $42 for 2 hrs) from **B.J.'s ATV Rentals** (197 Grand Ave., at Hwy. 1, tel. 805/481–5411). If tearing across the beach isn't your idea of fun, there are plenty of more benign ways to enjoy Pismo (*see* Outdoor Activities, *below*), not the least of which is simply lying on the usually uncrowded beaches and soaking up the world-renowned California sunshine.

**COMING AND GOING** On weekdays, **Central Coast Area Transit** (tel. 805/541–2228) runs buses from San Luis Obispo's City Hall to Pismo Beach; the trip takes 25 minutes and costs $1.25. Direct service to Avila Beach is available on Saturdays. Bikes are allowed on these buses.

**WHERE TO SLEEP** Avila Beach has a sole motel, located at the end of Front Street: **Surfside Motel** (256 Front St., tel. 805/595–2300), where a large but run-down double will cost you anywhere between $55–$85 depending on the season and the view. Unfortunately there are no public campgrounds, though **Avila Hot Springs** (*see above*) offers tent camping for $16.50 a night (campers also get a 40% discount on pool fees), but the sites are closer to the highway than to the beach. Campers would do better—though not by much—heading to Pismo Beach, which has three public campgrounds (*see below*).

**El Pismo Inn.** This turn-of-the-century hotel where Carole Lombard and Tyrone Power used to romp is stylishly cluttered with old furniture. Rooms range from $30 in the off-season to $58 in summer, making it one of the better deals on the coast. Try to get one of the rooms with large bay windows. *230 Pomeroy Ave., tel. 805/773–4529. 2 blocks east of pier. 30 rooms.*

➢ **CAMPING** • Pismo's campgrounds have great beach access, but they're the unfortunate targets of boisterous family reunions and ATV sand warriors. Open May through September, **North Beach State Campground** (off Hwy. 1) has 103 tightly packed tent sites in a grassy area near the beach. Try to get one near the sand dunes. **Oceano Campgrounds** (555 Pier Ave., off Hwy. 1), open year-round, offers access to a lagoon, but the 40 tent sites are too close to the 42 RV sites for true solitude. Both campgrounds have showers and charge $14 off-season and $16 in summer (RV sites are $20, $18 in the off-season). **Pismo Dunes** (on Pier Ave.) offers beach camping on soft sand in the same area where motor vehicles zoom around. Rangers claim no one's been run over yet. There are no sites here—simply drive or walk out onto the beach and pitch a tent for $6. To make reservations at any of these campsites, call MISTIX (tel. 800/444–PARK).

**FOOD** In Avila, your best bet is to head to the **Avila Grocery and Mercantile** (354 Front St., tel. 805/595–2098), where you'll find all the makings for a cheap picnic on the beach. In Pismo, **Chele's Food and Spirits** (198 Pomeroy Ave., 1 block east of pier, tel. 805/773–1020) serves up seafood as well as good breakfasts for a reasonable $4–$6. People come from miles around to devour the pricey seafood and steaks at **McLintock's** (750 Mattie Rd., 1½ mi north of Pismo, tel. 805/773–1892), a Western-style steak house with meals starting at $17.

**OUTDOOR ACTIVITIES** To go for a bike ride around town or along the boardwalk, come to **Pismo Bike Rental** (519 Cypress St., 3 blocks south of pier, tel. 805/773–0355), where beach cruisers rent for $15 per half day, $25 per full day; mountain bikes go for $21 per half day, $35 per full day (25% off during summer months). Most of Pismo's beaches are open to vehicular traffic, so don't be afraid to take your bike on the sand. On the right day, the surfing, body surfing, and body boarding next to the Pismo pier is excellent. One block east of the pier, **Pancho's** (181 Pomeroy Ave., tel. 805/773–7100) rents surfboards ($15 a day and up), body boards ($6), and wet suits ($6).

The **Pismo Dunes Preserve,** an area popular in the 1930s with proto–New Agers and the mystically inclined, was once thought to be the center of a powerful and benign energy. The last of the "dunites" disappeared in the early 1970s, but you can still experience the power of the dunes by taking a trek among its wildflowers and vegetation. No set trails exist, and hikers should be careful not to step on any plant life. Look for the preserve on Highway 1, just south of town at the end of Pier Avenue.

# Santa Barbara

**You cross an invisible line** as you enter Santa Barbara, and a small but noticeable change in attitude tells you this is no longer Northern California. Considered the northernmost coastal outpost of "SoCal" (Southern California), Santa Barbara is too wealthy and aloof to fit comfortably with the more genial towns of San Luis Obispo and Santa Cruz, yet it's too picturesque and relaxed to be seen as an extension of Los Angeles, only 92 miles south. While this may be an exceedingly wealthy and conservative community—Ronald Reagan has his ranch here, after all—the scenery is Riviera-esque in its beauty, and the locals all look as if they do nothing but sit on the beach and tan. There is a scruffier and less daunting contingent in town, too, ranging from mellow U.C. Santa Barbara students to the vagabond homeless, but the city works hard to retain its sanitized Mediterranean image. Everything here is designed around a Spanish-Moorish theme, with red-tile roofs, wrought-iron gates, and red adobe. Despite the fact that Santa Barbara takes itself much too seriously, it's still one of Southern California's most engaging coastal towns, buffered by golden beaches, a historic mission, a few museums, and tons of thriving outdoor cafés and restaurants. In the spring of 1995, the town was hit hard by floods and mud slides, resulting in $2 million worth of damages. All has since been repaired, and surfers, shoppers, and students alike seem to have only sunshine on their minds.

*The largest creature ever known to exist on the planet makes its home near Santa Barbara. The giant blue whales, at lengths of 100 feet and weights of 150 tons, are larger than any dinosaur ever discovered; their tongues alone weigh more than an elephant. About 3,000 of these fantastic creatures currently live in the waters off the coast of Santa Barbara.*

## BASICS

The **visitor center** stocks brochures, maps, and information on local accommodations. They also have guides to the "Red Tile" walking tour, which highlights Santa Barbara's architecture. *1 Santa Barbara St., at Cabrillo Blvd., tel. 805/965–3021. Open Mon.–Sat. 9–5, Sun. 10–5; July–Aug. until 6 PM and Dec.–Jan. until 4 PM.*

The **Gay and Lesbian Resource Center** has information on local gay and lesbian events, and they provide counseling for anyone who just wants to talk. *126 E. Haley St., Suite A-17, tel. 805/963–3636. Open weekdays 10–6 and by appointment.*

## COMING AND GOING

**BY CAR** **U.S. 101,** which connects Santa Barbara to Los Angeles (92 mi south) and San Luis Obispo (100 mi north), is the main highway through the city. Other arteries include **Highway 154** (San Marcos Pass Rd.), which leads north out of Santa Barbara to Lake Cachuma and Santa Ynez (*see* Cheap Thrills, *below*) and eventually rejoins U.S. 101 north of Buellton.

**BY BUS** **Green Tortoise** (tel. 800/867–8647) runs a bus from L.A. ($10) on Sunday nights that stops in Santa Barbara before heading on to San Luis Obispo ($15) and San Francisco ($30). In Santa Barbara, the bus stops in the parking lot behind Carrow's restaurant (210 W. Carrillo St., at De La Vina St., tel. 805/966–1227). **Greyhound** (34 Carrillo St., next to Transit Center, tel. 805/965–7551) has frequent service from Santa Barbara to San Francisco (7½ hrs, $34 one-way) and Los Angeles (2½–3 hrs, $11 one-way). The station is open weekdays 6 AM–8 PM, weekends until midnight; 24-hour lockers ($1) are available.

**BY TRAIN** **Amtrak** trains stop once daily at the Santa Barbara depot (209 State St., tel. 805/963–1040 or 800/USA-RAIL for reservations) on the way to San Francisco (9–10 hrs,

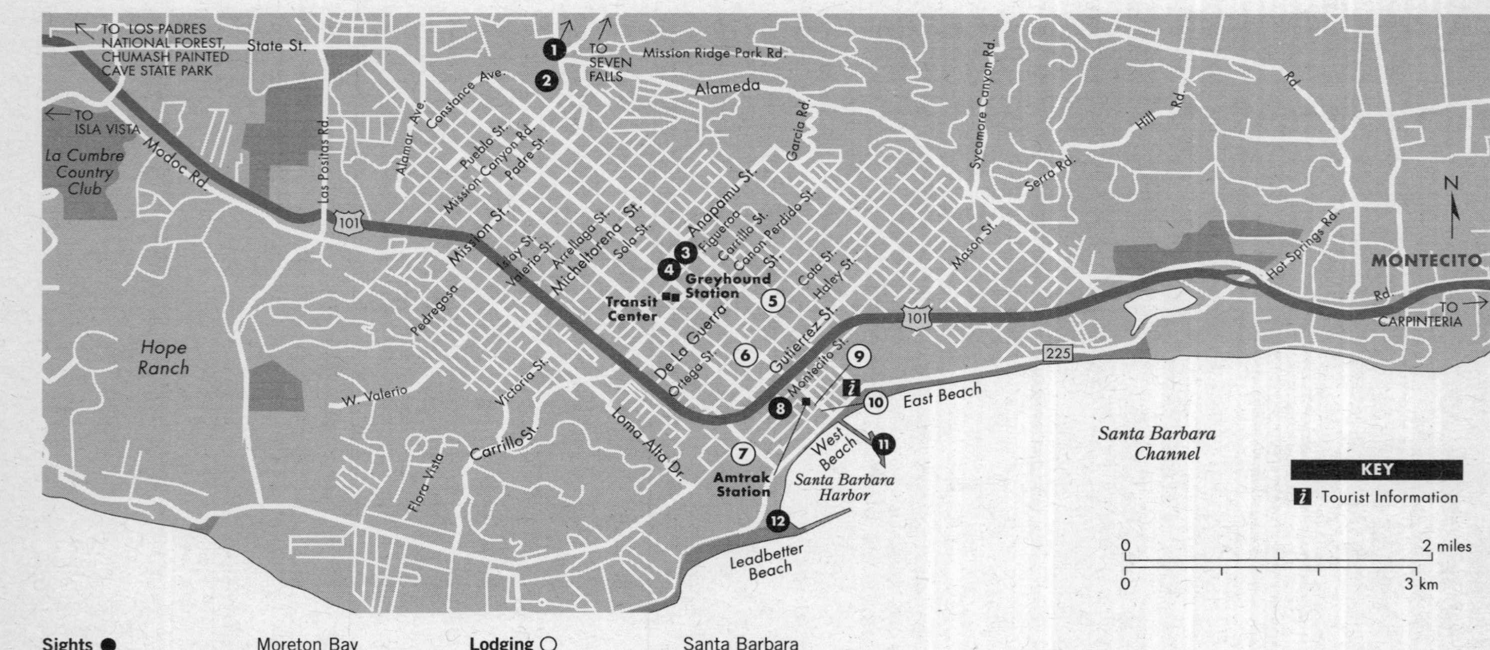


**Sights ●**
Botanical Gardens, **1**
County Courthouse, **3**
Mission Santa Barbara, **2**
Moreton Bay Fig Tree, **8**
Musuem of Art, **4**
Santa Barbara Yacht Harbor, **12**
Stearn's Wharf and Sea Center, **11**

**Lodging ○**
Californian Hotel, **10**
Hotel State Street, **9**
Inn at the Harbor, **7**
Santa Barbara International Hostel, **5**
Schooner Inn, **6**

# Santa Barbara

$67) or to L.A. (3 hrs, $20). The station is open daily 7 AM–11 PM, but the ticket window closes 2:15–2:45 PM, 6:30–7, and after 9. Luggage storage is available at $1.50 per bag for 24 hours.



## GETTING AROUND

The first thing to remember is that the Pacific Ocean is south, not west, and the mountains surrounding Santa Barbara run east–west, not north–south. Most restaurants, shops, and nightspots are densely concentrated on **State Street,** so the easiest way to orient yourself downtown is by this street, which starts at Stearn's Wharf and runs north toward the town of Goleta, where it becomes Hollister Avenue. The beach and Stearn's Wharf are less than a mile from downtown; walking is the best and easiest way to get around.

**BY BUS** All local bus routes pass through the **Transit Center** (1020 Chapala St., tel. 805/683–3702), which has info on routes and is open weekdays 6 AM–7 PM, Saturday 8–6, and Sunday 9–6. Buses run 6 AM–11:15 PM and cost 75¢; Bus 21 travels to the Amtrak depot, while Buses 6 and 11 take you from the Amtrak depot to upper State Street's budget hotels. Even more useful, a 25¢ shuttle travels daily along State Street between Stearn's Wharf and Sola Street downtown. Shuttles run daily 10–6 and until 8 PM on summer weekends; stops are marked SANTA BARBARA SHUTTLE. All buses are wheelchair accessible.

## WHERE TO SLEEP

Santa Barbara's Mediterranean climate draws a beach crowd year-round, and the city's hotels and motels are way overpriced, especially during summer, when prices jump by $3–$30 (ouch!). If all the cheap lodgings are booked, as they often are on summer weekends, you can usually find something affordable in **Carpinteria,** about 12 miles east. It's less flashy and more family-oriented, and motel prices are generally a bit lower. In Carpinteria, try **Casa Del Sol Motel** (5585 Carpinteria Ave., tel. 805/684–4307), which charges about $40 for a single or double with one bed; or the **Reef Motel** (4160 Via Real, tel. 805/684–4176), which has singles for $38 and doubles for $40 ($46 for four people). To get to Carpinteria, take Santa Claus Lane exit from U.S. 101 or Bus 20 from Transit Center.

In Santa Barbara, upper State Street is where you'll find the cheap—and truly indistinguishable—motels. Prices fluctuate madly depending on the season, but you can almost always find doubles in the $30–$40 range. If you want to be closer to the action downtown and on the beach, try to find something reasonable on lower State Street. If you're traveling in a pack of four, try the **Inn at the Harbor** (433 W. Montecito St., btw U.S. 101 and Cabrillo Blvd., tel. 805/963–7851 or 800/626–1986), which has large, elegant, nonsmoking rooms just 2 blocks from the beach, with kitchens, beautiful furniture, and plenty of floor space. A couple pays $89 for a room with two queen beds (add $10 on weekends), but extra guests pay only $5, and everyone gets to frolic in the pool and spa.

➢ **UNDER $60** • **Schooner Inn.** The pink and blue decor might make you go "hmm," but the central location and clean, comfortable rooms will make you go "mmm." Singles and doubles start at $50. *533 State St., at Cota St., tel. 805/965–4572. From Transit Center walk east to State St. Laundry. No reservations. Wheelchair access.*

➢ **UNDER $70** • **Californian Hotel.** This tall, ancient hotel is 1 block from the beach and half a block from the train tracks. When Amtrak thunders through at 2 AM you may go deaf, but the convenient locale makes up for the noise and the musty smell. Singles start at $50, doubles at $60 (add $10 in summer). *35 State St., at Mason St., tel. 805/966–7153.*

**Hotel State Street.** One block away from the Californian Hotel, this place is cursed with the same noise from the train tracks, but the rooms are spotless and close to the beach. The friendly management charges only $35 for a single and $55 for double rooms with shared bath. Continental breakfast is included. *121 State St., tel. 805/966–6586.*

**HOSTELS** **Santa Barbara International Hostel.** This former homeless shelter is now the town's new hostel, though it manages to retain that cramped and chaotic shelter feeling. A fun management and the fact that these are the cheapest beds ($15) in town—though maybe also the least comfortable—make it a good deal. They also have a host of cheap rental items ($4–$7 per day), including in-line skates, bikes, and surfboards. *210 E. Ortega St., at Santa Barbara St., tel. 805/963–0154. 40 beds. Curfew 2:15 AM, no lockout. Reception open 8 AM–2:15 AM. Laundry, security deposit ($5).*

**CAMPING** **Carpinteria State Beach.** Twelve miles east of Santa Barbara, Carpinteria offers 262 tent and RV spaces on a dirt-and-grass area beside the beach. Sites ($14–$16) are close together so privacy is a serious problem, as is the noise from both the highway and train tracks during the night. At least the beach is only a Frisbee throw away. Showers are available and a grocery store/restaurant is nearby. Crowds are a hassle during summer, so reservations through MISTIX (tel. 800/444–PARK) are advised. *U.S. 101, Carpinteria, tel. 805/684–2811. Bus 20 from Transit Center.*

**El Capitan State Beach.** Despite the shady palm trees and the pleasant beach nearby, the sardine-like conditions and 140 scraggly grass sites ($14–$16) are nearly enough to ruin El Capitan's appeal. Nonetheless, its location about 15 minutes north of Santa Barbara makes it more convenient than the campgrounds in the hills (*see below*). Showers and a grocery store (open summer only) are on the premises. It's crowded most of the year and reservations are highly recommended; call MISTIX (tel. 800/444–PARK). Two and a half miles north, **Refugio State Beach** has 82 sites indistinguishable from El Capitan. *El Capitan: U.S. 101, btw Gaviota and Santa Barbara. Tel. for both: 805/968–3294.*

*If you want to sack out in your car, park it in Isla Vista, where most UCSB students live. If you play your cards right, you can probably score a place on some newly made friend's couch.*

**Los Padres National Forest.** There are five developed campgrounds on Paradise Road in the forest outside of Santa Barbara, as well as unlimited acres of free camping, a perk available at all national forests. If you're looking for privacy and don't need bathrooms, a fire pit, or a picnic table, take U.S. 101 north to Highway 154 (San Marcos Pass Rd.), turn right on East Camino Cielo, and pick a spot—it's bare as a bone, but free. If you're not comfortable doing your thing in a bush, continue on Highway 154 to Paradise Road, hang a right, and follow the signs to the developed campgrounds ($8). The 15 sites at **Paradise** are ugly and crammed too close for comfort, but they're the most popular. Go figure. Most secluded are the 25 spacious sites at **Upper Oso.** Whatever your pleasure, you'll be surrounded by the Santa Ynez Mountains and more scrub brush than you ever imagined. *Tel. 800/280–CAMP for reservations.*

## FOOD

The Mexican food stands on **Milpas Street** are popular with UCSB students and others hard up for cash; authentic tacos and burritos go for less than $5. **El Escondido** (316 N. Milpas St., tel. 805/965–2690) is perhaps the best of the lot. Two weekly **farmers' markets** are good for stocking up on locally grown produce, flowers, and fish. The first is held on the 500 block of State Street Tuesdays 3–7, the second at Cota and Santa Barbara streets Saturdays 8:30–noon. For cheap eats, also try Isla Vista (*see* Near Santa Barbara, *below*).

➢ **UNDER $5** • **Natural Café.** On sunny afternoons (i.e., almost every day), Santa Barbara's granola contingent overflows onto the street in front of yet another healthy place to grab a bite. Try a big, fresh salad ($4.50–$5.25) or a tofu hot dog ($4.50) with a shot of wheatgrass juice ($1). *508 State St., at Haley St., tel. 805/962–9494. Open daily 11–11.*

➢ **UNDER $10** • **Esau's Coffee Shop.** The food is standard, but if you're hungry, Esau's serves up huge orders of eggs, hash browns, and pancakes to a mixed crowd of surfers and old-timers for $4–$6. *403 State St., tel. 805/965–4416. Open weekdays 6 AM–1 PM, weekends 7 AM–1 PM.*

**Sojourner Coffee House.** Healthy highlights here include homemade soups ($2.50) and tofu and brown-rice plates ($6). The Sojourner doubles as a coffeehouse popular with UCSB students—a place to play cards or chess, or read a good book. *134 E. Canon Perdido St., tel. 805/965–7922. 1½ blocks east of State St. Open daily 11–11. Wheelchair access.*

**New Yen Ching.** The best deal at this small Chinese restaurant is the daily all-you-can-eat buffet, $7 for lunch (11:30–2:30) or $7.95 for dinner (5:30–8). Otherwise, try the shark's fin soup with crab meat ($18). *613–615 State St., at Cota St., tel. 805/962–1796. Open daily 11:30–9:30 (Fri. until 10).*

➢ **UNDER $20** • **Palace Café.** Businesspeople in suits and students in Birkenstocks coexist here peacefully, drawn by the best Cajun and Creole cuisine in Santa Barbara—perhaps in all of California. Try the Cajun popcorn shrimp ($9) or any of the fish dishes ($13–$18). If you're daring, the Cajun martini is sure to sizzle your sinuses and put a spark in your step. For more moderate prices, look for the café's new spin-off, **Palace Express,** in the food court of the Paseo Nuevo Mall (State St., at Chapala St., tel. 805/899–9111). *8 E. Cota St., off State St., tel. 805/966–3133. Open daily 5:30 PM–10 PM (Fri.–Sat. until 11).*

**CAFES** If you're tired of staring at tanned bodies and neon clothing all day, you'll find the black-leather crowd well represented in Santa Barbara's cafés, most of which are concentrated downtown. Local artists use the **Green Dragon Espresso Bar and Art Studio** (22 W. Mission St., off State St., tel. 805/687–1902) as an informal exhibition space; there's live music Friday and Saturday nights, open mike poetry Sundays, and organic and decaf espresso drinks every day. The 24-hour **Hot Spots** (36 State St., ½ block from Stearn's Wharf, tel. 805/564–1637) plays host to students during the day, black-clothed teens in the early evening, and boisterous travelers late at night—all sipping $1.90 cappuccinos. The café doubles as a mini–visitor information center 9–9.

## WORTH SEEING

Any tour of Santa Barbara should begin with a stroll down palm-lined **State Street,** packed to the hilt with boutiques, import shops, bookstores, restaurants, and cafés. Even if you have no intention of buying, State Street provides great opportunities for people-watching and absorbing the local culture. The visitor center (*see* Basics, *above*) has a self-guided tour map covering historical sites downtown.

*Tune in to FM 104.7 (Q105) for rap, hiphop, and other dance grooves, or 92.9 (KJEE) for way-alternative rock. KTYD 99.9, the town's most popular radio station, mixes classic and modern rock.*

Santa Barbara's **Botanical Gardens** (1212 Mission Canyon Rd., tel. 805/682–4726) offer hundreds of trails and floral specimens for horticultural buffs willing to pay the $3 admission fee. Besides admiring the Joshua trees and redwoods, you can visit Mission Dam, constructed by the Chumash Indians in 1806. The mammoth **Moreton Bay Fig Tree** (Montecito and Chapala Sts.), transplanted from Australia in the late 1800s, is one of Santa Barbara's most striking sights. Check it out during the day, as its largely exposed root system makes it a popular homeless hangout at night.

**Stearn's Wharf** (Cabrillo and State Sts.), the oldest operating wharf on the West Coast, has one of the least touristed piers in California. Next to it are the aquariums and petting pools of the **Sea Center** (211 Stearn's Wharf, tel. 805/962–0885), a small hands-on museum that charges only $2 and is open daily 10–5. To the west of Stearn's Wharf lies the **Santa Barbara Yacht Harbor.** Walk to the end of its artificial breakwater for an outstanding view of the coast and shoreline. When you've had enough of the sights, head to **East Beach,** a wide, sweeping beach that rarely gets overcrowded—you can't miss it if you're at Stearn's Wharf.

**MISSION SANTA BARBARA** One of the city's best attractions, Mission Santa Barbara is considered the crown jewel of California's missions. Built in 1786 with the "help" of the local Chumash people, this Spanish Renaissance structure has come to define the Santa Barbara architectural style with its red tile roof, orange adobe facade, and wrought-iron gates and fixtures. If you visit during Memorial Day weekend you can catch the *I Madonnari,* a 3-day festival where internationally famous street artists, local artists, and children create elaborate chalk drawings in front of the mission. *Laguna St., at Los Olivos St., tel. 805/682–4149. Admission: $3. Open daily 9–5.*

**CHUMASH PAINTED CAVE STATE PARK** In the Los Padres National Forest 12 miles northwest of Santa Barbara, this state park houses the faded remains of centuries-old Chumash cave paintings. A locked metal screen keeps you from actually entering the cave, and the lack of light makes viewing the paintings a bit difficult, but you can still make out the colorful animal figures and decorative designs from outside. *Take U.S. 101 north to Hwy. 154 (San Marcos Pass Rd.), turn right on Painted Cave Rd. Admission free.*

**COUNTY COURTHOUSE** The 114-foot tower provides a 360°-view of the city, and the courthouse itself is full of ornate murals and elaborate Spanish tile work. You can wander around by yourself or take a free guided tour (call ahead for schedule). *Anapamu and Anacapa Sts., tel. 805/962–6464. Open weekdays 8–5, weekends 9–5.*

**MUSEUM OF ART** A modest collection of French impressionists and German expressionists—Monet to Kandinsky—are on display here, as well as classical Greek and Roman sculptures. *1130 State St., tel. 805/963–4364. Admission: $4, students $1.50; free Thurs. and first Sun. of month. Open Tues.–Sat. 11–5 (Thurs. until 9), Sun. noon–5.*

## CHEAP THRILLS

On Sundays between 10 AM and 4 PM, dozens of artisans display their wares on the boardwalk running along **East Beach.** Then at sunset on Sundays, a mellow drumming circle comes together at **Palm Park** (east of Stearn's Wharf, near Red Lion's Resort). If you're not feeling participatory, you can catch a free concert at **De la Guerra Plaza** between State and Anacapa streets at noon on Fridays. Cozy up to a tree and take a nap to the strains of big band music. Also, on summer Sundays at 3 PM, free concerts take place at **Alameda Park** (cnr Anacapa and Micheltorena Sts.).

To drink yourself silly for free, head 50 miles northwest of town on Highway 154 to the old pioneer towns of Santa Ynez and Los Olivos. Any local gas station or market can provide you with a free map of the region's eight wineries, which are best known for their chardonnays. North of Los Olivos off U.S. 101, **Firestone Vineyard** (5017 Zaca Rd., tel. 805/688–3940), one of California's largest, offers free tours, wine tasting, and a grassy picnic area. It's open daily 10–4.

If you'd rather watch rich folks having a good ol' time, make an appearance at the **Santa Barbara Polo and Racquet Club** (337 Foothill Rd., tel. 805/684–8667), east of the city off U.S. 101. In summer, you can catch the Pacific Coast Open polo tournament—the top polo event in the United States. Games are played on Sundays from April to October and cost $5 to watch. Finally, if you're feeling a bit wacky, hop in your car and make a beeline for **Santa Claus Lane** (U.S. 101, ½ mi west of Carpinteria), one of the strangest "theme malls" in the country. Santa Claus Lane is a symbol of California's determination to have it all—sun, surf, sand, and Christmas year-round.

## FESTIVALS

On the Saturday closest to June 21, the **Summer Solstice Celebration** (tel. 805/965–3396) offers Santa Barbara's fringe element a chance to let loose. No cars or promotional posters are permitted—just processions of people dressed in bizarre costumes, some dancing or performing short plays. At the end of the parade there's food and live music in one of the local parks.

Every summer, usually in July, thousands of people head to the beach to watch the **Sandcastle and Sculpting Contest** (tel. 805/965–0509), where artists from around the world make the most outlandish sand creations they can dream up. Dates change each summer, so call for details. The **Old Spanish Days Fiesta** (tel. 805/962–8101) is a big event in early August—five days of hardcore, citywide partying in celebration of Santa Barbara's Spanish and Mexican heritage. Highlights include a carnival, free music, parades, vociferous street vendors, and lots of beer drinking. In unofficial honor of the god of guacamole, the **California Avocado Festival** (tel. 805/684–0038) is held every October in Carpinteria. For two fun-filled days, exotic avocado concoctions are featured along with art exhibits and entertainment. Call ahead for the precise dates.



## AFTER DARK

Thanks to the 20,000 students at UCSB, the continuous influx of tourists, and an influential contingent of under-30 locals, Santa Barbara has a lively nightlife, especially if you like to drink. The action centers around lower State Street, where most bars feature live music—rock, reggae, folk, or funk—every weekend, and often on weekdays as well. For an events calendar, pick up a copy of *The Independent,* the county's free weekly, at any café or bookstore. Remember that live music usually means a $2–$5 cover charge.

A historic landmark, **Joe's Café** (536 State St., tel. 805/966–4638) is revered for its deadly stiff drinks and downhome charm. Joe's attracts all sorts, from locals to tourists to UCSB students. **Mel's** (6 W. De la Guerra St., in the Paseo Nuevo Mall, tel. 805/963–2211) is filled with some of Santa Barbara's grittiest barflies. Wild man Hunter S. Thompson used to hang out in Mel's back booth.

Part dance club and part bar, **Zelo** (630 State St., tel. 805/966–5792) is a favorite with hip, black-garbed clubbers drawn by the art-deco interior. Zelo's has a full bar with DJs every night. Come early: The cover charge slides from $1 to $5 as the evening progresses. Also call ahead, since some nights are 21-and-older only. Tiny, no-smoking **Joseppi's** (434 State St., tel. 805/962–5516) is the place to go for nightly jazz. The cover charge varies from $1 to $5, but mostly hovers around $2.

Gays and lesbians party free of charge on the small, friendly dance floor of **Gold Coast** (30 W. Cota St., tel. 805/965–6701), where the laid-back management plays whatever music the crowd clamors for. Hip straights and gays also flock to **Backstage** (18 E. Ortega St., tel. 805/730–7383), where the new management is dedicated to turning this old warehouse into *the* live dance venue in town. Each night has a different theme, and covers range from free to $5.

## OUTDOOR ACTIVITIES

**HIKING** There are literally hundreds of great walks in and around Santa Barbara. Close to downtown, one of the best trails takes you up a creek bed to a series of swimming holes and a seven-tiered waterfall known as **Seven Falls.** Although the falls dry up after low-rain winters, the pools remain year-round. To reach this choice spot, drive east on Mission Street, turn right on Foothill Road, veer left onto Mission Canyon Road and left at the next fork onto Tunnel Road; from the end of the road, follow the paved path to the bridge and either climb up the rocks for about 20 minutes or keep going on the path to the end. The walk takes 45 minutes to an hour.

For more serious hikes, head up to Los Padres National Forest in the sagebrush- and oak-covered hills behind Santa Barbara. There you'll find the **Santa Ynez Recreation Area,** rife with excellent trails. At the end of Paradise Road, the **Red Rock Trail** winds along and across the Santa Ynez River for 3½ miles—past rocky enclaves and some exceptional swimming holes—to the Gibraltar Dam. For a steeper climb, follow the **Santa Cruz Trail** for 6½ miles through oak and pine trees to the Happy Hollow campground on Little Pine Mountain, a beautiful spot to spend the night (pack your own water). To reach Los Padres, take U.S. 101 north to Highway 154 (San Marcos Pass Rd.) and turn right on Paradise Road. For more trail recommendations, call the Forest Service headquarters (tel. 805/683–6711).

**BIKING/IN-LINE SKATING** Whether you like to pedal along the coast or in the hills, you're in for a treat in Santa Barbara. Aside from the boardwalk and the two hiking trails listed above, which are both open to bikers, there's the short (about 2½ mi) bluffside dirt trail in Isla Vista (*see* Near Santa Barbara, *below*) and all sorts of fire roads off Highway 154 (San Marcos Pass Rd.). **Beach Rentals** (22 State St., tel. 805/966–6733) is the best place to rent cruisers ($5 an hour, $24 a day) or mountain bikes ($7 an hour, $26 a day). They also rent in-line skates by the day ($20). Bladers take off along the boardwalk and also skate from the end of Modoc Road in Goleta along the path to UCSB.

**SURFING** If the waves are breaking just the way you like 'em, rent boards from the hostel ($7 a day; *see* Where to Sleep, *above*) or from **Sundance Ocean Sports** (2026 Cliff Dr., tel. 805/966–2474) for $15 a day; the latter also has wet suits ($10 a day) for the thin-blooded. The most popular break near Santa Barbara—if not on the whole Central Coast—is Rincon, 3 miles south of Carpinteria on Highway 1.

# Near Santa Barbara

## ISLA VISTA

Built in the 1950s on the site of a military complex used in World War II, the University of California at Santa Barbara (UCSB) is perched on a bluff overlooking the Pacific Ocean 12 miles west of downtown Santa Barbara and dominates the town of Isla Vista. It's one of the country's few institutions of higher learning with its own surfing beach, known as Campus Point. The campus sits right on the ocean, and its enticing lawns, lagoon, and sandstone buildings are pleasant, if not exactly inspiring.

*To get an idea of how difficult it is to actually study at U.C. Santa Barbara, check out the main library—it's got ocean views and a third-floor sun deck, equipped with lounge chairs.*

Much more interesting than the UCSB campus is the town of Isla Vista (known to locals as I.V.), packed to the gills with thousands of raucous students hell-bent on exploring the boundaries of unmitigated hedonism. In the center of town, **Anisq'oyo Park** is the site of often excellent free concerts on spring and fall weekends, and a good place for a picnic otherwise. I.V. has a reputation for being a mindless party town that caters to the worst sort of postadolescent behavior. If you're in town on a weekend night during the school year, check out the mayhem centered around **Del Playa Street.** At all hours, thousands of bleary-eyed students stumble up and down the street, from one kegger to the

### *Seven Great Surfing Breaks in Central California*

***Although surfing is usually associated with the warm waters and sunny summers of Southern California, the Central Coast also has its fair share of killer breaks—the only difference being that the chilly waters require a wet suit (preferably a thick one) year-round. From north to south, here are the best spots to throw on a suit, jump on your board, and tear it up.***

***(1) Steamer's Lane: A Santa Cruz legend, some say the best break in California. (2) Morro Rock: In Morro Bay, just north of San Luis Obispo. (3) Pismo Beach: North of the pier in an age-old surf town south of San Luis Obispo. (4) Jalama Beach: A legendary break west of Solvang, off U.S. 101 between San Luis Obispo and Santa Barbara. (5) Refugio State Beach: A local favorite about 30 miles northwest of Santa Barbara. (6) Rincon: Off U.S. 101 between Santa Barbara and Ventura, it vies with Steamer's Lane as the Central Coast's most popular spot. (7) Ventura Pier: A popular day trip for L.A. surfers, in the gray area between Central and Southern California.***

next. Be forewarned that the scene mellows out considerably in summer, when the chilly fog chases most students out of town. The biggest event of the year at UCSB, even bigger than graduation, is the unofficial **Halloween** party in I.V. Costumed collegiates guzzle beer all night to live bands, while city officials futilely try to crush the party.

To reach UCSB from Santa Barbara, take U.S. 101 north to Los Carneros Road, head south (toward the ocean) 1 mile, then turn left on El Colegio Road and right on Embarcadero del Mar, a U-shaped street that serves as I.V.'s main drag. Otherwise, take Bus 11 from the Transit Center in Santa Barbara.

**FOOD** I.V. has some great places to eat cheaply. You can stuff yourself silly at **Freebird's** (879 Embarcadero del Norte, tel. 805/968–0123), where fat breakfast burritos with beans, potatoes, salsa, and eggs go for 95¢–$1.50. For lunch or dinner try the famous monster chicken burrito ($4.50), or—if you have two or three people—the super monster ($6.50). Also popular are the sandwiches ($3.50–$4.50) at **Sam's to Go** (6560 Pardall Rd., tel. 805/685–8895) and the pizza at **Woodstock's** (928 Embarcadero del Norte, tel. 805/968–6969). The I.V. crowd takes its java on the sun-drenched patio of **Espresso Roma** (6521 Pardall St., tel. 805/968–5101).

**AFTER DARK** In I.V. after nightfall? Do as the locals do: head into Santa Barbara or hang out around campus or at one of the restaurants until you get invited to a party. If you're looking for a game of pool or hard liquor, head over to **I.V. Beer Co.** (935 Embarcadero del Norte, tel. 805/961–4488), open until 1 AM. If it's Tuesday, make a beeline for the $1 drinks at **Safari** (643 State St., tel. 805/564–4862), where the cheap booze and deafening dance music draw dancing-on-the-bar UCSB students by the hundreds.

## OJAI

Hidden away in a shallow, oak-lined valley about 40 miles southeast of Santa Barbara, Ojai (pronounced "Oh, hi!") is a quintessentially Californian community: hot, scenic, laid back, and populated by an eclectic mix of beautiful people. Here, affluent made-it-in-L.A.-and-moved-to-the-country types drive $60,000 Range Rovers from their ranch-style homes to the town's posh mineral baths, while New Agers ramble around town in road-worn VW Beetles on their way to the **Krotona Institute** (off Hwy. 33, south end of town, tel. 805/646–2653)—the largest theophilosophical library on the West Coast—or the **Krishnamurti Library** (1130 McAndrew Rd., tel. 805/646–4948), part of a complex dedicated to the teachings of the eponymous Indian spiritual leader.

Even those who have trouble finding their third eye will enjoy **Bart's Books** (302 W. Marlija St., tel. 805/646–3755), a sprawling outdoor book stand filled with thousands of used paperbacks. You can soak up some culture at the studios of local artists willing to expose their work to the uninitiated public; check the listings of open studios at the **Ojai Visitor Center** (338 E. Ojai Ave., tel. 805/646–8126). If you find your stomach growling after dizzying discussions of chiaroscuro or color harmonies, head to the **Ojai Café Emporium** (108 S. Montgomery St., tel. 805/646–2723), which serves vegetable lasagna ($6) on a large outdoor patio. One of the best things about Ojai is the drive into town. From U.S. 101 south of Santa Barbara, follow Highway 150 for 20 miles past vast orchards, wooded hills, wide valleys, and Lake Casitas; then turn north on Highway 33 (Maricopa Hwy.) and go 2 miles.

## VENTURA AND THE CHANNEL ISLANDS

Halfway between Santa Barbara and Los Angeles is the unassuming town of **Ventura,** a beachside community being slowly engulfed by tract homes and mini-malls. At least Main Street and the historic downtown area—with a mission, museums, and endless thrift shops—retain some charm. For maps and information, stop by the **visitors' bureau** (89C S. California St., tel. 805/648–2075 or 800/333–2989). The **San Buenaventura Mission** (enter through gift shop at 225 Main St., tel. 805/643–4318) and tiny adjacent **museum** ($1) are located near the most interesting sight downtown, the **Albinger Archaeological Museum** (113 E. Main St., tel. 805/648–5823), open Wednesday–Sunday 10–4 (winters until 2). The museum features artifacts from over 200 years of the area's history. Ventura's raison d'être, though, is its endless miles of wide sand beaches; at the end of California Street you'll find **Main Beach,** complete with a pier, surfers, and sun worshipers. For food and drink, **Shield's Brewing Co.** (24 E. Santa Clara St., at Ventura Ave., tel. 805/643–1807) has tasty microbrews ($2.75), as well as burgers and veggie food in the $5–$11 range.

*The Albinger Archaeological Museum was a muffler shop until Chumash arrowheads were discovered in the backyard.*

If you're aching to explore the **Channel Islands,** one of California's least accessible—and most pristine—wildlife preserves, **Island Packers** (1867 Spinnaker Dr., tel. 805/642–1393) runs excursions from the Ventura harbor. Day trips start at $34, while overnight trips for those who want to camp on the islands start at $48. The island chain is situated where the warm waters of the tropics meet the cold waters of the Arctic, creating an exceptional breeding ground for endless types of plants and animals. Visitors who make their way out here will find 25 types of sharks, 27 species of whales and porpoises, five kinds of sea lions and seals, and one of the largest populations of brown pelicans in the world. The Channel Islands also contain ruins of Paleolithic villages, considered by some to be the oldest such settlements in North America. Primitive (no potable water) camping is allowed—and free—on any of the five islands except Santa Cruz, but you need a permit from park headquarters. For maps and information contact the visitor center at **Channel Islands National Park Headquarters** (1901 Spinnaker Dr., Ventura Harbor, tel. 805/658–5730), open daily 8–5:30 from Memorial Day to Labor Day and daily 8:30–4:30 off-season.

# U.S. 101

**If you choose to make your trip from San** Francisco to Los Angeles on U.S. 101, you'll find yourself in a long agricultural valley flanked on either side by rolling hills, some of which you drive through on the southernmost portion of the journey. Along the way you'll pass a series of small towns and minor attractions, none—save Pinnacles National Monument—true destinations in themselves, but some worthy of a quick stop.

*If you're driving U.S. 101, watch your speed, especially near King City, infamous for the incredible rate at which its police issue speeding tickets.*

All of the small towns along the way have heaps of cheap motels; get off at any highway exit marked LODGING and you should find a decent double for less than $35. One of the best overnight stops is San Luis Obispo (*see* The Central Coast Drive, *above*), about halfway into the drive. There are also a few places to camp, most in the vicinity of Pinnacles National Monument. Bring picnic supplies: Along the road you'll see some fast-food chains, but little else in the way of nourishment.

If you pass by at the right time of year, you can gorge yourself at one of the region's agricultural festivals. Best known is the **Garlic Festival** (tel. 408/842–1625), held each July in Gilroy, 35 miles south of San Jose and 27 miles north of Salinas. One of the largest food-based events in the country, the festival draws garlic lovers from all over California. Taste the garlic-based foods and drinks (including free garlic ice cream) or try bathing with garlic soaps and shampoos. Greenfield, a tiny hick town between Salinas and Soledad, hosts a **Broccoli Festival** (tel. 408/674–5410) each Labor Day. To the south, Templeton (between Paso Robles and Atascadero) is the site of a small **Apple Festival** (tel. 805/238–5634) every October. Finally—and perhaps best of all—the **Strawberry Festival** (tel. 805/489–1488) is held on Memorial Day weekend in Arroyo Grande, a small farming town between San Luis Obispo and Santa Maria.

**COMING AND GOING** As usual, the easiest way to make the 7- to 8-hour trip between San Francisco and L.A. on U.S. 101 is by car; if you don't have one, consider renting (*see* Coming and Going, in Chapters 1, 2, or 9). If you're hitchhiking, rides can be difficult to get; but once you find one, chances are it'll be going most if not all the way to either big city. **Greyhound** runs daily buses from San Francisco to Salinas (2½–4 hrs, $20 one-way) and to Paso Robles (5 hrs, $33 one-way). From Los Angeles the trip to Salinas takes about 6 hours ($38 one-way), 6 to 8 hours to Paso Robles ($34 one-way).

# Salinas

Driving U.S. 101 south from San Francisco or San Jose, the first major town you hit is Salinas, famed for its bountiful fields of lettuce and cabbage. However, what really put Salinas on the map was not its greenery but the success of native son John Steinbeck, the Pulitzer Prize–winning author of *Grapes of Wrath* and countless other novels and short stories, many of which use central California as a backdrop. The three small Steinbeck sights in town are all moderately interesting. The **Steinbeck Room** (350 Lincoln Ave., tel. 408/758–7311)—part of a public library—contains photos, an original manuscript, and some of the author's personal items. The **Steinbeck House** (132 Central Ave., tel. 408/424–2735), where the man himself was born, has been turned into a restaurant, open Tuesday–Saturday, that serves lunch (at 11:45 and 1:15) for $7.50, dessert for $3; the price also includes a tour. Call to make sure they're not hosting a group on the day you want to come. True fans should also check out the **Steinbeck Foundation** (371 Main St., tel. 408/753–6411), where several displays map out his life and work. The foundation also puts on a **Steinbeck Festival** the first weekend of August, popular among California's literati; the $5 registration gets you into as many lectures and movies about Steinbeck as you can stomach.

If you're hungry, experience the culinary expertise of the local Mexican American community at **Rosita's Armory Café** (231 Salinas St., tel. 408/424–7039), where $5–$7 will buy you a tasty plate of rice, beans, salad, and an entrée. To sample some of the famed local produce, head to a roadside stand on the outskirts of town along Highway 146 (a few can also be found along U.S. 101); not only are prices lower, but the stuff's grown 50 yards from the stand—deliciously fresh.

# Pinnacles National Monument

Pinnacles National Monument is a trippy-looking rocky outpost in the middle of the San Joaquin Valley, full of wickedly jagged spires (some over 600 feet high). Treacherous foot trails and dark caves wind through the remnants of an ancient volcano. Although most trails are not long (1–5 mi), they are steep and exposed—not pleasant in the hot summer sun. If you do visit in summer, be sure to hike only in the early morning or late afternoon. But the best time to come to Pinnacles is definitely in spring, when the weather is moderate and the valley surrounding the monument blooms with colorful wildflowers.

You can't drive from the west side of Pinnacles to the east—only hiking trails connect the two entrances. There is a **visitor center** (tel. 408/389–4485) on the east side and a helpful **ranger station** (tel. 408/389–4526) on the west, and both sides have campgrounds (*see below*). Those in the know claim that the west side has better hiking through the lava formations, while the east side is the place for cave exploration. The 5-mile **High Peaks Loop,** which takes you through the remnants of an extinct volcano to the Pinnacles formations, can be accessed from the east on **Condor Gulch Trail** and from the west on **Juniper Canyon Trail.** The round-trip takes 3 to 4 hours. Both trailheads are near the parking lots. Rock climbing is also popular, but only properly equipped and experienced climbers should attempt the **Balconies,** a massive shelf perched 200 feet off the valley floor. The west and east entrances to Pinnacles are both accessed from U.S. 101, via Soledad and King City, respectively (follow signs).

**WHERE TO SLEEP** Two campgrounds serve Pinnacles, a private one at the east entrance and a public one just inside the west entrance on Highway 146. Sites at both places are first-come, first-served, but the privately run campground to the east has more sites, more facilities, and—most importantly—more shade. The public one, **Pinnacles National Monument Chaparral Campground** (tel. 408/389–4526), offers 18 desolate sites in scrub brush, with about enough tree cover for a field mouse. There are no showers; but at $10 per site, at least it's cheap. This place is closed on weekends from Presidents' Day to Memorial Day, when the campsites are reserved for use as picnic areas.

Despite the corporate-sounding name—**Pinnacles Campground, Inc.** (408/389–4462)—shady trees, a small creek, a pool, and showers make this the better choice for campers. The

120 sites go for $6 per person, with a $24-per-site maximum. A small market on the premises is good for stocking up on bare necessities. Off Highway 146, drive 5 minutes from east entrance.

# Paso Robles

Midway between L.A. and San Francisco, an hour north of San Luis Obispo, Paso Robles is one of California's fastest-growing winery towns, with over 20 wineries in a 2-mile radius. One of the oldest and most attractive is **York Mountain** (off Hwy. 46, 7 mi west of U.S. 101, tel. 805/238–3925), with a dark, misty cellar and a wonderfully atmospheric tasting room. Tours and tastings are free. The region is predominantly known for its red wines, especially zinfandel. If you're just looking to get smashed, take Highway 46 east—in under 7 miles you'll come across five wineries, all with complimentary tasting.

Between November and March, bald and gold eagles come to **Lake San Antonio,** west of U.S. 101 between King City and Paso Robles, to escape the winters of northern California. You can picnic on the shore (day-use fee $6) and watch the rare creatures wing their way into the great unknown, or take a boat tour with the county parks department (tel. 805/472–2311 for info and reservations) for close-up views of the massive birds. Overdeveloped, and wheelchair-accessible, camping is available on the south shore of the lake ($15); drinking water and showers are available. To reach the lake from the north, take the Jolon exit (north of King City) west for 40 miles; from the south take the Bakersfield/24th Street exit (in Paso Robles) west for 30 miles.

# LOS ANGELES 9

By Sonia Perel

**Los Angeles: Aldous Huxley's "City of Dreadful Joy." Land of 24-hour celebrity** coverage, drive-through sushi bars, Drew Barrymore existentialism, *Baywatch* fantasies, and macabre Charles Manson and O.J. Simpson realities. The 44 Spanish, Native American, and African American settlers who founded El Pueblo de la Reina de Los Angeles on September 4, 1781, were cajoled into moving from northern Mexico by the Spanish crown's promise of free land, cash, and cows. Roughly 215 years later, their peaceful farming community has exploded into a drooling, unbounded megalopolis of more than 15 million people speaking some 120 tongues. This is the second-largest city in the United States, and it's still oozing out into new suburbs like a low-budget Hollywood *Blob* movie. If you ask for a map of L.A., you'll probably get something that includes most of Southern California. Within these vague boundaries exists a big, sweaty omelet of humanity, a mixture of diverse origins, wealth, and outlooks. Just consider the city's main districts: Hollywood, Watts, Beverly Hills, South Central, Bel Air, Malibu. These well-known names conjure images of everything from fabulous wealth and privilege to extreme poverty and oppression.

**ONLY IN L.A.:**

- *Alcoholics Anonymous meetings on the beach*
- *Gregorian chant-alongs*
- *Freeway-opening parties*
- *Fake car phones designed to look just like the real thing.*

The last three years have not been kind to Los Angeles. After enduring massive wildfires attributed to arsonists, heavy rains followed by mud slides, and renewed racial friction as police officers acquitted of beating black motorist Rodney King faced retrial, Angelenos were not—in the words of illustrious former V.P. Dan Quayle—happy campers. All they needed was the 6.6-magnitude earthquake of January 17, 1994, which caused more than $10 billion in damage—Angelenos are still paying off debts incurred from rebuilding costs, and many still break into a cold sweat at the slightest temblor. L.A.'s arid climate, inadequate drainage systems, and spider's web of earthquake faults make it fertile breeding ground for natural disasters. Malibu alone has endured an apocalyptic cycle of fires, mud slides, and floods over the past four years. The '95 floods incurred more than $4 million in damages, yet locals remain fiercely loyal to this paradisiacal enclave.

But Los Angeles's faults, geological and otherwise, should not deter you from visiting. For every tale of smog and traffic, there's a story of wide beaches, mild climate, superb museums, outrageously varied and bizarre nightlife, and, hey, surfboards for rent. Move beyond the tourist strips of Hollywood Boulevard, Universal Studios, and the Santa Monica Pier and you'll be rewarded; master the grid of freeways and avenues and you'll find an adventure. True Angelenos are used to traveling long distances in search of the coolest nightspot (heading to Malibu for dinner, Venice for drinks, West Hollywood for a movie, and Santa Monica for a snack),

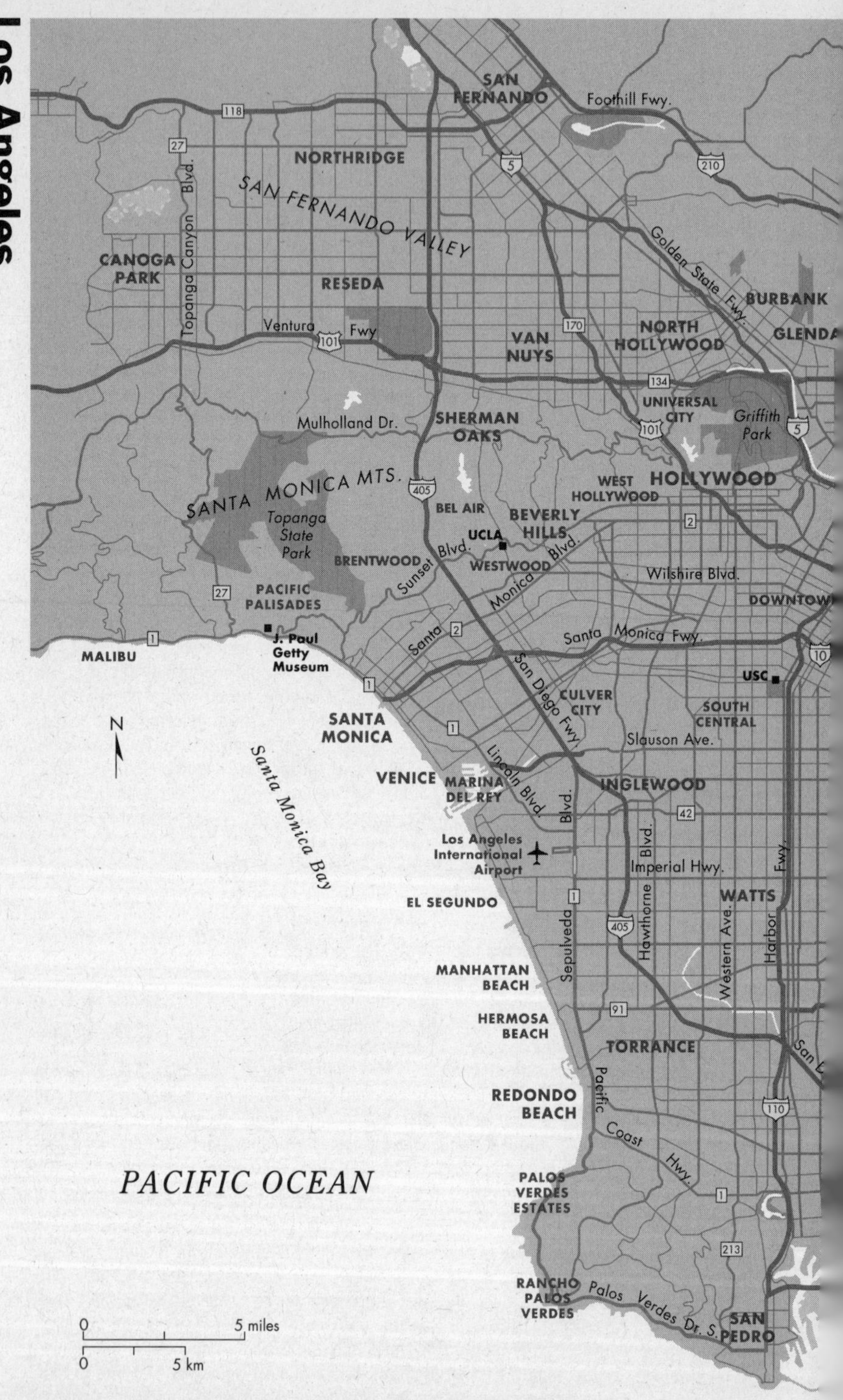

SAN FERNANDO
Foothill Fwy.
118
27
5
210
NORTHRIDGE
SAN FERNANDO VALLEY
Topanga Canyon Blvd.
CANOGA PARK
RESEDA
Golden State Fwy.
BURBANK
GLENDA
Ventura Fwy
101
170
VAN NUYS
NORTH HOLLYWOOD
134
UNIVERSAL CITY
Griffith Park
Mulholland Dr.
SHERMAN OAKS
SANTA MONICA MTS.
405
WEST HOLLYWOOD
HOLLYWOOD
BEL AIR
BEVERLY HILLS
2
Topanga State Park
UCLA
BRENTWOOD
Sunset Blvd.
WESTWOOD
Santa Monica Blvd.
Wilshire Blvd.
PACIFIC PALISADES
DOWNTOW
J. Paul Getty Museum
MALIBU
Santa Monica Fwy.
10
USC
San Diego Fwy.
CULVER CITY
SOUTH CENTRAL
SANTA MONICA
Slauson Ave.
N
Santa Monica Bay
Lincoln Blvd.
VENICE
MARINA DEL REY
INGLEWOOD
42
Los Angeles International Airport
Imperial Hwy.
EL SEGUNDO
WATTS
Harbor Fwy.
Sepulveda Blvd.
Hawthorne Blvd.
Western Ave.
MANHATTAN BEACH
91
HERMOSA BEACH
TORRANCE
San
REDONDO BEACH
Pacific Coast Hwy.
110
PACIFIC OCEAN
PALOS VERDES ESTATES
213
RANCHO PALOS VERDES
Palos Verdes Dr. S.
SAN PEDRO
0
5 miles
0
5 km

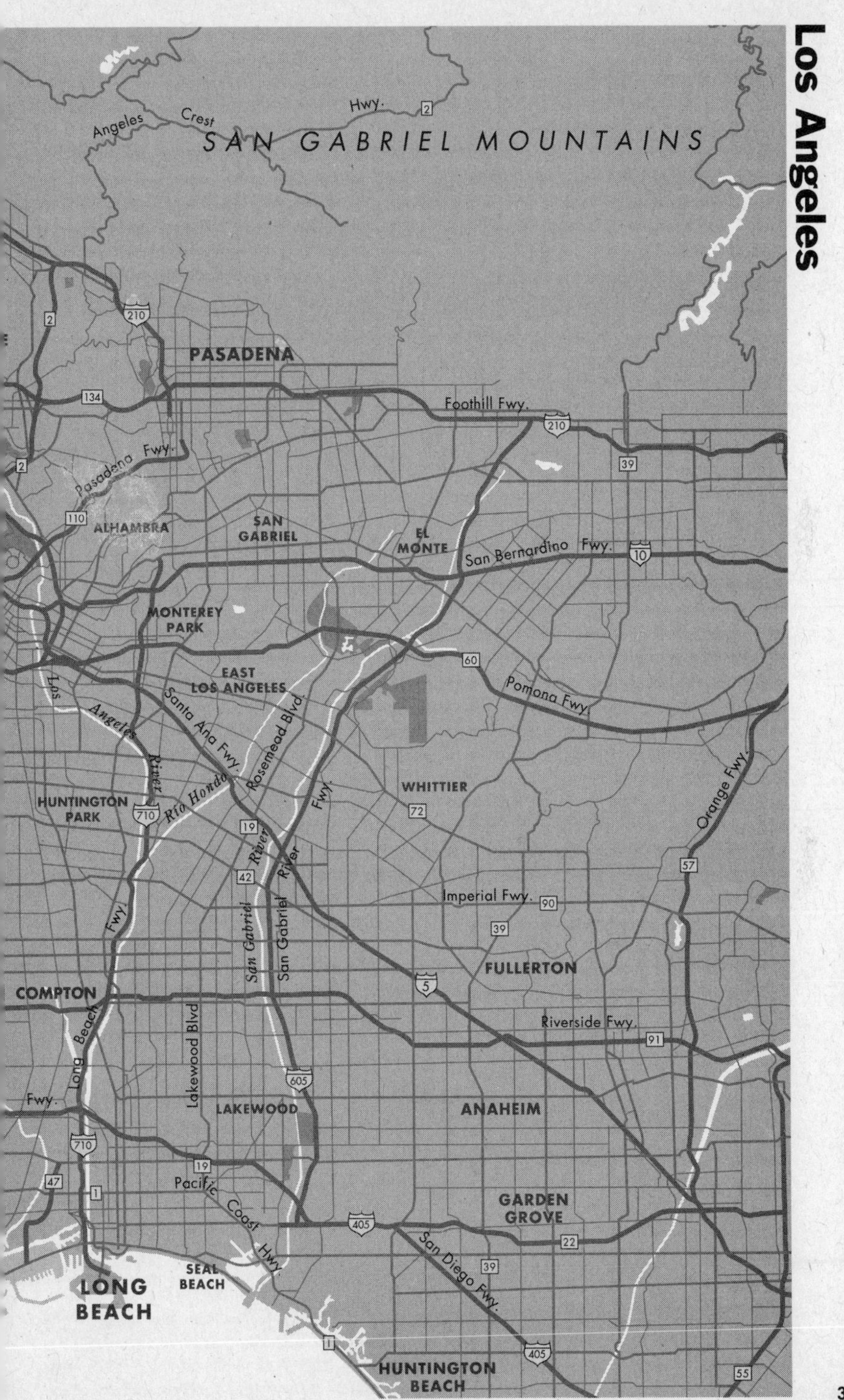
SAN GABRIEL MOUNTAINS
Angeles Crest Hwy.
PASADENA
Foothill Fwy.
Pasadena Fwy.
ALHAMBRA
SAN GABRIEL
EL MONTE
San Bernardino Fwy.
MONTEREY PARK
EAST LOS ANGELES
Pomona Fwy.
Los Angeles River
Santa Ana Fwy.
Rosemead Blvd.
Rio Hondo
HUNTINGTON PARK
WHITTIER
Orange Fwy.
San Gabriel River
Imperial Fwy.
San Gabriel River Fwy.
FULLERTON
COMPTON
Long Beach Fwy.
Lakewood Blvd
Riverside Fwy.
LAKEWOOD
ANAHEIM
Pacific Coast Hwy.
GARDEN GROVE
San Diego Fwy.
SEAL BEACH
LONG BEACH
HUNTINGTON BEACH

and visitors must be prepared to follow suit if they want to pierce the dark and exciting underbelly of the City of Angels. It'll sneak up on you, to be sure, but one morning you just might wake up and realize that you're addicted. "Leaving Los Angeles," noted one admirer of the city, "is like giving up heroin."

# Basics

**AMERICAN EXPRESS** **American Express has six offices** in Los Angeles County, where cardmembers may cash personal or traveler's checks and replace lost or stolen cards. *Downtown: 901 W. 7th St., 90017, tel. 213/627–4800. Open weekdays 8–6. At S. Figueroa St.*

**GAY AND LESBIAN RESOURCES** Los Angeles has a large and vocal gay and lesbian population, particularly in Hollywood and West Hollywood. Though public support is strong, violence toward homosexuals does occur. The **Gay and Lesbian Community Services Center** (1625 N. Schrader Ave., 4 blocks west of Vine St., tel. 213/993–7400), in Hollywood, offers information on community events, mental-health counseling, and support groups every Monday through Saturday 9 AM–10 PM and Sunday 10–6.

L.A.'s gay community finds quality reading material and the downlow on what's up in the city's numerous gay-oriented weeklies and microzines, available in bookstores and cafés, particularly in West Hollywood. Among the most widely distributed are *Edge, Frontiers, Planet Homo,* and *Spunk.* Specifically for lesbians are the monthly *Lesbian News* and *L.A. Girl Guide.* The *Gay and Lesbian Times* covers events and issues in Los Angeles and San Diego.

**MEDICAL AID** The **Los Angeles Free Clinic** (8405 Beverly Blvd., btw Fairfax Ave. and La Cienega Blvd., tel. 213/653–1990) provides free general medical services. Call weekdays 9 AM–11 AM for a same-day appointment. The **rape hotline** in the Los Angeles area is 310/392–8381.

**PUBLICATIONS** The *Los Angeles Times* (35¢, Sundays $1.50), widely considered the West Coast's best newspaper, is especially valuable on Sundays: The "Calendar" section contains a trove of entertainment info. For slightly hipper, up-to-the-minute entertainment listings, pick up a copy of *L.A. Weekly, L.A. Reader,* or *L.A. Village View,* three free weeklies available at cafés, supermarkets, and bookstores; new issues hit the stands on Thursdays. *L.A. Weekly* is the most comprehensive, often seeming to weigh more than a small child.

**VISITOR INFORMATION** The **Los Angeles Visitors and Convention Bureau** maintains two convenient offices. A multilingual staff dispenses free brochures and low-priced city maps from the downtown branch in the Hilton Hotel. They'll also set you up with an abbreviated but invaluable list of city bus routes. *685 S. Figueroa St., btw Wilshire Blvd. and 7th St., tel. 213/689–8822. Open weekdays 8–5, Sat. 8:30–5.*

The **Hollywood Visitor Information Center** occupies an elegant turn-of-the-century mansion in Janes Square. The multilingual staff distributes the same stuff as the downtown office; on occasion, they also have complimentary tickets to *The Tonight Show* and other TV marvels. *6541 Hollywood Blvd., near Hudson Ave., tel. 213/689–8822. Open Mon.–Sat. 9–5.*

If you're concentrating on the coast, you may want to drop by the **Santa Monica Convention and Visitor's Bureau,** north of the pier in Palisades Park. The staff has route information for the "Big Blue Bus" (*see* Getting Around, *below*) and can clue you in on special events. *1400 Ocean Ave., btw Broadway and Santa Monica Blvd., tel. 310/393–7593. Open summer, daily 10–5; winter, daily 10–4.*

## COMING AND GOING

**BY PLANE** **Los Angeles International Airport (LAX),** 17 miles southwest of downtown L.A. off I–405, is a snarl of traffic and tourists. It's the third-largest airport in the country, and every airline you can think of flies here. International terminals (2, 5, and the Bradley Terminal) have **currency exchange** offices and **information booths** open daily 7 AM–11 PM. In addition to dispensing the usual tourist pamphlets, the staff here can help you find accommodations. **Lug-**

**gage storage** is available in Terminals 1, 3, 4, 7, and the Bradley Terminal; prices range from $2 to $10 per bag per day, depending on size. Baggage storage facilities are generally open daily 6 AM–10 PM. All terminals have lockers, which cost $1 for the first 24 hours and $2 for each additional 24-hour period. The main information line for LAX is 310/646–5252.

Outside the baggage claim area in each of LAX's terminals is a Quick-Aid computer that provides ground transportation info (including public bus routes from the airport). More costly transport options include shuttle buses, such as **Super Shuttle** (tel. 213/775–6600) or **Airport Flyer Express** (tel. 818/376–1234). Both will take you anywhere in the greater L.A. area, 24 hours a day, for $10–$30 depending on pickup or drop-off location. Taxis, though convenient, are expensive. A ride to Santa Monica will set you back about $20, to Hollywood $26.

The smaller **Burbank Airport** (2627 N. Hollywood Way, at Thorton Ave. in Burbank, tel. 818/840–8847), close to Hollywood and only 1 mile south of I-5, is served by Alaska (tel. 800/426–0333), American (tel. 800/433–7300), America West (tel. 800/235–9292), Reno Air (tel. 800/736–6247), Sky West (tel. 800/453–9417), Southwest (tel. 800/435–9792), and United (tel. 800/241–6522). These airlines may offer the best fares on journeys up and down the West Coast (to San Francisco, say, or Seattle) because landing at small airports like Burbank costs less touching down at major hubs like LAX. To reach downtown from the Burbank Airport take Bus 94; to reach Hollywood take Bus 212.

**BY CAR** Just about every freeway in California seems to lead to Los Angeles eventually. From the north, take I-5, U.S. 101, or coastal Highway 1. From San Diego in the south, take I-405. From the east, I-10 leads into town (*also see* Getting Around by Car, *below*).

**BY BUS** Incontestably the cheapest—and potentially the most entertaining—way of getting to Los Angeles is by **Greyhound** (tel. 800/231–2222), which offers service to L.A.'s downtown station (1716 E. 7th St., at Central Ave., tel. 213/629–8400) from many U.S. and Canadian cities, including San Francisco (8–11 hrs, $65 round-trip) and San Diego (3 hrs, $20 round-trip). The station is in a blighted neighborhood, so try to arrive during daylight hours. The Greyhound station in Hollywood (1409 N. Vine St., btw Sunset Blvd. and De Longpre Ave., tel. 213/466–6384) offers roughly equivalent fares.

For perennially rootless road warriors, **Green Tortoise Adventure Travel** (tel. 800/227–4766) runs bus tours to San Francisco, Alaska, Baja California, the Grand Canyon, and the California desert (*also see box* Funky Deals on Wheels, in Chapter 1). Camper coaches cruise from sight to sight along a semi-flexible route, pausing to allow passengers time to swim, party, and cook meals. This is a great way to travel if you don't mind the smell of dirty socks—there's no on-board shower or toilet. From L.A., round-trip fare to San Francisco (12 hrs) is $60; for Seattle (2 days) you'll pay $138. Green Tortoise stops in Hollywood, downtown L.A., and Venice Beach once weekly; call for schedule and pickup locations.

**BY TRAIN** The slow but romantic way to reach L.A. is by train, arriving at the beautifully restored **Union Station** (800 N. Alameda St., at E. Macy St., tel. 213/683–6729), in a semi-sleazy neighborhood downtown. **Amtrak** (tel. 800/872–7245) sends several trains daily to San Francisco (12 hrs, $67), San Diego (3 hrs, $24), and Chicago (2 days, $217); round-trip fares are often only slightly higher. Several public transport lines link Union Station to the rest of L.A.: MTA Bus 434 heads to Santa Monica and Malibu; Bus 60 takes you to Sunset Boulevard, where you can catch Buses 1–4 to Hollywood; the Metro Red Line light-rail serves downtown; and **Metrolink** (tel. 213/808–5465) offers commuter service to far-flung communities.

## GETTING AROUND

**BY CAR** Traffic in L.A. is less apocalyptic than it's often portrayed in movies and on TV, though not by much. And while the popularity of drive-by shootings has waned, carjacking incidents are on the rise. The ***Thomas Guide to L.A. County*** ($26) is almost heavy enough to fill any self-defense needs, but its primary purpose is to help you figure out where the hell you are and how to get where you're going. Worshipped throughout the Southland, this comprehensive book of maps and indexes is available in area bookstores and gas stations, and should be the first thing a visiting driver buys.

Though you may not share the same enthusiasm for freeways that native Angelenos do, life's paved road will be much smoother if you can remember a few key routes: **I–5** (the Golden State Freeway) runs through downtown, continuing north to San Francisco and south to San Diego. **I–10** (the Santa Monica Freeway) runs east from Santa Monica, continuing through L.A.'s boring 'burbs to Palm Springs and points beyond. **I–405** (the San Diego Freeway) runs parallel to but west of I–5; take this to reach the L.A. International Airport and points south. **Highway 1,** also known as the **Pacific Coast Highway (PCH),** meanders along the coastline, passing through L.A.'s beach communities on its way north to San Francisco and south toward San Diego.

*L.A.'s freeways, shredded in the 1994 earthquake, were repaired in a frenzy of 24-hour workdays—while citizens of San Francisco continue to wait for repairs to roads damaged six years prior.*

➢ **RENTAL CARS** • Independent agencies are usually cheaper and give renters less attitude than the bigger corporations. When making a reservation at a smaller company, be sure to get a confirmation number, or at least the name of the person you speak with. Almost all rental agencies expect drivers to be over 25 and to possess a major credit card. Some will make exceptions, but you'll end up paying a lot more than the advertised rate (usually an extra $5–$20 per day). Almost all companies offer insurance (usually $9 per day), but check first with your own car-insurance company and your credit card company—chances are that the rental will already be covered. You may save cash if you're a member of AAA, or if you rent by the week rather than by the day. Some hostels (*see* Where to Sleep, *below*) offer rental discounts. Most companies without an office at LAX will send a shuttle to the airport to pick you up.

At LAX, **Bob Leech's** (4490 W. Century Blvd., tel. 310/673–2727 or 800/635–1240 for reservations) rents cars to those 23 and older for $20 a day or $120 a week. For an extra $50, you can drive the car up the coast and drop it off at their San Francisco office. You're allowed 150 free miles per day; it's 10¢ for each additional mile. **Capri** (8620 Airport Blvd., at LAX, tel. 310/641–2323 or 800/400–4736 for reservations) has rates of $23 a day or $140 a week; add $5 to the daily rate in August. **Fox** (10210 Glasgow Pl., at LAX, tel. 310/641–3838) rents economy cars for $30 a day or $150 a week. Those ages 21 to 24 pay an additional $10 per day.

**Avon** (8459 Sunset Blvd., near La Cienega Blvd. in West Hollywood, tel. 213/654–5533) charges $25 a day or $150 a week for low-end cars (something along the lines of a Yugo without radio or air-conditioning). Those under 21 (but at least 18 years old) pay an additional $15 a day, and 21- to 24-year-olds pay an additional $5 a day. Avon does not provide shuttle service to and from area airports. **Penny** and **Rent-a-Wreck** (14654 Oxnard St., at Van Nuys Blvd. in North Hollywood, tel. 818/786–1733) are jointly owned, and both rent nice, normal cars for $21–$27 a day or $129–$149 a week; 18- to 23-year-olds pay a $10 daily surcharge. They do not operate a shuttle service, but can arrange to pick up travelers at Burbank Airport free of charge.

## Driver's Ed: The Accelerated Course

***In Los Angeles, driving is as much a part of the daily routine as, say, breathing—and neither is easy. You and your car will feel right at home if you follow these few simple steps. First, get hip to L.A.'s driving lingo: Interstate 5 is "The Five" and U.S. 101 is "The One-oh-One." Next, rent a cellular phone, so you can conduct animated conversations while weaving recklessly. As you cruise, never ever concede space on the freeway to merging traffic. If you're pulled over by the California Highway Patrol, free yourself from the tedium of a ticket by casually mentioning that you're employed by Hollywood agencies ICM or CAA (and expect a cop-movie screenplay in the mail two weeks later). And finally, always have your auto "detailed"; never have it "washed." Now, drivers, you may start your engines.***

**BY BUS** The commonly spotted orange-and-white buses of the **Metropolitan Transit Authority (MTA)** (425 S. Main St., tel. 213/626–4455) provide thorough but plodding transportation through L.A. for a flat $1.35 (2-hr transfers 25¢). Carry exact fare, because drivers cannot make change. Generally, MTA buses numbered 1–99 serve downtown L.A., Buses 100–199 run east–west, and Buses 200–299 run north–south. Bus stops are well marked, and buses arrive every 10–30 minutes, depending on routes and days. Late-night service is skimpy, so stop by a visitor center (*see* Visitor Information, *above*) for a schedule. Most MTA buses have wheelchair access.

As its name suggests, **DASH** (Downtown Area Short Hop) buses serve the downtown area, including Chinatown, Little Tokyo, Olvera Street, and Union Station, during the daytime only. The 25¢ fare includes one free transfer. During rush hours (5–8 AM and 3–6 PM), express buses run from downtown to more distant destinations like Hermosa Beach (Bus 438, $1.10) and Westwood (Bus 431, $1.50). For more information call 800/2–LA–RIDE. All DASH buses have wheelchair access.

Though some MTA buses loop through the city of Santa Monica, more thorough service is provided by Santa Monica's **Big Blue Bus** (tel. 310/451–5444), which also takes passengers from the beach to LAX, Westwood, and downtown L.A. Fare is 50¢ ($1.25 to downtown), with one free transfer. Transfers to MTA bus lines are available for 25¢. Additionally, a city-operated shuttle called **The Tide** connects several downtown Santa Monica attractions, including the Promenade, the pier, and some motels. The shuttle operates daily from mid-May through September noon–10 PM, with departures every 30 minutes; fare is 50¢.

**BY SUBWAY** The city of Los Angeles recently debuted an extremely limited subway system connecting downtown with Long Beach. At this point, plans for extending it in 1996 only include Pasadena, Wilshire Boulevard, and Western Avenue in Koreatown. The **Metro Red Line** makes five stops in the downtown area, continuing on to Union Station, where it connects with Amtrak and Metrolink trains. The fare is 25¢. Red Line trains run every 10 minutes from 5 AM to 7 PM daily. The **Blue Line** makes the 1-hour journey from downtown L.A. to downtown Long Beach (*see* Chapter 10) daily 5 AM–10:40 PM; round-trip fare is $2.70. City officials unveiled a **Green Line** in June 1995; the route extends east from LAX to parts of L.A. you were planning to skip anyway. The Red and Blue lines converge at the **7th Street Metro Center** (cnr Flower and 7th Sts.). For more information on the Metro system, call **MTA** (tel. 213/626–4455).

*Even if you're not planning to take the Red Line subway, duck into the Civic Center Station (1st and Hill Sts.) to check out the mannequins suspended from the ceiling.*

**BY TAXI** Usually, you can't hail a taxi on the street; instead you phone for one. **L.A. Taxi** (tel. 213/627–7000) and **United Independent Cab Co.** (tel. 213/653–5050) charge an initial $1.90, plus $1.60 per mile. Most taxi companies operate 24 hours daily.

**HITCHHIKING** In general, don't do it. L.A. has more than its fair share of malignant people. Besides, you're far more likely to get a short ride in a police car—the city aggressively enforces its no hitchhiking law. If you're still determined, try median strips and curbs near freeway on-ramps. A much safer alternative is to check the **ride-sharing board** at UCLA, located on campus in Ackerman Union (*see* Westwood and Beverly Hills, Exploring L.A., *below*).

# Where to Sleep

**Hotels and motels range** from the grossly opulent to flea-infested, smelly joints where the bed linen is crunchy and yellow. Some of the most pleasant, safe, and convenient motels lie in the Wilshire District, along Beverly Boulevard and Fairfax Avenue. Hostels are an even better choice for those who want to save money and meet other travelers. Hollywood, Venice, and Santa Monica offer several hostels in key locations, some with private rooms similar in price and quality to those at standard inns. Figure out what you want to do and see in L.A. before choosing a hotel or hostel so that you don't spend half the day fighting traffic. If you're an AAA member or a student, ask about discounts; you could shave as much as 10% off your bill just by presenting ID. Many hotels recommend reservations during the busy summer months, as well as on weekends and holidays throughout the year. Keep in mind that a 12%–14% room tax will be added to listed prices.

## HOTELS AND MOTELS

**DOWNTOWN** Recently, city planners and private investors have poured large amounts of money into the downtown area, giving L.A. a long-needed center of business activity. As a result, the neighborhood now offers plenty of impressive hotels for executives on expense accounts, as well as a surviving host of dives unsafe for the budget traveler. Though staying downtown puts all the freeways at your fingertips, you're better off staying in the Wilshire District (*see below*). For a map of downtown lodging, *see* Exploring L.A., *below.*

➢ **UNDER $35** • **Orchid Hotel.** Amidst a sea of pricey Sheraton-types, the Orchid is a welcome respite. Clean, comfortable doubles are a refreshing $30 a night or $184 a week; triples (with three single beds) are $44, $228 a week. If one person in your group can produce a student ID, you'll receive a 15% discount. The clientele includes an odd mix of backpackers and pensioners; the 24-hour reception desk keeps the place safe and orderly 'round the clock. *819 S. Flower St., btw 8th and 9th Sts., tel. 213/624–5855 or 800/874–5855. From LAX, Bus 439 to 8th and Flower Sts. 60 rooms. Laundry. Wheelchair access.*

➢ **UNDER $50** • **Hotel Stillwell.** Framed East Indian prints line the halls of this freshly painted high-rise near the heart of downtown, and the rooms have tastefully matched curtains and linens. The management can be effusively friendly. You'll even find some families staying here, a testimony to the building's excellent security. Doubles are $49 a night, $45 with student ID. *838 S. Grand Ave., btw 8th and 9th Sts., tel. 213/627–1151 or 800/553–4774. From LAX, Bus 439 to 8th and Figueroa Sts. 350 rooms. Laundry. Wheelchair access.*

**HOLLYWOOD** This is a place of sin and excess. Drive along Hollywood Boulevard and you'll get a crash course in sexual appetites, from bondage shops to whirlpool-and-waterbed hotels with hourly rates. Even in Hollywood's nicer motels crime can be a problem, and at night muggings on the streets are common. But, hey, if you're fearless, stupid, or handy with Mace, you can see it all here: leather-clad Iron Maiden fans; glossy, giggling transvestites; between-gig glam rockers; and the assorted human driftwood that accumulates with each new wave of middle-America hopefuls seeking success in the City of Broken Dreams. For a map of Hollywood lodging, *see* Exploring L.A., *below.*

➢ **UNDER $55** • **Hollywood Towne House Motel.** The decor here is low-budget Gothic, with dark wood paneling, gilt mirrors, and antiquated rotary phones. You could heighten the effect by bringing along a tape of creepy organ music. Otherwise, this two-story motel, just blocks away from Sunset Boulevard's clubs, is clean and cheap: Doubles are $45 a night ($220 a week). *6055 Sunset Blvd., btw N. Gower and N. Bronson Sts., tel. 213/462–3221. Just west of U.S. 101. 32 rooms. Wheelchair access.*

➢ **UNDER $65** • **Liberty Hotel.** Quiet, charming, and unlike anything you'd expect to see in Hollywood, this low-rise hotel is the place to stay if you have high standards of personal hygiene. Though it's on a tree-lined residential street, it's only a block north of the everlasting carnival sideshow surrounding Mann's Chinese Theater (*see* Exploring L.A., *below*). Doubles start at $50. *1770 Orchid Ave., btw Franklin Ave. and Hollywood Blvd., tel. 213/962–1788. ½ block north of Hollywood Blvd. 20 rooms.*

*Even if you don't have $100 burning a hole in your pocket (and therefore can't afford a room at the Roosevelt), a subtle cruise through the hotel's lobby and pool area will give you a taste of legendary, but long-gone Hollywood.*

➢ **UNDER $120** • **Roosevelt Hotel.** Built in 1927, this hotel is an unofficial historic landmark. It reputedly hosted Marilyn Monroe, provided a trysting spot for Clark Gable and Carole Lombard, and was a hangout for Ernest Hemingway and F. Scott Fitzgerald. The first Academy Awards were held here in 1929. The Spanish-Moorish architecture, lush palm trees, and David Hockney–painted pool make for a luxurious retreat from the grime of Hollywood. Doubles start at $99, but call ahead to get the dope on special seasonal deals. *7000 Hollywood Blvd., btw. La Brea Ave. and Orange Dr., tel. 213/*

*466–7000 or 800/333–3333. 320 rooms. Exercise room, Jacuzzi, nightclub, pool, restaurant. Wheelchair access.*



**WILSHIRE DISTRICT** A string of ridiculously priced hotels lines Sunset Boulevard between Crescent Heights and La Cienega boulevards, most notably the 60-year-old **Chateau Marmont,** long a favorite of the rich and famous, and **Le Mondrian Hotel,** with a 60-foot painting in the style of the eponymous Dutch artist gracing the facade. Admire and move on; you'll find much cheaper lodging a few blocks south, around the intersection of Beverly Boulevard and Fairfax Avenue. Prices are a bit higher than in Hollywood or downtown L.A., but you're paying for comfort, security, and prime locale. Peruse the Melrose café scene, visit museums and the La Brea Tar Pits, or drive 20 minutes to downtown or Santa Monica Beach. To locate lodging, *see* the West L.A. map, in Exploring L.A., *below.*

➢ **UNDER $50** • **Bevonshire Lodge Motel.** This is a small and unremarkable motel with a chihuahua-size pool and fatigued furnishings. Quite a few twentysomethings reside here year-round, for reasons too difficult to explain. It does win bonus points for location; CBS is a block away. (But before you get excited, remember: Letterman broadcasts from New York City.) Doubles, all with refrigerators, are $43; an extra $6 will get you a room with a kitchenette. *7575 Beverly Blvd., btw Fairfax Ave. and Gardner St., tel. 213/936–6154. 25 rooms. Coin-op laundry across street. Wheelchair access.*

➢ **UNDER $75** • **Beverly Laurel Motor Hotel.** Tastefully furnished, spacious rooms make it a pleasure to stay at this well-situated three-story motel. All rooms have refrigerators; doubles are $57 a night, or $67 with kitchenette. Extras include a downstairs coffee shop (open daily 7:30 AM–2 AM, Fri.–Sat. until 4 AM), a pleasant tiled pool, and free underground parking. *8018 Beverly Blvd., 2 blocks west of Fairfax Ave., tel. 213/651–2441. 52 rooms. Wheelchair access.*

➢ **UNDER $85** • **Farmer's Daughter Motel.** This three-story motel, across from the Farmer's Market (*see* Exploring L.A., *below*), hasn't seen any real farmers—or their daughters—for decades. Large, immaculate doubles, complete with refrigerators, start at $65 in summer, $58 in winter. There's also a pool and sundeck. *115 S. Fairfax Ave., btw Beverly Blvd. and 3rd St., tel. 213/937–3930 or 800/334–1658. 64 rooms. Wheelchair access.*

**WESTWOOD AND BEVERLY HILLS** Unless you're traveling with your parents (or their credit cards), you're not likely to find lodging in Beverly Hills' illustrious 90210 zip code. You'll have better luck and more fun in Westwood, home to thousands of UCLA students. To locate lodging, *see* the West L.A. map, in Exploring L.A., *below.*

➢ **UNDER $65** • **Westwood Inn.** Don't be turned off by the shabby exterior. The rooms—equipped with phone, TV, and sofa—are spacious and comfortable. The motel is close to UCLA, with easy access to cheap eateries and student-filled bars. Doubles go for $54 a night ($340 a week). It's popular with young backpacking types, so you'll need to make reservations two to three weeks in advance during summer. *10820 Wilshire Blvd., btw Westwood and Beverly Glen Blvds., tel. 310/474–3118. From LAX, Bus 560. 21 rooms. Laundry. Wheelchair access.*

➢ **UNDER $95** • **Beverly Terrace Hotel.** On the border of West Hollywood and Beverly Hills, this motel is centrally located, decently furnished, clean, and welcoming. The clientele consists mainly of families and couples. If you feel daring, call ahead to reserve the Zebra Room. Doubles are $65–$85; anyone who mentions the *Berkeley Guides* or produces a student ID will get a 10% discount, subject to availability. *469 N. Doheny Dr., at Santa Monica Blvd., tel. 310/274–8141. 38 rooms. Italian restaurant, pool.*

**SANTA MONICA, VENICE, AND MALIBU** Malibu, remote and relatively inaccessible, has long been a favorite of the wealthy and famous. However, it's retained a laid-back air, and budget travelers will want to stay here if they're looking for a few days of solitude (and surfing). Santa Monica is ideal for beach lovers also looking to explore L.A.'s interior; the city has a range of motels and hotels, a huge number of young people, and easy freeway access. Also consider one of the excellent hostels in nearby Venice, a beach town that's a nonstop riotous carnival of skating Rastafarians, posing bodybuilders, and sidewalk shiatsu massage therapists. For a map of lodging, *see* the Santa Monica and Venice map in Exploring L.A., *below.*

➢ **UNDER $50** • **Palm Motel.** Palm trees, flower pots, and painted flags cheer up this bungalow-style motel. The rooms are airy and relatively clean, and doubles are only $40 a night ($256 a week). The clientele ranges from gregarious elderly residents to young hip-hop types. *2020 14th St., at Pico Blvd. in Santa Monica, tel. 310/452–3861. From LAX, Big Blue Bus 3 to Pico and Lincoln Blvds., transfer to Bus 7 eastbound on Lincoln Blvd. 26 rooms. Wheelchair access.*

➢ **UNDER $65** • **Jolly Roger Hotel.** Despite its colorful name, this three-story hotel is a bit on the bland side, with a decor that sticks too close to a beige-and-brown theme. But price (doubles $54) and location (5-minute drive to Venice Beach) are bonuses. *2904 Washington Blvd., btw Lincoln and Abbot Kinney Blvds. in Marina del Rey, tel. 310/822–2904 or 800/822–2904. From LAX, Big Blue Bus 3. 82 rooms. Courtyard café, Jacuzzi, pool. Wheelchair access.*

**Pacific Sands Motel.** Directly across from the Santa Monica Pier, this motel is peeling in some places and patched in others, but overall it's clean and comfortable. There's a pool, too, if you can find it. During summer, the Pacific Sands is usually packed with a college-age crowd, so reserve at least a week in advance. Doubles run $40 in winter, $55 the rest of the year; lower weekly rates are available. *1515 Ocean Ave., btw Broadway and Colorado Ave. in Santa Monica, tel. 310/395–6133. From LAX, Big Blue Bus 3 to 4th St. and Broadway. 40 rooms, 52 during summer. Wheelchair access.*

➢ **UNDER $85** • **Bayside Hotel.** The color tiles in the bathrooms might trigger a flashback, but you can't beat the location of this attractively landscaped motel, just across the street from the beach. Comfortable doubles without phones go for $44–$64 a night depending on season; some have kitchens and all come with plenty of free coffee. On Friday and Saturday nights, you'll pay $5 more. *2001 Ocean Ave., south of Pico Blvd. in Santa Monica, tel. 310/396–6000. From LAX, Big Blue Bus 3, get off at 4th St. and Pico Blvd. 45 rooms. Wheelchair access.*

**Hotel Carmel.** One of Santa Monica's original grand hotels, the Carmel has been carefully tended over the decades, as you'll see from the elegant lobby and well-appointed rooms. And its location in the heart of downtown Santa Monica, 2 blocks from the beach and around the corner from the Third Street Promenade (*see* Exploring L.A., *below*), can't be topped. Double rooms are $70. Though guests are primarily families and couples, the management (and multilingual staff) welcomes students; those with valid ID receive a 25% discount September 15–May 31. *201 Broadway, at 2nd St. in Santa Monica, tel. 310/451–2469 or 800/445–8695. From LAX, Big Blue Bus 3, get off at 4th St. and Broadway. 110 rooms. Wheelchair access.*

**Malibu Surfer Motel.** Ideally located across from Surfrider State Beach, this charming blue-and-white stucco motel has bright, clean rooms with refrigerators, king-size beds, and balconies. There's a small pool and sundeck, and a hilltop patio and picnic area. Singles and doubles range from $40 to $60 in winter, $60 to $90 in summer; the highest prices are for weekend stays. *22541 Pacific Coast Hwy., btw Tuna Canyon and Malibu Canyon Rds. in Malibu, tel. 310/456–6169. 17 rooms. Wheelchair access.*

**THE SOUTH BAY** The South Bay includes Manhattan Beach, Hermosa Beach, and Redondo Beach, all linked to the rest of Los Angeles by the Pacific Coast Highway (also known as PCH, Hwy. 1, or sometimes Sepulveda or Lincoln Boulevard). Budget lodgings here line the highway, and room rates get progressively higher as you near the water. But presumably, you're here for the beaches, so it might be worth it to fork over a few extra bucks. Manhattan and Redondo beaches are more commercialized than their quirky small-town neighbor Hermosa.

➢ **UNDER $50** • **East-West Inn.** A great bargain considering it's only a 5-minute walk from the beach, the East-West lets doubles for $37 a night or $200 for the week. Clean, newly furnished rooms, fresh paint, and scattered tubs of small palm trees save the hotel from generic blandness. *435 S. Pacific Coast Hwy., at Ruby St. in Redondo Beach, tel. 310/540–5998. South of Torrance Blvd. 40 rooms. Laundry. Wheelchair access.*

➢ **UNDER $65** • **Grandview Motor Hotel.** This tiny, modern three-story hotel sits steps from the beach; spacious rooms come complete with refrigerator and private balcony, and friendly managers give the place a comfortable feel. Doubles start at $58; weekly rates are available in winter. *55 14th St., off Hermosa Ave. in Hermosa Beach, tel. 310/374–8981. 17 rooms.*



**Sea Sprite Motel.** It lacks character, but this is nirvana for beach-seeking travelers: If it were any closer to the ocean, you'd need a life raft. All rooms have a microwave and refrigerator, and rates vary from $59 for economy one-bed rooms to $95 for ocean-view doubles; reserve at least a week in advance during summer. *1016 The Strand, at 10th St. in Hermosa Beach, tel. 310/376–6933. 89 rooms. Laundry, pool, sundeck.*

**Seahorse Motel.** Don't let the *Miami Vice* pink-and-aqua pastel exterior dissuade you: Rooms are large, clean, pleasantly furnished, and equipped with HBO. It's a 5-minute drive to the ocean and the Manhattan Beach Pier, and there's a pool on the premises. Double rooms are $59–$69 per night depending on season, or $324 a week, with lower rates in winter. *233 N. Sepulveda Blvd., btw 2nd St. and Manhattan Beach Blvd. in Manhattan Beach, tel. 310/376–7951 or 800/233–8057. 33 rooms. Closed Nov.–Jan.*

**NEAR THE AIRPORT** There's no reason to linger near the airport, unless you're fond of the sound of DC-10s. If you're concerned about making an early-morning flight, keep in mind that many beachside and Hollywood hostels offer free airport shuttle service.

➢ **UNDER $65 • Hacienda Hotel.** If you're determined to stay near the airport, head straight for this labyrinthine hotel. The modern rooms are almost antiseptically clean, and the fern- and fountain-bedecked ground floor might be mistaken for a Mediterranean palazzo. Free extras include movie channels, champagne and hors d'oeuvres at Happy Hour (weekdays 4:30–6:30), 24-hour airport shuttle service, and—if you're the type—free country-and-western dance lessons on Friday and Saturday nights. Double rooms start at $51. *525 N. Sepulveda Blvd., at Mariposa Ave. in El Segundo, tel. 310/615–0015 or 800/421–5900. 630 rooms. 24-hr coffee shop, Jacuzzi, laundry, pool. Wheelchair access.*

## HOSTELS

Hostels in Los Angeles usually offer a variety of sleeping options, from double rooms with private baths to warehouse-like dorms sleeping 20 or more. Many independent hostels hold their cheapest dormitory options for international and out-of-state travelers, particularly during summer. Passports are usually required, even of U.S. citizens. Despite these restrictions, hostels are an excellent lodging alternative: Most offer free airport pickup, and some even have arrangements with rental-car companies for discount car rentals.

**HOLLYWOOD** **Banana Bungalow Hotel and Hostel.** Near U.S. 101 and the Hollywood Bowl (*see* Exploring L.A., *below*), this well-run hotel/hostel offers so much that you may forget to venture down to frothy Hollywood Boulevard for fun. Dorms sleeping four to six people are $15 per person; doubles are $45 a night. There's always a crowd floating between the pool, weight room, basketball courts, sundeck, and arcade. Other extras include free airport pickup; free breakfast; free movie nights; free shuttles to the beach, studios, and amusement parks; and a reasonably priced café/restaurant. A passport (foreign or domestic) is required; international guests get preference for dormitory space. *2775 Cahuenga Blvd. W, 1 mi north of Franklin Ave., tel. 213/851–1129 or 800/4–HOSTEL. 250 beds. No curfew, no lockout. Reception open 24 hrs. Kitchen, laundry, free linens, luggage storage. Reservations advised in summer. Wheelchair access.*

**Hollywood International Hostel.** This small, intimate hostel—located in a two-story house—is the long-term residence of many aspiring young actors, directors, and screenwriters. A bed in a dorm sleeping two to four people goes for $12; show a *Berkeley Guide* for $3 off. If you're truly broke, ask about a work exchange. The hostel also offers free airport pickup. *6561 Franklin Ave., at Whitley Ave., tel. 213/850–6287 or 800/750–6561. 22 beds. No curfew, no lockout. Reception open 9 AM–1 AM. Kitchen, lounge, yard.*

**Hollywood Wilshire YMCA International Youth Hostel.** If you want to get in shape while you're visiting Hollywood, this newly renovated hostel offers free access to two swimming pools, a Jacuzzi, sauna, and fitness room. Dorm beds are $15 a night. *1553 N. Schrader Ave., btw*

*Selma Ave. and Sunset Blvd., tel. 213/467–4161. 44 beds. No curfew, lockout 10 AM–4 PM. Linen rental ($3), luggage storage. Wheelchair access.*

**SANTA MONICA AND VENICE** **Airport Hostel.** Recognizable from the road as the two-story structure with a perpetual string of drying laundry suspended from the balcony, the Airport Hostel offers a cheap place to sleep, free airport pickup, discount rentals on cars and bikes, and a reasonable standard of hygiene. There's one 30-bed dorm and several smaller ones that run $12–$14 a night or $84 a week; a handful of double rooms go for $32. The common room features a pool table and TV. The management gives preference to foreign and out-of-state visitors, particularly in summer; a passport is required. *221 Lincoln Blvd., near Venice Blvd. in Venice, tel. 310/305–0250. 70 beds. No curfew, no lockout. Reception open 24 hrs. Kitchen, laundry, free linens, luggage storage. Wheelchair access. No credit cards.*

**Cadillac Hotel.** The Cadillac is a stylishly renovated art deco hostel/hotel less than a block from Venice Beach. Thirty of the rooms are standard hotel-type and nine additional hostel rooms house four dorm-style beds each. Dorms are $16 per person; double rooms go for $49–$55. The hostel offers airport pickup for $5 and guests have access to a sauna, sundeck, gym, pool table, and laundry facilities; discount car rentals and studio tours are also available. *401 Ocean Front Walk, at Rose Ave. in Venice, tel. 310/399–8876. 85 beds. No curfew, no lockout. Reception open 24 hrs. Free linens, luggage storage. Wheelchair access.*

**Jim's at the Beach.** A stone's throw from the water, Jim's has a laid-back, homey atmosphere. Beds in six-person dorm rooms go for $16 a night, $90–$98 weekly, and $320–$340 monthly. Breakfast is included. A domestic or international passport is required. *17 Brooks Ave., at Pacific Ave. in Venice, tel. 310/399–4018. From LAX, take Apollo ($8) or Coast ($5) shuttle. 40 beds. No curfew, no lockout. Reception open 9 AM–midnight. Kitchen, laundry, free linens, lockers, lounge. Wheelchair access.*

**Santa Monica American Youth Hostel.** Perhaps the best hostel in L.A., this place is almost a self-sufficient community; its amenities include laundry machines, a spacious courtyard, kitchen facilities, and a travel store. The proprietors have preserved the brick-and-wood charm of the historic building, a former town hall. (It's quite a contrast to the neighboring Pussycat Adult Movie Theater, the only blemish in an otherwise respectable neighborhood.) The hostel, 1 block from the Third Street Promenade (*see* Exploring L.A., *below*), is open year-round to both AYH members and nonmembers on a first-come, first-served basis. Dorm rooms are $17 a night and doubles are $25 a person. Add $3 if you are not an HI member. *1436 2nd St., south of Santa Monica Blvd. in Santa Monica, tel. 310/393–9913. For free airport pickup call Westside Shuttle at 800/590–4243. 235 beds, all dorms single sex. No curfew, no lockout. Reception open 24 hrs. Kitchen, laundry, linens ($2), luggage storage, pool table. Reservations strongly advised in summer. Wheelchair access.*

**Share Tel Apartments.** Across the street from Jim's at the Beach (*see above*), this social hostel hosts free dinner-and-keg nights for guests. Dorm rooms cost $15 a night or $100 a week, and free airport pickup is provided. The management gives preference to foreign visitors; a domestic or foreign passport is required. *20 Brooks Ave., at Pacific Ave. in Venice, tel. 310/392–0325. 150 beds. No curfew, no lockout. Reception open 24 hrs. Kitchen, laundry, free linens.*

**Venice Beach Cotel.** Well-scrubbed and literally steps from the beach, the high-rise Cotel offers both dorm- and hotel-style accommodations. Studio tours, an inexpensive weekly shuttle to San Diego, and discount car rentals are all available. Dorms sleep three to four people; beds in rooms with a shared bath down the hall cost $13 ($15 with adjoining private bath and ocean view). Double rooms with ocean views are $30–$44. The management suggests that hostelers arrive soon after checkout time (11 AM) to get a bed; a foreign or domestic passport is required. *25 Windward Ave., 1 block west of Pacific Ave. in Venice, tel. 310/399–7649. From LAX, take Apollo Shuttle ($8). 70 beds. No curfew, no lockout. Reception open 24 hrs. Free linens, luggage storage.*

## STUDENT HOUSING

The only regularly available student housing in L.A. is administered by **University of Southern California Housing Services** (620 W. 35th St., 90089, tel. 800/872–4632). From the third week of May to mid-August, USC offers lodging on a first-come, first-served basis. Dorm accommodations with communal bathrooms are $35 a night for a single or $25 per person for a double. Lower weekly rates are sometimes available. Students who can prove that they are in L.A. for academic reasons (a registration card will suffice) can stay in apartments only 2 blocks north of campus in a relatively safe neighborhood. Minimum stay is 30 days; expect to pay $160–$350 a month, depending on how many roommates you have. Call or write for an application; you may reserve beginning in April with a $50 nonrefundable deposit.

### CAMPING

While it would indeed be a shock to find camping within L.A. city limits, a few oceanside state parks offer you a place to pitch your tent within striking distance of the city. Most are in or around Malibu and all offer fully developed sites; for reservations, contact MISTIX (tel. 800/444–PARK). At **Leo Carillo State Beach** (tel. 818/880–0350), 25 miles west of Santa Monica on PCH, you'll find 138 sycamore-shaded campsites ($16), as well as rugged cliffs, tide pools, hidden coves, and miles of hiking trails. **Malibu Creek State Park** (1925 Las Virgenes Rd., 4 mi south of U.S. 101 in Calabasas, tel. 800-533–PARK) has 60 sites in a pleasant clearing amidst the Santa Monica Mountains; fees are $14 per car (up to eight people, $5 each additional person).

### ROUGHING IT

A good place to try sleeping for free is Los Angeles International Airport (LAX): It's open 24 hours, with lots of room to stretch out among red-eye ticket holders. Consider securing your luggage in a locker ($1 a day, $2 each additional day); it has a tendency to wander off if not tied to your body. Although it's not the safest option and police do patrol, you'll see budget travelers catching z's on the beach in Santa Monica or Venice. More reliable and more comfortable than either of these options is sleeping in a car. For a $20–$40 daily rental charge (*see* Getting Around, *above*), you'll get padded, though not necessarily roomy, sleeping accommodations. Your best bet is to park near the beach on one of the canyon roads that feed PCH, north of Santa Monica. It's illegal, but the police will generally ignore you as long as you're low-key.

# Food

**Don't let drive-thrus with flashing signs or the smell of greasy** fries lure you into the fast-food trap. L.A. has a diverse, lively, and even affordable dining scene. The city's burgeoning selection of ethnic eateries reflects its large immigrant population: Thai, Peruvian, Mongolian, Japanese, Filipino, Cuban, Indian, Korean, Italian, and Mexican restaurants, among others, rub shoulders here. In addition, many cafés offer sandwiches and light, reasonably priced fare; scan *L.A. Weekly* or one of the many other free papers (*see* Basics, *above*) for news of the newest and best.

*Southern California is notorious for strip-mall eateries and fast-food joints; it is, after all, the birthplace of Carl's Jr., Jack-in-the-Box, and Taco Bell.*

If you're in L.A. for an extended period of time, consider obtaining radio station KABC's free booklet *Mostly Under $10 Dining,* written by Elmer Dills, a well-known L.A. restaurant reviewer. Send a self-addressed, double-stamped business-size envelope to: *Mostly Under $10 Dining,* Box A, Hollywood 90027. Even better is the annual *Zagat Survey* ($10) for L.A. and Southern California, which lists restaurants with ranking and commentary by L.A. residents. It's available at most bookstores.

### DOWNTOWN

Downtown L.A. has plenty to see on the cheap, but the area suffers from a dearth of inexpensive eateries. Most downtown restaurants are geared toward execs on power lunches and theatergoers with credit cards, but you'll find a few ancient hole-in-the-wall joints, as well as authentic ethnic cuisine in Little Tokyo, Koreatown, and Chinatown. In Grand Central Market, **Geraldine's Fresh Food and Juice Bar** (317 S. Broadway, btw 3rd and 4th Sts., tel. 213/626–

8394) serves 20 fresh-squeezed juices (including oddities like pomegranate, alfalfa, prune, and garlic) and inexpensive sandwiches.

➢ **UNDER $5** • **Clifton's Brookdale Cafeteria.** Clifton's dorm-style food and curious interior (a waterfall and a wallpaper redwood forest) give it cult status among young locals. The typical diner fare (hamburgers, hot dogs, etc.) at this 1930s relic generally runs less than $5. If you're really broke, try the macaroni and cheese for about $1—guaranteed to leave a greasy feeling in your mouth for at least a week. *648 S. Broadway, at 7th St., tel. 213/627–1673. Open daily 7–7. Wheelchair access.*

**Philippe the Original.** Across the street from Union Station, Philippe's (established 1908) is another beloved downtown institution, with faded photographs, communal tables, and sawdust on the floor. It's also the reputed birthplace of the French-dip sandwich (less than $4). You'll find all sorts lunching here, from bankers to beggars (and plenty of tourists). A cuppa joe is still just a dime. *1001 N. Alameda St., at Ord St., tel. 213/628–3781. Open daily 6 AM–10 PM. Wheelchair access. No credit cards.*

➢ **UNDER $10** • **Jeepney Grill.** A mini-mall filled with upscale Korean restaurants is probably not the first place you'd think of looking for Filipino food. Nonetheless, here it is—and with a gaudily painted Jeep from Manila parked right in the center of the small dining area. Traditional pork and beef barbecue dishes, many marinated in a surprisingly tasty concoction of banana sauce, honey, and spices, are $4.50 and up. *3470 W. 6th St., btw Western and Vermont Aves., tel. 213/739–2971. Open daily 8 AM–9 PM. Wheelchair access.*

**Original Pantry Café.** This classic American greasy spoon isn't the place to drag a vegetarian friend: They've been carving up about 7,200 cows a year since 1924. Pot roast ($6), stewed chicken ($6), and creamed tuna ($5) are menu staples. With red-vinyl stools, stainless-steel countertops, and employees with names like Vera, Flo, Mel, and Alice, the whole joint could qualify as a living museum. Next door, the **Pantry Bake Shoppe** is a less greasy alternative, serving decent, moderately priced sandwiches, soups, and salads. *875–877 S. Figueroa St., at 9th St., tel. 213/972–9279 (Original Café) or 213/627–6879 (Bake Shoppe). Original Café open daily 24 hrs; Bake Shoppe open weekdays 6–3, weekends 6–9. Wheelchair access.*

*The Original Pantry Café is owned by L.A. businessman and Republican mayor Richard Riordan—so if something's wrong with your order, go right to the top and ask for Dick.*

**Shabu Shabu House.** There's only one dish on the menu here, traditional Japanese *shabu shabu*. You cook the parchment-thin slices of beef yourself, in a broth of vegetables and noodles (it's a concept similar to French fondue). Though it's at the center of touristy Japanese Village, this is an authentic cultural experience. Lunchtime portions start at $5.75, dinner at $10. Wash it all down with Japanese beer ($2.50–$4.50) or sake ($3.75). *127 Japanese Village Plaza Mall, btw San Pedro and Center Sts. in Little Tokyo, tel. 213/680–3890. Open Tues.–Sun. 11:30–2:30 and 5:30–10. Wheelchair access.*

➢ **UNDER $15** • **El Cholo.** Tasty Mexican food and attentive service make this festive 67-year-old restaurant well worth the drive. Try the cheese-filled enchilada *suiza* ($8.75) or the carne asada ($10). To make your wait for a table fly by, grab a margarita ($5) at the bar. *1121 S. Western Ave., btw Pico and Olympic Blvds., tel. 213/734–2773. 2 mi west of downtown. Open Mon.–Thurs. 11–10, Fri.–Sat. 11–11, Sun. 11–9. Wheelchair access.*

**Mon Kee's Seafood Restaurant.** In the heart of Chinatown, Mon Kee's serves reasonably priced Cantonese poultry, pork, beef, and vegetable dishes ($6–$10). But this place is famed for its seafood—from exotics like sea cucumber and abalone ($12 and up) to more familiar dishes like oyster and crab ($7.25 and up). Residents from all over the city come here. *679 N. Spring St., btw Ord St. and Sunset Blvd., tel. 213/628–6717. Open Mon.–Thurs. 11:30–9:45, Fri.–Sat. 11:30–10:15. Wheelchair access.*

**Woo Lae Oak.** At this classic Korean barbecue, you grill your dinner at the table, choosing from chicken, squid, beef, pork, and other meats ($12.50 and up). Noodle dishes start at $9 and require no cooking skills. Cavernous ceilings and a fountain add a touch of grandeur. *623 S.*

*Western Ave., btw Wilshire Blvd. and 6th St., tel. 213/384–2244. Open daily 10:30–10:30. Wheelchair access.*



## HOLLYWOOD AND WEST HOLLYWOOD

Red-jacketed valet parking attendants signal a dangerously high concentration of pricey restaurants on just about every boulevard in Hollywood and West Hollywood. Fortunately, budget travelers can choose from an equally ample selection of quirky, inexpensive eateries—or succumb to one of the many cheap, greasy burger joints and taco stands. F. Scott Fitzgerald was once a regular customer at **The Musso and Frank Grill** (6667 Hollywood Blvd., at Highland Ave., tel. 213/467–7788), but don't let that tempt you into eating at "the oldest restaurant in Hollywood." Instead, pretend you *are* Fitzgerald, pass up the overpriced food (corned-beef sandwich $10, steak $20), and head straight for the cocktails. On Sundays from 8:30 to 1, pick up organic produce at the **Hollywood Farmers' Market** (Ivar Ave., btw Hollywood Blvd. and Selma Ave., tel. 213/463–3171).

➢ **UNDER $5** • For low-priced, high-viscosity chili concoctions, head to **Carney's** (8351 Sunset Blvd., at Sweetzer Ave. in West Hollywood, tel. 213/654–8300), which dispenses burgers and dogs (both less than $4) from a train caboose 11 AM–midnight (until 2 AM Friday and Saturday). The reputed birthplace of the hot-fudge sundae is **C.C. Brown's** (7007 Hollywood Blvd., at N. Orange Dr. in Hollywood, tel. 213/464–7062), open Monday–Thursday 11:30–10, Friday and Saturday 11:30 AM–midnight.

➢ **UNDER $10** • **Thai California Kitchen.** Items on the menu are labeled VERY MILD, SPICY, HOT, and NO, NO; only masochists should sample the chili sauce at each table, labeled LEAVE ME ALONE. The food is tasty and unique—try the drunkard's pasta ($5), a sweet-basil Thai dish with a slight mint flavor that allegedly counteracts drunkenness. The atmosphere is weirdly disco, with a strobe light and MTV. They also have free delivery. *414 N. La Cienega Blvd., btw Beverly Blvd. and Melrose Ave., tel. 310/652–6808. West Hollywood. Open daily 11:30–11:30 (Fri.–Sat. until 12:30). Wheelchair access.*

**The Flowering Tree.** Focusing on organic, no-artificial-anything dishes—from wheat-free waffles to sugarless chocolate mousse pie—this tiny, Formica-tabled joint features an inventive and surprisingly affordable menu. Turkey and tempeh burgers are $6, turkey-chili burritos $7.50. It's a friendly place where the staff greets longtime customers by name. *8253 Santa Monica Blvd., btw La Cienega Blvd. and N. Crescent Heights Blvd. in West Hollywood, tel. 213/654–4332. Open Mon.–Thurs. 8 AM–midnight, Fri. 8 AM–1 AM, Sat. 9 AM–1 AM, Sun. 9 AM–midnight. Wheelchair access.*

**Prizzi's Piazza.** Pick up a bottle of wine from the corner liquor store before going to Prizzi's, a charming restaurant serving giant portions of pasta (most plates under $10). They're justifiably famous for their garlic bread sticks. Sidewalk tables provide excellent people-watching opportunities, with the Scientology Center across the street and the Bourgeois Pig (*see* Cafés, *below*) nearby. *5923 Franklin Ave., btw Bronson and Tamarind Aves. in Hollywood, tel. 213/467–0168. Open daily 5:30 PM–11 PM (Fri.–Sat. until 1 AM). Wheelchair access.*

**Swingers Diner.** This '50s-style diner has recently become a trendy late-night hangout for the beautiful people of Melrose; recent sightings include cast members of *Beverly Hills 90210.* Besides teen-angst TV stars, you'll also find better-than-average diner fare (most dishes cost about $7) and smart drinks (about $6) with names like Thermite Bomb and Female Love. *8020 Beverly Blvd., at Laurel Ave. in Hollywood, tel. 213/653–5858. Open daily 6 AM–2 AM (Fri.–Sat. until 4 AM).*

**Toi on Sunset.** Toi offers Thai food as it's never been seen in Thailand. The creative menu caters to a vegetarian diet; the vegetable curries ($7) come highly recommended. The decor is definitely avant-grunge (note the giant papier-mâché cat suspended from the ceiling). Pierced and Puma-shod patrons complete the scene. Most dishes can be prepared meat-free for vegetarians. *7505½ Sunset Blvd., at Gardner St. in Hollywood, tel. 213/874–8062. Open daily 11 AM–4 AM. Wheelchair access.*

## MELROSE AND THE WILSHIRE DISTRICT

Between Santa Monica Boulevard and the Santa Monica Freeway (I–10), you'll find excellent dining options. Around trendy Melrose Avenue (btw Fairfax and La Brea Aves.), chic restaurants and sidewalk burgers-'n'-dogs stands predominate.

➢ **UNDER $5** • For the absolute best chili creations in town, come to **Pink's Famous Chili Dogs** (709 N. La Brea Ave., at Melrose Ave., tel. 213/931–4223). They've been stuffing buns daily until 2 AM (3 AM Fri.–Sat.) for over 20 years. At **Eat a Pita** (465 N. Fairfax Ave., at Rosewood Ave., tel. 213/651–0188), pick up a falafel sandwich ($2.75), a Greek salad ($2.95), or baklava ($1.50).

➢ **UNDER $10** • **California Chicken Café.** This casual restaurant is a favorite with the office lunch crowd and stray café types. Chicken—pita chicken sandwiches ($5.75–$6.75), chicken salad ($4.50–$7), and rotisserie chicken ($4 a half, $14 for a whole with side dishes)—dominates the menu, but vegetarians can choose from a few salads. *6805 Melrose Ave., btw La Brea and Highland Aves., tel. 213/935–5877. Open weekdays 11–10, Sat. noon–10. Wheelchair access. No credit cards.*

**El Coyote Café.** The only way to explain the enormous popularity of El Coyote is the abundance of cheap liquor ($2.50–$3.50). The food is almost awful, the decor a tacky Tinseltown approximation of Mexican. Nonetheless, it continually draws a crowd from every walk of life, including a fair number of celebrities. Combination plates (select from enchiladas, tacos, tamales, etc.) are $5. Weekend evenings the bar fills with clubgoers fueling up on frosted margaritas. *7312 Beverly Blvd., just west of La Brea Ave., tel. 213/939–2255. Open daily 11–10 (Fri.–Sat. until 11).*

**Flora Kitchen.** This corner café is a popular place to pick up the makings for a gourmet picnic at Hollywood Bowl (*see* Exploring L.A., *below*). It's also an ideal spot for a sit-down lunch at tables surrounded by the buckets of fresh-picked flowers from the adjacent florist. The quasi–California-cuisine menu includes sandwiches ($6–$10), salads ($5.25–$8), and sinful desserts ($4). *460 S. La Brea Ave., at 6th St., tel. 213/931–9900. Open daily 8 AM–11 PM (Fri.–Sat. until midnight). Wheelchair access.*

**Mario's Peruvian Seafood.** In an unassuming strip-mall near Paramount Studios (*see* Studios, Exploring L.A., *below*), Mario's serves excellent, generous portions of sautéed or fried red snapper, shrimp, and squid ($7–$11), with side orders of Peruvian-style rice and vegetables. *5786 Melrose Ave., at Vine St., tel. 213/466–4181. Open Mon.–Thurs. 11:30–8:30, Fri.–Sat. 11:30–10, Sun. 9:30–8:30. Wheelchair access.*

➢ **UNDER $15** • **Authentic Café.** The eclectic menu at this popular Southwestern-style eatery combines Latin American, Asian, and Middle Eastern cuisines to create some inspired dishes. Try the zesty, wood-grilled Yucatan marinated chicken breast with citrus and Mexican spices ($10) or the fresh corn tamales ($5.50). Be prepared to wait a half-hour or longer for a table in the company of a young and clean-cut, but casual, crowd. *7605 Beverly Blvd., at N. Curson Ave., tel. 213/939–4626. Open Mon.–Thurs. 11:30–10, Fri. 11:30–11, Sat. 10 AM–11 PM, Sun. 10–10. Wheelchair access.*

**Caffè Luna.** Luna keeps late hours for a good reason: There's always a crowd (including the occasional hoping-not-to-be-noticed celebrity). The menu includes a wide selection of pastas (buckwheat fettuccine, $8.75) and pizzas that feed two ($10). The best tables are on an outdoor patio designed to look like an Italian village square, but all come equipped with crayons for between-course scribbling. *7463 Melrose Ave., at Gardner St., tel. 213/655–8647. Open daily 9 AM–3 AM (Fri.–Sat. until 5 AM). Wheelchair access.*

**Louis XIV.** You could easily spend your entire dinner staring at the beautifully prepared dishes (appetizers $4–$9, entrées $8.50 and up) in front of you, without plucking up the nerve to disturb them. The darkly lit, narrow interior is impressively furnished with majestic carved chairs, gilt mirrors, and chandeliers. The waiters and much of the clientele are imported from France. The cuisine is continental, and a cool bar scene develops in late evening. *606 N. La*

*Brea Ave., at Melrose Ave., tel. 213/934–5102. Kitchen open daily 6 PM–midnight. Wheelchair access.*

## WESTWOOD AND BEVERLY HILLS

The majority of affordable restaurants in West L.A. cluster around Westwood Village and the UCLA campus. Farther south and east are a sprinkling of eclectic eateries worth the extra drive.

➢ **UNDER $5** • Walk southeast from the UCLA campus along Broxton Avenue and you'll pass almost all of Westwood's cheapest eats. **Tommy's** (970 Gayley Ave.) is a 24-hour grease shack notorious for its chili burgers (around $2). Nearby **Sepi's** (10968 Le Conte Ave., at Gayley Ave., tel. 310/208–7171) serves submarine sandwiches ($3–$5) in a frat/jock atmosphere; during Happy Hour (2–9) pitchers of beer are $2.50. **Stan's Donuts** (10948 Weyburn Ave., at Broxton Ave., tel. 310/208–1943) has recently diversified their donuts-only menu by offering all-you-can-eat Indian dishes ($5) from 11 to 11.

➢ **UNDER $10** • **The Apple Pan.** The Apple Pan's menu hasn't changed one iota since it opened in 1947—why bother, since it's widely considered the city's best burger joint? They serve up fries ($1.75) and homemade apple pie ($2.25) in addition to the much-loved burgers ($4). *10801 W. Pico Blvd., at Westwood Blvd. in Westwood, tel. 310/475–3585. Open daily 11 AM–midnight (Fri.–Sat. until 1 AM). Wheelchair access. No credit cards.*

**Mongols BBQ.** Almost all dishes are under $6 at this cafeteria-style joint, which is always mobbed by students who know a good deal when they eat one. For $5.50 you get your choice of meat, vegetables, or noodles—grilled Mongolian-style with a variety of spicy oils, and served with rice, soup, and a sesame bun. *1064 Gayley Ave., at Weyburn Ave. in Westwood, tel. 310/824–3377. Open Mon.–Fri. 11:30–10, Sat. noon–11, Sun. 4–10. Wheelchair access. No credit cards.*

**Versailles.** As you drive by, the perennial long line and delicious smells should tip you off to this local favorite. What looks like a Midwestern roadhouse is actually the purveyor of amaz-

### *So You Want to Sell Your Screenplay?*

***Or be discovered as an actor? A musician? Years ago, writers and starlets from Ohio hung around Schwab's Drugstore (made famous in the movie Sunset Boulevard), waiting to be noticed by the big movie execs who'd occasionally sweep in for aspirin. But since Schwab's no longer exists, a modern assault on the Hollywood elite requires a bit more cunning. A gross number of celebrities and behind-the-scenes power brokers frequent Morton's (8764 Melrose Ave., West Hollywood, tel. 310/276–5205) and Spago (1114 Horn Ave., at Sunset Blvd. in West Hollywood, tel. 310/652–4025). You won't be able to afford the food at these places, but you can down drinks at the bar, provided you act nonchalant and keep that dog-eared copy of Entertainment Weekly's annual "100 Most Powerful People in Hollywood" hidden. For a more low-key encounter, try Dalt's Grill (3500 Olive Blvd., in Union Bank Building, tel. 818/953–7752) in Burbank. You'll find affordable Mexican food, peons from the nearby studios, and DJs from KROQ (106.7 FM), a popular alternative radio station that broadcasts from upstairs—try slipping that long-haired dude your demo tape. If you just want to gawk at a celebrity (not be one), Patrick's Roadhouse in Santa Monica (106 Entrada Dr., at Pacific Coast Hwy., tel. 310/459–4544) offers mediocre grill food and great sightings of folks like Zsa Zsa Gabor, Sean Penn, and Arnold Schwarzenegger.***

ingly good Cuban food. The house special, garlic chicken ($7), comes with generous portions of rice, black beans, and fried plantains. *1415 S. La Cienega Blvd., south of Pico Blvd., tel. 310/289–0392. Open daily 11–10 (Fri.–Sat. until 11). Wheelchair access.*

➢ **UNDER $15** • **Crazy Fish.** The sushi chefs at Crazy Fish mold giant rolls ($4–$12) as big as footballs, filled with unusual combinations of fish, chicken teriyaki, asparagus, or Cajun spices. The names of dishes are equally strange: Crazy Rock 'n' Roll, Baked Hawaiian Volcano, or Oy Vey Salmon Sashimi. There's usually a wait for a seat in the small, brightly lit restaurant, which is extremely popular with L.A.'s sushi-mad populace. *9105 W. Olympic Blvd., at Doheny Dr. in Beverly Hills, tel. 310/550–8547. Open Mon.–Fri. 11:30–2:30 and 5:15–10:30, weekends 5:15–10:30. Wheelchair access.*

**Dive!** OK, OK, so Dive! is overpriced and designed with the tourist in mind—it's still fun. Built to resemble a giant yellow submarine, it has porthole windows offering diners views à la *20,000 Leagues Under the Sea,* and a giant TV screen that broadcasts aquarium shots. The menu, of course, is submarine sandwiches (most $8); investor Steven Spielberg's favorite is the spicy Nuclear Sicilian. *10250 Santa Monica Blvd., in Century City Shopping Mall, tel. 310/789– 8792. Open daily 11:30–11:30. Wheelchair access.*

## SANTA MONICA, VENICE, AND MALIBU

Aside from stands selling cheap and greasy food on the Venice boardwalk and the Santa Monica Pier, the dining scene in Venice and Santa Monica is quite tasteful. The restaurants that line **Main Street** in both neighborhoods range from elegantly expensive to funky and affordable; stroll south from Pico Boulevard if you've been stricken with diner's indecision.

➢ **UNDER $5** • Cheap eats in Venice are of the undistinguished, deep-fried, boardwalk variety. In Santa Monica, though, meat-eaters should head to **Jody Maroni's Sausage Kingdom** (2011 Ocean Front Walk, tel. 310/306–1995)—the self-proclaimed "home of the haut dog"—for all-natural and original variations on the frankfurter, such as the Toulouse Garlic ($4). Carnivores and herbivores alike will enjoy the tasty, thin-crust pizza ($1.80 a slice) at **Pizzarito** (1439 Third Street Promenade, Santa Monica, tel. 310/458–2838).

➢ **UNDER $10** • **Mio.** A favorite of Pepperdine University students and staff, Mio's is one of only a few affordable restaurants in Malibu. The food isn't stupendous, but it's filling and cheap, and the Italian menu is extensive. The *calzone secondo* ($8), stuffed with ricotta cheese, spinach, and mushrooms, will give you fuel to tackle the waves—the ocean is right across PCH. *22821 Pacific Coast Hwy., near Malibu Pier, tel. 310/456–3132. Open daily 11–11. Wheelchair access.*

**Rose Café.** More than a restaurant, the Rose is part of the daily routine for most Venice natives. You'll see bodybuilders and unemployed scriptwriters taking coffee at 10 AM; actors showing up for a bite around noon; and artists hunkering in for a meal after dark (a gallery displays local work). From croissants ($1.50) to chicken tacos ($7), the kitchen and bakery crank out a wide range of fresh, reasonably priced food in an open, social atmosphere. *220 Rose Ave., at Main St., tel. 310/399–0711. Open weekdays 7 AM–10 PM, Sat. 8 AM–10 PM, Sun. 8–5. Wheelchair access.*

**Van Go's Ear.** A visit to the Ear can provide unexpected entertainment: Mornings, bodybuilders fuel up before hitting Muscle Beach (*see* Exploring L.A., *below*), and café types filter in after midnight. Omelets, sandwiches, and salads range in price from $4.25 to $9. Desserts are baked in-house daily, and plenty of vegetarian dishes are available. *796 Main St., btw Rose and Brooks Aves. in Venice, tel. 310/314–0022. Open daily 24 hrs. Wheelchair access. No credit cards.*

**Wildflour Boston Pizza.** Come here if you crave traditional pizza in a city where guacamole often replaces pepperoni as the topping of choice. Voted as having the "Best Thin Pizza" by the *LA Times,* it's a great choice for a 15″ pie (cheese, $10.25) or a slice ($1.50). Inexpensive sandwiches and pastas ($4–$8) round out the menu. *2807 Main St., near Ocean Park Blvd.*

*in Santa Monica, tel. 310/392–3300. Open Mon.–Thurs. 11–10:30, Fri.– Sat. 11 AM–11:30 PM, Sun. noon–10:30. Wheelchair access.*

➢ **UNDER $15 • Nawab of India.** One of the best, most affordable Indian restaurants in L.A. is a short drive inland from Santa Monica Beach. Nawab offers tasty tandoori dishes ($8–$15), vegetarian plates ($7), and delicious curries ($10–$12); particularly good is the tandoori chicken *makhanwala* ($12). Though it's nothing fancy, the dining room is pleasantly serene. *1621 Wilshire Blvd., btw 16th and 17th Sts. in Santa Monica, tel. 310/829–1106. Open weekdays 11:30–2:30 and 5:30–10:30, Sat. noon–3 and 5:30–10:30, Sun. noon–3 and 5–10. Wheelchair access.*

## Beyond Mickey D's

***If the thought of dining at a chain restaurant makes you break out in hives, reconsider when visiting Los Angeles. A number of locally owned chains keep residents coming back for great, reliable eats.***

- ***California Pizza Kitchen. The main event is pizza ($6–$10) with unusual toppings like Peking duck, Thai chicken, guacamole, or smoked salmon. Downtown L.A.: 330 S. Hope St., btw 3rd and 4th Sts., tel. 213/626–2616. West Hollywood: 121 N. La Cienega Blvd., in Beverly Center, tel. 310/854–6555. Redondo Beach: 1815 Hawthorne Blvd., at Artesia Blvd., tel. 310/370–9931.***

- ***Chin Chin. L.A.'s hip come here for Chinese food, California-style. The Chinese chicken salad ($6) is a favorite. West Hollywood: 8618 Sunset Blvd., btw La Cienega Blvd. and Doheny Dr., tel. 310/652–1818. Marina del Rey (near Venice): 13455 Maxella Ave., at Lincoln Blvd., tel. 310/823–9999.***

- ***Gaucho Grill. This sparse but stylish nouveau Argentinean restaurant features moderately priced, garlicky grilled chicken and beef dishes (around $9), as well as sandwiches and salads. West Hollywood: 7980 Sunset Blvd., at Laurel Ave., tel. 213/656–4152. Santa Monica: 1253 Third Street Promenade, tel. 310/394–4966.***

- ***Jerry's Famous Deli. This 24-hour deli, popular after-hours with the clubbing crowd, serves massive sandwiches (around $8). Marina del Rey: 13181 Mindanao Way, at Lincoln Blvd., tel. 310/821–6626. Encino: 16650 Ventura Blvd., at Havenhurst Ave., tel. 818/906–1800.***

- ***Louise's Trattoria. Louise's dishes up sizable, reasonably priced Italian dishes with a California twist (around $9), served with freshly baked bread. There's usually outdoor seating. West Hollywood: 7505 Melrose Ave., at Gardner St., tel. 213/651–3880. Santa Monica: 1008 Montana Ave., btw 10th and 11th Sts., tel. 310/394–8888. Redondo Beach: 1430 Pacific Coast Hwy., at Ave. G, tel. 310/316–5236.***

- ***Tommy's. A 24-hour grease shack notorious for its chili burgers (around $2). Downtown L.A.: 2575 Beverly Blvd., at Rampart Blvd., tel. 213/389–9060. Santa Monica: 1900 Lincoln Blvd., at Pico Blvd., tel. 310/392–4820. Burbank: 1310 N. San Fernando Blvd., at Burbank Blvd., tel. 818/843–9150.***

## THE SOUTH BAY

Manhattan, Hermosa, and Redondo Beaches have excellent food, but you'll never find it if you stay on the Pacific Coast Highway. As you move closer to the shore, generic spots give way to locally owned kitchens offering fresh seafood and inexpensive California cuisine, particularly in health-conscious Hermosa Beach. In Manhattan Beach, the **Manhattan Beach Brewing Company** (*see* After Dark, *below*) serves up excellent entrées, such as wood-fired pizzas, burgers, and sandwiches ($5–$7.50), with their own freshly brewed beer.

➢ **UNDER $5** • In Manhattan Beach, filling and cheap burritos ($3.50) can be found 4 blocks in from the beach at the diminutive counter of **El Tarasco** (316 Rosecrans Ave., at Highland Ave., tel. 310/545–4241). Also in Manhattan Beach, **Sloopy's** (3416 N. Highland Ave., at 35th St., tel. 310/545–1373) has a garden patio, open fireplace, and tasty milkshakes, sandwiches, and salads ($3–$6). In Hermosa Beach, **Rosa's** (322 Pacific Coast Hwy., at 3rd St., tel. 310/374–9094) has served tasty, traditional Mexican dishes at reasonable prices for 25 years. Try the pork tacos *adobadas* (barbecued pork tacos, $2) or the bean-and-cheese burrito ($2).

➢ **UNDER $10** • **Dakota Café.** A local favorite, the Dakota serves up eclectic dishes among whimsically painted chairs and walls. Pig out on pasta, turkey burgers, garlic mashed potatoes, or "pizzadillas" (pizzas on a tortilla crust); all dishes are prepared with low-fat, low-salt ingredients. Dinner usually costs around $8. *316 Pier Ave., btw Pacific Coast Hwy. and Hermosa Ave. in Hermosa Beach, tel. 310/374–6577. Open weekdays 5 PM–10 PM, weekends 8 AM–10 PM. Wheelchair access.*

**Fat Face Fenner's Falloon.** More than just a local pub (though it serves that purpose quite nicely), "FFFF" has raised burger making to an art form. The half-pound Falloon Burger ($5) can be topped with 19 items, including pineapple and artichoke hearts. Weekends 9 AM–1 PM, chow down on brunch staples like eggs and home fries ($2–$4). *837 Hermosa Ave., at Pier Ave. in Hermosa Beach, tel. 310/376–0996. Open weekdays 11 AM–midnight, weekends 9 AM–midnight. Wheelchair access.*

**Good Stuff.** Home-cooked food, California-style (vegetarian burgers, massive burritos, omelets), tastes even better when served right on the beach. On weekend mornings the line for brunch can be formidable, but locals never seem to mind—it's just one more opportunity to tan. Lunch and dinner run about $5–$8, breakfast $2–$6. *1286 The Strand, at Pier Ave. in Hermosa Beach, tel. 310/374–2334. Open daily 7 AM–9 PM. Wheelchair access.*

**Ocean View Café.** A cross between a coffeehouse and a restaurant, the Ocean View serves up excellent salads and sandwiches ($4–$6), light breakfasts ($3–$4), and wonderful espresso drinks. Try the soup du jour with a baguette ($2) and freshly squeezed orange juice. Both the view of the Pacific from the outdoor patio and the staff's mellow attitude are big bonuses. *229 13th St., off Highland Ave. in Manhattan Beach, tel. 310/545–6770. Open Mon. 11–5, Tues.–Sun. 10–8:30. Wheelchair access. No credit cards.*

**Ragin' Cajun Café.** Mobbed by visitors and locals alike, this tiny restaurant dishes up authentic Cajun food—crawfish, catfish, gumbo, and jambalaya—cooked by a real Louisiana native. Menus are printed on brown paper bags. Entrées cost about $7–$9. *422 Pier Ave., btw Pacific Coast Hwy. and Hermosa Ave. in Hermosa Beach, tel. 310/376–7878. Open Tues.–Fri. 11–2 and 5:30–9:30, weekends 5:30 PM–9:30 PM. Wheelchair access.*

**The Spot.** The proprietors insist that you don't need to be a vegetarian to enjoy this very popular health-food/vegetarian restaurant, and they're right. Everything—from fresh-baked bread to soups, lasagna, and Mexican food—is made in-house without refined sugar or animal products, using purified water. Entrées cost about $8. *110 2nd St., at Hermosa Ave. in Hermosa Beach, tel. 310/376–2355. Redondo Beach location: Green at the Beach, 247 Avenida del Norte, at Via El Prado, tel. 310/316–9451. Both open daily 11–10. Wheelchair access. No credit cards.*

➢ **UNDER $15** • **Killer Shrimp.** They only serve one dish here, but they do it with gusto. For $11 you can gorge yourself on fresh, never frozen, Louisiana shrimp, with a hunk of bread to soak up the spicy sauce. *403 N. Pacific Coast Hwy., btw Beryl and Carnelian Sts. in Redondo Beach, tel. 310/798–0008. Open daily 11:30–10 (Fri.–Sat. until 11). Wheelchair access.*



# Cafés

Los Angeles has recently been Seattle-ized: It now bristles with quirkily decorated coffee bars offering a variety of entertainment to patrons quaffing espresso drinks strong enough to take lacquer off a wall. But as you might expect, few Angelenos are the type to fret over a volume of existentialist poetry. Instead, the café has been woven nicely into the fabric of the city's nightlife, a hip addition to clubbing in the era of Alcoholics Anonymous. Many cafés stay open until 4 AM, offering live music and poetry readings as well as backgammon boards, magazines, used paperbacks, and free local weeklies. And they generally don't give a damn how long you sit on that overstuffed couch. *Caffeine,* the café scene's own (free) magazine, prints poetry, art, fiction, and the praise of coffeehouses. Pick it up at any café. Prices for coffee drinks are fairly uniform; unless specified below, you'll pay $1–$3, depending on size, strength, and the number of frills (whipped cream, sprinkles, etc.).

**HOLLYWOOD AND WEST HOLLYWOOD** **All-Star Theatre Café and Speakeasy.** Located in the Hollywood Knickerbocker Hotel, the self-proclaimed "ultimate 1920s coffeehouse" has comfortably overstuffed club chairs and a menu of sandwiches and salads ($4–$6). *1714 N. Ivar Ave., ½ block north of Sunset Blvd. in Hollywood, tel. 213/962–8898. Open daily 7 PM–2 AM (Fri.–Sat. until 3 AM).*

*Old movies are shown for free at around 10 PM nightly at the All-Star Theatre Café and Speakeasy in Hollywood.*

**The Bourgeois Pig.** With cool blue lights illuminating the erotic-political paintings on the walls, and thrift store-clad patrons at the pool table, this is an achingly hip caffeine outlet. Despite the lack of alcohol, it's got a bar-like social quality, and its denizens are engaging in their own studied way. *5931 Franklin Ave., at Beachwood Dr. in Hollywood, tel. 213/962–6366. Open weekdays noon–2 AM, weekends 9 AM–2 AM. Wheelchair access.*

**Living Room Café.** Furnished with gold-painted mirrors and velvet thrift-shop chairs, the Living Room is the nighttime headquarters of L.A.'s poseur youth. Besides espresso, they have an extensive and appetizing menu of pizzas, pastas, and sandwiches (all about $8) and various breakfast items ($4–$7). *112 S. La Brea Ave., at 1st St. in West Hollywood, tel. 213/933–2933. Open daily 9 AM–midnight. Wheelchair access.*

**The Onyx.** This art gallery-cum-café is where L.A.'s small population of the unaffected gather to play card games with friends, write dissertations on laptop computers, or improvise on the piano. Poetry readings, live music, and comedy happen sporadically. The café serves veggie lasagna ($3.75) and a few daily specials, as well as desserts. *1804 N. Vermont Ave., btw Franklin Ave. and Hollywood Blvd. in East Hollywood, no phone. Open daily 9 AM–3 AM (Fri.–Sat. until 4 AM).*

**MELROSE AND WILSHIRE DISTRICT** **Betelgeuse.** With casually stylish chairs and couches, dim lighting, and a menu heavy on crêpes ($4–$7), Betelgeuse is the embodiment of Melrose Avenue cool. Most evenings there's some sort of live music (blues, acoustic guitar, rock), with a cover of around $5. *7160 Melrose Ave., 1 block west of La Brea Ave., tel. 213/936–0165. Open daily noon–2 AM (Sun. until midnight). Wheelchair access.*

**Highland Grounds.** Don't let the graffiti-covered exterior frighten you: This café is mellow and friendly, with excellent breakfasts (omelets and pancakes, $3–$6), and lunch and dinner items available after 11 AM. Come nightfall, it transforms into a demi-club, with art openings, open-mike poetry, and live music. There's an occasional small cover charge for some entertainment. *742 N. Highland Blvd., ½ block north of Melrose Ave., tel. 213/466–1507. Open Mon. 9 AM–6 PM, Tues.–Thurs. 9 AM–12:30 AM, Fri.–Sat. 9 AM–1 AM, Sun. 10 AM–9 PM. Wheelchair access.*

**Insomnia Café.** This velvet-couch-and-chandelier haunt is open till the wee hours. There's a small selection of pizzas and sandwiches ($2–$6), and the Thai iced tea ($2.50–$3.50) is heavenly. It's a friendly, social café, where the pick-up activity never gets out of hand. *7286 Beverly Blvd., at Poinsettia Pl., tel. 213/931–4943. Open daily 9 AM–4 AM. Wheelchair access.*

**Lou De Cris Café.** Set apart from most of the Melrose Avenue madness, this is the perfect place to rest and refuel after a day's window shopping, with comfy couches and messy stacks of recent magazines. Wednesdays at 8 PM the café hosts free screenings of original short films. Sandwiches and other snacks are about $6. *8164 Melrose Ave., btw Crescent Heights and La Cienega Blvds., tel. 213/655–3960. Open daily 8 AM–7 PM. Wheelchair access.*

**SANTA MONICA AND VENICE** **Café Collage.** Come here to get away from the Venice Beach circus. Modernist interpretations of renaissance paintings hang on the terra cotta walls, and wrought iron furnishings add to the funky atmosphere. There's the regular café cuisine as well as original espresso drinks like the Palermo (chocolate, espresso, orange peel, and nutmeg, $3.25). *1518 Pacific Ave., at Windward Ave. in Venice, tel. 310/399–0632. Open daily 7 AM–8:30 PM (Fri.–Sat. until 9 PM). Wheelchair access.*

**Congo Square.** In addition to good coffee, dense brownies, and tasty bagel sandwiches, Congo Square is also noted for its weekend entertainment. Past events have included everything from a "Clips Party," where you get your head shaved for free, to community forums on homelessness. *1238 Third Street Promenade, Santa Monica, tel. 310/395–5606. Open daily 8 AM–1 AM (Fri.–Sat. until 2 AM). Wheelchair access.*

**Lulu's Alibi.** Small and cheerful, Lulu's is a popular meeting place for those catching a show at the nearby Nuart Theater (*see* After Dark, *below*). Stop by for a poetry reading Sunday at 8:30 PM or come weekdays 5–7 for Happy Hour, when prices are slashed by half on caffeinated drinks. Brazilian appetizers and entrées ($2–$9) dominate the food menu. *1640 Sawtelle Blvd., at Santa Monica Blvd. in Santa Monica, tel. 310/479–6007. Open Mon.–Thurs. 10 AM–3 AM, Fri. 10 AM–4 AM, Sat. 9 AM–4 AM, Sun. 9 AM–1 AM. Wheelchair access.*

**COFFEE TALK:**

*Sizes aren't small or large, but short, tall, and grande. If you want decaf, ask for unleaded; if you like skim milk, call it a skinny; and if you want your drink to go, request it on a leash or with wings.*

**Newsroom Espresso Café.** Only at Newsroom can you catch CNN updates while sipping Bolt Coke ($2.25), a mix of espresso and cola. In other words, this is a habitat for tightly wired media junkies. Normal, well-adjusted types will enjoy the large magazine rack and tasty range of entrées, including tandoori chicken and pesto pizza (each about $6). *530 Wilshire Blvd., at 6th St. in Santa Monica, tel. 310/319–9100. Open Mon.–Sat. 8 AM–10 PM, Sun. 9–3. Wheelchair access.*

**Novel Café.** This is where the literati of Venice and Santa Monica congregate. Elegant, aging couches and floor-to-ceiling shelves of used hardbacks give the café/bookstore a clubby feel. Nosh on inexpensive soups, salads, and sandwiches while attempting to plow through Joyce or Faulkner. *212 Pier Ave., at Main St. in Santa Monica, tel. 310/396–8566. Open Mon.–Thurs. 7 AM–1 AM, Fri. 7 AM–2 AM, Sat. 7:30 AM–2 AM, Sun. 7:30 AM–1 AM. Wheelchair access.*

**Wednesday's House.** Its proximity to the Santa Monica Museum of Art (*see* Exploring L.A., *below*) makes this the perfect place to do the post-gallery java and art-crit thing. The outlandish collection of overstuffed furniture and the display of velvet Elvis paintings could only be the work of a gifted postmodernist decorator. On some evenings, musical friends of the owner drop by to jam. *2409 Main St., at Hollister St. in Santa Monica, tel. 310/452–4486. Open daily 8 AM–2 AM (sometimes later Fri.–Sat.). Wheelchair access.*

**THE SOUTH BAY** **Java Man.** Two blocks from the beach, this place has a homey feel—perhaps because it used to be somebody's house. It's also an art gallery, displaying works by local artists. Salads and sandwiches are about $6. *157 Pier Ave., at Manhattan Ave. in Hermosa Beach, tel. 310/379–7209. Open daily 7 AM–midnight (Fri.–Sat. until 1 AM).*

# Exploring L.A.

**Los Angeles has long been** characterized as "19 suburbs in search of a metropolis." One of the reasons this tag has stuck is that sights are incredibly spread out and public transit is slow and tedious. Unless you rent a car (*see* Getting Around, *above*) to drive between communities, you'll feel like a prisoner of the MTA bus system. There's plenty to see within certain neighborhoods, though, so if you have the time, don't try to tackle more than one neighborhood a day—unless sweating it out on the freeway is your idea of the L.A. experience.

## DOWNTOWN

To most, it's shocking to learn that somewhere amid L.A.'s strip-malls and tract houses there lurks a real downtown. But yes, the city's got it all: skyscrapers and sidewalk shoeshine stands, one-way streets bracketed by brass-and-marble shopping complexes, taxis, gaping potholes, and $5-an-hour parking garages. You'll probably want to explore downtown's attractions on foot or by DASH (*see* Getting Around, *above*). If the day is sunny and warm, consider picnicking in recently renovated **Pershing Square** (Hill St., btw 5th and 6th Sts.). Inexpensive parking lots ($2–$3.50 daily) can be found in the blocks around 9th Street, between Main and San Pedro streets on the fringes of downtown.

**BRADBURY BUILDING** Constructed in 1893, the Bradbury Building was designed by an obscure draftsman named George Wyman as a textile factory for mining millionaire Lewis Bradbury. Wyman created a masterpiece of light and form, later made famous by the films *Bladerunner* and *Citizen Kane.* The building was majestically restored to its original condition in 1991, and law offices replaced the sweatshops long ago. During business hours, visitors can enter the lobby to marvel at the glowing woodwork, wrought-iron open-cage elevators, and fifth-story glass roof. *304 S. Broadway, btw 3rd and 4th Sts., tel. 213/626–1893. Across from Grand Central Market; DASH Route D. Building open weekdays 9–5.*

**CHILDREN'S MUSEUM** At this colorful downtown museum, kids—and adults who think like kids—can construct forts and tunnels with giant Velcro cushions, create music in a professionally equipped recording studio, animate their own drawings, or learn more about recycling. Interactive entertainment and exhibits on history and multiculturalism abound. *310 N. Main St., in L.A. Mall, tel. 213/687–8800. Just south of U.S. 101; DASH Route B or D. Admission: $5. Open weekends 10–5 year-round; also Tues.–Fri. 9:15–1 in winter with advance prepaid reservations, Tues.–Fri. 11:30–5 in summer.*

**CHINATOWN** L.A.'s Chinatown, bordered by Yale, Bernard, Spring, and Ord streets, is actually in its second incarnation; much of the original neighborhood was razed in 1934 to make way for Union Station (*see below*). Today's small Chinese enclave is a 5-minute walk from downtown, north of U.S. 101—or an even shorter hop on DASH Route B. Along North Broadway you'll encounter Buddhist temples fragrant with burning incense; acupuncturists; vendors hawking live poultry and fish; and pungent shops purveying rare teas and dried herbs. Step into the **Teo Chow Association** (649 N. Broadway, at Ord St.), a temple and community organization, to make an offering of incense or fruit to one of the enigmatic Chinese idols. If you seek a meal, visit Mon Kee's (*see* Food, *above*). During February, Chinese New Year (*see* Festivals, *below*) culminates with a parade of dancing dragons and fireworks.

*Recently reopened after a seven-year hiatus forced by a devastating fire, the Los Angeles Public Library (630 W. 5th St., tel. 213/228–7000) houses exquisite murals depicting the founding of Los Angeles, as well as the third-largest library collection in the United States.*

**CITY HALL** Although the 1928 Los Angeles City Hall is now dwarfed by surrounding skyscrapers, as an icon it stands larger than life. Its gracious form contrasts markedly with the dreary architecture of most civic buildings. TV addicts have seen the building in many guises—it served a stint as the Daily Planet office in the *Superman* TV series and stood in for the Vatican in the TV movie *The Thorn Birds.* Though the observation area (27th–29th floors) is closed indefinitely for seismic

# Downtown Los Angeles

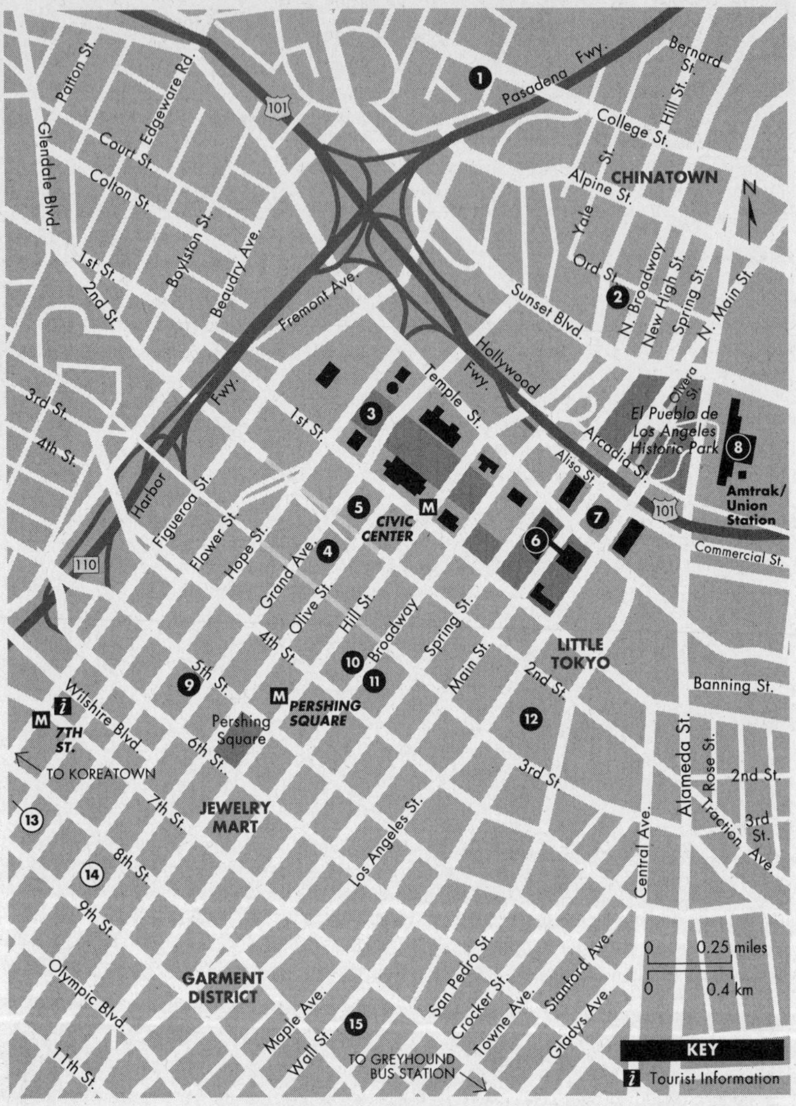


**Sights ●**

Bradbury Building, **11**

Children's Museum, **7**

City Hall, **6**

Dodger Stadium, **1**

Flower Mart, **15**

Grand Central, **10**

Japanese Village Plaza, **12**

Los Angeles Public Library, **9**

Museum of Contemporary Art, **4**

Music Center, **3**

Temporary Contemporary, **5**

Teo Chow Association, **2**

Union Station, **8**

**Lodging ○**

Hotel Stillwell, **14**

Orchid Hotel, **13**

renovation, you can still get a good look at the interior—and a peek inside the mayor's office (3rd floor)—by taking a free guided tour. The area around this grand pillar of justice tends to be iffy, especially after dark. Go figure. *200 N. Spring St., btw Temple and W. 1st Sts., tel. 213/485–4423. DASH Route A, B, or D. Free tours weekdays 10 AM and 11 AM; reserve at least 2–3 days in advance.*



**FLOWER MART** Each day before dawn, florists make a pilgrimage to this block-long series of fragrant shops and stalls, crowded into several large buildings on Wall Street (btw 7th and 8th Sts.). From 9 AM on, early risers jostle with wholesalers and florists to pick out enormous bouquets of every imaginable flower at wholesale prices. Most stalls close down by about 11 AM, with slightly longer hours on Wednesdays and Fridays.

**GARMENT DISTRICT** A slew of cut-rate clothing stores is wedged into the blocks between Santee Street, Maple Avenue, 12th Street and Pico Boulevard—though looking for stylish bargains can be akin to seeking the pony in the proverbial pile of manure. The six-floor **Cooper Building** (860 S. Los Angeles St., at 9th St., tel. 213/622–1139), open Monday–Saturday 9:30–5:30 and Sunday 11–5, is filled with ugly, overpriced department store leftovers, including garb by Calvin Klein and DKNY, but the prices don't promote impulse buying. It's at the smaller shops, like **Fashion Mart** (930 S. Santee St. #2, tel. 213/689–8700) and **Comedy Club** (930 S. Santee St. #7, tel. 213/891–9311) that you'll find cheap and decent stuff. Most stores close on Sundays.

**GRAND CENTRAL MARKET** Wander through this maze of produce and fishmongers' stalls, butcher shops, bakeries, and ethnic fast-food stands, and you'll rub elbows with Mexican housewives, chefs from ritzy Santa Monica restaurants, and just about every other kind of Angeleno imaginable. Recently renovated, the warehouse-size market has sawdust floors and a European feel. *317 S. Broadway, btw 3rd and 4th Sts., tel. 213/624–2378. DASH Route D. Open Mon.–Sat. 9–6, Sun. 10–5.*

**JEWELRY MART** Bounded by 5th and 8th streets and Spring and Olive streets, this cluster of shops is a must for anyone with a passion for wholesale and discounted jewelry (and credit enough to indulge). In addition to marked-down Cartier baubles and Rolex watches, this urban gold mine has wafer-thin gold-leaf pendants ($5) and a brilliant selection of loose gemstones.

**KOREATOWN** The boundaries of this Korean community just west of downtown are loosely defined by Wilshire Boulevard to the north and Pico Boulevard to the south. Because it's spread over so many blocks, Koreatown can be difficult to explore on foot. You'll want to start your visit at the **Korean Cultural Center** (5505 Wilshire Blvd., at Dunsmuir Ave., tel. 213/936–7141), host to an art gallery and museum. Exhibits range from a room furnished in the style of the ancient Choson Dynasty to a video installation by contemporary Korean artist Nam June Paik. The staff of the cultural center can provide tips for further exploration of the neighborhood. For authentic cuisine, head farther north to Woo Lae Oak (*see* Food, *above*), which serves reasonably priced classic Korean barbecue that you grill yourself.

**LITTLE TOKYO** Your first reaction to Little Tokyo (bordered by Temple, Los Angeles, 3rd, and Alameda Sts., and served by DASH Route A) may be disappointment. An overwhelming number of touristy gift shops tout pricey watches and plastic souvenirs. But you can look beyond these to find authentic shades of Japan. The **Japanese Village Plaza** (tel. 213/620–8861), on 1st and 2nd streets between San Pedro Street and Central Avenue, is the center of festivities such as *Hanamatsuri* (Buddha's Birthday), held the first weekend of April; *Tanabata* (Festival of Lovers), held the second weekend of July; and the Cherry Blossom Festival, which takes place the first weekend of May. When you get hungry, visit the plaza's Shabu Shabu House (*see* Food, *above*). Located on the plaza is the **Koyosan Buddhist Temple** (342 E. 1st St., at Central Ave., tel. 213/624–1267), one of L.A.'s most beautiful houses of worship; there's an English-language service open to the public on Sunday mornings at 10. Nearby, at the new **Japanese American National Museum** (369 E. 1st St., at Central Ave., tel. 213/625–0414), issues such as immigration and wartime internment are explored through film and photographs. Admission is $4 (students $3); the museum is open Tuesday–Thursday and Saturday–Sunday 10–5, Friday 11–8.

**MUSEUM OF CONTEMPORARY ART** The stark interior of MOCA is a startling contrast to the urban clutter of the outside world. The elegant red sandstone building—designed by Japanese architect Arata Isozaki—displays works from the museum's permanent collection, including paintings by abstract expressionists Mark Rothko and Jackson Pollock, along with special installations of contemporary pieces. A separate annex, the **Temporary Contemporary** (152 N. Central Ave.), had been scheduled for abandonment when MOCA was completed in 1986, but its popularity forced museum officials to reconsider. A free shuttle runs between the two buildings. *250 S. Grand Ave., at 3rd St., tel. 213/626–6222. DASH Route B. Admission: $6, $4 students; free Thurs. after 5 PM. Open Tues.–Sun. 11–5 (Thurs. until 8).*

**MUSIC CENTER** One of three performance spaces at the Music Center is the **Dorothy Chandler Pavilion** (named for the *L.A. Times* publisher's widow, who helped finance it), which plays host to the annual Academy Awards. For information on concert, ballet, and opera tickets at the center, *see* After Dark, *below. Grand Ave., at 1st St., tel. 213/972–7211. DASH Route B. Free tours available; call for schedule.*

**OLVERA STREET** On cobblestone, pedestrian-only **Olvera Street,** you'll find carts groaning with hand-tooled leather goods and open-air restaurants serving delicious *churros* (Mexican donuts), *carne asada* (grilled meat, usually on a tortilla with beans), and frosty margaritas. The street is part of **El Pueblo de Los Angeles Historic Park,** a collection of low wooden buildings that made up the original city, circa 1800. At around noon daily, the historic plaza becomes a stage for folkloric and Aztec dancers. The park also plays host to numerous special festivals (*see below*), including the springtime Blessing of the Animals, *Cinco de Mayo* (5th of May), and *Día de los Muertos* (Day of the Dead) in November. After catering to your worst tourist tendencies, visit the **Avila Adobe** on the east side of Olvera Street. Built in 1818, it's the oldest house in Los Angeles. The carefully restored rooms are open to the public Tuesday–Saturday 10–5, free of charge. The park is bordered by Alameda, Arcadia, Spring, and Macy streets; it's one block east of Union Station, where most MTA buses stop. *Visitor center: Sepulveda House, 622 N. Main St., tel. 213/628–1274. DASH Route B or D. Open Mon.–Sat. 10–3. Free park tours hourly Tues.–Sat. 10–1; call for reservations.*

*Philippe's (see Food, above), a wonderful ancient lunch counter across from Union Station, is filled with faded photos of people long since dead and buildings long since demolished. It's the perfect place to ponder where you've been and where you'll go, while slowly chewing a French-dip sandwich.*

**UNION STATION** Union Station and the Union Pacific Railroad helped transform Los Angeles from an underpopulated farming community into a bustling metropolis in the era before the superhighway. An eclectic mix of Spanish colonial, Southwestern, and art-deco styles, the station is also the best example of 1940s architecture in Los Angeles—a rare combination of marble floors, wrought-iron gas lamps, wood paneling, and engraved ceilings. It's now an Amtrak depot, linked with regional and local mass-transit lines. *800 N. Alameda St., north of U.S. 101. DASH Route B or D.*

## SOUTH CENTRAL L.A.

Most people's preconceptions about South Central, the area southwest of downtown L.A., involve images of gang warfare and riots. To be sure, gangs do operate here, though their main targets are usually other gangs. Generally, the middle-class neighborhoods north of **Slauson Avenue,** where most of South Central's attractions lie, are less troubled by urban violence than the areas to the south. Among the surprising sights here are the exclusive, private University of Southern California and Exposition Park, home to several museums and sporting stadiums. If you visit this area during the day you'll be relatively safe, but it's hard not to be disconcerted by the rampant evidence of poverty, from boarded-up delis to exhausted and sagging apartment complexes. You'll need to look closely for the small signs of hope—a flower-filled front yard or a carefully swept and painted corner store—that represent the area's untapped possibilities.

**EXPOSITION PARK** Created in 1880, Exposition Park is beginning to show signs of age and exhaustion (it hosted Olympic festivities in 1932 and 1984), but it's worth a visit nonetheless. Take a stroll in the 14-acre **Sunken Rose Garden** before tackling one of the park's fascinating museums. The free **Museum of Science and Industry** (700 State Dr., tel. 213/744–7400), open daily 10–5, houses everything from an authentic space capsule and fighter planes to hands-on computers and robots. At the museum's **IMAX Theatre** (tel. 213/744–2014) a larger-than-life movie experience is $6, $4.75 for students. The **Museum of Natural History** (900 Exposition Blvd., tel. 213/744–DINO), open Tuesday–Sunday 10–5, contains gems and minerals, fossils, and the obligatory stuffed mammals in lifelike poses. Admission is $6 ($3.50 students) and is free the first Tuesday of the month. The free **California Afro-American Museum** (600 State Dr., tel. 213/744–7432) explores the history, art, and culture of black people in the United States. Stop by Tuesday–Sunday 10–5. Sports fans will want to snap a few photos of the Olympic torch atop the **Coliseum.** The adjacent **Sports Arena,** like the Coliseum, is home to some pro sports teams (*see* Outdoor Activities, *below*).

**LEIMERT PARK** You might easily overlook this tiny triangle of shops and greenery in a middle-class community about a mile north of Slauson Avenue. But make the effort to find it. Leimert Park (cnr Crenshaw Blvd. and Vernon Ave.) is emerging as an oasis of solid African American culture amid the blight of South Central's boarded-up storefronts. The shops on 43rd Place and Degnar Boulevard feature African clothing, art, jewelry, and food. Stop by **5th Street Dick's Coffee Company** (3347½ W. 43rd Pl., tel. 213/296–3970) for a powerful cup of Ethiopian coffee ($3) and some of the best jazz in L.A., as well as poetry, drama, and rap. 5th Street Dick's is open Monday–Thursday 4 PM–2 AM, Friday 4 PM–5 AM, Saturday 1 PM–5 AM, and Sunday 1 PM–4 AM. Next door is **Final Vinyl** (tel. 213/296–1372), which sells old jazz, soul, and blues records, as well as contemporary CDs. The shoppers and the men playing dominoes in Leimert Park seem to go out of their way to be friendly, perhaps in an attempt to counteract South Central's menacing reputation. During the week after Christmas, Leimert Park is the site of the annual **Kwanzaa Festival** (*see* Festivals, *below*). To reach the park, take Crenshaw Boulevard south from I–10.

## *The Fire This Time*

***Government-sanctioned segregation ended in 1968 with the passage of the Civil Rights Act, but issues of race, ethnicity, and economics have lent the city of Los Angeles a segregated geography. In contrast to other major American cities like San Francisco and New York, Los Angeles's neighborhoods are fiercely stratified, and residents of various communities rarely do more than cross paths on their way to somewhere else. This separatist lifestyle exploded in the faces of Angelenos in April 1992, when devastating riots followed the acquittal of four white officers charged in the videotaped beating of black motorist Rodney King. While "justice" was delivered in 1993, when two of the acquitted officers finally received prison terms for violating King's civil rights, real restitution has yet to be seen by the 20,000 residents who lost jobs and businesses to the flames.***

***Four years later, the Rodney King riots have taken their place in the history books next to the riots that shook Watts in 1965. But while empty federal promises were able to extinguish fires in Watts, South Central has grown disillusioned with government "solutions." Instead, riot-engendered grassroots organizations are initiating their own revitalization programs. GED preparation courses, employment training, small business loans, job placement programs, and alliances with other economically depressed ethnic communities have recently been implemented in an attempt to strengthen the economy from the ground up.***

**UNIVERSITY OF SOUTHERN CALIFORNIA** Founded in 1880, USC (dubbed the "University of Spoiled Children" by rivals) is the West Coast's oldest major private college. Tree-shaded Spanish-style and contemporary brick buildings provide the backdrop for this enclave of wealth and white privilege—a gated and fenced village some 27,000 students strong—in a sea of relative poverty. The film school has graduated the likes of George Lucas, Ron Howard, and John Singleton, and the football team, the Trojans, once starred a young, less troubled O.J. Simpson. A stroll across campus can be rewarding for movie buffs: *The Graduate, The Hunchback of Notre Dame,* and parts of *Forrest Gump* were all shot here. Worthwhile stops include the beautiful main lobby and reading room of **Doheny Memorial Library,** the oddly shaped **Shrine Auditorium** (where Michael Jackson's hair caught fire during the making of a Pepsi commercial), and tiny clapboard **Widney Hall,** constructed in the early 1880s. The main gathering place for students is the quad, over which a statue of Tommy Trojan stands guard. Maps are available at all eight entrance gates. *Campus info: tel. 213/740–2311. From I–110, exit at Exposition Blvd. Enter campus at Gate 1 on Exposition Blvd., or turn right on Figueroa St. and enter at Gate 2. Free 1-hour walking tours year-round weekdays 10–2; for reservations call Alumni House (tel. 213/740–2300).*

**WATTS TOWERS** A masterpiece of Los Angeles folk art, the Watts Towers were constructed by Italian immigrant Simon Rodia entirely of discarded objects he collected between 1921 and 1954. The tallest of the three main structures stands an impressive 99½ feet tall. Art historians compare the steel and wire towers (embedded with colorful glass shards) to Gaudí's Barcelona cathedrals, but to the average traveler the Watts Towers are simply a striking and imaginative work looming over South Central L.A. with peculiar majesty. Despite several private and city-led efforts to raze them, the structures now stand in a state historic park. This is not a place you want to linger after dark. *1765 E. 107th St., at Graham Ave., tel. 213/847–4646. Take I–110 to I–105 east; exit north at S. Central Ave., turn right onto 108th St., left onto Graham Ave. Tours ($1) weekends 10–4.*

*Built of scrap iron, abandoned bedsteads, and shards of bottles and seashells, Watts Towers' strange spires are a symbol of hope in South Central L.A.—of something meaningful made from seemingly useless debris.*

## HOLLYWOOD

Modern Tinseltown came from inauspicious beginnings: The city's first movie was filmed in a barn at the corner of Sunset Boulevard and Gower Street in 1911. At the time, the area was called Hollywoodland, and most residents made a living farming fruit. Forty years later, Hollywood had shed the cumbersome last four letters of its name and emerged as the Movie Capital of the World—and an enviable playground for the rich and infamous. In the decades since, its star has dimmed slightly, as studio after studio has slipped over the hills to cheaper real estate in Burbank. People around the globe still dream of a glamorous Hollywood, and wanna-be starlets still flock to Tinseltown hoping to trade their pasts for more promising futures. But in reality, the only stars you'll see here are those embedded in the sidewalk along Hollywood Boulevard, which is littered with stumbling old men and discarded cigarette butts.

Just the same, this soiled and struggling area is full of hidden treasures. A few blocks from Hollywood Boulevard, innovative basement theater companies thrive in tight-knit ethnic enclaves. The eternal pimp-vs.-cop struggle of Hollywood Boulevard seems finally to have been won by the latter, and streets once dominated by boarded-up buildings are slowly being infiltrated by the *très chic* and their attendant string of hip cafés and taverns. The newly arrived naïf should still exercise caution, but don't be afraid to check out the experimental theaters on Santa Monica Boulevard (*see* After Dark, *below*) or explore the emerging, laid-back social scene on Franklin and North Vermont avenues in East Hollywood (*see below*).

To make a sweep through the obligatory tourist sights, take MTA Bus 1 along Hollywood Boulevard or park in one of the residential areas around Hollywood Boulevard and Highland Avenue (check signs first to see if it's legal; some areas are restricted to vehicles with residential permits). The bronze stars embedded in the pavement of Hollywood Boulevard will be your first clue that you've broached the much-ballyhooed **Hollywood Walk of Fame**—if the tour buses and snap-happy retirees didn't already give it away. You can easily do the walk in an afternoon.

# Hollywood

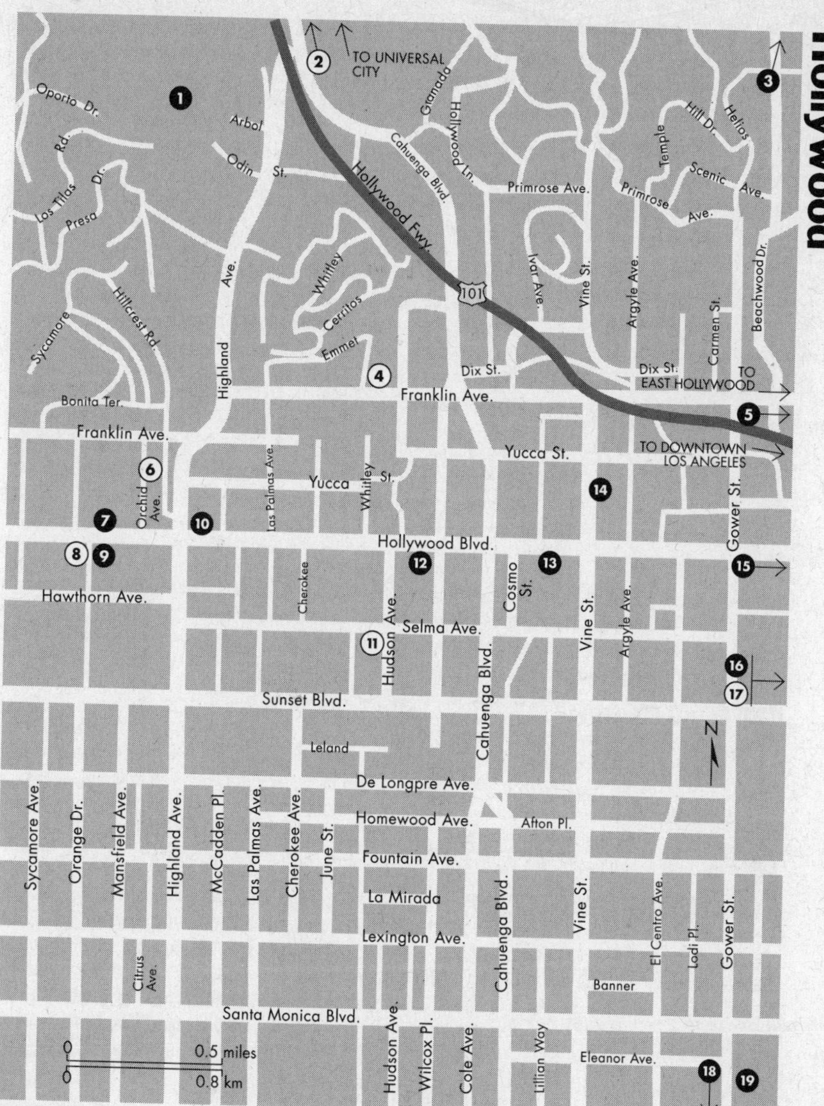


**Sights ●**

Capitol Records Building, **14**

Eco-Home, **5**

Fox Televison Studios, **16**

Frederick's of Hollywood, **12**

Hollyhock House, **15**

Hollywood Bowl, **1**

Hollywood Memorial Park Cemetery, **19**

Hollywood Sign, **3**

Hollywood Walk of Fame, **13**

Hollywood Wax Museum, **10**

Mann's Chinese Theater, **7**

Motion Picture Coordination Office, **9**

Paramount Studios, **18**

**Lodging ○**

Banana Bungalow Hotel and Hostel, **2**

Hollywood International Hostel, **4**

Hollywood Towne House Motel, **17**

Hollywood Wilshire YMCA International Hostel, **11**

Liberty Hotel, **6**

Roosevelt Hotel, **8**

Then head for the Hollywood Hills: If you have a map and some patience, you may stumble across a sliver of park northeast of the **Upper Hollywood Reservoir,** which offers a fantastic view of the legendary HOLLYWOOD sign. You'll also see some of L.A.'s architectural jewels, including homes designed by Frank Lloyd Wright, R. M. Schindler, and Richard Neutra.

**HOLLYWOOD BOWL** The Hollywood Bowl, a striking white band shell nestled in the Hollywood foothills, is the summer home of the **Los Angeles Philharmonic** and the **Hollywood Bowl Orchestra.** On clear summer nights, thousands of picnic-toting Angelenos head here for performances of classical, jazz, and contemporary music. Thirteen picnic areas surround the Bowl, and they get crowded; arrive an hour or two before the performance to claim a spot. You can pick up any supplies you forgot at the Bowl's concession stands: hot dogs, beer, pesto chicken, wine, whatever—though you'll pay for the convenience. Seat prices vary by type of performance and proximity, usually ranging from about $1 (the stage looks awfully small from here) to about $25. You can catch a rehearsal for free Tuesday–Friday 9:30–noon. Call ahead—some groups don't rehearse. *2301 N. Highland Ave., ¾ mi north of Hollywood Blvd., tel. 213/850–2000 for performance and Bowlexpress info. Bowlexpress Park & Ride service ($2.50 round-trip) from 15 locations in L.A. County; or MTA Bus 212 or 420. Performances June–Sept., Tues.–Sun.*

*Be it pâté and California chardonnay or Doritos and Schlitz, pre-performance picnicking has become a tradition among Hollywood Bowl attendees. So crunch all you want—just don't do it during the violin solo.*

Adjacent to the Bowl is the **Hollywood Bowl Museum,** which houses a permanent collection of photos and documents charting the history of the structure, as well as exhibits about guest composers and special performances. The museum is closed for remodeling until summer 1996. *Tel. 213/850–2058. Admission free. Open Tues.–Sat. 10–4 (until 8:30 concert nights).*

**MOTION PICTURE COORDINATION OFFICE** This is an invaluable resource if you're determined to see at least one celebrity (though you may have to settle for the cast and crew of a low-budget HBO thriller). Pick up the office's free "shoot sheet," which describes what's being filmed around town each day: It lists the kind of shoot (film, TV, music video, still photography), who's involved, and when and where it's happening. Once you find the set you may be allowed a closer inspection—perhaps even an autograph—if you remain polite and free of hysterics. *6922 Hollywood Blvd., Room 602, tel. 213/485–5324. Open weekdays 8–6.*

**MANN'S CHINESE THEATER** Built in 1927 as an outlandish approximation of a Chinese pagoda, Mann's Chinese is easily the most garish structure on Hollywood Boulevard. During the glorious '30s, opening nights drew enormous crowds anxious to glimpse arriving stars in person. Today—though movies are still shown in the opulent theater—the main attraction is a collection of some 160 cement imprints of celebrities' feet, hands, guns, cigars, and so forth outside the lobby. *6925 Hollywood Blvd., btw Highland and La Brea Aves., tel. 213/464–8111.*

*If you go up to anyone holding a clipboard at Mann's Chinese Theater, you'll likely walk away with a slew of free movie tickets.*

**HOLLYWOOD WAX MUSEUM** You need to be visually impaired or hallucinating to see any similarity between the wax figurines on display here and their intended subjects. Spend the admission price on a movie instead—at least in films the dummies move. *6767 Hollywood Blvd., btw Highland Ave. and Vine St., tel. 213/462–8860. Admission: $9. Open Sun.–Thurs. 10 AM–midnight, Fri.–Sat. 10 AM–2 AM.*

Across the street is the new **Hollywood Guinness World of Records** (6764 Hollywood Blvd., tel. 213/463–6433), worth the $9 admission only if you really, really crave Marilyn Monroe and Michael Jackson trivia. Down the street, you can't help noticing **Ripley's Believe It or Not!** (6780 Hollywood Blvd., at Highland Ave., tel. 213/466–6335); a full-scale Tyrannosaurus Rex protrudes from the roof. If you choose to pay the $9 admission, you'll find still more Marilyn (would you believe a Monroe sculpture made of 250,000 dollar bills?).

**FREDERICK'S OF HOLLYWOOD** Frederick's is a great place to pick up a pair of crotchless satin panties ($5) for the folks back home. The legendary purveyors of licentious lingerie also have a well-endowed **Bra Museum** (admission free) in the back of the store. Besides its "History of the Bra" display, there's a riveting "Celebrity Lingerie Hall of Fame," with undergarb once worn by Mae West, panties from Zsa Zsa Gabor, a Madonna bustier—even a bra of Milton Berle's. Though the museum was looted during the 1992 riots (what better way to show your rage than to make off with a used brassiere?), most stolen bras were later returned—one remorseful man turned in his loot to a bemused priest. *6608 Hollywood Blvd., at Wilcox Ave., tel. 213/466–8506. Open Mon.–Thurs. and Sat. 10–6, Fri. 10–9, Sun. noon–5.*

**CAPITOL RECORDS BUILDING** When Capitol Records needed new offices in 1956, singer Nat King Cole and songwriter Johnny Mercer suggested that the company build a cylindrical tower resembling a stack of records. And voilà, it was done—it's a shame they didn't press for a high-rise shaped like a guitar. If you peek through the window you can see the lobby, where numerous awards for gold and platinum albums (based on record sales) line the walls. The crowning bit of kitsch: The red beacon atop the tower spells out Hollywood nonstop in Morse code. *1750 North Vine St., at Hollywood Blvd.*

**HOLLYWOOD MEMORIAL PARK CEMETERY** Fame *is* immortal. Just ask the Memorial Park gardeners, who've seen countless tourists drive up in rented convertibles, stand on the gravesites of their favorite stars, and take snapshots of the tombstones with disposable cameras. The remains of Mel Blanc, Douglas Fairbanks Sr., Marion Davies, and other celebrities are here, denied anonymity even in death by a tour-of-the-dead-stars map available free in the cemetery office. *6000 Santa Monica Blvd., btw Gower St. and Van Ness Ave., tel. 213/469–1181. Open daily 8–5.*

**HOLLYHOCK HOUSE** Hollyhock House stands in the middle of **Barnsdall Art Park,** a small art community founded by oil heiress Aline Barnsdall. It is the first—and probably the most unusual—of the many L.A. projects designed by architect Frank Lloyd Wright. Built in the 1920s, the house is filled with quirky touches, like a water-filled moat surrounding the living-room fireplace and inward-sloping walls on the second floor. Mayan designs and hollyhock flowers are motifs used throughout the house. A few doorways measure only 5'7"—the "perfect" height for a door, according to short-of-stature Wright. The Art Park is also home to the **Los Angeles Municipal Art Gallery** (tel. 213/485–4581), known for its excellent contemporary art exhibits. *4800 Hollywood Blvd., at Vermont Ave., tel. 213/485–4581. Admission: $2. Tours on the hour, Tues.–Sun. noon–3.*

**ECO-HOME** Los Angeles, land of smog and excess, is hardly the place you'd expect to find Eco-Home, an ecologically sound household that features all sorts of low-cost, earth-friendly features, from solar energy panels to xeriscapes (low-water, low-maintenance landscaping). In order to see the house, you have to go on a 2-hour tour, given by the owner, during which you'll get tips on how you, too, can make your house an eco-home. *4344 Russell Ave., near Western Ave., tel. 213/662–5207. North of Franklin Ave. Admission: $7. Tours Oct.–June, Sun. 2–4:30; July–Sept., Sun. 4–6:30.*

**EAST HOLLYWOOD** If you're tired of Melrose attitude and Hollywood grime, head to East Hollywood, located roughly between Hollywood and Griffith Park. Here, around the intersection

## *The Walk of Fame Do-It-Yourself Tour*

***• ALFRED HITCHCOCK: 7013 Hollywood Blvd. • W. C. FIELDS: 7004 Hollywood Blvd. • MICHAEL JACKSON: 6927 Hollywood Blvd. • OLIVIA NEWTON-JOHN: 6925 Hollywood Blvd. • GRETA GARBO: 6901 Hollywood Blvd. • GROUCHO MARX: 6821 Hollywood Blvd. • ELVIS PRESLEY: 6777 Hollywood Blvd. • MARILYN MONROE: 6776 Hollywood Blvd. • CHARLIE CHAPLIN: 6751 Hollywood Blvd. • SYLVESTER STALLONE: 6712 Hollywood Blvd. • LUCILLE BALL: 6436 Hollywood Blvd. • BETTE DAVIS: 6225 Hollywood Blvd. • CLARK GABLE: 1608 Vine St. • JOHN LENNON: 1750 Vine St.***

of Franklin and North Vermont avenues, you'll find a newish café and club scene that has so far avoided the pretense and posing that accompany almost every emerging L.A. trend. On Franklin, have a coffee at the **Bourgeois Pig** (*see* Cafés, *above*) or dine at **Prizzi's Piazza** (*see* Food, *above*). On Vermont, wax critical about the art on the walls at **The Onyx** (*see* Cafés, *above*) while you wait for a spontaneous performance to develop out of thin air (and it will). If you're itching to reach deeper into your pocket, shop for vinyl coveralls at the **Ministry of Aesthetics** (1756 N. Vermont Ave., tel. 213/665–1735), or pick up a smart-ass T-shirt or an A-line dress at **X-Large** (1766 N. Vermont Ave., tel. 213/666–3483)—one in the chain of hip-hop stores fronted by Beastie Boy Mike D. After a hard day's window-shopping and people watching, stop by the **Dresden Room** (*see* After Dark, *below*), for liquid refueling to the accompaniment of Sinatra tunes.

## GRIFFITH PARK

Griffith Park's 4,213 acres in the Santa Monica Mountains, northeast of Hollywood, are part of a dwindling number of "nature zones" within L.A. county limits. Though portions have been developed for human pursuits, the bulk has been left in a relatively pristine state. Hiking, cycling, and horseback riding are all options (*see* Outdoor Activities, *below*); for safety, solo travelers should remain on maintained, populated trails. *Visitor center and ranger headquarters: 4730 Crystal Springs Dr., at Griffith Park Dr., tel. 213/665–5188. West of I–5, btw Hwy. 134 and Los Feliz Blvd. From I–5, exit at Los Feliz Blvd., Griffith Park, or Zoo Dr., and follow signs. From Hwy. 134, exit at Forest Lawn Dr. Park open daily 5:30 AM–10 PM.*

**GENE AUTRY WESTERN HERITAGE MUSEUM** If ever there were a politically correct cowboy museum, this is it. The huge, sophisticated collection of artifacts (and props from TV westerns) presents a fond look at the Old West without perpetuating myths and stereotypes about the era. It's located just across the parking lot from the zoo (*see below*). *4700 Western Heritage Way, tel. 213/667–2000. Enter at Griffith Park Dr. and follow signs. Or MTA Bus 96, 97, or 412. Admission: $7, $5 students. Open Tues.–Sun. 10–5.*

**GRIFFITH OBSERVATORY** The copper-domed observatory houses a science museum, a planetarium, a laserium, and a 12-inch telescope. Film crews love this place, as viewers of *Rebel Without a Cause* and *Barton Fink* can attest. If you're wondering how much you'd weigh on Mars, head to the **Hall of Science** (free), with interactive computers and exhibits designed for both kids and adults. In the main hall, you can buy tickets for the hour-long **Planetarium** presentation ($4) or for **Laserium** ($7), a laser art show set to the tunes of bands like Led Zeppelin, U2, and Pink Floyd. (Beware the hordes of red-eyed youths who flock here on Friday and Saturday nights; it's the unofficial meeting place of the "Just Say Yes" crowd.) On clear evenings from 7 to 9:45, peer through the telescope (free) at Jupiter or the Orion nebula. *2800 E. Observatory Rd., tel. 213/664–1191. Enter Griffith Park from Los Feliz Blvd. and follow signs. Call for Laserium and Planetarium show times. Observatory open summer, daily 12:30 PM–10 PM; winter, Tues.–Fri. 2 PM–10 PM, weekends 12:30–10.*

**L.A. ZOO** If you need a break from the urban jungle, head to the zoo. Considerable effort (and a hell of a lot of corporate money) has been expended to give the 2,000 animals here some semblance of a natural habitat, making L.A.'s zoo comparatively humane. The newest exhibits are **Tiger Falls,** where a pair of Bengals frolic in waterfalls, and **Adventure Island,** which houses bats, mountain lions, and other natives of the American Southwest. The vast zoo is well worth an afternoon's exploration, so wear comfortable shoes. *5333 W. Zoo Dr., tel. 213/666–4650. Enter Griffith Park at Los Feliz Blvd. or Zoo Dr. and follow signs. Admission: $8.25 (look for discount coupons at visitor centers). Open daily 10–5; ticket sales stop at 4.*

## WEST HOLLYWOOD

West Hollywood is home to some of L.A.'s best bars, cafés, clubs, and galleries, most of which line **Santa Monica Boulevard** between Doheny Drive and La Cienega Boulevard. This is a commercial and social center for the gay and lesbian community—most cafés and shops cater to this contingent—and on Saturday nights, the sidewalks are thronged with club-hopping couples both gay and straight. Begin your visit with a look at the landmark **Pacific Design Center** (south of Santa Monica Blvd. on San Vicente Blvd.), closed to the public but fun to admire from outside; locals refer to the colorful glass-and-steel structure as "the Blue Whale." Santa Monica Boulevard is served by MTA Bus 4.

At **A Different Light Bookstore** (8853 Santa Monica Blvd., near San Vicente Blvd., tel. 310/854–6601), you'll find an excellent selection of gay and lesbian literature. The tiny shop **Don't Panic** (802 N. San Vicente Blvd., at Santa Monica Blvd., tel. 310/287–3250) sells T-shirts with pro-queer messages for about $18 each. After hours, get wild at Micky's (*see* After Dark, *below*), where bare-chested bartenders pour the drinks. If that's not your taste, try fighting for a table at **Euro Coffee** (8941 Santa Monica Blvd., at San Vicente Blvd., tel. 310/246–0828), the café du jour. At the Troubador (*see* After Dark, *below*), some of the biggest names in rock have played as relative unknowns.

**SUNSET STRIP** Wild-child Sunset Strip (Sunset Blvd., btw Doheny Dr. and Crescent Heights Blvd.) was L.A.'s locus of hippie youth, anti-war protests, and rock and roll during the 1960s and '70s; though you'll still find an industrial-strength concentration of nightclubs, things are much tamer than they used to be (partly due to the subduing effect of the HIV/AIDS epidemic). Closed is the Dionysian den Gazzarri's, where the Doors, Van Halen, and Guns 'N Roses all climbed from obscurity. There's still the self-consciously cool **Roxy** and groupie-jammed **Whiskey A Go Go,** as well as the trendy new **House of Blues,** owned by actor Dan Ackroyd (for more on nightclubs, *see* After Dark, *below*). These days, though, you're more likely to encounter Wrangler-driving neo-preppies on their way to catch headline acts at the **Comedy Store** (8433 Sunset Blvd., tel. 213/656–6225) than beer-swilling glam rockers in leather. **Ben Frank's** (8585 Sunset Blvd., tel. 310/652–8808), a diner and late-night clubbers' lounge, is one of the few places where your meal will be served minus attitude.

## MELROSE AND THE WILSHIRE DISTRICT

The area bordered by Melrose Avenue to the north, Wilshire Boulevard to the south, and I–405 and I–110 to the west and east, respectively, is L.A.'s "midsection," the stuff most tourists skip over in their haste to get from Hollywood and Beverly Hills to coastal towns like Malibu and Santa Monica. Don't make the same mistake: This is archetypal L.A., where you can glimpse stars in their sneakers, be served lunch by an aspiring actor, and check out a large contingent of tattooed plastic-surgery recipients. It's also home to a growing number of excellent museums on Wilshire Boulevard. MTA Bus 10 serves Melrose Avenue, Bus 14 runs down Beverly Boulevard, and Buses 20–22, 320, and 322 travel Wilshire Boulevard.

**MELROSE AVENUE** The epicenter of L.A. hip, Melrose is lined with cafés, restaurants, avant-garde art galleries, and a jumble of stores purveying '60s and '70s furniture, clothing, and kitsch. Even if you lack the capital to purchase a studded leather bodysuit, it's fun to gawk at the duds and the youthful celebs attempting to shop incognito. (Yes, that does include the cast of *Melrose Place,* if you were waiting breathlessly to know.) Let the 6900–8200 blocks of

### *Pursuing the Hollywood Grail*

***Though years have passed since the last failed starlet did a swan dive from one of its 50-foot-tall O's, questions about the famous HOLLYWOOD sign are routinely intercepted by Griffith Park rangers with a curt "It's off-limits." Local opinions are mixed, from "You can't hike up there" to "Hell, yeah, you can hike up there, but you'll be slapped with a $103 fine." One look at the expressway-size trails blazing up the hillside from the ends of Deronda and Innsdale drives, and you just know that—despite the apparent illegality of the act—people are hiking up there.***

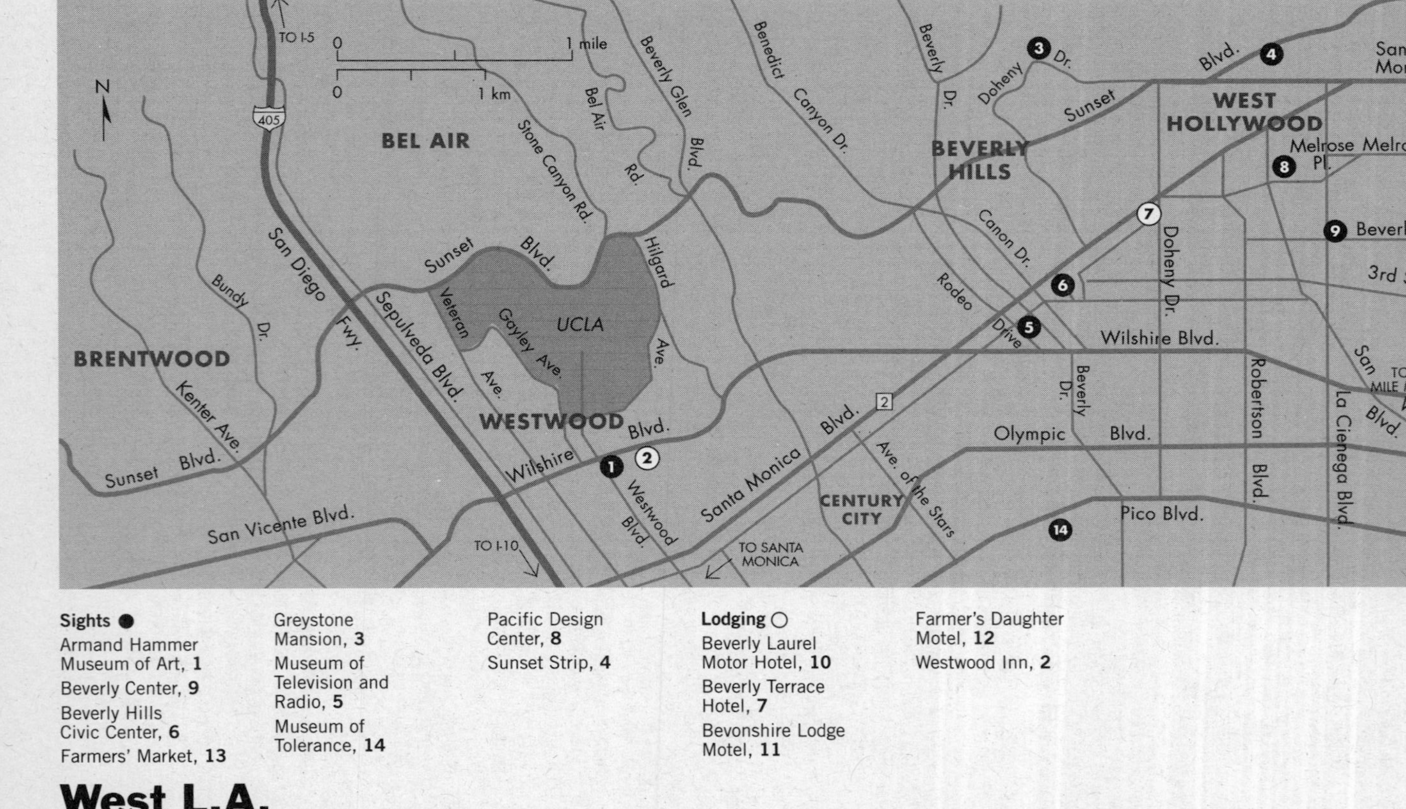


**Sights ●**
Armand Hammer Museum of Art, **1**
Beverly Center, **9**
Beverly Hills Civic Center, **6**
Farmers' Market, **13**
Greystone Mansion, **3**
Museum of Television and Radio, **5**
Museum of Tolerance, **14**
Pacific Design Center, **8**
Sunset Strip, **4**

**Lodging ○**
Beverly Laurel Motor Hotel, **10**
Beverly Terrace Hotel, **7**
Bevonshire Lodge Motel, **11**
Farmer's Daughter Motel, **12**
Westwood Inn, **2**

# West L.A.

Melrose (btw Highland Ave. and Crescent Heights Blvd.) be your starting point; you can park on surrounding residential streets, but pay attention to posted restrictions.

Pick up a glossy fashion rag—or the local paper, whichever you prefer—at **Melrose News** (647 N. Martel Ave., at Melrose Ave., tel. 213/655–2866). The **Cosmopolitan Book Shop** (7017 Melrose Ave., tel. 213/938–7119) has a good selection of used, 50¢ paperbacks perfect for a café read at Betelgeuse or the Lou De Cris Café (*see* Cafés, *above*). At **Off the Wall Antiques** (7325 Melrose Ave., tel. 213/930–1185), marvel at the latest pop trophy for sale; previous offerings have included Elvis Presley's Corvette convertible and several life-size fiberglass cows ($2,400 per heifer). **Spike's Joint West** (7263 Melrose Ave., tel. 213/932–7064) carries hats and such emblazoned with logos from filmmaker Lee's oeuvre, while **Condomania** (7306 Melrose Ave., tel. 213/933–7865) sells practical and playful prophylactics. Coordinate your condom purchase with an outfit from **Red Balls of Fire** (7365 Melrose Ave., tel. 213/655–3409), a velvet, leather, or whatever-your-pleasure kind of place.

Before heading south down La Brea Avenue to admire the ultra-chic furniture stores or to shop for used clothing, grab a chili dog at **Pink's** (*see* Food, *above*); then stop by **Fréwil** (605 N. La Brea Ave., tel. 213/934–8474), one of many havens of interior design along this street. Shop for reasonably priced '70s-style T-shirts and '60s-style mini-dresses at **Yellowstone Clothing** (712 N. La Brea Ave., tel. 213/931–6616); **American Rag** (150 S. La Brea Ave., tel. 213/935–3157) has retro ware at postmodern prices. Parallel to and south of Melrose is **Beverly Boulevard,** where you'll find lots of shops selling custom-made garb that looks street but costs steep. Admire and move on to **Insomnia** (*see* Cafés, *above*) for your third or fourth cappuccino of the afternoon.

**FAIRFAX AVENUE** It sure ain't Brooklyn, but the blocks surrounding Fairfax Avenue (btw Beverly and Santa Monica Blvds.) are the center of the orthodox Jewish community in Los Angeles. Unfortunately, the area has recently been discovered by the trendy kids of Melrose—who think kosher is a really cool food fad. You'll still find authentic kosher delis, including local favorite **Canter's** (419 N. Fairfax Ave., tel. 213/651–2030), which serves up matzo ball soup ($3) and other treats 24 hours a day. After midnight, club-crawlers can be found at the restaurant's bar, the **Kibitz Room** (*see* After Dark, *below*). Across the street, **Damiano** (412 N. Fairfax Ave., tel. 213/658–7611) serves up tasty New York–style pizza ($1.50 a slice) in a dark, club-like setting. Tucked into an unassuming mini-mall, **The Bagel Broker** (7825 Beverly Blvd., east of Fairfax Ave., tel. 213/931–1258) serves up authentic New York–style bagels for only 35¢ each. There's not much else to see around here, but this is an excellent place from which to tackle Melrose Avenue (*see above*).

➢ **FARMERS' MARKET** • Although you can still buy fresh produce here, this 60-year-old market has degenerated from a genuine farmers' market to a tacky tourist quagmire with everything from car tune-ups to "fun fashions for sophisticated ladies." The best of the ethnic food stands is **The Gumbo Pot** (tel. 213/933–0358), with authentic Cajun-Creole sandwiches and entrées (around $6). *6333 W. 3rd St., at Fairfax Ave., tel. 213/933–9211. Open summer, Mon.–Sat. 9–7, Sun. 10–6; winter, Mon.–Sat. 9–6:30, Sun. 10–5.*

**MIRACLE MILE MUSEUMS** You can spend at least a couple of days exploring the Wilshire District's plethora of museums. If you drive out here, however, be warned: Parking lots along Miracle Mile—the strip of Wilshire Boulevard between Fairfax and Curson avenues—can be expensive. Luckily, most lots will give discounts to those with validated museum tickets—check before you park. To reach the Miracle Mile museums from I–10 eastbound, exit north on Fairfax Avenue; from I–10 westbound, exit north on La Brea Avenue.

➢ **CRAFT AND FOLK ART MUSEUM** • The temporary exhibits at this excellent museum focus on particular geographical areas, from Okinawa to Guatemala, and aim to present art within its cultural context. The vividly colored masks, altars, and fabrics are truly engaging. *5800 Wilshire Blvd., at Curson Ave., tel. 213/937–5544. Admission $4, $2.50 students. Open Tues.–Sun. 11–5 (Fri. until 8).*

➢ **LA BREA TAR PITS** • About 10,000–40,000 years before freeways and tract houses, Los Angeles was a lush basin filled with strange mammals and exotic plants. Fossil remains of these early inhabitants were excavated from La Brea's subterranean tar pits when oil was discovered in the 1890s, and recovery of Ice Age remains continues today. Look for fossilized animal bones in the sticky pools by the observation area; the adjacent small museum displays re-creations of more spectacular finds, including California saber-toothed cats, an American mastodon, and a 9,000-year-old woman. Be sure to check out the trippy holograms that overlay flesh on restored skeletons. *5801 Wilshire Blvd., at Curson Ave., tel. 213/857–6311. Admission: $6, $3.50 students; free first Tues. of month. Open summer, daily 10—5; winter, Tues.–Sun. 10–5.*

➢ **LOS ANGELES COUNTY MUSEUM OF ART** • With the help of corporate money (Philip Morris, Chevron, etc.), LACMA has put Los Angeles on the art-world map. If you've got the stamina, you could easily pass an entire day exploring its four vast galleries. The **Pavilion for Japanese Art** is a soothing world of subdued light and gently flowing water; the collection features scrolls of paper and silk from the 13th to 16th centuries. The **Ahmanson Building** showcases a variety of ancient treasures. Permanent exhibits include ornamental gold and silver; Mayan statuary dating from AD 800; amazing collections of Egyptian, Greek, and Roman statuary; and neolithic and dynastic Chinese artifacts. The **Hammer Building** houses special exhibits that change seasonally. The **Anderson Building** features rotating displays and permanent collections of 20th-century art, including a Donald Judd minimalist sculpture and Andy Warhol's infamous *Brillo Boxes.* At the **Leo S. Bing Center,** take tea at the café, catch films and lectures at the theater (Wed. 1 PM), or visit a basement gallery of impressive local artwork. *5905 Wilshire Blvd., at Ogden Dr., tel. 213/857–6000. Admission: $6, $4 students; free second Wed. of month. Open Tues.–Thurs. 10–5, Fri. 10–9, weekends 11–6; call for hrs of individual galleries.*

Across the street, the new **Museum of Miniatures** (5900 Wilshire Blvd., tel. 213/937–6464) is full of tiny towns, tiny furniture, tiny famous people, tiny houses—you get the picture. Most interesting is the life-size violin in which a tiny violin workshop has been painstakingly re-created, complete with a half-dozen miniature instruments. Pop into the gift shop and check out the not-so-tiny prices; a miniature person retails for about $3,000. Admission is $7.50, $5 for students under 21; the museum is open Tuesday–Saturday 10–5 and Sunday 11–5.

➢ **PETERSEN AUTOMOTIVE MUSEUM** • You could call this new museum inevitable, given the city's fondness for auto travel. Fascinating even if your childhood never included Hot Wheels, it displays over 130 cars and motorcycles—including Joan Crawford's '33 Cadillac and a vehicle custom-built for Elvis's *Easy Come, Easy Go.* Some may actually weep when they see the museum's 1957 Ferrari 250 Testa Rossa, especially upon learning that test drives are not allowed. *6060 Wilshire Blvd., at Fairfax Ave., tel. 213/930–2277. Admission: $7, $5 students. Open Tues.–Sun. 10–6.*

## *Forget the Star Maps: Three Celebrity Houses You Need to Know*

- ***Aaron Spelling's château (the house that Charlie's Angels, Dynasty, and Melrose Place built): On the 500 block of North Mapleton Drive in Bel Air. With 123 rooms, it's only nine short of the White House.***
- ***Madonna's estate: On Canyon Lake Highway, near the Hollywood Reservoir. When the Material Girl moved into this former casino, she painted the entire thing in horizontal red and yellow stripes. Catch it while you can: Latest rumor is that she's having it repainted.***
- ***Ronald Reagan's house: On the 600 block of St. Cloud Road, in Bel Air. Wife Nancy created minor postal havoc by insisting on a number change—the original address was 666.***

## WESTWOOD AND BEVERLY HILLS

Beverly Hills has glitzy shops and showy houses with a nationally known zip code, and Westwood is full of UCLA students ditching classes to catch a flick. If you have a car, also consider a spin through exclusive **Bel Air** to pick out the mansion you'll purchase after you've made your first $10 million. Look for local kids hawking **Star Maps** ($3–$7), which allegedly—and usually inaccurately—identify movie stars' addresses. MTA Bus 8 travels Westwood Boulevard; Rodeo Drive is walkable, especially if you're only window-shopping and don't have to lug all those heavy purchases around.

**BEVERLY HILLS** Everything you've ever heard about the enormous wealth of Beverly Hills is true, so pack a lunch and make it a low-cost day trip of window-shopping and people watching. **Rodeo Drive** is the fabulous shopping avenue of the rich and famous; all the major names are here, including Gucci, Armani, and Chanel. Notice that very few people actually *shop* in these stores; instead, wistful visitors from Dubuque gaze through the windows. The **Counterspy Shop** (9557 Wilshire Blvd., near Rodeo Dr., tel. 310/274–7700) carries lie-detector telephones, bulletproof vests, and discreet personal microphones for James Bond aspirants. Eddie Murphy fans will recognize the facade of the opulent **Beverly Hills Civic Center** (444 N. Rexford Dr., at Santa Monica Blvd.), with its improbable pseudo-Spanish colonial tower and tile-mosaic dome. Still more shopping can be found at the **Beverly Center** (Beverly Blvd., at La Cienega Blvd., tel. 310/854–0070), an eight-story temple of fashion that's also home to the ubiquitous Hard Rock Café (*see* After Dark, *below*). Restore your inner tranquility with a stroll through the perfectly manicured gardens of beautiful **Greystone Mansion** (905 Loma Vista Dr., at Doheny Rd. north of Sunset Blvd., tel. 310/550–4796). Though the $100 million house is closed to the public, the grounds are open daily 10–6 in summer and 10–5 in winter, and admission is free.

*The dining court in the Beverly Center dishes up fast-food, Beverly Hills style: French cuisine and Godiva chocolates.*

➢ **MUSEUM OF TELEVISION AND RADIO** • This brand-new museum, scheduled to open in March 1996, houses 60,000 radio and TV programs covering a 70-year time span. Visitors have full access to this vast collection of 20th-century pop culture: You can march right in and say, "I want to see the *Brady Bunch* episode where Jan hides her glasses because she thinks she's ugly, and I want to see it now." The museum also has archives of news programs, documentaries, children's programming, sports, and advertising, and puts on regular special screening series. At press time, the museum had yet to hook up a phone line; call information in the 310 area code or ask at a visitor information center (*see* Basics, *above*) for more info. *465 N. Beverly Dr., near Santa Monica Blvd. Admission free ($6 donation requested). Open Wed.–Sun. noon–5 (Thurs. until 9).*

➢ **MUSEUM OF TOLERANCE** • Housed inside a mammoth glass-and-steel building is this unforgettable museum, asking tough questions about racism and prejudice. High-tech displays unflinchingly explore historical acts of oppression and genocide against groups as diverse as 18th-century Native Americans and World War II European Jews. Most exhibits encourage visitor participation and are designed to provoke—look for an authentic re-creation of a Holocaust gas chamber or the list of some 250 hate groups currently active in the U.S. There's also an examination of the issues underlying L.A.'s 1992 riots. It's a roller-coaster ride of revelation, revulsion, and self-doubt, occasionally heavy-handed but ultimately extraordinary. *9786 W. Pico Blvd., at Roxbury Dr., tel. 310/553–8403. Admission: $8, $5 students (advance ticket purchase recommended weekdays and mandatory Sun.). Open Nov.–March, Mon.–Thurs. 10–4, Fri. 10–1, Sun. 11–5; April–Oct., Mon.–Thurs. 10–4, Fri. 10–3, Sun. 11–5. Free, mandatory 10-min tour.*

**WESTWOOD/UCLA** The streets of Westwood Village teem with well-scrubbed kids from the University of California at Los Angeles (UCLA) out spending their parents' money. Most of the action takes place on **Broxton Avenue,** lined with student-oriented shops and eateries, as well as 10—count 'em, 10—movie theaters. Before visiting campus, stop by **Diddy Riese** (926 Broxton Ave., at Le Conte Ave., tel. 310/208–0448) for a cookie (25¢). On campus, worthwhile stops include **Ackerman Student Union,** which has a well-stocked bookstore and a ride-share board; the **Tree House** (main level), a popular place to pick up a snack; and **Melnitz Hall**

(tel. 310/206–8170), which often has free showings from the Department of Film and Television's extensive collection of old movie reels. At the campus's free **Fowler Museum of Cultural History** (tel. 310/825–4361), open Wednesday–Sunday noon–5 and until 8 on Thursday, you'll find fascinating exhibits of non-Western art. Stroll among works by Rodin and Matisse at the **Franklin D. Murphy Sculpture Garden.** Reserve ahead for a guided walking tour of the garden, weekdays only, at the Art Council (tel. 310/825–3264). *UCLA switchboard: tel. 310/825–4321. Visitor center: tel. 310/206–8147. Exit I–405 and follow signs to Westwood Blvd. Pass Westwood Village, cross Le Conte Ave. to UCLA parking lots. Free maps at kiosk, just past main entrance.*

➢ **ARMAND HAMMER MUSEUM OF ART** • The permanent collection at this richly endowed museum, located just south of campus, includes oils by van Gogh, Cassatt, Rubens, Monet, and Rembrandt, as well as some original manuscripts penned by Leonardo Da Vinci and an extensive collection of works by 19th-century French lithographer and sculptor Honoré Daumier. *10899 Wilshire Blvd., at Westwood Blvd., tel. 310/443–7000. Admission: $4.50, $3 students; free Thurs. after 6 PM. Open Tues.–Sat. 11–7 (Thurs. until 9), Sun. 11–5. Free tours daily at 1 PM.*

## SANTA MONICA AND VENICE

If you like the beach—and even if you don't—Santa Monica and Venice are full of diversions. At all hours, a stream of Beautiful People whiz by on the **Promenade/Ocean Front Walk,** a paved pathway for bicyclists, skaters, and pedestrians that links the two coastal communities. You have to wonder what these people do for a living. In each of these beach towns, Main Street is lined with shops, restaurants, art galleries, and museums aplenty.

**SANTA MONICA** Santa Monica is an ironic mixture of beach town and urban blight. On Main Street, crowds of cappuccino drinkers read the *New York Times* and bask in the glow of their own success; on strips of beach near the pier, a vaguely menacing throng makes the potential for mugging almost as good as that for getting a tan. The **Santa Monica Pier** (tel. 310/458–8900) is one of the main tourist destinations, though some may find the popularity of its arcade games and greasy fast-food stands unfathomable. Here you can ride a restored 1922 carousel (open June–Sept., Tues.–Sun.; Sept.–May, weekends only) for 50¢, or stare at the water over a fishing pole ($3 an hr) rented from **SM Pier Bait and Tackle** (tel. 310/576–2014). In the Fun Zone amusement area at the foot of the pier, a roller coaster with a 30-foot drop and an 11-story Ferris wheel that affords a great view of Santa Monica Bay are scheduled to open in summer '96. Exercise caution when hanging around the pier after dark. You can also stroll the adjacent shady **Palisades Park,** or rent in-line skates (*see* Outdoor Activities, *below*) and cruise the waterfront promenade. Watch for people with clipboards—they may be studio flunkeys distributing free movie tickets.

Beyond the beach, Santa Monica is a mecca of small museums and shops. The **Santa Monica Museum of Art** (2435 Main St., btw Hollister Ave. and Ocean Park Blvd., tel. 310/399–0433) hosts unusual exhibits of contemporary paintings; it's housed in the **Edgemar** complex of cafés and galleries, designed by acclaimed local architect Frank Gehry. Since the Edgemar's outdoor courtyard is overrun with *noir* aspirants sporting painstakingly clipped goatees, do your art criticism down the street at **Wednesday's House** (*see* Cafés, *above*), among the velvet Elvis paintings. Farther north, the **18th Street Arts Complex** (1639 18th St., at Olympic Blvd., tel. 310/453–3711) includes artists' residences, galleries, and a performance space, often featuring gay and lesbian events. A few more blocks northwest, look for **Bergamot Station** (2525 Michigan Ave., tel. 310/829–5854), an art gallery complex housed in a restored railroad depot, where you'll find a high concentration of intriguing works by young, up-and-coming artists.

If you're interested in Golden State history, step into the **California Heritage Museum** (2612 Main St., at Ocean Park Blvd., tel. 310/392–8537), housed in an 1894 American colonial revival home. Rotating displays of California history are on the second floor; the first floor has rooms furnished in turn-of-the-century styles. Admission is $4, $2 for students. If fighter planes get your blood pumping, pay $7 to see the **Museum of Flying** (2772 Donald Douglas

Santa Monica and Venice

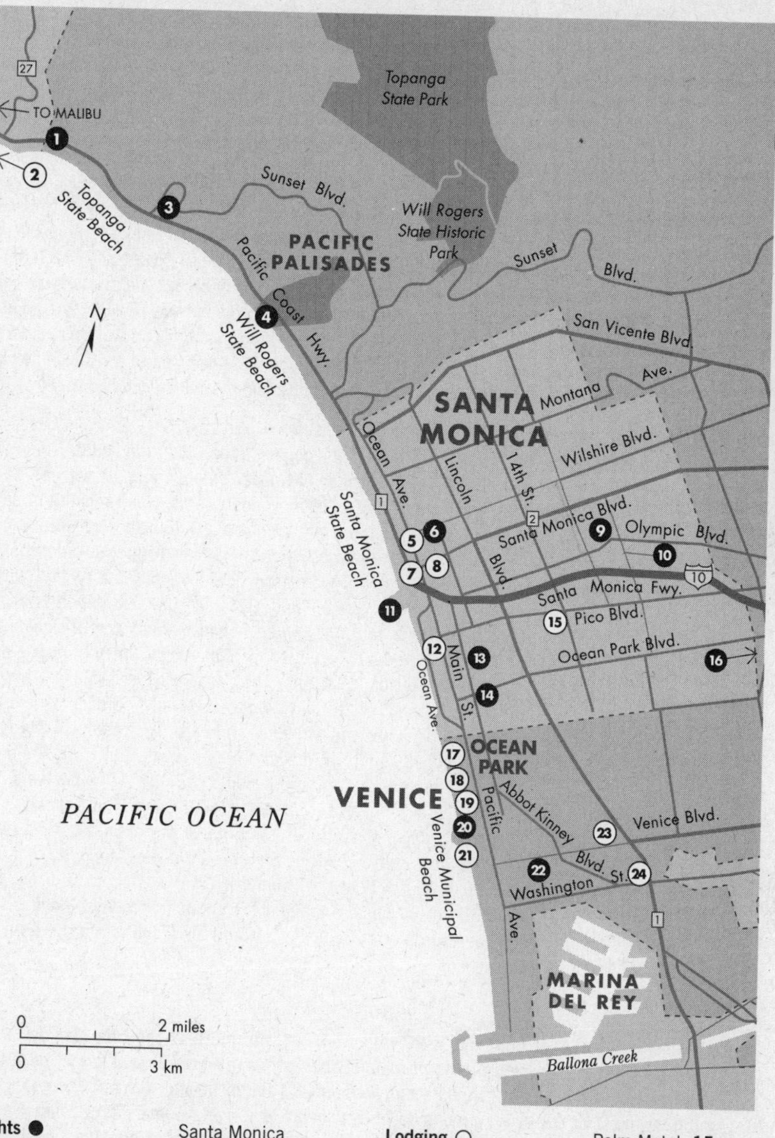


**Sights ●**

18th Street Arts Complex, **9**
Bergamot Station, **10**
California Heritage Museum, **14**
J. Paul Getty Museum, **1**
Muscle Beach, **20**
Museum of Flying, **16**
Palisades Park, **4**
Santa Monica Museum of Art, **13**
Santa Monica Pier, **11**
Self-Realization Fellowship Lake Shrine, **3**
Third Street Promenade, **6**
Venice Boardwalk, **20**
Venice Canals, **22**

**Lodging ○**

Airport Hostel, **23**
Bayside Hotel, **12**
Cadillac Hotel, **17**
Hotel Carmel, **5**
Jim's at the Beach, **18**
Jolly Roger Hotel, **24**
Malibu Surfer Motel, **2**
Pacific Sands Motel, **7**
Palm Motel, **15**
Santa Monica American Youth Hostel, **8**
Share Tel Apartments, **19**
Venice Beach Cotel, **21**

Loop N., at Santa Monica Airport, tel. 310/392–8822). You can check out Spitfires, Sopwith Camels, jet fighters, and the 1986 *Voyager,* the first plane to make a nonstop, unrefueled around-the-world flight. The stomach-turning Tornado jet-simulation ride is not to be missed. Admission is $7, $5 for students.

Two inland areas lend themselves to people watching. The **Third Street Promenade** is a Disneyfied version of hip, worth a quick walk-through. This pedestrians-only bazaar between Wilshire Boulevard and Broadway features topiary dinosaurs that look like giant Chia pets and Generation X chains like Z Gallerie and Urban Outfitters. Browse the shelves in the **Midnight Special Bookstore** (1318 3rd St., tel. 310/393–2923), which has Friday evening poetry readings (*see* Cheap Thrills, *below*). **Benita's Frites** (1437 3rd St., tel. 310/458–2889) serves up tasty Belgian-style fries with dipping sauces like peanut curry satay. The scene grows increasingly sophisticated as you move north toward **Montana Avenue** between Ocean Avenue and Lincoln Boulevard. Shops here sell artsy jewelry, one-of-a-kind furniture, and whimsical (if pricey) clothing. Montana's intersection with 7th Street is popularly referred to as "Caffeine Corner." Pick up a latte ($2) at **Odeon Breads and Pastries** (625 Montana Ave., tel. 310/451–9096).

**VENICE** The undisputed magnet for L.A. eccentrics is Venice Beach. Even its birth involved bizarre circumstances: At the turn of the century, cigarette manufacturer Abbot Kinney bought up land south of Santa Monica and built a replica of Italy's Venice, complete with a small-scale copy of St. Mark's Cathedral and 16 miles of saltwater canals. Alas, canal-making in California was an engineering hell, and gondola snobbery ran rampant in the new automobile age. Most of Kinney's underappreciated constructions were torn down when the city of Los Angeles annexed Venice in 1925. A few residence-lined canals remain, south of Venice Boulevard and east of Ocean Avenue. Only recently dredged of stinky algae, they're now a pleasant place for a stroll. The **Venice Boardwalk** is perennially thronged with bikini-clad skaters, T-shirt hucksters, street musicians and artisans, and New Age prophets; several characters, such as the chain-saw juggler and the Rollerblading Rastafarian guitarist, could qualify as boardwalk ambassadors. At **Muscle Beach** (1800 Ocean Front Walk), perfectly pumped bodybuilders from Gold's Gym flex and lift weights in the open air. If you yearn to become a part of the Venice scene, rent a bike or a pair of 'blades (*see* Outdoor Activities, *below*). Otherwise, grab a beer (about $3) at the **Sidewalk Café** (1401 Ocean Front Walk, at Horizon Ave., tel. 310/399–5547), sit back, and enjoy the show. Try to avoid the area between Lincoln and Abbot Kinney boulevards after dark: It's a notorious arena for gang warfare.

*In Venice, look for the offices of the Chiat/Day advertising agency (340 Main St.), designed by Frank Gehry. The conference rooms, which constitute the building's facade, are in the shape of giant four-story binoculars.*

## MALIBU

The city of Malibu extends along 27 miles of coastal cliffs and canyons. Besides sprawling estates and expensive restaurants, it includes one of the least developed stretches of beach in L.A.; nearby are acres of rugged state parklands. Though beach crowds can be annoying in summer, most of the area remains as undeveloped as it was 40 years ago, when Malibu and neighboring **Pacific Palisades** first became popular with reclusive celebrities. Local mailboxes still read like a *Who's Who* of the film world: Robert Redford, Shirley MacLaine, Dustin Hoffman, and Jack Lemmon live here, to name a few. You won't be able to see the stars' homes without a boat or a helicopter, though.

Who needs to look at aging celebrities anyway with these views of the Pacific? If the water looks tempting, check out **Malibu Surfrider State Beach** (tel. 818/880–0350), just east of Malibu Canyon Road on PCH. Here, locals carry on the tradition of longboard surfing, sometimes with antique wooden boards (for surfboard rentals, *see* Outdoor Activities, *below*). Or continue several miles farther west to **Zuma Beach County Park** (tel. 310/457–9891), a favorite escape for L.A. natives. Nudists gravitate to **Point Dume,** just north of Malibu.

**J. PAUL GETTY MUSEUM** One of the best classical art collections in the country lies in the foothills of the Santa Monica Mountains: Greek and Roman sculptures, statues, pottery, and antique jewelry amassed by L.A. collector J. Paul Getty. The estate in which they're housed, built to resemble the ancient Villa dei Papiri of the Bay of Naples in Italy, is itself a work of art, with mosaic fountains, ornate frescoes, columned walkways, and fragrant formal gardens. In 1996, additions will include an exhibit of Doris Ulmann's photography of Appalachia; illuminated manuscripts from the medieval and renaissance periods; and drawings of French masters Cézanne, Delacroix, Manet, and Degas, among others. (In 1997, all post-Greek and -Roman works will be moved to the separate Getty Center, under construction in nearby Brentwood.) Parking at the Getty is limited; you must make a reservation at least two days in advance. Otherwise, MTA Bus 434 stops a half-mile from the museum. The driver will give you a free museum pass, necessary for admission. *17985 Pacific Coast Hwy., btw Sunset and Topanga Canyon Blvds., tel. 310/458–2003. Parking and admission free. Open Tues.–Sun. 10–5.*

**MALIBU CREEK STATE PARK** If this park triggers TV or film flashbacks, it's probably because it served as a stand-in for Korean scenery in the hit series *M*A*S*H* and as alien landscape in *Planet of the Apes.* Film crews still make the trek out here for on-location shoots. Covering 6,000 acres of the Santa Monica Mountains, the park has over 20 miles of hiking and mountain-biking trails and a cliff face popular with rock climbers. You'll want to pick up a trail map ($1) at the park entrance station. Worth exploring is the easy 1-mile trail from the park entrance to the picnic area at **Century Lake,** where camping is available (*see* Where to Sleep, *above*). *1925 Las Virgenes Rd., Calabasas, tel. 818/880–0367. 4 mi south of U.S. 101. Admission: $5 per vehicle (includes all area state parks and beaches for one day). Park open summer, daily 8–8; winter, daily 8–5.*

*From the kick-us-while-we're-down file: Some Malibu homeowners survived the fires of October '93 and the mud slides of December '93, only to watch their houses finally collapse in the January '94 earthquake.*

**SELF-REALIZATION FELLOWSHIP LAKE SHRINE** A tiny pocket of paradise only occasionally punctured by the buzz of traffic from Sunset Boulevard, this 10-acre park is maintained by the Eastern-influenced Self-Realization Fellowship. Their doctrine promotes the universality of all religions—which may explain why the chapel is housed in a Dutch-style windmill, while across the small lake a lotus-topped arch flanks a stone sarcophagus containing a portion of Mahatma Gandhi's ashes. Along the gravel walkways, secluded benches encourage meditation. *17190 Sunset Blvd., Pacific Palisades, tel. 310/454–4114. ½ mi north of Pacific Coast Hwy. Admission free. Open Tues.–Sat. 9–4:45, Sun. 1–4:45.*

**WILL ROGERS STATE HISTORIC PARK** Cowboy, philanthropist, philosopher, actor, journalist, lasso artist, and naturalist Will Rogers lived at this sprawling ranch in the Santa Monica Mountains in the 1920s and '30s. In 1944, Rogers's house became a museum of the Old West, with displays of Navajo rugs, Native American arrowheads, antique saddles, cowboy boots, and a stuffed Texas longhorn bull. One wing is preserved with furnishings from Rogers's time here. Visitors can picnic on the polo grounds (for info on polo matches, *see* Outdoor Activities, *below*), or follow trails that lead from the lodge into the surrounding hills. The 1-mile hike up to **Inspiration Point** ends with a stunning view of the ocean. *14235 Sunset Blvd., btw Amalfi Dr. and Brooktree Rd. in Pacific Palisades, tel. 310/454–8212. Admission: $5 per vehicle. Park open summer, daily 8–7; winter, daily 8–6. House tours daily 10–4:30.*

## THE SOUTH BAY

The three beaches that make up the South Bay—Manhattan, Hermosa, and Redondo—embody many visitors' preconceptions about Southern California. The local attitude is laid-back (bordering on torpid near the water), and the pace of life is slow and undemanding. If you stick to the Pacific Coast Highway (PCH), you'll see nothing but car dealerships and mini-malls, but as you approach the water the distinctive features of each town emerge. Stop at any convenience store on PCH for a free copy of *Beach Reporter* or *Easy Reader*; both weeklies cover entertainment and news in the South Bay.

**MANHATTAN BEACH** Manhattan Beach Boulevard leads into the heart of Manhattan Beach, intersecting PCH 3 miles south of the airport and ending at the pier. More upscale than

Hermosa and less commercial than Redondo, Manhattan Beach has lots of condos, relatively few unemployed surfers, and plenty of attitude. At its northern boundary begins the **Strand,** part of a 22-mile, two-lane beachfront "highway" open to bicyclists, skaters, and pedestrians. This is *the* place to gawk and be gawked at along the South Bay coast. Stroll down the pier, blissfully devoid of tourist schlock, for a view of the seemingly endless string of beach volleyball courts. At the tip of the municipal pier is the free **Roundhouse Aquarium** (tel. 310/374–8117), where you can check out spiny lobsters, menacing crabs, and slinky sea slugs in an almost-natural environment.

**HERMOSA BEACH** If you're looking for the archetypal Southern California seaside town, head for **Hermosa Beach,** just south of Manhattan Beach. Though multimillion-dollar houses line the water, there's an antiestablishment, don't-worry-be-happy feel; even the Mercedes Benzes sport Grateful Dead stickers. To reach Hermosa's low-key jumble of shops and restaurants from PCH, look for Pier Avenue, 2 miles south of Manhattan Beach (it leads, naturally, to the municipal pier). You'll look out of place unless you're sporting equipment here: At **Jeffers Beach Rentals** (39 14th St., just off the Strand, tel. 310/372–9492), you'll find in-line skates ($6 an hr), body boards ($4–$5 an hr), and volleyballs ($2 an hr). Lower rates are available for full-day rentals. At **Hermosa Cyclery** (20 13th St., just off the Strand, tel. 310/376–2720) bike rentals are $6–$12 an hour.

If you tire of watching the take-no-prisoners volleyball being played by the pier, take a jaunt to **Hamilton Gregg Brewworks** (58 11th St., btw the Strand and Hermosa Ave., tel. 310/376–0406), where customers brew their own beer in giant steel kettles (about $100 gets you 48 bottles). If you're just passing through, you won't be able to brew; the beer requires two weeks of aging. It's fun to watch, however, and the display of witty personalized labels rivals many art galleries in creativity. Farther inland, the **Either/Or Bookstore** (124 Pier Ave., just east of Hermosa Ave., tel. 310/374–2060) offers stacks of fiction, nonfiction, and periodicals.

**REDONDO BEACH** Redondo Beach, just south of Hermosa, is the most family-oriented of the South Bay beaches, with more squealing children than volleyball players and more chain stores and greasy fish 'n' chips "shoppes" than plywood rental shacks or home-cooking cafés. From PCH, take Torrance Boulevard to **Veterans Park,** where you can picnic on the grass overlooking the Pacific (there's a farmers' market here Thursday mornings). The adjacent pier and King Harbor marina, a short walk north, are both cluttered with senior citizens and gift shops hawking tacky plastic souvenirs; proceed at your own risk.

*Amidst the tourist clutter of the Redondo Beach Pier, look for the simple bust of George Freeth, Southern California's first lifeguard and a pioneer of mainland surfing.*

## STUDIOS

Most of the movie and television studios, apart from Fox and Paramount, aren't actually in Los Angeles; they're in the San Fernando Valley (*see* Chapter 10). But because the studios are an integral part of the L.A. tourist experience, all are listed below. If you're itching to get past the tour guides and velvet ropes, *see box* So You Want to Sell Your Screenplay, *above.*

**FOX TELEVISION** Those hoping to be discovered as the next Shannen Doherty will be deeply disappointed to learn that Fox TV does *not* offer back-lot tours. The consolation prize: You can pick up free tickets to various TV programs taped here (*Home Improvement, Blossom, The Larry Sanders Show,* and *Roseanne*) at the Fox Television Center box office weekdays 8:30–6. Tickets are available beginning each Wednesday for the following week on a first-come, first-served basis. *5746 Sunset Blvd., 1 block west of U.S. 101 in Hollywood, tel. 213/856–1000 or 818/506–0067.*

**NBC STUDIOS** NBC's excellent tour takes you to working studios and sets; you might get a peek at *The Tonight Show* or an outdoor set for *Days of Our Lives.* The 1¼-hour guided walking tour of the network's facilities in Burbank also stops by the special effects, makeup, and wardrobe departments. If you're interested, free tickets for *The Tonight Show* (and other programs on occasion) are available weekdays on a first-come, first-served basis; you may also request tickets by mail (with an SASE) at least two weeks in advance. *3000 W. Alameda Ave., Burbank 91523, tel. 818/840–3537. Admission: $6. Ticket office open weekdays 8–5. Tours weekdays 9–3 on the hour (and 10–2 some summer Saturdays).*



**PARAMOUNT STUDIOS** Paramount, one of the last great movie studios remaining in Hollywood proper, offers a 2-hour guided walking tour through its back lots. You'll hear plenty of history and see whatever's happening around the lots on that particular day. From August through April you can join the live studio audience for one of several television shows, like *Frasier* or *Wings*; in the spring, sit in on the taping of a pilot show. Tickets, distributed on a first-come, first-served basis, are free at Paramount's box office weekdays 8:30–4. *860 N. Gower St., btw Melrose Ave. and Santa Monica Blvd. in Hollywood, tel. 213/956–5000. 2 blocks east of Vine St. Admission: $15. Tours hourly weekdays 9–2.*

**UNIVERSAL STUDIOS HOLLYWOOD** Many of Universal's past and present film props are displayed on the 420-acre grounds, but the emphasis is on thrilling the pants off visitors with high-tech extravaganzas and stunt shows involving explosions, mechanical monsters, and simulated gunfire. Scream through time on Back to the Future: The Ride, or get squirted by a Pterodactyl plane during the new Flintstones Show. Though there's no opportunity to see an authentic working studio, Universal is still jammed every summer; go early in the day if at all. Look for discount coupons at motels and visitor centers. *100 Universal City Plaza, Universal City, tel. 818/508–9600. Admission: $33. Summer: box office open daily 8 AM–9 PM; park closes at 11 PM. Winter: box office open daily 8:30–4:30; park closes at 7 PM. Park hrs vary, so call ahead.*

*Universal Studios is a visual Jolt Cola: Scream as you watch a lifelike King Kong squash tall buildings! Quiver as you experience the re-created carnage of San Francisco's subway in a major earthquake! Sweat as you're cast into the movie Backdraft without singeing a hair on your head!*

**WARNER BROTHERS STUDIOS** At Warner Brothers, there is no formal tour schedule; guides try to take you "behind the scenes" to wherever the action is on that particular day. You might drop by the old *Dukes of Hazzard* set (don't pretend you don't remember) before checking progress on the newest blockbuster mega-movie. Then stroll by set-construction facilities, sound stages, and the new costume warehouse. Walking tours last about 2 hours. *4000 Warner Blvd., at Olive Ave. in Burbank, tel. 818/954–1744. Admission: $27. Tours weekdays 9–4; call for schedule. Reservations advised.*

## CHEAP THRILLS

In L.A. comedy clubs, you can be pelted with the spittle of a famous stand-up for $30—or with that of an unknown for under $5. Gird yourself for the outrageous and occasionally gross. At

### *Take a Walk on the Mild Side*

***If you find real-life Hollywood disappointing, the folks at Universal Studios have manufactured a giddy Sani-Fresh version to satisfy your expectations. Universal CityWalk is Universal Studios' privately administered two-block "city"—a response to the fears of paranoid visitors and residents about L.A.'s carjackings, drugs, and gang warfare. Conveniently cleansing the "streets" of any undesirable urban elements, CityWalk provides a smiling, happy substitute. Your $6 parking fee (redeemable at any of the 18 cinema screens on the premises) is the only admission price for this weird world, where oversize, brilliantly lit signs and theme restaurants share space with Top 40–style rock bands, scripted street performers, and giant TV screens pulsing with the latest Universal Pictures release. It's enough to make you barf. For information, call 818/622–4455.***

the **West Hollywood Playhouse** (666 N. Robertson Ave., just south of Santa Monica Blvd. in West Hollywood, tel. 818/762–7547), Mice, the self-billed "Improv Comedy All-Stars," perform Saturdays at around 9 PM for free. At the **Wild Side Theater** (10945 Camarillo St., at Vineland Ave. in North Hollywood, tel. 818/506–8838) there's an open mike for comedians every Monday; sign-ups begin at 7:30 PM and the cover is $3. Check the *L.A. Weekly* (*see* Basics, *above*) for the latest acts.

In summer, music fills the air around Los Angeles. Besides practice sessions at the Hollywood Bowl (*see* Exploring L.A., *above*), you'll find free summer concerts at the **UCLA Summer Chamber Music Festival,** in the university's Schoenberg Auditorium (tel. 310/825–4401). Musicians from the L.A. Philharmonic, L.A. Chamber Orchestra, and UCLA's own Department of Music perform on Monday and Thursday afternoons. **Jazz at the Wadsworth** (tel. 310/794–8961), a series of free concerts that takes place the first Sunday of each month at UCLA's Veterans Wadsworth Theatre, has featured such artists as Tito Puente, Branford Marsalis, and Maceo Parker. The Santa Monica Pier's **Twilight Dance Concerts** (tel. 310/458–8900) feature a different sound each week, from big band to reggae; bands play Thursday evenings 7:30–9:30. At downtown's **California Plaza** (3rd St., btw Grand Ave. and Olive St., tel. 213/687–2159), you can catch local and international musicians Wednesday, Friday, and Sunday afternoons or Friday and Saturday evenings. Past performers have included the Japanese group Shoukichi Kina, and El Vez ("the Mexican Elvis") and his Memphis Mariachis.

Open-mike poetry readings draw the new beatniks of L.A.'s café society. They're usually freewheeling (and free) affairs—audience members stand up and read their own work while Wordsworth spins in his grave. In Beverly Hills, aspiring bards gather at art gallery/used bookstore/café **The Colloquy** (239 S. Robertson Blvd., at 3rd St., tel. 310/289–1989) on Wednesdays at 8:30 PM. On Santa Monica's Third Street Promenade, the **Midnight Special Bookstore** (1318 3rd St., tel. 310/393–2923) has open readings Fridays starting at 8 PM. And in Hollywood, the folks at **Highland Grounds** (*see* Cafés, *above*) open their café to musicians and poets at 7:30 PM Wednesdays. Participation is never required, but if you've composed a modern *Iliad* or an ode to sweat socks, arrive half an hour early to sign up for a reading time.

If you're aching to participate in Los Angeles's consumer culture but can't afford to play big spender, head to the **Melrose Weekend Market** (cnr Melrose and Fairfax Aves., tel. 213/934–2083), where on Sundays from 9 to 5 you'll find both junk and salvageable curios among the antiques, jewelry, and vintage clothing. Live jazz and fresh bread for sale are groovy extras.

## FESTIVALS

The Los Angeles **Cultural Affairs Department** (tel. 213/485–2433) publishes an annual "Festivals of Los Angeles" booklet, available at visitor centers (*see* Basics, *above*). It should be especially appealing to lovers of jazz and film, for which monthly festivals abound.

➢ **JANUARY** • During the first week of the month, look for the **Tournament of Roses Parade** and the **Rose Bowl** in Pasadena (*see* Chapter 10). In Little Tokyo, the **Oshogatsu Festival** (tel. 213/625–0414) ushers in the Japanese New Year.

➢ **FEBRUARY** • The Golden Dragon Parade—which falls on a different day in February each year—marks the height of the month-long **Chinese New Year** festivities (tel. 213/617–0396) in Chinatown.

➢ **MARCH** • The 26-mile **Los Angeles Marathon** (tel. 310/444–5544), held the first Sunday of the month, attracts international competitors and hordes of spectators. At the **St. Patrick's Day Parade** in Century City, expect green beer—and the sort of people green beer is likely to attract. There isn't a snowball's chance in hell you'll get invited to the **Academy Awards,** usually held the last week of the month, but you can lurk outside the Dorothy Chandler Pavilion (135 N. Grand Ave., at 1st St.) admiring arriving celebrities.

➢ **MAY** • The entire city comes alive for the celebration of **Cinco de Mayo** (tel. 213/625–5045), the anniversary of Mexico's independence from France. A 36-block section of downtown hosts Latino music, carnival rides, and traditional food and drink. At the end of the month, UCLA holds a free, two-day **Jazz and Reggae Festival** (tel. 310/825–6564).

➢ **JUNE** • The **Gay and Lesbian Pride Festival and Parade** (tel. 213/656–6553), in West Hollywood, commemorates the 1969 Stonewall riots in New York City and is a forum for the city's large gay population to show their solidarity and strength. The parade is preceded by a festival with live music, street vendors, and ethnic food.

➢ **JULY** • Watch the **Fourth of July Fireworks** from coastal communities such as Marina del Rey; most take place around sunset. The **Lotus Festival** (tel. 213/485–1310), held in Echo Park north of downtown, celebrates Pacific Rim cultures with crafts, music, and dragon boat races.

➢ **SEPTEMBER** • On the 5th, **Los Angeles's Birthday** (tel. 213/680–2821) is celebrated on Olvera Street in El Pueblo de Los Angeles Historic Park with a civic ceremony and festivities honoring the founders. At the end of the month, South Central's one-day, free **Watts Towers Jazz Festival** (tel. 213/485–1795) attracts top performers from all over the world. For more than 20 years, the annual **Koreatown Festival** (tel. 213/730–1495 or 213/730–1527), celebrated at the end of the month, has included a lavish parade, traditional dancing, and martial-arts demonstrations.

➢ **OCTOBER** • The three-day **Santa Monica Oktoberfest** (tel. 310/393–9287), which takes place at the beginning of the month, is an epic street fair, with German oompah bands, carnival rides—and maybe just a little beer.

➢ **NOVEMBER** • **Día de los Muertos** (tel. 213/628–1274), or Day of the Dead, is celebrated at the beginning of the month on Olvera Street with activities both silly and somber, from dancing humans dressed as skeletons to a candlelight procession at dusk.

➢ **DECEMBER** • Skip the traditional **Hollywood Christmas Parade** (tel. 213/469–8311) in favor of the annual African American **Kwanzaa Festival and Parade** (tel. 213/299–0964), held shortly after Christmas in Leimert Park.

# After Dark

**Most bars, clubs, and bistros in this go-**go-go city have a shelf life shorter than the vinyl skirts at Melrose boutiques. Sometimes, appearance in print—even in guidebooks as cool as this—equals instant social death. Of course, there's always the **Hard Rock Café** (8500 Beverly Blvd., in Beverly Center, tel. 310/276–7605), but you can go far beyond this type of tourist trap. Hollywood, the locus of L.A. nightlife, is without question the place to start your search; you can't help but stumble into a happening joint if you cruise its streets long enough. Check the **KROQ Concert Line** (tel. 818/566–ROCK); the popular alternative radio station (106.7 FM) occasionally sponsors free appearances by cool bands. Cafés are also an integral part of the evening scene, with live music, open-mike poetry readings, and screenings of cult and classic films; for more information, *see* Cafés, *above.* Tickets to many concerts and mainstream theater performances can be obtained directly through a venue's box office, or by calling **Ticketmaster** (tel. 213/480–3232), which adds an annoying $2–$6 service charge.

**BARS** **Barney's Beanery.** Half bar, half restaurant, the Beanery serves up over 300 different beers, including a few of their own brews. The crowd clustered at the long bar and near the pool tables is hip but not haughty. *8447 Santa Monica Blvd., btw La Cienega and Crescent Heights Blvds. in West Hollywood, tel. 213/654–2287.*

*L.A. bars and clubs have seen their share of tragedy: Janis Joplin partied at Barney's Beanery the night she died, and in October '93 young actor River Phoenix fatally overdosed on drugs at the Viper Room, an exclusive club on Sunset Boulevard.*

**Cat & Fiddle Pub and Restaurant.** You'll find a mixed crowd of yuppies and hipsters drinking pricey beers and espressos on the large, breezy outdoor patio. There's live jazz on Sunday evenings, and no cover. *6530 Sunset Blvd., btw Vine St. and Highland Ave. in Hollywood, tel. 213/468–3800.*

**Dresden Room.** This bar, a.k.a. Goatee Central, features occasional bouts of karaoke (Julia Roberts reportedly participated once). Otherwise, look for live piano music Monday–Saturday among furnishings unchanged since the '60s. *1760 N. Vermont Ave., at Hollywood Blvd. in East Hollywood, tel. 213/665–4294.*

**Formosa.** This is a Chinese restaurant and bar partially housed in a converted railroad car, with a photographic shrine to Hollywood's movie legends. The fun crowd is fittingly eclectic. *7156 Santa Monica Blvd., at Formosa Ave. in West Hollywood, tel. 213/850–9050.*

**Good Luck Club.** Chinese lanterns, comfy sofas, funky music, and a crowd that's willing to line up outside are sure signs this is a hot hangout. They stock powerful Chinese rose and melon whiskeys ($4.50) meant for sipping. *1514 Hillhurst Ave., at Hollywood Blvd. in East Hollywood, tel. 213/666–3524.*

**Hollywood Athletic Club.** Legend has it that a drunken John Wayne once pelted passing cars with the club's billiard balls. You, too, can pay $4–$14 (plus valet parking) for an hour of pool at this swank stomping ground for the see-and-be-seen crowd. Check out live blues on Monday nights. *6525 Sunset Blvd., just east of Highland Ave. in Hollywood, tel. 213/962–6600.*

**King's Head.** Guinness is on tap at this fish 'n' chips refuge for Irish and British ex-pats and other Anglophiles; on Saturday nights, the crowds are as thick as the accents. *116 Santa Monica Blvd., btw Ocean Ave. and 2nd St. in Santa Monica, tel. 310/451–1402.*

**Lava Lounge.** Occupying a two-tier strip-mall in a dicey neighborhood, this is the latest dimly lit den of L.A.'s chic society. Look for the faux lava-rock fountain and a variety of weird lounge acts (was that a xylophonist?). *1533 N. La Brea Ave., btw Sunset and Hollywood Blvds. in Hollywood, tel. 213/876–6612.*

**Manhattan Beach Brewing Company.** As the beach (2 blocks away) empties in late afternoon, this place fills. The homebrewed ales, bitters, and stouts go for $3 a pint, or you can sample the beers in shot-glass "tasters" ($1). *124 Manhattan Beach Blvd., at Ocean Dr. in Manhattan Beach, tel. 310/798–2744.*

**Micky's.** Bartenders at this packed and popular gay bar are more than occasionally bare-chested, and video screens dominate the walls. *8857 Santa Monica Blvd., btw La Cienega and San Vicente Blvds. in West Hollywood, tel. 310/657–1176.*

**San Francisco Saloon.** Magnanimously dedicated to L.A.'s main rival, the saloon has S.F. beer (Anchor Steam on tap) and S.F. baseball (Giants games on a big-screen TV); it's popular with a laid-back younger crowd. *11501 W. Pico Blvd., at Sawtelle Blvd. in West L.A., tel. 310/478–0152.*

**CLUBS** **Arena.** A favorite among the hip gay men of Hollywood, this 22,000-square-foot former ice-making factory literally thumps with house music under dramatic lights. *6655 Santa Monica Blvd., btw Highland Ave. and Vine St. in Hollywood, tel. 213/462–0714. Cover: $6–$10. Open Fri.–Sun. Usually 18 and up.*

**Checca.** This small, stylish, French-Italian restaurant hosts a different club every night of the week. B-side (Wednesday) is soul and funk; Club Prozak (Friday) is alternative music; High Society (Saturday) is house; and 45 Vibe (Sunday) is jazz and Latin. The crowd is young and groovy. Call ahead, since clubs are likely to change. *7323 Santa Monica Blvd. at Fuller Ave. in West Hollywood, tel. 213/850–7471. Cover: $3–$5.*

**Dragonfly.** Dragonfly offers different music nightly, always at the cutting edge of L.A.'s club scene. The current rage is Sellout, their Tuesday-night club, which revives '80s punk. You may even catch band members from the Chili Peppers in the crowd. *6505 Santa Monica Blvd., btw Highland Ave. and Vine St. in Hollywood, tel. 213/466–6111. Cover: $10.*

**Kingston 12.** Reggae reigns on the Kingston's two dance floors and is enjoyed by locals and visitors alike. Friday and Saturday nights feature live bands; Thursday and Sunday a DJ spins. *814 Broadway, at Lincoln Ave. in Santa Monica, tel. 310/451–4423. Cover: about $5. Open Thurs.–Sun.*

**Luna Park.** Dark, elegant, and elaborate, Luna has two stages, three bars, and a restaurant. Patrons are befittingly sleek. Nightly entertainment ranges from DJ'd world music to live bands and alternative comedy acts. *655 N. Robertson Blvd., btw Melrose Ave. and Santa Monica Blvd. in West Hollywood, tel. 310/652–0611. Cover: $5–$12.*



**Mayan.** This weekend venue is utterly dedicated to the dithyrambic powers of disco, retro, hip-hop, and salsa. Dress your best or the powers that be may not let you over the threshold of this renovated, former art-deco movie house. The downtown club has secured parking; take advantage, and be careful walking around here at night, as it can be a sketchy neighborhood. *1038 S. Hill St., near 11th St., tel. 213/746–4287. Cover: $12.*

**The Palms.** L.A.'s oldest lesbian nightclub (it's been around for 25 years) offers different DJs nightly, pool tables, and cheap drink nights (50¢ Wed., $1 Thurs.), and welcomes all comers. *8572 Santa Monica Blvd., at N. La Cienega Blvd. in West Hollywood, tel. 310/652–6188. Cover: $3–$5; no cover Mon., Thurs., and Sun.*

**The Probe.** There's a different club every night of the week, each with its own groupies. Tuesdays, Club Flex (tel. 818/980–4793 for info) is reggae and hip-hop; Stigmata (tel. 213/462–7442 for info) gives techno and industrial fans a place to party on Fridays; on Saturdays, Probe (tel. 310/281–6292 for info) is gay men's night with Euro-pop tunes; and the extremely popular Club '70s (tel. 213/957–4855) revives disco on Sundays. The crowd is a good mix of gay and straight folk. For some clubs, you must buy a $2 membership, good for one year. *863 N. Highland Ave., btw Santa Monica Blvd. and Melrose Ave. in Hollywood. Cover $10 and up.*

*If you insist on up-to-the-nanosecond nightlife, here's what to do: Cruise Melrose looking for a café that incorporates black lighting in its decor. Go in and (a) check for flyers at the door, (b) eavesdrop on the conversation of anyone multiply pierced, or (c) make friends by offering everyone within immediate arm span a cigarette. You can't fail.*

**LIVE MUSIC** Los Angeles had a cool music scene decades before Seattle became wired for sound. It's still one of the best cities in the country to catch promising rock acts, or to check out jazz, blues, and classical tunes.

➢ **ROCK** • **Al's Bar.** Every so often an unknown grunge, jazz, or neo-punk band shows up in this large brick warehouse downtown and blows you away. A popular hangout of the pierced and tattooed set, the bar hosts live music on Thursday, Friday, and Saturday nights. *305 S. Hewitt St., btw Alameda St. and Santa Fe Ave., tel. 213/625–9703. Cover: $5.*

**Anti-Club.** This was once the vanguard of L.A.'s underground music scene, when there still was one: Henry Rollins, the Red Hot Chili Peppers, and Soundgarden all played here early in their careers. Now you're most likely to find sub-thrash bands playing to crowds of hyperactive skatebrats. *4658 Melrose Ave., btw Western and Normandie Aves. in West Hollywood, tel. 213/661–3913 or 213/667–9762. Cover varies. All ages.*

*For tips on free (often random, sometimes good) shows, cheap beer nights, and the occasional apartment for rent, call 310/CUT–FOOT.*

**Jabberjaw Coffeehouse.** A surreal and retro dive that hosts pubescent punk and garage bands, the Coffeehouse is a favorite with the younger, horn-rimmed-glasses-wearing crowd. *3711 W. Pico Blvd., at Crenshaw Blvd., tel. 213/732–3463. Cover $5. All ages.*

**The Kibitz Room.** Adjoining the landmark kosher deli Canter's, the Kibitz Room often has jazz and blues in addition to rock acts. Sitting at the space-age Formica tables are intoxicated punkers, AA's hip crowd, CBS executives, and Hasidic Jews—a truly surreal scene. *419 N. Fairfax Ave., btw Melrose Ave. and Beverly Blvd. in West L.A., tel. 213/651–2030. No cover.*

**Roxy.** One of L.A.'s best-known and largest rock clubs, the Roxy has hosted the likes of David Bowie, Bruce Springsteen, Bob Marley, and Prince. Sadly, these days you'll probably find big-haired glam rockers trying too hard to impress talent scouts. *9009 Sunset Blvd., btw Doheny Dr. and San Vicente Blvd. in West Hollywood, tel. 310/276–2222. Cover: $3 and up. All ages.*

**Troubadour.** With a reputation for hosting some of the biggest names in rock when they were still relatively unknown, the multilevel Troubadour is an excellent place to catch budding and established alternative bands. *9081 Santa Monica Blvd., btw Doheny Dr. and San Vicente Blvd. in West Hollywood, tel. 310/276–6168. Cover: $6–$12.*

*The term "go-go girl" was supposedly coined at the Whiskey in the 1960s to refer to drugged-out dancers who enjoyed gyrating naked onstage.*

**Whiskey A Go Go.** Some of the city's best alternative rock bands play here, hoping to impress scouts; in past years, the club has hosted Led Zeppelin, the Doors, Jimi Hendrix, and Talking Heads, among others. *8901 Sunset Blvd., near San Vicente Blvd. in West Hollywood, tel. 310/652–4202. Cover: $3–$15. All ages.*

➢ **JAZZ/BLUES** • **The Derby.** This swank, retro club is housed in an impressive, domed room and comes complete with private booths, an oval-shaped bar, and plush furnishings. There's live jazz, blues, rockabilly, or swing. *4500 Los Feliz Blvd., at Hillhurst Ave. south of Griffith Park, tel. 213/663–8979. Cover: $5; no cover Tues.*

**Harvelle's.** Smoke and thick crowds are de rigueur for a great blues house, and Harvelle's proves no exception. Nightly sessions start at 8:30 PM. *1432 4th St., at Santa Monica Blvd. in Santa Monica, tel. 310/395–1676. Cover $3–$7; no cover Mon.*

**House of Blues.** This $9 million, newly opened plaything of actor Dan Aykroyd offers a glitzy interpretation of the South that might make it hard to concentrate on the quality blues, funk, and rock acts. Oh, there's a T-shirt shop, too. *8430 Sunset Blvd., east of La Cienega Blvd. in West Hollywood, tel. 213/650–1451 (info) or 213/650–0476 (box office). Cover: $10 and up. Some shows all ages.*

**Jack's Sugar Shack.** Is it a blues bar or a beach bungalow? The Sugar Shack has an all-out, faux-tropical decor with bamboo trellises, plastic birds, and beach landscapes painted on the walls. There's also 16 beers on tap (in addition to live music nightly). *1707 N. Vine St., at Hollywood Blvd. in Hollywood, tel. 213/466–7005. Cover: $5.*

**The Mint Lounge.** Drinks are cheap and soft (beer and wine only), the music hard and furious. This very un-L.A. hole-in-the-wall plays gritty blues and some indie rock. Shows happen every night, but Wednesdays are considered best. *6010 W. Pico St., btw Fairfax Ave. and La Cienega Blvd. in West L.A., tel. 213/937–9630. Cover: $5–$10.*

➢ **CLASSICAL** • The downtown Music Center's Dorothy Chandler Pavilion (135 N. Grand Ave., at 1st St.) offers student rush tickets an hour before show time. You'll pay $10 for the renowned **L.A. Opera** (tel. 213/972–7211) and $6 for the **Philharmonic** (tel. 213/850–2000) if you have a current student ID. The **Hollywood Bowl** (2301 N. Highland Ave., tel. 213/850–2000) also offers student rush tickets ($6) for weekday performances of classical, jazz, and contemporary music, available the day of (or one day prior to) the performance; for more info, *see* Exploring L.A., *above*. UCLA hosts a free **Summer Chamber Music Festival** with weekly performances (*see* Cheap Thrills, *above*).

**MOVIE HOUSES** The city that makes 'em is also the city that screens 'em—movie houses are a big part of life in L.A. Call 777–FILM in the 213 and 310 area codes for recorded info on movie times and locations. Offbeat flicks and revived classics can be found at UCLA's **Melnitz Theater** and the L.A. County Museum of Art's **Bing Theater** (for more on either, *see* Exploring L.A., *above*). The small but pleasant theater **Silent Movie** (611 N. Fairfax Ave., btw Melrose Ave. and Beverly Blvd., tel. 213/653–2389) runs lots of Charlie Chaplin and other 1920s classics. **Sunset 5** (8000 Sunset Blvd., at Crescent Heights Blvd. in West Hollywood, tel. 213/848–3500) is just another big movie complex—until midnight on weekends, when they screen five of the weirdest low-budget flicks they can find (like *Surf Nazis Must Die*).

**THEATER** The strip of Santa Monica Boulevard between Cole and Seward streets in Hollywood promotes itself as "Theater Row." Here, a loose federation of micro-theaters hosts an eclectic and usually obscure range of one-act and experimental plays with cheap ticket prices. **Actors' Gang** (6209 Santa Monica Blvd., btw Vine St. and El Centro Ave., tel. 213/465–0566) was founded by actor Tim Robbins, and is well known for both its original productions and its innovative adaptations of established plays; tickets cost $5–$10. In Santa Monica, **Highways**

(1651 18th St., tel. 310/453–1755) presents performance art, dance, theater, comedy, and any combination thereof; it's always avant-garde, wild, weird, and affordable ($10–$15). If you feel like splurging on a big Broadway-style production, check out downtown's **Ahmanson Theatre** (135 N. Grand Ave., btw 1st and 2nd Sts., tel. 213/365–3500).

*Look out for L.A. Connection, the comedy troupe that imposes hysterical improvisational plots and dialogue on cheap horror flicks; they appear sporadically at Nuart Theatre (11272 Santa Monica Blvd., at Sawtelle Blvd. in West L.A., tel. 310/478–6379) for $7.50.*

**Mark Taper Forum.** This theater in the downtown Music Center offers public rush tickets for some shows 10 minutes before curtain for $10 (regularly they're $30 and up). You'll want to get in line at least an hour early. Shows at the Forum often go on to New York City's Broadway; recent hits have included Tony Kushner's award-winning *Angels in America: Perestroika. 135 N. Grand Ave., at 1st St., tel. 213/972–0700.*

**Groundling Theater.** This is where Pee Wee Herman and many *Saturday Night Live* cast members got their start. The Groundling puts on several different shows a week, from scripted sketches to improvisational and audience-interaction pieces. *7307 Melrose Ave., near La Brea Ave., tel. 213/934–9700. Tickets: $10–$20.*

**Theatre/Theater.** The troupe here can always be counted on to come up with something witty and weird. Recent efforts include *The Dysfunctional Show,* which lampooned daytime talk shows. Audience participation is integral. *1713 Cahuenga Blvd., near Sunset Blvd. in Hollywood, tel. 213/871–0210. Tickets: around $10.*

# Outdoor Activities

**Even if you don't want to spend a day on the beach,** there are plenty of outdoor options in Los Angeles. Of course, smog can pose a serious threat to your health, but if it's any consolation, the air is clearer in the surrounding hills and along the coast. If you do plan to hit the sand, L.A. has over 20 public beaches from which to choose. Start on the Pacific Coast Highway (PCH) in Malibu and drive south along the ocean—you're sure to find your niche by the time you reach Venice. Especially attractive is **Leo Carillo State Beach** (tel. 818/880–0350), 25 miles west of Santa Monica on PCH, with rugged cliffs, tidal pools, hidden coves, and miles of hiking trails, as well as a developed campground (*see* Where to Sleep, *above*).

## PARTICIPANT SPORTS

**HIKING** In the Santa Monica Mountains, **Franklin Canyon** has beautiful hiking trails. To reach them, take Beverly Drive north to the stoplight in Coldwater Canyon Park. Continue on Beverly Drive (you'll have to turn left), then turn right onto Franklin Canyon Drive. During full moons, rangers lead two-hour night hikes through Franklin Canyon with views of the city lights far below. In **Griffith Park,** you can ascend to the summit of Mt. Hollywood, a trip with amazing views; the trail (3 mi round-trip) begins at the parking lot of the Griffith Observatory (*see* Exploring L.A., *above*). At the **Hollywood Reservoir** (Lake Hollywood Dr., tel. 213/481–4211)—in the Santa Monica foothills west of Griffith Park—a 3½-mile path loops the shore, blissfully secluded among stands of pine and eucalyptus. It's a popular circuit for racewalkers and runners, with a bonus view of Madonna's red-and-yellow–painted estate up the hill. From U.S. 101, take Cahuenga Boulevard north, go right on Barham Boulevard, and make a right on Lake Hollywood Drive.

*Before you lace up your hiking boots, check the newspaper for air-quality predictions. In the L.A. hills, pollution can reach unhealthy concentrations as many as 80 or more days per year.*

In the 9,000-acre **Topanga State Park** (tel. 818/597–1036), explore the Musch Trail, a 4-mile round-trip to a pleasant waterfall. Park admission is $5; you can reach the entrance on Topanga Canyon Boulevard from either PCH in Malibu or U.S. 101 in the San Fernando Valley.

There are also miles of trails in **Will Rogers** and **Malibu Creek state parks,** near Malibu (*see* Exploring L.A., *above*).

**BIKING** Despite the local addiction to autos, you'll find several worthwhile biking areas. Some 5 miles of gravel trails provide excellent mountain biking at **Sullivan Canyon** in the Santa Monica Mountains; from different points along the trails you'll find great views of the Pacific. To get here, take Sunset Boulevard to Mandeville Canyon Road (about 3 mi west of I–405 in Brentwood), turn north, and then go west on Westridge Road to the end. **Griffith Park** (*see* Exploring L.A., *above*) restricts bicyclists to paved paths. Try two unmaintained paved roads that are closed to vehicular traffic: the 5-mile **Mt. Hollywood Road,** which branches off Griffith Park Drive near the Travel Town Museum, and the 5-mile **Vista del Valle Road,** which you pick up from Commonwealth Avenue near the Roosevelt Golf Course. Both offer good views and solitude. Mountain bikers will also find miles of trails at **Malibu Creek State Park** in Malibu (*see* Exploring L.A., *above*).

If a cruise on the coast sounds more appealing, head to the strand of concrete that stretches 22 miles along the ocean; it's parallel to PCH, and connects the South Bay beaches to Pacific Palisades. Bike rentals cost $3–$6 per hour ($10–$22 per day) at **Rental on the Beach** (3100 Ocean Front Walk, at Washington Blvd. in Venice, tel. 310/821–9047) and **Spokes and Stuff** (1715 Ocean Front Walk, at Pico Blvd. in Santa Monica, tel. 310/395–4748). Near Griffith Park's southwest entrance, **Woody's Bicycle World** (3157 Los Feliz Blvd., just east of I–5, tel. 213/661–6665) rents mountain bikes by the day ($15) or the week ($60). For more info on biking in Southern California, contact the **L.A. County Transportation Commission** (818 W. 7th St., Suite 1100, tel. 213/244–6539), which distributes an invaluable full-color L.A. County bike map free of charge.

**IN-LINE SKATING** **Sea Mist Rentals** in Santa Monica rents roller skates and in-line skates, offering two ways to see and be seen on the 22-mile beachside bike path that winds south from Pacific Palisades. Beware: On summer weekends the route is completely clogged with knock-kneed Rollerblade virgins. Skates are $4 for the first hour ($3 each additional hr, $10 per day); blades are $5 for the first hour ($4 each additional hr, $14 per day). Photo ID is required as a deposit. *1619 Ocean Front Walk, across from Santa Monica Pier, tel. 310/395–7076. Open daily 9–8.*

**HORSEBACK RIDING** The **Griffith Park Equestrian Center** rents horses for a maximum of 2 hours at a mere $15 per hour. No riding test or reservations are required. *480 Riverside Dr., tel. 818/840–8401. From Hwy. 134, exit at W. Alameda Ave., turn right on Main St., and follow signs. Open daily 8–5.*

**SURFING AND BODY SURFING** Popular L.A. surf spots include Topanga, Zuma, and Leo Carillo beaches—but locals don't take kindly to being invaded by fumbling beginners. Novices should head to **Malibu Surfrider State Beach** for gentler breaks and kinder companions. The nearly clairvoyant recording of the **Surfline/Wavetrak** (tel. 714/976–SURF) is worth the $1.50-per-minute price; wave predictions are accurate to within a foot, up to 2 weeks in advance. If your interest in surfing is of the "sit on the beach and watch" variety, keep an eye out for the professional surfing competitions that surface during summer in Manhattan Beach and Malibu. For info on dates and locations, call the Association of Surfing Professionals (tel. 714/842–8826) or U.S. Surfing (tel. 714/443–6187). For more on area surfing, *see box* Go Ahead—Make My Wave, in Chapter 10.

Across from the pier in Malibu, **Natural Progression** (22935 Pacific Coast Hwy., tel. 310/456–6302) rents longboards and regular "sticks" for $20 a day, with a credit card or $400 cash deposit. Wet-suit and body-board rentals are $8 and $6 a day, respectively, and windsurfing boards go for $30 a day. In Venice, **Rental on the Beach** (*see* Biking, *above*) rents body boards for $4 an hour or $8 a day. **Spokes and Stuff** (*see* Biking, *above*) in Santa Monica has body boards for $3 an hour or $10 a day.

**WHALE WATCHING** **Redondo Sport Fishing,** on the pier at the Redondo Beach Marina, sends out two boats a day during whale-watching season (Jan.–Mar.). Trips last about three hours and cost $11 per person ($12 on weekends). *233 N. Harbor Dr., Redondo Beach, tel. 310/372–2111 or 213/772–2064. Reservations advised.*

## SPECTATOR SPORTS



**BASEBALL** Bundle up—preferably in the team colors blue and white—if you're headed to a night game. All the overpriced beer in the world can't keep you warm if the fog rolls into Dodger Stadium, beloved home of the beloved **Los Angeles Dodgers.** The stadium is just northwest of downtown, off Highway 110 north of U.S. 101. Call 213/224–1400 for game info, or 213/224–1448 for tickets. Seats start at $6 if you don't mind a nosebleed view.

**BASKETBALL** Although the **Los Angeles Lakers** are worshipped in their hometown, seats ($8 and up) are easily obtained for most home games. During intermissions, amuse yourself by scanning the crowd for actor and season-ticket holder Jack Nicholson; he'll be the only one in the indoor arena sporting sunglasses. Home court is the Great Western Forum in Inglewood, near Los Angeles International Airport. To reach the stadium, take I–405 to Manchester Avenue (Hwy. 42) east, then turn right on Prairie Avenue. The season runs October–April. Call 310/419–3100 for a schedule and tickets.

The **Clippers** is L.A.'s "other" basketball team. The city hasn't yet decided whether to love or hate them, and this won't change until they win a championship (or at least don't finish second to last). The Clippers play at the L.A. Sports Arena (3939 S. Figueroa St.) in Exposition Park and tickets start at $10. To reach the park from downtown, take I–110 to Exposition Boulevard and turn left onto Figueroa Street. For tickets and game info, call 213/748–8000.

**BEACH VOLLEYBALL** If you spend enough time in L.A., you can be sure to catch one of the professional, take-no-prisoners volleyball competitions that take place February–September on the sand in Manhattan Beach, Hermosa Beach, and Malibu. Tournament dates and sites change year to year; call the **Pro Women's Volleyball Association** (tel. 310/726–0700) or the **Association of Volleyball Professionals** (tel. 800/793–8687) for info.

**FOOTBALL** Now that the Rams have transplanted their franchise to St. Louis and the Raiders have headed back north to Oakland, Angelenos will have to rely on college pigskin. Luckily, one of the most heated college rivalries in the country—between the **USC Trojans** and the **UCLA Bruins**—provides ample entertainment. The competition culminates on the Saturday before Thanksgiving, when the two teams clash and the winner walks away with a year's worth of bragging rights. Tickets to see either team play cost about $20–$25. To reach the UCLA ticket office call 310/825–2101; the USC ticket office can be reached at 213/740–GOSC.

**ICE HOCKEY** Blood, gore, and random acts of violence: a **Los Angeles Kings** tradition. Ever since the club acquired all-star Wayne Gretzky, Angelenos have been flocking to the Forum to cheer a team that for years had been considered a joke. Despite a disappointing past season,

### *What Says Quack and Carries a Puck?*

***Though it sounds like a bad Jay Leno joke, there really is a professional ice hockey team called the Mighty Ducks, named after the 1992 movie starring Emilio Estevez and owned, naturally, by the savvy Walt Disney Corporation (the same folks who felt compelled to bring the French a theme park with Mickey Mouse). The Ducks play at the Pond in Anaheim, a $100 million stadium 28 miles south of downtown Los Angeles. With video screens, a dance group (the Decoys), their own anthem ("Rock the Pond"), and up to 17,000 rabid fans clad in Duck duds and blowing shrill duck-call whistles, it's more than just a hockey game—it's a trip to an alternate universe. In their inaugural season, the Mighty Ducks finished with an NHL record of 33 wins, 46 losses, 5 ties, and—despite sportswriters' snipes about "sitting" or "lame" ducks—the continued adoration of their fans. For info on tickets (starting at $14) and games, call 714/704–2701.***

they've turned in some rewarding recent performances. Tickets for Kings' games, held November–April at the Forum (for directions, *see* Basketball, *above*), start at $11. For tickets and game information, call 310/419–3100.

**POLO** Long ago, Will Rogers built a polo field so his friends could enjoy an afternoon chukker and barbecue. The polo field is still in use at **Will Rogers State Historic Park** (1501 Will Rogers State Park Rd., tel. 310/454–8212), where you can park ($5) and picnic on the sidelines. Games are played year-round, Saturday 1–5 PM and Sunday 10 AM–1 PM; rain cancels. The polo field is in the hills of Pacific Palisades, just off the 14000 block of Sunset Boulevard.

# NEAR LOS ANGELES 10

By Jim Stanley, with Sonia Perel

M

**Most people who live in or even near L.A. County will tell you that they're from** Los Angeles, when in fact they're from one of the myriad cities that surround it. Residents of the **San Fernando Valley,** for instance, often call themselves Angelenos, and with good reason—many would like to leave this tacky bit of suburbia for something more exciting. Though Valley residents vote in L.A. elections and are subject to most of L.A.'s ordinances, they're separated from the city by the Santa Monica Mountains. Here they've carved out a distinct cultural niche, with its own vernacular and an identity firmly based in the land of shopping malls and big hair.

Of course, Los Angeles sprawls in many directions, not all of it fertile territory for mall rats. In the South Bay, the clifftop estate community of **Palos Verdes** remains impervious to the encroachment of its less affluent neighbors to the east—**San Pedro** and the ever-expanding industrial town of **Long Beach.** Far enough from downtown L.A. to merit their own identities, these towns are still close enough to the city to serve as bedroom communities. They're also the most convenient departure point for **Santa Catalina Island,** 22 miles offshore and a world apart, with a profusion of marine activities and a rugged, undeveloped interior.

Oil rigs and port facilities line the shore near Long Beach and southern Los Angeles, but as you head farther south along the **Orange County** coast the scenery gives way to pristine stretches of beach and dramatic hillsides. Though notoriously conservative in parts—the pro-Clinton stance of the region's local paper during the 1992 presidential election was considered shocking enough to make national news—the coast is also immensely popular with surfers and artists. Galleries fill the streets of progressive Laguna Beach, a great place to spend some time on your way south toward San Diego or Mexico. The **Pacific Coast Highway (PCH)** is often congested with traffic during summer, so if you're in a hurry to reach San Diego you'll want to take I–5. But the coast road is the best way to discover Southern California's golden beaches firsthand, from healing ocean vistas to the tacky bric-a-brac of the tourist trail.

*Anaheim is about as exciting as static on a radio station, but even after 40 years the Magic Kingdom is one of California's—and the country's—best-loved attractions.*

**Disneyland,** contrary to popular belief, is not in Los Angeles but in Orange County, encircled by the inland city of **Anaheim.** As if the Magic Kingdom weren't enough wacky fun, Orange County also gives us the **Knott's Berry Farm** theme park in the city of Buena Park. It's true that inland Orange County is unwieldy suburbia that lacks any central focus—but it isn't nearly as bad as Angelenos make it out to be. So blaze your own trail through the tangle of freeways; most sights are within easy reach of L.A.

# Pasadena

**Pasadena has long been an uncomfortable** cousin to Los Angeles. While L.A. danced naked on the world's stage, Pasadena drank milk and brought home good grades. It's derided as traditional, residential, out-of-touch. (Poignantly, the town's comeback is to point with pride at being named the "most livable city in the United States"—in 1939.) But Pasadena does not deserve such harsh criticism, and after L.A.'s fires and riots, quite a few Pasadena-snubbing Angelenos have eaten their words. This is, after all, home to some of L.A. County's best museums and historic buildings. You can't see a Gutenberg Bible in L.A., because this priceless treasure is kept safe in Pasadena's marvelous Huntington Library.

*If the regular MTA buses don't float your boat, take a spin on one of Pasadena's ARTS buses, a city project that takes the concept of public art and makes it mobile. Each of six theme buses—including the New Year's Day bus and the Multicultural bus—travels daily along Colorado Boulevard, Green Street, and South Lake Avenue. As an added bonus, the fare is free.*

In fact, once-hokey Pasadena is slowly becoming cool. City planners have aided this transformation by gentrifying the hell out of **Old Pasadena,** an eight-block section of town bordered by Pasadena Avenue, Arroyo Parkway, and Green and Union streets. This is the place to check out historic bungalows on tree-shaded streets and restored two-story buildings that made up the city's business district at the turn of the century. The heart of Old Pasadena lies at the intersection of Colorado Boulevard and Fair Oaks Avenue; here you'll find a jumble of restaurants, bars, and shops—and a surprising number of guilty-looking L.A. natives enjoying the scene. Because Old Pasadena knows it's charming, expect to pay for parking at meters (until 8 PM) or at city-owned lots. Free parking, like Pasadena's dowdy image, is a thing of the past.

On New Year's Day, Pasadena is the site of the **Tournament of Roses Parade** and the **Rose Bowl** football game. If you're in town on Thanksgiving (the last Thursday in November), check out the **Doo Dah Parade,** a takeoff on the Tournament of Roses in which business executives march with their briefcases. For lodging and dining tips, plus schedules of current area events, pick up *Pasadena Weekly* or *In Pasadena* magazine; both are available free of charge at most bookstores, cafés, restaurants, and supermarkets. The **Pasadena Chamber of Commerce** offers free maps, restaurant listings, and a glossy community guide. *117 E. Colorado Blvd., at Arroyo Pkwy., tel. 818/795–3355. Open weekdays 9–5.*

## COMING AND GOING

From downtown Los Angeles, take Highway 110 north. From Orange County, take I–5 north to I–605 north to I–210 west. From the San Fernando Valley, take U.S. 101 east to Highway 134 east. **Metro Transit Authority (MTA)** provides frequent bus service from downtown L.A. to Old Pasadena daily 6 AM–10 PM. Catch Pasadena-bound Bus 401 at Olive and 7th streets in L.A.; fare is $2.35 for the 45-minute ride. The Pasadena **Greyhound** station (645 E. Walnut St., at N. El Molino Ave., tel. 818/792–5116) has a ticket office open weekdays 8:30–5 and Saturday 8:30–3.

Like most of the L.A. area, Pasadena is much too spread out to cover on foot. MTA provides bus service around town; the fare is $1.35, transfers 25¢ (disabled patrons pay 45¢ per ride and 10¢ for transfers). For local routes, pick up a schedule at the public library or the nearest Thrifty drugstore, or call MTA's **route information hotline** (tel. 800/252–7433).

## WHERE TO SLEEP

Most of Pasadena's budget motels lie along **East Colorado Boulevard,** just east of the city's happening area. Accommodations get more expensive as you head toward Fair Oaks Avenue and the heart of Old Pasadena. Rates are comparable to much of L.A., except during the week surrounding the January 1 Rose Bowl—the one time of year when prices soar and vacancy signs disappear.

Despite being a wide, palm-lined avenue, Colorado Boulevard is so ugly in places that it's physically painful to look at. Even the bold might grimace at the skanky **Pasadena Motor Inn** (2097

E. Colorado Blvd., at Hill Ave., tel. 818/796–3122) or the marginally hygenic **Swiss Lodge** (2800 E. Colorado Blvd., at San Gabriel Blvd., tel. 818/449–1122), both of which have doubles for about $35 and afford the opportunity to stay cheek by jowl with some truly shady characters. You can always head for the safety of **Travelodge** (2131 E. Colorado Blvd., west of Sierra Madre Blvd., tel. 818/796–3121), with doubles for $45 per night. However, an even better bet lies so far east it borders the neighboring town of Arcadia: The **Regal Inn Motel** (3800 E. Colorado Blvd., at Rosemead Blvd., tel. 818/449–4743) is extremely clean, with doubles for $32 ($160 per week) and kitchenettes for $5 extra.

## FOOD

Having increased its number of restaurants from three to around 100 since 1991, Old Pasadena has surely reached a zenith in its gustatory renaissance. People not only flock from L.A. to dine here—they actually wait in line to do so. In particular, walk-in customers at the reasonably priced Italian kitchen and bakery **Mi Piace** (25 E. Colorado Blvd., near Fair Oaks Ave., tel. 818/795–3131) face waits of up to an hour almost every night. Plan ahead and make reservations. If you're in the mood to splurge, head for the shaded patio and cool interiors of the **Clearwater Café** (168 W. Colorado Blvd., at Pasadena Ave., tel. 818/356–0959), where everything on the menu is grown organically. Seafood entrées start at $9, and vegan dishes go for $8. Otherwise, pick up a lengthy restaurant list at the Chamber of Commerce (*see above*) or simply peruse the blocks surrounding **Fair Oaks Avenue** and **Colorado Boulevard.** Another crop of restaurants lies just south of Colorado, along **Lake Avenue.**

**Burger Continental.** Part bar, part restaurant, and part belly-dancing venue, Burger Continental is popular with almost everyone in Pasadena—particularly the under-25 crowd. Besides cheap pitchers of beer, you'll find an excellent selection of Middle Eastern dishes; justifiably popular is the delicious chicken Corinthian ($9), baked in phyllo dough with spinach and feta cheese. Most nights, a quartet of Greek musicians delights diners on the outdoor patio. *535 S. Lake Ave., at California Ave., tel. 818/792–6634. 5 blocks south of Colorado Blvd. Open weekdays 6:30 AM–10:30 PM, weekends 6 AM–11:30 PM. Wheelchair access.*

**Ernie Jr.'s Taco House.** In a nutshell: fast, cheap, and tasty. Ernie's makes some of the best tacos and carne asada burritos in town ($4–$6). It may not look like much from the outside, but this little joint is top drawer. *126 W. Colorado Blvd., btw Pasadena Blvd. and De Lacey Ave., tel. 818/792–9957. Open daily 11–9:30 (Fri.–Sat. until 11:30).*

**Jake's Café.** A typical '50s diner with better-than-average burgers ($3.95) and yummy mozzarella sticks ($2.25), Jake's is a good choice if you don't mind the in-your-face service. *38 Colorado Blvd., at De Lacey Ave., tel. 818/568–1602. Open daily 1:30–1:30. Wheelchair access.*

## WORTH SEEING

If you tire of museums, check out the kitsch for sale at Pasadena's two well-known flea markets. **Pasadena City College** (1570 E. Colorado Blvd., at Hill St., tel. 818/585–7906) holds one the first Sunday of each month. The mother of all swap meets, though, takes place at the **Rose Bowl** (1001 Rosebowl Dr., tel. 818/577–3100 or 213/560–7469) the second Sunday of each month.

**GAMBLE HOUSE** This house was built for David and Mary Gamble (of Procter and Gamble fame) in 1908 by Pasadena's illustrious architects Charles and Henry Greene. Known for their love of open space and elaborately carved wood, the Greene brothers built the 8,400-square-foot mansion as a winter cottage, at a time when Pasadena was nothing more than a wild prairie of sagebrush. Next door, the **Unitarian church** at 2 Westmoreland Place is another Greene and Greene house, and nearby lies **Arroyo Terrace,** a curved street full of bungalows designed by the famous duo. Only the Gamble House gives tours, though. *4 Westmoreland Pl., tel. 818/793–3334. From Hwy. 134, take Orange Grove Blvd. exit north, first left after Walnut St., first right onto Westmoreland Pl. Admission: $4, $2 students. Tours several times an hour, Thurs.–Sun. noon–3.*

**HUNTINGTON LIBRARY** Built in 1919 on the grounds of Henry E. Huntington's 200-acre estate, the Huntington Library contains a gallery specializing in British and French art of the 18th and 19th centuries (including Gainsborough's *Blue Boy*); a library of rare books and manuscripts (featuring a Gutenberg Bible and the Ellesmore manuscript of Chaucer's *Canterbury Tales*); and 15 botanical gardens (including a Zen garden of raked gravel and a hemp-free herb garden). The Patio Restaurant on the grounds has sandwiches and salads for about $6—or join the flower-printed ladies at the flower-printed tables in the Rose Garden Tea Room, where you can nibble on nine kinds of finger sandwiches. *1151 Oxford Rd., San Marino, tel. 818/405–2100, or 818/405–2274 for directions. Suggested donation: $7.50, $4 students. Library, art collections, and gardens open Tues.–Fri. 1–4:30, weekends 10:30–4:30; garden tours at 1 PM or as posted. Wheelchair access.*

*Recently deceased industrialist Norton Simon used to rework the museum's displays to his liking, putting every flower painting he could find into one room, for example, and lavishing it with dozens of fresh tulips.*

**NORTON SIMON MUSEUM** The Norton Simon Museum contains one of the best collections of art on the West Coast, with more classic pieces than you'll find at L.A.'s Museum of Contemporary Art or the Los Angeles County Museum of Art (*see* Exploring Melrose and the Wilshire District, in Chapter 9). Rooms full of works by Rembrandt, Picasso, Van Gogh, Degas, Manet, Monet, and Rousseau are set among manicured parks, fountains, and sculpture gardens. Although the rather eccentric Norton Simon is no longer around to arrange the displays himself, the museum still has a personal, intimate charm. *411 W. Colorado Blvd., at Orange Grove Blvd., tel. 818/449–6840. Near intersection of I–210 and Hwy. 134. Admission: $4, $2 students. Open Thurs.–Sun. noon–6. Wheelchair access.*

**PACIFIC ASIA MUSEUM** Not only is this one of the few museums in California that specialize in Asian and Pacific Basin art, it's also housed in an amazing building constructed in the Chinese Imperial Palace style, complete with a center courtyard garden and a pond filled with koi fish the size of schnauzers. Exhibits include Japanese and Chinese woodworks, illuminated manuscripts, and pottery. *46 N. Los Robles Ave., ½ block north of Colorado Blvd., tel. 818/449–2742. Admission: $4, $2 students. Open Wed.–Sun. 10–5; tours Sun. 2 PM. Wheelchair access.*

### AFTER DARK

Old Pasadena is where several alternate universes collide. Weekend nights, the streets clog with everything from the white stretch limos of the nouveau riche to the Kustom Klass low riders of visiting gangstas. Slick sorts queue up at **Q's Billiard Club** (99 E. Colorado Blvd., one block west of Arroyo Pkwy., tel. 818/405–9777), where it costs up to $12 an hour just to play pool—*if* they find your attire suitable (no plain tees, tank tops, or torn items allowed). Otherwise, head across the street to **35er** (12 E. Colorado Blvd., tel. 818/356–9315), which has billiards and beer for less. **The Colorado** (2640 Colorado Blvd., at Altadena Dr., tel. 818/449–3485) has a dimly lit, well-worn ambience that's a far cry from the clean-cut veneer of Old Pasadena. In the afternoons you'll find old-timers who know each other by name, but at night a younger crowd prevails. South of Colorado Boulevard is **Crown City Brewery** (300 S. Raymond Ave., at Del Mar Blvd., tel. 818/577–5548), which pours 170 kinds of beer ($2–$6).

## Near Pasadena

### BIG BEAR LAKE

L.A. County's suburbs would probably continue to multiply like cancer cells were it not for the abrupt mountain ranges demarcating the **Angeles** and **San Bernardino national forests** (the two are divided by the ribbon of I–15). Though you may not believe it as you stand in smog-filled Los Angeles, an entirely different world awaits two to three hours northeast and 5,000–10,000 feet above sea level. Within this vast acreage lies Big Bear Lake, a source of year-round diversion for generations of grateful L.A. residents. On the south shore, **Big Bear Lake City** is home base for most vacationers.

**VISITOR INFORMATION** The **Big Bear Chamber of Commerce and Visitor Center** (633 Bartlett Rd., tel. 909/866–7000) has an excellent visitor's guide, many brochures, and limited information on campgrounds and hiking. The **Big Bear Ranger Station** (North Shore Dr., 3 mi east of Fawnskin, tel. 909/866–3437) has maps and detailed information on campgrounds and trails. The station also dispenses permits required for camping at undeveloped sites.

**COMING AND GOING** From L.A., take I–10 east to Redlands and pick up Highway 30 north; it becomes Highway 330 and then turns into Highway 18 at Running Springs. Here, turn right onto Highway 18 east, which takes you to Big Bear Lake City. The lake's north shore can be reached via Highway 38 (North Shore Dr.), which meets Highway 18 at the dam. To reach Big Bear Lake from Pasadena, take I–210 east to I–10 east and follow the directions above.

**WHERE TO SLEEP** The city of Big Bear Lake is chock-full of matchbox cottages tucked between pines, with names like Snuggler's Cove and Cuddly Inn. If the names don't make you gag, the prices will. A few budget options exist: **Motel 6** (42899 Big Bear Blvd., at Division Rd., tel. 909/585–6666) offers some of the cheapest lodging in the area, with doubles for $40 weekdays and $42 weekends. The nearby **Hillcrest Lodge** (40241 Big Bear Blvd., tel. 909/866–7330) is an appealing mountain cabin with 12 clean and comfortable rooms starting at $42.

Camping at one of Big Bear's seven campgrounds is your best option during summer months. **Pineknot** (south on Summit Blvd., near Snow Summit ski area, tel. 800/280–CAMP for reservations) has 48 pine-studded spots ($11) available from mid-May through the end of September. Two miles east of the north-shore community of Fawnskin, **Serrano** (North Shore Ln., off Hwy. 38, tel. 800/280–CAMP for reservations) has 132 spots ($15) open April–November, and more amenities than Pineknot (including showers and electrical hookups). The sparse foliage here means that privacy will be minimal. For info on Big Bear's other campgrounds (several are inaccessible to cars), contact the ranger station or Chamber of Commerce (*see* Visitor Information, *above*).

**FOOD** Local restaurants must rely on the appetite-inducing fresh mountain air to increase the appeal of their fare—less-than-fabulous cuisine abounds. **Boo Bear's Den** (572 Pine Knot Blvd., at Hwy. 18, tel. 909/866–2162) offers moderately priced American food—from $5 hamburgers to $9 grilled-chicken dinners—on a relaxing outdoor patio filled with shady trees. **Mongolian Palace** (40797 Lakeview Dr., west of Pine Knot Blvd., tel. 909/866–6678) lets carnivores and vegetarians alike fill up on all-you-can-eat Mongolian barbecue for lunch ($6) and dinner ($8). The area's most convenient and well-stocked market is **Vons** (Interlaken Shopping Center, Hwy. 18 near Stanfield Rd., tel. 909/866–8459).

**OUTDOOR ACTIVITIES** Look for the monthly newspaper *Big Bear Today* at motels and restaurants; it's an invaluable supplement if you plan to take part in Big Bear's many outdoor activities.

➢ **MOUNTAIN BIKING** • Mountain biking is also popular during summer; purchase a map of bike trails ($2) at the Big Bear Ranger Station (*see* Visitor Information, *above*) or at a local sporting goods store. For $7, a ride up the **Snow Summit** ski lift (Summit Blvd., south of Big Bear Blvd., tel. 909/866–5766) puts you and your bike on top of 40 miles of roads and trails. A full-day pass gives you unlimited runs for $18; bike rentals are an additional $6.50 an hour ($22 a day). Spectacular scenery is accessible to hikers on trails of varying difficulty, including the moderate 2-mile **Cougar Crest Trail,** which begins ½ mile west of the ranger station on Highway 38. This path ultimately leads to the **Pacific Crest Trail,** which meanders through California on its way from Canada to Mexico. To obtain maps of hiking trails, contact the ranger station.

➢ **FISHING AND BOATING** • During summer, you can fish for trout, bass, and silver salmon from any secluded spot along the shore, or struggle for casting space at **Dana Point** in the tiny north-shore community of Fawnskin, where some swear the fish bite better. **Jack's Tackle Shop** (39730 Big Bear Blvd., at Iris St., tel. 909/866–6525) rents gear ($6.50 a day,

$25 deposit), sells bait (about $4), and dispenses the required permit ($9 a day, $25 per season). You can rent a fishing boat at any of the lake's marinas, including **Pleasure Point Boat Landing** at Metcalf Bay (603 Landlock Landing Rd., at Cienega Rd., tel. 909/866–2455), where rates start at $14 an hour. The **Get Wet Water Sports Center** (38573 North Shore Dr., tel. 909/878–4FUN) rents Jet Skis and Waverunners (about $40–$55 an hour) and offers waterskiing packages ($78 an hour) that include optional instruction.

➢ **SKIING** • During winter, Big Bear fills up with skiers eager to shred the slopes of **Bear Mountain Ski Resort** (43101 Goldmine Dr., east of Big Bear Lake City, tel. 909/585–2519), **Snow Summit** (Summit Blvd., south of Big Bear Blvd., tel. 909/866–5766), and **Snow Valley** (Hwy. 18, 5 mi east of Running Springs, tel. 909/867–2751). Though they'll never be mistaken for the Swiss Alps, all three resorts offer downhill runs ranging in difficulty from novice to expert. Bear Mountain has the highest elevation, as well as several ungroomed, experts-only canyons (snow conditions permitting). Lift tickets sometimes sell out on weekends, so consider purchasing in advance by telephone; the smallest resort, Snow Valley, is least likely to have crowds. Lift tickets at all three places will set you back about $30, with equipment an extra $15. It's wise to call for snow conditions: Get the Bear Mountain ski report (tel. 909/585–2519) or county weather and road conditions (tel. 909/866–SNOW).

# The San Fernando Valley

**Ever since the movie *Valley Girl* was released in the** early '80s, the San Fernando Valley has basked in the spotlight of dubious international fame. Locals may not be proud that the phrases "oh my gawd," "gag me with a spoon," and "like, fer sure" were first coined here, but most residents don't mind the fact that people from around the world have heard of the Valley and its infamous shopping mall, the **Galleria** (cnr Ventura and Sepulveda Blvds., Sherman Oaks). By now, of course, even original Valleyspeak queen Moon Unit Zappa (daughter of Frank) wouldn't, like, be caught *dead* talking that way. Nevertheless, the San Fernando Valley maintains its relentlessly suburban personality in the shadow of très chic West Los Angeles and off-color Hollywood, both of which lie just over the Santa Monica Mountains.

It takes a certain suspension of aesthetics to embrace the Valley, an area carved from orchards and ranchlands during an unchecked postwar housing boom. The 1994 earthquake left scars on Sherman Oaks, Van Nuys, and Northridge, but these bedroom communities have kept busy rebuilding their frantic boulevards, strip centers, and tract houses. Most visitors have a limited tolerance for this particular brand of Americana. The eastern Valley's proximity to the rest of L.A.—including the movie studios—means you may want to take advantage of its cheap lodging and restaurants; do so if you must, but don't linger. Just north of the Valley is where you'll find most of the non-studio attractions, including **Six Flags Magic Mountain** (*see* Worth Seeing, *below*), with its gut-wrenchingly swift roller coasters.

## COMING AND GOING

**BY CAR** The Valley's main streets are **Ventura Boulevard,** which runs east–west, and **Van Nuys Boulevard,** which runs north–south. Traffic is at its worst 7–10 AM and 3–7 PM, but even at nonpeak hours the Valley's highways look much like parking lots. The main freeways are the north–south **I–5** and **I–405,** which follows the coast to San Diego. **U.S. 101** runs east–west through the southern edge of the Valley, eventually leading north to San Francisco. To get to the Valley from West L.A. take I–405 north or follow **Coldwater Canyon Boulevard, Laurel Canyon Boulevard,** or **Beverly Glen Boulevard.** These three streets can be accessed from Sunset Boulevard, and all eventually lead to Ventura Boulevard.

**BY BUS** **MTA** (tel. 818/781–5890) runs to almost every part of the Valley, but avoid the bus unless you have hours to kill (no joke). Fare is $1.35 ($2.35 to downtown L.A.). For long-distance travel, **Greyhound** has three stations in the Valley: North Hollywood (11239 Magnolia

Blvd.), Glendale (400 W. Cerritos Ave.), and San Fernando (1441 Truman St.). Call the general information number (tel. 800/231–2222) for tickets and timetables.

**BY METRO** **Metrolink** (tel. 800/371–5465) offers service to greater Los Angeles Monday through Friday from automated stations throughout the Valley. The trip from Burbank (201 N. Front St., at Olive St.) takes 20 minutes and costs $3.50; from Van Nuys (7720 Van Nuys Blvd.), it's 30 minutes for $4.50; and from Northridge (8775 Wilbur Ave.) it takes 40 minutes and costs a whopping $5.50.

**BY TRAIN** **Amtrak** (tel. 800/872–7245) has two stations that serve the Valley. In Glendale (400 W. Cerritos Ave., at San Fernando Rd., tel. 818/246–9681), you can catch trains departing for all points along the Pacific coast; prices and travel times are similar to those from Los Angeles's Union Station (*see* Coming and Going, in Chapter 9). From Burbank (3750 Empire Ave., near airport at Hollywood Way, no phone), trains run only to Santa Barbara (2 hrs, $18) and San Diego (4 hrs, $24).

**BY PLANE** The **Burbank Airport** (2627 N. Hollywood Way, at Thornton Ave., tel. 818/840–8847) offers service within and outside California. However, all international flights are handled by LAX (*see* Coming and Going, in Chapter 9). Rental cars are available at the airport. **Easy Rent-a-Car** (tel. 818/848–4885) is one of the cheapest agencies, with cars starting at $27 per day. They don't rent to anyone younger than 21, and there's a $5-a-day surcharge for renters ages 21–25.

## WHERE TO SLEEP

With few exceptions, lodging in the Valley falls into one of three categories: expensive, sleazy, or uncomfortably near earthquake damage. Avoid all three by staying in a similarly priced place in L.A. proper (you also won't spend half your day schlepping up and down U.S. 101). If you're fixated on staying in the Valley—you're shopping your screenplay at Warner, perhaps—your budget options lie along Sepulveda Boulevard, north of Ventura Boulevard.

**777 Motor Inn.** The combination of baroque headboards, tropical bedspreads, and bright carpets may make you dizzy, but the rooms are clean and in good repair. Doubles go for $38, and the motel is next door to that Valley-child mecca, the Galleria. *4781 Sepulveda Blvd., Sherman Oaks, tel. 818/788–3200. 1 block north of Ventura Blvd. 36 rooms.*

**Starlite.** Possibly the only motel along Sepulveda's budget strip where you don't have to worry about developing an inexplicable rash, this English country-style inn seems a fish out of water with its flower garden and neatly painted trim. Rooms are clean, fresh, and furnished with care. Basic singles go for $36, and doubles are $40; $10 extra puts you in a theme room (French cottage, safari, Ralph Lauren Polo). All room rates rise $5 on Friday and Saturday nights. *5450 Sepulveda Blvd., btw Magnolia Ave. and Burbank Blvd., tel. 818/997–9754. North of Ventura Blvd. in Sherman Oaks. 11 rooms. No check-in Sun.*

## FOOD

The Valley is blighted by countless indistinguishable chain eateries, as befits a land where communities are defined by proximity to various strip malls. (For a list of more worthwhile chains, *see box* Beyond Mickey D's, in Chapter 9). Stray west beyond Sherman Oaks and the food becomes expensive as well as generic. In the eastern part of the Valley, however, it's possible to eat cheaply. In Van Nuys, head to **Dr. Hogly Wogly's Tyler Texas BBQ** (8136 Sepulveda Blvd., south of Roscoe Blvd., tel. 818/782–2480) for L.A.'s undisputed best barbecue sandwiches ($6) on home-baked bread. If you can ignore the plastic booths and mirrored walls, **ZanKou Chicken** (5658 Sepulveda Blvd., at Burbank Blvd., tel. 818/781–0615) is an excellent place for falafel sandwiches ($2.50) or spicy roast chicken and pita ($5.25 for a half chicken).

In Sherman Oaks, you can get your Mexican-food fix from the friendly folks at **El Rancho** (15030 Ventura Blvd., 1 block east of Sepulveda Blvd., tel. 818/995–6466). It's not much to look at, but taco, burrito, and enchilada plates, complete with sides of rice and beans, are just $4–$6. If you've got a little money to blow, splurge at one of the nicer eateries along Ventura

Boulevard's budding "restaurant row." **La Pergola** (15005 Ventura Blvd., at Lemona Ave., tel. 818/905–8402) serves organic Italian dinners ($9.50 and up) made with produce grown in its own two nearby gardens. The excellent food at **The Great Greek** (13362 Ventura Blvd., near Woodman Ave., tel. 818/905–5250) is almost beside the point; it's the singing and dancing waiters that draw the crowds. Try the Macedonia shrimp pasta ($14), or share a few appetizers ($4–$9) with a friend.

## WORTH SEEING

Several of the major movie studios, including **Universal** and **Warner Brothers,** lie at the eastern end of the Valley. For more information, *see* Exploring the Studios, in Chapter 9.

**SIX FLAGS MAGIC MOUNTAIN** On these 260 acres in Valencia, north of the Valley off I-5, sit more than 100 roller coasters, rides, shows, and attractions that promise to either make you sick or throw your back out. Magic Mountain's coasters are fast and wicked; the newest is **Batman, the Ride,** where thrill-seekers dangle below the tracks rather than sitting in cars on top of them. Seven other "monster coasters," with names like **Viper, Colossus,** and **Psyclone,** should reduce you to a quivering, jelly-kneed lump. When you've had enough of roller coasters, head to the new **Hurricane Harbor** and cool off on more than 20 acres of water slides and rides. Look for coupons worth $2–$12 off the admission price in Six Flags brochures, available at L.A.-area tourist offices and some motels. *Magic Mountain Pkwy., off I-5 in Valencia, tel. 805/255–4100 or 818/367–5965 from L.A. From L.A., I-405 north to I-5 north to Valencia. Admission: $30, parking $6. For info on group discounts (10 or more) call 805/255–4500. Open year-round (Nov.–Mar., weekends and holidays only); hours vary, so call ahead.*

**MISSION SAN FERNANDO REY DE ESPANA** At the northern edge of the Valley, far from tourist haunts, lies this carefully restored 1797 mission. It's small, but its 35-bell carillon casts an enchanting spell over the surrounding gardens. If the grounds look familiar, it's because portions of Steve Martin's *L.A. Story* were filmed here. *15151 San Fernando Mission Blvd., Mission Hills, tel. 818/361–0186. From I-405, Mission Blvd. exit east. From I-5, Mission Blvd. exit west. Admission: $4. Open daily 9–5.*

*Steven Spielberg specifically requested that his recently deceased dog be buried away from the pets that he and ex-wife Amy Irving shared. That's divorce Hollywood-style.*

**LOS ANGELES PET MEMORIAL PARK** For those left unsatisfied by a dead-celebrity fix at the Hollywood Memorial Park Cemetery (*see* Exploring Hollywood, in Chapter 9), there is, thankfully, a celebrity pet cemetery. The rich and famous—Steven Spielberg among them—still bury their pets here, but recent markers are more likely to read "Fluffy" than "Bob Barker's Cat." If you stroll the hill bordering the riding academy, you'll see the final resting place of the African lion Tawny (1918–1940), and celeb companions like Mae West's monkey and Hopalong Cassidy's horse. The staff is friendly, but they can't do much more than point you in the general direction of a celebrity gravesite. Dead pets deserve privacy, too. *5068 N. Old Scandia Ln., Calabasas, tel. 818/591–7037. From U.S. 101, Parkway Calabasas exit to Ventura Blvd., left onto Old Scandia Ln. and follow signs. Admission free. Open daily 8–5.*

## AFTER DARK

Get in the car and drive to Los Angeles. The Valley is the land of dull and restless teens with shiny cars, shiny clothes, and midnight curfews. However, if you insist on staying after dark, you'll need to grit your teeth and slap on a ten-gallon hat—what Valleyites really like is country music and a good ol' two-step. The **Reseda Country Club** (18415 Sherman Way, Reseda, tel. 818/881–5601) is the most spacious of the Valley's country-and-western venues, with 3,000 feet of dance floor. They offer free dance lessons every Thursday 7 PM–8 PM. If this all seems like too much to handle, you only have a couple of other choices: Either head for the Valley outpost of L.A.'s too-hip **Insomnia Café** (13718 Ventura Blvd., Sherman Oaks, tel. 818/990–9945), and sip on a cappuccino for $3.25; or, if you insist on a Valley-style cultural odyssey, try **XIT** (21055 Ventura Blvd., at De Soto Ave. in Woodland Hills, tel. 818/887–6918), which tries hard to look "city" with its sleek decor—and would almost succeed if it weren't for the crowd.



# Disneyland and Inland

**Like apple pie, baseball, and Watergate,** Disneyland is a uniquely American phenomenon. It's far and away the most popular attraction that inland Orange County has to offer, though you will find a couple of noteworthy destinations nearby. Besides Knott's Berry Farm, the oldest theme park in the United States, there's Dr. Schuller's Crystal Cathedral, one of the world's largest churches, built almost completely out of glass. Fans of the late Richard "I cannot tell a lie" Nixon will enjoy the Richard M. Nixon Library and Birthplace, which presents a detailed history of the highs and lows of America's 37th president (he was buried on the grounds on April 27, 1994). Disney and Knott's lie in Anaheim and Buena Park, respectively, while the other sights are in surrounding suburbs easily reached by car. Accommodations are cheaper here than along the shore, but what you save in dollars you certainly lose in beauty—for the most part, this is a ghastly panorama of tedious suburbs, tightly buckled to the ailing defense industry.

*If you didn't get your fill of the good old U.S. of A. at Disneyland, hop in the Chevy and head over to Anaheim Stadium (tel. 714/254–3000). Despite earthquake damage to its upper level, the park still fills with fans cheering on the California Angels during baseball season.*

## COMING AND GOING

**BY CAR** The easiest way to reach Anaheim is via **I-5** (a.k.a. the **Golden State Fwy.** or the **Santa Ana Fwy.**). There are hundreds of signs once you get near Disneyland and Knott's Berry Farm. Traffic can be a serious problem during rush hour (7–10 AM and 3–7 PM); otherwise, it shouldn't take you more than an hour by car from downtown L.A., or about 2½ hours from San Diego.

**BY BUS** **Greyhound** (tel. 800/231–2222) has a station in Anaheim (100 W. Winston Rd., at Anaheim Blvd., tel. 714/999–1256), across I-5 from Disneyland. The trip from L.A. ($6 one-way) takes about an hour. From Los Angeles, **MTA** (tel. 213/626–4455) offers limited service to Orange County; Bus 460 leaves downtown L.A. for Anaheim, Disneyland, and Knott's Berry Farm ($3.35 one-way). Within Orange County, call the **Orange County Transportation Authority (OCTA)** (tel. 714/636–RIDE, ext. 10) for routes, schedules, and bus information. It's open weekdays 6 AM–8 PM, weekends 8–5.

**BY TRAIN** All **Amtrak** trains (tel. 800/872–7245) between Los Angeles and San Diego stop at **Anaheim Station** (2150 E. Katella Ave., tel. 714/385–1448), which lies at the east end of the Anaheim Station parking lot, a short drive east from Disneyland. The station, open 5:15 AM–11 PM, offers luggage storage. Amtrak also serves **Fullerton Station** (120 E. Santa Fe Ave., at Harbor Blvd., tel. 714/992–0530), 6 miles from Knott's Berry Farm and the city of Buena Park. Both stations are connected to the theme parks via public bus: 39 from Anaheim and 99 from Fullerton.

## WHERE TO SLEEP

You'll find ample lodging around Disneyland (Katella Ave. and Harbor Blvd. in Anaheim) and Knott's Berry Farm (south of Hwy. 91 on Beach Blvd. in Buena Park). However, most accommodations are run-down and depressing, and they're priced maddeningly like nicer hotels ($35–$100 a night). Even worse, you must reserve a room at least a week in advance, especially during summer, when hordes of tourists invade the area. Your best bet is the area's lone hostel (*see below*).

# Orange County

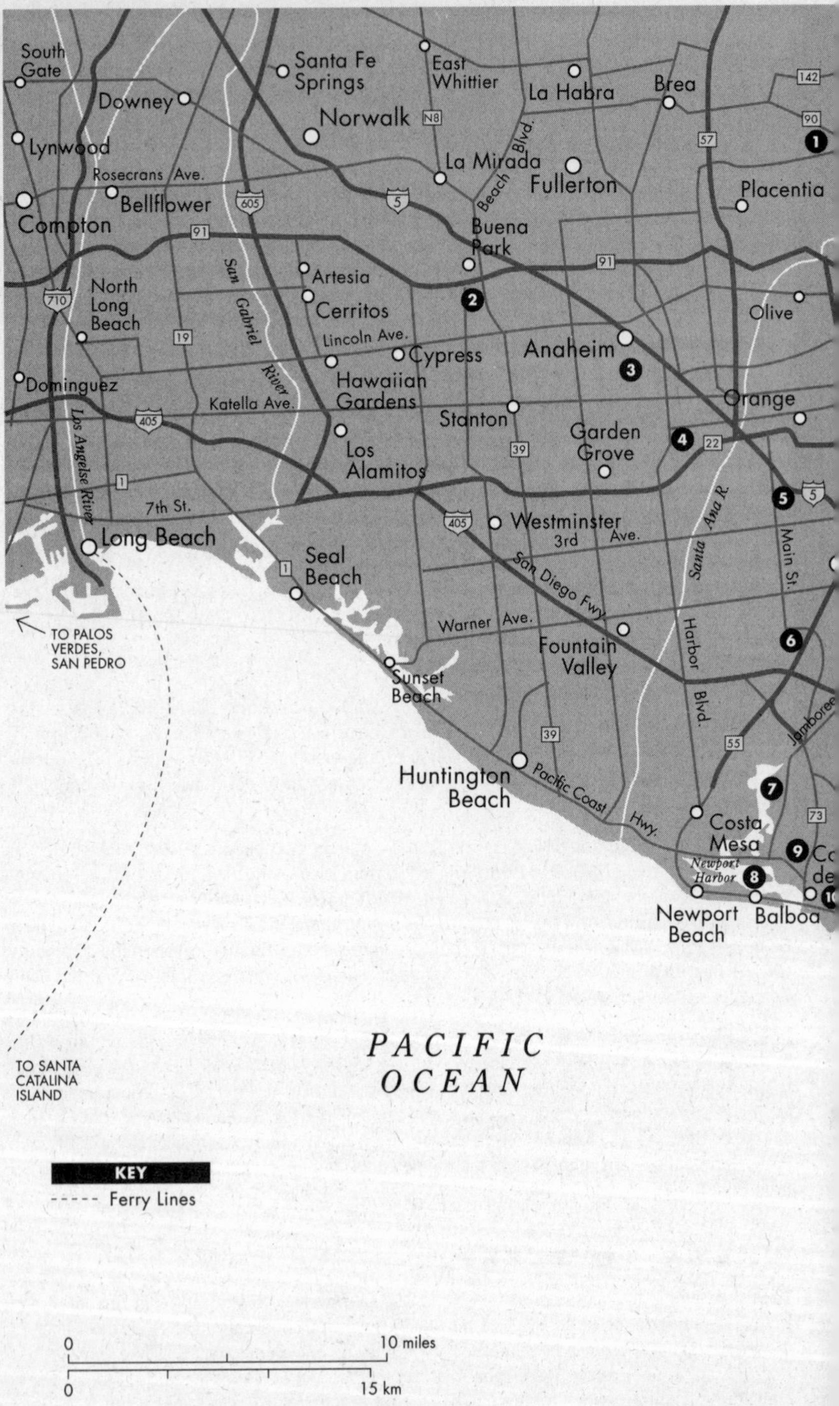

South Gate
Downey
Santa Fe Springs
East Whittier
La Habra
Brea
Norwalk
Lynwood
La Mirada
Beach Blvd.
Fullerton
Placentia
Rosecrans Ave.
Bellflower
Compton
Buena Park
Artesia
Cerritos
North Long Beach
San Gabriel River
Olive
Lincoln Ave.
Cypress
Anaheim
Dominguez
Hawaiian Gardens
Orange
Katella Ave.
Stanton
Garden Grove
Los Alamitos
Los Angelse River
7th St.
Westminster
3rd Ave.
Long Beach
Seal Beach
San Diego Fwy.
Santa Ana R.
Main St.
TO PALOS VERDES, SAN PEDRO
Warner Ave.
Fountain Valley
Harbor Blvd.
Sunset Beach
Jamboree
Huntington Beach
Pacific Coast Hwy.
Costa Mesa
Newport Harbor
Newport Beach
Balboa
PACIFIC OCEAN
TO SANTA CATALINA ISLAND
KEY
Ferry Lines
0
10 miles
0
15 km

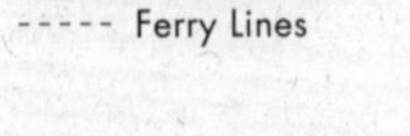

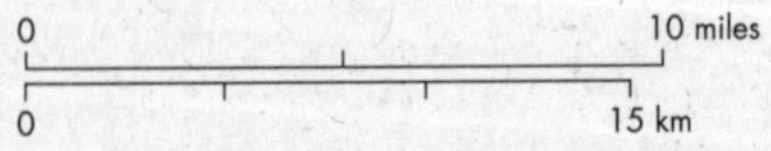

# Orange County

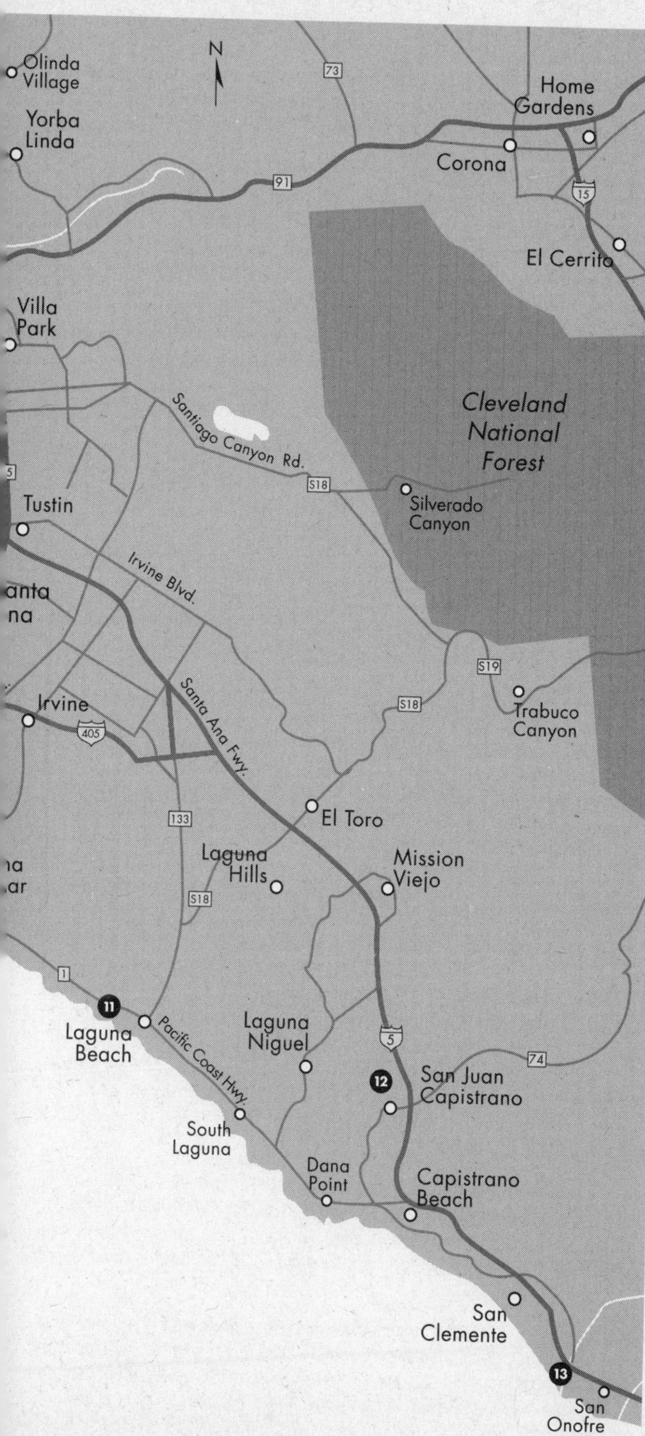


Balboa Island, **8**
Bowers Museum, **5**
Crystal Cathedral, **4**
Disneyland, **3**
Knotts Berry Farm, **2**
Laguna Beach Museum of Art, **11**
Mission San Juan Capistrano, **12**
Newport Harbor Art Museum, **9**
Orange County Performing Arts Center, **6**
Richard M. Nixon Library and Birthplace, **1**
San Onofre Nuclear Power Plant, **13**
Sherman Library and Gardens, **10**
Upper Newport Bay Ecological Reserve, **7**

**NEAR DISNEYLAND** **Anaheim Motel.** This average-looking motel is just far enough from the chaos of Disney (about a five-minute drive) to make a stay pleasant. And it has a pool and Jacuzzi to soothe your aching legs after a long day of walking around the theme parks. Doubles go for around $40. *426 W. Ball Rd., at Harbor Blvd. in Anaheim, tel. 714/774–3882. 46 rooms. Reservations advised. Wheelchair access.*

**Desert Palm Suites.** Just a few hundred yards from Disneyland, this very comfortable hotel offers spacious, clean rooms with refrigerators, microwaves, VCRs, and continental breakfast. Rooms run about $69; because they often fill with corporate types from the Convention Center just down the block, reservations are advised year-round. They also offer a free shuttle to Disneyland. *631 W. Katella Ave., at Harbor Blvd. in Anaheim, tel. 714/535–1133 or 800/635–5423. 103 rooms. Wheelchair access.*

**NEAR KNOTT'S BERRY FARM** **Covered Wagon Motel.** Although this motel looks like a charmless hole-in-the-wall from the outside, the rooms ($30 and up) are comfortable and you can't beat the location—directly across from Knott's. *7830 Crescent Ave., at Beach Blvd. (Hwy. 39) in Buena Park, tel. 714/995–0033. 20 rooms. Reservations advised.*

**Colony Inn.** Newly renovated and spanking clean, this blue-and-white inn feels fresher than most budget places. Doubles start at $36 in summer, $39 for weekend stays; for $58 you can get a mini-suite that sleeps up to six. The pool/sauna complex and a location across from Knott's Berry Farm attract colonies of hyperactive kids. *7800 Crescent Ave., at Beach Blvd. (Hwy. 39) in Buena Park, tel. 714/527–2201 or 800/982–6566. 130 rooms. Laundry. Wheelchair access.*

**HOSTEL** **Fullerton-Hacienda AYH-Hostel.** For price and location, the Fullerton-Hacienda is your best value. One mile from Amtrak's Fullerton Station (*see* Coming and Going, *above*), it's served by numerous public buses and is only a short car ride from both Disneyland and Knott's Berry Farm. There's no lockout and you can borrow a late key ($10 refundable deposit) if you plan to be out past 11 PM. The rate for members is $14, for nonmembers $17. To reach Disneyland from here, take OCTA Bus 41 south to Chapman and transfer to OCTA Bus 43 south. *1700 N. Harbor Blvd., tel. 714/738–3721. 3 mi north of Hwy. 91 on Harbor Blvd., in Brea Dam Park. From Fullerton Station, Bus 41 west to Brea Dam Park. 15 beds. Laundry, linen ($1), lockers, on-site parking. Reservations strongly advised. Wheelchair access.*

## FOOD

Most restaurants and food stands within the theme parks are overrated and overpriced—as in $3 ice-cream cones and $15 plates of leathery chicken and cold potatoes. The one exception is **Mrs. Knott's Chicken Dinner Restaurant** (8039 Beach Blvd., on Hwy. 39, tel. 714/220–5225), in the Berry Farm parking lot. The Knotts developed the first-ever boysenberry vine by crossbreeding raspberry and loganberry; today, the fresh-baked berry pies and fried chicken dinners ($10) still taste homemade. If you'd rather pack your lunch, the **K&C Market** (8465 Western Ave., at Crescent Ave., tel. 714/828–9141) near Knott's has basic items; near Disney, the behemoth **Food 4 Less** (1616 W. Katella Ave., at Euclid St., tel. 714/539–7497) is open 24 hours and carries whatever you desire in numbing quantities.

**PoFolks.** If you're in the mood for a hearty homestyle meal (in a slightly hokey setting), this is your place. Country-fried steak, barbecued ribs, and Southern-style catfish are all under $10. Finish your meal with a scrumptious Mississippi mud pie ($2.70). *7701 Beach Blvd. (Hwy. 39), btw Hwy. 91 and La Palma Ave. in Buena Park, tel. 714/521–8955. Open daily 7 AM–9 PM (weekends until 10 PM). Wheelchair access.*

**Restaurant Ararad.** Don't be dismayed by the unassuming exterior—delicious Armenian and Middle Eastern dishes are served at this family-owned establishment. Pick out a few appetizers ($2–$4) to share, or go for the generous kebab combination dinner ($8.75). Call ahead on weekend evenings to make sure the restaurant isn't closed for a private party. *1827A W. Katella Ave., btw Euclid and Brookhurst Sts. in Anaheim, tel. 714/778–5667. Open Tues., Thurs.–Sun. 2–8:30. Wheelchair access.*

## WORTH SEEING



**DISNEYLAND** Ever since it opened in 1955, Disneyland has been dazzling generations of children (and adults) from around the world. Everyone, it seems, has some connection with Disney—a song that's always stuck in their head, perhaps, or a lingering fondness for Mickey Mouse. If you haven't been here for a few years, you'll be surprised at how little it's changed: **Sleeping Beauty's Castle** still stands; the **Haunted Mansion** is still looking for its "1,000th ghost"; and, like clockwork, the **Main Street Electrical Parade** goes off without a hitch day in and day out. **Mickey's Toonland** is home to a host of well-known cartoon characters, and recent additions include the incredible laser-light symphony **Fantasmic**—staged several times each night from Tom Sawyer's Island—and the **Indiana Jones Adventure,** a thrilling ride through the Temple of the Forbidden Eye.

Long lines—sometimes two hours or longer—are a problem at all Disneyland attractions; your best bet is to visit the popular rides early in the morning or late at night. The park also has a number of bandstands and music venues—some free, some not. Stop by **City Hall** (near the entrance) for concert information and prices. Disney's best restaurant is the Southern-style **Blue Bayou,** in the Pirates of the Caribbean complex. Reservations are advised, and they must be made in person. A full dinner runs about $14. *1313 Harbor Blvd., Anaheim, tel. 714/999–4565. Admission: $33. Hrs vary, so call ahead.*

*In spring 1995, Disneyland finally started to go gender-neutral, after a park employee saw a woman skippering the Jungle Cruise ride at Disney World in Florida. When she returned to Anaheim, she asked to try the job. Park visitors may now be ferried through the "jungle" by women, as well as see men leading the children's Storybook Land ride, which traditionally had used female operators.*

**KNOTT'S BERRY FARM** What began as a temporary diversion for customers waiting for one of Mrs. Knott's famed chicken dinners (*see* Food, *above*) has now expanded into five different theme areas spread over 300 acres—the oldest theme park in America. In contrast to Disneyland, Knott's has an undeniable down-home charm that its neighbor lacks. The strong-stomached will enjoy **Jaguar,** a Mayan roller coaster adventure on one of the biggest tracks in California. Check out **Bigfoot Rapids,** a whitewater ride guaranteed to leave you soaking wet, or the park's $10 million **Mystery Lodge,** full of weird special effects (including a time-traveling Native American storyteller). At **Ghost Town,** modeled after an 1880s Old West mining town, you can pan for gold or take a train through a 19th-century gold mine complete with explosions and cave-ins. *8039 Beach Blvd. (Hwy. 39), ½ mi south of Hwy. 91 in Buena Park, tel. 714/220–5200 or 714/827–1776. Admission: $28.50. Hrs vary, so call ahead.*

**BOWERS MUSEUM** The Bowers Museum has numerous ethnographic displays from the Americas, the Pacific Rim, and Africa. Exhibitions include Native American arts and crafts, Colombian pottery, traditional African costumes and clothing, and an excellent display of international photography. *2002 N. Main St., Santa Ana, tel. 714/567–3600. Exit I–5 at 17th St., go ½ mi south. Admission: $4.50, $3 students. Open Tues.–Sun. 10–4 (Thurs. until 9 PM). Wheelchair access.*

**CRYSTAL CATHEDRAL** Designed by postmodern architect Phillip Johnson, the Crystal Cathedral is a 10,500-pane glass superstructure that looms over surrounding Garden Grove in peculiar majesty. Home to Dr. Robert Schuller and his *Hour of Power* ministry, it looks like something out of a bad science-fiction movie. And though the glass ceiling may afford an excellent view of the Garden Grove skyline (smog, tract housing, and mini-malls), it's about as inviting as a jail cell. You're free to inspect the cathedral at your leisure, but you may be followed by one of Dr. Schuller's vigilant sycophants if you don't look sufficiently respectable. Some say this modern-day Tower of Babel is worth visiting simply for its tacky extravagance. *12141 Lewis St., Garden Grove, tel. 714/971–4013. Admission free. Tours available; donation suggested. Wheelchair access.*

**RICHARD M. NIXON LIBRARY AND BIRTHPLACE** Built on the grounds of Nixon's childhood home, this 9-acre tribute to the life and times of the late 37th president was opened by Presidents Bush, Reagan, Ford, and Nixon on July 19, 1990. There are several things that are easy to mock: the 30-minute film *Never Give Up* (a sappy documentary focusing on Nixon's ability to triumph after his political disgrace); the "World Leaders" exhibit (littered with life-size bronze statues of Nixon's picks for the 20th century's greatest leaders); and carefully chosen snippets from the infamous Watergate tapes. But there's something both sad and stirring about the shiny marble headstone at the base of the Rose Garden. If you really want to get depressed, take a look at the line snaking out of the souvenir shop. *18001 Yorba Linda Blvd., Yorba Linda, tel. 714/993–3393. Follow signs from Hwy. 91. Admission: $6. Free parking available. Open Mon.–Sat. 10–5, Sun. 11–5. Wheelchair access.*

### AFTER DARK

Inland Orange County isn't known for its exciting nightlife. Except for a few dance clubs and Top 40 hangouts, you'll find your options sorely limited. You may want to see what's playing at the **Orange County Performing Arts Center** (600 Town Center Dr., Costa Mesa, tel. 714/556–ARTS); it frequently hosts the American Ballet Theatre, the L.A. Philharmonic, and the New York Opera. Performances cost a small fortune ($30–$70), but student discounts are available. In Irvine, the **Improv** (4255 Campus Dr., tel. 714/854–5455) offers live stand-up comedy nightly; the best acts appear on Friday and Saturday. You have to be at least 21 to get in, except on Wednesday, when the minimum age is 18. Since Irvine is home to a University of California campus, it's easy to find concerts and other college-type activities around here. For the latest, pick up the Orange County edition of *L.A. Weekly* at record stores and cafés.

**Fullerton Hofbrau.** Partly owned by the proprietor of the original Hofbrauhaus in Munich, this is a beer drinker's paradise. Aside from brewing vast amounts of beer on the premises, they also serve excellent, moderately priced Californian and German cuisine. Try pork schnitzel ($9) or the Hofbrau beef-eater sandwich ($6) with your choice of ale. Happy hour (weekdays 4–7) features two-for-one appetizers and beer at reduced prices, and there's live music nightly. *323 N. State College Blvd., at Chapman Ave. in Fullerton, tel. 714/870–7400. Wheelchair access.*

# Santa Catalina Island

**This small island resort 22** miles off the coast of San Pedro is perfect for a weekend respite from the smog, traffic, and bustle of Los Angeles and Orange County. The development of **Avalon,** Catalina's main hub, was carried out by the Wrigley family of Chicago (the gum magnates), who acquired majority ownership in the Santa Catalina Island Company in 1919. The Wrigleys made the mountainous island into a tourist resort and a spring training ground for their baseball team, the Chicago Cubs. The Cubs don't train here anymore, but the island has become a venue for world-class sailing meets, as well as competitive and recreational sportfishing. It's also a popular destination for boaters; during summer, the small marina overflows with luxury yachts, sailboats, and cruise ships from around the world. Catalina, however, is not an exclusive playground for the yachting set: Snorkeling, scuba diving, and backpacking are equally popular pursuits with reasonable price tags.

*Renowned writer Zane Grey spent much of his time on the island, and his biggest contributions—buffalo—are still evident today. For the movie version of Grey's book "The Vanishing America," buffalo had to be ferried across from the mainland. A small herd remains, grazing Santa Catalina's interior.*

Avalon's most famous sight is the **Casino Building,** an art-deco masterpiece built in 1929. Marking the end of **Crescent Avenue Walkway** on the north side of the bay, this enormous circular landmark once hosted live performances by top-notch big bands of the '30s and '40s. It now houses a movie theater (closed indefinitely for renovation), a historical museum ($1 entrance), and a tiny, free art gallery showcasing local talent. Ballroom dancing and evening concerts are still held here occasionally; check the Chamber of Commerce for schedules (*see below*). At the foot of the building is the **Underwater Dive Park,** a marine preserve with two shipwrecks, kelp forests, and school after school of fish. It's an excellent site for scuba diving, with some shallow areas suitable for snorkeling (for equipment rentals, *see* Outdoor Activities, *below*). In the hills above the Casino Building, look for the **Zane Grey Pueblo,** now a luxury hotel. A short walk up the road from the Pueblo is the **Chimes Tower,** commissioned by Ida Wrigley. The pleasant ringing of its bells every quarter hour can be heard throughout the streets of Avalon. About 1½ miles southwest of Avalon, at the end of Avalon Canyon Road, the **Wrigley Memorial and Botanical Gardens** ($1) feature a tribute to William Wrigley Jr. and a collection of the island's indigenous plant life.

The island's only other major outpost of civilization is **Two Harbors,** 23 miles by road (about 13 by boat) northwest of Avalon. The extra time and effort required to reach this remote but attractive village means that it's less likely to be overrun by day-trippers with loud radios and bad haircuts. Two Harbors offers outdoor activities comparable to Avalon's, as well as access to the island's five wilderness campgrounds (*see* Where to Sleep, *below*).

The **Catalina Island Chamber of Commerce** (tel. 310/510–1520), on Avalon's green Pleasure Pier, has maps, brochures, a visitor's guide, and information on hotel availability. The **visitor center** at the end of the pier in Two Harbors (tel. 310/510–7265) can advise you on the town's activities and amenities. For information on camping, hiking, and biking permits, *see* Where to Sleep or Outdoor Activities, *below.*

## COMING AND GOING

The ideal way to experience Santa Catalina is to sail over on your own and drop anchor in a secluded cove. For the rest of us, ferries depart regularly from Long Beach, San Pedro, and Newport. Newport's **Catalina Flyer** (400 Main St., Balboa, tel. 714/673–5245) is fast (75 min) but expensive ($33 round-trip). They don't permit excessive baggage, and reservations are required. **Catalina Cruises** (320 Golden Shore Blvd., Long Beach, tel. 800/228–2546) offers the cheapest round-trip fare to Avalon at $23. The trip takes two hours, and you depart from Catalina Landing in downtown Long Beach. Service to Two Harbors (spring and summer only) is the same price, but requires an additional 1¼ hours of travel time. Several ferries depart daily during summer; call ahead for schedule. For a few extra bucks, **Catalina Express** (tel. 310/519–1212) speeds over to Avalon in one hour from Berth 95 in San Pedro (follow signs from I–110) or from the Queen Mary in Long Beach (off Harbor Scenic Dr.). Round-trip tickets cost $35. They also have direct ferries to Two Harbors in high season; call ahead for the (erratic) schedule. All three ferry lines charge $6–$7 extra round-trip for bicycles and surfboards. Boats have both indoor and outdoor seating and snack bars. Reservations are a must, especially during summer, when the island becomes crowded. Since the waters around Santa Catalina can get rough, you may want to bring along some seasickness pills.

## GETTING AROUND

Only residents are allowed to have cars on Catalina, and an electronic key is required to drive through the gates of Avalon to outlying areas. The **Catalina Safari Bus** (tel. 310/510–2800) offers regular transportation between Avalon, Two Harbors, and several campgrounds for $29 round-trip. Buses depart from Island Plaza in Avalon and from the bus station just outside town in Two Harbors. **Catalina Express** (tel. 310/519–1212) has an express boat that shuttles between Avalon and Two Harbors for $25 round-trip. The town of Avalon is small enough to explore on foot, making the notion of renting a **golf cart** ($30 per hour) seem ridiculous; nonetheless, they're quite popular—distracted pedestrians beware. **Bicycles** are another option, though you'll need a $50 permit to ride outside the town limits of Avalon and Two Harbors. For information on bike rentals and permits, *see* Outdoor Activities, *below.*

## WHERE TO SLEEP

If you want to stay overnight and don't plan on camping, prepare to lay down a lot of cash. In Avalon, your cheapest option is the **Hermosa Hotel and Catalina Cottages** (131 Metropole St., btw Crescent Ave. and Beacon St., tel. 310/510–1010 or 800/666–3383), where you can get tidy, sparse rooms with shared bath for $35 in summer, or private cottages with kitchen and bath for $80. On weekends March–October there's a two-night minimum stay from. At **Hotel Atwater** (125 Sumner Ave., ½ block inland from Crescent Ave., tel. 800/851–0217), decent doubles in a slightly depressing, institutional building go for $65 weekdays and $83 weekends during summer. The cheerful, yellow **Catalina Lodge** (235 Sumner Ave., at Beacon St., tel. 800/974–1070) has only 15 rooms ($58 weekdays, $68 weekends, $89 daily in summer), but it's clean and cozy, and a jovial proprietor keeps things lively.

**CAMPING** Avalon's only campground is **Hermit Gulch** (tel. 310/510–TENT), 1½ miles southwest of town at the end of Avalon Canyon Road. With room for 240 people in 68 sites, this could hardly be classified as "getting away from it all"; the campground is usually filled with families and large groups. However, it's an easy walk into town (summer tram service available), and at $7.50 per person it's cheaper than any Avalon inn. Amusingly, they also rent tepees ($20–$25 per night). Reservations are recommended in summer and required in July and August.

If you can, hightail it out of Avalon and experience the island's rugged outback and secluded coves. Inland **Black Jack Campground,** midway between Avalon and Two Harbors, offers stunning mountain vistas, while **Little Harbor Campground,** 6 miles south of Two Harbors on the opposite coast, overlooks a serene beach. Both can be reached by shuttle (*see* Getting Around, *above*) or hiking, and have showers and chemical toilets. The **Two Harbors Campground,** ¼ mile outside the eponymous community, has tent cabins and tepees ($48–$72) as well as tent sites ($7.50 per person). Reservations for all these year-round campgrounds must be made through **Catalina Camping Reservations** (Box 5044, Two Harbors 90704, tel. 310/510–7265). If you plan to hike to your campground, you must also pick up a free hiking permit in Avalon or Two Harbors (*see* Outdoor Activities, *below*).

## FOOD

Santa Catalina's eateries seem secure in the knowledge that they play to a captive audience; the food ranges from decent to awful, and will sit best with those who enjoy a good dose of grease. The **Catalina Cantina** (311 Crescent Ave., tel. 310/510–0100) serves Mexican cuisine at moderate prices; try an enormous "big and wet" burrito for $9, and wash it down with a beer or a fresh-fruit margarita from the bar. Live bands play here on weekends. At the **Blue Parrot** (tel. 310/510–2465), on the second level in the Metropole Marketplace, you can get creole cuisine for $10–$14. Tropical drinks from the bar, views from all tables, and whimsical decor make up for the lackluster food. If you're on a tight budget, you'll find bread, cheese, fruit, and bottled water at the **Vons** supermarket on Metropole Avenue, half a block inland from Crescent Avenue.

## OUTDOOR ACTIVITIES

Santa Catalina's varied terrain makes it a great place to hike, bike, and get your feet wet; however, efforts to preserve the island have led to costly permits and limited trail access. **Wet Spot Rentals** (tel. 310/510–2229), next to the ferry landing, rents kayaks and paddleboats for $10–$17 an hour or $50 a day.

**BIKING AND HIKING** Mountain biking on the island can be a blast, but you'll need to buy a $50 permit if you want to ride outside Avalon or Two Harbors. In Avalon, permits are available at the **Catalina Island Conservancy** (125 Claressa St., at 3rd St., tel. 310/510–1421). Permits are valid from May 1 until April 30 of the following year, and applicants must have a mountain bike and helmet. You can rent both at **Brown's Bikes** (107 Pebbly Beach Rd., near ferry landing, tel. 310/510–0986) for about $25 a day. They also rent tandem and six-speed bikes ($6–$12 an hour) for in-town cruising. Compared to biking, hiking in the interior is hassle-free. The required hiking permit is free and available at the conservancy or at Hermit Gulch Campground (*see* Where to Sleep, *above*). In Two Harbors, both permits are available at the **visitor center** (tel. 310/510–7265) at the end of the pier. It's possible to hike or bike between Avalon and Two Harbors, starting at the Hogback gate above Avalon, though the 28-mile journey has an elevation gain of 3,000 feet and is not for the weak. For a pleasant 4-mile hike out of Avalon, take Avalon Canyon Road to Wrigley Gardens and follow the trail to Lone Pine. At the top you'll have an amazing view of the Palisades cliffs and, beyond them, the sea.

**FISHING** Year-round, the sportfishing is tremendous in the waters off Catalina, with an abundance of yellowtail, calico bass, and barracuda, as well as a pretty large shark population. In Avalon, **Catalina Mako** (17 Cabrillo Dr., tel. 310/510–2720) runs charter trips for up to six people, complete with gear, bait, tackle, and meals, for $95 per hour for the first three hours (prices decrease by $10 for each additional hour). They also can take you on a shark diving trip for $250 per person (cage included). If this is too rich for your wallet, you can rent fishing equipment ($5 plus for 4 hrs) at **Joe's Rent-a-Boat** (tel. 310/510–0455) on Avalon's Pleasure Pier. **Earl and Rose's Seafood,** at the pier's end, sells bait ($1–$3). For a small fee, they'll also fillet and freeze whatever you catch. No permit is necessary to fish off Pleasure Pier or from the end of the cement ferry landing. While barracuda, bonito, and mackerel bite at either location, the larger fish are found at the ferry landing.

**SNORKELING AND SCUBA DIVING** If you prefer your fish without hooks in their mouths, rent scuba or snorkeling gear in Avalon at **Catalina Diver's Supply** (end of Pleasure Pier, tel. 310/510–0330) for $56 and $11 per day, respectively. Only the certified can rent scuba equipment. The shop offers guided and package tours, but you can easily enjoy the Underwater Dive Park (*see* Catalina Island intro, *above*) on your own for free. Snorkelers should head to the shallow waters of **Lover's Cove Marine Preserve,** a short walk east past the ferry landing; this is also a good spot to swim, since it's free of the boat traffic that jams Avalon Bay.

# Near Santa Catalina

## PALOS VERDES

The Palos Verdes peninsula rises dramatically from the sea: a green-and-gold mass of rolling hills and steep cliffs peppered with elegant estates. Once a vast, treeless ranch owned by José Dolores Sepulveda—whose name graces one of the longest boulevards in Los Angeles—the peninsula was purchased for $1 million in 1913 by a wealthy businessman and turned into an exclusive residential community. Its pocket-size beaches, though difficult to reach, are worth a visit. You can get to Palos Verdes from L.A. by taking I–110 south to Highway 91 west (a.k.a. Artesia Blvd.). Take Artesia to Highway 1 (Pacific Coast Hwy.) and head south to **Palos Verdes Drive.**

Tiny beaches pocket the steep bluffs west of **Palos Verdes Estates**; one of the most attractive is **Bluff Cove,** accessible to the nimble via a winding trail from Paseo del Mar (at Flat Rock Point). The main inorganic attraction is the **Wayfayer's Chapel** (5755 Palos Verdes Dr. S, tel. 310/377–1650), designed by the son of famed architect Frank Lloyd Wright. This thrilling natural sanctuary, built almost entirely of glass and surrounded by redwoods, is open daily 9–5.

## SAN PEDRO

Quite a contrast to its ritzy neighbor Palos Verdes, this working-class neighborhood at the southern edge of the peninsula is home to **Los Angeles Harbor,** one of the major departure points for ferries to Santa Catalina (*see* Coming and Going, Catalina Island, *above*). Besides the **Cabrillo Marine Aquarium** (*see box,* Grunion Runs, *below*), the official main attraction here is **Ports O'Call Village** (Harbor Blvd. terminus, tel. 310/547–9977), a 15-acre cluster of pierside shops gussied up to look like New England. The city's real personality (cautiously avant-garde) can be found in the blocks surrounding the intersection of **Gaffey** and **6th streets**; inexpensive cafés and restaurants abound (*see* Food, *below*), and sidewalk plaques honor various athletes. Scuba divers may want to explore the **Underwater Dive Trail** just east of Royal Palm State Beach (Western Ave., at S. Paseo del Mar), which winds through kelp beds and sulfurous hot springs. **Pacific Wilderness and Ocean Sports** (1719 S. Pacific Ave., tel. 310/833–2422) rents scuba gear for about $40 a day. Stop by the **San Pedro Chamber of Commerce** (390 W. 7th St., 4 blocks east of Gaffey St., tel. 310/832–7272), open weekdays 9–5, to pick up a visitor's guide, trolley schedule, or detailed city map ($1). To reach San Pedro from downtown L.A., take I–110 south.

**GETTING AROUND** The **Electric Trolley** runs daily 10–6 between the Catalina Air and Sea Terminal and Cabrillo Beach, stopping at Ports O'Call Village, downtown San Pedro, the

Cabrillo Marine Aquarium, and other points of interest. Fare is 25¢; routes and schedules are available at the Chamber of Commerce (*see above*).

**WHERE TO SLEEP** **San Pedro International AYH-Hostel.** Set in Angel's Gate Park, with a panoramic view of the Pacific, this 60-bed hostel is one of the best deals in the area. You can't beat the location: It's near downtown San Pedro, it's easily accessible by bus, and it's only a 10-minute walk from the beach. Private rooms go for $27, semiprivate rooms (two beds) for $12.50 a person, and dorm beds for $11. There's a kitchen, a TV room with movies, a reading room, an extensive travel service, a volleyball court, a barbecue, and laundry facilities. In addition, the staff is friendly and there's no lockout. Backpackers and foreign travelers pack the place during summer, so make reservations. All guests must have a sleep sheet, which you can rent for $1.50. *3601 S. Gaffey St., Bldg. 613, tel. 310/831–8109. From LAX, Bus 232 to Anaheim St. and Avalon Blvd., catch southbound Bus 446 to Angel's Gate Park (hostel behind bell). From L.A. Greyhound station, Bus 446 south from 6th and Grand Sts., get off at Angel's Gate Park. By car, I–110 south to San Pedro, follow to end, then left on Gaffey St. 40 beds. Checkout 10 AM.*

**FOOD** For once, you don't have to avoid the "nice" restaurants if you're short on cash. Even the most highbrow places offer meals for around $10–$15. Top-rate Greek food and live Greek dancing have made **Papadakis** (301 W. 6th St., at Center St., tel. 310/548–1186) one of the most popular restaurants in San Pedro; catch one of two nightly informal performances (usually at 6 and 9) while you dine. Though the dining room lacks character, the moderately priced sushi at **Senfuku** (380 W. 6th St., east of Gaffey St., tel. 310/832–5585) makes it worth a visit. Stop by for lunch and dinner weekdays, dinner only (5–10 PM) Saturday. Across the street, **Sacred Grounds** (399 W. 6th St., tel. 310/514–0800) is the place to sample alternative tunes and fresh-brewed java.

## LONG BEACH

Long Beach, just across the Vincent Thomas Bridge from San Pedro, seems like a contradiction in terms—an industry-laden seaside resort. With its towering oil refineries and massive natural-gas processing plants, at first glance Long Beach appears to be a hideous eyesore just begging to be bypassed. Yet somehow (probably thanks to gross infusions of cash), parts of the city have shaken that tawdry image. There's plenty to explore in Long Beach, from the landmark deco buildings of downtown to a nascent artists' community to the cluster of funky cafés, shops, and restaurants that constitute the twentysomething haunt of Belmont Shore. The city is also one of Southern California's most socially diverse, and well worth a visit before catching the ferry to Catalina.

### Grunion Runs

***Gloria Steinem once observed that women need men about as much as fish need bicycles; take a look at the hundreds of Schwinn-less grunion fish struggling to spawn on the beaches of Southern California and make the call yourself. The silvery fish, which bear a strong resemblance to unhappy anchovies (without the can), head for the beach twice monthly from March through August. On evenings with a full or new moon, the grunion can be seen burrowing determinedly into the wet sand of numerous beaches, ready to procreate (their eggs hatch about two weeks later). As long as you have a license, it's legal to catch grunion during open season (Mar. and June–Aug.), but you may use only your hands. For further information, or to join an organized grunion-watching group, call or stop by San Pedro's fine Cabrillo Marine Aquarium (3720 Stephen White Dr., at Pacific Ave., tel. 310/548–7562; closed weekday mornings), which also houses an impressive 30-tank collection of indigenous marine life.***

**VISITOR INFORMATION** As is fitting in a city eager for tourist dollars, the **Long Beach Visitors Center** delights in distributing a comprehensive area map and guide, as well as the extremely helpful handout "101 Things to Do in the Long Beach Area." The staff is also knowledgeable about San Pedro and Palos Verdes. *1 World Trade Center, Suite 300, tel. 800/COAST–FUN. Btw Magnolia Ave. and Ocean Blvd. Open weekdays 8:30–5.*



**COMING AND GOING** To get to Long Beach from L.A., take I–710 south. From the south, take I–405 to I–710 or I–110. **Greyhound** (tel. 800/231–2222) has a station in downtown Long Beach (464 W. 3rd St., at Magnolia Ave., tel. 310/432–1842) with service to L.A. (45 min, $5), San Diego (3 hrs, $11), and San Francisco (10 hrs, $34). The Metro's **Blue Line** runs between L.A. and downtown Long Beach every 10–20 minutes, stopping at the Long Beach Transit Mall (*see* Getting Around, *below*) and 1st Street; the ride costs $1.10 each way. For more information, call 310/639–6800. Both **Catalina Express** (tel. 310/519–1212) and **Catalina Cruises** (tel. 800/228–2546) offer regular service to Santa Catalina Island (*see above*).

**Long Beach Airport** (4100 E. Donald Douglas Dr., tel. 310/570–2600) is served by American West (tel. 800/235–9292) and several charter services. Prices for in-state and national flights are the same as at LAX or slightly higher (all international travel is handled by LAX). Public buses shuttle every half hour on weekdays and hourly on weekends between the airport and the Long Beach Transit Mall.

**GETTING AROUND** Public buses are operated by **Long Beach Transit** (tel. 310/591–2301). Obtain schedules and catch most bus lines at the **Transit Mall** (1st St., btw Long Beach Blvd. and Pacific Ave.). Fare is 90¢, 75¢ for students. The **Runabout Shuttle** (no tel.) offers frequent free service from downtown (Ocean or Pine Blvd.) to the ferry terminal and the Queen Mary. Shuttles run 7–6 weekdays and 10–5 weekends.

**WHERE TO SLEEP** Long Beach has a large selection of motels, though many cater to the convention center's big spenders. The **Friendship Inn** (50 Atlantic Ave., ½ block from Ocean Blvd., tel. 310/435–8369) has immaculate, attractive rooms with refrigerators for $42–$48 a night. Farther from the center of town, the beachside **Surf Motel** (2010 E. Ocean Blvd., at Cherry Ave., tel. 310/437–0771) has a pool and small, clean rooms starting at $39 ($55 with ocean view).

**FOOD** In the area known as Belmont Shore, 2nd Street is lined with restaurants catering to the young but not necessarily rich. Locals jam into **Bondanna's Shore House Café** (5271 E. 2nd St., at LaVerne Ave., tel. 310/433–2266), open 24 hours, which has a lengthy list of sandwiches for $5–$7. Dinners, which come with soup or salad plus pasta or potato, range in price from $7.50 to $11. **Panama Joe's Café/Bar** (5100 E. 2nd St., tel. 310/434–7417) is best enjoyed during happy hour (daily 3–7), when umbrella-laden tropical drinks flow freely. The menu includes locally caught fresh fish (prices vary). At the tastefully named **Midnite Espresso** (4925 E. 2nd St., tel. 310/439–3978), pick up the namesake coffee drink (a mocha-cinnamon/whipped cream wake-up call) for about $3, and then cut the caffeine with a starchy snack (under $4).

A young artsy crowd fills the cluster of restaurants near the intersection of Pine Avenue and Broadway Street downtown. **System M** (213A Pine Ave., at Broadway St., tel. 310/435–2525) features an eclectic calendar of live music as well as delicious, skillfully prepared food. The menu includes a sautéed red-snapper sandwich ($7) and chicken with curried peas and potatoes ($9). The restaurant doubles as a gallery—they'll cheerfully sell you a painting off the wall for around $2,000. People flock to **Alegria** (115 Pine Ave., at Broadway St., tel. 310/436–3388) for the potent sangria ($16 a liter), the occasional live flamenco dancers, and the novel menu of hot and cold *tapas* (appetizers). For variety, try splitting a few tapas; good choices are the *salmón y aceitunas* (olives and roasted bell peppers wrapped with salmon sashimi; $4) or *gambas y alcachofas* (marinated artichoke hearts with ham, prawns, and Parmesan cheese in a cayenne sauce; $4.50).

**WORTH SEEING** If you enjoy architecture, head to the small residential community of **Belmont Shore,** at the east end of Ocean Boulevard (Bus 12 stops here). Developed in the 1940s, it has some of the town's oldest beach homes and bungalows. The unofficial inland boardwalk is **2nd Street** (btw Livingston Dr. and Bay Shore Ave.), a hot spot lined with bars, cafés, and nightclubs where twentysomethings gratefully shed job angst. Across from Belmont Shore in Alamitos Bay is the upscale island community of **Naples,** home to Long Beach's wealthiest families. Second Street crosses Naples' main island on its way to the Pacific Coast Highway (Hwy. 1); the two smaller islands are lined with a series of alleys, canals, and footbridges that create a pleasant Mediterranean feel.

To get a feel for the city's funkier side, explore **Broadway,** the downtown drag between Pacific and Cherry avenues. The art-deco feel is authentic; if you have any doubts check out the terra-cotta detailing and vibrant colors of the **Dr. Rowan Building** (201 Pine St.). Other landmarks include **Villa Riviera** (800 E. Ocean Blvd.), a 16-story high-rise built in 1929 with a schizophrenic mix of Gothic, Tudor, French, and Italianate architectural styles; and the **Breakers Hotel** (200 E. Ocean Blvd.), a Spanish Revival–style resort built in 1926. Covering the entire exterior of the Long Beach Arena (300 E. Ocean Blvd.) is **Planet Ocean,** whose life-size depictions of whales and other frolicsome sea creatures qualify it as the world's largest mural. A shuttle ride away (*see* Getting Around, *above*) lies the historic **Queen Mary,** permanently docked at the harbor and boardable for $5.

# Orange County Coast

**The 50-mile stretch of** coast between Seal Beach and San Clemente is fondly known as the "American Riviera," the most scenic and lively seaside region on California's coast. **Seal Beach,** only 10 miles south of Long Beach, is a quirky, uncommercial small town—the perfect place to begin your coastal odyssey. The adjacent **Sunset Beach** offers no-frills sand and surf and budget motels (some of the coast's only affordable lodging). A little farther south you'll come across **Huntington Beach,** a trendy enclave filled with bleached-blond surfers and their suntanned groupies. The average age here seems to be 18–25, so if you're looking to let loose and run wild in the sand, welcome to your new stomping grounds. Sprawling **Newport Beach,** one of Southern California's most exclusive seaside playgrounds, is just 40 miles south of downtown Los Angeles; its size makes it the unofficial coastal capital, particularly for boat trips of all types. At rugged **Laguna Beach,** the coast earns its Riviera nickname—it's beginning to resemble Princess Grace's cliffside Monaco. Laguna has also been a colorful coastal stop since

## *Go Ahead—Make My Wave*

***Surfing in Southern California is as popular today as it was back in 1966, when the cult-classic flick Endless Summer forever made the sport synonymous with cool. But not every beach is meant to be surfed, especially by neophytes. If you're just starting out, check the sets at mellow Redondo and Huntington beaches, both of which are wide enough to offer plenty of waves for beginners as well as experts. If you're confident in your ability, hit the landmarks: Malibu, Ventura County Line, San Clemente, and Carlsbad, all of which have a point break. A word of caution, though—these are largely "locals only" surf spots, and if you can't hold your own and stay out of the way, you may end up with a skagg mark on your forehead. Surf size and shape are usually prime during winter, but you'll need a full-body wet suit to handle the chilly water. During summer, a shorty suit will suffice, or you can "trunk it," as locals say, with no wet suit at all. Booties are highly recommended, since L.A. has more than its fair share of rocky beaches. Orange County maintains a recorded surf and weather report (tel. 714/494–6573) with details on area beaches.***

the '60s, when Timothy Leary and his hippie cronies hung out in the town's fast-food joints. The final two stops are **San Juan Capistrano** and **San Clemente,** both worth a short visit—the former for its historic mission and the latter for its narrow, crowd-free beaches. Wherever you go, pay attention to the brown COASTAL ACCESS signs; they may lead you to a completely untouristed stretch of sand.

Unfortunately, nothing comes cheap on this part of California's coast, including lodging. Orange County's beaches may look like good places to crash, but since they're bordered by expensive homes, someone will probably ask you to leave if you pitch a tent on the sand. Your best bet if you want to sleep for free is to park just north of Huntington Beach along the unpopulated stretch of the **Pacific Coast Highway (PCH),** a.k.a. Highway 1, and curl up in the backseat of your car. There are youth hostels in Huntington Beach and San Clemente, and you'll find excellent campgrounds near San Juan Capistrano. Otherwise, be prepared to spend upwards of $40 for lodging along the coast. You'll also pay anywhere from $2 to $10 for daytime parking at most beaches.

## COMING AND GOING

**BY CAR** The scenic stretch of Highway 1 called the Pacific Coast Highway traverses the coast from L.A. to San Juan Capistrano, where it merges with I–5. If you don't mind driving through Orange County's suburbs, you can take I–405 south from L.A., cross to the coast on Highway 55 (to Newport Beach) or Highway 133 (to Laguna), and continue south. This will save some time and still allow you to see some of Orange County's most rugged beachfront.

**BY BUS** The **Santa Ana Greyhound Station** (1000 E. Santa Ana Blvd., at Santiago Blvd., tel. 714/542–2215 or 800/231–2222) lies in the Transit Center just off the Santa Ana Freeway, 10 miles north of Newport Beach and the coast. Connections from this station include San Diego, Riverside, Los Angeles, Santa Barbara, San Luis Obispo, and San Francisco. The ticket office is open 7 AM–8 PM daily, and buses leave hourly throughout the day. To reach the coast from here you need to take OCTA Bus 85 to Main Street and Santa Ana Boulevard, and then Bus 53 south to Newport Beach; a taxi will run you about $25.

In **San Clemente,** Greyhound picks up and drops off passengers in front of the Carl's Jr. restaurant (3929 S. El Camino Real, near Cristianitos Rd.). Buses head north from here to Santa Ana, L.A., and beyond, and south to Oceanside and San Diego. You pay for the trip at the next station along your route.

Call the **Orange County Transportation Authority (OCTA)** for routes, schedules, and public bus information for all of Orange County. *Tel. 714/636–RIDE ext. 10. Open weekdays 6 AM–8 PM, weekends 8–5.*

**BY TRAIN** Between Los Angeles and San Diego, the main stop for Amtrak trains is the **San Juan Capistrano Depot.** Round-trip fare to Los Angeles is $16, to San Diego $22. Public buses run between this depot, Laguna, and San Clemente hourly 9–7. *26701 Verdugo St., west of Camino Capistrano, tel. 714/240–2972. Office open weekdays 6–12:30 and 1–3, weekends 6–12:30 and 1–6:30.*

Otherwise, you can get off the train at the **San Clemente Auxiliary Amtrak Station,** located at the Municipal Pier. There's no staff here, and outgoing passengers can't purchase tickets at the station; you must either already have a ticket or be prepared to pay for one in cash the moment you step on board. Call **Amtrak** (tel. 800/872–7245) for more information. To reach Laguna Beach from the San Clemente station, take OCTA Bus 91 south to the last stop, then hop on Bus 1 heading north; to reach Disneyland, take Bus 85 north to Main Street and Santa Ana Boulevard, then switch to Bus 51 north.

# Seal Beach

If you blink, you could easily miss this mellow seaside community 10 miles south of Long Beach. Even though it offers no real tourist attractions, Seal Beach has a wonderfully quirky,

1950s beach-town feel. **Main Street** has managed to ward off most of the evils of tourism (only one or two shops sell Seal Beach T-shirts). In the simply named **Book Store** (213 Main St., tel. 310/598–1818), you can browse among haphazard stacks of used books; behind one of them you may even uncover the proprietor. The **municipal pier,** Seal Beach's pride and joy despite recurrent electrical fires, sits in the center of a wide, sandy half shell of beach, bordered by houses big enough to make you question the legality of what these people do for a living. Though the view of oil rigs is less than inspiring, it's fun to stroll along the pier or pause to fish for rock cod. The sportfishing shop at the pier's end rents rods ($10) and sells bait ($3).

Seal Beach has recently begun a **Women's Pro Beach Volleyball Tournament,** held in mid-May. In late August, the week-long **Men's Pro Beach Volleyball Tournament** draws world-class competitors in two-person and team categories. For the exact dates of both events, call the **Seal Beach Chamber of Commerce** (13820 Seal Beach Blvd., tel. 310/799–0179) between 10 AM and 2 PM. The town's accommodations are few and cater to the very wealthy. You're better off in nearby Sunset or Huntington beaches (*see below*), where rooms go for about half the price.

Start with an Irish pub, fill it with surfers and lifeguards, then add a dash of country music and seaside charm, and you've got **Hennessy's Tavern** (140 Main St., tel. 310/598–4419), part of a small chain of beachside pubs and one of Seal Beach's popular hangouts. It has sandwiches ($5–$7) and salads (about $6), but most people prefer to down beers and make small talk at the bar. Line up at **Nick's** (223 Main St., tel. 310/598–5072) for beach fuel, including the tasty breakfast burrito ($2) and the vegetarian sandwich ($3.25). Otherwise, head to **Ruby's** (tel. 310/431–RUBY), at the end of Seal Beach's pier. This '50s-style diner has hefty burgers (beef, turkey, veggie, or chicken) starting at $4.

### NEAR SEAL BEACH

**SUNSET BEACH** Barely 2 miles long, this no-frills town is bordered by **Seal Beach Boulevard** (to the north) and **Warner Boulevard** (to the south). It's got the same sand and lifeguard towers you'll find in Huntington Beach in a more residential, less crowded setting. The shores are lined with a trim collection of two-story cottages, and you'll find free parking along North and South Pacific avenues, parallel to the PCH. You can't camp on the beach, but you can stay half a block from it at the reasonably clean, slightly seedy **Islander Motel** (16545 Pacific Coast Hwy., at 21st St., tel. 310/592–1993) for as little as $30 a night ($45 with kitchenette). The better-kept but misleadingly named **Oceanview Motel** (16196 Pacific Coast Hwy., tel. 310/592–2700) has rooms with no views starting at $38. Though you may be tempted to pay $30 more for a private Jacuzzi, the secret is that it's just a bathtub with jets. You're better off indulging yourself at the **Harbor House Café** (16341 Pacific Coast Hwy., at Anderson St., tel. 310/592–5404), which serves the best omelets in Orange County ($6–$8) 24 hours a day.

# Huntington Beach

Huntington Beach, 12 miles south of Seal Beach on the PCH, was once a quiet town, but robust development has left the city bustling with glittery, spanking-new shops and restaurants along **Main Street.** You'll also find heaps of pseudo-Spanish terra-cotta condo complexes—which look like giant Taco Bells with balconies and potted palms. Appropriately, beaches here are the sand-covered equivalent of a suburban shopping mall: huge and filled with conveniences (including tons of stands hawking slush puppies, soft tacos, firewood, boogie boards, and beach umbrellas). Pay $5–$6 for the privilege of parking near the action, or park for free on Beach Boulevard and walk. Huntington is also home to the **International Surfing Museum** (411 Olive Ave., 1 block west of Main St., tel. 714/960–3483), as if you didn't get enough of the real thing down at the shore.

You can catch some rays and get a little exercise playing pickup sand volleyball on the courts next to the pier. Be warned, though, that locals take their volleyball pretty seriously. **Wind and Sea**

**Surfboards** (520 Pacific Coast Hwy., at 6th St., tel. 714/536–9159) rents boards for $20 a day. They can set up lessons with a pro surfer for $40 per two hours; contact their second branch (127 Main St., tel. 714/374–0160) for information.

From mid-September until mid-November (but especially weekends in October), locals exhaustively celebrate **Oktoberfest** with German food, music, and, of course, beer. Lots of it. In late July and early August, the world's top surfers converge offshore for the **OP Pro Surfing Championship,** which is a prelude to the massive **U.S. Open of Surfing,** a leg of the world-championship circuit with over $150,000 in prizes. Catch the action from specially erected grandstands on the pier and adjacent beach. For further information on the festivities, contact the visitor's bureau.

*Huntington Beach is a haven for recently graduated working stiffs clinging to their youth. At any moment of the day, a steady stream of them can be found jaywalking across the PCH with surfboards, Rollerblades, and overexcited Labradors. At night the same throng packs into Main Street bars.*



**VISITOR INFORMATION** **Huntington Beach Visitors and Conference Bureau.** The staff will assail you with enough gushing, glossy material on restaurants, lodging, and activities to inspire your immediate and permanent defection to their fair city. *101 Main St., Suite 2A, tel. 714/969–3492. At Pacific Coast Hwy. Open weekdays 8:30–noon and 1–5 PM.*

**WHERE TO SLEEP** If you're willing to forgo beachside digs, reasonably priced motels abound along **Beach Boulevard** (a.k.a. **Hwy. 39**), about a mile inland. The visitor's bureau (*see above*) can refer you to several.

**Huntington Surf Inn.** With a second-story sundeck and the ocean just across the PCH, this is the place to be, especially if you're seeking contact with real-life surfers. Singles are $59, doubles $10 more (with a $5 charge per extra person). Other than a few stray surfing stickers, rooms are clean and well-kept, and the management aims to keep them that way. "Unregistered guests" (read: parties) are forbidden after 10 PM. *720 Pacific Coast Hwy., north of 8th St. pier, tel. 714/536–2444. 9 rooms. Laundry. Reservations advised 2 weeks in advance during summer.*

➢ **HOSTEL** • **Colonial Inn Youth Hostel.** In a cozy three-story building dating back to 1903, this privately owned, immaculate hostel offers three double rooms with twin beds ($14 per person) and three communal rooms ($12 per bed). The beach and downtown are a five-minute drive away, and several restaurants lie within easy walking distance. There's no curfew, and a late key is available for a $20 deposit. Reservations, especially during summer, are advised. A photo ID of some sort is also required. *421 8th St., tel. 714/536–3315. From Anaheim Greyhound station, Bus 50 or 50A to Katella, transfer at Beach Blvd. to Bus 29 or 29A toward Huntington Beach. Get off at Main St. (at the beach); hostel is 2 blocks to the right. From LAX, Bus 120 to Imperial and Beach Blvds., transfer to Bus 29 to Orange and Main Sts.; hostel is 2 blocks to the right. 48 beds. Free breakfast, kitchen.*

**FOOD** Depressingly, a giant **Burger King** sits at the north corner of Main Street and the PCH, commanding one of the best views of the beach. Express anguish and move on. Further inland, the **Huntington Beach Beer Company** (201 Main St., at Walnut Ave., tel. 714/960–5343) has views, too, as well as "armadillo eggs" (stuffed jalapeños, $4) and other fillers for less than $10. The pub, which overflows with revelers on weekend nights, brews ale with a name (Huntington Beach Blonde) that cries out for bad jokes—or a swift kick to the genius who thought up this moniker. Italian food with an attitude is dished up at **Mazzotti's** (412 Walnut Ave., at 5th St., tel. 714/536–8300); the pastas ($5–$12) and pizzas ($7–$14) are standard stuff, and the walls of the bar are covered with rock 'n' roll memorabilia. The ultimate budget meal awaits at **Java Jungle** (602 Pacific Coast Hwy., at 6th St., tel. 714/969–9697): For $1 they'll pour you a bowl from one of their 3-pound econo-boxes of Lucky Charms or some other cereal. Another $2 gets you cappuccino. A pool table and dog-eared copies of *Details* are yours to enjoy while you chow.

# Newport Beach

Newport Beach, 5 miles south of Huntington Beach on the PCH, is an aloof bastion of high society, yacht clubs, and multimillion-dollar beachfront homes. But, believe it or not, it's less stuffy than it sounds. During the summer, Newport's beaches are swamped with visitors, transforming the city's quiet boardwalk into a crowded and colorful promenade. It's the largest of Orange County's beachfront communities, with tons of organized scuba-diving, sportfishing, and whale-watching possibilities. There's also a daily ferry to Catalina Island (*see above*).

You can explore the happening parts of the city on foot, starting on the beach near the **Newport Pier.** If you want to blend in with the locals, rent a bicycle or a pair of Rollerblades from any of the shops along the waterfront. Otherwise, head for the **FunZone,** a small amusement park next to Newport Pier with an old-fashioned Ferris wheel and penny arcades. From here it's only a five-minute walk to the town's liveliest nightspot—the stretch of beach and bars between **Balboa Boulevard** and **Ocean Front Avenue.** Lunatics may want to check out **The Wedge** (end of Balboa Blvd., 20 min from the pier), one of the most famous—and dangerous—body-surfing breakwaters in the world. Be warned: The Wedge is for experienced swimmers only, and surfboards are not allowed. Waves range anywhere from 8 to 25 feet, and the water is extremely shallow. Any day of the week you can watch local body surfers getting knocked silly by the infamous swells. The mini-palazzos of the city's wealthy are shoehorned onto **Lido Island** in the center of Newport Harbor. Farther inland lies **Fashion Island** (which is neither fashionable nor an island), the location of the fine Newport Harbor Art Museum (*see below*).

**VISITOR INFORMATION** **Newport Beach Visitors and Conference Bureau.** It offers the usual: tourist brochures, maps, and sound advice. *3300A W. Coast Hwy., at Newport Blvd., tel. 714/722–1611 or 800/94–COAST. Open weekdays 8–5.*

**WHERE TO SLEEP** If you're willing to stay in the beach bum's equivalent of stadium nosebleed seats, you'll find a string of reasonably priced motels ($25–$40) along Newport Boulevard in dreary **Costa Mesa.** Of course, you won't have an ocean view (more likely a view of Highway 55), but Costa Mesa is only a 10-minute drive from the beach. The **Tern Inn Motel** (2154 Newport Blvd., near Victoria St., tel. 714/548–8173), where rooms start at $25, is probably the best of the bunch. The only two affordable hotels in Newport proper are the **Newport Channel Inn** (6030 W. Coast Hwy., btw Brookhurst and Superior Aves., tel. 714/642–3030), with rooms starting at $39 in winter and $57 in summer; and the **Newport Classic Inn** (2300 W. Coast Hwy., near Newport Blvd., tel. 800/633–3199), with rates from $65 on weekdays and from $76 on weekends. Both are well-maintained, clean, and about 1 mile from the beach. They're also popular with summer crowds, so reservations are advised.

➢ **CAMPING** • **Newport Dunes.** This privately owned facility is primarily an RV trailer park, but a limited number of tent sites go for a brutal $25 a night. Don't expect the great outdoors, either: The sites are made of cement, and there aren't any trees or verdant hillsides. However, Newport Dunes is only minutes away from Balboa Island and the peninsula, Newport Beach's hot spot. You'll find a few restaurants and stores near the campground, and the beach is a 10-minute walk away. *1131 Back Bay Dr., off Jamboree Rd., tel. 714/729–3863 or 800/288–0770. Reservations advised. Wheelchair access.*

**FOOD** Newport's cheapest eateries lie between **Balboa Boulevard** and **Ocean Front Avenue,** 1 block from the beach and pier. Along with ice-cream parlors and yogurt shops, there's a decent selection of breakfast and burger joints, as well as a healthy sampling of bars. You can indulge any long-repressed cravings for mediocre American food in a glam-rock setting here; in addition to the ubiquitous **Hard Rock Café** (451 Newport Center Dr., at San Miguel Dr., tel. 714/640–8844), there's now a **Planet Hollywood** (1641 W. Sunflower Dr., next to South Coast Plaza in Santa Ana, tel. 714/434–7827), where you can hope for the appearance of co-owners Stallone and Schwarzenegger or resign yourself to watching movie previews on big screens.

**C'est Si Bon.** This small seaside café, an ideal place to while away a lazy Sunday morning, serves one of the best cups of coffee between Newport Beach and Paris. It also has an excellent selection of croissants and other breads ($1–$2), as well as imported cheeses and pâté. *149 Riverside Ave., off Pacific Coast Hwy., tel. 714/645–0447. Open weekdays 6:30–6, Sat. 7–5, Sun. 7 AM–1:30 PM.*

**The Crab Cooker.** This place serves tasty seafood on no-frills paper plates, and offers the best clam chowder ($3 large, $1.70 small) for miles around. Entrées range from skewered cod ($5) to grilled salmon ($12). You can sit down in the restaurant or get your food to go from the adjoining market and eat as you stroll through Newport Beach. *2200 Newport Blvd., tel. 714/673–0100. Open daily 11–10. Wheelchair access.*

**WORTH SEEING** Newport's main attraction is **Balboa Island,** connected to the mainland by Jamboree Road. You can catch a ferry that shuttles between island and peninsula every 20 minutes, docking on the peninsula at the end of Palm Street (follow BALBOA FERRY signs from the PCH). The fun five-minute ride is a bargain at 95¢ per car, 40¢ per bike, or 25¢ per passenger. **Marine Avenue** is Balboa Island's main drag, with more than 70 shops and restaurants. It's too touristy, but it still has a seaside charm that most of California's overdeveloped beach towns lost years ago. Look for it in any ice-cream parlor along Marine Avenue. Back on the peninsula, the Victorian **Balboa Pavilion** (400 Main St., off Balboa Blvd.) is the architectural jewel of the city. Built in 1906 as a bathhouse, the pavilion became a haven for big-band sounds in the 1940s. Today, it's the place to go for deep-sea fishing ($23 a ½ day) and whale-watching (*see* Outdoor Activities, *below*).

The **Newport Harbor Art Museum,** near the business center of Fashion Island, occupies an unremarkable brown building with a remarkable large red plastic "ruby" jutting from one corner; the museum collects and displays the works of post–World War II California artists. If you're convinced coastal artists only paint pastel lighthouse landscapes, you'll be shocked. Some works of well-known modern artists also hang here. The outdoor **Sculpture Garden Café,** open 11:30–2:30, has sandwiches for about $6, if you don't mind granite-and-marble people watching you eat. *850 San Clemente Dr., tel. 714/759–1122. From Pacific Coast Hwy., Jamboree Rd. north and follow signs. Admission: $4, $2 students. Open Tues.–Sun. 10–5. Wheelchair access.*

*One of Newport's edible attractions is the Balboa Bar—a frozen, chocolate-dipped creation that was invented here (so locals claim) in the 1940s.*

The **Upper Newport Bay Ecological Reserve** (end of Back Bay Dr., tel. 714/640–6746) offers year-round viewing of a protected natural-wetland habitat—home to more than 30 species of indigenous and migratory birds. Some Newport Beach residents claim the reserve is a waste of good land (i.e., fit for a shopping mall), but luckily it hasn't been built on or developed—at least not yet. You'll get a good sense here of what the California coast looked like 100 years ago: lush flora and chattery fauna accompanied by the peaceful rumble of the sea. The road that follows the shore is popular among bicyclists, joggers, and Rollerbladers. To get to the preserve from the PCH, turn onto Jamboree Road, veer left on Back Bay Drive, and follow it to the end.

**AFTER DARK** Newport Beach has long had a reputation as *the* oceanside playground of Orange County's young and relentlessly hormonal. Many have defected lately for the crush of new bars in Huntington Beach, but Newport—like Elvis—will always be the King. Most of the late-night action takes place on the Balboa peninsula, particularly in the strip of restaurants and bars near **Newport Pier** and in **Lido Village.** Women traveling alone and those who don't enjoy exchanging sexual *bons mots* might prefer to explore the area's cafés, which are a bit more low-key.

➢ **BARS** • Across the street from the Newport Pier, **Blackies by the Sea, Inc.** (no phone), the apotheosis of all things Californian, dispenses cheap beer with an attitude; the sign on the door reads SORRY—WE'RE OPEN. On the other side of the peninsula and a world apart, **The Cannery** (3010 La Fayette Ave., at Newport Blvd., tel. 714/675–5777) draws crowds into its maw for happy hour (weekdays 4–6:30) and that exhibitionist's staple, karaoke (Mon. and Wed.). Weekends bring bands playing rock classics, as well as a $5 cover.

*Most state beaches allow barbecues and campfires in designated areas (those with fire pits), so find a quiet spot at sunset and build a fire with friends.*

➢ **CAFÉS** • Jazz lovers should make a beeline for the **Studio Café** (100 S. Main St., at Balboa Blvd., tel. 714/675–7760), which presents top-rate jazz and blues musicians nightly. The café has a full-service bar and dining room; try the excellent grilled-shrimp platter ($14) or the barbecued ribs ($11). The **Alta Coffee Warehouse and Roasting Co.** (506 31st St., off Newport Blvd., tel. 714/675–0233) has jazz, folk, and blues singers weekly and open mike on Tuesday night (closed Mon.). The food is simple, the coffee strong.

**OUTDOOR ACTIVITIES** Newport Beach seems to revolve around sporting activities, most of which take advantage of the town's prime coastal location.

➢ **FISHING** • Fishing is allowed from either of Newport's two piers without a permit. At Newport Pier, **Baldy's Tackle Store** (100 McFadden Pl., tel. 714/673–4150) rents gear for $2 an hour ($7.50 a day) and sells bait ($2–$3). Both **Davey's Locker** (400 Main St., tel. 714/673–1434) and **Newport Landing** (309 Palm St., Suite F, tel. 714/675–0550) organize fishing trips year-round for rock cod, mackerel, bonito, barracuda, or whatever else is biting at the moment (about $22 per half day). Both are located in the Balboa Pavilion (*see* Worth Seeing, *above*).

➢ **SNORKELING AND SCUBA DIVING** • In Newport Beach, the **Aquatic Center** (4537 W. Coast Hwy., at Balboa Blvd., tel. 714/650–5440) rents scuba gear ($50 a day) and snorkeling equipment ($10 a day). Photo ID and a deposit are required, and scuba divers must bring certification papers. Call their 24-hour hotline (tel. 714/650–5783) for diving conditions. But the best dive spots along this stretch of coastline are not in Newport; they're farther south in Corona del Mar and Laguna Beach.

➢ **WHALE WATCHING** • If you're in the area between December and March, check out the gray-whale migration, during which herds of grays head from Alaska to Mexico and back along the California coast. Whale-watching boats ($12 per person) are run by Davey's Locker (*see above*) at the Balboa Pavilion.

### NEAR NEWPORT BEACH

**CORONA DEL MAR** Only 3 miles south of Newport, this small coastal community has an exceptional beach and some of the county's toniest stores and ritziest restaurants. You can search for starfish and anemones in the tide pools around the breakwater, or walk clear out into the bay on a rough-and-tumble rock jetty and watch local anglers reel in barracuda and perch. Corona del Mar is off-limits to boats *and* it has two colorful reefs, making it an ideal place for snorkeling and diving. Unfortunately, no one rents gear, so bring your own or stop first in Newport Beach's Aquatic Center (*see* Outdoor Activities, *above*). The **Sherman Library and Gardens** (2647 E. Coast Hwy., at MacArthur Blvd., tel. 714/673–1880), a botanical garden and library specializing in Southwestern flora, offers a fun diversion from sun and sand. Colorful seasonal flowers adorn the grounds, and you can have pastries and coffee in the tea garden. Corona del Mar's golden beaches are ideal for a late-afternoon walk, but past sunset there isn't much to do. Unless you're prepared to pay $50 for a suit-and-tie meal in one of the town's swank restaurants, you're better off stopping here for an hour or two on your way somewhere else.

# Laguna Beach

Laguna Beach, 17 miles south of Corona del Mar, is home to one of Southern California's largest gay communities and is one of the state's largest artist colonies. Of course, this is not to say you won't find the BMW crowd well represented. Rather, Laguna has somehow managed to maintain a balance between luxury tourism and communal values. The county's largest housing project for AIDS patients, for example, is under construction only blocks from the town's $200-a-night hotels.

*Laguna is an "alternative" city tailor-made for artists, hippies, and counterculture dropouts, a place where even Jaguar drivers are likely to have a SAVE THE HARBOR SEALS bumper sticker.*

If you like art, be sure to visit some of Laguna's 60 galleries, where you'll find everything from traditional seascapes to 6-foot Day-Glo marlin sculptures made by Todd the Fish Man. The **Laguna Beach Museum of Art** (307 Cliff Dr., at Pacific Coast Hwy., tel. 714/494–6531), one block north of Main Beach, has some spectacular temporary exhibits of offbeat and ultramodern local artists. Laguna has plenty of outdoor diversions, too: At **Main Beach,** you can join a game of pickup basketball or volleyball, or watch the ubiquitous guitar-strumming beachniks. Some of the best scuba diving in the county is here; join an organized expedition originating in Newport (*see* Outdoor Activities, Newport Beach, *above*), or rent equipment at one of the many local dive shops, including **Laguna Sea Sports** (925 N. Coast Hwy., at Wave St., tel. 714/494–6965). A complete rental will cost you $30–$32 a day. In particular, **Moss Point** (off Pacific Coast Hwy. at Moss St., south of Main Beach) is an excellent and rarely crowded dive spot. Only a few short miles north of Laguna Beach, **Crystal Cove State Park** (8471 Pacific Coast Hwy., tel. 714/494–3539) has a 1,000-acre **underwater park** for scuba divers and snorkelers. Park rangers can guide you to the best areas for viewing marine life. The inland portion of the park, almost destroyed in an October 1993 fire, has become popular again with hikers and mountain bikers.

Though Laguna Beach is home to Orange County's hipsters, that doesn't mean they party here. To find out where the action really is, stop by **Underdog Records** (812 S. Coast Hwy., at St. Ann's Dr., tel. 714/494–9490). It's the de facto counterculture headquarters, and usually posts flyers for bars, bands, and other alternative goings-on in the area.

**VISITOR INFORMATION** **Laguna Beach Visitor Information Center.** Call for recorded info on lodging, restaurants, and activities, or stop by for maps and brochures. *252 Broadway, tel. 800/877–1115. Open summer, weekdays 8–5:30, Sat. 9–4, Sun. 10–3; shorter hrs winter.*

**WHERE TO SLEEP** Laguna is the most popular stopover south of Newport, but it's priced way out of the budget traveler's reach. The **Crescent Bay Inn** (1435 N. Coast Hwy., at Crescent Bay Dr., tel. 714/494–2508) isn't the classiest place in town, but it is one of the cheapest. The rooms ($40–$65 weekdays, $55–$95 weekends) are clean and comfortable, and some even have kitchens and partial views of the ocean. On the other side of town, the **Trade Winds Motor Lodge** (2020 S. Coast Hwy., at Diamond St., tel. 714/494–5450) has summer rates of $55 weekdays and $65 weekends. A large sundeck and proximity to a beautiful pocket-size beach compensate for the annoying roar of cars on the PCH, audible from every room.

**FOOD** Laguna's hotels and galleries may be prohibitively expensive, but finding a cheap, well-prepared meal is easy. In the center of town are more than 30 restaurants, ranging from greasy spoon to china-and-crystal. **Royal Thai Cuisine** (1750 S. Coast Hwy., tel. 714/494–8424) has delicious, authentic dishes for less than $10, and the inexpensive **Wahoo's Fish Tacos** (1133 S. Coast Hwy., tel. 714/497–0033), a popular local hangout, serves the best—repeat, the *best*—Mexican seafood on the coast. Another local favorite is stylish **Café Zinc** (350 Ocean Ave., tel. 714/494–6302), which does brisk business at lunch (pizzettas, $6) and brunch (granola with fresh berries, $5). The outdoor tables are wonderful for lingering.

**FESTIVALS** Laguna's many festivals give it a worldwide reputation in the arts community. The **Pageant of the Masters** (tel. 714/494–1145), held in July and August, is by far the town's most impressive event. Each evening at a park on Laguna Canyon Road actors re-create some of the world's most famous paintings in stunning detail. Participants must hold a perfectly still pose while on stage; though you may not realize it at first, every figure in these life-size paintings is alive—from the man in the bathtub in Jacques-Louis David's *Death of Marat* to the picnickers in Georges Seurat's *Sunday on La Grande Jatte.* Tickets for the pageant start at $15. The **Sawdust Festival** (tel. 714/494–3030), also held in July/August on Laguna Canyon Road, is not an event that pays tribute to wood shavings but a raucous "Auld Tyme Faire" featuring handmade arts and crafts, strolling minstrels, mimes, and hearty tankards of ye olde ale and wine. Tickets are $5. Parking for both events is limited, and it's recommended that you park in one of the marked lots along Laguna Canyon Road. A $1 shuttle runs between the lots and the festival grounds. Advance ticket purchases are advised for both events. Call the visitor center (*see* Visitor Information, *above*) for exact locations.

# San Juan Capistrano

Just 6 miles south of Laguna, San Juan Capistrano is a serene inland town with an old-world look—a welcome respite from the frenzied commercialism so common in other coastal towns. Aside from visiting surfers who sometimes meet on the shores of **Capistrano Beach** at dawn, most people see San Juan only from the freeway. Don't make that mistake: The town's clean beaches and historic **Mission district** deserve a day's visit if only so that you can contrast real

Spanish architecture with the dreadful adobe imitations cropping up in other cities. The **Mission San Juan Capistrano** (Camino Capistrano and Ortega Hwy., tel. 714/248–2049), founded in 1776 by Father Junípero Serra, was once the major Roman Catholic outpost between Los Angeles and San Diego. Although an 1812 earthquake left the great stone church in ruins, many of the mission's adobe outbuildings have been restored. One of them, the **Serra Chapel,** is believed to be the oldest building in California in continuous use. In the week surrounding St. Joseph's Day (Mar. 19), the mission hosts the ***Fiesta de las Golindrinas*** (Festival of the Swallows), celebrating the springtime return of the swallows from Argentina. The tradition dates to the days of the mission padres, and includes a parade, a rodeo, traditional music, and the strangely out-of-place "hairiest beard" contest. One block north of the mission is the striking **San Juan Capistrano Library** (31495 El Camino Real, tel. 714/493–1752), built in 1983 by postmodern architect Michael Graves. It has a wonderfully peaceful and shady courtyard with private spots for reading. The library is open to the public Monday–Tuesday 11–9, Wednesday 1–9, Thursday noon–6, and Saturday 10–5.

**WHERE TO SLEEP** **Mission Inn.** It's close enough to the mission (architecturally and geographically) to be mistaken for part of it, and it's only two blocks from the train station. Rooms are clean, the service is friendly, and guests have use of a pool, Jacuzzi, and a VCR (videos, $4). You're encouraged to pick fruit from the orange trees on the premises. Double rooms start at $48 during winter weekdays, $58 summer weekends. *26891 Ortega Hwy., tel. 714/493–1151. 21 rooms.*

➢ **CAMPING • Doheny State Beach.** Forget about wasting your money on an expensive hotel; if you have a tent, come straight here. Overlooking the ocean, the campground sits on Dana Point, nestled among sand dunes and trees. Facilities include fishing areas, swimming, a general store, and food service. During the peak season (Mar.–Nov.), an inland site fetches $16, a beachfront site $21. This campground is popular with backpackers and families, so call MISTIX (tel. 800/444–PARK) to make advance reservations. *25300 Harbor Dr., Dana Point, tel. 714/496–6172. Near intersection of I–5 and Pacific Coast Hwy. at entrance to Dana Point Harbor. 121 sites (87 RV or tent spaces, 34 beachfront sites, several hike/bike sites). Firewood ($4).*

**Ronald W. Caspers Wilderness Park.** Believe it or not, no one under 18 is allowed to camp here because of the presence of mountain lions. Otherwise, this is a great place for car campers and RVs. Tents are allowed, but the ground is uneven and strewn with rocks. Hordes of retired folks flock here, so excessive noise isn't tolerated. All campers must obtain a free wilderness-use permit, available on the premises. Camping costs around $10 a vehicle per day. Numerous hiking trails and scenic walks surround the campground, but the beach is a disappointing 8 miles away. *33401 Ortega Hwy., tel. 714/728–0235 or 714/728–3420. Off Hwy. 74 (Ortega Hwy.) 7½ mi east of I–5. 50 developed sites.*

**FOOD** Those who are camping or broke should head to the **Marbella Plaza Farmers Market** (31109 Rancho Viejo Rd., north of Ortega Hwy., tel. 714/248–0838), which has the usual staples, plus artfully arranged produce, a full deli and bakery (sandwiches $5), and several indoor tables. Near the mission lies a string of unremarkable taco shops, but the delicious Mexican entrées at **El Adobe** (31891 Camino Capistrano, south of Ortega Hwy., tel. 714/493–1163) are worth the extra $5–$10; portions of the romantic, honeycombed interior were once the town's *juzgados* (jails). The crowd at **Sarducci's Café** (31751 Camino Capistrano, across from Amtrak station, tel. 714/493–9593) may look like tourists, but they're natives. This place has outdoor seating and serves light, original pasta dishes like the Thai chicken pasta in peanut sauce ($6.25). Lunch is affordable, but prices jump for dinner.

# San Clemente

San Clemente, the southernmost city in Orange County, is only 15 miles south of Laguna Beach on I–5, but in lifestyle and spirit it's a world apart. If summer crowds are getting on your nerves, make a beeline for San Clemente's clean, undeveloped, and virtually deserted beaches. The town is probably best remembered as the site of **Casa Pacifica,** Nixon's "Western White

House." The massive 25-acre estate is visible from San Clemente State Beach; just look up to the cliffs for a large Spanish-style mansion (one of several) perennially surrounded by flowers. Because of its proximity to **Camp Pendleton,** one of the largest military bases in the state, San Clemente is a popular weekend beach retreat for military personnel. The town's main street is **Avenida del Mar,** which winds through picturesque hills of stucco-and-tile houses, eventually reaching the **Municipal Pier.**

*San Clemente's narrow beaches would be perfect were it not for the San Onofre Nuclear Power Plant, 3 miles down the coast. Billed as "the safest nuclear station in the world," it nevertheless makes the nearby shore seem eerie, especially in areas where towering reactors dominate the horizon. Environmentalists claim that even a small leak could render nearly 30% of Southern California barren—thankfully, there's never been a reported accident.*

**WHERE TO SLEEP** **Motel San Clemente.** This spotless and incredibly comfortable motel lies inland from the coast, but its hilltop location means that many rooms still have ocean views. Rooms cost $45 during the week, $55 on weekends. There's a $5 charge per extra person. *1819 S. El Camino Real, near exit off I–5, tel. 714/492–1960.*

➢ **HOSTEL** • **San Clemente Beach AYH-Hostel.** This hostel provides affordable, clean, and safe lodging only 2½ blocks from a quiet beach. There's even an Amtrak stop nearby, the San Clemente Auxiliary (*see* Coming and Going, Orange County Coast, *above*), where you can catch a bus to Disneyland or Laguna Beach. Members pay $9 a night, nonmembers $12. *233 Av. Granada, tel. 714/492–2848. From Amtrak stop, walk 5 blocks uphill on Av. Granada; it's on right-hand side. 50 beds. Curfew 11 PM, lockout 11 AM–4:30 PM. Reception open 9–11 AM and 4:30–11 PM, checkout 10 AM. Kitchen, laundry.*

➢ **CAMPING** • **San Clemente State Beach.** Developed sites at this campground, atop bluffs overlooking the beach, are open to both tent and RV campers, and additional undeveloped sites are available to those who don't mind sleeping on hilly ground without water hookups or fire rings. During peak season (Mar.–Nov.) fees are $16, $20 with hookups. Facilities include picnic areas, hiking trails, and fishing. Bring your own food, since there are no stores (although the county beach immediately to the north has a snack shack). Reservations (tel. 800/444–PARK) are recommended during summer. *3030 Av. del Presidente, tel. 714/492–3156. From I–5 south, Av. Calafia exit and follow signs. 157 developed sites, 72 with hookups. Reservations advised.*

**FOOD** The **Fisherman's Restaurant** (San Clemente Pier, tel. 714/498–6390) serves up mediocre seafood but offers stunning views of the ocean below. The prices are steep—dinner will run you $15. Across the street, the **Tropicana Grill** (610 Av. Victoria, tel. 714/498–TROP) has standard restaurant fare (burgers, salads, pasta) for less than $10; you'll also hear live jazz and local rock bands most weekend evenings—and this is the only place in town where you'll have a slim chance of seeing other young people. Vegetarian dishes—including the delectable Bali veggie burger with ginger lime sauce ($4.25) and delicious fruit-and-yogurt drinks ($2.75)—can be found at the small counter of **Captain Culver's Counter Culture** (149 Av. del Mar, at Ola Vista, tel. 714/498–8098).

# SAN DIEGO 11

By Laura Burgardt, with Shayna Samuels

**Cool ocean breezes and more than 300 days of sunshine a year give San Diego a** sublime Mediterranean climate. And like many Mediterranean cities, San Diego—the genesis of Southern California's stereotype of sun, surf, and sand—moves at a pace that would have New Yorkers beating their heads against the palm trees. San Diegans spend a great deal of their time outside; even at night, you'll find a lot of people kicking back on the beach rather than sweating it out in nightclubs. But don't get too enchanted with San Diegans' laid-back attitude. Remember, this is the constituency that sent Richard Nixon and Ronald Reagan to the White House.

Peaceniks beware: The U.S. military is a major local presence. Warships are visible in San Diego Bay every day, as are fighters overhead. The navy's Top Gun program, made famous in the movie that stars Tom Cruise, operates out of the Miramar Naval Air Station near La Jolla. Even after a period of downsizing brought on by the end of the Cold War, the military continues to be San Diego's second-largest revenue generator.

*In 1996, San Diego will host both the Super Bowl (January) and the Republican National Convention (August). There's a joke there, but we don't know what it is yet.*

San Diego has one of the highest growth rates of any city in the country and, as the entire country is now aware, the population explosion is fueled in part by the human flow across the Mexican border. Like it or not (and many Anglo San Diegans do not), San Diego and Mexico are tightly tied economically and culturally. Untold numbers of Mexicans and Central Americans cross the border at Tijuana—legally or illegally—every day in search of higher wages (*see box* Border Trouble, *below*). Just 150 years ago, Americans would have been considered the illegal immigrants, but Mexico surrendered California to the United States in 1848, after a brief war. During the negotiations, it was a toss-up which side of the border San Diego would fall on. Today, the Mexican influence is still very visible in the architecture, the cuisine, and the sizable Latino population.

San Diego's Mexican-influenced architecture and the hilly terrain conspire to give the city an enduring charm. To the north is the wealthy enclave of La Jolla, home of U.C. San Diego; at the other end you have Balboa Park with its museums and world-famous zoo; in between are neighborhoods like Mission Bay (otherwise known as Sea World) and Hillcrest, a hip gay and lesbian day- and night-spot. If you're like many visitors, though, you won't give a damn about anything but plunking your body on the beach and listening to the crash of the surf.

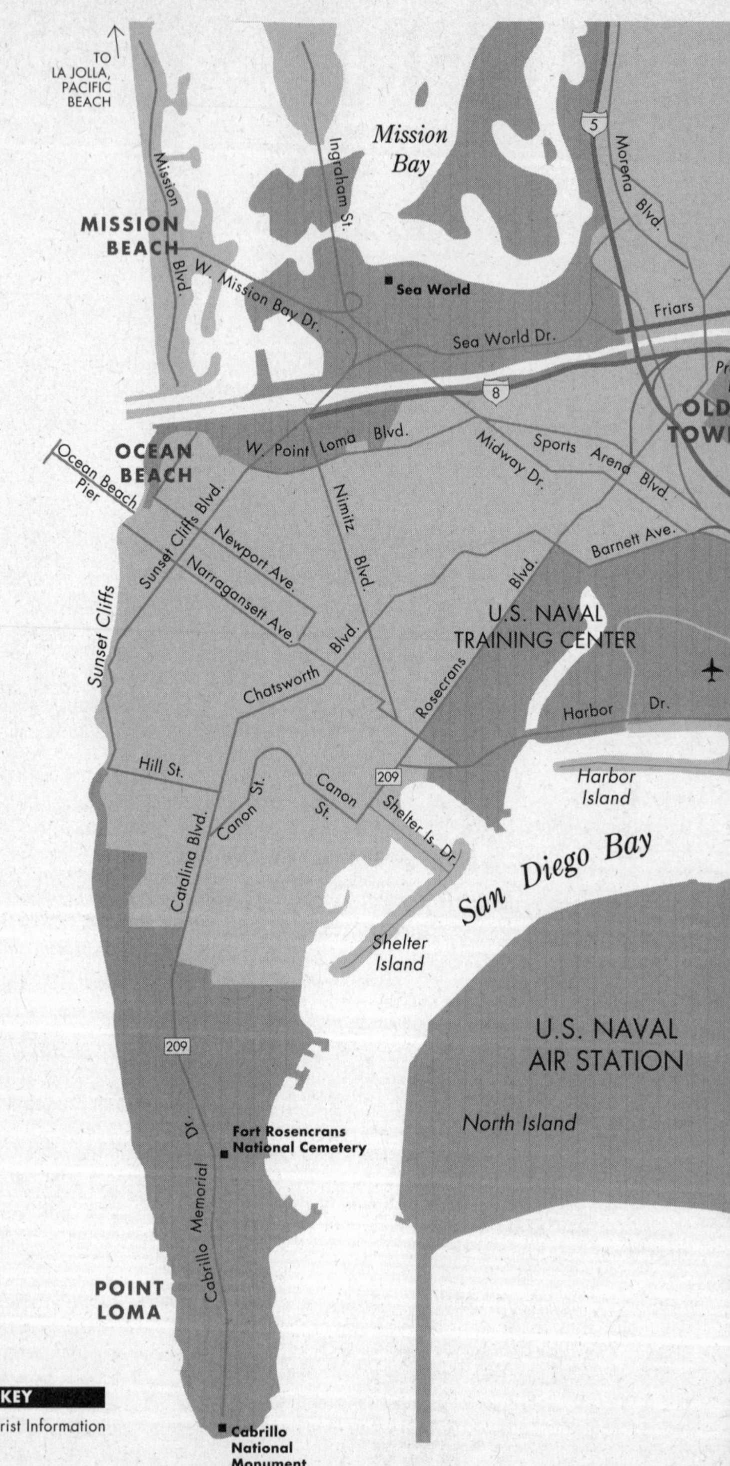

TO
LA JOLLA,
PACIFIC
BEACH
N
Mission Bay
5
Ingraham St.
Morena Blvd.
Mission Blvd.
MISSION BEACH
W. Mission Bay Dr.
Sea World
Friars
Sea World Dr.
8
OLD TOWN
OCEAN BEACH
W. Point Loma Blvd.
Midway Dr.
Sports Arena Blvd.
Ocean Beach Pier
Sunset Cliffs Blvd.
Nimitz Blvd.
Newport Ave.
Barnett Ave.
Narragansett Ave.
Rosecrans Blvd.
Sunset Cliffs
U.S. NAVAL TRAINING CENTER
Chatsworth Blvd.
Harbor Dr.
Hill St.
209
Harbor Island
Canon St.
Catalina Blvd.
Shelter Is. Dr.
San Diego Bay
Shelter Island
U.S. NAVAL AIR STATION
North Island
209
Cabrillo Memorial Dr.
Fort Rosencrans National Cemetery
POINT LOMA
KEY
Tourist Information
Cabrillo National Monument

# San Diego

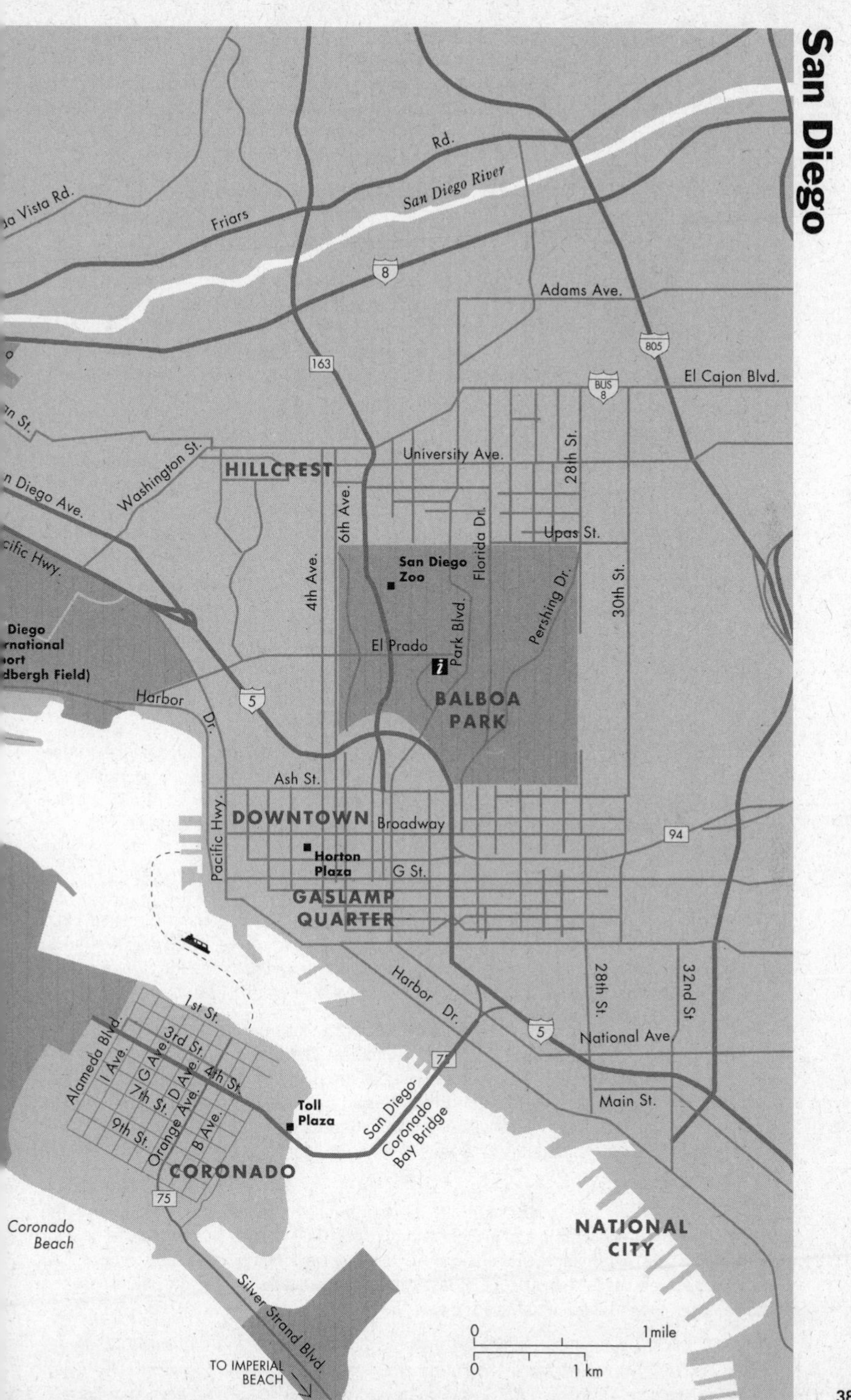
Rd.
San Diego River
Friars
8
Adams Ave.
805
163
El Cajon Blvd.
BUS 8
Washington St.
HILLCREST
University Ave.
28th St.
6th Ave.
Upas St.
Florida Dr.
San Diego Zoo
4th Ave.
Park Blvd.
Pershing Dr.
30th St.
El Prado
BALBOA PARK
Harbor
Dr.
5
Ash St.
DOWNTOWN
Broadway
Pacific Hwy.
Horton Plaza
G St.
94
GASLAMP QUARTER
Harbor
Dr.
28th St.
32nd St
1st St.
5
National Ave.
Alameda Blvd.
I Ave.
3rd St.
G Ave.
D Ave.
4th St.
7th St.
Orange Ave.
75
Toll Plaza
San Diego-Coronado Bay Bridge
Main St.
9th St.
B Ave.
CORONADO
75
Coronado Beach
NATIONAL CITY
Silver Strand Blvd.
TO IMPERIAL BEACH
0
1 mile
0
1 km

# Basics

**AMERICAN EXPRESS** **AmEx has three offices in San** Diego: in **Downtown** (258 Broadway, San Diego 92101, tel. 619/234–4455); in **La Jolla** (1020 Prospect St., La Jolla 92037, tel. 619/459–4161); and just north of downtown in **Mission Valley** (7610 Hazard Center Dr. No. 515, Mission Valley 92108, tel. 619/297–8101), the only one open Saturday (10–3). All are open at least weekdays 10–5, and all accept client mail.

**MEDICAL AID** While San Diego has no free clinics, the **San Diego Council of Community Clinics** (4646 Mission Gorge Pl., at Mission Gorge Blvd., tel. 619/265–2100) provides referrals to local clinics that charge on a sliding scale based on income level.

**PUBLICATIONS** For a window onto San Diegan life, pick up a copy of the free weekly ***Reader,*** available throughout the city. It has extensive restaurant and entertainment listings and well-written articles on local issues. The local daily, the ***Union-Tribune,*** is a pathetic hodgepodge of wire-service reports and *L.A. Times* reruns. The "Night and Day" section, which appears every Thursday, gives a pretty good picture of what's going on in San Diego each week.

**RESOURCES FOR GAYS AND LESBIANS** Though San Diego is undeniably a conservative town, the gay and lesbian community has a visible presence, especially in the Hillcrest neighborhood. For information on gay resources, contact the **Lesbian and Gay Community Center** (3916 Normal St., at University Ave., tel. 619/692–4297). Publication-wise, look for ***Update,*** a weekly with an insert section that serves as a community bulletin board for social events; and the weekly ***Gay & Lesbian Times,*** Southern California's most widely distributed lesbian and gay publication, with extensive calendar listings. Pick up the papers in cafés and bookstores downtown and in Hillcrest; both are free.

**RESOURCES FOR WOMEN** The **Center for Women's Studies and Services** operates a 24-hour live hotline (tel. 619/233–3088) to address women's needs. In addition, the **Women's Resource Center** (1963 Apple St., at Oceanside Blvd. in Oceanside, tel. 619/757–3500) provides counseling, information, and referrals for victims of violence, sexual assault, and homelessness.

**VISITOR INFORMATION** The multilingual staff at the downtown **International Visitor Information Center** (111 1st Ave., at F St., tel. 619/236–1212), on the first level of Horton Plaza, offers free maps and information on local activities, attractions, and places to stay. The office is open year-round Monday–Saturday 8:30–5, as well as Sunday 11–5 in summer.

## COMING AND GOING

**BY PLANE** **San Diego International Airport** (tel. 619/231–2100), commonly called Lindbergh Field, lies about 2 miles northwest of downtown and is served by all major airlines. Although the airport does not have lockers, it's open 24 hours and has restaurants, snack bars, and ATMs, as well as a **Traveler's Aid** info desk that stays open until 11 PM.

➢ **AIRPORT TRANSIT** • **San Diego Transit Bus 2** (a.k.a. the "30th and Adams bus") goes from the airport to downtown in about 10 minutes. The fare is $1.50 and buses leave every 10–15 minutes from 5:30 AM to 1 AM. The bus drops you off at 3rd Avenue and Broadway downtown, putting you near Horton Plaza, Seaport Village, the Amtrak and Greyhound terminals, and the AYH hostel. Otherwise, the **Public Shuttle** (tel. 619/990–8770) can whisk you downtown in about 15 minutes for $4 per person, 24 hours a day. Taxis to downtown cost $7–$8, plus tip.

**BY CAR** **I-5,** which runs north–south all the way through California, passes through the heart of downtown and terminates in San Ysidro at the U.S.–Mexico border. Farther inland, **I-15** acts as the unofficial eastern border of the city, and heads northeast through San Bernardino to Las Vegas. **I-8,** the main east–west freeway, starts at Mission Bay (where the beaches and Sea World are) and travels toward the desert.

**BY BUS** The **Greyhound** station is a bit scummy, but at least it's in the heart of the downtown lodging area, just a few blocks east of the train station. You can rent lockers for $4 a day. The station is open 24 hours, but if you're going to crash here you should keep your luggage closely tethered. Several buses leave for L.A. daily (2½ hrs, $11 one-way). *120 W. Broadway, at 1st Ave., tel. 619/239–3266 or 800/231–2222 for reservations.*



**BY TRAIN** Daily, eight **Amtrak** trains make the three-hour trek between San Diego and Los Angeles ($24 one-way). The **Santa Fe Depot,** easily accessible by bus and trolley, is open 4:30 AM–12:15 AM, and luggage storage is available for passengers ($1.50 per day). A tourist booth offers info on transportation and area attractions. *1050 Kettner Blvd., at Broadway, tel. 619/239–9989 or 800/USA–RAIL for recorded info on reservations and train schedules. Ticket office open daily 4:40 AM–9 PM.*

## GETTING AROUND

Balboa Park, downtown, the Gaslamp Quarter, and Hillcrest form the heart of San Diego. Beyond that, the beaches and the city's sprawling neighborhoods can be a pain to reach unless you have a car. Even if you're driving, San Diego is bound to give you problems. Outside the more densely populated areas of the city, you won't be able to find your way around the wide, anonymous boulevards, freeway ramps, and miles of condo hell without a map.

**BY CAR** Cars are essential in San Diego unless you're willing to stick to small, walkable areas or spend a good deal of travel time standing on a hot road, wondering where the hell the bus is. For rentals, it's best to use an obscure local company—they're usually less expensive and more flexible. Most rental places will charge an extra fee ($5–$10) if you're under 25. Rental car insurance can cost up to $10 extra per day, but if you have a major credit card and auto insurance, you're probably already covered. If you're planning to venture into Mexico, though, you should unquestionably buy one-day (or longer) insurance, widely available near the border.

The rates listed here are for budget or compact cars. At **Payless Car Rental** (2367 India St., at Kalmia St. next to airport, tel. 619/239–2886), you pay $24 a day or $139 a week with a major credit card. They'll rent to people aged 21–25 for an extra $7 a day. **Pacific Beach Auto Rentals** (861 Garnet Ave., near Mission Blvd., tel. 619/581–6500) charges $17 a day or $95 a week, but you must have a credit card and you'll pay $8 extra a day if you're 18–20 ($4 extra if you're 21–25).

**BY BUS** **San Diego Transit** is neither cheap nor reliable, but if you wait long enough and pay enough, you can eventually get where you're going. Instead of fussing with bus maps, call the folks at the **San Diego Transit Information Line** (tel. 619/233–3004) 5:30 AM–8:30 PM daily to find out which buses you need to catch. Otherwise, pick up a bus map at the International Visitor Information Center (*see* Basics, *above*). The regular fare is $1.50, $1.75 for express buses, and $2 for certain longer routes. If you have to switch buses, be sure you get a transfer when you first board. At the **Transit Store** (449 Broadway, at 5th Ave., tel. 619/234–1060) you can buy several types of bus passes, as well as maps and bus schedules.

*The $5 Day Tripper Transit Pass gives one day's unlimited use of city buses, the San Diego Trolley, and the San Diego–Coronado Ferry.*

The **Handicap Pass** ($12.25 per month) allows disabled passengers unlimited rides on trolleys and most buses. Buses with a wheelchair lift serve each route at least hourly. In addition, **Dial-a-Ride** provides special services, including pick-up, for qualifying disabled passengers. *Dial-a-Ride: in San Diego, tel. 619/236–6200; in North County, tel. 619/726–1111 or 619/436–5632; in Coronado, East County, Imperial Beach, and National City, tel. 619/297–3947.*

**BY TROLLEY** The two lines of the **San Diego Trolley** (tel. 619/231–8549) are generally faster and more comfortable than the bus. The **East Line** begins at the Convention Center in the Gaslamp Quarter, circles through downtown, and extends into the East County. The **South Line** leads from Old Town to the U.S.–Mexico border, where Tijuana is but a hole in the fence away. Trolleys run weekdays every 10–15 minutes from 5 AM to 8 PM and every 30 minutes until midnight (after which you should check a schedule). Service on weekends is more limited, but the trolley to the border runs all night Saturday. Fares range from $1 to $1.75 each way, depending on the distance traveled. Purchase tickets from the vending machines at each station before boarding. For information about trolley passes, *see* Getting Around by Bus, *above.*

# Where to Sleep

**San Diego has plenty of budget hotels, many** easily accessed by public transport. Staying anywhere near the water will always cost you dearly—especially during the peak summer season—but if you live to surf or sunbathe, you may want to shell out a few extra bucks. The cheapest places are generally downtown, but the area can be sketchy after dark; be careful, especially when traveling alone. San Diego slaps a 10.5% tax on hotel rooms, and many hotels require a key deposit when you pay with cash.

There are no public campgrounds within city limits, but the surrounding towns and parks (*see* Near San Diego, *below*) offer a variety of terrain—including beach, woodlands, and desert—where you can pitch your tent. Sleeping on the beach is both illegal and dangerous. The airport is probably the safest and most comfortable place to spend the night if you can't pay for a bed.

## DOWNTOWN

While staying here puts you a ways from the beach, downtown is the social and commercial center of the city, and the Gaslamp Quarter, Hillcrest, and the Embarcadero are all nearby. If the heart of downtown seems too hectic, you can always try one of the national chains in the quiet residential area just north of Balboa Park. For a map of downtown hotels, *see* Exploring San Diego, *below.*

➢ **UNDER $30** • **Astor Hotel.** The location is ideal—right next to Horton Plaza in the heart of downtown—and the price is unbeatable if you're going to stay a while (singles $80 a week, doubles $100 a week; no nightly rates). It's mostly a residential hotel, with refrigerators and TVs in all the rooms. The brick-wall view in most rooms imbues the place with a *Barton Fink*-like character. *421 E St., at 4th Ave., tel. 619/232–4642. Deposit ($50), kitchen, laundry, luggage storage. No credit cards.*

**Golden West Hotel.** One of the cheapest downtown flophouses, Golden West is surprisingly clean and well kept. Doubles with private bath (translation: a bathtub in the closet) go for $26; singles with shared bath are $16 a night and $80 a week. *720 4th Ave., at G St., tel. 619/233–7594. Laundry, luggage storage. Wheelchair access. No credit cards.*

**La Pensione Hotel.** This hotel offers clean rooms with kitchenette and cable TV, near the Embarcadero and between Horton Plaza and the airport. Singles are $25 a day or $110 a week, and doubles are $30 a day or $140 a week. Watch out for the second hotel of the same name; it is both more visible and more expensive. *1654 Columbia St., at Date St., tel. 619/232–3400. Deposit ($15), laundry. Wheelchair access.*

**Pacifica Hotel.** It's mostly for long-term tenants on Social Security and there are no private bathrooms available, but it's right in the Gaslamp Quarter and it's cheap ($20 a night or $85 a week). The rooms are dark, but real art by local artists graces the walls. Rooms facing the street are brighter but get noise from the nightspot below. *551 4th Ave., at Market St., tel. 619/235–9240. Deposit ($2), laundry.*

➢ **UNDER $40** • **Pickwick Hotel.** At first glance, this classic downtown establishment looks a bit shabby, but you'll find yourself in a clean room for only $32 a night. Unless you're partial to discolored, peeling paint, try to get one of the remodeled rooms. The hotel is almost inside the Greyhound station. *132 W. Broadway, tel. 619/234–9200 or 800/826–0009. Laundry. Wheelchair access.*

➢ **UNDER $50** • **Hotel Churchill.** The trolley runs right in front of this hotel, which lies about 5 blocks east of Horton Plaza and looks like it was designed by Walt Disney's less-talented brother. Check out the medieval castle decor in the lobby before heading to the Chrome-a-Rama room or one of 29 other atrociously over-themed lairs (starting at $42). Run-of-the-mill singles with shared bath start at around $27. *827 C St., tel. 619/234–5186. From Amtrak or Greyhound, East or South Line trolley to 5th Ave., walk 3 blocks east on C St. Laundry.*

**La Pacifica.** The pleasant rooms at this clean residential hotel come with microwave, fridge, and private bath. Prices fluctuate based on time of year and other forces beyond human comprehension, but if you mention *The Berkeley Guides* you can get a room for $30; otherwise they run $40–$60. Weekly rates are $150–$165—more for a harbor view. *1546 2nd Ave., btw Cedar and Beech Sts., tel. 619/236–9292. Laundry, luggage storage. Wheelchair access.*

➢ **UNDER $85** • **U.S. Grant Hotel.** *The* hotel in downtown San Diego, the U.S. Grant has played host to many a visiting dignitary over the years. In summer (which is their off-season, strangely enough) they offer a deal: $79 for a single or double. You get free parking, but most of the other extras will cost you. *326 Broadway, btw 3rd and 4th Aves., tel. 619/232–3121. From Greyhound station, walk 2 blocks east to 3rd Ave. Deposit ($50), laundry, luggage storage. Wheelchair access.*

*The U.S. Grant Hotel is old, but it's got style—and one of the biggest New Year's Eve parties in San Diego.*

## OLD TOWN

The area around Old Town isn't scenic or serene (an interstate freeway plows through the area), and you can't just walk out of your hotel and find the action, though you are near the Sports Arena and Old Town. You'll pay more for less, but at least it's a short bus ride to most major attractions. Lodging is concentrated on **Hotel Circle,** along I–8 near the Fashion Valley and Mission Valley shopping centers. One of the cheaper choices is **Hotel Circle Budget Motel** (445 Hotel Circle S, tel. 619/692–1288), which charges $35 in summer or $30 in winter for 2 people. For a map of Old Town hotels, *see* Exploring San Diego, *below.*

**Old Town Inn.** The rooms here look like little cottages and rates start at $29, higher in summer. You can't walk to Old Town from this hotel without passing beneath a creepy I–5 underpass, and the isolated neighborhood should be avoided after nightfall. *4444 Pacific Hwy., btw Taylor St. and Rosecrans Blvd., tel. 619/260–8024 or 800/225–9610. Bus 4 from downtown. Free continental breakfast, laundry. Wheelchair access.*

## MISSION BAY AND THE BEACHES

You'll pay more to be near the water, but you can't go wrong here if you want to catch some rays and hang out with surfers. Sea World is nearby, Mission Bay Park is a cool place to ride a bike, and you're near the nightlife on Garnet Avenue in Pacific Beach.

➢ **UNDER $50** • **Ocean Villa Motel.** Only 1½ blocks to Ocean Beach and a short drive from Mission Bay, this place is nothing fancy; but it does offer peace, quiet, and a pool. Rates for up to two people start at $45 in summer, and rooms with full kitchen are $58 per night. Winter rates are $10 cheaper. There's no air-conditioning. *5142 W. Point Loma Blvd., tel. 619/224–3481 or 800/759–0012. From I–5 south, Sea World Dr. west, left on Sunset Cliffs Blvd., right on W. Point Loma Blvd. Or Bus 35 from downtown to Cable and Voltaire Sts., walk 3 blocks NW on Voltaire St. Laundry.*

**Point Loma Inn.** The area south of Mission Bay is dominated by sleazy dives, but this place is an exception. The rooms have been recently refurbished, the management is amiable, and the location is central: Mission Bay and the Point Loma marinas are only a short drive away. Singles run $43 a night, doubles $46. *2933 Fenelon St., at Rosecrans Blvd., tel. 619/222–4704. From I–5 south, Rosecrans Blvd. 3 mi SW. Or Bus 29 from downtown.*

**Western Shores.** The management here is haggard but friendly, Mission Bay is a 10-minute walk, and the recently redecorated rooms are clean and even a bit homey, with free coffee, TV, a phone, and blessed air-conditioning. Singles are $26–$31 and doubles $37–$43, depending on the season and day of the week (summer and weekends are more expensive). *4345 Mission Bay Dr., tel. 619/273–1121. From I–5 south, Garnet exit (Mission Bay Dr.). Or Bus 30 from downtown (no weekend or holiday service). Deposit ($10). Wheelchair access.*

## LA JOLLA

Stay in La Jolla if you want to be near the ocean but don't want to be surrounded by scruffy people. Most accommodations near La Jolla Cove are prohibitively expensive for budget travelers, but there are a few reasonably priced beach motels along La Jolla Boulevard.

➤ **UNDER $65** • **La Jolla Biltmore Hotel.** It's a bit grimy, but close to the beach, and it's probably the cheapest lodging you'll find in La Jolla. Rooms are the sort you don't mind tracking sand into, and the dim interior feels like a time-warped East Berlin flat. In summer, singles run $58, doubles $78; rates plummet during winter. *5385 La Jolla Blvd., tel. 619/459–6446. Bus 30 from downtown (no weekend or holiday service). Wheelchair access.*

➤ **UNDER $85** • **La Jolla Travelodge.** Staying in a large chain motel may be nothing to write home about, but at least you know what you're in for. The location is ideal for shopping and cruising, and it's just a ten-minute walk to the beach. Doubles start at $69, but the price can as much as double depending on season, day of the week, and who you talk to (call a couple of times and take the lowest price you're quoted). *1141 Silverado St., at Herschel St., tel. 619/454–0791. From downtown, Bus 34. Wheelchair access.*

## HOSTELS

In keeping with San Diego's easygoing attitude, none of the following hostels has a curfew or lockout; all have kitchens and TV rooms.

**AYH-Hostel on Broadway.** This hostel, on the second floor of the Armed Services YMCA, is conveniently located between the bus and train stations, close to the trolley and city buses, and within easy walking distance of downtown's major sights. The neighborhood is sprinkled with panhandlers and other street life that may make you uncomfortable. But, hell, it's cheap—$12 for members, $15 for nonmembers; "for couples only" rooms are $14 per person (sheets included). The YMCA also offers some rather dingy private rooms. *500 W. Broadway, tel. 619/525–1531. 1 block east of Amtrak, 3 blocks west of Greyhound. 84 beds. Reception open 7 AM–midnight. Laundry, linen rental ($1), lockers. Wheelchair access.*

**Grand Pacific Hostel.** Depending on the time of year, $12–$16 will get you a bed in a dorm, $30 for a private room with microwave and fridge. The spacious hostel, a newly renovated Victorian in the Gaslamp Quarter, welcomes international travelers and accepts Americans with travel documents. They'll pick up two or more people from the airport, train depot, or bus station. Organized fun includes weekly keg parties, $5 all-you-can-drink Tijuana nights, and Sunday beach barbecues. *437 J St., at 5th Ave., tel. 619/232–3100 or 800/GET–TO–CA. 60 beds. Laundry, luggage storage.*

**Jim's San Diego.** This place is in a deserted downtown neighborhood, but it's just 2 blocks from the trolley and 10 blocks east of Horton Plaza. More like a home than a dorm, the hostel has a sunny patio and welcomes all travelers with valid passports. Beds are $13 the first night, $12 for multiple nights, $1 off with student ID, HI card, or flyer; breakfast is included. *1425 C St., at 14th Ave., tel. 619/235–0234. East or South Line trolley to City College, walk 2 blocks east. Deposit ($20), laundry, lockers. No credit cards.*

**Ocean Beach International Backpacker Hostel.** This newly opened hostel—formerly a historic hotel, Hell's Angels hangout, and rehabilitation center—has been miraculously cleaned up, with a front porch for watching the scruffy-surfer scene on Newport Avenue, and it's just 1½ blocks from the beach. The friendly management welcomes all hostelers with proof of international travel. A bed in a dorm room costs $12.50, in a double room $15. *4961 Newport Ave., at Cable St., tel. 619/223–SURF or 800/339–SAND. From I-5, Sea World Dr. west to Sunset Cliffs Blvd., right on Newport Ave. Or Bus 35. 60 beds. Reception open 7 AM–11 PM. Laundry, lockers. Free pickup from airport, bus, or train station. Wheelchair access.*

**Point Loma–Elliot AYH-Hostel.** Spacious, with a large kitchen, common area, and outdoor patio, this hostel offers lots of peace and quiet. It's in the boonies, but the hostel is great if you don't mind walking or biking—a challenging day's ride leads to Sunset Cliffs and Ocean Beach. Beds are $12 for members, $15 for nonmembers. *3790 Udall St., tel. 619/223–4778. From the end of I-8, Sunset Cliffs Blvd. SW, left on Voltaire St., right on Worden St. Or Bus 35 to Worden St. and Voltaire St.; walk 1 block south on Worden St. 60 beds. Office open 8 AM–11 AM and 5:30 PM–11 PM; reception open 4 PM–midnight. Laundry, luggage storage. Wheelchair access.*

**San Diego Beach Banana Bungalow.** This friendly, bright-yellow hostel offers the best location for the price in coastal San Diego, just inches from the sand at Mission Beach. The bunk rooms ($11–$18 per night) are always packed; private "couple" rooms are available in winter for $35. You get free breakfast, a sand volleyball area, and a weekly free party. If all 70 beds are occupied they'll put you up on the floor for $5. Show up early (around 9 AM) or call a day ahead to get bunk space; reservations are advised for private rooms. *707 Reed Ave., tel. 800/5–HOSTEL. From bus or train station, Bus 34 to Mission Blvd. and Reed Ave.; walk ½ block to beach. Deposit ($5), laundry, luggage storage. Wheelchair access.*

# Food

**San Diego has a wide enough variety of excellent, inventive** restaurants to keep anyone's mouth watering. Budget travelers are especially lucky here, since the cheapest and most satisfying places to stuff your face are also some of the best—the city's innumerable, quality taco shops. Two of the better chain taquerías are **Roberto's,** open 24 hours, and **Rubio's,** which specializes in fish tacos.

Quality eateries can be found downtown in the Gaslamp Quarter and in Little Italy (around India and Date streets); on Garnet Avenue in Pacific Beach; on Mission Boulevard near the beaches; and around University Avenue and 5th Street in Hillcrest, near Balboa Park. Only eat in places that receive an A rating from the city's Environmental Health Services; the grade will appear on a small white sign with a large blue letter. For fresh produce and baked goods, head for the daily **Farmers' Bazaar** at the corner of 7th Avenue and K Street downtown.

## DOWNTOWN

Downtown's main eating center is the Gaslamp Quarter, where you'll find everything from trendy bistros to slick, tourist-savvy bar-and-grills. Though it sometimes seems like nothing here is affordable, inexpensive restaurants do exist—no need to do anything rash, like eating at the overpriced Horton Plaza food stalls.

➢ **UNDER $5** • **El Indio.** Another in San Diego's infinite series of well-under-$5 taquerías, El Indio apparently coined the term "taquito" to refer to flautas (rolled tacos) in 1940, though the name seems highly irrelevant as you snort the little tacos down at 60¢ a pop. Try the fish-taco plate ($3.75)—beans, rice, and chips accompany the two fish tacos. There's also an extensive vegetarian menu. *409 F St., at 4th Ave., tel. 619/239–8151. Open Mon.–Thurs. 11–8, Fri.–Sat. 11 AM–2 AM. Other locations: 3695 India St., btw Old Town and Hillcrest, tel. 619/299–0333; 4120 Mission Blvd., Pacific Beach, tel. 619/272–8226.*

**Home Quest Coffee House.** At this comfortable, no-frills kind of place you can get a basic eggs-bacon-toast breakfast for just $2. Sandwiches and burgers run about $2–$3, and Home Quest delivers for free with no minimum charge. Entertain yourself with pool, pinball, or darts, but be careful throwing sharp objects when you're blurry-eyed at 7 AM. *1020 8th Ave., btw Broadway and C St., tel. 619/232–3222. Open daily 7 AM–6 PM (Fri.–Sat. until 8). Wheelchair access.*

*Long a Baja California staple, the fish taco is now a San Diego phenomenon. It's basically a few chunks of fish (grilled, or more frequently fried, "Baja style") folded with cabbage and tomato salsa into a soft flour tortilla, and served with a wedge of lime.*

➢ **UNDER $10** • **Kansas City Barbecue.** Napkins ain't gonna cut it after you've finished slobbering over the ribs at this place—ideally, patrons should be washed down with a fire hose. If the neon signs look familiar, it's because scenes from *Top Gun* were filmed here. Dinner plates cost around $9, sandwich plates $5; lunch prices are slightly lower. *610 W. Market St., near Seaport Village, tel. 619/231–9680. Kitchen open daily 11 AM–1 AM (bar until 2 AM).*

**La Tazza.** In the heart of downtown, La Tazza bills itself as an "espresso and wine café," but it's also an excellent place to take in a light, inexpensive meal at a sidewalk table. Try the spicy Mediterranean sausage and pesto lasagna ($6), served with garlic bread and a green salad.

*823 5th Ave., btw E and F Sts., tel. 619/238–8010. Open weekdays 10 AM–midnight (Fri. until 2 AM), Sat. noon–2 AM, Sun. 5 PM–midnight. Wheelchair access.*

**Sushi-Deli.** The huge, beautifully assembled sushi plates and other Japanese dishes will make you float away on a cloud of fish-inspired ecstasy. Sushi combination plates cost $5–$12; teriyaki chicken is $4. Watch out—the bill adds up quicker than you think. *828 Broadway, near 8th Ave., tel. 619/231–9597. Open Mon.–Thurs. 11:30–2 and 5–9:30, Fri. 11:30–2 and 5–10:30, Sat. 5–10:30. Wheelchair access.*

➢ **UNDER $15** • **Fio's Cucina Italiana.** If you're sick of sitting on the sidewalk eating fish tacos, dust off that one clean, respectable outfit and make a beeline for Fio's. The pizza à la Genovese (spicy shrimp with pesto, mozzarella, and goat cheese; $11) feeds one easily, two with dainty appetites. Also try the rich, filling *cappellini al basilico con pollo* (pasta with chicken, basil, and sun-dried tomatoes; $11). *801 5th Ave., at F St., tel. 619/234–3467. Open Mon.–Thurs. 11:30–3 and 5–11, Fri. 11:30–3 and 5–midnight, Sat. 5–midnight, Sun. 5–10. Wheelchair access.*

## HILLCREST

Hillcrest, just northwest of Balboa Park, is a common mealtime destination for suburban kids, gourmet foodies from San Diego's wealthier districts, and AWOL downtown businesspeople desperate for decent and reasonably priced food. The short stretch of 5th Avenue near University Avenue offers tasty but pricey eateries.

➢ **UNDER $5** • For utterly dependable, cheap Mexican food 24 hours a day, locals stop by **La Posta #8** (3980 Washington St., at 3rd Ave., tel. 619/295–8982). The tasty, filling bean burrito is just $1.25. For an inexpensive breakfast or lunch, grab a bagel at **Top of the Bagel** (658 University Ave., at 6th Ave., tel. 619/298–4201). The pastrami and corned beef "bagelwiches" ($4) are favorites.

➢ **UNDER $10** • **Kung Food.** Stop in here for one of the most diverse and unique menus in the city, with healthy, tasty, all-vegetarian food. You can't go wrong with the garden burger ($5.50) and a papaya smoothie with protein powder ($3.70). You're welcome to peruse the New Age crystals and scented oils in the adjoining gift shop while you wait for your food. *2949 5th Ave., near main Balboa Park entrance, tel. 619/298–7302. Open weekdays 11:30–9 (Fri. until 10), Sat. 8:30–10, Sun. 8:30–9. Wheelchair access.*

**Pasta al Dente.** The fresh, authentic Italian pasta dishes make up for the uninspired decor. Ask about specials ($8 and up), or try fettuccine athena (sun-dried tomatoes, feta cheese, scallions, sweet basil; $10). Entrées come with garlic bread and salad. *420 Robinson Ave., at 4th Ave., tel. 619/295–2727. Open Mon.–Thurs. 11–10:30, Fri. 11–11, Sat. noon–11, Sun. noon–10:30. Wheelchair access.*

**Taste of Thai.** At the local favorite for Thai food in Hillcrest, pick the basic form of your meal (chicken, roast duck, vegetarian, etc.), then choose one of 13 ways to have it prepared—including hot basil (green peppers, chili, garlic, onions, and shredded carrots), red curry, and choochi curry (sweet and mild curry, coconut milk, peas, and carrots). Lunch entrées are around $5, dinner $6–$9. *527 University Ave., at 6th Ave., tel. 619/291–7525. Open Mon.–Sat. 11:30–3 and 5–11, Sun. 5–11. Wheelchair access.*

## OLD TOWN

Restaurant prices are inflated in this touristy area, but Old Town nevertheless offers culinary quality and good atmosphere. The Bazaar del Mundo in Old Town State Historic Park has three restaurants with reasonable prices that attract long lines every weekend: **Rancho El Nopal** (tel. 619/295–0584), **Lino's Italian Restaurant** (tel. 619/299–7124), and **Casa de Pico** (tel. 619/296–3267), one of the city's most popular margarita spots.

➢ **UNDER $5** • **Carne Estrada's.** There used to be a Taco Bell here, and Carne Estrada's still looks like a fast-food joint, although the taste and quality are a cut above. Owned and operated by the same guys that run the overcrowded Old Town Mexican Café (2489 San Diego Ave., 2 blocks east of Old Town Plaza, tel. 619/297–4330), this place offers excellent food—the carne asada in particular—for less money, in less time. *2502 San Diego Ave., at Harney St., tel. 619/296–1112. Open daily 8 AM–9 PM (Fri.–Sat. until 10 PM). Wheelchair access. No credit cards.*

➢ **UNDER $10 • El Fandango.** Facing historic Old Town Plaza, El Fandango is named for the two- to three-day, food-laden parties that once marked weddings or christenings in the homes of wealthy Spanish-Californian families. The menu reflects the diverse cultures that influenced San Diego in the mid-1800s, ranging from huevos rancheros (eggs with salsa, guacamole, and a tortilla; $6) to flower-plum Cornish hen ($13), with most entreés running about $8. Eat on the lush outdoor patio, a welcome retreat on hot summer afternoons. *2734 Calhoun St., in Old Town State Historic Park, tel. 619/298–2860. Open daily 8 AM–9 PM. Wheelchair access.*

➢ **UNDER $15 • Casa de Bandini.** In a mansion that was once the center of Old Town's social life (rumor has it that the first tango in San Diego was danced here), this restaurant is decorated with colorful murals and tapestried chairs. Ask locals to name a good restaurant in Old Town, and they'll probably mention this one first. The fajita dinner plate is $9; enchilada plates go for around $7. *2754 Calhoun St., tel. 619/297–8211. In Old Town State Historic Park. Open summer, Mon.–Thurs. 11–9:30, Fri.–Sat. 11–10, Sun. 10–9:30; shorter hours winter. Wheelchair access.*

## THE BEACHES

You'll be pleasantly surprised if the word "beach" makes you think of boring, grease-shack American fare. Pacific, Mission, and Ocean beaches have several casual restaurants that serve excellent, inexpensive food. In Mission Beach, your best bet for price and quality is the **Mission Coffeehouse** (*see* Cafés, *below*).

➢ **UNDER $5 • Ichiban PB.** Very popular with beach locals and UCSD students, Ichiban serves complete Japanese meals for unbelievably low prices. Try one of the specials ($4.50), or the Ichiban stamina noodles ($5). Sodas are free ad infinitum with a $4 purchase. Arrive early—the place is often busy, and you'll have to wait 20 minutes or more if you get here after 5:30. It's a longish walk from the water (10–15 minutes), but it's by far the best deal near the beach. *1441 Garnet Ave., Pacific Beach, tel. 619/270–5755. Open Mon.–Sat. 11–2:30 and 5–9:30, Sun. 5–9:30. Wheelchair access. No credit cards.*

**Old Town House.** If you're famished from carving up the early morning sets and don't have a $10 bill to your name, Old, Town, and House are the only words you need to know. Three delicious plate-size pancakes cost a mere $2.75, with friendly countertop or booth service in a divey diner-meets-the-beach setting. *4941 Newport Ave., at Cable St. in Ocean Beach, tel. 619/222–1880. Open daily 6 AM–4 PM. Wheelchair access.*

➢ **UNDER $10 • Newport Bar & Grill.** A welcome change from the San Diego bar-and-grills that focus on the bar to the detriment of the grill, the Newport has a full menu of sandwiches, soups, and salads in addition to a good selection of microbrews on tap. Try the zesty fish tacos ($5.50), served with rice and black beans, or the stout-beer chili ($5.25). *4935 Newport Ave., at Cable St. in Ocean Beach, tel. 619/222–0168. Open Mon.–Wed. 11 AM–midnight, Thurs.–Fri. 11 AM–2 AM, Sat. 8 AM–2 AM, Sun. 8 AM–midnight. Wheelchair access.*

## CORONADO ISLAND

➢ **UNDER $5 • Nite & Day Café.** As the name suggests, it's a 24-hour greasy spoon—a cheap, friendly place where you can brood unmolested over coffee and scrambled eggs at 4 AM while mournful '30s music plays on the jukebox. The Belgian waffle with blueberries ($3) is a good breakfast bet. *847 Orange Ave., at 8th St., tel. 619/435–9776. Wheelchair access.*

➢ **UNDER $10 • Mexican Village.** This famous Mexican restaurant has long been a favorite with the military and the old Hollywood crowd—Ronald Reagan, Red Skelton, Vincent

Price, and Liberace, among others. The Village admirably maintains its commitment to reasonable prices (most items are under $10), but the nightly entertainment is only for the desperate. A veggie burrito costs $6.25. *120 Orange Ave., tel. 619/435–1822. Open daily 11–10 (Fri.–Sat. until 11). Wheelchair access.*

### LA JOLLA

Unless you've been dying to see the Hard Rock Café, don't even bother trying to eat on Prospect Street. You'll find more sensible options along Pearl Street and La Jolla Boulevard. Otherwise, eating in La Jolla usually involves a chain restuarant in some shopping center.

➢ **UNDER $5 • Don Carlos Taco Shop.** For those in the know, this is *the* La Jolla taco shop. First in the area to include black beans on its menu, Don Carlos serves up great vegetarian burritos ($2.50) and other tasty dishes, including the *Don Carlos especial*—five rolled tacos with guacamole, rice, and beans ($3). Don Carlos's specialty is the 69¢ potato taco, which tastes a lot better than it sounds. *737 Pearl St., Suite 113, tel. 619/456–0462. Open Sun. 9 AM–10:30 PM, Mon.–Sat. 9 AM–11 PM (Fri.–Sat. until 2 AM). Wheelchair access.*

➢ **UNDER $10 • The Cottage.** This upscale breakfast joint (which also serves lunch and dinner) offers some of the best and most creative omelets in town. Dishes are expensive, but portions are huge—try the Californian, with avocado, jack cheese, and sour cream ($6). Sandwiches cost about $6. If you go for brunch on Sunday, bring the newspaper—you're in for a wait. *7702 Fay Ave., at Kline St., tel. 619/454–8409. Open Mon. 7:30–5, Tues.–Sat. 7:30–9, Sun. 8 AM–9 PM. Wheelchair access.*

**Pannikin's Brockton Villa.** Located near La Jolla Cove in an 1894 beach cottage overlooking the ocean, the popular Pannikin puts out good grub and outstanding coffee drinks, with a menu ranging from granola to red chili nachos. Try the cove cakes (whole-wheat pancakes with banana chunks; $6) with a Keith Richards (four shots of espresso with Mexican hot chocolate and a shot of milk; $3.50). Most of the better cafés and restaurants in San Diego use Pannikin's beans for their coffee. *1235 Coast Blvd., tel. 619/454–7393. Open daily 8–8.*

➢ **UNDER $15 • Aesop's Tables Greek Café.** Despite its setting in a sterile shopping center, this restaurant offers quality dinner entrées like falafel and gyros for $7–$15; lunch offers a similar menu at lower prices. *8650 Genesee Ave., tel. 619/455–1535. Open Mon.–Sat. 11–10, Sun. 4–10. Wheelchair access.*

## Cafés

Within the past few years the number of cafés in San Diego has skyrocketed, though many seem to be just a brief flash in the pan—gone as quickly as they came on the scene. Besides serving up espresso drinks and café cuisine, coffeehouses serve as nonalcoholic nightspots; they provide gallery spaces for struggling artists and venues for local bands, poetry readings, and open-mike nights. A thin tabloid called *The Espresso,* available in most coffeehouses, lists café happenings and openings alongside the usual angst-ridden commentary on the wretched state of the world.

**DOWNTOWN Café Bassam.** This café is spacious and decorated with elegant antiques, but you won't be able to see the antiques if you show up on a weekend after 2 AM, when a well-dressed crowd—anybody not ready to call it a night—packs the place from wall to wall. Bassam usually stays open until 4, and some nights they don't even bother to close. *401 Market St., at 4th Ave., tel. 619/557–0173. Open daily 8 AM–4 AM.*

**The Gas Haus.** You'll have to vie with young, painfully hip regulars for a stint at the pool tables, but at least you'll wait in comfort—there are enough soft old armchairs to make you think you're in your own living room. Coffee drinks ($2) and breakfast cereals ($2) are the nourishment of choice. *640 F St., at 7th Ave., tel. 619/232–5866. Open weekdays 8 AM–2 AM (Fri. until 4 AM), Sat. 10 AM–4 AM, Sun. 4 PM–2 AM.*

**HILLCREST** **Better World Galeria.** The Galeria, at the edge of Hillcrest, includes a café, a bookstore, a concert space, and several eclectic shops, and does more than its share to showcase local acoustic musicians and poets. For their almost nightly entertainment they request a $5–$8 donation. *4010 Goldfinch St., at Washington St., tel. 619/260–8007. Open daily 7 AM–11 PM (Fri.–Sat. until 2 AM).*

**Wikiup Café.** Dedicated to "tilting consciousness," the Wikiup is mostly a huge, airy gallery space hosting displays of local art, artists' receptions, and exhibition openings, with some well-made coffee thrown in for good measure. If the swirls of psychedelic acrylics are melting your mind, regress to childhood with the café's Lincoln Logs set or a game of Battleship. *4247 Park Blvd., at El Cajon Blvd., tel. 619/574–6454. Open Mon.–Thurs. 7 AM–11 PM, Fri. 7 AM–midnight, Sat. 9 AM–midnight.*

**THE BEACHES** **Mission Coffeehouse.** The Mission is a large, sunny space with overstuffed furniture and the best espresso drinks on the San Diego beaches. It's also a popular breakfast spot, and for good reason—try the blackberry pancakes with real maple syrup ($4.75). All bread and pastries are baked fresh on the premises. *3795 Mission Blvd., Mission Beach, tel. 619/488–9060. Open daily 6:30 AM–1 AM.*

**Zanzibar.** Angst meets the beach: Shaved heads and black leather mix genially with bottle-blondes and neon surfwear at this Pacific Beach coffeehouse. Zanzibar has a good selection of teas and coffee drinks, along with a range of salads and sandwiches ($4–$6) and the obligatory overpriced pastries. Best of all, they're open daily 24 hours. *976 Garnet Ave., Pacific Beach, tel. 619/272–4762.*

**LA JOLLA** **Bernini's.** Decorated like a country kitchen, Bernini's serves breakfast, as well as pasta ($5), salads ($5–$6), and sandwiches ($4–$5). Browse through the well-stocked newsstand as you sip your coffee. It's located in downtown La Jolla, and the crowd gets younger as the day progresses—from businesspeople to escapees from the local high school to UCSD students too young to go out to a bar. *7550 Fay St., near Pearl St., tel. 619/454–5013. Open weekdays 7 AM–midnight, weekends 8 AM–midnight.*

# Exploring San Diego

**Within each of San Diego's very different neigh**borhoods, walking is the most sensible—and cheapest—way to get around, but you'll probably need to hop on a bus or trolley to get from one community to another. If you only have a couple of days, spend one of them in central San Diego, checking out downtown, Balboa Park (including the San Diego Zoo), Old Town, and Hillcrest. The rest of San Diego's attractions are strung out along the coast, and they emphasize fun in the sun—beaches, water parks, swimming, and lots of brown bodies. Pick a beach and enjoy yourself, but leave time for Sea World and Mission Bay, and for picturesque La Jolla a little farther north.

## DOWNTOWN AND THE EMBARCADERO

Modern downtown began when Alphonso Horton visited what is now Old Town, decided San Diego was in the wrong place, and bought up 1,440 acres of land near San Diego Bay for 26¢ an acre to begin building the city as we now know it. Today, despite the efforts that have been made at revitalization, downtown San Diego hardly has the bustling feeling you'd expect from the center of a growing city: Businesspeople are generally outnumbered by street people. The centerpiece of the redevelopment program is the inescapable, confection-colored, 11.5-acre **Horton Plaza** (btw Broadway and G St. and 1st and 4th Aves., tel. 619/239–8180), a shopping mall masquerading as a tourist attraction. A more recent—and decent—downtown addition is the **Museum of Contemporary Art** (cnr Broadway and Kettner Blvd., tel. 619/454–3541), the sister gallery to

*The unusual architectural style of Horton Plaza combines the open-air, breezy feeling of a Mediterranean plaza with elements of early Romper Room—large, primary-color shapes and other big objects that don't make any apparent sense.*

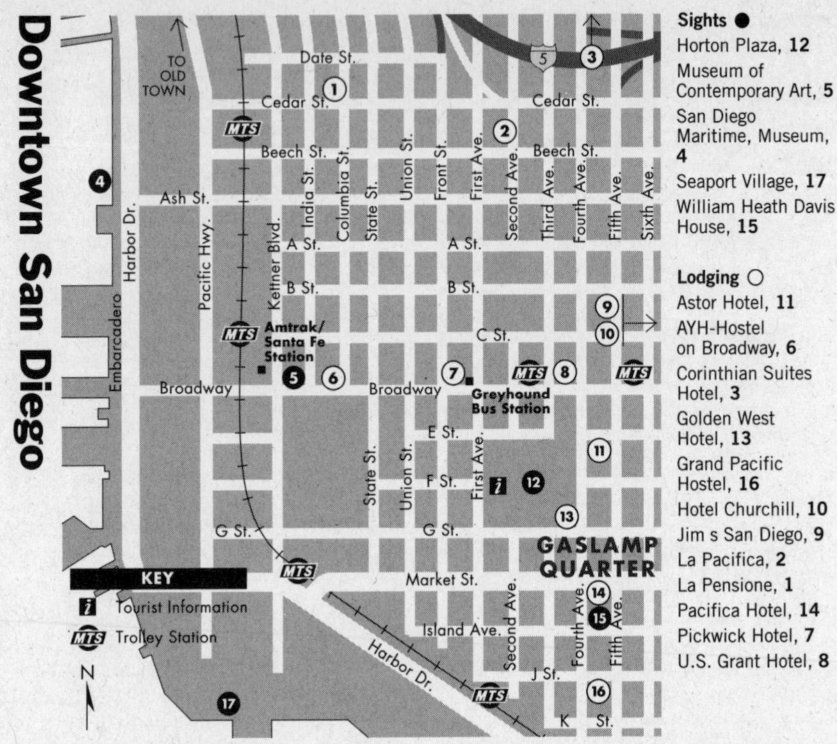


the one in La Jolla (*see below*). It costs $2 ($1 students) to view the special exhibitions and selections from the permanent collection; admission is free Thursday after 5. The museum is open Tuesday–Sunday 11–6, Thursday until 9.

Also hard to miss is the **Embarcadero,** the section of downtown waterfront that follows Harbor Drive along the curve of San Diego Bay. The strip's main attractions are its views of the bay and its docked boats, ranging from huge cruise ships to old sailing vessels. The **San Diego Maritime Museum** (1306 N. Harbor Dr., at Ash St., tel. 619/234–9153) displays three restored ships, including the *Berkeley,* an 1898 riverboat that ferried passengers between Oakland and San Francisco after the 1906 earthquake. It's open every day 9–8 (until 9 in summer), and admission is $6.

**Seaport Village** (849 W. Harbor Dr., at Kettner Blvd., tel. 619/235–4014) is a touristy shopping mall, where more than 65 specialty shops vie to sell out-of-towners fudge, cookies, nautical kitsch, and expensive souvenirs. Check out the **Boardwalk Flying Horses Carousel,** whose handcrafted horses were brought from Coney Island. A ride costs $1. If you make a trip down here, save it for after dark, when the views of downtown and the Coronado Bridge are excellent. Once you're here, also drop by **Upstart Crow** (tel. 619/232–4855), a cozy bookstore/café with lots of fancy coffee drinks.

**GASLAMP QUARTER** Named for the elegant gas lamps (now electric) that line the streets, the Gaslamp Quarter was a flourishing business center in the 19th century and features some of the city's finest Victorian commercial architecture. When the business center moved west at the turn of the century, the Gaslamp Quarter declined and became the city's seedy underbelly for more than 60 years. After some concerted clean-up efforts, the whorehouses and gambling parlors have been replaced by trendy restaurants and clubs, art galleries, and boutiques. If you're interested in the historical aspect, contact the **Gaslamp Quarter Foundation** (tel. 619/233–4692) about their Saturday morning neighborhood tours that leave from the **William**

**Heath Davis House** (410 Island Ave.), the oldest building in the quarter. If you're allergic to tour guides, check out the Mini Photo Museum at **Gaslamp Antiques** (413 Market St., tel. 619/237–1492).

The Gaslamp's collection of art galleries have suffered some fiscal setbacks in recent years, but a couple places are still worth visiting. **Galería Dos Damas** (415 Market St., tel. 619/231–3030) represents local culture, with contemporary art from Mexico and California. The **Rita Dean Gallery** (548 5th Ave., tel. 619/338–8153), with its new Museum of Death, wins the "Most Eccentric" award. The gallery exhibits anything that will mess with your head, including a live two-headed turtle. The best places to wade into the cultural morass of the Gaslamp, though, are its bars and cafés, which bring out both the best and worst of San Diego. Stop in at **Johnny M's** (801 4th Ave., formerly the Golden Lion Tavern, tel. 619/233–1131), which features a beautiful stained-glass dome ceiling, and a mahogany bar. Life doesn't really start around here until after dark, so you'll have to come back then to see the Gaslamp's other face (*see* After Dark *below*).

## BALBOA PARK

Straddling two mesas that overlook downtown, Balboa Park offers visitors a gorgeous respite from urban San Diego. Its 1,000 acres hold a world-famous zoo, a complex of 13 museums, and a handful of colorful gardens, including the **Japanese Friendship Garden,** a **Sculpture Garden,** and a **Rose Garden.** Most museums are grouped around **El Prado,** the park's central pedestrian mall, and are housed in big Spanish–Moorish buildings that were constructed for the Panama-California International Exposition of 1915. On any given day, you'll see lots of strolling families, young skateboarders, and street performers on El Prado, which acts as the park's spine. The **visitor center** (Plaza de Panama, tel. 619/239–0512) offers general park information as well as the "Passport to Balboa Park," which allows weeklong entry to nine museums for $18. Many museums give discounts to students with ID.

Blundering along downtown's thoroughfares, it's almost impossible *not* to slam into Balboa Park, or at least a sign pointing the way. From the west side of downtown, take any east–west street to Park Boulevard, and drive north into the park. From Old Town, take I–8 east to Highway 163 south into the park. From I–5, take any of the well-marked exit signs. Inside the park, numerous signs along El Prado point the way to the attractions. It's easy to walk from one place to another, but if you're feeling particularly lazy you can catch the **Balboa Park Tram,** which runs regularly during the day from the Inspiration Point parking lot off Park Boulevard to all museums.

**SAN DIEGO ZOO** The most visited sight in the city contains 3,900 animals (not counting tourists), representing 800 species. The zoo, off Park Boulevard in the northwest corner of the park, is famous for its botanical collection and its many rare and exotic animals, as well as its barless cages, designed to simulate the natural habitats of the various critters. Walking around the hilly 100-acre park can get tiring, and disabled travelers may have trouble without an electric wheelchair. For $4, you can see most of the zoo from an open-air double-decker bus, complete with a disgustingly cheery tour guide. The **Skyfari Tram** ($2), an aerial tramway that carries riders 170 feet above the zoo, is another good way to see the animals, and also offers tremendous views of downtown, the bay, and the ocean. On Zoo Founder Day, the first weekend in October, everyone is admitted free. *Tel. 619/234–3153 or 619/231–1515. Admission: $13. Open Labor Day–Apr., daily 9–4; May–Labor Day, daily 9–9.*

*If you want to see lions, tigers, and bears (not to mention cobras, emus, orangutans, and mynah birds), mornings are the best time to visit. The zoo isn't as crowded then, and the animals are more likely to be out and about.*

**MUSEUMS** **Centro Cultural de la Raza.** Covered with murals, this cultural center stands apart from its neighboring museums. The Centro exhibits contemporary Chicano, Mexican, and Native American art, and also hosts literary, performing arts, and film events. *2125 Park Blvd., near Pepper Grove, tel. 619/235–6135. Admission free. Open Wed.–Sun. noon–5.*

**Museum of Photographic Arts.** This is one of the few museums in the world dedicated solely to photography. Excellent rotating exhibits, ranging from the artistic to the journalistic, greatly augment a small permanent collection. The museum store sells a plethora of photography books. *Casa de Balboa, tel. 619/239–5262. Admission: $3. Open daily 10–5.*

*Every Tuesday, select museums in Balboa Park will let you in for free; call the visitor center to find out which freebies are available on the day you want to visit.*

**Natural History Museum.** In the halls of Ocean, Shore, and Desert Ecology, you'll find lots of stuffed animals (the kind that used to be alive, that is); the Hall of Mineralogy has a variety of pretty rocks; and the Insect Zoo has live insects and lots of signs pointing out that many of the exhibits are not insects at all. Confused? Well, no one ever said learning would be easy. There are lots of hands-on and interactive exhibits to help you rediscover your inner child. *Tel. 619/232–3821. Admission: $5, half-price Thurs. 4:30–6:30 PM. Open daily 9:30–5:30 (Thurs. until 6:30).*

**Reuben H. Fleet Space Theater and Science Center.** The Omnimax theater here can simulate a wild roller-coaster ride through the desert, on the space shuttle, along the ocean floor, or inside the human body. In the evening, catch a laser show on a giant domed screen in the Laserium—a popular pastime for stoned teenagers. The science center, a futuristic playhouse filled with interactive exhibits, is only mildly entertaining if you're more than nine years old. *Park Blvd., tel. 619/238–1233. Admission to science center only $2.50; to space theater $6 ($1 more for science center); laser shows $7 ($1 more for science center); 20% off with student ID. Open Sun.–Tues. 9:30–6:30, Wed.–Thurs. 9:30–9:30, Fri.–Sat. 9:30 AM–10:30 PM; longer hrs summer. Wheelchair access.*

**San Diego Aerospace Museum and International Aerospace Hall of Fame.** A thin line of blue neon outlines this round building at night, making it look like a grounded UFO. If you grew up assembling model airplanes and dreaming of becoming a pilot, this is the place for you. Low-flying commercial jets overhead unintentionally enhance the effect. *Tel. 619/234–8291. Admission: $5. Open summer, daily 9–5:30; winter, daily 10–4:30. Wheelchair access.*

**San Diego Museum of Art.** The museum features a notable permanent collection of Spanish baroque and Italian renaissance works, including the only authenticated Giorgione in America, as well as Dutch, American, and Asian art. The temporary exhibits—ranging from big-name modern art to an exhibit of Fabergé eggs—are very popular, and you'll pay a couple dollars more to see them. Come play with the new IMAGE system, which allows you to see and research many of the museum's works on computer; for a few dollars you can print out a color copy of your favorite. *Tel. 619/232–7931. Admission: $6, $2 students with ID. Open Tues.–Sun. 10–4:30.*

**Timken Museum of Art.** This small collection includes some impressive samples of European Old Master paintings, as well as 18th- and 19th-century American paintings. *Tel. 619/239–5548. Admission free. Open Tues.–Sat. 10–4:30, Sun. 11–4:30.*

*Stray businesspeople looking for lunch in Hillcrest mix with interns in hospital scrubs from the nearby UCSD Medical Center, and lost-looking sailors pass by fashionable young gay men.*

## HILLCREST

A few freeway exits north of downtown proper, just northwest of Balboa Park, lies Hillcrest, an oasis of cafés, bookstores, record shops, and restaurants—and the most visible center of San Diego's gay and lesbian community. Hillcrest centers around the intersection of University and 5th avenues, although interesting shops stretch all the way down to Park Boulevard. For that elusive '70s concept album you've been seeking, check **Off The Record** (3849 5th Ave., at University Ave., tel. 619/298–4755). Not only do they have a good selection of new and used records, CDs, and tapes, the staff is a great source of information about the local music scene, both underground and mainstream. Nearby, **Blue Door Bookstore** (3823 5th Ave., tel. 619/298–8610) stocks a number of books with a lesbian and gay emphasis, as well as general-interest titles. If you want to cool your heels for a bit, stop by

Quel Fromage (523 University Ave., tel. 619/295–1600) and order a giant iced cappuccino ($3.25), made with 11 ingredients. Or catch a flick at the **Guild Theater** (3827 5th Ave., at University Ave., tel. 295–2000); they show old and new artsy movies, with an emphasis on camp. If you're looking to put down a little more cash, head to Park Avenue, south of Univeristy, where you'll find a number of vintage—don't call them "thrift"—stores. For duds from the late-1800s to the mid-1970s, stop by **Life's Little Pleasures** (4219 Park Blvd., near El Cajon Blvd., tel. 619/296–6222). Hillcrest is best accessed from the Washington Street exit off I–5.



## OLD TOWN

Old Town, a few miles north of downtown off I–5, is simply a collection of remnants from the original San Diego, the first European settlement in California. The former pueblo is now preserved as a state historic park, containing several original and reconstructed buildings. Old Town is a favorite with tourists and is predictably ringed with numerous "Apache Trading Post Shoppe"–type stores. Avoid the schlocky **Bazaar del Mundo** unless you're a sucker for dubiously Mexican and Native American novelty items. If you ignore Old Town's commercial aspects, though, it can be a fascinating afternoon trip into California's past. Buses 4 and 5 and the North line trolley serve Old Town from downtown. Visitors in wheelchairs may find it difficult to get around the area, and access to some of the buildings is well-nigh impossible.

The settlement began as a suburb of California's first mission, **San Diego de Alcalá** (10818 San Diego Mission Rd., tel. 619/281–8449), founded by Padre Junípero Serra in 1769. It's now located east of town near the San Diego River. The peaceful gardens and cool adobe structures are pleasant enough, although the Padre Luis Jayme Museum's exhibits are limited. Masses are held daily, and private weddings book the chapel on Saturdays—during these times no admission is charged; otherwise, it's $2. The mission is open daily 9–5; take Bus 43 from downtown, or take I–8 east, take Mission Gorge Road north, then go left on Twain Avenue for a half mile.

**CASA DE ESTUDILLO** Despite the earthquakes that have rattled Southern California, many of Old Town's first adobe buildings, erected in the early and mid-1800s by Spanish military officers from the nearby Presidio, are still standing. The largest remaining adobe is Casa de Estudillo, built in the early 1800s by Captain José M. Estudillo. For $2, you can view the mansion's 13 luxurious rooms. *Across Mason St. from the plaza. Open daily 10–5.*

**OLD TOWN PLAZA** This clearing at the center of Old Town was used in the mid-19th century for assemblies, festivals, and periodic bullfights. The American flag was first raised over the plaza after the brief massacre known as the Mexican-American War (1846–48), but the only bodies laid out beneath the flag today belong to napping tourists. Park rangers lead free, informative tours of Old Town starting at 2 PM daily from the **Robinson-Rose House/State Park Visitor Center,** on the Wallace Street side of the plaza. An info-packed booklet for a self-guided tour is also available here for $2.

**PRESIDIO PARK** In 1769 a Spanish presidio (fort) was built next to the original site of Padre Serra's mission, in what is now Presidio Park. The park is a short, vigorous hike (or a brief car ride) up a hill from the core of Old Town. Its 40-odd acres, covered with grass and trees, offer a great view of Old Town, the freeways, and the golf course below. The actual Presidio was used only briefly—in Spain's attempt to subdue the resistant indigenous people—but would have been useless against foreign invasions. Constructed in 1929, the **Junípero Serra Museum** (2727 Presidio Dr., tel. 619/297–3258) is one of San Diego's most well-known landmarks. Although small, the museum does an excellent job of outlining San Diego's Native American, Spanish, and Mexican history, with displays of furniture, clothing, tools, and household items. If you dig archaeology, check out the excavation of the Presidio next to the museum; during summer you can pay $50 to do the archaeologists' work for them. Admission to the museum is $3.

**WHALEY HOUSE** The oldest brick structure in Southern California houses a surprisingly interesting collection of early California photographs and other antique trinkets. Built by Thomas Whaley in 1856, the building is one of the only two houses in California listed by the U.S. Department of Commerce as haunted. Come find out why. *2482 San Diego Ave., at Harney St., tel. 619/298–2482. Admission: $4. Open daily 10–5.*

Old Town San Diego

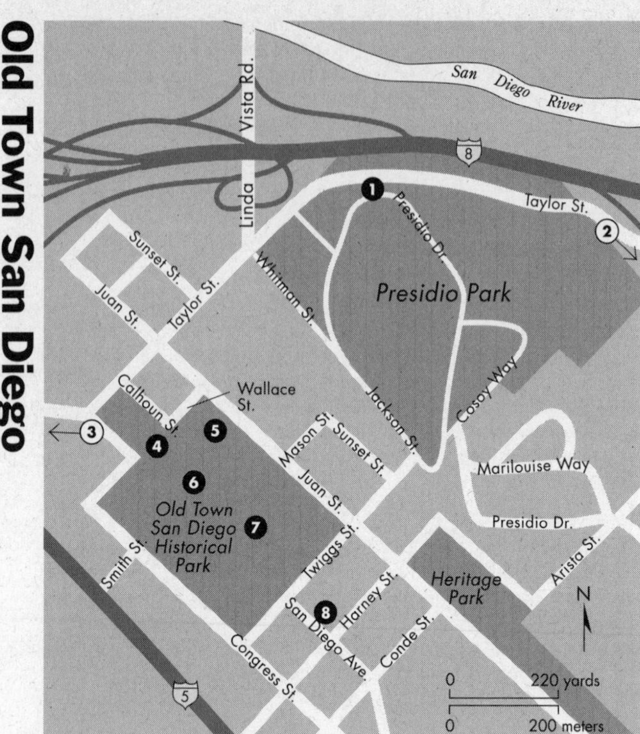


**Sights ●**

Bazaar del Mundo, **5**

Casa de Estudillo, **7**

Junípero Serra Museum, **1**

Old Town Plaza, **6**

Robinson-Rose House/State Park Visitor Center, **4**

Whaley House, **8**

**Lodging ○**

Hotel Circle Budget Motel, **2**

Old Town Inn, **3**

## MISSION BAY

Locals and visitors looking to do some boating, running, sunning, or jet skiing head to this 4,600-acre aquatic park in droves. Terrestrial types can jog, play basketball, toss a Frisbee, or fly a kite along 27 miles of bayfront beach or on one of two main islands, Vacation Isle and Fiesta Island. The winds striking the Tecolote Shores area near East Mission Bay Drive are known to produce especially good kite-flying conditions. The **Mission Bay Visitor Information Center** (2688 East Mission Bay Dr., tel. 619/276–8200) is a clearinghouse for promotional and informational pamphlets about Mission Bay and San Diego as a whole that will greatly help the befuddled visitor. It's open Monday–Saturday 9–5:30, Sunday 9:30–5. One note: Mission Bay is absolutely clogged with cars and people on summer weekends. Save your sanity and go during the week if possible.

**SEA WORLD** Easily the most famous attraction in Mission Bay, and possibly all of San Diego, Sea World displays fish and captive marine mammals, including sea otters, dolphins, seals, and the trademark killer whales. If you're not thrilled by contrived shows in which your fellow mammals do tricks for bribes of fish, check out the park's diverse aquarium displays; skip the disappointing **Shark Encounter,** though. There's an impressive waterskiing show, redundantly named **Ski! Ski! Ski!** For $2, you can be hydraulically shoved 320 feet into the air on Southwest Airlines' **Skytower,** which offers an excellent view of greater San Diego. Look for coupons at visitor centers, hotels, McDonald's, and the like, to chop a couple dollars off admission. *Sea World Dr., 1 mi west of I–5, tel. 619/226–3901. Bus 9 from downtown. Admission: $29. Open summer, daily 10 AM–11 PM; winter, daily 10 AM–6 PM. Parking ($5). Wheelchair access.*

**BELMONT PARK** Near the ocean at the end of West Mission Bay Drive, Belmont Park is fun for the family by day; by night, it's a gangland (in other words, you do not want to be here after dark). The park's three main attractions: The rather tame **Giant Dipper** rollercoaster, the reconstructed **Liberty Carousel,** and **The Plunge** pool are the relics of a 1925 amusement park built on the present site. **The Plunge** (tel. 619/488–3110) was once a saltwater showplace that hosted the likes of Esther "Vaseline" Williams and Johnny Weismuller. It's now a public pool, and admission is $2.50.



## THE BEACHES

The San Diego coast stretches from Pacific Beach, where a "no shirt, no shoes, no problem" attitude prevails, all the way to the tip of Point Loma, where the Naval Reservation and National Cemetery set the tone. In between, you're likely to find a scene you can deal with.

**PACIFIC BEACH** Known locally as "P.B.," Pacific Beach is one of San Diego's most popular "just hanging out" spots. You'll find ample quantities of sunburned flesh and kids on rented body boards, and a smattering of longboard surfers. Adolescents whiz along the concrete strip that runs parallel to the beach on bicycles, skateboards, in-line skates, and LSD. Longhaired, bare-chested young men sit on the porches of rented beach bungalows, and hippie girls sell handmade necklaces and offer to wrap your hair in yarn. If you feel an urge to join this kaleidoscope of humanity, you can rent all manner of beach-bumming equipment, including in-line skates ($5 an hour, $15 a day) and body boards ($5 an hour, $10 a day), at **Skates Plus** (735 Seagirt Ct., at Mission Blvd., tel. 619/488–PLUS). Bus 34 or Express Bus 30 will get you here from downtown.

The only strip of ocean in San Diego devoted exclusively to surfing, **Tourmaline Surfing Park** teems with boards, although the waves can be scant. Surf veterans sit like tribal elders on the park's benches, bragging about the gigantic waves they rode decades ago. Take Tourmaline Street off Mission Boulevard to reach the beach.

At the very edge of the beach, the hippest of locals regularly mob **Lahaina Beach House** (710 Oliver Ave., near Pacific Beach Dr., tel. 619/270–3888), the social center of the beach scene first, and a burger-and-beer joint second. Head inland a bit to the **Pacific Beach Brew House** (4475 Mission Blvd., tel. 619/274–2537) for a tasty ale and your ESPN fix. **Garnet Avenue** (pronounced gar-NET) is the undisputed main drag of P.B.'s business district, with hip new and used clothing stores, campy novelty shops, and the inevitable surfwear boutiques. The very best of P.B.'s eateries, for quantity, quality, and price, is **Ichiban P.B.** (*see* Food, *above*). P.B. also has a happening nightlife, from mellow bars to cheesy discos.

*If you don't want to come face-to-face with a dollop of je ne sais quoi, keep an eye out for signs warning about pollution, particularly on beaches in the southern areas. San Diego has had its fair share of sewage leaks in recent years.*

**MISSION BEACH** Mission Beach is P.B. with attitude, or else Ocean Beach (*see below*) plus tourists. You get teenage skateboard punks in stocking caps in addition to the more common varieties of beachgoer. Bikers, joggers, and sun-bleached teenagers all flow along the concrete strip of **Ocean Front Walk,** running the length of the 3-mile beach all the way to Pacific Beach. The laissez-faire street scene may be enhanced by the proximity of the **Get-It-On Smoke Shop** (3219 Mission Blvd., at W. Mission Bay Dr., tel. 619/488–9753), the best place in Mission Beach to procure a toke-stone, a red plastic water pipe, or other items having nothing whatsoever to do with drugs. If you'd rather mix it up with the folks on the Ocean Front Walk, **Mike's Bikes** (tel. 619/488–1444), on the beachfront block of West Mission Bay Drive, can rent you blades or a bike for $4 an hour, a body board for $4 a day, or a surfboard for $7 a day. Bus 35 from downtown goes to Mission Beach.

**OCEAN BEACH** Occasionally called "O.B.," this community is among San Diego's liveliest. Adolescent boys with tattoos reading "White Trash" watch the surf, while huge commercial jets from San Diego International roar overhead regularly. Take a walk out onto **Municipal Pier,** where you can watch a phalanx of better-than-average regulars carving up the wave sets. Near the end of the pier, the **Bait Shop** will rent you a fishing pole and give you bait for $8.50 a day plus $20 deposit, but you'll be lucky to catch anything. Don't miss **Newport Avenue,** Ocean Beach's main drag, where you'll find a plethora of bars and restaurants, a few clothing boutiques, and, of course, surf shops. Check out **The Black** (5017 Newport Ave., at Bacon St., tel.

619/222–5498), one convenient location for all your water-bong and throwing-knife needs. Bus 35 serves Ocean Beach from downtown.

**POINT LOMA** Acting as a buffer against the temperamental Pacific, Point Loma curves along San Diego Bay and extends south into the sea. If you stick to the main streets, you'll see only plastic fast-food joints, parking lots, tacky neon signs, and flophouses catering to navy sailors. Away from the main strips, though, Point Loma is one of San Diego's wealthiest and most established enclaves, a favorite retirement spot for naval officers. From the bay side you have a terrific view of downtown San Diego, and the point is a good place to watch the parade of ships and aircraft from the U.S. Naval Air Station on North Island.

*Point Loma's Sunset Cliffs, between Mission Beach and Point Loma, are a prime spot for watching the sunset, and then for nighttime wave watching and whatever other nocturnal activities you can comfortably accomplish on the gritty sandstone.*

➢ **CABRILLO NATIONAL MONUMENT** • Perched at the end of the peninsula, the 144-acre park's rugged cliffs and shoreline offer truly spectacular views of the harbor and coastline, and the park is a prime viewing spot for the migration of the California gray whale from mid-December to mid-March. The visitor center offers films and lectures about the monument, the sea-level tide pools, and the gray whale migration. Also check out the **Old Point Loma Lighthouse,** which began operating in 1855. The light from its lens was visible for 25 miles on a clear day, but ships' navigators were usually unable to see it in the fog. The lighthouse stopped operating in 1891, but visitors can still tour it. *Tel. 619/557–5450. From downtown, Bus 2 to Redwood St. and transfer to Bus 6. Admission: $4 per vehicle, $1 on foot or bike. Open daily 9–5:15.*

## CORONADO ISLAND

Across the water from the Embarcadero in downtown San Diego lies Coronado Island, a combination of wealthy suburb and naval air base. Coronado—actually the tip of the peninsula that creates San Diego Bay—attracts a lot of retirees and stiff military types who love the smell of aviation fuel in the morning (the North Island U.S. Naval Air Station takes up the northern tip of the island). Anarchists who look hard will find all kinds of evil connections between the military and the island's obvious wealth. The easiest way to reach Coronado is on the **Bay Ferry** (tel. 619/234–4111). The 15-minute ride from the Broadway Pier to the Old Ferry landing in Coronado costs $2 each way, and an additional 50¢ for bicycles. Ferries leave every hour 9 AM–9 PM, except on Friday and Saturday, when they run until 10 PM. The ferry docks at the touristy **Old Ferry Landing** (tel. 619/435–8895); from there a trackless trolley (50¢) runs down Orange Avenue, the island's main strip, to the Hotel del Coronado (*see below*) and the beach.

If you have a car, you can cross the San Diego–Coronado Bay Bridge, but rush-hour traffic may cause hellish delays. The toll into Coronado is $1, but cars with two or more passengers cross for free. The **Coronado Visitor Information Center** (1111 Orange Ave., Suite A, tel. 619/437–8788 or 800/622–8300) offers brochures on shopping, dining, and lodging.

**HOTEL DEL CORONADO** Referred to as the "Hotel Del" by locals, this place offers the ultimate example of Victorian architecture. Its tall circular turrets, hand-carved wooden pillars, and sheer size represent the pinnacle of San Diego affluence and clout. Opened in 1888, the Hotel Del has hosted a veritable *Who's Who* of the world's elite, including the Prince of Wales and several U.S. presidents (including the Clintons); and it was the backdrop for Marilyn Monroe's *Some Like It Hot.* Explore at night for maximum effect: Rumor has it that one of the rooms is haunted. *1500 Orange Ave., tel. 619/435–6611. From Coronado Bridge, left on Orange Ave., and drive 6 blocks. Open to public 5 AM–10 PM. Wheelchair access.*

**SILVER STRAND BEACH** Follow Highway 75 east from Coronado (or take Bus 901 from downtown) and you'll hit the slim, unique, 2-mile-long **Silver Strand Beach State Park,** which connects the mainland at Imperial Beach to the south with Coronado. Named for the silver shells found at the water's edge, the beach offers calm bay on one side and pounding surf on the other. The park is open 8 AM–9 PM and charges a $4 day-use fee. South of Silver Strand on

Highway 75, also on Bus 901's route, lies **Imperial Beach,** home to the famous and elaborate sand castles constructed at the annual **Sand Castle Days Festival** (*see below*).



## LA JOLLA

La Jolla—in Spanish, "the jewel"—lives up to its name in both beauty and expense, with dramatic ocean coves, spectacular views, and huge, expensive homes. Boutiques and restaurants cater to the affluent local gentry, but the largely unspoiled scenery is still free. La Jolla is the best place in San Diego to see marine life from underwater or examine the results of centuries of oceanic erosion. In addition, U.C. San Diego, the Museum of Contemporary Art, and the world-famous Scripps Institute of Oceanography, with a new aquarium-museum, are clustered here, all within a few minutes' driving time of one another. **Prospect Street** and **Girard Avenue** are the two main drags, with plenty of pricey restaurants and boutiques. To reach them, take Bus 30 or 34 from downtown; within La Jolla, walking is easy. If you're driving north on I–5, exit at Ardath Road; from I–5 southbound take the La Jolla Shores Village Drive exit to Torrey Pines Road.

*If you want to get a good feel for how Windansea locals feel about tourists, read Tom Wolfe's 1960s story* The Pump House Gang; *the characters and their beachside hangout were based on this small stretch of La Jolla's coast.*

**Windansea Beach,** known throughout the region for its excellent surfing conditions, was once a viciously enforced "locals only" surfers' beach (*see box* The Ways of the Waves, *below*). Take Nautilus Street west from La Jolla Boulevard to Neptune Place to check it out. If you're feeling a little more daring, try **Black's Beach,** where only about half of the mostly male sunbathers wear clothes. Although the beach is beautiful and the waves are usually excellent for surfing, it's almost never crowded because there's no road in. The closest you can get by car is the Torrey Pines Glider Port (2800 Torrey Pines Scenic Dr.), from which you'll have to hike down a steep cliffside trail.

**U.C. SAN DIEGO** UCSD students are remarkably studious, especially considering that their classes have to compete with the sun and the sea. The campus has a reputation for blandness, but a hike through its eucalyptus groves may surprise you with some unique features. Pick up a map at the info booth in the **Price Center** (9500 Gilman Dr., tel. 619/534–3362) or at the booths at the north and south entrances. The campus features lots of harsh, parking garage–like structures built in the style known as "brutalism." More architecturally interesting is the **Central Library** (tel. 619/534–3336), which may remind you of a spaceship. It lies diagonally across from an even wackier campus building, the Structural Systems Laboratory, lit by night with neon that flashes the names of the Seven Sins (avarice, greed, and the rest) and the Virtues (hope, charity, faith, etc.). The "decoration" is part of an attempt to spice up the campus with public artwork. Two more pieces, in the thinning stand of eucalyptus trees nearby, are the **Singing Tree** and the **Talking Tree.** One tree sings everything from country and western to opera, while the other chants or whispers poetry; both work via speakers implanted by the Visual Arts department.

*Buddhas watch the boob tube as part of a campus-wide outdoor arts project that also includes the Singing and Talking Trees.*

For a bite to eat, the **Food Co-op** (tel. 619/546–8339), in the Student Center just off Gilman Drive, has a variety of organic items at unbeatable prices. You can get two vegetarian rice-noodle egg rolls and a decent bag of carob chips for less than $2. For a less conventional scene, make your way to the southern edge of campus behind the La Jolla Playhouse and visit **Ché Café** (tel. 619/534–2311). The Ché serves soup, salads, and sandwiches in a comfortable, casual setting. Look for the artwork on the outside celebrating leftist revolutionaries of the past two centuries, and stop by on Wednesdays for the all-you-can-eat $4 special.

**MT. SOLEDAD** Several miles south of campus and east of downtown La Jolla is Mt. Soledad, the highest point in the area. Soledad's peak has long been topped by a cross, first a rickety wooden affair in the early part of the century, then a concrete version dedicated in 1954 as a tribute to the U.S. Armed Forces. In 1991, the more devoutly secular of San Diego's populace began an effort to remove the cross, since it stood on public land, technically in violation of the American division of church and state. Eventually, the city transferred ownership of the few square feet beneath the cross to a nonprofit historical society to get around the problem. All of downtown and most of greater San Diego are clearly visible from Mt. Soledad's peak, though the horizon is sometimes obscured by looming L.A.-like smog. From I-5 north, take Ardath Street exit and make a left at the third light.

**SCRIPPS PARK** Strolling along the walkway that borders Coast Boulevard and Scripps Park, you'll understand why people are willing to pay so much to live in La Jolla. The park, a sea-cooled patch of manicured grass, makes a great site for a seaside picnic, attracting everyone from wet-suited scuba divers to the tassel-loafered lunch crowd. The ocean is stunningly clear, and La Jolla Cove's largest beach—usually just called **The Cove**—hosts sunbathers, snorkelers, and divers attracted by the good underwater visibility and swirling schools of fish (*see* Outdoor Activities, *below*). Would-be swimmers take note: The wave action here is sometimes strong and often unpredictable, and the rocky reef nearby can make ocean play very hazardous. Keep your eyes peeled for sea lions and harbor seals sunning themselves on the rocks, as you continue south towards the tide pools—with anemones, crabs, sea urchins, and small fish—that dot the coast farther south.

**MUSEUM OF CONTEMPORARY ART SAN DIEGO** Sister to a gallery of the same name downtown, MCA displays a small permanent collection of modern American works—including some Warhol soup cans and Lichtenstein lithographs—dating from the 1950s to the present. Try to come on Free Day (Thursday 5–9 PM). The La Jolla branch is scheduled to reopen after renovation in early 1996—call ahead to make sure. *700 Prospect St., tel. 619/454–3541. Admission $3, $1 students. Open Tues.–Sun. 11–6 (Thurs. until 9).*

**SCRIPPS INSTITUTE** The new Stephen Birch Aquarium-Museum puts emphasis on the educational, in an attempt to promote the Scripps Institute's work and oceanography in general. Among the more popular exhibits is the floor-to-ceiling kelp-forest aquarium: The living spectacle of leopard sharks, giant sea bass, and other species cruising serenely around a tangle of swaying kelp is trance-inducing. Skip the "Deep Diver" simulation, though—it certainly can't compete with Disneyland. For a spectacular view of La Jolla Cove and the Pacific, walk out to the observation deck by the artificial tide pool, itself an excellent example of the teeming life that inhabits these miniature marine ecosystems. Try to arrive after 2 PM, when school groups have dispersed. *Tel. 619/534–FISH. From La Jolla Village Dr., take North Torrey Pines Rd. and follow signs. Admission: $6.50, $4.50 students; parking $2.50. Open daily 9–5.*

**TORREY PINES STATE RESERVE** Home to one of only two groves of Torrey pines in the world, the hilly reserve lies on the coast just north of La Jolla; you can hike or bike in its day-use park (no camping). The adjacent **Torrey Pines State Beach** is often mobbed with sunbathers by day, but as the afternoon wears on, body boarders and surfers take over.

## CHEAP THRILLS

Cheap thrills are most abundant near San Diego's beaches; the whole coastal strip is one big people-watching opportunity on most days. But if you're creative, you can find ways to entertain yourself for next to nothing all over San Diego. But if you can't tear yourself away from the sand, kill time San Diego style with a bonfire on the beach. Bring fuel and refreshments (in cans, not bottles) to Pacific, Mission, or Ocean beaches, get the fire going, and tell all the fishy stories you like.

Shop for necessities, or simply fulfill your own sick fantasies at **Kobey's Swap Meet** (tel. 619/226–0650), a big flea market in the parking lot of the San Diego Sports Arena that takes place Thursday–Sunday 7–3. Admission is a mere 50¢ Thursday and Friday, $1 on weekends.

In Balboa Park (*see above*), the road that branches off south from El Prado at the parking lot by the Museum of Art leads to the **Spreckels Organ Pavilion** (tel. 619/226–0819). Proclaimed the "world's largest outdoor musical instrument," the 5,000-pipe organ is played for the public free of charge every Sunday afternoon 2–3. Monday-evening concerts are also held during summer. The concerts are a fun way to relax, if you can drown out the sounds of aircraft landing downtown.

If you'd like to hang with the collegiate crowd, **U.C. San Diego** shows movies for $1 on Tuesday and Thursday nights during the school year. Films are usually second-run, and the crowd knows the meaning of audience participation. For a schedule, call or stop by the information booth at the Price Center (9500 Gilman Dr., tel. 619/534–3362).



## FESTIVALS

**APRIL** The **San Diego Crew Classic** (tel. 619/488–0700) is a collegiate competition at Crown Point Shores in Mission Bay that attracts more than 2,000 athletes from the United States and Canada.

**MAY** The **Cinco de Mayo Festival** (tel. 619/296–3161) commemorates Mexico's victory over France at the battle of Puebla with entertainment and booths in Old Town State Park. Join P.B. locals at the **Pacific Beach Block Party** (tel. 619/483–6666), a yearly fiesta with live music, prizes, arts and crafts, and food, held near the beginning of the month.

**JUNE–SEPTEMBER** Through the summer, the **Old Globe Festival** (tel. 619/239–2255) features contemporary plays, Shakespearean works, and other classics at the Simon Edison Centre for Performing Arts in Balboa Park. Tickets cost $20–$36.

**JULY** The **Over-the-Line Tournament** (tel. 619/688–0817) is basically an excuse for thousands of people to get stinking drunk and extremely sunburned, while competing in a sport that's a cross between softball and stickball; it happens on Fiesta Island in Mission Bay.

**AUGUST** The Navy's Blue Angels flying team headlines the **Miramar Naval Air Station Show** (tel. 619/537–6289), five hours of breathtaking stunts and flying formations straight out of *Top Gun.* Admission and parking are free. At **Sand Castle Days** (tel. 619/424–6663), America's largest sand castle–building event, you can enter your own replica of the Acropolis or the USS *Enterprise.*

**SEPTEMBER** The **Street Scene** festival (tel. 619/557–8490) transforms the Gaslamp Quarter into a rollicking three-day music show, with 12 stages showcasing more than 100 bands playing every type of music under the sun. Tickets run about $23.

**DECEMBER** The first Friday and Saturday of the month, **Christmas on El Prado** (tel. 619/292–8592) features a candlelight procession, carolers, and free admission to all museums after 5 PM.

# After Dark

**San Diego has tried hard in recent years to** establish a nightlife fit for a true city, and has actually succeeded here and there. The Gaslamp Quarter jumps on weekends, with DJ and live music on every block, but since the clientele tends to sport tight black dresses and European suits, budget travelers might feel a bit out of place. For a more jeans-and-beer crowd, head to Garnet Avenue in Pacific Beach, or for even less pretense to Newport Avenue in Ocean Beach.

Where San Diego comes into its own after dark, though, is at its coffeehouses—many showcase local musicians (*see* Cafés, *above*) and are more popular than bars. For events listings, consult the *Reader,* San Diego's free arts-and-news weekly, which comes out every Thursday and disappears from most newsstands by Friday (look for it in 7-Eleven stores). *Revolt in Style,* a small underground publication with local listings, is available at most cafés and some trendy boutiques, as are flyers for roving dance clubs. For lesbian and gay clubs and bars, check either *Update* or *Gay & Lesbian Times,* both free and available in shops and cafés in Hillcrest.

**BARS** **The Alibi.** The doorwoman wears a pink polyester pantsuit and reads *Soap Opera Digest,* Patsy Cline's on the jukebox, and a casual combination of young, hip kids and old-time regulars sip 23-ounce Buds ($1.75) side by side. This is the ultimate cheap dive, red lights and all. *1403 University Ave., at Richmond St. in Hillcrest, tel. 619/295–0881.*

**Bullfrog's.** This bar is as unpretentious as they come. Rowdy Ocean Beach locals are drawn by the pool tables and the 4–7 happy hour. *5046 Newport Ave., Ocean Beach, tel. 619/222–5300.*

**La Jolla Brewing Company.** Popular with the trendy UCSD crowd, this place isn't so much a bar as a social scene. They do serve tasty pints of ale, though, and they serve typical pub munchies. If you want to get rip-roaring drunk, consider going elsewhere: A whole pitcher of beer will either make you feel elated about your drinking skills or cheated by the seemingly nonexistent alcohol content. *7536 Fay Ave., at Pearl St. in La Jolla, tel. 619/456–2739.*

**Numbers.** A small neighborhood place located across the street from Flame (*see* Clubs, *below*), Numbers is a friendly gay bar popular with a mix of younger and older men. Numbers comes complete with a patio and a plethora of pool tables, where you'll usually find some serious games going on. *3811 Park Blvd., near University Ave. in Hillcrest, tel. 619/294–9005. Wheelchair access.*

**Society Billiard Café.** At this very '80s pool hall, the lighting is indirect and lots of things are laminated black. A large selection of beers and a decent menu complement the 15 pool tables. An hour of pool costs $3 during the day and up to $10 an hour at night, depending on the day of the week and the number of people shooting stick. *1051 Garnet Ave., Pacific Beach, tel. 619/272–POOL.*

*Stingers in Pacific Beach opens at 6 AM for those on a bender.*

**Stingers.** Stingers attracts the bold and the beautiful (with a taste of the alternative). Loud house music—mostly college-radio chart toppers—blasts nightly. Tables are pretty easy to come by on weeknights, but expect a short wait to get in on weekends, and a serious lack of space and fresh air inside. *1038 Garnet Ave., at Cass St. in Pacific Beach, tel. 619/581–1234.*

**CLUBS** The best way to find out about new or underground dance clubs is to look for flyers or ask around at alternative record shops and cafés, especially in Hillcrest or downtown.

**The Flame.** This multiroom, women-only club (except on Tuesday, which is "boys' night") features events like salsa night, Monday-night football, country-western night, and soul night. Lose some cash at one of the pool tables or get funky under the two gleaming disco balls. *3780 Park Blvd., near Cypress Ave. in Hillcrest, tel. 619/295–4163. Cover: up to $3.*

**Green Circle Bar.** Green Circle's impressive DJ keeps this place hopping all week long. In addition to house music, live jazz is featured one night a week and a dance party goes on every Sunday. The mostly straight crowd here is young, fashionable, and noticeably sexy. *827 F St., at 9th St. downtown, tel. 619/232–8080. Cover: up to $5. Closed Mon.*

**Olé Madrid.** A Spanish-inspired tapas bar, this downtown joint has live and DJ music in the basement. You'll hear everything from '70s disco and deep house to reggae to salsa, depending on the night. *755 5th Ave., btw F and G Sts., tel. 619/557–0146. Cover: $3–$7.*

**West Coast Production Company.** This gay club is for the seasoned disco veteran only. It's extra-loud and extra-bright, the music is extra-synthesized, and there's one too many spinning disco balls. Locals give Wednesdays—with thumping thrash disco—rave reviews. Fridays and Saturdays, the beat goes on until 4 AM. *2028 Hancock St., btw Old Town Ave. and Washington St. in Hillcrest, tel. 619/295–3724. Cover varies. Closed Mon.–Tues.*

*Some of the bigger bands to come out of San Diego in the past few years include a Miniature, 3 Mile Pilot, Rocket from the Crypt, Drive Like Jehu, and Inch—all of whom have played the Casbah.*

**LIVE MUSIC** San Diego has been dubbed "the next Seattle" by several national music publications. Whether this is a blessing or a curse is hard to tell, but now's the chance to check out a large number of excellent local bands just gaining the limelight.

➤ **ROCK • Bodie's.** Formerly San Diego's rockabilly nightspot catering to boys and girls with slicked-back hair and chunky black shoes, Bodie's has now expanded to include blues, rock, and punk acts. *528 F St., btw 5th and 6th Sts. downtown, tel. 619/236–8988. Cover: $5 weekends.*

**The Casbah.** A key venue in San Diego's burgeoning alternative music scene, the Casbah headlines cream-of-the-crop local bands nightly, with smaller nationally acclaimed acts every now and again. A tight-knit group of regulars frequents the small club (which is underneath an apartment complex), but everyone is friendly. *2501 Kettner Blvd., at Laurel St. downtown, tel. 619/232–4355. Cover: up to $10.*

**SOMA Live.** The lack of age restrictions draws lots of 18- to 20-year-olds, and the bands that play here aren't much older. The music is predominately punk rock, though some touring college-radio bands round out the roster. *5305 Metro St., off Marina Blvd. in Mission Bay, tel. 619/239–SOMA. Cover: $7–$10.*

➢ **JAZZ AND BLUES** • While there are few exclusively jazz joints in San Diego, somewhere usually has it going on—check the *Reader.* The local favorite is **Croce's Restaurant and Jazz Bar** (802 5th Ave., tel. 619/233–4355), which has a $5 cover, plus a $5 minimum on drinks or food. Next door, **Croce's Top Hat Bar and Grille** offers nightly R&B. **Dick's Last Resort** (345 4th Ave., btw J and K Sts., tel. 619/231–9100) occasionally puts on New Orleans jazz.

Blues offerings are similarly limited. **Blind Melons** (710 Garnet Ave., Pacific Beach, tel. 619/483–7844) offers blues, reggae and zydeco, or other tunes for between $5 and $25, even if you don't catch the allusion. In Ocean Beach, **Winston's** (1921 Bacon St., Ocean Beach, tel. 619/222–6822) features live blues with no cover, giving over other nights to reggae, Dead covers, and anything else that will promote their nightly drink specials.

The best sources of information about blues clubs, concerts, and festivals throughout Southern California are *Southland Blues Magazine,* a monthly available in record stores and the **Blues Hotline** (tel. 310/498–8052).

➢ **LATIN** • Venues with a Latin theme are a dime a dozen in San Diego, as befits a city with a strong Latino heritage. **Café Sevilla** (555 4th Ave., at Market St., tel. 619/233–5979) attracts a fun and friendly international crowd for its nightly music, which ranges from samba to flamenco to Spanish rock-and-roll. The music is accompanied by appropriate food and drink (i.e., tapas and margaritas) and dance lessons some evenings. For Latin jazz, try **Café Bravo** (4th Ave. and E St., tel. 619/234–8888).

➢ **CLASSICAL** • The **San Diego Symphony** (1245 7th Ave., tel. 619/699–4205) performs October–May at Copley Symphony Hall, and during summer outdoors at Embarcadero Marina Park South. **La Jolla Chamber Music Society** (tel. 619/459–3724) offers classical music throughout the year. For half-price tickets contact **Art Tix** (*see below*).

**THEATER** Don't overlook San Diego's great theater offerings. A good way to take advantage without paying an arm and a leg is through **Art Tix** (Horton Plaza, 3rd St. and Broadway, tel. 619/497–5000). The group, sponsored by the San Diego Theater League, offers half-price admission tickets (cash only) for same-day shows at all area theaters. The box office is open Tuesday–Saturday 10–7; the best time to go is weekday mornings, since shows during the week don't usually sell out. Some of the major theaters include the **La Jolla Playhouse** (2910 La Jolla Village Dr., tel. 619/550–1010), which has sent several productions to Broadway; the **San Diego Repertory Theatre** (79 Horton Plaza, tel. 619/235–8025); and the **Old Globe** (Balboa Park, tel. 619/239–2255), famous for its Shakespearean productions and top-flight actors.

# Outdoor Activities

**With an ideal climate year-round, San Diego offers** lots of ways to get your couch-potato body out into the sun. Most beaches have at least one shop or waterfront shack that rents in-line skates, bikes, and body boards. Many coastal communities with piers also have bait shops that rent fishing gear. For more information, *see* The Beaches, in Exploring San Diego, *above.*

**BIKING** Biking is huge in San Diego. The **California Department of Transportation** (tel. 619/688–6699) puts out a free map of all county bike paths. Probably the most popular route is **Old Highway 101,** the coastal road that runs from La Jolla north to Oceanside. Although the road is narrow and windy, experienced riders like to follow **Lomas Santa Fe Drive** in Solana Beach (*also see* Near San Diego, *below*) east into beautiful Rancho Santa Fe. For more leisurely rides, Mission Bay, San Diego Harbor, and the Mission Beach boardwalk are all flat and scenic. You can rent bikes all over town for $20 a day or less. Try **Mike's Bikes** in Mission Beach (756A Ventura Pl., near Mission Blvd. across the street from the roller coaster, tel. 619/488–1444).

**SURFING** Contrary to popular mythology, you need a wet suit if you're going to surf in San Diego any time other than the summer months. If you have personally experienced the meaning of "tubular," you should head for the pier at Ocean Beach, Tourmaline Surfing Park in Pacific Beach, Windansea Beach near La Jolla, or Swami's (Sea Cliff Roadside Park) in Encinitas. You can rent boards at **Star Surfing Company** (tel. 619/273–7827) in Pacific Beach, **La Jolla Surf Systems** (*see* Snorkeling and Scuba Diving, *below*) in La Jolla, and **Hansen's Sporting Goods** (tel. 619/753–6595) in Encinitas. Boards rent for about $4 an hour, or $17 a day, and you need a major credit card to rent one. Beginners should definitely stick to beach breaks; ask at these surf shops about lessons.

**SNORKELING AND SCUBA DIVING** The ecological reserve at La Jolla Cove provides some of the best snorkeling in Southern California. Look out for the bright-orange garibaldi, California's unofficial state fish, known for its friendliness. **La Jolla Surf Systems** (3132 Avenida de la Playa, tel. 619/456–2777) will rent you a full snorkeling rig (mask, flippers, snorkel) for $4 an hour, and it's within spitting distance of the beach. If you're certified for scuba diving, **San Diego Divers Supply** (4004 Sports Arena Blvd., near I–8, tel. 619/224–3439; 5701 La Jolla Blvd., La Jolla, tel. 619/459–2691) can fix you up with all the equipment you need, including fins, snorkel, tank, and mask, for $35 a day. You'll need a boat to access the best scuba diving; contact **Seaforth Boat Rentals** (*see* Boating, *below*) about charters.

**BOATING** Mission Bay's smooth water and consistent winds provide easy sailing, especially for beginners. However, if you want views (of downtown and big Navy ships), head to San Diego Bay. **Seaforth Boat Rentals** (1641 Quivira Rd., Mission Bay, tel. 619/223–1681; or 1715 Strand Way, Coronado, tel. 619/437–1514) rents sailboats from $20 an hour, as well as motorboats ($40 an hour) and canoes and kayaks ($5 an hour). **Mission Bay SportCenter** (1010 Santa Clara Pl., Mission Bay, tel. 619/488–1004) has a wide selection of aquatic gear, including sailboats from $12 an hour and sailboards from $16 an hour.

**SPORT FISHING** Several sportfishing fleets and individual boats operate out of San Diego, fishing in both U.S. and Mexican waters. **Seaforth Sportfishing** (1717 Quivira Rd., tel. 619/224–3383) has a good variety of trips: A shark-boat ticket runs $30, a twilight boat goes for $18, and a full day trip to the Coronado Islands is $45. Rod and reel rental costs an extra $6–$10, and a one-day California fishing license is $6.

**WHALE WATCHING** The best terrestrial vantage point for watching California gray whales on their annual southern migration (late Dec.–Mar.) is the Cabrillo National Monument at the tip of Point Loma (*see* The Beaches, in Exploring San Diego, *above*). If you want to get closer,

## The Ways of the Waves

***Considering the beauty of San Diego's beaches, the quality of the local breaks, and veteran surfers' general disdain for novices, it's little wonder that a "locals-only" wave territorialism developed some time ago at the better surf beaches around town. In particular, Windansea Beach, a few miles south of La Jolla, gained a reputation in the early 1960s for harshly punishing violations of the unwritten rules of surfing etiquette. At the time, interloping beginners who made mistakes—dropping in on someone else's wave, or cutting in front of someone more experienced—were summarily dealt with through verbal abuse, an "accidental" flip of the board, or a mysteriously slashed tire in the parking lot. Although threats of litigation have somewhat softened Windansea's traditional hard line, it's still not the best place for a beginner to learn.***

**Helgren's Sportfishing** (315 Harbor Drive S, Oceanside, tel. 619/722–2133) offers narrated tours of the San Diego migratory route December 17–March 31 for $12 a person. Helgren's also offers a variety of sportfishing tours throughout the year.



# Near San Diego

## TIJUANA

San Diego likes to bill itself as "a two-nation vacation destination," and nearly every visitor to San Diego makes at least a day trip to Tijuana to shop for *artesanía* (crafts), or a night trip to join in the hedonism. If you're looking for an authentic Mexican vacation you'll have to go a lot farther than "TJ," where popular wisdom holds that the sprawling town is more a mixture of many Mexican and gringo cultures than a "real" Mexican city; oh yeah, it's also a lawless den of hedonism. Travelers left cold by crowds, made-for-export *artesanía* (crafts), dollar beers, eyebrow-raising sex shows, and prostitutes may want to avoid the main tourist drag of Avenida Revolución; instead, head one block west to Avenida Constitución, where the buzzing pace, microphone-wielding salesmen, and strolling families with father and son in cowboy hats could be part of any Mexican city.

**BASICS** Anyone can visit a Mexican border town for up to 72 hours without a border card: U.S. and Canadian citizens should present a driver's license or birth certificate at the border; citizens of Hong Kong, South Africa, Brazil, and Taiwan need a visa; citizens of other countries need a passport.

### *Border Trouble*

***In 1994, California voters passed Proposition 187, which seeks to deny public services to undocumented immigrants and requires teachers and health-care workers to report them to the Immigration and Naturalization Service. Proponents hope that this legislation will staunch the flow of illegal immigrants across the border, and argue that social service agencies are already struggling to provide for native Californians. They deny racism as a motivation, although critics feel the proposition incites racial tensions and discrimination. While unlikely to be enforced because of its potential unconstitutionality, the legislation speaks volumes about the curent public opinion in California toward its neighbor to the south.***

***Nowhere in California are anti-immigrant sentiments—usually tied to economic worries—more rampant than in San Diego, whose border with Tijuana is the busiest in the United States. Since October 1994, "Operation Gatekeeper" has attempted to curb illegal crossings by jacking up funding for agents and surveillance equipment; whether it's helped is anybody's (and everybody's) guess. Opponents of Operation Gatekeeper charge that the border is becoming a war zone, citing increases in human rights violations. Within this antagonistic climate, there have been several cases of racially motivated murders of Mexican immigrants in recent years. But without the cheap labor they provide, it is difficult to imagine how California's economy would function efficiently. It seems that today's immigrants, like the generations before them, are willing to weather the hostility to pursue the "American Dream."***

➢ **CHANGING MONEY** • All prices below are listed in U.S. dollar values due to the instability of the Mexican economy. While dollars are accepted, and often encouraged, you'll generally get a better value if you change dollars into pesos: when you get to Tijuana, simply look around for a place with competitive rates. For pesos to dollars, try moneychangers on San Ysidro Boulevard in San Ysidro. To buy or change traveler's checks, try the **American Express office** (Sánchez Taboada, at Clemente Orozco, tel. 66/34–36–60), open weekdays 9–6 and Sat. 9:30–1; you do not have to be a cardmember. ATMs accepting Visa and Mastercard can be found at most banks. Try **Bancomer** (on Constitución, at Calle 5a) or **Bital** (on Revolución and Calle 2a.

➢ **VISITOR INFORMATION** • The most centrally located tourist office is run by **CANACO** (Revolución, at Calle 1a, tel. 66/88–16–85), the Tijuana Chamber of Commerce. It has friendly, English-speaking staff, decent maps, and a public phone and restroom; open daily 9–7.

**COMING AND GOING** If your plans only include Tijuana proper, public transportation into and around the city is your best bet. The tourist areas are compact and walkable, and buses are affordable and straightforward. The wheelchair-accessible **San Diego Trolley** (*see* Getting Around, San Diego, *above*) runs from downtown San Diego to the border at San Ysidro. Many trolley stations along the line provide free parking, which can save you $7 in parking expenses at San Ysidro. Be sure to park in a guarded and lighted parking lot. The easiest way to get to downtown from the border is via taxi ($3); the easiest way to get from downtown back to the border is on a **Mexi-Coach** bus ($1), which leaves from Revolución (btw Calle 6 and 7) every half hour between 9 AM and 9 PM.

Otherwise, **Greyhound/Trailways** (tel. 66/21–29–48) travels to Tijuana from San Diego (50 min, $4 one-way), stopping at one of two bus stations: **Central Viejo** (Madero, at Calle 1a 1 block east of Revolución, tel. 66/88–07–52) is more conveniently located than **Central Camionera.**

If you do cross by car, the less central **Otay Mesa** border crossing (10 minutes east of San Diego) has shorter lines but is only open 6 AM–10 PM. On weekends and holidays, the wait to enter the United States by car at the main **San Ysidro–Tijuana** crossing can be two hours. While only required for trips further south, it is recommended that you purchase one-day (or more) Mexican car insurance at the border (less than $10 a day), since other countries' insurance is not valid.

**WHERE TO SLEEP AND EAT** At clean, quiet **Hotel Catalina** (Calle 5a, at Madero, tel. 66/85–97–48) you can get a single ($10) or a double ($15) in the heart of the tourist area. Reservations are advised on weekends. Tijuana is a great place to sample the diversity of Mexican cuisine, because people move here from all over Mexico. The fabulous **La Vuelta** (Revolución, at Calle 11a, tel. 66/85–72–09) doubles as an all-hours nightclub featuring live mariachi music at 8 PM Monday–Saturday and 6:30 PM on Sunday. If you've reached taco overload, head to the 24-hour **Restaurant Los Norteños** (Constitución 530, near Calle 2a, tel. 66/85–68–55), where breakfast costs less than $2 and meat or veggie sandwiches go for $2–$3. The outdoor tables here provide a clear line of sight to the nonstop action on Plaza Revolución.

*If you can't afford the grilled meats ($7–$10) at La Vuelta, nurse a beer ($2) or try the 2-for-1 margaritas (weekdays 7 AM–10 PM), and plunge into the free chips, salsa, and atmosphere.*

**WORTH SEEING** The popular Basque game of jai alai is played at **El Palacio Frontón** (Revolución, near Calle 7a, tel. 66/38–43–07 or 66/85–25–24 for game times), a dramatic Moorish-style palace. Something like racquetball, the game is played with curved, wicker baskets, three walls, and a balsawood, goatskin-wrapped ball moving at about 250 kph.

Tijuana is also home to the second-largest bullring in the world, the beachside **Plaza de Toros Monumental.** Fights take place May–September on Sundays at 4 PM; tickets start at $7 for seats in the sun, $10 for shade. Buy tickets at the *caseta,* or ticket office (Revolución, btw Calles 3a and 4a, tel. 66/85–22–10), open weekends 10 AM–7 PM, or at the ring (Highway 1D, by the ocean). To reach the Plaza take a Mexi-Coach bus (½ hr, $2) at 3:30 PM from Revolución, between Calle 6a and 7a. Get there early to guarantee yourself a ticket.

**AFTER DARK** Finding something to do at night is not a problem here. Revolución (between Calle 1 and 7) is jam-packed with blaring discos; happily, none charges a cover, so you can scope out each club until you find your niche or become too drunk to care. Typically, a margarita costs $3–$4, a beer about $2.50. If you want to party down with Americans, head to **People's** (Calle 2a, at Revolución, tel. 66/85–45–72). If you get tired of dancing with the under-dressed and underage, try to keep up with the locals at the restaurant/nightclub **La Vuelta** (*see* Where to Sleep and Eat, *above*). The most popular gay disco in town is **Mike's Disco** (Revolución 1220, near Calle 6a, tel. 66/85–35–34); the main draw here is the midnight and 3 AM shows, where men dress up like famous Mexican actresses and sing torch songs.

## NORTH COUNTY COAST

The North County's seaside towns each have a distinct history and character, and all are manageable day-trips from San Diego if you're looking for a change of scenery. **Solana Beach** is a small, very beach-oriented town with a mellow demeanor and scads of sand. **Encinitas** is justly famous for its fabulous fields of flowers and gardens, which extend inland from excellent surfing waters, and **Oceanside** shows off its nature preserve and restored mission, as well as offering the marines stationed at nearby Camp Pendleton a town-size support group. If you want to stay the night coastside, Oceanside is probably a budget traveler's best bet. Other North County coastal towns include **Del Mar,** with inordinately expensive lodging and exclusive boutiques; and **Carlsbad,** which lures visitors on package tours with its history as a spa town.

*If possible, stay in Del Mar at Les Artistes (944 Camino del Mar, tel. 619/755–4646), just 2 blocks from the water. The rooms (from $45) include refrigerators and kitchenettes, and are all delightfully decorated to reflect the motifs and personal styles of significant artists, from Monet to Georgia O'Keeffe.*

**COMING AND GOING** The coastal portion of North County is best accessed via I–5, but traveling along **Highway S21** (Old Highway 101) once you reach the general area will give you a better feel for the individuality of each town. If you're without a car, **Amtrak** (tel. 619/239–9021 or 800/USA–RAIL) stops regularly in Solana Beach and Oceanside en route to L.A. and San Diego. The newest way to get to the North County seaside towns is on Amtrak's *Coaster* (800/COASTER). Currently it's strictly a weekdays commuter train, running southbound in the morning and northbound in the evening, but there are plans to expand the schedule. **Greyhound-Trailways** (tel. 800/231–2222) stops in Oceanside on the L.A.–San Diego route. Bus 800 of the **San Diego County Transit Express** takes I–5 as far north as Oceanside from downtown San Diego. Bus 30 meanders along the coast from downtown up to La Jolla, whereupon you must transfer to Bus 301, which also ends up in Oceanside. The **North County Transit District** also operates a network of bus routes within the North County coastal area (tel. 619/722–6283).

**SOLANA BEACH** Dwarfed in size and population by its North County neighbors, Solana is a classic—and relatively untouristed—beach town. **Fletcher Cove,** at the western terminus of Lomas Santa Fe Drive (past where it becomes Plaza Street), provides the powdery sand; it's also known as Pillbox by locals because of its lifeguard station, shaped like a bunker. Slightly less crowded than Pillbox is **Tide Beach County Park,** to the north on Pacific Avenue. The nearly level beach is perfect for sunbathing and skim boarding.

Drop in for a box of fresh, locally grown fruit at **Solana Beach Produce** (343 S. Hwy. 101, tel. 619/259–3866). For more substantial grub, try **Gia's** (145 S. Hwy. 101, tel. 619/792–7521), a casual Italian restaurant where individual Sicilian pizzas run $3.50–$5. Ask anyone in North County where to go for Mexican food, and they're sure to tell you **Fidel's** (607 Valley Ave., at Genevieve St., tel. 619/755–5292). Gorge yourself on a combination plate, including rice, beans, and tortillas ($8), in an old Spanish-style villa. After nightfall, check out always-hopping **Belly Up** (143 E. Cedros Ave., tel. 619/481–9022), a UCSD favorite featuring nightly live rock, blues, funk, rhythm-and-blues, or reggae.

**ENCINITAS** Encinitas is worth a stop for its numerous natural attractions. Foremost among them is **Quail Botanical Gardens** (230 Quail Gardens Dr., tel. 619/436–3036), a conservation

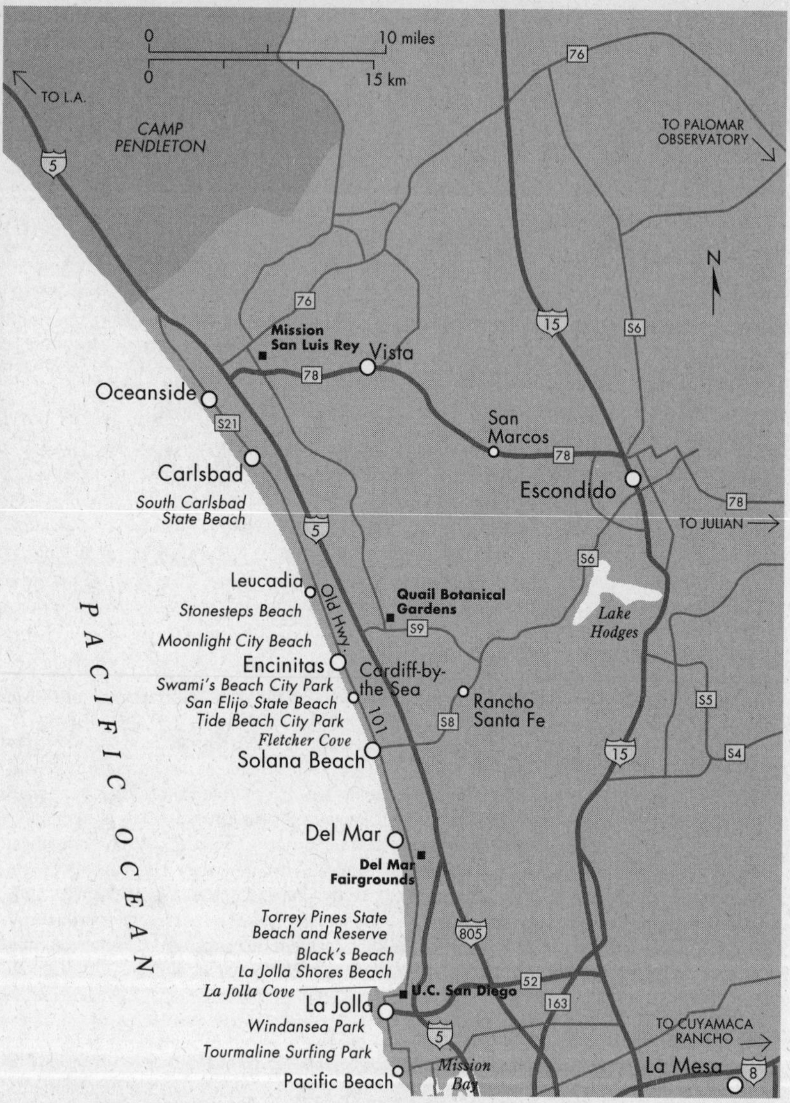

## The San Diego North Coast

*If you want to get around Encinitas without damaging its natural appeal, rent a bike at Coast Schwinn Cyclery (553 1st St., tel. 619/753–5867) for $6 an hour, $23 a day.*

preserve for threatened or rare plants. Take Encinitas Boulevard east from I–5 and follow signs; the park is open 9–5 daily and admission is $2.

Encinitas also has a number of notable beaches. **Stonesteps,** so-called despite the newer wooden ones, is rocky and pebbly; but you get an excellent view of the water from halfway down the stairs, which are located along the 1600 block of Neptune Avenue just past Grandview Street. Slightly south of Stonesteps is **Moonlight Beach** (4th and B Sts.), with a lot of white, fluffy sand for the family-picnic-and-barbecue set. Farther south lies the beach known as **Swami's** (1st St., just past K St.), in dubious deference to the adjacent Encinitas branch of the Self Realization Fellowship. The "beach" at Swami's is much like Stonesteps—only the few and the brave surf, swim, or sunbathe here.

Stop by **Kim's Restaurant** (745 1st St., in Lumberyard Shopping Plaza, tel. 619/942–4816) for inexpensive Vietnamese food, like the filling rice sticks with chicken skewer ($5). The iced French coffee with condensed milk ($2) is a wonder. In general, most of what's worthwhile in Encinitas is on or near 1st Street, which turns into Old Highway 101 as it crosses the town's other main drag, Encinitas Boulevard. If you want to stay the night, **San Elijo State Beach** (look for signs off Old Hwy. 101, Cardiff, tel. 619/753–5091 for info or 800/444–PARK for reservations) has 171 sites ($14–$21); if these are full or don't appeal, the 226 sites at nearby **South Carlsbad State Park** (Carlsbad Blvd., at Poinsettia Ln., tel. 619/438–3143) are indistinguishable. For more information on local events or lodging, contact the **Encinitas Chamber of Commerce** (345 1st St., tel. 619/753–6041).



**OCEANSIDE** Oceanside would probably not exist were it not for Camp Pendleton, the enormous U.S. Marine base just to the north, but it does have other charms. Among them is the 1798 **Mission San Luis Rey** (4050 Mission Ave., tel. 619/757–3651), the largest of California's Spanish missions. For $3, you can walk through a small museum and reconstructions of the mission's past, getting a good sense of the asceticism of the friars and their patronizing attitude toward the native residents.

Also check out the **Buena Vista Audubon Society Nature Center** (2202 S. Hill St., tel. 619/439–2473). You can visit native plants in their natural lagoon habitat, look for animal tracks, or peruse the still-life exhibits within the center itself. Admission is free. For fishing, venture westward to the pleasant **Oceanside Municipal Pier** (end of 3rd St. downtown). You can rent a pole for $2 an hour (with $25 deposit and ID) at the **Bait Shop** on the pier, but there are no public benches (chair rentals are $10 a day, plus $100 deposit and ID). Surfers frequent the water near the pier; if you'd like to take a shot at the waves or bike along the beach, **Action Beach** (310 W. Mission Ave., tel. 619/722–7101) will rent you a surfboard or mountain bike for $5 an hour or $20 a day; volleyball sets run $10 a day.

If all this activity is wearing you down, stop in at the **Hill Street Coffee House** (524 S. Hill St., tel. 619/966–0985), *the* caffeine depot in Oceanside. For serious travel fuel, the inexpensive, down-home **BB's Café** (1938 S. Hill St., tel. 619/722–7337) will serve you french toast, eggs, and bacon for $3. Oceanside has some of the cheapest lodging in the San Diego area. The **Dolphin Hotel** (133 S. Hill St., tel. 619/722–7200) bills itself as "Oceanside's Grand Hotel," and the narrow rooms with vintage furnishings do suggest at least a faded grandeur. Rooms start at $33 a night, plus TVs and refrigerators; and it's only 4 blocks from the beach. If you absolutely have to be closer to the water and you're on a tight budget, try the **Beachwood Motel** (210 6th St., tel. 619/722–3866) at around $32 a night. It's grimy and dilapidated in a comfortable sort of way, and only 1½ blocks from the beach.

For more information on Oceanside, contact the **Visitor Information Center** (940 N. Hill St., tel. 619/721–1101 or 800/350–7823). Oceanside's two main drags are Hill Street, running north–south, and Mission Avenue, running east–west.

## INLAND NORTH COUNTY

When you venture east of the coast, the tourist trappings of fun-in-the-sun California fall away. At first, the hills are covered with oak and pine, and interspersed with wineries, missions, and freshwater lakes. As you go farther east, the land breaks down into arid desert and scrub. Linked only by winding, hilly country highways, the small and scattered towns of the inland north are infrequently served by the **Northeast Rural Bus System** (tel. 619/765–0145). Fare is $2.50, and the system doesn't include the town of Palomar Mountain; but it does serve Escondido, Julian, and Borrego Springs. Buses are small, so you should make reservations. The **Escondido Transit Center** (700 W. Valley Pkwy., Escondido) serves as the hub for buses of the **North County Transit District** (tel. 619/743–6283) and **Greyhound** (tel. 619/745–6522), both of which offer service from San Diego.

*Much of the land is devoted to farms and ranches, and the region has a bucolic feel very different from the rest of the San Diego area.*

**ESCONDIDO** This quiet lake community 18 miles east of the Pacific and 30 miles north of San Diego is more isolated than the beach communities that dominate San Diego's North

Coast. Located at the intersection of Highway 78, which heads east from Oceanside, and I–15, which connects San Diego to Riverside and points north, Escondido is a major transport hub for trips inland to Palomar Mountain and Julian (*see below*). Other than that, it has little to offer. Cheap lodging can be found near the transit center (*see* Coming and Going, *above*), including a **Motel 6** (509 W. Washington Ave., at Center City Pkwy., tel. 619/743–6669) with doubles for about $31. Most motels are on Washington Avenue; to get there from the transit center, walk north on Quince Avenue. For more information, contact the **Escondido Convention and Visitors Bureau** (720 N. Broadway, tel. 619/745–4741).

➢ **SAN DIEGO WILD ANIMAL PARK** • Opened in 1972 as an extension of the San Diego Zoo in Balboa Park, this 2,200-acre park allows the animals to roam freely in natural-looking habitats with other species normally found in their environments. Humans view the area via a 50-minute, 5-mile monorail trip. The park is also fun to explore on foot: With plenty of steep hills, the 1¾-mile **Kilimanjaro Hiking Trail** can prove exhausting. While not as "hands-on" as the San Diego Zoo, the Wild Animal Park is more for the animals than for humans, and therein lies its beauty. *Tel. 619/234–6541 or 619/480–0100. I–15 north to Via Rancho Parkway, follow signs. Or NCTD Bus 307 from downtown Escondido. Admission: $19, parking $3. Open Sept.–May, daily 9–4; June–Aug., daily 9–6 (Thurs.–Sun. until 8).*

**PALOMAR OBSERVATORY** About 30 miles northeast of Escondido along Highway S6 is the Hale Telescope at the Palomar Observatory. With its 200-inch diameter mirror, the telescope is one of the largest Peeping-Tom devices in the world, with a range of approximately one billion light-years. Images taken by the telescope are shown at the observatory museum, as is a video history of the telescope. *North end of Hwy. S6, tel. 619/742–2119. Admission free. Open daily 9–4, disabled access 9:30–2.*

At the town of Palomar Mountain, if you turn off onto S7 instead of continuing on S6 to the observatory, you'll come to **Palomar Mountain State Park** (tel. 619/742–3462). Camping among pine and cedar forests is allowed in the park at **Doane Valley,** which has 31 sites, three of which have wheelchair access. The campground has restrooms and showers, and the $14 small sites each have table, stove, and fire ring. You should reserve in summer through MISTIX (tel. 800/444–PARK). The **Palomar Mountain General Store** (tel. 619/742–3496), at the intersection of Highways S6 and S7 in Palomar Mountain, is really a *general* store, selling everything from art and chocolates to astronomy-related items. **Mother's Kitchen** (tel. 619/742–4233) next door has inexpensive salads and burgers.

**JULIAN** A two-hour drive east of San Diego is Julian, one of the last places with any fertile landscape before the vast expanses of desert start. At an elevation of 4,220 feet, this little town sees snow during winter, but people don't come here for the seasons, nor for the town's cute shops and handmade crafts—they come for the homemade pies. People from all over the country (literally) make a beeline to **Dudley's Bakery** (junction Hwys. 78 and 79, tel. 800/225–3348) for pastry, bread, and the infamous pies. To reach Julian from San Diego, take I–8 east and then Highway 79 north; if you don't have a car, take Bus 878 of the Northeast Rural Bus System (*see above*) from Escondido.

*As bagels are to Brooklyn, apple pie is to Julian.*

Lodging in Julian is too expensive for most budget travelers, but you can camp cheaply in nearby Cuyamaca Rancho State Park (*see below*). **William Heise County Park,** 5 miles outside of town, is another nearby camping option, with about 80 sites going for $11 each. Make reservations (tel. 619/565–3600 for reservations) in summer and in fall during the **Fall Harvest Festival** and **Apple Days,** when three months' notice is not too much. To get to the campground from Julian, follow Highway 78 east to Pine Hills Road, go south 2 miles to Frisius Road, head east 2 miles to park entrance. Call 619/694–3049 for park information.

**CUYAMACA RANCHO STATE PARK** A little more than an hour's drive east of San Diego and just west of Anza-Borrego Desert State Park (*see* Chapter 12), Cuyamaca Rancho is a richly forested area that you would never expect to find tucked into the surrounding desert. More than half the park's 25,000 acres are classified as wilderness, which prohibits all vehicles in order to preserve the park's natural beauty. The hiking can be quite challenging: **Cuyamaca Peak Trail** is a reasonably difficult trek that climbs 3½ miles to the 6,500-foot summit, where you can gaze at the desert and the ocean on clear days. The difficult **Harvey Moore Trail** (9 mi round-trip) begins a half-mile north of the Green Valley campground, goes to the Oceanic East Mesa, and continues through Harper Creek Canyon. If you don't feel up to the challenge, the short **Paso Self-Guided Nature Trail** at the Paso Picacho campground is an easy introduction to the area's native plants.

With all its cheap campgrounds, Cuyamaca Rancho is a great place to stay if you can't afford to pay the premium rates of Julian (*see above*). Reservations through MISTIX (tel. 800/444–PARK) are advised, especially if you plan on visiting during one of Julian's many festivals. The 85 sites at **Paso Picacho,** a secluded, tree-covered campground, are $12–$14. **Arroyo Seco** (about 2 mi west of Green Valley) and **Granite Springs** (about 4 mi east of Green Valley) are primitive sites—essentially clearings with no facilities. The only way to get there is on your own two feet, but you pay only $3 a night, so who can complain? The easiest way to get to the park from San Diego is to take I–8 east to Highway 79 north. If you're using the Northeast Rural Bus System (*see* Coming and Going, *above*), you want Bus 878 from Escondido. The **park headquarters** (tel. 619/765–0755) on Highway 79 provides information on trails, camping, and other sights in and near the park.

# PALM SPRINGS AND THE DESERT 12

By Michael Rozendal

**Exploring the California desert is like entering a pentathalon: The conditions may** be harsh, but the rewards are great. From a distance, the desert seems merely sun-scorched, brown, and lumpy—the geographic equivalent of a plate of refried beans. But with preparation and the right temperament, visitors can grow to appreciate the stark beauty of this seemingly barren world, which extends along California's eastern border from Mexico to the area south of Fresno. Some return year after year to explore its soulful solitude and discover still more of its hidden natural wonders.

*In 1994, the U.S. Congress passed the California Desert Protection Act, upgrading Joshua Tree and Death Valley to the status of national parks and the Mojave to a national preserve. The deserts will get more protection, but also more visitors. Environmentalists hope this won't prove to be a contradiction in terms.*

In geologic time, the California desert is a recent development. Only a few thousand years ago lakes and rivers covered the area, creating lush valleys populated by an assortment of now-extinct giant mammals. In some ways, this arid land is the ideal place for contemplating the passage of time. While sweating through 100° heat to the top of a 700-foot sand dune in Death Valley, consider that this was once the floor of an ancient lake. When the climate was milder, people lived here, too: On the canyon walls of almost every desert, prehistoric pictographs and petroglyphs (stone etchings) provide clues to early civilizations.

Though the climate is now anything but mild, a few people still scratch out a living here: ranch families who fled to the desert a century ago when Los Angeles boomed; refugees from crowded coastal cities; and a few crusty prospectors still searching the desolate buttes and washes for elusive wealth. Though annual rainfall rarely exceeds a few inches, certain animals and plants have adapted to the overheated terrain. Look for colorful beetles, giant tarantulas, kangaroo rats, rattlesnakes, roadrunners, and jackrabbits. At higher elevations, you may even find bighorn sheep.

If you think desert plant life is just a bunch of stumpy cacti, you'll be in for a pleasant surprise. During spring, the valleys are covered with a riotous carpet of blooms that attract a swarm of amateur photographers. Since the show changes from week to week and location to location, you may want to check the Thomas Payne Society's **wildflower hotline** (tel. 818/768–3533) before planning a trip. Wildflower viewing is particularly popular at **Anza-Borrego Desert State Park** and **Joshua Tree National Park.** The twisting, tufted plants that give Joshua Tree its name offer a dramatic vista year-round; the park is also a mecca for rock climbers from around the world, drawn by the challenge of scaling the huge granite massifs.

When night rolls around, you'll most likely camp (free in many locations) or flop down in a forgettable motel in **Barstow,** the de facto desert capital. Avoid the desert in summer unless you're truly masochistic. If you do show up in July or August, at least reward yourself by shacking up in a motel with a swimming pool in the sunny resort town of **Palm Springs** or the collegiate playground of **Lake Havasu,** on the Arizona border.

## BASICS

**COMING AND GOING** The vast desert is poorly served by public transportation; the best way to see it is by car. Carry a few extra gallons of water at all times (for your car radiator and for yourself), and keep the gas tank full and the engine in good working order. Remember, you've just come to visit the desert—not to end up there permanently. Two interstate freeways traverse the desert, meeting at Barstow: I–40 heading east to Lake Havasu and beyond, and I–15 from San Diego on its way to Las Vegas.

**DESERT SURVIVAL** To survive in such heat, you need a constant supply of water. Drink 1–3 gallons per day, depending on the season and whether your plans include strenuous exercise. Don't wait until you're thirsty before taking a gulp—by then, you may already be dehydrated. Avoid caffeine and alcohol, which only make you more dehydrated. Desert hikers should consume plenty of high-sugar, carbohydrate-rich foods (dried banana chips are excellent). Skip high-protein or fatty foods, which require a lot of water to digest.

If you're going to spend time outdoors (especially during summer), you must also protect your skin. Thick-soled shoes are a must, as ground temperatures can reach a blistering 200°F. Wear a hat, sunglasses, and a high-SPF sunscreen, and remain fully clothed at all times—a sweat-soaked T-shirt, though uncomfortable, may be the only thing slowing the evaporation of your bodily fluids. In the evenings, especially during winter, temperatures may drop to near freezing, so bring extra layers for warmth. Whether you're hiking or camping, always let someone know where you're headed. It's a good idea to register at a ranger station before beginning your trip. Bring a small signal mirror with you. Even if its reflection doesn't draw help, it might annoy the buzzards.

Wait, there's more: Just when you got used to the absence of water, you have to deal with the possibility of flash floods. Don't linger in low-lying washes and canyons; a storm can blow in without warning and dump thousands of gallons of precipitation onto the desert floor in less than a minute. Watch out for rattlesnakes and scorpions—both are potentially deadly. They reserve their venom for unexpected annoyances, like being stepped on. They often pass the hottest part of the day under rocks and brush where they are difficult to spot. Other desert dangers include abandoned mines with unstable structures and hidden shafts—admire these from a safe distance. A great deal of military training has taken place here over the past four decades. If you see something metallic glittering in the sun, don't think "souvenir." Think "unexploded shell," leave it plenty of room, and report your findings to a ranger or the local police department.

# Death Valley National Park

**It's a wasteland in the middle of** nowhere with searing summer temperatures and a nasty tendency to be fatal to the ill-prepared, yet Death Valley still draws a crowd, intrigued by its fierce reputation as one of the least hospitable places on earth. Each year, more than a million adventurous or macabre travelers come away moved by the valley's stark beauty and the legends of its crumbling ghost towns. It all began nearly three million years ago when plates under the earth's crust separated, creating a sunken valley almost 100 miles long and up to 25 miles wide. This open-face geological taco consists of craggy mountains, sand dunes, inhospitable salt flats, natural oases, and volcanic craters. Human history here began around 6000 BC, when Native-American tribes inhabited the Grapevine Canyon. At the time, the valley floor was covered with water and big game roamed freely. Today, the rivers and lakes have all but vanished, and less than 5 inches

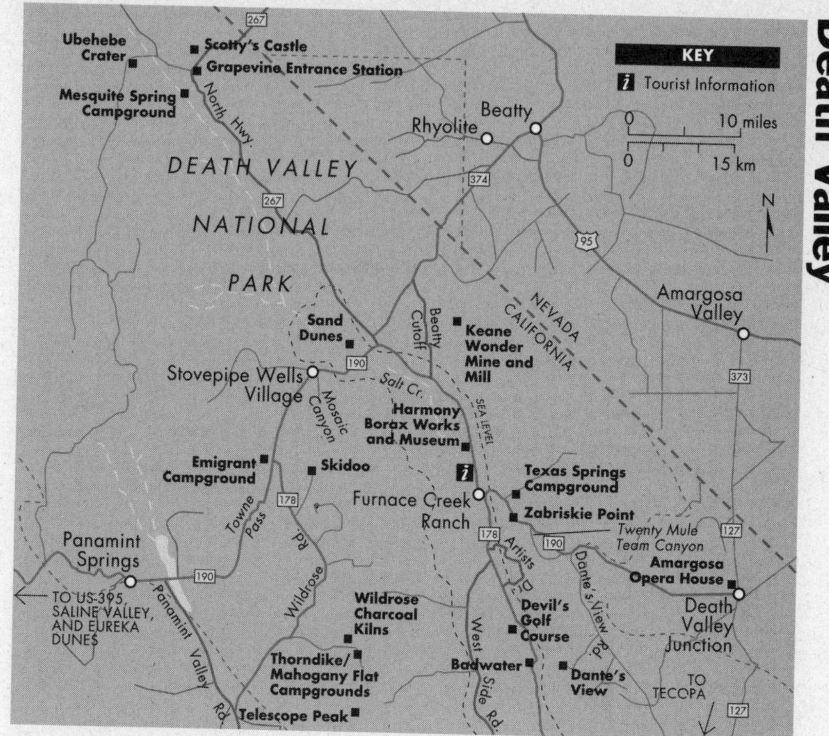


of rain fall every year. Birds dropped dead in mid-flight on July 10, 1913, when the temperature in Furnace Creek reached 134°, the hottest weather ever recorded outside the Sahara.

*Death Valley's weather lives up to its melodramatic name. When the average temperature in July hits a hibachi-like 116°, it's not hard to understand hyperbolic headlines like a recent one from the* National Enquirer: *"Man's Nose Melts in the Sun."*

Death Valley's modern era began in 1849, when about 100 emigrant families stumbled onto it in search of a route to gold country in the Sierra Nevada mountain range. They found a way out only after one died and the rest had burned their wagons and eaten their gaunt oxen; hence the name. Though myths, rumors, and occasional successes brought waves of prospectors searching for gold and silver, the real find was the rich boron deposits that are still mined to this day at the edge of the valley. In 1933 Death Valley was declared a national monument, and in 1994, with the addition of 1.3 million acres and a change in name, it became the largest national park, at three million acres, outside of Alaska.

The best way to enjoy Death Valley in the summer is to stay in the shade during the day and trek along the dunes and trails in early morning or late afternoon. A winter trip requires less pre-planning, since temperatures are comfortable during the day, though sometimes very cold at night. Civilization (restaurants, lodging, gas stations, and potable water) exists in three places: **Furnace Creek Ranch, Stovepipe Wells Village,** and **Panamint Springs,** though food and gas are also available at **Scotty's Castle.** Prices at all these places run as high as the temperatures.

## BASICS

**VISITOR INFORMATION** The **Furnace Creek Visitor Center** (3 mi north of junction of Hwys. 178 and 190, tel. 619/786–2331), near the center of the park, is the best starting point for visitors. For a quick overview of the park, check out the small adjacent museum and 18-minute orientation film. Rangers lead evening programs and daytime walks on a regular basis in high season, November to March, and on a more limited basis in off-season. Pick up a free guide, maps, and lists of bike routes, campsites, and trails. During the summer, request the free pamphlet "Hot Weather Hints: How to Survive Your Summer Trip Through Death Valley." (For a crash course on dealing with the desert, *see* Desert Survival, in chapter Basics, *above*.) The visitor center is open daily 8–6 in summer, 8–7 in winter.

**FEES** Entrance permits, valid for seven days, are $5 per vehicle, $3 for hikers and cyclists. Fees are collected at the Furnace Creek Visitor Center (*see above*).

**PUBLICATIONS** The **Death Valley Natural History Association** (Box 188, Death Valley 92328, tel. 619/786–2331) has maps and guides that you can order in advance if you want to read up on the park before you leave home; all are also available at the visitor center (*see above*).

**WHEN TO GO** The best times to visit are in fall and spring, when temperatures hover in the mid-70s. The park can be busy in winter, particularly during Thanksgiving and Christmas, when daytime temperatures are in the low 60s and nighttime temps can dip below freezing. During summer, temperatures are unbearably hot (up to 120°); some campgrounds and lodgings close altogether.

**GENERAL STORES** The general store at **Furnace Creek Ranch** (tel. 619/786–2345), open daily 7 AM–9 PM, and the store at **Stovepipe Wells** (tel. 619/786–2387), open daily 7 AM–8 PM, sell groceries, camping goods, cold drinks, and ice at inflated prices. You'll need to buy your charcoal or firewood here; collecting wood in the park is not permitted.

## COMING AND GOING

It's difficult to see Death Valley without your own wheels, as no mass transportation runs through the valley. To reach **Furnace Creek Ranch,** the center of civilization and the starting point for most excursions, take I–10 east from L.A. to I–15 north. At Baker, 60 miles northeast of Barstow, take Highway 127 north for 84 miles to Death Valley Junction, then drive 30 miles north on Highway 190. If you're coming from Northern California, take Highway 99 south to Highway 178 near Bakersfield, then travel east on 178 to U.S. 395 north, where you'll connect to Highway 190 east.

*It may seem like torture, but when driving up the steep grades in the park, turn off your air conditioner to avoid overheating the engine.*

Fill up with gas before going to Death Valley; the few stations here charge about 30¢ more per gallon than you'll pay near the interstate. Also check your oil and tire pressure and bring extra radiator water and antifreeze to soothe an overheated engine. If the temperature gauge in your car gets close to the red line, roll down the windows and turn on the heater full blast. Sounds like fun? Read on. Should your car overheat anyway, pull to the side of the road but leave your engine and the heater on. Get out of the car, find or make some shade, and allow the engine to cool. If you break down, stay with the car until someone comes by.

## WHERE TO SLEEP

Camping is the best alternative for price and location—if you can bear the heat. Accommodations at Stovepipe Wells Village and Furnace Creek Ranch are operated by the concessionaire **Fred Harvey, Inc.** (tel. 619/786–2345); prices generally range from expensive to ridiculous. On the western edge of the park, Panamint Springs is independently owned and offers more reasonable prices, but it's a lengthy drive away from the park's main sights. The visitor center (*see above*) has a partial list of area motels.

**HOTELS** **Panamint Springs Resort.** Don't be alarmed by the fancy moniker: This is really a plain and simple roadside motel, just inside the park's western boundary. You'll pay $42–$57 for a clean, comfortable room with a TV; the restaurant on the premises is actually well worth the money. The only problem is, you can't call your parents for more money—there are no telephones in the rooms and no pay phones. *Tel. 702/482–7680. On Hwy. 190, 48 mi east of Lone Pine and 35 mi west of Stovepipe Wells. 14 rooms. Gas station, general store, restaurant.*

**Stovepipe Wells Village.** This is as cheap as it gets for a solid, centrally located roof over your head. Extremely clean, attractive rooms with two beds and a shower, but without TV, phone, or drinkable water, are $53—you'll pay $76 or more if you want a room with water you can drink. Take a refreshing swim in the adjacent swimming pool. *Tel. 619/786–2387. 24 mi northwest of Furnace Creek Visitor Center on Hwy. 190. Gas station, general store, gift shop, restaurant. Reserve 2 weeks ahead. Wheelchair access.*

**HOSTEL** **Desertaire Home Hostel.** Actually located in the town of Tecopa, a one-hour drive south of Death Valley, this small hostel offers visitors free access to hot springs, nearby hiking and mountain-biking trails, a volleyball court, and a watchtower to observe the starry nighttime sky. Dorm-style beds cost $12; one private room is available. Though the hostel accepts walk-ins, the manager requests that people reserve in advance (with a deposit) or call one day in advance if possible. *Mailing address: Box 306, Tecopa 92389. Street address: 2000 Old Spanish Trail Hwy. (off Hwy. 127). Tel. 619/852–4580. 12 beds. Curfew 9 PM, no lockout. Reception open 5 PM–9 PM. Linen rental ($1.50). No credit cards.*

**CAMPING** All of the designated campgrounds operate on a first-come, first-served basis except Furnace Creek. Many camppgrounds on the valley floor are closed April–October, and some at higher elevations are closed in winter. During hot weather, head for higher elevations, where campgrounds are cooler, more isolated, and sometimes even wooded. Showers, a swimming pool, and a laundromat are all available for a fee at Furnace Creek Ranch.

**Emigrant.** On Highway 190, 9 miles west of Stovepipe Wells Village, this small, free campground may be just a patch of flat gravel, but it's much cooler than Stovepipe, thanks to its 2,100-foot elevation. Fires are not allowed. *10 sites. Drinking water, flush toilets, picnic tables. Open Mar.–Nov.*

**Furnace Creek.** This uninspiring campground is quite popular, thanks to its location: The entrance is a half mile north of Furnace Creek Ranch. To get a spot ($10), shaded with a handful of spindly cottonwood trees, arrive by 8 AM. From October to April you may make reservations up to eight weeks in advance through MISTIX (tel. 800/365–CAMP). *136 tent and RV sites. Drinking water, fire grills, flush toilets; elev. -196 ft. Open year-round. Wheelchair access.*

**Mesquite Spring.** In contrast to the barren campsites nearby, this shaded year-round campground ($6) is surrounded by shrubbery. But there's a catch—its location, near the park's northern boundary, is far from most of the park's attractions. *Off Hwy. 267 near Scotty's Castle, 52 mi north of Furnace Creek. 30 sites. Drinking water, fire rings, flush toilets, picnic tables; elev. 1,800 ft.*

**Stovepipe Wells.** This is nothing more than an open, treeless patch of ground parceled into campsites ($6), but it is adjacent to Stovepipe Wells Village, which consists of a motel, a restaurant, a general store, and—most important—a swimming pool. You may use the pool and showers for $2. *24 mi NW of Furnace Creek on Hwy. 190. 200 sites. Drinking water, no fires, flush and pit toilets; elev. sea level. Open Sept.–May.*

**Texas Springs.** Located 1½ miles south of Furnace Creek off Highway 190, Texas Springs is a designated "quiet" campground: Since RVs may not use their generators, many rely on solar paneling. The parking lot looks like a scene from *Mad Max,* but there is a tents-only section of about 40 sites ($6). *92 sites. Drinking water, fire rings, flush and pit toilets, picnic tables; elev. sea level. Closed May–Sept.*

**Thorndike** and **Mahogany Flat.** These adjacent free campgrounds are for serious solitude-seekers only, or for hikers planning a trip to the top of 11,000-foot Telescope Peak (*see* Longer Hikes, *below*). At 7,500 and 8,200 feet respectively, these sites are at much higher elevations than other campgrounds in the park. They are accessible only via several miles of rough, unpaved road that isn't passable by RVs or by cars that don't have four-wheel drive. *From Emigrant Campground, follow signs 25 mi south of Hwy. 190 on Wildrose Rd. Thorndike: 8 sites. Mahogany Flat: 10 sites. Both have fire rings, picnic tables, pit toilets, no potable water. Both closed Dec.–Feb.*

➢ **BACKCOUNTRY CAMPING** • Backcountry camping is permitted anywhere in the park, as long as you're at least 1 mile from maintained roads, a quarter-mile from any water source, and 5 miles from developed areas, including campgrounds. Fires are not permitted. You may follow trails or strike out cross-country; in either case you'll want to pick up topographic maps and check conditions at the Furnace Creek Visitor Center first. While you're there, fill out a voluntary backcountry registration form so someone knows your whereabouts; you may also register at ranger stations at Stovepipe Wells Village and Grapevine (the north entrance). Water found in the valley is an undrinkable concoction of salts and minerals, so plan on packing in at least a gallon per person per day. (For hot-weather hiking tips, consult rangers; *also see* Desert Survival, in chapter Basics, *above*.) **Hanaupah, Johnson,** and **Warm Springs canyons**—all off the unpaved West Side Road—are excellent destinations if you're looking for a day or more of desert solitude. West Side Road branches southwest from Highway 178 about 10 miles south of Furnace Creek Ranch, and is accessible to high-clearance vehicles like jeeps and pickups; conditions may require four-wheel drive—ask at the ranger station.

## FOOD

Unfortunately, unless you've discovered a way to digest creosote bushes, you'll need to lay out a lot of cash for a meal. You'll find food in only four locations in Death Valley, or at the two grocery stores in the park (*see* General Stores, *above*). **Furnace Creek Ranch** and **Stovepipe Wells Village** each contain a handful of sit-down or buffet-style restaurants; the best of the lot are in Furnace Creek, where **Coyote's International Restaurant,** open 5 PM–9 PM, serves burgers and vegetarian sandwiches for—can you believe this?—about $10 each. The **Coffee Shop** in Furnace Creek, open October–June, 7 AM–9 PM, has breakfast and basic dinner-style lunches and dinners at the same ungodly prices. At the remote northern boundary, a snack bar at **Scotty's Castle** (*see* Exploring Death Valley, *below*), open 8:30–5:30, serves spicy fries and good grilled sandwiches for under $5, though they don't sell hamburgers May–October, due to the heat.

The best deal on quality chow is at **Panamint Springs Resort** (tel. 702/482–7680), open daily 6:30 AM–midnight. Unfortunately, in addition to an exceptional view, the restaurant is exceptionally far from the centers of activity. But if you make it out here, you can get a bowl of spicy vegetable soup for $3.50 or a burger for about $6. If you're thinking you'll beat the bloodsuckers by providing for yourself, think again: prices at the two grocery stores in the park (*see* General Stores, *above*) are also worthy of hyperbole. You'd be wisest to stock up before your trip.

## EXPLORING DEATH VALLEY

Though high temperatures often make Death Valley seem like hell on earth, travelers who prepare accordingly will be intrigued by the park's unique sights, including 200 square miles of crusty salt beds, a string of 11,000-foot peaks, and whipped mounds of weirdly hued soil. The intense heat often makes lengthy hikes impossible; fortunately, the park is packed with shorter trails that can be explored during early morning or late afternoon and evening, when desert sands assume luminous purple, orange, and gold hues. Most points of interest are accessible from the paved main roads.

*Created when ancient lakes dried up and their sandy bottoms were teased into stiff peaks by the wind, Death Valley's awe-inspiring sand dunes tower up to eight stories high. Wandering among the windswept slopes may be a mesmerizing experience, but don't lose sight of your car. Should an abrupt gust of wind cover your tracks with sand, you may suddenly become lost.*

**HIKING** The Furnace Creek Visitor Center (*see* Visitor Information, *above*) has a comprehensive list of day hikes, as well as trail guides and topo maps for sale. Most trails lie near Furnace Creek or farther north. Remember to carry plenty of water.

➢ **SHORT HIKES** • In addition to established trails, you may want to explore the valley's **sand dunes,** which reach heights of nearly 100 feet. They aren't particularly tough to climb, though you'll find the experience most pleasant when the sands are cool (in early morning or evening). A parking and picnic area is accessible from Highways 190 and 267, near their intersection with Mid-Canyon Road. To reach the tallest dunes, look for a roadside marker on Highway 190 about 4 miles east of Stovepipe Wells Village; park and hike 1 mile north.

**Golden Canyon.** From the trailhead on Badwater Road, 3 miles south of Furnace Creek, take this relatively easy trail (2 mi round-trip), which climbs through colorful layers of rock bearing the ripple marks of an ancient lake. After a half mile, you have two options for magnificent views of the valley: A short trek to the sheer cliffs of **Red Cathedral,** or a steep and strenuous two-mile ascent to **Zabriskie Point** (*see* Scenic Drives and Views, *below*).

**Keane Wonder Mine and Mill.** This steep two-mile round-trip trail follows a defunct aerial tramway to the abandoned remains of one of Death Valley's most successful mines. A one-eyed butcher and his prospector partner discovered gold here in 1904; by 1911 they'd hauled out almost $1 million worth. Don't enter the mine—Indiana Jones isn't around to rescue you in case you tumble down a hidden vertical shaft. You can, however, safely enjoy spectacular views of the valley floor below. To reach the trail from Furnace Creek, drive 16 miles north on Highway 190, then go east on Beatty Cutoff Road. Turn south onto a marked, but unpaved, access road and continue 3 miles to the parking area.

**Mosaic Canyon.** Take this easy uphill trail (2 mi one-way) to see the unique geologic mosaic for which the canyon is named. Portions of the narrow canyon walls have been polished to marble-like smoothness by draining water; in other places, the workings of time have "glued" rock fragments together. Follow signs to the trailhead 3 miles west of Stovepipe Wells Village off Highway 190. Use caution: The unpaved access road can be rough.

**Salt Creek.** From a wheelchair-accessible boardwalk, check out this briny, spring-fed creek. In spring, look for a rare relative of the minnow, the tiny desert pupfish, which thrives in water that ranges from just above freezing to well over 100°. A guide (50¢) to this half-mile round-trip nature walk is available at either the trailhead or the visitor center. From Furnace Creek, drive 14 miles north on Highway 190, then follow signs to the parking area at the end of a one-mile access road.

➢ **LONGER HIKES** • If it's not too hot (i.e., below 95°), you have a choice of several day hikes. Let your water supply and internal thermometer—not your ego—help you decide when to turn back (*also see* Desert Survival, in chapter Basics, *above*). Experienced hikers in excellent physical condition may want to purchase topographic maps at the visitor center and plan a cross-country trek through isolated **Johnson, Warm Springs,** and **Hanaupah canyons** (*see* Backcountry Camping, *above*).

**Telescope Peak.** If you have abundant energy and six to nine hours to spare, the strenuous seven-mile hike to the summit of 11,049-foot Telescope Peak affords panoramic views of Death Valley and the High Sierra. In winter, the last ice-covered mile to the summit requires special preparation and equipment. The trailhead is comfortably above the valley floor, about 25 miles south of Highway 190 on Emigrant Canyon Road; follow signs from Mahogany Flat Campground or, if you lack four-wheel drive, from the Wildrose Charcoal Kilns (*see* Scenic Drives and Views, *below*); the kilns are an additional two miles from the summit.

**Ubehebe Crater.** Around 3,000 years ago, molten lava oozed into contact with groundwater under the valley floor, creating explosions of steam and gas that spewed debris over six square miles—a massive Maalox moment. From the wreckage was born this crater, nearly half a mile wide and 600 feet deep. Though the three-mile trail to the bottom may be a lark, bear in mind that it will take you twice as long to climb back up. The trail is at the northern edge of the park, 5 miles west of the Grapevine Entrance Station; follow signs from Highway 267.

**SCENIC DRIVES AND VIEWS** The valley's attractions are spread out over hundreds of miles, so you won't be able to see everything unless you stick around for at least three days. A great drive begins at **Badwater,** 18 miles south of the visitor center on Highway 178. This brackish pool is the remnant of an ancient lake. At 279.8 feet below sea level, it's nearly the lowest point in the United States. (The actual lowest point is a half mile away and 2 feet farther down.) Drive 4 miles north of Badwater on Highway 178 to the whimsically named **Devil's Golf Course,** a craggy expanse of crystallized salt beds crisscrossed by chasms several stories deep. Wear thick-soled shoes if you walk out onto the flats—the sharp salt crystals can easily cut unprotected feet. Another 4 miles farther north, turn onto **Artist's Drive,** which loops through colorful rock and mineral deposits. The most vibrant ones are at **Artist's Palette,** an overlook about halfway along the drive. The scenic detour rejoins Highway 178 about 5 miles south of the visitor center.

Immortalized by the orgiastic Michelangelo Antonioni film of the same name, **Zabriskie Point,** 4 miles south of Furnace Creek Ranch on Highway 190, provides a striking panorama of weathered, cinnamon-colored hills from a height of 710 feet. One mile farther south, a three-mile unpaved drive loops through **Twenty-Mule Team Canyon** before returning to Highway 190. The canyon is named for the teams once used to haul wagons laden with boron (20 tons at a time) out of the desert. Tunnels made by prospectors are still visible from the road. Continue 4 miles south to a marked 13-mile paved road leading through the Black Mountains to **Dante's View** scenic lookout, 5,000 feet above the valley floor. From here, the bleak landscape includes the Devil's Golf Course (*see above*), the green oasis of Furnace Creek, and the incongruous, snow-capped Telescope Peak (*also see* Longer Hikes, *above*). On a clear day, look for Mt. Whitney's imposing profile on the western horizon.

The **Saline Valley,** 130 miles west of Stovepipe Wells Village on Highway 190, is chock-full of eerie mine ruins, shaggy wild burros, waterfalls, and the crumpled towers of an abandoned aerial salt tram. But the real reason people come to this site at Death Valley's far northwestern corner is for the clothing-optional hot springs (yes, most people do take that option). Over the years, **Lower Warm Spring** and **Palm Spring** have been modified so that their naturally heated waters flow into stone and cement soaking tubs; team labor has also provided crude showers, toilets, and a semi-official primitive campground. During spring it's crowded but always congenial—as long as you respect the fragile environment. *From Hwy. 190, pass Panamint Springs, right on unpaved Saline Valley Rd. for 4 mi, right when the road forks, left at the Painted Rock, left again after 4 miles.*

**HISTORIC BUILDINGS** **Harmony Borax Works and Museum.** The abandoned adobes and weathered buildings here are not the remains of a typical ghost town: This is the former site of a boron processing plant that operated through the early 20th century. You'll also see the wagons immortalized in ads for the radio and TV show *Death Valley Days,* hosted by none other than Ronald Reagan. *Off Hwy. 190, 2 mi north of Furnace Creek Ranch.*

**Scotty's Castle.** This sprawling Spanish-style compound seems as incongruous in the desert as an igloo would be in Tahiti. The castle was built with no expenses spared between 1922 and 1933 as a vacation retreat for Chicago millionaire Albert Johnson and his wife, Bessie; the Johnsons entertained Hollywood types here, including Will Rogers and Betty Grable. The name sprang from Johnson's unusual friendship with local eccentric Walter Scott, a.k.a. Death Valley Scotty, who was allowed to live on the property and brag that it was his own. The castle's lavish interiors are worth seeing, but the crowds, especially on holidays, can be maddening. If you don't feel like parting with $8, or waiting one to two hours for the privilege of doing so, take a walk around the grounds instead. *Tel. 619/786–2392. 3 mi north of Grapevine Entrance Station on Hwy. 267. Tours on the hour (sometimes more often) daily 9–5; grounds open until 6.*

**Wildrose Charcoal Kilns.** The kilns, which look like a row of monstrous beehives, are 10 huge ovens (each about 25 feet high and almost 10 yards across) used by miners to turn wood into the coal needed to process silver and borax ores. You can still get a whiff of the acrid wood resins left behind in the burning process. To get here, drive east on Wildrose Canyon Road from the Wildrose Campground. After 4 miles the pavement ends; you may want to hike the final 1½ miles rather than risk damage to your car. Pick up a brochure about the kilns on-site or at the Furnace Creek Visitor Center.

## PARK ACTIVITIES

**BIKING** Bicycles are permitted on anything cars and trucks may drive upon, but are banned from hiking trails and may not be ridden cross-country. Be sure to bring lots of extra water, food, tools, a first-aid kit, and maps, as a backcountry breakdown could equal a huge ordeal. Oh yeah, and bring your own mountain bike—there's no place to rent within a hundred-mile radius.

For a moderate, mostly level workout, try the 12-mile round-trip to the once-booming ghost town of **Skidoo.** Little is left of the town (you may see a few tin cans), though the stamp mill that once crushed gold-impregnated rock is still fairly intact. The key word is fairly: Use caution; one day it might collapse on some hapless tourist. Pick up the unpaved road to Skidoo about 12 miles south of Highway 190 on Wildrose Road. Ambitious cyclists may want to explore **Cottonwood Canyon.** The fairly level road, sandy in spots, extends westward for 20 miles from the Stovepipe Wells campground. You'll see Native-American petroglyphs 15 miles in; otherwise, enjoy the occasional shade of cottonwood trees.

**HORSEBACK RIDING** In fall, winter, and spring, **Furnace Creek Ranch** (tel. 619/786–2345) offers guided horseback rides, starting at $15 per person for one hour. During the full moon, they have one-hour moonlight rides ($20 per person). Carriage rides go for $6 per person. Make reservations for all activities.

# Near Death Valley

## EUREKA SAND DUNES

Spectacular and unspoiled, these are the tallest sand dunes in California—some of them reach heights of nearly 700 feet. Fifty plant species thrive here, including three that grow nowhere else in the world. At dawn, look for the tracks of sidewinder snakes and tiny mammals on the windswept dunes. Now for the bad news: Though the dunes lie within Death Valley's boundaries, to reach them you must take a staggering 182-mile semicircular detour, through the town of Big Pine and part of the Inyo National Forest. Not surprisingly, few tourists make this trek, so the dunes are not only spectacular, but also uncrowded. Because getting here can be a trek, you'll probably want to camp a night or two, though the only nod to human needs is a single pit toilet off the roadside as you approach the dunes. To reach them from Big Pine (*see* Bishop, in The Eastern Sierra and Inyo National Forest, in Chapter 7) on U.S. 395, go 2.3 miles east on Highway 168, south on Death Valley Road, and past the Saline Valley turnoff to South Eureka Valley Road (40 mi from U.S. 395). The dunes are 10 miles away. Though you'll travel on unpaved roads, you probably won't need four-wheel drive.

## RHYOLITE

In 1904, two miners stumbled across a "crackerjack" of a hill, bursting with nuggets of pure gold. The ensuing scramble to lay claims and collect ore spawned the desert city of Rhyolite (named for the type of rock in which the gold was embedded). In its heyday, this was a classic boomtown, with a reputation that drew enterprising whores from as far away as San Francisco.

### *Best Little Opera House in Death Valley*

***The desert snags wandering souls the way barbed-wire fences collect tumbleweeds. Case in point: New York artist and dancer Marta Becket's car broke down near the all-but-dead burg of Death Valley Junction years ago. Once the gaskets were fixed, Becket's travel fuse had blown out: She stayed. The town lacks necessities like a gas station and restaurant, but damned if they don't have some of the highest culture west of Manhattan, in the form of the one-woman ballet at Becket's Amargosa Opera House. Marta's repertoire of 47 different characters is world famous (well, almost), as are her murals on the walls and ceilings of the theater. She often plays to sell-out crowds, so call ahead for reservations (tel. 619/852–4441). Admission is $8; shows happen Friday, Saturday, and Monday at 8:15 PM in November and February to April, Saturday only in October, December, January, and May.***

But in 1916, a combination of financial misfortune and waning mine profits put the lights out in Rhyolite for good. Though the town has been empty since, the train depot and the **Bottle House,** built of 50,000 beer and liquor bottles, are still intact, and a portion of the jail remains. Caretakers lead tours of the town October–April whenever people arrive; during the summer months, tours are more infrequent. To get here, drive 37 miles northeast of the Furnace Creek Visitor Center on Highway 374, and follow signs north on the short paved road.

# Mojave Desert

**If you've only flipped to** this page because you're zooming through the desert en route to somewhere else and you're hungry and/or need a place to shack up for the night, consider this: For some, the Mojave Desert is a place to visit by choice rather than by necessity. There's a whole subculture of desert groupies who make annual pilgrimages to see a particular flower that blooms for one week in the year; who have been panning for gold for years, convinced they will soon strike the mother lode; or who caravan in ATVs (all-terrain vehicles) to the Mojave to get the rush that comes from a jolting ride over sand dunes. While you may not become a desert regular, take some time to contemplate the beauty of arid, stark plains and the desert's maddening vastness. In particular, the 600-foot-high **Kelso Dunes,** 95 miles east of Barstow in the **East Mojave National Preserve,** are worth a detour.

## Barstow

On holidays and weekends, some 4,000 people pass through this high-desert town, halfway between Los Angeles and Las Vegas at the intersection of I–15 and I–40, but few do more than stretch their legs and slap on some sunscreen. You would be wise to follow their example. There's not much here besides the Santa Fe Railroad and Fort Irwin, a Marine training base. The **California Desert Information Center** (831 Barstow Rd., btw Virginia Way and Mountain View St., tel. 619/255–8313), open daily 9–5, has indoor exhibits about desert life and brochures on nearby attractions.

If you're stuck in Barstow overnight, at least you won't have to pay a lot for the privilege. Try the **Barstow Inn Motel** (1261 E. Main St., tel. 619/256–7581), where doubles start at $33, or the **Economy Motel** (1590 Coolwater Ln., tel. 619/256–1737), which has cheap but uninspiring one-bed doubles for $29. Perhaps the most interesting place to eat here is, well, **McDonald's** (1611 E. Main St., tel. 619/256–8023), open 5 AM–11 PM. This location is built like an old rail car and has a candy shop, a bakery and deli, a liquor store, and a gift shop. But if you can't bear to choke down another burger, check out the **Muchos Munchies Snack Bar** (208 E. Main St., tel. 619/255–3713), open Monday–Saturday 10–8. Prices on the menu at this hamburger stand/snack-shack rarely rise above $2; you'll have to eat outside, though, since there's no indoor seating.

### NEAR BARSTOW

**CALICO GHOST TOWN** The town of Calico was abandoned for 44 years before suffering a worse fate—in 1951, it was taken over by Walter Knott, owner of the Knott's Berry Farm theme park in Los Angeles. The ghost town is cheesy, but the museum exhibits, silver mine, and gold-panning school make for an enjoyable afternoon's break from desert driving. *Tel. 619/254–2122. Exit I–15 12 mi NE of Barstow at Calico Ghost Town Rd. and follow signs. Admission: $5. Open daily 7 AM–dusk; rides open 9–5.*

**CALICO EARLY MAN ARCHAEOLOGICAL SITE** This is the site of perhaps the most significant archaeological find in the United States. More than 200,000 years ago, this stretch of desert was an idyllic lakeside quarry, campsite, and workshop where Pleistocene people—the earliest-known Americans—made utensils for cutting, scraping, and drilling. Excavations begun in 1964, under the direction of noted archaeologist Louis Leakey, have yielded thousands of stone tools (but no skeletons). The site is accessible by guided tour only; public and

# Mojave Desert

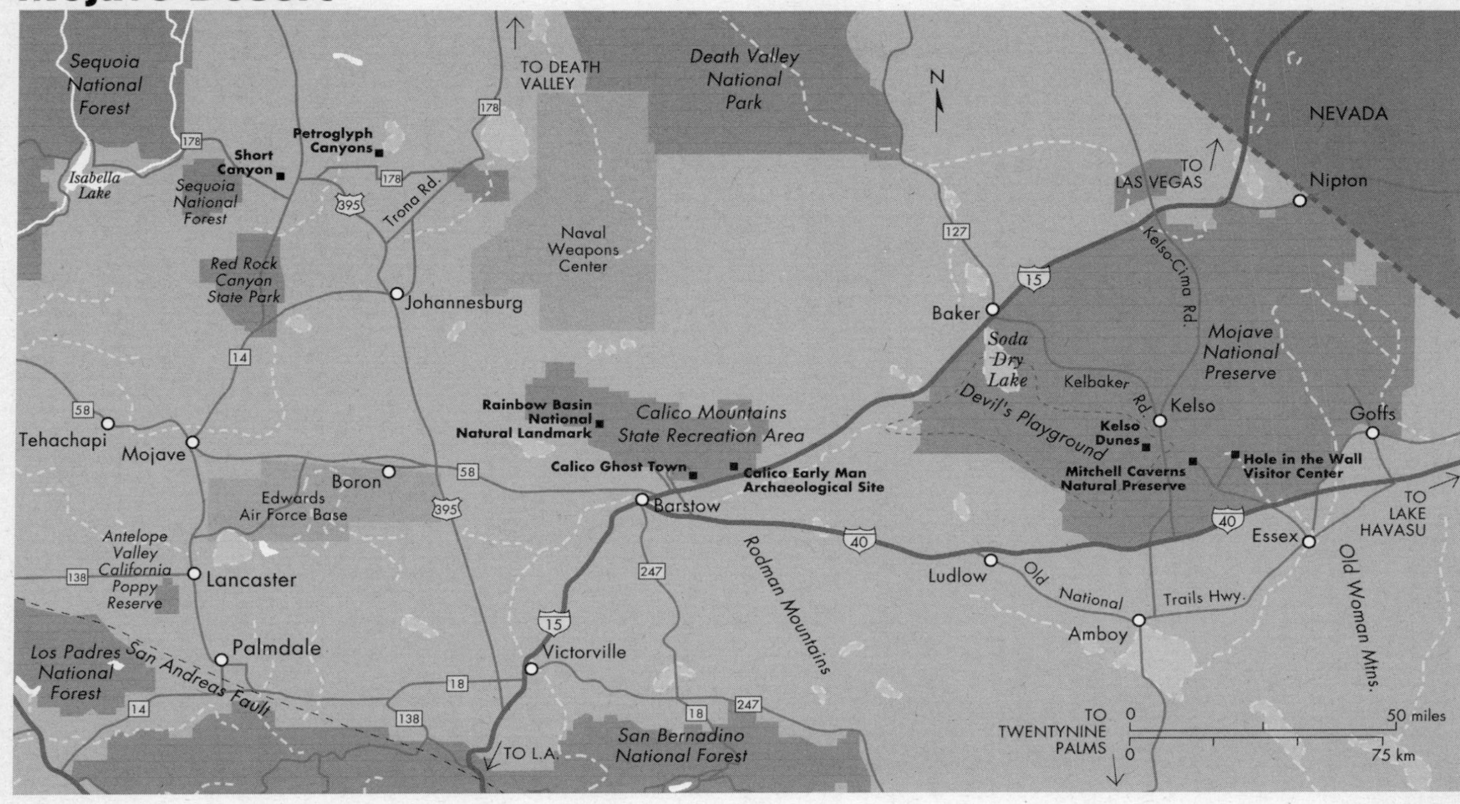

private camping is available near the site. *15 mi NE of Barstow. From I–15, exit Minneola Rd. and follow dirt road north 2½ mi. Suggested donation: $1. Tours Wed.–Sun. 9:30–4. Limited drinking water available.*

**RAINBOW BASIN NATIONAL NATURAL LANDMARK** Twelve to 16 million years ago, the basin was the bottom of a large lake, its shores grazed by a circus of creatures, including three-toed horses, camels, dog-bears, and mastodons. When these animals died, their skeletons stuck in the mud; the resulting fossils have been perfectly preserved in the cliff walls. Visitors will also be fascinated by the red, orange, and green hued striations on the walls of the basin. The six-mile round-trip scenic drive on a dirt road is perfect for an afternoon's visit. The more ambitious can meander in one of the many washes, the most interesting of which is **Owl Canyon Wash,** just off the scenic drive. If one day is simply not enough, you can stay in one of the 31 sites in the **Owl Canyon Campground** ($4), though there is only limited drinking water and there are only pit toilets. *8 mi north of Barstow. Hwy. 58 west to Fort Irwin Rd., go north 5½ mi to Fossil Bed Rd. (a graded dirt road), and head west 3 mi.*

# East Mojave National Preserve

Mojave's rock spires, sand dunes, and bare mesas, combined with the nearly total absence of human life, either inspire or torment visitors. Stretching more than 50 miles east and about 40 miles south from the flyspeck town of Baker to the Arizona and Nevada borders, the 1.4-million-acre national preserve can be accessed from several points along I–15 to the north and I–40 to the south. As always, avoid visiting during the sweltering summer months and make sure to fill the gas tank and several water jugs before leaving civilization. Information on the area is available Wednesday–Sunday 9–5 at the new **Hole in the Wall Visitor Center** (Black Canyon Rd., 19 mi north of I-40, tel. 619/928–2572); follow the Essex Road to Black Rock Canyon Road.

*Thought the official California state reptile was Governor Pete Wilson? Think again. The title is actually held by the slow-moving, camouflaged desert tortoise, common in the East Mojave National Preserve.*

Those wishing to be immersed in the solitude of the Mojave should try camping at the **Hole in the Wall Campground** near the visitor center. The 35 unshaded, open-desert sites ($8), located near volcanic-rock towers and canyons, are all wheelchair accessible. Facilities include water, pit toilets, and grills. The first-come, first-served campground is open year-round and is never crowded; temperatures are most pleasant between February and May. You may want to stay away during hunting season (Oct. and Nov.). From the nearby Hole in the Wall picnic area, the strenuous quarter-mile **Rings Trail** descends into Banshee Canyon via iron rings.

At the preserve's western boundary, the extraordinary **Kelso Dunes** involve a detour but are well worth the effort. More than 600 feet high, these are some of the tallest sand dunes in the United States. From I–15 at Baker, drive 43 miles south on Kelbaker Road, pass the almost nonexistent town of Kelso, and follow signs 3 miles west on the dirt road to the parking area. From there, you walk a half mile to the pristine dunes, but be sure to remember where you parked. There are no facilities at the dunes or in the town, which consists of six shacks, some trailers, and a handful of people no doubt looking to sell some real estate. Also off Kelbaker Road (look for the parking area and small sign on the right 9 miles south of I–15) is the **Teutonia Peak Trail,** leading 2 miles through a Joshua tree forest to a 5,755-foot peak that overlooks more than 30 young volcanic cones and the 75-square-mile Cima Dome.

Another worthwhile diversion is **Mitchell Caverns Natural Preserve,** 116 miles from Barstow in a patch of mountainous desert designated as the Providence Mountains State Recreation Area. Driving up the steep inclines to your destination, you'll have a spectacular view of the desert valleys that stretch all the way to Kingman, Arizona. The underground caves are sculpted with astonishing rock and mineral formations, and you can expect cool 65° temperatures in the caverns year-round—a great break from the desert heat. The 4,200-foot elevation also makes the six campsites ($12), which come complete with running water and flush toilets, more bearable in the summer heat. *Tel. 619/928–2568. From Barstow, I–40 100 mi east to Essex Rd., fol-*

*low signs NW 16 mi. Guided tours ($4) Sept.–mid-June, weekdays 1:30, weekends and holidays 10, 1:30, and 3; mid-June–late Aug., weekends 1:30.*



# Lake Havasu

Formed when the Colorado River was blocked by Parker Dam in 1938, Lake Havasu—off I–10 160 miles south of Las Vegas and 330 miles east of Los Angeles—provides water for the thirsty city of Los Angeles. In 1968 Robert P. McCulloch, founder of Lake Havasu City, negotiated with the British government to purchase the slightly used, 150-year-old **London Bridge,** which had been slowly sinking into the Thames River. At $2.46 million it was, according to the *Guinness Book of Records,* the most expensive antique ever sold.

For almost 30 years, the bridge has drawn more than one million visitors annually from all over the globe, ranking it second only to the Grand Canyon among Arizona's tourist attractions (of course, that isn't saying a whole lot). In the last decade or so, Lake Havasu has become immensely popular with a new breed of lake lover—party-minded college students. Particularly during spring break (late March through early May), the area is clogged from shore to shore with zillions of bobbing houseboats and overtanned teenagers. If you want to hang with this crowd, get a trust fund—you'll have to muster a fistful of dollar bills for the requisite houseboat. At **Havasu Springs Resort** (Hwy. 2, tel. 520/667–3361), 20 miles south of Lake Havasu City off Highway 95, rental rates are $1,200–$2,150 per week March–September, and $800–$1,495 a week October–February.

*Hard-core hikers, off-roaders, and other desert enthusiasts gather at the Nellie E. Saloon, 35 miles south of Lake Havasu City in the Buckskin Mountains. Look for the dirt turnoff to Cienega Springs Road off the east side of Highway 95. This isn't an urban version of a cowboy saloon; the bar has no electricity or plumbing, and its entire water supply is stored in a 500-gallon fire truck.*

**VISITOR INFORMATION** The **Lake Havasu Area Chamber of Commerce** offers camping, motel, and dining guides, city maps, and a barrage of brochures on water sports; some of the brochures include discount coupons. *420 English Village, Lake Havasu City, tel. 520/855–5655. North of London Bridge. Open summer, Tues.–Sat. 9–5 and Sun.–Mon. 9–4; winter, daily 9–5.*

**WHERE TO SLEEP** Moderate evening temperatures nearly year-round make camping a more inviting option than a cheap motel. For the real Havasu experience, though, try to muster up eight to 12 people to rent a houseboat (*see above*). If your ship (or houseboat) has failed to come in, the **Windsor Inn** (451 London Bridge Rd., ¾ mi north of London Bridge, tel. 520/855–4135 or 800/245–4135) has clean doubles for $29–$36 weekdays, $45–$49 weekends. Guests have use of a pool and spa, and the inn is within walking distance of Windsor State Beach.

➢ **CAMPING** • The **Windsor Beach Unit of Lake Havasu State Park** (2 mi north of London Bridge, tel. 520/855–2784) has 75 first-come, first-served lakeside campsites ($10). Though the boat launches to the north and south are dominated by beer-guzzlin', testosterone-charged powerboaters, the grounds themselves draw a more mellow crowd. Amenities include flush toilets, showers, and a swimming beach. The grounds are open year-round.

**FOOD** Restaurants abound in the **English Village,** but the Brits were never noted for culinary genius—transplantation to Arizona hasn't helped matters. Unless you're a glutton for overpriced tourist chow, leave the lakeside.

**Scotty's Broasted Chicken and Ribs** (410 El Camino Way, near S. Palo Verde Blvd., tel. 520/680–4441), open Tuesday–Saturday 11–8 and Sunday–Monday 11–7, may look like your average rubber-chicken pit stop from Highway 95, but the food is excellent and cheap. A two-piece chicken dinner with potatoes, roll, and slaw will set you back just $3.75. **Uncle Kenny's Café** (362 London Bridge Rd., in London Bridge Shopping Center, tel. 520/680–

7100), open daily 6 AM–2 PM, is a local favorite for breakfast at reasonable prices ($2.75 for three pancakes).

**OUTDOOR ACTIVITIES** Most people come to Lake Havasu to frolic in the water, and the lake buzzes year-round with Jet Skis, speedboats, waterskiers, and fishing boats. But unless you've brought your own equipment, all this aquatic fun can be costly. **Arizona Jet Ski Rentals** (635 Kiowa Blvd., tel. 520/453–5558) rents tandem Jet Skis ($35 an hour) and 15-foot motorboats ($50 an hour), and will deliver equipment to the dock. Ascetics and the thin-walleted may eschew the pricey floating stuff in favor of a dip in the lake at **Rotary Community Park** (west end of Smoke Tree Ave., off Hwy. 95), open daily until 10:30 PM. The beach has a $5 day-use fee and is furnished with volleyball courts and picnic tables.

# Palm Springs

**Between a string of burlap-**colored mountains and the barren desert, this incongruous resort community has garnered a reputation as a playground for the rich and famous. It became a haven for Hollywood stars when Ginger Rogers, Humphrey Bogart, and Clark Gable joined the Palm Springs Racquet Club in the 1930s. The celebrity contingent is still present, cowering behind the high hedges that screen their huge houses from stargazing bus tours. However, most of Palm Springs' recent growth has come from a potpourri of less tinseled visitors. Retirees from San Diego and Los Angeles with big bank accounts are drawn by the sunny skies and clean air. The Palm Springs area has also become a hot vacation spot for gays and lesbians from as far away as New York City, who enjoy being pampered at expensive, exclusively gay resorts.

*Palm Springs' popularity as a collegiate spring break party zone has fallen off in recent years, thanks mostly to crackdowns by the local government and police department. Lake Havasu (see Mojave Desert, above) is now king of the hill.*

Palm Springs and the seven neighboring cities of the Coachella Valley, collectively called "The Springs," have the climate—and, unfortunately, the high prices—of a true resort. Even in the dead of winter, when snow dusts the top of San Jacinto Peak, temperatures are regularly in the 70s and rarely dip below freezing at night. Notwithstanding the fact that this is the desert, developers have built more than 80 golf courses. Three times that many tennis courts and thousands of swimming pools fill whatever land is left, and golf, tennis, and poolside lounging are the primary pursuits of visitors. There are other options, however, from hiking the palm oases of Indian Gardens to ascending a Swiss-style tram for a view of the desert from 10,000-foot peaks in the San Jacinto Wilderness. During summer, motel prices fall as temperatures rise, so if you can take the heat (90°–100°), you'll be able to negotiate outrageous bargains.

## VISITOR INFORMATION

The **Palm Springs Visitor Information Center** makes gratis lodging reservations (often at cut-rate prices) and distributes a free city map, a visitors' guide, and brochures. Here you can pick up a copy of the biweekly *Bottom Line,* which lists gay hotels, bars, restaurants, and nightclubs in Palm Springs and surrounding communities. *2781 N. Palm Canyon Dr., btw Racquet Club Rd. and Tram Way, tel. 619/778–8418 or 800/34–SPRINGS. Open daily 9–5.*

## COMING AND GOING

Palm Springs lies 110 miles southeast of Los Angeles, a drive of approximately two hours; take I–10 east to Highway 111 south. From San Diego, it's a 2½-hour drive (about 140 mi) northeast; from I–15 north, take Highway 215 north to Highway 60 east, which connects with I–10 east. You can also reach Palm Springs by plane, bus, or train. **Palm Springs Regional Airport** (tel. 619/323–8161), 2 miles east of downtown, is served by Alaska Airlines, America West Express, American, American Eagle, Delta, United, and U.S. Air Express. **Greyhound** (311 N. Indian Canyon Dr., tel. 619/325–2053, or 800/231–2222 for ticket info) has direct service

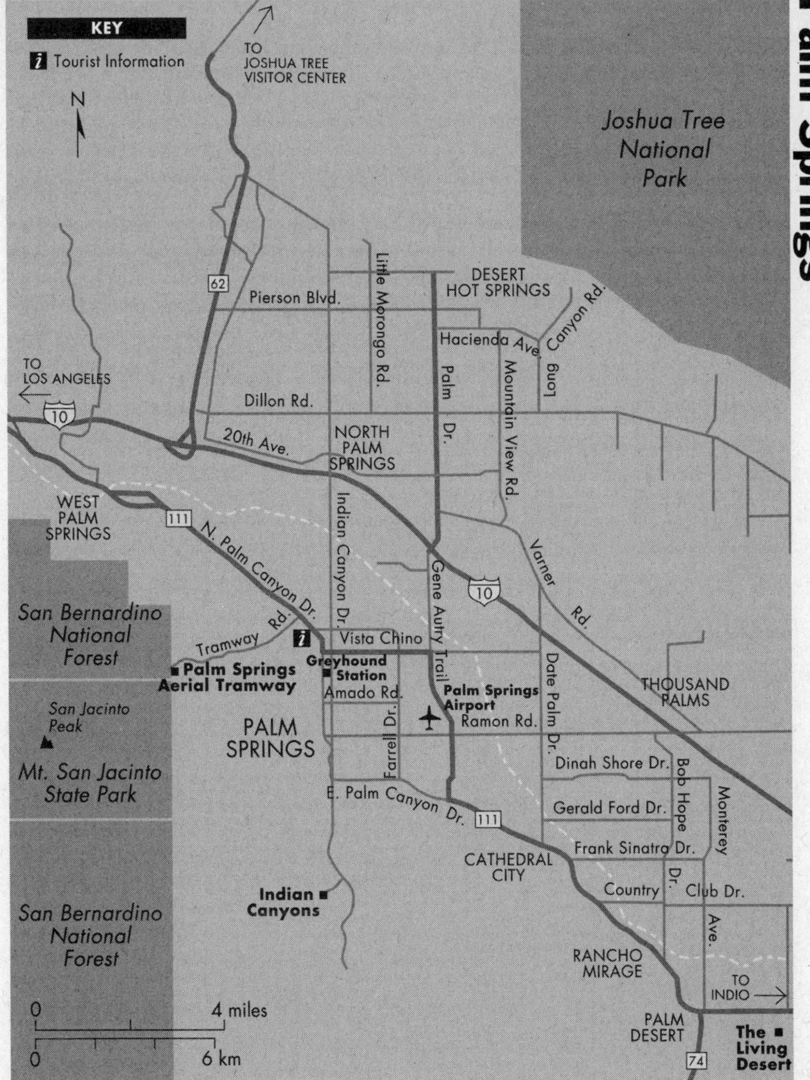


between Palm Springs and Los Angeles (3 hrs, $12 one-way). **Amtrak** (45050 Jackson St., Indio, tel. 800/USA–RAIL) runs three trains weekly from Los Angeles to Indio, 20 miles east of Palm Springs (2½ hrs each way, $46–$60 round-trip). From Indio, **Sunbus** (*see below*) provides public transportation to Palm Springs.

Within the city limits, Highway 111 is known as **Palm Canyon Drive**; the section of the highway between Amado and Ramon roads constitutes the town center and is open to southbound traffic only (Indian Canyon Drive, one block east, handles downtown's northbound flow). South of Ramon Road, Palm Canyon splits; continue on East Palm Canyon Drive (Hwy. 111) to reach other desert resort communities, including Cathedral City and Rancho Mirage. **Sunbus** (tel. 619/343–3451) serves the entire Palm Springs area from Desert Hot Springs to Coachella, including Indio, for only 75¢. The buses, which are powered by natural gas, run 6 AM–11 PM. Schedules and route guides are available at the visitor center (*see above*) and most other tourist locations.

*The springs referred to in the name Palm Springs can mostly be found underneath the fancy, expensive hotels, effectively making them inaccessible for travelers with thin wallets. If you're on a budget, consider staying at the Ambassador Health Spa Motel.*

## WHERE TO SLEEP

Admire the luxury resorts from afar, then check into one of the area's reasonably priced inns, hotels, or resorts (a lot of which are really motels, but don't tell anyone we told you). Rest assured that almost any establishment comes with a heated pool. Room rates are steepest in high season, October–May, and on summer holiday weekends; reservations are a must during these times. Camping isn't an option unless it sounds appealing to hike 3 miles from the top of the Aerial Tramway (*see* Worth Seeing, *below*) or drive half an hour to **Lake Cahuilla County Park** (tel. 619/564–4712) in Indio.

➢ **UNDER $50** • **Ambassador Health Spa Motel.** Rooms (and most guests) appear to be ancient and a bit frayed around the edges, but at $39–$45 for a roomy double, consider this motel, located about 10 miles north of Palm Springs, a budget resort. Water is piped into the Jacuzzi and pool from hot mineral springs below the AstroTurf. Après-soak, slip into the sauna. *12921 Tamar Dr., Desert Hot Springs, tel. 619/329–1909. From I–10, Palm Dr. north to Hacienda Ave. east, then left onto Tamar Dr. 20 rooms, all with kitchens.*

**Dunes Hotel.** This three-story hotel in the center of town draws a young crowd that spends most of its time at the two outdoor swimming pools and the oversize Jacuzzi. The rooms are drab and seedy, but they are inexpensive; doubles average $49 and drop to $29 on summer weekdays, including a continental breakfast. Prices may increase if the new management slaps a new name and a much-needed coat of paint on the place. *390 S. Indian Canyon Drive, btw Ramon and Arenas Rds., tel. 619/322–8789 or 800/59–DUNES. 6 blocks from Greyhound station. 108 rooms.*

**Mira Loma Hotel.** This tiny, affordable oasis has immaculate and luxurious rooms, some with private patios. Guest quarters encircle a small pool in which Marilyn Monroe purportedly swam, and the congenial management provides plenty of thick, nubby towels for sunbathing. Rates start at around $35 in summer and $45 the rest of the year. *1420 N. Indian Canyon Dr., btw Vista Chino and Alejo Rd., tel. 619/320–1178. 15 rooms. Airport transit, free morning newspaper, refrigerators. Wheelchair access.*

➢ **UNDER $65** • **Avanti Resort.** Gay men should treat themselves to a splurge at this beautiful, secluded retreat; the lushly landscaped garden creates an alternative vision of a clothing-optional Eden—this time, it's Adam and *Steve.* Located on a quiet street near three other gay resorts, Avanti's rates start at $49 Monday–Wednesday, $59 Thursday–Sunday. *715 San Lorenzo Rd, tel. 619/325–9723 or 800/572–2779. From S. Palm Canyon Dr., left on Mesquite Ave., left on Random Rd., right on San Lorenzo Rd. 14 rooms.*

## FOOD

➢ **UNDER $5** • The resort set may be sucking down overpriced pasta at swanky bistros, but you needn't join them. Satiate sandwich cravings at the **Burger Factory** (333 S. Indian Canyon Dr., btw Ramon and Arenas Rds., tel. 619/322–7678), open daily 10–9. This tiny shop has a choice of at least 45 different things to put on hot buns for less than $5. After spending the day swimming upstream, try the salmon burger ($4) and finish with chocolate-dipped cheesecake on a stick ($3). The best bet for breakfast is at **Bit of Country** (418 S. Indian Canyon Dr., tel. 619/325-5154), which serves down-home fare daily 5:45–2, with $3 specials before 8:30.

➢ **UNDER $10** • **Edgardo's Café Veracruz.** Edgardo's serves traditional Mexican food in a casual atmosphere. This is the kind of place where the owner will take time out to discuss the home-grown herbs and cacti in his desert cactus soup ($3.50). The tamales ($6–$9) are not to be missed. *233 S. Indian Canyon Dr., btw Baristo and Arenas Rds., tel. 619/864–1551. Open Thurs.–Tues. 11–3 and 5–10; reduced hours in summer.*

**Nature's Express.** This café and market serves vegan food and sells a small supply of organic vegetables in a friendly atmosphere. For a meal just like mom used to make (or never made, whichever), try an avocado sandwich ($5) with a delicious date shake ($4). *555 S. Sunrise Way, at Ramon Rd., tel. 619/323–9487. Open Mon.–Sat. 8–8, Sun. 10–6. Wheelchair access.*

**Shame on the Moon.** This roomy, comfortable restaurant serves Continental-style meals ($12–$17) to a well-dressed, older gay crowd; recently, increasing numbers of "breeders" have gotten wind of the high quality of meals and service. *69950 Frank Sinatra Dr., at Hwy. 111, tel. 619/324–5515. In Rancho Mirage. Open Mon.–Fri. 11:30–2 and 5:30–10, Sat. and Sun. 5:30–10. Closed Aug.*

## WORTH SEEING

On Thursday evenings from September through mid-July, check out the **Palm Springs Village-Fest** (tel. 619/320–3781), a sprawling street fair covering Palm Canyon Drive between Baristo and Amado roads. Bands play live music while merchants sell everything from velvet jester's hats to Guatemalan jewelry and decorative dried gourds. Look for the professional massage booth ($1 a minute) and plenty of barbecued eats.

**INDIAN CANYONS** The Agua Caliente Indians thrived in the inhospitable desert because they settled in cool, palm-shaded canyon oases. Today the tribe manages this preserve as a day-use area for hikers and horseback riders. The **Andreas Canyon** oasis has dozens of pools and shallow falls. To escape its occasional crowds, follow the easy 1½-mile trail southwest from the Andreas Canyon parking lot to **Murray Canyon.** The creek here flows only after a season's rainfall, but stands of fan palms always provide a pleasant picnic spot. The large **Palm Canyon** oasis, also accessible by car, stretches 15 miles and contains over 3,000 palm trees. From the Trading Post parking lot, follow the steep West Fork Trail south 3 miles; at its juncture with West Fork Trail North, you'll see pre-Columbian petroglyphs and, if you're lucky, wild horses and desert bighorn sheep. *Tel. 619/325–5673. Follow signs from S. Palm Canyon Dr. Admission: $5. Open Sept.–mid-July, daily 8–6.*

**THE LIVING DESERT** To see some of the desert's nocturnal residents, check out this 1,200-acre wildlife park, located fifteen miles east of Palm Springs. Eagle Canyon, the park's newest addition, houses golden eagles, mountain lions, and Mexican wolves in landscaped natural settings. The park also has an assortment of exotics from around the world, including zebras, gazelles, and Arabian oryx. Abundant nature trails offer many views of the park and its inhabitants. *47900 Portola Ave., Palm Desert, tel. 619/346–5694. From Hwy. 111, south 1½ mi on Portola Ave. Admission: $7. Open Sept.–mid-June, daily 9–5.*

**PALM SPRINGS AERIAL TRAMWAY** This Swiss-built tramway, a 10-minute drive from downtown Palm Springs, makes a dizzying one-mile ascent from the desert floor into the mountains of the **San Jacinto Wilderness**—a state park with 13,000 alpine acres and 54 miles of hiking trails (*see* Outdoor Activities, *below*). The mountaintop station house has postcard views, a moderately priced cafeteria/restaurant (full dinners $10), and a free 20-minute flick

### *What the Truck?!*

***No truck stop in the nation is quite as strange as the creepily avant-garde Wheel-In, which greets you with gigantic, proto–Jurassic Park models of a brontosaurus and a tyrannosaurus rex looming over the parking lot. Don't forget to take photos of your friend being eaten alive by a creature that bit the dust 65 million years ago. In the belly of the big green one, the Dinosaur Gift Shop (tel. 909/849–8309) sells dino trinkets daily 9 AM–sunset. Immortalized by Pee Wee Herman in his 1985 movie Pee Wee's Big Adventure, Wheel-In is on I–10 in Cabazon (between Palm Springs and Los Angeles). The diner next door serves up hot and hearty truck-stop fare 'round the clock.***

on Francis Crocker, the man who planned the tram. Best of all, it's always 30° cooler up here than in the city below. Worst of all is the steep admission price. *Tel. 619/325–1391 or 619/325–4227 (for weather). From Hwy. 111, Tramway Rd. uphill 3½ mi. Admission: $16. Open weekdays 10–9:45, weekends 8 AM–9:45 PM. Trams depart every half hour; last tram at 8 PM (1 hr later during daylight savings time).*

## AFTER DARK

Nightlife in the desert is eclectic—there's something for just about everyone. Gay nightlife centers around the many bars and clubs of Cathedral City, just south of Palm Springs on Highway 111. **C.C. Construction Co.** (68449 Perez Rd., Cathedral City, tel. 619/324–4241) is the Coachella Valley's largest gay nightclub; on Sundays it goes country and western. The **Wolf's Den** (67625 E. Palm Canyon Dr., Cathedral City, tel. 619/321–9688) is a more hard-core cruise bar that appeals mostly to the leather-bound, body-pierced biker-crowd, though a diverse group mingles in the dim, smoky interior. For other gay venues, consult the free biweekly publication *The Bottom Line* (*see* Visitor Information, *above*).

**Zelda's Nightclub and Beach Club** (168 N. Indian Canyon Dr., Palm Springs, tel. 619/325–2375) attracts a young, mostly straight crowd with dancing, nightly drink specials, and contests for limbo squads and limber bods. **Harley's Coffee and Beers Café** (168 N. Palm Canyon Dr., tel. 619/778–5750) serves, uh, coffee and beers. International and microbrewed ales cost $3.50–$5. Reggae, jazz, blues, and acoustic-guitar players drop in to jam on weekend evenings beginning at around 8 PM.

## OUTDOOR ACTIVITIES

**HIKING** Head for the hills when you tire of the heat and glitter of Palm Springs. At the top of the Aerial Tramway (*see* Worth Seeing, *above*), the **San Jacinto Wilderness** offers a surreal view of the desert below from cool, rugged peaks (8,000–10,000 feet high). Get maps and mandatory free hiking permits and info at the **Long Valley Ranger Station** (tel. 619/327–0222 for recorded weather and trail info), just below the tram's mountaintop station. Many hikers make the 12-mile ascent to **San Jacinto Peak** (10,804 ft), a strenuous, six hour round-trip beginning at the foot of the ranger station. Your reward: to stand astride the summit, queasily admiring the near-vertical drop of the mountain's north face. Acrophobes may feel more at ease on the moderate five-mile loop to **Long Valley Camp**; the hike begins at the ranger station and affords good views of the backcountry. For a shorter trek with breathtaking panaromas, try the **Desert View Trail,** a 1½-mile loop. Hike-in camping is also available; stop by the ranger station for the required free permits and camping suggestions.

**GOLF AND TENNIS** The **Tahquitz Creek Golf Course** (1885 Golf Club Dr., btw Highway 111 and Ramon Rd., tel. 619/328–1005) keeps a parking spot reserved for golf king Arnold Palmer, but prices are egalitarian. Greens fees start at $35 during peak season, $18 in other months; clubs rental costs $25. At the **Tennis Center** (1300 East Baristo Rd., btw Sunrise Way and Ramon Rd., tel. 619/320–0020), court fees are about $5 per person and racket rental is $6.

**CROSS-COUNTRY SKIING** The **Palm Springs Nordic Ski Center** (tel. 619/327–6002), at the top of the Aerial Tramway (*see* Worth Seeing, *above*), is generally open from mid-November to early April. Here you can rent equipment ($9 an hour, $18 a day) to tour the two miles of beginners' trails in adjacent Long Valley. Lessons start at $15 for 1½ hours. Experienced cross-country skiers will want to blaze their own trails in the San Jacinto Wilderness (*see* Hiking, *above*). To do this, obtain a free permit at the ranger station next to the tramway.

# Joshua Tree National Park

**Most people approach Joshua Tree** with the vague feeling that it must be cool: After all, Irish rockers U2 did name an album for it in 1987. But to visit this desert preserve, which encompasses more than 790,000 acres of spiky, twisted Joshua trees and boulders piled high like giant bowling pins, is to encounter a sublime, unexpected, and almost surreal beauty. There are actually two types of desert here, joined raggedly together at the center of the park. To the west, in the higher-elevation **Mojave Desert,** grow the Joshuas and other thick vegetation; to the east, the drier **Colorado Desert** bristles with spindly clumps of ironwood, ocotillo, and creosote. Throughout the park, granite monoliths rise from the landscape like the product of a strangely fertilized garden. The majority of campgrounds and trails lie within the Mojave sector, though both types of desert support an incredible variety of life, despite extreme temperatures and sparse precipitation. Don't skip the less colorful Colorado portion—two of the park's cool, green palm oases lie to the east, near the south entrance station.

*Joshua trees are not really trees, but a large type of yucca plant. The name came about when turn-of-the-century Mormon settlers saw in their reaching branches the beckoning arms of the prophet Joshua.*

For humans, the deserts have been inhospitable; early explorers expressed their disgust by giving mountainside washes unappealing names like Fried Liver, no doubt cursing the rumors of a hidden mother lode. More recently, though, angst-ridden Angelenos have rediscovered the value of a weekend's desert escape, as have RV drivers hell-bent on seeing all of America, springtime wildflower enthusiasts, and an international crowd of thrill-hungry rock climbers. The greatest present-day difficulty may be the struggle for a campsite during the peak season (late fall through spring), but if you're willing to hike a mile or so away from the road to pitch your tent, you can have any patch of ground your heart desires.

Summer can bring temperatures in excess of 100°, but it's considerably less crowded than spring, when desert blooms draw capacity crowds. Winter and fall are the best times for solitude and reasonable weather (daytime highs in the 60s, lows of around 35° at night). Water sources are very limited within the park, so bring lots (*also see* Desert Survival, in chapter Basics, *above*). You can fill your canteen at the visitor centers, Indian Cove ranger station, and Cottonwood and Black Rock Canyon campgrounds.

## BASICS

**VISITOR INFORMATION** At the **Oasis Visitor Center,** you can pick up the informative free park map and newspaper, purchase detailed rock-climbing and hiking guides, and check backcountry camping regulations. On weekends from mid-October to mid-December and mid-February to May, rangers lead nature walks and short hikes. *74485 National Park Dr., Twentynine Palms 92277, tel. 619/367–7511. Just south of Hwy. 62 at northern park boundary. Open daily 8–5.*

Smaller visitor centers are located in the northwest part of the park at **Black Rock Canyon** (4½ mi south of Hwy. 62, on Joshua Ln., tel. 619/365–9585), open most days October–May, and at **Cottonwood** (South Entrance Rd., 7 mi north of I–10, no phone), open daily 8–4. Both are subject to occasional closures due to staff shortage, so call ahead.

**FEES** Park entrance fees, good for seven days, are $5 per car or $3 for hikers, cyclists, and bus passengers.

**GENERAL STORES** The town of **Twentynine Palms** is full of small convenience stores, but you'll find the best selection of supplies in **Yucca Valley,** 23 miles east of the Oasis Visitor Center along Twentynine Palms Highway. Try the **Vons** supermarket (57590 Twentynine Palms Hwy., Yucca Valley, tel. 619/365–8998), open daily 6 AM–11 PM.

**MEDICAL AID** In an emergency, contact the 24-hour **Ranger Dispatch Center** (tel. 909/383–5651); you may call collect. Pay telephones are located at the Oasis and Black Rock Canyon visitor centers.

## COMING AND GOING

The park is 140 miles east of L.A. Take I–10 east to the Twentynine Palms Highway (Hwy. 62), which leads to the two northern entrances: The West Entrance Station, in the town of Joshua Tree; and the Oasis Visitor Center, in Twentynine Palms. The park is about an hour from Palm Springs; take I–10 to the southern entrance at Cottonwood Springs, 25 miles east of Indio. The park's main paved road—Park Boulevard—loops westward through the park from the Oasis Visitor Center to the town of Joshua Tree. A second paved road branches off from Park Boulevard and heads south to the Cottonwood Visitor Center.

The only way to get to Joshua Tree without a car is via **Morongo Basin Transit** (tel. 619/367–7433), which provides service to Twentynine Palms from Palm Springs (1½ hrs, $9 one-way) five days a week; reserve 24 hours in advance. Considering the size of the park, though, it's really difficult to get around without a car.

## WHERE TO SLEEP

The streets of Twentynine Palms are lined with a slew of forgettable motels that mostly accommodate traffic from the nearby military base. The **Sunset Motel** (73842 Twentynine Palms Hwy., 2 blocks east of Adobe Rd., tel. 619/367–3484) has nine spacious rooms starting from $35 ($10 extra for kitchenette). **El Rancho Dolores** (73352 Twentynine Palms Hwy., tel. 619/367–3528) has rooms in pleasant Spanish-style buildings from $26 weekdays, higher on weekends. Both motels has swimming pools. Neither has wheelchair access.

**CAMPING** Most of the 500 campsites in the park are free. Campgrounds have pit toilets, picnic tables, and fire pits, though you must bring your own wood and kindling. Only Cottonwood and Black Rock Canyon have flush toilets and water. The latter is also the only campground that accepts reservations; call MISTIX (tel. 800/365–2267). All others are first come, first served, so arrive well before noon during winter and spring, particularly on weekends and holidays. During summer, rangers may close some campgrounds—seek out those at higher elevations and you should have no trouble finding a space.

Backcountry camping is the best way to experience Joshua Tree's untrammeled vastness. You may pitch your tent anywhere that's at least one mile from the road, 500 feet from any trail, and a quarter mile from all water sources. Avoid making camp in the valley washes, where there

### *Dumping in the Desert*

***The world's largest solid-waste dump may soon sit only 8,000 feet from the border of Joshua Tree National Park. The desert, in its barren flatness, might seem like the ideal large-scale garbage bin, and it was probably in that spirit that the Eagle Mountain Landfill was envisioned as the final resting place for garbage from all over Southern California. The dump would receive 20,000 tons of trash each day, totaling more than eight million tons of trash over the landfill's projected 115-year life. So what's the problem? Better to dump it on a dry patch of earth than in a flower-covered meadow or the ocean, right? Maybe so, but many experts fear that the smog, noise, and blowing trash caused by this dump would mar a pristine desert environment and attract large numbers of ravens to feed on the park's already endangered tortoise population.***

is a danger of flash flooding. Check with rangers for further regulations and weather conditions. You must also register at one of 12 backcountry boards, located at trailheads throughout the park. Fires are not permitted in the backcountry.

**Black Rock Canyon.** Scattered piñon pines provide some shade and the high elevation gives relief from the heat. This campground is close to several trails, including the High View Nature Trail (*see* Short Hikes, in Exploring Joshua Tree, *below*), and fills quickly during winter and spring. To be sure of getting a spot, reserve ahead. The fee is $10 per night. *Joshua Ln., 4½ mi south of Hwy. 62. 100 sites. Drinking water, flush toilets; elev. 4,000 ft. 1 site wheelchair accessible.*

**Cottonwood.** The lowest-elevation campground in the park has unshaded sites ($8) in the open desert with views of Eagle and Hexie mountains. A moderate, 7½-mile round-trip hike leads from the camp to Lost Palms Oasis, the largest of the park's oases. *South entrance, 7 mi north of I–10. 62 sites. Drinking water, flush toilets; elev. 3,000 ft. 1 site wheelchair accessible.*

**Hidden Valley.** Legend has it that this was once a favorite hideout of cattle rustlers; nowadays, this tiny, enclosed valley is popular with rock climbers. Joshua trees and towering rock formations provide a spot of shade, and sites are free. The Barker Dam Trail (*see* Exploring Joshua Tree, *below*) begins nearby. *From Oasis Visitor Center, go 20 mi south on Park Blvd., follow signs to the 1½-mi winding road into Hidden Valley. 39 sites. Elev. 4,200 ft.*

**Jumbo Rocks.** This secluded, free campground is ideally located among the enormous granite boulders and Joshua trees of Queen Valley, at the center of the park. A short nature trail leads to the aptly named Skull Rock. *12 mi south of Oasis Visitor Center on Park Blvd. 125 sites. Elev. 4,400 ft. 1 site wheelchair accessible.*

## FOOD

The coolest place in the desert—in attitude as well as temperature—is **Jeremy's Cappuccino Bar** (61597 Twentynine Palms Hwy., near Park Dr. in Joshua Tree, tel. 619/366–9799), open daily 6 AM–midnight. Vegetarian and other sandwiches on pita bread go for about $4.50; for breakfast, try the bagel with hummus ($2.50). When MTV isn't issuing from the ancient television above the counter, musicians (some with gold and platinum albums) drop by to play rock, blues, ska, reggae, or classical music. For breakfast and burgers, stop by **Andrea's Charbroiled Burgers** (73780 Twentynine Palms Hwy., near Adobe Rd., tel. 619/367–2008), open daily 6 AM –10 PM, which serves buffalo burgers and three-egg omelets for less than $4. It may be too expensive to stay at the **Twentynine Palms Inn** (73950 Inn Ave., Twentynine Palms, tel. 619/367–3505), but it's an excellent place to dine. Lunch items, including the black-bean tostada ($5), feature healthy ingredients. Dinner can be pricey, with entrées running about $9–$13. To reach the inn, follow signs south from Highway 62 at National Park Drive.

## EXPLORING JOSHUA TREE

Hikers, rock climbers, and a hardy band of mountain bikers are big fans of the park. If you only have a few hours or for some reason are loath to leave the confines of your car, traverse Park Boulevard (about 34 mi total) for a scenic overview. Informative exhibits explain the sights at frequent roadside pullouts.

**HIKING** Five palm oases lie within the park. To reach the manmade one at **Cottonwood Springs,** drive to the parking lot 1 mile east of the Cottonwood Visitor Center. More secluded is the **Lost Palms** oasis, the park's largest group of fan palms. A moderate to strenuous 7½-mile round-trip hike to this lovely spot begins from Cottonwood Campground.

➢ **SHORT HIKES** • The park has two wheelchair-accessible trails: The half-mile **Oasis of Mara** loop at the Oasis Visitor Center, and **Cap Rock,** a ½-mile loop beginning southeast of Hidden Valley Campground at Keys View Road. The 1.1-mile **Barker Dam Trail Loop** leads to a turn-of-the-century reservoir at the Wonderland of Rocks (*see* Scenic Drives and Views, *below*). Migrating birds liven the scene in the spring and fall, but the reservoir's not much to look at during summer—unless you're interested in mud. The return portion passes Native American petroglyphs; if you think they look odd, it's because they were recently painted over by a film crew for *The Doors* movie who didn't think they looked exciting enough to inspire Jim Morrison's spiritual visions. To reach the trailhead, follow the dirt road from Hidden Valley Campground approximately 1 mile.

The painless, quarter-mile **Cholla Cactus Garden** nature trail is ideal for a leisurely desert stroll. Be sure to wear thick-soled shoes: The barbed spines of the *bigelow cholla* almost reach out and grab you. Grab a brochure about the area at the trailhead, 20 miles north of the Cottonwood Visitor Center off the main park road. You get excellent views at the midpoint of the **High View Nature Trail,** near Summit Peak (4,500 ft). The trail starts at the South Park parking area, just northwest of Black Rock Canyon Campground; the trail is moderately steep, but at 1.3 miles, it's not too taxing. A brochure about the plant life and views along the trail is available at the Black Rock Canyon Visitor Center.

*Prior to becoming a protected preserve, the Joshua Tree area was mined for gold and ore. You'll notice abandoned structures like the Lost Horse Mine along hiking trails and unpaved roads—don't attempt to rappel down into them, as one overzealous climber did.*

➢ **LONGER HIKES** • The ruins of one of the park's most successful gold mines can be seen at the end of the **Lost Horse Mine Trail.** The site was abandoned in 1936, 11 years after the owner was found—dead, mummified, and clutching a single piece of bacon. The 4-mile round-trip is only moderately strenuous, so you won't suffer the same fate as the former owner. If you continue an additional quarter-mile beyond the mine, you'll reach the summit of **Lost Horse Mountain** (5,278 ft). The hike begins at the parking area 1.2 miles east of Keys View Road.

The strenuous but rewarding hike up **Ryan Mountain** is a three-mile, three-hour haul with a total elevation gain of about 1,000 feet. Once you're at the summit, you can sit back and enjoy 360° views of Lost Horse, Queen, and Pleasant valleys. Start the trail at the Ryan Mountain parking area or slightly farther east at Sheep Pass Campground. The three-mile hike to **Mastodon Peak,** which begins at Cottonwood Springs Oasis or Cottonwood Campground, is easier than the one up Ryan Mountain and provides similar stunning views. In the distance, look for the Salton Sea, a vast, salty inland lake with a maximum depth of 12 feet.

**SCENIC DRIVES AND VIEWS** **Keys View.** As long as the L.A. smog doesn't choke the sky, you can see clear to Mexico (Signal Mountain, to be specific) from here. Below, you'll notice topographic proof of the writhings of the San Andreas Fault. To reach the viewpoint from Quail Spring Road, go south on Keys View Road to the parking lot.

*If your interest in rock-climbing is that of an acrophobe, the area around Hidden Valley Campground (see Camping, above) is a good spot to watch experts leverage their bodies up the sheer rock faces.*

**Wonderland of Rocks.** Weird stone massifs abound inside the park, but the most impressive collection of giant granite boulders lies to the north, covering roughly 20 square miles between the Indian Cove and Hidden Valley campgrounds. It's a mazelike jumble of caves and boulder piles, with a resident population of bighorn sheep. Off-trail exploring without a compass and topographic map is foolhardy; instead, take a walk along the Barker Dam Trail (*see* Hiking, *above*).

**PARK ACTIVITIES** During cooler months, mountain biking is popular, but you'll need to bring your own bike; rentals are not available in the park. Bikes are restricted to paved or unpaved roads and may not be taken on trails or ridden cross-country through the desert. The 13-mile dirt road in **Covington Flats** passes some of the park's largest Joshua trees. For magnificent views, continue 3.8 miles beyond the Lower Covington Flats picnic area along a steep path to get to **Eureka Peak.** To reach Lower Covington Flats from Highway 62 in Yucca Valley, follow Yucca Trail Road to La Contenta Road. The self-guided **Geology Tour Road** passes through a variety of remarkable desert terrain. Descriptive pamphlets are available at the trailhead for the 18-mile round-trip on a sandy, occasionally bumpy track. Look for the road marker on the south side of Park Boulevard, 2 miles west of Jumbo Rocks Campground.

Joshua Tree is one of the world's most popular rock-climbing destinations, with hundreds of evocatively named climbs (Up Chuck, Bloody Knuckles, Heart of Darkness), and the highest density of established routes anywhere—more than 3,500. The **Saddle Rocks** formation at Ryan Mountain (*see* Hiking, *above*) has some of the longest climbs, and **Astro Dome** in the Wonderland of Rocks (*see* Scenic Drives and Views, *above*) contains some of the most extreme terrain. These and other established routes are serious endeavors, suitable only for climbers with proper equipment and training. Climbing virgins should find a gently sloping giant boulder on which to engage in a bit of innocuous "scrambling" or take a class: **Wilderness Connections** (tel. 619/366–4745) in Joshua Tree offers a two-day introductory rock climbing class for $150.

# Anza-Borrego Desert State Park

**About 90 miles east of San** Diego and 70 miles southwest from Palm Springs lie the 660,000 acres of desert that make up the largest and perhaps most rewarding state park in the United States. At first glance, the terrain could be mistaken for a barren moonscape with scraggly, pasted-on brush—until you catch sight of a nimble-footed bighorn grazing on a mountain slope, a jackrabbit nibbling scrub at the foot of your tent, or a hummingbird going about its business in the shade of a palm oasis. The dozens of plant species seem almost indistinguishable until wildflower season in spring (usually from March to mid-April), when multicolored blooms literally carpet the desert floor. Viewing the spring blossoms is one of the most popular activities in the park. For info on the peak blooming period, call or send a stamped, self-addressed postcard to **Wildflowers** (Box 299, Borrego Springs 92004, tel. 619/767–4684). High temperatures (100° plus) make it tough to enjoy the park in summer, but during the rest of the year this is a popular destination for hikers, fearless four-wheel-drive explorers of the unpaved roads, and, to a lesser degree, mountain bikers.

## BASICS

**VISITOR INFORMATION** Obtain detailed maps, self-guided trail brochures, and a schedule of park activities at the **Anza-Borrego Visitor Center** (tel. 619/767–4205 or 619/767–5311), 2 miles west of Highway S3 off Highway S22. Rangers post updates on the condition of unpaved roads here daily. The center is open October to May, daily 9–5; in summer, weekends and holidays 9–5.

**FEES** The day-use fee for Anza-Borrego State Park is $5 per vehicle, collected only if you use one of the developed campgrounds where all facilities, including potable water, are located.

## COMING AND GOING

*Sharpen your wit at the annual Peg Leg Liar's Contest, held at dusk on the Saturday nearest April 1 at the Peg Leg Monument, east of Borrego Springs.*

The town of **Borrego Springs** lies at the center of Anza-Borrego on Highway S22, which bisects the park. Borrego Springs and Highway S22 are accessible from Palm Springs via Highway 86, which skirts the brown, malodorous Salton Sea. From San Diego, take Highway S22 east from Highway 79 or catch a ride on the **Northeast Rural Bus System** (tel. 619/765–0145). Fares run about $3; service is infrequent and some stops require prior registration, so be sure to call at least 24 hours in advance. You need a healthy car (four-wheel drive very strongly advised), since almost all attractions require some travel on graded dirt roads. Throughout the year, the state of the park's unpaved roads varies widely due to washouts and erosion, and during the bighorn sheep summer mating season some unpaved roads are closed altogether; check road conditions at the visitor center (*see* Basics, *above*).

## WHERE TO SLEEP

You'll find a few reasonably priced inns in Borrego Springs; most are booked several weeks in advance during the spring. The **Whispering Sands** (2376 Borrego Springs Rd., tel. 619/767–3322), a quarter mile north of Highway S22, has eight cramped but clean rooms. The atmosphere consists of limp lace curtains, cutesy names on the doors, and bad landscape paintings. Rates are $35 in summer, $45 the rest of the year. At the **Oasis Motel** (366 W. Palm Canyon Dr., tel. 619/767–5409), clean rooms with ceiling fans and photos of wildflowers on the wall start at $35 during summer and $55 at other times. Both motels have pools.

**CAMPING** The best way to explore this vast park is by camping, either in open terrain or at one of the handful of primitive sites. If you prefer to set up camp at an established campground, head for **Borrego Palm Canyon,** one mile north of the visitor center, or **Tamarisk Grove,** near the intersection of Highways 78 and S3. These campgrounds are wheelchair accessible and have flush toilets, showers, water, and fire rings. Rates for both are $14 per night during peak season, $10 during summer. Tamarisk has 27 sites set among shady trees, while Borrego Palm Canyon offers 65 tent sites and 52 RV hook-ups in open desert.

You can pitch your tent almost anywhere in the park for free, as long as you remain at least one car length away from roads, trails, flood-prone washes, water sources, and developed campgrounds; also take care not to destroy native plants. Before you go, check weather conditions and regulations with a ranger and be sure to register on the backcountry board at the visitor center (*see above*). The **Mountain Palm Springs** area, in the south part of the park off Highway S2, makes an excellent overnight destination: It's a pleasant, uncrowded oasis with 54 primitive sites where camping is free. In the sweltering summer months, check out the 10 free campsites in **Culp Valley,** west of Borrego Springs on S22; the 3,400-foot elevation may offer some respite from the painful intensity of the sun.

## FOOD

Eating in Borrego Springs will not be your primary fond memory of the desert, but you can at least find a passable and cheap meal here. In the shopping mall west of Christmas Circle on Highway S22, **Kendall's Café** (528 The Mall, at Palm Canyon Dr., tel. 619/767–3491) serves hearty Mexican and American fare for less than $10 daily 6 AM–8 PM (Wed. until 2 PM). The local favorite is the tasty, low-fat buffalo burger ($4.75)—yup, it's made from ground-up bison buttocks. At the same location, **Chefs For You** (551 The Mall, tel. 619/767–3522), open Sunday–Thursday 5 AM–6 PM and Friday–Saturday 10–8, is a delicatessen that has pizzas (vegetarian $10.75), hot and cold sandwiches ($3–$5), doughnuts (45¢), and other breakfast delights (85¢–$1.75). Both restaurants are wheelchair accessible.

## EXPLORING ANZA-BORREGO

You'll see some rare 10-foot trees with swollen branches on the **Elephant Tree Discovery Trail,** south of Highway 78 on Split Mountain Road. The one-mile loop makes for a short and easy hike. To glimpse your first palm oasis and, if you're lucky, bighorn sheep, take the three-mile round-trip **Borrego Palm Canyon Nature Trail,** which begins at the Borrego Palm campground. More experienced backpackers will enjoy the miles of trail-less canyons and ridges at **Bow Willow Creek** and **Mountain Palm Springs,** both located in the southern sector of the park off Highway S2. Off-trail exploration offers the possibility of discovering unmapped Native American petroglyphs and completely isolated oases; rangers at the visitor center can help you plan your trip.

Though many of the park's unpaved roads are too sandy for cyclists, mountain bikers might try exploring **Indian Gorge,** which branches west of Highway S2 about 25 miles south of its intersection with Highway 78. The canyon road extends for several miles, but the curious should look for a side canyon 2 miles in and to the north, where a group of elephant trees was recently found.

**SCENIC DRIVES AND VIEWS** For breathtaking views of the Borrego Valley and the Borrego Badlands, stop at **Font's Point,** just east of Borrego Springs on a four-mile dirt road south of Highway S22. Nearby is a self-guided auto tour known as **Erosion Road,** which offers views of the corroded landscape along an active fault that runs from 240 feet below sea level to the 8,700-foot Toro Peak. In **Blair Valley,** you can see prehistoric Native American pictographs in red and yellow hues at the end of a four-mile dirt road off Highway S2 (south of Highway 78).

# LAS VEGAS AND THE GRAND CANYON 13

By Laura Burgardt and Ray Klinke

**Almost everyone reacts the same way at the first sight of Las Vegas. Shimmering** in the distance—even during the day—the city grows brighter as you approach, eventually turning into street after street of flashing electric lights and frantic commotion. Instantly, you're like a 14-year-old, moved at once by innocent awe and lustful hormones. You may think it's kitschy, you may think it's sleazy, you may think it's corrupt—but suddenly you feel lucky. Standing at a roulette wheel in one of the more than 50 casinos, you may find yourself between a fresh-faced bride whose dress still sports a 7-foot train, and a boneheaded drunk in a pin-striped suit jacket and gym shorts. The booze is flowing, and if you feel a bit bewildered, the casinos have done their job. Some people grow to cherish their Las Vegas experience; others depart in disgust, never to return. If you lose all your money, you can always throw yourself into the Grand Canyon, 300 miles to the east. Most of the annual five million visitors, though, are content to babble in amazement from the rim of what is surely one of the country's most deservedly famous attractions, with its stunning views, countless buttes and pillars, and seemingly bottomless chasms.

# Las Vegas

**They call themselves professional gamblers**, honeymooners, cultural critics, or plain old tourists. In whatever guise, more than 28 million people visit Nevada's biggest city each year, making Las Vegas one of the top tourist attractions in the world. Apparently not content with having nine of the ten largest hotels on the planet, Las Vegas continues to develop at a dizzying pace. The latest trend is toward family-oriented entertainment—the mega-resorts all have kid-sized attractions, and magic shows are proliferating on the Strip. But if the casinos are catering to kids and non-gambling spouses, it's only to get someone in the family to empty his or her wallet into a slot machine. Gambling so permeates Nevada culture that you can play slot machines almost anywhere, including the airport, most restaurants, and even supermarkets. Gambling pays for the neon signs on Fremont Street and the lavish hotels on Las Vegas Boulevard, and allows the state of Nevada not to impose any personal, business, or corporate income taxes on its residents.

*Vegas breeds strange attitudes toward money. Minutes after you add a $5 chip to your blackjack wager because you "feel good" about the cut of the deck, you'll pass up a $5 buffet because it's too expensive.*

You need not be discouraged, though, by the statistic that casinos keep about 70¢ of every dollar wagered in a machine and about 30¢ of every dollar risked at the tables. If you accept at

# Las Vegas

Bonanza Rd.
95
N. Highland Dr.
Downtown Transportation Center
Squire's Park
Gragson Hwy.
Union Station
Stewart Ave.
Greyhound Bus Station
Main St.
E. Fremont St.
Rancho Dr.
Alta Dr.
Discovery Dr.
DOWNTOWN
Carson St.
Bonneville Ave.
TO RED ROCK CANYON
Charleston Blvd.
Circle Park
Las Vegas Blvd.
Oakey Blvd.
Industrial Rd.
St. Louis Ave.
15
Sahara Ave.
604
Karen Ave.
Circus Circus La.
Riviera Blvd.
Las Vegas Country Club
Maryland Pkwy.
Convention Center Dr.
THE STRIP
Stardust Rd.
Paradise Rd.
Desert Inn Rd.
Sierra Vista Dr.
Spring Mountain Rd.
Twain Ave.
Sands Ave.
Swenson St.
Cambridge St.
Algonquin Dr.
605
Flamingo Rd.
Koval La.
Harmon Ave.
University of Nevada Las Vegas
Tropicana Ave.
Reno Ave.
McCarran International Airport
Hacienda Ave.
N

**KEY**

Tourist Information

0 1 mile
0 1 km

**Sights ●**

Cashman Field, **7**
Graceland Wedding Chapel, **8**
Imperial Palace Auto Cellection, **20**
Liberace Museum, **29**
Little White Chapel, **10**
Virtual World, **17**

**Lodging ○**

Las Vegas Independent Hostel, **9**
Sunbird Inn, **31**

**Hotel-Casinos ●**

Aladdin, **23**
Binion's Horseshoe, **4**
Caesars Palace, **22**
Circus Circus, **13**
Excalibur, **27**
Flamingo Hilton, **21**
Golden Nugget, **5**
Gold Spike, **6**
Hacienda, **30**
Hard Rock, **24**
Las Vegas Club, **3**
Las Vegas Hilton, **15**
Luxor, **28**
MGM Grand, **25**
Mirage, **19**
Jackie Gaugan's Plaza, **2**
Riviera, **14**
Sahara, **12**
Santa Fe, **1**
Stardust, **16**
Stratosphere 2000, **11**
Treasure Island, **18**
Tropicana, **26**

the outset that you'll probably lose any money you convert into chips, you can have a great time here. You can even make your trip a relatively inexpensive one by taking advantage of cheap rooms, free drinks while you play, and all-you-can-eat buffets offered by casinos eager to attract your gaming dollars.

Beyond the vagaries of the gaming tables, Las Vegas remains an unparalleled cultural spectacle, a city of profound paradoxes. This town, where marriages and divorces are a snap, liquor flows all night long, legal bordellos are nearby, and "anything goes," is also the paragon of control and surveillance—security mirrors abound in every casino, and both gamblers and dealers are monitored night and day. Once dominated by mobsters and still associated with the shady side of American life, Vegas nonetheless hosts countless sales conventions and national gatherings of Elks and Rotarians.

If you tear yourself away from the Strip and downtown, you'll notice a sprawling metropolitan area of about one million people, many of whom have only minimal direct contact with the gaming industry. For many, this is a city characterized by shopping malls and about 300 days of clear, sunny skies every year. Las Vegas is also home to the University of Nevada at Las Vegas, whose high-profile basketball team, the Runnin' Rebels, usually plays to capacity crowds at the Thomas and Mack Center. Yet over in the casinos, their games hardly count: State law prohibits wagering on Nevada teams. In keeping with their name, the Rebels were, until recently, an outlaw team; former coach Jerry "Tark the Shark" Tarkanian fought a long battle with the NCAA over allegations of recruiting violations. At one point in the investigation, the university was embarrassed by the release of photos of basketball players in a hot tub with a noted gambler.

Though the casinos never close, and there's really no slow season, you may want to time your visit with care. The surreal world that is Las Vegas was built in the middle of the desert, and temperatures soar well over the 100° mark during summer and rarely drop below 50° even during the coldest days of winter. Summer heat can force you into the climate-controlled casinos more than you can afford, and hotel prices double on weekends and holidays. If you're here for the bargains, don't pull into town on Friday or Saturday.

## BASICS

Many agencies in Las Vegas bill themselves as "official tourist centers," offering hotel reservations, bus tours, and show tickets. These offices are really travel agencies in disguise, making their money off commissions from casinos and motels. Still, their services don't cost you anything, and you can pick up maps, information, and a "fun" (coupon) booklet. A reliable source of info is the **Las Vegas Tourist Bureau** (5191 Las Vegas Blvd. S, tel. 800/522–9555), open daily 7 AM–11 PM. Detailed and up-to-date information on shows, buffets, and the casino scene, as well as coupons galore, can be found in publications like *What's On in Las Vegas* and *Today in Las Vegas,* available free in hotels, gift shops, tourist centers, and newspaper machines.

## COMING AND GOING

**BY PLANE** Slot machines are spread throughout **McCarran International Airport** (5757 Wayne Newton Blvd., tel. 702/261–5743), which is serviced by all major U.S. carriers. McCarran serves as a hub for **America West** (tel. 800/235–9292), which offers vacation packages that include discounted hotel stays. The south end of the Strip is just a mile from the airport; head north on Paradise Road and turn left on Tropicana Avenue.

➢ **AIRPORT TRANSIT** • Apart from courtesy buses for guests of major hotels, the cheapest way to get to the casinos is on a **Citizens Area Transit (CAT)** bus (*also see* Getting Around, *below*). Bus 109 runs to downtown every 20 minutes, and Bus 108 runs on Paradise Road to the north end of the Strip. Either bus will connect you to Bus 201, which runs along Tropicana Avenue to the south end of the Strip. Private shuttles cost $3.50–$4. A cab costs a minimum of $10.

**BY CAR** Las Vegas sits along **I–15** in southern Nevada. There's a steady flow of traffic on the interstate and on the two other highways that serve the city, **U.S. 93** and **U.S. 95,** which merge near downtown. From Los Angeles (293 mi), take I–10 east and pick up I–15 north near Ontario. From San Francisco (570 mi), take I–580 east to I–5 south, pick up Highway 58 at Buttonwillow, and follow it east through Bakersfield and over to Barstow and I–15.

**BY BUS** Buses heading to destinations throughout the United States leave from the **Greyhound Bus Station** (200 S. Main St., tel. 702/384–8009 or 800/231–2222 for reservations). Lockers are available for a small price. Buses run to and from Los Angeles (5–7½ hrs, $69 round-trip) and San Francisco (16 hrs, $99 round-trip) several times daily.

**BY TRAIN** **Amtrak** (tel. 800/872–7245) serves **Union Station** downtown (1 Main St., behind Jackie Gaughan's Plaza, tel. 702/386–6896); the station is open 6 AM–7:30 PM. Passengers can check luggage at the station for $1.50 per 24 hours. Trains head west to Los Angeles every morning, and trains from Los Angeles to Salt Lake City, Denver, and Chicago pass through Las Vegas in the early evening. Round-trip fares from L.A. start at $70 (advance purchase) and the trip lasts 7½ hours. There is no direct service to Las Vegas from San Francisco, but with a connecting bus in Bakersfield, you can get there for $124 round-trip (more than 12 hrs each way).

## GETTING AROUND

Most of the action is concentrated in two parts of town: The Strip (a 3-mile stretch of Las Vegas Boulevard South) and downtown (near the bus and train stations). Downtown is easily navigated on foot; it's served by U.S. 95/93 (take the Casino Center exit). Distances between casinos can be considerable on the congested Strip, which is accessible from four well-marked exits off I–15. If you're headed more than a few blocks north–south, try one of the parallel thoroughfares, such as Paradise Road (east of the Strip), Industrial Road, or the interstate (west of the Strip). The major east–west streets are named for the big hotels they pass when they hit the Strip. Parking at most casinos is plentiful and free. As you move about the city, be extra vigilant at night—especially around Fremont Street and the less populated blocks of the Strip, where even the bus stop signs warn of pickpockets.

**BY BUS** **CAT** (tel. 702/228–7433) runs buses from 5:30 AM to 1:30 AM, with 24-hour service between downtown and the Strip. Normal fares are $1, but you pay $1.50 to travel along the Strip (transfers are free). All buses are wheelchair accessible. Most routes originate from

### *The Road to Riches*

***It seems fitting that the largest U.S. city founded in this century is Las Vegas. When the Nevada legislature legalized gambling in 1931, ostensibly to finance school construction, the town was merely a 7-block-long railroad stop. But mobster Bugsy Siegel had a dream. In 1946, Siegel and his partners opened the first hotel casino on the Strip, the Fabulous Flamingo. Vegas soon became the preferred getaway for Hollywood's elite—the 1951 debut of Frank Sinatra, followed by the rest of the Rat Pack (including Dean Martin and Sammy Davis, Jr.), helped make Vegas the "Entertainment Capital of the World." Since then, Vegas has been a mecca for every sort of swingin' entertainment, ranging from sophisticated British songwriter Noel Coward in the 1950s to the Grateful Dead and Bob Dylan in the 1990s. Sadly, Bugsy never lived to see modern-day Las Vegas, an oasis of unrestrained glamour, architectural marvels, and relentless kitsch. Within a few months of his hotel's grand opening, Bugsy was rubbed out by his associates, a fitting end for the creator of a place where dreams come true—and then come back to haunt you.***

the **Downtown Transportation Center** (300 N. Casino Center Blvd., at Stewart Ave.), which is within walking distance of all the downtown hotel-casinos. Bus 301 (every 10 min) serves the Strip from the downtown station.

## WHERE TO SLEEP

During the week, budget rooms are easy to find in fancy hotels, chain motels, and at the hostel. Plan ahead if you're arriving on a weekend, or you may face high prices and a round of neon NO VACANCY signs. If you're in a bind, call **Room Reservations** (tel. 800/332–5333), which provides last-minute availability information for hotels around town. The price categories below refer to weekday rates; on weekends, you'll generally pay double. Rates are lowest in mid-December and early August. Because room rates are so fluid, it's a good idea to ask about special promotions or discounts when making a reservation.

You'll find many of the best deals at the giant hotel-casinos, where rates are kept low to attract vacationing gamblers. These places have comfortable rooms and sometimes offer special promotions, contingent upon a specific number of hours spent at the tables or on the slots; do the math first, though, since you can sometimes end up staking more cash than you save on the hotel room.

➢ **UNDER $35** • **Hacienda.** The rooms at this large Spanish-style hotel-casino are nothing special, but they are clean and comfy—and there's a nice outdoor pool. The hotel, located just south of the Luxor, has a more relaxed ambiance than some of the more centrally located places, and the rates are quite low (most singles and doubles go for around $30 during the week, $60 on weekends). *3950 Las Vegas Blvd. S, tel. 702/739–8911 or 800/634–6713. Laundry. Wheelchair access.*

**Jackie Gaughan's Plaza.** At Jackie Gaughan's (formerly known as the Union Plaza), the rooms are slightly older and less fancy than the imposing edifice might suggest, but spacious singles and doubles run $30 on weekdays most of the year, there's a pool, and the location is great. The hotel is next door to the bus and train stations and is only a couple of blocks from all the downtown casinos. Reserve ahead, and prepare for crowds and lines. *1 Main St., tel. 702/386–2110 or 800/634–6575. Wheelchair access.*

➢ **UNDER $45** • **Binion's Horseshoe.** This Western-style hotel-casino was built in 1931 and was bought by a Texan named Binion in 1947. Doubles in the east wing run $28–$35; newer rooms start at $40 on weekdays. The adjoining Binion's Horseshoe Coffee Shop (*see* Food, *below*) offers a cheap Late-Night Steak Dinner. *128 E. Fremont St., tel. 702/382–1600 or 800/622–6468. Wheelchair access.*

➢ **UNDER $50** • **Aladdin.** This 1,100-room hotel is the site of one of the major events in American history—Elvis married Priscilla here in 1967. The hotel has aged somewhat since then, but it is situated between the major concentrations of casinos on the Strip, it has two large pools to help guests beat the heat, and its Arabian theme is thankfully less than pervasive. Doubles start at $35 during the week and $45 on the weekend most of the year. *3667 Las Vegas Blvd. S, tel. 702/736–0111 or 800/634–3424. Wheelchair access.*

**Circus Circus.** In *Fear and Loathing in Las Vegas,* Hunter S. Thompson took massive doses of psychedelics to help him get through his stay at Circus Circus. With abundant weirdness that includes acrobats swinging on trapezes high above hordes of weekend visitors, you can go drug free and still feel as if you're hallucinating. Everything about the place is immense, including the number of rooms—nearly 3,000. Room rates sink as low as $25 per night (single or double) for a week or two during December, but are generally in the $30–$40 range on weekdays and as much as $90 on weekends. *2880 Las Vegas Blvd. S, tel. 702/743–0410 or 800/634–3450. Laundry, pool. Wheelchair access.*

**Sunbird Inn.** For a break from the mega-hotels, try this family-run place; rates vary wildly, but the lowest rates are real bargains: Recently remodeled rooms start at $35 ($65 on weekends). There's an English-style pub next door, with 15 draft beers. *3969 Las Vegas Blvd. S, tel. 702/739–1915.*

➢ **UNDER $65** • **Excalibur.** This enormous 4,032-room Arthurian castle is the supreme middle-class family resort. The medieval motif is hammered home endlessly, from lavish dinner shows to a Canterbury wedding chapel and regularly scheduled jousting tournaments. The rooms are more polished and modern than those at Circus Circus, and the rates are higher ($39–$59 for a double on weekdays, $74–$84 on weekends). *3850 Las Vegas Blvd. S, tel. 702/597–7700 or 800/937–7777. Wheelchair access.*

**HOSTEL** **Las Vegas Independent Hostel.** This popular and well-managed hostel draws a refreshingly international crowd of backpackers and young travelers. You need an AYH card or a student ID to stay here, a condition that keeps these inexpensive accommodations from being completely booked. The hostel also offers a popular three-day tour of Grand, Bryce, and Zion canyons (*see* Near the Grand Canyon, *below*) for $125. Beds go for $9; a private room for two is $21; this includes free lemonade, coffee, and tea. *1208 Las Vegas Blvd. S, tel. 702/385–9955. No curfew, no lockout. Reception open 7 AM–11 PM, checkout 10 AM. Key deposit ($5), kitchen, laundry.*

**CAMPING** If you prefer starlight to the refracted neon glow of Strip, drive to the **Toiyabe National Forest,** where you can camp for free anywhere that's more than 100 feet from an improved road. There are designated campsites with fire pits and tables, but they cost $8. Better just to drop by the ranger station (Hwy. 157, tel. 702/872–5486; open May–Sept.), for info on good free sites and fire regulations. Contact the Las Vegas office of the Toiyabe National Forest (2881 S. Valley View Blvd., Suite 16, tel. 702/873–8800) for conditions during the winter months, and for general camping and hiking info. To reach the forest, take U.S. 95 about 18 miles north and pick up Highway 157 west toward Mt. Charleston and Kyle Canyon. After 17 miles, you'll see the ranger station.

## FOOD

For many, Vegas dining is synonymous with the all-you-can-eat buffet, a perverse combination of thrift and conspicuous consumption. It's tempting to dismiss buffets as greasy, heartburn-inducing gimmicks, but many buffets offer a mind-boggling range of items, and the quality may pleasantly surprise you. You can also find great savings in the casinos' cocktail lounges, snack bars, and regular restaurants (the ones that actually dare to restrict your portions).

**CASINO BUFFETS AND DINNER SPECIALS** Most major casinos offer some sort of buffet, which draw long lines of tourists. **Circus Circus** (*see* Where To Sleep, *above*) is renowned for the cheapest buffets ($3–$5) and lines that resemble those at Disneyland. Unless you really want to save a few bucks, you'll probably prefer **Rio Suite** (3700 W. Flamingo Rd., tel. 702/252–7777) or **Palace Station** (2411 W. Sahara Ave., tel. 702/367–2411), two newer casinos just west of the Strip, which offer better quality, a bigger selection, and less waiting time.

### Gamblers' Guru

***In Vegas, almost everyone you meet will claim to know how to take the casinos for a ride. If you're having trouble wading through all the claims, an excellent resource is Anthony Curtis's "Las Vegas Advisor," a thin monthly newsletter ($5) that lists the best deals on everything from seafood buffets to slot tournaments to airport transportation. Curtis is not a travel agent or casino P.R. man; he's a young gambling enthusiast who has extended the gospel of beating the system beyond card-counting to the entire spectrum of Vegas attractions. If you're trying to get by in Las Vegas on a small bankroll, this is your bible. Copies of the Advisor can be purchased by phone or picked up at Curtis's office (5280 S. Valley View Blvd., Suite B, tel. 702/597–1884), open weekdays 9–5.***

➢ **UNDER $5** • **Binion's Horseshoe Coffee Shop—Late-Night Steak Dinner.** Even if you're not staying at the adjoining Western-style hotel-casino (*see* Where to Sleep, *above*), this is *the* big bargain in a town of big bargains. Hostelers and baccarat players alike head downtown nightly for the $3 meal, which features a tasty 10-ounce steak, salad, a large baked potato, and rolls. Beverages are extra. *128 E. Fremont St., tel. 702/382–1600. Served nightly 10 PM–5:45 AM.*

➢ **UNDER $10** • **Flamingo Buffet.** As long as a few days in town haven't convinced you that $9 is too much to spend on a meal, you'll find the fresh fruit and vegetables at this quiet gourmet salad bar a welcome break from the heavier fare at most buffets. You'll also find smoked fish, marinated chicken breast, hearts of palm, and a variety of other delicacies intended to put you in the mood to lose some serious coin. *3555 Las Vegas Blvd. S, tel. 702/733–3111. Open daily 4:30 PM–10 PM.*

**Golden Nugget.** Turkey breast for turkey breast, this is probably the best all-around buffet in town. You can't go wrong with the delicious roasted vegetables, the huge salad bar, the dynamite pork chops, and some of the yummiest desserts in Nevada, though the price ($5.25 breakfast, $7.50 lunch, $9.50 dinner) is about double what you'd pay at Circus Circus or other cheap joints. *129 E. Fremont St., downtown, tel. 702/385–7111. Open daily 7–3 and 4–10.*

**Santa Fe.** A good 12 miles north of the crowds and hubbub, this hard-to-miss hotel-casino serves an $8 Sunday brunch that is one of the area's hidden treasures. While most buffets offer a limited palate of meat options, here you can chow down on unlimited quantities of lox and smoked whitefish. The desserts are tremendous, with a mind-boggling array of choices. To top it off, you get a steady flow of champagne. They also have a regular buffet throughout the week. *4949 N. Rancho Dr., tel. 702/658–4900. U.S. 95 north to northern end of Rancho Dr. business loop. Open Mon.–Sat. 7:30–10:30, 11:30–2:30, and 4–9, Sun. 7:30–2:30.*

**RESTAURANTS** Though nowhere near as cheap as the buffets, non-casino eateries are a good way to avoid the gaming tables for a while. Vegetarians can take cover at **Rainbow's End Natural Foods** (1100 E. Sahara Ave., near S. Maryland Pkwy., tel. 702/737–7282), a health-food store that also serves sandwiches, salads, and hot dishes in the $3–$6 range. The restaurant is open daily 9–9 (Sunday 11–6); the deli has shorter hours. For a sit-down meal, visit **Battista's Hole in the Wall** (4041 Audrie Ln., at Flamingo Rd., tel. 702/732–1424), where Italian dinners (from $14) come with all the house wine you can drink; the restaurant is open daily 4:30–10:30 (Fri.–Sat. until 11).

**CAFES** If you're overdosing on the garish and cheesy, Las Vegas has a couple of good cafés that offer some tranquillity. Only a short walk from the hostel, **Enigma Garden Café** (918½ S. 4th St., 1 block north of Charleston Blvd., tel. 702/386–0999) is a neighborly place that showcases local artists and hosts live music on an outdoor patio; they also serve nourishing eats in the $3–$5 range. Across from the University of Nevada at Las Vegas campus, **Café Copioh** (4550 S. Maryland Pkwy., Suite 17, tel. 702/739–0305) attracts local intellectuals who find the plush seating conducive to their literary pursuits. Fruit smoothies ($3.25) and mocha slushes ($3.50) are refreshing drink choices to combat the desert heat.

## WORTH SEEING

**CASINOS** Las Vegas casinos may seem disorienting to the first-time visitor: The walls are mirrored, bright lights shine from the ceilings, coins clang everywhere, time and direction are confused, and the exits seem hard to locate. Part of the intended effect is to sap your will to gawk and stroll and encourage you to make yourself comfortable at a table or machine. Vegas hotel-casinos, which get more ridiculous and extravagant each year, remain the focus of tourist interest even among non-gamblers, and you inevitably have to walk across the casino floor to get to any of the indoor attractions.

No trip to Las Vegas would be complete without spending a couple of hours at these cultural shrines. The newest, most dramatic addition to the Vegas skyline is the needle-shaped observation tower of the **Stratosphere Hotel and Casino** (2000 Las Vegas Blvd. S, tel.

*The MGM Grand (3799 Las Vegas Blvd. S, tel. 702/891–1111), the largest resort hotel-casino in the world, boasts 5,005 rooms and encompasses 112 acres, including its own 33-acre amusement park.*

702/382–4446), rising 135 stories above the north end of the Strip. Daring souls can ride the Space Shot, launching themselves up the tower at dizzying speed, or race around the outside of the tower on an elevated roller coaster 100 stories above the ground. The south end of the Strip is dominated by the upper-class **Luxor** (3900 Las Vegas Blvd. S, tel. 800/627–6667), a 30-story bronze pyramid fronted by a 10-story replica of the Sphinx.

Another newcomer is the **Hard Rock Hotel** (4455 Paradise Rd., tel. 702/693–5000), luring a younger crowd with loud music, Sex Pistols slot machines, and music memorabilia. A portion of the proceeds from some of the slots go to help preserve the rain forests. Beginning late 1996, you can beam aboard *Star Trek: The Experience* at the **Las Vegas Hilton** (3000 Paradise Rd., tel. 702/732–5111); the attraction is said to include interactive voyages with the Starfleet, virtual reality games, and a Cardassian restaurant and lounge.

"Cultural mainstays" may be the wrong phrase, but the more established casinos on the Strip include **Caesars Palace** (3570 Las Vegas Blvd. S, tel. 702/731–7110), Las Vegas's preeminent theme casino replete with Greco-Roman statuary, Centurion doormen, fountains, and the upscale Forum Shops. The opulent **Mirage** (3400 Las Vegas Blvd. S, tel. 800/627–6667) features a 60-foot rain-forest atrium, habitually amorous white tigers, and an outdoor volcano that erupts every 15 minutes after dark.

*A number of years ago, a man walked into Binion's Horseshoe Club with $770,000 and took it to a $1 craps table. He bet the whole stash at even money, won, and walked away. Several years later, the man returned and reenacted the scene. This time he lost, then went up to his hotel room and shot himself in the head.*

While the Strip is home to the glitziest hotels and big-name entertainment, downtown has a sadder, more Western ambiance. Walking down the outrageously illuminated Fremont Street, between the neon cowboy of the Pioneer and showgirl of the Glitter Gulch, you're more likely to catch yourself humming Tom Waits than Frank Sinatra. In an effort to compete with the affluence of the Strip, the major downtown casinos recently unveiled the **Fremont Street Experience,** which includes a space frame arching 90 feet above the pedestrian mall and stretching from Main Street to Fourth Street. In keeping with the traditional aesthetics of Glitter Gulch, this "experience" features a multisensory light show, complete with two million lights. The fanciest hotel downtown is the **Golden Nugget** (129 E. Fremont St., tel. 702/385–7111), where you'll see a lot of the frenetic big-money gambling portrayed in the movies. When you've cashed out, you can wade through the shutter-happy tourists and stare at the world's largest gold nugget (a 63-pound chunk found in Australia), stored in a glass case near the casino.

**IMPERIAL PALACE AUTO COLLECTION** On display are more than 200 rare and exotic cars, including Elvis's '76 Cadillac, an experimental car with a Naugahyde exterior, and cars dating back to the 1880s. In a special section, you can check out cars owned by Hitler and Mussolini—take a rare glimpse into the lifestyles of the dead and fascist. Look for free-admission coupons in tourist magazines. *3535 Las Vegas Blvd. S, tel. 702/731-3311. Admission: $7. Open daily 9:30 AM–11:30 PM.*

**LIBERACE MUSEUM** Until his death in 1987, Liberace entertained legions of Las Vegas audiences with some of the purest camp ever concocted. Savage beasts were lulled by his fluid piano playing, blue-haired grandmothers were charmed by his bubbly personality, and most everybody else was moved—either to awe or mirth—by his spectacular collection of diamond-studded costumes, wacky pianos, and trademark candelabra. Look for the red, white, and blue hot pants he wore to celebrate the American bicentennial. *1775 E. Tropicana Ave., at Spencer St., tel. 702/798–5595. Admission: $6.50, $3.50 students. Open Mon.–Sat. 10–5, Sun. 1–5.*

**VIRTUAL WORLD** Technophiles and Luddites alike will enjoy the interactive battles waged on futuristic virtual worlds at this cyberpark. Once briefed on your "mission," you'll enter a pod where you engage in an exciting 10-minute adventure. Afterward, assess your performance in the Explorers' Lounge, a Victorian-style parlor with ancient and futuristic battle implements on display. *3053 Las Vegas Blvd. S, tel. 702/369-3583. Admission: $7 weekdays before 5 PM, $8 Mon.–Thurs. after 5, $9 all other times; additional one-time $1 fee. Open daily 11 AM–midnight (Fri. and Sat. until 2 AM).*

**WEDDING CHAPELS** In Las Vegas, marriage is more than an institution—it's an industry. Tying the knot couldn't be easier: Under Nevada law, if you're at least 18 years old and have identification, you can obtain a license at the **Clark County Marriage License Bureau** (200 S. 3rd St., downtown, tel. 702/455–4415) for $35 (cash only). The bureau is open weekdays 8 AM–midnight, weekends 24 hours (i.e., they open 8 AM Friday morning and don't close again until midnight on Sunday). Once you've got the license, you're ready for that special wedding ceremony that only happens once (or twice or three times) in a person's life. Most chapels are open every day. Be aware that on special occasions—like Valentine's Day and New Year's Eve—lines can stretch around the block. If you're not ready for a lifelong commitment, there's no harm in merely sitting through a ceremony or two—just ask. The price of a wedding depends on its extravagance ($50 and up). At the **Graceland Wedding Chapel** (619 Las Vegas Blvd. S, near Charleston Ave., tel. 702/474–6655), an Elvis impersonator will perform the ceremony for an extra $120 (ceremonies start at $50, plus a $30 "donation" to the ministry). Michael Jordan and Joan Collins were married (not to each other) at the **Little White Chapel** (1301 Las Vegas Blvd. S, tel. 702/382–5943), which performs drive-up ceremonies for $30.

## GAMBLING

You can have a lot of fun trying to squeeze a few bucks out of the house in Vegas if you adopt the attitude that you're buying entertainment and a very small chance at an unexpected windfall. In picking a casino, look for low table minimums that will enable you to get cheap entertainment and free alcohol for your money. You get free drinks if you're gambling; just tell the cocktail waitresses what you want when they come by (infrequently) to take your order. If you want to make friends with the server, a tip of 50¢ to $1 is customary.

Downtown, the cheap casinos are clustered within a couple of blocks of one another. At the low-key and slightly depressing **Gold Spike** (400 E. Ogden Ave., tel. 702/384–8444), penny slots and dollar blackjack tables are the norm, and you won't find yourself intimidated by impatient dealers or high-stakes players. The action at **Jackie Gaughan's Plaza** (1 S. Main St., tel. 702/386–2110) is more lively, and they have lots of low-minimum tables, including 25¢ craps, which makes it easy to learn this fast game without risking the rent money. Once you've mastered the intricacies of the game, the most liberal blackjack rules can be found at the **Las Vegas Club** (18 E. Fremont St., tel. 702/385–1664). Feel confident in your gambling abilities before heading to one of the bigger casinos, where you won't find a blackjack table with a minimum lower than $5.

On the Strip, the budget choices are even greater, though the long distances between casinos can complicate matters. If you want to stay put for awhile, the **Hacienda,** at the south end of the Strip, offers a friendly gambling environment with low minimums. Farther north, the **Stardust** is particularly attractive to sports gamblers, who can take advantage of the "Sports Handicappers' Library," a small room where every relevant statistic for the day's games is posted. For non-smokers, one consideration in selecting a casino is finding an environment you can breathe in. Several of the bigger casinos on the Strip, including the **Tropicana,** the **Flamingo Hilton,** and the **Mirage,** have nonsmoking areas for slots and blackjack.

For many visitors, the casino matters less than the game. You can get free instruction in all the Las Vegas games through daily classes offered in the major casinos, or on your TV set in many of the hotels. You might even find a sympathetic dealer who will discreetly offer tips during the slower hours. Some games offer slim shots at major payoffs (slots, roulette, big-six), while others give you better odds but no chance to win much more than you wager (blackjack, baccarat, pai gow). Some games are festive and group-oriented (craps and roulette) while others are more private (video poker). And then there's Keno, which has terrible odds but is such a passive game that you can play it while noshing at the buffet. Sports betting is an excellent value, since the games last a long time and the house edge is minimal. Blackjack (*see box, below*) remains the game of choice for most young people visiting Las Vegas. The pace of the game is fairly controlled, and with patience, preparation, and a little bit of luck, you can last a while without having to pawn any treasured belongings.

## CHEAP THRILLS

The resourceful traveler can be inexpensively entertained by taking the bait casinos use to lure and keep patrons. "Funbooks" usually feature food and drink coupons, discounts on shows, and a couple of bucks of free gaming action. The funbooks at the **Sahara** (2535 Las Vegas Blvd. S., tel. 702/737-2111) and the **Riviera** (2901 Las Vegas Blvd. S., tel. 702/734-5110) get the highest marks from the local cognoscenti.

### Blackjack Tips

***The game favors the dealer; if both you and the dealer bust (i.e., exceed 21), you lose. Still, many people do win money at blackjack, and self-proclaimed experts on the subject are everywhere. If you want to prolong your ride at the table, the following elementary rules may prove useful:***

***(1) In picking a table, consider rule variations that help the player, like the option of doubling down on any two cards, or the requirement that the dealer stand on "soft" 17 (a hand that includes an ace, which counts as 1 or 11). Even if you don't completely understand them, these rule variations can work to your advantage.***

***(2) Start with the basics: Since the dealer has to hit (take a card) on any hand 16 or lower, you'll never win with less than 17 unless the dealer busts. Take a hit on any hand below 17 when the dealer shows Ace, K, Q, J, 10, 9, or 8, all of which are unlikely to make the dealer bust. Stand on any hand above 11 when the dealer shows a 4, 5, or 6, cards that will cause the dealer to bust more than 40% of the time.***

***(3) When you "double down," you double your bet and get one additional card. This is the player's chief advantage, so don't ignore this option. Double with 10 against a 9 or lower and with any hand of 11. Rules permitting, double with 9, or with "soft" hands totaling 13–17 against a 4, 5, or 6.***

***(4) If you are dealt two cards of the same value, you may "split" them, doubling your bet and playing two hands. Never split 5s, 10s, or face cards. Always split 8s or 7s against a dealer's card of equal or lower value. Always split 2s or 3s against a 4, 5, or 6. Always split aces.***

***(5) Tip (or "toke") the dealers, as they are not unionized, work for lousy wages, and depend upon your generosity. Unless you're winning serious stakes, a dollar chip every twenty or so hands is generally appropriate. If you want to make sure the dealer has your best interests at heart, place the tip right in front of your wagering circle, essentially turning it into a side bet on your hand. If you win, the dealer's tip doubles.***

The best free entertainment on the Strip is the live-action cannon battle between a pirate ship and a British frigate at **Treasure Island** (3300 Las Vegas Blvd. S., tel. 702/894-7111). The show, which always results in the same victor, takes place daily every 90 minutes 4 PM–10 PM, until 11:30 on Fridays and Saturdays.

The natural splendor of **Red Rock Canyon,** 15 miles west of Las Vegas, might help you forget your gambling losses for a while. Created by a thrust fault, the red sandstone formations afford scenic views and can be explored on any one of several short hikes located along the 13-mile Loop Drive. To get there, take Charleston Boulevard (Highway 159) west and follow signs. The visitor center (tel. 702/363–1921), 11 miles past Rainbow Boulevard, is open daily 8–5.

Baseball fans can watch high-quality minor-league ball April–September at **Cashman Field** (850 Las Vegas Blvd. N., tel. 702/386–7200), home of the Class AAA **Las Vegas Stars,** an affiliate of the San Diego Padres. General admission is $4.

## AFTER DARK

Las Vegas is renowned for its elaborate and gaudy stage shows. Sadly, ticket prices for headline acts are prohibitive, and even the regular revues (burlesque, celebrity impersonators, magic shows) tend to run at least $20. The free magazines all offer plenty of info on these shows, but unless you've always wanted to see Rich Little or David Copperfield, you'll probably have more fun exploring the less famous side of Vegas nightlife. Away from the Strip, a sizable bar and club scene attracts young people of various cultural predilections. Both the self-consciously hip monthly *Scope Magazine* and the weekly *Las Vegas New Times,* which is aimed at a broader readership, provide excellent directories of local hangouts and live music events. Both are free and can be found in cafés and record stores.

The **Palladium** (3665 S. Industrial Rd., near Spring Mountain Rd., tel. 702/733–6366) is Las Vegas's largest dance club. They play a mix of rock, techno, and disco Wednesday, Friday, and Saturday nights for a casual crowd; Thursday is country night. Cover here is $5. Just off the Strip, the **Shark Club** (75 E. Harmon Ave., tel. 702/795–7525) is an aptly named pick-up joint that stays open as late as 6 AM. Cover charges run as high as $10 to bust a move on the club's two dance floors. Of the city's various gay bars, the unpretentious **Gipsy** (4605 Paradise Rd., near Naples St., tel. 702/731–1919) is the liveliest dance spot. Doors open at 10 PM, seven nights a week. There's no cover before midnight, $4 thereafter.

**Drink.** The funky, innovative design of this recently opened restaurant and club has established it as the hottest nightspot in town. The interior courtyard is enclosed by two stories of adjoining rooms ranging in style from psychedelic to swank, with most favoring earth tones and incorporating a look of faux dilapidation. The hip crowd will even line up on occassion to dance to the sounds of a DJ and occasional live acts. Thursday–Saturday arrive before 9 PM to avoid the $5 cover. *200 E. Harmon Ave., at Koval Ln., tel. 702/796–5519. Closed Mon.*

**Fremont Street Reggae and Blues.** This popular downtown hangout for the progressive crowd is split into two sections, one featuring live reggae, the other live blues. Covers run $5 during the week and $10 on weekends at each venue. The place tends to be packed on weekends; you may have to stand to enjoy the local band. *400 Fremont St., at 4th St., tel. 702/594–4640. Just off Las Vegas Blvd., across from the Fitzgerald Hotel and Casino. Wheelchair access.*

**Sports Pub.** Right across from the University of Nevada, this is a 24-hour college hangout with cheap or free live music, dancing when the stage is empty, pool tables, and the inevitable video poker machines at the bar. The music is mostly progressive modern rock. *4440 S. Maryland Pkwy., tel. 702/796–8870.*

# Near Las Vegas

## LAKE MEAD

Las Vegas is a completely artificial environment in the middle of the desert. Fittingly, the nearest watersport paradise is also manmade—110-mile-wide Lake Mead, created by the construction of the Hoover Dam. The lake is less than an hour's drive south of Vegas on U.S. 93; the recreation area also includes nearby Lake Mohave, stretching for 67 miles below the dam. Even if you don't have the money to rent a boat at one of the nine marinas along the two lakes, you'll have no problem finding a quiet, sandy beach for camping and swimming. In summer, the water gets close to 80°.

You may want to begin your visit at the **Lake Mead National Recreation Area Visitor Center** (U.S. 93, at Hwy. 166 4 mi east of Boulder City, tel. 702/293–8906), which has maps, brochures, and information on boating and camping. The center is open daily 8:30–5 in summer, 8:30–4:30 in winter. All Lake Mead campsites cost $8 a night. Campers seeking solitude might want to ignore large, developed **Boulder Beach,** 2 miles from the visitor center, and head to **Echo Bay,** where sites sit right on the water. To get there, go straight on Highway 166, which becomes Lakeshore Scenic Drive, make a right on Northshore Road, and follow signs for 45 miles. At **Lake Mead Resort and Marina** (tel. 702/293–3484), you can rent anything from waterskiing equipment ($20 a day) to patio boats ($175 a day). For swimming, several access roads lead to the water; the most popular is Northshore Road (Hwy. 167). **Crawdad Cove** and **Ridge Road,** off Northshore Road, are the nearest (very unofficial) gay, lesbian, and nude beaches.

### HOOVER DAM

This Depression-era public works project is considered to be one of the great manmade wonders of the world. At its tallest, Hoover Dam is 70 stories high; at its widest, it spans the length of two football fields. Spanning the mouth of Black Canyon, the 1,244-foot-long dam successfully regulates the flow of the Colorado River in its intermittent periods of flooding and drought. It was even completed on schedule and under budget. *U.S. 93, 7 mi east of Boulder City, tel. 702/293–8391. Admission: $5 (includes parking). Tours Memorial Day–Labor Day, daily 8:30–6:30; off-season, daily 9–5.*

*Fifty-six percent of the hydroelectric power generated by Hoover Dam is consumed by the folks in Southern California—only 4% goes to nearby Las Vegas, which at the time of the dam's construction was little more than a railway stop.*

**Lake Mead Cruises** (707 Wells Rd., Boulder City, tel. 702/293–6180) ferries you right up to the foot of Hoover Dam. The 90-minute tour ($14.50) lets you see up close the amazing contrast between the lake and the surrounding desert terrain. Tours leave three times daily (twice daily in winter) from Lake Mead Marina; to get there, take U.S. 93/95 south, exit left on Lake Mead Drive, go straight, and take Lake Shore Road (to the right) at the fork. The marina is on your left. The **Boulder City/Hoover Dam Museum** (1305 Arizona St., Boulder City, tel. 702/294–1988) gives you an in-depth look at the difficulties faced daily by the people building the dam in the 1930s, a process that claimed 96 lives. A $1 donation is requested, and the museum is open daily 10–4.

## The Grand Canyon

**Still growing deeper and wider every day** (thanks to the winds and the Colorado River, which runs along its floor), the Grand Canyon is much more than the world's finest example of erosion. Native Americans inhabiting the canyon and the surrounding Kaibab Plateau have likened this breathtaking chasm to a "mountain lying upside down." It's a striking comparison. The park covers 1,900 square miles, and the "big crack" itself averages 1 mile deep and 10 miles wide. A considerable chunk of the vast, largely unexplored canyon is inaccessible to travelers, while the tourist centers on the North and South rims are connected only by a circuitous 215-mile road. The canyon is, well, grand—especially in the morning and at dusk, when the sun's rays create a dazzling display of changing colors and patterns on the rock.

Most people visit the South Rim, which turns into a giant RV park during the hot, dusty summers, when camcorder-toting travelers can make sightseeing a sort of sweaty human-slalom

# Grand Canyon National Park

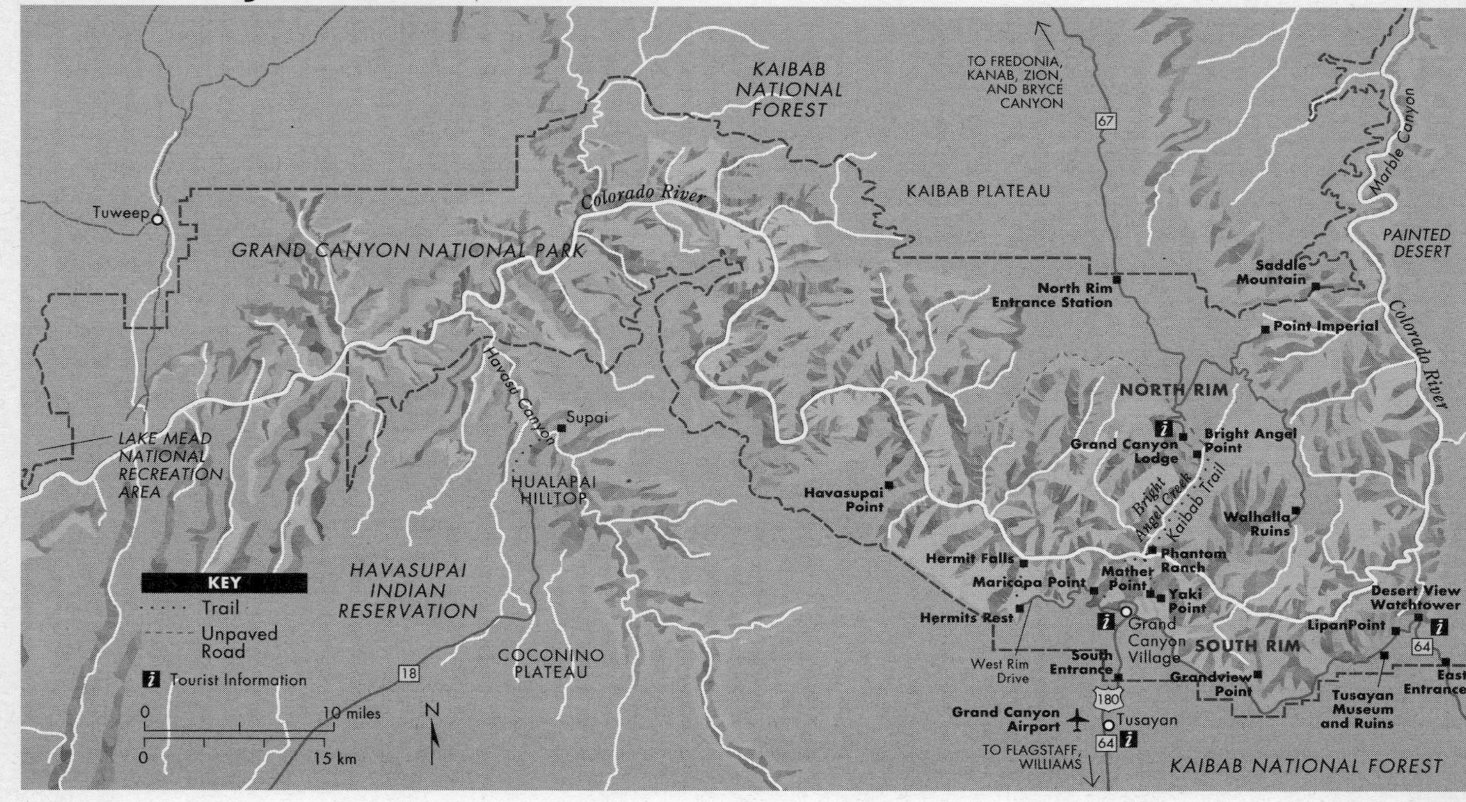

KAIBAB NATIONAL FOREST
TO FREDONIA, KANAB, ZION, AND BRYCE CANYON
67
KAIBAB PLATEAU
Colorado River
Tuweep
GRAND CANYON NATIONAL PARK
Marble Canyon
PAINTED DESERT
Saddle Mountain
North Rim Entrance Station
Point Imperial
NORTH RIM
Havasu Canyon
Supai
LAKE MEAD NATIONAL RECREATION AREA
HUALAPAI HILLTOP
Grand Canyon Lodge
Bright Angel Point
Havasupai Point
Bright Angel Creek
Kaibab Trail
Walhalla Ruins
Hermit Falls
Phantom Ranch
Maricopa Point
Mather Point
Yaki Point
HAVASUPAI INDIAN RESERVATION
Hermits Rest
Grand Canyon Village
Desert View Watchtower
LipanPoint
SOUTH RIM
KEY
Trail
Unpaved Road
Tourist Information
COCONINO PLATEAU
18
West Rim Drive
South Entrance
Grandview Point
64
East Entrance
Tusayan Museum and Ruins
0
10 miles
15 km
N
180
Grand Canyon Airport
Tusayan
TO FLAGSTAFF, WILLIAMS
KAIBAB NATIONAL FOREST

*In the last 30 years, the canyon has become less grand and more grimy. A nearby generating station belches some 10 tons of sulfur dioxide into the air hourly, while torrents of water from the Glen Canyon Dam wash away beaches. These hazards are now being regulated, but it may be too little too late—only one native fish species still survives.*

event. During these months you'll have a better chance at solitude and serenity on the less accessible North Rim, where services are comparable but smaller in scale. It lies a thousand feet higher than the South Rim and has a more alpine climate, with twice as much annual precipitation. Due to severe winters all North Rim facilities—as well as the road in—close between November and mid-May.

Spring and fall, when the weather is mild and the crowds aren't so heavy, are the best times to visit the South Rim. Even though this part of the canyon is at a lower elevation, it still suffers wet, cold winters. Don't let snow on the rim stop you from hiking down to the canyon floor, though; even when there's a blizzard up top, it may be just drizzling below.

The canyon itself is five million years old, and the Colorado River's fantastic erosions have exposed rock dating back billions of years. The oldest human artifacts found within the canyon are animal-shaped figurines and arrowheads dating back 4,000 years, but little is known about the people who made them. The Anasazi, who populated the region 1,500 years ago, are the earliest known group to dwell in the area around the canyon; only a few of their artifacts and cliff drawings remain in the canyon today. However, Native Americans (the Hopi, Havasupai, Navajo, Hualapai, and the southern Paiute) continue to inhabit much of the canyon and its surroundings.

The first Europeans came this way in the 16th century, when Spanish explorer Francisco Vázquez de Coronado forged north in search of the fabled Seven Cities of Cíbola. After a four-day attempt to find a crossing, the expedition finally gave up, wisely concluding "it must be as wide as the Indians had said." Few visited the canyon again for some 300 years, until Major John Wesley Powell boated 1,000 miles down the dangerous Colorado in 1869. The true tourism boom began in 1901, when the Santa Fe Railroad reached the South Rim from Williams, Arizona, shortening the trip to three hours from the 11 it took by horse.

You can still take the train from Williams, but most people today arrive by car or plane. Once you've arrived, you can hike into the canyon on several trails, maintained or rough, and camp on the canyon floor. For the best perspectives from above and below, there are scenic air tours and Colorado River rafting trips, most of which originate in nearby towns and require a moderate to frightening outlay of cash. Finally, there's the possibility of riding a pack animal into the canyon. For 200 hard-earned bucks, you'll travel down a narrow trail reeking of mule dung with a cliff on one side and a sheer drop on the other, while placing all your trust in an ass. Survivors claim the experience is incredible.

## BASICS

Arizona is in the Mountain Standard Time Zone, but does not observe Daylight Savings Time. This means that Grand Canyon National Park is on the same time as California in April through October, but is an hour ahead during winter. However, Utah and the Navajo Indian Reservation do recognize Daylight Savings Time, so these areas are always an hour ahead of California time.

**VISITOR INFORMATION** For general information, maps, brochures, and brief orientation programs, contact **Grand Canyon National Park Visitor Services** (Box 129, Grand Canyon, AZ 86023, tel. 520/638–7888). The **visitor center** (tel. 520/638–7771) in Grand Canyon Village, 6 miles north of the South Entrance Station, is open daily 8–6 in summer, 9–5 in winter. The **Desert View Information Center** (tel. 520/638–7893), 23 miles from Grand Canyon Village on East Rim Drive, offers similar services during the same hours to visitors arriving at the East Entrance Station. Tips on North Rim services and activities are available at the information desk (staffed daily 8–5 from mid-May through mid-October) in the lobby of the **Grand Canyon Lodge.**

For more detailed information on South Rim lodging, restaurants, rafting trips, and scenic flights, try the **Grand Canyon Chamber of Commerce** (Hwy. 64, in Imax Theater, tel. 520/638–

2901). The office, in Tusayan (2 miles south of the South Entrance Station), is open daily 9–5 in summer. For similar information about the North Rim, contact the **Kane County Travel Council** (78 S. 100 East, Kanab, UT 84741, tel. 801/644–5033), open daily 8–6 in summer, until 5 in winter.



**FEES** There's a $10 entrance fee for each car, good for seven days (bus passengers, hikers, and bikers pay only $4). If you plan to stay longer, the Grand Canyon Passport ($15) allows you to come and go as you please all year long. The Golden Eagle Passport ($25), available at access stations, is good in all federal recreation areas and national parks throughout the United States for one year.

**PUBLICATIONS** The *Grand Canyon Guide* is published in two editions, one for the North Rim and the other for the South. The guides tell you all you need to know about park activities, regulations, facilities, and ranger programs. Pick up free copies at the entrance stations, the visitor center in Grand Canyon Village on the South Rim, or the information desk in the lobby of the North Rim's Grand Canyon Lodge. Disabled visitors should request the free *Accessibility Guide,* available at the same locations. To purchase complete listings of maps, trail guides, and other publications, write the **Grand Canyon Association** (Box 399, Grand Canyon, AZ 86023, tel. 520/638–2481).

**GENERAL STORES** **Babbitt's General Store** (tel. 520/638–2262), in the Mather Business Center at Grand Canyon Village, has groceries, camping supplies, and equipment rentals. The in-store deli sells hot and cold sandwiches (about $3) and other picnic edibles. The store is open 8–8 in summer; the deli closes at 7 PM. Other locations are in Tusayan (Hwy. 64, tel. 520/638–2854) and Desert View (near the East Entrance, tel. 520/638–2393). In Flagstaff, **Mountain Sports** (1800 S. Milton Rd., at University Dr., tel. 520/779–5156 or 800/286–5156) rents mountain bikes ($20–30 a day), tents ($10 a day), and other helpful stuff. The store is open Monday–Saturday 9–8 and Sunday 11–5.

On the North Rim, the **Camper Store** (across from North Rim Campground, tel. 520/638–2611, ext. 270) has groceries, camping supplies, and a small snack bar serving pizza and sandwiches (under $5). It's open daily 7 AM–9 PM, from mid-May to October. Five miles north of the park boundary, the **Country Store and Gas Station** (across Hwy. 67 from Kaibab Lodge, tel. 520/638–2383) carries groceries, automotive supplies, and camping and backpacking equipment. It's open daily 7–7.

**LAUNDRY AND SHOWERS** Coin-operated laundry ($1 wash, 25¢ dry) and shower facilities (5 min 75¢) can be found on the South Rim in the Camper Services Building (open daily 6 AM–11 PM) near Mather Campground. The last wash load is at 9 PM. Similar facilities near the North Rim Campground are open daily 7 AM–9 PM. All are wheelchair accessible.

## COMING AND GOING

The routes to the North and South rims are very different thanks to one small obstacle—namely, the Grand Canyon itself. There are more options for getting to the South Rim and more people using them. In contrast, the North Rim is only easily accessible by car, unless you care for a five-hour shuttle ride from the South Rim (*see below*).

**BY CAR** The South Rim is almost exactly 500 miles from Los Angeles. From either Southern or Northern California, take I–40 east from Barstow to Williams, Arizona (322 mi). From Williams, head north 60 miles on Highway 64. If you're arriving from the east, take I–40 to Flagstaff, Arizona, and then head north on Highway 180.

To reach the North Rim from either Southern or Northern California, take I–15 east through Barstow and Las Vegas to southern Utah (about 350 mi from L.A.). Fifteen miles north of St. George, Utah, leave the interstate for scenic Highway 9, which runs east through the spectacular Zion National Park. About 50 miles later, Highway 9 intersects Highway ALT89, which you follow south 54 miles through Kanab, Utah, to Jacob Lake, Arizona. From there, Highway 67 (closed in winter) takes you directly to the North Rim. The drive takes you past pine-covered mountains and lush green meadows, a welcome change from the rugged desert vegetation of the South Rim.

**BY BUS** The nearest **Greyhound** station is in Flagstaff, Arizona (399 S. Malpais Ln., at Milton Rd., tel. 520/774–4573 or 800/231–2222 for reservations). The journey from L.A. to Flagstaff takes about 12 hours and costs $99 round-trip. **Nava-Hopi Tours, Inc.** (114 Hwy. 66, at Beaver St. in Flagstaff, tel. 520/774–5003 or 800/892–8687) provides round-trip service between Flagstaff and the South Rim for $25, and to Williams for $14 round-trip. Call to arrange morning pick-ups from the bus or train station, or from motels in Flagstaff. During the months when the North Rim is open, **Trans Canyon Van Service** (Box 348, Grand Canyon, AZ 86023, tel. 520/638–2820) links it to the South Rim (5 hrs, $60 one-way). There's one round-trip daily that leaves the North Rim's Grand Canyon Lodge at 7 AM and the South Rim's Bright Angel Lodge at 1 PM. Reservations are required. This service is used mainly by hikers making the 24-mile rim-to-rim trek.

**BY TRAIN** **Amtrak** (1 U.S. 66, at Leroux Ave., tel. 800/USA–RAIL for reservations) makes daily stops in Flagstaff, where you can catch a bus to Williams or the South Rim (*see above*). You'll pay $87 for the 10-hour trip from L.A. to Flagstaff; round-trip prices run $94–$174, depending on how far in advance you book. The **Grand Canyon Railway** (233 N. Grand Canyon Blvd., tel. 800/843–8724) winds its way through the wilderness to the historic log depot in Grand Canyon Village. Passengers ride in an early–20th-century restored steam locomotive, just as most travelers did before the automobile took over. Round-trip fare is $57 for adults (including park entrance fee), $20 for those under 16; reservations are advised. To reach the depot in Williams from I–40, take Exit 163 (Grand Canyon Blvd.) south ½ mile.

**BY PLANE** The **Grand Canyon Airport** (near Tusayan, 4 mi south of park entrance, tel. 520/638–2446) is served by several airlines, some of which also offer air tours of the canyon (*see* Park Activities, *below*). **Scenic Airlines** (tel. 520/638–2436 or 800/634–6801) and **Air Nevada** (tel. 520/736–8900 or 800/634–6377) connect with Las Vegas. Tri-Star (tel. 800/218–8777) flies into the Grand Canyon Airport from both San Francisco and Los Angeles. Round-trip fares can drop as low as $120, and average $250 from either city. You'll pay $300 round-trip from Los Angeles if you fly via Las Vegas on **Delta** (tel. 800/221–1212). If you fly **America West** (tel. 800/2-FLY-AWA) to Flagstaff, Nava-Hopi tours (*see above*) will pick you up at the airport, 15 miles south of town. From L.A., prices vary a lot depending on time of travel and how far in advance tickets are purchased—from $168 to $882 round-trip—so be sure to plan far in advance.

From the Grand Canyon airport, you can catch the **Grand Canyon–Tusayan Shuttle** (tel. 520/638–0821), which departs hourly 8:15 AM–7:15 PM for stops in Tusayan and at the Bright Angel and Maswik lodges in Grand Canyon Village. One-way fare is $7. Those who prefer to drive can rent economy cars from **Budget** (tel. 520/638–9360), located at the airport, for $42 a day.

## GETTING AROUND

**SOUTH RIM** Roads are crowded and parking spots are in short supply. Take advantage of the numerous free or low-cost shuttles that tool around the area in May through September. The free **Village Loop** shuttle operates daily 6:30 AM–10:30 PM, stopping at the visitor center and other village facilities at 15-minute intervals—look for the blue signs designating shuttle stops. The **West Rim Loop** shuttle, also free, begins service at the West Rim interchange and continues to Hermits Rest (*see* Scenic Drives, *below*). Brown signs designate shuttle stops. A **hiker's shuttle** connects several points in Grand Canyon Village (Bright Angel Lodge, Maswik Lodge, the Backcountry Office) with the South Kaibab trailhead near Yaki Point. Service is $3 to the trail; the return trip is free. There are three morning pickups daily. Look for schedule information at pickup points or in the *Grand Canyon Guide.*

**NORTH RIM** A **hiker's shuttle** travels between Grand Canyon Lodge and the North Kaibab trailhead daily between 6 AM and 8 PM. Purchase tickets ($5; $2 for each additional person) at the lodge's front desk.

## WHERE TO SLEEP

**SOUTH RIM** Hotels at the South Rim are expensive and are usually booked months in advance. Contact **Grand Canyon National Park Lodges** (Box 699, Grand Canyon, AZ 86023, tel. 520/638–2401) about advance reservations for all park accommodations. It's possible to pick up a room because of a canceled reservation, but don't count on it. Call the park's same-day reservation number (tel. 520/638–2631) or go to the lodge you want to stay at and inquire at the front desk. The most reasonably priced options within the park are **Maswik Lodge** (the canyon's newest addition) and the rustic **Bright Angel Lodge,** situated right on the rim. At Maswik, cabins are $48 and rooms start at $69. At Bright Angel, rooms with shared bath cost $53, and the knotty-pine cabins ($61) can sleep two or more; extra persons pay $7–$9 each.

**Phantom Ranch** (tel. 520/638–2401) at Bright Angel Creek, accessible by mule or on foot (*see* Longer Hikes or Park Activities, *below*), has the only non-camping accommodations below the rim. Cozy cabins for two ($56) can actually sleep 4–10; extra guests pay $11 each per night. Another option is single-sex dormitory beds ($22). You can either haul your cookstove and supplies down the trail or reserve a meal in the canteen (breakfast $12, dinners $17–$27). The food may be pricey, but it's damn good all-you-can-eat grub. Reservations are required and rooms are often booked almost a year in advance; the Bright Angel Lodge transportation desk resells Phantom Ranch cancellations (usually for the next two to four nights) to those who inquire in person.

Flagstaff (79 miles south of the Grand Canyon) is hardly the town next door, but with a hip mountain atmosphere it makes a great base camp. Hostels, outdoor equipment stores, and cheap eats–cum–indie rock venues can be found in the historic blocks surrounding the railroad depot (*see* Coming and Going, *above*). The **Western Hill Hotel** (1580 E. Hwy. 66, at Enterprise Rd., tel. 520/774–6633) has a pool; a Thai restaurant, open Monday–Saturday 11–9 and Sunday 4–9; and wheelchair-accessible rooms starting at $30. Williams, 56 miles south of the park, is a more reasonable commute. The drawback is that most of its budget motels cater mainly to senior-citizens. In a pinch, the **Arizona Motor Hotel** (315 W. Bill Williams Ave., tel. 520/635–4552) has cramped but clean doubles starting at $35, and offers weekly rates and kitchenettes.

➢ **HOSTELS** • The **Du Beau International Hostel** in Flagstaff attracts a new bohemian crowd. It offers both dorm-style ($12) and private ($25) rooms; breakfast is included, and the hostel picks you up for free from the Flagstaff airport, bus, or train station. The downside is the racket—huge freight trains roll by nearly every hour. *19 W. Phoenix Ave., at Beaver St., tel. 520/774–6731. 70 beds. No curfew, no lockout. Reception open 6 AM–midnight. Kitchen, luggage storage. Wheelchair access. No credit cards.*

The **Grand Canyon International Hostel** in downtown Flagstaff is also known as the Downtowner because of the sign out front, left over from the building's previous life as a motel. At about five stories tall it is reputed to be the tallest hotel sign in the world. This meticulously decorated, too-nice-to-be-a-hostel hostel can sleep 65 people—options include a dorm ($10–12) or a private double ($30), breakfast included. The hostel provides free pickup from the Flagstaff bus or train station. *19 S. San Francisco St., at Phoenix Ave., tel. 520/779–9421. No curfew, no lockout. Reception open 6 AM–2 AM. Kitchen, laundry, lockers. Wheelchair access.*

The **Grey Hills Inn and Hostel** lies between the South and North rims, on the Navajo reservation 60 miles east of the Grand Canyon. Extremely clean, motel-style doubles with shared bath cost $16 per person for HI members. Nonmembers pay $42 and up for a double. *Box 160, Tuba City, AZ 86045, tel. 520/283–6271, ext. 141. From U.S. 89, U.S. 160 east 10 mi to Tuba City, left on Warrior Dr. 62 beds. No curfew, no lockout. Reception open 24 hrs. Laundry. No credit cards.*

The **Weatherford Hotel** is an AYH lodging in downtown Flagstaff that has 64 dorm-style beds for $12, as well as a few hotel rooms that go for $32 with private bath and $24 without. They'll also pick you up from the local Greyhound station. The hostel is directly above Charly's Pub and Restaurant, a drinking spot beloved by locals. *23 North Leroux St., at Santa Fe Ave., tel.*

*520/774–2731. Curfew 1 AM, no lockout. Reception open 7 AM–10 AM and 5 PM–11 PM. Kitchen, luggage storage.*

➢ **CAMPING ABOVE THE RIM** • A word to the wise regarding park campgrounds: Arrive at your site before noon if you have not reserved in advance. **Mather Campground** is conveniently located right in Grand Canyon Village, just south of the visitor center. Towering pine trees disguise the fact that this 319-site tent city (six sites have wheelchair access) is within spitting distance of the business center's tourist throngs. It's also an easy walk to the rim of the canyon. Sites ($10) have toilets and drinking water. From March to November, reserve through MISTIX (tel. 800/365–CAMP) up to eight weeks in advance.

Near the East Entrance Station, the first-come, first-served **Desert View Campground** (tel. 520/638–7893) operates from mid-May to early October and has drinking water and toilets. The 50 sites seem shoehorned in, but if you take a short hike past the community campfire, you'll be rewarded with an incredible view of the canyon. Sites go for $10; no RVs over 40 feet are allowed.

The U.S. Forest Service maintains the **Ten-X Campground** in the Kaibab National Forest, 3 miles south of Tusayan off Highway 180. In an enchantingly secluded forest, the campground (open May–Oct.) has yet to be discovered by the usual whey-faced mob. The 70 first-come, first-served sites ($10) fill up quickly in summer; the sites have picnic tables, water, and toilets. Dispersed camping is available in the forest (*see* Camping, in Chapter 1)—there's no fee and no permit is required. The basic rule is that you can pitch a tent or toss down a sleeping bag anywhere at least a quarter mile from a paved road. Contact the **U. S. Forest Service** (Box 3088, Tusayan, AZ 86023, tel. 520/638–2443) for more info.

➢ **CAMPING BELOW THE RIM** • To protect the inner canyon from overuse, backcountry camping is restricted. Anyone wishing to stay overnight at developed or primitive campsites below the rim must first get a free permit from the **Backcountry Reservations Office (BRO)** (Box 129, Grand Canyon, AZ 86023, tel. 520/638–7888), a quarter mile south of the visitor center near Mather Campground. Permit requests are taken no more than four months in advance, by mail or in person only. Rangers are available to field questions by telephone weekdays 11–5. Request the free ***Backcountry Trip Planner,*** an invaluable introduction to the permit procedure and the trails, with tips on pre-trip preparations. Though competition for reservations is fierce, it's still possible to obtain a campsite on the in-person waiting list. The first-come, first-served permits are issued every morning at 8 AM. In summer it usually takes two or more days to reach the top of the list. Persistence is key.

Once you get the permit, you can camp inside the rim at **Bright Angel, Indian Gardens,** or **Cottonwood,** which have drinking water, chemical toilets, and emergency telephones. Indian Gardens and Cottonwood both have about 15 sites in canyon oases that stay green year-round. Bright Angel's 31 sites, next to Phantom Ranch along the Colorado River, offer few trees, but if you bring a swimsuit, you can splash around in Bright Angel Creek. If you don't feel like hauling out the Coleman, reserve ahead (tel. 520/638–2401) and you can dine at nearby Phantom Ranch (*see* Where to Sleep, *above*). A number of more primitive, less crowded sites are located along unmaintained trails. **Horseshoe Mesa,** at the end of Grandview Trail, has great views, but only pit toilets and no water. **Hermit Creek** and **Hermit Rapids** are designated camping areas along Hermit Trail. They offer pit toilets, water at year-round creeks (remember to purify), and shade in the form of cottonwood trees. For directions to these sites, *see* Longer Hikes, *below.*

**NORTH RIM** The only North Rim hotel accommodations within the park are at the **Grand Canyon Lodge** (tel. 801/586–7686), which has 163 rim-side cabins—amazing life-size replicas of a kid's Lincoln Log project. Cabins that sleep two start at $49; unexciting motel-style units start at $59. The lodge is open mid-May through mid-October and tends to book up three to four months in advance. For same-day reservations, present your charming self at the registration desk at random times throughout the day in the hope that someone has canceled.

Travelers on a tight budget have to trek 74 miles from the North Rim to Fredonia, Arizona. The **Blue Sage Motel** (330 S. Main St., tel. 520/643–7125) offers standard doubles for $30–$35 in summer, $5 less in winter. About 10 miles farther in Kanab, Utah, there's a wide choice of slightly pricier digs. The **Parry Lodge** (89 E. Center St., tel. 801/644–2601 or 800/748–4104) is your best bet if you're looking for a little more than a bed and a roof over your head. This colonial-style lodge has all the services you'd expect from an upscale hotel, as well as rooms named after movie actors—John Wayne, James Arness, and Ronald Reagan all slept here while filming in the nearby high desert. Regular doubles start at $43 in summer; prices are about $10 lower in winter.

➢ **HOSTELS** • The **Grey Hills Inn and Hostel** lies between the South and North rims, on the Navajo reservation 60 miles east of the Grand Canyon (*see* Where to Sleep, in the South Rim, *above*). Otherwise, the **Canyonlands International Hostel** is a great place to stay. It has an extensive travel center and free buffet breakfast, coffee, tea, and lemonade. Best of all, you can relax in friendly company on the shaded patio. The hostel costs $9 per night and has 36 beds; reservations are advised. *143 E. 100 South, Kanab, tel. 801/644–5554. No curfew, no lockout. Reception open 7 AM–midnight. Kitchen, laundry. Wheelchair access. No credit cards.*

➢ **CAMPING ABOVE THE RIM** • The sites at **North Rim Campground** are interspersed between stands of tall pine trees. The ground is adorned with pine cones, and layers of pine needles make your bed soft and altogether pleasant. Showers, a Laundromat, and a general store are nearby. The 82 sites ($10) are open mid-May to mid-October. Since this is the only North Rim campground inside the park, it fills up fast; be sure to make reservations at least two weeks in advance through MISTIX (tel. 800/365–CAMP). Your only alternative is to join the near-futile waiting list; sign up before 10 AM at the camp's registration kiosk. Two sites and the restroom are wheelchair accessible.

The U.S. Forest Service maintains two campgrounds in the **Kaibab National Forest,** which stretches for miles on either side of Highway 67, between Highway ALT89 and the North Rim Entrance Station. Stop by the **visitor center** (junction Hwys. ALT89 and 67, 30 mi north of entrance station, tel. 520/643–7298) in Jacob Lake for tips on forest activities or dispersed camping (*see below*). The area closes from mid-October to mid-May due to snow. **Jacob Lake Campground,** in a shaded pine setting, sits at the junction of Highways ALT89 and 67. Be prepared for the roar of the adjacent highway, visible from many of the 56 first-come, first-served sites ($10). The campground is open mid-May to the end of October. Gas, food, firewood ($5), and groceries are available; toilets and some campsites are wheelchair accessible. **DeMotte Park Campground** is near a lush green meadow, 5 miles north of the North Rim Entrance Station off Highway 67. Depending upon your point of view, you'll regard its rutted dirt road as wildly rustic, or a huge pain in the ass. The 25 tent sites, with drinking water and pit toilets, go for $10 per night on a first-come, first-served basis. Pick up supplies at the nearby Country Store and Gas Station (*see* General Stores, *above*).

Primitive camping is available in the forest free of charge from May through mid-October. Stop by the information center (*see above*) for current information and a look at the list of regulations. Then pull off on one of the dozens of dirt fire trails that branch off the highway and pitch your tent. There's no registration and no facilities—just you, a forest of pine trees, and an occasional deer or two for company. Some basic rules: Camp at least a quarter mile away from any paved road or water source and use existing fire rings whenever possible.

➢ **CAMPING BELOW THE RIM** • Hikers spending the night below the rim must first obtain a free permit from the **North Rim Backcountry Reservations Office** at the North Rim Ranger Station. The same restrictions apply as for the South Rim (*see above*). The North Rim BRO is open daily 7:30 AM–noon. The major backcountry campgrounds—**Bright Angel, Indian Gardens,** and **Cottonwood**—are accessible via both the North and South rims (for directions, see Longer Hikers, *below*); the closest one to the North Rim is Cottonwood, 7 miles along the North Kaibab Trail.

## FOOD

The Canyon's best food will cost you blood, sweat, and tears—it lies at the end of the long hike to Phantom Ranch (*see* Where to Sleep, *above*). Anywhere else, expect an all-American menu of hamburgers, soups, sandwiches, and salads, served with a dollop of grease and a grin.

**SOUTH RIM** Within the park, stop at the **Bright Angel Fountain,** open daily 6 AM–8 PM from May to September, for ice cream and sandwiches (about $3). You can eat while sitting on a rock near neighboring Bright Angel Lodge, trying to avoid the pesky squirrels hungrily eyeing your Canyon Crunch ice cream. The **Maswik Cafeteria,** in the Maswik Lodge (at the Village's west end), and the **Canyon Café,** in the Yavapai Lodge, offer the same food (cafeteria-style American) at the same prices ($3–$7) and are open the same hours (daily 6 AM–10 PM). Picnickers may want to purchase hot or cold sandwiches ($5) at the deli in Babbitt's General Store (*see* General Stores, *above*).

In Flagstaff, **Monsoon's** (22 E. Hwy. 66, near Beaver St., tel. 520/774–7929) serves barbecued eats for less than $7, but is best-loved for the bands that play all kinds of dance music (except country-and-western) Wednesday to Sunday nights. After 9 on Fridays and Saturdays, the cover charge cover is sometimes as much as $20, but it's usually closer to $3–$5; Wednesday and Thursday are usually free. **El Charro** (409 S. San Francisco St., tel. 520/779–0552) is the local favorite for Mexican food. Enchiladas and tacos go for about $2 each; combo plates run $7–$9. El Charro is open Monday through Thursday 11–9, until 10 Friday and Saturday. In Williams, the **Fireside Restaurant and Bar** (106 S. 9th St., tel. 520/635–4130) serves lunch and dinner for under $10; one-person pizzas are about $3, and pasta dishes run $5–$9. Fireside is open Monday through Saturday 11:30–3:30 and 5–9. Be forewarned that the evening's live entertainment usually consists of a senior citizen playing country tunes on the guitar.

**NORTH RIM** Maybe it's the higher altitude, but food at the North Rim just tastes better. The **Grand Canyon Lodge Dining Room** (tel. 520/638–2611) serves such delicacies as fillet of Utah red trout ($12), but you could eat tuna straight from the can and still be happy in this impressive room with rock walls, cathedral ceilings, and sweeping views. Lunch at the lodge ranges from the expected (burger; $5) to the unusual (smoked-trout spinach salad; $4.50). Even the Formica-laden snack bar isn't bad, serving up surprisingly good pizza slices ($3) and pies ($10). They make (or, more likely, thaw) the same pizza at a counter in the **General Store** by the North Rim campground (*see* General Stores, *above*); both places also serve the usual hot dogs and sandwiches. In Kanab, **Nedra's Too** (Hwy. ALT89, at Hwy. 89, tel. 801/644–2030) serves decent Mexican food (for Utah, anyway), with breakfast, lunch, and dinner for under $10. The eatery, open daily 7 AM–11 PM, is wheelchair accessible.

## EXPLORING THE GRAND CANYON

**ORIENTATION PROGRAMS** In addition to its walk-through exhibits, the South Rim's **visitor center** (tel. 520/638–7888) in Grand Canyon Village runs free 15-minute slide shows daily on the canyon's geology, discovery, and development. If groups don't bother you, join one of the free ranger-led talks or hikes at the canyon's rim. North Rim park rangers hold a variety of informative talks daily (mid-May to mid-October) at Point Imperial, the Campground Amphitheater, and the east patio of the Grand Canyon Lodge. They also lead short hikes throughout the park. Check the North or South Rim version of the *Grand Canyon Guide* (*see* Publications, *above*) for schedules.

**GUIDED TOURS** For information on raft, air, and mule tours of the canyon, *see* Park Activities, *below.*

➢ **SOUTH RIM** • **Fred Harvey Transportation Co.** (tel. 520/638–2401) has several narrated, wheelchair-accessible bus tours to various locations west and east of Grand Canyon Village, including a sunset tour. The tours cost $7.50–$20 and last anywhere from 90 minutes to half a day. Tickets are available at the transportation desks at the Yavapai, Maswik, and Bright Angel lodges. **Nava-Hopi Tours** (114 Hwy. 66, Flagstaff, tel. 520/774–5003 or 800/892–8687) has bus tours of the Grand Canyon and other northern Arizona attractions, including Monument Valley, the Petrified Forest, and the prehistoric dwellings at Montezuma Castle National Monument. Tours cost about $35–$75 and originate in downtown Flagstaff.

**Hopi Polewyma Travel and Tours** (Box 210, Polacca, AZ 86042, tel. 520/737–2534) has an interesting approach to touring the canyon. You get to drive the guide around on a tour that costs $15 an hour and originates in Flagstaff. The Hopi owned-and-operated tour can also include villages, cultural centers, and artisans' workplaces within the Hopi reservation.

➢ **NORTH RIM** • **TW Recreational Services** (tel. 801/586–7686) has a three-hour van tour of Cape Royale, Angel's Window, and other scenic viewpoints for $20. Reservations and information are available at the reservations desk of the Grand Canyon Lodge.

**SHORT HIKES** You may want to start off with a shorter hike before tackling a below-the-rim trail, in order to acclimate yourself both to the high elevation and the specific hazards associated with canyon hiking (*see box, below*).

➢ **SOUTH RIM** • The level, paved, and wheelchair-accessible **South Rim Trail** runs 1½ miles from the Yavapai Observation Station to the historic district of Grand Canyon Village. All along the trail, you'll see spectacular views of the inner gorge—but there'll be lots of other people in the way. The less-trafficked, moderately challenging **West Rim Trail** begins where the South Rim trail ends. The path sometimes veers close to the edge of the canyon; in some parts it rises and falls several feet as it follows the rim 8 miles west, past Maricopa Point (where the pavement ends) and the Abyss Overlook to Hermits Rest.

➢ **NORTH RIM** • The paved **Bright Angel Point Trail** ascends a steep quarter mile to a toe-curling view of the inner gorge. Far below, you can hear **Roaring Springs,** which supplies water and hydroelectric power to both rims. The trail begins at the log structure alongside the Grand Canyon Lodge parking lot and doubles back to end at the lodge's east patio. Pamphlets describing the half-mile loop are available at the trailhead for a 25¢ donation. The **Cape Royal Trail,** an easy ⅔-mile paved path with partial wheelchair access, begins at the Cape Royal parking area, 25 miles southeast of the lodge (follow signs). In

*On North Rim trails, look for the Kaibab squirrel, a rare species found only in the pine forests of this plateau. It's a small grey animal with bizarre, Spock-like tufts of fur sprouting from the tip of each ear.*

## *Hiking in the Grand Canyon*

***If you've ever lugged your gym's Stairmaster into the sauna and then performed at level 9 for, oh, four or more hours—congratulations, you're already prepped to hike the canyon. Otherwise, read on. The most important thing to do is bring a gallon of water per person per day. Carry a canteen rather than stuffing an oversize jug into your backpack, so that you can frequently and easily replace body fluids lost through copious perspiration. Raisins and banana chips are ideal trail eats because they're high in carbohydrates and natural sugars.***

***Other helpful hints: Unless you want to fall to a grisly death, mind the edge; there are no guardrails. Wear sturdy, broken-in hiking boots (you can get by with running shoes and the like for day hikes on the well-maintained corridor trails). Keep your shoes on in the backcountry campsites, as scorpions are regular below-the-rim residents; though rarely fatal, their sting is extremely painful. Avoid hiking during summer's hottest hours (10 AM–3 PM) by rising early and finding a shaded midday picnic spot. Day hikers especially should take care to allow extra time for the return trip. The rule of thumb is that it takes twice as long to go up as it does to descend, regardless of your physical condition. You may be tempted to trek to the river and back again in one day, but rangers—and anyone who's lived to tell about trying it—will strongly discourage you.***

addition to impressive views of the canyon, the Colorado River, and high-desert plateaus, look for **Angel's Window,** a huge trapezoidal hole in a rock wall. It's a product of erosion, not—as you might think—of tour operators' sledgehammers. Several signs describe the local vegetation and explain how the Anasazi Indians used it for medicinal purposes centuries ago.

**LONGER HIKES** Unless you've had experience hiking canyon terrain, cut your teeth on the corridor trails—**Bright Angel, North Kaibab,** and **South Kaibab.** These well-maintained, ranger-patrolled paths have water available year-round, but they're hardly sissy trails. At the top, the trails are crowded with day hikers, but the most obnoxious child- and camcorder-toting tourists rarely stray more than 2 or 3 miles below the rim. The rest of the way, you'll have the trails (and views) to yourself. Call or visit the BRO (*see* Backcountry Camping, *above*) for trip-planning assistance, maps, and information on these and other trails.

➢ **SOUTH RIM** • The 9½-mile **Bright Angel Trail,** which begins just west of Bright Angel Lodge, is the most heavily traveled route into the inner gorge. Water is available year-round at Indian Garden Campground (halfway down), and from May to September at the two rest houses (1½ and 3 mi down). For an excellent day hike, continue 1½ miles beyond Indian Gardens to **Plateau Point** (3,120 feet below the rim), where you can gaze at the Colorado River another 3,000 feet below. The return is strenuous: Allow 8–12 hours round-trip. Farther down, the trail terminates at Bright Angel Campground and Phantom Ranch after crossing the Colorado via suspension bridge.

The **South Kaibab Trail,** beginning near Yaki Point on East Rim Drive, is a steeper and shorter (6½ mi) route to the Colorado River, but there's no water and little shade along the way. Your reward? The views are spectacular. Day hikers with strong calf muscles will enjoy the 3-mile round-trip journey part way down the trail to **Cedar Ridge,** requiring 2½–4 hours total. Overnight hikers heading to Bright Angel Campground and Phantom Ranch will want to take South Kaibab down and return on the easier Bright Angel Trail. Though overnight parking is possible at Yaki Point, you may want to leave your car in Grand Canyon Village and take the hiker's shuttle (*see* Getting Around, *above*) to the trailhead to avoid the extra 5-mile trek back.

Steeper still is the unmaintained **Grandview Trail** (3 mi one-way), beginning at Grandview Point on East Rim Drive. It's possible to make a day hike to the campgrounds at **Horseshoe Mesa**—just set aside 4–11 hours for the round-trip, depending upon your physical condition (or lack thereof). There is no water along Grandview Trail. **The Hermit Trail** (8½ mi from rim to river), also steep and unmaintained, begins just south of Hermits Rest on West Rim Drive. At the turn of the century, it was the property of the Santa Fe Railway; portions of the company's tramway and camp are still visible along the trail. Day hikers should follow signs for the 6-mile hike to **Dripping Springs** (6–9 hours round-trip). Overnight hikers can continue to the Hermit Creek and Hermit Rapids camps; the Colorado River is another 1½ miles away along Hermit Creek. Springs along this trail mean that water is available year-round—just remember to purify before drinking.

All of the above trails are intersected by the **Tonto Trail,** which meanders east–west along the plateaus above the Colorado River. Overnight hikers planning to spend several days below the rim may want to descend by one trail and then follow Tonto to another trail for the return hike.

*To hike rim-to-rim, rangers recommend descending on North Kaibab and climbing out on Bright Angel; the total trip is 24 miles.*

➢ **NORTH RIM** • **North Kaibab Trail** is the only corridor trail from the North Rim into the inner canyon. The 14-mile trail begins 2 miles north of the Grand Canyon Lodge (for info on shuttle service *see* Getting Around, *above*) and ends at Bright Angel Campground and Phantom Ranch on the Colorado River after a 6,000-foot descent. The last 5 miles follow **Bright Angel Creek,** named by an early explorer after a character in Milton's *Paradise Lost.* About 7 miles down lies Cottonwood Campground; day hikers in excellent physical condition may want to continue 2½ miles more to **Roaring Springs**—allow 6–8 hours total for the round-trip from the trailhead. A worthy 3-mile round-trip detour leads to the small waterfall and emerald pools at **Ribbon Falls**; look for the **Spur Trail** a mile below Cottonwood Campground.

A pleasant contrast to the crowded trails below the rim, the **Widforss** and **Ken Patrick trails** offer the tranquillity of cool glens and ridge-top views, but are still lengthy enough to provide a workout. The Ken Patrick Trail meanders north from the North Kaibab parking area to Point Imperial, a distance of 10 miles. The Widforss Trail (10 mi round-trip) follows the canyon rim for a short distance, then retreats into the forest before emerging at stunning **Widforss Point.** Pick up a brochure (25¢ donation) at the trailhead, which lies at the end of a dirt road 2¾ miles north of Grand Canyon Lodge, opposite the paved road to Cape Royal. It's possible to camp among the pines of the Widforss Trail, but you'll need a permit from the BRO (*see* Backcountry Camping, *above*).



### SCENIC DRIVES AND VIEWS

➢ **SOUTH RIM** • The **West Rim Drive** runs 8 miles west from Grand Canyon Village to Hermits Rest. Along this tree-lined, two-lane drive are several scenic overlooks with panoramic views of the inner canyon. The road is closed to automobile traffic during summer (exemptions available from the visitor center for disabled drivers), but you can catch the free shuttle bus at the West Rim Interchange near Bright Angel Lodge every 15 minutes (7:30 AM–6:45 PM). The shuttle stops at all eight scenic viewpoints, making a complete round-trip every 90 minutes.

The **East Rim Drive,** relatively uncluttered by cars and tour buses, also affords some beautiful views of the canyon and the raging river. The 23-mile (each way) drive takes you past **Lipan Point,** the widest part of the canyon. The road continues to the **Tusayan Museum and Ruins,** where you'll see partially intact Anasazi rock dwellings (*also see* Worth Seeing, *below*). The drive ends at the **Desert View Watchtower,** which clings precariously to the lip of the chasm (*also see* Worth Seeing, *below*).

➢ **NORTH RIM** • The road to **Point Imperial** and **Cape Royal** intersects Highway 67 about 3 miles north of Grand Canyon Lodge. The road winds 8 miles through stands of quaking aspen combed neatly into a forest of unkempt conifers; it's most impressive after fall's first frosts, when the aspen leaves turn golden. From the intersection, continue 3 miles north to Point Imperial—the views of the eastern canyon and desert are spectacular at sunrise. Or head south 15 miles to Cape Royal for the North Rim's only views of the Colorado River (*see* Shorter Hikes, *above*). On this leg of the drive, you'll pass an Anasazi ruin (*see* Worth Seeing, *below*) and several canyon overlooks perfect for picnicking.

**WORTH SEEING** About 30 Anasazi, ancestors of the modern Hopi and other Pueblo cultures, hunted and farmed here until the 12th century, when they were forced to move east (possibly by drought). The free **Tusayan Museum and Ruins** (3 mi west of Desert View on East Rim Drive, tel. 520/638–2305) has exhibits about the various Native American tribes who have inhabited the region in the past 2,000 years. The museum is open daily 8:30–6 (9–5 off-season).

The 70-foot **Desert View Watchtower,** built in 1932 to resemble southwestern Native American architecture, is the highest point on the South Rim; not surprisingly, the views are spectacular. A stairway inside leads to viewing windows, and replicas of petroglyphs, Native American paintings, and a unique Hopi altar. The watchtower is located at the end of the 25-mile East Rim Drive. *Admission: 25¢. Open daily 8–7:30 (summer), daily 9–4:30 (winter).*

The **Walhalla Ruins,** along the road that ends at Cape Royal, 20 miles from the Grand Canyon Lodge, are thought to have been the summer living quarters of the Kayenta Anasazi Indians 900 years ago. Though the excavation itself isn't much to look at, it's awe-inspiring to think of the courage of the Anasazi, who made the arduous two-day ascent from the delta every summer because beans and squash grew better in the warm air here. Pick up a brochure (25¢ donation) just outside the Walhalla Overlook parking lot.

## PARK ACTIVITIES

**MOUNTAIN BIKING** While mountain bikes are permitted on all of the park's paved and unpaved roads (not the trails), the amount of auto and bus exhaust you'll inhale touring the South Rim will quickly negate any health benefits. Avid bikers should plan to spend most of their time at the North Rim instead, where roads are less crowded and the air is cleaner. If you're hell-bent on biking here, you can rent a bike at **Mountain Sports** in Flagstaff (*see* General Stores, *above*) by the day ($20) or the week ($75).

In addition to park roads on the North Rim, the adjacent **Kaibab National Forest** has miles of dirt track. Some, like Road 461 (just below the intersection of Hwys. 67 and ALT89), lead to abandoned copper mines. You can purchase a map of the forest ($3) and get additional information at the Jacob Lake visitor center (*see* Camping, *above*). The "closest" place to rent mountain bikes is in St. George, Utah, more than 100 miles west of here. There, **Swen's Cyclery** (1060 E. Tabernacle St., off I–15, tel. 801/673–0878) charges $25 a day or $60 a week.

**MULE RIDES** Mules do not come equipped with air conditioning, shock absorbers, or antilock brakes, but they provide efficient and exhilarating (if expensive) transportation down steep canyon trails. Several mule trains depart daily from the South Rim's Bright Angel Lodge for day trips to Plateau Point ($102) or overnight trips to Phantom Ranch at the canyon bottom ($250 per night). Trips book months in advance, but spontaneous sorts can place their names on a waiting list at the Bright Angel transportation desk. For the mule's safety, there's a 200-pound weight limit so strictly enforced that Sylvester Stallone is rumored to have been forced to walk. Contact the **Grand Canyon National Park Lodges** (Box 699, Grand Canyon, AZ 86023, tel. 520/638–2401) for further information.

Mule trains on the North Rim don't descend to the canyon bottom, but they do spend a full day traveling to Roaring Springs ($85); half-day trips are $35. A one-hour trip along the rim is mere mule feed at $12. Reservations are advised; write Box 128, Tropic, Utah 84776, or call the **Grand Canyon Lodge** (tel. 520/638–2292).

**HORSEBACK RIDES** If you feel that $250 ought to buy the mule, not just a mule ride, you might be happier on horseback. The disadvantage is that horses don't go into the canyon, they just ride along the rim. **Apache Stables** (Box 158, Grand Canyon, AZ 86023, tel. 520/638–2891) offers short and affordable horseback rides through the Kaibab National Forest and along the canyon rim. Rates start at $22 for one hour; rides originate at Moqui Lodge just below the South Rim entrance station on Highway 64.

*Rock climbing at the Grand Canyon is only for the experienced; the loose shale is extremely dangerous. At 7,136 feet, Zoroaster Temple—shaped like a Mexican sombrero and visible from the North Rim and Kaibab trails—challenges even expert mountaineers. Those who succeed may inscribe their names on a plaque at its peak.*

**Allen's Outfitters** (584 E. 300 South St., Kanab, Utah 84741, tel. 801/644–8150) offers guided horseback rides through the North Kaibab Forest and along the North Rim for $15 per hour, $45 per half-day, or $75 per day. Rides originate at Jacob's Lake, near the forest service visitor center (*see* Camping Above the Rim, *above*).

**RAFTING** The Colorado River's course through the Grand Canyon incorporates both rushing rapids and slow-moving stretches of crystal-clear water perfect for swimming. Guided rafting tours range from day trips to extensive (and expensive) two-week outings, and are available from over 20 companies in both motorized (smooth water) and oar-propelled (white-water) boats. Trips originate in Flagstaff, Page, or Las Vegas, and the price usually includes transportation to the river. Trips of less than one week generally explore only half of the Colorado River's course through the canyon, starting or ending at Phantom Ranch. Be prepared to hike one leg of the journey. You must reserve well in advance; for a list of all rafting companies, consult the *Grand Canyon Guide*.

**Canyoneers, Inc.** (Box 2997, Flagstaff, AZ 86003, tel. 520/526–0924 or 800/525–0924) offers a three-day trip into the canyon with all meals and gear included for $495 per person. **Hualapai River Runners** (Box 247, Peach Springs, AZ 86434, tel. 520/769–2219 or 800/622–4409) runs trips that begin at Diamond Creek and end at Pierce Ferry; transportation is provided from Peach Springs, about 2½ hours west of Grand Canyon Village. A one-day trip with no accommodations costs $192 per person; the same trip with food and sleeping arrangements for two nights costs around $245. Discounts are offered for groups (generally 10 or more people).

**SCENIC FLIGHTS** Helicopter and airplane tours of the canyon leave from the Grand Canyon Airport just south of Tusayan. Rates start at around $50 for 30- to 50-minute plane rides, $80 for helicopter rides. The visitor center (*see* Basics, *above*) can supply you with the names and phone numbers of various companies. Try **Windrock Aviation** (Box 3399, Grand Canyon, AZ 86023, tel. 520/638–9591 or 800/24–ROCKY) for plane flights or **Kenai Helicopters** (Box 1429, Grand Canyon, AZ 86023, tel. 520/638–2412 or 800/541–4537) for helicopter rides.

*If you're considering "flightseeing," check your conscience first. Many environmentalists would like to see air tours—and the attendant pollution and noise—banned from the Grand Canyon. While park officials consider their options, flights continue at a rate of 80,000 a year.*

Scenic flights originate near the North Rim at **Lake Mead Air** in Kanab, Utah (2378 S. Hwy. ALT89, tel. 801/644–2299) offers 40-minute plane tours of the Grand Canyon for $79 per person (two-person minimum), originating at Kanab Airport. **Grand Canyon AirTours** (475 S. Donlee Dr., St. George, Utah 84770, tel. 801/644–2904) offers two-hour flights from the Kanab Airport, beginning at $129 per person (two-person minimum).

# Near the Grand Canyon

## HAVASUPAI INDIAN RESERVATION

As an alternative to crowded Grand Canyon National Park, explore the **Havasupai Indian Reservation,** four hours west of the South Rim's Grand Canyon Village. The views from the 8-mile riverbed trail leading to the remote village of **Supai** at times rival those in the park. Life for the agrarian Havasupai hasn't changed much; this is the only town in the United States that still receives mail by mule train. The tribe maintains a campground for hikers (with pit toilets and water) 2 miles north of Supai, near a series of spectacular waterfalls that fill the narrow, red-walled canyon with a surprising abundance of greenery. There's a $15-per-person entrance fee, plus a campsite fee of $10 per person per night. Reservations are required, and it's best to schedule several weeks in advance. Contact **Havasupai Tourist Enterprises** (Supai, AZ 86435, tel. 520/448–2141). To reach the trailhead, follow Highway 18 north from historic **Old Route 66** (parallel to I–40 between Kingman and Seligman). Parking is on Hualapai Hilltop at the end of Highway 18.

## CAMERON AND THE PAINTED DESERT

Since 1916, Native Americans have been bringing their crafts to the **Historic Cameron Trading Post** at the intersection of Highways 64 and 89, 50 miles north of Flagstaff and 30 miles east of the Grand Canyon's east entrance. These days, though prices are occasionally inflated, it's still an ideal place to find finely crafted turquoise jewelry, kachina dolls, woven rugs, and pottery. For information on any of the above facilities, contact the Cameron Trading Post (Box 339, Cameron, AZ 86020, tel. 800/338–7385).

Stretching for 70 miles north of Cameron, on either side of Highway 89, is the Technicolor sandstone of the **Painted Desert.** The lavender, red, saffron, and pink hues of the rocks, exposed by millions of years of erosion, are most spectacular at sunset. This is also the best place to shop for Native American jewelry—Navajo artists sell their crafts from roadside stands to passing motorists, but you'll have to haggle to get the best price. This portion of the desert is on the Navajo Reservation, but the Painted Desert extends more than 100 miles southeast to the **Petrified Forest National Park.** Pieces of "wood turned to stone" from the Triassic period are scattered throughout the park, ranging in size from tiny bits to "Old Faithful," a log nearly 10 feet in diameter at the base. A number of short hiking trails show off the variety of rock formations, as well as Anasazi ruins and petroglyphs. The Painted Desert Visitor Center (tel.

520/524–6228) is located 115 miles east of Flagstaff on I–40. Camping is permited in two wilderness areas, as long as you have a (free) permit from one of the visitor's centers.

## BRYCE CANYON AND ZION NATIONAL PARKS

There seems to be no end to the bizarre contortions and colors that nature has wrought from solid rock. At **Zion National Park** (119 miles northwest of the North Rim), red- and pink-hued canyon walls of fragile sandstone are fissured to create checkerboard patterns and striations reminiscent of a giant esophagus. Those passing through should pause long enough to climb the 2-mile round-trip trail to Canyon Overlook, beginning just east of the first of two park tunnels. To get to Zion from the Grand Canyon, take U.S. 89 north, which intersects Highway 9 at Fredonia. Highway 9 crosses the park before joining I–15. For more info on camping and other park activities, contact the Zion National Park Ranger Headquarters (Springdale, UT 84767, tel. 801/772–3256). The visitor center, open daily 9–4:30, is located a mile north of Springdale. Admission ($5 per vehicle, $3 per person) gives you access to the park for one week.

**Bryce Canyon National Park,** 155 miles north of the North Rim, is a land of rock minarets. The spires that rise from the canyon floor are impressive year-round, but become outrageously photogenic in fall and winter, when they're topped with snow. If you only have a day to sample the park's unique vistas, hike the strenuous 8-mile Fairyland Loop from Sunrise Point, near the visitor center. To reach Bryce from the Grand Canyon, take U.S. 89 north to Highway 12. For more info contact Bryce Canyon National Park (Bryce Canyon, UT 84717, tel. 801/834–5322). Admission (good for one week) is $5 per vehicle, $3 for those on bus, bicycle, or foot.

# Index

# Notes

# Notes

## TELL US WHAT YOU THINK

We're always trying to improve our books and would really appreciate any feedback on how to make them more useful. Thanks for taking a few minutes to fill out this survey. We'd also like to know about your latest find, a new scam, a budget deal, whatever . . . Please print your name and address clearly and send the completed survey to: The Berkeley Guides, 515 Eshelman Hall, U.C. Berkeley, CA 94720.

**1.** Your name ______________________________

**2.** Your address ______________________________

______________________________ Zip __________

**3.** You are: Female Male

**4.** Your age: under 17 17–22 23–30 31–40 41–55 over 55

**5.** If you're a student: Name of school __________ City & state __________

**6.** If you're employed: Occupation ______________________________

**7.** Your yearly income: under $20,000 $21,000–$30,000 $31,000–$45,000 $46,000–$60,000 $61,000–$100,000 over $100,000

**8.** Which of the following do you own? (Circle all that apply.)

Computer CD-ROM Drive Modem

**9.** What speed (bps) is your modem?

2400 4800 9600 14.4 19.2 28.8

**10.** Which on-line service(s) do you subscribe to apart from commercial services like AOL?

______________________________

**11.** Do you have access to the World Wide Web? If so, is it through a university or a private service provider? ______________________________

**12.** If you have a CD-ROM drive or plan to have one, would you purchase a Berkeley Guide CD-ROM? ______________________________

**13.** Which Berkeley Guide(s) did you buy? ______________________________

**14.** Where did you buy the book and when? City __________ Month/Year __________

**15.** Why did you choose The Berkeley Guides? (Circle all that apply.)

Budget focus
Outdoor emphasis
Off-the-beaten-track emphasis
Resources for gays and lesbians
Resources for people with disabilities
Resources for women

Design
Attitude
Writing style
Organization
More maps
Accuracy
Price

Other ______________________________

**16.** How did you hear about The Berkeley Guides? (Circle all that apply.)

Recommended by friend/acquaintance  Bookstore display  TV

Article in magazine/newspaper (which one?) ____________________

Ad in magazine/newspaper (which one?) ____________________

Radio program (which one?) ____________________

Other ____________________

**17.** Which other guides, if any, have you used before? (Circle all that apply.)

| | | |
|---|---|---|
| Fodor's | Let's Go | Rough Guides |
| Frommer's | Birnbaum | Lonely Planet |

Other ____________________

**18.** When did you travel with this book? Month/Year ____________________

**19.** Where did you travel? ____________________

**20.** What was the purpose of your trip?

| | | |
|---|---|---|
| Vacation | Business | Volunteer |
| Study abroad | Work | |

**21.** About how much did you spend per day during your trip?

| | | | |
|---|---|---|---|
| $0–$20 | $31–$45 | $61–$75 | over $100 |
| $21–$30 | $46–$60 | $76–$100 | |

**22.** After you arrived, how did you get around? (Circle all that apply.)

| | | | |
|---|---|---|---|
| Rental car | Personal car | Plane | Bus |
| Train | Hiking | Bike | Hitching |

**23.** Which features/sections did you use most? (Circle all that apply.)

| | | |
|---|---|---|
| Book Basics | City/region Basics | Coming and Going |
| Hitching | Getting Around | Where to Sleep |
| Camping | Roughing It | Food |
| Worth Seeing | Cheap Thrills | Festivals |
| Shopping | After Dark | Outdoor Activities |

**24.** The information was (circle one): V = very accurate  U = usually accurate
S = sometimes accurate  R = rarely accurate

| | | | |
|---|---|---|---|
| Introductions | V U S R | Worth Seeing | V U S R |
| Basics | V U S R | After Dark | V U S R |
| Coming and Going | V U S R | Outdoor Activities | V U S R |
| Where to Sleep | V U S R | Maps | V U S R |
| Food | V U S R | | |

**25.** I would ______ would not ______ buy another Berkeley Guide.

**26.** Which of the following destinations are you planning to visit in the next five years?

**The Americas**
Chicago
Washington, D.C.
New Orleans
Los Angeles
Boston
Austin
The Midwest
The South
The Southwest
New England
The Pacific Northwest
Hawaii
Canada
South America

**Middle East/Africa**
Turkey
Israel
Egypt
Africa

**Europe**
Spain
Portugal
Greece
Russia
Scandinavia
Berlin
Prague
Rome

**Australia/Asia**
Australia
New Zealand
Vietnam
Philippines
Indonesia
Thailand
Singapore
Malaysia
Cambodia
India/Nepal